CONSUMER BANKRUPTCY

Third Edition

CONSUMER BANKRUPTCY

Third Edition

By

David Gray Carlson

VANDEPLAS PUBLISHING

UNITED STATES OF AMERICA

Consumer bankruptcy, Third Edition

Carlson, David Gray

Published by:

Vandeplas Publishing – December 2013

801 International Parkway, 5th Floor
Lake Mary, FL. 32746
USA

www.vandeplaspublishing.com

ISBN: 978-1-60042-214-0

Table of Contents

INTRODUCTION

After October 17, 2005, when the Bankruptcy Abuse Prevention and Consumer Protection Act (BAPCPA) became effective, bankruptcy for individuals became so specialized as to warrant a course separate and apart from what is usually called "Creditor's Remedies and Debtor's rights" or "Bankruptcy," conceived as covering primarily business or generic issues of debt collection.

The idea of the Consumer Bankruptcy course is to introduce students to chapter 7 and 13 as these apply to ordinary consumers. For the consumer, the promise of chapter 7 is (1) discharge of debt and (2) retention of all exempt property (which is usually the only property a consumer debtor has, apart from an overencumbered house and car). In addition, a chapter 7 debtor gets to keep all postpetition wages free and clear of prepetition claims (provided a discharge is legally appropriate).

In chapter 13, the debtor is offered a bargain. If the debtor agrees to surrender postpetition wages (otherwise not available to prepetition creditors in chapter 7), the debtor gets to keep all her property--exempt or not. In chapter 13, a debtor basically buys back non-exempt assets with postpetition wages.

When the Bankruptcy Code was first enacted in 1978, few realized how revolutionary and powerful a piece of legislation this was. By the 1990s, in spite of favorable economic circumstances, about 1.5 million bankruptcy petitions were being filed, almost all filed by consumers who felt overwhelmed by credit card debt. Since 1978, when the vulture eye of Congress turns toward bankruptcy legislation, it moves to restrict access to chapter 7 for consumers, while increasing the amount of wages a debtor must pay in chapter 13 to buy back all assets.

This retrenchment came to a head in 2005 with BAPCPA. The legislation accomplishes many things, almost all of which are pro-creditor reforms. This course focuses on what this legislative reform accomplishes.

Bankruptcy reform has become highly political and has penetrated even presidential politics. This case book, however, aims to take a non-polemical approach. It attempts to explore how the bankruptcy system works for consumers after 2005, without drawing political conclusions. Nevertheless, it cannot be denied that the craftsmanship of BAPCPA leaves something to be desired. Much effort is spent in the following pages exploring the contradictory nature of Congress's latest reform. Because of BAPCPA, consumer bankruptcy has turned out to be a very technical and complex specialty.

Chapter 1 begins by examining the barriers to entry that any individual faces in commencing a federal bankruptcy proceeding. These include the new credit counseling requirement, which conditions any bankruptcy petition by an lender on providing a certificate from a qualified provider that the debtor has been "counseled" as to the options to seeking a discharge in bankruptcy. Attempts to prevent bankruptcy petitions by abusive multiple filing debtors is also covered.

Chapter 2 examines what is required of a consumerdebtor by way of submissions in order to sustain a bankruptcy petition. Included is the remarkable new doctrine of automatic dismissal in case certain submissions are not paid. Also, failure to make some submissions may or may not eliminate the "automatic stay" the Bankruptcy Code's injunction preventing creditor collections once a bankruptcy petition is filed. This too is covered in chapter 2.

Chapter 3 covers the "means test." This is a mechanical and very technical test to determine whether consumer debtors have too much surplus income. If they have too much, debtors are invited out of chapter 7. They are permitted to substitute a chapter 13 procedure, if they wish. Dismissal of chapter 7 cases involving individuals whose debts are not primarily consumer debts is also discussed. Nonconsumer debtors are not means-tested.

Chapter 4 assumes that the debtor has qualified for chapter 7 and has not been dismissed. In such an event, the debtor is deemed to have transferred all prepetition property to a chapter 7 bankruptcy trustee. The debtor, however, is invited to claim exemptions. In the main, these exemptions are provided for in applicable non-bankruptcy law. For instance, every state prohibits the sheriff, under a writ of execution stemming from a money judgment, from levying certain property. These items, exempt from execution, become the basis of exemptions in bankruptcy. Also discussed is a debtor's unique federal right to avoid liens (including certain consensually created liens) to the extent they impair an exemption right.

Chapter 5 discusses the golden ring for consumer debtors--discharge from debt. The chapter discusses what the concept of discharge means--a surprisingly metaphysical notion, as it turns out. It also describes how certain debts are never discharged, and how the debtor might forfeit the right to a discharge (without being expelled from chapter 7) for various forms of bad prepetition and postpetition behavior. The chapter also covers the opposite of discharge--the debtor's carefully regulated right to waive discharge and reaffirm selected debts in a "reaffirmation agreement."

Chapter 6 discusses the consumer's alternative of a chapter 13 proceeding. It discusses who is eligible to file in chapter 13. It also discusses the minimum things the chapter 13 plan must accomplish. As stated earlier, the idea of the chapter 13 plan is that the debtor surrenders postpetition wages (not part of the bankruptcy estate in a chapter 7 case) in exchange for all property--exempt or not. The debtor, however, is required to dedicate all "disposable income" to the plan for a minimal period. BAPCPA heavily regulates what "disposable income" means, tying the concept most intimately together with the means test in chapter 7 for consumer debtors. In the main, the means test of chapter 7 is designed to force debtors out of chapter 7 in the hope that they will choose chapter 13 where the disqualifying surplus income of chapter 7 becomes disposable income of chapter 13 which will be paid to the creditors. The two most important assets of a consumer debtor will be her home and her car. Chapter 13 severely limits the amount of relief a debtor can have against the home mortgage lender. BAPCPA has added similar (but conceptually different) protections for creditors claiming a security interest on the debtor's car or truck.

It turns out that three-fourths of all chapter 13 plans fail. So the ultimate destination of most chapter 13 debtors is chapter 7 after all. Accordingly, the last chapter of this book covers the phenomenon of the converted case, which differs rather interestingly from the case that begins in (and never leaves) the jurisdiction of chapter 7.

Cast of Characters

The way the Bankruptcy Code works is that anything in chapters 1, 3, and 5 universally apply to all the chapters. Chapter 7 is liquidation, chapter 11 is general reorganization for everyone (except stock brokers), and chapter 13 is the chapter for persons with modest debt and regular income. Much of what ensues are interpretations of chapters 3 and 5. Since we cannot present chapter 7 and chapter 13 procedure in advance, here is a cast of characters that will appear in the early chapters.

The debtor or debtors. Although involuntary bankruptcy petitions are possible, 11 U.S.C. § 303, they are virtually unknown in consumer cases. In this book involuntary petitions will be largely ignored. The debtor is the one who commences a case by filing a bankruptcy petition under chapter 7 (liquidation) or chapter 13 (reorganization). 11 U.S.C. § 301. Married couples are permitted to commence joint cases. Id. § 302.

The chapter 7 trustee. In chapter 7 cases, an interim chapter 7 trustee is appointed by the United States trustee for the judicial district in question. Id. § 701. The United States trustee convenes a mandatory creditors' meeting where the permanent chapter 7 trustee is appointed. The chapter 7 trustee marshals the assets of the debtor and distributes the proceeds to the unsecured creditors. In a consumer case, the proceeds are typically zero.

The United States trustee. The United States Trustee is a member of the Justice Department. Every judicial district has one, who in turn has many assistants. (This is a great entry-level job for anyone who is interested in bankruptcy litigation or who aspires to be a bankruptcy judge). North Carolina and Alabama, however, do not have United States trustees. Instead they have bankruptcy administrators, who are court employees. Bankruptcy Judges, United States Trustees, and Family Farmer Bankruptcy Act of 1986, § 302(d)(3). The existence of bankruptcy administrators was to terminate on October 1, 1992, but Congress extended this deadline first to October 1, 2002. Act of December 1, 1990, P.L. 101-650, 104 Stat. 5115, § 317(a)(1). In 2000, the deadline was entirely omitted. Federal Courts Improvement Act of 2000, 106 P.L. 518, 114 Stat. 2410 § 501. As a result, bankruptcy administrators still roam the hills of North Carolina and Alabama. See Federal Rules of Bankruptcy Procedure § 9035 History: Ancillary Laws and Directives.

In St. Angelo v. Victoria Farms, Inc., 38 F.3d 1525 (9th Cir. 1994), the United States trustee sought a fee in a chapter 11 case. The debtor resisted on the grounds that the United States trusteeship is unconstitutional, since this institution does not exist in Alabama and North Carolina. The United States Constitution, it seems, requires a uniform national bankruptcy law. The Ninth Circuit permitted the fee but took the trouble to advise those two states that their bankruptcy administrator program was unconstitutional. Congress, however, has chosen to ignore the studied advice of the Ninth Circuit and has perpetuated this unconstitutional regime. See generally Dan J. Shulman, The Constitution, Interest Groups, and the Requirements of Uniformity: The United States Trustee and the Bankruptcy Administrator Programs, 74 NEB. L. REV. 91, 127-29 (1995).

The standing chapter 13 trustee. Every district appoints a standing chapter 13 trustee. The job of the trustee is to receive the wages that the debtor promises to pay pursuant to a confirmed reorganization plan. The trustee represents the unsecured creditors and will keep watch over the debtors' performance under the plan.

In consumer cases, the debtor typically is engaged in litigation with either the United States trustee, the chapter 7 trustee or the chapter 13 trustee.

CHAPTER 1 BARRIERS TO ENTRY

Bankruptcy proceedings are commenced by the filing of a petition. By far the most common type of petition (almost exclusively in consumer cases) is the voluntary petition. Bankruptcy Code § 301. Married copies may commence joint cases under Bankruptcy Code § 302.

Bankruptcy Code § 109 describes eligibility for bankruptcy. For example, only a person who "resides or has a domicile, a place of business, or property in the United States, or a municipality, may be a debtor under this title." Bankruptcy Code § 109(a). Some entities may not file in chapter 7. These include railroads, insurance companyies and banks. Bankruptcy Code § 109(a). From the perspective of consumer debtors, they are eligible for chapter 7, 11, or 13. Bankruptcy Code § 109(b), § 109(d), § 109(e). With regard to chapter 13, the debtor must have limited debt and regular income. These matters are described in chapter 6.

The present chapter discusses new limitations on who may be a consumer debtor in a bankruptcy case.

A. CREDIT COUNSELING

ADAMS v zARNEL (IN RE ZARNEL)

619 F.3d 156 (2d Cir. 2010)

LIVINGSTON J.

This case requires us to interpret the interplay of provisions of the Bankruptcy Code that arises when an individual or entity files a petition for bankruptcy without complying with the credit counseling requirements created by the Bankruptcy Abuse Prevention and Consumer Protection Act of 2005 ("BAPCPA"), Pub. L. No. 109-8, 119 Stat. 23. In the course of our analysis, we interpret the credit counseling requirement, 11 U.S.C. § 109(h), the provisions that govern the commencement of bankruptcy cases, 11 U.S.C. §§ 301, 302, and 303, and the statutory section governing automatic stays, 11 U.S.C. § 362.

Petitioner-appellant Diana G. Adams, United States Trustee ("Trustee"), appeals from a final judgment entered November 8, 2006 in the United States District Court for the Southern District of New York (Brieant, J.) dismissing her appeal for lack of standing and in the alternative affirming the bankruptcy court's decision to strike the bankruptcy petitions filed by respondents-appellees ("debtors") rather than to dismiss their cases. We determine that the Trustee has standing to bring this appeal; that the appeal is not moot; and that the filing of a bankruptcy petition by a debtor who has failed to satisfy credit counseling requirements commences a bankruptcy case and invokes the automatic stay. We do not, however, pronounce on the question of what action a bankruptcy court may take with respect to such a petition given these determinations.

The appeal before this Court is of a consolidated matter, generated by three unrelated filings of bankruptcy in the United States Bankruptcy Court for the Southern District of New York. As the facts are not in dispute, we take them largely from the bankruptcy court's opinion. See In re Elmendorf, 345 B.R. 486 (Bankr. S.D.N.Y. 2006).

Lena Elmendorf, represented by counsel, filed a voluntary Chapter 7 petition on November 29, 2005. Although this proceeding was her first bankruptcy filing and her petition was accompanied by the correct schedules, she neither filed a credit-counseling certificate, see 11 U.S.C. § 521(b), nor sought an extension of time to do so, see id. § 109(h)(3)(A). The United States Trustee's Office ("Trustee") moved to dismiss the case on February 1, 2006. In re Elmendorf, 345 B.R. at 491.

Diana Finlay filed a Chapter 13 petition on April 3, 2006, as a pro se debtor, attaching none of the requisite schedules. She sought an extension of time to file her credit-counseling certificate, which the bankruptcy court denied for failure to state that the debtor sought counseling within five days of filing. Id. at 492. Finlay had recently filed two prior Chapter 13 petitions: one on August 31, 2005, and one on November 28, 2005. Both were dismissed for failure to file the appropriate bankruptcy schedules. Id. The Trustee filed a motion to dismiss the case on May 3, 2006.

Shayna Zarnel, the third relevant debtor, filed a Chapter 13 petition on March 13, 2006. Although this was Zarnel's first bankruptcy filing, her husband had filed five bankruptcy petitions with the court since January 2004. Id. She sought an extension of time to file her credit counseling certificate but failed to allege exigent circumstances meriting a waiver; the bankruptcy court therefore denied the extension. Id. at 493. On April 3, 2006, nonetheless, Zarnel filed a credit counseling certificate attesting that she had received counseling on March 21, 2006. The Trustee then moved to dismiss the case.

After holding a hearing on the motions in the Elmendorf and Zarnel proceedings, and reserving decision on the motions in all three cases, the bankruptcy court determined in a July 18, 2006 opinion to "strike" the case of each debtor rather than to dismiss each case as requested by the Trustee.[1] Id. at 504-05. It arrived at this decision by examining the credit-counseling requirement codified at 11 U.S.C. § 109(h). The court observed that the provision, which it said "was intended to provide debtors with education as to all of their options when experiencing financial difficulty, before a resort to bankruptcy protection was necessary," had as a policy matter "not proven to be of assistance to debtors in seeking relief outside of the bankruptcy context." Id. at 490. The court nonetheless concluded that compliance with § 109(h)'s requirement that a debtor seek credit counseling before obtaining bankruptcy relief was "an absolute pre-requisite to individual bankruptcy eligibility." Id. at 495. The court acknowledged that debtors may in certain circumstances obtain an extension of time to receive counseling under § 109(h)(3)(A). The court noted, however, that

[1] To "strike" a case is peculiar terminology. The District Court felt that only a case that was actually "commenced" by the filing of a petition could be "dismissed." In the opinion of the District Court, a bankruptcy petition without credit counselling never "commences" a case, and so the word "dismissal" is inappropriately used.-ed.]

the difficulties of satisfying each of the statutory factors necessary to have a request for extension granted are substantial, particularly for a pro se debtor.[2] Id. at 496.

Relying on its reasoning in a previous case, In re Rios, 336 B.R. 177 (Bankr. S.D.N.Y. 2005), the bankruptcy court found that the statutory language of § 109(h), which provides that an individual "may not be a debtor" without prior credit counseling, bars such filers from commencing a case under 11 U.S.C. § 301. In re Elmendorf, 345 B.R. at 497. Moreover, if a case is not commenced, the court determined, the automatic stay against creditor actions provided for in 11 U.S.C. § 362 does not operate to protect the ineligible filer. Id. at 497-98. Nonetheless, it found that it still had jurisdiction over the matter even if a case was not properly commenced by the filing. Id. at 499. Therefore, under the equitable powers granted by 11 U.S.C. § 105(a), the bankruptcy court determined that because Congress had not explicitly directed the action a court should take in response to a bankruptcy petition failing to commence a case, it had the power to strike the petitions before it rather than to dismiss the cases, as urged by the Trustee.[3] Id. at 503. The court noted that in its view dismissal, which has the potential effect of limiting access to or the duration of § 362's automatic stay in a subsequent filing, is for the most part "an inappropriate remedy for a debtor's innocuous failure to obtain counseling, prior to filing a bankruptcy petition," id. at 491, and it concluded that it could always strike a case with prejudice to future filings if it found such a measure to be warranted by a filer's bad faith or other such circumstances, id. at 504.

Because Elmendorf had not filed any previous bankruptcy petitions nor were there other indications of bad faith, the court ordered her case stricken without prejudice. Id. In the case of Finlay, the bankruptcy court noted that the debtor had filed "three back-to-back bankruptcy petitions," and that she "sought, and obtained, an extension of time to file her credit counseling certificate in her prior case," and was thus "not ignorant of the requirement." Id. Noting that "[t]he circumstances in Ms. Finlay's filings are indicative of a pattern of delay and an abuse of the provisions of Section 362," relating to the automatic stay, the court suggested that it might have been "inclined to grant some sort of preclusive relief," but because the Trustee had not requested any relief other than dismissal, the court merely struck the case without prejudice. Id. at 504-05. Finally, it also struck Zarnel's case without prejudice on the ground that, although her husband had repeatedly filed for bankruptcy, this was Zarnel's first filing. Id. at 505.

---

[2] The court noted that before an extension of time to receive credit counseling may be granted, "a debtor must submit to the court (1) a certification (2) describing exigent circumstances that (3) merit a waiver of the requirement, (4) states that the debtor requested credit counseling from an approved nonprofit budget and credit counseling agency, but was unable to obtain services during the five day period beginning on the date that debtor made the request and (5) which is satisfactory to the Court." Id. at 496 (footnotes omitted).

[3] 11 U.S.C. § 105(a) provides as follows:

> The court may issue any order, process, or judgment that is necessary or appropriate to carry out the provisions of this title. No provision of this title providing for the raising of an issue by a party in interest shall be construed to preclude the court from, sua sponte, taking any action or making any determination necessary or appropriate to enforce or implement court orders or rules, or to prevent an abuse of process.

Acting on its own volition, the bankruptcy court then certified its orders for direct appeal to this Court under 28 U.S.C. § 158(d)(2). On November 17, 2006, we consolidated and dismissed those appeals because no party had filed a petition for permission to appeal under Federal Rule of Appellate Procedure 5(a).

The Trustee appealed the bankruptcy court's decision in each instance to the district court on the issue of whether the bankruptcy court had erred in ruling that the petitions of ineligible debtors had not commenced cases and that the petitions could thus be struck rather than dismissed. Adams v. Finlay, No. 06 civ. 6039, 2006 U.S. Dist. LEXIS 81591, 2006 WL 3240522 (S.D.N.Y. Nov. 3, 2006). In its opinion of November 3, 2006, the district court sua sponte raised the issue of the Trustee's standing to appeal the denials of its motions to dismiss. Applying the bankruptcy standing test of this Court that requires an appellant to be a "person aggrieved," meaning "a person 'directly and adversely affected pecuniarily by' the challenged order of the bankruptcy court,'" Int'l Trade Admin. v. Rensselaer Polytechnic Inst., 936 F.2d 744, 747 (2d Cir. 1991) (quoting In re Cosmopolitan Aviation Corp., 763 F.2d 507, 513 (2d Cir. 1985)), the district court found that the Trustee was not aggrieved because no creditor's rights were affected by these decisions and no substantive actions had been taken between the filing and the striking of the cases. Therefore, it held, the Trustee lacked standing to appeal. It nonetheless proceeded to decide the merits in the alternative after confessing that it had "no great confidence" in its standing determination. Finlay, 2006 U.S. Dist. LEXIS 81591, 2006 WL 3240522.

The district court concluded that the bankruptcy court's interpretation of the interplay between §§ 109(h), 301, and 362(a) was the correct one -- that a case is not commenced nor does the automatic stay come into existence when a bankruptcy petition is filed by an individual who fails to fulfill the credit-counseling requirement. It then expounded on the court's equitable powers, noting that motions to strike pleadings, although fallen from favor, were once common in the federal courts and have not since that time been prohibited. Furthermore, it added, Federal Rule of Civil Procedure 12(f) permits a court to strike a pleading, as do Bankruptcy Rules 7012(b) and 9011. Given the latitude provided the bankruptcy court under § 105(a), the district court found it was not beyond the bankruptcy court's judicial powers to strike the petition of a debtor who has not satisfied the credit counseling requirement and thus has not commenced a case. Therefore, in the alternative to dismissing the appeals for want of standing, it affirmed the bankruptcy court's orders in all respects.

The Trustee timely appealed the district court's decision to this Court. In order to assist in the development of arguments on appeal, this Court appointed Sanford I. Weisburst, Esq. amicus curiae on behalf of the pro se debtors ("Amicus"). The debtors have not appeared in this appeal.

DISCUSSION

Before reaching the merits of this appeal, we must first determine whether we have jurisdiction. Issues arise both from the Trustee's standing to take this appeal and its potential mootness. We review these legal issues de novo. N.Y. Civil Liberties Union v. Grandeau, 528 F.3d 122, 128 (2d Cir. 2008); Cent. States Se. & Sw. Areas Health & Welfare Fund v. Merck-Medco Managed Care, L.L.C., 433 F.3d 181, 197 (2d Cir. 2005).

I. Standing

Section 307 of the Bankruptcy Act authorizes the Trustee to "raise and [ ] appear and be heard on any issue in any case or proceeding under this title." 11 U.S.C. § 307. Despite that broad authorization, cf. In re Columbia Gas Sys., 33 F.3d 294, 296 (3d Cir. 1994) ("[i]t is difficult to conceive of a statute that more clearly signifies Congress's intent to confer standing"), the district court concluded that the Trustee did not have standing to appeal the denial of its motions to dismiss. We disagree with that determination.

As the district court correctly noted, in determining whether a party has standing to appeal from a particular ruling of a bankruptcy court, we have frequently looked to whether an appellant is a "person aggrieved" that is, "a person 'directly and adversely affected pecuniarily by' the challenged order of the bankruptcy court." Int'l Trade Admin., 936 F.2d at 747 (quoting In re Cosmopolitan Aviation Corp., 763 F.2d at 513); see also 11 U.S.C. § 67(c) (1976) (repealed 1978) (permitting appeal by a "person aggreived by an order of a referee"). Applying that standard, the district court determined that the Trustee had no direct pecuniary interest in the outcome of this litigation and accordingly lacked standing. We disagree.

While the "pecuniary interest" formulation is an often used and often useful test of standing in the bankruptcy context, it "is not the only test." In re Revco D.S., Inc., 898 F.2d 498, 499 (6th Cir. 1990). Instead, even absent a direct pecuniary interest in the litigation, "a public interest may also give a sufficient stake in the outcome of a bankruptcy case to confer appellate standing." Id. (emphasis in original); see also In re Clark, 927 F.2d 793, 796 (4th Cir. 1991) ("[S]tanding to appeal under the Bankruptcy Act as a 'party aggrieved' may arise from a party's official duty to enforce the bankruptcy law in the public interest"). The Supreme Court has thus determined, for instance, that the Securities and Exchange Commission's interest in "the maintenance of its statutory authority and the performance of its public duties" was sufficient to give the Commission standing to pursue a bankruptcy appeal. SEC v. U.S. Realty & Improvement Co., 310 U.S. 434, 459-60 (1940).

Applying U.S. Realty and the "public interest" standard, several of our sister circuits have concluded that the U.S. Trustee has just such an interest and thus standing to pursue bankruptcy appeals. As the Sixth Circuit explained in reasoning adopted by the First and Third Circuits, "the U.S. trustees are responsible for 'protecting the public interest and ensuring that bankruptcy cases are conducted according to law.' That is the interest the U.S. trustee has pursued in this case, and that interest gives him standing to appeal." In re Revco D.S., Inc., 898 F.2d at 499 (internal citation omitted); see also In re United Artists Theatre Co., 315 F.3d 217, 225 (3d Cir. 2003) ("U.S. Trustees are officers of the Department of Justice who protect the public interest by aiding bankruptcy judges in monitoring certain aspects of bankruptcy proceedings."); In re Plaza de Diego Shopping Center, Inc., 911 F.2d 820, 824 (1st Cir 1990) (standing derives from "the U.S. Trustee's interest from his statutory responsibility to represent and protect the public"). The Fourth Circuit similarly concluded, in reliance on U.S. Realty, that the U.S. Trustee had standing in the matter before that court because the "trustee [was] attempting, as was the SEC in United States Realty, to enforce the law in the public interest--in this case the interest of the public in avoiding substantial abuse of the bankruptcy process." In re Clark, 927 F.2d at 796.

We find the reasoning of those courts to be persuasive and conclude that the U.S. Trustee's responsibility to represent and protect the public interest affords it a substantial interest in, and therefore standing to proceed with, this appeal.

II. Mootntess

Mootness is a doctrinal restriction stemming from the Article III requirement that federal courts decide only live cases or controversies; a case is moot if "the parties lack a legally cognizable interest in the outcome" of the case. Fox v. Bd. of Trustees of State Univ. of N.Y., 42 F.3d 135, 140 (2d Cir. 1994) (quoting County of L.A. v. Davis, 440 U.S. 625, 631 (1979)) (internal quotation marks omitted). This occurs "when interim relief or events have eradicated the effects of the defendant's act or omission, and there is no reasonable expectation that the alleged violation will recur." Irish Lesbian & Gay Org. v. Giuliani, 143 F.3d 638, 647 (2d Cir. 1998). A bankruptcy case may also be mooted based on "jurisdictional and equitable considerations" related to difficulty in fashioning "fair and effective judicial relief." AmeriCredit Fin. Servs., Inc. v. Tompkins, 604 F.3d 753, 755 (2d Cir. 2010) (quoting In re Sasso, 409 B.R. 251, 254 (B.A.P. 1st Cir. 2009)) (internal quotation marks omitted).

The debtors, by failing to appeal the bankruptcy court's order striking their cases, have waived any argument that they have satisfied the credit counseling requirements of 11 U.S.C. § 109(h) and should have been allowed to proceed with their bankruptcies. Therefore, neither party has a legally cognizable interest in this appeal related to its effect on the proceedings that initiated the case. However, the effects of the bankruptcy court's decision to strike the petitions rather than dismissing the cases, the question on appeal, extend beyond the matter immediately at hand. Under 11 U.S.C. § 362(c)(3), the automatic stay protecting the debtor's assets, which comes into being when a petition is filed, terminates after thirty days if "a single or joint [bankruptcy] case of the debtor was pending within the preceding 1-year period but was dismissed." Similarly, if the debtor has had two bankruptcy cases pending within the preceding year that were dismissed, the automatic stay does not go into effect upon a third filing.[4] Id. § 362(c)(4). Because, under the plain language of § 362(c)(3) and (c)(4), only the "dismiss[al]" of a prior bankruptcy case triggers these provisions," the manner in which the bankruptcy court disposes of the matter appears likely to affect whether the limitations on the automatic stay for subsequent proceedings take effect. Within a year of the striking of their petitions, therefore, the debtors clearly had a legally cognizable interest in the outcome of this appeal, as did the Trustee, whose duty to protect the public interest is affected by debtors avoiding what it alleges are the appropriate legal consequences of their actions.

The bankruptcy court struck the petitions at issue here on July 28, 2006. More than a year has passed since that decision. Both the Trustee and Amicus argue that the case is nonetheless not moot, but provide different reasons. The Trustee suggests that the word "pending" in § 362(c)(3) and (c)(4) encompasses the time during which the case is on appeal, and hence that the year period given

[4] With regard to both of these provisions, the debtor may seek relief from the bankruptcy court, which is authorized to institute or extend an automatic stay, as appropriate, if the debtor demonstrates that the filing of the later case was in good faith as to the creditors to be stayed. 11 U.S.C. § 362(c)(3)(B), (c)(4)(B).

in the statute has not yet even begun. The debtors and the Trustee would therefore maintain their legally cognizable interests in the outcome for the duration of the appeal. Amicus, however, argues that "pending" covers only the period in which the case is pending in the bankruptcy court and that the automatic stay repercussions for a debtor end a year after the case is dismissed, even if that dismissal is appealed. It invokes the exception to mootness for cases "capable of repetition, yet evading review." Van Wie v. Pataki, 267 F.3d 109, 113 (2d Cir. 2001) (quoting Knaust v. City of Kingston, 157 F.3d 86, 88 (2d Cir. 1998)) (internal quotation marks omitted). This exception applies when "(1) the challenged action [is] in its duration too short to be fully litigated prior to its cessation or expiration, and (2) there [is] a reasonable expectation that the same complaining party [will] be subjected to the same action again." Id. at 114 (alterations in original) (quoting Weinstein v. Bradford, 423 U.S. 147, 149 (1975)) (internal quotation marks omitted).

We conclude that we need not interpret § 362(c) at the present time. The parties present the only two logical possibilities for the meaning of the word "pending" in this context, and we agree with each party that under its interpretation of the statute the case is not moot. If a case is pending for the purpose of § 362(c)(3) and (c)(4) during the period on appeal, then each party continues to have a legally cognizable interest because the manner in which the bankruptcy court disposed of the debtors' cases is likely to affect any subsequent proceedings in which they may be involved for a year after this appeal is concluded. If, on the other hand, the year period delineated in the statute has already expired, then we conclude that the "capable of repetition, yet evading review" doctrine applies. The first element is clearly fulfilled under this interpretation, because a year is too short to pursue an appeal to its conclusion. The second element is also satisfied because the bankruptcy court will apply its interpretation of the relevant statutory provisions in future cases. See Storer v. Brown, 415 U.S. 724, 737 n.8 (1974) ("[T]his case is not moot, since the issues properly presented, and their effects on independent candidacies, will persist as the California statutes are applied in future elections.") Thus, the bankruptcy court will persist in striking petitions rather than dismissing cases, causing repeated injury to the Trustee's interest. This indicates that under Amicus's interpretation of the statute, the appeal is not moot. Because we need only assure ourselves that we are deciding a live case or controversy, and because Article III jurisdiction exists under both interpretations of the statute, we pass on to the merits of the appeal before us.

III. Whether a case is Commenced

The question before us arises primarily from the interplay of two statutory sections of the Bankruptcy Code: 11 U.S.C. § 301 and 11 U.S.C. § 109(h). Section 301(a), part of the subchapter entitled "Commencement of a Case," reads as follows: "A voluntary case under a chapter of this title is commenced by the filing with the bankruptcy court of a petition under such chapter by an entity that may be a debtor under such chapter." Section 109, titled "Who may be a debtor," contains a list of requirements that must be satisfied before an entity or individual, as the case may be, is eligible for bankruptcy. As part of BAPCPA, Congress amended § 109 to add subsection (h). Pub. L. No. 109-8, § 106, 119 Stat. 23, 37 (2005). Subsection (h) begins as follows: "Subject to paragraphs (2) and (3), and notwithstanding any other provision of this section, an individual may not be a debtor under [the Bankruptcy Code] unless such individual has, during the 180-day period preceding the date of filing of the petition by such individual, received [credit counseling]." 11 U.S.C. § 109(h)(1). The remaining paragraphs provide exceptions for debtors who reside in areas where there is no such available credit counseling, for debtors who can certify that they have exigent circumstances and have made appropriate efforts to obtain counseling, and for those incapacitated, disabled, or on active military duty in a combat zone. Id. § 109(h)(2)-(4).

As the bankruptcy court's decision noted, these two provisions may be read to suggest that, since an individual "may not be a debtor" unless he has received credit counseling congruent with the requirements of § 109(h) and under § 301 he may not commence a case unless he "may be a debtor," a debtor who fails to obtain pre-petition credit counseling and yet files a bankruptcy petition has not actually commenced a case. In re Elmendorf, 345 B.R. at 497. Informed by this conclusion, the bankruptcy court reasoned further that striking the petition was the appropriate procedural method to dispose of the filing, rather than "dismiss[ing] the case" as provided for in 11 U.S.C. § 707.[5] Amicus argues for this interpretation on appeal; the Trustee contends instead that a case is commenced when an ineligible individual files for bankruptcy, and that the case must be dismissed.

An additional twist arises from the automatic stay provision. Section 362(a) of the Code states that "a petition filed under section 301, 302, or 303 of [the Bankruptcy Code] . . . operates as a stay." Section 362(c)(3)-(4), in turn, sets forth limitations on the automatic stay applicable to subsequent cases by the same petitioner. Under § 362(c)(3), where a "case of the debtor was pending within the preceding 1-year period but was dismissed," the automatic stay is limited to 30 days unless the debtor is able by clear and convincing evidence to rebut a presumption that the later case was not filed in good faith. Moreover, § 362(c)(4) states that "if 2 or more . . . cases of the debtor were pending within the previous year but were dismissed, . . . the stay . . . shall not go into effect upon the filing of the later case," and the debtor may obtain a stay only if he is able to demonstrate that the filing of the later case is in good faith. The bankruptcy court, interpreting the interplay among §§ 109(h), 301, and 362(a), concluded "that the automatic stay comes into existence only when a case is filed in accordance with §§ 301, 302, or 303 of the [Code]." In re Elmendorf, 345 B.R. at 498. Under this reading, when a petition is filed but no case is commenced, the automatic stay does not come into effect. Amicus urges us to reject this interpretation and instead find that the filing of the petition, not the commencing of a case, is sufficient to institute the automatic stay.

Of the bankruptcy and district courts to consider this statutory tangle so far, a majority have sided with the Trustee and found that debtors such as the ones in the case at bar should have their cases dismissed. See, e.g., In re Crawford, 420 B.R. 833, 838 & n.7 (Bankr. D.N.M. 2009) (collecting cases); In re Jones, 352 B.R. 813, 821 (Bankr. S.D. Tex. 2006) (same); In re Seaman, 340 B.R. 698, 703, 706 n.3 (Bankr. E.D.N.Y. 2006). Of the minority of courts that recognize the option of striking the petition of a debtor ineligible under § 109(h), some agree with the bankruptcy court in this case that such a petition "does not trigger the protections

[5] Section 707 provides that a bankruptcy court "may dismiss a case" for cause after notice and a hearing. 11 U.S.C. § 707(a).

of the automatic stay" under § 362(a), In re Elmendorf, 345 B.R. at 498-502. See, e.g., In re Salazar, 339 B.R. 622, 632-33 (Bankr. S.D. Tex. 2006). Finally, some courts have ruled in line with Amicus's conclusion that the petition's filing does trigger an automatic stay but does not commence a dismissible case when the petitioner is ineligible under § 109(h). See In re Thompson, 344 B.R. 899, 905-08 (Bankr. S.D. Ind. 2006), vacated as moot by 249 F. App'x 475 (7th Cir. 2007).

In constructing its argument, Amicus places emphasis on the language of § 301, which provides that a "voluntary case under a chapter of [the Bankruptcy Code] is commenced by the filing with the bankruptcy court of a petition under such chapter by an entity that may be a debtor under such chapter." 11 U.S.C. § 301(a) (emphasis added). Amicus suggests that the phrase "may be a debtor" should be interpreted as barring a debtor ineligible for bankruptcy under § 109(h) from commencing a "case." The Trustee, citing authority rejecting this position, counters that "the word 'may' as used in the § 301 of the Bankruptcy Code means 'might' or is meant to express a 'possibility.'" In re Tomco, 339 B.R. 145, 159 (Bankr. W.D. Pa. 2006). We conclude that § 301, as well as §§ 302 and 303 ("Voluntary cases," "Joint cases," and "Involuntary cases," respectively), define the prerequisites for relief under particular chapters of the Bankruptcy Code, rather than the existence in a jurisdictional sense of a voluntary, joint, or involuntary case. We thus reject the position of Amicus that a debtor ineligible for bankruptcy pursuant to § 109(h) does not commence a case by filing a petition pursuant to § 301.

Each of the three parallel sections implicated here contains limiting language indicating that it is referencing a particular type of case, whether voluntary, joint, or involuntary, that in turn is treated in a separate chapter of the Bankruptcy Code. Sections 301, 302 and 303 thus each provide that a case under a given chapter is commenced by the filing of a petition by a petitioner "that may be a debtor under such chapter." See 11 U.S.C. §§ 301-03 (emphasis added). This limiting language in all three sections suggests that the sections are not concerned with determining the existence of a "case" in the broader sense -- i.e., "[a] civil or criminal proceeding, action, suit, or controversy at law or in equity." BLACK'S LAW DICTIONARY 243 (9th ed. 2009) (defining "case"). Rather, they clarify that, when a debtor commences a case, the debtor is not eligible for relief under a particular chapter of the Bankruptcy Code unless it meets the requirements to be a debtor under that chapter. Other provisions in the Code place similar emphasis on the existence of chapter-specific requirements for debtors. See, e.g., 11 U.S.C. §§ 706(d), 1112(f), 1307(g) ("[A] case may not be converted to a case under another chapter of this title unless the debtor may be a debtor under such chapter."); see also H.R. Rep. 95-595, at 380, 406, 428 (Sept. 8, 1977), 1978 U.S.C.C.A.N. 5963, 6336, 6362, 6384 (providing that the limitations on conversion are meant to reinforce § 109).

The reading of § 301 proposed by Amicus, moreover, is inconsistent with other provisions of the Bankruptcy Code. While claiming that the interpretation of § 301 permitting dismissal "ignores the distinction between 'case' and 'petition,'" Amicus itself ignores the Bankruptcy Code's definition of petition: "The term 'petition' means petition filed under section 301, 302, 303, or 304 of this title, as the case may be, commencing a case under this title." 11 U.S.C. § 101(42) (emphasis added). Thus, a petition filed under §§ 301, 302, or 303 both "operates as a stay," id. § 362(a), and commences a bankruptcy case, id. § 101(42). See, e.g., Michael Newman, Comment, BAPCPA's New Section 109(h) Credit Counseling Requirement: Is It Having the Effect Congress Intended?, 2007 UTAH

L. REV. 489, 511. And while Amicus's theory that the automatic stay may come into effect upon the filing of a petition, even though a case is not commenced, is superficially plausible pursuant to the language of § 362(a) (providing that "a petition filed under section 301, 302, or 303 . . . operates as a stay"), this theory falls apart when one attempts to determine the date that such a stay terminates. Under § 362(c)(2), most actions remain stayed under § 362(a) "until the earliest of (A) the time the case is closed; (B) the time the case is dismissed; or (C) if the case is a case under chapter 7 of this title concerning an individual or a case under chapter 9, 11, 12, or 13 of this title, the time a discharge is granted or denied." 11 U.S.C. § 362(c)(2) (emphasis added). We determine, therefore, that although an individual may be ineligible to be a debtor under the Bankruptcy Code for failure to satisfy the strictures of § 109(h), the language of § 301 does not bar that debtor from commencing a case by filing a petition; it only bars the case from being maintained as a proper voluntary case under the chapter specified in the petition.

Although our conclusion in this respect comes into conflict with the reasoning in this Court's decision in In re BDC 56 LLC, 330 F.3d 111 (2d Cir. 2003), which held that the eligibility requirements of § 303 were jurisdictional in nature, we conclude that as a result of recent Supreme Court precedent, that case is no longer good law. Section 303 provides, in relevant part, as follows:

> (a) An involuntary case may be commenced . . . only against a person, except a farmer . . . that may be a debtor under the chapter under which such case is commenced.
>
> (b) An involuntary case against a person is commenced by the filing with the bankruptcy court of a petition . . . by three or more entities, each of which is either a holder of a claim against such person that is not contingent as to liability or the subject of a bona fide dispute as to liability or amount . . . .
>
> (c) After the filing of a petition under this section but before the case is dismissed or relief is ordered, a creditor . . . may join in the petition with the same effect as if such joining creditor were a petitioning creditor under subsection (b) of this section.
>
> . . .
>
> (h) If the petition is not timely controverted, the court shall order 16 relief against the debtor in an involuntary case under the chapter 17 under which the petition was filed. . . .
>
> . . .
>
> (j) Only after notice to all creditors and a hearing may the court dismiss a petition filed under this section -- (1) on the motion of a petitioner; (2) on consent of all petitioners and the debtor; or (3) for want of prosecution.

11 U.S.C. § 303. As discussed above, under the interpretation we grant to the language "may be a debtor under the chapter under which such case is commenced," a case is commenced under § 303 even if the debtor is ineligible by virtue of, for example, being a farmer. Similarly, the ineligibility of creditors under the restrictions in § 303(b) does not prevent the case from being commenced. This reading is supported, moreover, by the provisions of § 303(c), (h), and (j). Under § 303(c), a creditor may join in the petition after it is filed -- before the case is dismissed -- with the effect being as if the creditor had been part of the initial filing. Were there no case in existence because of an insufficiency of eligible creditors at the outset, it would be impossible for new creditors to join it by joining the petition. Moreover, § 303(h) and (j) provide for the bankruptcy court to order relief or dismiss a case based on whether debtors and creditors take given actions. Surely relief cannot be so granted, or the matter not dismissed in the absence of a motion to do so, if a case did not exist in the

first place.

Subject matter jurisdiction under title 11 proceedings in the bankruptcy courts is provided by 28 U.S.C. § 1334(a), which states that, with some given exceptions, "the district courts shall have original and exclusive jurisdiction of all cases under title 11." District courts may, under 28 U.S.C. § 157(a), "provide that any or all cases under title 11 . . . shall be referred to the bankruptcy judges for the district." The most straightforward reading of these provisions is that if a case exists under title 11, the district court (and the bankruptcy court, if so invoked by § 157(a)) has jurisdiction over it. The contrapositive of this statement, then, is also true: if the court has no jurisdiction, then there is no case under the Bankruptcy Code. In In re BDC 55 LLC, we stated:

> At least one circuit . . . has held that the requirement that a petitioning creditor's claim not be subject to a bona fide dispute[, found in § 303(b),] is not jurisdictional, but is "an element that must be established to sustain an involuntary proceeding."
>
> We believe the more sound view is that the requirement is subject matter jurisdictional, and now so hold. Whether an alleged debtor is properly before the bankruptcy court in an involuntary case is a threshold determination that should be made at the earliest possible stage of the proceedings. One of the requirements to bringing such a petition is that the petitioning creditors' claims are free from bona fide dispute. Any creditor wishing to invoke the bankruptcy court's jurisdiction in an involuntary case should be required to demonstrate at the earliest practicable point that its petition satisfies this requirement. Otherwise, creditors could, on the basis of relatively untested claims, haul a solvent debtor with whom they have legitimate disputes into bankruptcy court and force it to defend an involuntary proceeding while the bankruptcy court leaves for a later merits determination whether the debtor is even properly before it.

330 F.3d at 118-19 (quoting In re Rubin, 769 F.2d 611, 615 (9th Cir. 1985)) (internal citations and footnote omitted). This holding, then, necessarily indicates that if the requirements of § 303 are not met, no case exists -- nor, presumably, was commenced -- under title 11.

This panel is "bound by the decisions of prior panels until such time as they are overruled either by an en banc panel of our Court or by the Supreme Court." United States v. Wilkerson, 361 F.3d 717, 732 (2d Cir. 2004). However, if "there has been an intervening Supreme Court decision that casts doubt on our controlling precedent," one panel of this Court may overrule a prior decision of another panel. Gelman v. Ashcroft, 372 F.3d 495, 499 (2d Cir. 2004) (quoting Union of Needletrades, Indus. & Textile Employees v. U. S. I.N.S., 336 F.3d 200, 210 (2d Cir. 2003)) (internal quotation marks omitted). The intervening decision need not address the precise issue decided by the panel for this exception to apply. Wojchowski v. Daines, 498 F.3d 99, 106 (2d Cir. 2007).[6] Since our holding in In re BDC 56 LLC, the Supreme Court has clarified the distinction between "two sometimes confused or conflated concepts: federal-court 'subject-matter' jurisdiction over a controversy; and the essential ingredients of a federal claim for relief." Arbaugh v. Y&H Corp., 546 U.S. 500, 503 (2006). In a unanimous decision, the Court held that a clear statement by Congress was required to construe a

---

[6] In addition, prior to filing this opinion has been circulated to all the judges of this Court. See Shipping Corp. of India Ltd. v. Jaldhi Overseas Pte Ltd., 585 F.3d 58, 67 & n.9 (2d Cir. 2009); United States v. Crosby, 397 F.3d 103, 105 n.1 (2d Cir. 2005).

threshold limitation on the scope of a statute as jurisdictional. Id. at 515-16. "But when Congress does not rank a statutory limitation on coverage as jurisdictional, courts should treat the restriction as nonjurisdictional in character." Id. at 516. Therefore, a limitation on Title VII claims based on whether the defendant-employer had a particular number of employees was nonjurisdictional because the limitation "does not speak in jurisdictional terms or refer in any way to the jurisdiction of the district courts," the statute contains an express jurisdictional provision in a different portion from the limitation, there was no evidence in the statutory text that Congress intended the requirement to be sua sponte monitored by the courts, and consideration of the limitation after a judgment on the merits would be unfair and wasteful. Id. at 514-16; see also In re Trusted Net Media Holdings, LLC, 550 F.3d 1035, 1043 (11th Cir. 2008). This "readily administrable bright line," Arbaugh, 546 U.S. at 516, now guides our consideration of whether § 303 contains restrictions on the bankruptcy court's jurisdiction.

We find that, in light of Arbaugh, In re BDC 56 LLC can no longer be considered good law on this point. As the Eleventh Circuit noted in evaluating the same question, § 303 "contains no explicit reference to its requirements being jurisdictional in nature and never uses the word 'jurisdiction.'" In re Trusted Net Media Holdings, LLC, 550 F.3d at 1043.[7] Nor does the text of the statute suggest that the bankruptcy court should sua sponte raise the issue of whether the requirements of § 303 are satisfied; in fact, § 303(h) provides the opposite, since the bankruptcy court should order relief if the petition is not timely controverted. Moreover, the Bankruptcy Code is governed by a separate jurisdictional provision, 28 U.S.C. § 1344, which contains other restrictions and exclusions. In sum, the restrictions of § 303 fall decisively on the nonjurisdictional side of Arbaugh's bright line.

Similarly, we find that the restrictions of § 301 and § 109(h) are not jurisdictional, but rather elements that must be established to sustain a voluntary bankruptcy proceeding. Restricting whether an individual may be a debtor either under the Bankruptcy Code in general or under a given chapter does not speak in jurisdictional terms or invoke the jurisdiction of the district court, delineated in 28 U.S.C. § 1344 as discussed above. Certainly, consideration of these limitations after other decisions on the merits have taken place would be wasteful and unfair; because bankruptcy is a swift-moving process involving multiple parties, "creditors and other parties in interest have a considerable interest in being able to rely on the existence of a case, the bankruptcy court's jurisdiction, and the validity of actions taken in the case" in order to facilitate asset-preserving transactions. In re Ross, 338 B.R. 134, 140 (Bankr. N.D. Ga. 2006). This decision, moreover, is in line with pre-BAPCPA decisions from our sister circuits and in this circuit finding that other provisions of § 109 are not jurisdictional. See, e.g., Rudd v. Laughlin, 866 F.2d 1040, 1042 (8th Cir. 1989) ("Nor do we believe that 11 U.S.C. § 109 is meant to restrict the jurisdiction granted under [28 U.S.C. §§ 1334, 157]."); In re Phillips, 844 F.2d 230, 235 n.2 (5th Cir. 1988) (finding § 109(g) nonjurisdictional); In re Flores, 291 B.R. 44, 52-53 (Bankr. S.D.N.Y. 2003) (same), superseded by BAPCPA, Pub. L. No. 109-8, § 303(b), 119 Stat. at 78.

[7] The Fifth and Eighth Circuits held that the requirements of § 303(a) were not jurisdictional pre-Arbaugh; the Ninth Circuit similarly so held for § 303(b). See In re Marlar, 432 F.3d 813, 814-15 (8th Cir. 2005) (per curiam); In re McCloy, 296 F.3d 370, 375 (5th Cir. 2002); In re Rubin, 769 F.2d 611, 615 (9th Cir. 1985).

Some additional support for our conclusion that a case has been commenced when debtors ineligible for relief under § 109(h) file a bankruptcy petition may be gleaned from cases interpreting 11 U.S.C. § 342(b), which provides that "[b]efore the commencement of a case under this title by an individual whose debts are primarily consumer debts, the clerk shall give to such individual written notice containing . . . a brief description of" bankruptcy proceedings, credit counseling services, and legal consequences from fraudulent findings. If we were to interpret the language regarding commencement of a case in this section as the bankruptcy court did the language of § 301 and § 109(h), the provision would suggest that a case is not commenced if the would-be debtor is not given the statutorily required notice. Courts considering the question have not so held. See, e.g., In re Guth, No. 02-02121, WL 31941460, at (Bankr. D. Idaho Nov. 8, 2002); In re Bryant, 51 B.R. 729, 731-32 (Bankr. N.D. Miss. 1985).

IV. Whether the Automatic Stay is Triggered

Having determined that a case is commenced, we turn to the question whether the automatic stay takes effect when a petition is filed by a debtor ineligible under § 109(h). We conclude that it does. Section 362, which outlines the basic commencement, effect, and termination of the automatic stay, provides significant indications to that effect. As an initial matter, the section contains language suggesting that the stay accompanies a commenced case:

> [A] petition filed under section 301, 302, or 303 of this title . . . operates as a stay . . . of -- (1) the commencement or continuation . . . [of an] action or proceeding against the debtor that was or could have been commenced before the commencement of the case under this title, or to recover a claim against the debtor that arose before the commencement of the case under this title; (2) the enforcement, against the debtor . . . , of a judgment obtained before the commencement of the case under this title.

11 U.S.C. § 362(a). Section 362(b) lists circumstances under which the filing of a petition does not operate as a stay, but the debtor's ineligibility is not among them. Moreover, none of the mechanisms outlined in the remainder of the statute for confirming the existence of a stay or for granting relief from one address anything related to the ineligibility of a debtor.

In addition, the bankruptcy court's interpretation of § 362 renders a nullity BAPCPA's enactment of § 362(b)(21)(A). Section 362(b)(21)(A) provides that certain actions against real property are not stayed when "the debtor is ineligible under section 109(g) to be a debtor in a case under this title."[8] As In re

[8] Section 109(g) provides as follows:

> Notwithstanding any other provision of this section, no individual or family farmer may be a debtor under this title who has been a debtor in a case pending under this title at any time in the preceding 180 days if--
>
> (1) the case was dismissed by the court for willful failure of the debtor to abide by orders of the court, or to appear before the court in proper prosecution of the case; or
>
> (2) the debtor requested and obtained the voluntary dismissal of the case following the filing of a request for relief from the automatic stay provided by section 362 [**41] of this title.

Ross notes, if an action by a person ineligible under § 109(g) were "void ab initio and did not result in an automatic stay under existing law, such an amendment would not have been necessary." 338 B.R. at 139; see also In re Racette, 343 B.R. 200, 203 (Bankr. E.D. Wis. 2006). As discussed above, no such exception is provided for debtors ineligible under § 109(h), which leads us to the conclusion that the automatic stay commences in such cases. The bankruptcy court purported to distinguish § 109(h) from § 109(g) by characterizing ineligibility under the latter provision as a failure that may be cured or "waived" by the court, rendering it possible that the automatic stay could go into effect notwithstanding such a failure -- and thus conceivable that a provision specifying circumstances in which it should not would be necessary. See In re Elmendorf, 345 B.R. at 499-500. We agree with the Trustee that this is not a tenable distinction. The wording of § 109(g) is no less mandatory that the wording of § 109(h). Moreover, even assuming that the legislative history cited by the bankruptcy court for its description of § 109(g) is properly considered, it does not support the conclusion that the requirements of the subsection are curable.

Amicus and the Trustee both correctly observe that our decision in In re Casse, 198 F.3d 327 (2d Cir. 1999), does not undermine the conclusion that an ineligible debtor's petition gives rise to an automatic stay. Under separate but analogous circumstances, Casse affirmed the bankruptcy court's dismissal of a case "nunc pro tunc" to the date of filing and approved of annulling a stay per § 362(d), id. at 332, 342, rulings that indicate Casse recognized the stay as having initially gone into effect. See Ross, 338 B.R. at 137 n.4; In re Flores, 291 B.R. at 57-58; Robert Lefkowitz, Note, The Filing of a Bankruptcy Petition in Violation of 11 U.S.C. § 109(g): Does It Invoke the Automatic Stay?, 26 CARDOZO L. REV. 297, 309 (2004).

Finally, we note that having the automatic stay commence even when a debtor fails to satisfy the credit-counseling requirements both fits into the overall purpose and framework of the stay and ensures that eligible debtors receive protection from the bankruptcy system. The automatic stay serves a number of purposes: "providing debtors with a fresh start, protecting the assets of the estate, and allowing the bankruptcy court to centralize disputes concerning the estate." MBNA Am. Bank, N.A. v. Hill, 436 F.3d 104, 109 (2d Cir. 2006). Much of the value of the stay is in the clarity of its implementation; once a debtor files for bankruptcy and the stay is in effect, creditors must cease their individual attempts to gain repayment and operate only through the bankruptcy court. This centralization ensures a fair distribution of assets if the debtor proceeds through bankruptcy. If it were unclear whether the stay was in place immediately following a debtor's filing for bankruptcy, creditors would likely continue their collection efforts "in hopes that the bankruptcy court would find no merit in the debtor's petition. Thus, rather than providing the debtor with automatic breathing space, the Code would pressure the debtor to file correctly in the first instance or risk losing the protections of Title 11 due to the actions of several unscrupulous creditors." Shaw v. Ehrlich, 294 B.R. 260, 268 (Bankr. W.D. Va. 2003). Even a debtor who filed correctly might face challenges outside the bankruptcy court from particularly aggressive creditors hoping that a filing correct on its face had an underlying flaw that would redound to their advantage. Construing a debtor's ineligibility pursuant to § 109(h) as creating an exception to the automatic stay provision, therefore, is a tenuous proposition given the statutory framework provided by Congress. Our interpretation, in contrast, we believe supports and furthers that framework.

V. Whether the Bankruptcy Court Must Dismiss the Cases

Having concluded that no case had commenced and no automatic stay had been triggered in the cases of the three debtors here, the bankruptcy court chose as the appropriate method of disposing of the matters to exercise its equitable powers under 11 U.S.C. § 105(a) and strike the debtors' petitions. See In re Elmendorf, 345 B.R. at 503-05. The Trustee urges us to determine that the only proper method of disposing of the matter of a debtor ineligible under § 109(h) is dismissal. At this time, we need not, and do not, determine what actions the bankruptcy court may have taken on the petitions. Rather, we remand to the bankruptcy court for it to consider in the first instance the ramifications of our determination in the circumstances presented here that cases have commenced. The bankruptcy court's determination that its equitable powers included striking the petitions was premised on the belief that there were no cases to dismiss. While we note that we are unaware of any case similar to this one in which a court has determined that a case has commenced and yet taken an action other than dismissal, the bankruptcy court did not address whether other actions, including striking a petition, might be appropriate in these circumstances. We thus conclude that this is a question for the bankruptcy court to address initially. See In re Morgan, 182 F.3d 775, 780 (11th Cir. 1999) ("Since the applicability and use of § 105(a) is a decision that is typically left to the bankruptcy court, we leave the decision to the bankruptcy court in this case.").

CONCLUSION

For all of the foregoing reasons, the judgment of the district court is VACATED and the case is REMANDED to the district court with instructions to remand to the bankruptcy court for further proceedings consistent with this opinion. We thank amicus counsel, Sanford I. Weisburst and William B. Adams of Quinn Emanuel Urquhart & Sullivan, LLP, for their helpful brief and oral argument.

Notes and Questions

1. The reason a debtor files for bankruptcy is because something bad is about to happen. When a debtor files, the automatic stay, 11 U.S.C. §362(a), prevents virtually any sort of creditor action except filing a claim or motions in the bankruptcy court. Therefore, the court's insinuation that an automatic stay does arise in consumer cases (in spite of no credit counseling) is of the utmost importance.

Typically, a result of violating the automatic stay is that the legal actiion wrongly taken by a creditor is considered a nullity. David Gray Carlson, Bankruptcy's Acephalous Moment: Postpetition Transfers Under the Bankruptcy Code, 21 EMORY BANKR. DEV. J. 113, 128-31 (2004). So a mortgage foreclosure procedure in violation of the automatic stay would have to be re-done once the automatic stay has lapsed. In re Brown, 342 B.R. 248 (Bankr. D. Md. 2006).

IN RE HOSHAN

2008 U.S. Dist. LEXIS 1139 (E.D. Pa. January 28, 2008)

MCLAUGHLIN, J.

Appellant Rehap Hoshan appeals from the bankruptcy court's dismissal of her chapter 13 bankruptcy petition on April 23, 2007, its denial of her application to vacate the dismissal order on May 3, 2007, and its denial of her motion for reconsideration on June 4, 2007 . . . .

The issue on appeal is whether the bankruptcy court has abused its discretion in dismissing the appellant's petition and denying her motion for reconsideration. The Court concludes that the bankruptcy court has not abused its discretion and will affirm the bankruptcy court's decision.

Under the Bankruptcy Abuse Prevention and Consumer Protection Act of 2005 ("BAPCA"), an individual debtor filing for bankruptcy under chapter 13 must receive credit counseling from an approved agency during the 180 days before she files her petition. 11 U.S.C. § 109(h)(1) (2006). To demonstrate compliance with this new requirement, a debtor must file with her petition a certificate identifying the agency, describing the services provided, and including a copy of any debt repayment plan. Id. § 521(b).

There are three exemptions to this requirement: First, those debtors who live in a district where the United States trustee or bankruptcy administrator determines that the nonprofit agencies are not reasonably able to provide adequate services are exempt. Id. § 109(h)(2). Second, a debtor can file for an exemption describing exigent circumstances and a failed request for counseling. Id. § 109(h)(3). Third, there is an exemption for those who are incapacitated, disabled, or on active military duty. Id. § 109(h)(4).

The appellant filed her petition on March 30, 2007, without attaching the credit counseling certification, bankruptcy schedules (except for Schedule D), statement of financial affairs, statement of current monthly income, or her proposed chapter 13 plan. She did not request an exigent circumstances exemption or an extension. That same day, the bankruptcy court issued an order informing the appellant of the filing defects and instructing her to provide some of the required documents by April 6, 2007, and other required documents by April 14, 2007. On April 23, 2007, when none of the documents had arrived, the court dismissed the case. Between April 25, 2007, and April 30, 2007, the appellant filed the required documents . . .

On April 30, 2007, the appellant filed an "Application to Reinstate Chapter 13 Petition," explaining that she had seven children at home, which made it difficult to get her documents in order. The bankruptcy court denied her application on May 3, 2007, pointing out that she had neither timely filed her documents nor filed for an extension. Bankr. Mem. at 6.

On May 14, 2007, the appellant filed a Motion for Reconsideration, arguing that her delay in filing the required documents should not be cause for dismissal. She said that her husband had been injured in a fall and needed extra help at the time when she should have sought an extension. The bankruptcy court denied the appellant's motion on June 4, 2007, pointing out that the documents belatedly filed were still defective: the appellant had never filed her creditor mailing matrix and her credit counseling certificate showed that she received counseling on April 3, 2007, after she filed her bankruptcy petition, rather than before she filed the petition, as required by § 109(h)(1).

The appellant filed her appeal with this Court on October 12, 2007. She argues that the bankruptcy court has abused its discretion in dismissing her bankruptcy petition and denying her motions. She points to Bankruptcy Rule 9006(b)(1), which allows a court discretion to allow late filing where failure to timely file "was the result of excusable neglect" and to Pioneer Inv. Servs. Co. v. Brunswick Assocs. Ltd. P'ship, 507 U.S. 380, 388 (1993), which holds that "excusable neglect" includes inadvertence and mistake, not just circumstances beyond a party's control. The appellant contends that her family situation caused her to miss the filing deadlines and that her lateness should have been considered excusable neglect by the bankruptcy court.

The appellant makes a persuasive case that her situation could have excused her from timely filing all of her documents. See In re Schultz, 254 B.R. 149, 154 (B.A.P. 6th Cir. 2000) (holding that the failure of an attorney to timely file bankruptcy papers because his wife was seriously ill was due to excusable neglect). The real issue in this case, however, is not the late filing. The real issue is that the appellant did not receive credit counseling before she filed her bankruptcy petition on March 30, 2007, as required under § 109(h)(1).

The credit counseling requirement is not jurisdictional. Montgomery v. Ryan, 37 F.3d 413, 415 n.5 (8th Cir. 1994) ("Section 109 determines eligibility for bankruptcy relief, not jurisdiction."). Most courts have concluded that dismissal is mandated when a debtor has not complied with the credit counseling requirements. See In re Hedquist, 342 B.R. 295, 301 (B.A.P. 8th Cir. 2006); In re Ruckdaschel, 364 B.R. 724, 730 (Bankr. D. Idaho 2007); In re Seaman, 340 B.R. 698, 706 (Bankr. E.D.N.Y. 2006); In re Wallace, 338 B.R. 399, 401 (Bankr. E.D. Ark. 2006); In re Ross, 338 B.R. 134 (Bankr. N.D. Ga. 2006).

Some courts have waived the credit counseling requirements to avoid manifest injustice. See In re Manalad, 360 B.R. 288, 296 (Bankr. C.D. Cal. 2007) (debtor's counsel mistakenly advised him that his non-consumer debts were not subject to the requirements); In re Vollmer, 2007 Bankr. LEXIS 587, 2007 WL 541747 (Bankr. E.D. Va. 2007) (debtor was incarcerated at the time he filed his petition and had no access to a credit counselor); In re Petit-Louis, 344 B.R. 696 (Bankr. S.D. Fla. 2006) (debtor spoke only Creole and no Creole-speaking credit counselor was available); In re Bricksin, 346 B.R. 497 (Bankr. N.D. Cal. 2006) (debtors had set up a payment plan with a credit counseling agency and had been making payments but failed to file the certificate with their bankruptcy petition).

The Court is sympathetic to the challenges the appellant faces as the mother of seven children and as the primary caretaker for her injured husband. The law is clear, however, that a debtor must get credit counseling before filing the bankruptcy petition. If a debtor faces exigent circumstances and cannot comply with the requirements, she may request a waiver. The appellant did not get credit counseling until after she had filed her petition, and she did not seek an exigent circumstances waiver. Her family situation, while difficult, does not rise to the level of those cases in which courts avoid manifest injustice by waiving the credit counseling requirements.

The bankruptcy court did not abuse its discretion when it dismissed the appellant's bankruptcy petition and denied her motion for reconsideration on the ground that she had not complied with the credit counseling requirements in § 109(h). . .

Notes and Questions

1. Which of these cases must be dismissed?

(a) D completes credit counsel on January 2, 2008. D files for bankruptcy 182 days later. Must the case be dismissed? Yes. §109(h)(1) requires receipt of credit counseling within 180 days of bankruptcy. In re Williams, 359 B.R. 590 (Bankr. E.D.N.Y. 2006); In re Jones, 352 B.R. 813 (Bankr. S.D. Tex. 2006) (counseling was 190 days before the bankruptcy petition).

(b) D had credit counseling prior to the 180 day period and chose a credit management agreement, with which D was complying during the 180-day period prior to bankruptcy. Must the case be dismissed? No. D was within the spirit of the law. In re Bricksin, 346 B.R. 497 (Bankr. N.D. Cal. 2006).

(c) D obtained credit counseling, but the agency was not qualified to issue a certificate because it was not an authorized providor. D filed a bankruptcy petition and attended credit counseling four days later. Must the case be dismissed? No. In re Hess, 347 B.R. 489 (Bankr. D. Vt. 2006).

(d) D obtains credit counseling in the morning and files for bankruptcy in the afternoon. Has D complied with §109(h)(1)? Courts differ. Compare In re Gossett, 369 B.R. 361 (Bankr. N.D. Ill. 2007) (credit counseling may not occur the same day as bankruptcy) with In re Barbaran, 365 B.R. 333 (Bankr. D.D.C. 2007). These courts disagree on the interpretation of this language from §109(h)(1): "an individual may not be a debtor under this title unless the individual has, during the 180-day period preceding the date of filing of the petition by such individual, received [credit counseling]" (emphasis added).

(e) In a joint case, the husband received credit counseling and the wife did not. Must the wife be dismissed from bankruptcy? Yes. In re Piontek, 346 B.R. 126 (Bankr. W.D. Pa. 2006).

2. The bankruptcy courts have been unable to resist the temptation to editorialize about the credit counseling requirement in BAPCPA. In In re Raymond, 2006 Bankr. LEXIS 604 (Bankr. D.N.H., April 12, 2006), the court remarked:

> It is a mystery to the Court why Congress granted the Court the authority to waive all filing fees for persons such as the Filer, but not waive the credit counseling requirement. The Filer qualified for a waiver of fees which means the Court and the chapter 7 trustee would have received no payment for the processing of the Filer's bankruptcy case. However, the credit counseling agency would still receive payment for a counseling session.[1] Exactly what form of credit counseling could be useful, or necessary, to a person who qualifies for a waiver of fees under 28 U.S.C. § 1930(f) is even more of a mystery. The rationale for many of the provisions in BAPCPA, the language used in those provisions, and the coordination among them are likely to remain an enigma for a long time.

Id. at *3. And in In re Elmendorf, 345 B.R. 486 (Bankr. S.D.N.Y. 2006), rev'd sub nom. Adams v. Zarnel (In re Zarnel), 619 F.3d 156 (2d Cir. 2010), the court wrote:

> In this opinion, the Court again determines the proper means of disposing of a bankruptcy petition filed by a debtor who has not undergone the requisite credit briefing required by Section 109(h) of the Bankruptcy Abuse Prevention and Consumer Protection Act of 2005 (hereinafter "BAPCPA"). One of the watermark provisions of this much heralded legislation, which took several years to enact, is the credit counseling requirement of 11 U.S.C. § 109(h). Credit counseling was a significant aspect of the new bankruptcy legislation because the requirement was intended to provide debtors with education as to all of their options when experiencing financial difficulty, before a resort to bankruptcy protection was necessary. Congress envisioned that credit counseling would provide individuals with the skills necessary to lead financially responsible lives. This facially well-intentioned[2] section of the BAPCPA has evolved into an expensive, draconian gate-keeping requirement that has prevented many deserving individuals from qualifying for bankruptcy relief. The credit counseling requirement has not proven to be of assistance to debtors in seeking relief outside of the bankruptcy context, as shown by a recent survey[3] of credit counseling agencies performed by the National Association of

---

[1] The Court is aware that credit counseling agencies are required to provide free credit counseling services to "qualified" persons. However, anecdotal information indicates that such free credit counseling services are difficult and time consuming to obtain, if they are available at all.

[2] As Clare Boothe Luce is quoted to have remarked, "No good deed goes unpunished."

[3] See generally Press Release, National Association of Consumer Bankruptcy Attorneys, STUDY: CONTROVERSIAL BANKRUPTCY LAW REFORMS NOT WORKING? 97 PERCENT UNABLE TO REPAY DEBTS, MOST PUSHED TO BRINK BY CRISIS -- NACBA Analysis of More

> Consumer Bankruptcy Attorneys. That study determined that of 66,335 consumers served by the participating credit counseling agencies, a paltry 3.3 percent qualified for alternative (i.e. non-bankruptcy) debt management treatment. Additionally, many of these same credit-counseling agencies have come under fire for fraudulent practices; some have lost their not-for-profit status.[4] The requirement that a debtor seek "credit counseling" before being eligible for bankruptcy relief is quickly becoming the most outrageous fleecing of consumer debtors in this Court's memory -- a perfunctory exercise with little or no substance which leaves a putative debtor $50-$100 the poorer. The Court has seen at least one example of a "Client Action Plan" provided to a consumer debtor before this Court. See In re Anthony Rios, Case No. 05-55002, ECF Docket No. 11. The Client Action Plan proposed in that case is repetitive, advising the debtor twice to track expenses, and tends to state the obvious, such as recommending that debtor seek a job making higher wages, and referring debtor to the local library for resources on bankruptcy.

Id. at 489.

3. In one of the earliest cases on credit counseling, a sophisticated individual proprietor argued that §109(h) violates the equal protection clause of the Fifth Amendment, in that the debtor could have organized an LLC or partnership, in which case there would be no individual debtor to whom §109(h). The court, however, found a rational basis for the discrimination and dismissed the debtor's bankruptcy, in spite of his sophistication. In re Watson, 332 B.R. 740 (Bankr. E.D. Va. 2005).

4. Suppose D has not received credit counseling and no party in interest objects? Is there a bankruptcy case? In Mendez v. Salven (In re Mendez), 367 B.R. 109 (Bankr. 9th Cir. 2007), the court held yes. In Mendez, neither the creditor nor the trustee moved to dismiss. Rather, D regretted the bankruptcy petition (because she feared losing her house) and sought to dismiss because she did not receive credit counseling. The court ruled that credit counseling is not "jurisdictional" and that D had waived credit counseling by filing the bankruptcy petition without it. Accord, In re Parker, 351 B.R. 790 (Bankr. N.D. Ga. 2006).

5. Although the vast majority of bankruptcy cases are commenced by a voluntary petition filed by the debtor, a debtor can be placed into bankruptcy by the creditors pursuant to Bankruptcy Code § 303. Suppose a debtor is subject to an involuntary petition. She moves to dismiss because she has not had credit counseling. May the case proceed? Although the plain meaning of §109(h)(1) does not distinguish between voluntary and involuntary cases, courts have permitted the involuntary proceeding in the absence of credit counseling. In re Allen, 378 B.R. 151, 153 (Bankr. N.D. Tex. 2007) ("interpreting this provision as requiring that an involuntary debtor comply with section 109(h)(1) would lead to an absurd result").

6. D is facing a foreclosure sale at 1 p.m. D begins credit counseling at 12:10 p.m. She completed it at 1:36 p.m. After speaking to D at 12:10, D's attorney files a bankruptcy petition at 12:28 p.m. Can the attorney be sanctioned for filing frivolous papers under bankruptcy's version of Rule 11? In re Bolling, 2009 Bankr. LEXIS 340 (Bankr. D.D.C. February 6. 2009) (yes).

6. The honor of the first debtors to be booted from bankruptcy for failure to obtain credit counseling goes to John and Linda Booth, residents of northern Florida, who filed for bankruptcy on October 20, 2005, three days after BAPCPA went effective. By October 20, they were out of court. In re Booth, 2006 Bankr. LEXIS 2769 (Bankr. N.D. Fla., October 25, 2005).

---

than 60,000 Consumers Processed Under New Law Asks: "Where Are the Deadbeats" Congress Expected to Find and Stop With Onerous Rule Changes? (Feb. 22, 2006) (available at http://nacba.com/news/releases/022206.php) (last visited June 30, 2006) (quoting Senatorial comments regarding fiscal irresponsibility as a major cause of bankruptcy filings).

[4] In May, 2006, the Internal Revenue Service revoked the tax exempt status held by the nation's largest educational credit counseling services, representing 41 % of the $1 billion credit counseling industry, after IRS audits revealed that the credit counseling agencies "... exist mainly to prey on debt-ridden customers." I.R.S. Ends Tax Exempt Status For Some Credit Counselors, N.Y. Times, May 16, 2006, at C6. It is into the hands of "predators" such as these that the consumer debtor has been entrusted before resort to bankruptcy protection may be had. As the filing statistics show bankruptcy is still available -- but now the credit counseling agencies are guaranteed a piece of the action. Perhaps Congress should have taken a closer look at this industry before placing it between a debtor and the succor of the federal bankruptcy court.

IN RE ROMERO

349 B.R. 616 (Bankr. N.D. Cal. 2006)

THOMAS E. CARLSON, J.

This case turns upon what constitutes "exigent circumstances" permitting a debtor to file for bankruptcy relief before obtaining credit counseling. I determine that such circumstances generally exist where the debtor faces serious and immediate creditor action before the debtor can obtain credit counseling. The wage garnishment faced by Debtors in this case qualifies under this standard.

FACTS

Ana and Javier Romero ("Debtors") filed a chapter 7 bankruptcy petition on July 10, 2006. Concurrently with their petition, Debtors filed a request for a temporary waiver of the prepetition credit counseling requirement (the "Certification"). The Certification states under penalty of perjury that Javier was the sole wage earner for the family, and that he faced imminent garnishment of his wages. Debtors certified that they needed to file bankruptcy immediately, prior to the wage garnishment taking effect, and that they tried to get credit counseling before filing their bankruptcy petition but were unable to do so.

On July 13, 2006, the court filed an Order Re Debtors' 109(h) Exigent Circumstances Declaration (the "Order"). The Order gave Debtors until August 9, 2006 to file a sworn declaration as to whether Debtors requested prepetition credit counseling services from an approved agency but were unable to obtain such services during the five-day period beginning on the date of their request.

On July 14, 2006, Debtors obtained credit counseling from Money Management Int'l Inc. ("Money Management"), an agency approved to provide such counseling in this district. On July 17, 2006, the United States Trustee filed her Motion to Dismiss Under Section 109(h). On the same day, Debtors filed proof of having completed the credit counseling.

On July 24, 2006, Debtors filed an additional sworn declaration (the "Supplemental Certification") regarding their prepetition efforts to obtain credit counseling. The Supplemental Certification states that on July 7, 2006, three days prior to the petition date, Debtors telephoned Money Management to obtain the required prepetition counseling services, but that Debtors were unable to obtain the required counseling until July 14, seven days after their request.

At the hearing on the Motion to Dismiss, the United States Trustee argued that the Supplemental Certification did not state exigent circumstances because Debtors would have had adequate prior notice of the wage garnishment.

DISCUSSION

Bankruptcy Code section 109(h)(1) conditions an individual debtor's eligibility for bankruptcy relief on obtaining credit counseling from an approved agency before filing. If a debtor files a bankruptcy petition without obtaining such counseling, the case must be dismissed unless the debtor obtains a temporary or permanent waiver of the credit counseling requirement. See 11 U.S.C. § 109(h). To obtain a temporary waiver, the debtor must submit to the court a certification that satisfies the following conditions: (1) it must describe "exigent circumstances" meriting a short-term exemption; (2) it must state that the debtor requested credit counseling services from an approved agency, but was unable to obtain the services during the five-day period beginning on the date the debtor made the request; and (3) it must be satisfactory to the court. 11 U.S.C. § 109(h)(3)(A). The Bankruptcy Code does not define exigent circumstances, and courts have not agreed upon an interpretation.

One line of cases concludes that the exigent circumstances standard is a high one that is generally not satisfied when the debtor has sufficient advance knowledge of the threatened creditor action to obtain the credit counseling before the creditor action takes effect. See, e.g., In re DiPinto, 336 B.R. 693 (Bankr. E.D. Pa. 2006) (debtor's imminent loss of home to foreclosure scheduled to occur on petition date not exigent circumstances); In re Anderson, 2006 Bankr. LEXIS 136, 2006 WL 314539, at *2 (Bankr. N.D. Iowa Feb. 6, 2006) (existing wage garnishment of husband's income plus wife's recent loss of employment not exigent circumstances); In re Rodriguez, 336 B.R. 462, 474-76 (Bankr. D. Idaho 2005) (boilerplate allegations re impending third garnishment insufficient); In re Valdez, 335 B.R. 801, 803 (Bankr. S.D. Fla. 2005) (filing bankruptcy to prevent foreclosure scheduled two days later not exigent circumstances because foreclosure did not prevent debtor from obtaining counseling).

The other line of cases holds that exigent circumstances exist when the debtor is unable to obtain credit counseling within five days of requesting such counseling, and faces immediate creditor action before the credit counseling can be obtained. See, e.g., In re Henderson, 339 B.R. 34, 39 (Bankr. E.D.N.Y. 2006) (impending sale of home or sole means of transportation are examples of potentially exigent circumstances warranting temporary relief) (dictum); In re Hubbard, 333 B.R. 377, 384 (Bankr. S.D. Tex. 2005) (exigent circumstances exist when debtor faces loss of family home or permanent loss of sole means of transportation unless immediate bankruptcy relief granted); In re Childs, 335 B.R. 623, 630-31 (Bankr. D. Md. 2005) (imminent sale of property at foreclosure and/or imminent eviction from residence are exigent circumstances).

I find the second line of cases more persuasive, and conclude that the threat of serious creditor action before credit counseling can be obtained generally is sufficient to establish exigent circumstances.[1]

Advance knowledge of the threatened creditor action should not preclude a finding of exigent circumstances. The statutory language chosen does not suggest such a limitation. As noted in the Childs decision, requiring the debtor to explain why she or he did not seek credit counseling earlier is more akin to an excusable neglect standard than to an exigent circumstances standard.

The standard for exigent circumstances set forth in the statute is minimal. It requires only that the debtor state the existence of some looming event that renders prepetition credit counseling to be infeasible. The standard is not one of "excusable neglect" that would require the Court to delve into the reasons why the exigent circumstances occurred. Childs, supra, 335 B.R. at 630 . Nor is such a limitation required by the statutory purpose of credit counseling enunciated by Congress.

> Most importantly, [section 109(h)] requires debtors to participate in credit counseling programs before filing for bankruptcy relief (unless special circumstances do not permit such participation). The legislation's credit counseling provisions are intended to give consumers in financial distress an

[1] Serious creditor action could include foreclosure, eviction, wage garnishment, or repossession of an automobile.

> opportunity to learn about the consequences of bankruptcy-such as the potentially devastating effect it can have on their credit rating.

H.R. REP. NO. 109-31, pt.1, at 75 (2005). The Committee Report states that this stop-and-think requirement was intended for the benefit of the debtor. A statute with such a purpose should not be read to impose a significant financial loss on a debtor because that debtor did not anticipate that she or he might not be able to get credit counseling within five days of requesting it.

It must be remembered that exigent circumstances are relevant only if the debtor has been unable to obtain credit counseling within five days of requesting it. The presence of this five-day provision in the statute represents a Congressional determination that a debtor's expectation of obtaining counseling within that period is reasonable.

In this case, Debtors faced imminent garnishment of their only income. The only way to stop the wage garnishment from taking effect was for Debtors to file bankruptcy by July 10. Debtors requested credit counseling from an approved agency on July 7, but were unable to obtain the requested services until seven days later. I determine that the looming wage garnishment constitutes exigent circumstances permitting a temporary waiver of the credit counseling requirement. Accordingly, the United States Trustee's Motion to Dismiss is denied.

Notes and Questions

1. The court in Romero was exceptionally generous. Probably the weight of authority agrees with In re Dixon, 338 B.R. 383 (Bankr. 8th Cir. 2006), which found the immanence of a mortgage foreclosure was no excuse for skipping credit counseling.

2. Which of the following exigent circumstances are good enough to defer or defeat the credit counseling requirement?

(a) In jail. Bristol v. Ackerman (In re Bristol), 2009 Dist. LEXIS 7107 (E.D.N.Y. Feburary 2, 2009) (no); In re Anderson, 397 B.R. 363 (Bankr. 6th Cir. 2008) (no); In re Hubel, 395 B.R. 823 (N.D.N.Y. 2008) (no).

(b) Has dementia. In re Myers, 350 B.R. 760 (Bankr. N.D. Ohio 2006) (yes).

(c) Was about to be evicted but had not sought credit counseling five days prior to the bankruptcy petition, as required by §109(h)(3)(A)(ii). In re Carey, 341 B.R. 798 (Bankr. M.D. Fla. 2006) (no).

(d) Needed the automatic stay to prevent a foreclosure that had been scheduled well before the bankruptcy petition. In re Kimsel, 2006 Bankr. LEXIS 1874 (Bankr. D. Hawaii August 16, 2006) (no).

(e) The debtor's lawyer was stricken with cancer and her office mistakenly filed the debtor's bankruptcy petition without arranging for credit counseling. In re Hess, 347 B.R. 489 (Bankr. D. Vt. 2006) (yes).

(f) Attended credit counseling with a counselor not yet approved by the United States trustee's office. In re Hess, 347 B.R. 489 (Bankr. D. Vt. 2006) (yes).

(g) 81 years old and hard of hearing. In re Hall,. 347 B.R. 532 (Bankr. N.D. W. Va. 2006) (yes).

(h) Could only speak Creole, and no credit counselor could speak it. In re Petit-Louis, 344 B.R. 696 (Bankr. S.D. Fla. 2006) (yes).

(i) Bank account frozen by garnishment and could not pay the $50 credit counseling fee. In re Morales, 2006 Bankr. LEXIS 1562 (Bankr. E.D.N.Y., August 24, 2006) (yes).

(j) Request for a deferral not signed under oath. In re Cobb, 343 B.R. 204 (Bankr. D. Ark. 2006) (no); cf. In re Graham, 336 B.R. 292 (Bankr. W.D. Ky 2005) (debtor's certification must be signed but need not be under oath).

(k) Debtor was a farmer, and credit councilors know aught of agronomics. Bogedain v. Eisen, 2006 Bankr. LEXIS 59926 (E.D. Mich., August 24, 2006) (no).

(l) 97% deaf, on oxygen and had consulted with a family friend who was a lawyer. In re Tulper, 345 B.R. 322 (Bankr. D. Colo. 2006) (yes).

(m) All credit counselors were swamped, and the debtor could not get counseling within five days of the bankruptcy. In re Hubbard, 332 B.R. 288 (Bankr. S.D. Tex. 2005) (no).

(n) Debtor filed without credit counseling and then died a month later. In re Trembulak, 362 B.R. 205 (Bankr. D.N.J. 2007) (yes).

(o) Debtor husband recently left nursing home and has heart problems; wife has breast cancer. In re Farrell, 2008 Bankr. LEXIS 546 (Bankr. D.S.C. February 21, 2008) (no).

B. REPETITIVE FILERS

MONTGOMERY v RYAN (IN RE MONTGOMERY)

37 F.3d 413 (8th Cir. 1994)

BEAM, J.

George C. Montgomery appeals from an order of the district court affirming the section 109(g) dismissal of his second bankruptcy petition. We affirm.

On March 24, 1992, Montgomery filed for bankruptcy protection under Chapter 13 of the Bankruptcy Code. The case was dismissed on June 8, 1992, because Montgomery did not attend a section 341 creditors meeting. On August 11, 1992, Montgomery filed a second Chapter 13 petition. Norah Ryan, a creditor, moved to dismiss the second petition arguing that Montgomery was not eligible for bankruptcy relief because he was not a "debtor" within the meaning of 11 U.S.C. § 109. After a hearing, the bankruptcy court granted Ryan's motion to dismiss and the district court affirmed.

I. DISCUSSION

Under 11 U.S.C. § 109 (g) (1), no individual may be a "debtor" if he or she has been a debtor in the preceding 180 days and the previous case was dismissed for "willful failure . . . to abide by orders of the court . . . ." Failure to attend a creditors meeting is a failure to obey a court order within the meaning of section 109(g) (1). See, e.g., In re Pappalardo, 109 Bankr. 622, 625 (Bankr. S.D.N.Y. 1990). Montgomery argues that dismissal of his second petition was not proper because the bankruptcy court, in its order dismissing the first petition, did not specifically find a "willful failure."[1] He also argues that the party moving for dismissal bears the burden of establishing such a "willful failure" and that Ryan has not done so. Like the district court, we review the bankruptcy court's legal conclusions de novo and its factual findings under the clearly erroneous standard. In re Commonwealth Cos., Inc., 913 F.2d 518, 521 (8th Cir. 1990).

Montgomery's first argument is without merit. No specific finding of willfulness was necessary in the order dismissing the first petition. Section 109(g)

---

[1] The order of dismissal provided as follows:

> Debtor(s) having failed to show cause, after notice, IT IS
> ORDERED AND YOU ARE HEREBY NOTIFIED THAT this Chapter 13 case is DISMISSED for Debtor(s) failure to appear for examination at the 11 U.S.C. § 341 Creditors Meeting . . . .

was not at issue until Ryan moved to dismiss the second petition. A finding of willfulness must be made when a sanction is imposed, but need not be made earlier. Here, a finding of willfulness was necessary only when the bankruptcy court dismissed the second petition.[2] Montgomery's arguments to the contrary amount to "no more than technical and/or semantic game playing." In re Ward, 78 Bankr. 914, 916 (Bankr. E.D. Ark. 1987).[3]

The remaining issue involves allocation of the burden of proving (or disproving) willfulness under section 109(g) (1). There is no evidence in the record (other than a copy of the first dismissal order of the bankruptcy court) regarding the circumstances of Montgomery's failure to attend the creditors meeting. Thus, the allocation issue is dispositive. If the burden is Montgomery's, his appeal fails. If the burden falls to Ryan, we must reverse.

The district court found that Montgomery bears the burden of showing that his failure to attend the creditors meeting was not willful.[4] We agree. The burden of establishing eligibility in bankruptcy lies with the party filing the bankruptcy petition. In In re Tim Wargo & Sons, Inc., 869 F.2d 1128, 1130 (8th Cir. 1989), we required the filing debtor to prove its eligibility for relief under Chapter 12. In Jenkins v. Petitioning Creditor--Ray E. Friedman & Co., 664 F.2d 184, 186 (8th Cir. 1981), a pre-Code case, we placed the burden of establishing eligibility on the creditor who filed the involuntary petition. Though this court has not previously addressed an eligibility issue specifically involving section 109(g), we believe our previous holdings are applicable here.

As Montgomery asserts, some lower courts have placed the burden on the creditor to show willfulness when the issue is raised by the creditor in a motion to dismiss. See, e.g., In re Arena, 81 Bankr. 851 (Bankr. E.D. Pa. 1988); In re Inesta Quinones, 73 Bankr. 333, 336 (Bankr. D. P.R. 1987). They have done so without discussion,[5] however, and are inconsistent with the precedent in this circuit. In Tim Wargo & Sons, Inc., we found the burden of establishing eligibility to fall on the filing debtor even though the issue was raised by the

---

[2] This finding was made when the bankruptcy court found that "the facts herein warrant imposition of sanctions pursuant to 11 U.S.C. § 109 (g)." Though the term "willful" was not used, we agree with the district court that this language is properly read to constitute a finding of willfulness.

[3] Montgomery contends that the court in In re Lawless, 79 Bankr. 850 (W.D. Mo. 1987), reached a contrary result. We disagree. In Lawless, the district court considered a bankruptcy court order which both dismissed the bankruptcy petition and barred additional bankruptcy filings for 180 days. Because a section 109(g) sanction was imposed as part of the order dismissing the original petition, the court properly required a finding of willfulness. Id. at 853. Both Lawless and our holding in this case are consistent with the fundamental proposition that required factual findings must be made before a sanction is imposed.

[4] Specifically, the district court held that Montgomery "bears the burden of demonstrating that jurisdiction in the bankruptcy court is proper." To the extent the district court characterized section 109(g) (1) as a jurisdictional provision, it was in error. We have held that 11 U.S.C. § 109 is not meant to restrict the jurisdiction of the federal courts. Rudd v. Laughlin, 866 F.2d 1040, 1042 (8th Cir. 1989). See also In re Phillips, 844 F.2d 230, 235 n.2 (5th Cir. 1988) (discussing negative consequences of interpreting section 109(g) as a limit on subject matter jurisdiction of bankruptcy courts). Section 109 determines eligibility for bankruptcy relief, not jurisdiction.

[5] Also without discussion, some courts have placed the burden on the debtor. See In re Huerta, 137 Bankr. 356, 375 (Bankr. C.D. Cal. 1992) ("The burden of proof under 109(g) is on debtor to show his inability to obey the prior court order."); In re Fulton, 52 Bankr. 627, 634 (Bankr. D. Utah 1985) ("In this case the burden is on the debtors to show that they are eligible for relief under the Bankruptcy Code.").

creditor. 869 F.2d at 1130.

Thus, we hold that where a section 109(g) issue is properly raised, the filing party must establish that the failure to obey a court order was not willful. This result is supported by policy considerations. Section 109(g) was enacted as part of a scheme to "curb abuses of the bankruptcy code and make its use truly a last resort." 130 Cong. Rec. 8894, reprinted in 1984 U.S.C.C.A.N. 590, 598 (statement of Sen. Hatch). It would frustrate this purpose to require a creditor to prove a "willful failure" while a debtor who failed to comply with a court order stands silent.

In this case, the burden was on Montgomery to explain his failure to attend the creditors meeting. Since he has offered no evidence on this point, the bankruptcy court's finding was not clearly erroneous.

For the foregoing reasons, the order of the district court is affirmed.[6]

Notes and Questions

1. Attorneys who file second petitions in violation of §109(g) can be sanctioned by the courts. Moran v. Frisard (In re Ulmer), 19 F.3d 234 (5th Cir. 1994).

2. Section 109(g) ended up being a disappointment. First, the six month duration of the sanction did little to stem the avalanche of multiple filings. Second, many courts ruled that the automatic stay arises from a bankruptcy petition filed in violation of § 109(g). Robert Lefkowitz, Note, The Filing of a Bankruptcy Petition in Violation of 11 U.S.C. § 109(g): Does It Invoke the Automatic Stay?, 26 CARDOZO L. REV. 297 (2004). Therefore, debtors willing to face sanctions continued to have the power to disrupt foreclosure sales. To rectify the matter BAPCPA initiated a new exception to the automatic stay. According to §362(b):

> The filing of a petition. . . does not operate as a stay– . . .
>
> (21) under subsection (a), of any act to enforce any lien against or security interest in real property--
>
> (A) if the debtor is ineligible under section 109(g) to be a debtor in a case under this title; or
>
> (B) if the case under this title was filed in violation of a bankruptcy court order in a prior case under this title prohibiting the debtor from being a debtor in another case under this title . . . .

As the court pointed out in In re Brown, supra, the fact that there is an exception for foreclosing mortgagees helps to prove that there is an automatic stay for all other purposes when a bankruptcy petition is filed in violation of § 109(g).

2. BAPCPA also takes a different approach toward abusive multiple filings. It attempts to limit or eliminate the automatic stay in such cases. 11 U.S.C. § 362(c)(3) & (4). How good a job does BAPCPA do? The next case suggests, "Not very good."

WHITAKER v BAXTER (IN RE WHITAKER)

341 B.R. 336 (Bankr. S.D. Ga. 2006).

JOHN S. DALIS, J.

By motion filed January 17, 2006, the debtors Jonathan and Angie Whitaker (the "Debtors" or "Movants") seek to reinstate the automatic stay of 11 U.S.C. § 362(a). The Debtors seek this relief pursuant to § 362(c)(4) of the Bankruptcy Code.[1] The Debtors are not entitled to a reinstatement of the

---

[6] [A concurring opinion is omitted. -Ed.]

[1] As to debtors who have had "2 or more" cases dismissed in the preceding 1-year period, 11 U.S.C. § 362(c)(4)(B) provides:

automatic stay (the "stay") under that subsection. Nor does subsection 362(c)(3)(B) authorize its reinstatement.[2] Instead, I rely on the authority conferred by § 105(a) of the Bankruptcy Code to order the stay reinstated as to all creditors.[3] I do not employ § 105 lightly, but only to "prevent an abuse of process," that is impermissibly severe. . . .[4]

> [I]f, within 30 days after the filing of the later case, a party in interest requests the court may order the stay to take effect in the case as to any and all creditors (subject to such conditions or limitations as the court may impose), after notice and a hearing, only if the party in interest demonstrates that the filing of the later case is in good faith as to the creditors to be stayed; . . .

[2] As to debtors who have had only one case dismissed in the preceding 1-year period, 11 U.S.C. § 362(c)(3)(B) provides:

> [O]n the motion of a party in interest for continuation of the automatic stay and upon notice and a hearing, the court may extend the stay in particular cases as to any or all creditors (subject to such conditions or limitations as the court may impose) after notice and a hearing completed before the expiration of the 30-day period only if the party in interest demonstrates that the filing of the later case is in good faith as to the creditors to be stayed; . . .

[3] 11 U.S.C. § 105(a) provides:

> The court may issue any order, process, or judgment that is necessary or appropriate to carry out the provisions of this title. No provision of this title providing for the raising of an issue by a party in interest shall be construed to preclude the court from, sua sponte, taking any action or making any determination necessary or appropriate to enforce or implement court orders or rules, or to prevent an abuse of process.

[4] Section 362(c) raises compelling issues of due process and equal protection under the United States Constitution. The Movants have not raised the constitutional issues, and only an Article III court has authority to declare an act of Congress unconstitutional. N. Pipeline Constr. Co. v. Marathon Pipe Line Co., 458 U.S. 50, 57-76 (1982). I raise these issues only to demonstrate the "abuse of process" §§ 362(c)(3) & (4) invite. See 11 U.S.C. § 105(a).

Because § 362(c)(3)(B) requires that "notice [to all creditors] and a hearing be completed before the expiration of the 30-day period [from the filing date]," it creates unprecedented requirements of process that burden the court and the creditors effected, no less than the debtor. Nowhere else does the Bankruptcy Code condition a right or privilege on a party's ability to ensure a hearing with notices to so many interested parties within so brief a period of time.

Given the administrative difficulties of providing timely notice to all creditors of the bankruptcy estate, the actual window in which the hearing may be set is considerably less than thirty days. Depending on the timeliness of the motion, the notice required, and the available space on the docket calendar, it may be as few as two days or less. It may be impossible, as in this case.

When bankruptcy courts hear motions to alter the § 362 stay, the debtor and other parties have property interests sufficient to trigger a Fifth Amendment right to procedural due process. Normally, hearings require a minimum of 20 days notice. F.R.B.P. 2002(a). However, where there is cause shown, a court may reduce this requirement. F.R.B.P. 9006(c)(1). Section 362(c)(3)(B) motions nearly always create a need for expedited process. Nevertheless, notice must be sufficient to provide due process to all interested parties. With regard to § 362(c) motions, [*339] other courts have held that as much as 16 days notice to creditors violates their due process rights. In re Taylor, 334 B.R. 660 (Bankr. D. Minn. 2005) (5 or 8 days notice is insufficient process); In re Wilson et al., 336 B.R. 338 (Bankr. E.D. Tenn 2005) (9 or 16 days notice is insufficient process).

Since all parties' due process rights must be satisfied within a 30-day window, § 362(c)(3)(B) requires the moving party -- usually, though not necessarily, the debtor -- to have near perfect timing. It is not enough that the movant can demonstrate by clear and convincing evidence that the debtor filed her most recent case in good faith. The movant must ensure that the

FACTS

The Debtors filed their present case within a year of the dismissal of their only previous case, also a joint chapter 13 plan. They had filed their prior case on

---

required hearing is completed in time. However, this is not within the movant's proximate control. Besides the usual reliance on the diligence of counsel, the movant must rely on the Bankruptcy Clerk's ability to schedule the hearing and serve interested parties. Not the movant, but rather the court is the gatekeeper who determines when hearings may be set. This removes control from the party affected. It also places a severe burden on court administrators. They are required to treat § 362(c)(3)(B) motions as urgent priorities. In many cases, this has required the Bankruptcy Clerk to serve notices by hand at considerable public expense.

The Supreme Court relies on a balancing test to determine whether a procedure provides constitutional due process:

> [D]ue process generally requires consideration of three distinct factors: First, the private interest that will be affected by the official action; second, the risk of an erroneous deprivation of such interest through the procedures used, and the probable value, if any, of additional or substitute procedural safeguards, and finally, the Government's interest, including the function involved and the fiscal and administrative burdens that the additional or substitute procedural requirements would entail.

Mathews v. Eldridge, 424 U.S. 319, 335 (1976).

Generally, the Government's interest in administrative efficiency counter-balances the private interests affected and the risks of erroneous deprivation. Mathews, 424 U.S. at 335, 347-49, 96 S. Ct. 893, 909-910; see also Grayden v. Rhodes, 345 F.3d 1225, 1233-37 (11th Cir. 2003) That is not the case here. With respect to § 362(c)(3)(B), the Government's fiscal and administrative burden would be substantially reduced if hearings were permitted beyond the statute's "30-day period."

Were this insufficient to raise serious concerns over its constitutionality, §§ 362(c)(3) & (4) also raise an issue of equal protection. Although the equal protection clause of the Fourteenth Amendment specifically applies to acts of the states, the Supreme Court recognizes an inferred right to equal protection under the Fifth Amendment. Bolling v. Sharpe et al., 347 U.S. 497, 499 (1954). The Supreme Court has held that with regard to bankruptcy discharges,"the applicable standard in measuring the propriety of Congress' classification, is that of rational justification." United States v. Kras, 409 U.S. 434, 446 (1973). Arguably, a greater degree of protection is required to safeguard the various property interests preserved by the automatic stay. Not just the debtor, but also the secured and unsecured creditors rely on the estate's preservation for the orderly distribution of assets. All of these parties are entitled to due process.

Even simply applying the standard of rational justification, the classification created by § 362(c) is troublesome. The statute separates debtors who file more than a single case in a one-year period into two classes: one-time repeat filers subject to § 362(c) (3) and multiple repeat filers subject to § 362(c)(4). For no apparent reason, § 362(c) creates different burdens of notice for these two classes.

Mysteriously, the due process predicament created by § 362(c)(3)(B) only occurs if the debtor has had just one case dismissed in the past year, but not if the debtor has repeatedly re-filed. If an individual debtor has had "2 or more . . . cases . . . pending within the previous year but were dismissed," a hearing is required to impose the automatic stay, but there is no fixed period by which it must be completed. 11 U.S.C. § 362(c)(4)(A) &(B). The statute only requires that "within 30 days [from the petition date] . . . a party in interest requests" the relief. Id. The hearing may be held at some later, unspecified time.

Because the automatic stay provided to single-repeat filers is temporary, there may be some justification for more burdensome notice and hearing requirements to extend the stay before it expires. However, there is no rational justification to deny first-time repeat filers the same process to impose the stay that BAPCPA gives to multiple repeat filers. To deny first-time repeat filers an equivalent process subjects them and their creditors to greater "risks of an erroneous deprivation" than are applied to multiple repeat filers and their creditors. Mathews v. Eldridge, 424 U.S. 319, at 335.

July 25, 2003, and it was dismissed November 5, 2005. On December 21, 2005, they filed this case. The automatic stay commenced on the filing date, but terminated by operation of law 30 days later. See 11 U.S.C. § 362(c)(3)(A).[5] Twenty-seven (27) days after filing this case, the Debtors filed this motion. Even while the stay was still in effect, they moved this court to "order the stay to take effect in this case as to . . . all creditors."

All creditors and the chapter 13 trustee were served with the motion. None filed a response. A hearing was held on February 13, 2006, fifty-four (54) days after the petition date. No creditors appeared. At the hearing, the Debtors presented evidence that they had filed their most recent case in good faith. Based on the evidence presented at the hearing, I determined that they met the applicable burden of proof under 11 U.S.C. § 362(c)(3)(C).[6]

---

[5] 11 U.S.C. § 362(c)(3)(A) provides:

> . . . if a single or joint case is filed by or against [a] debtor who is an individual in a case under chapter 7, 11, or 13, and if a single or joint case of the debtor was pending within the preceding 1-year period but was dismissed, other than a case filed under a chapter other than chapter 7 after dismissal under section 707(b) --
>
> (A) the stay under subsection (a) with respect to any action taken with respect to a debt or property securing such debt or with respect to any lease shall terminate with respect to the debtor on the 30th day after the filing of the later case. . .

[6] 11 U.S.C. § 362(c)(3)(C) provides that:

> (C) for purposes of subparagraph (B) [§ 362 (c)(3)(B)], a case is presumptively filed not in good faith (but such presumption may be rebutted by clear and convincing evidence to the contrary) --
>
> (i) as to all creditors, if --
>
> (I) more than 1 previous case under any chapters 7,11, and 13 in which the individual was a debtor was pending within the preceding 1-year period;
>
> (II) a previous case under any chapters 7, 11, and 13 in which the individual was a debtor was dismissed within such 1-year period, after the debtor failed to --
>
> (aa) file or amend the petition or other documents as required by this title or the court without substantial excuse (but mere inadvertence or negligence shall not be a substantial excuse unless the dismissal was caused by the negligence of the debtor's attorney);
>
> (bb) provide adequate protection as ordered by the court; or
>
> (cc) perform the terms of a plan confirmed by the court; or
>
> (III) there has not been a substantial change in the financial or personal affairs of the debtor since the dismissal of the next most previous case under chapter 7, 11, or 13 or any other reason to conclude that the later case will [not] [sic]* be concluded --
>
> (aa) if a case under chapter 7, with a discharge; or
>
> (bb) if a case under chapters 11 or 13, with a confirmed plan that will be fully performed; and
>
> (ii) as to any creditor that commenced an action under subsection (d) in a previous case in which the individual was a debtor if, as of the date of dismissal of such case, that action was still pending or has been resolved by terminating, conditioning, or limiting the stay as to

By clear and convincing evidence, these Debtors rebut the statutory presumption that they filed their present case "not in good faith." The Debtors are not abusing the Bankruptcy Code by re-filing. After dutifully adhering to their first chapter 13 plan, which had lasted 16 months, the Whitakers faced an unexpected impediment to completing their chapter 13 plan: Jonathan Whitaker was laid off. At the time, Angie Whitaker was devoting her time to taking care of her ill father and the Whitaker's three school-age children. Before they filed this case, both Debtors established steady employment. Their current plan provides for a 100% dividend to unsecured creditors.

Nevertheless, for the reasons set forth here, I may not rely on § 362(c)(3)(B) to "extend the stay." Nor do I have authority under § 362(c)(4)(B) to "order the stay to take effect." By their plain language, neither of those provisions apply to the Debtors. They have no recourse under any specific statute to move this court to re-impose the stay.

THE AUTOMATIC STAY AS APPLIED TO REPEAT FILERS

Cases in this same posture have recurred regularly on this court docket's since the Bankruptcy Abuse Prevention and Consumer Protection Act of 2005 (BAPCPA) became effective on October 17, 2005. That Act established fundamental changes to the Bankruptcy Code, including numerous changes to the automatic stay provisions in 11 U.S.C. § 362.

Traditionally, the automatic stay has served to "prevent dismemberment of the [bankruptcy] estate and insure its orderly distribution." SEC v. First Financial Group, 645 F.2d 429, 439 (5th Cir. 1981), citing S. Rep. No. 95-989, 95th Cong., 2d Sess. 50 (1978), H.R. Rep. No. 95-595, 95th Cong., 2d Sess. 341 (1977). In that capacity, the automatic stay serves the interests of both the debtor and the creditors of the bankruptcy estate. For the debtor, it provides a "breathing spell" by "stopping all collection efforts, all harassment, and all foreclosure actions." S. Rep. No 95-989, 95th Cong. 2d Sess. 54-55 (1978); H.R. Rep. No 95-595, 95th Cong., 1st Seas. 340 (1977). However, the stay also serves the interest of creditors, insofar as it "eliminate [s] the impetus for a race of diligence by fast-acting creditors." SEC v. First Financial Group, at 439. The stay ensures that assets are distributed according to the order of priorities established by Congress.

The BAPCPA amends the stay provisions with respect to individual debtors who file new cases within a year of the dismissal of their previous case or cases. For individual debtors who have had just one previous case dismissed in the preceding year, the automatic stay has a limited duration of 30 days. For convenience, I will refer to such debtors as "one-time repeat filers."

The Bankruptcy Code clearly distinguishes them from debtors who have had "2 or more single or joint cases . . . pending within the previous year but were dismissed."[7] Throughout this decision, I refer to these debtors as "multiple repeat

---

> actions of such creditor. . .

* Were § 362(c)(3)(C) not sufficiently complicated, it also contains this obvious scrivener's error; compare the otherwise identical language in § 362(c)(4)(D)(i)(III).

[7] 11 U.S.C. § 362(c)(4)(A)(i) provides:

> if a single or joint case is filed by or against a debtor who is an individual under this title, and if 2 or more single or joint cases of the debtor were pending within

filers." For them, the stay does not go into effect automatically.

Most individual debtors who file a new case within a year of having had a previous case (or cases) dismissed will be subject to a statutory presumption that the most recent case is not filed in good faith.[8] However, "a party in interest" may rebut this presumption. In which event, the court "may extend the stay" or "may order the stay to take effect" as to any or all creditors (as to one-time repeat and multiple repeat filers, respectively).[9]

However, the Debtors are no longer entitled to the § 362(c)(3)(B) safe harbor. Its applicable window is very narrow, requiring "notice and a hearing [be] completed before the expiration of the 30-day period [from the date the petition was filed]."[10]

The Whitakers' problem, quite simply, is that their counsel failed to file a motion to extend the stay quickly enough. This Motion to Reinstate the Automatic Stay was filed 27 days after the filing date -- just three days before the

---

> the previous year but were dismissed, other than a case refiled under section 707(b); the stay under subsection (a) shall not go into effect upon the filing of the later case; and . . .

[8] The statutes that trigger the "not in good faith" presumption are quite broad. See 11 U.S.C. § 362(c)(3)(C)(I); compare 11 U.S.C. § 362(c)(4)(D), which provides:

> (D) for purposes of subparagraph (B) [§ 362(c)(4)(B)], a case is presumptively filed not in good faith (but such presumption may be rebutted by clear and convincing evidence to the contrary) --
>
> (i) as to all creditors, if --
>
> (I) 2 or more previous cases under this title in which the individual was a debtor were pending within the preceding 1-year period.
>
> (II) a previous case under this title in which the individual was a debtor was dismissed within the time period stated in this paragraph after the debtor failed to file or amend the petition or other documents as required by this title or the court without substantial excuse (but mere inadvertence or negligence shall not be substantial excuse unless the dismissal was caused by the negligence of the debtor's attorney), failed to provide adequate protection as ordered by the court; or failed to perform the terms of a plan confirmed by the court; or
>
> (III) there has not been a substantial change in the financial or personal affairs of the debtor since the dismissal of the next most previous case under this title, or any other reason to conclude that the later case will not be concluded if a case under chapter 7, with a discharge, and if a case under chapter 11 or 13, with a confirmed plan that will be fully performed; or
>
> (ii) as to any creditor that commenced an action under subsection (d) in a previous case in which the individual was a debtor if, as of the date of dismissal of such case, such action was still pending or has been resolved by terminating, conditioning, or limiting the stay as to such action of such creditor . . .

[9] See 11 U.S.C. §§ 362(c)(3)(B) & 362(c)(4)(B).

[10] See 11 U.S.C. § 362(c)(3)(B). The "30-day period" refers to two related, but nevertheless separate events. Firstly, as to first-time repeat filers, the automatic stay has a duration of thirty days. Section 362(c)(3)(A) provides that, the stay "shall terminate with respect to the debtor on the 30th day after the filing of the case." 11 U.S.C. § 362(c)(3)(A) (reprinted supra note 5). Secondly, § 362(c)(3)(B) proscribes the court's authority to extend the stay. It provides that "the court may extend the stay . . . after notice and a hearing completed before the expiration of the 30-day period." 11 U.S.C. § 362(c)(3)(B) (reprinted supra note 2).

expiration of the 30-day period. As a result, the required notice and a hearing could not be completed in time.

Presumably, Debtors' counsel apprised his clients' situation, since this motion cites § 362(c)(4) as authority for reinstating the stay. However, that statute is also inapplicable.

It is true that § 362(c)(4)(B) provides repeat filers an opportunity to protect the estate under § 362. Unlike § 362(c)(3)(B), it does not require that notice and a hearing be completed within 30 days of the filing of the petition. The court may order the stay to take effect "if within 30 days after the filing of the later case, a party in interest requests [it]." Although notice and a hearing are required, no limitation is fixed, and so they may occur outside of a thirty-day period.

The problem is that this separate safe harbor is only available to multiple repeat filers.[11] The Whitakers are ineligible for the simple reason that they filed just one prior case in the previous year. The very brief safe harbor provided to one-time repeat filers has passed. The Debtors now wish to move this court using the extended safe harbor separately reserved for multiple repeat filers. This they may not do. The plain language of § 362 (c)(4) does not apply to them.

THE PLAIN MEANING RULE APPLIED TO § 362(c)(4)

In construing a statute, "it is . . . axiomatic that [my] first step 'is to determine whether the language at issue has a plain and unambiguous meaning.'" D'Angelo v. Conagra Foods, 422 F. 3d 1220, 1235 (11th Cir. 2005) quoting Robinson v. Shell Oil Co., 519 U.S. 337, 340 (1997). "[T]he preeminent canon of statutory interpretation requires [me] to 'presume that [the] legislature says in a statute what it means and means in a statute what it says there." BedRoc Ltd., LLC v. United States, 541 U.S. 176, 183 (2004) quoting Connecticut Nat'l Bank v. Germain, 503 U.S. 249, 253-54 (1992). This inquiry requires me to "begin[] with the statutory text, and end[] there as well if the text is unambiguous." Id.

By its plain and unambiguous language, section 362(c)(4) applies only to multiple repeat filers. It is only triggered "if a single or joint case is filed by or against a debtor who is an individual under this title, and if 2 or more single or joint cases of the debtor were pending within the previous year but were dismissed."[12]

The relief available under § 362(c)(4)(B) also indicates its limited application to multiple repeat filers: "the court may order the stay to take effect." This implies that the stay is otherwise nonexistent, which makes sense since § 362(c)(4)(A)(i) states that the "stay does not go into effect." Contrast this with § 362 (c)(3)(B), which states that "the court may extend the stay." This indicates that the stay is present only temporarily, as is the case for one-time repeat filers.

THE INAPPLICABILITY OF § 362(c)(4)(B) TO ONE-TIME REPEAT FILERS

The Bankruptcy Code, as amended by BAPCPA, divides debtors who file more than one case in a one-year period into two classes: first-time repeat filers

[11] 11 U.S.C. § 362(c)(4)(A)(i).
[12] 11 U.S.C. § 362(c)(4)(A)(i).

described in § 362(c)(3), and multiple repeat filers described in § 362(c)(4). Each class has its own applicable safe harbor provision.

However, at least one court has held that one-time repeat filers are entitled to the § 362(c)(4) safe harbor. In re Toro-Arcila, 334 B.R. 224 (S.D. Texas 2005). I find the arguments supporting this holding unpersuasive. In re Toro-Arcila states that if § 362(c)(4)(B) applied only to multiple repeat filers, then virtually all of § 362(c)(4)(D) would be "meaningless surplusage." Id. at 227. I disagree.

Section 362(c)(4)(D) describes the circumstances in which there is a presumptive absence of good faith. It lists three disjunctive factors that create such a presumption. However, first among these is simply: "if . . . 2 or more previous cases under this title in which the individual was a debtor were pending within the 1-year period."[13] Plainly, any debtor described under § 362(c)(4)(A) (i.e., any multiple repeat filer) is automatically presumed to have filed "not in good faith."[14]

According to In re Toro-Arcila, a court might therefore dispense with any further consideration of the other independent tests of bad faith listed in § 362(c)(4)(D)(i)(II) & (III). But were that so, § 362(c)(4)(D) would be largely superfluous. According to In re Toro-Arcila, that would violate "'a cardinal principal of statutory construction' that 'a statute ought, upon the whole, . . . be so construed that, if it can be prevented, no clause, sentence, or word shall be superfluous, void, or insignificant." Id., quoting TRW, Inc. v. Andrews, 534 U.S. 19, 31 (2001) (quoting Duncan v. Walker, 533 U.S. 167, 174 (2001)).

According to the opinion, not just one word would be rendered superfluous, but no less than all 278 words of § 362(c)(4)(D). In re Toro-Arcila, at 227 n.2 and accompanying text. To rectify this purported surplusage, the opinion holds that debtors described in § 362(c)(3)(A) are entitled to the safe harbor in subparagraph (c)(4)(B). In its own words, this opinion "creates a statutory structure where certain provisions of § 362(c)(4) apply to §§ 362(c)(3) and (4)." In re Toro-Arcila, at 228.

There is no basis for this construction. The customary separation of distinct sub-paragraphs does not render § 362(c)(4)(D) meaningless surplusage. Rather, the disjunctive factors listed in § 362(c)(4)(D) place consecutive burdens on the multiple repeat filer to establish good faith.

If an interested party moves for imposition of the stay under section 362(c)(4)(B), then the burden of rebutting the presumption of filing "not in good faith" arises automatically, since "2 or more cases under this title in which the individual was a debtor were pending in the 1-year period."[15]

The movant cannot fully meet this burden unless she provides a "substantial excuse" for failing to file or amend documents required in previous cases.[16]

The burden persists at least until the debtor demonstrates "a substantial change in [her] financial or personal affairs" sufficient to indicate that either a chapter 7 discharge is permissible or "a confirmed plan . . . will be fully

[13] 11 U.S.C. § 362(c)(4)(D)(i)(I).
[14] 11 U.S.C. § 362(c)(4)(A)(i).
[15] 11 U.S.C. § 362(c)(4)(D)(i)(I).
[16] 11 U.S.C. § 362(c)(4)(D)(i)(II).

performed."[17]

Lastly, an additional burden must be met with respect to each creditor who moved to lift the stay in a previous case.[18]

The statute thus serves hybrid roles. As In re Toro-Arcila recognizes, "[s]ection 362(c)(4)(D) creates a presumption that certain cases are not filed in good faith." In re Toro-Arcila, at 226-27. In this capacity, the statute casts its net so wide that effectively all cases by multiple repeat filers are "presumptively filed not in good faith." But the statute also establishes how "such presumption may be rebutted." Congress' use of the disjunctive 'or' confers the necessary flexibility to provide separate, sequential burdens for the different kinds of failures that some repeat filers experienced in their previous cases.

DETERMINING 'GOOD FAITH' UNDER § 362(c)(3)(B)

Based on the evidence presented at the hearing on February 13, I find that the Debtors do rebut, by clear and convincing evidence, the statutory presumption that they filed their most recent case "not in good faith."[19] In other words, they "demonstrate[] that the filing of the later case is in good faith to the creditors to be stayed."[20]

The appropriate test for rebutting the presumption of "not in good faith" (i.e., bad faith) is provided in § 362 (c)(3)(C). Like § 362(c)(4)(D), this statute does not simply state the various circumstances that trigger a presumption of bad faith. In several places, it also indicates how those presumptions may be rebutted.

If the debtor "failed to file or amend the previous petition or other documents as required," she must now provide a "substantial excuse" for failing to do so.[21]

Also, as to each creditor who successfully moved to lift the stay in the prior case, there is an additional, presumably weightier, burden that the movant must meet, although the statute does not establish a definitive test.[22]

However, the chief means of rebutting the presumption of bad faith requires the movant to establish "a substantial change in the financial or personal affairs of the debtor . . . or any other reason to conclude" that the instant case will be successful.[23] If the instant case is one under chapter 7, a discharge must now be permissible.[24] If it is a case under chapters 11 or 13, there must be some substantial change indicating that a "confirmed plan . . . will be fully performed."[25]

Because I find that the statute provides the evidentiary burden required to rebut the presumption of bad faith, I do not apply the tests of good faith developed under § 1325 (a) (good faith proposal of a chapter 13 plan for the purpose of confirmation) or § 1307 (c) (dismissal or conversion of a chapter 13 case for cause including lack of good faith). See, respectively, Kitchens v. Ga. RR

[17] 11 U.S.C. § 362(c)(4)(D)(i)(III).
[18] 11 U.S.C. § 362(c)(4)(D)(ii).
[19] 11 U.S.C. § 362(c)(3)(C).
[20] 11 U.S.C. § 362(c)(3)(B).
[21] 11 U.S.C. § 362(c)(3)(C)(i)(II)(aa).
[22] 11 U.S.C. § 362(c)(3)(C)(ii).
[23] 11 U.S.C. § 362(c)(3)(C)(i)(III).
[24] 11 U.S.C. § 362(c)(3)(C)(i)(III)(aa).
[25] 11 U.S.C. § 362(c)(3)(C)(i)(III)(bb).

Bank & Trust Co. (In re Kitchens), 702 F.2d 885, 888-89 (11th Cir. 1983); Leavitt v. Soto (In re Leavitt), 209 B.R. 935, 939 (9th Cir. 1999).

Not only are these tests superceded by the language of § 362(c)(3)(C), their application here would result in considerable confusion. They deal with very different provisions of the Bankruptcy Code, generally implemented later in the case. But see In re Montoya, 333 B.R. 449, 458 nn. 14-16 and accompanying text (Bankr. D. Utah 2005); In re Ball, 336 B.R. 268 (Bankr. M.D. N.C. 2006); In re Galanis, 334 B.R. 685 (Bankr. D. Utah 2005). These opinions all struggle to identify the "totality of the circumstances" factors that might apply, discard those that obviously cannot, and also add new factors not indicated by § 362(c)(3).

The better approach simply requires the Debtors to meet the dictates of the statute. The uncontested evidence presented by the Debtors, and supported by the chapter 13 trustee, establishes that their first case failed because Mr. Whitaker lost his job. As a result the Debtors "failed to perform the terms of a plan confirmed by the court."[26] Between the dismissal of their previous case and filing their instant case, both of the Debtors have found employment. Mr. Whitaker has returned to work at his previous employer, where other than his brief lapse, he has worked for five years. Ms. Whitaker currently works part-time at a video store. Their income appears sufficient to support a plan that will provide a 100% dividend to unsecured creditors.

Based on this evidence, I find that there has "been a substantial change in the financial or personal affairs of the debtor[s] since the dismissal of the next most previous case" sufficient "to conclude that the later case [under chapter 13] will be concluded. . . with a confirmed plan that will be fully performed."[27] The other burdens established by § 362(c)(3)(C) are not applicable here.

Therefore, the Debtors, by clear and convincing evidence, rebut the presumption that they filed their most recent case "not in good faith."[28] Stated otherwise, they "demonstrate[] that the filing of the later case is in good faith to the creditors to be stayed."[29]

RELIANCE ON § 105 TO REIMPOSE THE § 362 STAY

With respect to first-time repeat filers, there is no specific grant of authority to reimpose the stay once it has lapsed under § 362 (c)(3)(A). Although the Debtors meet the statutory burden of good faith, their opportunity to use the § 362(c)(3)(B) safe harbor has passed. My only authority for reinstating the stay is to use the equitable powers conferred by § 105(a).

The powers conferred by § 105(a) are unambiguously broad. Courts elsewhere have held that the statute grants authority to reimpose the stay if the court has lifted the stay under § 362(d) or after the stay has lapsed by operation of law -- typically by § 362 (e). Chrysler Capital Corp. V. Official Comm. Of Unsecured Creditors (In re Twenver), 149 B.R. 950, 953-54 (D. Colo. 1993); In re Bogosian, 112 B.R. 2, 4 (Bankr. D. R.I. 1990); Smith v. Citifed (In re Smith). 111 B.R. 102, 104-05 (Bankr. E.D. Pa. 1990); Wedgewood Investment Fund, Ltd. V. Wedgewood Realty Group, Ltd. (In re Wedgewood Realty Group, Ltd.), 878 F.2d

---

[26] 11 U.S.C. § 362(c)(3)(C)(i)(II)(cc).
[27] 11 U.S.C. § 362(c)(3)(C)(i)(II).
[28] 11 U.S.C. § 362(c)(3)(C).
[29] 11 U.S.C. § 362(c)(3)(B).

693, 701 (3rd Cir. 1989); ML Barge Pool VII Partners -- Series A v. United States (In re ML Barge Pool VII Partners, et al.), 71 B.R. 161, 164, P 8(E. D. Mo. 1987); In re Clark, 69 B.R. 885, 893 (Bankr. E.D. Pa. 1987); In re Kozak Farms Inc., 47 B.R. 399, 402-03 (Bankr. W.D. Mo. 1985); In re McNeely, 51 B.R. 816, 821 (Bankr. D. Utah 1985); Explorer Drilling Co. V. Martin Exploration Co. (In re Martin Exploration Company), 731 F.2d 1210, 1214 (5th Cir. 1984); Bank Hapoalim B.M., Chicago Branch v. E.L.I., Ltd., 42 B.R. 376, 378 (Bankr. N.D. Ill. 1984); In re Rolanco, Inc., 43 B.R. 150, 152-53 (Bankr. E.D. Mo. 1984); In re Small, 38 B.R. 143, 147-48 (Bankr. D. Md. 1984); In re Pirsig Farms, Inc., 41 B.R. 835, 835 (Bankr. D. Minn. 1984); In re Brusich & St. Pedro Jewelers, Inc., 28 B.R. 545, 549-50 (Bankr. E.D. Pa. 1983); In re Wilmette Partners, 34 B.R. 958, 11 B.R. 958, 961-62 (Bankr. N.D. 111. 1983); In re Codesco, Inc., 24 B.R. 746, 751 (Bankr. S.D. N.Y. 1982). Contra, Canter v. Canter (In re Canter), 299 F.3d 1150, 1155 n.1 (9th Cir. 2002); citing Andreiu v. Reno, 223 F.3d 1111, 1121 n. 4 (9th Cir. 2000) (The addition by BAPCPA of specific provisions providing for the reinstatement of the automatic stay places in question the viability of the Ninth Circuit precedents.)

Section 105(a) grants me the authority to "issue any order, process, or judgment that is necessary or appropriate to carry out the provisions of [Title 11]." Under the circumstances and facts of this case, I find that re-imposition of the automatic stay is appropriate, and necessary to ensure an orderly payment to creditors under the Debtors' chapter 13 plan. In granting the Debtors' request to reimpose the stay, I am influenced by a variety of factors.

First, I am reluctant to deprive the Whitakers of a decision on the merits, since they can clearly and convincingly carry their statutory burden under § 362(c)(3)(B) & (C). See Mitchell v. Brown & Williamson Tobacco Co., 294 F.3d 1309, 1316-17 (11th Cir. 2002), quoting Wahl v. McIver, 773 F.2d 1169, 1174 (11th Cir. 1985) (stating the "usual preference that cases be heard on the merits").

Secondly, notice of this motion was served on the chapter 13 trustee and all creditors of the estate. None objected or even filed a response.

Thirdly, I am concerned that parties not suffer merely because of the inadvertence of their counsel. Sections 362(c)(3)(C)(i)(II)(aa) & 362(c)(4)(D)(i)(II) indicate that "negligence by the debtor's attorney" does not require "substantial excuse" by the party seeking to establish the good faith of a repeat filing.

The Debtors might just dismiss this case, file another, and move for imposition of the stay under § 362(c)(4)(B). They could then submit evidence that their counsel failed to ensure a § 362(c)(3)(B) hearing within the required 30-day period. See 11 U.S.C. § 362(c)(4)(D)(i)(II). The In re Toro-Arcila court also considered this strategy, noting that "Congress could not have meant to create such gamesmanship." In re Toro-Arcila, at 228-29. Indeed, this would only further prolong payment to creditors and burden the debtors with unnecessary expense.

Applying the traditional test for injunctive relief, the Movants demonstrate that they merit relief. See McDonald's Corp. v. Robertson, 147 F.3d 1301, 1306 (11th Cir. 1998); In re Wedgewood Realty Group. Ltd., 878 F.2d 693, 701 (3rd Cir. 1989). If the stay is not imposed, both they and the bankruptcy estate would be susceptible to irreparable injury. In this case, the creditors also will benefit from the stay's reimposition. Because the debtors' plan provides a 100% dividend to unsecured creditors, imposing the stay will permit the orderly payment of claims in full. It is in the public interest that creditors be paid what is owed them in an orderly fashion. Furthermore, the creditors enjoined retain the usual means to move for relief from the stay under 11 U.S.C. § 362(d). The Movants have no equivalent fail-safe. The balance of hardships favors the Movants.

It is therefore ORDERED that the stay described at 11 U.S.C. § 362(a) is reimposed as to all creditors.

Notes and Questions

1. In In re Frazier, 339 B.R. 516 (Bankr. N.D. Fla. 2006), a multiple filer filed again on February 17, 2006, one week before a scheduled foreclosure sale. Accompanying the bankruptcy petition was a motion to reimpose the automatic stay under §362(c)(4)(B). This was served on creditor's counsel on February 21. Creditor's counsel was notified of the hearing by fax and telephone, but creditor's counsel denied receiving these. The court scheduled a hearing on February 22. Creditor's counsel did not show up. The court reinstated the automatic stay. Later, creditor's counsel protested the lack of due process. According to the court:

> There is no question but that Centex did not receive much advance notice of the hearing on Debtor's emergency motion. This situation was unfortunate however, under the circumstances unavoidable. Had the Court waited longer to schedule the hearing on Debtor's emergency motion, the foreclosure sale scheduled for February 24 would have been completed and any relief for the Debtor would have been rendered meaningless. While § 362(c)(4)(B) requires notice and hearing before the Court can impose the stay, the Bankruptcy Code's definition of "notice and hearing" as contained in § 102(1) leaves it to the Court to determine what is appropriate in the particular circumstance. In re Collins, 334 B.R. 655 (Bankr. D. Minn. 2005). Given the exigencies of this situation, I find that the notice given to Centex was appropriate under the circumstances. At the hearing on reconsideration, Centex's counsel conceded that their opposition to the imposition of the automatic stay would have consisted primarily of the Debtor's history of filings and the dealings between the Creditor and the Debtor. All of this information is within the possession of Centex attorneys or immediately available online through the Court's electronic dockets. Notwithstanding the fact that the law office of Daniel Consuegra is located in Tampa, the advent of electronic filing under CM/ECF permits them to view documents that are filed immediately as they are docketed and to file documents online without any delay. Any lack of opportunity to respond, prepare, and attend the emergency hearing is a result of the internal practice of the law office coupled with the Creditor's decision to use a law firm located in Tampa, Florida to handle cases in the Northern District of Florida. While there is nothing wrong with law firms in one part of the state handling cases all over the state,[1] this is not a justification for not being able to promptly respond to emergency matters as they arise. The apparent lack of organization to deal with this type of matter in the Creditor's attorney's office was exemplified at this hearing by the submission by Debtor's counsel of a facsimile he received from the Law Offices of Daniel Consuegra asking if he (Debtor's counsel) could cover this hearing for them as local counsel.
>
> The limited automatic stay for repeat filers is a major feature of BAPCPA which was passed by Congress at the behest of the credit industry. Now that they have it, the credit industry, and especially the mortgage servicing companies and the law firms they retain to represent them, need to adapt their practices in order to deal with what they have created. Since the effective date of BAPCPA, this Court has conducted evidentiary hearings on fifteen (15) Motions for the Extension or Imposition of the Stay in cases involving repeat filers. In only one of those hearings did an attorney appear on behalf of the mortgagee, and that attorney was a local consumer debtor lawyer who had been

[1] This Court accommodates such practice by conducting all preliminary hearings on Motions for Relief from the Automatic Stay telephonically.

> retained at the last minute to make an appearance and argue against the extension of the stay. While in this case, notice was admittedly short, the experience of this Court in other cases suggests that even with another week's notice nothing would have changed. The Creditor has made no demonstration of any prejudice due to the short notice for the hearing. Accordingly, the Motion for Rehearing or Reconsideration is hereby DENIED.

Id. at 518.

2. Suppose D files a bankruptcy petition without credit counseling. The case is dismissed. D immediately files a second case after obtaining credit counseling. Is a court justified in extending the automatic stay pursuant to §632(c)(3)(B)? In re Ferguson, 376 B.R. 109 (Bankr. E.D. Pa. 2007) (yes).

HOLCOMB v HARDEMAN (IN RE HOLCOMB)

380 B.R. 813 (Bankr. 10th Cir. 2008)

MCFEELEY, J.

Appellants/Debtors, Aleshia Holcomb and Bradley Holcomb, appeal an order of the bankruptcy court of the Western District of Oklahoma contending that the bankruptcy court erred under 11 U.S.C. § 362(c)(3)(A) when it concluded that the stay imposed on the filing of their case terminated with respect to the property of the estate on the thirtieth day after the initiation of their case. Because the language of § 362(c)(3)(A) terminates the stay only with respect to the debtor, we reverse and remand to the bankruptcy court.

I. Background

On June 3, 2005, Debtors Bradley and Aleshia Holcomb ("Debtors") filed a proceeding under Chapter 13 of the Bankruptcy Code. Their plan was confirmed. The self-employed Debtors became unable to make their plan payments. On March 2, 2007, their case was dismissed for failure to make payments.

After the Debtors found new employment, on April 26, 2007, they again filed a petition under Chapter 13. The primary asset in the case is their home. On May 25, 2007, the Debtors filed a Motion to Determine the Automatic Stay Remains in Effect to Property of the Estate Pursuant to § 362(c)(4)(B) ("Motion"). In the Motion the Debtors asked the bankruptcy court to determine that the automatic stay remained in effect with regard to the property of the estate or in the alternative to impose the automatic stay under 11 U.S.C. § 362(c)(4)(B). No objections were filed.

The bankruptcy court heard the Motion on June 26, 2007. The court orally denied the Motion on that date. The court held that the language in § 362(c)(3)(A) when read in conjunction with the statutory scheme and the concurrent requirement that a stay may be extended only upon motion of the debtor within the named thirty day period, indicated that Congress must have meant the stay to expire with regard to property of the debtor's estate, the debtor and any property of the debtor not included in the estate.

The Order denying the Motion was entered on July 9, 2007. On July 18, 2007, the Debtors timely filed their notice of appeal. The parties have consented to this Court's jurisdiction because they did not elect to have the appeal heard by the United States District Court for the Western District of Oklahoma. 28 U.S.C. § 158(c)(1); Fed. R. Bankr. P. 8001; 10th Cir. BAP L. R. 8001-1. At issue in this appeal is the meaning of language in § 362(c)(3)(A) . . . .

II. Discussion

Section § 362(c)(3)(A) was added to the Bankruptcy Code by the Bankruptcy Abuse Prevention and Consumer Protection Act of 2005, Pub. L. No. 109-8 § 302, 119 Stat. 23 (2005). Under § 362(c)(3)(A), if a debtor has had a case pending within the preceding one year period that was dismissed,

> (A) the stay under subsection (a) with respect to any action taken with respect to a debt or property securing such debt or with respect to any lease shall terminate with respect to the debtor on the 30th day after the filing of the later case[.]

11 U.S.C. § 362(c)(3)(A). The debtor may obtain an extension of the stay if he can rebut the presumption that the subsequent case was not filed in good faith. The motion to extend the stay must be filed and a hearing must be held before the expiration of the thirty day period. 11 U.S.C. § 362(c)(3)(B). The thirty day period begins on the filing date of the later case. 11 U.S.C. § 362(c)(3)(A).[1]

At issue in this appeal is the language in § 362(c)(3)(A) that mandates that "the stay . . . shall terminate with respect to the debtor." The Debtors argue that the bankruptcy court erred when it concluded that this phrase ends the stay with respect to the debtor, the debtor's property, and property of the estate on the thirtieth day after they filed their second bankruptcy petition. They contend that pursuant to this language, the stay terminates only with respect to any actions against the debtor.

On this issue, courts have taken two different approaches. A minority of courts have concluded that under § 362(c)(3)(A) the stay terminates in its entirety. These courts begin with the premise that the plain language rule does not apply because the language of § 362(c)(3)(A) is capable of more than one interpretation and is inconsistent with the overall statutory scheme. See, e.g., In re Curry, 362 B. R. 394, 400-01 (Bankr. N. D. Ill 2007). Using the "broader context of BAPCPA changes" and the legislative history, the minority approach concludes that in § 362(c)(3)(A) Congress intended to terminate the stay in its entirety. Id. at 398, 401-02.

The minority approach reasons that the term "with respect to the debtor" is an ambiguous phrase because it appears to run contrary to the statutory scheme. They reason that the term "property of the estate" incorporates virtually all property. Only property that is abandoned or exempt or otherwise is excluded from the definition "property of the estate." They state that if the phrase "with respect to the debtor" is read to refer only to the debtor and the debtor's property, then the rest of the sentence which reads "the stay . . . with respect to any action taken with respect to a debt or property securing such debt or with respect to any lease shall terminate" does not make sense and the phrase is superfluous. These courts conclude that the phrase "with respect to the debtor," must be meant to address situations where there are co-debtors and one debtor has filed a successive case and the other has not.

Agreeing with the minority approach, the bankruptcy court concluded that the language of § 362(c)(3)(A), when read in conjunction with the statutory guidelines in that same paragraph regarding termination of the stay, indicates that the phrase within that subsection "with respect to the debtor" must mean the

---

[1] The Debtors filed their Motion one day prior to the expiration of the thirty day limit.

debtor, the debtor's property, and property of the estate.

In contrast, a majority of courts have relied on the plain language of the phrase "with respect to the debtor," concluding that there is no ambiguity in its application. See, e.g., In re Jumpp, 356 B.R. 789, 796 (1st Cir. BAP 2006) (concluding that the stay continued with regard to property of the estate). According to these courts, the automatic stay terminates under § 362(c)(3)(A) only with respect to the debtor and the debtor's property but not as to property of the estate. Id.; In re Paschal, 337 B.R. 274, 278-79 (Bankr. E.D.N.C. 2006); In re Jones, 339 B.R. 360, 364-65 (Bankr. E.D.N.C. 2006). These courts reason that if Congress meant to terminate the stay in its entirety, it would have done so in plain language as it did in § 362(c)(4)(A)(i).[2]

The Court of Appeals for the Tenth Circuit has not yet addressed this issue. We find the majority approach better reasoned and more faithful to the language of the statute and the policies behind the Bankruptcy Code.

First, we see no ambiguity in the language of the statute. "Statutory construction must begin with the language employed by Congress and the assumption that the ordinary meaning of that language accurately expresses the legislative purpose." Park 'N Fly, Inc. v. Dollar Park & Fly, Inc., 469 U.S. 189, 194 (1985). Nowhere in § 362 does Congress use the phrase "with respect to the debtor" as incorporating the debtor, the debtor's separate property, and property of the estate. In fact, "[s]ection 362(a) differentiates between acts against the debtor, against property of the debtor and against property of the estate." Jones, 339 B. R. at 363. As observed in Jones, "a plain reading of those words ['with respect to the debtor'] makes sense and is entirely consistent with other provisions of § 362 and other sections of the Bankruptcy Code." Id.

Reading this statute according to its plain meaning is also consistent with the policies behind bankruptcy law. At the core of bankruptcy law is the policy of "obtaining a maximum and equitable distribution for creditors." BFP v. Resolution Trust Corp., 511 U.S. 531, 563 (1994); Research-Planning, Inc. v. Segal (In re First Capital Mortgage Loan Corp.), 917 F.2d 424, 428 (10th Cir. 1990) (noting that the preference provisions found in 11 U.S.C. § 547 further this important policy). The minority approach circumvents this policy by allowing a single creditor, who may be oversecured, full access to property that would otherwise be property of the estate. Such property may be necessary to implement a debtor's Chapter 13 plan; or, in a Chapter 7 case, equity in the property above the creditor's security interest could be realized by the trustee to pay a dividend to creditors. This dividend could potentially be lost if we adopt the reasoning of the bankruptcy court. Maintaining the stay with respect to such property is an important creditor protection.

On this basis, we conclude that the language of § 362(c)(3)(A) terminates the stay only as to the debtor and the debtor's property.

For the reasons set forth above, the order of the bankruptcy court is

---

[2] That section reads:

> if a single or joint case is filed by or against a debtor who is an individual under this title, and if 2 or more single or joint cases of the debtor were pending within the previous year but were dismissed, other than a case refiled under section 707(b), the stay under subsection (a) shall not go into effect upon the filing of the later case[.]

reversed and the case is remanded for proceedings consistent with this Opinion.

Notes and Questions

1. The import of the court's holding is that the mortgage lender claiming the debtor's house must move to lift the automatic stay (as usual) even after the 30 day lapse. But §362(c)(3)(A) says that the automatic stay lapses "with respect to any action taken with respect to a debtor or property securing such debt. . ." Why doesn't this free up the mortgage lender to foreclose after 30 days?

2. If the Holcomb court has read §363(c)(3) aright, then §363(c)(3) is of virtually no help to foreclosing creditors, who are the very victims of multiple filings in order to obtain the automatic stay. Reswick v. Reswick (In re Reswick), 2011 Bankr. LEXIS 873 (Bankr. 9th Cir., February 4, 2011) (disagreeing with Holcomb because of this consequence).

3. Under §362(a)(3), even if the automatic stay lapses, the bankruptcy continues. The debtor's house may have a valuable equity in it, which the trustee can sell to reimburse unsecured creditors. 11 U.S.C. § 363(f)(3). In such a case, the trustee, as a "party in interest," may move to extend or reimpose the automatic stay. 11 U.S.C. §§ 362(c)(3)(B), 362(c)(4)(B).

4. Suppose D is subject to § 362(c)(3). Thirty days pass, and the court has not extended the stay. Which of the following is permitted to a creditor?

(a) Pursuant to a prior money judgment, serve an execution on the sheriff.

(b) Pursuant to a writ of execution, have the sheriff garnish D's bank account.

(c) Commence an action to evict D for failing to pay rent.

CHAPTER 2 DEBTOR DUTIES

A. AUTOMATIC DISMISSALS

COMMUNITY BANK, N.A. v RIFFLE

617 F.3d 171 (2d Cir. 2010)

PER CURIAM

Appellant Community Bank, N.A. ("Community Bank"), appeals the August 15, 2008, judgment of the United States District Court for the Western District of New York (Siragusa, J.). The district court affirmed the bankruptcy court's denial of Community Bank's motion to, inter alia, obtain an order confirming the automatic dismissal of the bankruptcy case of Stephen Riffle pursuant to 11 U.S.C. § 521(i)(1) on the grounds that Stephen and Lora Riffle (collectively, "Appellees") failed to file copies of all payment advices received by Stephen Riffle within 60 days before the date of the filing of the bankruptcy petition as required by 11 U.S.C. § 521(a)(1)(B)(iv). We hold that because Appellees provided information reflecting "payment received" from Stephen Riffle's employer in the 60 days prior to the petition, they satisfied the requirements of § 521(a)(1)(B)(iv). We therefore affirm the judgment of the district court.

I. STATUTORY REQUIREMENTS

Appellees filed a petition for bankruptcy under Chapter 13 of the Bankruptcy Code. Schedules and statements filed by the Appellees indicated that Community Bank was a fully secured creditor that held a mortgage on their residence. Prior to the bankruptcy filing, Stephen Riffle was employed by YB Sales and Distribution. During the 60-day period before the filing, Stephen Riffle received from his employer four payment advices with respect to his compensation. According to the Appellees' Schedule I of Current Income, Lora Riffle had no income during this time.

Within the 45-day period for filing "copies of all payment advices or other evidence of payment received within 60 days before the date of the filing of the petition, by the debtor from any employer of the debtor," 11 U.S.C. § 521(a)(1)(B)(iv), the Appellees filed the last payment advice that Stephen Riffle received during that 60-day period. The advice was dated September 14, 2007, covered the pay period ending September 8, 2007, included Stephen Riffle's earnings and deductions for that pay period, and identified his year-to-date earnings and payroll deductions in various categories. Stephen Riffle claims that he had thrown the other payment advices away. The Appellees also filed a chart entitled "Sales Earnings Report." This document was issued by Stephen Riffle's employer and showed his gross earnings for each pay period from January 5, 2007, through August 31, 2007.

After the 45-day period for filing had passed, Community Bank moved to confirm the automatic dismissal of Stephen Riffle's petition for failure to file all of the payment advices received within the 60-day period and, upon dismissal of Stephen Riffle's petition, to dismiss Lora Riffle's petition because she had no income and could not fund a Chapter 13 plan. The Trustee opposed the dismissal on the grounds that the evidence submitted by the Appellees represented full compliance with the statutory requirements of 11 U.S.C. § 521(a)(1)(B)(iv).

The bankruptcy court denied Community Bank's motion to dismiss Stephen Riffle's case on the basis that the filed payment advice and sales earning report were "other evidence of payment" as required under Section 521(a)(1)(B)(iv) and provided year-to-date gross and net pay, including every category of gross pay and applicable deductions. The court also stated that it did not "believe that detailed information per pay period with respect to deductions is critical under Section 521(a)(1)(B)(iv), as long as the year-to-date evidence, as supplied here by the last Pay Stub received before the filing of the petition, provides a complete list of the categories of the deductions from the Debtor's pay for the sixty-day period in question." The court accordingly also denied the motion to dismiss Lora Riffle's case.

Community Bank appealed to the district court, which affirmed on the opinion of the bankruptcy court. On appeal to this Court, Community Bank challenges only the district court's affirmance of the bankruptcy court's denial of the motion to dismiss.

II. DISCUSSION . . .

B. Obligations under 11 U.S.C. § 521(a)(1)(B)(iv)

. . . Under 11 U.S.C. § 521(a)(1)(B)(iv), a bankruptcy debtor must, "unless the court orders otherwise," file "copies of all payment advices or other evidence of payment received within 60 days before the date of the filing of the petition, by the debtor from any employer of the debtor." If a voluntary filer under Chapter 7 or Chapter 13 does not comply with this requirement within 45 days after the filing of the petition, the case is automatically dismissed. 11 U.S.C. § 521(i)(1).[1]

We have not previously decided what obligations 11 U.S.C. § 521(a)(1)(B)(iv) imposes upon a debtor, and the statute, to put it mildly, is not a model of syntactical clarity. At least two grammatically valid readings of the statute are possible, each of which would place a different requirement on the debtor.

"Statutory analysis begins with the text and its plain meaning, if it has one." Green v. City of New York, 465 F.3d 65, 78 (2d Cir. 2006) (quoting Gottlieb v. Carnival Corp., 436 F.3d 335, 337 (2d Cir. 2006)). This text lacks a plain meaning. What makes the statute ambiguous is that it is not clear how the

[1] 11 U.S.C. § 521(i)(1) provides that "[s]ubject to paragraphs (2) and (4) and notwithstanding section 707(a), if an individual debtor in a voluntary case under chapter 7 or 13 fails to file all of the information required under subsection (a)(1) within 45 days after the date of the filing of the petition, the case shall be automatically dismissed effective on the 46th day after the date of the filing of the petition."

participle "received" functions in context. On one possible reading, the clause "received within 60 days" could be understood to refer to the compound subject "all payment advices or other evidence" (with the word "all" modifying both "payment advices" and "other evidence"). Were we to adopt this reading, which we may call the document-focused interpretation, the effect would be to require the debtor to turn over all payment advices that he received in the 60 days leading up to the filing of his bankruptcy petition, or, if he received no such payment advices, all other evidence he received. On this understanding of the statute, we would have to conclude that the Riffles failed to comply, because it is undisputed that Stephen Riffle received some payment advices that he did not file.

A second possible reading would read "received" to modify "payment." This reading would thus treat the phrase "of payment received" as a unit that: (1) is modified by the phrase "within 60 days of before the date of the filing of the petition, by the debtor from any employer of the debtor"; and (2) so modified, itself modifies the phrase "all payment advices or other evidence" (with the word "all" modifying "payment advices" but not "other evidence"). This approach may feel somewhat more awkward than the first, but it is grammatical, and becomes easily intelligible if one reads "of" as "in respect to," which is among that preposition's definitions. See Webster's Third New International Dictionary 1565 (2002). Under this approach, which we may term the payment-focused interpretation, the statute requires a debtor alternatively to file either (1) "all payment advices . . . of payment received within 60 days before the date of the filing of the petition," or (2) "other evidence of payment received within 60 days before the date of the filing of the petition." If we adopt this approach, a debtor will be in compliance so long as he files credible evidence that sets forth all "payment received" from his employer in the 60 days prior to the petition. This reading has been embraced by the bankruptcy appellate panel for the Tenth Circuit. See In re Miller, 383 B.R. 767, 770-71 (B.A.P. 10th Cir. 2008). On this interpretation, the Riffles prevail, because, as the bankruptcy court found, the documents the Riffles filed provided adequate information regarding all payments from his employer in the required period.

Although neither reading is perfectly satisfying, we conclude that the payment-focused interpretation is superior. The document-focused interpretation may have the benefit of requiring less grammatical parsing, but it also makes less sense according to principles of statutory construction. Under the document-focused approach, where the word "received" modifies "payment advices or other evidence," then either type of document also must be received "from the employer" to satisfy the requirement of the statute. And in that case, it is unclear what type of "other evidence" -- received from an employer and reflective of the same time period as the payment advice for which it is substituting -- would not itself constitute a "payment advice." In other words, the document-focused interpretation of the statute seems to render the term "other evidence" meaningless. See In Re Miller, 383 B.R. at 771; Triestman v United States, 124 F.3d 361, 376 (2d Cir. 1997) ("[W]e assume that Congress intended that language which it chose to employ actually was to have meaning; effect must be given, if possible, to every word, clause and sentence of a statute . . . so that no part will be inoperative or superfluous, void or insignificant." (brackets and ellipsis in original)(quoting Consolidated Rail Corp. v. United States, 896 F.2d 574, 579, 283 U.S. App. D.C. 47 (D.C. Cir. 1990))).

The term "payment advice," of course, is not defined in the statute, and it might be suggested instead that only documents generated contemporaneously with the delivery of payment constitute payment advices. "Other evidence" then might include non-contemporaneous documentation of payment generated by an employer at the debtor's request (for example, a letter generated by the employer's accounting department because the debtor was missing a pay stub). But in that case, there would be no necessary relationship between the time at which the missing payment advice should have been received and the time at which the substitute other evidence was ultimately received. That is, the time at which the documents were received would not ensure that one was a useful substitute for the other, and the statute's focus on what documents the debtor happened to receive in the period immediately prior to his petition would be quite arbitrary. See Troll Co. v. Uneeda Doll Co., 483 F.3d 150, 160 (2d Cir.2007) ("[I]t is an elemental principle of statutory construction that an ambiguous statute must be construed to avoid absurd results.")

The payment-focused interpretation, on the other hand, has the benefit of consistency with the other requirements listed under § 521(a)(1)(B), each of which demands information about the finances of the debtor at the time of his bankruptcy petition that might be relevant to the petition. See, e.g., 11 U.S.C. § 521(a)(1)(B)(i) (directing debtor to file "a schedule of assets and liabilities"); id. at (ii) (requiring "a schedule of current income and current expenditures"); id. at (v) (requiring "a statement of monthly net income, itemized to show how the amount is calculated"). To the extent that the text of § 521(a)(1)(B)(iv) is ambiguous, the context of these surrounding provisions suggests that subsection (iv) also should be read to focus on relevant information -- the actual compensation received by the debtor from his employer immediately prior to his petition -- rather than specific documents. See Natural Res. Def. Council v. Muszynski, 268 F.3d 91, 98 (2d Cir. 2001) ("[W]hen determining which reasonable meaning [of an ambiguous text] should prevail, the text should be placed in the context of the entire statutory structure."). The fact that automatic dismissal is mandated only in the event of a failure to file "all of the information required," 11 U.S.C. § 521(i)(1) (emphasis added), also suggests a statutory emphasis on the filing of information relevant to the debtor's petition, rather than a requirement for specific documents.

With the "plain language" of the statute being anything but, we are guided by the foregoing canons to reach the most sensible interpretation. See Green, 465 F.3d at 78 ("Only if an attempt to discern the plain language fails because the statute is ambiguous, do we resort to canons of construction."). The canons favor a conclusion that § 521(a)(1)(B)(iv) is better interpreted to require disclosure of certain relevant information than to require production of specific pieces of paper. We accordingly join the Tenth Circuit Bankruptcy Appellate Panel in holding that: (1) the word "received" in § 521(a)(1)(B)(iv) modifies the word "payment," and thus it is the date of receipt of any relevant payment, not the date of receipt of any particular document, that establishes the debtor's obligations under the subsection; and (2) a debtor may satisfy the subsection's requirements by filing either (a) "copies of all payment advices . . . of [such] payment received . . . by the debtor from any employer" or (b) "copies of . . . other [credible] evidence of [such] payment received . . . by the debtor from any employer." In re Miller, 383 B.R. at 771.

Community Bank also argues that the Appellees did not meet their obligation under § 521(i)(1) to "file all of the information required under subsection (a)(1)." It contends that:

> [t]he Sales Earning Report filed by Mr. Riffle disclosed his gross pay over the four pay periods in question, but provided no information on net pay or his payroll withholdings and deductions. The one payment advice filed provided cumulative year to date data on payroll deductions and net pay. However, it was not possible to extrapolate from that data all of the information contained on the three missing payroll documents.

The Bankruptcy Code does not require a breakdown of gross and net income on a perpay period basis.

As discussed above, under § 521(a)(1)(B)(iv), evidence must be submitted of payment for the 60-day period prior to the date that the petition is filed. Further, pursuant to § 521(a)(1)(B)(v), the debtor must identify monthly net income. Community Bank points to no language in the Bankruptcy Code that compels a debtor to provide gross and net income on a per-pay-period basis.

We conclude that by presenting the September 14, 2007, payment advice, which included Stephen Riffle's earnings and deductions for that pay period, and identified his year-to-date earnings and payroll deductions for various categories, and by submitting the "Sales Earnings Report," which showed his gross earnings for each pay period from January 5, 2007, through August 31, 2007, Appellees "create[d] a very clear picture as to the amount of income [the] [d]ebtor[s] received in the sixty days prepetition," In re Miller, 383 B.R. at 772, and thus met their obligations under § 521(a)(1)(B)(iv).

We affirm the judgment of the district court.

Notes and Questions

1. For some slam poetry denouncing automatic dismissal, see In re Riddle, 344 B.R. 702 (Bankr. S.D. Fla. 2006).

2. Suppose a debtor asks for more time to file the information required by § 521(a). The request is made 50 days after the bankruptcy petition. Does the court have power to prevent autoamtic dismissal? In re Williams, 339 B.R. 794 (Bankr. M.D. Fla. 2006) (no).

3. Suppose the debtor gives a set of pay stubs to the standing chapter 13 trustee the day after she files a bankruptcy petition. Forty-six days later, is the case dismissed? In re Rubio, 2006 Bankr. LEXIS 2846 (Bankr. S.D. Tex. Sept. 25, 2006).

4. Suppose tax returns are missing. Automatic dismissal? In re Ring, 341 B.R. 387, 389 n.4, 390 (Bankr. D. Me. 2006) (no). Why not?

5. Suppose a debtor is late filing a tax return with the court. The debtor supplied the tax return to his lawyer and the lawyer did not file it. Was this event "beyond the control of the debtor" within the meaning of §521(e)(2)(B)? In re Merrill, 340 B.R. 671 (Bankr. D.N.H. 2006) (no).

SEGARRA-MIRANDA v ACOSTA-RIVERA (IN RE ACOSTA-RIVERA)

557 F.3d 8 (1st Cir. 2009)

SELYA, J.

This appeal, which requires us to decide an issue of first impression at the federal appellate level, turns on the construction of a provision of [BAPCPA]. Writ large, the provision in question expands the debtor's duties of financial disclosure to the extent that he or she must now file with the bankruptcy court, "unless the court orders otherwise," six traunches of financial information (including payment advices and an itemized statement of monthly net income). 11 U.S.C. § 521(a)(1)(B)(iv), (v). The issue centers on whether the bankruptcy court may enter an order excusing non-disclosure after the time for filing the required information has expired. The bankruptcy court thought that it had the authority to enter such an order. It proceeded to exercise that power, thus avoiding dismissal of the debtors' petition under section 521(i)(1) (BAPCPA's so-called "automatic dismissal" provision). The district court construed the "orders otherwise" provision differently. Consequently, it determined that the order excusing the failure to file was beyond the scope of the bankruptcy court's authority. See Rivera v. Miranda, 376 B.R. 382, 386 (D.P.R. 2007).

We conclude that the bankruptcy court acted in consonance with the statutory scheme and within the realm of its discretion. Accordingly, we reverse the district court's order and remand for further proceedings.

The procedural background is uncomplicated. The debtors, Ivan Acosta-Rivera and Ana Balseiro-Chacon, are married to each other. They originally filed a joint Chapter 13 petition and later converted that filing to a Chapter 7 petition.[1] The debtors' estate included an unresolved employment discrimination suit brought by Acosta-Rivera against his quondam employer. In that suit, which had been pending for roughly eight years and had twice been appealed to the Supreme Court of Puerto Rico, Acosta-Rivera sought reinstatement, backpay, and compensatory damages.

At this point, the plot thickens. Although this chose in action was plainly an asset of the debtors' estate, it did not appear on their original bankruptcy schedules, their first amended schedules, or their second amended schedules.

Six months after the filing of the bankruptcy petition, the debtors revealed the existence of the chose in action, listing its value as "unknown," in their third amended set of schedules. Even then, they failed to disclose that the suit demanded pecuniary relief (e.g., backpay and money damages). After several further amendments (not material here), the debtors valued the chose in action at $2,700,000 and claimed an exemption of $350,000.

Eventually, the Chapter 7 trustee moved for leave to settle the suit for $200,000 (a sum that would have generated enough cash to pay all allowed claims and produce some surplus funds for the debtors). Balking at this proposal, the debtors moved under the automatic dismissal provision, 11 U.S.C. § 521(i)(2), to confirm the dismissal of their petition. In support of their motion, they claimed not to have filed or otherwise provided the payment advices and statement of monthly net income required by BAPCPA. As their attorney acknowledged, the debtors wanted to dismiss the bankruptcy case so that they could "continue prosecuting the state court action" for damages.

We pause at this juncture to discuss the Act's "automatic dismissal" provision. When a debtor fails to file all the information required by section 521(a)(1)(B) within the prescribed period -- that is, within forty-five days of the filing date of the bankruptcy petition -- BAPCPA provides that "the case shall be automatically dismissed."[2] 11 U.S.C. § 521(i)(1). The term "automatic dismissal"

---

[1] In brief, a Chapter 13 bankruptcy allows individuals who have a regular source of income to submit to the bankruptcy court a plan to repay all or part of their debts over a three to five year period. During the repayment period creditors are stayed from starting or continuing collection efforts. See 11 U.S.C. §§ 1321-1330. Chapter 7 is a liquidation. See 11 U.S.C. §§ 701-784. A bankruptcy trustee collects and sells the debtor's non-exempt assets and uses those proceeds to pay creditors.

[2] The automatic dismissal deadline can be extended by another forty-five days upon timely request. See 11 U.S.C. § 521(i)(3). Moreover, the automatic dismissal provision is subject to an explicit statutory exception: a timely motion by the trustee to forestall dismissal based on the best

is something of a misnomer. Typically, dismissal under this provision takes place at the instance of a "party in interest." Id. § 521(i)(2); see, e.g., In re Spencer, 388 B.R. 418, 421 (Bankr. D.D.C. 2008). Dismissal is, therefore, hardly "automatic."[3]

We return to what transpired below. In due season, the bankruptcy court denied the debtors' motion to dismiss, finding that "facts peculiar to this case do not require dismissal under section 521." In support, the court noted that the debtors' motion stemmed from their "disagreement with the proposed settlement." That was significant because the putative settlement would have satisfied all allowed claims; thus, neither the creditors nor the trustee needed the missing (undisclosed) information. Based on that reasoning, the court entered "an order nunc pro tunc . . . excusing the debtors from filing the payment advices mentioned in section 521(a)(1)(B)(iv)."[4] In short, the court excused the detailed disclosure by ordering the debtors to do "otherwise" under section 521(a)(1)(B).

In a subsequent order, the court approved the trustee's revised recommendation to settle the discrimination case for $600,000, citing the likelihood of delay from further litigation, uncertainties surrounding collection, and the fact that Acosta-Rivera stood to receive nearly $400,000, less mortgage arrearages, after the allowed claims were paid.

The debtors appealed the denial of their motion to dismiss to the district court. The district judge ruled that the bankruptcy court lacked authority to excuse compliance with the disclosure requirement more than forty-five days after the debtors filed their bankruptcy petition. See Rivera, 376 B.R. at 386. In the judge's view, the strictures of the Act left the bankruptcy judge "with no discretion to fashion any reasonable or equitable solution." Id. at 386-87. The judge stated: "'After the expiration of the specified period set forth in 11 U.S.C. § 521(i)(1), there are no exceptions, no excuses, only dismissal and the consequences that flow therefrom.'" Id. at 386 (quoting In re Ott, 343 B.R. 264, 268 (Bankr. D. Colo. 2006)). This timely appeal followed. . . .[5]

Having cleared away the underbrush, what remains is the question of the bankruptcy court's authority to waive the disclosure requirement after the expiration of the filing deadline. The statute provides that the debtor "shall . . . file" the required disclosures "unless the court orders otherwise." 11 U.S.C. § 521(a)(1)(B). The grant of judicial power to "order[] otherwise" predated BAPCPA.[6] In overhauling section 521, Congress left this familiar language intact. We do not regard that as a mere fortuity. Nor do we think that a slip of the pen

---

interests of the creditors and the debtors' good-faith efforts to effect the required filing. Id. § 521(i)(1), (4). That exception does not apply here.

[3] A few courts have conceptualized dismissal under this section as a matter involving only the counting of the days. See, e.g., In re Fawson, 338 B.R. 505, 510 (Bankr. D. Utah 2006). To decide this case, we need not resolve that question.

[4] Although not explicitly mentioned, the court evidently meant to excuse as well the filing of the monthly net income statement. We proceed on that assumption.

[5] Only the United States Trustee filed an answering brief in the district court. That court, however, designated both the United States Trustee and the Chapter 7 trustee as appellees. The Chapter 7 trustee has taken the instant appeal. We are satisfied that he has standing to do so.

[6] The pre-BAPCPA version of section 521(1) provided:

> The Debtor shall . . . file a list of creditors, and unless the court orders otherwise, a schedule of assets and liabilities, a schedule of current income and current expenditures, and a statement of the debtor's financial affairs.

accounts for the fact that the provision does not now contain an explicit deadline for ordering otherwise. In this context, we have a high regard for congressional silence.

Sharing this regard, a few courts have held that the bankruptcy court possesses authority to waive the disclosure requirement even after the forty-five-day filing deadline has expired. See, e.g., In re Parker, 351 B.R. 790, 801-02 (Bankr. N.D. Ga. 2006); In re Jackson, 348 B.R. 487, 499-500 (Bankr. S.D. Iowa 2006); cf. In re Bonner, 374 B.R. 62, 64-65 (Bankr. W.D.N.Y. 2007) (suggesting that "special circumstances can justify nunc pro tunc relief" under section 521(i)). Other courts, however, have taken the view that BAPCPA's new forty-five-day deadline applies to courts and debtors alike. See, e.g., In re Spencer, 388 B.R. at 422; Warren v. Wirum, 378 B.R. 640, 647 (N.D. Cal. 2007); In re Hall, 368 B.R. 595, 599 (Bankr. W.D. Tex. 2007); In re Brickey, 363 B.R. at 64-65 (Bankr. N.D.N.Y. 2007); In re Calhoun, 359 B.R. 738, 740 (Bankr. E.D. Mo. 2007). That view reads into the filing deadline a restriction on bankruptcy courts' authority gleaned by implication from the "automatic dismissal" provision.

Neither reading satisfies both head and heart in equal measure. The former (more flexible) reading honors the policy behind the Act by vesting bankruptcy courts with greater discretion to discourage bankruptcy abuse. Because any party in interest may request an order of automatic dismissal, debtors with something to hide are liable to treat dismissal as an escape hatch to be opened as needed. See Parker, 351 B.R. at 802; see also Hall, 368 B.R. at 602 (dismissing case on motion of debtor whom court describes as "the poster child for a bad faith debtor"). In such cases, the court has no occasion to address non-disclosure until long after the forty-five-day period has elapsed. That timetable rubs uneasily against the strictures of an inflexible reading--and bankruptcy courts are, after all, courts of equity.

But the story has another side. The stricter reading of the statute, though inflexible, gives sharper teeth to the automatic dismissal provision. It ensures that dismissal at a party's request is all but guaranteed once the forty-five days have passed. Given Congress's concern with "the recent escalation of consumer bankruptcy filings," H.R. Rep. No. 109-31, at 3-4, reprinted in 2005 U.S.C.C.A.N. 90, it can be argued that the stricter reading has some implicit support in the legislative history. See, e.g., Warren, 378 B.R. at 647; see also Rivera, 376 B.R. at 386 (voicing concern that retroactive relief from the filing requirement "would render the automatic dismissal provision in § 521(i) meaningless").

This position has a certain superficial appeal. Still, we must caution against trying to stretch a morsel into a meal. The amendments to section 521 are part of an abuse-prevention package. With Congress's core purpose in mind, we are reluctant to read into the statute by implication a new limit on judicial discretion that would encourage rather than discourage bankruptcy abuse. It is safe to say that Congress, in enacting BAPCPA, was not bent on placing additional weapons in the hands of abusive debtors.[7]

In all events, we believe that it is possible to give effect to all of section 521, preserving the bankruptcy court's discretion to forgive compliance with disclosure requirements after the fact while at the same time preserving the

[7] By definition, such debtors are unfit for the "good faith" exception in section 521(i)(4). See supra note 2. Moreover, under 11 U.S.C. § 707(a), a chapter 7 debtor has no absolute right to dismiss his petition but must instead show cause. See In re Smith, 507 F.3d 64, 72 (2d Cir. 2007).

authentic value of automatic dismissal. When a party moves under section 521(i)(2) for the entry of an order dismissing an incomplete petition, the court can do one of three things: dismiss the case, decline to dismiss the case if the good-faith exception for payment advices applies, see supra note 2; or determine, in its discretion, that the missing information is not "required under subsection (a)(1)." 11 U.S.C. § 521(i)(1). In the last-mentioned event, the court can deny the motion to dismiss. Some courts in "strict" jurisdictions seem to assume that the second and third of these options cover the same ground. That thinking underlies the opinions construing the forty-five-day deadline for automatic dismissal as an implicit temporal limitation upon the court's authority to order otherwise. See, e.g., Spencer, 388 B.R. at 422; Warren, 378 B.R. at 646; Hall, 368 B.R. at 599; Brickey, 363 B.R. at 64-65; Calhoun, 359 B.R. at 740.

We find that mechanical reading unwise. While it may be textually plausible, it fails to harmonize the letter and purpose of the statute. There is another, equally plausible reading--a reading that avoids this vice.

The approach that we endorse recognizes that missing information may or may not be required, in a practical sense, depending upon what is deemed material by the court many months (or even years) after the bankruptcy petition has been filed. This would seem to be a likely reason for Congress to have entrusted the bankruptcy court with discretion to modify disclosure requirements on the fly. Where, as here, a previously hidden asset has more than enough value to cover the entire universe of creditors' claims, dollar for dollar, dispensing with the disclosure of statements reflecting payment advices and/or monthly net income is both pragmatic and reasonable. Common sense suggests that Congress never intended to strip the bankruptcy court of the flexibility needed to respond intelligently to the emergence of such a circumstance after the forty-five-day filing deadline has expired.

This intuition is reinforced by our certain knowledge that this degree of flexibility existed in the Bankruptcy Code prior to BAPCPA's passage. As we have said, BAPCPA did not expressly curtail this aspect of the bankruptcy court's authority and, given the practical realities, we are reluctant to step in where Congress has elected not to tread. Automatic dismissal may be a new twist, but the importance of the judiciary's ability to assess needs and respond to exigencies free of artificial constraints has not changed. In our view, Congress must have recognized that bankruptcy courts would still need a meaningful opportunity to gauge whether missing information is "required" in a particular case. We conclude, therefore, that when the missing information has become irrelevant or extraneous and the court, in lieu of dismissal on that account, "order[s] otherwise," section 521(i) does not compel dismissal of the case.[8]

On the same reasoning, we also reject the assertion that the exceptions to automatic dismissal contained in section 521(i), see supra note 2, were meant to supplant the bankruptcy court's discretion to order otherwise more than forty-five days after the filing date. Those exceptions apply when the court does not choose to waive the disclosure requirement either ex ante or ex post; they do not apply when the court does so elect. So understood, the exceptions operate within

[8] To be sure, the time line for the entry of an order of automatic dismissal suggests an impatience with delay. When a party in interest requests dismissal and the case is one that falls within section 521(i)(1), "the court shall enter an order of dismissal not later than 5 days after such request." 11 U.S.C. § 521(i)(2). Nothing in our holding today diminishes this mandate.

their own statutory ambit and do not cabin the bankruptcy court's discretion in other areas.

Let us be perfectly clear. We do not decide today whether bankruptcy courts possess unfettered discretion to waive the disclosure requirements ex post. Where, however, there is no continuing need for the information or a waiver is needed to prevent automatic dismissal from furthering a debtor's abusive conduct, the court has discretion to take such an action. This case is of that genre.[9]

To sum up, the great divide in section 521 is between information that is required and information that is not. The Act allows courts to do the sifting suggested by that divide without rigid adherence to the forty-five-day deadline.

We need go no further. In this case the bankruptcy court, acting with care and restraint, was faithful to the evolving statutory scheme. Its order was, therefore, within the compass of its discretion.

The judgment of the district court is reversed and the matter is remanded for further proceedings consistent with this opinion.

Notes and Questions

1. So-called automatic dismissal applies if the debtor does not file the items required in Bankruptcy Code §521(a)(1). See 11 U.S.C. § 521(i)(1). Other sections require the debtor to file items, but these are required in subsection other than § 521(a)(1). Here is an informal list of items that result in automatic dismissal if the debtor does not file

- List of creditors.
- Schedule of assets and liabilities
- Schedule of current income and expenditures
- Statement of financial affairs
- Statement of an attorney or petition preparer signing the petition that a § 342(b) notice was served; § 342(b) requires the court clerk to provide a notice describing the various bankruptcy chapters, the services available from credit counseling, and warnings against committing bankruptcy crimes
- Pay stubs.
- Statement of monthly net income.
- Statement as to whether income will increase in the near future.

Here is a list of items which the debtor must supply but which do not result in dismissal.

- A statement whether the debtor will retain or surrender collateral encumbered by a security interest. § §362(a)(2).
- Records pertaining to the debtor's prepetition property. § 521(4)
- Credit counseling certificate. § 521(b)(1).
- A debt repayment plan development by a cred counseling agency.
- A debtor's uinterest in an education IRA. § 521(c).
- Tax returns. § 521(e).

Failure to file items on the second list do not result in automatic dismissal. In re Ring, 341 B.R. 387, 389 n.4, 390 (Bankr. D. Me. 2006).

[9] It would serve no useful purpose for us to attempt to sketch the full range of circumstances that might justify the exercise of this discretion.

B. ENCUMBERED CARS AND REAL ESTATE

IN RE NORTON
347 B.R. 291 (Bankr. E.D. Tenn. 2006)

RICHARD STAIR, J.

. . . The Debtor filed the Voluntary Petition commencing her Chapter 7 bankruptcy case on May 2, 2006. On that date, she also filed the Chapter 7 Individual Debtor's Statement of Intention (Statement of Intention), stating that she was surrendering to CIT its collateral consisting of a commercial building, 100% of the Debtor's interest in Carol Ann's, Inc., and a 2-acre lot in Gurley, Alabama. The Statement of Intention also provides that "Debtor will retain collateral and continue to make regular payments" to Tennessee Bank and Washington Mutual with respect to real property located at 8742 Wimbledon Drive, Knoxville, Tennessee (Residence), and to Knoxville TVA Employees Credit Union (Credit Union) on a 2001 PT Cruiser (PT Cruiser). The Debtor's statements and schedules value the Residence at $172,000.00, subject to liens in the aggregate amount of $187,000.00, and the PT Cruiser at $4,500.00, subject to a lien in the amount of $1,900.00. She has claimed an exemption in the PT Cruiser in the amount of $2,389.00.

The Trustee filed the Motion on June 22, 2006, requesting additional time to investigate the Debtor's case more closely to determine if there are unencumbered, non-exempt assets, unperfected liens, and/or assets available for liquidation, arguing that doing so is in the best interests of creditors. . . .

II

The Trustee first asks the court to extend the time within which the Debtor must perform her Statement of Intention with respect to secured personal property under § 521(a)(2). Under the Bankruptcy Abuse Prevention and Consumer Protection Act of 2005 (BAPCPA), debtors have responsibilities and requirements that, if not followed, will result in the automatic stay being terminated with respect to certain property of the estate . . . .

As it relates to § 521(a)(2) and this case, § 362(h) provides, in material part:

> (h)(1) In a case in which the debtor is an individual, the stay provided by subsection (a) is terminated with respect to personal property of the estate or of the debtor securing in whole or in part a claim . . . and such personal property shall no longer be property of the estate if the debtor fails within the applicable time set by section 521(a)(2) --
>
> (A) to file timely any statement of intention required under section 521(a)(2) with respect to such personal property or to indicate in such statement that the debtor will either surrender such personal property or retain it and, if retaining such personal property, either redeem such personal property pursuant to section 722 [or] enter into an agreement of the kind specified in section 524(c) applicable to the debt secured by such personal property. . .; and
>
> (B) to take timely the action specified in such statement, as it may be amended before expiration of the period for taking action, unless such statement specifies the debtor's intention to reaffirm such debt on the original contract terms and the creditor refuses to agree to the reaffirmation on such terms.

> (2) Paragraph (1) does not apply if the court determines, on the motion of the trustee filed before the expiration of the applicable time set by section 521(a)(2), after notice and a hearing, that such personal property is of consequential value or benefit to the estate, and orders appropriate adequate protection of the creditor's interest, and orders the debtor to deliver any collateral in the debtor's possession to the trustee. If the court does not so determine, the stay provided by subsection (a) shall terminate upon the conclusion of the hearing on the motion.

11 U.S.C. § 362(h).

In summary, unless extended by the court, § 521(a)(2)(A) requires an individual debtor to file a statement of intentions "within thirty days after" the bankruptcy filing or "on or before the date of the meeting of creditors," whichever is earlier, specifying whether property will be retained through redemption or reaffirmation or will be surrendered. Section 521(a)(2)(B) then requires a debtor to perform the stated intention within thirty days after the first scheduled meeting of creditors unless the court grants an extension that was sought during the original thirty-day performance period. Pursuant to § 362(h)(1), if a debtor fails to comply with both subsections of § 521(a)(2) with respect to personal property, and the failure to comply is not due to a creditor refusing to agree to a reaffirmation under the original contract terms, the automatic stay is terminated, and the personal property is no longer property of the estate.

There is a caveat, however, found within § 362(h)(2). The automatic stay will not terminate, and property will remain in a debtor's bankruptcy estate if the Chapter 7 trustee files a motion "before the applicable time set by section 521(a)(2)," and the court determines, after notice and a hearing, that the affected personal property is "of consequential value or benefit to the estate." 11 U.S.C. § 362(h)(2).[1] The statute does not expressly state which of the § 521(a)(2) deadlines controls.

In this case, the Debtor filed the Voluntary Petition commencing her Chapter 7 case on May 2, 2006, and June 6, 2006, was the first date set for her meeting of creditors. Pursuant to § 521(a)(2)(A), the Debtor was required to file a statement of intentions expressly stating, with respect to her encumbered real and personal property, whether she would be surrendering or retaining such property by redemption or reaffirmation no later than thirty days from the date upon which she filed her petition, or June 1, 2006. Then, pursuant to § 521(a)(2)(B), the Debtor was required to perform her statement of intention no later than thirty days after the first date scheduled for her meeting of creditors, or not later than July 6, 2006.[2] Pursuant to § 362(h), if the Debtor failed to comply with both subsections of § 521(a)(2) by failing to file her statement of intention, failing to specify her intended treatment in the statement of intention, and failing to timely perform the stated intention, the automatic stay would terminate by operation of law "with respect to personal property of the estate," and the affected personal property would cease to be property of the estate. Accordingly, the Debtor had until June 1, 2006, to file a statement of intention

---

[1] This section also requires "appropriate adequate protection of the creditor's interest" and contains a directive that the collateral be turned over to the trustee.

[2] The court takes judicial notice, pursuant to Rule 201 of the Federal Rules of Evidence, that as of July 7, 2006, the Debtor had not filed either a motion to redeem or a reaffirmation agreement with respect to the PT Cruiser, nor has she filed either as of the date of this Memorandum.

specifying her desired intentions with respect to her property, and she had until July 6, 2006, to perform under the statement of intention as to personal property.

Pursuant to § 521(a)(2) and § 362(h), the automatic stay would have terminated by operation of law on July 7, 2006, but only as to the PT Cruiser. However, the Trustee filed her Motion on June 22, 2006. Albeit this was fifty-one days after the Debtor filed her petition, and thus presumably outside the time limit imposed by § 521(a)(2)(A),[3] it was sixteen days prior to the § 521(a)(2)(B) statement of intention performance deadline of July 6, 2006. Section 362(h) does not expressly state which of the two § 521(a)(2) deadlines applies; however, because subsections (A) and (B) of § 362(h)(1) are in the conjunctive, thus requiring that both subsections (A) and (B) of § 521(a)(2) be met prior to termination of the automatic stay, the court finds the § 521(a)(2)(B) deadline to be determinative, since § 362(h)(1) cannot be triggered until the expiration of that particular deadline. As such, the Trustee's Motion was timely and precluded termination of the automatic stay on July 7, 2006, until after the court's resolution of the Motion.

The Trustee did not introduce any proof at the July 13, 2006 hearing with respect to the value of the PT Cruiser, but based upon the Debtor's statements and schedules and the Credit Union's proof of claim, the court determines that the PT Cruiser is of consequential value or benefit to the Debtor's estate, thus precluding application of the stay termination provisions of § 362(h)(1). On her Schedule D, the Debtor values the PT Cruiser at $4,500.00, subject to a lien in the amount of $1,900.00. However, the Credit Union filed a proof of claim on June 6, 2006, in the minimal amount of $497.34, and while it does not provide a value for the PT Cruiser, the attached documentation evidences an original loan amount of $24,741.21 on May 29, 2001. Per the Debtor's Schedule C, she has claimed an exemption in the PT Cruiser in the amount of $2,389.00 which has not been objected to by the Trustee. Accordingly, based upon the documents filed in the Debtor's case, the PT Cruiser is valued at $4,500.00, less the Credit Union's claim of $497.34, less the Debtor's exemption of $2,389.00, leaving apparent equity of $1,613.66.

Having determined that the PT Cruiser is of consequential value, § 362(h)(2) also requires that the court order appropriate adequate protection of the Credit Union's interest and order the Debtor to deliver the vehicle to the Trustee.

Adequate protection safeguards a secured creditor's interest in its depreciating collateral during the pendency of the automatic stay. See United Sav. Ass'n of Tex. v. Timbers of Inwood Forest Assocs., Ltd., 484 U.S. 365 (1988). In addition to the statutory forms specified in 11 U.S.C. § 361 (2005), adequate protection is also accomplished through the existence of an "equity cushion," which is defined as "the value in the property, above the amount owed to the [secured] creditors . . ., that will shield that interest from loss due to any decrease in the value of the property during [the] time the automatic stay remains in

[3] Section 521 (a)(2)(A) 's requirement that the statement of intentions must be filed "within thirty days after" the bankruptcy filing or "on or before the date of the meeting of creditors" is ambiguous because creditors meetings are often continued from the originally scheduled date. This ambiguity is not continued to § 521(a)(2)(B) where the requirement is that the statement of intentions must be performed within thirty days after the "first date set for the meeting of creditors." Given the ambiguity in § 521(a)(2)(A), the court concludes that the "thirty days after the filing of a petition" will be determinative of the time lines of a debtor's filing of his or her statement of intentions.

effect." Sumitomo Trust & Banking Co. v. Holly's Inc. (In re Holly's Inc.), 140 B.R. 643, 697 n.87 (Bankr. W.D. Mich. 1992)(quoting Pistole v. Mellor (In re Mellor), 734 F.2d 1396, 1400 n.2 (9th Cir. 1984)). "While an equity cushion is generally considered prima facie evidence of adequate protection, the absence of an equity cushion does not establish the converse. . . . the concept of adequate protection was not designed or intended to place an undersecured or minimally secured creditor in a better post-filing petition [sic] that it was in before the stay." In re Planned Sys., Inc., 78 B.R. 852, 865 (Bankr. E.D. Ohio 1987) (quoting United States v. Smithfield Estates, Inc. (In re Smithfield Estates, Inc.), 48 B.R. 910, 914-15 (Bankr. D.R.I. 1985)).

Because the Credit Union's claim is $497.34, and the Debtor valued the PT Cruiser at $4,500.00, the court finds the Credit Union to be adequately protected by an equity cushion of almost $4,000.00. Additionally, the Debtor will be directed to immediately deliver possession of the PT Cruiser to the Trustee.

The Trustee also requested an extension of time pursuant to 11 U.S.C. § 521(a)(6), which provides as follows:

> (A) The debtor shall . . .
>
> (6) in a case under chapter 7 of this title in which the debtor is an individual, not retain possession of personal property as to which a creditor has an allowed claim for the purchase price secured in whole or in part by an interest in such personal property unless the debtor, not later than 45 days after the first meeting of creditors under section 341 (a), either --
>
> (A) enters into an agreement with the creditor pursuant to section 524(c) with respect to the claim secured by such property; or
>
> (B) redeems such property from the security interest pursuant to section 722.
>
> If the debtor fails to act within the 45-day period referred to in paragraph (6), the stay under section 362(a) is terminated with respect to the personal property of the estate or of the debtor which is affected, such property shall no longer be property of the estate, and the creditor may take whatever action as to such property as is permitted by applicable nonbankruptcy law, unless the court determines on the motion of the trustee filed before the expiration of such 45-day period, and after notice and a hearing, that such property is of consequential value or benefit to the estate, orders appropriate adequate protection of the creditor's interest, and orders the debtor to deliver any collateral in the debtor's possession to the trustee[.]

11 U.S.C. § 521(a)(6).

As an initial matter, based upon the statutory language of § 521(a)(6), BAPCPA extinguished the "ride-through" option, by which some courts allowed debtors to keep their secured property without reaffirming or redeeming, as long as they-made their regular contract payments. See Garske v. Arcadia Fin., Ltd. (In re Garske), 287 B.R. 537, 542 (B.A.P. 9th Cir. 2002).[4] Although the "ride-through" was not a statutory pre-BAPCPA alternative, those courts considered this a "fourth option" concerning treatment of a debtor's property, along with redemption, reaffirmation, and surrender. Nevertheless, "Congress by amending

[4] The Sixth Circuit did not weigh in on either side of this issue; however, this court has previously held that "redemption or reaffirmation are the exclusive methods by which debtors under Chapter 7 may retain possession of secured property." In re Whitaker, 85 B.R. 788, 793 (Bankr. E.D. Tenn. 1988).

§§ 521 and 362 intended to and was successful in eliminating the 'fourth option,' under which a Chapter 7 individual debtor having possession of personal property subject to a purchase money lien by performing all obligations under the security agreement and note could retain the property and be protected by the stay without either redemption of the property or reaffirmation of the secured debt." In re Rowe, 342 B.R. 341, 351 (Bankr. D. Kan. 2006); see also In re Craker, 337 B.R. 549, 551 (Bankr. M.D.N.C. 2006) ("[P]ursuant to § 362(h)(1) the Debtor was also required to indicate on her timely filed Statement of Intention that she was either surrendering or retaining the Vehicle, and if retaining the Vehicle, that she was either redeeming the Vehicle or reaffirming the underlying debt.").

Section 521(a)(6), which makes no mention of the statement of intentions, has limited applicability, however, as it only applies to creditors holding "allowed claims" for personal property that are subject to purchase money security interests. See Rowe, 342 B.R. 347-49 (citing H.R. Rep. No. 109-31, Pt. 1, at 70-71 (2005)). If those restrictions apply, § 521(a)(6) directs that unless a debtor enters into a reaffirmation agreement or redeems the personal property within forty-five days "after the first meeting of creditors," the automatic stay is terminated, the property is no longer property of the estate, and the creditor may take whatever action is allowed under nonbankruptcy law, unless the trustee files a motion within that forty-five day period, and the court determines, after notice and a hearing, that the property is of consequential value or benefit to the estate.[5]

Clearly, there are inconsistent time restrictions in § 521(a)(2) and (a)(6). Subsection (a)(2), in conjunction with § 362(h), requires a debtor to file a statement of intention indicating reaffirmation, redemption, or surrender at a point no later than thirty days after the debtor's case is filed and to perform such intention within thirty days after the first date of the meeting of creditors to avoid termination of the automatic stay as to personal property, which then ceases to be property of the debtor's bankruptcy estate. On the other hand, subsection (a)(6) requires a debtor to actually enter into a reaffirmation agreement or to redeem personal property subject to a purchase money security interest within forty-five days after the first meeting of creditors, or else the automatic stay is terminated, the property is no longer property of the estate, and the creditor is authorized to pursue its non-bankruptcy remedies to obtain possession of the property. There is no explanation for the fifteen-day differential between these two statutory requirements,[6] which raises serious questions as to statutory interpretation in light of the fact that the court is not aware of any statutory authority for reinstating the automatic stay once it has terminated by

[5] Once again, as under § 362(h)(2), the court is required to order adequate protection to the affected creditors and to order the debtor to deliver the affected personal property to the trustee.

[6] Invariably, an individual debtor's failure to perform his or her statement of intention within thirty days of the "first date set for the meeting of creditors" will, as to personal property, trigger the stay termination provisions of § 362(h)(1), thereby trumping the forty-five day stay termination provisions of § 521(a)(6). To further compound the issue, the performance period under § 521(a)(2)(B) is fixed at "within 30 days after the first date set for the meeting of creditors" while the forty-five day performance requirement of § 521(a)(6) is fixed at "not later than 45 days after the first meeting of creditors." The "first date" of the meeting of creditors requirement of § 521(a)(2)(B) will be clearly identified and established in each chapter 7 case. The date "after the first meeting of creditors" provided for in § 521(a)(6) can properly be construed to provide a forty-five day performance window from the date the first creditor's meeting is completed, which may or may not be on the "first date set" for the meeting of creditors.

operation of law,[7] or for re-vesting personal property into a bankruptcy estate once it has been removed therefrom.

Fortunately, or unfortunately, depending upon one's point of view, the court need not attempt to resolve the § 521(a)(2) and (a)(6) inconsistent time restrictions within the context of the present bankruptcy case. In the first place, the Debtor's Statement of Intention does not comply with the mandatory requirements of § 521(a)(2)(A) that a debtor shall specify whether property to be retained is to be retained by redemption or reaffirmation but instead recites with respect to the PT Cruiser that "Debtor will retain collateral and continue to make regular payments." Therefore, reaffirmation and redemption were never an option, and § 521(a)(6) cannot apply. Secondly, the Trustee timely filed her Motion under § 362(h)(2), which prevented the automatic stay from terminating due to the Debtor's failure to comply with § 521(a)(2). Because the stay termination provisions of both § 521(a)(2) and (a)(6) are the same, and because the relief available to the Trustee is also identical under both statutes, the filing of the Trustee's Motion under § 362(h) would, were § 521(a)(6) applicable, sufficiently serve to negate the automatic stay termination provisions of § 521(a)(6) pending resolution of the Motion.

III

The Trustee also asks the court to grant the Debtor additional time to provide her tax returns to the Trustee. In addition to the expanded filing requirements set forth in § 521(a), BAPCPA [§ 521(e)(2)(A)] also imposes additional disclosure duties upon debtors, including the requirement to produce tax returns as follows:

> The debtor shall provide --
>
> (i) not later than 7 days before the date first set for the first meeting of creditors, to the trustee a copy of the Federal income tax return required under applicable law (or at the election of the debtor, a transcript of such return) for the most recent tax year ending immediately before the commencement of the case and for which a Federal income tax return was filed . . . .
>
> (B) If the debtor fails to comply with clause (i). . . of subparagraph (A), the court shall dismiss the case unless the debtor demonstrates that the failure to so comply is due to circumstances beyond the control of the debtor.

The first date set for the Debtor's first meeting of creditors was June 6, 2006. Based upon the Trustee's Motion requesting additional time for the Debtor to do so, the court can presume that she did not produce the required tax returns at least a week prior to that date, and that she still had not supplied them to the

[7] See also 11 U.S.C. § 362(c), which states in material part:

> (c) Except as provided in subsections (d), (e), (f), and (h) of this section [not applicable] --
>
> (1) the stay of an act against property of the estate under subsection (a) of this section continues until such property is no longer property of the estate[.]

11 U.S.C. § 362(c)(1)(2005).

Trustee as of June 22, 2006, the date upon which the Trustee filed her Motion. In support of her Motion, the Trustee states that she has no evidence that the Debtor has not attempted to provide her tax returns in good faith, based upon the Debtor's testimony at the meeting of creditors.

In the only two cases thus far examining this issue, it has been held that "[w]here, as here, dismissal is contrary to the interest of the estate and of creditors, the Trustee has the authority to waive an untimely delivery of documents simply by declining to file a motion." In re Duffus, 339 B.R. 746, 748 (Bankr. D. Ore. 2006).

> This Court agrees with the reasoning of the Duffus decision. If the Trustee has no discretion to waive an untimely filing under § 521(e)(2)(A), then dismissal would be automatic upon the Trustee's motion coming to the Court's attention, unless the debtor can satisfy § 521(e)(2)(B). Congress simply did not impose such a requirement. There is nothing in the language of § 521(e)(2) that suggests that Congress intended to limit the discretion traditionally exercised by trustees in performing their duties under federal bankruptcy law. This Court will not limit such discretion by implication. If anything, the language of § 521(e)(2)(B) was likely intended to limit the Court's discretion regarding the dismissal of a case for failure to timely deliver tax returns to the trustee as required under § 521(e)(2)(A). If a trustee or other party in interest brings a debtor's failure to timely comply with § 521(e)(2)(A) to the Court's attention, the Court must dismiss the case, unless the debtor can establish that such failure is excused as being due to circumstances beyond the debtor's control within the meaning of § 521(e)(2)(B).

In re Grasso, 341 B.R. 821, 824-25 (Bankr. D.N.H. 2006).

The court disagrees with these holdings, however, as being contrary to the wording of § 521(e)(2). The statute expressly states that debtors "shall" provide their most recent tax return to the trustee "no later than" one week prior to the first date set for the first meeting of creditors, and if the debtor does not do so, the court "shall" dismiss the case "unless the debtor demonstrates that the failure to so comply is due to circumstances beyond the control of the debtor." 11 U.S.C. § 521(e)(2). This language does not instruct or authorize the Trustee to file a motion requesting an extension of time to allow compliance. Nowhere within this provision are motions or extensions mentioned. Similarly, based upon the clear wording of § 521(e)(2)(B), the court has little discretion, and, in fact, the statute clearly provides that it is only the Debtor who may prevent dismissal for failure to comply with subsection (e)(2)(A). Other than being the party to whom the tax return is to be provided, the Trustee is not implicated in this statute. There is simply nothing within § 521(e)(2) to allow the Trustee to request an extension on the Debtor's behalf, and in any event, the Trustee has not provided the court with any reasons behind her request to demonstrate that the Debtor's failure to comply was due to circumstances beyond the Debtor's control.

Pursuant to § 521(e)(2)(A), the Debtor was required to produce her 2005 Form 1040 Individual tax return to the Trustee by May 30, 2006, seven days before the June 6, 2006 initial meeting of creditors. Unless the Debtor is able to show cause otherwise, i.e., establish that her failure to comply was due to circumstances beyond her control, the court "shall" be required to dismiss the Debtor's case. Accordingly, the Trustee's Motion will be denied, and the court will require the Debtor to appear and show cause why her case should not be dismissed for failure to comply with § 521(e)(2)(A) . . . .

In summary, the Trustee's Motion will be granted in part and denied in part as follows: (A) With respect to her request that the automatic stay continue in effect, the Motion will be granted as to the PT Cruiser, and the Debtor will be required to immediately turn over possession of this vehicle to the Trustee. (B) With respect to her request for an extension of time within which the Debtor must provide tax returns to the Trustee pursuant to § 521(e)(2)(A)(i), the Motion will be denied. The Debtor will, however, be required to appear and show cause why this bankruptcy case should not be dismissed upon her failure to comply with § 521(e)(2)(A)(i) . . . .

Notes and Questions

1. Suppose D is current on mortgage payments and then files for bankruptcy. D declares an intent to retain her home but does not declare an intent to reaffirm the mortgage. Can the mortgage lender foreclose thirty days later? See 11 U.S.C. §§ 362(h), 521(a)(2). Is the underlying bankruptcy automatically dismissed? 11 U.S.C. § 521(i)(1) ("if an individual debtor in a voluntary case under chapter 7 or 13 fails to file all of the information required under subsection (a)(1) within 45 days after the date of the filing of the petition, the case shall be automatically dismissed on the 46th day after the date of the filing of the petition").

2. Suppose D files in chapter 13 but does not state his intention to reaffirm, redeem or abandon his encumbered car, as §521(a)(2)(A) requires. May the car lender repossess the car thirty one days later? In re Schlitzer, 332 B.R. 856 (Bankr. W.D.N.Y. 2005) (no). Why not?

3. Imagine the following chronology:

March 1:	D files a chapter 7 bankruptcy petition.
March 5:	D declares her intent to enter into a reaffirmation agreement with SP, who claims a security interest in D's car.
April 10:	Schedule date of the first creditors' meeting.

It is now April 20. D has not lifted a finger to obtain a reaffirmation agreement. Does the automatic stay prevent SP from repossessing the car? See Bankruptcy Code §§ 521(a)(2), (6), 362(h).

4. The Norton court ruled that § 521(a)(6) (45 day deadline) did not apply because D missed the deadline of § 521(a)(2)(A). Is that a good reading of § 521(a)(6)?

3. In Norton, D did not file a valid statement of intent by the deadline of § 521(a)(2)(A) (30 days). The trustee asked for an extension of the stay 22 days after the 521(a)(2)(A) deadline. The court was at least prepared to grant that motion. Is this a good reading of § 521(a)(2) and § 362(h)?

5. No equity in a car. BAPCPA seems to be written on the assumption that there is no valid equity in an encumbered car, once the outstanding security interest and exemption is accounted for. In such a case, the trustee cannot benefit the unsecured creditors by administering the car and so ought to abandon it. 11 U.S.C. § 554(a) ("After notice and a hearing, the trustee may abandon any property of the estate that is burdensome to the estate or that is of inconsequential value and benefit to the estate").

6. Valuable equity in the car. The contradictions in BAPCPA, as exhibited in Norton, arose because there was equity in the car even after the oustanding security interest and D's exemption was accounted for. In such a case, the trustee must intervene to extend the automatic stay. The trustee can then sell the car, free and clear of the security interest. Bankruptcy Code § 363(f)(3). The secured lender has a "proceeds" security interest in the money received. Bankruptcy Code § 552(b)(1). This must be distributed to the secured lender, to the extent of the security interest. Bankruptcy Code § 725. The surplus may then be distributed pursuant to Bankruptcy Code § 726(a). There we learn that the first priority goes to family law claims. Bankruptcy Code § 507(a)(1). The second priority goes to adminsitrative claims, including the trustee's own claim for compensation, plus attorneys the chapter 7 trustee may have retain. Bankruptcy Code § 507(a)(2). The trustee directly benefits herself and her professionals if she captures the equity in the car. These matters are further described in chapter four.

COASTAL FEDERAL CREDIT UNION v HARDIMAN

398 B.R. 161 (E.D.N.C. 2008)

DEVER, J.

. . . This case presents the question whether BAPCPA contains a modified version of the "ride-through" option where debtors without legal counsel timely enter into a reaffirmation agreement concerning personal property with their creditor and submit the reaffirmation agreement to the bankruptcy court, but the bankruptcy court refuses to approve the reaffirmation agreement. The bankruptcy court analyzed BAPCPA and held that under the plain meaning of the relevant BAPCPA provisions, such a modified version of the "ride-through" option exists within BAPCPA. Thus, after refusing to approve the reaffirmation agreement, the bankruptcy court held that the debtors could retain the car that was the subject of the reaffirmation agreement and continue to make payments on the car loan.

Coastal Federal Credit Union ("Coastal") appeals and contends that the bankruptcy court erred in analyzing BAPCPA. Coastal argues that BAPCPA's plain meaning leads to absurd results and contravenes clearly expressed Congressional intent in BAPCPA's legislative history. On August 29, 2008, the court held oral argument. As explained below, this court disagrees with Coastal and affirms the bankruptcy court's judgment.

I.

In February 2005, Landon and Daffney Hardiman ("debtors" or "Hardimans") bought a 2005 Chevrolet Equinox. The Hardimans financed the purchase through Coastal. Under the loan agreement with Coastal, the Hardimans are obligated to make a monthly car payment of $479.69 to Coastal, and Coastal has a senior, perfected first lien on the car. . . . As of May 2007, the Hardimans were upside down on their loan--the car was worth about $9,000, but the Hardimans owed Coastal over $20,000. See id. Moreover, the loan agreement contains an "ipso facto" clause (which declares the debtors in default on the secured obligation simply by virtue of filing for bankruptcy). See id. at 2-3.[1]

On May 2, 2007, the Hardimans filed for bankruptcy under Chapter 7 of the Bankruptcy Code. As part of the bankruptcy, the Hardimans desired to reaffirm the automobile loan with Coastal because they have three children and the Chevrolet is their only reliable means of transportation. The Hardimans (without legal counsel) timely signed a reaffirmation agreement with Coastal. According to the reaffirmation agreement, the Hardimans have $3,925 in monthly income and $2,535 in monthly expenses, leaving $1,390 to make the required monthly car payment of $479.69 to Coastal. Because the reaffirmation agreement did not include an attorney affidavit or declaration under 11 U.S.C. § 524(c)(3),[2] the bankruptcy court had to decide whether to approve the reaffirmation agreement as (1) not imposing an undue hardship, and (2) in the Hardimans' best interest. See 11 U.S.C. § 524(c)(6)(A).

The bankruptcy court held a hearing under section 524(d). At the hearing,

[1] Ipso facto clauses are also called "default-on-filing" and "bankruptcy default" clauses.

[2] This section, and the other Bankruptcy Code provisions relevant to this appeal, are explained in detail below.

the bankruptcy court noted that the Hardimans' Schedule I filed with their Chapter 7 petition showed an average monthly income of $4,454.93 and their Schedule J showed average monthly expenses of $5,689, resulting in a net monthly income of -$1,234.07. Nonetheless, with the "fresh start" arising from their bankruptcy, the Hardimans told the bankruptcy court that their expenses would be reduced to $2,535 and that they thought they could make the monthly payments on the Chevrolet.[3] The Hardimans acknowledged, however, that it would be hard sometimes. On August 15, 2007, the bankruptcy court rejected the reaffirmation agreement as imposing an undue hardship on the Hardimans and not in the Hardimans' best interest. Because the bankruptcy court did not approve the reaffirmation agreement, Coastal believed that the automatic stay no longer applied, that the ipso facto clause became operative, that Coastal could seek to repossess the car under state law, and that Coastal could seek a deficiency judgment against the Hardimans for the difference between the value of the car and the amount owed. However, the bankruptcy court interpreted BAPCPA and held that the automatic stay still applied, and that Coastal could not seek to repossess the vehicle under state law so long as the Hardimans remained current on their payments and complied with the other requirements of the contract and lien.

Coastal filed a motion for reconsideration. On October 31, 2007, the bankruptcy court held a hearing on the motion. On November 20, 2007, the bankruptcy court denied the motion for reconsideration. The bankruptcy court summarized its judgment as follows:

> Because court approval of a reaffirmation agreement is not an element of §§ 521(a)(2) and 362(h)(1), the debtors complied with the requirements of the Code by doing everything within their control to reaffirm the debt to Coastal. While "ride-through" is not a stand-alone option in addition to surrender, redemption, or reaffirmation of a debt secured by personal property, it may, in limited circumstances, occur as a result of a debtor's attempt to reaffirm . . . . The automatic stay remains in place with respect to Coastal, and as long as the debtors remain current in their payments, Coastal may not repossess the vehicle or declare default based on the debtors' bankruptcy filing.

Coastal timely appeals to this court.

II.

. . . Coastal argues: (1) the bankruptcy court erred in determining that section 521(a)(6) does not apply to this case and thereby refusing to lift the automatic stay, and (2) the bankruptcy court erred in determining that sections 521(a)(2)(C) and 362(h) do not mandate the termination of the automatic stay. Coastal's arguments are premised on two exceptions to the plain meaning rule of statutory construction. Essentially, Coastal argues that the court should reject the plain meaning of the BAPCPA provisions at issue because (1) they lead to absurd results, and (2) they run manifestly counter to clearly expressed Congressional intent in BAPCPA's legislative history.

---

[3] The reaffirmation agreement indicated that the Hardimans' monthly income would be $3,925, but their Schedule I filed with their bankruptcy petition indicated that their monthly income was $4,454.93. Regardless, the debtors' expenses would be reduced by the bankruptcy discharge, so they thought they would have enough money to make the payments on the Chevrolet.

"In interpreting a statute, 'a court should always turn first to one, cardinal canon [of construction] before all others': the plain meaning rule." Ayes v. U.S. Dep't of Veterans Affairs, 473 F.3d 104, 108 (4th Cir. 2006) (alteration in original) (quoting Conn. Nat'l Bank v. Germain, 503 U.S. 249, 253 (1992)). In applying the plain meaning rule, courts must "consider the context in which the statutory words are used because [courts] do not construe statutory phrases in isolation; [courts] read statutes as a whole." Id. (quotation & alterations thereof omitted). However, "[t]he [statutory construction] inquiry ceases if the statutory language is unambiguous and the statutory scheme is coherent and consistent." Barnhart v. Sigmon Coal. Co., 534 U.S. 438, 450 (2002) (quotation omitted); see Ayes, 473 F.3d at 108.

Coastal acknowledges the plain meaning rule, but notes that the plain meaning rule is subject to "two narrow exceptions." In re Sunterra Corp., 361 F.3d 257, 265 (4th Cir. 2004). According to the Fourth Circuit:

> The first such exception, premised on absurdity, exists when literal application of the statutory language at issue results in an outcome that can truly be characterized as absurd, i.e., that is so gross as to shock the general moral or common sense. The second exception is premised on legislative intent, and it exists only when literal application of the statutory language at issue produces an outcome that is demonstrably at odds with clearly expressed congressional intent. A reviewing court may look beyond the plain language of an unambiguous statute only when one of these exceptions is implicated. And [the Fourth Circuit] ha[s] recognized that the instances in which either of these exceptions to the Plain Meaning Rule apply are, and should be, exceptionally rare.

Id. (internal citations & quotations omitted).

To invoke the absurdity exception, the outcome mandated by the plain language must be "so gross as to shock the general moral or common sense." Md. State Dep't of Educ. v. U.S. Dep't of Veterans Affairs, 98 F.3d 165, 169 (4th Cir. 1996). . . .

As for the intent exception to the plain meaning rule, a court should not apply a statute's plain language if "the literal application of a statute will produce a result demonstrably at odds with the intentions of its drafters." United States v. Ron Pair Enters., Inc., 489 U.S. 235, 242 (1989) (quotation omitted) . . . .

In analyzing this case under the plain meaning rule, the absurdity exception, and the intent exception, the court recognizes that the party challenging the plain meaning of a statute bears an exceptionally heavy burden. See, e.g., Sunterra, 361 F.3d 265 ("[T]he instances in which either of these exceptions to the Plain Meaning Rule apply are, and should be, exceptionally rare.") (quotation omitted). Moreover, as this case illustrates, "burdens of proof . . . matter." Thorn v. Jefferson-Pilot Ins. Co., 445 F.3d 311, 324 (4th Cir. 2006).

III.

To understand the current dispute about BAPCPA, the court begins with the so-called "ride-through" option in the Bankruptcy Code pre-BAPCPA. See In re Belanger, 118 B.R. 368 (Bankr. E.D.N.C. 1990) (Small, J.).[4] In the 1980s, a

[4] The Third Circuit has recognized Judge Small's "compelling" analysis in Belanger of the Bankruptcy Code provisions in section 521. See In re Price, 370 F.3d 362, 375 n.9 (3d Cir. 2004).

coalition of secured creditors lobbied for changes to the Bankruptcy Code. See id. at 370. The secured creditors were concerned because the bankruptcy automatic stay prohibited them from contacting debtors who filed for Chapter 7 bankruptcy. See id. at 370-71. Because they could not contact the debtors due to the automatic stay, the secured creditors often had no information on what was going to happen to their collateral during the bankruptcy. Id. at 370. Secured creditors would therefore be forced to file adversary proceedings against debtors in order to get this information. Id. at 370-71.

In 1984, Congress responded to these concerns and added what is now section 521(a)(2)(A) to the Bankruptcy Code. See id. (discussing former section 521(2)(A)).[5] This section was "essentially a notice requirement to permit secured creditors to ascertain the debtor's intentions early in the case." Id. at 370. This section reads almost exactly the same today as it did when first enacted. It currently provides:

> (2) if an individual debtor's schedule of assets and liabilities includes debts which are secured by property of the estate--
>
> (A) within thirty days after the date of the filing of a petition under chapter 7 of this title or on or before the date of the meeting of creditors, whichever is earlier, or within such additional time as the court, for cause, within such period fixes, the debtor shall file with the clerk a statement of his intention with respect to the retention or surrender of such property and, if applicable, specifying that such property is claimed as exempt, that the debtor intends to redeem such property, or that the debtor intends to reaffirm debts secured by such property . . . .

11 U.S.C. § 521(a)(2)(A). This language gave rise to litigation as to whether Congress intended this list of three options--claim the collateral as exempt, redeem the collateral, or reaffirm the debt--to be exclusive. See, e.g., Belanger, 118 B.R. at 369.

Belanger presented this question within the Fourth Circuit. In Belanger, a couple filed for Chapter 7 bankruptcy. The couple lived in a mobile home purchased via an installment sales contract, which included a senior, perfected first lien on the mobile home. Id. Therefore, section 521(a)(2)(A) required the couple to file a "[s]tatement of [i]ntention" to give the creditor notice of what they intended to do with the mobile home. In their statement of intention, the debtors stated that they would simply retain the mobile home and continue making monthly payments, without actually reaffirming the debt. This option was not one of the three options expressly listed in section 521(a)(2)(A).

The debtors argued that they could take this approach for three reasons. First, under Fourth Circuit precedent, the ipso facto clause in their loan agreement was unenforceable. See id. & n.1 (citing Riggs Nat'l Bank of Washington, D.C. v. Perry, 729 F.2d 982 (4th Cir. 1984)). Because the ipso facto clause in their loan agreement was unenforceable, they were not in default on their loan, even though they filed for bankruptcy. See id. at 369. Second, the language of the statute provides that a Chapter 7 debtor must declare his intention with respect to the three options "if applicable." Id. (quotation omitted). The debtors argued that they did not select any of the three options because none was "applicable." See id. at 369-70. Further, they argued that the three options

[5] Because this statute reads almost the same today as it did historically, court hereafter refers to it by its current code designation, 11 U.S.C. § 521(a)(2)(A).

were nonexclusive, and they could select another option. Finally, the debtors noted that the statute at that time expressly stated that it should not be interpreted to "alter the debtor's . . . rights with respect to [encumbered] property." See id. at 371-72 (discussing former 11 U.S.C. § 521(2)(C)).

In Belanger, the bankruptcy court agreed with the debtors. In so doing, the bankruptcy court rejected the reasoning of several other courts, including the Seventh Circuit. See id. at 372 (rejecting In re Edwards, 901 F.2d 1383 (7th Cir. 1990)). Because the debtors did not select any of the three options, this approach became known as the "fourth option." See, e.g., In re Price, 370 F.3d 362, 372 (3d Cir. 2004). It has also been labeled "ride-through" and "pay and drive" (because debtors used this option to keep their cars and continue to make payments on their car loans). See, e.g., In re Donald, 343 B.R. 524, 526 (Bankr. E.D.N.C. 2006).

The mobile home creditor appealed to this court. This court affirmed on Judge Small's reasoning. See In re Belanger, 128 B.R. 142, 143 (E.D.N.C. 1990) (Dupree, J.). The mobile home creditor appealed to the Fourth Circuit, which affirmed. See In re Belanger, 962 F.2d 345, 346 (4th Cir. 1992). In doing so, the Fourth Circuit rejected the Seventh Circuit's conclusion that the three options in section 521(a)(2)(A) were exclusive. The Fourth Circuit noted, inter alia, that the Seventh Circuit's analysis rested on another case which reasoned in part from the premise that ipso facto clauses were enforceable in that circuit. See id. at 347-48 (rejecting Edwards and its reliance on In re Bell, 700 F.2d 1053 (6th Cir. 1983)).

In so holding, the Fourth Circuit chose its side in a vigorous circuit split. This circuit split persisted for over fifteen years. See Donald, 343 B.R. at 530-31. The Supreme Court never resolved whether the three options listed in section 521(a)(2)(A) were exclusive, or whether there was a "fourth option." Rather, this issue was the subject often different decisions of the courts of appeals. Five courts of appeals held that a debtor is not limited by the options enumerated in current section 521(a)(2)(A).[6] Five others held to the contrary.[7]

---

[6] In re Price, 370 F.3d 362, 379 (3d Cir. 2004) (explaining that current section 521(a)(2)(A) is merely a notice provision); In re Parker, 139 F.3d 668, 673 (9th Cir. 1998) ("The debtor's other options remain available . . . ."); In re Boodrow, 126 F.3d 43, 51 (2d Cir. 1997) (explaining that current section 521(a)(2)(A) "appears to serve primarily a notice function, not necessarily to restrict the substantive options available to a debtor"); Belanger, 962 F.2d at 347-48 ("Nothing in [current] section 521[a](2)(A) requires the debtor to choose redemption, reaffirmation or surrender of the property to the exclusion of all other alternatives . . . ."); Lowry Fed. Credit Union v. West, 882 F.2d 1543, 1547 (10th Cir. 1989) ("[W]e do not believe those provisions make redemption or reaffirmation the exclusive means by which a bankruptcy court can allow a debtor to retain secured property.").

[7] Four courts of appeals rejected the ride-through option. In re Burr, 160 F.3d 843, 849 (1st Cir. 1998) ("[W]e believe that [current] 11 U.S.C. § 521[(a)](2) unambiguously requires chapter 7 debtors wishing to retain property of the estate that secures a consumer debt to elect one of the retention options specified . . . ."); In re Johnson, 89 F.3d 249, 252 (5th Cir. 1996) (per curiam) ("[D]ebtors are limited to the three options set forth in the statute."); In re Taylor, 3 F.3d 1512, 1517 (11th Cir. 1993) ("[W]e hold the plain language of [current] 11 U.S.C. § 521[(a)](2) does not permit a Chapter 7 debtor to retain the collateral property without either redeeming the property or reaffirming the debt . . . ."); Edwards, 901 F.2d at 1387 ("[W]e hold that [current] 11 U.S.C. § 521[(a)(2)] requires a debtor to choose between the reaffirmation, redemption or surrender of property . . . ."). Additionally, the Sixth Circuit rejected an argument that approximated ride-through shortly before Congress amended the Bankruptcy Code in 1984 to include the language that gave rise to the ride-through dispute. See Bell, 700 F.2d at 1054-55, 1058 (rejecting argument that debtor may "redeem" property by making installment payments); see also Taylor, 3 F.3d at 1515 n.3 ("The Sixth Circuit decided Bell the year before Congress passed the 1984 Amendments to the Bankruptcy Code.").

IV.

In 2005, Congress enacted BAPCPA and made many changes to the Bankruptcy Code. The question in this case is whether BAPCPA contains a modified version of the "ride-through" or "fourth option" where debtors without counsel timely enter into a reaffirmation agreement concerning personal property with their creditor and submit the reaffirmation agreement to the bankruptcy court for approval, but the bankruptcy court refuses to approve the reaffirmation agreement. Answering this question requires an analysis of 11 U.S.C. §§ 362, 521, and 524.

A.

Just like the Bankruptcy Code pre-BAPCPA, the Bankruptcy Code post-BAPCPA still presents a Chapter 7 debtor with the three enumerated options with respect to secured personal property--claim the property as exempt, redeem the property, or reaffirm the debt. BAPCPA requires that the debtor file "a statement of his intention with respect to the retention or surrender of [encumbered] property." Id. § 521(a)(2)(A). From there, the BAPCPA amendments address both aspects of what a secured creditor must show before the secured creditor may seek to repossess such collateral under state law: termination of the automatic stay and default on the underlying obligation.

Under BAPCPA, termination of the automatic stay may occur through either of two independent provisions: section 521(a)(6) or the combination of sections 521(a)(2)(C) and 362(h). These provisions use some similar terminology, but differ in important respects.

1.

The first BAPCPA provision under which the automatic stay may be terminated is section 521(a)(6). That section provides that the debtor shall:

> in a case under chapter 7 of this title in which the debtor is an individual, not retain possession of personal property as to which a creditor has an allowed claim for the purchase price secured in whole or in part by an interest in such personal property unless the debtor, not later than 45 days after the first meeting of creditors under section 341(a), either--
>
> (A) enters into an agreement with the creditor pursuant to section 524(c) with respect to the claim secured by such property; or
>
> (B) redeems such property from the security interest pursuant to section 722.

Id. § 521(a)(6). Section 521(a) goes on to state:

> If the debtor fails to so act within the 45-day period referred to in paragraph (6), the [automatic] stay under section 362(a) is terminated with respect to the personal property of the estate or of the debtor which is affected, such property shall no longer be the property of the estate, and the creditor may take whatever action as to such property as is permitted by applicable nonbankruptcy law . . . .

Id. § 521(a).

Section 521(a)(6) makes three things clear. First, it applies when the creditor has an "allowed claim" for the "purchase price" of an individual debtor's personal property. Second, if it applies, and if the debtor does not redeem the encumbered personal property, but desires to retain the encumbered personal property, the debtor must timely "enter[] into an agreement . . . pursuant to section 524(c)" (which discusses reaffirmation agreements) in order to do so. Finally, if section 521(a)(6) applies and the debtor does not obey it, the automatic stay is terminated, the property is no longer part of the estate, and "the creditor may take whatever action as to such property as is permitted by applicable nonbankruptcy law." Id. § 521(a). Such action would include invoking an ipso facto clause and (1) seeking to repossess the encumbered personal property in state court under state law and (2) seeking to obtain a deficiency judgment against the debtor for the difference between the value of the collateral and the amount due on the note.

2.

The second provision under which BAPCPA may terminate the automatic stay as to personal property is a combination of two statutory provisions. The first of these is section 521(a)(2)(C). That section now reads:

> [N]othing in subparagraphs (A) or (B) of this paragraph [11 U.S.C. § 521(a)(2)] shall alter the debtor's . . . rights with regard to [encumbered] property under this title, except as provided in section 362(h).

Id. § 521(a)(2)(C). Turning to the internal cross-reference, section 362(h) provides:

> In a case in which the debtor is an individual, the [automatic] stay provided by [11 U.S.C. § 362](a) is terminated with respect to personal property of the estate or of the debtor securing in whole or in part a claim . . . , and such personal property shall no longer be the property of the estate if the debtor fails within the applicable time set by section 521(a)(2)--
>
> (A) to file timely any statement of intention required under section 521(a)(2) with respect to such personal property or to indicate in such statement that the debtor will either surrender such personal property or retain it and, if retaining such personal property, either redeem such personal property pursuant to section 722, enter into an agreement of the kind specified in section 524(c) applicable to the debt secured by such property . . . and
>
> (B) to take timely the action specified in such statement [of intentions], as it may be amended before expiration of the period for taking action, unless such statement specifies the debtor's intention to reaffirm such debt on the original contract terms and the creditor refuses to agree to the reaffirmation on such terms.

Id. § 362(h)(1).

Sections 521(a)(2)(C) and 362(h) make three things clear. First, the debtor must timely enter into an agreement "of the kind specified in section 524(c)." Id. § 362(h)(1)(A). Second, the debtor must timely take the action that the debtor specified in the required statement of intentions. Third, if the debtor does not obey these provisions, then the automatic stay is terminated with respect to the encumbered personal property and the property is no longer part of the estate. The creditor may then seek remedies against the debtor in state court under state law, including (1) seeking to repossess the encumbered personal property and (2) seeking to obtain a deficiency judgment against the debtor for the difference between the value of the collateral and the amount due on the note.

B.

Both stay-termination provisions refer to section 524(c), though they do so in different ways. Section 521(a)(6) discusses agreements "pursuant to" section 524(c), while section 362(h) discusses agreements "of the kind specified in" section 524(c). Although the court discusses this difference in statutory language infra at Part VII.B, the court initially analyzes section 524(c).

Section 524(c) does not directly terminate the automatic stay, nor does it directly affect whether the debtor is in default. Rather, it lists numerous requirements for reaffirmation agreements. It also contains, inter alia, two internal regimes for determining whether a reaffirmation agreement is enforceable. These regimes differ based on whether an attorney represented the debtor during the course of negotiating the reaffirmation agreement and, if so, whether the attorney submitted a declaration or affidavit consistent with BAPCPA.

Where an attorney represented the debtor during the course of negotiating the reaffirmation agreement, the reaffirmation agreement is enforceable if it is:

> accompanied by a declaration or an affidavit of the attorney that represented the debtor during the course of negotiating an agreement under this subsection, which [affidavit or declaration] states that--
>
> (A) such agreement represents a fully informed and voluntary choice by the debtor;
>
> (B) such agreement does not impose an undue hardship on the debtor or a dependent of the debtor; and
>
> (C) the attorney fully advised the debtor of the legal effect and consequences of--
>
> (i) an agreement of the kind specified in this subsection; and
>
> (ii) any default under such an agreement . . . .

Id. § 524(c)(3).

By contrast, "in a case concerning an individual who was not represented by an attorney during the course of negotiating an agreement under this subsection," the agreement is enforceable if "the court approves such agreement as--(i) not imposing an undue hardship on the debtor or a dependent of the debtor; and (ii) in the best interest of the debtor." Id. § 524(c)(6)(A).

In sum, under section 524(c), whether a reaffirmation agreement is enforceable depends in part on whether an attorney represented the debtor during the course of negotiating the reaffirmation agreement. If so, then the agreement is enforceable so long as the debtor's attorney files a compliant declaration or affidavit. See id. § 524(c)(3). If an attorney did not represent the debtor during such negotiations, then the bankruptcy court must hold a hearing and independently scrutinize the reaffirmation agreement. See id. § 524(d).[8] The

[8] BAPCPA fails to contemplate a scenario where a debtor is represented by an attorney during the course of negotiating a reaffirmation agreement, but the attorney fails or refuses to provide an affidavit or declaration in accordance with section 524(c)(3). See, e.g., In re Husain, 364 B.R. 211, 215-16 (Bankr. E.D. Va. 2007). Because an attorney did not represent the Hardimans during

reaffirmation agreement is not enforceable without the bankruptcy court's approval. See id. § 524(c).

C.

Under BAPCPA, a debtor who is current on his payments on a secured obligation can still be in default on the secured obligation. Although the Fourth Circuit once held that ipso facto clauses were unenforceable as a matter of law,[9] BAPCPA partially abrogated the Fourth Circuit's holding in Riggs by adding 11 U.S.C. § 521(d). See In re Wilson, 372 B.R. 816, 820 (Bankr. D.S.C. 2007). Under that section:

> If the debtor fails timely to take the action specified in [section 521(a)(6)], or in [section 362(h)], with respect to property . . . as to which a creditor holds a [valid, enforceable] security interest . . . , nothing in this title shall prevent or limit the operation of a provision in the underlying . . . agreement that has the effect of placing the debtor in default under such . . . agreement by reason of the occurrence, pendency, or existence of a proceeding under this title or the insolvency of the debtor.

11 U.S.C. § 521(d).

In other words, if a debtor fails to comply with whichever automatic-stay-termination regime applies, the automatic stay is terminated, and any ipso facto clause in the contract and lien becomes enforceable. The creditor would then be able to seek relief against the debtor in state court under state law, including (1) seeking to repossess the encumbered personal property and (2) seeking to obtain a deficiency judgment against the debtor in personam.

V.

Shortly after BAPCPA became law, Judge Small analyzed the foregoing BAPCPA provisions. See In re Donald, 343 B.R. 524 (Bankr. E.D.N.C. 2006). The debtors in Donald, a married couple, owned a 1999 Lexus encumbered by a lien held by Coastal. 343 B.R. at 528. The debtors' loan agreement contained an ipso facto clause. Id. The debtors filed a Chapter 7 petition, and the debtors' counsel negotiated a reaffirmation agreement for the Lexus with Coastal on essentially the same terms as the original loan. See id. at 527-28. However, the debtors' counsel did not file an affidavit or declaration stating that he had advised the debtors about the consequences of the agreement as discussed under 11 U.S.C. § 524(c)(3). See id. at 528.

Judge Small reviewed the BAPCPA amendments to determine whether the debtors could still exercise the pre-BAPCPA fourth option. In doing so, Judge Small observed that the BAPCPA amendments "are confusing, overlapping, and sometimes self-contradictory. They introduce new and undefined terms that resemble, but are different from, established terms that are well understood. Furthermore, the new provisions address some situations that are unlikely to arise." Id. at 529. However, after analyzing the relevant BAPCPA amendments, Judge Small concluded that BAPCPA eliminated the pre-BAPCPA fourth option.

---

the course of negotiating the reaffirmation agreement, the court need not address that scenario.

[9] See Riggs Nat'l Bank of Washington, D.C. v. Perry, 729 F.2d 982, 985 (4th Cir. 1984).

Id. at 539-40.

In reaching this conclusion, Judge Small analyzed section 521(a)(6)--one of the BAPCPA provisions under which the automatic stay may be terminated. He concluded that "[i]n most chapter 7 cases, § 521(a)(6) will have very little application." Id. at 534. Reviewing the language of the statute, Judge Small noted that "[f]or the redemption/reaffirmation requirement of § 521(a)(6) to come into play, the creditor must have 'an allowed claim for the purchase price.'" Id. at 535 (emphasis added). Creditors file proofs of claim in Chapter 7 cases when there are assets to be distributed, and filing a proof of claim is the primary way that a claim becomes "allowed." See id. at 536 & n.7. Judge Small noted, however, that "[i]n no-asset chapter 7 cases, creditors do not file proofs of claim and [thus] do not have 'allowed' claims," and that "prior to the addition of § 52[1](a)(6), [creditors] have had no reason to file proofs of claim [in such cases]." Id. at 536. Because Coastal had not filed a proof of claim, Judge Small found that the case did not involve an "allowed" claim, and that section 521(a)(6) did not apply.

Judge Small further concluded that section 521(a)(6) did not apply because Coastal's claim was not for the "purchase price." See id. at 536-37. Citing Black's Law Dictionary, Judge Small concluded that the term "purchase price" used in section 521(a)(6) meant the full purchase price. Id. at 536 ("The term 'purchase price' is defined in Black's Law Dictionary (6th ed. rev. 1990) as being the '[p]rice agreed upon as consideration for which the property is sold and purchased.'" (alteration in original)). Judge Small noted that the term "purchase price" in the statute was not the same as the term "purchase money obligation" or "purchase money security interest." Id. Judge Small observed that Congress had used "purchase money security interest" elsewhere in BAPCPA, but did not do so in section 521(a)(6). Id. at 536-37. Judge Small concluded that Congress knew how to use commercial-law terms of art, and chose not to do so in section 521(a)(6). Because the debtors had paid some money towards the debt they owed Coastal on the Lexus, Judge Small held that Coastal did not have a claim for the full purchase price; therefore, section 521(a)(6) did not apply. Id. at 537-38.

Having concluded that section 521(a)(6) did not apply, Judge Small considered whether sections 521(a)(2)(C) and 362(h) applied and thereby terminated the automatic stay. See id. at 533-34, 540. Judge Small noted that, unless the debtors had timely "entered into" a reaffirmation agreement, and had taken the action specified in their statement of intentions for purposes of section 362(h), then section 362(h) would terminate the automatic stay, section 521(d) would allow the ipso facto clause in the loan agreement to activate, and Coastal would be able to seek to relief against the debtor in state court under state law. See id. at 538-41. Such relief would include the possibility of repossession and a deficiency judgment.

Judge Small turned to whether the debtors had "entered into" a reaffirmation agreement within the meaning of section 362(h). As mentioned, the debtors had signed a reaffirmation agreement with Coastal, but the debtors' attorney did not file a declaration or affidavit under section 524(c)(3). Judge Small therefore had to decide whether to approve the reaffirmation agreement under section 524(c)(6)(A). Section 524(c)(6)(A) mandates that a bankruptcy court must consider whether the reaffirmation agreement is (1) an undue burden on the debtors, and (2) in the debtors' best interest. See 11 U.S.C. § 524(c)(6)(A).

On this point, the debtors argued "that disapproval by the court of their reaffirmation agreement is in their best interest." Donald, 343 B.R. at 526 (emphasis supplied). The debtors' theory was that, by signing the reaffirmation agreement with Coastal, they had "entered into" it as required by 11 U.S.C. § 362(h)(1)(A). The debtors then argued that bankruptcy court approval was not an element of "entering into" the agreement. In the debtors' view, they had done all that they could do under BAPCPA, and even if the bankruptcy court did not approve the reaffirmation agreement, they still had complied with BAPCPA. Moreover, if the bankruptcy court did not approve the reaffirmation agreement, the debtors argued that the car would remain a part of the bankruptcy estate. Thus, they argued that the bankruptcy court would discharge the debt on the balance of the car loan, and that they could keep their car and continue making payments to Coastal without entering into an enforceable reaffirmation agreement. Further, the discharge of the car loan debt would prevent the creditor from later obtaining a deficiency judgment against the debtors but would not prevent the creditor from enforcing its rights under the contract and lien. One of those rights would be repossession if the debtors failed to make timely payments on the loan. In sum, the debtors argued that the BAPCPA amendments had created a new, modified fourth option on these particular facts. See id. at 526, 540. Coastal disagreed and argued that the court had to approve the reaffirmation agreement for it to have been "enter[ed] into" under section 524(c)(6)(A). Id. at 540. Absent such approval, Coastal argued that it could invoke all state law remedies, including filing a state court action seeking repossession and a deficiency judgment against the debtors. Id. at 528.

Judge Small rejected the debtors' theory on the facts of that case. Id. at 540. Instead, Judge Small found that the reaffirmation agreement was not an undue hardship and was in the debtors' best interest, and approved it. Id. However, Judge Small noted:

> This does not mean that the debtors' argument will always fail. Section 524(c) sets forth the requirements that must be met for a re affirmation agreement to be enforceable. Several of these requirements do not involve the debtor, and whether or not an agreement is enforceable may often be beyond the debtor's control.

Id. In particular, Judge Small noted that "disapproval by the court is beyond the debtors' control." Id. at 541.

Courts have cited Donald many times, both positively[10] and negatively.[11] Donald is the leading case for the "modified fourth option" position. See, e.g., Christopher M. Hogan, Note, Will the Ride-Through Ride Again?, 108 COLUM. L. REV. 882, 905 (2008). Basically, Donald reopened the pre-BAPCPA fourth option split in a small category of cases by concluding that BAPCPA contains a "modified fourth option," even though Donald did not actually apply the modified fourth option on its facts.

Neither party appealed in Donald. Thus, in Donald, neither this court nor the Fourth Circuit addressed these BAPCPA issues.

VI.

Initially, Coastal argues that the bankruptcy court erred in analyzing

---

[10] See, e.g., In re Steinhaus, 349 B.R. 694, 704-07 (Bankr. D. Idaho 2006).

[11] See, e.g., In re Moustafi, 371 B.R. 434, 438 (Bankr. D. Ariz. 2007); In re Husain, 364 B.R. 211, 219 nn.14, 15 (Bankr. E.D. Va. 2007); In re Blakeley, 363 B.R. 225, 229 n.7 (Bankr. D. Utah 2007).

section 521(a)(6). The crux of the dispute is whether the word "allowed" in "allowed claim" in section 521(a)(6) should be ignored, and whether the claim must be for the full purchase price. Basically, Coastal argues that the court should read the statute "holistically," invoke the absurdity exception and the intent exception to the plain meaning rule, and conclude that (1) the word "allowed" makes no sense and should be disregarded, and (2) requiring the claim to be for the full purchase price makes no sense, either.

A.

Coastal does not have an "allowed claim." Nevertheless, Coastal contends that it is absurd to enforce section 521(a)(6) as written so that it only applies to an "allowed claim." In support, Coastal cites In re Rowe, 342 B.R. 341, 347-49 (Bankr. D. Kansas 2006), and Steinhaus, 349 B.R. at 705-06.

Contrary to what Coastal argues, applying section 521(a)(6) only to an "allowed claim" is not absurd. Under 11 U.S.C. § 501, parties and parties in interest are permitted to file proofs of claim. "A claim or interest, proof of which is filed under [11 U.S.C. § 501], is deemed allowed . . . ." 11 U.S.C. § 502(a). "A proof of claim or interest should be filed only when some purpose would be served." 4 Collier on Bankruptcy § 501.01 (Alan N. Resnick & Henry J. Sommer, eds., 15th ed. rev. 2008) (quotation omitted). There are at least two possible purposes to be served in applying the phrase "allowed claim" in section 521(a)(6) as written. Each purpose revolves around documentation that creditors generally attach when they file a proof of claim. First, filing a proof of claim will establish whether the creditor has an ipso facto clause that it can invoke. Second, filing a proof of claim will establish whether the underlying contract and lien are valid, enforceable, and perfected. As Judge Small reasoned in Donald, "it is not too much to require that the secured creditor file a proof of claim" before it attempts to take property from a debtor who is not behind on payments. See 343 B.R. at 536 ("At a minimum, the proof of claim would establish the amount of the claim and would provide documentation that supports the creditor's invocation of an ipso facto clause."); see also In re Openshaw, No. 06C-24120, 2007 Bankr. LEXIS 3489, 2007 WL 2916294 (Bankr. D. Utah Mar. 12, 2007) (unpublished); In re Hinson, 352 B.R. 48, 51-52 (Bankr. E.D.N.C. 2006); In re Norton, 347 B.R. 291, 299 (Bankr. E.D. Tenn. 2006). Because there are plausible reasons that Congress might have chosen the statutory language in section 521(a)(6), the absurdity exception does not apply. See, e.g., Sunterra, 361 F.3d at 268-69; Md. State Dep't of Educ., 98 F.3d at 169-71.

Alternatively, Coastal cites Rowe and Steinhaus, and argues that it is demonstrably against Congressional intent to enforce the plain meaning of section 521(a)(6) to apply only to an "allowed claim." In Rowe, the bankruptcy court noted that most Chapter 7 debtors have no assets that can be liquidated for the benefit of creditors; therefore, most creditors have no reason to file a proof of claim. 342 B.R. at 348. In support, the Rowe court examined the House Report on BAPCPA,[12] and concluded that the House Report did not limit section

[12] See The Bankruptcy Abuse Prevention and Consumer Protection Act of 2005, H.R. Rep. No. 109-31, pt. 1 (2005), as reprinted in 2005 U.S.C.C.A.N. 88 [hereinafter "House Report"]. The House Report is practically BAPCPA's only legislative history. See, e.g., Jean Braucher, Rash and Ride-Through Redux: The Terms for Holding on to Cars, Homes and Other Collateral Under the 2005

521(a)(6)'s applicability to "allowed claims." Id. at 349. Thus, the Rowe court concluded that it should disregard the word "allowed" in section 521(a)(6). Id. Steinhaus adopted Rowe's analysis. See 349 B.R. at 706.

For the intent exception to apply, a party must show that Congress clearly expressed a contrary intent. E.g., Sunterra, 361 F.3d at 268-70; Md. State Dep't of Educ., 98 F.3d at 169. Coastal relies on the fact that Congress did not clearly state in the legislative history that it wanted to have section 521(a)(6) apply only to an "allowed claim," and from there reasons that Congress must have desired section 521(a)(6) to apply to all claims, whether "allowed" or not. See, e.g., Rowe, 342 B.R. at 349 ("[The House R]eport does not use the phrase 'allowed claim.'"). Coastal's reasoning, however, turns the intent exception on its head. Congress used the phrase "allowed claim" in section 521(a)(6). Coastal essentially argues that the court should disregard the plain language in section 521(a)(6) because Congress failed to clearly express its intent in favor of the plain language in BAPCPA's legislative history. However, simply because the legislative history fails to mention the phrase "allowed claim" does not negate the statutory language. Both the House and Senate voted to enact the statute. Neither the House nor the Senate voted to enact the House Report. Cf. In re First Merchants Acceptance Corp., 198 F.3d 394, 401 (3d Cir. 1999) (finding no "basis to assume the Senate was aware of the one sentence in [another] House Report on which [other] parties rely"). The plain language in section 521(a)(6)--including the phrase "allowed claim"--is the best evidence of Congress' intent. See, e.g., Sunterra, 361 F.3d at 268-70. Accordingly, the court rejects Coastal's argument.

B.

Next, Coastal contends that Congress did not intend for section 521(a)(6) to apply only to claims for the full "purchase price." First, Coastal argues that the plain language leads to an absurd result because there is no plausible reason that Congress would intend section 521(a)(6) to apply only where the debtor has not paid any money towards the debt. In support, Coastal again cites Steinhaus. There, the bankruptcy court reasoned that the plain language in section 521(a)(6) leads to an absurd result because "the [c]ourt can divine no cogent, or even plausible, reason why Congress would have intended to limit § 521(a)(6) relief to only those creditors who have secured claims for the 'full' purchase price." Steinhaus, 349 B.R. at 706; accord In re Dumont, 383 B.R. 481, 487-88 (B.A.P. 9th Cir. 2008).

The court disagrees with Coastal. Congress could have chosen to make section 521(a)(6) apply as written to curb the most abusive of bankruptcy practices: buying personal property on credit by taking advantage of a "no money down, no payments for X days" offer, enjoying the personal property while making no payments whatsoever, and then filing for bankruptcy immediately before repossession. See In re Blakeley, 363 B.R. 225, 229 (Bankr. D. Utah 2007) ("While instances where a creditor would hold a claim for the purchase price of property are rare, it does occur in situations of abuse when a debtor, knowing full well that they are about to file bankruptcy, will take advantage of 'no down payment' offers to purchase vehicles or other property."); accord House Report

Act, 13 Am. Bankr. Inst. L. Rev. 457, 460 n.13 (2005). Neither party cites any legislative history other than this report.

15 ("[BAPCPA] also addresses abusive practices by consumer debtors who, for example, knowingly load up with credit card purchases or recklessly obtain cash advances and then file for bankruptcy relief."). Because curbing this most abusive bankruptcy practice is a plausible reason that Congress might have chosen to write section 521(a)(6) using the term "purchase price," the plain language does not lead to an absurd result. Accordingly, Coastal has failed to demonstrate that the absurdity exception applies. See, e.g., Sunterra, 361 F.3d at 268; Md. State Dep't of Educ., 98 F.3d at 169-71.

Alternatively, Coastal maintains that interpreting the phrase "purchase price" to mean the full purchase price conflicts with Congressional intent. Coastal again cites Steinhaus, which noted that the House Report speaks of "'personal property securing, in whole or in part, a purchase money security interest.'" 349 B.R. at 705 n.21 (quoting House Report 71); accord Dumont, 383 B.R. at 488 & n.11.

Although this sentence in the House Report arguably provides some evidence in support of Coastal's position, it is not enough to invoke the intent exception. First, although the quoted language from the House Report might suggest one view of Congress' intent, it is not clear that the result mandated by the plain language in section 521(a)(6) contravenes the legislative intent. See United States v. Ron Pair Enters., Inc., 489 U.S. 235, 242-43 (1989) (analyzing whether the plain language "contravene[s] the intent of the framers of the Code"); Sunterra, 361 F.3d at 269 ("[A] court is obliged to apply the Plain Meaning Rule unless the party otherwise can demonstrate that the result would be contrary to that intended by Congress."). Indeed, all claims for the full purchase price will involve a purchase money security interest. Thus, the legislative history is arguably consistent with, not contrary to, the statutory text.

Second, and more importantly, Coastal asks the court to insert one legal term of art from the House Report (i.e., "purchase money security interest") and to delete another legal term of art in the statute (i.e., "purchase price"). Congress, however, knows how to say "purchase money security interest," and used that phrase in other places in BAPCPA. See Donald, 343 B.R. at 537 ("Clearly, if Congress intended in § 521(a)(6) for a 'claim for the purchase price' to mean something less than the full purchase price, it would have said so as it did in § 522(f)(1)(B), § 524(k)(3)(G), § 1325(a)(4) and § 1326(a)(4)."). That Congress elsewhere used the term that Coastal desires the court to insert into section 521(a)(6) is evidence in favor of the result mandated by the plain language, not against it. See id.

Finally, although it might be wiser policy to apply section 521(a)(6) to all purchase money security interests, whether for the full purchase price or not, the intent exception does not apply so whimsically. See, e.g., Sunterra, 361 F.3d at 269. The Fourth Circuit has said that federal courts cannot "ignore the plain language of the statute in order to effectuate what [a litigant] claim[s] to be the overarching purpose of Congress." First S. Prod. Credit Ass'n v. Farm Credit Admin., 926 F.2d 339, 346 (4th Cir. 1991). "Judges are not free to take the general purpose of a statute and choose the means to implement it, because it is in the delineation of means as well as in the prescription of purposes that Congress makes its intentions clear." Id. Rather, the party challenging the plain language must affirmatively show that the plain language is demonstrably contrary to the legislature's intentions. See Sunterra, 361 F.3d at 269; First Merchants Acceptance Corp., 198 F.3d at 403. This Coastal has not done. Thus, section 521(a)(6) does not apply.

VII.

Alternatively, Coastal argues that the combination of sections 521(a)(2)(C) and 362(h) terminates the automatic stay. In making this argument, Coastal contends that the plain language of section 362(h), which requires that the debtors "enter into" an agreement (not "enter into and receive court approval of" an agreement), leads to absurd results and contravenes clearly expressed Congressional intent. In making this argument, Coastal also contends that there is no difference between an agreement "of the kind specified in" section 524(c) (as used in section 362(h)) and an agreement "pursuant to" section 524(c) (as used in section 521(a)(6)). Further, according to Coastal, if there is a difference between the language in section 362(h) and section 521(a)(6), then the plain-meaning implications of an agreement "of the kind specified in" section 524(c) lead to absurd results and contravene clearly expressed Congressional intent.

A.

As discussed, the bankruptcy court analyzed sections 521(a)(2)(C) and 362(h) to determine whether they applied and thereby terminated the automatic stay. Judge Small concluded that the Hardimans had "entered into" a reaffirmation agreement with Coastal within the meaning of section 362(h)(1)(A). Id. at 7-8. Further, because the Hardimans "entered into" the reaffirmation agreement without legal counsel, the bankruptcy court had to decide whether to approve the agreement as "'(i) not imposing an undue hardship on the debtor or a dependant of the debtor; and (ii) in the best interest of the debtor.'" Id. at 5 (quoting 11 U.S.C. § 524(c)(6)(A)). If Judge Small approved the reaffirmation agreement, then the agreement would be "enforceable." See 11 U.S.C. § 524(c); see also id. § 524(k)(3)(J)(i).

After holding a hearing, Judge Small found that the reaffirmation agreement did impose an undue hardship on the debtors and was not in their best interest. Bankr. Thus, Judge Small refused to approve the agreement. In reaching this conclusion, Judge Small rejected Coastal's argument that the phrase "enter into" a reaffirmation agreement in section 362(h)(1)(A) means enter into an enforceable reaffirmation agreement. On appeal, Coastal contends that it is absurd for Congress to use "enter into an agreement" in section 362(h)(1)(A) to mean anything less than "enter into a valid, enforceable contract." In support, Coastal cites a variety of North Carolina cases for the proposition that, without mutuality of obligation, there can be no contract enforceable at law.

The court rejects Coastal's reliance on North Carolina contract law, because whether North Carolina contract law requires mutuality of obligation is irrelevant to construing BAPCPA's statutory language. Notably, a contractual agreement that is unenforceable can still be an "agreement." "The term 'agreement,' although frequently used synonymously with the word 'contract,' is really an expression of greater breadth of meaning and less technicality. Every contract is an agreement; but not every agreement is a contract." Black's Law Dictionary 74 (8th ed. 2004) (definition of "agreement"; quotation omitted).

People often enter into unenforceable "agreements." For example, contracts that do not comply with the statute of frauds are unenforceable, but that does not mean that they are not "agreements." Moreover, such "agreements" are sometimes enforceable in equity--as, for example, by promissory estoppel. Likewise, in other circumstances, people enter into "agreements" which are not enforceable either at law or in equity. For example, an accepted invitation to dinner is an "agreement," but not one that creates any enforceable obligation between the parties. See id. Congress could plausibly have chosen to require uncounseled debtors to "enter into" an agreement within the meaning of 11 U.S.C. § 362(h)(1)(A)--not to "enter into" an enforceable contract--because whether the contract is enforceable is not within the debtors' control. See, e.g., In re Baker, 390 B.R. 524, 529-30 (Bankr. D. Del. 2008); In re Tran, No. 07-12512-SSM, 2007 Bankr. LEXIS 3997, 2007 WL 4210559, at n.2 (Bankr. E.D. Va. Nov. 27, 2007) (unpublished); In re Husain, 364 B.R. 211, 218-19 (Bankr. E.D. Va. 2007); In re Bower, No. 07-60126-fra7, 2007 Bankr. LEXIS 2580, 2007 WL 2163472, at (Bankr. D. Or. July 26, 2007) (unpublished); Openshaw, 2007 Bankr. LEXIS 3489, 2007 WL 2916294, at *5-*6; Blakeley, 363 B.R. at 232 ("To rule otherwise would potentially penalize a debtor for actions outside the control of the debtor."); Donald, 343 B.R. at 540-41; cf. Black's Law Dictionary 572 (8th ed. 2004) ("[E]nter" means "[t]o become a party to.").

Coastal complains that here, because the bankruptcy court did not approve the reaffirmation agreement, the agreement is not enforceable at law or in equity. But that fact does not render it any less an "agreement." The question is not whether the debtors would be bound by some form of legal compulsion, but whether it is absurd for Congress to have used the phrase "enter into an agreement" to mean what it says.

Coastal contends that Congress could not have done so. In Coastal's view, Congress would never write a statute to permit an uncounseled debtor whose reaffirmation agreement was rejected by the bankruptcy court to be able to keep secured personal property without the threat of repossession and personal liability for a deficiency judgment should the debtor damage or mistreat the collateral. Coastal argues that a hypothetical debtor who was permitted to do what the plain language allows could simply stop paying insurance on the car, stop maintaining the car, and mistreat the car without concern for the consequences, because the debtor does not face the prospect of a personal deficiency judgment. Coastal argues that such a policy would eviscerate individual responsibility and is absurd.

Coastal underestimates the real-world consequences to a debtor who engages in such foolish practices. Coastal admits that, under the bankruptcy court's decision in this case, all portions of the Hardimans' vehicle contract (including the lien), save for the threat of a personal deficiency judgment, "ride through" the bankruptcy. Indeed, "'[i]t is well-settled that a bankruptcy discharge extinguishes only one mode of enforcing a claim--namely, an action against the debtor in personam--while leaving intact another--namely, an action against the debtor in rem.' 'Thus, liens on property remain enforceable after discharge . . . .'" In re Anderson, 348 B.R. 652, 655 (Bankr. D. Del. 2006) (quoting Johnson v. Home State Bank, 501 U.S. 78, 84, 111 S. Ct. 2150, 115 L. Ed. 2d 66 (1991) & In re Holloway, 81 F.3d 1062, 1063 n.1 (11th Cir. 1996), respectively (internal citations omitted)); see Estate of Lellock v. Prudential Ins. Co. of Am., 811 F.2d 186, 188-189 (3d Cir. 1987); Chandler Bank of Lyons v. Ray, 804 F.2d 577, 578-79 (10th Cir. 1986) (per curiam). Should a debtor fail to uphold a contractual duty to make timely payments, insure the collateralized vehicle, or otherwise violate any other provision of the underlying contract (including the lien), the creditor would be able to seek to repossess the vehicle under state law if the contract permits. See, e.g., Belanger, 962 F.2d at 349.

Moreover, and significantly, even if the bankruptcy court refuses to approve the uncounseled debtor's reaffirmation agreement, that result does not mean that in all cases the debtor will be allowed to "ride through" the bankruptcy with the collateral. Rather, just like pre-BAPCPA, a "creditor can obtain relief under § 362(d) for 'cause.' Cause is not defined in the Code and a bankruptcy court has broad discretion to lift the stay in 'appropriate circumstances.'" In re Cooper, 296 B.R. 410, 412 (Bankr. E.D. Va. 2002) (footnote omitted) (quoting In re Holtkamp, 669 F.2d 505, 508 (7th Cir. 1982)). In attempting to demonstrate "cause," a creditor usually would need to show some "affirmative harm." Cooper, 296 B.R. at 412. In evaluating "cause," a bankruptcy court would examine "the debtor's 'previous payment record, a comparison of the value of the collateral and the amount of debt, and other relevant facts.'" Id. at 412 (quoting In re Boodrow, 126 F.3d 43, 52 (2d Cir. 1997)); accord Price, 370 F.3d at 373, 377; Am. Nat'l Bank & Trust Co. v. DeJournette, 222 B.R. 86, 92-97 (W.D. Va. 1998). Further, if the debtor had no equity in the property, the bankruptcy court could terminate the automatic stay. See 11 U.S.C. § 362(d) ("On request of a party in interest and after notice and a hearing, the court shall grant relief from the stay . . . if . . . the debtor does not have an equity in such property; and . . . such property is not necessary to an effective reorganization . . . ."). Thus, the creditor is not as helpless as Coastal implies.

Additionally, a rational debtor would not only have to be concerned with the legal consequences of the contract including the lien, but also with the practical consequences of mistreating the vehicle. "The automobile is a crucial piece of property for many individuals and integral to most Americans' daily lives." Christopher M. Hogan, Note, *Will the Ride-Through Ride Again?*, 108 Colum. L. Rev. 882, 907 (2008) (citation omitted). "[T]he automobile is [often] the only way to retain employment or seek education anywhere far from the home. When a debtor files for bankruptcy, his car will be one of the most, if not the most, important pieces of property that he will want to keep." Id. (citation omitted). A debtor cannot simply mistreat such a vehicle without serious consequences. If a debtor mistreats the vehicle, the debtor will very likely need to purchase another vehicle, which will very likely require a new loan at far more unfavorable terms than the previous one, given the debtor's status as formerly bankrupt. And the debtor cannot expect to simply refile for bankruptcy to escape this new debt. See 11 U.S.C. § 727(a)(8) (prohibiting a Chapter 7 discharge where "the debtor has been granted a discharge . . . in a case commenced within 8 years before the date of the filing of the petition").

Ultimately, it is not this court's role to analyze whether the language in BAPCPA constitutes good policy. See, e.g., Sunterra, 361 F.3d at 268-69. Likewise, it is not this court's role to determine whether Congress could have done a better job in drafting BAPCPA. See id. at 269. Rather, under the governing principles of statutory construction, this court must analyze whether it is plausible that Congress could have chosen to spare uncounseled debtors whose reaffirmation agreements were not approved by the bankruptcy court from automatically losing the protection of the automatic stay, becoming subject to any applicable ipso facto clause, and becoming subject to both repossession and a personal deficiency judgment. For the reasons discussed, Congress could plausibly have chosen the result that flows from BAPCPA's plain language. Accordingly, the absurdity exception does not apply.

B.

Next, Coastal argues that the plain-meaning implications of the phrase "enter into an agreement" in section 362(h)(1)(A) contravene clearly expressed Congressional intent in the legislative history. However, the legislative history actually appears to support the bankruptcy court's interpretation of the phrase "enter into" a reaffirmation agreement. The House Report consistently speaks about what "the debtor" must do. For example, it states that "the automatic stay is terminated if *the debtor* fails to take the action specified in the statement of intention." House Report 71 (emphasis added). It is a basic principle of contract law that an offer requires an act which a reasonable person would believe manifests an intent to enter into an agreement. Once the offer is made and the offeree accepts, the parties have done all that they can do to enter into the agreement. Neither party controls whether the agreement is enforceable.

Where "the debtor" manifests an intent to enter into an agreement , "the debtor" has "take[n] the action specified in the statement of intention." See House Report 71. Nowhere does the House Report state that court approval is a necessary aspect of entering into a reaffirmation agreement. Nor could it logically do so, because court approval is not within an uncounseled debtor's control. See 11 U.S.C. § 524(c)(6); Baker, 390 B.R. at 529-30; Donald. The statutory scheme is consistent with this interpretation in that section 524(c) distinguishes between an agreement and an "enforceable" agreement with respect to debtors who enter reaffirmation agreements without counsel. 11 U.S.C. § 524(c). Further, section 524(f) contemplates a debtor voluntarily repaying a debt, which is what happens when a debtor pays on a car loan that has been discharged. See id. § 524(f) ("Nothing contained in [sections 524(c) or 524(d)] prevents a debtor from voluntarily repaying any debt."); see In re Hellums, 772 F.2d 379, 381 (7th Cir. 1985) (per curiam). In sum, the plain-meaning implications of the phrase "enter into an agreement" in section 362(h)(1)(A) do not contravene clearly expressed Congressional intent. See Sunterra, 361 F.3d at 268-69.

Next, Coastal argues that the court should look to the phrase "enter into" an agreement in both section 362(h)(1)(A) and section 521(a)(6) and conclude that both sections require the same interpretation. Coastal's argument hinges on equating the phrase "pursuant to" in section 521(a)(6) and the phrase "of the kind specified in" section 362(h)(1)(A). Compare 11 U.S.C. § 521(a)(6) (describing one option for a Chapter 7 debtor as "enter[ing] into an agreement with the creditor *pursuant to section 524(c)* with respect to the claim secured by such property" (emphasis added)) with id. § 362(h)(1)(A) (describing one option for debtor as "enter[ing] into an agreement *of the kind specified in section 524(c)* applicable to the debt secured by such personal property") (emphasis added)). In essence, Coastal argues an agreement "pursuant to" section 524(c) means an agreement that complies with *every subsection* of 524(c), including the subsection addressing bankruptcy court approval of the reaffirmation agreement for uncounseled debtors. See id. § 524(c)(6)(A). Further, Coastal argues that this court should import the "pursuant to" language found in section 521(a)(6) into section 362(h)(1)(A). In making this argument, Coastal contends that there is no difference between the phrases "pursuant to" as found in section 521(a)(6), and "of the kind specified in" as found in section 362(h)(1)(A). Thus, Coastal maintains that, to be an agreement "of the kind specified in" section 524(c), a reaffirmation must comply with every subsection of 524(c), including the provision governing court approval of the reaffirmation agreement.

The court rejects this argument. Even if the court equates the phrases "enter into an agreement pursuant to section 524(c)" and "enter into an agreement of the kind specified in section 524(c)," the court's analyses of the phrase "enter into an agreement" in section 521(a)(6), the phrase "enter into an agreement" in section 362(h)(1)(A), and the term"agreement" in section 524(c) demonstrate that with respect to debtors proceeding without counsel the phrase "enter into an agreement" does not equal "enter into an enforceable agreement." See Fees v. Ford Motor Credit Co., No. CV07-389-S-EJL, 2008 U.S. Dist. LEXIS 83937, 2008 WL 4630668, at n.9 (D. Idaho Oct. 17, 2008); Moustafi, 371 B.R. at 439 n. 10. Indeed, section 524(c) recognizes that where an individual who is not represented by an attorney negotiates and signs a reaffirmation agreement that a creditor has signed, that reaffirmation agreement is not enforceable unless the bankruptcy court holds a hearing and approves it. See 11 U.S.C. § 524(c)(6)(A). Thus, the court rejects Coastal's argument that, under section 524(c) the phrase "enter into an agreement pursuant to section 524(c)" and the phrase "enter into an agreement of the kind specified in section 524(c)" can only mean "enter into an agreement that the bankruptcy court has approved." See, e.g., In re Chim, 381 B.R. 191, 197-98 (Bankr. D. Md. 2008).

Next, Coastal argues that if the phrase "of the kind specified in" as used in section 362(h)(1)(A) does not equate to the phrase "pursuant to" as used in section 521(a)(6), then the result is absurd because this interpretation destroys the alleged parallelism between section 362(h)(1)(A) and section 521(a)(6). Coastal decries the plain-meaning reading because under it, a party could comply with section 362(h) even when the bankruptcy court refuses to approve the reaffirmation agreement, while a party under section 521(a)(6) could never comply with that section's dictates absent actual approval of the reaffirmation agreement by the bankruptcy court.

For the reasons given earlier, the court rejects the premise that either entering into an agreement pursuant to section 524(c) or entering into an agreement of the kind specified in section 524(c) requires bankruptcy court approval. Such approval is necessary for an uncounseled debtor's reaffirmation agreement to be enforceable, but entering into an enforceable agreement is different than entering into an agreement. Congress could plausibly have chosen the statutory framework set forth in section 524(c), including the discretionary authority for a bankruptcy court to disapprove a debtor's uncounseled reaffirmation agreement. See 11 U.S.C. § 524(c)(6)(A).[13]

Coastal next argues that the sum total of the BAPCPA amendments indicates that Congress wanted court approval of a reaffirmation agreement to be a necessary condition of compliance .... However, even if Congress eliminated the pre-BAPCPA fourth option, that intent does not mean that Congress did not intend to create a modified version of the fourth option that applies to certain uncounseled debtors in certain cases:

> While BAPCPA has done away with simple "ride through" in bankruptcy, it has not entirely eliminated the possibility that a debtor can "ride through" a

[13] The Hardimans contend that it is Coastal's interpretation of the statute--not the plain meaning reading--that leads to absurd results. See Hardimans Initial Br. 9-11; Hardimans Supp. Br. 6-7. According to the Hardimans, it is impossible for any debtor comply with every provision of section 524(c), because that section contains differing deadlines. See Hardimans Initial Br. 10-11; Hardimans Supp. Br. 6-7. The court need not address this argument.

> bankruptcy and retain possession of secured personal property. Under the limited circumstances stated above, where a debtor timely complies with all requirements under §§ 521 and 362(h), the debtor can "ride through" the bankruptcy notwithstanding a bankruptcy court's refusal to approve the reaffirmation agreement.

Blakeley, 363 B.R. at 232; see Baker, 390 B.R. at 529-30; Chim, 381 B.R. at 199 ("[W]here a court rejects a reaffirmation agreement that was timely entered into by a debtor, the debtor is left in the same position as a debtor who elected to have the loan contract ride through bankruptcy prior to the adoption of the creditor relief provisions in BAPCPA, and the rationale of Belanger continues to apply."); Donald, 343 B.R. at 540-41.

C.

Finally, the court addresses Coastal's reliance on section 521(d) and the ipso facto clause in the loan agreement. Section 521(d) reads, "If the debtor fails timely to take the action specified in [section 521(a)(6) or in section 362(h) and 521(a)(2)] . . . , nothing in this title shall prevent or limit the operation of [an ipso facto clause] . . . ." 11 U.S.C. § 521(d). Relying on the plain language of section 521(a)(6) and section 521(d), Judge Small first held that section 521(a)(6) simply did not apply. As for sections 362(h) and 521(a)(2), Judge Small held that the debtors timely took the action specified in sections 362(h) and 521(a)(2). Specifically, "[b]y signing the [reaffirmation a]greement, the debtors 'entered into' an agreement to reaffirm the debt to Coastal. This constitutes 'performing their intention' to reaffirm, as required by § 521(a)(2)(B), as well as 'entering into an agreement of the kind specified in § 524(c),' as required by § 362(h)(1)." Once again, Coastal argues that this plain-meaning reading of "timely . . . tak[ing] the action specified" in the applicable BAPCPA provisions leads to absurd results and contravenes clearly expressed Congressional intent.

First, Coastal contends that the bankruptcy court's interpretation of "take the action specified" in BAPCPA to not require court approval of the reaffirmation agreement in order to avoid the effect of section 521(d) and any ipso facto clause has "the absurd result of creat[ing] a 'class within a class' of Chapter 7 debtors seeking to retain their encumbered property." Coastal Initial Br. 11. However, as discussed, Congress could have chosen to retain a modified version of the "fourth option" for certain uncounseled debtors who sought to reaffirm their debt, but whose attempt to reaffirm was thwarted by the expertise of the bankruptcy court. Because a plausible rationale exists for the result mandated by BAPCPA's plain language, the absurdity exception does not apply. See, e.g., Sunterra, 361 F.3d at 268.

Second, Coastal contends that Congress wanted to eliminate the fourth option "for all Chapter 7 debtors," and that the House Report says so. In support, Coastal cites the background part of the House Report, which states, "[BAPCPA] terminates the automatic stay with respect to personal property if the debtor does not timely reaffirm the underlying obligation or redeem the property." House Report 17. Coastal places the emphasis on "timely reaffirm," and argues that this means that a debtor must in fact reaffirm by getting court approval if necessary. However, the House Report fails to address the scenario in this case concerning uncounseled debtors who timely enter into a reaffirmation agreement, but who have to get bankruptcy court approval for the reaffirmation agreement to be enforceable. Further, even looking at the House Report for what it does say, the emphasis could just as easily be placed on "the debtor," implying that where the debtor did everything that the debtor could to timely reaffirm the debt, then the debtor has complied with BAPCPA.

The burden to overcome the plain language in BAPCPA is "extraordinary." Garcia v. United States, 469 U.S. 70, 75, 105 S. Ct. 479, 83 L. Ed. 2d 472 (1984); Sunterra, 361 F.3d at 268-69. Coastal's citation to one arguably ambiguous sentence in the House Report is not enough to successfully mount an intent exception challenge to BAPCPA's plain language. See, e.g., Sunterra, 361 F.3d at 270. Accordingly, Coastal has failed to show that the intent exception applies. In sum, section 521(d) provides no relief to Coastal.[14]

D.

The court has carefully considered the statutes at issue in this case as a whole, and concludes that neither narrow exception to the plain meaning rule applies to the provisions at issue in this case. See, e.g., Ayes, 473 F.3d at 108; Sunterra, 361 F.3d at 265. The statutory scheme is coherent and consistent, and must be applied as written. At bottom, Coastal attempts to mix the absurdity exception, the intent exception, and the circumstances surrounding BAPCPA's passage to concoct a "this is what Congress really should have done" exception to the plain meaning rule. There is no such exception. See Garcia, 469 U.S. at 78 (noting that courts should not change the plain meaning of a statute "on the basis of a gestalt judgment as to what Congress probably intended"); Sunterra, 361 F.3d at 269 ("[P]ut simply, the modification of a statutory provision to achieve a preferable policy outcome is a task reserved to Congress."); First South, 926 F.2d at 346-47.

Therefore, the automatic stay remains in place with respect to the Hardimans' loan concerning the Chevrolet, the Chevrolet remains part of the bankruptcy estate, and the Hardimans are not in default. The Hardimans may continue to possess the car and make payments to Coastal. If the Hardimans fail to make timely payments, or if they violate any other provision of the contract (including the lien), Coastal retains whatever rights it possesses under the terms of the underlying contract (including the lien). Those rights include seeking to repossess the car under state law. As part of any such in rem action, however, Coastal may not obtain a deficiency judgment against the Hardimans in personam.

VIII.

The court has examined the parties' arguments about the plain meaning of the BAPCPA provisions at issue in this case and the possible application of either the absurdity exception or the intent exception. Coastal has failed to meet the extraordinary burden of overcoming the plain meaning rule of statutory construction. Accordingly, for the reasons explained in this order, the judgment of the bankruptcy court is affirmed.

---

[14] This order does not address any state law limitations that might prevent repossession under section 521(d). Cf. Dumont, 383 B.R. at 489-90.

Notes and Questions

1. In Hardiman, D had not yet received or been denied a discharge. What happens to the car if the debtors ultimately receive a discharge? Bankruptcy Code § 362(c)(1)(C).

2. Does Bankruptcy Code § 362(a)(h) not apply just because SP has not filed a proof of claim. One court refuses to reach this conclusion:

> The Court does not believe that Congress could have intended the phrase "allowed claim" to have the clear meaning ascribed to it by operation of § 502, since this construction of "allowed claim" renders the section applicable only in asset chapter 7 cases when a secured creditor files a proof of claim after the clerk has given notice that assets are available for distribution.

In re Rowe, 342 B.R. 341, 348 (Bankr. D. Kan. 2006). In most cases, the flaw in § 521(a)(6) will not matter, since neither §521(a)(2) or § 362(h) refer to "allowed secured claims."

C. LAW SUITS

CANNON-STOKES v POTTER
453 F.3d 446 (7th Cir. 2006)

EASTERBROOK, J.

Traci Cannon-Stokes contends that the Postal Service, which hired her as a letter carrier, violated the Rehabilitation Act, 29 U.S.C. § 791, by not accommodating her mental aversion to making residential deliveries and by retaliating against her for asserting her statutory rights. At the same time as Cannon-Stokes was pursuing an administrative claim for $300,000 from the Postal Service, she filed a Chapter 7 bankruptcy petition asserting that she had no assets; her petition expressly denied that she had any valuable legal claims ("contingent and unliquidated claims of every nature", the schedule calls them, leaving no room for quibbles). The bankruptcy court believed that assertion and discharged all of her approximately $98,000 in unsecured debts.

After the bankruptcy was over, Cannon-Stokes filed this suit. Naturally enough, the Postal Service contended that judicial estoppel forecloses the action. Cannon-Stokes had represented that she had no claim against the Postal Service (or anyone else); that representation had prevailed; she had obtained a valuable benefit in the discharge of her debts. Now she wants to assert the opposite in order to win a second time. That satisfies the requirements of judicial estoppel. See, e.g., New Hampshire v. Maine, 532 U.S. 742, 749 (2001); Astor Chauffeured Limousine Co. v. Runnfeldt Investment Corp., 910 F.2d 1540, 1547-48 (7th Cir. 1990). Cannon-Stokes blamed the false statement on her bankruptcy lawyer; accepting this explanation, the district court declined to dismiss the proceeding but later granted summary judgment to the Postal Service on the merits - which on appeal defends its judgment by relying, once again, on judicial estoppel.

All six appellate courts that have considered this question hold that a debtor in bankruptcy who denies owning an asset, including a chose in action or other legal claim, cannot realize on that concealed asset after the bankruptcy ends. See Payless Wholesale Distributors, Inc. v. Alberto Culver (P.R.) Inc., 989 F.2d 570 (1st Cir. 1993); Krystal Cadillac-Oldsmobile GMC Truck, Inc. v. General Motors Corp., 337 F.3d 314 (3d Cir. 2003); Jethroe v. Omnova Solutions, Inc., 412 F.3d 598 (5th Cir. 2005); United States ex rel. Gebert v. Transport Administrative Services, 260 F.3d 909, 917-19 (8th Cir. 2001); Hamilton v. State Farm Fire & Casualty Co., 270 F.3d 778 (9th Cir. 2001); Barger v. Cartersville, 348 F.3d 1289,

1293-97 (11th Cir. 2003). We reserved that question in Biesek v. Soo Line R.R., 440 F.3d 410 (7th Cir. 2006), while holding that judicial estoppel has aproviso: bankruptcy fraud designed to hide an asset from creditors does not prevent the creditors themselves from realizing on the claim after its discovery.

Judicial estoppel is an equitable doctrine, and it is not equitable to employ it to injure creditors who are themselves victims of the debtor's deceit. Moreover, as a technical matter the estate in bankruptcy, not the debtor, owns all pre-bankruptcy claims, and unless the estate itself engages in contradictory litigation tactics the elements of judicial estoppel are not satisfied. But if the estate (through the trustee) abandons the claim, then the creditors no longer have an interest, and with the claim in the debtor's hands the possibility of judicial estoppel comes to the fore. That is what has happened here: the trustee abandoned any interest in this litigation, so the creditors are out of the picture and we must decide whether Cannon-Stokes may pursue the claim for her personal benefit.

The answer is no, as the other circuits (cited above) have concluded. "By making [litigants] choose one position irrevocably, the doctrine of judicial estoppel raises the cost of lying." Chaveriat v. Williams Pipe Line Co., 11 F.3d 1420, 1428 (7th Cir. 1993). A doctrine that induces debtors to be truthful in their bankruptcy filings will assist creditors in the long run (though it will do them no good in the particular case) - and it will assist most debtors too, for the few debtors who scam their creditors drive up interest rates and injure the more numerous honest borrowers. Judicial estoppel is designed to "prevent the perversion of the judicial process," In re Cassidy, 892 F.2d 637, 641 (7th Cir. 1990), a fair description of the result if we were to let Cannon-Stokes conceal, for her personal benefit, an asset that by her reckoning is three times the value of the debts she had discharged. It is impossible to believe that such a sizeable claim - one central to her daily activities at work - could have been overlooked when Cannon-Stokes was filling in the bankruptcy schedules. And if Cannon-Stokes were really making an honest attempt to pay her debts, then as soon as she realized that it had been omitted, she would have filed amended schedules and moved to reopen the bankruptcy, so that the creditors could benefit from any recovery. Cannon-Stokes never did that; she wants every penny of the judgment for herself.

In the district court Cannon-Stokes filed an affidavit asserting that her false statement on the bankruptcy schedules was the result of good-faith reliance on legal advice. She main-tained that in 2000 she told Erik Martin, her bankruptcy lawyer, about her administrative claim under the Rehabilitation Act and that he instructed her to omit the information. Martin certainly was not above shady dealings. In 2001 he was indicted on multiple counts of perjury committed in the course of his bankruptcy practice, and in 2003 he resolved that proceeding by pleading guilty to contempt of court. Martin is not currently authorized to practice law in either state or federal court, and a bankruptcy court recently found him complicit in tax fraud. See Claxton v. United States, 335 B.R. 680 (Bankr. N.D.Ill. 2006).

Yet bad legal advice does not relieve the client of the consequences of her own acts. A lawyer is the client's agent, and the client is bound by the consequences of advice that the client chooses to follow. Cannon-Stokes might as well say that she is free to ignore any contract that a lawyer advised her to sign with her fingers crossed behind her back. The lawyer's role as agent is why the Supreme Court held in United States v. Boyle, 469 U.S. 241 (1985), that a taxpayer could not avoid paying interest and penalties occasioned by his lawyer's mishandling of the return. Just so here: a debtor in bankruptcy is bound by her own representations, no matter why they were made, at least until the debtor moves to amend the disclosures and pay the creditors their due (a step that, to repeat, Cannon-Stokes has not taken). The remedy for bad legal advice lies in malpractice litigation against the offending lawyer.

What is more, Cannon-Stokeshas repudiated the core of her affidavit. Asked at her deposition about her dealings with Martin, she replied that she could not remember meeting or talking with him. Maybe with other lawyers in his office, Cannon-Stokes said, but not Martin. Yet her affidavit maintained that Martin personally had told her not to list the Rehabilitation Act claim on her bankruptcy schedules.

Whether the bankruptcy fraud was Martin's suggestion, some other lawyer's, or Cannon-Stokes's own bright idea does not matter in the end. The signature on the bankruptcy schedule is hers. The representation she made is false; she obtained the benefit of a discharge; she has never tried to make the creditors whole; now she wants to contradict herself in order to win a second case. Judicial estoppel blocks any attempt to realize on this claim for her personal benefit.

AFFIRMED

Notes and Questions

1. Could the bankruptcy trustee in Cannon-Stokes chapter 7 case re-open the bankruptcy case, 11 U.S.C. § 350(b), and bring the law suit, free and clear of estoppel claims? After all, the cause of action belong to the trustee, at least while the bankruptcy case was ongoing, and the trustee made no misrepresentations to the court.

CHAPTER 3 CHAPTER 7 MEANS TESTING

A. CONSUMER DEBTS

STEWART v UNITED STATES TRUSTEE (IN RE STEWART)

175 F.3d 796 (10th Cir. 1999)

BRORBY, J.

Appellant Jeffrey D. Stewart appeals from the Bankruptcy Appellate Panel's ("the Panel") decision affirming the dismissal of his Chapter 7 bankruptcy petition. The bankruptcy court dismissed the petition pursuant to 11 U.S.C. § 707 (b) for substantial abuse of the provisions of Chapter 7. In re Stewart, 201 B.R. 996 (Bankr. N.D. Okla. 1996) (Stewart I). In a related decision, the bankruptcy court determined 11 U.S.C. § 707 (b) is constitutional. In re Stewart, 204 B.R. 780 (Bankr. N.D. Okla. 1997) (Stewart II). On appeal, Dr. Stewart challenges several rulings of the bankruptcy court as affirmed by the Panel. In Re Stewart, 215 B.R. 456 (B.A.P. 10th Cir. 1997) (Stewart III). He contends the bankruptcy judge erred in: (1) [omitted]; (2) concluding his debts constituted "primarily consumer debts;" (3) concluding the filing of his Chapter 7 petition constituted "substantial abuse" of Chapter 7 provisions; and (4) holding § 707(b) is not void for vagueness and does not violate the equal protection guarantees of the Fourteenth and Fifth Amendments of the United States Constitution. We exercise our jurisdiction under 28 U.S.C. § 158 (d) and affirm.

I. BACKGROUND

Jeffery Stewart and Barbara Teichner married in 1978, and produced four children. During this time, Mr. Stewart performed various odd jobs and periodically attended college. They maintained a minimal standard of living, relying in part on money provided by Barbara's parents. Mr. Stewart also obtained student loans from commercial lenders under government-sponsored programs.

In 1988, Mr. Stewart entered medical school and became romantically involved with another medical student, Patricia Hill. In 1990, he and Barbara divorced. The marital settlement agreement required Mr. Stewart to: (1) pay Barbara $500 monthly alimony until he completed his medical residency, and $25,000 in annual alimony thereafter, with a cap of $2 million or in the event she remarried, a cap of $250,000, and (2) pay child support totaling $2,000 per month, as well as the children's medical and future college expenses. In order to meet these support obligations, Mr. Stewart borrowed over $100,000 in student loans from 1990 to 1992, of which he gave Barbara $60,000 for support and paid $3,000 toward the children's medical expenses; the rest he spent on his living expenses, tuition, and loan processing fees. Prior to, and independent from, the divorce decree and marital settlement, Mr. Stewart agreed to sign two promissory notes to Barbara's parents for $150,000 and $50,000 for loans they made to him and Barbara during their twelve-year marriage.

In 1992, after graduating from medical school, Dr. Stewart began an internship and residency program in obstetrics-gynecology. At the same time, he ceased making support payments to Barbara and began a proceeding to vacate the marital settlement agreement. Although Barbara defended the agreement and counter-sued for past support, she agreed to reduce Dr. Stewart's child support obligation to $586.82 per month. In 1993, during the pendency of that lawsuit, Barbara remarried. The same year, her father, Mr. Teichner, sued Dr. Stewart on the $150,000 note in a state court proceeding.

In 1994, Patricia Hill began her medical residency. In 1995, she successfully filed a voluntary petition for relief under Chapter 7. Later the same year, she married Dr. Stewart.

In late 1995, while Dr. Stewart remained in arrears for approximately $26,000 in past spousal support and unpaid medical bills for his children, he purchased a 1990 Range Rover for $26,466. In January 1996, the state court denied Dr. Stewart's motion to vacate the divorce decree and granted Barbara a judgment of $26,077.95 for breach of the marital settlement agreement. In April 1996, the state court granted Mr. Teichner a judgment with interest against Dr. Stewart on the $150,000 promissory note.

Just weeks after the divorce court denied his motion for a new trial, Dr. Stewart filed his voluntary petition for relief under Chapter 7 and filed bankruptcy schedules showing debt totaling $2,548,440.37. In this figure, Dr. Stewart included a sum of $2 million owed Barbara under the marital settlement agreement, rather than the $250,000 actually owed as a result of her remarriage. Dr. Stewart sought discharge of: (1) all his debt obligations to his ex-wife and her parents; (2) his children's medical expenses; (3) all future, contractual post-secondary education expenses for his four children; and (4) other incidental debts including taxes and attorney fees. Dr. Stewart listed, but did not seek to discharge, his student loan debt of $218,000. While Dr. Stewart listed himself as "married," he did not apportion his percentage of the total household expenses or list his wife's income. He listed his occupation as a "physician" at three hospitals, with his monthly income totaling $3,358. He provided captions for the legal proceedings involving Barbara and her father, but did not list the amount owed to Barbara under the judgment against him. On his petition, Dr. Stewart characterized his debts as non-business/ consumer debts.

Days later, Barbara filed for relief from the automatic stay of the bankruptcy, under 11 U.S.C. § 362, to allow her to enforce the terms of the divorce decree, the marital settlement agreement and the judgment for support arrears, and to modify child support. The bankruptcy court modified the stay to allow Barbara to commence an action to collect and modify child support, and to exercise her rights to enforce the judgment and take action in connection with Dr. Stewart's appeal of that judgment.

One month after filing his bankruptcy petition, Dr. Stewart completed his residency program and opted to enter a two- to three-year fellowship program specializing in perinatology rather than begin an obstetrics/gynecology practice.

His fellowship salary ranged from $34,292 to $37,000 a year. The monetary consequences of his entering a fellowship are appreciable. Had Dr. Stewart entered directly into practice rather than opting for a fellowship, his estimated starting salary as a non-board-certified, perinatology graduate would have ranged from $100,000 to $140,000 - substantially more than his fellowship. However, on completing his fellowship, his estimated earning power increased substantially with the average annual earnings for board-certified obstetrics/gynecology specialists ranging between $175,000 and $325,00, and the highest salaries exceeding $500,000. Dr. Stewart forewent immediate employment as an obstetrics/gynecology physician and instead chose specialization in the treatment of high-risk pregnancies in order to "help desperately-ill and needy mothers and babies," and because he is "passionately interested in research" which he intends to pursue "regardless of remuneration." Stewart I, 201 B.R. at 1002.

In July 1996, Dr. Stewart submitted an amended petition. In amending his schedules, Dr. Stewart slightly increased his expenses and decreased the value of his assets; he also increased his liabilities to $2.6 million. He projected his average monthly income from his new fellowship position at $3,403, and his monthly expenses at $7,966, for a monthly deficit of $4,563. His revised monthly expenses schedule reflected his share of the total household expenses, but still did not list his wife's income. He again characterized his debts as nonbusiness/ consumer debt.[1]

Based on his revised schedule and after adjusting the inaccurate $2 million alimony debt, Dr. Stewart's actual total debt reached $837,009,[2] including $250,000 marital debt,[3] $218,000 in student loans from commercial lenders, $320,000 debt to his former in-laws[4], and $59,009 for other obligations including medical bills for his children, attorney fees for litigation of his various suits, and taxes. See Stewart III, 215 B.R. at 460. As to the debt owed to his in-laws, Dr. Stewart testified his wife received her parents' checks and used the money to support the family while he attended school; she used the money on house payments, groceries, pre-school, children's activities, moving expenses, and family vacations. Similarly, Barbara testified her parents loaned them money for living expenses to maintain a "certain life style," thus facilitating Dr. Stewart's education. She noted, however, her parents continued to support them even when Dr. Stewart did not attend college.[5]

---

[1] At a subsequent hearing, Dr. Stewart testified his living expenses are high because he rents an apartment in Oklahoma City while also renting a home in Tulsa where his physician wife is in residency. He economized by dropping a health club membership, trying to cut food and gas expenses, and dropping disability insurance.

[2] The schedules show total unsecured, nonpriority debt of $582,509 and, after adjusting the $2 million alimony debt, a priority debt of $254,500, for a total debt of $837,009. See Stewart III, 215 B.R. at 460 n.3.

[3] The actual debt owed Barbara is $238,000, consisting of the $250,000 alimony award minus $12,000 alimony previously paid. This amount apparently includes Barbara's judgment against Dr. Stewart for $26,077.95 for unpaid alimony and children's medical expenses. The Bankruptcy Appellate Panel, for the sake of simplicity, used the $250,000 figure in its calculations, stating the same result occurs using either figure. Stewart III, 215 B.R. at 460 n.4. To avoid confusion on appeal, we do the same.

[4] This amount includes the judgment for the original $150,000 promissory note to Mr. Teichner, and the $50,000 promissory note to Mrs. Teichner, both with ten percent interest.

[5] Dr. Stewart questions the credibility of his ex-wife's testimony on this subject, stating her testimony substantially differed from that in the proceeding involving her father. Having read that portion of her bankruptcy testimony in which Dr. Stewart's counsel attempted to rebut it with her

Ten days prior to the filing of Dr. Stewart's amended petition, the United States Trustee, through an Assistant Trustee, filed a motion to dismiss Dr. Stewart's petition under 11 U.S.C. § 707 (b) as "substantial abuse" of Chapter 7. The Trustee alleged Dr. Stewart's sole purpose in filing for bankruptcy centered on discharging marital and family obligations, even though he retained the ability to pay a substantial portion of his debts. . . .

Following the hearing, the bankruptcy court granted the motion and dismissed Dr. Stewart's Chapter 7 petition for "substantial abuse." Stewart I, 201 B.R. at 1008. In reviewing the dismissal, the Panel found the bankruptcy court relied on the following findings of fact in reaching the conclusion "substantial abuse" occurred:

> (1) Dr. Stewart and his doctor wife possess considerable future earning potential;
>
> (2) The student loan debts are not dischargeable, so the main effect of the case is discharge of Dr. Stewart's debts to his former wife, her parents, and his children, which he appears to have "no intention of honoring;"
>
> (3) Dr. Stewart exaggerated his debts and expenses and minimized his income. While he was not required to include his non-debtor wife's income in his schedules, his failure to do so presented a "seriously misleading picture of his actual financial status;"
>
> (4) Dr. Stewart's lifestyle was extravagant - "he spends $4,500 more than he takes home every month";
>
> (5) His new wife obtained a Chapter 7 discharge under effectively fraudulent circumstances just prior to marrying Dr. Stewart;
>
> (6) Although Dr. Stewart is ineligible for Chapter 13 relief, Chapter 11 is available to him;
>
> (7) No emergency, disaster or untenable situation existed when he filed bankruptcy; and
>
> (8) Chapter 7 relief would result in little or no dividend to creditors, and would amount to a reward for Dr. Stewart's own financial improvidence and judicial blessing of an unconscionably one-sided, opportunistic adjustment of his relationship with his domestic creditors.

Stewart III, 215 B.R. at 460-61 (quoting Stewart I, 201 B.R. at 1006-08).

On appeal to the Panel, Dr. Stewart contested the facts supporting findings 2, 3, 5 and 6. After review of the bankruptcy court's findings, the Panel found support for finding 2, but agreed with Dr. Stewart and rejected findings 3, 5 and 6. Stewart III, 215 B.R. at 461-62. . . .

B. Primarily Consumer Debt

We next turn to the issue of whether Dr. Stewart's debt is "primarily consumer debt." Under § 707(b), a court "may dismiss a case filed by an individual debtor . . . whose debts are primarily consumer debts if it finds that the granting

---

prior testimony, we disagree her testimony substantially differed. Moreover, credibility determinations are within the sound discretion of the trial judge. See Anderson v. City of Bessemer City, 470 U.S. 564, 575 (1985). In this case, the bankruptcy court relied on Barbara's testimony that the money loaned by her parents went toward facilitating Dr. Stewart's education while maintaining the family in a "certain life style" beyond their reach, thus evidencing the court's belief her testimony was credible. Stewart I, 201 B.R. at 1002.

of relief would be a substantial abuse of the provisions" of Chapter 7.[6] 11 U.S.C. § 707 (b) (emphasis added). The Bankruptcy Code defines "consumer debt" as "debt incurred by an individual primarily for a personal, family, or household purpose." 11 U.S.C. § 101(8). Courts consistently have applied this definition for the purposes of § 11 U.S.C. § 707 (b). See In re Krohn, 886 F.2d 123 at 126 (applying § 101(7) - the predecessor to § 101(8), which contained the same language); In re Kelly, 841 F.2d at 912 (same); In re Booth, 858 F.2d 1051, 1054-55 (5th Cir. 1988) (same). " Consumer debt" is further distinguished from "non- consumer " debt as a debt incurred with a "profit motive." Citizens Nat'l Bank v. Burns (In re Burns), 894 F.2d 361, 363 (10th Cir. 1990); accord Cypher Chiropractic Ctr. v. Runski (In re Runski), 102 F.3d 744, 747 (4th Cir. 1996); In re Booth, 858 F.2d at 1054-55.

In his initial and amended petition and schedules, Dr. Stewart categorized his debt as "nonbusiness/ consumer " debt. Notably, in response to the § 707(b) motion to dismiss, Dr. Stewart seeks to recharacterize his debts as not "primarily consumer debts" to avoid dismissal. In support of this recharacterization, he argues he used the $320,000 owed his ex-in-laws and $218,000 owed in student loans principally for financing his education; thus, those debts constitute "non-consumer debt" incurred "for the purpose of completing a higher and professional level of education." As to the $250,000 owed his wife for alimony, he contends this is not the kind of debt Congress envisioned when the consumer credit card industry lobbied it to write § 707(b).[7] He admits, however, no published decision supports his characterization of alimony as "non- consumer " debt.

In support of his argument, Dr. Stewart relies on two bankruptcy court decisions, In re Gentri, 185 B.R. 368 (Bankr. M.D. Fla. 1995), and First Trust Co. v. Frisch (In re Frisch), 76 B.R. 801 (Bankr. D. Colo. 1987), insisting we must follow a per se rule that monies received by a debtor from his father-in-law constitute "non- consumer " debt. Despite Dr. Stewart's insistence, these cases are distinguishable and constitute non-persuasive, non-binding authority. The court in both cases failed to examine the purpose for which the debtor incurred the loans. In Gentri, the court based its finding that medical education loans to the debtor from his former father-in-law constituted "business debt" solely on the Trustee's admission of that characterization. 185 B.R. at 373. In Frisch, the court summarily concluded an intra-family loan between the debtor and his former father-in-law was not " consumer debt" in light of the creditor's failure to provide any authority for the proposition intra-family loans constitute consumer debt. 76 B.R. at 803.

Unlike these cases, the record in this case shows the actual purpose for which Dr. Stewart used the intra-family loans. In fact, Dr. Stewart's own testimony supports the finding he used the money predominantly for family living expenses rather than for direct educational costs. Stewart III, 215 B.R. at

---

[6] Congress promulgated § 707(b) as part of the 1984 consumer credit amendments to the Bankruptcy Code. In re Krohn, 886 F.2d 123, 125-26 (6th Cir. 1989); see also In re Lamanna, 153 F.3d at 3-4. Congress passed these amendments in response to an increasing number of Chapter 7 bankruptcies filed each year by non-needy debtors. See In re Krohn, 886 F.2d at 125-26 (relying on In re Walton, 866 F.2d 981, 983 (8th Cir. 1989)); In re Lamanna, 153 F.3d at 3-4 (relying also on In re Walton, 866 F.2d 981).

[7] While the credit card industry may have lobbied Congress to pass § 707(b), we note Congress did not expressly confine § 707(b) 's use to "credit card" debt, thus giving the courts flexibility to determine potential abuse beyond credit card misuse.

465. Dr. Stewart testified his ex-wife used the money to support their family, including use for house payments, groceries, pre-school, children's activities, moving expenses, and family vacations. Nothing in the record convinces us the main purpose of these loans was to finance Dr. Stewart's actual educational expenses. Rather, Dr. Stewart used the money to support his family because he did not earn enough for his family to live comfortably. Notably, this support continued even during those times when Dr. Stewart did not attend college. Thus, the intra-family loans Dr. Stewart received for household and family expenses are " consumer debt."

The Panel concluded Dr. Stewart's student loans totaling $218,000 constitute " consumer debt" because the money was used for dual family and personal purposes. Due to the lack of evidence in the record and authority to guide us, we are unwilling to characterize the entire $218,000 as consumer debt. However, based on the evidence in the record, we can comfortably conclude a substantial portion of Dr. Stewart's student loan debt is indeed " consumer debt."

We start by noting nothing in the record indicates the actual cost of Dr. Stewart's tuition, books, or other direct educational expenses as compared to the portion of student loans used for personal, family, and household expenses. Moreover, little or no binding or persuasive authority exists to help us determine the characterization of educational expenses such as books, tuition, and room and board as either consumer or business debt.[8]

The record does, however, establish a substantial amount of Dr. Stewart's loans went toward his family's expenses. As to student loans received during their marriage, Dr. Stewart's testimony, read in its entirety, together with his brief on appeal, establishes he used a portion of the money on family expenses in addition to any direct educational costs. Specifically, in his brief, Dr. Stewart admits he used his student loan money during his marriage to pay for tuition and books as well as to support "his five dependents." Finally, the record shows during the two years following their divorce, Dr. Stewart obtained over $100,000 in student loans, paying Barbara $60,000 of it for support obligations and $3,000 on his children's medical expenses. Under these circumstances, an appreciable portion - $63,000 - of his student loans went toward family expenses, which fairly may be characterized as " consumer debt."

Finally, as to the alimony debt of $250,000, the weight of the case law on this issue conclusively shows it is a " consumer debt" if it is based on a non-profit motive. See, e.g., In re Kestell, 99 F.3d 146, 149 (4th Cir. 1996) (alimony, child support, and lump-sum award are considered " consumer debt" as they were not incurred with a profit motive or in connection with a business transaction); In re Traub, 140 B.R. 286, 290 (Bankr. D. N.M. 1992) (property settlement owed ex-wife is consumer debt as it is a distribution of the net value of the community interest of the debtor's medical practice and not owed because of a profit-seeking activity); In re Palmer, 117 B.R. 443, 447 (Bankr. N.D. Iowa 1990) (lump-sum alimony award is consumer debt because the debt was created to allow the debtor to retain ownership of the home and his pension). In this case, the weight of the evidence suggests the alimony owed to Dr. Stewart's ex-wife is for her support and benefit, and not for any profit motive. Therefore, it constitutes " consumer

[8] Dr. Stewart testified the student loans received prior to his 1978 marriage went solely toward tuition, books, and room and board. However, the record shows he received only $660 in student loans prior to that time. This is a mere fraction of the $218,000 owed on student loans.

debt" for the purposes of § 707(b).

Having conclusively determined the debt owed Dr. Stewart's ex-wife and her parents, and at least a portion of the student loan debt, are " consumer debt," we next must determine whether Dr. Stewart's total debt is primarily " consumer debt" for the purposes of a § 707(b) dismissal. Dr. Stewart suggests that even if some of the debt owed to his creditors is " consumer debt" it is not "primarily" consumer debt as required under § 707(b). Dr. Stewart suggests "primarily" means the overall "ratio" of " consumer debt" to "total debt" must exceed fifty percent.

The Bankruptcy Code does not define "primarily," and only a few of our sister circuits have defined "primarily" under § 707(b). Noting the word "primarily" is not an ambiguous or difficult word to understand, and is defined in Webster's Dictionary as "for the most part," the Ninth Circuit determined it to mean consumer debt must exceed more than half the total debt for dismissal under § 707(b). See In re Kelly, 841 F.2d at 913, 916. [9]In a non-bankruptcy context, we similarly defined "primarily" as meaning more than fifty percent. Bohn v. Park City Group, Inc., 94 F.3d 1457, 1461 (10th Cir. 1996) (recognizing the Department of Labor, as a "good rule of thumb," defines "primary duty" to mean the major part, or over fifty percent, of the employee's time). Finding no cases to the contrary, we therefore define "primarily" in the context of § 707(b) as meaning consumer debt exceeding fifty percent of the total debt.

Applying this definition to the instant case, Dr. Stewart's actual total debt is $837,009. Of that amount, $633,000 is " consumer debt" ($320,000 owed to his former in-laws, at least $63,000 of the $218,000 in student loan debt, and $250,000 in alimony). This amount exceeds fifty percent of the total debt. Hence, we determine Dr. Stewart's debt is "primarily consumer debt" for the purposes of § 707(b), and, therefore, his petition may be dismissed under § 707(b), but only if substantial abuse occurred.

C. Substantial Abuse

Under the provisions of § 707(b), a court "may dismiss a case filed by an individual debtor . . . if it finds that the granting of relief would be a substantial abuse of the provisions" of Chapter 7. See 11 U.S.C. 707 (b) (emphasis added).[10] The bankruptcy statutes do not define "substantial abuse," and this court has never undertaken to define the phrase in the context of § 707(b). Consequently, we look to other circuits, which agree the debtor's ability to repay his debts out of future earnings is a primary factor in determining if substantial abuse occurred. See In re Kornfield, 164 F.3d at 784; In re Lamanna, 153 F.3d at 4-5; In re Koch, 109 F.3d 1285, 1288 (8th Cir. 1997); In re Green, 934 F.2d 568, 572 (4th Cir. 1991); In re Krohn, 886 F.2d at 126; In re Kelly, 841 F.2d at 914. To a certain degree, however, these courts differ on what, if any, other factors should be considered in determining if "substantial abuse" occurred.

Some courts regard ability to repay debt as dispositive in determining

[9] The Fifth Circuit agrees, but goes one step further by also requiring that the actual number of individual consumer debts must exceed at least half the total number of debts. See In re Booth, 858 F.2d at 1055. In other words, even if the debt owed to one creditor is " consumer debt" and constitutes ninety-nine percent of the entire debt, if the remainder of the debt is owed to ten other creditors, the total debt is not "primarily" " consumer debt." Believing this requirement is illogical, we reject it.

[10] [BAPCPA deletes the word "substantial." Section 707(b) now requires "an abuse."--ed.]

whether substantial abuse occurred. See In re Kelly, 841 F.2d at 914-15 (only factor overriding primary factor of inability to pay is "bad faith"); In re Koch, 109 F.3d at 1288 (substantial ability to repay, measured by the debtor's ability to repay debts under a hypothetical Chapter 13 filing, alone is sufficient to warrant a § 707(b) dismissal).

The Fourth Circuit relies on a "totality of the circumstances" standard. See In re Green, 934 F.2d at 572-73. It believes that while the debtor's ability to repay his debts is a primary factor, other factors must be considered. Id. These other factors include, but are not limited to: (1) sudden illness, calamity, disability, or unemployment; (2) cash advances and consumer purchases in far excess of ability to repay; (3) excessive or unreasonable family budget; (4) accurate reflection of true financial condition in the debtor's schedules and statements of income and expenses; and (5) the debtor's good faith. Id.

Other courts appear to use a hybrid standard. They believe the debtor's ability to pay may alone be sufficient to warrant dismissal, but in evaluating the "totality of the circumstances," acknowledge it may be appropriate to consider other relevant factors. See In Re Lamanna, 153 F.3d at 5; In re Krohn, 886 F.2d at 126. Those factors may include: (1) whether the debtor enjoys a stable source of future income; (2) whether the debtor is eligible for adjustment of debt through Chapter 13; (3) whether state remedies exist to ease the financial predicament; (4) the degree of relief obtainable through private negotiation; and (5) whether the debtor's expenses can be significantly reduced without depriving him of adequate food, clothing, shelter and other necessities. See In re Krohn, 886 F.2d at 126-27; In re Lamanna, 153 F.3d at 4-5 (factors in Krohn regarded as nonexclusive list of relevant considerations).

After careful consideration, we adopt the "totality of the circumstances" standard. While we agree ability to pay is a primary factor in determining whether "substantial abuse" occurred, we believe other relevant or contributing factors, such as unique hardships, must also be examined before dismissing a Chapter 7 petition. Conversely, where an inability to pay exists, we believe other factors may nevertheless establish substantial abuse. We recognize the factors articulated by the other courts as instructive, but conclude they are not inclusive of all factors considered. A substantial-abuse analysis must be made on a case-by-case basis.

In applying this standard, we begin by looking at whether Dr. Stewart can repay his debts. See In re Green, 934 F.2d at 572. During his fellowship, Dr. Stewart's monthly expenses of $8,000 clearly exceeded his income of $3,400, so his ability to repay his debt was greatly diminished for the two- to three-year length of his fellowship. However, having instead chosen and then completed his fellowship, Dr. Stewart's earning potential increased to $175,000 - $325,000 a year, so his monthly earning potential well exceeds his monthly expenses. Hence, Dr. Stewart possesses the financial ability to pay his expenses and repay his debt within a reasonable time. See In re Kornfield, 164 F.3d at 784. Seeking a discharge of debt under these circumstances evidences "substantial abuse" under § 707(b).

Under the "totality of the circumstances" standard, we must also look at other relevant factors to see if "substantial abuse" occurred. One factor to consider is whether Dr. Stewart suffered any unique hardships, such as sudden illness, calamity, disability, or unemployment. See In re Green, 934 F.2d at 572-73. He did not. Dr. Stewart suffered no emergency, disaster, or untenable situation when he filed his bankruptcy petition. Stewart I, 201 B.R. at 1007; Stewart III, 215 B.R. at 461. Another factor is whether his cash advances and consumer purchases far exceeded his ability to pay at that time. Id. They did. Dr. Stewart lived an extravagant lifestyle, spending $4,500 more than his monthly take-home pay. Stewart I, 201 B.R. at 1007; Stewart III, 215 B.R. at 461. [11]Bankruptcy relief is not intended to remedy the consequences of extravagant spending.

Another factor to consider is whether Dr. Stewart will enjoy a stable source of future income. See In re Krohn, 886 F.2d at 126-27. This factor is met through Dr. Stewart's successful completion of his fellowship and resulting appreciable earning power as a specialty physician. The next factor is whether Dr. Stewart's expenses can be significantly reduced without depriving him of adequate food, clothing, shelter, and other necessities. Id. Dr. Stewart's actual expenses are clearly excessive and can be reduced. See Stewart III, 215 B.R. at 462. Moreover, given his current earning power, even these excessive expenses can clearly be met without depriving him of any necessities. We further note Dr. Stewart does not qualify for Chapter 13 relief, see id., which weighs against dismissal. See In re Kohn, 886 F.2d at 126-27. However, Dr. Stewart fails to show he is unable to obtain relief through private negotiation, which weighs in favor of dismissal. See id.

Finally, we look to the debtor's good faith as a factor under "the totality of the circumstances." See In re Green, 934 F.2d at 572-73. We note Dr. Stewart filed his petition immediately after unsuccessful litigation with his wife and former father-in-law in an attempt to discharge judgments he is legally obligated to pay. Ironically, he also seeks to discharge his legal obligation to pay his children's college expenses even though his in-laws provided him money over a twelve-year period so he could pursue his own education. Moreover, he now attempts to discharge those intra-family loans.

Just as ironic is Dr. Stewart's contention he opted for a low-paying fellowship for the humanitarian reason of servicing needy children and mothers, while disregarding his own children's medical expenses and the financial support of their mother. In fact, Dr. Stewart purchased a $26,000 vehicle rather than pay these expenses at the time they became due and owing. In filing his petition, Dr. Stewart sought discharge of his family obligations, while (1) pursuing a fellowship that paid substantially less than his earning potential, and (2) knowing he could, and now will, enjoy a substantially higher income. We are reminded of the old adage, "having your cake, and eating it too." Indeed, under "the totality of the circumstances," we question Dr. Stewart's good faith in filing his petition and conclude his actions constitute "substantial abuse" within the meaning of § 707(b). For these reasons, the bankruptcy court correctly dismissed his petition under § 707(b).

D. Constitutionality

As an alternative argument, Dr. Stewart asserts § 707(b) is unconstitutional because it is (1) void for vagueness and (2) in derogation of the equal protection guarantees of the Fourteenth and Fifth Amendments. Specifically, Dr.

[11] The bankruptcy court and Panel disagreed on whether Dr. Stewart's petition and schedules accurately reflected his true financial condition. Compare Stewart I, 201 B.R. at 1006 with Stewart III, 215 B.R. at 461. This is another factor to consider under "the totality of the circumstances" standard. See In Re Green, 934 F.2d at 572-73. Regardless of which position is correct, under "the totality of the circumstances," other factors we consider sufficiently establish "substantial abuse."

Stewart laments the words "substantial abuse" and "primarily consumer debts" are so vague as to render the statute meaningless and unenforceable. Dr. Stewart further contends no "rational basis" exists for Congress to choose to discriminate against only consumer debtors under § 707(b), to the exclusion of business debtors.

Section 707(b) has survived similar constitutional challenges in the Ninth Circuit and several bankruptcy courts in this and other circuits. See In re Kelly, 841 F.2d at 916-17 (challenged for vagueness); Heller v. Foulston (In re Heller), 160 B.R. 655, 661 (Bankr. D. Kan. 1993) (same); In re Higginbotham, 111 B.R. 955, 965 (Bankr. N.D. Okla. 1990) (challenged for vagueness and violation of equal protection guarantees); In re Wilkes, 114 B.R. 551, 553 (Bankr. W.D. Tenn. 1989) (reviewed for vagueness and violation of due process and equal protection guarantees); In re Keniston, 85 B.R. 202, 204-05 (Bankr. D. N.H. 1988) (same).

One of the main purposes of bankruptcy law is to relieve honest debtors from the weight of oppressive indebtedness, thereby allowing them to start afresh. See In re Krohn, 886 F.2d at 125. While Congress promulgated bankruptcy laws to assist needy debtors, a constitutional right to bankruptcy discharge does not exist. United States v. Kras, 409 U.S. 434, 446 (1973). Bankruptcy laws regulating economic activity do not involve constitutionally protected conduct and, thus, are subject to "a quite lenient test for constitutional sufficiency." In re Kelly, 841 F.2d at 915 (considering constitutionality of § 707(b)). See also Kras, 409 U.S. at 446; Otasco, Inc. v. United States (In re South), 689 F.2d 162, 165 (10th Cir. 1982), cert. denied, 460 U.S. 1069 (1983). With this in mind, we proceed to the constitutional issues raised.

1. Vagueness

[The court found §707(b) to be unvague.]

2. Equal Protection

The bankruptcy court, applying a "rational basis" standard, held § 707(b) does not violate the equal protection provisions of the Constitution. Stewart II, 204 B.R. at 782. However, in reviewing the bankruptcy court's decision, the Panel avoided the equal protection issue by construing the statute no more broadly than other statutes that generally permit dismissal of bankruptcy petitions.[12] Stewart III, 215 B.R. at 463-64. The Panel concluded, without giving thorough, delineated examples, that the case-by-case analysis applied to motions to dismiss under § 707(b) is substantially similar to the case-by-case analysis given dismissal motions under other, more general bankruptcy provisions that apply to business debtors.

On appeal, the Trustee asserts an equal protection analysis is necessary because a difference does exist between the treatment of consumer and business debtors under the bankruptcy code. The Trustee contends a rational basis exists

[12] The Panel compared § 707(b) motions to dismiss with motions to dismiss under 11 U.S.C. §§ 105 and 707(a). These statutes give bankruptcy courts general jurisdiction to dismiss abusive petitions under other provisions of the Bankruptcy Code, without regard to classification. See, e.g., 11 U.S.C. § 105 (granting courts sua sponte power to "prevent an abuse of process"), and 11 U.S.C. § 707 (a) (granting general jurisdiction to dismiss petitions, but not specifically mentioning "abuse"); see also Stewart II, 204 B.R. at 782.

justifying the dissimilar treatment given consumer and business debtors.

We acknowledge those cases instructing us to avoid resolution of the constitutionality of a statute if a reasonable, alternative statutory interpretation poses no constitutional question. See Hall v. Commissioner of Internal Revenue, 30 F.3d 1304, 1306 (10th Cir. 1994); Turner v. United States Parole Comm'n, 934 F.2d 254, 257 (10th Cir.), cert. denied, 502 U.S. 885 (1991). However, where, as here, the legislature clearly intended to separately classify consumer debtors, and the constitutional issue can be easily resolved, we determine it more prudent to resolve the constitutional issue than "press statutory construction 'to the point of disingenuous evasion.'" United States v. Locke, 471 U.S. 84, 96 (1985) (quoting George Moore Ice Cream Co. v. Rose, 289 U.S. 373, 379 (1933)). Specifically, we find it prudent to refrain from applying a statutory interpretation that might pervert the clear purpose of § 707(b) to separately classify consumer debtors and broaden the judiciary's ability to dismiss consumer petitions for substantial abuse. Cf. Heckler v. Mathews, 465 U.S. 728, 741-42 (1984). Therefore, we proceed to the constitutional issue and review § 707(b) to determine if it impermissibly discriminates against consumer debtors in violation of the equal protection provisions of the Constitution.

We review § 707(b) and its distinction between consumer and business debtors under a "rational basis" analysis. This is because the distinction between consumer and business debtors does not implicate a fundamental right or affect a suspect classification. See generally Kras, 409 U.S. at 446 (finding "bankruptcy legislation is in the area of economics and social welfare," and no constitutional right exists to obtain a discharge of one's debts in bankruptcy). A classification involving neither a fundamental right nor a proceeding along suspect lines is accorded a strong presumption of validity. Heller v. Doe, 509 U.S. 312, 319 (1993). "A statute is presumed constitutional . . . and 'the burden is on the one attacking the legislative arrangement to negative every conceivable basis which might support it.'" Id. at 320 (quoting Lehnhausen v. Lake Shore Auto Parts Co., 410 U.S. 356, 364 (1973)).

Keeping § 707(b)'s strong presumption of validity in mind, we must determine if a rational relationship exists between the disparity of treatment between consumer and business debtors and some legitimate governmental purpose. Heller, 509 U.S. at 320. Section 707(b) must be upheld against Dr. Stewart's equal protection challenge if "any reasonably conceivable state of facts" exists providing a rational basis for the separate classification of consumer and business debtors. FCC v. Beach Communications, Inc., 508 U.S. 307, 313 (1993). An economic classification such as that applied in § 707(b) does not fail rational basis review merely because in practice it results in some inequality. See Dandridge v. Williams, 397 U.S. 471, 485 (1970).

Congress enacted § 707(b) for two reasons. First, it wanted to address the problem of consumer debtors taking inordinate advantage of modern easy-credit practices, running up consumer debt, and then seeking discharge of that debt through Chapter 7 bankruptcy. See In re Lamanna, 153 F.3d at 3. Congress apparently felt § 707(b) would remedy the problem of consumer debtors unfairly taking advantage of Chapter 7 even though they are able over time to pay off their debts. See id.; In re Kornfield, 164 F.3d at 781. Second, Congress wanted to give the courts a specific mechanism to more readily dismiss petitions by abusive consumer debtors. As the bankruptcy court aptly noted, § 707(b) was not enacted to narrow and discourage court review of abuse cases to those involving consumer debt, but to broaden and encourage such review in light of the fact many bankruptcy courts were not dismissing abusive consumer petitions. Stewart II, 204 B.R. at 781-82. Thus, "section 707(b) was enacted in response to . . . judicial abdication of authority." Id.

Congress' legitimate concern over consumer abuse of Chapter 7 continues today given easy-credit practices involving signature loans and credit cards. As the bankruptcy court in this case reasoned, § 707(b) addresses a type of bankruptcy case - consumer debt - especially liable to abuse and deserving review. Id. at 782.

> That type of case involves an individual debtor who . . . takes advantage of modern easy-credit practices to accumulate debts, for the immediate purpose of satisfying his private appetites and maintaining or enhancing his personal qualities and lifestyle, or those of his dependents,often in circumstances which offer creditors little security, because the benefits acquired by the debts are used up ("consumed") by the debtor himself and assimilated to his person-and who effectively avoids repayment by keeping his unconsumed property and his income from wages or professional earnings to himself and from his creditors.

Stewart I, 201 B.R. at 1004. While consumer debtors for the most part "consume" the benefits acquired by their debt, it is reasonable to assume most business debtors accrue debt to obtain tangible, secured business assets, which thereby gives creditors more protection in recovering those assets and conceivably lessens the possibility of bankruptcy abuse. Therefore, in enacting § 707(b), Congress addressed the more immediate concern it had with consumer abuse of Chapter 7 and the bankruptcy courts' failure to dismiss abusive consumer petitions. In doing so, it was not necessary for Congress to similarly address business debtor abuse. See, e.g., Dandridge, 397 U.S. at 486-87; Williamson v. Lee Optical of Okla., 348 U.S. 483, 489 (1955).

Based on the above, we conclude a "reasonably conceivable state of facts" exists providing a rational basis for the separate classification and treatment of consumer and business debtors under 11 U.S.C. § 707. Specifically, we find it reasonable Congress enacted § 707(b) to counter Chapter 7 abuse by consumers who amass debt through easy credit practices, consume the items purchased, and then seek discharge of their debt even when able to pay. A rational relationship exists between Congress singling out consumer debtors for dismissal for substantial abuse under § 707(b) and the government's legitimate purpose in preventing consumer abuse, reasonably protecting creditors and empowering the courts with a mechanism to more readily dismiss substantially abusive consumer petitions. Accordingly, we hold 11 U.S.C. § 707 (b) does not violate the equal protection provisions of the Constitution.

For the foregoing reasons, we AFFIRM the dismissal of Dr. Stewart's Chapter 7 petition for substantial abuse.

Notes and Questions

1. The court says Congress could reasonably assume that business debtors acquire assets while consumers simply live beyond their means; therefore, creditors are adequately protected in business bankruptcies, if the debtor maintains a lavish life style from postpetition wages. But what if the debtor is bankrupt because she has guaranteed loans to an incorporated business. What protection do creditors have in such a case? In re Copeland, 2006 Bankr. LEXIS 2200 (Bankr. S.D. Tex. September 5, 2006) (debtor was bankrupt because she guaranteed the debts of a corporation).

2. Stewart is a pre-BAPCPA case, but its holdings will still be relevant for two reasons. First, it is a leading case on what "primarily consumer debts" means in Bankruptcy Code §707(b)(1), a phrase BAPCPA does not change. Second, it discusses the "totality of the

circumstances" test. This is the same phrase that BAPCPA invokes in new §707(b)(3). Whatever the mechanical means test of §707(b)(2) means, the United States trustee apparently can still move to dismiss a case under §707(b)(3) if the case is an abuse of the bankruptcy process, even where the debtor has passed the means test.

Form B22A

3. The means test is administered according to Form B22A. This form is available from the internet and can be Googled easily. Please retrieve this form and consider the following notes and questions.

Current Monthly Income

4. Form B22A makes numerous references to the IRS National Standards for Living Expenses. This is a manual, available on the internet, that advises IRS officials (and, by implication, taxpayers) how much the IRS will write off in bad tax debt, given levels of income and expenses of the taxpayer.

5. BAPCPA establishes a 60 month means test for above-median debtors. 11 U.S.C. § 707(b)(2)(A)(i). The 60 month means test applies only to gross income. It entails current monthly income as reduced by expenses, in a manner to be described. Significantly, the debtor is not required to prove 60 months of expenses but can use snapshot pictures of those expenses at the time of the bankruptcy petition.

The test to be applied is a kind of minimum-maximum test. In order to avoid the connotation of bankruptcy abuse, the multiplicand (net monthly income times 60) must be less than $12,475[13] or the maximum of two criteria: 25% of D's nonpriority secured claims or $7,475. So, for example, suppose D has net income of $40 per month. Multiplying by 60 produces $2400. This is less than $12,475 and less than $7,475. Our debtor is not a bankruptcy abuser under the means test.

Suppose the debtor's net income is $130 per month. Now the multiplicand is $7,800. This is less than $12,475 but more than $7,475. D must now show that unsecured claims against her exceed $31,200. In other words, the more bad debts such D has, the more "good faith" she has–a counter-intuitive result.

Finally, suppose net income is $200 a month. Since the multiplicand ($12,500) exceeds $12,475, D is disqualified from a chapter 7 proceeding.

What is the significance of the number 60? Presumably, this is related to the duration of a chapter 13 plan for households above the median. 11 U.S.C. § 1325(b)(4)(A)(ii).

The 60 month test, however, turns on a monthly test, which in turn depends on a 12 month average. One might suspect that the number 60 could have largely been dispensed with, but this is not so. Means testing boils down to this. If net current monthly income exceeds $207.92, the debtor's chapter 7 case will always be dismissed. If it is under $124.58, the case will not be dismissed on the mechanical means test alone. Only if monthly income is between $124.58 and $207.92 does the multiplicand of $60 really relevant. For such net monthly incomes, the debtor will have to show the following inequality:

$$x < u \div 240$$

where $124.58<x<207.92$ is net current monthly income and u is the total amount of unsecured claims against the debtor. The denominator 240 is the product of 4x60. The "4" represents the 25% requirement of § 707(b)(2)(A)(i)(I) (("25 percent of the debtor's non-priority unsecured claims in the case, or $7,475, whichever is greater . . . "); that is, by multiplying both the numerator and denominator by 4, .25u becomes u, and 60 becomes 240. The 60 in the denominator product comes from the 60 multiplicand of § 707(b)(2)(A)(i), and so 60 cannot entirely be eliminated from the calculation. It is relevant whenever $124.58<x<207.92$, where x is current monthly income. For example, in In re Praleikus, 248 B.R. 140 (Bankr. W.D. Mo. 2000), the debtor's current monthly

[13] Any dollar amount to be found in § 707(b) is subject to increase according to the rules of Bankruptcy Code § 104(b). This provision provides for automatic adjustments every three years to reflect the Consumer Price Index for All Urban Consumers, published by the Department of Labor.

income was $154. Her debt was about $31,894. Therefore, u/240=132.89, so the debtor would be an abuser under BAPCPA (as she was prior to BAPCPA).

A related observation based on the above inequality is that $207.92 for net current monthly income is the only relevant test where unsecured claims against the debtor exceed $49,900.80 ($207.92 x 240). $124.58 is the only relevant test where unsecured debts are less that $29,899.20 ($124.58 x 240). The multiplicand of 60 is relevant only where $29,899.20<u<$49,900.80.

6. According to the above formula, where 124.58<x<207.92, a debtor can actually gain eligibility for chapter 7 if he or she increases her unsecured debt. As we shall see, there are other opportunities to game the system by increasing debts just before filing a chapter 7 petition. To prevent this from happening, BAPCPA makes it illegal for a "debt relief agency" to

> advise an assisted person or prospective assisted person to incur more debt in contemplation of such person filing a case under this title or to pay an attorney or bankruptcy petition preparer fee or charge for services performed as part of preparing for or representing a debtor in a case under this title.

Bankruptcy Code § 526(a)(4). A "debt relief agency" is "any person who provides any bankruptcy assistance to an assisted person in return for the payment of money or other valuable consideration . . . " Bankruptcy Code § 101(12A). In Milavetz, Gallop & Milavetz, P.A. v. United States, 559 U.S. 229 (2010), the Supreme Court ruled that bankruptcy lawyers fall within this definition. It also ruled that § 526(a)(4) is no infringement on the first amendment rights of bankruptcy lawyers, because what is prohibited is advice that constitutes an abuse of the bankruptcy system.

7. Notice that Form B22A makes no reference to how much money D has in the bank. This is solely a test of income going forward. However, regardless of how the test works out, courts have the ability to dismiss cases for abuse under § 707(b)(3), as we shall see in due course. See In re Tamecki, 229 F.3d 205 (3d Cir. 2000) (in a pre-BAPCA case, the court could dismiss a consumer debtor under § 707(a) for having a substantial asset which, once a divorce was concluded, would not longer be exempt property). In fact, the rigorous means test is a flop, for various reasons. Courts will have to rely on § 707(b)(3) to get rid of cases where D manipulates the means test to get the result he wants. Witcher v. Early (In re Witcher), 702 F.3d 619 (11th Cir. 2012 (debtors who passed the mechanical test could be booted from chapter 7 for continuing to retain luxury items encumbered by secured claims).

How is it that Congress passed an extremely detailed means test, but courts can kick out any D they want? The answer to this requires a look at the structure of § 707(b). Subsection (1) authorizes the court to dismiss chapter 7 cases, where the debts are primarily consumers debts, if the case constitutes an abuse. Subsection (2) sets forth the means test. If D flunks the test, the court must presume that abuse exists. Meanwhile, subsection (3) provides:

> In considering under paragraph (1) whether the granting of relief would be an abuse of the provisions of this chapter in a case in which the presumption in subparagraph (A)(i) does not arise[14] or is rebutted, the court shall consider–
>
> (A) whether the debtor filed the petition in bad faith; or
>
> (B) the totality of the circumstances (including whether the debtor seeks to reject a personal services contract and the financial need for such rejection as sought by the debtor) of the debtor's financial situation demonstrates abuse (emphasis added).

The emphasized language indicates that courts can ignore the means test in subparagraph (2) when dismissing cases under subparagraph (3), where D passes the test. But courts must dismiss under subparagraph (1) is D flunks the test.

8. Current monthly income is defined in Bankruptcy Code § 101(10A) to be a monthly average of income from all sources. To find this average, we are to take a six month period stretching backward. In re Love, 350 B.R. 611, 613 (Bankr. M.D. Ala. 2006) ("One may readily see

[14] This is a mis-reference. There is no subparagraph (a)(i) to "such paragraph"--i.e., paragraph (1). Presumably Congress meant to refer to subparagraph (a)(i) to paragraph (2). For literalists, no harm is done, since the non-existent presumption of subparagraph (1)(A)(i) never arises, as it does not exist. The statute works perfectly well with the bad cross-reference.

that the term 'current monthly income' is something of a misnomer in that it is historical data and not a projection of the amount of income that the debtor may expect to receive in the future"). One starts counting from the last day of the month preceding the bankruptcy petition. 11 U.S.C. § 101(10A)(A)(i). But this rule applies only if the debtor has filed a schedule of current income under § 521(a)(1)(B)(ii). Interestingly, § 521(a)(1)(B)(ii) requires only a "schedule of current income and current expenditures." There is no requirement of a monthly schedule here. But § 707(b)(2)(C) requires

> [a]s part of the schedule of current income and expenditures required under section 521, . . . a statement of the debtor's current monthly income, and the calculations that determine whether a presumption arises under subparagraph [707](b)(2)(A)(i), that show how each such amount is calculated (emphasis added).

Oddly, if the debtor has not made this filing, the court is authorized by Section 101(10A)(A)(ii) to calculate six months back from the "date on which current income is determined. . . " D's failure to file Form B22A is perhaps not grounds to dismiss the case, because Form B22A is not required by § 522(a)(1), as both § 522(i)(2) and (arguably) § 707(a)(3) require. The fact that the court does not need this form to accomplish means testing is further evidence on this inability to dismiss the debtor for not filing Form B22A. On the other hand, according to § 521(i)(A), if it is agreed § 707(b)(2)(C) is "under" § 521(a)(1) (in spite of no cross reference there), the debtor's bankruptcy case is automatically dismissed after 45 days. One of the things § 521(a)(1)(B)(ii) requires is "a schedule of current income and current expenditures," and this plausibly includes Form B22A under § 707(b)(3)(C). If the above reasoning follows, there will be little need for the court to establish the six month reach-back period.

9. D earns much less than his spouse. They agree that D will cover household expenses with his income, while the non-debtor spouse will simply bank her much larger salary. She therefore contributes nothing to the household, within the definition of "current monthly income" in § 101(10A). Because of this ruse, D passes the means test. Can the chapter 7 case go forward? In In re Springirth, 2008 B.R. LEXIS (Bankr. S.D.Ind. February 29, 2008), the court skipped to the chase and threw the case out under § 707(b)(3).

10. Whatever spousal income must be added, there are exclusions. Social security payments need not be added. 11 U.S.C. § 101(10A)(B). Unemployment compensation is a state-provided benefit. Yet, under the Social Security Act, grants are provided to the states if states choose to offer unemployment benefits, provided the state comply with federal mandates. 42 U.S.C. §§ 1101-05, 1321. Do the indirect subsidies mandated by the Social Security Act make state unemployment benefits excludible under the definition of "current monthly income"? In In re Sorrell, 359 B.R. 167 (Bankr. 2007), the court ruled that these benefits are excludible, because the indirect federal subsidies. The court's major point was a "knew how to" argument. In several section of BAPCPA, Congress knew how to invoke limited portions of the Social Security Act. E.g., 11 U.S.C. §§ 362(b)(2)(D) & (E) & (F), 704(c)(1)(A)(i). But in defining "current monthly income," Section 101(10A) excludes "benefits received under the Social Security Act." Congress must have intended, the court induced, that indirect benefits stemming from the Social Security Act were included in the expansive language of §101(10A). Sorrell, supra, at 181.

Also to be excluded are "payments to victims of war crimes or crimes against humanity on account of their status as victims of such crimes, and payments to victims of international terrorism or domestic terrorism. . . " 11 U.S.C. § 101(10A)(B). So the scant consolation to the victims of man's inhumanity to man is an invitation to commit acts which, if performed by a non-victim, would constitute a bankruptcy abuse. Two wrongs (one monumental, the other petty) make a right, according to Congress. Exclusions such as these imply that D's real income may be higher than his BAPCPA income. In re Casey, 356 B.R. 519 (Bankr. E.D. Wash. 2006). Meanwhile, exempt income (such as worker's compensation payments in states like South Dakota, Stuart v. Koch (In re Koch), 109 F.3d 1285 (8th Cir. 1997), or social security or disabled veteran benefits, In re Shields, 322 B.R. 894 (Bankr. M.D. Fla., 2005), are not excluded; the expectation is that these must be used to fund chapter 13 plans.

11. The six month test gives rise to anomalies with regard to seasonal workers. For example, a teacher who is not paid in the summer may find that a bankruptcy petition filed in December is in good faith. In re Beasley, 342 B.R. 280 (Bankr. C.D. Ill. 2006). The same petition filed in March is in bad faith. For such workers, there is a seasonal aspect to bankruptcy abuse. High income workers who have been fired and who could easily find new employment may find that, by taking an unpaid leave, they can qualify for chapter 7 bankruptcy, where they can walk

away from their credit card debts. In re Pak, 343 B.R. 239 (Bankr. N.D. Cal. 2006). Such tricky debtors, however, can still be dismissed under § 707(b)(3)(B), which applies to those who have passed the means test if "the totality of the circumstances. . . of the debtor's financial situation demonstrates abuse." Thus, in In re Quintana, 2006 Bankr. LEXIS 2256 (Bankr. D. Ariz., September 12, 2006), a striking worker could show a very low current monthly income and could still be invited out of chapter 7.

12. Another difficulty with "current monthly income" is that "income from all sources," 11 U.S.C. § 101(10A)(A), is not a defined term. So it presumably includes proceeds from the sale of assets. Judge Eugene Wedoff gives the example of a debtor who sells her home within six months of bankruptcy. Eugene R. Wedoff, Means Testing in the New 707(b), 79 AM. BANKR. L.J. 231, 251 (2005). This sale might even constitute a capital loss. The sale would in general fund chapter 7 dividends for unsecured creditors. Perhaps it would fund a very high bankruptcy dividend indeed. Nevertheless, it must be included in income, thus raising the average for purposes of the 60 month calculation and making a chapter 7 proceeding an abuse. On the other hand, a debtor who sells the house seven months before the bankruptcy and then indulges in a luxury vacation is fully eligible for chapter 7, if the lower income allows the debtor to meet the means test. Similarly, a debtor may have received a bonus in the prior six months, but no adjustment is appropriate because bonuses are, by definition, not mandatory. In re Oliver, 350 B.R. 294, 300 (Bankr. W.D. Tex. 2006).

On the other side of the coin, money withdrawn from a tax-deferred retirement account (although being taxed for the first time) is not income received within six months of bankruptcy. In re Wayman, 351 B.R. 808 (Bankr. E.D. Tex. 2006).

JOHNSON v ZIMMER
686 F.3d 224 (4th Cir. 2012), cert. denied, 133 S.Ct. 846 (2013)

AGEE, J.

In this direct appeal from the United States Bankruptcy Court for the Eastern District of North Carolina, we address a question of first impression in the circuit courts of appeal: in light of the 2005 amendments to the Bankruptcy Code . . . , how is the "household" size of a debtor seeking bankruptcy relief to be calculated under Chapter 13. Finding no error in the bankruptcy court's method of calculating the Debtor's household size based on how many individuals operate as an "economic unit" with the Debtor, we affirm the order of the bankruptcy court denying the Debtor's motion for confirmation with leave to amend the Debtor's "disposable income calculation and plan to reflect the household size [of five]." (J.A. 100.) See In re Johnson, No. 10-07244-8-JRL, 2011 Bankr. LEXIS 4636 (Bankr. E.D.N.C. July 21, 2011).

I.

The facts are not in dispute. Tanya Rene Johnson ("the Debtor") filed a voluntary petition for Chapter 13 bankruptcy in September 2010. Robert R. Browning was appointed as Trustee. Upon receiving notice of the Debtor's motion for confirmation of a plan, the Debtor's ex-husband, William H. Zimmer ("the Creditor"), objected. The basis for the Creditor's objection was that the proposed plan overstated the Debtor's household size, resulting in an inaccurate calculation of her monthly expenses. The Creditor maintained that as a result of this alleged error, the Debtor's proposed Chapter 13 plan improperly showed a "disposable monthly income" insufficient to make payments on two unsecured loans for which the Creditor was jointly liable with the Debtor.

Prior to the bankruptcy court's consideration of the objections, the parties stipulated to the following facts: the Debtor and Creditor share joint custody of their two minor sons. Neither party pays child support; they share "expenses for clothing, school supplies, and other incidental expenses for their sons based on where the sons live when an expense is necessary." (J.A. 92-93.) Out-of-pocket medical expenses are divided equally. By oral agreement, the Debtor's sons reside with her and are in her care and custody for 204 days each year. The Debtor's current husband has joint custody of three children from his previous marriage: two minor sons and a nineteen-year-old daughter. The Debtor's step-children reside with her and her husband approximately 180 days per year.[15]

The Debtor's proposed Chapter 13 plan claimed a household of seven members, counting individually each person who resided in her home for any period of time within the past six months (i.e., the Debtor, her husband, her two children, and her three step-children). The Creditor asserted that the Debtor did not actually have seven members of her household because the five children and step-children did not live at her residence full-time. He contended that rather than simply counting the number of "heads on the bed" to determine household size, the Debtor's plan should use a method that better approximated the actual economic impact of each individual on the Debtor's expenses. He asserted that such an approach would result in a lower calculation of her monthly expenses such that she would have income available with which to pay toward her unsecured debts as part of a proper Chapter 13 plan.

In examining the parties' dispute, the bankruptcy court observed that the Code does not define "household," there was no binding precedent on point, and that other bankruptcy courts followed three different approaches to define that term. As described in greater detail below, those three approaches are: the "heads-on-beds" approach that follows the Census Bureau's broad definition of a household as "all the people who occupy a housing unit," without regard to relationship, financial contributions, or financial dependency; the "income tax dependent" method derived from the Internal Revenue Manual's ("IRM") definition that examines which individuals either are or could be "included on the debtor's tax return as dependents"; and the "economic unit" approach that "assesses the number of individuals in the household who act as a single economic unit by including those who are financially dependent on the debtor, those who financially support the debtor, and those whose income and expenses are intermingled with the debtor's." (J.A. 96-98.)

The bankruptcy court adopted a variation of the "economic unit" approach, first assessing the number of individuals whose income and expenses are intermingled with the Debtor's, and then calculating how much time any part-time residents were members of the Debtor's household. In adopting the "economic unit" approach, the bankruptcy court noted that the other two definitions were inconsistent with the purpose of the Code and were the least flexible in terms of adapting to an individual debtor's circumstances.

In deciding that part-time residents should count as part-time members of the Debtor's "household," the bankruptcy court acknowledged that "[d]ividing children into fractions is not ideal," but concluded that this additional step in applying the economic unit approach best "capture[d] the nuances of familial support and bonds" and enabled the court to "account for dependents who reside with the debtor on a part-time basis . . . in calculating variable costs such as food, utilities, and out-of-pocket health care expenses." (J.A. 98, 99.) In re Johnson, 2011 Bankr. LEXIS 4636, 2011 WL 5902883, at *2-*3. Accordingly, the court

[15] It is not apparent in the record before us who claims the Debtor's children or step-children as dependents for federal income tax purposes.

relied on the parties' stipulated facts to determine that each of the Debtor's two sons constituted 0.56 members of the Debtor's household (residing with her 204 days out of a possible 365), and that each of the Debtor's three step-children constituted 0.49 members of her household (residing with her 180 days out of a possible 365).[16] Id. 2011 Bankr. LEXIS 4636, [WL] at *3.

Implementing this fractional economic unit approach thus resulted in the Debtor having a total of 2.59 children in her household full-time, which the court then rounded up to three children. Thus, the Debtor, her husband, and the deemed three children yielded a "household" of five persons. The bankruptcy court also noted that the Debtor could claim "any particular expenses . . . that the debtor must meet given the family's total size of seven" as itemized costs in an amended proposed plan. (J.A. 99-100.) Id. Consequently, it denied the Debtor's motion for confirmation of a plan, but granted leave to amend the plan based on re-calculation of the Debtor's disposable income based on a household size of five.

The bankruptcy court certified the issue of the determination of the "household" size for direct interlocutory appeal. We granted the Debtor's petition for permission to appeal, thus satisfying the requirements for the appeal under 28 U.S.C. § 158(a)(3), (d), and Fed. R. Bankr. P. 8003(d).[17]

II.

A. Statutory Framework

We review "the appropriate statutory interpretation of the Bankruptcy Code . . . de novo." Botkin v. DuPont Cmty. Credit Union, 650 F.3d 396, 398 (4th Cir. 2011). In undertaking this review, we first set forth the relevant statutory provisions, and then describe the approaches bankruptcy courts have adopted as well as the parties' arguments relating to each. For the reasons then articulated, we conclude that there is no statutorily mandated approach and that the Code's purposes were best served in this case by the "economic unit" approach as applied by the bankruptcy court to calculate the Debtor's "household" size. Accordingly, we affirm the order of the bankruptcy court.

In Hamilton v. Lanning, 130 S. Ct. 2464 (2010), the Supreme Court summarized the key features of a Chapter 13 bankruptcy proceeding:

> Chapter 13 . . . provides bankruptcy protection to "individual[s] with regular income" whose debts fall within statutory limits. 11 U.S.C. §§ 101(30), 109(e). Unlike debtors who file under Chapter 7 and must liquidate their nonexempt assets in order to pay creditors, see §§ 704(a)(1), 726, Chapter 13 debtors are permitted to keep their property, but they must agree to a court-approved plan under which they pay creditors out of their future income, see §§ 1306(b), 1321, 1322(a)(1), 1328(a). A bankruptcy trustee oversees the filing and execution of a Chapter 13 debtor's plan. § 1322(a)(1); see also 28 U.S.C. § 586(a)(3).
>
> . . .
>
> [I]f a trustee or an unsecured creditor objects to a Chapter 13 debtor's plan, a bankruptcy court may not approve the plan unless it provides for the full repayment of unsecured claims or "provides that all of the debtor's projected

---

[16] The bankruptcy court further noted that although the Debtor's step-daughter was over the age of 19, it appeared from the stipulated facts that she was "financially dependent" on the Debtor. (J.A. 99 n.5.)

[17] The Trustee is an intervenor in this appeal, on the side of the Creditor. For purposes of simplicity, we address their joint arguments as those of the Creditor.

> disposable income to be received" over the duration of the plan "will be applied to make payments" in accordance with the terms of the plan. 11 U.S.C. § 1325(b)(1); see also § 1326(b)(1) (2000 ed.).

Id. at 2468-69.

One of the many changes to the Code arising from the BAPCPA was the tightening of how a Chapter 13 debtor's "projected disposable income" is calculated. Although "projected disposable income" remained an undefined term in the Code, the BAPCPA "specified in some detail how 'disposable income' is to be calculated." Id. at 2469. "'Disposable income' is now defined as 'current monthly income received by the debtor' less 'amounts reasonably necessary to be expended' for the debtor's maintenance and support, for qualifying charitable contributions, and for business expenditures. § 1325(b)(2)(A)(i) and (ii)." Id. "The phrase 'amounts reasonably necessary to be expended' in § 1325(b)(2) is . . . newly defined" and how it is calculated depends on whether the debtor's current monthly income is above or below the median for his or her state. Id. at 2470. The determination of how to calculate a debtor's "amounts reasonably necessary to be expended" is based, in part, on the size of a debtor's "household." See § 1325(b).[18] "Household" is not defined in the Code.

Rather than including "the full amount for 'maintenance or support'" (the calculation for below-median-income debtors), an above-median-income debtor can only include "certain specified expenses." Hamilton, 130 S. Ct. at 2470 (citing §§ 707(b)(2), 1325(b)(3)(A)). Section 1325 directs above-median-income debtors to use the "means test" set forth in § 707(b)(2) as the basis for calculating those expenses. The "means test" formulation "is reflected in a schedule (Form 22C) that a Chapter 13 debtor must file." Id. at 2470 n.2. Section 707(b)'s means test uses standardized expenditure figures in lieu of an above-median income debtor's actual monthly living expenses. Those amounts are derived from the Internal Revenue Service (IRS) National Standards and Local Standards tables for the geographic area in which the debtor resides. Debtors are also permitted to include their actual monthly expenses for certain categories of expenditures falling under the IRS's "Other Necessary Expenses." The calculations under § 707(b) are based on a fixed number of individuals: "the debtor, the dependents of the debtor, and the spouse of the debtor in a joint case, if the spouse is not otherwise a dependent." § 707(b)(2)(A)(ii)(I). The term "dependent" as used in § 707(b) is not defined in the Code either.

The means test "supplants the pre-BAPCPA practice of calculating debtors' reasonable expenses on a case-by-case basis, which led to varying and often inconsistent determinations." Ransom v. FIA Card Services, N.A., 131 S. Ct. 716, 722 (2011). Adopting the means test was "'[t]he heart of [BAPCPA's] consumer bankruptcy reforms,'" Id. at 721 (quoting H.R. Rep. No. 109-31, pt. 1, p.2 (2005)), and was designed "to help ensure that debtors who can pay creditors do pay them." Id. (emphasis in original).

---

[18] Specifically, a debtor's "household" size is relevant to determining how much the debtor can deduct for two portions of his "amounts reasonably necessary to be expended": the amounts "for the maintenance or support of the debtor or a dependent of the debtor, or for a domestic support obligation . . ." and, "if the debtor is engaged in business, for the payment of expenditures necessary for the continuation, preservation, and operation of such business." § 1325(b)(2)(A)(i), (iii); § 1325(b)(3). "Dependent," as used in this subsection is not defined.

B. Statutory Analysis
1. Overview

As an initial matter, the Debtor briefly posits that resolving which method should be used to calculate her household size may not ultimately be determinative of her case. This is so, in her view, because under either parties' method of calculating household size (i.e., five or seven members), the Debtor remains an above-median-income debtor under § 1325. Consequently, she must use the means test set forth in § 707(b)(2), which directs a debtor to include herself, her "dependents," and in appropriate cases her spouse, in the required calculations. And she observes that the sum of those individuals may not be the same as her "household" size, depending on how "dependents" and "household" are each defined. The Debtor contends that the "dispositive" issue in her case will be the application of § 707(b)'s means test, which requires a determination of who are her "dependents." On this matter, the Debtor contends the Court should "adopt an ordinary and common meaning of the word dependent" and that the meaning of "household" is irrelevant. (Br. for Appellant at 14-15.)

The Creditor agrees that "[t]he Court could recognize that the definition of 'dependent' [in § 707(b)(2)] is the real issue," but does not develop this idea further. (Br. for Appellee at 24.) Instead, he focuses on why § 707(b)(2)'s use of the term "dependent" should not be used as a basis for defining "household" according to the IRS definition of "dependents."

While the Debtor is correct that her "household" size may not be the "dispositive" inquiry in determining her disposable income, the determination of "household" remains a significant component of the § 1325(b) scheme. The purpose of § 1325(b) is to determine a debtor's ability to pay creditors by determining his or her projected disposable income. The complex formula used for that calculation deducts the debtor's expenses ("amounts reasonably necessary to be expended") from his or her monthly income. As an initial step in determining the debtor's "amounts reasonably necessary to be expended," § 1325(b)(3) directs debtors to calculate the relevant median family income for his or her geographic area based on the debtor's "household" size. Accordingly, we decline the Debtor's invitation to ignore how the bankruptcy court calculated her "household" size.

The bankruptcy court's order is limited to the § 1325(b) determination of how the Debtor should calculate her "household" size. It resolved that issue and ordered the Debtor to file an amended Form 22C and proposed plan based on the court's conclusion that she has a household of five. In so doing, it did not specifically address how the § 707(b) means test calculation should be performed. Accordingly, what the Debtor identifies as the "dispositive" means test calculations have not yet been performed or ruled upon in the bankruptcy proceedings. It would be premature for us to consider that issue now.[19]

In deciding whether the Debtor is an above-median income debtor, she

[19] Although the Debtor discounts the significance of the § 1325(b) "household" size in her case, the calculation is an important preliminary step in assessing the "amounts reasonably necessary to be expended" for purposes of determining her projected disposable income. As discussed in greater detail below, the "amounts reasonably necessary to be expended" deduction from the Debtor's monthly income includes an amount "for the maintenance or support of the debtor or a dependent of the debtor." § 1325(b)(2)(A)(i). This amount, in turn is determined by the means test if the Debtor is an above-median income Debtor. § 1325(b)(3).

must identify whether her "current monthly income, when multiplied by 12, [is] greater than" "the highest median family income of the applicable State for a family of 4 or fewer individuals, plus $625 per month for each individual in excess of 4." In making this calculation, the Debtor must use either a household size of five or seven. Whether she uses five or seven will alter her final calculation by $1,250 per month, or a total of $15,000 for the twelve-month period. While in either case, the result may be that she is an above-median income debtor, she still must go through the required calculations to reach the § 707(b) means test alternative method of calculating her "amounts reasonably necessary to be expended." In turn, as discussed above, the Debtor's "household" size under § 1325(b) will impact how she calculates her "amounts reasonably necessary to be expended" under the § 707(b) means test.

We also observe that the language in § 707(b)(2)(A)(ii)(I) referring to "the debtor, the dependents of the debtor, and the spouse of the debtor in a joint case, if the spouse is not a dependent," is not the totality of the means test calculation.[20] In addition to the word "household" being used in other parts of § 707(b), see, e.g., § 707(b)(2)(A)(ii)(II), a debtor is also permitted to claim certain itemized deductions based on actual expenses for items such as "housing and utilities" if they are "reasonable and necessary." E.g., § 707(b)(2)(A)(ii)(V). At various times, both §§ 1325(b) and 707(b) refer alternatively to a debtor's "dependents," "dependent child[ren]," "household," "family," and "immediate family." As discussed infra, in order to understand what Congress meant by each of these undefined terms, they must be understood in context and in light of each other. Our interpretation of "household"--one of the first of these terms used in a Chapter 13 debtor's calculation of his or her disposable income--will impact how these other terms are understood as well.

In sum, a debtor's entire § 707(b) means test calculation will be affected by the threshold determination of how many people are part of her "household," as determined for purposes of § 1325(b). Moreover, the bankruptcy court's review of the appropriateness of a debtor's means test calculations, e.g., whether the debtor is claiming "reasonable and necessary" additional sums for his or her "housing and utilities," will likely also be informed by the debtor's § 1325(b) "household" size. The bankruptcy court appears to have recognized such nuances to the means test calculations when noting that the Debtor could include "any particular expenses [that] exist that the [D]ebtor must meet given the family's total size of seven" "in an amended Form 22C and provide documentation of those costs." (J.A. 100.) In re Johnson, 2011 Bankr. LEXIS 4636, 2011 WL 5902883, at *3. For all of these reasons, we conclude that it is necessary for us to resolve whether the bankruptcy court properly calculated the Debtor's "household" size under § 1325(b).

2. Calculating "Household" Size

As noted, § 1325(b)(2) contains the provisions for calculating a debtor's "disposable income" in order to assess his or her ability to pay debts as part of a Chapter 13 plan. At its most basic level, the relevant formula is that the debtor's disposable income equals the debtor's "current monthly income" "less amounts

[20] Because it is beyond the scope of the bankruptcy court's order, we do not address what "dependents" means for purposes of § 707(b)'s means test calculations.

reasonably necessary to be expended." § 1325(b)(2). A debtor's "household" size is relevant to determining how to calculate certain parts of the debtor's "amounts reasonably necessary to be expended." § 1325(b)(3).

Despite the centrality of the term to the requisite analysis, the Code does not state how the size of a debtor's "household" under § 1325(b) is to be calculated for determining his or her disposable income. From this void comes the primary issue before us: whether the bankruptcy court erred in using a fractional economic unit approach to determine the Debtor's "household" size for purposes of conducting its review of the disposable income calculation.

a. The Party's Arguments

The Debtor would have us answer this query in the affirmative, contending that the bankruptcy court erred in looking past the "ordinary and common meaning of statutory words that Congress declined to define." (Br. for Appellant 16.) She asserts that her proffered methodology, the heads-on-beds approach, is consistent with "[t]he expansive [dictionary] definition of household" and that it is "logical and 'fair'" to rely on the Census Bureau's correspondingly broad definition of "household" because § 1325 refers debtors to Census Bureau statistics to determine a "median family income."[21] (Id. at 18.) She also posits that if Congress had intended to require familial or economic ties to limit the definition of "household," it could have used a word that connotes such limits, such as the terms "family" or "dependents," which are used elsewhere in the Code. (Id. at 17-19.) She thus concludes that the heads-on-beds approach best reflects what Congress intended by "household," and that the bankruptcy court usurped Congress' legislative function by utilizing any other definition of "household." (Id. at 20-23.)

In response, the Creditor asserts that undefined terms are construed by the terms that surround it, and that the bankruptcy court correctly rejected the heads-on-beds approach and adopted the economic unit approach. He contends that the Code's purpose and text are best served by using a definition of "household" that is based on the financial interdependence of the debtor and those persons comprising the debtor's "household." (Br. for Appellee 14-16.) The Creditor argues that the heads-on-beds approach is too broad and "can lead to anomalies that are inconsistent with the purpose of the means test" and the Code because it merely counts individuals based on presence in the debtor's residence without examining whether they are part of the debtor's financial situation. (Id. at 16.) Furthermore, he submits that the Census Bureau's expansive definition of "household" is not incorporated into the Code and that adopting it does not make sense given the different objectives of the Census and bankruptcy proceedings. In conclusion, the Creditor posits that the bankruptcy court's approach "provides an accurate snapshot of the Debtor's household size when considered over a period of time," and thus was an appropriate method to calculate her household "given the complexities of today's family structure." (Id. at 19.)

Neither party advocates that the bankruptcy court should have used the income tax dependent method of calculating household size. Indeed, other than defining the approach, the Debtor does not address it at all. The Creditor posits

[21] The Code defines "median family income" as "the median family income both calculated and reported by the Bureau of the Census." 11 U.S.C. § 101(39A)(A).

that this approach is inconsistent with the purpose of the Code, but submitted during oral argument that it was at least a better approach than the "heads on beds" definition, should the court not adopt the "economic unit" approach.

b. Analysis

As always, we begin with the statute, "bearing in mind that we should give effect to the legislative will as expressed in the language." United States v. Murphy, 35 F.3d 143, 145 (4th Cir. 1994) . . . .

Although the Debtor relies on the expansive definition of the word to support her argument, by doing so, she necessarily overlooks other aspects of these dictionary definitions that are narrower, and would cut against her interpretation. Thus while the heads-on-beds approach looks solely to how many individuals reside under one roof, that definition ignores other components of the dictionary definitions of "household" that limit it to individuals who comprise a "family" or "a domestic establishment." These components of the "ordinary" dictionary definition suggest that a "household" also consists of something beyond co-residency. It is therefore not evident from the word "household" alone which common and ordinary definition Congress intended to apply in the § 1325(b) analysis. A statutory interpretation of "household" could be crafted in several different ways that would yield different household sizes depending on which dictionary definition is used.

As noted, it is a "cardinal rule" of statutory interpretation that "statutory language must be read in context [because] a phrase gathers meaning from the words around it." Gen. Dynamics Land Sys., Inc. v. Cline, 540 U.S. 581, 596 (2004) (citation and internal quotation marks omitted). In some cases, "[t]he meaning of a word that appears ambiguous if viewed in isolation may become clear when [it] is analyzed in light of the terms that surround it." Smith v. United States, 508 U.S. 223, 229 (1993).

Context provides some guidance in this case, but ultimately does not resolve the fundamental uncertainty of what Congress intended "household" to mean. On the one hand, Congress used the word "household" as opposed to "family," "dependent child," or "dependent," all of which are used elsewhere in the surrounding and cross-referenced Code provisions. Consistent with the principle that "[t]he use of different terms within related statutes generally implies that different meanings were intended," this would often mean that Congress intended the term "household" to mean something other than what those terms mean. See Cunningham v. Scibana, 259 F.3d 303, 308 (4th Cir. 2001) (quoting 2A Norman J. Singer, Sutherland's Statutes and Statutory Construction, § 46.06, at 195 (6th ed. 2000)). On the other hand, as set forth above, the dictionary definitions of "household" overlap with each of these terms to varying degrees, as "household" may or may not be defined to include the concept of familial connection or domestic interconnectedness.

Further muddying the waters is the statute's own use of different terms for aspects of the same calculation. Section 1325(b)(3) states that a debtor should use his or her "household" size and determine the "median family income" for "1 earner" if the household size is one; for "a family of the same number or fewer individuals" for a "household size of 2, 3, or 4 individuals"; or for "a family of 4 or fewer individuals, plus $625 per month for each individual in excess of 4" for a "household exceeding 4 individuals." It is not entirely clear from this language whether Congress intended for the additional references to "family" to serve as qualifiers to the definition of "household," or whether "family" simply refers to the cross-referenced "median family income" statistics the debtor is supposed to use when comparing his independently defined "household" size. In either event, it is not immediately clear how to define "family" even as part of the determination of a "household."

Similarly, § 1325(b)(3) uses the number in the debtor's "household" to explain how a debtor is to calculate two components of the "amounts reasonably necessary to be expended" under § 1325(b)(2)(A)(i) and (B). For example, subsection (A)(i) includes expenses the debtor may have for the "maintenance or support of the debtor or a dependent of the debtor, or for a domestic support obligation." (Emphasis added.) In addition, § 1325(b)(3) instructs above-median income debtors to use § 707(b)'s means test to perform their "amounts reasonably necessary to be expended" calculation, and § 707(b) also refers to a debtor's "dependents" as opposed to his or her "household." Congress' use of "dependents" in both of these other statutory provisions that directly relate to the same calculation that is to occur in § 1325(b)(3) would tend to suggest that although Congress used "dependent" and "household" at different points, they may nonetheless have related meanings.

In addition to and arising from these immediate contextual conundrums, bankruptcy courts have offered reasoned explanations for why one method of defining "household" is more or less appropriate than others based on the context within § 1325(b), the BAPCPA amendments, and the Code as a whole.[22] However, none of these approaches is directly required by the statutory language and is consequently based on inference and implication to one degree or another.

The bankruptcy court in In re Law, 2008 Bankr. LEXIS 1198 (Bankr. D. Kan. 2008), concluded that § 1325(b)'s cross-reference to § 707(b)--which only allows debtors to claim "dependents" and refers to the IRS tables--meant that the Code "consistently limits allowable expenses to those of the debtor, the debtor's dependents, and the spouse of the debtor," and thus the term "household" should be restricted to those individuals a debtor can claim as dependents on his or her income tax filings. In contrast, the bankruptcy court in In re Jewell, 365 B.R. 796 (Bankr. S.D. Ohio 2007), was "unwilling to accept the broad definitions of [household] suggested by the Debtors of 'heads on beds'" because it believed that definition was "inconsistent with the methodology and purpose" of the test to "calculate[e] a debtor's 'disposable income.'" Id. at 800. It also noted that the income tax dependent method was too narrow "inasmuch as it fails to recognize

[22] Most of the bankruptcy courts to address the issue have noted the lack of a definition of "household" in the Code, and have provided some explanation for why one or another approach is most consistent with congressional intent. As discussed infra, the bankruptcy court in In re Ellringer, 370 B.R. 905 (Bankr. D. Minn. 2007), concluded that the Census Bureau definition of "household" should be used because that is the definition used in the Census Bureau's creation of the median family income statistics. Id. at 910-11. Other bankruptcy courts to apply this approach have noted that while the "economic unit" approach may have appealing aspects to it, nothing in the word "household" or the relevant statutory text suggests that the individuals in a household be financially interconnected. E.g., In re Epperson, 409 B.R. 503, 506-07 (Bankr. D. Ariz. 2009) ("Congress does not require courts to take into account financial contribution of the household member, relationship to the debtor, and dependency when determining household size. Absent Congressional direction, it is inappropriate to consider a household member's dependency on the [d]ebtor when determining household size; accordingly, household should be understood in the ordinary sense of the word.") (internal quotation marks and citation omitted).

those instances when a debtor may be actually providing support for a household member, but the circumstances do not fall neatly within the parameters envisioned by the [tax code]." Id. at 801. It also noted that even the IRS recognized "reasonable exceptions" to the principle that "the number of household members allowed should generally be the same as those claimed as dependents on the taxpayer's tax returns." Id. Consistently, the bankruptcy courts that have applied the "economic unit" approach over the other methods have pointed to its flexibility to the financial status of the debtor, and how its results provide the courts with the best tools to achieve the Code's goal of providing a realistic assessment of the debtor's financial obligations. See In re Herbert, 405 B.R. 165, 169 (Bankr. W.D.N.C. 2008); see also In re Robinson, 449 B.R. 473, 478-82 (Bankr. E.D. Va. 2011) (same, and delineating similar reasons for rejecting the other methods); Morrison, 443 B.R. 378, 384-87 (Bankr. M.D.N.C. 2011) (same).

These are the hallmarks of statutory language that is anything but plain. Because the term "household" "lends itself to more than one reasonable interpretation," it is ambiguous. See Newport News Shipbuilding & Dry Dock Co., 376 F.3d at 248 (quoting United States ex rel Wilson v. Graham Cnty., 367 F.3d 245, 248 (4th Cir 2004).[23] Accordingly, "our obligation is to find that interpretation which can most fairly be said to be imbedded in the statute, in the sense of being most harmonious with its scheme and the general purposes that Congress manifested." Id. Put differently, where statutory language is ambiguous, we "turn to other evidence to interpret the meaning of the provision," interpreting provisions harmoniously, where possible, or by reference to the legislative history, and always with the goal of ascertaining congressional intent. See New Cingular Wireless PCS, LLC v. Finley, 674 F.3d 225, 249 (4th Cir. 2012) (internal quotation marks and citations omitted). Our next step, then, is to determine which approach best corresponds to Congress' intent despite the ambiguous meaning of the precise text it has used.

We begin by examining whether the heads-on-beds approach best reflects Congress' intent in requiring a debtor to determine his or her "household" size, as the Debtor contends. A handful of bankruptcy courts have adopted the heads-on-beds approach, using the Census Bureau definition of "household," although they use different--and in some cases no--reasons to explain why. Some bankruptcy courts have stated that this definition of "household" is simply its plain meaning. E.g., In re Smith, 396 B.R. 214, 215-18 (Bankr. W.D. Mich. 2008). For the reasons set forth above, we reject that conclusion. Other bankruptcy courts do not specifically identify how they reach that conclusion, but base their use of the heads-on-beds approach upon § 1325(b)'s reference to Census Bureau statistical data. In Ellringer, for example, the bankruptcy court concluded that because § 1325(b)(2) refers to the "median family income," and 11 U.S.C. § 101(39A)(A) defines "median family income" by reference to the Census Bureau's reports, "the Census Bureau provides the most appropriate definition of 'household.'" Id. at 910-11; see also, e.g., In re Bostwick, 406 B.R. 867, 872-73 (Bankr. D. Minn. 2009); In re Fleishman, 372 B.R. 64, 67-68 (Bankr. D. Or. 2007).

[23] As one bankruptcy court noted, if § 1325(b) was "so plain, so clear, so unambiguous that the [c]ourt need look no further to determine its meaning . . . then how could [so many] courts have interpreted it one way and [so many other] courts have interpreted it in exactly the opposite way? Doesn't the concept of 'plain' meaning carry with it the implication that the same meaning would be 'plain'--ordinary, literal and obvious--to every reader?" Morrison, 443 B.R. at 387 n.6 (quotation marks and citation omitted).

We are not persuaded that Congress intended for "household" to be so broadly defined. At the outset, nothing in § 1325(b) directly or indirectly incorporates the Census Bureau's definition of "household." Although there is a cross-reference to the Census Bureau's median income tables, that is not sufficient to demonstrate a congressional intent to adopt the usage utilized by the Census Bureau in its wholly separate sphere of government work. Moreover, while the use of "household" as opposed to "family" or "dependents" (terms used elsewhere in § 1325(b)(2)) would indicate that the term means something different from those words, that does not automatically indicate that Congress intended for the term "household" to be synonymous with the Census Bureau's definition and refer to any person living in a particular residence. Nothing in § 1325(b) supports the conclusion that a bankruptcy court is required or intended to use such a broad definition.

In the absence of clear direction in the Code to use the heads-on-beds approach, the question becomes whether the bankruptcy court erred in failing to choose that method over other possible approaches. On this point, we agree with the majority of bankruptcy courts in concluding that the heads-on-beds approach using the Census Bureau's expansive definition of "household" is inconsistent with the purpose and objectives of the Code. As noted, the Census Bureau defines a "household" as "all of the people, related and unrelated, who occupy a housing unit." Ellringer, 370 B.R. at 911 (internal quotation marks and citation omitted). This definition serves the Census Bureau's need to compile demographic information identifying the number of people in a particular geographic region. It is wholly unrelated to any bankruptcy purpose and does not serve the Code's objective of identifying a debtor's deductible monthly expenses and, ultimately, his or her disposable income.

As the Jewell bankruptcy court observed, the Census Bureau definition is at odds with the purpose of § 1325(b) because "[i]f a person lives in the home with the debtor but the debtor does not support that person, then inclusion of that person for purposes of calculating the applicable median family income and disposable income would give rise to a faulty calculation and would result in an inaccurate figure for both." 365 B.R. at 800; see also Herbert, 405 B.R. at 169 (criticizing the heads-on-beds approach as being "too broad").

The calculation of a debtor's monthly income and expenses is aimed at ensuring that debtors pay the amount they can reasonably afford to pay to creditors. It makes little sense to allow debtors to broadly define their "households" so as to include individuals who have no actual financial impact on the debtor's expenses. The over-inclusion of individuals in a debtor's household size would lead to an artificially high calculation of the debtor's "amounts reasonably necessary to be expended" each month, and thus to an incorrect determination of the debtor's disposable income and ability to pay creditors.[24] This result would be entirely at odds with the stated purpose of the BAPCPA: "The heart of the bill's consumer bankruptcy reforms consists of the implementation of an income/expense screening mechanism ('needs-based

---

[24] While the heads-on-beds approach runs a substantial risk of being over-inclusive for purposes of § 1325(b)'s calculations, we note that in certain cases it may also be under-inclusive. There may be situations in which a bankruptcy court determines it is appropriate to include within a debtor's "household" an individual who does not live with the debtor, but is part of the debtor's reasonably necessary expenses, such as a dependent relative in a nursing home or assisted medical care facility.

bankruptcy relief' or 'means testing'), which is intended to ensure that debtors repay creditors the maximum they can afford." H.R. Rep. No. 109-31(I), Because "household" should be interpreted consistent with the context of § 1325(b), the BAPCPA, and the Code as a whole, we conclude the bankruptcy court did not err in rejecting the heads-on-beds approach.

Next, we consider whether the bankruptcy court erred in using the "economic unit" approach. As set forth above, because the text does not define "household" and leaves room for different connotations, the economic unit approach does not inherently contradict the language of § 1325(b). And unlike the heads-on-beds approach, the economic unit approach is consistent with § 1325(b), the BAPCPA, and the Code as a whole. By examining the financial interdependence of individuals to determine whether someone is an economic part of the debtor's household, bankruptcy courts are able to avoid over- and under-inclusive results that would result by artificially defining "household" according to factors unrelated to which individuals within a residence impact the debtor's financial situation. The approach is flexible because it recognizes that a debtor's "household" may include non-family members and individuals who could not be claimed as dependents on the debtor's federal income tax return, but who nonetheless directly impact the debtor's financial situation. See Morrison, 443 B.R. at 388; Herbert, 405 B.R. at 169; Robinson, 449 B.R. at 481-82. Accordingly, it is consistent with § 1325(b)'s purpose of identifying a debtor's disposable income by identifying a debtor's "amounts reasonably necessary to be expended" each month and determining what amount a debtor is able to pay to his or her creditors.

Under this method, a debtor's "household" would include individuals who operate as an "economic unit" with the debtor: those the debtor financially supports and those who financially support the debtor. In other words, those whose income and expenses are interdependent with the debtor's are part of his or her "household" for purposes of § 1325(b). Such financial intermingling is an appropriate factor in determining "household" size under § 1325(b)(2) because the debtor's finances are the focal point of the Code. Indeed, § 1325(b) is specifically directed at determining a debtor's disposable income, which is defined as currently monthly income less "amounts reasonably necessary to be expended." § 1325(b)(2). The "amounts reasonably necessary to be expended" are calculated based, in part, on the relevant median family income for the size of the debtor's household. Thus, the entire purpose of identifying a debtor's household size is to use that number to determine his or her financial obligations and ability to pay. A definition of "household" that is also tailored to reflect a debtor's financial situation focuses directly upon the ultimate purpose of the Code.

The "economic unit" approach is also consistent with other components of the § 1325(b)(2) analysis. For example, a debtor's disposable income is based, in part, on the debtor's "current monthly income," a term that is defined in 11 U.S.C. § 101(10A) to mean "the average monthly income from all sources that the debtor receives (or in a joint case the debtor and the debtor's spouse receive) without regard to whether such income is taxable income, derived during [a specified period of time]" "and" "any amount paid by any entity other than the debtor (or in a joint case the debtor and the debtor's spouse), on a regular basis for the household expenses of the debtor or the debtor's dependents (and in a joint case the debtor's spouse if not otherwise a dependent) . . . ." Id. (emphases added). Since the "plus" side of the current monthly income part of the equation would include financial contributions from various outside sources, it is also logical to include in the amount deducted therefrom the financial liability of the debtor for the members of the debtor's "household" on the opposing side of the equation. The relevance on either side of the equation is established by the actual financial connection to the debtor, not mere physical presence or a federal income tax status. Therefore, it makes sense to define "household" with reference to whether the person's "income or expenses are inter-mingled or interdependent with [the] debtor," and whether the individuals "are acting as a single economic unit." See Morrison, 443 B.R. at 386. The extent to which that household member increases the debtor's "current monthly income" due to financial contributions set forth under § 101(10A) or increases the debtor's "amounts reasonably necessary to be expended" under § 1325(b)(2) would then be determined according to each provision. For each of these reasons, we conclude that the bankruptcy court did not err in adopting the economic unit approach in its § 1325(b) analysis.

As noted, neither party directly advances the third approach--the IRM definition and income tax dependent model--as the best method of defining "household" for § 1325(b) purposes. We agree with the Creditor that there are numerous limitations that this approach would place on the bankruptcy court's ability to accurately determine a debtor's household size. While there might be a case where the income tax dependent model could be feasible for § 1325(b) purposes, the case at bar ably demonstrates why that case would be a rare case indeed. In contrast to the "economic unit" approach, the income tax dependent approach fails to match the goals of the BAPCPA and the Code.

Bankruptcy courts have articulated the income tax dependent method to define a "household" as the same number of individuals as "those allowed as dependents on the taxpayer's tax returns," Jewell, 365 B.R. at 800, or "the people who could be or are included on the debtor's tax return as dependents." Morrison, 443 B.R. at 385.[25] The reason some courts have concluded that using this definiion is appropriate or even required is because of § 1325(b)'s cross-reference to § 707(b). Above-median income debtors (a status determined, in part, by debtor's "household" size) must use § 707(b)'s means test to determine their "amounts reasonably necessary to be expended," and the means test includes in its formula "the debtor, the debtor's dependents, and the spouse of the debtor in a joint case, if the spouse is not otherwise a dependent." § 707(b)(2)(A)(ii)(I) (Emphasis added.) The means test specifically refers debtors to use certain IRS tables (the National and Local Standards) as part of their calculations in determining deductible monthly expenses.[26] Because these provisions contain two parts of the same calculation, and because § 1325(b) refers to "household" while § 707(b) refers to "dependents," there is some logic to defining the terms consistently.

---

[25] The IRS defines "dependent" as a qualifying child or relative and takes into consideration numerous factors, unrelated to any bankruptcy purpose, as set forth in 26 U.S.C. § 152 (defining "dependent" for federal income tax purposes).

[26] A debtor using the means test is permitted to deduct not only the "applicable monthly expense amounts specified" in the tables, but also "the debtor's actual monthly expenses for the categories specified as Other Necessary Expenses [by the IRS] for the area in which the debtor resides . . . ." § 707(b)(2)(A)(ii)(I). Thus, in requiring above-median income debtors to use the means test to assess their "amounts reasonably necessary to be expended," the BAPCPA moved away from permitting such debtors to claim their actual expenses and toward requiring them to use a more standardized amount. See Ransom, 131 S. Ct. at 721-22; Baud v. Carroll, 634 F.3d 327, 333-34 (6th Cir. 2011).

That said, there are three factors that--as with the Census Bureau definition--negate the appropriateness of using this definition for purposes of § 1325(b). First, neither § 707(b) nor § 1325(b) (nor any other Code provision) expressly incorporates the IRS definitions. Indeed, the Supreme Court's decision in Ransom v. FIA Card Services, N.A., 131 S. Ct. 716 (2011), while referencing the IRS's explanatory guidelines to clarify a point regarding how another aspect of § 1325(b) should be interpreted, expressly "emphasize[d] . . . that the statute does not 'incorporate' or otherwise 'import' the IRS's guidance." Id. at 726 n. 7 (internal alterations omitted). Second, the IRM definition of "dependent" was created with a markedly different purpose from the Code's definition of "household." As the bankruptcy court in Morrison observed, "[t]he Internal Revenue Code is designed to collect tax revenue for the government" by ensuring that each person is accounted for, and that those claimed as dependents are only claimed by one individual for federal income tax purposes. 443 B.R. at 387-88. As demonstrated above, a debtor's "household" size for bankruptcy purposes is determined in order to assess his disposable income and ability to pay creditors: a goal unrelated to tax collection. Third, § 1325(b)(2) refers to "dependents" at one point in the provision and "household" in another, even setting aside § 1325(b)'s subsequent cross-reference to § 707(b), which in turn uses both "dependents" and "household." If Congress had intended for "household" to refer exclusively to the debtor and his or her dependents as defined for income tax purposes, it could have done so. Congress did not, and instead referred to a debtor's "household."

As the parties recognize, and as we explain further below, the income tax dependent approach tends to be under-inclusive for purposes of ascertaining a debtor's household size and disposable income. Thus, for example, if narrowly defined as actually claimed dependents on the debtor's income tax return, this approach would not permit a debtor to include minor children who live with the debtor, but whom by formal or informal agreement the debtor does not claim on his or her tax return. Nor would it necessarily allow a debtor to claim as a member of his or her "household" step-children, a cohabiting fiance, live-in elderly parents, and the like. This would be so regardless of the actual financial contributions to the debtor's monthly income and regardless of the real financial obligations the debtor incurred regarding those individuals. If the individual did not satisfy the IRS definition of a "dependent," the person would not be included in the debtor's "household" for § 1325(b) purposes, even though Congress never expressly indicated such an intent, and even though it results in an inaccurate assessment of the debtor's financial situation.[27]

Just as the heads-on-beds approach poses the risk of skewing the calculation by being over-inclusive and thus risks misrepresenting a debtor's ability to pay, the income tax dependent method poses an unnecessary risk of skewing the calculation by "undercounting legitimate deductions due to a debtor who financially provides for individuals he or she does not claim as dependents" on his or her tax return. Robinson, 449 B.R. at 481. Neither the income tax

[27] As with the heads-on-beds approach, although the income tax dependent approach tends to skew one way, in some circumstances it may also create a false picture in the other direction. We can readily contemplate situations in which the income tax dependent method would be over-inclusive, such as where divorcing spouses agree who will claim a child for purposes of filing federal income taxes irrespective of the degree of financial support or where the child predominantly lives.

dependent nor the "heads-on-beds" approach best reflect the purposes of the Code--and specifically the BAPCPA amendments and § 1325--as to how a debtor's disposable income is to be calculated. Rather than the choice between Scylla and Charybdis that these other methods pose, the economic unit approach affords bankruptcy courts the ability to calculate a debtor's disposable income under § 1325(b) in a way that satisfies the language of the Code, all the while steering clear of creating an unrealistic assessment (in either direction) of the debtor's disposable income.

3. Part-Time "Household" Members

The foregoing analysis does not end our inquiry, however, because the bankruptcy court opted to further refine the economic unit approach to account for the part-time members of the Debtor's "household." The Debtor contends that even if the bankruptcy court did not err in using an economic unit analysis to determine her household size, it nonetheless erred in dividing individuals (the Debtor's children and step-children) into "fractions and percentages" of her "household" when the Code "only speak[s] in terms of whole 'person[s]' and 'individuals.'" She points to the majority of courts that have used the economic unit approach to contend that the bankruptcy court relied on the outlier case of Robinson to "carve[ ] children into fractions" and thus lead to "a contrived result." (Br. for Appellant 23-25.)

We find no error in the bankruptcy court's method of applying the economic unit approach in a manner that accounted for part-time members of the Debtor's household. The cases apart from Robinson that have used the economic unit approach were asked to determine whether an individual who resided full-time with the debtor should be considered part of his or her "household." E.g., Morrison, 443 B.R. at 388 (using the economic unit approach to determine that the boyfriend of a debtor who lived with that boyfriend full-time was a member of the debtor's "household" under § 1325(b)); Jewell, 365 B.R. at 802 (using the economic unit approach to determine whether the debtors' adult daughter and her children, and the debtors' adult son, who resided full-time with the debtors were members of the debtors'"household").[28]

The situation in those cases is not what was presented in Robinson or here, where individuals do not live with the debtor on a full-time basis. See 449 B.R. at 482 (determining whether children who lived part-time with the debtor were part of his "household"). We recognize, as the bankruptcy courts in Robinson and this case have, that dividing individuals into fractional members of a household is less than ideal. At the same time, we recognize that the Debtor's situation is increasingly common in modern American life, and that the number

---

[28] In criticizing the bankruptcy court's application of the fractional economic unit approach, the dissent notes that the bankruptcy court in Jewell "did not treat [the debtors' son] as a fractional member of the household based on the ratio of his parents' [limited financial support] to his total income." Supra, at 37. Jewell did not ever resolve the issue of whether the debtors' son should have been part of the debtors' household because that was not the overarching issue in the case. 365 B.R. at 802 ("Even if this Court agreed . . . that [the son] should be included as a member of the Debtors' household . . . ."). Moreover, each of the individuals at issue in Jewell resided with the debtors full-time, so the bankruptcy court was not faced with the circumstance presented here, where the Debtor has individuals who reside regularly, but only part-time, with her and for whom she provides primary support only during the periods in which they reside with her.

of individuals with a financial relationship to a debtor may well vary depending on the day of the week and other circumstances.[29]

Contrary to the view expressed in the dissenting opinion, this result is consistent with the statutory language precisely because Congress did not define "household" or instruct bankruptcy courts how to make the determination as to a debtor's "household" size. Despite this lack of clear guidance, the bankruptcy court carefully considered the specific financial circumstances of the parties involved, and ably recognized that the Debtor's "household" size fluctuated from two to seven depending on what day or days were used to assess it. Requiring the bankruptcy court to pick between these extremes, which, although conveniently allowing for consideration of "whole" dependents, would also result in an inaccurate financial snapshot that has no basis in reality or the capacity of a debtor to pay creditors. The Code and the economic unit approach are flexible enough to permit the bankruptcy court's conclusion that a composite number best reflected the debtor's true "household" size. To be sure, the bankruptcy court's task was made easier in this case given the parties' stipulations as to the amount of time each child and step-child resided with the Debtor and the financial support the Debtor provides to them.[30] As the dissent points out, such mathematical precision may be more difficult in other cases. That it was possible here does not mean that every bankruptcy court must undertake the same level of precision in future cases. But it seems to us that the better model of § 1325(b)'s analysis is for the bankruptcy court to try to get to the bottom of the debtor's true financial circumstances, rather than merely to ballpark a figure based on the approximate number of "whole" dependents. Such a result would lead to similar under- and over-inclusive problems to those addressed above with respect to the heads-on-beds and income tax dependent methods, while simultaneously eliminating the flexibility and advantages of the economic unit approach. Section 1325(b), and the Code in general, is focused on assessing a debtor's financial obligations and ability to pay creditors; in some cases, it may be necessary for the bankruptcy court--as the court did in this case--to recognize that a debtor has part-time members of the household who can neither be wholly excluded or wholly counted, but should be included for the fraction of time during which they are a part of the debtor's household expenses. Bankruptcy courts are capable of reviewing and making the requisite findings to permit such a determination

---

[29] While both we and the bankruptcy court acknowledge this social shift as a factor in why it may be consistent with the intent of the Code to divide individuals into fractional members of a household, this recognition would not justify the approach used if it were inconsistent with the language Congress used. It is only because we conclude that the statutory text does not preclude this methodology that we recognize that it may be increasingly appropriate to use in light of the rising number of households with part-time residents.

Given the language Congress chose to use and has left undefined, it may be that Congress recognized the bankruptcy court would be in the best position to determine a debtor's "household" size and that a practical, fact-based definition best served the Code's purposes. In either event, Congress did not provide a clear definition such as it has to define terms in other contexts, so we are tasked with assessing whether the bankruptcy court's interpretation is an unreasonable interpretation of the language Congress did use. We conclude it is not.

[30] The dissent may well be correct that the time spent in a debtor's "household" is not always true reflection of how much financial support a debtor provides. But this is not the case here, and that concern is something bankruptcy courts and the parties can argue in an appropriate case in which the economic unit method is applied. Because of the parties' stipulations in this case, however, the bankruptcy court appropriately determined that the one reflected the other.

of a debtor's household size that reflects a just approximation of the debtor's true financial situation.

This result is consistent with the Supreme Court's recognition in Hamilton that bankruptcy courts possess flexibility to look beyond a mechanical application of § 1325(b)'s calculations in order to account for variations readily apparent in the record, even after the BAPCPA. See 130 S. Ct. at 2471-78; see also id. at 2478 ("[W]hen a bankruptcy court calculates a debtor's projected disposable income [under § 1325(b)], the court may account for changes in the debtor's income or expenses that are known or virtually certain at the time of confirmation."). Consistent with that approach, we conclude that the bankruptcy court did not err in recognizing that the Debtor's actual household size fluctuated based on the changing number of part-time members of her household. Nor did the bankruptcy court err in exercising its discretion to accommodate this reality in the debtor's situation by representing the individuals as fractional full-time members of the household and then rounding to a whole number.[31]

III.

Congress did not make determining a debtor's "household" size a straightforward component of his or her disposable income calculation. As discussed above, the Census Bureau's "heads-on-beds" approach is too removed from the purpose of § 1325(b) to be an appropriate measure of a debtor's "household" size. We further conclude that there are significant concerns with the income tax dependent method and the bankruptcy court here was correct not to rely on that approach in this case. Because Congress' intent will most often be best implemented through a definition of "household" that is based on whether individuals operate as a single economic unit and are financially interdependent, we conclude the bankruptcy court did not err in applying this method to determine the Debtor's "household" size. Accordingly, we affirm the order of the bankruptcy court.

WILKINSON, J. DISSENTING. [Omitted.]

Notes and Questions

1. In dissent, Judge Harvey Wilkerson's makes these points: (1) Fractionalizing children is not founded on the text of the Bankruptcy Code. (2) Fractionalizing is never used in defining "dependent" or "individual." (3) Fractionalization is too much work for the overburdened courts.

2. Household expenses will vary according to the number of people in the household. Accordingly, it is relevant that §707(b)(2)(A)(ii)(I) refers to the expenses "for the debtor, the dependents of the debtor, and the spouse of the debtor in a joint case, if the spouse is not otherwise a dependent." In In re Napier, 2006 Bankr LEXIS 2248 (Bankr. D.S.C., September 18, 2006), debtors sought to expand their deductible expenses in a chapter 13 case, but the court ruled that the household, for purposes of choosing the national standards was defined by the number

[31] The bankruptcy court did not explain its decision to round from the fraction of 2.59, which resulted from the calculations of how much time each child and step-child lives with the Debtor, to the round number of three "children" for purposes of § 1325(b). The Debtor does not specifically raise any challenge to this specific component of the bankruptcy court's decision. We find nothing about doing so that conflicts with the Code's provisions and thus do not find that the court abused its discretion in deciding to round off to the nearest whole individual for the purpose of determining a household size that could be cross-referenced to the median family income tables.

of dependents in the household, not the number of persons in the household. The debtors could therefore not claim more expenses due to the presence of boarders in the house. Id,. at *4 ("While the debtor's acts are admirable, debtors should not be allowed to voluntarily put the needs of these non-dependents above the obligations. . . to their unsecured creditors . . . To the extent that the official Form B22C indicates that debtors may include the boarders in the means test calculation, it must yield to the plain language of §707(b)(2) which only allows debtors to include dependents.").

The provision for the National Standards is one of many which invokes the concept of "dependents." 11 U.S.C. §§ 101(10A)(B), §523(a)(2)(C)(II), 524(c)(3)(B), 1114(a), 1225(b)(2)(A), 1325(b)(2)(A), §1329(a)(4). As with "family" and "household," "dependent" is an undefined terms. But §707(b)(2)(A)(ii)(I) contains a clue. The spouse of a debtor is includeable in the household for the purposes of expanding the National Standard deduction if the case is a joint case and "the spouse is not otherwise a dependent." This particular wrinkle suggests that Congress had in mind the Internal Revenue Code definition of dependent. 26 U.S.C. § 152(a). At least where a married couple files a joint return, the spouse cannot be a dependent for tax deduction purposes. 26 U.S.C. § 152(b)(2).

If this clue is followed, the Internal Revenue Code defines two types of dependents: qualifying children and qualifying relatives. 26 U.S.C. § 152(a). Qualifying child means an individual who (i) bears a relationship to the taxpayer, (ii) has the same abode for more than half the year, (iii) is less than 19, 24 (if a student), 26 U.S.C. § 152(c)(3), or any age (if disabled), 26 U.S.C. § 152(c)(3)(B), and (iv) has not provided more than half his own support. 26 U.S.C. § 152(c)(1). "Bears a relationship" means being the child, sub-child, sibling, step-sibling, descendent of a sibling or step-sibling. 26 U.S.C. § 152(c)(2). A hierarchy exists as to who may claim the child, where multiple taxpayers compete for the deduction. 26 U.S.C. § 152(c)(4).

A qualifying relative is one who (i) bears a relationship with the taxpayer, (ii) has less gross income than the exemption amount (currently $3,300). 26 U.S.C. §151(d). (iii) receives from the taxpayer over half of the individual's support, and (iv) is not a qualifying child. 26 U.S.C. § 152(d)(1). "Bears a relationship" means a child, sub-child, sibling, step-sibling, ancestor, step-parent, niece of nephew, close in-law, or any individual living in the household with the taxpayer. 26 U.S.C. § 152(d)(2). Particularly this last point contradicts the holding in Napier supra, if the excluded boarders had virtually no gross income and is supported by the debtor.

Pre-BAPCPA case law has addressed the concept of "dependent." Offspring at college,[1] adult children and the grandchildren,[2] mothers,[3] fathers in nursing homes,[4] and stepchildren[5] have qualified as dependents, whose expenses may be deducted. Stepchildren,[6] grandchildren,[7] mother,[8] fiance and children,[9] girlfriend and her dependents,[10] illegitimate children living with the debtor[11] have been disallowed.

Expenses

3. For the purpose of the means test, net income is discovered by subtracting allowed expenses from gross income. Section 707(b)(2)(A)(ii) incorporates by reference in the Internal

---

[1] In re Smith, 269 B.R. 686, 689-90 (Bankr. W.D. Mo. 2001).

[2] In re Tefertiller, 104 B.R. 513, 515 n.1 (Bankr. N.D. Ga. 1989).

[3] In re Bauer, 307 B.R. 47 (Bankr. D. Idaho 2004) (chapter 13 case); In re Tracy, 66 B.R. 63, 67 (Bankr. D. Md. 1986).

[4] In re Vansickel, 309 B.R. 189, 199 (Bankr. E.D. Va. 2004).

[5] In re Dempton, 182 B.R. 38 (Bankr. W.D. Mo. 1993).

[6] Shulz v. Gano (In re Gano), 2001 Bankr. LEXIS 2167 (Bankr. D. Kan. January 17, 2001); In re Davidoff, 185 Bankr. 631, 635-36 (Bankr. S.D. Fla. 1995) (dismissing where wife received child support payments); In re Beharry, 164 B.R. 396 (Bankr. D. Md. 1986).

[7] In re Richmond, 144 Bankr. 539, 542 (Bankr. W.D. Okla. 1992).

[8] In re Cox, 249 B.R. 29, 32 (Bankr. N.D. Fla. 2000).

[9] In re Cox, 249 B.R. 29, 32 (Bankr. N.D. Fla. 2000).

[10] United States Trustee v. Meler (In re Meler), 295 B.R. 625 (D. Ariz. 2003); In re Mastromarino, 197 B.R. 171, 178 (Bankr. D. Me. 1996) ("This is not a moral judgment, but a legal one. Mastromarino has no obligation to support them. But he is legally obligated to his creditors. To grant such voluntary expenditures priority over existing legal obligations would be to permit Mastromarino unilaterally to subordinate his creditors to his personal lifestyle choices.").

[11] United States Trustee v. Meler (In re Meler), 295 B.R. 625 (D. Ariz. 2003).

Revenue Service Financial Analysis Handbook, which itself is part of the Internal Revenue Service's Internal Revenue Manual. H.R. Rep. No. 109-31 at 13-14 (2005). This handbook can be retrieved on the IRS website. http://www.irs.gov/irm/. It can be retrieved from Lexis under the source "Internal Revenue Manual (IRM)". The purpose of the handbook is to aid IRS tax collectors in assessing how much tax can be extracted from delinquent tax payers. See Internal Revenue Manual 5.15.1.35 ("Making the Collection Decision"). Prior to BAPCPA, the IRS guidelines were informally used to determine expenses in connection with chapter 13's requirement that all disposable income must be dedicated to the plan. In re Beckel, 268 B.R. 179 (Bankr. N.D. Iowa 2001); but see In re DeGross, 277 B.R. 309 (Bankr. M.D. Fla. 2001) (declining to use IRS standards for § 707(b) dismissal).

4. National Standards. National standards cover food, clothing, household supplies, personal care and miscellaneous. The allowable amounts vary according to gross income of the debtor. On B22A, this is an easy amount to fill in. Form B22A Line 19. For instance, a two person household with a gross income of $5834 or more is entitled to deduct $1306. The same household with a gross income of $578 is entitled to deduct $578. The poor are expected to sacrifice more than the rich, in terms of producing disposable income for their benefit. Populists protest this phenomenon. Professor Tabb asks, "Do wealthier people have to eat more?" Charles Jordan Tabb, The Death of Consumer Bankruptcy in the United States?, 18 BANKR. DEV. J. 1, 29 (2001). Of course they do not. They simply require a better grade of claret.

If the debtor shows that it is necessary, she can have an additional 5% of the food and clothing categories as specified by the National Standards of the Internal Revenue Service. Bankruptcy Code § 707(b)(2)(A)(ii)(I). The 5% number is directly retrievable in the IRS National Standards. For a family of two, food and clothing are designated to cost $1000 out of the total $1306 allocable if the household's gross income exceeds $5834, and 5% yields an additional $50 deduction. This claim, however, must be documented, as B22A warns. Form B22A Line 39. Meanwhile, the fact that an extra amount if allowed for documented clothing expense suggests that extra amounts for other expenses, such as gasoline, are not permitted. In re Tranmer, 355 B.R. 234 (Bankr. D. Mont. 2006).

5. D is a homemaker with no income of her own. Her spouse grossed $7,225 a month, well in excess of the median for North Carolina. So D entered $7,225 on Line 16 of B22A. She then estimated her husband's personal expenses at $2,121.45 So Line 18 (her "current monthly income") amounted to $5,103.55. D then used line 16 ($7,225) to calculate allowable living expenses ($5,833), according to the IRS National Standards. Using this deduction, D qualified for chapter 7. The Administrator[12] insisted that D had to use line 18 ($5,103.55) to calculate living expenses

---

[12] North Carolina and Alabama do not participated in the United States trustee program, pending the decision of the judges of those districts to participate in it. Bankruptcy Judges, United States Trustees, and Family Farmer Bankruptcy Act of 1986, § 302(d)(3). The existence of bankruptcy administrators was to terminate on October 1, 1992, but Congress extended this deadline first to October 1, 2002. Act of December 1, 1990, P.L. 101-650, 104 Stat. 5115, § 317(a)(1). In 2000, the deadline was entirely omitted. Federal Courts Improvement Act of 2000, 106 P.L. 518, 114 Stat. 2410 § 501. As a result, bankruptcy administrators still roam the hills of North Carolina and Alabama. See Federal Rules of Bankruptcy Procedure § 9035 History: Ancillary Laws and Directives. Oddly, BAPCPA eliminates bankruptcy administrators from § 1112(b) but freely alludes to them in numerous bankruptcy provisions. Meanwhile, an uncodified statute provides, "A bankruptcy administrator may raise and appear and be heard on any issue in any case under title 11, United States Code, but may not file a plan pursuant to section 1121(c) of such title." Act of December 1, 1990, P.L. 101-650, Title III, § 317h), 104 Stat. 5115. This uncodified law closely resembles Bankruptcy Code § 307, pertaining to the power of United States trustees.

In St. Angelo v. Victoria Farms, Inc., 38 F.3d 1525 (9th Cir. 1994), the United States trustee sought a fee in a chapter 11 case. The debtor resisted on the grounds that the United States trusteeship is unconstitutional, since this institution does not exist in Alabama and North Carolina. The United States Constitution, it seems, requires a uniform national bankruptcy law. The Ninth Circuit permitted the fee but took the trouble to advise those two states that their bankruptcy administrator program was unconstitutional. Congress, however, has chosen to ignore the studied advice of the Ninth Circuit and has perpetuated this unconstitutional regime. See generally Dan J. Shulman, The Constitution, Interest Groups, and the Requirements of Uniformity: The United States Trustee and the Bankruptcy Administrator Programs, 74 NEB. L. REV. 91, 127-29 (1995).

under line 19 ($4,167). Under this assumption, D did not qualify for chapter 7. Who wins? Lynch v. Parrish, 382 B.R. 907 (E.D.N.C. 2008) (D prevails). Delving deeply in to § 707(b)(2)(A)(ii), the Administrator highlighted this language: "and the spouse of the debtor in a joint case." (Note this was not a joint case.) According to the administrator this language refers to income. As a result, D must use joint income (line 16), not just D's income, in finding the properly allowed expenses. In a case of first impression, the court held that "and the spouse of the debtor in a joint case" modified expenses, not income. As a result, D calculated rightly and was entitled to higher expenses. Notice that D's income was net of her spouse's income. But her expenses were not based on her net current income, but on her spouse's gross income. Was the court comparing apples and oranges here?

6. Local standards. Local standards cover housing and transportation. They are not actually in the Manual but are available on the IRS and Department of Justice (United States Trustee) website. To my knowledge, this is the first time the United States Code defers to the fluctuating content of internet websites.

7. Housing. Form B22A Line 20A first bids the debtor to record non-mortgage expenses. This is easily retrieved from the UST website. The Local Standard has two entries, one for "non-mortgage." These are listed by county. In Manhattan (New York County), for example, the amount listed is $632.

B22A line 20B then requires an entry for mortgage/rent. This too is broken out in the Local Standards. Yet § 707(b)(2)(A)(ii)(I) also states that, "[n]otwithstanding any other provision of this clause, the monthly expenses of the debtor shall not include any payment for debts." This overrides the Local Standards with regard to mortgages and car loans. Separately, however, as we shall see, the debtor is permitted average monthly payments to all secured creditors, under § 707(b)(2)(A)(iii)(I). Accordingly, B22A line 20B(b) requires that mortgage payments be subtracted from the Local Standard amount. Numbers below zero are abolished for this purpose. The actual deduction permitted is the difference (if any) between the Local Standards amount and actual mortgage payments.

14. An enhancement is permitted to housing and utilities expense, but only with regard to "actual expenses for home energy costs." 11 U.S.C. § 707(b)(2)(i)(V). The debtor must also show that the additional amount is "reasonable and necessary." This gives an opening for the court to rule that debtors must adjust their thermostats on behalf of their creditors.

If energy costs are to be enhanced, the debtor must know what percentage of non-mortgage expenses are allocable to energy and what part to other expenses. Form B22A gives no help on this allocation question. Form B22A Line 37. Judge Wedoff, however, draws from the Bureau of Labor Statistics (which the IRS uses to devise its National and Local Standards) to suggest that 24% is an appropriate allocation. Eugene R. Wedoff, Means Testing in the New 707(b), 79 AM. BANKR. L.J. 231, 269 (2005).

14. Transportation. The Local Standards permit a debtor to own two cars. Form B22A Line 22. This is so even if the debtor is a single person with no family. So, for the singles, it is possible to maintain a regular car and perhaps a motorcycle for the weekend. In re Casey, 356 B.R. 519 (Bankr. E.D. Wash. 2006) (motorcycles are cars).

There are two types of transportation expenses. The first is "operating costs and public transportation costs." The Local Standards organize this category by region. Within a region, high expense urban areas are singled out for favored treatment. For the Northeast Census Region, New York is designated to include counties in New Jersey, Connecticut and even Pennsylvania, as well as designated counties in New York. Not all New York Counties are listed, however. For example, in Manhattan, allowed transportation expenses are as follows:

No Car	One Car	Two Cars
$313	$402	$484[13]

A resident of, say, Chautauqua County (a rural location) must use the generic regional figure and so does less well:

No Car	One Car	Two Cars
$238	$311	$393

[13] In a joint case, the two debtors with two cars cannot both claim this higher amount but rather must take the lesser combined two-car deduction. In re Lara, 347 B.R. 198, 202-03 (Bankr. N.D. Tex. 2006).

This Local Standard arguably benefits persons who, like myself, who walk to work and own no car. In my case, a deduction of $313 per month substantially exceeds the amount I spend on subway trips and taxis.

Separately, the Local Standards permit a deduction for ownership and lease expenses. Here there is no regional variation. All debtors are allocated $471 for the first car and $332 for the second car. Form B22A Line 23-24 (first and second car). As with home mortgages, the Local Standards for cars is overridden by the admonition in § 707(b)(2)(A)(ii)(I) that, "[n]otwithstanding any other provision of this clause, the monthly expenses of the debtor shall not include any payment for debts." Accordingly, a deduction must be made for scheduled payments on car loans. Again, the negative numbers are abolished for this purpose. As with home mortgages, the debtor will be able to claim the full monthly payment on cars under § 707(a)(iii), covering payments on secured debts. The net result is that car renters are disfavored. If their actual rental payments exceed the local standard, they are not permitted the deduction. But car owners with secured car loans are permitted the deduction.

RANSOM v FIA CARD SERVICES, N.A.

131 S. Ct. 716 (2011)

KAGAN, J.

Chapter 13 of the Bankruptcy Code enables an individual to obtain a discharge of his debts if he pays his creditors a portion of his monthly income in accordance with a court-approved plan. 11 U.S.C. § 1301 et seq. To determine how much income the debtor is capable of paying, Chapter 13 uses a statutory formula known as the "means test." §§ 707(b)(2) (2006 ed. and Supp. III), 1325(b)(3)(A) (2006 ed.). The means test instructs a debtor to deduct specified expenses from his current monthly income. The result is his "disposable income" -- the amount he has available to reimburse creditors. § 1325(b)(2).

This case concerns the specified expense for vehicle-ownership costs. We must determine whether a debtor like petitioner Jason Ransom who owns his car outright, and so does not make loan or lease payments, may claim an allowance for car-ownership costs (thereby reducing the amount he will repay creditors). We hold that the text, context, and purpose of the statutory provision at issue preclude this result. A debtor who does not make loan or lease payments may not take the car-ownership deduction.

I-A

"Congress enacted the Bankruptcy Abuse Prevention and Consumer Protection Act of 2005 (BAPCPA or Act) to correct perceived abuses of the bankruptcy system." Milavetz, Gallop & Milavetz, P. A. v. United States, 559 U.S. 229 (2010)). In particular, Congress adopted the means test -- "[t]he heart of [BAPCPA's] consumer bankruptcy reforms," H. R. Rep. No. 109-31, pt. 1, p. 2 (2005) (hereinafter H. R. Rep.), and the home of the statutory language at issue here -- to help ensure that debtors who can pay creditors do pay them. See, e.g., id. (under BAPCPA, "debtors [will] repay creditors the maximum they can afford").

In Chapter 13 proceedings, the means test provides a formula to calculate a debtor's disposable income, which the debtor must devote to reimbursing creditors under a court-approved plan generally lasting from three to five years.

§§ 1325(b)(1)(B) and (b)(4).[1] The statute defines "disposable income" as "current monthly income" less "amounts reasonably necessary to be expended" for "maintenance or support," business expenditures, and certain charitable contributions. §§ 1325(b)(2)(A)(i) and (ii). For a debtor whose income is above the median for his State, the means test identifies which expenses qualify as "amounts reasonably necessary to be expended." The test supplants the pre-BAPCPA practice of calculating debtors' reasonable expenses on a case-by-case basis, which led to varying and often inconsistent determinations. See, e.g., In re Slusher, 359 B. R. 290, 294 (Bkrtcy. Ct. Nev. 2007).

Under the means test, a debtor calculating his "reasonably necessary" expenses is directed to claim allowances for defined living expenses, as well as for secured and priority debt. §§ 707(b)(2)(A)(ii)-(iv). As relevant here, the statute provides:

> "The debtor's monthly expenses shall be the debtor's applicable monthly expense amounts specified under the National Standards and Local Standards, and the debtor's actual monthly expenses for the categories specified as Other Necessary Expenses issued by the Internal Revenue Service [IRS] for the area in which the debtor resides." § 707(b)(2)(A)(ii)(I).

These are the principal amounts that the debtor can claim as his reasonable living expenses and thereby shield from creditors.

The National and Local Standards referenced in this provision are tables that the IRS prepares listing standardized expense amounts for basic necessities.[2] The IRS uses the Standards to help calculate taxpayers' ability to pay overdue taxes. See 26 U.S.C. § 7122(d)(2). The IRS also prepares supplemental guidelines known as the Collection Financial Standards, which describe how to use the tables and what the amounts listed in them mean.

The Local Standards include an allowance for transportation expenses, divided into vehicle "Ownership Costs" and vehicle "Operating Costs."[3] At the time Ransom filed for bankruptcy, the "Ownership Costs" table appeared as follows:

---

[1] Chapter 13 borrows the means test from Chapter 7, where it is used as a screening mechanism to determine whether a Chapter 7 proceeding is appropriate. Individuals who file for bankruptcy relief under Chapter 7 liquidate their nonexempt assets, rather than dedicate their future income, to repay creditors. See 11 U.S.C. §§ 704(a)(1), 726. If the debtor's Chapter 7 petition discloses that his disposable income as calculated by the means test exceeds a certain threshold, [***9] the petition is presumptively abusive. § 707(b)(2)(A)(i). If the debtor cannot rebut the presumption, the court may dismiss the case or, with the debtor's consent, convert it into a Chapter 13 proceeding. § 707(b)(1).

[2] The National Standards designate allowances for six categories of expenses: (1) food; (2) housekeeping supplies; (3) apparel and services; (4) personal care products and services; (5) out-of-pocket health care costs; and (6) miscellaneous expenses. Internal Revenue Manual § 5.15.1.8 (Oct. 2, 2009), http://www.irs.gov/irm/part5/irm_05-015-001.html#d0e1012 (all Internet materials as visited Jan. 7, 2011, and available in Clerk of Court's case file). The Local Standards authorize deductions for two kinds of expenses: (1) housing and utilities; and (2) transportation. Id., § 5.15.1.9.

[3] Although both components of the transportation allowance are listed in the Local Standards, only the operating-cost expense amounts vary by geography; in contrast, the IRS provides a nationwide figure for ownership costs.

*3*Ownership Costs

National	First Car	Second Car
	$471	$332

App. to Brief for Respondent 5a. The Collection Financial Standards explain that these ownership costs represent "nationwide figures for monthly loan or lease payments," id., at 2a; the numerical amounts listed are "base[d] . . . on the five-year average of new and used car financing data compiled by the Federal Reserve Board," id., at 3a. The Collection Financial Standards further instruct that, in the tax-collection context, "[i]f a taxpayer has no car payment, . . . only the operating costs portion of the transportation standard is used to come up with the allowable transportation expense." Id.

B

Ransom filed for Chapter 13 bankruptcy relief in July 2006. App. 1, 54. Among his liabilities, Ransom itemized over $82,500 in unsecured debt, including a claim held by respondent FIA Card Services, N. A. (FIA). Id., at 41. Among his assets, Ransom listed a 2004 Toyota Camry, valued at $14,000, which he owns free of any debt. Id., at 38, 49, 52.

For purposes of the means test, Ransom reported income of $4,248.56 per month. Id., at 46. He also listed monthly expenses totaling $4,038.01. Id., at 53. In determining those expenses, Ransom claimed a car-ownership deduction of $471 for the Camry, the full amount specified in the IRS's "Ownership Costs" table. Id., at 49. Ransom listed a separate deduction of $338 for car-operating costs. Id. Based on these figures, Ransom had disposable income of $210.55 per month. Id., at 53.

Ransom proposed a 5-year plan that would result in repayment of approximately 25% of his unsecured debt. Id., at 55. FIA objected to confirmation of the plan on the ground that it did not direct all of Ransom's disposable income to unsecured creditors. Id., at 64. In particular, FIA argued that Ransom should not have claimed the car-ownership allowance because he does not make loan or lease payments on his car. Id., at 67. FIA noted that without this allowance, Ransom's disposable income would be $681.55 -- the $210.55 he reported plus the $471 he deducted for vehicle ownership. Id., at 71. The difference over the 60 months of the plan amounts to about $28,000.

C

The Bankruptcy Court denied confirmation of Ransom's plan. App. to Pet. for Cert. 48. The court held that Ransom could deduct a vehicle-ownership expense only "if he is currently making loan or lease payments on that vehicle." Id., at 41.

Ransom appealed to the Ninth Circuit Bankruptcy Appellate Panel, which affirmed. In re Ransom, 380 B. R. 799, 808-809 (2007). The panel reasoned that an "expense [amount] becomes relevant to the debtor (i.e., appropriate or applicable to the debtor) when he or she in fact has such an expense." Id., at 807. "[W]hat is important," the panel noted, "is the payments that debtors actually make, not how many cars they own, because [those] payments . . . are what actually affect their ability to" reimburse unsecured creditors. Id.

The United States Court of Appeals for the Ninth Circuit affirmed. In re

Ransom, 577 F.3d 1026, 1027 (2009). The plain language of the statute, the court held, "does not allow a debtor to deduct an 'ownership cost' . . . that the debtor does not have." Id., at 1030. The court observed that "[a]n 'ownership cost' is not an 'expense' -- either actual or applicable -- if it does not exist, period." Id.

We granted a writ of certiorari to resolve a split of authority over whether a debtor who does not make loan or lease payments on his car may claim the deduction for vehicle-ownership costs.[4] We now affirm the Ninth Circuit's judgment.

II

Our interpretation of the Bankruptcy Code starts "where all such inquiries must begin: with the language of the statute itself." United States v. Ron Pair Enterprises, Inc., 489 U.S. 235, 241 (1989). As noted, the provision of the Code central to the decision of this case states:

> "The debtor's monthly expenses shall be the debtor's applicable monthly expense amounts specified under the National Standards and Local Standards, and the debtor's actual monthly expenses for the categories specified as Other Necessary Expenses issued by the [IRS] for the area in which the debtor resides." § 707(b)(2)(A)(ii)(I).

The key word in this provision is "applicable": A debtor may claim not all, but only "applicable" expense amounts listed in the Standards. Whether Ransom may claim the $471 car-ownership deduction accordingly turns on whether that expense amount is "applicable" to him.

Because the Code does not define "applicable," we look to the ordinary meaning of the term. See, e.g., Hamilton v. Lanning, 130 S. Ct. 2464 (2010)). "Applicable" means "capable of being applied: having relevance" or "fit, suitable, or right to be applied: appropriate." Webster's Third New International Dictionary 105 (2002). See also New Oxford American Dictionary 74 (2d ed. 2005) ("relevant or appropriate"); 1 Oxford English Dictionary 575 (2d ed. 1989) ("[c]apable of being applied" or "[f]it or suitable for its purpose, appropriate"). So an expense amount is "applicable" within the plain meaning of the statute when it is appropriate, relevant, suitable, or fit.

What makes an expense amount "applicable" in this sense (appropriate, relevant, suitable, or fit) is most naturally understood to be its correspondence to an individual debtor's financial circumstances. Rather than authorizing all debtors to take deductions in all listed categories, Congress established a filter: A debtor may claim a deduction from a National or Local Standard table (like "[Car] Ownership Costs") if but only if that deduction is appropriate for him. And a deduction is so appropriate only if the debtor has costs corresponding to the category covered by the table--that is, only if the debtor will incur that kind of expense during the life of the plan. The statute underscores the necessity of making such an individualized determination by referring to "the debtor's

[4] Compare In re Ransom, 577 F.3d 1026, 1027 (CA9 2009) (case below), with In re Washburn, 579 F.3d 934, 935 (CA8 2009) (permitting the allowance), In re Tate, 571 F.3d 423, 424 (CA5 2009) (same), and In re Ross-Tousey, 549 F.3d 1148, 1162 (CA7 2008) (same). The question has also divided bankruptcy courts. See, e.g., In re Canales, 377 B. R. 658, 662 (Bkrtcy. Ct. CD Cal. 2007) (citing dozens of cases reaching opposing results).

applicable monthly expense amounts," § 707(b)(2)(A)(ii)(I) (emphasis added)--in other words, the expense amounts applicable (appropriate, etc.) to each particular debtor. Identifying these amounts requires looking at the financial situation of the debtor and asking whether a National or Local Standard table is relevant to him.

If Congress had not wanted to separate in this way debtors who qualify for an allowance from those who do not, it could have omitted the term "applicable" altogether. Without that word, all debtors would be eligible to claim a deduction for each category listed in the Standards. Congress presumably included "applicable" to achieve a different result. See Leocal v. Ashcroft, 543 U.S. 1, 12 (2004) ("[W]e must give effect to every word of a statute wherever possible"). Interpreting the statute to require a threshold determination of eligibility ensures that the term "applicable" carries meaning, as each word in a statute should.

This reading of "applicable" also draws support from the statutory context. The Code initially defines a debtor's disposable income as his "current monthly income . . . less amounts reasonably necessary to be expended." § 1325(b)(2) (emphasis added). The statute then instructs that "[a]mounts reasonably necessary to be expended . . . shall be determined in accordance with" the means test. § 1325(b)(3). Because Congress intended the means test to approximate the debtor's reasonable expenditures on essential items, a debtor should be required to qualify for a deduction by actually incurring an expense in the relevant category. If a debtor will not have a particular kind of expense during his plan, an allowance to cover that cost is not "reasonably necessary" within the meaning of the statute.[5]

Finally, consideration of BAPCPA's purpose strengthens our reading of the term "applicable." Congress designed the means test to measure debtors' disposable income and, in that way, "to ensure that [they] repay creditors the maximum they can afford." H. R. Rep., at 2. This purpose is best achieved by interpreting the means test, consistent with the statutory text, to reflect a debtor's ability to afford repayment. Cf. Hamilton, 130 S. Ct. 2476 (rejecting an interpretation of the Bankruptcy Code that "would produce [the] senseless resul[t]" of "deny[ing] creditors payments that the debtor could easily make"). Requiring a debtor to incur the kind of expenses for which he claims a means-test deduction thus advances BAPCPA's objectives.

Because we conclude that a person cannot claim an allowance for vehicle-ownership costs unless he has some expense falling within that category, the question in this case becomes: What expenses does the vehicle-ownership category cover? If it covers loan and lease payments alone, Ransom does not qualify, because he has no such expense. Only if that category also covers other costs associated with having a car would Ransom be entitled to this deduction.

The less inclusive understanding is the right one: The ownership category encompasses the costs of a car loan or lease and nothing more. As noted earlier, the numerical amounts listed in the "Ownership Costs" table are "base[d] . . . on

[5] This interpretation also avoids the anomalous result of granting preferential treatment to individuals with above-median income. Because the means test does not apply to Chapter 13 debtors whose incomes are below the median, those debtors must prove on a case-by-case basis that each claimed expense is reasonably necessary. See §§ 1325(b)(2) and (3). If a below-median-income debtor cannot take a deduction for a nonexistent expense, we doubt Congress meant to provide such an allowance to an above-median-income debtor -- the very kind of debtor whose perceived abuse of the bankruptcy system inspired Congress to enact the means test.

the five-year average of new and used car financing data compiled by the Federal Reserve Board." App. to Brief for Respondent 3a. In other words, the sum $471 is the average monthly payment for loans and leases nationwide; it is not intended to estimate other conceivable expenses associated with maintaining a car. The Standards do account for those additional expenses, but in a different way: They are mainly the province of the separate deduction for vehicle "Operating Costs," which include payments for "[v]ehicle insurance, . . . maintenance, fuel, state and local registration, required inspection, parking fees, tolls, [and] driver's license." Internal Revenue Manual §§ 5.15.1.7 and 5.15.1.8 (May 1, 2004), reprinted in App. to Brief for Respondent 16a, 20a; see also IRS, Collection Financial Standards (Feb. 19, 2010), http://www.irs.gov/individuals/article/0, id=96543,00.html.[6] A person who owns a car free and clear is entitled to claim the "Operating Costs" deduction for all these expenses of driving -- and Ransom in fact did so, to the tune of $338. But such a person is not entitled to claim the "Ownership Costs" deduction, because that allowance is for the separate costs of a car loan or lease.

The Collection Financial Standards -- the IRS's explanatory guidelines to the National and Local Standards -- explicitly recognize this distinction between ownership and operating costs, making clear that individuals who have a car but make no loan or lease payments may claim only the operating allowance. App. to Brief for Respondent 3a; see supra, at 4. Although the statute does not incorporate the IRS's guidelines, courts may consult this material in interpreting the National and Local Standards; after all, the IRS uses those tables for a similar purpose -- to determine how much money a delinquent taxpayer can afford to pay the Government. The guidelines of course cannot control if they are at odds with the statutory language. But here, the Collection Financial Standards' treatment of the car-ownership deduction reinforces our conclusion that, under the statute, a debtor seeking to claim this deduction must make some loan or lease payments.[7]

Because Ransom owns his vehicle free and clear of any encumbrance, he incurs no expense in the "Ownership Costs" category of the Local Standards. Accordingly, the car-ownership expense amount is not "applicable" to him, and the Ninth Circuit correctly denied that deduction.

III

Ransom's argument to the contrary relies on a different interpretation of the key word "applicable," an objection to our view of the scope of the "Ownership Costs" category, and a criticism of the policy implications of our

---

[6] In addition, the IRS has categorized taxes, including those associated with car ownership, as an "Other Necessary Expens[e]," for which a debtor may take a deduction. See App. to Brief for Respondent 26a; Brief for United States as Amicus Curiae 16, n. 4.

[7] Because the dissent appears to misunderstand our use of the Collection Financial Standards, and because it may be important for future cases to be clear on this point, we emphasize again that the statute does not "incorporat[e]" or otherwise "impor[t]" the IRS's guidance. Post, at 1, 4 (opinion of SCALIA, J.). The dissent questions what possible basis except incorporation could justify our consulting the IRS's view, post, at 4, n., but we think that basis obvious: The IRS creates the National and Local Standards referenced in the statute, revises them as it deems necessary, and uses them every day. The agency might, therefore, have something insightful and persuasive (albeit not controlling) to say about them.

approach. We do not think these claims persuasive.

A

Ransom first offers another understanding of the term "applicable." A debtor, he says, determines his "applicable" deductions by locating the box in each National or Local Standard table that corresponds to his geographic location, income, family size, or number of cars. Under this approach, a debtor "consult[s] the table[s] alone" to determine his appropriate expense amounts. Reply Brief for Petitioner 16. Because he has one car, Ransom argues that his "applicable" allowance is the sum listed in the first column of the "Ownership Costs" table ($471); if he had a second vehicle, the amount in the second column ($332) would also be "applicable." On this approach, the word "applicable" serves a function wholly internal to the tables; rather than filtering out debtors for whom a deduction is not at all suitable, the term merely directs each debtor to the correct box (and associated dollar amount of deduction) within every table.

This alternative reading of "applicable" fails to comport with the statute's text, context, or purpose. As intimated earlier, Ransom's interpretation would render the term "applicable" superfluous. Assume Congress had omitted that word and simply authorized a deduction of "the debtor's monthly expense amounts" specified in the Standards. That language, most naturally read, would direct each debtor to locate the box in every table corresponding to his location, income, family size, or number of cars and to deduct the amount stated. In other words, the language would instruct the debtor to use the exact approach Ransom urges. The word "applicable" is not necessary to accomplish that result; it is necessary only for the different purpose of dividing debtors eligible to make use of the tables from those who are not. Further, Ransom's reading of "applicable" would sever the connection between the means test and the statutory provision it is meant to implement -- the authorization of an allowance for (but only for) "reasonably necessary" expenses. Expenses that are wholly fictional are not easily thought of as reasonably necessary. And finally, Ransom's interpretation would run counter to the statute's overall purpose of ensuring that debtors repay creditors to the extent they can -- here, by shielding some $28,000 that he does not in fact need for loan or lease payments.

As against all this, Ransom argues that his reading is necessary to account for the means test's distinction between "applicable" and "actual" expenses -- more fully stated, between the phrase "applicable monthly expense amounts" specified in the Standards and the phrase "actual monthly expenses for . . . Other Necessary Expenses." § 707(b)(2)(A)(ii)(I) (emphasis added). The latter phrase enables a debtor to deduct his actual expenses in particular categories that the IRS designates relating mainly to taxpayers' health and welfare. Internal Revenue Manual § 5.15.1.10(1), http://www.irs.gov/irm/part5/ irm_05-015-001.html#d0e1381. According to Ransom, "applicable" cannot mean the same thing as "actual." Brief for Petitioner 40. He thus concludes that "an 'applicable' expense can be claimed [under the means test] even if no 'actual' expense was incurred." Id.

Our interpretation of the statute, however, equally avoids conflating "applicable" with "actual" costs. Although the expense amounts in the Standards apply only if the debtor incurs the relevant expense, the debtor's out-of-pocket cost may well not control the amount of the deduction. If a debtor's actual expenses exceed the amounts listed in the tables, for example, the debtor may claim an allowance only for the specified sum, rather than for his real expenditures.[8] For the Other Necessary Expense categories, by contrast, the debtor may deduct his actual expenses, no matter how high they are. [9] Our reading of the means test thus gives full effect to "the distinction between 'applicable' and 'actual' without taking a further step to conclude that 'applicable' means 'nonexistent.'" In re Ross-Tousey, 368 B. R. 762, 765 (Bkrtcy. Ct. ED Wis. 2007), rev'd, 549 F.3d 1148 (CA7 2008).

Finally, Ransom's reading of "applicable" may not even answer the essential question: whether a debtor may claim a deduction. "[C]onsult[ing] the table[s] alone" to determine a debtor's deduction, as Ransom urges us to do, Reply Brief for Petitioner 16, often will not be sufficient because the tables are not self-defining. This case provides a prime example. The "Ownership Costs" table features two columns labeled "First Car" and "Second Car." See supra, at 4. Standing alone, the table does not specify whether it refers to the first and second cars owned (as Ransom avers), or the first and second cars for which the debtor incurs ownership costs (as FIA maintains) -- and so the table does not resolve the issue in dispute.[10] See In re Kimbro, 389 B. R. 518, 533 (Bkrtcy. App. Panel CA6 2008) (Fulton, J., dissenting) ("[O]ne cannot really 'just look up' dollar amounts in the tables without either referring to IRS guidelines for using the tables or imposing pre-existing assumptions about how [they] are to be navigated" (footnote omitted)). Some amount of interpretation is necessary to decide what the deduction is for and whether it is applicable to Ransom; and so we are brought back full circle to our prior analysis.

[8] The parties and the Solicitor General as amicus curiae dispute the proper deduction for a debtor who has expenses that are lower than the amounts listed in the Local Standards. Ransom argues that a debtor may claim the specified expense amount in full regardless of his out-of-pocket costs. Brief for Petitioner 24-27. The Government concurs with this view, provided (as we require) that a debtor has some expense relating to the deduction. See Brief for United States as Amicus Curiae 19-21. FIA, relying on the IRS's practice, contends to the contrary that a debtor may claim only his actual expenditures in this circumstance. Brief for Respondent 12, 45-46 (arguing that the Local Standards function as caps). We decline to resolve this issue. Because Ransom incurs no ownership expense at all, the car-ownership allowance is not applicable to him in the first instance. Ransom is therefore not entitled to a deduction under either approach.

[9] For the same reason, the allowance for "applicable monthly expense amounts" at issue here differs from the additional allowances that the dissent cites for the deduction of actual expenditures. See post, at 3-4 (noting allowances for "actual expenses" for care of an elderly or chronically ill household member, § 707(b)(2)(A)(ii)(II), and for home energy costs, § 707(b)(2)(A)(ii)(V)).

[10] The interpretive problem is not, as the dissent suggests, "whether to claim a deduction for one car or for two," post, at 3, but rather whether to claim a deduction for any car that is owned if the debtor has no ownership costs. Indeed, if we had to decide this question on the basis of the table alone, we might well decide that a debtor who does not make loan or lease payments cannot claim an allowance. The table, after all, is titled "Ownership Costs" -- suggesting that it applies to those debtors who incur such costs. And as noted earlier, the dollar amounts in the table represent average automobile loan and lease payments nationwide (with all other car-related expenses approximated in the separate "Operating Costs" table). See supra, at 9-10. Ransom himself concedes that not every debtor falls within the terms of this table; he would exclude, and thus prohibit from taking a deduction, a person who does not own a car. Brief for Petitioner 33. In like manner, the four corners of the table appear to exclude an additional group -- debtors like Ransom who own their cars free and clear and so do not make the loan or lease payments that constitute "Ownership Costs."

B

Ransom next argues that viewing the car-ownership deduction as covering no more than loan and lease payments is inconsistent with a separate sentence of the means test that provides: "Notwithstanding any other provision of this clause, the monthly expenses of the debtor shall not include any payments for debts." § 707(b)(2)(A)(ii)(I). The car-ownership deduction cannot comprise only loan and lease payments, Ransom contends, because those payments are always debts. See Brief for Petitioner 28, 44-45.

Ransom ignores that the "notwithstanding" sentence governs the full panoply of deductions under the National and Local Standards and the Other Necessary Expense categories. We hesitate to rely on that general provision to interpret the content of the car-ownership deduction because Congress did not draft the former with the latter specially in mind; any friction between the two likely reflects only a lack of attention to how an across-the-board exclusion of debt payments would correspond to a particular IRS allowance.[11] Further, the "notwithstanding" sentence by its terms functions only to exclude, and not to authorize, deductions. It cannot establish an allowance for non-loan or -lease ownership costs that no National or Local Standard covers. Accordingly, the "notwithstanding" sentence does nothing to alter our conclusion that the "Ownership Costs" table does not apply to a debtor whose car is not encumbered.

C

Ransom finally contends that his view of the means test is necessary to avoid senseless results not intended by Congress. At the outset, we note that the policy concerns Ransom emphasizes pale beside one his reading creates: His interpretation, as we have explained, would frustrate BAPCPA's core purpose of ensuring that debtors devote their full disposable income to repaying creditors. See supra, at 8-9. We nonetheless address each of Ransom's policy arguments in turn.

Ransom first points out a troubling anomaly: Under our interpretation, "[d]ebtors can time their bankruptcy filing to take place while they still have a few car payments left, thus retaining an ownership deduction which they would lose if they filed just after making their last payment." Brief for Petitioner 54. Indeed, a debtor with only a single car payment remaining, Ransom notes, is eligible to claim a monthly ownership deduction. Id., at 15, 52.

But this kind of oddity is the inevitable result of a standardized formula like the means test, even more under Ransom's reading than under ours. Such formulas are by their nature over- and under-inclusive. In eliminating the pre-BAPCPA case-by-case adjudication of above-median-income debtors' expenses, on the ground that it leant itself to abuse, Congress chose to tolerate the occasional peculiarity that a brighter-line test produces. And Ransom's alternative reading of the statute would spawn its own anomalies -- even placing to one side the fundamental strangeness of giving a debtor an allowance for loan

---

[11] Because Ransom does not make payments on his car, we need not and do not resolve how the "notwithstanding" sentence affects the vehicle-ownership deduction when a debtor has a loan or lease expense. See Brief for United States as Amicus Curiae 23, n. 5 (offering alternative views on this question); Tr. of Oral Arg. 51-52.

or lease payments when he has not a penny of loan or lease costs. On Ransom's view, for example, a debtor entering bankruptcy might purchase for a song a junkyard car -- "an old, rusted pile of scrap metal [that would] si[t] on cinder blocks in his backyard," In re Brown, 376 B. R. 601, 607 (Bkrtcy. Ct. SD Tex. 2007) -- in order to deduct the $471 car-ownership expense and reduce his payment to creditors by that amount. We do not see why Congress would have preferred that result to the one that worries Ransom. That is especially so because creditors may well be able to remedy Ransom's "one payment left" problem. If car payments cease during the life of the plan, just as if other financial circumstances change, an unsecured creditor may move to modify the plan to increase the amount the debtor must repay. See 11 U.S.C. § 1329(a)(1).

Ransom next contends that denying the ownership allowance to debtors in his position "sends entirely the wrong message, namely, that it is advantageous to be deeply in debt on motor vehicle loans, rather than to pay them off." Brief for Petitioner 55. But the choice here is not between thrifty savers and profligate borrowers, as Ransom would have it. Money is fungible: The $14,000 that Ransom spent to purchase his Camry outright was money he did not devote to paying down his credit card debt, and Congress did not express a preference for one use of these funds over the other. Further, Ransom's argument mistakes what the deductions in the means test are meant to accomplish. Rather than effecting any broad federal policy as to saving or borrowing, the deductions serve merely to ensure that debtors in bankruptcy can afford essential items. The car-ownership allowance thus safeguards a debtor's ability to retain a car throughout the plan period. If the debtor already owns a car outright, he has no need for this protection.

Ransom finally argues that a debtor who owns his car free and clear may need to replace it during the life of the plan; "[g]ranting the ownership cost deduction to a vehicle that is owned outright," he states, "accords best with economic reality." Id., at 52. In essence, Ransom seeks an emergency cushion for car owners. But nothing in the statute authorizes such a cushion, which all debtors presumably would like in the event some unexpected need arises. And a person who enters bankruptcy without any car at all may also have to buy one during the plan period; yet Ransom concedes that a person in this position cannot claim the ownership deduction. Tr. of Oral Arg. 20. The appropriate way to account for unanticipated expenses like a new vehicle purchase is not to distort the scope of a deduction, but to use the method that the Code provides for all Chapter 13 debtors (and their creditors): modification of the plan in light of changed circumstances. See § 1329(a)(1); see also supra, at 17.

IV

Based on BAPCPA's text, context, and purpose, we hold that the Local Standard expense amount for transportation "Ownership Costs" is not "applicable" to a debtor who will not incur any such costs during his bankruptcy plan. Because the "Ownership Costs" category covers only loan and lease payments and because Ransom owns his car free from any debt or obligation, he may not claim the allowance. In short, Ransom may not deduct loan or lease expenses when he does not have any. We therefore affirm the judgment of the Ninth Circuit.

SCALIA, J. DISSENTING. I would reverse the judgment of the Ninth Circuit. I agree with the conclusion of the three other Courts of Appeals to address the question: that a debtor who owns a car free and clear is entitled to the car-ownership allowance. See In re Washburn, 579 F.3d 934 (CA8 2009); In re Tate, 571 F.3d 423 (CA5 2009); In re Ross-Tousey, 549 F.3d 1148 (CA7 2008).

The statutory text at issue is the phrase enacted in the Bankruptcy Abuse Prevention and Consumer Protection Act of 2005 (BAPCPA), "applicable monthly expense amounts specified under the National Standards and Local Standards," 11 U.S.C. § 707(b)(2)(A)(ii)(I). The Court holds that the word "applicable" in this provision imports into the Local Standards a directive in the Internal Revenue Service's Collection Financial Standards, which have as their stated purpose "to help determine a taxpayer's ability to pay a delinquent tax liability," App. to Brief for Respondent 1a. That directive says that "[i]f a taxpayer has no car payment," the Ownership Cost provisions of the Local Standards will not apply. Id., at 3a.

That directive forms no part of the Local Standards to which the statute refers; and the fact that portions of the Local Standards are to be disregarded for revenue-collection purposes says nothing about whether they are to be disregarded for purposes of Chapter 13 of the Bankruptcy Code. The Court believes, however, that unless the IRS's Collection Financial Standards are imported into the Local Standards, the word "applicable" would do no work, violating the principle that "'we must give effect to every word of a statute wherever possible.'" Ante, at 8 (quoting Leocal v. Ashcroft, 543 U.S. 1, 12 (2004)). I disagree. The canon against superfluity is not a canon against verbosity. When a thought could have been expressed more concisely, one does not always have to cast about for some additional meaning to the word or phrase that could have been dispensed with. This has always been understood. A House of Lords opinion holds, for example, that in the phrase "'in addition to and not in derogation of'" the last part adds nothing but emphasis. Davies v. Powell Duffryn Associated Collieries, Ltd., [1942] A. C. 601, 607.

It seems to me that is the situation here. To be sure, one can say "according to the attached table"; but it is acceptable (and indeed I think more common) to say "according to the applicable provisions of the attached table." That seems to me the fairest reading of "applicable monthly expense amounts specified under the National Standards and Local Standards." That is especially so for the Ownership Costs portion of the Local Standards, which had no column titled "No Car." Here the expense amount would be that shown for one car (which is all the debtor here owned) rather than that shown for two cars; and it would be no expense amount if the debtor owned no car, since there is no "applicable" provision for that on the table. For operating and public transportation costs, the "applicable" amount would similarly be the amount provided by the Local Standards for the geographic region in which the debtor resides. (The debtor would not first be required to prove that he actually operates the cars that he owns, or, if does not own a car, that he actually uses public transportation.) The Court claims that the tables "are not self-defining," and that "[s]ome amount of interpretation" is necessary in choosing whether to claim a deduction at all, for one car, or for two. Ante, at 14-15. But this problem seems to me more metaphysical than practical. The point of the statutory language is to entitle debtors who own cars to an ownership deduction, and I have little doubt that debtors will be able to choose correctly whether to claim a deduction for one car or for two.

If the meaning attributed to the word by the Court were intended, it would have been most precise to say "monthly expense amounts specified under the National Standards and Local Standards, if applicable for IRS collection purposes." And even if utter precision was too much to expect, it would at least have been more natural to say "monthly expense amounts specified under the National Standards and Local Standards, if applicable." That would make it clear that amounts specified under those Standards may nonetheless not be applicable, justifying (perhaps) resort to some source other than the Standards themselves to give meaning to the condition. The very next paragraph of the Bankruptcy Code uses that formulation ("if applicable") to limit to actual expenses the deduction for care of an elderly or chronically ill household member: "[T]he debtor's monthly expenses may include, if applicable, the continuation of actual expenses paid by the debtor that are reasonable and necessary" for that purpose. 11 U.S.C. § 707(b)(2)(A)(ii)(II) (emphasis added).

Elsewhere as well, the Code makes it very clear when prescribed deductions are limited to actual expenditures. Section 707(b)(2)(A)(ii)(I) itself authorizes deductions for a host of expenses -- health and disability insurance, for example -- only to the extent that they are "actual . . . expenses" that are "reasonably necessary." Additional deductions for energy are allowed, but again only if they are "actual expenses" that are "reasonable and necessary." § 707(b)(2)(A)(ii)(V). Given the clarity of those limitations to actual outlays, it seems strange for Congress to limit the car-ownership deduction to the somewhat peculiar category "cars subject to any amount whatever of outstanding indebtedness" by the mere word "applicable," meant as incorporation of a limitation that appears in instructions to IRS agents.[12]

I do not find the normal meaning of the text undermined by the fact that it produces a situation in which a debtor who owes no payments on his car nonetheless gets the operating-expense allowance. For the Court's more strained interpretation still produces a situation in which a debtor who owes only a single remaining payment on his car gets the full allowance. As for the Court's imagined horrible in which "a debtor entering bankruptcy might purchase for a song a junkyard car," ante, at 17: That is fairly matched by the imagined horrible that, under the Court's scheme, a debtor entering bankruptcy might purchase a junkyard car for a song plus a $10 promissory note payable over several years. He would get the full ownership expense deduction.

Thus, the Court's interpretation does not, as promised, maintain "the connection between the means test and the statutory provision it is meant to implement -- the authorization of an allowance for (but only for) 'reasonably necessary' expenses," ante, at 12. Nor do I think this difficulty is eliminated by the deus ex machina of 11 U.S.C. § 1329(a)(1), which according to the Court would allow an unsecured creditor to "move to modify the plan to increase the amount the debtor must repay," ante, at 17. Apart from the fact that, as a practical

[12] The Court protests that I misunderstand its use of the Collection Financial Standards. Its opinion does not, it says, find them to be incorporated by the Bankruptcy Code; they simply "reinforc[e] our conclusion that . . . a debtor seeking to claim this deduction must make some loan or lease payments." Ante, at 10. True enough, the opinion says that the Bankruptcy Code "does not incorporate the IRS's guidelines," but it immediately continues that "courts may consult this material in interpreting the National and Local Standards" so long as it is not "at odds with the statutory language." Ibid. In the present context, the real-world difference between finding the guidelines incorporated and finding it appropriate to consult them escapes me, since I can imagine no basis for consulting them unless Congress meant them to be consulted, which would mean they are incorporated. And without incorporation, they are at odds with the statutory language, which otherwise contains no hint that eligibility for a Car Ownership deduction requires anything other than ownership of a car.

matter, the sums involved would hardly make this worth the legal costs, allowing such ongoing revisions of matters specifically covered by the rigid means test would return us to "the pre-BAPCPA case-by-case adjudication of above-median-income debtors' expenses," ante, at 16. If the BAPCPA had thought such adjustments necessary, surely it would have taken the much simpler and more logical step of providing going in that the ownership expense allowance would apply only so long as monthly payments were due.

The reality is, to describe it in the Court's own terms, that occasional overallowance (or, for that matter, underallowance) "is the inevitable result of a standardized formula like the means test . . . . Congress chose to tolerate the occasional peculiarity that a brighter-line test produces." Id. Our job, it seems to me, is not to eliminate or reduce those "oddit[ies]," id., but to give the formula Congress adopted its fairest meaning. In my judgment the "applicable monthly expense amounts" for operating costs "specified under the . . . Local Standards," are the amounts specified in those Standards for either one car or two cars, whichever of those is applicable.

Notes and Questions

1. Ransom is a chapter 13 case, but it interprets the meaning of § 707(b)(2)(A)(ii)(I), which permits debtor's to deduct "applicable" car ownership costs.

2. The debtor in Ransom claimed a $471 ownership expense (as set forth the the IRS manual) but in actuality had zero expense. Suppose the debtor had only a $1 expense. Could he claim all $471 or only $1?

3. The issue of deductions when D owns the car outright is of the highest significance. Two commentators predict that this one issue alone will have a 50% impact on debtors' ability to survive a means test challenge. Marianne B. Culhane & Michaela M. White, Catching Can-Pay Debtors: Is the Means Test the Only Way, 13 AM. BANKR. INST. L. REV. 665, 676 (2005).

4. As with cars, some people have no rent or mortgage expense. Some courts have allowed the housing deduction under the Local Standard under these conditions. In re Farrar-Johnson, 353 B.R. 224 (Bankr. N.D. Ill. 2006) (debtors lived free in military housing). Ransom, supra, clearly implies that the housing deduction is not "applicable" to the debtor and cannot be claimed. According to § 707(b)(2)(A)(ii)(I), the debtor is entitled to "applicable monthly expense amounts specified under the. . . Local Standards . . . " (emphasis added).

KRAWCZYK v LYNCH

2013 U.S. Dist LEXIS 138591 (E.D.N.C. June 17, 2013)

FLANAGAN, J.

This matter comes before the court on appeal by debtors John and Michelle Krawczyk ("appellants"), from an order of the bankruptcy court entered July 27, 2012, granting the motion to dismiss of Bankruptcy Administrator, Marjorie K. Lynch ("appellee"), based on a presumption of abuse pursuant to 11 U.S.C. § 707(b). The matter is fully briefed and the issues presented are ripe for ruling.[13]

BACKGROUND

On December 20, 2011, appellants filed a voluntary petition for relief

[13] Although appellee requested oral argument in advance of the court's ruling, the court dispenses with oral argument because the facts and legal contentions are adequately presented in the materials before this court and argument would not aid the decisional process.

under Chapter 7 of the Bankruptcy Code. In connection with the petition, appellants filed schedules and statements, which included itemizations of assets, liabilities, income, and expenditures. In pertinent part, appellants identified (1) an ownership interest in three properties (Schedule A), (2) five separate secured debts relating to these three properties (Schedule D), (3) no current or projected monthly expenses related to secured debt payments on these three properties (Schedule J), (3) and a "means test" calculation (Form B22A), listing deductions from current monthly income for future payments on secured claims related to these three properties. At the same time, appellants filed a statement of intention to surrender their interest in these three properties.

On February 29, 2012, appellee filed a motion to dismiss, arguing that deductions from current monthly income for secured debt payments in the means test calculation were improper because they related to property appellants intended to surrender. Removing the improper deductions, appellee argued, would result in the means test calculating 60 month disposable income of positive $354,554.40, instead of negative $204,551.40, as asserted by debtors, thus triggering a presumption of abuse under the bankruptcy code. Appellants filed a memorandum of law in opposition to the motion to dismiss, arguing, as they do on appeal, that the means test allows Chapter 7 debtors to deduct secured debt payment on properties that they intend to surrender. Accordingly, appellants argued, the means test calculation resulting in disposable income of negative $204,551.40 was proper, and no presumption of abuse is triggered.

On July 9, 2012, the bankruptcy court held a hearing on appellee's motion to dismiss. During the hearing, appellants confirmed that their Schedule J includes no expense related to secured debt payments on their real property. Appellants also confirmed that they had no intention to keep their real property, and they had not made any secured debt payments on their real property since August, 2010. (Id. 17-23). In addition, one of the properties was foreclosed upon prior to the bankruptcy filing.

On July 27, 2012, the bankruptcy court entered an order granting appellee's motion to dismiss. In pertinent part, the court concluded that appellants improperly listed deductions for secured debt payments where appellants had not made payments on their real property since 2010 and do not intend to make payments again. While the bankruptcy court recognized that this court previously had interpreted the means test to allow an expense deduction where a debtor intends to surrender collateral, the bankruptcy court noted that recent Supreme Court and Fourth Circuit cases now shed new light on the issues raised. The bankruptcy court also found persuasive a more recent decision of the bankruptcy court, analyzing the recent Supreme Court and Fourth Circuit precedent. On August 21, 2012, the bankruptcy court granted appellants' motion for stay of the dismissal order pending this appeal.

Discussion

... Under 11 U.S.C. § 707(b), the bankruptcy court may dismiss a Chapter 7 bankruptcy case, or convert it to a Chapter 13 case with the debtor's consent, "if it finds that the granting of relief would be an abuse of the provisions of [Chapter 7]." 11 U.S.C. § 707(b)(1). In considering whether granting of relief would be an abuse of Chapter 7 provisions, "the court shall presume abuse exists" if the debtor's "current monthly income" exceeds a statutory minimum amount, under a mathematical formula in the statute known as the "means test." §

707(b)(2)(A); Ransom v. FIA Card Services, N.A., 131 S.Ct. 716, 721 (2011). The means test requires the court to deduct specified categories of expenses as set forth in the statute from the debtor's current monthly income. See id. As pertinent here, the means test provides a deduction for "[t]he debtor's average monthly payments on account of secured debts," which "shall be calculated as . . . the total of all amounts scheduled as contractually due to secured creditors in each month of the 60 months following the date of the filing of the petition. . . . divided by 60." 11 U.S.C. § 707(b)(2)(A)(iii).

The issue in this case is whether appellants are entitled to a deduction for "average monthly payments on account of secured debts" where appellants intend to surrender the collateral securing the debt and appellants did not make for ten months, and will not make again in the future, any payments on the debt. Appellants argue that the deduction applies by virtue of the language of the means test, the purposes underlying the means test, and policy considerations, regardless of the debtors' stated intention to surrender the collateral and never make payments again. Appellee argues that the bankruptcy court properly determined appellants were not entitled to the deduction, in light of recent Fourth Circuit and Supreme Court law shedding light on the proper interpretation of the means test.

The court recognizes that the issue presented on appeal has been encountered by this court before, and that there is a sharp division of authority between courts that have allowed the deduction despite a debtor's stated intention to surrender collateral, and those that have not.[14] Following recent Supreme Court and Fourth Circuit cases, however, which were decided after this court's earlier ruling on this issue, the court finds reason to revisit application of the deduction under the circumstances presented here.

The court's "interpretation of the Bankruptcy Code starts where all such inquiries must begin: with the language of the statute itself." Ransom, 131 S.Ct. at 723 (quotations omitted). "[W]hen the statute's language is plain, the sole function of the courts -- at least where the disposition required by the text is not absurd -- is to enforce it according to its terms." Lamie v. U.S. Trustee, 540 U.S. 526, 534 (2004). Where, by contrast, the statute "lends itself to more than one reasonable interpretation, and thus does not have a 'plain' meaning," the court must look to other factors bearing on the meaning of the text. In re Maharaj, 681 F.3d 558, 568-70 (4th Cir. 2012). The court must "find that interpretation which can most fairly be said to be imbedded in the statute, in the sense of being most harmonious with its scheme and with the general purposes that Congress manifested." Comm'r of Internal Rev. v. Engle, 464 U.S. 206, 217 (1984).

For example, in In re Maharaj, the Fourth Circuit recently addressed the interpretation of two provisions in the Bankruptcy Code, §§ 1115 and § 1129(b)(2)(B)(ii), as amended by Bankruptcy Abuse Prevention and Consumer Protection Act of 2005 (BAPCA), related to property included in the bankruptcy estate. Noting that "the courts that have considered this issue have arrived at plausible, competing arguments as to why their respective approaches are consistent with Congressional purpose in enacting BAPCPA," the court first held

[14] Compare, for example, In re Rivers, 466 B.R. 558 (Bankr. M.D. Fla. 2012) (allowing deduction); Lynch v. Haenke, 395 B.R. 346 (E.D.N.C. 2008) (same, collecting caes), with In re Sterrenberg, 471 B.R. 131 (Bankr. E.D.N.C. 2012) (not allowing deduction, collecting cases); In re Fredman, 471 B.R. 540 (Bankr. S.D. Ill. 2012) (same).

that the language at issue was ambiguous because it was susceptible to more than one reasonable interpretation. Maharaj, 681 F.3d at 569. The court then looked "to the specific context in which that language is used, and the broader context of the statute as a whole," as well as canons of statutory construction, and the purpose of the statute, in determining the proper interpretation of the statutory text. See Maharaj, 681 F.3d at 570-575.

The provision at issue in this case, which also resulted from BAPCA amendments, is ambiguous in several respects. First, the term "scheduled" is susceptible to more than one reasonable interpretation with respect to the circumstances presented in this case. On the one hand, it can be interpreted, as some courts have along with appellants here, to mean that payments are specified to be paid under a loan contract. See Lynch, 395 B.R. at 349 (collecting cases); see also Appellants' Br. at 9-10. In this respect, payments on secured debts are "scheduled" because they are contractually due. See id. On the other hand, "scheduled" can be interpreted, as some courts have, to require reference to the bankruptcy schedules and statements upon which debtors list their financial affairs. See Sterrenberg, 471 B.R. at 133-34 (collecting cases); see, e.g., In re Fredman, 471 B.R. 540, 551 (Bankr. S.D.Ill. 2012). For example, in this case, appellants list on Schedule J an estimate of monthly expenses which includes no payments on secured debts. See Schedules and Statements dated 12/28/2011 at 25 (DE 2-5); Hr'g Tr. 26. In this respect, payments on secured debts are not "scheduled" because they are not included among the Schedule J estimate of monthly expenses and appellants have filed a statement of intent to surrender the collateral.

An additional ambiguity arises because of the requirement that payments be "on account of secured debts" and that amounts be due to "secured creditors." These terms can be interpreted, as some courts have, to refer to the type of debt existing at the time of the filing of the petition. See e.g., In re Walker, 05-15010-WHD, 2006 WL 1314125 (Bankr. N.D. Ga. May 1, 2006). In this respect, even if the debts may at some point change character because of surrender of collateral or foreclosure, their status at time of filing determines applicability of the deduction. By contrast, these terms can be interpreted, as some courts have, to mean that the amounts claimed must be for debts that will remain secured by collateral following the date of filing. See e.g., In re Lipford, 397 B.R. 320, 337 (Bankr. M.D.N.C. 2008); In re Harris, 353 B.R. 304, 309 (E.D. Okla. 2006). Thus, after debtors surrender the collateral underlying the debt, or after a foreclosure has taken place, the debts will not remain secured debts, even though they may remain contractually due. See id.

Another way to describe the ambiguity in the language of § 707(b)(2)(A)(iii) concerns whether the provision involves a "forward-looking" calculation, taking into account changes taking place after the filing of the petition, or a "snapshot" of the debtor's financial state as of the date of the petition. See Sterrenberg, 471 B.R. at 134 (collecting cases); Lynch, 395 B.R. at 348-49 (collecting cases). Under the snapshot view, the amount of payments claimed is dependent not on what the debtor intends to pay but solely on what payments are specified in the loan contract at the time of the date of filing. The forward-looking interpretation, by contrast, takes into account the debtor's stated intentions and whether the debtor will have expenses on account of secured debts in the "60 months following the date of the filing of the petition." § 707(b)(2)(A)(iii). In this respect, if a debtor is not making secured debt payments, and does not intend to make any secured debt payments in any of the 60 months following filing, then there are no "payments" upon which to make an average monthly payment calculation.

Given that § 707(b)(2)(A)(iii) is susceptible to differing interpretations, the court's next task is to determine which interpretation to adopt. Maharaj, 681 F.3d at 569. This process is simplified in this case because the Fourth Circuit has already applied the provision in accordance with the forward-looking interpretation. In particular, the Fourth Circuit, in In re Quigley, 673 F.3d 269 (4th Cir. 2012), applied § 707(b)(2)(A)(iii) in the context of approval of a Chapter 13 reorganization plan, which requires payment of "projected disposable income" to unsecured creditors, less certain amounts qualifying as expense deductions under the Chapter 7 means test. Quigley, 673 F.3d at 272 (quoting 11 U.S.C. § 1325(b)). The deduction at issue in Quigley was, as in this case, the § 707(b)(2)(A)(iii) deduction for "average monthly payments on account of secured debts." Quigley, 673 F.3d at 272 (quoting § 707(b)(2)(A)(iii)). The court held that in the context of determining "projected disposable income" for a Chapter 13 plan, the debtor could not deduct under § 707(b)(2)(A)(iii) payments for secured debts that the debtor knew she would not be making because of her stated intent to surrender the vehicles securing the debts. Quigley, 673 F.3d at 273.

Given that the Fourth Circuit did not permit application of the § 707(b)(2)(A)(iii) deduction where the debtor intended to surrender the collateral securing the debts, the court is constrained here to interpret the same provision, albeit in a different context, consistently. If § 707(b)(2)(A)(iii) did not apply in Quigley, even though secured debt payments were contractually due, then they also do not apply in this case, even though appellants' payments are contractually due here.

In Quigley, the Fourth Circuit discussed two Supreme Court cases that provided further support for its decision, Hamilton v. Lanning, 560 U.S. 505 (2010), and Ransom v. FIA Card Services, N.A., 131 S.Ct. 716 (2011), which also shed further light on the proper interpretation of the statute here. In Lanning, the Supreme Court held that "when a bankruptcy court calculates a debtor's projected disposable income, the court may account for changes in the debtor's income or expenses that are known or virtually certain at the time of confirmation." 130 S.Ct. at 2478. In Ransom, the Supreme Court held that a debtor who does not make loan or lease payments may not take a car-ownership deduction available under the means test provision for "applicable monthly expense amounts." 131 S.Ct. at 724 & 730.

Of particular relevance here, Ransom confirmed that "[b]ecause Congress intended the means test to approximate the debtor's reasonable expenditures on essential items, a debtor should be required to qualify for a deduction by actually incurring an expense in the relevant category." 130 S.Ct. at 725. Likewise, "[r]equiring a debtor to incur the kind of expenses for which he claims a means-test deduction thus advances BAPCPA's objectives." Id. The Supreme Court's confirmation that a debtor should be required to qualify for a deduction by actually incurring an expense under the means test further supports the forward-looking interpretation of § 707(b)(2)(A)(iii).

Appellants suggest that Quigley, Lanning, and Ransom are inapposite because these cases involved application of the means test in Chapter 13 proceedings as opposed to Chapter 7 proceedings, and the means test in Chapter 7 cases serves a different function from the means test in Chapter 13 cases. The court finds this argument unpersuasive, however, because the provisions that comprise the means test in Chapter 13 proceedings are the same provisions that comprise the means test in Chapter 7 cases. See 11 U.S.C. § 1325(b)(3). As noted in Ransom, "Chapter 13 borrows the means test from Chapter 7." 131 S.Ct. at 721 n.1. Likewise, as stated in Quigley, the Chapter 13 inquiry into "amounts reasonably necessary to be expended" are "determined by reference to the Chapter 7 'Means Test.'" 673 F.3d at 272 (citing 11 U.S.C. § 707(b)(2), 1325(b)(3)).

Furthermore, Quigley applied the same § 707(b)(2)(A)(iii) expense deduction at issue here, and Ransom applied one of the other expense deductions that is also present in the Chapter 7 means test. Indeed, the Supreme Court in Ransom, "granted a writ of certiorari to resolve a split of authority" over the application of the means test expense deduction for vehicle-ownership costs. Ransom, 131 S.Ct. at 723. Notably, the Supreme Court identified four circuit court cases included in the split of authority, see id. at 723 n. 4, two of which involved Chapter 7 debtors, In re Tate, 571 F.3d 423, 424 (5th Cir. 2009) and In re Ross-Tousey, 549 F.3d 1148, 1162 (7th Cir. 2008).

Thus, while appellants suggest that the same provisions should be applied differently depending on whether the case arises under Chapter 7 or Chapter 13, this suggestion runs contrary to the "standard principle of statutory interpretation [that] provides that identical words and phrases within the same statute should normally be given the same meaning." Powerex Corp. v. Reliant Energy Servs., Inc., 551 U.S. 224, 232 (2007). As a result, even though the Fourth Circuit applied § 707(b)(2)(A)(iii) in the context of a Chapter 13 proceeding, the language of the provision is the same in a Chapter 7 proceeding, and should thus be applied in the same manner. Similarly, the principles announced in Lanning and Ransom for application of the means test apply equally in Chapter 13 and Chapter 7 cases because the language of the means test is identical in each.

Finally, appellants raise a policy argument in favor of their position, arguing that they should not be penalized for honestly stating their intentions to surrender property. Appellants point out that under the interpretation adopted by the bankruptcy court, a debtor "could simply indicate their plans to retain the property and perhaps even pay the applicable mortgage for 1-3 months after filing and then promptly stop paying once the chapter 7 discharge was entered."

The Supreme Court addressed and rejected similar policy arguments in Ransom and Lanning. In Ransom, the debtors argued that under the court's interpretation "[d]ebtors can time their bankruptcy filing to take place while they still have a few car payments left, thus retaining an ownership deduction which they would lose if they filed just after making their last payment." 131 S.Ct. at 729. In rejecting this argument, the court observed "this kind of oddity is the inevitable result of a standardized formula like the means test," and the court noted that the debtor's "alternative reading of the statute would spawn its own anomalies--even placing to one side the fundamental strangeness of giving a debtor an allowance for loan or lease payments when he has not a penny of loan or lease costs." Id.

The same can be said here. Under appellants' interpretation of the statute, two separate debtors with identical income and expenses would receive different results in Chapter 7. One, who amassed secured debts prior to filing bankruptcy, could claim deductions for secured debt payments that will never actually be paid, and would satisfy the means test and be allowed to proceed in Chapter 7. The other, who amassed no secured debts prior to filing bankruptcy, could claim no deductions and would be required to proceed to Chapter 13 and make payments to unsecured creditors without deductions from income.

Moreover, debtors' hypothetical scenario presumes circumstances that may not be realistic in the context of a Chapter 7 filing. As the facts of this case illustrate, where foreclosure proceedings took place and appellants ceased making all secured debt payments several months before they filed for bankruptcy, it is questionable they would have to been inclined to "pay the applicable mortgage for 1-3 months after filing," in order to take advantage of the secured debts deduction. The Supreme Court addressed a similar hypothetical in Lanning, where it was suggested that a debtor could delay a petition to impact the calculation of income under the means test. The court observed that "delay is often not a viable option for a debtor sliding into bankruptcy," and "even when a debtor is able to delay filing a petition, such delay could be risky if it gives the appearance of bad faith." 130 S.Ct. 2476. Similarly here, Chapter 7 debtors who attempt to circumvent means test requirements through dishonest activity face significant deterrent consequences. 11 U.S.C. § 707(b)(3)(A). Thus, in light of all these considerations, the court finds appellants' policy arguments unavailing.

In sum, where the language of § 707(b)(2)(A)(iii) is ambiguous, the court is compelled to interpret the provision in accordance with Fourth Circuit and Supreme Court interpretations of the means test, such that this expense deduction is not applicable to a debtor who intends to surrender collateral and never intends to make secured debt payments.

Based upon the foregoing, the bankruptcy court's decision allowing appellee's motion to dismiss is AFFIRMED.

EGEBJERG v ANDERSON (IN RE EGEBJERG)

574 F.3d 1045 (9th Cir. 2009)

HAWKINS, J.

In this direct appeal from the bankruptcy court, Scott Lee Egebjerg ("Egebjerg") challenges the bankruptcy court's dismissal of his Chapter 7 petition for abuse under 11 U.S.C. § 707(b)(3). In an issue of first impression in this circuit under the Bankruptcy Abuse Prevention and Consumer Protection Act of 2005 ("BAPCPA"), we consider whether a debtor's repayment of a 401(k) loan constitutes a "monthly payment on account of secured debts" or an "[o]ther [n]ecessary [e]xpense" that can be deducted from a debtor's monthly income for purposes of calculating the debtor's disposable monthly income under § 707(6)(2). Because we conclude it is not, the debtor's filing in this case was presumptively abusive under the "means test" of § 707(b)(2). We therefore affirm the bankruptcy court's dismissal of his Chapter 7 petition.

FACTS AND PROCEDURAL HISTORY

Egebjerg filed a voluntary Chapter 7 bankruptcy petition on December 31, 2006. At the time, he had been employed by Ralph's grocery store for twenty-seven years and earned a gross income of $ 6,115.56 per month. Egebjerg was single with no assets. His only secured property was an automobile he used for work and a timeshare. He had unsecured consumer debt of about $ 31,000.

Approximately two years before he filed for bankruptcy, Egebjerg had taken a loan from his 401(k) plan. The plan automatically deducted $ 733.90 from his paycheck each month to repay this loan, which was scheduled to be fully repaid by September 2008. According to Egebjerg's amended schedule of necessary expenses (in which he included the 401(k) repayment), he was left with a monthly disposable income of $ 15.31.[1]

The U.S. Trustee moved to dismiss Egebjerg's Chapter 7 petition, arguing that Egebjerg had improperly included the 401(k) repayment in his necessary expenses. If, the Trustee urged, this amount were not subtracted from income as a necessary expense, Egebjerg's filing was presumptively abusive under the "means test" of § 707(6)(2). The Trustee further argued that even if the presumption of abuse did not arise under § 707(b)(2), the court should still dismiss the case because, under the totality of the circumstances, Egebjerg had sufficient means to repay a meaningful portion of his debts, especially once his 401(k) loan was repaid.

The bankruptcy court rejected the Trustee's first argument, concluding that the 401(k) loan was a "secured debt" and could be deducted from income for purposes of the means test. By including this figure, no presumption of abuse arose under § 707(b)(2).

Still, agreeing with the Trustee on the totality of the circumstances ground, the bankruptcy court dismissed the Chapter 7 petition under § 707(b)(3), noting that, at the time of the court's order in June 2007, the 401(k) loan would be repaid in just over a year, leaving $ 525 a month to repay unsecured creditors. The court concluded that the debtor could therefore pay a significant amount of his debts in a Chapter 13 proceeding and that, because of his ability to pay, it would be an abuse to permit the case to continue as a Chapter 7 proceeding. The court ordered the case to be dismissed unless the debtor converted to a Chapter 13 within ten days, which Egebjerg did not do.

Egebjerg filed a notice of appeal and requested that the bankruptcy court enter an order certifying the decision for direct appeal pursuant to 28 U.S.C. § 158(d)(2). The bankruptcy court entered the certification, and a motions panel of this court granted Egebjerg's petition for direct appeal and stayed the district court appeal pending circuit review.

DISCUSSION

I. Statutory Background

Prior to BAPCPA, there was a presumption "in favor of granting the relief requested by the Debtor." 11 U.S.C. § 707(b) (2004). This presumption could be overcome if the court found that "granting of relief would be a substantial abuse" of Chapter 7. Id. (emphasis added). Courts looked to the "totality of the circumstances" to make this substantial abuse determination. In re Price, 353 F.3d 1135, 1139-40 (9th Cir. 2004).

BAPCPA produced a sea change. There is now no presumption favoring Chapter 7 relief, but an emphasis on repaying creditors as much as possible. H.R. Rep. No. 109-31, pt. I at 2 (2005), reprinted in 2005 U.S.C.C.A.N. 88, 89. BAPCPA introduced a mathematical formula, commonly referred to as the "means test," to determine whether a debtor's financial circumstances create a

[1] Egebjerg's estimated monthly disposable income on the amended schedule was $ 170.31, less a $ 155 deduction for the difference between his actual rent and the applicable monthly rent expense specified in the IRS's Housing and Utility Standards, which debtors are required to use for means test purposes. Egebjerg listed this rent differential as a necessary "Other Expense[]" on line 56 of his amended means test form. The government does not challenge this deduction and we express no opinion on its propriety. Instead, we assume, without deciding, that the deduction was proper.

presumption against granting relief under Chapter 7. 11 U.S.C. § 707(6)(2) (2008). A presumption of abuse may be rebutted if the debtor demonstrates "special circumstances" such as "a serious medical condition or a call or order to active duty in the Armed Forces." § 707(b)(2)(B). Even if a debtor's financial situation does not create a presumption of abuse (or if the presumption is rebutted), the bankruptcy court may still dismiss the petition if the debtor filed the petition in bad faith or if the "totality of the circumstances" demonstrates "abuse" of Chapter 7. § 707(6)(3); Blausey v. U.S. Trustee, 552 F.3d 1124, 1127 n.1 (9th Cir. 2009).

This case potentially implicates both § 707(b)(2) and § 707(6)(3). However, because the statute is framed to consider the presumptive abuse question first, and resorts to the totality of circumstances analysis only if the debtor survives the means test, we have chosen to address the proper interpretation of § 707(b)(2) first. We review the bankruptcy court's legal conclusions de novo. In re Fowler, 394 F.3d 1208, 1212 (9th Cir. 2005).

II. Presumption of Abuse under § 707(b)(2)

A. Secured Debt

In calculating the debtor's current monthly income, § 707(b)(2) permits the debtor to deduct "the average monthly payments on account of secured debts." § 707(b)(2)(A)(iii) (emphasis added). In the Bankruptcy Code, the term "debt" means "liability on a claim." § 101(12). "Claim" is defined very broadly within the Code to mean any "right to payment," whether fixed, contingent, matured, disputed, secured, and so on. § 101(5). The terms "debt" and "claim" are coextensive, "flip sides to the same coin." In re Rifkin, 124 B.R. 626, 628 (Bankr. E.D. N.Y. 1991); S. Rep. No. 989, 95th Cong. 2d Sess., 23 (1978), reprinted in U.S.C.C.A.N. 5787, 5809. Therefore, Egebjerg's 401(k) loan constitutes a "debt" only if the plan administrator has a "claim" for repayment.

We join the vast majority of courts in holding that the debtor's obligation to repay a loan from his or her retirement account is not a "debt" under the Bankruptcy Code. See, e.g., In re Villarie, 648 F.2d 810 (2d Cir. 1981) (loan drawn on employee's contributions to retirement system not a "debt" because plan has no right to sue a member for the amount of the advance, it is simply offset against future benefits); Bolen v. Adams, 2009 WL 605270, (N.D. Miss. 2009) (vast majority of courts have held a debtor's obligation to repay retirement account loan is not a "debt" under the Code); Eisen v. Thompson, 370 B.R. 762, 769 (N.D. Ohio 2007) (majority view is that retirement plan loans are not secured debts); In re Esquivel, 239 B.R. 146, 152 (Bankr. E.D. Mich. 1999) ("clear consensus" that borrowing from retirement account does not give rise to either secured or unsecured "claim" under the Bankruptcy Code); see also McVay v. Otero, 371 B.R. 190, 195 (W.D. Tex. 2007); In re Fulton, 211 B.R. 247, 264 (Bankr. S.D. Ohio 1997); In re Scott, 142 B.R. 126, 131-32 (Bankr. E.D. Va. 1992); In re Jones, 138 B.R. 536, 537-38 (Bankr. S.D. Ohio 1991).

The reasoning behind these decisions is straightforward. Egebjerg's obligation is essentially a debt to himself -- he has borrowed his own money. In re Smith, 388 B.R. 885, 887 (Bankr. C.D. III. 2008); see also McVay, 371 B.R. at 197 (collecting cases). Egebjerg contributed the money to the account in the first place; should he fail to repay himself, the administrator has no personal recourse against him. In re Villarie, 648 F.2d at 812. Instead, the plan will deem the outstanding loan balance to be a distribution of funds, thereby reducing the amount available to Egebjerg from his account in the future. See In re Mowris,

384 B.R. 235, 238 (Bankr. W.D. Mo. 2008); see also Mullen v. United States, 696 F.2d 470, 472 (6th Cir. 1983). This deemed distribution will have tax consequences to Egebjerg, but it does not create a debtor-creditor relationship. In re Smith, 388 B.R. at 888 ("Nonpayment comes with liability for income taxes and penalties, but nonpayment is a valid, lawful alternative.").

As succinctly explained by one district court:

> Retirement plan loans are qualitatively different than secured debts such as home mortgages and car loans. The retirement plan administrator does not loan the plan participant the administrator's money. It simply deducts the requested loan amount from the participant's own account, and credits the loan payments and interest back to the participant's account. If the participant defaults on the loan, the plan administrator deducts the amount owed from the vested account balance, and repays the loan with this deduction. The participant must treat this deduction as a distribution which is taxable as income to the participant in the default year. The participant may also be subject to an early withdrawal penalty. But, the plan administrator has no right to payment under the Bankruptcy Code.

Thompson, 370 B.R. at 768 n.10.

Because the debtor's loan repayment obligation is not a "claim" or "debt" under the Bankruptcy Code, the debtor may not include payments on such loans as a deduction for purposes of the means test under § 707(b)(2). See, e.g., In re Smith, 388 B.R. at 888; In re Mowris, 384 B.R. at 237-38; McVay, 371 B.R. at 203; Thompson, 370 B.A. at 768-72. This conclusion under BAPCPA is not only supported by the definitions of "claim" and "debt" within the Code, but also by two basic canons of statutory construction.

First, we presume that when Congress legislates, it is aware of past judicial interpretations and practices. See Dewsnup v. Timm, 502 U.S. 410, 419 (1992) ("When Congress amends the Bankruptcy laws, it does not write on a clean slate.") (internal quotation marks omitted). "Because overwhelming case law preceding [BAPCPA] held that 401(k) loans were not 'debts' under the Code, and because Congress has not expressly said otherwise, the Court must presume that 'debt' retains its pre-2005 Act meaning." Thompson, 370 B.R. at 771; see also In re Mowris, 384 B.R. at 238 ("The overwhelming majority of pre-BAPCPA opinions held that a debtor's obligation to make payments on a loan taken from a qualified retirement account was not a claim or debt under the Code, and the court must assume that Congress was aware of this judicial interpretation when it enacted BAPCPA.").

Second, we also presume that if Congress includes particular language in one section of a statute but omits it in another, Congress acted intentionally in that exclusion. KP Permanent Make-Up, Inc. v. Lasting Impression I, Inc., 543 U.S. 111, 118 (2004). Here, in BAPCPA, Congress expressly gave Chapter 13 debtors the ability to deduct 401(k) payments from their disposable income calculation, § 1322(f), but did not include any similar exemption for Chapter 7 debtors. Congress also added a section which provides that the automatic stay does not apply to automatic deductions to repay a retirement plan loan, but expressly stated that the provision shall not be construed to provide that such a loan constitutes a "claim" or "debt." § 362(b)(19). "In light of the amendments sprinkled throughout the Code [addressing 401(k) loans] -- especially section 1322(f) -- the lack of a 401(k) provision in section 707 is a glaring indication that Congress did not intend 401(k) loan repayments to be deducted in Chapter 7." In re Turner, 376 B.R. 370, 376 (Bankr. D. N.H. 2007).

Although Egebjerg contends that this construction creates anomalous results, "[t]he explanation for the lack of such a provision in section 707 is that Congress intended to steer many would-be Chapter 7 debtors toward Chapter 13." Id. As one court explained:

> First, 401(k) loan repayments are finite; a loan will eventually be paid off. Second, a Chapter 13 case is prospective, i.e., it encompasses a debtor's current and future financial circumstances for a period of three to five years . . . . Excluding 401(k) loans from the means test evidences a "wait and see" approach that would channel debtors with such expenses into the longer period of bankruptcy supervision of Chapter 13 rather than the relatively short tenure of a Chapter 7 case, notwithstanding that doing so might result in a zero payment plan. However, because, as here, 401(k) loans might be paid off within the commitment period of a Chapter 13 case, the ability to increase the monthly plan payment would direct newly available funds to creditors. Such an approach serves both the Congressional intent to protect retirement contributions and "ensure that debtors repay creditors the maximum they can afford," a primary goal of BAPCPA.

In re Lenton, 358 B.R. 651, 660 (Bankr. E.D. Penn. 2006).

B. Other Necessary Expense

In addition to maintaining that his 401(k) loan to himself is a "secured debt," Egebjerg also contends that his loan repayments are an "other necessary expense" for the purposes of applying the means test. We reject that argument as well.

Under the statutory provisions governing the means test, debtors may deduct, in addition to payments on secured debt, their "actual monthly expenses for the categories specified as Other Necessary Expenses issued by the Internal Revenue Service." 11 U.S.C. § 707(b)(2)(A)(ii). In turn, the Internal Revenue Manual ("IRM") lists fifteen categories of expenses which may be considered necessary under certain circumstances, such as child care, education and court-ordered payments such as alimony and child support. IRM § 5.15.1.10.

The IRM list of categories appears to be nonexhaustive. See IRM § 5.15.1.10(1) (noting that other expenses may be considered if they meet the necessary expense test -- i.e., if they "provide for the health and welfare of the taxpayer and/or his or her family or [provide] for the production of income."). However, some bankruptcy courts have held that this list is exhaustive for purposes of the bright-line means test, because, by the plain language of § 707(b)(2)(A)(ii)(1), Congress expressly limited a debtor's deductions for other expenses to "the categories specified" by the Internal Revenue Service. See In re Turner, 376 B.R. at 375; In re Lara, 347 B.R. 198, 204 (Bankr. N.D. Tex. 2006); In re Mordis, 2007 WL 2962903, (Bankr. E.D. Mo. 2007); In re Whitaker, 2007 WL 2156397, (Bankr. N.D. Ohio 2007). Other courts have looked beyond the enumerated categories and considered the applicability of IRM § 5.15.1.10(1)'s "necessary expense test" on a case-by-case basis. See In re Mowris, 384 B.R. at 238-39; In re Lenton, 358 B.R. at 658.

We need not resolve this debate in this case, however, because we conclude that under either interpretation, Egebjerg's repayment of his 401(k) loan does not qualify as an "Other Necessary Expense." Such payments do not fit within any of the IRM's listed categories. See, e.g., In re Barraza, 346 B.R. 724, 730 (Bankr. N.D. Tex. 2006) (rejecting argument that repayment could be considered an "involuntary deduction" because it is not a condition of the debtor's employment); see also In re Lenton, 358 B.R. at 657-58 (same). As discussed above, the 401(k) loan repayments themselves are voluntary in the sense that Egebjerg can simply ask the loan administrator to treat his outstanding loan balance as an early withdrawal from his 401(k) and thereby relieve himself of a future repayment obligation. Doing so would have tax consequences, but Egebjerg would retain the use of most of the money loaned.

According to Egebjerg, the replenishment of his 401(k) plan is necessary to his long-term "health and welfare," because he is approaching retirement and his 401(k) plan is his only significant asset.[2] But even if we were to look beyond the specified categories to consider the more general "necessary expense test" in the IRM, 401(k) repayments are simply not of the same kind and character as those expenses allowed elsewhere under § 5.15.1.10. For example, dependent care expenses (for care of the elderly or handicapped) are permitted only if there is no alternative to paying the expense, and "[e]ducation" costs are necessary expenses only if they are "required for a physically or mentally challenged child and no public education providing similar services is available," or if they are "required as a condition of [the debtor's] employment." Id. We also note that the IRS guidelines themselves provide that "[c]ontributions to voluntary retirement plans are not a necessary expense." IRM § 5.15.1.23; see also In re Lenton, 358 B.R. at 658 ("[i]f future voluntary contributions to the 401k plan are not necessary expenses, it is hard to argue that the replenishment of past voluntary contributions to the 401k account by repaying loans is a necessary expense.").[3]

Arguing to the contrary, Egebjerg cites Hebbring v. United States Trustee, 463 F.3d 902 (9th Cir. 2006), In re Hill, 328 B.R. 490 (Bankr. S.D. Tex. 2005), and In re Vansickel, 309 B.R. 189 (Bankr. E.D. Va. 2004), for the proposition that voluntary 401(k) contributions are not per se unnecessary expenses for the purposes of calculating a debtor's disposable income under § 707(b)(2). What Egebjerg fails to note is that each of these cases either pre-dates the BAPCPA (and therefore pre-dates the means test) or applies pre-BAPCPA law. See, e.g., Hebbring, 463 F.3d at 904 n.1. This point is critical because the pre-BAPCPA § 707(6)(2) "totality of circumstances" test for abuse, which now appears (as modified by BAPCPA) as part of § 707(b)(3), is distinct from the current § 707(b)(2) means test. When it introduced the means test, Congress provided, by reference to the IRS guidelines, specific guidance as to what qualifies as a necessary expense for the purposes of applying that test. Our holding in Hebbring, which concerns only the former "totality of circumstances" test, is

[2] Egebjerg does not actually provide his age. He states only that "[s]ince he has been employed with Kroger for 27 years he is not someone who is many years from retirement."

[3] We do not hold that § 5.15.1.23 11is controlling, but that it is useful and persuasive in the context of this case -- defining the parameters of § 5.15.1.10(1) and what was considered to provide for "health and welfare" at the time Congress cross-referenced the IRM's "Other Necessary Expenses" provisions. We recognize that the extent of the manual's "incorporation" and/or usefulness in interpreting § 707(b)(2)(A)(ii)(I) is a subject of extensive debate, particularly with respect to interpreting the "applicable monthly expense amounts specified under the National Standards and Local Standards." See In re Ross-Tousely, 549 F.3d 1148, 1156-57 (7th Cir. 2008) (discussing split in authority). By our narrow decision today, we do not mean to imply that the IRS standards have been incorporated wholesale into the Bankruptcy Code or that they control outcomes on other issues.

simply not applicable.[4]

For all the foregoing reasons, the bankruptcy court erred by allowing Egebjerg to deduct his 401(k) repayment from disposable income for purposes of the means test. If the amount of his loan repayment is included in Egebjerg's income, then a presumption of abuse arises under § 707(6)(2).

III. Special Circumstances

The bankruptcy court also held, in the alternative, that even if the amount of Egebjerg's loan repayment obligation should not be included as a secured debt or necessary expense, it could be properly included as a "special circumstance" which could rebut the presumption of abuse, citing In re Thompson, 350 B.R. 770 (Bankr. N.D. Ohio 2006). However, Thompson was reversed by the district court on this very point on appeal, Thompson, 370 B.R. at 772-73, and the majority of courts agree that the mere obligation to repay a 401(k) loan is not itself a special circumstance. See, e.g., Smith, 388 B.R. at 888; In re Mowris, 384 B.R. at 240; In re Turner, 376 B.R. at 378.

Section 707(b)(2)(B) provides:

> In any proceeding brought under this subsection, the presumption of abuse may only be rebutted by demonstrating special circumstances, such as a serious medical condition or a call or order to active duty in the Armed Forces, to the extent such special circumstances . . . justify additional expenses or adjustments of current monthly income for which there is no reasonable alternative.

Thus, Congress did not provide an exhaustive list of "special circumstances," but did indicate examples of situations it would consider sufficient to rebut the presumption of abuse. As one court has noted, both examples given by Congress share "a commonality; they both constitute situations which not only put a strain on a debtor's household budget, but they arise from circumstances normally beyond the debtor's control." In re Castle, 362 B.R. 846, 851 (Bankr. N.D. Ohio 2006).

We need not explore the outside parameters of the special circumstance provision, however, for we agree that "retirement plan loans are neither extraordinary nor rare; many individuals take loans for many different reasons, and they are all required to repay the loans. Without more, a situation as common as the withdrawal of one's retirement funds cannot be a 'special circumstance' within the accepted definition of this term." Thompson, 370 B.R. at 773.

While there may be situations in which the debtor's underlying reason for taking out a 401(k) loan may constitute a special circumstance, see In re Tauter, 402 B.R. 903, 906-7 (Bantu. M.D. Fla. 2009), Egebjerg's only explanation was that he was using the money to "pay off bills" in the hope of avoiding bankruptcy in the first instance. Although a commendable goal, "the fact that he borrowed from those retirement funds and now wishes to pay the loans back is not a life altering circumstance of the kind referenced in the statute. It is simply the consequence of a prior financial decision." Smith, 388 B.R. at 888.

---

[4] Egebjerg also argues that our failure to recognize his 401(k) repayments as a "necessary expense" would create a conflict with the Bankruptcy Code's automatic stay provisions. We reject this argument for the reasons already stated in Part II.A.

It appears that borrowing from a 401(k) is not an uncommon approach for many debtors, usually stemming from their "longstanding general inability to keep up with their obligations to creditors." Thompson, 370 B.R. at 773; see also In re Mowris, 384 B.R. at 240; In re Turner, 376 B.R. at 378. Indeed, if the original unsecured consumer obligation could not be considered a special circumstance, it would seem problematic to find "special circumstances" for the 401(k) loan that merely replaced those debts. See In re Jackson, 2008 WL 5539790 at n.20 (Banta. D. Kan. 2008); cf. Turner, 376 B.A. at 378-79 (401(k) repayment may be special circumstance if taken out for a "special" reason other than general financial problems preceding almost every bankruptcy).

Thus, on this record, while we agree with the bankruptcy court's bottom line conclusion, it erred by concluding Egebjerg had demonstrated special circumstances under § 707(b)(2)(B). Because Egebjerg thus did not rebut the presumption of abuse under § 707(b)(2)(A), the bankruptcy court properly dismissed Egebjerg's Chapter 7 petition.

AFFIRMED.

Notes and Question

1. Suppose D owes $1,000 a month for the next twelve months on her secured car loan. How much may she deduct from current monthly income under § 707(b)(2)(iii)(I)?

2. Other Necessary Expenses. Earlier notes drew attention to IRS National and Local Standards. There is a third IRS category mentioned in § 707(b)(2)(A)(ii)(I): Other Necessary Expenses. The IRS Manual lists 18 such expenses: (1) accounting and legal fees, (2) charitable contributions,[1] (3) child care, (4) court-ordered payments (such as alimony and child support), (5) dependent care, (6) health care, (7) involuntary wage deductions (such as for union dues or uniforms), (8) life insurance, (9) secured debts, (10) unsecured debts, (11) current taxes,[2] (12) optional telephones and telephone services (such as cell phones and pagers),[3] (13) student loans, (14) internet service, and (15) repayment of loans made for payment of federal taxes.[4] Another portion of the Manual adds (16) education, (17) disability insurance, and (18) professional association dues.[5] A third list gives further definition of some of the categories already set forth.[6]

---

[1] Courts have rejected the idea that voluntary tithing is a Necessary Expense. In re Tranmer, 355 B.R. 234 (Bankr. D. Mont. 2006); In re Diagostino, 347 B.R. 116 (Bankr. N.D.N.Y. 2006). The IRS manual requires a charitable contribution to be a condition of employment: "Example: a minister is required to tithe according to his employment contract." IRS Manual § 5.15.1.10.

[2] This would include income tax withholding. Over-withholding, however, is not allowed. Boynton v. Boynton (In re Lawson), 361 B.R. 215 (Bankr. D. Utah 2007); Baxter v. Johnson (In re Johnson), 346 B.R. 256, 268-69 (Bankr. S.D. Ga. 2006); see In re Risher, 344 B.R. 833 (Bankr. W.D. Ky. 2006) (tax refunds are to be considered income for purposes of disposable income test in chapter 13). A difficulty arises when a debtor files for bankruptcy in February and is overwithholding; how can the debtor know what may happen for the balance of the year that might increase the debtor's taxes? In In re Balcerowski, 353 B.R. 582 (Bankr. E.D. Wis. 2006) (chapter 13), Judge Pamela Pepper ruled that the debtor may not over-withhold and must simply use the best estimate available at the time the form is filled out.

[3] Dial up internet is not allowed, where the debtor also claims an expense for high speed internet access. In re Lara, 347 B.R. 198 (Bankr. N.D. Tex. 2006). Thus expense is limited to "the debtor, the dependents of the debtor, and the spouse of the debtor in a joint case." 11 U.S.C. § 707(b)(2)(A)(ii)(I). Therefore, cell phones for a non-dependent adult child (even if chronically ill) is not permitted. In re Haley, 354 B.R. 340, 344-45 (Bankr. D.N.H. 2006) (chapter 13). Meanwhile, there is redundency between this item and the Local Standards for housing and utilities (which includes telephone bills). In re Carlton, 362 B.R. 402 (Bankr. C.D. Ill. 2007) (allowing the debtor the full telecommunications deduction nevertheless).

[4] Iinternal Revenue Manual 5.15.1. 10 P 3.

[5] IRM 5.19.1.4.3. 5 P 3.

[6] IRM Exhibit 5.19.1-12.

Form B22A includes several lines for "other necessary expenses"[7] but gives scanty hints with regard to the rich array of categories. With regard to Other Necessary Expenses, the debtor must confirm under oath that call waiting, caller identification and internet services are "necessary for the health and welfare of you and your dependents."[8] Of course, it can be argued that a loss of "call waiting" is per se a loss of "welfare," so perhaps a debtor can risk his sacred oath on such propositions.[9]

These Other Necessary Expenses exclude expenses for housing and transportation, which are fully provided for elsewhere. Also, to the extent Other Necessary Expenses cover the payment of debts, it must be remembered that § 707(b)(2)(A)(ii)(I) provides: "Notwithstanding any other provision of this clause, the monthly expenses of the debtor shall not include any payments for debts."

3. In Egebjerg, the court disallowed payback of 401(k) loans as a secured debt expense under Bankruptcy Code § 707(b)(2)(iii)(I). It also ruled that these paybacks cannot be categorized as an Other Necessary Expense. But such expenses include involuntary wage deductions. In In re Barraza, 346 B.R. 724 (Bankr. N.D. Tex. 2006), the court held that the ERISA loan repayments from wages are not mandatory.

> Both plans provide that the loans must be repaid via payroll deductions. . . However, the requirement to repay the 401(k) loans is not a job requirement in the sense that union dues, uniforms, and workshoes are. The consequence of a debtor's failure to comply with the requirement to pay union dues, ear a particular uniform, or wear certain shoes is, in all likelihood, loss of employment. By contrast, the consequences of the debtor defaulting on his 401(k) loans is that the loans are treated as taxable distributions. Consequently, the plan loan repayments do not qualify as 'involuntary deductions' under the Internal Revenue Manual.

346 B.R. at 730. This conclusion can certainly be challenged. Nothing the IRS Manual makes the manditoriness of the withholding be the sine qua non of continued employment. If ERISA withholding constitutes an assignment of wages, then indeed it is mandatory, in the sense that the ERISA plan has a fiduciary duty to enforcement the assignment mechanism. For this reason, Judge Nelms's conclusion should be rejected as based on an unnecessary predicate of manditoriness.

5. The Egebjerg court states that ERISA loans are not debts, because the debtor simply borrows from herself. Yet Bankruptcy Code § 523(a)(19) (new to BAPCPA) directly refers to such ERISA claims as "debts." (See the preamble to § 523(a).

6. Health and disability insurance. The lack of social health care programs was certainly in the air in 2005, and so Congress has permitted deductions for "reasonably necessary health insurance, disability insurance, and health savings account expenses for the debtor, the spouse of the debtor, or dependents of the debtor." Bankruptcy Code § 707(b)(ii)(I) (second sentence). Form B22A does not limit these amounts to "reasonably necessary" insurance but simply asks straight out what the debtor pays on average per month for these items. Form B22A Line 34.

Amounts contributed to health savings accounts are deductible from federal income tax. 26 U.S.C. § 223. This deduction was added or at least refined by the Medicare legislation in 2003. Medicare Prescription, Drug Improvement and Modernization Act of 2003 § 1201. See generally Edward J. Larson & Marc Dettman, The Impact of HSAs on Health Care Reform: Preliminary Results After One Year, 40 WAKE FOREST L. REV. 1187 (2005). It is part of a neo-conservative solution to rising health costs. The premise is that Americans (with insurance) are over-insured and so they visit the doctor too often. The scheme is to get American taxpayers to buy "high deductible health plans" in exchange for which the taxpayer may establish a tax-deferred savings account to cover the increased personal medical expense that result.

These new health savings accounts are not to be confused with annual use-it-or-lose-it flexible spending accounts that are part of a cafeteria plan offered by employers. Regina T. Jefferson, Medical Savings Accounts: Windfalls for the Healthy, Wealthy and Wise, 48 CATH. U.L.

---

[7] Form B22A Part IV Lines 25-32.

[8] Form B22A Line 32. See In re Napier, 2006 Bankr. LEXIS 2248 (Bankr. D.S.C., September 18, 2006) (debtor reduced to $175 a month from $330; $90 internet justified by the nature of debtor's employment).

[9] The word "welfare" appears in the IRS Manual, ¶707.030, and so is justifiably used in Form B22A.

REV. 685, 704 (1999). Because nothing is "saved" in these plans, Congress could not have meant to include these contributions within the scope of § 707(b)(ii)(I).

7. Family violence. BAPCPA permits a debtor to deduct whatever is spent to protect the debtor from family violence, "as identified under section 309 of the Family Violence Prevention and Services Act, or other applicable law." Bankruptcy Code § 707(b)(2)(A)(ii)(I). The court is enjoined to keep this last amount confidential. Id. § 707(b)(ii). Section 309 of this act, redesignated as § 320 in 1995, Act of June 25, 2003, P.L. 108-36, defines "family violence" as

> any act or threatened act of violence, including any forceful detention of an individual, which--
>
> (A) results or threatens to result in physical injury; and
>
> (B) is committed by a person against another individual (including an elderly person) to whom such person is or was related by blood or marriage or otherwise legally related or with whom such person is or was lawfully residing.

42 U.S.C. § 10421(1). To be noted is the last clause which is broad enough to cover expenses to guard against any former roommate as well as against family members. It does not, however, cover stalking unless it involves existing or previous cohabitation.

What expenses may be deducted in the name of warding off family violence? The expense of keeping a watchdog might qualify, but before deducting the expenses of the family's pet poodle, the debtor will presumably have to document a threat from a relative or roommate.

8. Chronic illness. The debtor may add actual expenses for "the continuation of actual expenses paid by the debtor that are reasonable and necessary" for the care of elderly, chronically ill, or disabled household member or member of the immediate family who is unable to pay such expense. Bankruptcy Code § 707(b)(2)(A)(ii)(II). The word "continuation" is problematic, suggesting the care for the infirm relative somehow precede the chapter 7 proceeding in some way, though it is still possible for a debtor to introduce purely prospective care as a "special circumstance" to rebut the appearance of bankruptcy abuse, pursuant to § 707(b)(2)(B)(i). Where the aged relative is entitled to welfare payments, the phrase "reasonable and necessary" could justify a court in declaring it an abuse if the debtor's aged relative fails to seek such relief.

The infirm recipient of debtor charity must either be a member of the household or a member of the debtor's immediate family, which "includes" siblings, parents, etc., but does not specifically mention step-children out of the household or parents-in-law. Presumably the non-exclusive nature of this definition is broad enough to include these more extended relations. Aged servants and loyal retainers out of the household are not deductible.

9. Chapter 13 expenses. A seemingly curious item is that a debtor eligible for chapter 13 (yet nevertheless in chapter 7) may include the "actual" administrative expense of administering as chapter 13 plan. Bankruptcy Code § 707(b)(2)(A)(ii)(II). By "actual," Congress apparently meant the hypothetical expenses the debtor would have borne in his judicial district had she filed in chapter 13 instead of chapter 7. The requirement makes sense in that the 60 month test ultimately aims to see if, in the 60 months following the bankruptcy test, the debtor could generate substantial payments to the unsecured creditors. Since a chapter 13 proceeding is a likely mode for achieving these payments, the debtor is permitted to deduct the chapter 13 administrative expense, even though the debtor may qualify for chapter 7, where no such expense will be borne.

Debtors may not in fact be eligible for chapter 13. For instance, too much debt may eliminate such an option. 11 U.S.C. § 109(e). Currently, these amounts are $307,675 for unsecured debts and $922,975 for secured debts. In case of ineligibility, no chapter 13 expense can be deducted. Such a debtor might be eligible for chapter 11. Chapter 11 cases generate quarterly fees to the United States trustee. 28 U.S.C. 1930 (a)(6). But there is no provision for any deduction of such expenses. Although chapter 11 expenses would be a priority claim under § 507(a)(2), they would be claims against the bankruptcy estate, not against the debtor and so not eligible for deduction under the priority concept in § 707(b)(2)(iii)(iv).

The chapter 13 fee is set by the attorney general. It may not exceed 10% of plan disbursements through the standing chapter 13 trustee. But chapter 13 is embroiled in a controversy as to whether such things as mortgage payments must be made through the trustee, or whether these payments can be made "outside the plan." Since the debtor can write what plan she pleases, it is open for the debtor to hypothesize no payments outside the plan, thereby inflating the deductions by 10% of mortgage and car payments.

10. Priority claims. Under § 707(b)(2)(iv), a debtor may deduct payment of priority claims. Taxes will be covered by this concept, if they qualify for priority under § 507(a)(8). Section

707(b)(2)(iv) specifically mentions child support and alimony. In fact, the relevant priority is new § 507(a)(1)(A), which accords priority to "domestic support obligations."

BAPCPA newly and expansively defines this term to include any amount owed to a spouse, former spouse of the debtor (presumably including business loans). Bankruptcy Code § 101(14A)(A)(i). Also covered are any amount "owed to or recoverable by. . . (ii) a governmental unit." Grammatically, these amounts are not tied to a family aspect at all, although courts may be tempted to stray from the literal meaning of the statute to link such debts to family matters. If they are not so tied, out of a literalist "plain meaning" attitude, then all sorts of spousal and government loans can be used to reduce net monthly income. Of course, the total debt must be divided by 60 in order to make the amount comparable to the monthly standard on which means testing is based.

Why did Congress make the pro rata amounts of priority claims deductions? In chapter 13, priority creditors must be paid in full over the life of the plan. Bankruptcy Code § 1322(a)(2). This rule is an obstacle to ordinary unsecured creditors being paid in chapter 13. It therefore makes sense to make these priority claims a deduction in the means test, as these are amounts the unsecured creditors will not get anyway.

Perhaps the most important priority expense is the cost of bankruptcy administration. Bankruptcy Code § 507(a)(2). This is partially provided for in § 707(b)(2)(A)(ii)(III), as we have seen, but this is limited to the mandatory fee due to the standing chapter 13 trustee. Another important expense is the debtor's lawyer, who, in chapter 13 cases, is an administrative claimant. This is not typically the case in chapter 7. Lamie v. United States Trustee, 540 U.S. 526 (2004). In contrast, § 330(a)(4)(B) directly mentions the debtor's attorney in chapter 13 cases. And § 503(b)(2) defines as an administrative claim "compensation and reimbursement awarded under section 330(a) of this title."

Can the debtor claim the hypothetical expense of an attorney in a chapter 13 case as part of means testing for chapter 7? The answer is probably no. In re Amato, 366 B.R. 348 (Bankr. D.N.J. 2007). According to § 707(b)(2)(A)(iv):

> The debtor's expenses for payment of all priority claims (including priority child support and alimony claims) shall be calculated as the total amounts of debts entitled to priority, divided by 60.

This language apparently requires the priority claim to exist at the time of the bankruptcy proceeding. The expense of the chapter 13 attorney is entirely hypothetical.

To be compared is the standing chapter 13 trustee deduction in § 707(b)(2)(A)(ii)(III):

> In addition, for a debtor eligible for chapter 13, the debtor's monthly expenses may include the actual administrative expenses of administering a chapter 13 plan for the district in which the debtor resides, up to an amount of 10 percent of the projected plan payments, as determined under the schedules issued by the Executive Office for United States Trustees.

Here the expense is expressly hypothetical.

If hypothetical attorneys' fees cannot be deducted, it is unfortunate. The idea of the means test is to project the payout over the life of a chapter 13 plan. For this reason, § 707(b)(2)(A)(ii)(III) makes sense. But, because § 707(b)(2)(A)(iv) seems to exclude hypothetical expense of the chapter 13 attorney, the means test is skewed to over-report how much will really be available in chapter 13.

Suppose a debtor owes court-ordered child support but this obligation lapses a few months after the bankruptcy petition. May the debtor list the full amount as if this expense will continue throughout the period of a hypothetical chapter 13 plan? If the debtor relies on § 707(b)(2)(iv), the answer is apparently no. The debtor must estimate the total due over time and divide by 60. So where a debtor's child support obligation is $600 per month, but it ends in 24 months, the debtor must take the total amount due ($14,400) and divide it by 60 to obtain $240 per month. In re Casey, 356 B.R. 519, 525-26 (Bankr. E.D. Wash. 2006). If this is so, then suppose the debtor owes child support of $600 per month for 17 years. Presumably the debtor must take the total amount due ($122,400) and divide by 60 to obtain a deduction of $2,040. Thus, BAPCPA discriminates in favor of dads who walk out on their infant children, compared to dads who walk out when the child is just short of the age of majority.

Furthermore, court-ordered child support payments is an Other Necessary Expense within the meaning of § 707(b)(2)(A)(ii)(I). May the debtor who owes $600 a month in court-ordered child support also deduct $600 in addition to the above deduction under § 707(b)(2)(iv)? Here the answer is assuredly no. According to the third sentence of § 707(b)(2)(A)(ii)(I), "[n]otwithstanding any other provision of this clause, the monthly expenses of the debtor shall not include any payments for debts." If we consider child support a "debt," it may not qualify as an Other Necessary Expense.

11. Tuition. A debtor may add $1500 per year per dependent child, to the extent of actual expenses to attend a private or public elementary or secondary school. Bankruptcy Code § 707(b)(2)(A)(IV). The debtor must document the expenses and explain why they are reasonable and necessary and not already accounted for in the National Standards, Local Standards referred to § 707(b)(2)(A)(ii)(II). This requirement should embroil the courts in such inquiries as whether parochial schools teaching religion is reasonable or necessary.

In In re Cleary, 357 B.R. 369 (Bankr. D.S.C. 2006), the court permitted a debtor to exceed the limit of $1,500 per child on the grounds that tuition was an Other Necessary Expense. It cautioned, however, that the holding was limited to the circumstance of a non-debtor spouse who was willing to work in order to pay tuition, but was not willing to work for the coarser purpose of paying her spouse's credit card debt. The extra deduction was permitted because it was not at the expense of the unsecured creditors.

12. Charitable contributions. According to § 707(b)(1),

> In making a determination whether to dismiss a cause under this section, the court may not take into consideration whether a debtor has made, or continues to make, charitable contributions (that meet the definition of "charitable contribution" under section 548(d)(3)) to any qualified religious or charitable entity or organization (as that term is defined in section 548(d)(4)).

This sentence is unamended by BAPCPA.

Suppose a debtor is close to passing the means test but faces dismissal. It is feared that the debtor could increase his contribution to Jerry Falwell in sufficient sums to meet the test. Since "the court may not take into consideration" such religious donations, the debtor enters into chapter 7 bankruptcy.

Charitable contributions do not appear in the list of allowed expenses in § 707(b)(2)(A)(ii). Therefore, it is open for a debtor who flunks the test to show that the charitable contributions are just high enough to qualify the debtor for chapter 7. Of course, the televangelist amendment requires that the debtor "has made, or continue to make" the contributions. So presumably some sort of historical record will have to be established. If the chapter 7 proceeding is permitted, it will be up to the good conscience of the debtor whether he will live up to the representations made to the bankruptcy court, though it should be remarked that revoking discharges under § 727(d) is a possible remedy for the televangelist who does not receive his weekly fraudulent transfer.

There is, however, a counter-argument. Means testing is in general a mandatory presumption of abuse, if the debtor flunks the test. The means test appears within § 707(b)(2). Gross income is defined in subsection (A)(i), and allowable expenses are defined in subsection (A)(ii)-(iv). Nowhere in subsection (a)(ii-iv) are charitable contributions mentioned as an allowable expense. So it is open for the bankruptcy court to conduct the test and find the debtor in bad faith, without any reference to the charitable contributions. If a court does this, it has conformed to § 707(b)(1), which orders the court not to take into consideration the religious contribution. In re Diagostino, 347 B.R. 116 (Bankr. N.D.N.Y. 2006) (in the context of above-median chapter 13 debtors); accord, In re Tranmer, 355 B.R. 234 (Bankr. D. Mont. 2006) (same). A debtor may claim the deduction as an expense, but § 707(b)(1) bids the court not to consider this. So just as the devil may quote the scriptures to his own purposes and o'ersugar the truth to his own end, so may he cite the Bankruptcy Code to defeat televangelism in the name of preventing bankruptcy abuse.

13. Rebuttals. If the debtor flunks the 60 month test, she is given a chance to rebut the presumption of bad faith abuse of the system. The debtor must demonstrate "special circumstances, such as a serious medical condition or a call or order to active duty in the Armed Forces." Bankruptcy Code § 707(b)(2)(B)(i). These circumstances must generate extra expenses or reduce income which explain away the too-large multiplicand in the 60 month test. Bankruptcy Code § 707(b)(2)(B)(i). The debtor is required to itemize each additional expense under oath.

In Egebjerg, the court rejected the idea that the need to pay back a 401(k) loan was a special circumstance. Which of the following might qualify as such?

(a) D had extra car expense because he kept crashing into deer. In re Batzkiel, 349 B.R. 581 (Bankr. N.D. Iowa 2006) (yes).

(b) A long commute caused extra gas expenses. In re Tranmer, 355 B.R. 234 (Bankr. D. Mont. 2006) (no).

(c) Extra housing expense so each child could have his or her own room. In re Delunas, 2007 Bankr. LEXIS 803 (Bankr. E.D. Mo. March 6, 2007) (no).

(d) A pregnant unmarried daughter lived at home and there was a terminally ill puppy. In re Olson, 2005 Bankr. LEXIS 395 (Bankr. Utah 2005) (pre-BAPCA) (yes).

(e) High nondischargeable student loan debt. In re Champagne, 2008 Bankr. LEXIS 953 (Bankr. D. Kan., April 4, 2008) (no).

B. STANDING

IN RE PARET
347 B.R. 12 (Bankr. D. Del. 2006)

MARY F. WALRATH, J.

. . . Before the Court is the Motion of the United States Trustee ("the UST") to dismiss the Debtor's chapter 7 case based upon the totality of the Debtor's financial circumstances. The Debtor opposes the motion. For the reasons outlined below, the Court concludes that the totality of the Debtor's financial circumstances (including the Debtor's ability to repay his debts) is the applicable standard. Having determined the legal standard, the Court will schedule an evidentiary hearing on that issue.[1]

I. BACKGROUND

Matthew J. Paret ("the Debtor") owes $43,938 in nonpriority unsecured claims, the bulk of which are credit card debts. On March 22, 2006, the Debtor filed a voluntary petition for relief under chapter 7 of the Bankruptcy Code. On April 19, 2006, the UST filed a motion to dismiss the Debtor's case under section 707(b)(1). 11 U.S.C. § 707(b)(1). In a response filed May 4, 2006, the Debtor asserted that the "totality of the circumstances" test under section 707(b)(3) does not apply and that the Debtor's ability to pay creditors is not relevant because his income falls below the median income level under section 707(b)(7). The parties have briefed the issue, and the matter is ripe for decision. . . .

III. DISCUSSION

The UST asserts that the Debtor's filing under chapter 7 constitutes an abuse of the provisions of the Code, because the Debtor has the ability to repay his creditors in full in fewer than sixty months. The Debtor argues, however, that because his income falls below the relevant median income level, he is deemed

---

[1] At the initial hearing, the UST offered into evidence the Debtor's schedules, which it argues proves that the Debtor has almost $875 per month in excess income from which he can repay his creditors in full under a five-year plan. In his reply brief, the Debtor submitted an affidavit putting at issue his employment history and prospects for continued employment. The UST opposes the Court's consideration of the Debtor's affidavit because the Debtor failed to appear at the hearing and the UST was unable to cross-examine. Accordingly, the Court will schedule an evidentiary hearing to address these disputed facts.

not to have the ability to pay under section 707(b)(7). Essentially, the Debtor claims that paragraphs (b)(2) and (b)(7) constitute the only provisions of section 707(b) that address a debtor's ability to pay. Any inquiry under paragraph (b)(3), argues the Debtor, cannot include the Debtor's ability to pay his creditors.

A. Section 707(b)

Section 707(b)(1) provides that "a court . . . may dismiss a case if it finds that the granting of relief would be an abuse of the provisions of this chapter." In paragraph (b)(2) is outlined the "means test," perhaps the most noteworthy feature of the Bankruptcy Abuse Prevention and Consumer Protection Act of 2005 ("BAPCPA"). When the means test is triggered, a presumption of abuse arises that can only be rebutted by a debtor on a showing of "special circumstances." Paragraph (b)(3) states that "in considering under paragraph (1) whether the granting of relief would be an abuse in a case in which the presumption in subparagraph (A)(i) of such paragraph[2] does not arise or is rebutted, the court shall consider whether the debtor filed his petition in bad faith or whether the totality of the circumstances of the debtor's financial situation demonstrates abuse."

Paragraph (b)(7), on which the Debtor relies, provides that "no judge, United States trustee, . . . trustee, or any other party in interest may file a motion under paragraph (2) if the current monthly income of the debtor is equal to or less than (i) the median family income of the applicable State." This "safe harbor" provision prevents all parties, including the UST and the Court,[3] from moving to dismiss a chapter 7 case based on a presumption of abuse resulting from the application of the means test outlined in paragraph (b)(2). If no one can file a motion under section 707(b)(2) and the Court cannot presume abuse sua sponte, no presumption of abuse can arise.

Even where no presumption of abuse arises under section 707(b)(2), however, the Court must still determine under paragraph (b)(1) whether the granting of relief under chapter 7 would constitute an abuse. Dismissal under paragraph (b)(1) depends on the guidelines established by Congress in paragraph (b)(3), namely fraud or the totality of the circumstances.

The Debtor argues that dismissal based on "the totality of the circumstances of the debtor's financial situation" set forth in paragraph (b)(3) cannot include a debtor's ability to pay as a factor. Ability to pay, argues the Debtor, has been subsumed post-BAPCPA under paragraphs (b)(2) and (b)(7). The Debtor contends that the totality of the circumstances test should be limited to prevent the granting of relief under chapter 7 to debtors who file serial bankruptcies, load up on secured debt or manipulate their current monthly income to pass the means test.

The UST asserts that consideration of the totality of the circumstances test in paragraph (b)(3) includes determining the Debtor's ability to repay his creditors. The UST refers to pre-BAPCPA cases that interpreted a similar test

[2] It appears that Congress actually meant to refer to subsection (A)(i) of paragraph (2) ; there is no subsection (A)(i) of paragraph (1).

[3] Of course, no Bankruptcy Judge "files motions" in proceedings before her. It appears the intent of Congress in drafting paragraph (b)(7) was to preclude the Court from sua sponte applying the means test and dismissing a failing debtor's case.

under former section 707(b). See, e.g., In re Roth, 108 B.R. 78, 81 (Bankr. W.D. Pa. 1989).

B. Explicit Language of the Statute

"It is axiomatic that statutory interpretation begins with the language of the statute itself." Virgin Islands v. Knight, 989 F.2d 619, 633, 28 V.I. 249 (3d Cir. 1993). A statutory language analysis must precede any resort to legislative history or case law as "there is, of course, no more persuasive evidence of the purpose of a statute than the words by which the legislature undertook to give expression to its wishes." United States v. Am. Trucking Ass'ns, 310 U.S. 534, 543 (1930). Where a statute's language is plain, the court's function is to enforce the statute according to its terms. See United States v. Ron Pair Enters., Inc., 489 U.S. 235, 241 (1989) (citation omitted).

Paragraph (b)(3) explicitly mandates[4] that the totality of the circumstances of the Debtor's financial situation be considered in determining whether there is an abuse when the presumption of abuse under paragraph (b)(2) does not arise or is rebutted.[5] There is nothing in the language of section 707 to suggest that the test in paragraph (b)(3) is less than "total" if a debtor's income falls below the median income level in paragraph (b)(7).

The Debtor argues nonetheless that paragraphs (b)(2) and (b)(7) already test the Debtor's ability to pay his creditors. Because paragraph (b)(7) is applicable here, the Debtor asserts that the Court must conclude he is not able to pay his creditors.

The Court disagrees with the Debtor's argument. Under the Debtor's theory, if a debtor's income were to fall below the median income level, no motion to dismiss based on ability to pay could be brought. That is not what paragraph (b)(7) states. Rather, it simply precludes any presumption of abuse from arising under paragraph (b)(2). No presumption of abuse does not mean there is no abuse. Section 707(b)(7) makes no reference, or changes, to paragraph (b)(3).

Also unpersuasive is the Debtor's argument that the UST is trying to "bypass" the safe harbor outlined in paragraph (b)(7). The UST's motion to dismiss is based on paragraph (b)(3) and, therefore, does not skirt paragraph (b)(7)'s prohibition on motions to dismiss under paragraph (b)(2). Debtors within the protection of paragraph (b)(7) are only safe from a presumption of abuse that might otherwise arise under paragraph (b)(2) and are not beyond the reach of paragraph (b)(3)'s comprehensive, statutorily-mandated inquiry into their fitness for chapter 7 relief.

As is manifest in section 707, a safe harbor upon entry into which neither one's motives nor fitness for chapter 7 relief are questioned is hardly one Congress sought to dredge. When no presumption of abuse arises under paragraph (b)(2), the Court concludes that the Code mandates consideration of a debtor's ability to pay his creditors within the test articulated in paragraph

---

[4] Section 707(b) (3) states "the court shall consider . . . the totality of the circumstances."

[5] Also of note is that Congress did explicitly limit the exercise of the Court's discretion in granting motions to dismiss under paragraph (b)(1) : the Court may not consider any charitable contributions made by a debtor. This provision suggests that Congress knew how to exclude factors and chose not to exclude a debtor's ability to pay his creditors from consideration under paragraph (b)(3).

(b)(3). Accord In re Pak, 343 B.R. 239, 244 (Bankr. N.D. Cal. 2006).

C. Statutory Construction

The Debtor argues that the rules of statutory construction support his contention that ability to pay may not be considered under paragraph (b)(3) because his income falls below the median income level in paragraph (b)(7). The Debtor cites the proposition that "it is a commonplace of statutory construction that the specific govern the general." See Morales v. Trans World Airlines, Inc., 504 U.S. 374, 384 (1992). Paragraphs (b)(2) and (b)(7), argues the Debtor, are more specific determinants of one's ability to pay than the general provisions of paragraph (b)(3). See Marianne B. Culhane and Michaela M. White, Catching Can-Pay Debtors: Is the Means Test the Only Way?, 13 AM. BANKR. INST. L. Rev. 665, 678-80 (2005).

The Court concludes, however, that paragraph (b)(7)'s safe harbor provision does not conclusively determine that the Debtor is unable to pay his creditors. For example, a debtor with an adjusted annual income one dollar below the median income level may nonetheless have the ability to repay trivial debts. Therefore, the Court cannot conclude that paragraph (b)(7) is the more specific provision on this point. Pak, 343 B.R. at 243 (holding that for below-median income level debtor, there is no more specific provision on ability to pay than section 707(b)(3)). See also Eugene Wedoff, Means Testing in the New 707(b), 79 Am Bankr. L.J. 231 (2005) (concluding that passing means test does not preclude finding of abuse under section 707(b)(3) based on ability to pay).

D. Congressional Intent

The Debtor also argues that dismissal of his case based on ability to pay is contrary to the intent of Congress in passing the BAPCPA amendments to the Bankruptcy Code. He cites several statements from Congressmen during the debates on BAPCPA that the Act will not bar debtors with below-median income from filing chapter 7 cases.

While the plain language of the statute is sufficiently clear that an inquiry into the intent of Congress is not warranted, the Court concludes that the Debtor's method of discerning Congressional intent and the conclusions he draws are misguided. The Debtor attempts to discern Congressional intent from an assortment of statements made by individual legislators. The Supreme Court has stated, however, that "[i]n surveying legislative history . . . the authoritative source for finding the Legislature's intent lies in the Committee Reports on the bill, which represent the considered and collective understanding of those Congressmen involved in drafting and studying proposed legislation.'... We have eschewed reliance on the passing comments of one member . . . and casual statements from the floor debates." Garcia v. United States, 469 U.S. 70, 76 (1984) (internal citations omitted).

In fact, the Committee Reports on BAPCPA unequivocally indicate Congress' intent that the Court consider a debtor's ability to pay his creditors under paragraph (b)(3), even where the safe harbor provision of paragraph (b)(7) operates to prevent a presumption of abuse from arising under paragraph (b)(2). See Bankruptcy Reform Act of 2000 -- Conference Report, 146 Cong. Rec. S11683-02, S11703.

> Dismissal under 707(b) is also authorized when there is "abuse." It is intended that by changing the standard for dismissal from "substantial abuse" to "abuse," stronger controls will be available . . . to limit the abusive use of Chapter 7 based on a wide range of circumstances. The "bad faith" and "totality of the circumstances" of the debtor's situation is adopted as an appropriate standard. It is intended that all forms of inappropriate and abusive debtor use of Chapter 7 will be covered by this standard, whether because of the debtor's conduct or the debtor's ability to pay. . . . Cases which have decided that a debtor's ability to pay should not be considered when determining abuse, or can be outweighed if the debtor is otherwise acting in good faith, are intended to be overruled. In dealing with ability to pay cases which are abusive, the presumption of abuse and the safe harbor protecting debtors from application of the presumption will not be relevant.

Id. (emphasis added).

In fact, the Debtor admits that the means test is not an accurate indicator of a debtor's ability to pay. See, e.g., In re Walker, 2006 Bankr. LEXIS 845, 2006 WL 1314125, at *13 (Bankr. N.D. Ga. 2006) ("Section 707(b)'s presumption of abuse was not intended to and does not produce the most accurate prediction of the debtor's actual ability to fund a Chapter 13 plan."). The Walker Court noted that "whether the debtor passes or fails the means test is relevant only to the question of whether the U.S. Trustee will benefit from a presumption of abuse. In cases in which the presumption of abuse does not arise or is rebutted, the U.S. Trustee may pursue dismissal of a debtor's case under section 707(b)(3)." 2006 Bankr. LEXIS 845, at *25, [WL] at 17.

The Court agrees and concludes that, even where application of the means test or paragraph (b)(7)'s safe harbor provision prevents a presumption of abuse from arising, section 707(b)(3) requires the Court to consider the Debtor's ability to pay his creditors.

Thus, the Court will consider the totality of the circumstances of the Debtor's financial situation, including the Debtor's ability to pay his creditors, in considering the Trustee's motion to dismiss under section 707(b)(1) and (3).

The Court concludes that, where the safe harbor of section 707(b)(7) applies and no presumption of abuse arises under section 707(b)(2), the Court nonetheless must determine if the Debtor's case is an abuse under section 707(b)(3). The Court further concludes that the totality of the circumstances test under section 707(b)(3) includes consideration of the Debtor's ability to repay his creditors. The Court will schedule a further hearing to consider the motion to dismiss in light of the Court's ruling.

Notes and Questions

1. If the court in Paret is correct, what is the utility of Bankruptcy Code §707(b)(7), and how does it differ from §707(b)(6)?

2. Notice that if D is below the state median, given the size of her household, Form B22A line 15 excuses D from listing expenses. The implication is that the means test does not apply to below-median debtors.

3. Overriding the partial and even the (perhaps) total immunities of below-median debtors is § 707(c)(2), which invites victims of violent or drug-trafficking crime to move to dismiss a case "[e]xcept as provided in paragraph (3)." The partial immunity accorded the below-median debtors is an immunity for a motion to dismiss "under section 707(b)." The total immunity may or may not likewise refer to motions under § 707(b). Neither of these bar motions by crime victims under § 707(c). Therefore, the immunities of below-median debtors can never be complete, as dismissals under subparagraph (c) are always possible.

The crime victim, however, will have to show a criminal conviction and that dismissal "is in the best interest of the victim." 11 U.S.C. § 707(c)(2). It will not be necessary, however, for the victim to be a creditor of the debtor, though it is hard to imagine how the dismissal of the case helps the victim unless the victim is a creditor. Even so, the criminal debtor can defend herself by showing "by a preponderance of the evidence" that a chapter 7 case is "necessary to satisfy a claim for a domestic support obligation." For example, a domestic support claimant is entitled to a high priority under § 507(a)(1). If this claim could be paid in chapter 7 but not outside it, then criminal debtor can resist the dismissal. Outside bankruptcy, the domestic support claimant may have no priority compared to the crime victim. Some states, however, do provide such a priority. E.g., N.Y.C.P.L.R. § 5234(b).

Why crime victims should have standing to move for dismissal is questionable in light of § 523(a)(6) since claims "for willful and malicious injury by the debtor to another entity or to the property of another entity" are never dischargeable. One answer might be that drug trafficking harms may not be malicious (though typically they will be willful). Another answer is that, even if the crime is malicious and willful, the automatic stay still applies to prevent the victim from enforcing a tort judgment during the pendency of the case. Therefore, early dismissal would be in the interest of the victim.

TURNER v CLOSE (IN RE CLOSE)

384 B.R. 856 (D. Kan. 2008)

JULIE A. ANDERSON, J.

This matter comes before the Court on appeal by the United States Trustee ("Trustee") from an order of the bankruptcy court denying as untimely the Trustee's motion to dismiss the underlying bankruptcy case pursuant to 11 U.S.C. § 707(b)(2) and the subsequent order granting the Debtors a discharge. For the reasons explained in detail below, the Court affirms the bankruptcy court's orders.

I. Statutory Framework

Prior to the enactment of the Bankruptcy Abuse Prevention Consumer Protection Act of 2005 ("BAPCPA"), 11 U.S.C. § 704 was concerned with duties of Chapter 7 trustees. The 2005 amendments added a new subsection (b) that sets forth duties of the United States Trustee in cases of all individual debtors. These duties pertain to the determination of whether a Chapter 7 case is an abuse as defined by section 707(b) and, in particular, the presumption of abuse under section 707(b)(2). In BAPCPA, Congress sought to limit the discretion previously exercised by bankruptcy judges by creating a mechanical formula for presuming abuse in the filing of a Chapter 7 case.[1] Congress implemented this policy by requiring debtors to file documentation on their financial condition and history in addition to the schedules of income and expenses and to prepare calculations to determine whether the new statutory presumption of abuse arises (the "Means Test"). Highly simplified, the Means Test can be explained as follows: when a debtor's monthly disposable income is above the amount of $ 166.66, a "presumption of abuse" arises. If his monthly disposable income is less than $ 100, the presumption does not arise. If his monthly disposable income is between those amounts, then the presumption arises only if the amount, taken over 60 months, is sufficient to pay at least 25% of the debtor's nonpriority secured debt.

Section 704(b)(1)(A) requires the Trustee to review the materials filed by the debtor and to file a statement as to whether the debtor's case would be presumed to be an abuse under § 707(b). The materials to be reviewed for the §

[1] In re Hartwick, 359 B.R. 16, 21 (Bankr. D.N.H. 2007).

704(b)(1) statement include the schedules and statements filed by the debtor, which would include calculations of current monthly income and, if the debtor's income is over the applicable state median income, calculations regarding the Means Test presumption of abuse. Each debtor with primarily consumer debts is required to file, in conjunction with his or her bankruptcy schedules and statement of financial affairs, a Statement of Current Monthly Income and Means Test Calculation, Official Form B22A of the Federal Rules of Bankruptcy Procedure.[2] The materials also include evidence of payment from employers and a tax return. As discussed in more detail below, the Trustee's statement must be filed not later than ten days after "the date of the first meeting of creditors.

If a debtor does not satisfy the Means Test, the case is presumed to be an abuse under § 707(b)(2). At a hearing on a motion to dismiss under § 707(b)(2), a debtor may rebut the presumption only by demonstrating "special circumstances" as prescribed in § 707(b)(2)(B). However, at a hearing to dismiss a case where the presumption of abuse does not arise, the burden of proof is on the moving party to establish that the case was filed in bad faith or that the totality of the circumstances of a debtor's financial situation demonstrate abuse.

If a presumption of abuse arises under the Means Test, it "may only be rebutted by demonstrating special circumstances, such as a serious medical condition or a call or order to active duty in the Armed Forces."[3] If the debtor cannot rebut the presumption, he has the option of having his case dismissed or converted to a Chapter 13 proceeding, in which he may obtain a discharge only after repaying a set amount to his creditors.[4] Even if the presumption of abuse does not arise or is rebutted, however, the court may find abuse based on the debtor's bad faith in filing the bankruptcy petition or the totality of the circumstances of the debtor's financial situation.[5]

Under BAPCPA, § 707(b)(2) allows not only the Trustee, but also other parties in interest and private trustees to move for dismissal of Chapter 7 cases where the debtor's net income "passes" the means test.[6]

II. Factual Background

Debtors filed their petition for Chapter 7 relief on February 28, 2006. Included in the initial filing was Debtors' Form B22A. Debtors reported $ 55,536.48 in annualized gross income. The median income for a family of two in Kansas is $ 50,258.00. Debtors completed the remaining sections of Form B22A because they are above median. In Part VI of Form B22A, entitled "Determination of § 707(b)(2) Presumption," Debtors stated that their monthly disposable income was $ 192.96, or $ 11,577.60 over sixty months. Because that amount of disposable income creates a presumption of abuse under 11 U.S.C. § 707(b)(2), the bankruptcy software used by Debtors' counsel automatically checked the box at the top of the form that states, "The presumption arises."

---

[2] Id. Although the Form is currently known as Form "22A," since the Form was known as "B22A" at the time the Debtors filed this case, the Court will continue to use that name.

[3] Id. § 707(b)(2)(B)(i).

[4] Id. § 707(b)(1).

[5] Id. § 707(b)(3).

[6] Under § 707(b)(7), creditors may only file a motion to dismiss if the debtor's current monthly income is above a certain income threshold.

The 11 U.S.C. § 341 meeting of creditors was scheduled for March 30, 2006. On March 14, 2006, the Trustee sent a letter to Debtors' counsel requesting, among other things, pay stubs for the full six-month Certified Monthly Income ("CMI") period and inquiring about any health insurance expenses that may have been omitted as deductions on their Official Form 22A. The Chapter 7 Trustee called the first meeting of creditors on its scheduled date but continued it at the Trustee's request to April 27, 2006, pending additional information to be supplied by the Debtors. Debtors responded to the requests on March 30, 2006, and the continued meeting of creditors was concluded on April 27, 2006, without the parties actually meeting.

Debtors contend that they did not know their case was being analyzed for presumptive abuse until May 1, 2006, when the Trustee filed a notice of presumptive abuse under 11 U.S.C. § 704(b)(1)(A), followed by a Motion to Dismiss on May 30, 2006. The Trustee sought dismissal under two subsections: § 707(b)(2) for abuse based on the presumption of abuse arising under the Form B22A, and § 707(b)(3), under the "totality of circumstances" standard.

Debtors filed an Amended Form B22A on June 20, 2006, indicating a presumption of abuse does not arise. Although debtors' amendment reported $ 55,223.16 in annualized gross income, which remained above the median, the amendments to Debtors' expenses no longer indicated a presumption of abuse. The Amended Form B22A corrected several errors in the original Form, which were attributed to error of counsel rather than the Debtors.

Debtors asserted that the Trustee's motion to dismiss was time-barred by § 704(b)(1)(A) because the notice of presumed abuse was filed ten days after the conclusion of the § 341 meeting rather than the date of the first § 341 meeting of creditors. The parties agreed to bifurcate the timeliness issue from the merits of the § 707(b)(3) totality of the circumstances issue.

On October 18, 2006, the bankruptcy court entered an Order denying the motion to dismiss on the § 707(b)(2) grounds, ruling that the plain language of § 704(b)(1)(A) supported the Debtors' interpretation that the "first" meeting was the first meeting date, and thus the motion to dismiss based on § 707(b)(2) was untimely. Because the timeliness requirement to bringing a motion under § 707(b)(3) is 60 days from the first date set for the meeting of creditors,[7] the bankruptcy court determined that portion of the motion could proceed.

On October 27, 2006, the Trustee moved for reconsideration of the bankruptcy court's order, which the court denied on February 7, 2007. In the interim, the Trustee withdrew that portion of the motion to dismiss based on the totality of the circumstances under § 707(b)(3). On February 16, 2007, the bankruptcy court entered an order of discharge. On February 20, 2007, the Trustee filed a notice of appeal from the order denying the motion to dismiss and the order denying the motion to reconsider. Later that day, the bankruptcy court entered an order vacating the discharge order stating that it had been entered in error. The next day, however, the bankruptcy court vacated the order vacating the discharge order and reinstated the discharge order, retroactive to the original date of February 16, 2007. The Trustee filed a second notice of appeal from order of discharge and order setting aside order vacating discharge, and the two appeals were later consolidated by this Court . . .

---

[7] Fed. R. Bankr. P. 1017(e).

V. Analysis . . .

B. Timeliness of Motion to Dismiss

. . . Section 704, denominated "Duties of Trustee," provides in subsection (b)(1)(A),

> [T]he United States trustee . . . shall review all materials filed by the debtor and, not later than 10 days after the date of the first meeting of creditors, file with the court a statement as to whether the debtor's case would be presumed to be an abuse under section 707(b) . . . . (Emphasis added.)

In turn, § 704(b)(1)(B) directs that, "not later than 5 days after receiving a statement under subparagraph (A), the court shall provide a copy of the statement to all creditors."

Section 704(b)(2), which governs the timing of the filing of a motion to dismiss, provides,

> The United States trustee . . . shall, not later than 30 days after the date of filing a statement under paragraph (1), either file a motion to dismiss or convert under section 707(b) or file a statement setting forth the reasons the United States trustee . . . does not consider such a motion to be appropriate . . . . (Emphasis added.)

Although the parties each claim that the language of § 704(b)(1)(A) is plain and unambiguous, they nonetheless arrive at starkly different interpretations. The Debtors read "the date of the first meeting of creditors" to mean the date on which the meeting is first scheduled, March 30, 2006. The Trustee argues the language means the entire § 341 meeting of creditors as it may be continued from time to time, and that "date" refers to the date the meeting is concluded, April 27, 2006. The Trustee asserts that "first meeting of creditors" is synonymous with "341 meeting," no matter how many dates "first meeting of creditors" may take. The Trustee argues that "first meeting of creditors" was a vestige of pre-Code practice, is widely used in practice by courts and parties to refer to multiple meetings, and therefore does not refer to the "date" of the meeting but to the series of meetings. The Trustee also cites to 11 U.S.C. § 102(7), which directs that "the singular includes the plural."

The Court begins its analysis with some historical context. The Bankruptcy Act of 1898 that preceded the modern Bankruptcy Code provided for a "first meeting of creditors."[8] It also contained provisions for optional interim meetings after the "first meeting" and for a final meeting in some cases.[9] The pre-BAPCPA Bankruptcy Code did not use the phrase "first meeting of creditors." Section 341(a) of the pre-BAPCPA Bankruptcy Code provides that the Unites States Trustee shall "convene and preside at a meeting of creditors."[10] Subsection 341(c) prohibits the court from presiding or attending "any meeting under this section including any final meeting."[11] Subsection 341(d) provides that the trustee

[8] Id. § 55(a).
[9] Id. § 55(d) and (e).
[10] 11 U.S.C. § 341(a) (emphasis added).
[11] Id. § 341(c) (emphasis added).

shall orally examine the debtor "[p]rior to the conclusion of the meeting."[12] Other Bankruptcy Code sections also refer to "the meeting of creditors."[13] In 1999, Congress amended the Federal Rules of Bankruptcy Procedure to define the deadlines for objections to discharge and dischargeability as 60 days after "the first date set for the meeting of creditors under § 341."[14] Thus, prior to BAPCPA, the Bankruptcy Code and Rules recognized a distinction between (1) "the meeting," meaning the first meeting and any meeting thereafter until the meeting is concluded or final, (2) "the first date set for the meeting," and (3) the "conclusion of" or "final meeting."

BAPCPA, however, added several deadlines triggered by the § 341 meeting, using var-ied syntax. For example, § 521 requires that a debtor perform his statement of intent within "30 days after the first date set for the meeting of creditors;"[15] that the debtor reaffirm or redeem "not later than 45 days after the first meeting of creditors;"[16] and that the debtor pro-vide tax returns "not later than 7 days before the date first set for the first meeting of cred-itors."[17] Section 1308(a) requires a debtor to file tax returns not later than the day before "the date on which the meeting of creditors is first scheduled to be held."[18] Section 1324(b) requires a confirmation hearing to be held not earlier than 20 days and not later than 45 days "after the date of the meeting of creditors under section 341(a)."[19] And, of course, the language before us, the requirement that the Trustee file the statement of abuse "not later than 10 days after the date of the first meeting of creditors."[20] But, BAPCPA did not amend § 341 or the other Code sections that continue to reference "the meeting." Unfortunately, Congress did not define the new triggers in a clear and consistent manner. Thus, the issue becomes, what did Congress intend by the phrase "date of the first meeting of creditors?"

This is an issue of first impression in this District. Neither the Tenth Circuit nor any other circuit court of appeals has addressed the issue of the deadline for the Trustee to file a statement under § 704(b)(1)(A). In support of her position, the Trustee attaches two unpublished opinions that decline to follow Judge Berger's ruling in this case.[21] In In re Williams,[22] the bankruptcy court in the Southern District of Texas reconsidered its reliance on the order in this case based on its perceived erroneous presumption that the ten-day period to file the § 704(b)(1)(A) statement could be extended.[23] The court also cited Collier on

---

[12] Id. § 341(d) (emphasis added).

[13] See id. § 702(b) (addressing the right of creditors to elect a trustee "[a]t the meeting of creditors held under section § 341;" § 705(a) ("[a]t the meeting under section 341(a) of this title . . . ."); former § 521(2) (addressing debtor's duty to file the statement of intention "on or before the date of the meeting of creditors. . . .")

[14] Fed. R. Bankr. P. 4004(a), 4007(c) (emphasis added). As the bankruptcy court noted, the fact that these rules of bankruptcy procedure provide dates tied to the meeting of creditors does not control the interpretation of § 704(b)(1)(A).

[15] 11 U.S.C. § 521(a)(2)(B) (emphasis added).

[16] Id. § 521(a)(6) (emphasis added). This section does not include the word "date."

[17] Id. § 521(e)(2)(A)(i) (emphasis added).

[18] Id § 1308(a) (emphasis added).

[19] Id. § 1324(b) (emphasis added).

[20] Id. § 704(b)(1)(A) (emphasis added).

[21] The Trustee also cites an unpublished slip opinion that follows In re Close, without attaching a copy for the Court, in violation of Fed. R. App. P. 32.1(6).

[22] Case No. 06-20116 (Bankr. S.D. Tex. May 14, 2007).

[23] Id. slip op. at 2.

Bankruptcy in support of its decision.[24] In In re Sloan,[25] the bankruptcy court in the Western District of Oklahoma also declined to follow the ruling in this case, citing Collier.[26] The Sloan court reasoned that if Congress meant for the Trustee's statement to be filed within ten days of the "first date set," it would have so specified.[27] The court 'also concluded that "meeting of creditors" encompasses multiple meeting dates, apparently equating that phrase with "first meeting of creditors."[28]

The Trustee also submitted supplemental authority post-briefing. In In re Cadwallder,[29] an unpublished opinion from the Southern District of Texas, the bankruptcy court embarked on an extensive discussion of § 704(b) in holding that the ten days by which the Trustee must file his statement runs from the end of the creditors' meeting, not the commencement of the creditors' meeting.[30] As with the previously mentioned cases, in support of its conclusion the bankruptcy court cites Collier on Bankruptcy:

> The statement must be filed within 10 days after the date of the "first meeting of creditors." The "first meeting of creditors" is a term sometimes used in the past to refer to the section 341(a) meeting of creditors. The language is somewhat unclear, but logically it makes sense to read this deadline as running from the conclusion of the meeting of creditors, rather than the first date set for the meeting of creditors, which is specifically referenced in some other Code provisions enacted at the same time. Otherwise, if the debtor is unable to attend the meeting on the first date set, or provide all necessary documents, the United States trustee might not have all the materials necessary to make an accurate determination.[31]

Contrary to the decision in the instant case, the Cadwallder bankruptcy court found that the function of "first" in section 704 is "ambiguous, at best," and that it could not determine the "plain meaning."[32] The court concluded that the "most reasonable interpretation is to recognize the essential equivalence of 'first meeting of creditors' and 'meeting of creditors' in general parlance. This interpretation would make the word 'first' surplusage."[33] Remarkably, the court went on to acknowledge that this interpretation clearly violated principles of statutory construction, but it was "not aware of any better alternative."[34] Reading the term "date" as "dates" to include the entire period that the § 341 meeting convenes, the court concluded that the deadline refers to all dates of the first meeting of creditors, including continuances or resets.[35]

The Cadwallder bankruptcy court also held that "§ 704(b) is a mandate for U.S. Trustee action imposed for the benefit of the Court and the other parties in interest, not a deadline. Therefore, even if the U.S. Trustee had not met the §

[24] Id. slip op. at 3.
[25] Case No. 06-11490-WV (W.D. Okla. Feb. 6, 2007).
[26] Id. slip op. at 4.
[27] Id.
[28] Id. slip op. at 5.
[29] No. 06-36424, 2007 Bankr. LEXIS 2260, 2007 WL 1864154 (Bankr. S.D. Tex., June 28, 2007).
[30] 2007 Bankr. LEXIS 2260, [WL] at
[31] Id. (citing 6 Collier on Bankruptcy P 704.17[2] (15th rev. ed. 2006)).
[32] 2007 Bankr. LEXIS 2260, [WL] at *12.
[33] Id.
[34] Id.
[35] Id.

704(b) deadlines, the motion [to dismiss] would not be time barred merely for that reason."[36] The court found that although § 704(b) sets a time for the Trustee to file a statement of presumed abuse, it specifies no consequence for tardy action.[37]

The Court is not persuaded by either the Trustee's arguments on appeal or the cases cited in support of her position, as they utilize incomplete or questionable applications of statutory construction. Moreover, although Collier on Bankruptcy is a well respected, oft-quoted resource for bankruptcy courts and practitioners, it does not employ any statutory construction in its blanket conclusion on this issue. Instead, the Court is persuaded by the bankruptcy court's reasoning that the statutory language of § 704(b)(1)(A) supports a plain language interpretation that "first" means "first." In other words, the plain meaning of the phrase "date of the first meeting of creditors" refers to the first meeting date and not some later date. The language is not vague or ambiguous and does not need extraneous verbiage to clarify its meaning. The Court agrees with the bankruptcy court that the Trustee reads more into the statute than what it unambiguously states, both by reading "conclusion" into the statute to support her own position, or by requiring "first date set for" by attacking Debtors' position. Under either alternative, the Trustee must add words to the statute to make her interpretation work. Similarly, the fact that "first meeting of creditors" was commonly understood pre-Code to refer to multiple meetings, ignores the express use of the word "date" to refer to the first meeting. Again, the Trustee's interpretation either derogates from or adds to the plain language of § 704(b)(1)(A).

Nor is the Court persuaded by the Trustee's reliance on § 102(7), the rule of construction providing that the singular includes the plural, to support its argument that a meeting of creditors can occur on multiple "dates." If the word "date" in § 704(b)(1)(A) is to be read as the plural "dates," so should the word "meeting," as in "not later than 10 days after the dates of the first meetings of creditors. . . ." The Trustee's interpretation would render the word "first" meaningless, which the Court declines to adopt.[38] the Court rejects the Trustee's argument that the bankruptcy court's interpretation would require her to file statements of abuse "during" the meeting of creditors and not "after." This argument is valid only if the Court reads the plain language of the statute to include multiple meetings and omits the word "first."

The Court finds some support for its holding from analogous rulings of other courts dealing with the related question of whether a timely unequivocal statement of abuse is a prerequisite to the Trustee's § 707(b) motion to dismiss. The bankruptcy court did not have the benefit of these decisions, as they were issued after the briefing was completed in the instant appeal, and several opinions were submitted by Debtors to the Court as supplemental authority.

The bankruptcy court in In re Robertson[39] held that § 704(b)(1)(A) requires the Trustee to timely file an unequivocal statement that a case is or is not

[36] Id. 2007 Bankr. LEXIS 2260, [WL] at *9.

[37] Id. 2007 Bankr. LEXIS 2260, [WL] at *6.

[38] Lopez-Soto v. Hawayek, 175 F.3d 170, 174 (1st Cir. 1999) (It is a "time-honored tenet that [a]ll words and provisions of a statute are intended to have meaning and are to be given effect, and no construction should be adopted which would render statutory words or phrases meaningless, redundant or superfluous.") (quotation omitted).

[39] 370 B.R. 804, 810-11 (Bankr. D. Minn. 2007).

presumptively an abuse under § 707(b). In Robertson, the Trustee filed a statement ten days after the date first set for the meeting of creditors issued by the clerk's office upon filing of the debtors' petition that stated:

> The United States Trustee has determined that the debtor has not filed nor transmitted all of the required means testing documents and that without these documents, the United States Trustee cannot make a determination as to whether the debtor's case is presumed abusive under section 707(b).[40]
>
> This statement was followed within 30 days by a motion to dismiss under § 707(b)(2). Debtors raised a threshold issue that the motion was barred because the Trustee had never filed a "statement as to whether the debtors' case would be presumed to bean abuse under [11 U.S.C. §] 707(b)," as required under § 704(b)(1)(A).[41]

Turning to the plain meaning of the statute, the bankruptcy court held that the phrase "the United States Trustee . . . shall review all materials filed by the debtor," means materials filed with the court; there is no reference to materials to be obtained from the debtor or third-party sources via formal discovery, informal exchange, or independent investigation.[42] Thus, in conducting the

> statutorily-mandated early evaluation of a case for the prospect of a presumption of abuse, the [United States Trustee] ultimately is relegated to relying on what the debtor "filed" in the case. The statute seems to contemplate that this will present sufficiently reliable information on which to make an evaluation--at least when debtors and their counsel have complied with the newly-heightened duties of verification as to accuracy that BAPCPA has imposed."[43]

The court further found that the statute is equally clear that the Trustee's statement requires an election between two specific representations, which are to go in an unequivocal fashion to the Trustee's estimation of the legal posture of the case in light of § 707(b)(2).[44] In short, "[t]here either is or is not a presumption of abuse based on a detail-busy analysis of the debtor's monthly income, reduced by the expenses and secured debt payments and so forth, both general in nature and fussily pinpoint-specific, that are laid out in §§ 707(b)(2)(A)-(B)."[45] The court concluded that "[u]nder the common, every-day meaning of the statutory verbiage there is no room for an equivocal placeholder, the planting of a stake that is somehow to reserve the right to draw a conclusion for later exercise, to toll the period under § 704(b)(2) for the filing of a motion under § 707(b)(2), or both."[46] the Trustee did not timely put of record his unequivocal conclusion that the presumption lies in Robertson, he was precluded from filing his motion to dismiss.[47]

In its examination of the issue, the Robertson court noted that the timeliness elements of § 704(b) are consistent with the policies sought to be engendered by BAPCPA. "The language of §§ 704(b)(1)-(2) tracks with a more

[40] Id. at 807.
[41] Id. at 807-08.
[42] Id. at 809 (emphasis in the original).
[43] Id. The court noted that the new text seems to be designed to "put some teeth" into this assumption." Id. at 809 n.8.
[44] Id. at 810.
[45] Id.
[46] Id. at 810.
[47] Id. at 811.

general intent behind BAPCPA, to reduce delay in the fixing of rights and statuses during the court of bankruptcy cases, and in particular to expedite the basic determination of whether a party should be in bankruptcy at all."[48] the court explained,

> This is one instance, however, where the onus of acting quickly, clearly, and decisively falls on a party other than the debtor. BAPCPA contained a number of ostensibly strict-compliance, zero-tolerance measures that weigh heavily on debtors in bankruptcy. This one happens to impact on a constituency that stands in opposition to a debtor.[49]

The decision in Robertson has garnered support from several courts.[50] Although decided in the context of the content of the statement, these cases all require the statement filed pursuant to § 704(b)(1)(A) to be both unequivocal and "timely."[51] In each of these cases, as in Robertson, the Trustee filed the § 704(b)(1) statement within ten days of the date originally set for the meeting of creditors, based on the filing of the bankruptcy petitions.[52] And, as in Robertson, the Trustee's statement was to be based on what the debtor filed with the court, not on additional documentation requested by the Trustee. Indeed, the Form B22A is quite comprehensive, the apparent purpose of which is to determine whether a presumption does or does not arise in the debtor's case.[53] these courts seem to have imposed upon the Trustee a deadline for filing a § 704(b)(1) statement of abuse.[54]

Although the proper interpretation of § 704(b)(1)(A) is dictated by the language of the statute itself, the Court notes that its interpretation comports with the purposes of BAPCPA.[55] legislative history for BAPCPA reveals that "[t]he heart of the bill's consumer bankruptcy reforms consists of the implementation of an income/expense screening mechanism ('needs-based bankruptcy relief or 'means testing'), which is intended to ensure that debtors repay creditors the maximum they can afford."[56] The new consumer bankruptcy provisions were intended to respond to several factors, including the escalation

---

[48] Id. (citing H.R. Rep. No. 109-31, pt. 1.(2005)).

[49] Id. (citations omitted).

[50] See, e.g., In re Ansar, B.R. , 2008 Bankr. LEXIS 544, 2008 WL 623136, at *3 (Bankr. D. Minn. Mar. 5, 2008) (adopting decision in Robertson as a careful and sound analysis with respect to the ten-day statement requirement); In re Byrne, 376 B.R. 700, 703 (Bankr. W.D. Ark. 2007) ("In the absence of a timely filed statement under § 704(b)(1), the UST is precluded from filing a motion to dismiss based on a presumption of abuse, i.e., a § 707(b)(2) motion."); In re Perrotta, 378 B.R. 434, 438 (Bankr. D.N.H. 2007) ("[F]ailure to timely file a statement of presumed abuse by the deadline in § 704(b)(1) results in the UST being unable to pursue dismissal of a case for presumed [*30] abuse under § 707(b)(1) and (2)."). But see In re Cadwallder, No. 06-36424, 2007 Bankr. LEXIS 2260, 2007 WL 1864154, at *9 (Bankr. S.D. Tex. 2007) (holding that because Congress did not specify consequences for failure to meet the § 704(b) deadlines, there would be none).

[51] Id.

[52] See Ansar, 2008 Bankr. LEXIS 544, 2008 WL 623136, at *1; Perrotta, 378 B.R. at 436; Byrne, 376 B.R. at 701.

[53] Byrne, 376 B.R. at 703-04.

[54] See Perrotta, 378 B.R. at 437.

[55] Notwithstanding the determination that statutory language is clear on its face, the court may look to legislative history to reinforce its conclusion that the statute is, indeed, unambiguous. 2A Sutherland Statutory Construction § 46:4 (7th ed. 2007); see also Wieland v. Thomas, 382 B.R. 793 (D. Kan. 2008).

[56] H.R. Rep. No. 109-31(1), 2005 U.S.C.C.A.N. 88, 89.

of consumer bankruptcy filings and the "growing perception that bankruptcy relief may be too readily available and is sometimes used as a first resort, rather than a last resort;" the adverse financial consequences for the economy as a whole resulting from increased filings; loopholes and incentives in the prior system "that allow and sometimes even encourage opportunistic personal filings and abuse;" and the fact that "some bankruptcy debtors are able to repay a significant portion of their debts."[57] The report accompanying the act notes that the prior "substantial abuse" standard for dismissal was inherently vague, and thus the new statute replaces the prior presumption in favor of discharge with a mandatory presumption of abuse arising under a certain formula.[58] As noted above, those amendments were intended to reduce delay and in particular, to expedite the basic determination of whether a party should be in bankruptcy. If the Trustee were permitted to postpone filing the § 704(b)(1)(A) statement until after she decides to conclude the § 341 meeting, the purpose of the statute would be frustrated. Moreover, Fed. R. Bankr. P. 1017(e) clearly establishes a-60-day deadline for any party to file a motion-to dismiss under § 707(b), except to the extent that § 707(b)(2) sets the deadline for the Trustee to act. The 60 days runs from the first date set for the meeting of creditors.[59] If the § 704(b)(1)(A) deadline ran from the conclusion of the meeting of creditors, as argued by the Trustee, the consequence might be that the § 704(b) deadline could be longer than the Rule 1017(e) deadline.[60]

Furthermore, the fact that this deadline might be burdensome to the Trustee is of no consequence in the Court's analysis.[61] As another bankruptcy court recently explained, "[t]he loss of the benefit of the presumption is the consequence Congress intended on the [United States Trustee] for failure to meet the deadline."[62] Supreme Court has clearly instructed bankruptcy courts to not consider whether particular phraseology makes good policy sense, to the extent a court can ascertain policy, but instead to apply the statute as written, leaving it to Congress to amend the statute if a contrary interpretation was intended.[63] As the Court explained, "[o]ur unwillingness to soften the import of Congress' chosen words even if we believe the words lead to a harsh outcome is longstanding."[64]

Nor would the Court's interpretation permit debtors to escape the consequences of failing to file the required materials or withholding information for the Trustee to review. As the bankruptcy court noted, the. Trustee has options

---

[57] Id. at 90-92.

[58] Id. at 98-99, 119.

[59] Fed. R. Bankr. P. 1017(e).

[60] As Debtors point out, the court is to provide a copy of the statement filed by the Trustee to all creditors within five days after it is filed. 11 U.S.C. § 704(b)(1)(B). Presumably, this is to give creditors an opportunity to file their own motions to dismiss under § 707(b)(2), if they are eligible to do so. Thus, it is likely that most creditors will wait and see if the Trustee files a motion, saving them the expense. The Court notes that if the Trustee is permitted to postpone filing of the statement, it might [*33] negatively impact a creditor's deadline for doing so.

[61] The Court questions the Trustee's claim of a burden in this particular case, as Debtors' Form B22A, although apparently erroneous, clearly stated on its face that the presumption applied and they responded to the Trustee's inquiry letter with information in time for the Trustee to have met the ten-day deadline after the first meeting of creditors.

[62] Perrotta, 378 B.R. at 438.

[63] See Lamie v. United States Trustee, 540 U.S. 526, 542 (2004).

[64] Id. at 538.

when faced with an uncooperative debtor and time constraints.[65] In addition, § 707(a)(3) provides for dismissal of the case for cause upon motion of the Trustee for failure of the debtor to timely file the information required by § 521(1), including Form B22A.[66] Under BAPCPA, § 707(b) imposes Rule 9011 standards on the debtor's attorney in preparing the schedules, statements and Form B22A's and attorneys can be sanctioned if they file these documents without sufficient legal or factual basis or inquiry. Moreover, it is important to note that even if there is no presumption of abuse, the Trustee is not precluded from taking action when she finds a case to be abusive under a "totality of the circumstances" or bad faith analysis.[67] Where no presumption of abuse arises, the 30-day deadline imposed by § 704(b)(2) does not apply and a § 704(b)(1)(A) statement is not a prerequisite for filing.[68]

The Court concludes that because the date of the first meeting of creditors was March 30, 2006, the Trustee should have filed the statement on or before April 10, 2006, and should have filed the motion to dismiss under § 707(b)(2) within 30 days, or by May 10, 2006. The Trustee did not do so, and accordingly, the motion to dismiss was untimely. The bankruptcy court's order denying the Trustee's motion to dismiss on, this basis is therefore affirmed.

C. Entry of Discharge Order

Nine days after the bankruptcy court entered its order denying reconsideration of its order denying the Trustee's motion to dismiss, the bankruptcy court entered an order granting Debtors a discharge. The Trustee contends that this was in error under Bankruptcy Rule 4004(c)(1), which provides that the bankruptcy court "shall forthwith" grant a discharge unless a motion to dismiss the case under § 707 is pending.[69] According to the Trustee, this rule precludes a discharge not only before the bankruptcy court has ruled on a motion to dismiss, but also during the time in which the Trustee is pursuing an appeal of the ruling. The Trustee further asserts that the bankruptcy court lacked jurisdiction to enter the order reinstating the vacated discharge order by reason of her filing a notice of appeal.

Given its aforementioned decision affirming the bankruptcy court's order denying the Trustee's motion to dismiss, the Court questions the need to address this issue.[70] Nevertheless, the Court finds that the Trustee cites no support for the proposition that her motion to dismiss was pending after the bankruptcy court entered its final order denying the motion to reconsider. Accepting the Black's

[65] These suggested options include moving to continue the first date set for the § 341 hearing or filing the presumption of abuse based on the debtor's failure to provide sufficient information. Bankruptcy Court Order at 6. In addition, the Debtors suggest that the Trustee can file a motion to extend the ten day deadline pursuant to Fed. R. Bankr.P. 9006 or 11 U.S.C. § 105(a). The Court mentions these options by way of example only, and leaves the merits of any such issues for the bankruptcy courts.

[66] 11 U.S.C. § 707(a)(3).

[67] 11 U.S.C. § 707(b)(3).

[68] In re Byrne, 376 B.R. 700, 704 (Bankr. W.D. Ark. 2007) (holding if the United States trustee fails to file a definitive § 704(b)(1) statement, she is not precluded from filing a motion to dismiss based on § 707(b)(3) for bad faith or a totality of the circumstances [*36] surrounding a debtor's financial situation that indicates abuse).

[69] Fed. R. Bankr. P. 4004(c)(1).

[70] See McVay v. Olero, 371 B.R. 190, 205 (Bankr. W.D. Tex. 2007).

Law Dictionary of "pending" as cited by the Trustee--that a matter is pending from inception until final judgment--the motion to dismiss was pending until February 7, 2007. The order became final on that date, and the Trustee was entitled to file an appeal of right.[71] There is no stay of execution preventing immediate finality from an order denying a motion to dismiss under § 707(b),[72] and the Trustee did not move for a stay pending appeal. Moreover, under the Trustee's theory, the order vacating the discharge order was itself void, and thus the original discharge order entered before any notice of appeal should stand. Accordingly, the order granting Debtors a discharge is also affirmed.

IT IS THEREFORE ORDERED BY THE COURT that the Order of the bankruptcy court denying the United States Trustee's motion to dismiss pursuant to § 707(b)(2) and the subsequent Order granting Debtors a discharge are AFFIRMED.

Notes and Questions

1. Suppose the first creditors' meeting is scheduled on March 1. The United States trustee files a notice of presumptive abuse on March 12 (too late). The trustee then moves to dismiss on March 31 (within the time limit if the notice had been timely filed). Is the trustee timely? In re Robertson, 370 B.R. 804, 810-11 (Bankr. D. Minn. 2007).

2. Suppose the trustee files a timely notice of no presumptive abuse on March 9 and then, in a change of mind, moves to dismiss on March 30. Is the trustee's motion appropriate? In re Jasper, 414 B.R. 83 (Bankr. E.D. Va. 2009).

3. Suppose the United States trustee is too late to move to dismiss on the grounds of presumptive abuse and instead moves to dismiss under § 707(b)(3) because of the totality of the circumstances. Is this permitted? Fokkena v. Draisey (In re Draisey), 395 B.R. 79 (Bankr. 8th Cir. 2008).

C. DISMISSAL UNDER § 707(a)

PERLIN v HITACHI CAPITAL AMERICA CORP. (IN RE PERLIN)

497 F.3d 364 (3th Cir. 2007)

COWEN, J.

Hitachi Capital America Corporation ("Hitachi") appeals from the Bankruptcy Court's order denying its motion to dismiss the voluntary joint bankruptcy petition filed by Steven J. Perlin and Cristine A. Perlin under Chapter 7 of the Bankruptcy Code. Hitachi sought dismissal of the petition under 11 U.S.C. § 707(a), on the ground that the Perlins had filed the petition in bad faith. The Bankruptcy Court denied Hitachi's motion, reasoning that the Perlins had been truthful with the court and their creditors and had not engaged in the kind of manipulative conduct at issue in In re Tamecki, 229 F.3d 205 (3d Cir. 2000). In considering the motion to dismiss, however, the Bankruptcy Court refused to consider the Perlins's substantial income and expenses as evidence of bad faith. The Bankruptcy Court reasoned that the negative implication of the substantial modifications made to section 707(b) by the Bankruptcy Abuse Prevention and Consumer Protection Act of 2005 ("BAPCPA" or "the 2005 Act"), Pub. L. No. 109-8, § 102, 119 Stat. 23 (2005), which created a presumption of abuse against

[71] 28 U.S.C. § 158(a)(1).

[72] See Fed. R. Bankr. P. 9014 (governing which of the federal rules of civil procedure apply to contested matters) and Fed. R. Civ. P. 62 as incorporated by Fed R. Bankr. P. 7062 (imposing a stay of execution on judgments only in adversary proceedings filed under Rule 7000).

debtors having primarily consumer debts who have sufficient income to repay their debts, is that a bankruptcy court may not consider a debtor's income and expenses in deciding a motion to dismiss brought under section 707(a).

In this appeal, which the Bankruptcy Court certified directly to us pursuant to 28 U.S.C. § 158(d)(2)(B), Hitachi challenges the Bankruptcy Court's refusal to consider the Perlins's high income and expenses in assessing good faith. As explained more fully below, we hold that in adjudicating a motion to dismiss asserting bad faith under 11 U.S.C. § 707(a), it is within the sound discretion of the bankruptcy court to consider a debtor's monthly income and expenses together with any other factors relevant to a debtor's good faith in filing for bankruptcy. Nevertheless, because we conclude that the facts and circumstances of this case do not support a finding of bad faith, we will affirm the Bankruptcy Court's order denying Hitachi's motion to dismiss.

I.

Dr. Steven J. Perlin is a licensed radiologist. In recent years, working only part-time, he has earned an annual income of approximately $370,000. At all relevant times, Dr. Perlin's wife, Cristine A. Perlin, owned and operated Centre Medical Imaging, LLC ("CMI"), the medical imaging company where Dr. Perlin practiced. Together, the Perlins expended a considerable amount of money on certain luxury items, such as two Lexus automobiles and private school tuition totaling $5,000 per month. In addition, they have saved more than $430,000 for their retirement.

In July of 2004, three months before CMI's opening, CMI entered into a lease agreement ("Lease") with Hitachi, whereby Hitachi leased to CMI medical diagnostic equipment and other property in exchange for the payment of rent. Dr. and Mrs. Perlin executed a personal guaranty ("Guaranty") in favor of Hitachi, whereby they agreed to guarantee CMI's obligations under the Lease subject to a limit of $1,271,588.00.

Under the Lease, CMI's payments were due on a graduated payment schedule. Under that schedule, CMI's monthly payments ranged from $2,000 in the first few months of the schedule to $70,000 beginning with the seventh month and continuing through the end of the Lease.

For the first six months of the schedule, CMI met its payment obligations in accordance with the terms of the Lease. During that time, however, CMI began experiencing financial difficulties. It failed to meet its own income projections and failed to pay Dr. Perlin a salary. Beginning with the seventh month and forward, CMI failed to generate sufficient cash flow to make the payments due under the Lease.

In February of 2005, CMI engaged a medical imaging consultant to reevaluate the income potential of the business. The consultant determined that the original income projections were flawed. Around the same time, CMI asked Hitachi to renegotiate the payment terms of the Lease on two separate occasions. Hitachi refused to do so.

In June of 2005, Hitachi advised CMI by letter that it had defaulted under the terms of the Lease by failing to make the payments due. After an agreed-upon period of forbearance, Hitachi demanded that CMI pay the full amount of the indebtedness under the Lease and that the Perlins pay the full amount of the Guaranty limit. CMI and the Perlins failed to pay the amounts owed.

On or about August 2, 2005, Hitachi filed suit against the Perlins and other defendants seeking repossession of the leased equipment and damages. Soon thereafter, the Perlins filed an answer to the complaint. On or about January 13, 2006, Hitachi filed a motion for default judgment against CMI. Days later, this bankruptcy case ensued.

II.

On January 19, 2006, the Perlins filed a voluntary joint petition under Chapter 7 of the Bankruptcy Code, seeking discharge of their obligation under the Guaranty, which stayed the litigation against them. In response to the petition, Hitachi filed a motion to dismiss under 11 U.S.C. § 707(a), alleging that the Perlins had filed the petition in bad faith. Hitachi claimed that the following factors supported a finding of bad faith: (1) the Perlins had submitted allegedly misleading schedules to the court; (2) they had timed the filing of their bankruptcy petition around Hitachi's exercise of its legal rights against them; (3) they had artificially inflated their expenses in order to insulate their substantial income; (4) they enjoyed a substantial annual income and a lavish lifestyle, which included two luxury automobiles, private school tuition, and substantial retirement savings; and (5) they failed to make a good faith effort to repay Hitachi as an alternative to seeking discharge.

The Bankruptcy Court heard evidence and argument of counsel on Hitachi's motion to dismiss. Applying the Tamecki framework, the Bankruptcy Court found that Hitachi had presented sufficient information to shift the burden to the Perlins to prove that their petition was brought in good faith. Upon hearing testimony from the Perlins, the Bankruptcy Court concluded that the Perlins had met their burden of proving good faith and, therefore, denied the motion to dismiss.

In reaching its conclusion, the Bankruptcy Court reasoned that the Perlins had been "straightforward in their schedules," App. at 104, and "forthcoming with the Court and their creditors," id. at 107. The Bankruptcy Court found that the Perlins's substantial expenses were "[a]ctual, but inflated." Id. In addition, the Bankruptcy Court found that this case was distinguishable from Tamecki, where the debtor had manipulated the timing of his filing of his petition. The Bankruptcy Court observed that it "d[id]n't see Tamecki factors here," id. at 108, and "d[id]n't see a manipulation," id.

With regard to the Perlins's substantial income and expenses, the Bankruptcy Court opined that based upon the legislative history to section 707(a) and our comments in Tamecki, a debtor's ability to repay is not, in and of itself, sufficient to support a bad faith finding. Moreover, going one step further, the Bankruptcy Court suggested that as a result of the recent amendments to section 707(b) made by BAPCPA, a bankruptcy court is now precluded from giving any consideration to a debtor's income and expenses in deciding a motion to dismiss brought under subsection (a) of section 707. Relying upon a theory of negative implication, the Bankruptcy Court opined that the newly-created presumption of abuse under section 707(b), which arises when a consumer debtor meets a specified income/expense test, excludes the possibility that a debtor's ability to repay may be considered under section 707(a). In assessing good faith, therefore, the Bankruptcy Court did not consider the Perlins's substantial income and high expenses.

Upon certification of the Bankruptcy Court, this Court granted Hitachi's petition, pursuant to 28 U.S.C. § 158(d)(2)(A), to appeal the Bankruptcy Court's order denying Hitachi's motion to dismiss as to the following issue: "Whether, in deciding a motion to dismiss for cause under 11 U.S.C. § 707(a), a bankruptcy court is prohibited from considering a debtor's monthly income and expenses when assessing a debtor's good faith in filing a bankruptcy petition."

III.

Section 707(a) provides, in pertinent part, that "[t]he court may dismiss a case under this chapter only after notice and a hearing and only for cause," and provides three non-exclusive examples of "cause" warranting dismissal. 11 U.S.C. § 707(a). Although a debtor's lack of good faith is not mentioned in the statute, in Tamecki, we held that a debtor's lack of good faith in filing a bankruptcy petition is a proper cause for dismissal under section 707(a). 229 F.3d at 207. Here, the Bankruptcy Court has certified the question of whether in assessing good faith under section 707(a), a bankruptcy court may consider a debtor's income and expenses, to which we turn below.

A.

The first issue we must decide is whether the newly-added provisions in section 707(b), which create a presumption of abuse against consumer debtors who have an ability to repay, imply that a bankruptcy court may not consider a debtor's income and expenses in adjudicating a motion to dismiss under section 707(a). Because the canon of negative implication does not apply in this case, as explained below, we conclude that the new provisions of section 707(b) do not impliedly prohibit a bankruptcy court from considering a debtor's income and expenses under section 707(a).

The principle that the enumeration of one case excludes another is a canon of statutory interpretation. The canon applies only when the expressed and unmentioned items are part of a "commonly associated group or series," United States v. Vonn, 535 U.S. 55, 65 (2002), "justifying the inference that items not mentioned were excluded by deliberate choice, not inadvertence." Barnhart v. Peabody Coal Co., 537 U.S. 149, 168 (2003). In other words, the expressed item and the unmentioned item should be understood to go "hand in hand," thus supporting a sensible inference that Congress must have meant to exclude the unmentioned item. Id. (citation and internal quotation marks omitted). The canon is "only a guide, whose fallibility can be shown by contrary indications that adopting a particular rule or statute was probably not meant to signal any exclusion of its common relatives." Vonn, 535 U.S. at 65; see Burns v. United States, 501 U.S. 129, 136 (1991) ("An inference drawn from congressional silence certainly cannot be credited when it is contrary to all other textual and contextual evidence of congressional intent.").

By virtue of the 2005 Act, Congress enacted an income/expense test for consumer filings under section 707(b), and in doing so, has expressed a clear intention to permit bankruptcy courts to consider a consumer debtor's income and expenses in deciding a motion to dismiss under that subsection. Congress has not created an income/expense test for filings under section 707(a). The Bankruptcy Court suggested that Congress's singular expression of an intention to authorize bankruptcy courts to consider income and expenses under section 707(b) justifies the inference Congress did not intend for bankruptcy courts to consider income and expenses under section 707(a). As explained below, such an inference cannot be made because Congress has not treated consumer filings under section 707(b) and consumer/non-consumer filings under section 707(a) as part of a "commonly associated group or series." Vonn, 535 U.S. at 65.

As an initial matter, two separate subsections govern the dismissal of bankruptcy petitions filed under Chapter 7: subsection (a) governs the dismissal of all bankruptcy filings, when adequate "cause" has been shown, and subsection (b) governs the dismissal of only those bankruptcy filings involving primarily consumer debts, when granting relief would be an "abuse" of Chapter 7. 11 U.S.C. § 707(a), (b). As indicated below, Congress codified these two subsections at different times and for different reasons.

Subsection (a) was enacted first, as part of the Bankruptcy Reform Act of 1978 (the "1978 Act"). At that time, there was no analogous provision to what is now subsection (b), relating only to consumer filings. See In re Padilla, 222 F.3d 1184, 1194 (9th Cir. 2000); Pub. L. No. 95-598, 92 Stat. 2549 (codified as amended at 11 U.S.C. § 707(a)). It was not until six years later that Congress added subsection (b) through the Bankruptcy Amendments and Federal Judgeship Act of 1984 ("the 1984 Act"). Pub. L. No. 98-353, 98 Stat. 333 (codified as amended at 11 U.S.C. § 707(b)). Moreover, unlike subsection (a), subsection (b) was enacted as part of a package of consumer credit amendments in response to perceived abuses by consumer filers. See 6 Collier on Bankruptcy, P 707.LH[2] (Matthew Bender 15th ed., rev. 2006); see also S. Rep. No. 98-65 (1983) (observing that there had been a dramatic increase in the number of consumer bankruptcy case filings since the enactment of the 1978 Bankruptcy Act). Hence, from a historical perspective, Congress has treated consumer filings under section 707(b) and consumer/non-consumer filings under section 707(a) differently, not as part of a package or "commonly associated group or series." Vonn, 535 U.S. at 65.

Furthermore, the legislative history to the 2005 Act does not indicate that the modifications to section 707(b) imply anything about the dismissal of bankruptcy cases under section 707(a). As stated in the House report, the amendments were intended to "respond to many of the factors contributing to the increase in consumer bankruptcy filings, such as lack of personal financial accountability, the proliferation of serial filings, and the absence of effective oversight to eliminate abuse in the system." H.R. Rep. No. 109-31, at 2 (2005), as reprinted in 2005 U.S.C.C.A.N. 88, 89 (emphasis added). The amendments to section 707(b) effectively tightened the dismissal procedures for consumer filings. There is no indication that Congress intended, contrarily, to restrict a bankruptcy court's discretion in deciding motions to dismiss under section 707(a).

In summary, we conclude that Congress would not have considered its treatment of dismissal procedures for consumer filings under section 707(b) "to go hand in hand" with the dismissal provisions under section 707(a). See Peabody Coal, 537 U.S. at 168 (citation and internal quotation marks omitted). As a result, we conclude that Congress's adoption of an income/expense test applicable to consumer filings under section 707(b) was not meant to signal any exclusion of income-and-expense factors from a bankruptcy court's consideration of motions to dismiss under section 707(a).

B.

Having concluded that the 2005 Act amendments to section 707(b) do not, by negative implication, preclude a bankruptcy court from considering income-

and-expense factors in deciding whether to dismiss a bankruptcy petition under section 707(a), there remains the more salient question of whether consideration of income-and-expense factors is consonant with section 707(a) itself, as informed by our precedent and the legislative history.

Hitachi asserts that in deciding whether to dismiss a bankruptcy petition for lack of good faith under section 707(a), a bankruptcy court should consider a debtor's ability to repay his debts. Specifically, Hitachi contends that a bankruptcy court should consider whether a debtor has substantial income or maintains a lavish lifestyle entailing excessive and continued expenditures, the adjustment of which would result in a substantial amount of net discretionary income. Hitachi posits that a debtor who has an ability to repay his debts is not the "honest but unfortunate debtor" that the Bankruptcy Code was intended to protect. In response, the Perlins contend that the legislative history to section 707(a) makes clear that in deciding whether to dismiss a petition for cause, a bankruptcy court may not consider a debtor's ability to repay his debts. For the reasons stated below, we hold that, in deciding a motion to dismiss under section 707(a), a bankruptcy court may consider a debtor's substantial income and expenses together with other factors in assessing good faith.

In answering a question of statutory interpretation, we normally begin with the statutory language, but because section 707(a) does not touch on the question presented, we will begin our analysis by looking to the legislative history to discern congressional intent. See United States v. Gregg, 226 F.3d 253, 257 (3d Cir. 2000) ("Where the statutory language does not express Congress's intent unequivocally, a court traditionally refers to the legislative history and the atmosphere in which the statute was enacted in an attempt to determine the congressional purpose."). Here, the House and Senate committee reports indicate that Congress did not intend for a debtor's ability to repay his debts to be adequate cause for dismissal of a bankruptcy petition:

> The section does not contemplate, however, that the ability of the debtor to repay his debts in whole or in part constitutes adequate cause for dismissal. To permit dismissal on that ground would be to enact a non-uniform mandatory chapter 13, in lieu of the remedy of bankruptcy.

H.R. Rep. No. 95-595, at 380 (1977), as reprinted in 1978 U.S.C.C.A.N. 5963, 6336; S. Rep. No. 95-989, at 94 (1978), as reprinted in 1978 U.S.C.C.A.N. 5787, 5880. As in Tamecki, we read the legislative history to mean that a debtor's ability to repay his debts out of disposable income is not a sufficient reason to dismiss a bankruptcy petition under section 707(a). As stated by one court, "[i]t is difficult to contemplate how Congress could more emphatically have stated that the debtor's net worth or future prospects is not 'cause' as the word is used in Section 707 for dismissal." In re Goulding, 79 B.R. 874, 876 (Bankr. W.D. Mo. 1987).

While the legislative history makes clear that a debtor's ability to repay his debts is inadequate cause for dismissal, we do not read the history as prohibiting a bankruptcy court from considering a debtor's substantial income and expenses in determining whether the debtor filed his bankruptcy petition in good faith. The legislative history establishes only that a debtor's ability to repay is an invalid cause for dismissal. It does not indicate that a bankruptcy court must ignore the economic reality of a debtor's financial situation in determining whether a valid cause for dismissal exists.

As with the legislative history, we do not read our precedents as prohibiting a bankruptcy court from considering a debtor's income and expenses as part of a good faith analysis. As noted above, in Tamecki, we held that a debtor's lack of good faith in filing a bankruptcy petition is a proper cause for dismissal under section 707(a). 229 F.3d at 207. Although we stated that a debtor's "ability to repay is not in and of itself sufficient proof of bad faith," id. at 208, we did not rule out the possibility that a debtor's income may be considered as part of a good faith analysis. Rather, we instructed that courts should assess a debtor's good faith on an "ad hoc basis," considering the "honest intention" of the debtor and "whether the debtor has abused the provisions, purpose, or spirit of bankruptcy law." Id. at 207. Moreover, we emphasized that the good-faith determination rests within the sound discretion of the bankruptcy court. Id.

Our non-restrictive approach in Tamecki reflects the fact-intensive nature of the good-faith inquiry. An assessment of a debtor's good faith requires consideration of all of the facts and circumstances surrounding the debtor's filing for bankruptcy. See In re Integrated Telecom Express, Inc., 384 F.3d 108, 118 (3d Cir. 2004) (Chapter 11 case) ("Whether the good faith requirement has been satisfied is a 'fact intensive inquiry' in which the court must examine 'the totality of facts and circumstances' and determine where a 'petition falls along the spectrum ranging from the clearly acceptable to the patently abusive.'" (citation and internal quotation marks omitted)). Indeed, "[t]he facts required to mandate dismissal based upon a lack of good faith are as varied as the number of cases." In re Bingham, 68 B.R. 933, 935 (Bankr. M.D. Pa. 1987).

Of course, a bankruptcy court's discretion in making a good-faith determination is not without limitations. In Tamecki, we acknowledged certain limitations on that discretion. First, we noted that a finding of lack of good faith "should not [be] lightly infer[red]." 229 F.3d at 208. Second, we cautioned that dismissal should be "confined carefully" and utilized only in "egregious cases that entail concealed or misrepresented assets and/or sources of income, lavish lifestyles, and intention to avoid a large single debt based upon conduct akin to fraud, misconduct or gross negligence." Id. (quoting In re Zick, 931 F.2d 1124, 1129 (6th Cir. 1991)); see also 229 F.3d at 209 ("[B]ankruptcy and district courts have reserved bad faith dismissal for the truly egregious case, often involving individuals with substantial means who have flaunted their wealth, have continued their lavish lifestyles, and are engaging in creative, elaborate schemes to conceal their assets and cheat their creditors or to otherwise inflict harm on third parties.") (Rendell, J., dissenting). But other than delineating these general limitations, we were careful not to restrict the bankruptcy court's discretion.

So too in this case, we favor an approach to the certified question that does not restrict a bankruptcy court's consideration of entire categories of facts and circumstances in a case, which restriction could lead to a skewed good-faith analysis. At the same time, however, to avoid undercutting congressional intent as expressed in the legislative history to section 707(a), we believe that articulation of some parameters to guide a bankruptcy court's consideration of income-and-expense factors is entirely appropriate.

As an initial matter, there are certain situations in which a bankruptcy court's consideration of income-and-expense factors do not implicate the concerns Congress expressed in the legislative history. One such example is where the bankruptcy court considers evidence that the debtor "concealed or misrepresented assets and/or sources of income." Tamecki, 229 F.3d at 207 (internal quotation marks omitted); see In re Marks, 174 B.R. 37, 41 (E.D. Pa.

1994) ("Most instances of dismissal for bad faith filing under § 707(a) involve concealment, misrepresentation, or unexplained transfers to place assets beyond the reach of creditors." (citing cases)); see also In re Brown, 88 B.R. 280, 284 (Bankr. D. Hawaii 1988) (finding a lack of good faith where the debtor earned a substantial income and transferred the profits of his medical practice to avoid paying a malpractice judgment). Another example is where a creditor raises allegations that the debtor has artificially inflated expenses to disguise a state of financial well-being. In re Keobapha, 279 B.R. 49, 52 (Bankr. D. Conn. 2002) (internal quotation marks and citation omitted) (setting forth a variety of factors for bankruptcy courts to consider in assessing good faith). As these examples illustrate, a bankruptcy court may properly and unqualifiedly consider a debtor's income and expenses as an analytical step in assessing allegations of debtor misconduct.

Hitachi also argues that a bankruptcy court should consider a debtor's substantial earnings and lavish lifestyle as evidence of a debtor's bad faith in filing a bankruptcy petition. We agree that in deciding a motion to dismiss based upon a debtor's lack of good faith, a bankruptcy court may consider these factors together with any other facts and circumstances surrounding the debtor's filing for bankruptcy. Our conclusion flows not only from the fact-intensive nature of the good-faith inquiry, see Integrated Telecom Express, 384 F.3d at 118, but also from our recognition in Tamecki that dismissal should be utilized only in "egregious cases that entail concealed or misrepresented assets and/or sources of income, lavish lifestyles, and intention to avoid a large single debt based upon conduct akin to fraud, misconduct or gross negligence." Id. (emphasis added) (quoting Zick, 931 F.2d at 1129).

However, to avoid undercutting congressional intent, a bankruptcy court's ultimate finding of bad faith may not be based exclusively or primarily on a debtor's substantial financial means. Otherwise, dismissal would essentially be based upon a debtor's mere ability to repay, which is expressly prohibited by the legislative history. We note that several other courts have adopted a similar approach. Compare McDow v. Smith, 295 B.R. 69, 81 (E.D. Va. 2003) (holding that debtor's annual income of $454,000 and lavish lifestyle, which included annual private school tuition of $68,000, were insufficient cause for dismissal under section 707(a)), with In re Cappuccetti, 172 B.R. 37, 38-41 (Bankr. E.D. Ark. 1994) (finding that debtors filed Chapter 7 case in bad faith where in addition to the debtors' high income and expenses and lavish lifestyle, there were numerous inaccuracies and misstatements on their schedules and they had attempted to transfer assets out of reach from their creditors), and In re Hammonds, 139 B.R. 535, 542-43 (Bankr. D. Col. 1992) ("While some ability to repay debts is certainly not, in and of itself, adequate cause for dismissal of a Chapter 7 case . . ., when considered in conjunction with (1) the transfer of non-exempt corporate assets, without fair consideration, to Debtor's non-debtor spouse, (2) a continuing comfortable life-style, (3) a deliberate and persistent pattern of evading a single major creditor, (4) less than candid, full disclosure, and (5) Debtor's prior procedural gymnastics in Bankruptcy Court, this Court must find that the Debtor lacks the requisite good faith . . . [under § 707(a)]."), and In re Jones, 114 B.R. 917, 926 (Bankr. N.D. Ohio 1990) (finding lack of good faith where the debtor could repay his debts, engaged in fraudulent conduct, and attempted to conceal income).

As these cases illustrate, although a debtor's ability to repay is not, itself, sufficient cause for dismissal, "[w]hen a debtor capable of at least partial repayment has made every effort to avoid payment of an obligation, lack of good faith sufficient to justify dismissal may be found." Zick, 931 F.2d at 1127 n.3 (citation, internal quotation marks, and brackets omitted). Indeed, we need look no further than the facts in Tamecki for a good example of this principle. 229 F.3d 205.

In Tamecki, the debtor had filed for Chapter 7 protection seeking the discharge of approximately $35,000 in credit card debt. Id. at 206. The trustee sought dismissal of the debtor's petition for lack of good faith under section 707(a), arguing that the debtor acted in bad faith in filing his petition while knowing that he would soon be in a position to repay his debts. Id. at 206-07. The bankruptcy court granted the trustee's motion and entered an order dismissing the case for lack of good faith, and the district court affirmed. Id. at 207. After applying a burden-shifting framework, we too affirmed. Id. at 208. In affirming, we explained that while a debtor's ability (or, as in that case, future ability) to repay his debts is not itself sufficient proof of bad faith, there were two aggravating facts which had the effect of shifting the burden to the debtor, namely, the reasonableness of the debt accrual and the timing of filing. Id. First, when the debtor accrued the $35,000 debt, he was earning a small amount of income and did not have an urgent need to accrue a large consumer debt. Id. at 207. Second, at the time of filing for bankruptcy, the debtor was involved in a divorce proceeding which would soon leave him with approximately $50,000. Id. Based upon those circumstances, we concluded that there was no error in the bankruptcy court's ruling that the debtor failed to prove good faith. Id. at 208.

Hence, as Tamecki illustrates, in deciding a motion to dismiss based upon a debtor's lack of good faith, a bankruptcy court may consider all of the facts and circumstances surrounding the debtor's filing of the bankruptcy petition, including the reality of the debtor's financial situation.

For all of the foregoing reasons, we conclude that, in deciding a motion to dismiss under section 707(a), a bankruptcy court may consider a debtor's income and expenses together with other factors in assessing good faith. The recent modifications to counterpart-section 707(b) do not impliedly preclude a bankruptcy court from considering income-and-expense factors, and, as discussed and qualified above, consideration of income-and-expense factors is consonant with section 707(a) itself.

C.

Although a bankruptcy court may consider a debtor's income and expenses in assessing whether a debtor filed a bankruptcy petition in bad faith, we conclude that no reasonable factfinder would find that the evidence in this case demonstrates bad faith. There is no evidence that the Perlins schemed to conceal or misrepresent income, inflated their expenses to hide income, filed misleading statements or schedules in an effort to defraud their creditors, unduly interfered with the judicial process, or engaged in any other misconduct. On the contrary, the Bankruptcy Court found that the Perlins were "straightforward in their schedules" and "forthcoming with the Court and their creditors," and Hitachi has not appealed these factual determinations. Furthermore, unlike the debtor in Tamecki, the Perlins did not time the filing of their bankruptcy petition to shield a future source of income. Likewise, the accrual of their debt to start a medical imaging company, which had a business plan with definite income projections, was not unreasonable.

Although, it is true, that the Perlins have a substantial income and a comfortable lifestyle, those factors are insufficient, at least in this case, to demonstrate their bad faith in filing the bankruptcy petition. Hence, we ultimately agree with the Bankruptcy Court that this is not the kind of "egregious case" which warrants dismissal for lack of good faith under § 707(a).

For the foregoing reasons, we will affirm the Bankruptcy Court's order denying Hitachi's motion to dismiss.

Notes and Questions

1. In Sherman v. Securities & Exchange Commission (In re Sherman), 441 F.3d 794 (9th Cir. 2006), the Ninth Circuit reversed a district court decision dismissing a chapter 7 case under § 707(a) because the debtor sought to sustain a lifestyle funded by bilking investors in a Ponzi scheme. The Sherman court conceded that "cause" exceeds the confines of § 707(a), but an asserted cause could not be something specifically addressed by other Bankruptcy Code sections. Since the movant could not cite a reason for dismissal that was not addressed by other code sections, dismissal was not appropriate. A stylish life specifically did not suffice as cause to dismiss. As one appellate court put it, with regard to a non-consumer debtor earning $454,000 a year:

> The result reached here may understandably offend some on the ground that this debtor, given his income and lifestyle, is a member of a class of people who are undeserving of the privileges and benefits of the Bankruptcy Code. i.e. the class of people who can pay their debts, but choose instead to spend their substantial incomes on what most would consider luxuries. Importantly, however, § 707(a) does not embody this sentiment. Any dissatisfaction with this result should therefore be addressed to Congress for it is that body, and not the courts, that has the power to alter the result reached here.

McDow v. Smith, 295 B.R. 69, 82-83 (E.D. Va. 2003) (footnotes omitted).

CHAPTER 4 BANKRUPTCY BASICS

A. THE AUTOMATIC STAY

WEBER v SEFCU (IN RE WEBER)

719 F.3d 72 (2d CIr. 2013)

CARNEY, J.

Defendant SEFCU, a lender, appeals from a judgment of the United States District Court for the Northern District of New York (Suddaby, J.) reversing an order of the United States Bankruptcy Court for the Northern District of New York (Littlefield, J.) and remanding the case to the Bankruptcy Court for further proceedings. The District Court concluded that SEFCU violated the automatic stay provision of the Bankruptcy Code, 11 U.S.C. § 362, when, after lawfully repossessing a vehicle belonging to the debtor, plaintiff Christopher Weber, it failed to deliver the vehicle to him notwithstanding its knowledge of the debtor's pending petition under Chapter 13 of the Bankruptcy Code. The District Court affirmed, holding that, by declining to surrender the vehicle absent a turnover order and protection SEFCU considered adequate, the lender wrongfully "exercised control" over the vehicle in contravention of section 362 and was liable for Weber's related damages, attorneys' fees, and costs.

On appeal to our Court, SEFCU challenges the District Court's interpretation of section 362 and other relevant provisions of the Bankruptcy Code, and argues that, under the authority of Manufacturers & Traders Trust Co. v. Alberto (In re Alberto), 271 B.R. 223 (N.D.N.Y. 2001), it was entitled to retain the vehicle notwithstanding the pending bankruptcy proceedings. For the reasons set forth below, we AFFIRM the judgment of the District Court and REMAND the cause to the district court for a determination of the amount of damages, costs, and attorneys' fees that SEFCU owes Weber under section 362(k), and any other proceedings consistent with this opinion.

Background

The relevant facts are undisputed. In August 2006, Weber and SEFCU (identified in Bankruptcy Court pleadings as the "State Employees Federal Credit Union") entered into a loan agreement pursuant to which SEFCU obtained a security interest in Weber's vehicle, a pickup truck. The loan agreement entitled SEFCU to repossess Weber's vehicle upon default.

In 2009, SEFCU became entitled to proceed against Weber. As a result, on January 10, 2010, SEFCU took possession of Weber's vehicle pursuant to the loan agreement, and, by notices dated January 10 and 11, 2010, advised him of his right under New York law to redeem the vehicle upon payment of amounts due and certain costs. Four days after the seizure, on January 14, Weber filed a voluntary petition for relief under Chapter 13 of the Bankruptcy Code in the United States Bankruptcy Court for the Northern District of New York. Weber's attorney concurrently gave SEFCU written notice of Weber's bankruptcy filing, and, invoking the stay imposed by Bankruptcy Code section 362, 11 U.S.C. § 362(a), requested the vehicle's return.

One week later, SEFCU still had the vehicle, and accordingly, on January 22, Weber filed an adversary proceeding against SEFCU seeking its return so that, as later explained by his counsel to the Bankruptcy Court, he could "continue his construction business" during the pendency of his petition. On March 1, with the vehicle still in SEFCU's possession, the Bankruptcy Court entered an order requiring SEFCU to show cause why it should not return the vehicle and why the court should not grant Weber an award of damages for SEFCU's violation of section 362 and for other relief. On March 4, the court heard argument on the order to show cause, and, although the record does not reflect entry of a related order at that time, SEFCU is reported to have returned the vehicle to Weber the following day.

The proceedings in the Bankruptcy Court continued, as Weber sought damages for his inability to use the vehicle between January 14 and March 5, attorneys' fees, and sanctions. In November 2010, SEFCU moved for summary judgment, putting to the Bankruptcy Court the question of law whether SEFCU's failure to release the vehicle promptly after the petition was filed constituted a "willful" violation of the automatic stay under subsections (a) and (k)(1) of section 362 (providing for recovery of damages, costs, and attorneys' fees for "any willful violation of a stay"). SEFCU maintained that there was no violation, and that an earlier district court decision in other proceedings, Alberto, 271 B.R. 223 (N.D.N.Y. 2001), gave it a reasonable basis for declining to release the vehicle absent a court order issued pursuant to Bankruptcy Code section 542, 11 U.S.C. § 542 (relating to "Turnover of property to the estate"). Weber, for his part, argued that Alberto was wrongly decided, and that section 362 required SEFCU to release the vehicle promptly after the petition was filed. The Bankruptcy Court, in a brief Order, granted summary judgment for SEFCU.

Weber appealed to the District Court. Relying primarily on the Supreme Court's decision in United States v. Whiting Pools, Inc., 462 U.S. 198 (1983), and rejecting the reasoning of the Alberto court, the district court concluded that SEFCU was bound to release the vehicle to Weber, the debtor-in-possession, upon learning of Weber's pending Chapter 13 proceedings. The district court further determined that, having failed to do so, SEFCU violated section 362. Because it knew of the petition and retained the vehicle, SEFCU's violation was willful, making it liable for damages and attorneys' fees. Weber v. SEFCU, 477 B.R. 308, 311 (N.D.N.Y. 2012). SEFCU timely appealed.

Discussion

. . . Under Bankruptcy Code section 541, governing "Property of the estate," the act of filing a petition for bankruptcy creates an estate comprised of (as relevant here) "all legal or equitable interests of the debtor in property as of the commencement of the [bankruptcy] case." 11 U.S.C. § 541(a)(1). Section 541 gathers into the estate all such interests in property, "wherever located and by whomever held." Id. § 541(a).

To assemble the bankruptcy estate, section 542 of the Code requires that, during bankruptcy proceedings, an entity "in possession, custody, or control" of certain property in the estate "shall deliver" that property to the trustee, "unless such property is of inconsequential value or benefit to the estate." 11 U.S.C. § 542(a) (emphasis added). The property subject to this delivery obligation is "property that the trustee may use, sell, or lease under section 363," which grants broad powers over the estate's property to the trustee.[1] Id. In a Chapter 13 bankruptcy, the debtor "remain[s] in possession of all property of the estate"--acting in effect as trustee under section 542(a) --unless the debtor's reorganization plan provides otherwise. 11 U.S.C. § 1306(b).[2] The delivery obligation of section 542(a) thus contemplates the debtor-in-possession as the recipient of the property of the estate.

While bankruptcy proceedings are pending, the automatic stay provisions of section 362 work with sections 541 and 542 to shelter the debtor's estate from action by creditors, enabling the debtor to get the relief and fresh start that are among the goals of the bankruptcy regime. Thus, under section 362, filing a bankruptcy petition automatically effects a stay of "any act to obtain possession of property of the estate . . . or to exercise control over property of the estate." 11 U.S.C. § 362(a)(3). Those who violate section 362 are liable for related damages and costs: under section 362(k), a debtor "injured by any willful violation of a stay provided by [section 362] shall recover actual damages, including costs and attorneys' fees, and, in appropriate circumstances, may recover punitive damages." Id. § 362(k)(1) (emphasis added).

We first consider whether SEFCU's refusal to return the vehicle to Weber promptly upon learning of his Chapter 13 bankruptcy filing constituted an unlawful "exercise [of] control" over the "property" of his estate, in violation of the automatic stay. We then examine whether SEFCU may be excused from promptly surrendering the vehicle because Weber had not provided "adequate protection" for SEFCU's security interest in the vehicle. Finally, because we conclude that SEFCU's actions did violate section 362, we then turn to the question whether, in light of its reliance on Alberto, SEFCU's violation was nonetheless "willful" under section 362(k), making it liable for Weber's actual damages, costs, and attorneys' fees under that section.

I.

As observed above, section 541(a) provides that a bankruptcy estate is comprised of "all legal or equitable interests in property as of the commencement

---

[1] Section 363, as applicable here, provides: "[U]nless the court orders otherwise, the trustee may enter into transactions, including the sale or lease of property of the estate, in the ordinary course of business, without notice or a hearing, and may use property of the estate in the ordinary course of business without notice or a hearing." 11 U.S.C. § 363(c)(1); see also United States v. Whiting Pools, Inc., 674 F.2d 144, 149 (2d Cir. 1982) (Friendly, J.), aff'd, 462 U.S. 198 (1983). The trustee may also use, sell, or lease property of the estate outside the ordinary course of business, upon notice and a hearing before the bankruptcy court. 11 U.S.C. § 363(b)(1); see also Motorola, Inc. v. Official Comm. of Unsecured Creditors and JPMorgan Chase Bank, N.A. (In re Iridium Operating LLC), 478 F.3d 452, 466 (2d Cir. 2007).

[2] The debtor-in-possession may exercise many of the rights and powers of a bankruptcy trustee, including the right to use, sell, or lease property of the estate. 11 U.S.C. §§ 1303, 1304(b) "Unless the court orders otherwise, a debtor engaged in business may operate the business of the debtor and, subject to any limitations on a trustee under sections 363(c) and 364 of this title and to such limitations or conditions as the court prescribes, shall have, exclusive of the trustee, the rights and powers of the trustee under such sections.").

of the case." Although SEFCU's repossession of the vehicle before Weber filed his petition lawfully overrode Weber's immediate possessory rights, the parties agree that New York law afforded Weber at least a continuing equitable interest in the vehicle. See Wornick v. Gaffney, 544 F.3d 486, 490 (2d Cir. 2008) ("Whether the debtor has a legal or equitable interest in property such that it becomes property of the estate under section 541 is determined by applicable state law." (internal quotation marks omitted)). That interest arose from Weber's right pursuant to the state Uniform Commercial Code to redeem the vehicle before sale. See N.Y. U.C.C. § 9-623.[3] It was this right that SEFCU acknowledged and identified for Weber in its notice to him dated January 11. Weber's equitable interest thus constituted "property" of the bankruptcy estate under section 541. Neither party seriously challenges the scope of that definition.

Rather, Weber and SEFCU dispute whether, by failing to surrender the vehicle immediately upon receiving notice of the petition's filing, SEFCU "exercise[d] control" over Weber's equitable interest in the vehicle and thereby violated the stay imposed by section 362. The Supreme Court's decision in United States v. Whiting Pools, Inc., 462 U.S. 198 (1983), provides important guidance for our resolution of this issue.

The dispute in Whiting Pools arose when, to satisfy a tax lien, the IRS seized all of the tangible personal property of the corporation. One day after the seizure, the corporation filed for bankruptcy. The IRS moved for relief from the automatic stay, wishing to be free to sell the personal property that it had seized in satisfaction of the tax debts owed. The debtor corporation counterclaimed and, in the bankruptcy court, successfully sought an order under section 542 that required the IRS to return the property to the estate. Id. at 199-201.

The Supreme Court affirmed the bankruptcy court's turnover order. Characterizing the IRS's interest in the seized property as "its lien"--not ownership--and analogizing the Service's right to effect a seizure to the remedies available to private secured creditors, the Court described the seizure as "not determin[ing] the Service's rights to the seized property, but merely bring[ing] the property into the Service's legal custody." Id. at 210-11. It explained that "[i]n effect, § 542(a) grants to the estate a possessory interest in certain property of the debtor that was not held by the debtor at the commencement of reorganization proceedings," id. at 207, and "requires an entity . . . holding any property of the debtor that the trustee can use under § 363 to turn that property over to the trustee." Id. at 205-06.

The Court underscored the Congressional intent, in shaping the definition of "property" set forth in section 541(a), to include "a broad range" of property in the estate, and indeed, to capture "any property made available to the estate by other provisions of the Bankruptcy Code." Id. at 204-05. Section 542(a) is such a

---

[3] Weber retained other rights under state law consistent with his status as the equitable owner of the vehicle. These rights included a right to notification before the creditor disposed of the vehicle, N.Y. U.C.C. § 9-611, and a right to receive any surplus from the sale of the vehicle, id. § 9-615(d)(1). In addition, we observe that Weber may have retained legal title to the vehicle. See, e.g., N.Y. U.C.C. § 9-609; N.Y. Veh. & Traf. Law § 2115. But the parties have not briefed this question and we do not decide it here. That Weber has a colorable claim to have retained legal title to the truck, in addition to his acknowledged equitable interests in the vehicle, arguably serves to distinguish this case, however, from those in which legal title transferred to the creditor automatically upon repossession (or never was in the debtor to begin with). We express no view about the bearing of section 362 upon the latter situations.

provision. It requires delivery to the trustee of "any property of the debtor that the trustee can use under § 363," including property repossessed by a secured creditor. Id. at 205-06. "Any other interpretation of § 542(a)," the Court declared, "would deprive the bankruptcy estate of the assets and property essential to its rehabilitation effort and thereby would frustrate the congressional purpose behind the reorganization provisions." Id. at 208.

For these reasons, the Court restricted the IRS--like any other creditor seizing property in which it held a security interest--to seeking protection of its interests "according to the congressionally established bankruptcy procedures, rather than by withholding the seized property from the debtor's efforts to reorganize." Id. at 212.

Similarly, here, SEFCU seized Weber's vehicle before Weber filed for bankruptcy, but under New York law, Weber retained at least an equitable interest in the property notwithstanding its repossession. SEFCU did not automatically obtain an ownership interest in the vehicle: its rights to seize and sell were subject to U.C.C. provisions of state law, including certain continuing rights held by Weber, and also subject to the rights and remedies established by the Bankruptcy Code. Whiting Pools teaches that, upon Weber's filing of his bankruptcy petition, Weber's equitable interest under state law gave the bankruptcy estate a possessory right in the secured property, as property that the trustee could use under section 363. Under section 542, that right took precedence over the state law possessory right of SEFCU. See id. at 207.

It is true that Whiting Pools involved a Chapter 11 corporate reorganization, and that the Supreme Court expressly reserved judgment as to whether its analysis would also apply to Chapter 13 personal reorganizations like Weber's. 462 U.S. at 208 n.17. But, like other courts to have addressed the issue, we observe that the language of sections 541, 542, and 362 applies to the "estate," not just the "reorganization estate." See Austein v. Schwartz (In re Gerwer), 898 F.2d 730, 734 (9th Cir. 1990) (cited in In re Velichko, 473 B.R. 64, 67 (Bankr. S.D.N.Y. 2012)). We see no reason--and the parties have presented none--to restrict application of the reasoning of the Whiting Pools Court to corporate reorganizations: the same concerns apply fully in the Chapter 13 context as well. See, e.g., Thompson v. General Motors Acceptance Corp., 566 F.3d 699, 705-06 (7th Cir. 2009) (applying Whiting Pools in Chapter 13 setting and observing that the "purpose of reorganization bankruptcy, be it corporate or personal, is to allow the debtor to regain his financial foothold and repay his creditors") (emphasis added). As noted above, Weber required his vehicle to conduct his construction business; Whiting Pools required its equipment and other personal property to conduct its business. In each case, the reorganization's chances for success would seem markedly improved if operations could be maintained during the pendency of the petition and formulation of the plan.

Whiting Pools does not resolve, however, whether by demanding a turnover order of the bankruptcy court or "adequate protection" as a condition of its relinquishment, SEFCU "exercise[d] control" over the vehicle in contravention of the stay. In Whiting Pools, the IRS--unlike SEFCU--moved for relief from the stay, and did not simply wait for the debtor to initiate an adversary proceeding or seek a turnover order under section 542. Id. at 201. Thus, the Court there held only that the bankruptcy court properly ordered the IRS to return the seized property to the estate under section 542. Id. at 212.

The district court's decision in Alberto, relied upon by SEFCU here, directly addressed the question left unanswered by Whiting Pools. The Alberto court concluded that a secured creditor did not violate the automatic stay when, after learning of the debtor's bankruptcy, it failed immediately to return a debtor's repossessed vehicle. 271 B.R. at 228. Rather, the court held that before such a secured creditor was obligated to surrender the collateral to the estate, the debtor must "take[ ] an affirmative step," such as obtaining a turnover order under section 542. Id. at 227. Because (as it found) a repossessed vehicle was not part of the debtor's estate until such an action had occurred, the court reasoned that a creditor that had taken possession of its security did not "exercise control" over "property" of the estate by declining to surrender the possessory interest to the estate. Id. at 228. Since the debtor no longer had a possessory interest, the court concluded, the creditor "did not 'act to obtain possession . . . or to exercise control' of the vehicle in violation of the stay, since it already lawfully possessed and controlled the vehicle when the stay went into effect." Id. at 226 (alteration in original) (quoting 11 U.S.C. § 362(a)(3)).

We find the Alberto court's reasoning unpersuasive. Section 541 expressly provides that the "property" of Weber's estate includes equitable interests, and Weber's right to redeem and other rights catalogued above, together with his lingering claim to ownership of title, comprise such an interest. That SEFCU had already effected a repossession does not alter the conclusion that the equitable interest is property of the estate: section 541 provides further that the estate is comprised of property "wherever located and by whomever held." 11 U.S.C. § 541(a). Nor was Weber obligated to initiate an additional proceeding. Section 542 requires that any entity in possession of property of the estate deliver it to the trustees, without condition or any further action: the provision is "self-executing." Collier on Bankruptcy § 542.02 (16th ed. 2012) ("By its express terms, [section 542] is self-executing, and does not require that the trustee take any action or commence a proceeding or obtain a court order to compel the turnover."). And Whiting Pools teaches that the filing of a petition will generally transform a debtor's equitable interest into a bankruptcy estate's possessory right in the vehicle.

As for whether SEFCU's refusal to return the vehicle to the estate violated the stay, section 362 forbids any act to "obtain possession" or "exercise control" over the property of the estate. We need consult only an ordinary dictionary to confirm that a typical definition of "control" is: "To exercise authority over; direct; command." Webster's New World College Dictionary (4th ed. 2002). In light of that definition, we see no way to avoid the conclusion that, by keeping custody of the vehicle and refusing Weber access to or use of it, SEFCU was "exercising control" over the object in which the estate's equitable interest lay, and its retention of the vehicle violated the stay.

The Bankruptcy Amendments and Federal Judgeship Act of 1984 (the "1984 Amendments") confirms our conclusion. The 1984 Amendments, passed after the Whiting Pools decision in 1983, broadened the already sweeping provisions of the automatic stay even further to prohibit expressly not only "acts to obtain possession" of property of the estate, but also "any act . . . to exercise control over the property of the estate." Pub. L. No. 98-353, 98 Stat. 333, 371. This significant textual enlargement is consonant with our understanding and the Supreme Court's interpretation that Congress intended to prevent creditors from retaining property of the debtor in derogation of the bankruptcy procedure and the broad goals of debtor protection discussed above, without regard to what party was in possession of the property in question when the petition was filed. As the Seventh Circuit has pointed out, "Although Congress did not provide an explanation of that amendment, the mere fact that Congress expanded the provision to prohibit conduct above and beyond obtaining possession of an asset suggests that it intended to include conduct by creditors who seized an asset pre-petition." Thompson, 566 F.3d at 702 (citation omitted).

The rule adopted by the Alberto court and urged on us by SEFCU--that some additional act by the debtor is required before the creditor is obligated to surrender the property--would, in contrast, place on the debtor or trustee the burden of undertaking a series of adversary proceedings to pull together the bankruptcy estate, and thereby increase the costs of administering the estate and decrease the assets available to effect a successful reorganization. In our view, the plain language of section 542 (directing that those in custody of assets of the estate "shall deliver" them to the trustee); the approach of the Whiting Pools Court to equitable interests and bankruptcy estates; and the broad language of the 1984 Amendments enlarging the scope of the automatic stay point unmistakably away from any Congressional desire to impose such an additional burden on debtors seeking bankruptcy protection. As the Eighth Circuit wrote,

> [I]f persons who could make no substantial adverse claim to a debtor's property in their possession could, without cost to themselves, compel the debtor or his trustee to bring suit as a prerequisite to returning the property, the powers of a bankruptcy court . . . to collect the estate for the benefit of creditors would be vastly reduced.

Knaus v. Concordia Lumber Co. (In re Knaus), 889 F.2d 773, 775 (8th Cir. 1989) (internal quotation marks omitted). SEFCU has identified no basis for concluding that Congress intended this result.

The district court's decision in Alberto also runs counter to the strong trend of decisions from our sister Circuits. For example, the Seventh Circuit has bluntly ruled that "a plain reading of the Bankruptcy Code's provisions, the Supreme Court's decision in [Whiting Pools], and various practical considerations require that a creditor immediately return a seized asset in which a debtor has an equity interest to the debtor's estate upon his filing of Chapter 13 bankruptcy." Thompson, 566 F.3d at 700; see also Knaus, 889 F.2d at 775. Bankruptcy Appellate Panels from other Circuits agree. E.g., Unified People's Fed. Credit Union v. Yates (In re Yates), 332 B.R. 1, 7 (B.A.P. 10th Cir. 2005); TranSouth Fin. Corp. v. Sharon (In re Sharon), 234 B.R. 676, 682 (B.A.P. 6th Cir. 1999); Abrams v. Sw. Leasing & Rental Inc. (In re Abrams), 127 B.R. 239, 243 (B.A.P. 9th Cir. 1991).

Only the Eleventh Circuit has adopted a contrary approach, and those decisions have largely relied on readings of state law with regard to the relative legal property interests of debtor and secured creditor after a lawful repossession. See Bell-Tel Fed. Credit Union v. Kalter (In re Kalter), 292 F.3d 1350, 1356-60 (11th Cir. 2002) (applying Florida law); Charles R. Hall Motors, Inc. v. Lewis (In re Lewis), 137 F.3d 1280, 1284-85 (11th Cir. 1998) (applying Alabama law).

In our view, the majority rule adheres more faithfully to the text of the Bankruptcy Code and the reasoning of Whiting Pools. In addition, sound policy supports the majority's reading of the statutory text:

> The primary goal of reorganization bankruptcy is to group all of the debtor's property together in his estate such that he may rehabilitate his credit and pay off his debts; this necessarily extends to all property, even property lawfully seized pre-petition. An asset actively used by a debtor serves a greater purpose to both the debtor and his creditors than an asset sitting idle on a creditor's lot.

We therefore join the majority of other Circuits to have addressed this issue and conclude that section 362 requires a creditor in possession of property seized as security--but subject to a state-law-based residual equitable interest in the debtor--to deliver that property to the trustee or debtor-in-possession promptly after the debtor has filed a petition in bankruptcy under Chapter 13.

II.

SEFCU argues that even if the Code did not permit SEFCU to await a turnover order before relinquishing the vehicle, SEFCU was entitled to withhold the vehicle until Weber offered or the court ordered Weber to provide SEFCU "adequate protection" for SEFCU's security interest. Appellant's Br. 15. We need not pause long over this argument, for the plain text of the Bankruptcy Code contradicts this position. As we have observed, section 542(a) provides without qualification that anyone in possession of the property of the estate "shall deliver" it to the trustee. 11 U.S.C. § 542(a). The Code requires the creditor first to surrender the property. Only then or in conjunction with that surrender may it proceed to "request" from the Bankruptcy Court "adequate protection" for its interests. 11 U.S.C. §§ 362(d), 363(e). The provisions authorizing imposition of such protection operate only upon application of the creditor to the Bankruptcy Court. Unlike section 542(a), these are not self-executing.

SEFCU points to no provision of the Code permitting a creditor to withhold property of the estate until the debtor has offered protection that is "adequate" in the creditor's view, separate from any formal proceeding before the Bankruptcy Court. Rather, the Code provides for protection that the court deems adequate: "[O]n request of an entity that has an interest in property used . . . by the trustee, the court . . . shall prohibit or condition such use . . . as is necessary to provide adequate protection of such interest." 11 U.S.C. § 363(e). See Sharon, 234 B.R. at 683 (holding that [t]here is no 'exception' . . . that excuses [the creditor's] refusal to deliver possession of the Debtor's car based on [the creditor's] subjective opinion that adequate protection offered by the Debtor was not 'adequate'"). To hold otherwise would permit a creditor holding the debtor's property at the time of the debtor's bankruptcy filing to "negotiat[e] a better security package" than other creditors, thereby ensuring that creditor "a position above other secured creditors" and circumventing the bankruptcy court's authority to approve the debtor's plan to repay his or her debts. Thompson, 566 F.3d at 707.

SEFCU points principally to the Fourth Circuit's decision in Tidewater Finance Co. v. Moffett (In re Moffett), 356 F.3d 518 (4th Cir. 2004), in support of the proposition that a secured creditor may await delivery of what it deems adequate protection before surrendering the debtor's property to the estate. But Moffett is inapposite. That case did not concern the creditor's assessment of whether the debtor's proffered protection was "adequate." Rather, there, the creditor moved in the bankruptcy court for relief from the stay, seeking permission to sell the previously repossessed vehicle. Id. at 520. The Fourth Circuit agreed with the bankruptcy court that the debtor's reorganization plan provided "adequate protection" to the creditor and declined to lift the stay, requiring the creditor to return the vehicle to the debtor. Id. at 523.

We easily conclude that SEFCU's belief that Weber had not provided "adequate protection" for SEFCU's security interest in the vehicle does not cure SEFCU's violation of section 362.

III.

Finally, SEFCU asserts that even if its actions violated section 362, its violation was not "willful" within the meaning of section 362(k), and therefore the court may not require it to pay Weber's damages, costs, or attorneys' fees, or to impose any sanction. SEFCU asserts primarily that, because it relied in good faith on the Alberto decision and the "rule and custom" of the Northern District of New York, any violation that it committed should not be deemed "willful" under section 362(k). Appellant's Br. at 3.

We appreciate that, since one district court rendered its decision in Alberto, a practice may have developed in the Northern District of New York under which creditors felt entitled to await a turnover order and that SEFCU may therefore have felt justified in failing to surrender Weber's vehicle absent a court order. Nothing prevented SEFCU from surrendering the vehicle in response to Weber's request, however: it always was free to do so, and free concurrently to move the Bankruptcy Court for entry of an order that would--in the court's view--provide "adequate protection" to SEFCU. The creditor's error in this regard does not justify placing costs related to the vehicle's retention on the debtor.

Indeed, SEFCU misconstrues the meaning of "willful" as our Circuit law has construed the term in the context of section 362. A creditor willfully violates section 362 when it knows of the filing of the petition (and hence of the automatic stay), and has the general intent simply to perform the act found to violate section 362; no specific intent to violate section 362 is necessary. As we wrote over twenty years ago, "any deliberate act taken in violation of a stay, which the violator knows to be in existence, justifies an award of actual damages." Crysen/Montenay Energy Co. v. Esselen Assocs., Inc. (In re Crysen/Montenay Energy Co.), 902 F.2d 1098, 1105 (2d Cir. 1990); see also In re Dominguez, 312 B.R. 499, 508 (Bankr. S.D.N.Y. 2004) ("[S]o long as the violator possessed general intent in taking actions which have the effect of violating the automatic stay the intent required by § 362(h) is satisfied."); Yates, 332 B.R. at 7 ("Whether the party believes in good faith that it had a right to the property is not relevant to whether the act was willful or whether compensation must be awarded." (internal quotation marks omitted)). Section 362(k) operates to compensate the debtor who has been injured by the violation, in line with the distribution of the procedural burden struck by the statute, as discussed above, in favor of the estate and the bankruptcy mechanism. Because it intended to retain Weber's vehicle, SEFCU acted "willfully," and is liable for damages, costs, and attorney's fees under section 362(k)(1).

Although its good faith is insufficient to excuse SEFCU from liability for Weber's actual damages, it may prevent the imposition of punitive damages, which in any event Weber's counsel has conceded he no longer seeks. See Crysen/Montenay Energy Co., 902 F.2d at 1105 ("An additional finding of maliciousness or bad faith on the part of the offending creditor warrants the further imposition of punitive damages . . . ."); see also In re Velichko, 473 B.R. at 69-70 (imposition of punitive damages premised on finding that secured creditor acted in bad faith by forcing debtors to sign reaffirmation agreement before relinquishing their vehicle).

For the foregoing reasons, we conclude that by failing to deliver the repossessed vehicle to the debtor-in-possession promptly after receiving notice of the pending petition, SEFCU willfully violated section 362(a), and is liable under section 362(k) for Weber's actual damages, costs, and attorney's fees. The order of the district court is affirmed, and the cause remanded to the district court for further proceedings consistent with this opinion. The district court may, if it chooses, remand the cause to the bankruptcy court for adjudication of the remaining issues, including Weber's costs.

Notes and Questions

1. An interesting argument of the court is that adequate protection does not begin until the creditor actually requests it. This claim is based on a reading of Bankruptcy Code § 363(e), which provides:

> [A]t any time, at the request of an entity that has an interest in property used , , , by the trustee, the court, without or without a hearing, shall prohibit or condition such use, sale, or lease as is necessary to provide adequate protection.

Emphasis added. On whether this is a correct reading of § 363(e), see 2 GRANT GILMORE & DAVID GRAY CARLSON, GILMORE AND CARLSON ON SECURED LENDING: CLAIMS IN BANKRUPTCY chapter 18 (2000).

2. In Bell-Tel Fed. Credit Union v. Kalter (In re Kalter), 292 F.3d 1350, 1356-60 (11th Cir. 2002), debtors sought sanctions for automatic stay violations because car lenders who lawfully repossessed would not return cars on demand to the bankruptcy estate. Once SP repossessed, the court reasoned, SP was the owner of the car. D was not. True, SP had a duty to take care of the collateral. UCC 9-207. But this proved nothing. D is benefited by a reduced deficiency if SP takes good care of the collateral.

True, UCC §9-504 [now §9-617(a)(1)] states that, in a foreclosure sale, "all of the debtor's rights therein" pass to the buyer. But the UCC defines "debtor" to mean owner of the collateral, even if the owner owes no debt. SP is therefore an Article 9 debtor! The right to redeem does not prove D is the owner. Redemption changes "the otherwise dormant right to redeem repossession into a meaningful ownership interest." Pending redemption, the debtor's ownership right is dormant--hence nonexistent.

Florida's certificate of title legislation also indicates that the car is not property of the bankruptcy estate. Fla. Stat. § 319.28(1)(a) provides that when SP repossesses, the DMV may issue a certificate of title to SP. "With this language, the Florida Certificate of Title statute expressly recognizes that ownership transfers upon repossession." See § 319.28 ("In case of repossession . . . an affidavit by the party to whom possession has passed stating that the vehicle . . . was repossessed upon default . . . shall be considered satisfactory proof of ownership"). True, D can get a court order preventing the DMV from issuing the certificate of title if the repo is unlawful, but this just proves that title passes to SP unless D takes action. In any case, SP can sell the car even without a certificate of title from the DMV. And the Florida courts have held that the certificate of title is merely evidence of ownership, not ownership itself.

CITIZENS BANK v. STRUMPF

516 U.S. 16 (1995)

SCALIA, J.

We must decide whether the creditor of a debtor in bankruptcy may, in order to protect its setoff rights, temporarily withhold payment of a debt that it owes to the debtor in bankruptcy without violating the automatic stay imposed by 11 U.S.C. § 362(a).

I

On January 25, 1991, when respondent filed for relief under Chapter 13 of the Bankruptcy Code, he had a checking account with petitioner, a bank conducting business in the State of Maryland. He also was in default on the remaining balance of a loan of $5,068.75 from the bank. Under 11 U.S.C. § 362(a), respondent's bankruptcy filing gave rise to an automatic stay of various types of activity by his creditors, including "the setoff of any debt owing to the debtor that arose before the commencement of the [bankruptcy case] against any claim against the debtor." § 362(a)(7).

On October 2, 1991, petitioner placed what it termed an "administrative hold" on so much of respondent's account as it claimed was subject to setoff -- that is, the bank refused to pay withdrawals from the account that would reduce the balance below the sum that it claimed was due on respondent's loan. Five days later, petitioner filed in the Bankruptcy Court, under § 362(d), a "Motion for Relief from Automatic Stay and for Setoff." Respondent then filed a motion to hold petitioner in contempt, claiming that petitioner's administrative hold violated the automatic stay established by § 362(a).

The Bankruptcy Court ruled on respondent's contempt motion first. It concluded that petitioner's "administrative hold" constituted a "setoff" in violation of § 362(a)(7) and sanctioned petitioner. Several weeks later, the Bankruptcy Court granted petitioner's motion for relief from the stay and authorized petitioner to set off respondent's remaining checking account balance against the unpaid loan. By that time, however, respondent had reduced the checking account balance to zero, so there was nothing to set off.

The District Court reversed the judgment that petitioner had violated the automatic stay, concluding that the administrative hold was not a violation of § 362(a). The Court of Appeals reversed. "An administrative hold," it said, "is tantamount to the exercise of a right of setoff and thus violates the automatic stay of § 362(a)(7)." 37 F.3d 155, 158 (CA4 1994). We granted certiorari. 514 U.S. 1035 (1995).

II

The right of setoff (also called "offset") allows entities that owe each other money to apply their mutual debts against each other, thereby avoiding "the absurdity of making A pay B when B owes A." Studley v. Boylston Nat. Bank, 229 U.S. 523, 528 (1913). Although no federal right of setoff is created by the Bankruptcy Code, 11 U.S.C. § 553(a) provides that, with certain exceptions, whatever right of setoff otherwise exists is preserved in bankruptcy. Here it is undisputed that, prior to the bankruptcy filing, petitioner had the right under Maryland law to set off the defaulted loan against the balance in the checking account. It is also undisputed that under § 362(a) respondent's bankruptcy filing stayed any exercise of that right by petitioner. The principal question for decision is whether petitioner's refusal to pay its debt to respondent upon the latter's demand constituted an exercise of the setoff right and hence violated the stay.

In our view, petitioner's action was not a setoff within the meaning of § 362(a)(7). Petitioner refused to pay its debt, not permanently and absolutely, but only while it sought relief under § 362(d) from the automatic stay. Whether that temporary refusal was otherwise wrongful is a separate matter -- we do not consider, for example, respondent's contention that the portion of the account subjected to the "administrative hold" exceeded the amount properly subject to setoff. All that concerns us here is whether the refusal was a setoff. We think it was not, because -- as evidenced by petitioner's "Motion for Relief from Automatic Stay and for Setoff" -- petitioner did not purport permanently to reduce respondent's account balance by the amount of the defaulted loan. A requirement of such an intent is implicit in the rule followed by a majority of jurisdictions addressing the question, that a setoff has not occurred until three steps have been taken: (i) a decision to effectuate a setoff, (ii) some action accomplishing the setoff, and (iii) a recording of the setoff. See, e. g., Baker v. National City Bank of Cleveland, 511 F.2d 1016, 1018 (CA6 1975) (Ohio law); Normand Jo-sef Enterprises, Inc. v. Connecticut Nat. Bank, 230 Conn.486, 504-505, 646 A.2d 1289, 1299 (1994). But even if state law were different, the question whether a setoff under § 362(a)(7) has occurred is a matter of federal law, and other provisions of the Bankruptcy Code would lead us to embrace the same requirement of an intent permanently to settle accounts.

Section 542(b) of the Code, which concerns turnover of property to the estate, requires a bankrupt's debtors to "pay" to the trustee (or on his order) any "debt that is property of the estate and that is matured, payable on demand, or payable on order . . . except to the extent that such debt may be offset under section 553 of this title against a claim against the debtor." 11 U.S.C. § 542(b) (emphasis added). Section 553(a), in turn, sets forth a general rule, with certain exceptions, that any right of setoff that a creditor possessed prior to the debtor's filing for bankruptcy is not affected by the Bankruptcy Code. It would be an odd construction of § 362(a)(7) that required a creditor with a right of setoff to do immediately that which § 542(b) specifically excuses it from doing as a general matter: pay a claim to which a defense of setoff applies.

Nor is our assessment of these provisions changed by the fact that § 553(a), in generally providing that nothing in the Bankruptcy Code affects creditors' prebankruptcy setoff rights, qualifies this rule with the phrase "except as otherwise provided in this section and in sections 362 and 363." This undoubtedly refers to § 362(a)(7), but we think it is most naturally read as merely recognizing that provision's restriction upon when an actual setoff may be effected–which is to say, not during the automatic stay. When this perfectly reasonable reading is available, it would be foolish to take the § 553(a) "except" clause as indicating that § 362(a)(7) requires immediate payment of a debt subject to setoff. That would render § 553(a)'s general rule that the Bankruptcy Code does not affect the right of setoff meaningless, for by forcing the creditor to pay its debt immediately, it would divest the creditor of the very thing that supports the right of setoff. Furthermore, it would, as we have stated, eviscerate § 542(b)'s exception to the duty to pay debts. It is an elementary rule of construction that "the act cannot be held to destroy itself." Texas & Pacific R. Co. v. Abilene Cotton Oil Co., 204 U.S. 426, 446 (1907).

Finally, we are unpersuaded by respondent's additional contentions that the administrative hold violated §§ 362(a)(3) and 362(a)(6). Under these sections, a bankruptcy filing automatically stays "any act to obtain possession of property of the estate or of property from the estate or to exercise control over property of the estate," 11 U.S.C. § 362(a)(3), and "any act to collect, assess, or recover a claim against the debtor that arose before the commencement of the case under this title," § 362(a)(6). Respondent's reliance on these provisions rests on the false premise that petitioner's administrative hold took something from respondent, or exercised dominion over property that belonged to respondent. That view of things might be arguable if a bank account consisted of money belonging to the depositor and held by the bank. In fact, however, it consists of nothing more or less than a promise to pay, from the bank to the depositor, see Bank of Marin v. England, 385 U.S. 99 (1966); Keller v. Frederickstown Sav. Institution, 193 Md. 292, 296, 66 A.2d 924, 925 (1949); and petitioner's temporary refusal to pay was neither a taking of possession of respondent's property nor an exercising of control over it, but merely a refusal to perform its promise. In any event, we will not give § 362(a)(3) or § 362(a)(6) an interpretation that would proscribe what § 542(b)'s "exception" and § 553(a)'s general rule were plainly intended to permit: the temporary refusal of a creditor to pay a debt that is subject to setoff against a debt owed by the bankrupt.[1]

The judgment of the Court of Appeals for the Fourth Circuit is reversed.

Notes and Questions

1. An interesting holding in Strumpf is that a bank account is not property--to D. A bank account represents D's right of performance of a contract with her bank. A bank account is, however, D's property insofar as a levying sheriff is concerned, and for this reason a postpetition levy would violate the automatic stay. The Supreme Court, then, agrees with Kant, who said of a right to contractual performance:

> This right of mine is, however, only a right against a person, namely a right against a specific physical person, and indeed a right to act upon his causality (his choice) to perform something for me it is not a right to a thing.

IMMANUEL KANT, THE METAPHYSICS OF MORALS 59 (Mary Gregor trans., 1991).

2. Setoff is the right of any debtor or creditor to proclaim that a countervailing debt is canceled. Under state law, any visible manifestation of an intent to set off suffices for the cancellation of the mutual debt.

State law is strictly according to the rule of "use it or lose it." Suppose D owes C $100 and C owes D $100. D demands payment. C can either pay or manifest a setoff. If C elects to pay, C has "lost" the set off right (as has D). The rule is quite otherwise in bankruptcy. To the extent of the "setoff opportunity," C is a secured creditor, even if C is required to turn over funds to the bankruptcy trustee.

3. At the time of his petition, D's checking account had a credit of $11,279.86. The Bank's loan to D was for $5,086. Citizens Bank v. Strumpf (In re Strumpf), 37 F.3d 155, 157 (4th Cir. 1994), rev'd, 516 U.S. 16 (1995). Was the bank oversecured or undersecured? See Bankruptcy Code § 506(b) (oversecured creditors are entitled to postpetition interest).

4. Why does Bankruptcy Code § 542(b) support the notion that the administrative hold on the checking account is permissible.

5. In Weber, supra, SP repossessed a car prior to bankruptcy and violated the stay by not returning the car to D at D's request. Is the Weber result consistent with Strumpf? See Thomas E. Plank, The Outer Boundaries of the Bankruptcy Estate, 47 Emory L.J. 1193, 1254-59 (1998).

6. In the second footnote, the Strumpf court refused to consider the effect of confirmation of the chapter 13 plan, on the feeble ground that it was not argued in the court below. Suppose the chapter 13 plan ignores the setoff right of the bank and treats the bank as an unsecured creditor. Would that properly have an effect on this case? See Bankruptcy Code § 1327(a) ("The provision of a confirmed plan bind the debtor and each creditor, whether or not the claim of such creditor is provided for by the plan, and whether or not such creditor has objected to, has accepted, or has rejected the plan").

7. Suppose a debtor files for bankruptcy and owes tax to the IRS. The debtor is entitled to a refund of some postpetition wages. The IRS refuses to pay. Has the IRS violated the automatic stay? See United States v Harchar, 371 B.R. 254 (D. Ohio 2007) (yes). What is the difference between a checking account and a tax refund?

FLEET MORTGAGE GROUP, INC. v KANEB
196 F.3d 265 (1st Cir. 1999)

LIPEZ, J.

Fleet Mortgage, Inc. ("Fleet"), appeals from the order of the Bankruptcy

[1] We decline to address respondent's contention, not raised below, that the confirmation of his Chapter 13 Plan under 11 U.S. C. § 1327 precluded petitioner's exercise of its setoff right. See Granfinanciera, S. A. v. Nordberg, 492 U.S. 33, 39, 106 L. Ed. 2d 26, 109 S. Ct. 2782 (1989).

Appellate Panel for the First Circuit affirming an award of damages and attorneys' fees by the bankruptcy court to Kenneth A. Kaneb pursuant to 11 U.S.C. § 362 (h).[1] We review directly the bankruptcy court's findings of fact and conclusions of law. See Brandt v. Repco Printers & Lithographics, Inc. (In re Healthco Intl'l, Inc.), 132 F.3d 104, 107 (1st Cir. 1997). The bankruptcy court found that Fleet willfully violated the automatic stay provision of the Bankruptcy Code and awarded Kaneb $25,000 for emotional distress and $18,220.68 for attorneys' fees and costs. Fleet contests the finding that the violation of the automatic stay was willful and challenges the award of damages for emotional distress. Fleet also seeks relief from its pretrial stipulation relating to a violation of the stay. We affirm the decision of the Bankruptcy Appellate Panel ("BAP").

I.

In 1993, Kaneb filed a voluntary petition for bankruptcy under Chapter 13 of the Bankruptcy Code. An eighty-five year old retiree and widower, Kaneb spent the cold-weather months in Florida and the balance of the year in Massachusetts.[2] After the sale of his Massachusetts residence to pay secured creditors, he converted to Chapter 7 bankruptcy. Shawmut Bank, N.A. ("Shawmut"), was the original mortgagee of Kaneb's second residence, a Florida condominium.

Shawmut sought relief from the automatic stay in order to initiate foreclosure proceedings. The bankruptcy court denied Shawmut's petition. Kaneb and Shawmut entered into settlement negotiations without success. After the failed negotiations, Shawmut forwarded Kaneb's file to the Florida law firm of Shapiro & Fishman ("Fleet's counsel") to initiate foreclosure proceedings. Shawmut and Fleet merged on November 15, 1995.

The file forwarded from Shawmut contained the order of discharge, dated January 31, 1996, which relieved Kaneb from personal liability for all debts dischargeable under 11 U.S.C. § 523. The file also contained an unsigned order granting relief from the automatic stay. The attorney from Shapiro & Fishman testified that she knew Kaneb was in bankruptcy but she thought that the unsigned order for relief from the automatic stay meant that the bankruptcy judge had granted relief. Further, she erroneously believed that Fleet could initiate foreclosure proceedings lawfully because the bankruptcy court had issued an order of discharge.[3] On behalf of Fleet, Shapiro & Fishman filed a complaint for foreclosure in Florida state court on June 4, 1996.

Shortly after the initiation of the foreclosure, Kaneb's attorney informed Fleet's counsel of the automatic stay and faxed documents confirming this information. Fleet's counsel placed Kaneb's file on "hold" status. Six weeks later, in response to a letter from Kaneb strenuously protesting the violation of the automatic stay, Fleet's counsel dismissed the foreclosure suit.

---

[1] Section 362(h) provides: "An individual injured by any willful violation of a stay provided by this section shall recover actual damages, including costs and attorneys' fees, and, in appropriate circumstances, may recover punitive damages." [This provision now appears as Bankruptcy Code § 362(k)(1).-Ed.]

[2] Mr. Kaneb died on July 23, 1999.

[3] A discharge order " operates as an injunction against the commencement or continuation of an action, the employment of process, or an act, to collect or recover from, or offset any [discharged] debt as a personal liability of the debtor." 11 U.S.C. § 524(a)(2).

During the six weeks that Fleet allowed the foreclosure suit to languish on "hold" status, Kaneb's neighbors learned of the foreclosure proceeding. As a result of a foreclosure notice published in a local Florida newspaper, Kaneb received a barrage of colorful mail offering legal and investment services. These solicitations, known as "dayglow mail," accumulated in Kaneb's Florida mailbox. Neighbors who regularly held his mail for him when he was in Massachusetts learned of the foreclosure action. In addition, one of Kaneb's neighbors erroneously received a solicitation addressed to Kaneb.

Once Kaneb's neighbors learned of the foreclosure suit, they began to avoid him. The condominium where Kaneb lived is a "gated community" populated by affluent retirees. Prior to the initiation of the foreclosure, he socialized frequently with his neighbors. As a widower and retiree, Kaneb's life in Florida revolved around recreational activities within the condominium complex. After his neighbors became aware of the legal proceedings, they stopped inviting him to social outings.

Kaneb brought suit for compensatory and punitive damages for willful violation of the automatic stay in the District of Massachusetts Bankruptcy Court. The court awarded him damages for emotional distress and attorneys' fees, and the Bankruptcy Appellate Panel affirmed. On appeal, Fleet argues for the first time that there was no violation of the automatic stay despite its pretrial stipulation to the contrary. Fleet seeks relief from its pretrial stipulation and contests the sufficiency of the evidence of Kaneb's emotional suffering.

II.

In examining Fleet's pretrial stipulation, we find that Fleet stipulated to a set of uncontested facts from which the bankruptcy judge found a violation of the automatic stay. However, the stipulation merely recites historical facts. Nowhere in the agreement does Fleet concede that, as a legal matter, it violated the automatic stay.[4] Fleet's request for relief from its supposed stipulation to a violation is, in reality, a request for permission to argue a legal issue that it failed to raise below. That is, Fleet raises on appeal Judge Votolato's sua sponte argument in his dissent to the decision of the Bankruptcy Appellate Panel that there was no violation because the foreclosure occurred after Kaneb's discharge from bankruptcy and the automatic stay does not apply because Kaneb excluded the Florida property from the bankruptcy estate by claiming it as exempt. We will not address issues raised for the first time on appeal.[5] See Teamsters Local No.

---

[4] The pretrial stipulation includes a series of uncontested facts relevant to the alleged stay violation: "On November 8, 1995, Shawmut Bank, N.A., the predecessor in interest to Fleet, filed for Relief from the Automatic Stay;" "On December 6, 1995 this Court denied the Motion for Relief from Stay with Prejudice for failure to cooperate;" "On June 4, 1996 a Complaint for foreclosure was initiated by Fleet National Bank to foreclosure [sic] on the Debtor's property;" "On June 11, 1996 a call was made by the Plaintiff's Counsel to the Defendant's attorneys, indicating the automatic stay was still in effect; " "Fleet's counsel placed the Debtor's file on hold on June 11, 1996 and informed Fleet of the status of the File;" "On July 23, 1996, after receipt of the facsimile transmission [from Kaneb's attorney] Fleet filed a Voluntary Dismissal and Discharge of Lis Pendens Without Prejudice."

[5] Because we decline to review issues raised for the first time on appeal, we describe Judge Votolato's argument for the sake of completeness rather than addressing it on the merits. Judge Votolato took the view that the condominium property was no longer part of the bankruptcy estate and not subject to the automatic stay:

59 v. Superline Transp. Co., 953 F.2d 17, 21 (1st Cir. 1992) ("If any principle is settled in this circuit, it is that, absent the most extraordinary circumstances, legal theories not raised squarely in the lower court cannot be broached for the first time on appeal."). We decline to address Fleet's "no violation" argument.

Instead, we accept the conclusion that there was a violation of the automatic stay and review the trial court's determination that this violation was willful. The trial court found that, "Despite knowing that the stay was still in force, on April 26, 1996 Shawmut forwarded its file to the law firm of Shapiro & Fishman . . . for the purpose of initiating foreclosure on the property." Fleet argues that this action was simply an innocent mistake. Further, Fleet contends that its actions were not willful because they were not taken with "flagrant or reckless disregard" for its legal obligations.

Fleet cites no authority for its "flagrant or reckless disregard" standard and our research discloses none. We decline to create a new standard for willfulness. We similarly reject Fleet's argument that it is immune from sanctions because it made a mistake. A good faith belief in a right to the property is not relevant to a determination of whether the violation was willful. See Tsafaroff v. Taylor (In re Taylor), 884 F.2d 478, 483 (9th Cir. 1989), (quoting INSLAW, Inc. v. United States (In re INSLAW, Inc.), 83 B.R. 89, 165 (Bankr. D.D.C. 1988)). A willful violation does not require a specific intent to violate the automatic stay. The standard for a willful violation of the automatic stay under § 362(h) is met if there is knowledge of the stay and the defendant intended the actions which constituted the violation. See Goichman v. Bloom (In re Bloom), 875 F.2d 224, 227 (9th Cir. 1989); see also Crysen/Montenay Energy Co. v. Esselen Assocs., Inc. (In re Crysen/Montenay Energy Co.), 902 F.2d 1098, 1105 (2d Cir. 1990); Cuffee v. Atlantic Bus. and Community Dev. Corp. (In re Atlantic Business and Community Corp.), 901 F.2d 325, 329 (3d Cir. 1990). In cases where the creditor received actual notice of the automatic stay, courts must presume that the violation was deliberate. See Homer Nat'l Bank v. Namie, 96 B.R. 652, 654 (W.D. La. 1989). The debtor has the burden of providing the creditor with actual notice. Once the creditor receives actual notice, the burden shifts to the creditor to prevent violations of the automatic stay. See Mitchell Constr. Co., Inc. v. Smith (In re Smith), 180 B.R. 311, 319 (Bankr. N.D. Ga. 1995).

The parties do not contest that Shawmut received actual notice of the automatic stay. Indeed, the record reveals that Shawmut unsuccessfully filed a motion for relief from the stay. After the bankruptcy court's denial of the motion

> I am unable to agree with the majority's decision to leave undisturbed a stipulation that is invalid as a matter law, in light of the fact that as of the date of the alleged stay violation: (1) the discharge had already entered; and (2) the debtor had claimed his condominium as exempt, thereby terminating its status as property of the estate.

The BAP majority, although insisting that Fleet was bound by its supposed stipulation, concluded that whether the condominium was property of the bankruptcy estate, and hence subject to the automatic stay, depended on whether there was equity in the condominium: "When as here we have realty with little or no information as to its value, encumbrances and exemption, we cannot know whether it is valueless, outside the purview of the estate." Kaneb asserted in a July 19, 1996, letter to Fleet that, "Since there is equity in this asset for the estate, it remains part of the bankruptcy estate and I have a claim of exemption in this asset." Judge Votolato acknowledged that Fleet's failure to raise the exemption issue before the bankruptcy court was "incomprehensible."

for relief, Shawmut retained the law firm of Shapiro & Fishman to initiate foreclosure proceedings. Although Fleet received notice of a violation when Kaneb's attorney informed Shapiro & Fishman of the stay, Fleet's counsel failed to dismiss the suit for six weeks. Under the applicable standard, Fleet's actions constitute a willful violation of the automatic stay.

III.

Fleet challenges generally the sufficiency of the evidence of harm and causation for the $25,000 award for mental anguish and argues specifically that a showing of mental anguish requires physical injury or corroborating medical testimony. We decline to address Fleet's specific arguments about evidentiary requirements because Fleet has once again waived these arguments by failing to raise them below. The BAP majority noted: "Our examination of the lengthy record shows Fleet did not question the appropriateness of the [damages award] on grounds that there was no corroborating evidence. Therefore, Fleet is precluded from raising the issue of corroboration now . . . ." Similarly, our review of the record reveals that Fleet did not raise before the lower court the argument that a plaintiff must have suffered concomitant physical harm in order to receive damages for mental anguish.

In responding to Fleet's general challenge to the sufficiency of the damages evidence, we note that emotional damages qualify as "actual damages" under § 362(h). See Holden v. IRS (In re Holden), 226 B.R. 809, 812 (Bankr. D. Vt. 1998) ("Emotional distress is an actual injury . . . . Legitimate human emotions are brought to bear when one's rights are trampled on."); In re Carrigan, 109 B.R. 167, 170 (W.D.N.C. 1989) ("The debtor's actual injury here is somewhat imprecise, but it is real -- and, it is certainly the result of [the creditor's actions].); but see In re McPeck, 1991 Bankr. LEXIS 100, 1991 WL 8405 at *3 (Bankr. D. Minn. Jan. 29, 1991). In the instant case, Kaneb provided specific information about the sharp decline in social invitations and outings following Fleet's violation of the automatic stay rather than "generalized assertions" of his emotional state. See In the Matter of Robinson, 228 B.R. 75, 85 (Bankr. E.D.N.Y. 1998) (finding insufficient evidence of debtor's claim of emotional harm based on unsworn and generalized assertion that debtor was concerned and upset). He then testified about the emotional distress he experienced because of these changes in his life: "Its very irritating. I don't sleep well. My eating habits have changed. I -- I don't feel that ambitious about getting out and doing things and meeting people. It's -- it's not a pleasant situation to be in . . . . I'm worried concerning where am I going to live." An honest accounting of actual damages under § 362(h) must include the psychological suffering of this eighty-five year old retired widower. We affirm the bankruptcy court's award of damages for mental anguish.

IV.

In his cross-appeal, Kaneb challenges the Bankruptcy Appellate Panel's deferment of an award of attorneys' fees pending appeal, arguing that § 362(h)'s mandate that an injured individual "shall recover actual damages" requires a prompt award of attorneys' fees. Further, Kaneb asserts that deferment of fees discourages attorneys from filing suits to vindicate debtors' rights under the automatic stay provision and creates a burdensome cycle of "satellite" appeals over fees. However, Kaneb cites no authority for the proposition that an award by the trial court of attorneys' fees may not be held in abeyance under § 362(h) until the trial court's determination that there was a willful violation of the automatic stay is affirmed on appeal. The BAP's order was within its discretion and not contrary to law.

Affirmed.

Notes and Questions

1. In this case, the debtor had claimed his Florida condo as exempt and had received a discharge. Was the automatic stay still in effect? See Bankruptcy Code § 362(c). The mortgage lender, however, forgot to cite § 362(c) to the bankruptcy court, and the Court of Appeals refused to hear "new arguments" not raised at the trial level.

2. Suppose C challenges D's discharge pursuant to some part of § 523(a), and the court declares C's claim is not discharged. Even though the bankruptcy case still continues, C garnishes D's bank account. Has C violated the automatic stay? Boatmen's Bank v. Embry (In re Embry), 10 F.3d 401 (6th Cir. 1993) (no).

B. PROPERTY OF THE BANKRUPTCY ESTATE

IN RE SZEKELY

936 F.2d 897 (7th Cir. 1991)

POSNER, J.

This bankruptcy appeal raises a surprisingly fundamental, and difficult, question . . . on which we are unable to find any authority. The question is whether if a debtor continues to occupy his home after declaring bankruptcy, the trustee can charge rent to him, notwithstanding the homestead exemption. The debtors in this case–a married couple named Szekely, living in Zion, Illinois–declared bankruptcy (originally under Chapter 13, later converted to Chapter 7 -- liquidation) on December 5, 1988. One of the assets of the bankrupt estate was the couple's home, on which there were both a first and a second mortgage. The Bankruptcy Code allows a state to require debtors to use the state's exemptions rather than the exemptions set forth in the Code itself. 11 U.S.C. § 522 (b)(1); First National Bank v. Norris, 701 F.2d 902, 904 (11th Cir. 1983). Illinois has taken up this option, and as a result each of the Szekelys was "entitled to an estate of homestead to the extent in value of $7,500," for a total of $15,000. Ill. Rev. Stat. ch. 110, paras. 12-901, 12-1201.

The Szekelys continued living in their home, though they made no payments on either mortgage. In April, the trustee asked the bankruptcy judge to order the couple to pay rent. Two months later the bankruptcy judge granted the trustee's request and fixed the rent at $600 a month, though it was understood that since the Szekelys couldn't pay, the rent would accrue, and would be deducted from their homestead exemption when the house was sold. In September, although the house hadn't been sold yet, the Szekelys vacated it, owing eight months' accrued rent -- $4,800. In February of the following year, the district judge affirmed the bankruptcy judge's rent order. 111 Bankr. 681 (N.D. Ill. 1990). The Szekelys now appeal the district judge's order to us. We were told at argument that the house has now been sold, for about $135,000, which is $30,000 more than the amount owing on the two mortgages and therefore enough to cover the entire homestead exemption. Yet if we affirm, the trustee will give the Szekelys only $10,200 ($15,000-$4,800). . .

In defending the judgment that he won below, the trustee points out correctly that the debtors' home became an asset of the bankrupt estate upon the declaration of bankruptcy. 11 U.S.C. § 541. Thus, by continuing to live in the house, the Szekelys were using an asset that belonged to the bankrupt estate, not to them. Therefore–the trustee argues–they should be required to pay rent for its use, just as anyone else leasing assets of the estate would be required to pay rent to the trustee. The argument is fine as far as it goes, but it doesn't leave much in the way of a homestead exemption. Imagine a case–this case, in fact–in which the debtors live in a relatively expensive home. They go broke, and naturally they want to live more modestly. If they move out, then under the trustee's view of the case they get nothing until the house is sold, at which time they get their $15,000. But since they get nothing till then, they will find it hard to arrange for substitute accommodations if they move out now. (Of course they can rent housing out of their current income, if they have any. But this would be true even if there were no homestead exemption, so it is a better argument against the exemption–though not an argument properly addressed to us, for we of course have no authority to abolish the exemption–than it is in favor of allowing the trustee to charge rent.) If, therefore, they decide to remain in their house–their house that was, now the property of the estate–they will, if the trustee prevails, be forced to pay rent based on the value of the house, a value geared to the debtors' standard of living before they went bankrupt. As the months pass, the accruing rent will dig a deeper and deeper hole in the homestead exemption; in this case it reduced it by a third. When the debtors finally move out they will have substantially diminished resources with which to find alternative housing.

This is looking at the case from the debtors' point of view, and thus emphasizing the "fresh start" rationale of bankruptcy -- that is, bankruptcy as a debtor's cushion against the effects of financial misfortune. Bankruptcy is equally a creditor's remedy, however, in particular a remedy of unsecured creditors, represented by the trustee. The house was an asset of the estate and did have a positive rental value that the debtors impaired by continuing to live in the house. If the house had been sold right after the Szekelys had declared bankruptcy, they would have gotten $15,000, period. If they prevail on this appeal, they will have got $15,000 -- plus free housing (well, almost free) for eight months. This overstates the windfall, because the present receipt of $15,000 is worth more in real terms than the receipt of $15,000 eight months later. Nevertheless the Szekelys are seeking a windfall. And the more valuable the house, the greater the windfall (for the greater the housing value is). But some degree of inequity is built into the homestead exemption: people too poor to own a house have no homestead exemption. This may be an argument against the exemption; and another argument, one not even limited to the homestead exemption, is that anything which impairs creditors' rights in bankruptcy drives up interest rates (for creditors will seek compensation in advance for any added risks of default), to the ultimate detriment of the debtor class. Indeed, the higher that interest rates are (other things being equal), the greater the risk of bankruptcy is, since interest is a fixed expense. But these are academic speculations, because we are not authorized to restructure bankruptcy law.

The competing thrusts of that law, as a debtor's and as a creditor's remedy respectively (though, as we have just said, it may only be in the short run that bankruptcy is really a debtor's remedy), are mirrored in the competing characterizations of the homestead exemption that the parties press on us. The Szekelys conceive of the exemption as a right to remain in one's home, rent-free, until the trustee either through sale or otherwise can pay the debtor the value of the exemption. They point out that Illinois law describes the exemption as an "estate of homestead," Ill. Rev. Stat. ch. 11, para. 12-901 (emphasis added), rather than using the humbler designation "homestead exemption," which is the formula in the list of federal statutory exemptions applicable in states that do not want their own exemptions applied in bankruptcy, 11 U.S.C. § 522 (d)(1), and is also the formula found in most state statutes . . . . They cite cases which hold that even though the title of the Illinois statute is "Exemption of Homestead" (Ill. Rev. Stat. ch. 11, art. 12, pt. 9), the term in the body of the statute, "estate of homestead," is not an archaic sonority but denotes a right to possession.

The trustee argues that the homestead exemption (or "estate") is not a possessory interest at all, but merely a lien -- a claim to $15,000 if and when the house is sold or the claim, which is freely alienable, Dixon v. Moller, 42 Ill. App. 3d 688, 690, 356 N.E.2d 599, 602, 1 Ill. Dec. 411 (1976), is otherwise transferred.

The cases support the debtors' characterization. Wiegand v. Wiegand, 410 Ill. 533, 535, 103 N.E.2d 137, 139 (1952) ("homestead is an estate in land and not a mere exemption"); Dixon v. Moller, supra, 42 Ill. App. 3d at 690, 356 N.E.2d at 602 (it is a "possessory freehold estate"); Willard v. Northwest National Bank, 137 Ill. App. 3d 255, 264, 484 N.E.2d 823, 828, 92 Ill. Dec. 92 (1985) ("a freehold estate in land"). But none involves the precise issue here, the trustee's right to receive rent for the debtors' occupancy of their (former) house. Not even Mix v. King, 55 Ill. 434 (1870), on which the debtors principally rely. That case holds that the homestead exemption is possessory, all right; but it was not an insolvency case; it was a case of improper ejectment of the holder of an express right of homestead, and thus was analogous to the wrongful eviction of a tenant. See also In re Nye, 133 F. 33 (8th Cir. 1904). The trustee does not contest the Szekelys' right to occupy the house until it is sold or he pays them the amount of the homestead exemption; all he wants is rent; and since the cases are emphatic that the "estate" is limited by the value of the exemption, it is a little hard to see why the debtors should obtain in effect the full rental value of the house, over and above the exemption, without paying rent for that surplus comfort. On the other hand, the case on which the trustee principally relies holds only that if there is a right of ejectment (as there was not in Mix), the owner must pay off the homestead exemption before ejecting the homesteader. Hotchkiss v. Brooks, 93 Ill. 386 (1879). That is common ground among the parties to this suit.

Precedent does not decide our case. We must consider principle.

Because the house belongs to the estate, the trustee can pay the Szekelys their $15,000 and tell them to skedaddle, and then rent the house to whomever he pleases until he sells it. That much is clear. And he can raise the $15,000 either by liquidating other assets of the bankrupt estate or, if there are insufficient other assets (as we may assume to be the case here), by taking out another mortgage on the house. The Szekelys' house, though, was already encumbered by two mortgages, and although in the end the house was sold for an amount that yielded enough equity over and above the mortgages (with all their arrearages) to pay the homestead exemption in full, the value of the house may have been too uncertain for the trustee to have been able to obtain a third mortgage, for $15,000, at a tolerable rate of interest. In that event he would (under the Szekelys' view of the case) have had to let them stay there rent free until he sold the house.

Some brokers believe that it is more difficult to sell a house with a tenant in it than with the house vacant, partly because it is easier to show a house when no one is living there and it is uncluttered with personal possessions and partly because the presence of a tenant will make it difficult for the owner to promise immediate possession to the buyer. (The argument contra is that a vacant house is uninviting.) So the trustee may not have wanted the Szekelys living there and paying rent, but may instead have wanted them out, and of course they were more likely to leave if they had to pay rent (eventually they did leave, perhaps for that reason, before the house was sold). If this is right, then had they moved out the trustee would not have rented the house to someone else. It would have stood vacant, yielding no income to him until he sold it. This suggests that he too is seeking a windfall, and that the real purpose of his charging rent was to induce the Szekelys to leave, so that the house could be sold more easily. To cast them out into the cold, as it were, without giving them the $15,000 to which the homestead exemption entitled them, undermined the purpose of the exemption, which is to assure the debtor adequate housing despite the economic disaster that has overtaken him. The harm to the debtor depends on how long it takes to sell the house. If it is sold right off, he gets the cash value of the exemption; but if there is a delay in selling it, he must arrange for substitute housing without the assistance that Illinois meant him to have through the homestead exemption.

We are just speculating that the trustee wanted the Szekelys out (though they did move out eventually, before the house was sold). But the speculation is not critical to our decision. The important thing is that whether they paid rent and stayed, or left before being cashed out of the homestead exemption, the value of the exemption to them was diminished. And while it is true that if the debtor can live rent-free in the house until it is sold he will have an incentive to delay the sale if he can, by the same token if the debtor can't live there rent-free the trustee has no incentive to sell the house as quickly as possible, and in addition the bankruptcy court must step in and fix a reasonable rental. The hardship to the debtor should have the greater weight in decision. The homestead exemption, perhaps especially when as here it is capped at a relatively modest sum of money, is designed to assist the debtor to the extent of the exemption to obtain more modest living quarters. That aim is blunted if the trustee can in effect expel the debtor from the homestead (whether directly or by charging a rent geared to a standard of living that the debtor no longer can maintain) without giving him a penny of benefit from the homestead exemption.

There is an analogy to tenancy in common. Neither tenant can charge the other rent, but either can demand that the property be partitioned between them. Massman v. Duffy, 333 Ill. App. 30, 40, 76 N.E.2d 547, 551-52 (1947). The interaction of bankruptcy law and the homestead exemption made the Szekelys in effect cotenants, with the trustee, of the Szekelys' former house. The trustee was entitled to obtain sole rights to the property by paying off the homestead exemption -- in effect a partition of the property in which the Szekelys would receive $15,000 -- but until then he had no right to disturb the Szekelys in their possession of the property. We hold that the homestead exemption in Illinois entitles the debtor to remain in his home rent free until he receives the cash value of the exemption. We therefore reverse the decisions below with directions to allow the debtors their full $15,000 from the proceeds of the sale of the house.

Notes

1. Do you agree that, by virtue of their homestead rights, the debtors were cotenants with the trustee? If this is true, is the trustee a trespasser in the debtors' home when he drops by to use

the guest room?

2. The Szekeley court seems to assume that a bankruptcy trustee owns a debtor's home in fee simple absolute. If so, the debtor is a trespasser, and rent is the remedy the debtors owe for their trespass. But is it so clear that the trustee's interest in the house is a fee simple interest? See 11 U.S.C. § 544(a). For the view that the trustee is simply a lien creditor against the home, see Vladimir Elgort, Note, Do Debtors Owe Rent to Their Bankruptcy Trustee for Remaining in the Home After Filing and Prior to Foreclosure, Notwithstanding a Homestead Exemption?, 23 CARDOZO L. REV. 2253 (2002).

3. Under New York law, a debtor possessing a house owes no rent to the mortgage lender following default. Holmes v. Gravenhorst, 263 N.Y. 148, 188 N.E. 285 (1933). Does this say anything about what the rule should be in bankruptcy? See Bankruptcy Code § 544(a)(3).

DEWSNUP v. TIMM,
502 U.S. 410 (1992)

BLACKMUN, J.

We are confronted in this case with an issue concerning § 506(d) of the Bankruptcy Code, 11 U.S.C. § 506(d).[1] May a debtor strip down a creditor's lien on real property to the value of the collateral, as judicially determined, when that value is less than the amount of the claim secured by the lien?

I

On June 1, 1978, respondents loaned $119,000 to petitioner Aletha Dewsnup and her husband, T. LaMar Dewsnup, since deceased. The loan was accompanied by a Deed of Trust granting a lien on two parcels of Utah farmland owned by the Dewsnups.

Petitioner defaulted the following year. Under the terms of the Deed of

---

[1] Section 506 provides in full:

> (a) An allowed claim of a creditor secured by a lien on property in which the estate has an interest, or that is subject to setoff under section 553 of this title, is a secured claim to the extent of the value of such creditor's interest in the estate's interest in such property, or to the extent of the amount subject to setoff, as the case may be, and is an unsecured claim to the extent that the value of such creditor's interest or the amount so subject to setoff is less than the amount of such allowed claim. Such value shall be determined in light of the purpose of the valuation and of the proposed disposition or use of such property, and in conjunction with any hearing on such disposition or use or on a plan affecting such creditor's interest.
>
> (b) To the extent that an allowed secured claim is secured by property the value of which, after any recovery under subsection (c) of this section, is greater than the amount of such claim, there shall be allowed to the holder of such claim, interest on such claim, and any reasonable fees, costs, or charges provided for under the agreement under which such claim arose.
>
> (c) The trustee may recover from property securing an allowed secured claim the reasonable, necessary costs and expenses of preserving, or disposing of, such property to the extent of any benefit to the holder of such claim.
>
> (d) To the extent that a lien secures a claim against the debtor that is not an allowed secured claim, such lien is void, unless–
>
> (1) such claim was disallowed only under section 502(b)(5) or 502(e) of this title; or
>
> (2) such claim is not an allowed secured claim due only to the failure of any entity to file a proof of such claim under section 501 of this title.

Trust, respondents at that point could have proceeded against the real property collateral by accelerating the maturity of the loan, issuing a notice of default, and selling the land at a public foreclosure sale to satisfy the debt. See also Utah Code Ann. §§ 57-1-20 to 57-1-37 (1990 and Supp. 1991).

Respondents did issue a notice of default in 1981. Before the foreclosure sale took place, however, petitioner sought reorganization under Chapter 11 of the Bankruptcy Code, 11 U.S.C. § 1101 et seq. That bankruptcy petition was dismissed, as was a subsequent Chap-ter 11 petition. In June 1984, petitioner filed a petition seeking liquidation under Chapter 7 of the Code, 11 U.S.C. § 701 et seq. Because of the pendency of these bankruptcy procee-dings, respondents were not able to proceed to the foreclosure sale. See 11 U.S.C. § 362.

In 1987, petitioner filed the present adversary proceeding in the Bankruptcy Court for the District of Utah seeking, pursuant to § 506, to avoid" a portion of respondents' lien. App. 3. Petitioner represented that the debt of approximately $120,000 then owed to respondents exceeded the fair market value of the land and that, therefore, the Bankruptcy Court should reduce the lien to that value. According to petitioner, this was compelled by the interrelationship of the security-reducing provision of § 506(a) and the lien-voiding provision of § 506(d). Under § 506(a) ("An allowed claim of a creditor secured by a lien on property in which the estate has an interest . . .. is a secured claim to the extent of the value of such creditor's interest in the estate's interest in such property"), respondents would have an allowed secured claim" only to the extent of the judicially determined value of their collateral. And under § 506(d) ("To the extent that a lien secures a claim against the debtor that is not an allowed secured claim, such lien is void"), the court would be required to void the lien as to the remaining portion of respondents' claim, because the remaining portion was not an allowed secured claim" within the meaning of §506(a).

The Bankruptcy Court refused to grant this relief. In re Dewsnup, 87 Bankr. 676 (1988). After a trial, it determined that the then value of the land subject to the Deed of Trust was $39,000. It indulged in the assumption that the property had been abandoned by the trustee pursuant to § 554, and reasoned that once property was abandoned it no longer fell within the reach of § 506(a), which applies only to property in which the estate has an interest," and therefore was not covered by § 506(d).

The United States District Court, without a supporting opinion, summarily affirmed the Bankruptcy Court's judgment of dismissal with prejudice. App. to Pet. for Cert. 12a.

The Court of Appeals for the Tenth Circuit, in its turn, also affirmed. In re Dewsnup, 908 F.2d 588 (1990). Starting from the fundamental premise" of § 506(a) that a claim is subject to reduction in security only when the estate has an interest in the property, the court reasoned that because the estate had no interest in abandoned property, § 506(a) did not apply (nor, by implication, did § 506(d)). 908 F.2d at 590-591. The court then noted that a contrary result would be inconsistent with § 722 under which a debtor has a limited right to redeem certain personal property. Id., at 592.

Because the result reached by the Court of Appeals was at odds with that reached by the Third Circuit in Gaglia v. First Federal Savings & Loan Assn., 889 F.2d 1304, 1306-1311 (1989), and was expressly recognized by the Tenth Circuit as being in conflict, see 908 F.2d at 591, we granted certiorari.

II

As we read their several submissions, the parties and their amici are not in agreement in their respective approaches to the problem of statutory interpretation that confronts us. Petitioner-debtor takes the position that § 506(a) and § 506(d) are complementary and to be read together. Because, under § 506(a), a claim is secured only to the extent of the judicially determined value of the real property on which the lien is fixed, a debtor can void a lien on the property pursuant to § 506(d) to the extent the claim is no longer secured and thus is not an allowed secured claim. In other words, § 506(a) bifurcates classes of claims allowed under § 502 into secured claims and unsecured claims; any portion of an allowed claim deemed to be unsecured under § 506(a) is not an allowed secured claim" within the lien-voiding scope of § 506(d). Petitioner argues that there is no exception for unsecured property abandoned by the trustee.

Petitioner's amicus argues that the plain language of § 506(d) dictates that the proper portion of an undersecured lien on property in a Chapter 7 case is void whether or not the property is abandoned by the trustee. It further argues that the rationale of the Court of Appeals would lead to evisceration of the debtor's right of redemption and the elimination of an undersecured creditor's ability to participate in the distribution of the estate's assets.

Respondents primarily assert that § 506(d) is not, as petitioner would have it, rigidly tied" to § 506(a), Brief for Respondents 7. They argue that § 506(a) performs the function of classifying claims by true secured status at the time of distribution of the estate to ensure fairness to unsecured claimants. In contrast, the lien-voiding § 506(d) is directed to the time at which foreclosure is to take place, and, where the trustee has abandoned the property, no bankruptcy distributional purpose is served by voiding the lien.

In the alternative, respondents, joined by the United States as amicus curiae, argue more broadly that the words allowed secured claim" in § 506(d) need not be read as an indivisible term of art defined by reference to § 506(a), which by its terms is not a definitional provision. Rather, the words should be read term-by-term to refer to any claim that is, first, allowed, and, second, secured. Because there is no question that the claim at issue here has been allowed" pursuant to § 502 of the Code and is secured by a lien with recourse to the underlying collateral, it does not come within the scope of § 506(d), which voids only liens corresponding to claims that have not been allowed and secured. This reading of § 506(d), according to respondents and the United States, gives the provision the simple and sensible function of voiding a lien whenever a claim secured by the lien itself has not been allowed. It ensures that the Code's determination not to allow the underlying claim against the debtor personally is given full effect by preventing its assertion against the debtor's property.[2]

[2] Respondents expressly stated in their brief and twice again at oral argument that they adopted as an alternative position the United States' interpretation of § 506(d). Brief for Respondents 40, n. 33; Tr. of Oral Arg. 14, 20. In dissent, however, JUSTICE SCALIA contends that respondents have not taken the same position as the United States on this issue. According to the dissent, the United States has taken the position that a lien only secures' the claim in question up to the value of the security that is the object of the lien--and only up to that value is the lien subject to avoidance under § 506(d)." Post, at 5. In fact, the United States says: Under [petitioner's] reading, Section 506(d) would operate to reduce the creditor's lien to the value of the allowed secured claim described in Section 506(a). In our view, this reading makes no sense." Brief for United

Respondents point out that pre-Code bankruptcy law preserved liens like respondents' and that there is nothing in the Code's legislative history that reflects any intent to alter that law. Moreover, according to respondents, the fresh-start" policy cannot justify an impairment of respondents' property rights, for the fresh start does not extend to an in rem claim against property but is limited to a discharge of personal liability.

III

The foregoing recital of the contrasting positions of the respective parties and their amici demonstrates that § 506 of the Bankruptcy Code and its relationship to other provisions of that Code do embrace some ambiguities. See 3 Collier on Bankruptcy, ch. 506 and, in particular, para. 506.07 (15th ed. 1990). Hypothetical applications that come to mind and those advanced at oral argument illustrate the difficulty of interpreting the statute in a single opinion that would apply to all possible fact situations. We therefore focus upon the case before us and allow other facts to await their legal resolution on another day.

We conclude that respondents' alternative position, espoused also by the United States, although not without its difficulty, generally is the better of the several approaches. Therefore, we hold that § 506(d) does not allow petitioner to strip down" respondents' lien, because respondents' claim is secured by a lien and has been fully allowed pursuant to § 502. Were we writing on a clean slate, we might be inclined to agree with petitioner that the words allowed secured claim" must take the same meaning in § 506(d) as in § 506(a).[3] But, given the ambiguity in the text, we are not convinced that Congress intended to depart from the pre-Code rule that liens pass through bankruptcy unaffected.

1. The practical effect of petitioner's argument is to freeze the creditor's secured interest at the judicially determined valuation. By this approach, the creditor would lose the benefit of any increase in the value of the property by the time of the foreclosure sale. The increase would accrue to the benefit of the debtor, a result some of the parties describe as a windfall."

We think, however, that the creditor's lien stays with the real property until the foreclosure. That is what was bargained for by the mortgagor and the mortgagee. The voidness language sensibly applies only to the security aspect of the lien and then only to the real deficiency in the security. Any increase over the judicially determined valuation during bankruptcy rightly accrues to the benefit of the creditor, not to the benefit of the debtor and not to the benefit of other unsecured creditors whose claims have been allowed and who had nothing to do with the mortgagor-mortgagee bargain.

Such surely would be the result had the lienholder stayed aloof from the bankruptcy proceeding (subject, of course, to the power of other persons or entities to pull him into the proceeding pursuant to § 501), and we see no reason why his acquiescence in that proceeding should cause him to experience a forfeiture of the kind the debtor proposes. It is true that his participation in the bankruptcy results in his having the benefit of an allowed unsecured claim as well as his allowed secured claim, but that does not strike us as proper

States as Amicus Curiae 5.

[3] Accordingly, we express no opinion as to whether the words allowed secured claim" have different meaning in other provisions of the Bankruptcy Code.

recompense for what petitioner proposes by way of the elimination of the remainder of the lien.

2. This result appears to have been clearly established before the passage of the 1978 Act. Under the Bankruptcy Act of 1898, a lien on real property passed through bankruptcy unaffected. This Court recently acknowledged that this was so. See Farrey v. Sanderfoot, 500 U.S. 291 (1991) (slip op. 6) (Ordinarily, liens and other secured interests survive bankruptcy"); Johnson v. Home State Bank, 501 U.S., (1991) (slip op. 5) (Rather, a bankruptcy discharge extinguishes only one mode of enforcing a claim -- namely, an action against the debtor in personam -- while leaving intact another -- namely, an action against the debtor in rem.").[4]

3. Apart from reorganization proceedings, see 11 U.S.C. §§ 616(1) and (10) (1976 ed.), no provision of the pre-Code statute permitted involuntary reduction of the amount of a creditor's lien for any reason other than payment on the debt. Our cases reveal the Court's concern about this. In Long v. Bullard, 117 U.S. 617, 620-621 (1886), the Court held that a discharge in bankruptcy does not release real estate of the debtor from the lien of a mortgage created by him before the bankruptcy. And in Louisville Joint Stock Land Bank v. Radford, 295 U.S. 555 (1935), the Court considered additions to the Bankruptcy Act effected by the Frazier-Lemke Act, 48 Stat. 1289 (1934). There the Court noted that the latter Act's avowed object is to take from the mortgagee rights in the specific property held as security; and to that end to scale down the indebtedness' to the present value of the property. Id., at 594. The Court invalidated that statute under the Takings Clause. It further observed: No instance has been found, except under the Frazier-Lemke Act, of either a statute or decision compelling the mortgagee to relinquish the property to the mortgagor free of the lien unless the debt was paid in full. Id., at 579.

Congress must have enacted the Code with a full understanding of this practice. See H. R. Rep. No. 95-595, p. 357 (1977) (Subsection (d) permits liens to pass through the bankruptcy case unaffected).

4. When Congress amends the bankruptcy laws, it does not write "on a clean slate." See Emil v. Hanley, 318 U.S. 515, 521 (1943). Furthermore, this Court has been reluctant to accept arguments that would interpret the Code, however vague the particular language under consideration might be, to effect a major change in pre-Code practice that is not the subject of at least some discussion in the legislative history. See United Savings Assn. of Texas v. Timbers

---

[4] Section 67d of the 1898 Act, 30 Stat. 564, made this explicit:

> Liens given or accepted in good faith and not in contemplation of or in fraud upon this Act, and for a present consideration, which have been recorded according to law, if record thereof was necessary in order to impart notice, shall not be affected by this Act.

The Court, with respect to this statute, has said: Section 67d . . .. declares that liens given or accepted in good faith and not in contemplation of or in fraud upon this Act, shall not be affected by it. City of Richmond v. Bird, 249 U.S. 174, 177, 63 L. Ed. 543, 39 S. Ct. 186 (1919).

This precise statutory language did not appear in a reorganization of the section in the Chandler Act of 1938, 52 Stat. 840. A respected bankruptcy authority convincingly explained that this was done not to remove the rule of validity but because the draftsmen of the 1938 Act desired generally to specify only what should be invalid. 4B Collier on Bankruptcy para. 70.70, p. 771 (14th ed. 1979) (emphasis in original). The alteration had no substantive effect. Oppenheimer v. Oldham, 178 F.2d 386, 389 (CA2 1949).

of Inwood Forest Associates, Ltd., 484 U.S. 365, 380 (1988). See also Pennsylvania Dept. of Public Welfare v. Davenport, 495 U.S. 552 (1990) (slip op. 9); United States v. Ron Pair Enterprises, Inc., 489 U.S. 235, 244-245 (1989). Of course, where the language is unambiguous, silence in the legislative history cannot be controlling. But, given the ambiguity here, to attribute to Congress the intention to grant a debtor the broad new remedy against allowed claims to the extent that they become unsecured for purposes of § 506(a) without the new remedy's being mentioned somewhere in the Code itself or in the annals of Congress is not plausible, in our view, and is contrary to basic bankruptcy principles.

The judgment of the Court of Appeals is affirmed.[5]

Notes and Questions

1. The meaning of Dewsnup is that valuations are never final; bifurcation can always be revisited. But there are two exceptions.

> (a) If the collateral is sold free and clear of a lien pursuant to § 363(f), the bifurcation is final. The undersecured creditor obtains the proceeds. 11 U.S.C. § 552(b). Any remaining deficit is an unsecured claim (if a proof of claim was timely filed).
>
> (b) A plan of reorganization may be confirmed. If so, the bifurcation memorialized in the plan is frozen forever, even if the plan goes into default. 2 GRANT GILMORE & DAVID GRAY CARLSON, GILMORE AND CARLSON ON SECURED LENDING: CLAIMS IN BANKRUPTCY § 27.07 (2000). Plan confirmation in chapter 13 is a different matter. The 2005 amendments make clear that, if the plan goes into default (as it usually does), the bifurcation is undone; the creditor's two claims merge, and this claim encumbers all of the collateral. Bankruptcy Code §348(f)(1)(C) (as to cases converted from chapter 13 to chapter 7) §1325(a)(5)(B)(II) (as to conversions or dismissals).

2. Suppose D grants a perfected security interest to SP more than 90 days before bankruptcy. D then files for bankruptcy. SP never files a proof of claim. Clearly §506(d)(2) prevents disallowance of the security interest. However, what if SP does file a proof of claim, but files late–after the bar date. Does §506(d)(2) still protect SP? Hamlett v. Amsouth Bank, 322 F.3d 342 (4th Cir. 2003) (yes).

LITZLER v. SHOLDRA (IN RE SHOLDRA)

270 B.R. 64 (Bankr. N.D. Texas 2001)

LYNN, J.

This adversary proceeding is before the Court by reason of a motion filed by Plaintiff John Litzler as trustee ("Plaintiff" or "Trustee") seeking summary judgment against Eugene Peter Sholdra ("Defendant" or "Sholdra"), debtor in the underlying Chapter 7 bankruptcy case . . . .

I. Background

Sholdra, an ophthalmologist, filed for relief under Chapter 7 of the Bankruptcy Code (the "Code") on August 4, 1998. Shortly thereafter Plaintiff was appointed Trustee and has acted in such capacity ever since. Prior to filing bankruptcy and at least until July of this year, Sholdra conducted his practice through a professional corporation, the Eugene P. Sholdra, M.D., P.A. (the

---

[5] [The dissenting opinion is omitted.-ed.]

"P.A."), organized under Subchapter S of the Internal Revenue Code. Besides Sholdra, the P.A. employed only his wife as office manager and a part-time clerk. Sholdra has at all times been the only professional employed by the P.A.

As a result of the filing of Sholdra's Chapter 7 case, the stock of the P.A. (the "Stock") became property of the estate created pursuant to Section 541 of the Code. Because state law prohibits one who is not licensed to practice the profession for which a professional corporation is organized from owning its stock (see TEX. REV. CIV. STAT. art. 1528f § 10 (2000); see also Eikenhorst v. Eikenhorst, 746 S.W.2d 882, 887 (Tex. App.-- Houston [1st Dist] 1988)), the Trustee did not take title to the Stock. Thus, Sholdra continues to hold the Stock and serve as an officer of the P.A.

Prior to and since the commencement of the bankruptcy, Sholdra caused the P.A. to pay him a salary. Until 1999 the salary was equal to 20% of the P.A.'s profits. In addition the P.A. directly paid certain expenses of Sholdra and made distributions of profits to Sholdra. In 1999, Sholdra directed his accountant to increase the percentage of profits devoted to his salary, and for 1999 Sholdra's salary equaled 24.81% of the P.A.'s income. In 2000, Sholdra's salary was again increased as a percentage of the P.A.'s income.

II. The Positions of the Parties

The Trustee filed his original complaint on October 18, 2000 seeking recovery under Section 549 of the Code of payments other than his salary (the "Payments") made by the P.A. since January 1, 1999 to or on behalf of Sholdra.[1] As Plaintiff, it is the Trustee's contention that the Payments constituted property of the estate as "profits" generated by estate property (i.e., the Stock) within the meaning of Section 541(a)(6) of the Code.

Defendant, on the other hand, argues that the Payments fall within the exception provided by Section 541(a)(6) for "earnings from services performed by an individual debtor after the commencement of the case."

Plaintiff contends that Defendant is bound by his tax returns and the Statement of Financial Affairs filed in his bankruptcy case. These documents are dispositive, argues Plaintiff, of what is, for Sholdra, a reasonable salary, which represents all Sholdra was entitled to under the earnings exception. The Payments therefore must be turned over to the Trustee.

Defendant takes the position that the distributions from the P.A. reflected on his tax returns and Statement of Financial Affairs as other than salary are nevertheless earnings falling within the exception provided in Section 541(a)(6) of the Code. He argues this is so since all of the P.A.'s receipts are attributable to Sholdra's personal services. . . .

---

[1] In the original complaint the Trustee relied entirely on Section 549. On March 2, 2001, the Trustee filed an amended complaint asserting that Sholdra had "converted" property of the estate by increasing his salary beyond 20% of the P.A.'s profits. Perhaps realizing that many (if not all) of the "transfers" complained of were made by the P.A., and so (as discussed infra) were not transfers of property of the estate, in the Motion for Summary Judgment Plaintiff characterizes all his claims as arising from the conversion of estate property, a trend continued in the pretrial order, filed after oral argument, which couches the issues presented by this adversary wholly in terms of "conversions" (though P D.1 of the pretrial order lists as a contested issue of law whether the Trustee is entitled to judgment under Section 550 of the Code - a provision applicable only if the Trustee's cause of action arises under Section 549 of the Code).

IV. Discussion

A. Has Plaintiff Stated a Valid Claim for Relief?

As discussed, supra, note 1, the Trustee's claims have metamorphosed over time. When he began this action, he sought relief under Section 549 of the Code, which allows the Trustee to "avoid a transfer of property of the estate. . . made after the commencement of the case." By the time of the filing of the Motion for Summary Judgment, his claims were premised on Defendant's "conversion" of estate property, and no mention was made of Section 549 (the first mention of "conversion" came in the Trustee's amended complaint, in which Plaintiff used the term to attack Sholdra's instructions to his accountant to increase his salary).

The P.A. is a separate entity from the estate. Halverson v. Funaro (In re Funaro), 263 B.R. 892 (B.A.P. 8th Cir. 2001); see also Parker v. Saunders (In re Bakersfield Westar, Inc.), 226 B.R. 227, 234 (B.A.P. 9th Cir. 1998). Any profits from the P.A.'s operations were property of the P.A. until it distributed them. Thus, the Payments by the P.A. were not transfers of property of the estate and are not avoidable by Plaintiff. 5 COLLIER ON BANKRUPTCY P549.04[1] (15th ed. rev. 2001); see also E.A. Martin Mach-ine Co. v. Williams (In re Newman), 875 F.2d 668, 670 (8th Cir. 1989); see also Dominican Fathers of Winona v. Dreske (In re Dreske), 25 B.R. 268, 271 (Bankr. E.D. Wis. 1982).

If, however, the Payments represent "profits" from property of the estate (the Stock) within the meaning of Section 541(a)(6), then, upon their receipt, Sholdra was obligated to turn them over to the Trustee. 11 U.S.C. § 542(a). If, therefore, the Payments, upon reaching Sholdra, constituted property of the estate and Sholdra converted them to his own use, the Trustee would have a cause of action against Sholdra.[2]

B. Are the Payments Property of the Estate or Earnings Excepted from Section 541(a)(6)? . . .

2. The Bankruptcy Code

The proper place to begin in interpreting language of the Bankruptcy Code is with the plain meaning of the words at issue. The most obvious way to read Section 541(a)(6) is that it includes within the estate of an individual debtor profits of estate property unless the profits are earned through the personal services (i.e., labor) of the debtor.

Plaintiff, however, contends that "earnings from services performed by an individual debtor," as the term is used in Section 541(a)(6), is limited to the salary or wages earned by the debtor. Thus, argues Plaintiff, the Payments, not being salary or wages, are income of the P.A., which becomes property of the estate pursuant to Section 541(a)(6) when distributed, since they must be the dividends on the Stock.

This ignores the use by Congress of the terms "earnings", "salary" and

[2] The Court will not at this time address whether "conversion" of the Payments to his own use by Sholdra could be a transfer subject to avoidance under Section 549; or, if not, whether the Trustee's original complaint or the amended complaint was sufficient to state a cause of action for conversion. Instead the Court will assume that the amended complaint states a cause of action for recovery of any property of the estate received by Sholdra and proceed to a determination of whether the Payments fell within the exception to Section 541(a)(6)

"wages" elsewhere in the Code. Congress acts intentionally in its choice of words. See, e.g., BFP v. Resolution Trust Corp. 511 U.S. 531, 537 (1994), citing Chicago v. Environmental Defense Fund, 511 U.S. 328, 338 (1994). Congress clearly intended by the term "earnings" something broader than salary or wages. Sections 503(b)(1)(A) and 507(a)(3)(A) refer to "wages, salary and commissions," and sections dealing with collective bargaining agreements make reference only to "wages." 11 U.S.C. § 1113 (c), § 1167. On the other hand see Sections 1207(a)(2), 1306(a)(2) and § 522(d)(11)(E) of the Code which, like Section 541(a)(6), use the term "earnings."

Reading "earnings" as broader in scope (or at least something other) than salary or wages is consistent with both the common meanings accorded the words and the meanings given in Black's Law Dictionary. Wages are paid for time actually worked.[3] Salary refers to a periodic payment for services rendered without regard to time worked.[4] Earnings refers to all income generated by an individual.[5]

In Section 541(a)(6), the Court concludes that Congress meant to except from the estate and reserve to the debtor post petition earnings to which the estate might otherwise have a claim if they were not attributable to the debtor's personal services. In Carter v. Anderson, 182 F.3d 1027 (9th Cir. 1999), a case dealing with a pre-bankruptcy distribution by a Subchapter S Corporation to its stockholder,[6] the Ninth Circuit construed California Civil Procedure Code § 706.011 which defines earnings as follows:

> (a) "Earnings means compensation payable by an employer to an employee for personal services performed by such employee, whether denominated as wages, salary, commission, bonuses, or otherwise."

Carter, 182 F.3d at 1029 (citing CAL. CIV. PROC. CODE § 706.011). The Court of Appeals in Carter noted that, whatever the definition encompassed, it was "at least clear that a primary criterion [to qualify as earnings] is that the payments must be for 'personal services performed.'" 182 F.3d at 1032-33. This Court believes the allocation of "earnings" as used in Section 541(a)(6) also turns primarily on who performed the services creating them.

3. Other Case Law

. . . The one case cited by Plaintiff which sheds light on the application of Section 541(a)(6) to the Payments is the Ninth Circuit's decision in [In re FitzSimmons, 725 F.2d 1208 (9th Cir. 1984).] FitzSimmons involved the Chapter

[3] "Wage" is defined as "payment for labor or services, usually bases on time worked or quantity produced." BLACK'S LAW DICTIONARY 1373 (7th ed. 1999).

[4] "Salary" is "an agreed compensation for services...usually paid at regular intervals on a yearly basis, as distinguished from an hourly basis." Id. at 1337.

[5] Black's defines "earnings" as "revenue gained from labor or services, from the investment of capital, or from assets." Id. at 526.

[6] Carter involved a Chapter 7 debtor's claim that income from a wholly-owned Subchapter S Corporation was exempt as "earnings" under California law. The court rejected the trustee's claim that the debtor's characterization of revenues of the corporation as "net profits" meant they could not be earnings (182 F.3d at 1033). While the Carter court's analysis is not of Section 541(a)(6), its discussion of income from a Subchapter S Corporation as "earnings" is useful and supportive of this Court's reading of the Bankruptcy Code.

11 case of an attorney who operated a sole proprietorship[7] that employed other lawyers. The Court of Appeals held that the debtor was entitled to except from the estate "the portion of the law practice's earnings that were attributable to [his] personal efforts." 725 F.2d at 1212. Earnings from the work of other lawyers would be property of the estate. This result is consistent with the position taken by Defendant, since Defendant claims all earnings of the P.A. were attributable to his personal services.

In addition to the cases cited by Plaintiff (Defendant cited no legal authorities in support of his position), the Court has found several decisions which are helpful . . . In re Cooley, 87 B.R. 432 (Bankr. S.D.Tex. 1988), another sole proprietorship case, involved a debtor surgeon who employed other surgeons. The court there took an even broader view than the Ninth Circuit of the earnings exception in Section 541(a)(6), allowing the debtor to except from the estate earnings of the sole proprietorship beyond revenue derived solely from surgeries he performed or advised or assisted in. The court reasoned that Dr. Cooley produced (earned) additional revenues because his reputation as a heart surgeon resulted in referrals to his colleagues. See Cooley, 87 B.R. at 435.

More promising for Plaintiff is In re Herberman, 122 B.R. 273 (Bankr. W.D. Tex. 1990). That case involved a urologist operating as a sole proprietor who filed Chapter 11. The court determined that the debtor was entitled to a salary of 75% of the income of the practice. In *Herberman* the court considered the debtor's fiduciary duty as a Chapter 11 debtor and the "enterprise value" of the debtor's practice in setting aside 25% of the profits for the estate.

The *Herberman* court's decision, however, did not equate "salary" with "earnings" as the term is used in Section 541(a)(6). In fact, the court concluded that the earnings exception to Section 541(a)(6) did not apply because the debtor's earnings did not constitute income from property of the estate. Rather, the court determined that Section 541(a)(7) of the Code controlled, and the income produced by the debtor's urology practice was property acquired by the estate after the commencement of the case.

In the instant case, where the Payments were clearly produced through the operation of the P.A., the Stock of which is property of the estate, *Herberman*'s reliance on Section 541(a)(7) is inapplicable. Moreover, the *Herberman* court's emphasis on a Chapter 11 debtor's fiduciary duty is not relevant in the context of Sholdra's Chapter 7 case.

The Court does find *Herberman*'s distinction between income from the debtor's personal services and that from "enterprise value" useful. Thus, the Court concludes that the P.A. may have generated some income other than purely through Sholdra's services. Equipment, corporate goodwill or other assets of the P.A. may account for part of the Payments.[8]

---

[7] Under the reasoning of *FitzSimmons* (and *Cooley, infra*), the distinction between a sole proprietorship and a Subchapter S Corporation is immaterial for purposes of construing Section 541(a)(6) of the Code. The *FitzSimmons* court considered the sole proprietorship to be the "property of the estate," just as the P.A., through the Stock, is owned by the estate.

[8] For example, Sholdra may perform procedures requiring specialized equipment owned by the P.A. To the extent the charges for these procedures are attributable to the equipment, the P.A. may realize income other than from Sholdra's services.

IV. Conclusion

A professional corporation is a device allowed under state law to give professionals the protection of corporate status. Subchapter S of the Internal Revenue Code permits individuals to obtain the benefit of corporate status without incurring the penalty of a corporate tax. While the way in which a Subchapter S Corporation allocates income - as between salaries and other distributions - may have consequences under the tax laws, it is, at most, one factor to be considered in distinguishing between income to the estate and earnings from personal services under the Bankruptcy Code.

The test of whether earnings are excluded from the estate pursuant to Section 541(a)(6) is whether they are produced by the debtor's personal services or by something else.

Plaintiff has presented no evidence that the Payments resulted other than from Defendant's personal services. Defendant has produced affidavits stating that his work was the source of the Payments. This is not to say that some part of the Payments was not the product of assets of the P.A. rather than just Sholdra's labor. However, even aside from the questions raised about the legal viability of the Trustee's claims, in the absence of any evidence that there is property of the estate at issue, Summary Judgment must be DENIED.

Notes

1. The ability of a debtor to keep postpetition wages is considered one of the key elements of the debtor's "fresh start." Indeed, the phrase "fresh start" comes from a wage case, Local Loan Co. v. Hunt, 292 U.S. 234 (1934). In this case, a debtor assigned wages as security for a debt. The debtor then filed for bankruptcy and obtained a discharged. The court ruled that the bankruptcy discharge disencumbered the wages from the creditor's security interest. Discharges have no similar effect on any other kind of security interest.

HILL v DOBIN

358 B.R. 130 (D.N.J. 2006)

JOEL A. PISANO, J.

Pursuant to 28 U.S.C. § 158(a)(1), Debtor Phyllis Hill ("Hill") has appealed the United States Bankruptcy Court's June 14, 2006 orders granting summary judgment in favor of the Trustee and denying Hill's request that her interest in two annuities be excluded from her bankruptcy estate. The issue presented here is whether Hill's interest in the annuities qualifies for exclusion from the bankruptcy estate pursuant to 11 U.S.C. § 541(c)(2). Resolving some disagreement among the bankruptcy courts in this district, the Court holds that an asset is excluded from the bankruptcy estate under § 541(c)(2) if (1) the asset represents the debtor's beneficial interest in a trust, (2) there is a restriction on transfer, and (3) the restriction is enforceable under an applicable non-bankruptcy law. See 11 U.S.C. § 541(c)(2). This involves a case-by-case approach requiring the bankruptcy courts to analyze the terms of the particular annuity at issue and determine whether it satisfies the elements necessary for exclusion. As explained below, the Court finds that Hill's annuities do not satisfy the requirements of § 541(c)(2) because they do not qualify as trusts. Accordingly, Hill's annuities are not excluded from her bankruptcy estate and the orders of the Bankruptcy Court are affirmed.

I. BACKGROUND

On June 16, 2004, Hill filed a voluntary bankruptcy petition under Chapter 7 of the Bankruptcy Code. Among the assets Hill listed in her original petition was an annuity with Guardian Insurance and Annuity Company, Inc. ("GIAC"), which she improperly identified as Park Avenue Securities. As of June 30, 2004, the GIAC Annuity had a value of $73,202.79. Hill later amended her petition to include an American Express Privileged Asset Annuity Certificate ("AMEX Annuity"), which had a value of $31,415.05 as of June 30, 2004. In her petition, Hill stated her belief that both annuities were excluded from her bankruptcy estate pursuant to 11 U.S.C. § 541(c)(2).

The Trustee filed a complaint on June 13, 2005 seeking a determination that both annuities were property of the bankruptcy estate. After Hill filed an answer on September 23, 2005, both parties filed motions for summary judgment wherein the Trustee requested an order that the annuities were assets of the debtor estate and Hill sought an order that the annuities were excluded from the estate. At the close of oral argument on June 12, 2006, the Bankruptcy Court rendered a decision in favor of the Trustee. After reviewing the terms of the AMEX Annuity, the Bankruptcy Court determined that the annuity was not excluded from Hill's bankruptcy estate because it had none of the indicia of a trust. Specifically, the Court found that the annuity was not a trust because "it doesn't have a fiduciary relationship, there's no manifest intent to create a trust, and there's no duty on the part of [AMEX] to deal with the property for the benefit of any person." Transcript of Hearing at 17, Dobin v. Hill (In re Hill), Ch. 7 Case No. 04-30325, Adv. No. 05-19401 (Bankr. D.N.J. June 12, 2006). Similarly, upon examining the GIAC Annuity documents, the Court noted that the annuity did not give rise to a fiduciary relationship, there was no trustee, and GIAC held the funds as an asset of the company, not as trust property. Id. at 22-23. The Court concluded, therefore, that Hill had no more than a "contractual debtor creditor relationship" with GIAC. Id. On June 14, 2006, the Court entered orders granting summary judgment in favor of the Trustee and denying Hill's cross-motion for summary judgment. Hill timely filed an appeal of these orders on July 19, 2006.

II. DISCUSSION . . .

B. Section 541 of the Bankruptcy Code

Pursuant to Section 541(a)(1) of the Bankruptcy Code, 11 U.S.C. § 541(a)(1), a bankruptcy estate includes "all legal or equitable interests of the debtor in property" as of the creation of the bankruptcy estate "[e]xcept as provided in subsections (b) and (c)(2)." Subsection (c)(2) states that "[a] restriction on the transfer of a beneficial interest of the debtor in a trust that is enforceable under applicable nonbankruptcy law is enforceable in a case under this title." Several courts have addressed the question of whether § 541(c)(2) covers annuities and the results vary. Compare In re Barnes, 264 B.R. 415 (Bankr. E.D. Mich. 2001) (finding that TIAA annuity did not qualify as a trust and thus was not excluded from the debtor estate under § 541(c)(2)); In re Neto, 215 B.R. 939 (Bankr. D.N.J. 1997) (finding that lottery annuity is part of debtor estate); In re Simon, 170 B.R. 999 (Bankr. S.D. Ill. 1994) (concluding that annuity, which court determined was not a trust, is part of debtor estate); Walro v. Striegel, 131 B.R. 697 (S.D. Ind. 1991) (same) with In re Quinn, 327 B.R. 818 (W.D. Mich. 2005) (finding a pension plan annuity excluded from the bankruptcy estate under § 541(c)(2); In re Schuster, 256 B.R. 701 (Bankr. D.N.J. 2000) (finding the annuities at issue were trusts and thus excludable under § 541(c)(2)). Further, neither the Supreme Court nor the Third Circuit has dealt squarely with this issue.

In Patterson v. Shumate, 504 U.S. 753 (1992), the Supreme Court analyzed § 541(c)(2) and held that the antialienation provision in an ERISA-qualified plan "consti-tute[d] an enforceable transfer restriction for purposes of § 541(c)(2) 's exclusion of property from the bankruptcy estate." Patterson, 504 U.S. at 757-60 . In so holding, the Court noted that the "natural reading of [§ 541(c)(2)] entitles a debtor to exclude from property of the estate any interest in a plan or trust that contains a transfer restriction enforceable under any applicable nonbankruptcy law." Id. at 758 . Focusing on the Court's use of the phrase "plan or trust," some courts have concluded that § 541(c)(2)'s trust requirement no longer applies when the asset at issue is an ERISA-qualified plan.[1] Another line of cases espouses the view that non-ERISA qualified employer pension plans are not subject to a strict trust requirement.[2] There is, however, nothing in Patterson, or the statute for that matter, suggesting that the trust requirement does not apply to a non-ERISA annuity. See generally id.; Barnes, 264 B.R. at 425 ("Rather than 'categorically' eliminating § 541(c)(2) 's trust requirement,. . . the most that one can plausibly infer from Shumate . . . is that the requirement is not applicable to ERISA-qualified plans.").

In In re Yuhas, 104 F.3d 612, 613 (3d Cir. 1997), the Third Circuit held that a New Jersey statute "that protects a qualified individual retirement account (IRA) from claims of creditors constitutes a 'restriction on the transfer of a beneficial interest of the debtor in a trust' within the meaning of 11 U.S.C. § 541(c)(2) and thus result[ed] in the exclusion of the IRA from a bankruptcy estate." Notably, the Court did not address the issue of whether IRAs qualify as trusts for the purpose of § 541(c)(2); instead, the Court assumed that the IRA satisfied the trust requirement because the parties did not raise that issue on appeal. Subsequent to Yuhas, however, some bankruptcy courts within the Third Circuit have concluded that IRAs are not trusts and thus not eligible for exclusion under § 541(c)(2). See, e.g., In re Haney, 316 B.R. 827, 829 (Bankr. E.D. Pa. 2004); In re Williams, 290 B.R. 83, 87 (Bankr. E.D. Pa. 2003); In re Fulton, 240 B.R. 854, 865-66 (Bankr. W.D. Pa. 1999).

In any event, there is no doubt that the Yuhas decision preserves the trust requirement set forth in § 541(c)(2). In deciding whether the IRA at issue was

---

[1] See, e.g., Arkison v. UPS Thrift Plan (In re Rueter), 11 F.3d 850, 852 (9th Cir. 1993) ("Under Shumate, a court need look no further than whether the ERISA-qualified plan at issue has an anti-alienation provision that satisfies the literal terms of § 541(c)(2)."); Mfrs. Bank & Trust Co. v. Holst, 197 B.R. 856, 859 (N.D. Iowa 1996) ("Once the plan is determined to be ERISA-qualified, the inquiry is finished.").

[2] See, e.g., Morter v. Farm Credit Servs., 937 F.2d 354, 357 (7th Cir. 1991) (finding that courts have exhibited a "willingness to exclude [a pension] plan if it is employer-created and controlled and, therefore, analogous to a spendthrift trust"); Matter of Goff, 706 F.2d 574, 589 (5th Cir. 1983) (finding that employer-created and controlled retirement plans may be characterized as spendthrift trusts for the purposes of § 541(c)(2) even though they are not traditional spendthrift trusts); In re Atallah, 95 B.R. 910, 919 (Bankr. E.D. Pa. 1989) ("Section 541(c)(2) is not limited to traditional spendthrift trusts, but also applies to pension funds which exhibit the characteristics of a spendthrift trust."). But see Barnes, 264 B.R. at 428 ("There is no statutory support for the notion that in determining whether a trust was created, employee benefit plans are subject to a less stringent standard than are other assets in which the debtor holds an interest.").

excluded from the bankruptcy estate, the Yuhas Court employed a five-part test, which states that:

> (1) the IRA must constitute a "trust" within the meaning of 11 U.S.C. § 541(c)(2); (2) the funds in the IRA must represent the debtor's "beneficial interest" in that trust; (3) the IRA must be qualified under Section 408 of the Internal Revenue Code;[3] (4) the[re] . . . must be a "restriction on the transfer" of the IRA funds; and (5) this restriction must be "enforceable under nonbankrupcty law."

Yuhas, 104 F.3d at 614 . The Court notes that, contrary to the interpretation of some bankruptcy courts, the Yuhas five-part test is not one of general applicability. Specifically, there is no requirement in § 541(c)(2) that the asset be qualified under Section 408 of the Internal Revenue Code. The Yuhas Court added that prong because the restriction on transfer upon which the debtor relied in that case–N.J.S.A. § 25:2-1(b)–applied only to qualifying trusts, defined in N.J.S.A. § 25:2-1(b) as "trust[s] created or qualified and maintained pursuant to . . . section 408 . . . of the federal Internal Revenue Code of 1986." Yuhas, therefore, does not suggest that for an asset to be excluded from a bankruptcy estate under § 541(c)(2) it must be qualified under Section 408 of the Internal Revenue Code. Rather, that requirement simply addressed whether the particular restriction on transfer applied to the asset at issue in Yuhas.

This Court holds that, in order to demonstrate that an asset is excluded from a bankruptcy estate pursuant to § 541(c)(2), the debtor must establish that: (1) the asset represents the debtor's beneficial interest in a trust, (2) there is a restriction on transfer, and (3) the restriction is enforceable under an applicable non-bankruptcy law. See 11 U.S.C. § 541(c)(2); Yuhas, 104 F.3d at 614; see also In re Wilcox, 233 F.3d 899, 904 (6th Cir. 2000). The debtor bears the burden of establishing that these requirements are met. In re Adams, 302 B.R. 535, 540 (B.A.P. 6th Cir. 2003). The nature of this test does not allow for a bright line rule resolving the issue of whether annuities, in general, are excluded from the bankruptcy estate under § 541(c)(2). Rather, a case-by-case approach is necessary: the bankruptcy courts must examine the annuity documents in each case to determine whether the specific annuities at issue satisfy the three elements set forth above.

The Court notes that the likely result of this test--particularly because of the trust requirement--will be that many annuities do not qualify for exclusion from bankruptcy estates. Such a result, however, is not inconsistent with the congressional policy "encouraging retirement savings, as reflected in the statutes which have given us ERISA, Keogh plans, and IRAs." Velis v. Kardanis, 949 F.2d 78, 82 (3d Cir. 1991). Indeed, there is no federal statute evincing a goal to encourage or protect investments in annuities.[4] Moreover, to the extent that Congress wants to protect annuities from the claims of bankruptcy creditors, it has the ability to amend the Bankruptcy Code. As it stands now, the plain language of § 541(c)(2) makes clear that only a debtor's "beneficial interest in a trust" is eligible for exclusion under that section. 11 U.S.C. § 541(c)(2).

---

[3] [This is not part of §541(c)(2). Why did the court mention it?-Ed.]

[4] It should be noted that an annuity is not necessarily a vehicle for retirement savings. There are many reasons why one might choose to purchase an annuity, not the least of which is to achieve the tax benefits that annuities typically provide.

1. The Elements of a Trust

The Bankruptcy Code does not define the term trust. Consequently, the Court relies on the common understanding of the term to discern the elements of a trust. Williams v. Taylor, 529 U.S. 420, 431 (2000) ("We give the words of a statute their ordinary, contemporary, common meaning, absent an indication Congress intended them to bear some different import.") (citations and internal quotation marks omitted). Pursuant to the Restatement of Trusts, a trust is a

> fiduciary relationship with respect to property, arising from a manifestation of intention to create that relationship and subjecting the person who holds title to the property to duties to deal with it for the benefit of charity or for one or more persons, at least one of whom is not the sole trustee.

RESTATEMENT (THIRD) OF TRUSTS § 2 (2003). Borrowing from that definition, the elements of a trust are: (1) a manifestation of intention to create a trust; (2) a trust res; (3) a trustee who is bound by a fiduciary duty to deal with the property for another's benefit; and (4) a division of title between the trustee who holds legal title to the property and the beneficiary who retains equitable title.

2. Restriction on Transfer

The Bankruptcy Code broadly defines "transfer" as "every mode, direct or indirect, absolute or conditional, voluntary or involuntary, of disposing of or parting with property or with an interest in property, including retention of title as a security interest and foreclosure of the debtor's equity of redemption." 11 U.S.C. § 101(54). Thus, "[a]ny procedure by which funds in [a trust] might be reached to satisfy the claims of creditors would seem to fall within this broad definition . . . ." Yuhas, 104 F.3d at 614 (citations and internal quotation marks omitted). The source of the restriction may be state law, see id. at 614-15, federal law, see Patterson, 504 U.S. at 760, or the annuity itself, see Barnes, 264 B.R. at 437.

3. Enforceable Under Applicable Non-bankruptcy Law

Though some courts previously held the view that only state law could be the source of the "applicable non-bankruptcy law" under § 541(c)(2), Patterson established that "any relevant non-bankruptcy law," whether state or federal, satisfies the requirement. Patterson, 504 U.S. at 759 ("Plainly read, [§ 541(c)(2)] encompasses any relevant nonbankruptcy law, including federal law . . . ."); see also Yuhas, 104 F.3d at 614 n.1 ("Applicable nonbankruptcy law includes both federal law such as ERISA, . . . and state law . . . .") (internal citations omitted).

C. Hill's Annuities

At the outset, the Court notes that the annuities at issue are neither ERISA-qualified plans nor pension plans created and controlled by an employer. Therefore, even assuming that ERISA-qualified plans and pension plans are subject to a less exacting test, there is no basis upon which to relax the requirements of § 541(c)(2) in this case.

Both the AMEX Annuity and the GIAC Annuity are subject to a "restriction on transfer . . . that is enforceable under applicable nonbankrutpcy law." In fact, N.J.S.A. 17B:24-7 is the source of both the restriction on transfer and the applicable nonbankruptcy law. See Yuhas, 104 F.3d at 614-16 (relying on New Jersey statute as the source of the restriction on transfer and the applicable nonbankruptcy law). The statute, which expressly protects annuities from the claims of creditors, states:

> The benefits, rights, privileges, powers and options which under any annuity contract heretofore or hereafter issued are due or prospectively due the annuitant, shall not be subject to execution, garnishment, attachment, sequestration or other legal process nor shall the annuitant be compelled to exercise any such rights, privileges, powers, or options, nor shall creditors be allowed to interfere with or terminate the contract . . . .

N.J.S.A. 17B:24-7(a). Therefore, the only issue in dispute is whether the annuities qualify as trusts.

Hill argues that both of her annuities should be excluded from the estate under § 541(c)(2) because all annuities are trusts or, in the alternative, the annuities satisfy all of the elements of a trust. The Trustee counters that Hill's annuities do not qualify as trusts and that Hill has not carried her burden of demonstrating that the annuities are excluded from her bankruptcy estate. As explained above, this Court does not take the view that all annuities are trusts. Courts must review the annuity documents to determine whether the particular annuity at issue satisfies the statutory requirements of § 541(c)(2), including the trust requirement. As explained below, having reviewed the annuity documents for both the AMEX Annuity and the GIAC Annuity, the Court concludes that neither annuity qualifies as a trust. Accordingly, the annuities are not excludable from Hill's bankruptcy estate.

1. The AMEX Annuity

The terms of the AMEX Annuity, a fixed annuity, describe it as a long-term savings plan into which the owner (Hill) deposits monthly contributions. AMEX, in turn, agrees to repay those deposits plus interest to Hill or a designated beneficiary beginning on an agreed upon date in the future. AMEX determines the applicable interest rate depending upon current economic conditions, yields on AMEX's current investments, and projected yields on future investments. Hill has the right to withdraw funds from the annuity and to send extra payments at any time. AMEX owns and controls the monthly contributions and has unrestricted use of those funds. Moreover, the use of the funds has no bearing on the final value of the Annuity. To the extent that AMEX neglected to make the scheduled payments to Hill or the designated beneficiary, the owner would have a contract claim against AMEX, and if it became insolvent, the annuity owner would become a creditor.

Tellingly, Hill spends no more than four sentences of her sixteen page brief explaining why the AMEX Annuity should be excluded from her bankruptcy estate under § 541(c)(2). Further, Hill does not identify any evidence demonstrating her manifestation of an intention to create a trust, the existence of a trust res, a division of title between beneficiary and trustee, or the existence of a trustee. Nor could she, because the annuity documents reveal that the AMEX Annuity does not satisfy the elements of a trust. The documents demonstrate that the AMEX Annuity creates a debtor-creditor relationship, not a trust, in which AMEX "contractually guarantees" Hill's "contributions and . . . interest earnings." Thus, there is no evidence of a manifested intention to create a trust. Nor is there an identifiable res: AMEX has unrestricted use of the premium payments and is bound only to pay Hill an amount similar to her contributions plus interest at a specified date in the future.

Further, there is no division of title. AMEX holds legal and equitable title[5] to Hill's premium payments because AMEX, by contract, bears the risk of loss arising out of its use of the premium payments. See Barnes, 264 B.R. at 434 . Finally, the annuity documents do not identify a trustee; indeed, AMEX does not assign itself the role of trustee or undertake an obligation to invest the owner's premium payments for her benefit. Therefore, the AMEX Annuity is not a trust. It represents no more than a debtor-creditor relationship and thus is not excluded from Hill's bankruptcy estate under § 541(c)(2).

2. The GIAC Annuity

Under the terms of the GIAC Annuity, Hill could select either a fixed rate option or a variable option. The variable option, which Hill chose, allowed her to allocate her premiums to certain investment vehicles--mostly mutual funds--and have her funds kept in The Guardian Separate Account E ("Account E"). As with the AMEX Annuity, Hill had the right to withdraw funds from the GIAC Annuity. GIAC owns the assets held in Account E, but those assets are kept separate from GIAC's general and other accounts. Though "[a]ssets equal to the reserves and contract liabilities of Account E [are] not charged with liabilities that arise from any other business GIAC may conduct," GIAC maintains the right to "transfer assets in excess of the reserves and contract liabilities to its general account." Thus, although not entirely clear, it appears that, were GIAC to become insolvent, the Account E assets would become subject to receiver control and/or liquidation. The size of the payments that Hill would receive beginning on the annuity commencement date--the date on which GIAC would begin sending monthly payments to Hill--depended upon the success of Hill's investments. Also, Hill had the right to withdraw funds from the annuity account.

The GIAC Annuity presents a closer question than the AMEX Annuity, principally because there is evidence of a division of title: GIAC, by the terms of the annuity documents, holds legal title and Hill retains an equitable interest in the funds she has paid into the annuity because she bears the risk of loss. See id. at 434. Indeed, her payments were used to purchase variable annuity units, the value of which could increase or decrease depending upon the performance of the annuity portfolio. Unlike the Barnes court, however, this Court does not adopt the view that division of title conclusively establishes that the asset is a trust. See id. at 432 ("The sine qua non of a trust is the division of ownership rights in the subject property--the trust beneficiary holding equitable title thereto but the trustee holding legal title.").

Further, there are three factors that counsel against a finding that the GIAC Annuity qualifies as a trust. First, the annuity documents consistently refer

[5] "'Equitable title' may be defined as 'the beneficial interest of one person whom equity regards as the real owner, although legal title is vested in another.'" Arachnid, Inc. v. Merit Indus., Inc., 939 F.2d 1574, 1578 n.3 (Fed. Cir. 1991) (quoting BLACK'S LAW DICTIONARY (6th ed. 1990)).

to the GIAC Annuity as a contract. Though the Court will not afford controlling weight to the parties description of their relationship without analyzing its substance, the Court finds that the parties' consistent and repeated use of the word contract is persuasive evidence that the parties did not intend to create a trust. See Walro, 131 B.R. at 701 ("[C]ourts will not simply assume that an annuity is a trust in the absence of evidence that the parties had the specific intent to create a trust . . . .").

Second, there is no indication in the annuity documents that GIAC has assumed the role of trustee. Although, as Hill points out, GIAC reserved the right "to serve the best interests of the owner and any beneficiary," GIAC is not bound by a fiduciary duty to do so. Thus, the Court finds that there is no trustee. Third, it appears that there is no trust res. It is true that GIAC purported to hold Hill's payments in Account E, keeping them separate from their other accounts and shielding the funds from any liabilities that could result from GIAC's other business activities. The annuity documents indicate, however, that GIAC could remove assets equal to those in Account E. Thus, the implication is that GIAC did have access the funds purportedly kept separately in Account E. In sum, the GIAC Annuity does not meet all of the elements of a trust. Therefore, Hill has failed to carry the burden of establishing that the GIAC Annuity is excluded from her bankruptcy estate under § 541(c)(2). See Adams, 302 B.R. at 540 .

Notwithstanding the fact that the GIAC and AMEX Annuities fail to satisfy § 541(c)(2), Hill suggests that her interest in the annuities should be excluded from her bankruptcy estate because there is a policy favoring the "[u]niform treatment of property interests," to prevent "a party from receiving a windfall merely by the reason of happenstance of bankruptcy." Butner v. United States, 440 U.S. 48, 55 (1979) (internal quotation marks and citation omitted); Patterson, 504 U.S. at 764 . A decision not to exclude the annuities in this case violates that policy, according to Hill, because it means that the happenstance of bankruptcy allows her creditors to access funds that would be otherwise be protected under N.J.S.A. 17B:24-7(a). The flaw in Hill's argument is that she requests uniform treatment of assets which she characterizes differently depending on the applicable law. Specifically, Hill suggests that her assets are trusts for the purpose of federal law (§ 541(c)(2)) and annuities for the purpose of state law (N.J.S.A. 17B:24-7(a)). Hill cannot have it both ways, and the Court declines her invitation to give two different names--each with legal significance--to the same asset in order to achieve what she calls "uniform treatment."[6]

She further argues that failure to exclude the annuities under § 541(c)(2) will encourage creditors to "engage in the strategic manipulation of the bankruptcy laws in order to gain access to otherwise inaccessible funds." Patterson, 504 U.S. at 764. That concern, however, is not valid where, as here, the debtor filed a voluntary bankruptcy petition.

For the reasons explained above, the Court finds that Hill's annuities do not satisfy the requirements of § 541(c)(2) because they are not trusts. Therefore,

---

[6] The Bankruptcy Court reached a similar conclusion: "[I]f [Hill were] able to convince me that the contracts were actually trusts, I don't think they'd get the benefit of the state law because the state law exclusion only applies to annuities. So it seems to me that you can't have it a trust for federal law and an annuity for state law purposes." Transcript of Hearing at 17, Dobin v. Hill (In re Hill), Ch. 7 Case No. 04-30325, Adv. No. 05-19401 (Bankr. D.N.J. June 12, 2006).

the AMEX Annuity and the GIAC Annuity are not excluded from Hill's bankruptcy estate.

Notes and Questions

1. According to §541(c)(2), spendthrift trusts were excluded from the bankruptcy estate, a great boon to the drunken scions of industrial robber barons. E.g., Swartz v. Fetter (In re Fetter), 354 B.R. 242 (Bankr. C.D. Ill. 2006). Typically, however, self-settled trusts are invalid under state law, although, recently, Delaware and Alaska have permitted them in an endeavor to get business away from the Cayman Islands. Prior to 1992, there was substantial doubt as to whether ERISA pensions were excludable from the bankruptcy estate. ERISA requires a spendthrift clause in the trust instrument. 29 U.S.C. § 1056 (d)(1) ("Each pension plan shall provide that benefits provided under the plan may not be assigned or alienated"). An argument existed, however, that these clauses were unenforceable under state law and so the ERISA plan was part of the bankruptcy estate. In Patterson v. Shumate, 504 U.S. 753 (1992), the Supreme Court held that ERISA was out of the estate because ERISA preempts state law. To make assurance double sure and to take a bond of fate, Congress has added §541(b)(7) to make ERISA plans expressly excluded.

2. Once classic 401(k) plans won status under §542(c)(2), because they were valid, if self-settled, spendthrift trusts, the pressure was on to extend this protection, as ERISA permitted tax deferral for annuities, which arguably were not trusts, and government programs, which were not spendthrfited. Accordingly, BAPCPA added §541(b)(7), which extends bankruptcy exclusion to these retirement schemes.

2. In Hill, the debtor bought an annuity, which was held not to be a trust. BAPCPA has added §541(b)(7)(A) to protect annuities, if tax deferred under 26 U.S.C. §403(b). But such annuities are funded directly from wages transferred from employer of a taxpayer to the issuer of the annuity.

In Teachers Insurance & Annuity Assoc. v. Breham (In re Quinn), 327 B.R. 818 (Bankr. W.D. Mich. 2005), the court considered an annuity which qualified for tax deferral under 26 U.S.C. §403(b). Today, of course, this annuity would be excluded under §362(b)(7)(A)(III). But in 2005, the issue was, as in Hill, whether annuities are trusts. The Quinn court took a much more casaul approach toward the definition of "trust:"

> The term "trust" is not defined in § 541(c)(2) or elsewhere in the Bankruptcy Code. In concluding that the TIAA annuity is not a trust, the bankruptcy court cited the decision in In re Barnes, 264 B.R. 415 (Bankr. E.D. Mich. 2001), and concluded that there was no trust relationship between Quinn and TIAA because Quinn's interest in the annuity is "simply contractual." In Barnes, the debtor, like Quinn, was an employee of MSU and a participant the Plan. The debtor had an interest in both a TIAA annuity and a CREF annuity. In a lengthy opinion, the court held that the CREF annuity was excluded from the estate under § 541(c)(2) but the TIAA annuity was not because only the CREF annuity constituted a trust. In its analysis of the issue, the court first determined that, although several courts, including the Supreme Court in Patterson, arguably dispensed with the trust requirement of § 541(c)(2) and instead focused their inquiries solely upon whether the plans at issue were "ERISA-qualified" plans with anti-alienation provisions, § 541(c)(2) still requires the existence of a trust that meets the requirements of an express trust. See 264 B.R. at 421-29. The court then examined the provisions of the CREF annuity contract and found that it exhibited sufficient indicia of a trust because the value of the annuity was not guaranteed, but rather depended, at least in part, upon the performance of CREF's investments. See id. at 434 . The court reasoned that the transfer of risks and benefits to the debtor was a "strong indication that the 'transferee' -- i.e., the Debtor -- holds an equitable interest in CREF's portfolio." Id. On the other hand, the court concluded that the TIAA contract did not reflect a trust relationship because each premium payment purchased a guaranteed annuity amount and the benefit was not tied to the performance of TIAA's investment portfolio. Id. at 435 . In light of that fact, the court concluded that there was no basis for concluding that TIAA was under any obligation to use the premium payments for the benefit of the debtor because the value of the debtor's interest was fixed at the time TIAA received the premium and "TIAA was under no contractual

obligation to invest the payments in such a manner as to protect or benefit the Debtor's economic well-being." Id. at 436.

The Bankruptcy Appellate Panel for the Sixth Circuit followed Barnes in Rhiel v. Adams (In re Adams), 302 B.R. 535 (B.A.P. 6th Cir. 2003). The debtors in that case participated in separate 403(b) retirement plans that used qualified annuities. The plans were ERISA plans but, as 403(b) plans, were not subject to ERISA's trust requirements. The court found no basis in either ERISA or the IRC for concluding that the annuities were trusts because "the federal statutory framework does not compel, or even imply, the existence of a trustee in plans funded by tax-sheltered annuities." Id. at 544.[7]

In contrast to the literal interpretation of the term "trust" espoused in Barnes and Adams, other courts have held that annuities, and in particular, TIAA annuities, are excluded by § 541(c)(2) because they constitute, or are equivalent to, trusts. For example, in Morter v. Farm Credit Services, 937 F.2d 354 (7th Cir. 1991), the court held that the debtor's interest in Purdue University's TIAA-CREF retirement plan was excluded from the estate. Essentially, the court concluded that so long as a retirement plan possesses the characteristics of a spendthrift trust, it should be excluded from the estate:

> The plain language of section 541(c)(2) does not require that a retirement plan be a "traditional" spendthrift trust. We agree with the Fourth Circuit's reasoning in [McLean v. Central States. Southeast and Southwest Areas Pension Fund, 762 F.2d 1204 (4th Cir. 1985)] that section 541(c)(2)
>
>> should [not] be confined in its recognition of enforceable transfer restrictions to those found in "traditional" spendthrift trusts. The language of § 541(c)(2) does not suggest such a limitation, and the legislative history reveals only that the provision has the unambiguous purpose of preserving enforceable transfer restrictions in spendthrift trusts. . . .
>
> 762 F.2d at 1207 n.1 . Even in cases in which courts have included retirement plans within the bankruptcy estate, there has been a willingness to exclude the plan if it is employer-created and controlled and, therefore, analogous to a spendthrift trust.
>
> Moreover, in every decision we could find that addressed the very pointed question whether TIAA is a spendthrift trust under New York law, the answer was a resounding "yes." See, e.g., In re Reynolds, 1989 Bankr. LEXIS 2719, No. 87-1515311F, slip op. (Bankr. W.D. Ark., September 18, 1989); In re Montgomery, 104 B.R. 112 (Bankr. N.D. Iowa 1989); In re Woodward, 1988 Bankr. LEXIS 2683, No. 3-86-03344(3), A.P. No. 3-87-0036, slip op. (Bankr. W.D. Ky., February 16, 1988), aff'd, 1988 U.S. Dist. LEXIS 17622, No. 3-86-03344(3)7 Civil Action C88-0161-L(A), slip op. (W.D. Ky., June 24, 1988); In re Braden, 69 F.R. 93 (Bankr. E.D. Mich. 1987). In addition, two New York state courts have held that the TIAA-CREF plan has all the characteristics of a spendthrift trust necessary to allow the plan to be excluded under section 541(c)(2). See Aurora G. v. Harold G., 98 Misc. 2d 695, 414 N.Y.S.2d 632 (1979); Alexandre v. Chase Manhattan Bank, 61 A.D.2d 537, 403 N.Y.S.2d 21 (1978).
>
> The proper inquiry under section 541(c)(2), then, is not whether the accumulated funds are in a "traditional" spendthrift trust, but whether the retirement plan bars the beneficiary and his creditors from reaching the funds. If it does, the plan is tantamount to a spendthrift trust under state law. When we look at a retirement plan to determine whether it is a spendthrift trust, the fact that the plan administrators might have to dip into the fund to make up any shortfall is not as important to the analysis

[7] Because Adams was a decision of a Bankruptcy Appellate Panel, it is equivalent to review by a district court and thus is not binding upon this court. See Specker Motor Sales Co. v. Eisen, 393 F.3d 659, 663 n.3 (6th Cir. 2003).

as the extent of access to the plan and who has that access.

Id. at 357-58 (citations in first paragraph omitted). See also In re Hipple, 225 B.R. 808, 815 (Bankr. N.D. Ga. 1996) (concluding that the debtor's TIAA/CREF accounts satisfied the requirements for valid and enforceable spendthrift trusts under Georgia law); In re Lyons, 148 B.R. 88, 93 (Bankr. D.D.C. 1992) (noting that courts have routinely "determined that TIAA/CREF retirement plans are 'spendthrift trusts' under New York law and thus were excluded from the debtor's estate pursuant to 11 U.S.C. § 541(c)(2) "); In re Bennett, 185 B.R. 4, 6 (Bankr. E.D.N.Y. 1995) (holding that the debtor's interests in TIAA/CREF retirement annuities were excluded under § 541(c)(2) because the retirement plans were ERISA plans that contained enforceable anti-alienation provisions).[8] In In re Schuster, 256 B.R. 701 (Bankr. D.N.J. 2000), the court held that two annuities were trusts as defined by the Restatement of Trusts because "when the Debtor purchased these annuities from the insurance companies, he did so with the expectation that the money would be paid to him at some later date in accordance with the terms of the annuity contract." Id. at 703 . There is no indication in the court's opinion that the annuities were issued pursuant to a tax qualified retirement plan, but rather, it appears that debtor purchased the annuities outside of such a plan. The court rejected as contrary to Patterson the trustee's suggestion that the absence of restrictions on transfer in the annuities themselves and the debtor's ability to surrender the annuities precluded the annuities from being excluded under § 541(c)(2). Other courts, when addressing the trust requirement, have found that while annuities issued in connection with a tax-qualified 403(b) plan are not trusts, they should be excluded under § 541(c)(2) in light of the policies identified in Patterson.

> We see no reason to treat a corporate pension plan differently than a 403(b) annuity pension plan. Both are set up by a third party, utilize the tax vehicles provided by the Internal Revenue Code to accumulate funds on a tax-free basis and contain antialienation clauses to prevent creditors from reaching a debtor's interests in the plan. We further conclude that this broader view of § 541(c)(2) is supported by the Congressional goal of protecting pension benefits. See Guidry v. Sheet Metal Workers Nat. Pension Fund, 493 U.S. 365 (1990).

Skiba v. Gould (In re Gould), 322 B.R. 741, 744 (Bankr. W.D. Pa. 2005). The Gould court echoed Judge Latta's dissent in Adams explaining why there is no practical reason to treat employer-sponsored ERISA plans that use trusts differently from those plans that do not use trusts:

> The majority's reading is inconsistent with the clear intent of Congress that ERISA-qualified pension plans not be subject to creditor claims.
>
> Outside of bankruptcy law, I find no functional distinction between the protections afforded to beneficiaries of ERISA-qualified pension plans in which assets are held in trust and those in which assets are used to purchase annuity contracts. Outside of bankruptcy, no creditor of the Adams would be able to reach the debtors' beneficial interests in their

[8] In fact, to this Court's knowledge, with the exception of the court in Barnes, the bankruptcy court in this case, and the court in Richardson v. TIAA/CREF, 123 B.R. 540 (E.D.N.C. 1991), every court that has considered a TIAA annuity has found that it is excluded under § 541(c)(2). The Richardson court concluded that the TIAA/CREF annuities were not excluded under § 541(c)(2) because they had provisions allowing for cash surrender at any time before annuity payments began and the debtor could withdraw funds at any time, thus giving the debtor "effective control over the distribution or termination of the trust in that he may reach the funds of the trust and may surrender the annuities for cash." Id. at 543. As noted below, the TIAA annuity in this case does not provide for cash surrender or loans and Quinn's access to the funds is severely limited, thus distinguishing this case from Richardson. Moreover, the Richardson court acknowledged that the annuities were trusts.

> pension plans to satisfy claims, and this is true not because these interests are exempt from execution pursuant to state law, but because they are exempt from execution pursuant to federal law. See Guidry v. Sheet Metal Workers Nat. Pension Fund, 493 U.S. 365 (1990) (permitting no equitable exception to ERISA's anti-alienation provision). The filing of a bankruptcy case should not change this result.
>
> In Patterson v. Shumate, the Supreme Court held that "the antialienation provision required for ERISA qualification . . . constitutes an enforceable transfer restriction for purposes of § 541(c)(2) 's exclusion of property from the bankruptcy estate." 504 U.S. at 759, 112 S.Ct. 2242 . Earlier in that opinion, the Court pointed out that "the natural reading of the provision [§ 541(c)(2)] entitles a debtor to exclude from property of the estate any interest in a plan or trust that contains a transfer restriction enforceable under any relevant nonbankruptcy law." Id. at 758, 112 S. Ct. 2242 . (emphasis added). While it is true that the specific issue before this Panel was not before the Court in Shumate, and thus that the reference to "the plan" may be merely dicta, I think that the reference actually illumines the Court's understanding of the intent of Congress expressed both in ERISA and the Bankruptcy Code. The Court, recalling its previous refusal in Guidry to recognize any exceptions to ERISA's anti-alienation provisions outside the bankruptcy context, asserted that its holding gave "full and appropriate effect to ERISA's goal of protecting pension benefits," and that it furthered the important policy underlying ERISA of uniform treatment of pension benefits. Id. at 764-65, 112 S. Ct. 2242 . Each of these considerations applies with respect to plans that are not required to hold certain assets in trust.
>
> The majority has advanced no policy considerations that support their more restrictive reading of 541(c)(2). Instead their conclusion rests solely upon the literal requirement that a debt's beneficial interest be held "in a trust." This emphasis on the asserted plain meaning of one section of the Bankruptcy Code fails to give proper deference to the unqualified prohibition on alienation found in ERISA. "Where there is no clear intention otherwise, a specific statute will not be controlled by a general one." Morton v. Mancari, 417 U.S. 535, 550-51 (1974) quoted in Guidry, 493 U.S. at 375. It is not section 541(c)(2) that excludes a debtor's beneficial interest in an ERISA-qualified plan from the bankruptcy estate, but rather the anti-alienation provision itself which excludes it.

Adams, 302 B.R. at 547-48 (Latta, J., dissenting).

This Court agrees with Judge Latta's observations and finds them applicable in this case. Because of the transfer restrictions contained in the annuity contract and the state law statutory restrictions, no creditor could reach Quinn's interest in the annuity outside of bankruptcy. Also, the contract places significant restrictions upon Quinn's ability to access the funds. As required by IRC § 403(b)(11), the annuity provides for distributions only when the participant: (1) reaches age 59 1/2; (2) ceases his employment; (3) dies; (4) becomes disabled; or (5) suffers a "financial" hardship. (TIAA Retirement Annuity Contract at 995.1 -DA, E5.) Moreover, the contract does not provide for cash surrender or loans. (Id. at 1000.17.) These features render the TIAA annuity functionally indistinguishable from a spendthrift trust, or at least from an ERISA trust. Thus, it is of no consequence to either Quinn or his creditors (outside of bankruptcy) whether or not his interest in the retirement plan is held in a formal or traditional trust.[9]

---

[9] As Judge Latta noted in Adams, the Court in Patterson stressed the importance of the anti-alienation requirement while impliedly suggesting by its use of the phrase "plan or trust" that an actual trust is not essential to the operation of § 541(c)(2). Although the reference to a "plan" was dicta because the Court was not confronted with the trust issue, in rejecting the trustee's argument that its interpretation of § 541(c)(2) rendered § 522(d)(10)(E) superfluous, the Court noted that "§ 522(d)(10)(E) exempts from the bankruptcy estate a much broader category of interests than § 541(c)(2) excludes." Patterson, 504 U.S. at 762, 112 S. Ct. at 2249 . As examples

> The fact that the MSU Plan is not an ERISA plan should not affect the application of § 541(c)(2), even though Congress left the States to regulate their own retirement plans, because protecting state employees' retirement benefits is consistent with Congress' policy concerns for protecting the retirement benefits of employees, whether public or private. The result of excluding the TIAA annuity from Quinn's bankruptcy estate is also consistent with the policy expressed in Patterson of preventing creditors from "engaging in strategic manipulation of the bankruptcy laws in order to gain access to otherwise inaccessible funds." Patterson, 504 U.S. at 764, 112 S. Ct. at 2250 . That is, it would make no sense to preclude creditors from using bankruptcy against private-sector employees in order to gain access to protected retirement funds while allowing creditors to use bankruptcy for that purpose against public employees. Accordingly, given that the TIAA annuity is tantamount to a trust, the Court concludes that it is excluded from Quinn's estate under § 541(c)(2).

3. Suppose a debtor violates the terms of a plan and treats it as a private bank, thereby forfeiting the tax exempt status of contributions made to the plan. Is the ERISA account now part of the bankruptcy estate? In re Handel, 301 B.R. 421 (Bankr. S.D.N.Y. 2003) (no).

4. Are IRAs excluded under §541(c)(2)? Courts are divided. See Walsh v. Benson, 2006 U.S. Dist. LEXIS 59251 (W.D. Pa. 2006) (no trustee of the IRA account). But the question will arise whether IRAs are exempt property within the meaning of §522(b). Exempt property comes into the bankruptcy estate under §542(a) and is taken back out when the debtor claims an exemption under § 522(l). For the moment, we are concerned with property that never enters the bankruptcy estate.

5. Employee stock ownership plans are schemes where an employer places stock in trust for employees for withdrawal upon retirement. In In re Kane, 336 B.R. 575 (Bankr. S.D. Fla. 2006), the debtor had equities in an ESOP that had a spendthrift clause in it, valid under Florida law. The debtor withdrew the equities and placed them in an IRA, which was not exempt. Was the ESOP securities in or out of the bankruptcy estate? The Kane court held, surprisingly, they were out of the estate, although the IRA was not spendthrifted.

6. Suppose a debtor has a 401(k) plan but is fired just before the bankruptcy petition. The 401(k) plan administrator still has the funds, but the debtor has the right to withdraw the funds and "roll them over" to another 401(k) plan or an IRA. Are these funds in or out of the estate. Corzin v. Larson (In re Larson), 340 B.R. 852 (Bankr. N.D. Ohio 2006).

7. The above authorities discuss whether retirement benefits and other spendthrift trusts are in or out of the bankruptcy estate. If the item in question was included in, there is the separate question of whether this property of the estate can be exempted under state or federal law. Exemption of property in the bankruptcy estate is analytically different from property that never enters the bankruptcy estate because of §541(b) or (c).

C. EXEMPT PROPERTY

1. Procedure for exemption

SCHWAB v REILLY

130 S. Ct. 2652 (2010)

THOMAS, J.

When a debtor files a Chapter 7 bankruptcy petition, all of the debtor's assets become property of the bankruptcy estate, see 11 U.S.C. § 541, subject to

---

of interests included in § 522(d)(10)(E) but not in § 541(c)(2), the Court cited government and church plans exempted from Subchapter I of ERISA, including the anti-alienation requirement of ERISA § 206(d)(1), and individual retirement accounts under IRC § 408 that are specifically exempt from ERISA's antialienation requirement. See id. at 762-63, 112 S. Ct. at 2249 . It is interesting to note that Court did not also cite what would be obvious if an actual trust is required -- that § 522(d)(10)(E) would include any retirement plan (both ERISA and non-ERISA) not maintained pursuant to a trust.

the debtor's right to reclaim certain property as "exempt," § 522(l). The Bankruptcy Code specifies the types of property debtors may exempt, § 522(b), as well as the maximum value of the exemptions a debtor may claim in certain assets, § 522(d). Property a debtor claims as exempt will be excluded from the bankruptcy estate "[u]nless a party in interest" objects. § 522(l).

This case presents an opportunity for us to resolve a disagreement among the Courts of Appeals about what constitutes a claim of exemption to which an interested party must object under § 522(l). The issue is whether an interested party must object to a claimed exemption where, as here, the Code defines the property the debtor is authorized to exempt as an interest, the value of which may not exceed a certain dollar amount, in a particular type of asset, and the debtor's schedule of exempt property accurately describes the asset and declares the "value of [the] claimed exemption" in that asset to be an amount within the limits that the Code prescribes. Fed. Rule Bkrtcy. Proc. Official Form 6, Schedule C (1991) (hereinafter Schedule C). We hold that, in cases such as this, an interested party need not object to an exemption claimed in this manner in order to preserve the estate's ability to recover value in the asset beyond the dollar value the debtor expressly declared exempt.

I

Respondent Nadejda Reilly filed for Chapter 7 bankruptcy when her catering business failed. She supported her petition with various schedules and statements, two of which are relevant here: Schedule B, on which the Bankruptcy Rules require debtors to list their assets (most of which become property of the estate), and Schedule C, on which the Rules require debtors to list the property they wish to reclaim as exempt. The assets Reilly listed on Schedule B included an itemized list of cooking and other kitchen equipment that she described as "business equipment," and to which she assigned an estimated market value of $10,718. App. 40a, 49a-55a.

On Schedule C, Reilly claimed two exempt interests in this equipment pursuant to different sections of the Code. Reilly claimed a "tool[s] of the trade" exemption of $1,850 in the equipment under § 522(d)(6), which permits a debtor to exempt his "aggregate interest, not to exceed $1,850 in value, in any implements, professional books, or tools, of [his] trade." See also 69 Fed. Reg. 8482 (2004) (Table). And she claimed a miscellaneous exemption of $8,868 in the equipment under § 522(d)(5), which, at the time she filed for bankruptcy, permitted a debtor to take a "wildcard" exemption equal to the "debtor's aggregate interest in any property, not to exceed" $10,225 "in value."[1] See App. 58a. The total value of these claimed exemptions ($10,718) equaled the value Reilly separately listed on Schedules B and C as the equipment's estimated market value, see id., at 49a, 58a.

Subject to exceptions not relevant here, the Federal Rules of Bankruptcy Procedure require interested parties to object to a debtor's claimed exemptions

[1] The 1994 version of 11 U.S.C. § 522(d)(5) allowed debtors to exempt an "aggregate interest in any property, not to exceed in value $800 plus up to $7,500 of any unused amount of the [homestead or burial plot] exemption provided under [§ 522(d)(1)]." In 2004, pursuant to § 104(b)(2), the Judicial Conference of the United States published notice that § 522(d)(5) would impose the $975 and $9,250 ($10,225 total) limits that governed Reilly's April 2005 petition.

within 30 days after the conclusion of the creditors' meeting held pursuant to Rule 2003(a). See Fed. Rule Bkrtcy. Proc. 4003(b). If an interested party fails to object within the time allowed, a claimed exemption will exclude the subject property from the estate even if the exemption's value exceeds what the Code permits. See, e.g., § 522(l); Taylor v. Freeland & Kronz, 503 U.S. 638, 642-643 (1992).

Petitioner William G. Schwab, the trustee of Reilly's bankruptcy estate, did not object to Reilly's claimed exemptions in her business equipment because the dollar value Reilly assigned each exemption fell within the limits that §§ 522(d)(5) and (6) prescribe. App. 163a. But because an appraisal revealed that the total market value of Reilly's business equipment could be as much as $17,200,[2] Schwab moved the Bankruptcy Court for permission to auction the equipment so Reilly could receive the $10,718 she claimed as exempt, and the estate could distribute the equipment's remaining value (approximately $6,500) to Reilly's creditors.

Reilly opposed Schwab's motion. She argued that by equating on Schedule C the total value of the exemptions she claimed in the equipment with the equipment's estimated market value, she had put Schwab and her creditors on notice that she intended to exempt the equipment's full value, even if that amount turned out to be more than the dollar amount she declared, and more than the Code allowed. Citing § 522(l), Reilly asserted that because her Schedule C notified Schwab of her intent to exempt the full value of her business equipment, he was obliged to object if he wished to preserve the estate's right to retain any value in the equipment in excess of the $10,718 she estimated. Because Schwab did not object within the time prescribed by Rule 4003(b), Reilly asserted that the estate forfeited its claim to such value. Reilly further informed the Bankruptcy Court that exempting her business equipment from the estate was so important to her that she would dismiss her bankruptcy case if doing so was the only way to avoid the equipment's sale at auction.[3]

The Bankruptcy Court denied both Schwab's motion to auction the equipment and Reilly's conditional motion to dismiss her case. See In re Reilly, 403 B. R. 336 (Bkrtcy. Ct. MD Pa. 2006). Schwab sought relief from the District Court, arguing that neither the Code nor Rule 4003(b) requires a trustee to object to a claimed exemption where the amount the debtor declares as the "value of [the debtor's] claimed exemption" in certain property is an amount within the limits the Code prescribes. The District Court rejected Schwab's argument, and the Court of Appeals affirmed. See In re Reilly, 534 F.3d 173 (CA3 2008).

The Court of Appeals agreed with the Bankruptcy Court that by equating on Schedule C the total value of her exemptions in her business equipment with the equipment's market value, Reilly "indicate[d] the intent" to exempt the equipment's full value. Id., at 174. In reaching this conclusion, the Court of

[2] Schwab concedes that the appraisal occurred before Rule 4003(b)'s 30-day window for objecting to the claimed exemptions had passed. See Brief for Petitioner 15.

[3] Reilly's desire to avoid the equipment's auction is understandable because the equipment, which Reilly's parents purchased for her despite their own financial difficulties, has "'extraordinary sentimental value.'" Brief for Respondent 5. But the sentimental value of the property cannot drive our decision in this case, because sentimental value is not a basis for construing the Bankruptcy Code. Because the Code imposes limits on exemptions, many debtors who seek to take advantage of the Code are, no doubt, put to the similarly difficult choice of parting with property of "extraordinary sentimental value."

Appeals relied on our decision in Taylor:

> "[W]e believe this case to be controlled by Taylor. Just as we perceive it was important to the Taylor Court that the debtor meant to exempt the full amount of the property by listing 'unknown' as both the value of the property and the value of the exemption, it is important to us that Reilly valued the business equipment at $10,718 and claimed an exemption in the same amount. Such an identical listing put Schwab on notice that Reilly intended to exempt the property fully.
>
> . . .
>
> "'[A]n unstated premise' of Taylor was 'that a debtor who exempts the entire reported value of an asset is claiming the "full amount," whatever it turns out to be.'" 534 F.3d at 178-179.

Relying on this "unstated premise," the Court of Appeals held that Schwab's failure to object to Reilly's claimed exemptions entitled Reilly to the equivalent of an in-kind interest in her business equipment, even though the value of that exemption exceeded the amount that Reilly declared on Schedule C and the amount that the Code allowed her to withdraw from the bankruptcy estate. Id.

As noted, the Court of Appeals' decision adds to disagreement among the Circuits about what constitutes a claim of exemption to which an interested party must object under § 522(l).[4] We granted certiorari to resolve this conflict. We conclude that the Court of Appeals' approach fails to account for the text of the relevant Code provisions and misinterprets our decision in Taylor. Accordingly, we reverse.

II

The starting point for our analysis is the proper interpretation of Reilly's Schedule C. If we read the Schedule Reilly's way, she claimed exemptions in her business equipment that could exceed statutory limits, and thus claimed exemptions to which Schwab should have objected if he wished to enforce those limits for the benefit of the estate. If we read Schedule C Schwab's way, Reilly claimed valid exemptions to which Schwab had no duty to object. The Court of Appeals construed Schedule C Reilly's way and interpreted her claimed exemptions as improper, and therefore objectionable, even though their declared value was facially within the applicable Code limits. In so doing, the Court of Appeals held that trustees evaluating the validity of exemptions in cases like this cannot take a debtor's claim at face value, and specifically cannot rely on the fact that the amount the debtor declares as the "value of [the] claimed exemption" is within statutory limits. Instead, the trustee's duty to object turns on whether the

[4] Compare In re Williams, 104 F.3d 688, 690 (CA4 1997) (holding that interested parties have no duty to object to a claimed exemption where the dollar amount the debtor assigns the exemption is facially within the range the Code allows for the type of property in issue); In re Wick, 276 F.3d 412 (CA8 2002) (employing reasoning similar to Williams, but stopping short of articulating a clear rule), with In re Green, 31 F.3d 1098, 1100 (CA11 1994) ("A debtor who exempts the entire reported value of an asset is claiming the [asset's] 'full amount,' whatever it turns out to be"); In re Anderson, 377 B. R. 865 (Bkrtcy. App. Panel CA6 2007) (similar); and In re Barroso-Herrans, 524 F.3d 341, 344 (CA1 2008) (focusing on "how a reasonable trustee would have understood the filings under the circumstances"); In re Hyman, 967 F.2d 1316 (CA9 1992) (applying an analogous totality-of-the-circumstances approach).

interplay of various schedule entries supports an inference that the debtor "intended" to exempt a dollar value different than the one she wrote on the form. 534 F.3d at 178. This complicated view of the trustee's statutory obligation, and the strained reading of Schedule C on which it rests, is inconsistent with the Code.[5]

The parties agree that this case is governed by § 522(l), which states that a Chapter 7 debtor must "file a list of property that the debtor claims as exempt under subsection (b) of this section," and further states that "[u]nless a party in interest objects, the property claimed as exempt on such list is exempt." The parties further agree that the "list" to which § 522(l) refers is the "list of property . . . claim[ed] as exempt" currently known as "Schedule C." See Schedule C.[6] The parties, like the Courts of Appeals, disagree about what information on Schedule C defines the "property claimed as exempt" for purposes of evaluating an exemption's propriety under § 522(l). Reilly asserts that the "property claimed as exempt" is defined by reference to all the information on Schedule C, including the estimated market value of each asset in which the debtor claims an exempt interest. Schwab and the United States as amicus curiae argue that the Code specifically defines the "property claimed as exempt" as an interest, the value of which may not exceed a certain dollar amount, in a particular asset, not as the asset itself. Accordingly, they argue that the value of the property claimed exempt, i.e., the value of the debtor's exempt interest in the asset, should be judged on the value the debtor assigns the interest, not on the value the debtor assigns the asset. The point of disagreement is best illustrated by the relevant portion of Reilly's Schedule C:

Schedule C-Property Claimed as Exempt

Description of Property	Specify Law Providing Each Exemption	Value of Claimed Exemption	Current Market Value of Property Without Deduction Exemptions
Schedule B Personal Property			
. . .	. . .	. . .	. . .
See attached list of business equipment.	11 U.S.C. § 522(d)(6)	1,850	10,718
	11 U.S.C. § 522(d)(5).	8,868	

According to Reilly, Schwab was required to treat the estimate of market value she entered in column four as part of her claimed exemption in identifying the "property claimed as exempt" under § 522(l). See Brief for Respondent 22-28. Relying on this premise, Reilly argues that where, as here, a debtor equates the total value of her claimed exemptions in a certain asset (column three) with her

[5] The forms, rules, treatise excerpts, and policy considerations on which the dissent relies, see post, at 4-16, must be read in light of the Bankruptcy Code provisions that govern this case, and must yield to those provisions in the event of conflict.

[6] Bankruptcy Rule 4003 specifies the time within which the debtor must file Schedule C, as well as the time within which interested parties must object to the exemptions claimed thereon.

estimate of the asset's market value (column four), she establishes the "property claimed as exempt" as the full value of the asset, whatever that turns out to be. See ibid. Accordingly, Reilly argues that her Schedule C clearly put Schwab on notice that she "intended" to claim an exemption for the full value of her business equipment, and that Schwab's failure to oppose the exemption in a timely manner placed the full value of the equipment outside the estate's reach.

Schwab does not dispute that columns three and four apprised him that Reilly equated the total value of her claimed exemptions in the equipment ($1,850 plus $8,868) with the equipment's market value ($10,718). He simply disagrees with Reilly that this "identical listing put [him] on notice that Reilly intended to exempt the property fully," regardless whether its value exceeded the exemption limits the Code prescribes. 534 F.3d at 178. Schwab and amicus United States instead contend that the Code defines the "property" Reilly claimed as exempt under § 522(l) as an "interest" whose value cannot exceed a certain dollar amount. Brief for Petitioner 20-26; Reply Brief for Petitioner 3-6; Brief for United States as Amicus Curiae 12-18. Construing Reilly's Schedule C in light of this statutory definition, they contend that Reilly's claimed exemption was facially unobjectionable because the "property claimed as exempt" (i.e., two interests in her business equipment worth $8,868 and $1,850, respectively) is property Reilly was clearly entitled to exclude from her estate under the Code provisions she referenced in column 2. See supra, at 8 (citing §§ 522(d)(5) and (6)). Accordingly, Schwab and the United States conclude that Schwab had no obligation to object to the exemption in order to preserve for the estate any value in Reilly's business equipment beyond the total amount ($10,718) Reilly properly claimed as exempt.

We agree. The portion of § 522(l) that resolves this case is not, as Reilly asserts, the provision stating that the "property claimed as exempt on [Schedule C] is exempt" unless an interested party objects. Rather, it is the portion of § 522(l) that defines the target of the objection, namely, the portion that says Schwab has a duty to object to the "list of property that the debtor claims as exempt under subsection (b)." (Emphasis added.) That subsection, § 522(b), does not define the "property claimed as exempt" by reference to the estimated market value on which Reilly and the Court of Appeals rely. Brief for Respondent 22-23; 534 F.3d at 178. Section 522(b) refers only to property defined in § 522(d), which in turn lists 12 categories of property that a debtor may claim as exempt. As we have recognized, most of these categories (and all of the categories applicable to Reilly's exemptions) define the "property" a debtor may "clai[m] as exempt" as the debtor's "interest" -- up to a specified dollar amount -- in the assets described in the category, not as the assets themselves. §§ 522(d)(5)-(6); see also §§ 522(d)(1)-(4), (8); Rousey v. Jacoway, 544 U.S. 320, 325 (2005); Owen v. Owen, 500 U.S. 305, 310 (1991). Viewing Reilly's form entries in light of this definition, we agree with Schwab and the United States that Schwab had no duty to object to the property Reilly claimed as exempt (two interests in her business equipment worth $1,850 and $8,868) because the stated value of each interest, and thus of the "property claimed as exempt," was within the limits the Code allows.[7]

Reilly's contrary view of Schwab's obligations under § 522(l) does not

[7] Schwab's statutory duty to object to the exemptions in this case turns solely on whether the value of the property claimed as exempt exceeds statutory limits because the parties agree that Schwab had no cause to object to Reilly's attempt to claim exemptions in the equipment at issue, or to the applicability of the Code provisions Reilly cited in support of her exemptions.

withstand scrutiny because it defines the target of a trustee's objection -- the "property claimed as exempt" -- based on language in Schedule C and dictionary definitions of "property," see Brief for Respondent 24-25, 40-41, that the definition in the Code itself overrides.[8] Although we may look to dictionaries and the Bankruptcy Rules to determine the meaning of words the Code does not define, see, e.g., Rousey, supra, at 330, the Code's definition of the "property claimed as exempt" in this case is clear. As noted above, §§ 522(d)(5) and (6) define the "property claimed as exempt" as an "interest" in Reilly's business equipment, not as the equipment per se. Sections 522(d)(5) and (6) further and plainly state that claims to exempt such interests are statutorily permissible, and thus unobjectionable, if the value of the claimed interest is below a particular dollar amount.[9] That is the case here, and Schwab was entitled to rely upon these provisions in evaluating whether Reilly's exemptions were objectionable under the Code. See Lamie v. United States Trustee, 540 U.S. 526, 534 (2004); Hartford Underwriters Ins. Co. v. Union Planters Bank, N. A., 530 U.S. 1, 6 (2000). The Court of Appeals' contrary holding not only fails to account for the Code's definition of the "property claimed as exempt." It also fails to account for the provisions in § 522(d) that permit debtors to exempt certain property in kind or in full regardless of value. See, e.g., §§ 522(d)(9) (professionally prescribed health aids), (10)(C) (disability benefits), (7) (unmatured life insurance contracts). We decline to construe Reilly's claimed exemptions in a manner that elides the distinction between these provisions and provisions such as §§ 522(d)(5) and (6), see, e.g., Duncan v. Walker, 533 U.S. 167, 174 (2001), particularly based upon an entry on Schedule C -- Reilly's estimate of her equipment's market value -- to which the Code does not refer in defining the "property claimed as exempt." [10]

---

[8] The dissent's approach suffers from a similar flaw, and misstates our holding in critiquing it. See post, at 1-2 (asserting that by refusing to subject "challenges to the debtor's valuation of exemptible assets" to the "30-day" objection period in Federal Rule of Bankruptcy Procedure 4003(b), we "drastically reduc[e] Rule 4003's governance"). Challenges to the valuation of what the dissent terms "exemptible assets" are not covered by Rule 4003(b) in the first place. Challenges to "property claimed as exempt" as defined by the Code are covered by Rule 4003(b), but in this case that property is not objectionable, so the lack of an objection did not violate the Rule. Our holding is confined to this point. Accordingly, our holding does not "reduc[e] Rule 4003's governance," nor does it express any judgment on what constrains objections to the type of "market value" estimates, the dissent equates with the dollar value a debtor assigns the "property claimed as exempt" as defined by the Code.

[9] Treating such claims as unobjectionable is consistent with our precedents. See, e.g., Rousey, 544 U.S., at 325. It also accords with bankruptcy court decisions holding that where, as here, a debtor claims an exemption pursuant to provisions that (like § 522(d)(6)) permit the debtor to exclude from the estate only an "interest" in certain property, the "property" that becomes exempt absent objection, § 522(l), is only the "partial interest" claimed as exempt and not "the asset as a whole," e.g., In re Soost, 262 B. R. 68, 72 (Bkrtcy. App. Panel CA8 2001).

[10] The dissent's approach does not avoid these concerns. The dissent insists that "a debtor's market valuation [of the equipment in which she claims an exempt interest] is an essential factor in determining the nature of the 'interest' [the] debtor lists as exempt" (and thus in determining whether the claimed exemption is objectionable), because "without comparing [the debtor's] market valuation of the equipment to the value of her claimed exemption" the trustee "could not comprehend whether [the debtor] claimed a monetary or an in-kind 'interest' in [the] equipment." This argument overlooks the fact that there is another way the trustee could discern from the "face of the debtor's filings," whether the debtor claimed as exempt a "monetary or an in-kind 'interest' in" her equipment: The trustee could simply consult the Code provisions the debtor listed as governing the exemption in question. Here, those provisions, §§ 522(d)(5) and (d)(6), expressly describe the exempt interest as an "interest" "not to exceed" a specified dollar amount.

For all of these reasons, we conclude that Schwab was entitled to evaluate the propriety of the claimed exemptions based on three, and only three, entries on Reilly's Schedule C: the description of the business equipment in which Reilly claimed the exempt interests; the Code provisions governing the claimed exemptions; and the amounts Reilly listed in the column titled "value of claimed exemption." In reaching this conclusion, we do not render the market value estimate on Reilly's Schedule C superfluous. We simply confine the estimate to its proper role: aiding the trustee in administering the estate by helping him identify assets that may have value beyond the dollar amount the debtor claims as exempt, or whose full value may not be available for exemption because a portion of the interest is, for example, encumbered by an unavoidable lien. See, e.g., 3 W. Norton, Bankruptcy Law and Practice § 56:7 (3d ed. 2009); Brief for United States as Amicus Curiae 16; Dept. of Justice, Executive Office for U.S. Trustees, Handbook for Chapter 7 Trustees, p. 8-1 (2005), http:// www.justice.gov /ust/eo/private_trustee/library/chapter07/ docs/7handbook1008/Ch7_Handbook.pdf (as visited June 14, 2010, and available in Clerk of Court's case file). As noted, most assets become property of the estate upon commencement of a bankruptcy case, see 11 U.S.C. § 541, and exemptions represent the debtor's attempt to reclaim those assets or, more often, certain interests in those assets, to the creditors' detriment. Accordingly, it is at least useful for a trustee to be able to compare the value of the claimed exemption (which typically represents the debtor's interest in a particular asset) with the asset's estimated market value (which belongs to the estate subject to any valid exemption) without having to consult separate schedules.[11]

Accordingly, it was entirely appropriate for Schwab to view Reilly's schedule entries as exempting an interest in her business equipment in the (declared and unobjectionable) amounts of $1,850 and $8,868. Viewing the entries otherwise, i.e., as exempting the equipment in kind or in full no matter what its dollar value, would unnecessarily treat the exemption as violating the limits imposed by the Code provisions that govern it, as well as ignore the distinction between those provisions and the provisions that "authoriz[e] reclamation of the property in full without any cap on value." And it would do all of this based on information (identical dollar amounts in columns three and four of Schedule C) that Schwab and one of his amici say often result from a default setting in commercial bankruptcy software.

[11] The dissent's argument that the estimate plays a greater role, and is "vital," to determining whether the value a debtor assigns the "property claimed as exempt" (here, an interest in certain business equipment) is objectionable, lacks statutory support because the governing Code provisions phrase the exemption limit as a simple dollar amount. The dissent's view, might be plausible if the Code stated that the debtor could exempt an interest in her equipment "not to exceed" a certain percentage of the equipment's market value, because then it might be necessary to "compar[e] [the debtor's] market valuation of the equipment to the value of her claimed exemption" to determine the exemption's propriety. But the Code does not phrase the exemption cap in such terms. Moreover, even accepting that the equivalent Schedule C entries the dissent relies upon represent a claim to exempt an asset's full value, the dissent does not explain why this equivalence precludes a trustee from relying on the dollar amount the debtor expressly assigns both entries. According to the dissent, a trustee faced with such entries should assume not only that the debtor reclaims from the estate what she believes to be the full value of an asset in which the Code allows her to exempt an interest "not to exceed" a certain dollar amount, e.g., § 522(d)(6), but also that the debtor would continue to claim the asset's full value as exempt even if that value exceeds her estimate to a point that would cause her claim to violate the Code. The schedule entries themselves do not compel this assumption, and the Code provisions they invoke undercut it. The evidence that the debtor in this case would have chosen that course is external to her exemption schedule. And in the ordinary case, particularly if the equivalent entries the dissent relies upon result from a software default, see n. 10, supra, there is no reason to assume that a debtor would want to violate the Code or jeopardize other exemptions if her market value

Our interpretation of Schwab's statutory obligations is not only consistent with the governing Code provisions; it is also consistent with the historical treatment of bankruptcy exemptions. Congress has permitted debtors to exempt certain property from their bankruptcy estates for more than two centuries. See Act of Apr. 4, 1800, ch. 19, § 5, 2 Stat. 19.[12] Throughout these periods, debtors have validly exempted property based on forms that required the debtor to list the value of a claimed exemption without also estimating the market value of the asset in which the debtor claimed the exempt interest. See Brief for Respondent 46, n. 7 (citing Sup. Ct. Bkrtcy. Form 20 (1877)).[13] Indeed, it was not until 1991 that Schedule B-4 was redesignated as Schedule C and amended to require the estimate of market value on which Reilly so heavily relies. See Schedule C. This amendment was not occasioned by legislative changes that altered the Code's definition of "the property claimed as exempt" in this case as an "interest," not to exceed a certain dollar amount, in Reilly's business equipment.[14] Accordingly, we agree with Schwab and the United States that this recent amendment to the exemption form does not compel Reilly's view of Schwab's statutory obligations, or render the claimed exemptions in this case objectionable under the Code. See Reply Brief for Petitioner 9-11; Brief for United States as Amicus Curiae 16-17.[15]

III

The Court of Appeals erred in holding that our decision in Taylor dictates a contrary conclusion. See 534 F.3d at 178. Taylor does not rest on what the debtor "meant" to exempt. 534 F.3d at 178. Rather, Taylor applies to the face of

estimate turns out to be wrong.

[12] See also Act of Aug. 19, 1841, ch. 9, § 3, 5 Stat. 440; Act of Mar. 2, 1867, ch. 176, § 11, 14 Stat. 517, amended by Act of June 22, 1874, 18 Stat., Pt. 3, p. 182; Bankruptcy Act of July 1, 1898, ch. 541, § 6, 30 Stat. 544, 11 U.S.C. § 24 (1926 ed.); Chandler Act, ch. 575, § 1, 52 Stat. 840, 11 U.S.C. § 24 (1934 ed., Supp. IV); § 522 (1976 ed., Supp. II); § 522 (2000 ed. and Supp. V).

[13] See also General Forms in Bankruptcy, Official Form 1, Schedule B. (5) (1898); Fed. Rule Bkrtcy. Proc. Official Form 6, Schedule B-4 (1971).

[14] The precise reason for the amendment is unclear. See Communication from THE CHIEF JUSTICE of the United States Transmitting Amendments to the Federal Rules of Bankruptcy Procedure Prescribed by the Court, Pursuant to 28 U.S.C. 2075, H. R. Doc. 102-80, p. 558, reprinted in 11 Bankruptcy Rules Documentary History (1990-1991) (referencing only the fact of the amendment). It may have been to consolidate and reconcile the separate forms debtors were previously required to file in Chapter 7 and Chapter 13 cases, see, e.g., In re Beshirs, 236 B. R. 42, 46-47 (Bkrtcy. Ct. Kan. 1999), or simply to make it easier for trustees to evaluate whether certain assets were viable candidates for liquidation. Whatever the case, it did not result from statutory changes to the Code provisions that govern this dispute.

[15] Because the Code provisions we rely upon to resolve this case do not obligate trustees to object under Rule 4003(b) to a debtor's estimate of the market value of an asset in which the debtor claims an exempt interest, our analysis does not depend on whether the schedule of "property claimed as exempt" (currently Schedule C) calls for such an estimate or not. We engage the point only because Reilly suggests that the 1991 schedule revisions requiring debtors to provide such an estimate on the schedule of "property claimed as exempt" means that the estimate must be viewed as part of the exemption and is therefore subject to the Rule. See Brief for Respondent 40-41. The dissent ranges far beyond even this unavailing argument in suggesting that the market value estimate served as "an essential factor in determining the nature of the 'interest' a debtor lists as exempt," even before 1991 when that estimate did not appear on the schedule of "property claimed as exempt" (former Schedule B->4), but rather appeared on former "Schedule B-2," which merely listed the debtor's "personal property" as of the date of the petition filing. Interim Fed. Rule Bkrtcy. Proc. Official Form 6, Schedules B-2, B-4 (1979).

a debtor's claimed exemption the Code provisions that compel reversal here.

The debtor in Taylor, like the debtor here, filed a schedule of exemptions with the Bankruptcy Court on which the debtor described the property subject to the claimed exemption, identified the Code provision supporting the exemption, and listed the dollar value of the exemption. Critically, however, the debtor in Taylor did not, like the debtor here, state the value of the claimed exemption as a specific dollar amount at or below the limits the Code allows. Instead, the debtor in Taylor listed the value of the exemption itself as "$unknown":

Schedule B-4.-Property Claimed Exempt

Type of Property	Location, Description, and, So Far As Relevant to the Claim of Exemp-tion, Present Use of Property	Specify the Statute Creating the Exemption	Value claimed Exempt
Proceeds from Lawsuit	Winn v. TWA Claim for lost wages	11 U.S.C. 522(b)(d)	$unknown

The interested parties in Taylor agreed that this entry rendered the debtor's claimed exemption objectionable on its face because the exemption concerned an asset (lawsuit proceeds) that the Code did not permit the debtor to exempt beyond a specific dollar amount. See 503 U.S., at 642. Accordingly, although this case and Taylor both concern the consequences of a trustee's failure to object to a claimed exemption within the time specified by Rule 4003, the question arose in Taylor on starkly different facts. In Taylor, the question concerned a trustee's obligation to object to the debtor's entry of a "value claimed exempt" that was not plainly within the limits the Code allows. In this case, the opposite is true. The amounts Reilly listed in the Schedule C column titled "Value of Claimed Exemption" are facially within the limits the Code prescribes and raise no warning flags that warranted an objection.[16] See supra, at 8.

Taylor supports this conclusion. In holding otherwise, the Court of Appeals focused on what it described as Taylor's "'unstated premise'" that "'a debtor who exempts the entire reported value of an asset is claiming the "full amount," whatever it turns out to be.'" 534 F.3d at 179. But Taylor does not rest on this premise. It establishes and applies the straightforward proposition that an interested party must object to a claimed exemption if the amount the debtor lists as the "value claimed exempt" is not within statutory limits, a test the value ($unknown) in Taylor failed, and the values ($8,868 and $1,850) in this case pass.

[16] See, e.g., Barroso-Herrans, 524 F.3d at 345 (explaining that Schedule C entries listing the value of a claimed exemption as "unknown," "to be determined," or "100%" are "'red flags to trustees and creditors,' and therefore put them on notice that if they do not object, the whole value of the asset -- whatever it might later turn out to be -- will be exempt" (quoting 1 Collier on Bankruptcy P8.06[1][c][ii] (15th ed. rev. 2007); citation and some internal quotation marks omitted)). The dissent concedes that a debtor's exemption schedule "must give notice sufficient to cue the trustee that an objection may be in order," and rightly observes that the sufficiency of a particular cue, or "' warning flag,'" may lie "in the eye of the beholder." In this case, however, the Code itself breaks the tie between what might otherwise be two equally tenable views.

We adhere to this test. Doing otherwise would not only depart from Taylor and ignore the presumption that parties act lawfully and with knowledge of the law, cf. United States v. Budd, 144 U.S. 154, 163 (1892); it would also require us to expand the statutory definition of "property claimed as exempt" and the universe of information an interested party must consider in evaluating the validity of a claimed exemption. Even if the Code allowed such expansions, they would be ill advised. As evidenced by the differences between Reilly's Schedule C and the schedule in Taylor, preprinted bankruptcy schedules change over time. Basing the definition of the "property claimed as exempt," and thus an interested party's obligation to object under § 522(l), on inferences that party must draw from evolving forms, rather than on the facial validity of the value the debtor assigns the "property claimed as exempt" as defined by the Code, would undermine the predictability the statute is designed to provide.[17] For all of these reasons, we take Reilly's exemptions at face value and find them unobjectionable under the Code, so the objection deadline we enforced in Taylor is inapplicable here.

IV

In a final effort to defend the Court of Appeals' judgment, Reilly asserts that her approach to § 522(l) is necessary to vindicate the Code's goal of giving debtors a fresh start, and to further its policy of discouraging trustees and creditors from sleeping on their rights. See Brief for Respondent 21, 55-68. Although none of Reilly's policy arguments can overcome the Code provisions or the aspects of Taylor that govern this case, our decision fully accords with all of the policies she identifies. We agree that "exemptions in bankruptcy cases are part and parcel of the fundamental bankruptcy concept of a 'fresh start.'" Brief for Respondent 21 (quoting Rousey, 544 U.S., at 325); see Marrama v. Citizens Bank of Mass., 549 U.S. 365, 367 (2007). We disagree that this policy required Schwab to object to a facially valid claim of exemption on pain of forfeiting his ability to preserve for the estate any value in Reilly's business equipment beyond the value of the interest she declared exempt. This approach threatens to convert a fresh start into a free pass.

As we emphasized in Rousey, "[t]o help the debtor obtain a fresh start, the Bankruptcy Code permits him to withdraw from the estate certain interests in property, such as his car or home, up to certain values." 544 U.S., at 325 (emphasis added). The Code limits exemptions in this fashion because every asset the Code permits a debtor to withdraw from the estate is an asset that is not available to his creditors. See § 522(b)(1). Congress balanced the difficult choices that exemption limits impose on debtors with the economic harm that exemptions visit on creditors, and it is not for us to alter this balance by requiring trustees to object

[17] Reilly insists that our conclusion should nonetheless be avoided because "procedures that burden the debtor's exemption entitlements, like those that impair a debtor's discharge generally, are to be construed narrowly." Brief for Respondent 33 (citing Kawaauhau v. Geiger, 523 U.S. 57, 62 (1998)). This argument misses the mark for two reasons. First, the only burdens our conclusion imposes are burdens the Code itself prescribes, specifically, the burdens the Code places on debtors to state their claimed exemptions accurately and to conform such claims to statutory limits. Second, and in any event, Geiger and the other cases Reilly cites emphasize in the discharge context the importance of limiting exceptions to discharge to "those plainly expressed," a principle that supports our approach here. Id. (internal quotation marks omitted).

to claimed exemptions based on form entries beyond those that govern an exemption's validity under the Code. See Lamie, 540 U.S., at 534, 538; Hartford, 530 U.S., at 6; United States v. Locke, 471 U.S. 84, 95 (1985).

Reilly nonetheless contends that our approach creates perverse incentives for trustees and creditors to sleep on their rights. See Brief for Respondent 64, n. 10, 67-69. Again, we disagree. Where a debtor intends to exempt nothing more than an interest worth a specified dollar amount in an asset that is not subject to an unlimited or in-kind exemption under the Code, our approach will ensure clear and efficient resolution of competing claims to the asset's value. If an interested party does not object to the claimed interest by the time the Rule 4003 period expires, title to the asset will remain with the estate pursuant to § 541, and the debtor will be guaranteed a payment in the dollar amount of the exemption. If an interested party timely objects, the court will rule on the objection and, if it is improper, allow the debtor to make appropriate adjustments.[18]

Where, as here, it is important to the debtor to exempt the full market value of the asset or the asset itself, our decision will encourage the debtor to declare the value of her claimed exemption in a manner that makes the scope of the exemption clear, for example, by listing the exempt value as "full fair market value (FMV)" or "100% of FMV."[19] Such a declaration will encourage the trustee to object promptly to the exemption if he wishes to challenge it and preserve for the estate any value in the asset beyond relevant statutory limits.[20] If the trustee fails to object, or if the trustee objects and the objection is overruled, the debtor will be entitled to exclude the full value of the asset. If the trustee objects and the

[18] We disagree that Reilly's approach to exemptions would more efficiently dispose of competing claims to the asset. On Reilly's view, a trustee would be encouraged (if not obliged) to object to claims to exempt a specific dollar amount of interest in an asset whenever the value of the exempt interest equaled the debtor's estimate of the asset's market value. Where the debtor genuinely intended to claim nothing more than the face value of the exempt interest (which is rational if a debtor wishes to ensure that his aggregate exemptions remain within statutory limits), such an approach would engender needless objections and litigation, particularly if the equation that would precipitate the objection often results from a default software entry. See Reply Brief for Petitioner 15; Brief for Nat. Assn. of Bankruptcy Trustees 13, n. 15.

[19] The dissent's observations about the poor fit between our admonition and a form entry calling for a dollar amount, simply reflect the tension between the Code's definition of "property claimed as exempt" (i.e., an interest, not to exceed a certain dollar amount, in Reilly's business equipment) and Reilly's attempt to convert into a dollar value an improper claim to exempt the equipment itself, "'whatever [its value] turns out to be.'" In re Reilly, 534 F.3d 173, 178-179 (CA3 2008). As the dissent concedes, "[s]ection 522(d) catalogs exemptions of two types." "Most exemptions -- and all of those Reilly invoked -- place a monetary limit on the value of the property the debtor may reclaim," and such exemptions are distinct from those made pursuant to Code provisions that "authoriz[e] reclamation of the property in full without any cap on value." Nothing about Reilly's Schedule entries establishes that Schwab should have treated Reilly's claim for $10,718, an unobjectionable amount under the Code provisions she expressly invoked, as an objectionable claim for thousands of dollars more than those provisions allow, or as a claim for an uncapped exemption under Code provisions she did not invoke and the dissent admits are "not at issue here."

[20] A trustee will not always file an objection. As the United States observes, Schwab did not do so in this case with respect to certain assets (perishable foodstuffs from Reilly's commercial kitchen) that could not be readily sold. See Brief for United States as Amicus Curiae 28, n. 7 (explaining that Schwab could have objected to Reilly's claim of a wildcard exemption for an interest in the food totaling $2,036 because this claim, combined with her wildcard claims for an interest of $8,868 in her business equipment and interests totaling $26 in her bank accounts, placed the total value of the interests she claimed exempt under the wildcard provision $975 above then-applicable limits).

objection is sustained, the debtor will be required either to forfeit the portion of the exemption that exceeds the statutory allowance, or to revise other exemptions or arrangements with her creditors to permit the exemption. See Fed. Rule Bkrtcy. Proc. 1009(a). Either result will facilitate the expeditious and final disposition of assets, and thus enable the debtor (and the debtor's creditors) to achieve a fresh start free of the finality and clouded-title concerns Reilly describes. See Brief for Respondent 57-59 (arguing that "[u]nder [Schwab's] interpretation of Rule 4003(b), a debtor would never have the certainty of knowing whether or not he or she may keep her exempted property until the case had ended"); id., at 66.[21]

For all of these reasons, the policy considerations Reilly cites support our approach. Where, as here, a debtor accurately describes an asset subject to an exempt interest and on Schedule C declares the "value of [the] claimed exemption" as a dollar amount within the range the Code allows, interested parties are entitled to rely upon that value as evidence of the claim's validity. Accordingly, we hold that Schwab was not required to object to Reilly's claimed exemptions in her business equipment in order to preserve the estate's right to retain any value in the equipment beyond the value of the exempt interest. In reaching this conclusion, we express no judgment on the merits of, and do not foreclose the courts from entertaining on remand, procedural or other measures that may allow Reilly to avoid auction of her business equipment.

We reverse the judgment of the Court of Appeals for the Third Circuit and remand this case for further proceedings consistent with this opinion.

GINSBURG, J., DISSENTING. In Chapter 7 bankruptcies, debtors must surrender to the trustee-in-bankruptcy all their assets, 11 U.S.C. § 541, but may reclaim for themselves exempt property, § 522. Within 30 days after the meeting of creditors, the trustee or a creditor may file an objection to the debtor's designation of property as exempt. Fed. Rule Bkrtcy. Proc. 4003(b). Absent timely objection, "property claimed [by the debtor] as exempt . . . is exempt." § 522(l).

The trustee in this case, petitioner William G. Schwab, maintains that the obligation promptly to object to exemption claims extends only to the qualification of an asset as exemptible, not to the debtor's valuation of the asset. Respondent Nadejda Reilly, the debtor-in-bankruptcy, urges that the timely objection requirement applies not only to the debtor's designation of an asset as exempt; the requirement applies as well, she asserts, to her estimate of the asset's

[21] Reilly's clouded-title argument arises only if one accepts her flawed conception of the exemptions in this case. According to Reilly, "once the thirty-day deadline passed without objection" to her claim, she was "entitled to know that she would emerge from bankruptcy with her cooking equipment intact." Brief for Respondent 57. There are two problems with this argument. First, it assumes that the property she claimed as exempt was the full value of the equipment. That assumption is incorrect for the reasons we explain. Second, her argument assumes that a claim to exempt the full value of the equipment would, if unopposed, entitle her to the equipment itself as opposed to a payment equal to the equipment's full value. That assumption is at least questionable. Section 541 is clear that title to the equipment passed to Reilly's estate at the commencement of her case, and §§ 522(d)(5) and (6) are equally clear that her reclamation right is limited to exempting an interest in the equipment, not the equipment itself. Accordingly, it is far from obvious that the Code would "entitle" Reilly to clear title in the equipment even if she claimed as exempt a "full" or "100%" interest in it (which she did not). Of course, it is likely that a trustee who fails to object to such a claim would have little incentive to do anything but pass title in the asset to the debtor. But that does not establish the statutory entitlement Reilly claims.

market value. That is so, she reasons, because the asset's current dollar value is critical to the determination whether she may keep the property intact and outside bankruptcy, or whether the trustee, at any time during the course of the proceedings, may sell it.

The Court holds that challenges to the debtor's valuation of exemptible assets need not be made within the 30-day period allowed for "objection[s] to the list of property claimed as exempt." Rule 4003(b). Instead, according to the Court, no time limit constrains the trustee's (or a creditor's) prerogative to place at issue the debtor's evaluation of the property as fully exempt.

The Court's decision drastically reduces Rule 4003's governance, for challenges to valuation have been, until today, the most common type of objection leveled against exemption claims. See 9 Collier on Bankruptcy P4003.04, p. 4003-15 (rev. 15th ed. 2009) (hereinafter Collier) ("Normally, objections to exemptions will focus primarily on issues of valuation."). In addition to departing from the prevailing understanding and practice, the Court's decision exposes debtors to protracted uncertainty concerning their right to retain exempt property, thereby impeding the "fresh start" exemptions are designed to foster. In accord with the courts below, I would hold that a debtor's valuation of exempt property counts and becomes conclusive absent a timely objection.

I

Nadejda Reilly is a cook who operated a one-person catering business. Unable to cover her debts, she filed a Chapter 7 bankruptcy petition appending all required schedules and statements. Relevant here, her filings included a form captioned "Schedule B - Personal Property," which called for enumeration of "all personal property of the debtor of whatever kind." App. 40a. On that all-encompassing schedule, Reilly listed "business equipment," i.e., her kitchen equipment, with a current market value of $10,718.

Reilly also filed the more particular form captioned "Schedule C - Property Claimed as Exempt." Schedule C contained four columns, the first headed "Description of Property"; the second, "Specify Law Providing Each Exemption"; the third, "Value of Claimed Exemption"; and the fourth, "Current Market Value of Property Without Deducting Exemptions." In the first column of Schedule C, Reilly wrote, as she did in Schedule B's description-of-property column: "See attached list of business equipment." On the list appended to Schedules B and C, Reilly set out by hand a 31-item inventory of her restaurant-plus-catering-venture equipment. Next to each item, e.g., "Dough Mixer," "Gas stove," "Hood," she specified, first, the purchase price and, next, "Today's Market Value," which added up to $10,718 for the entire inventory.[22]

As the laws securing exemption of her kitchen equipment, Reilly specified in the second Schedule C column, § 522(d)(6), the exemption covering trade tools, and § 522(d)(5), the "wildcard" exemption.[23] In the value-of-claimed-

[22] Reilly's Schedules B and C, and the inventory she attached to the forms, are reproduced in an Appendix to this opinion.

[23] Unlike exemptions that describe the specific property debtors may preserve, e.g., 11 U.S.C. § 522(d)(6) (debtor may exempt her "aggregate interest, not to exceed [$1,850] in value, in any implements, professional books, or tool[s] of [her] trade"), the "wildcard" exemption permits a debtor to shield her "aggregate interest in any property" she chooses, up to a stated dollar limit, § 522(d)(5); In re Smith, 640 F.2d 888, 891 (CA7 1981).

exemption column, she listed $1,850, then the maximum trade-tools exemption, and $8,868, drawn from her wildcard exemption, amounts adding up to $10,718. And in the fourth, current-market-value, column, she recorded $10,718, corresponding to the total market value she had set out in her inventory and reported in Schedule B.

Before the 30-day clock on filing objections had begun to run, an appraiser told Schwab that Reilly's equipment was worth at least $17,000. Brief for Petitioner 15; App. 164a. Nevertheless, Schwab did not object to the $10,718 market value Reilly attributed to her business equipment in Schedule C and the attached inventory. Instead, he allowed the limitations period to lapse and then moved, unsuccessfully, for permission to sell the equipment at auction.[24]

From Reilly's filings, the Bankruptcy Judge found it evident that Reilly had claimed the property itself, not its dollar value, as exempt . . . .

The District Court and Court of Appeals similarly concluded that, by listing the identical amount, $10,718, as the property's market value and the value of the claimed exemptions, Reilly had signaled her intention to safeguard all of her kitchen equipment from inclusion in the bankruptcy estate. In re Reilly, 403 B. R. 336, 338-339 (MD Pa. 2006); In re Reilly, 534 F.3d 173, 178 (CA3 2008). Both courts looked to § 522(l) and Federal Rule of Bankruptcy Procedure 4003(b), which state, respectively:

> "The debtor shall file a list of property that the debtor claims as exempt . . . . Unless a party in interest objects, the property claimed as exempt on such list is exempt." § 522(l).
>
> "A party in interest may file an objection to the list of property claimed as exempt only within 30 days after the meeting of creditors held under § 341(a) is concluded . . . . The court may, for cause, extend the time for filing objections if, before the time to object expires, a party in interest files a request for an extension." Rule 4003(b).[25]

Schwab having filed no objection within the allowable 30 days, each of the tribunals below ruled that the entire inventory of Reilly's business equipment qualified as exempt in full. App. 168a; 403 B. R., at 339; 534 F.3d at 178. The leading treatise on bankruptcy, the Court of Appeals noted, id., at 180, n. 4, is in accord:

> "Normally, if the debtor lists property as exempt, that listing is interpreted as a claim for exemption of the debtor's entire interest in the property, and the debtor's valuation of that interest is treated as the amount of the exemption claimed. Were it otherwise -- that is, if the listing were construed to claim as exempt only that portion of the property having the value stated -- the provisions finalizing exemptions if no objections are filed would be rendered meaningless. The trustee or creditors could [anytime] claim that the debtor's interest in the property was greater than the value claimed as exempt and [then]

---

[24] Schwab informed Reilly at the meeting of creditors that he planned to sell all of her business equipment. App. 137a. She promptly moved to dismiss her bankruptcy petition, stating that her "business equipment . . . is necessary to her livelihood and art, and was a gift to her from her parents." She "d[id] not desire to continue with the bankruptcy," she added, because "she wishe[d] to continue in restaurant and catering as her occupation." Id. The Bankruptcy Court denied Reilly's dismissal motion simultaneously with Schwab's motion to sell Reilly's equipment.

[25] In 2008, this prescription was recodified without material change and designated Rule 4003(b)(1).

object to the debtor exempting his or her entire interest in the property after the deadline for objections had passed." 9 Collier P4003.02[1], pp. 4003-4 to 4003-5.

Agreeing with the courts below, I would hold that Reilly, by her precise identification of the exempt property, and her specification of $10,718 as both the current market value of her kitchen equipment and the value of the claimed exemptions, had made her position plain: She claimed as exempt the listed property itself -- not the dollar amount, up to $10,718, that sale of the property by Schwab might yield. Because neither Schwab nor any creditor lodged a timely objection, the listed property became exempt, reclaimed as property of the debtor, and therefore outside the bankruptcy estate the trustee is charged to administer.

II-A

Pursuant to § 522(l), Reilly filed a list of property she claimed as exempt from the estate-in-bankruptcy. Her filing left no doubt that her exemption claim encompassed her entire inventory of kitchen equipment. Schwab, in fact, was fully aware of the nature of the claim Reilly asserted. At the meeting of creditors, Reilly reiterated that she sought to keep the equipment in her possession; she would rather discontinue the bankruptcy proceeding, she made plain, than lose her equipment. See supra, at 4, n. 3. Bankruptcy Rule 4003(b) requires the trustee, if he contests the debtor's exemption claim in whole or part, to file an objection within 30 days after the meeting of creditors. Absent a timely objection, "the property claimed as exempt . . . is exempt." § 522(l); Rule 4003. That prescription should be dispositive of this case.

The Court holds, however, that Schwab was not obliged to file a timely objection to the exemption Reilly claimed, and indeed could auction off her cooking equipment anytime prior to her discharge. In so holding, the Court decrees that no objection need be made to a debtor's valuation of her property.

To support the conclusion that Rule 4003's timely objection requirement does not encompass the debtor's estimation of her property's market value, the Court homes in on the language of exemption prescriptions that are subject to a monetary cap.[26] Those prescriptions, the Court points out, "define the 'property' a debtor may 'clai[m] as exempt' as the debtor's 'interest' -- up to a specified dollar amount -- in the assets described in the category, not as the assets themselves." Ante, at 10. So long as a debtor values her claimed exemption at a dollar amount below the statutory cap, the Court reasons, the claim is on-its-face permissible no matter the market value she ascribes to the asset. To evaluate the propriety of Reilly's declared "interest" in her kitchen equipment, the Court concludes, Schwab was obliged promptly to inspect "three, and only three, entries on Reilly's Schedule C: the description of the business equipment . . .; the Code provisions

[26] Section 522(d) catalogs exemptions of two types. Most exemptions -- and all of those Reilly invoked -- place a monetary limit on the value of the property the debtor may reclaim. See, e.g., § 522(d)(2) ("motor vehicle"); § 522(d)(3) ("household furnishings, household goods, wearing apparel, appliances, books, animals, crops, or musical instruments"); § 522(d)(4) ("jewelry"). For certain exemptions not at issue here, the Bankruptcy Code authorizes reclamation of the property in full without any cap on value. See, e.g., § 522(d)(7) ("unmatured life insurance contract"); § 522(d)(9) ("[p]rofessionally prescribed health aids"); § 522(d)(11)(A) ("award under a crime victim's reparation law").

governing the claimed exemptions; and the amounts Reilly listed in the column titled 'value of claimed exemption.'"[27]

The Court's account, however, shuts from sight the vital part played by the fourth entry on Schedule C -- current market value -- when a capped exemption is claimed. A debtor who estimates a market value below the cap, and lists an identical amount as the value of her claimed exemption, thereby signals that her aim is to keep the listed property in her possession, outside the estate-in-bankruptcy. In contrast, a debtor who estimates a market value above the cap, and above the value of her claimed exemption, thereby recognizes that she cannot shelter the property itself and that the trustee may seek to sell it for whatever it is worth.[28] Schedule C's final column, in other words, alerts the trustee whether the debtor is claiming a right to retain the listed property itself as her own, a right secured to her if the trustee files no timely objection.[29]

Because an asset's market value is key to determining the character of the interest the debtor is asserting in that asset, Rule 4003(b) is properly read to require objections to valuation within 30 days, just as the Rule requires timely objections to the debtor's description of the property, the asserted legal basis for the exemption, and the claimed value of the exemption. See 4 Collier P522.05[1], p. 522-28 (rev. 15th ed. 2005) ("[T]o evaluate the propriety of the debtor's claim of exemption," trustees need the information in all four columns of Schedule C; "[market] value" is "essential" to judging whether the claim is proper because "[e]xemption provisions often are limited according to . . . [the property's] value.").[30]

---

[27] In support of its view that market value is not relevant to determining the "property claimed as exempt" for purposes of Rule 4003(b)'s timely objection mandate, the Court observes that Schedule C did not require the debtor to list this information until 1991. Ante, at 14-15. Prior to 1991, however, debtors recorded market value on a different schedule. See Interim Fed. Rule Bkrtcy. Proc. Official Form 6, Schedule B-2 (1979) (requiring debtor to list the "[m]arket value of [her] interest [in personal property] without deduction for . . . exemptions claimed"). Trustees assessing the "property claimed as exempt," therefore, have always been able, from the face of the debtor's filings, to compare the value of the claimed exemption to the property's declared market value. See Brief for National Association of Consumer Bankruptcy Attorneys et al. as Amici Curiae 34.

[28] By authorizing exemption of assets that a debtor would want to keep in kind, such as her jewelry and car, but limiting the exemptible value of this property, Congress struck a balance between debtors' and creditors' interests: Debtors can reclaim items helpful to their fresh start after bankruptcy, but only if those items are of modest value. Assets of larger worth, however, are subject to liquidation so that creditors may obtain a portion of the item's value. Cf. In re Price, 370 F.3d 362, 378 (CA3 2004) ("[B]ankruptcy law is bilateral, replete with protections and policy considerations favoring both debtors and creditors.").

[29] The significance of market value is what differentiates capped exemptions from uncapped ones that permit debtors to exempt certain property in kind regardless of its worth. See supra, at 7, n. 5. For uncapped exemptions, the nature of the property the debtor has reclaimed is clear: If the exemption is valid, the debtor gets the asset in full every time. For capped exemptions, however, market value is a crucial component in determining whether the debtor gets the item itself or a sum of money representing a share of the item's liquidation value. Reading Bankruptcy Rule 4003(b) to require objections to valuation thus does not, as the Court contends, "elid[e] the distinction" between capped and uncapped exemptions, ante, at 12 (emphasis added), but instead accounts for that distinction.

[30] Suggesting that this interpretation of Rule 4003(b) "lacks statutory support," the Court repeatedly emphasizes that the Bankruptcy Code defines the "property claimed as exempt," to which a trustee must object, as "the debtor's 'interest' -- up to a specified dollar amount -- in the assets described in [capped exemption] categor[ies]," But the commonly understood definition of a property "interest" is "[a] legal share in something; all or part of a legal or equitable claim to or

C

Requiring objections to market valuation notably facilitates the debtor's fresh start, and thus best fulfills the prime purpose of the exemption prescriptions. See, e.g., Burlingham v. Crouse, 228 U.S. 459, 473 (1913) (Bankruptcy provisions "must be construed" in light of policy "to give the bankrupt a fresh start."). See also Rousey v. Jacoway, 544 U.S. 320, 325 (2005); United States v. Security Industrial Bank, 459 U.S. 70, 72, n. 1 (1982). The 30-day deadline for objections, this Court has recognized, "prompt[s] parties to act and . . . produce[s] finality." Taylor v. Freeland & Kronz, 503 U.S. 638, 644 (1992). As "there can be no possibility of further objection to the exemptions" after this period elapses, the principal bankruptcy treatise observes, "if the debtor is not yet in possession of the property claimed as exempt, it should be turned over to [her] at this time to effectuate fully the fresh start purpose of the exemptions." 9 Collier P4003.03[3], p. 4003-13.

With the benefit of closure, and the certainty it brings, the debtor may, at the end of the 30 days, plan for her future secure in the knowledge that the possessions she has exempted in their entirety are hers to keep. See 534 F.3d at 180. If she has reclaimed her car from the estate, for example, she may accept a job not within walking distance. See Brief for National Association of Consumer Bankruptcy Attorneys et al. as Amici Curiae 2-3 (hereinafter NACBA Brief). Or if she has exempted her kitchen equipment, she may launch a new catering venture. See App. 138a (Reilly "wishe[d] to continue in restaurant and catering as her occupation" postbankruptcy.).

By permitting trustees to challenge a debtor's valuation of exempted property anytime before discharge, the Court casts a cloud of uncertainty over the debtor's use of assets reclaimed in full. If the trustee gains a different opinion of an item's value months, even years, after the debtor has filed her bankruptcy petition,[31] he may seek to repossess the asset, auction it off, and hand the debtor a check for the dollar amount of her claimed exemption.[32] With this threat looming until discharge, "[h]ow can debtors reasonably be expected to restructure their affairs"? NACBA Brief 25. See In re Polis, 217 F.3d 899, 903 (CA7 2000) (Posner, J.) ("If the assets sought to be exempted by the debtor were not valued at a date early in the bankruptcy proceeding, neither the debtor nor the creditors would know who had the right to them.").

---

right in property . . . . Collectively, the word includes any aggregation of [such] rights." Black's Law Dictionary 828 (8th ed. 2004). Schwab, therefore, could not comprehend whether Reilly claimed a monetary or an in-kind "interest" in her kitchen equipment without comparing her market valuation of the equipment to the value of her claimed exemption. In line with the statutory text, a debtor's market valuation is an essential factor in determining the nature of the "interest" a debtor lists as exempt. Bankruptcy "forms, rules, treatise excerpts, and policy considerations," corroborate, rather than conflict with, this reading of the Code.

[31] Schwab states that "[c]ases in which there are assets to administer . . . can take 'one to four years' to complete." Brief for Petitioner 32 (quoting Dept. of Justice, U.S. Trustee Program, Preliminary Report on Chapter 7 Asset Cases 1994 to 2000, p. 7 (June 2001)).

[32] Money generated by liquidation of an asset will often be of less utility to a debtor, who will have to pay more to replace the item. See H. R. Rep. No. 95-595, p. 127 (1977) (noting that "household goods have little resale value" but "replacement costs of the goods are generally high").

III

The Court and Schwab raise three concerns about reading Rule 4003 to require timely objection to the debtor's estimate of an exempt asset's market value: Would trustees face an untoward administrative burden? Would trustees lack fair notice of the need to object? And would debtors be tempted to undervalue their property in an effort to avoid the monetary cap on exemptions? In my judgment, all three questions should be answered no.

A

The Court suggests that requiring timely objections to a debtor's valuation of exempt property would saddle trustees with an unmanageable load. See ante, at 18 (declining to "expand . . . the universe of information an interested party must consider in evaluating the validity of a claimed exemption"). See also Brief for Petitioner 32-33; Brief for United States as Amicus Curiae 24.[33] But trustees, sooner or later, must attempt to ascertain the market value of exempted assets. They must do so to determine whether sale of the items would likely produce surplus proceeds for the estate above the value of the claimed exemption, see § 704(a)(1); the only question, then, is when this market valuation must occur -- (1) within 30 days or (2) at any time before discharge? Removing valuation from Rule 4003's governance thus does little to reduce the labors trustees must undertake.

The 30-day objection period, I note, does not impose on trustees any additional duty, but rather guides the exercise of existing responsibilities; under Rule 4003(b), a trustee must rank evaluation of the debtor's exemptions as a priority item in his superintendence of the estate.[34] And if the trustee entertains any doubt about the accuracy of a debtor's estimation of market value, the procedure for interposing objections is hardly arduous. The trustee need only file with the court a simple declaration stating that an item's value exceeds the amount listed by the debtor.[35]

---

[33] This concern is questionable in light of the prevailing practice, for, as earlier noted, valuation objections are the most common Rule 4003(b) challenge. By lopping off valuation disagreements from the timely objection requirement, the Court so severely shrinks the Rule's realm that this question arises: Why are trustees granted a full 30 days to lodge objections? Under the Court's reading of the Rule, trustees need only compare a debtor's Schedule C to the text of the exemption prescriptions to assess an exemption claim's facial validity, with no further investigation necessary. That comparison should take no more than minutes, surely not a month.

[34] Trustees, it bears noting, historically had valuation duties far more onerous than they have today. Rule 4003's predecessor required trustees in the first instance, rather than debtors, to estimate the market value of property claimed as exempt. See Rule 403(b) (1975). Trustees had to provide this valuation to the court within 15 days of their appointment.

[35] The leading bankruptcy treatise supplies an illustrative valuation objection:

> "[Name of Trustee], the duly qualified and acting trustee of the estate of the debtor, would show the court the following:
>
> "1. The debtor is not entitled under [the automobile exemption] to an interest of more than $3,225 in an automobile. The automobile claimed by debtor as exempt . . . has a value substantially greater than $3,225.
>
> . . . .
>
> "WHEREFORE Trustee prays that the court determine that debtor is not entitled to . . . the exemptio[n] claimed by him, that the [property claimed as

If the trustee needs more than 30 days to assess market value, moreover, the time period is eminently extendable. Rule 4003(b) prescribes that a trustee may, for cause, ask the court for an extension of the objection period. Alternatively, the trustee can postpone the conclusion of the meeting of creditors, from which the 30-day clock runs, simply by adjourning the meeting to a future date. Rule 2003(e). A trustee also may examine the debtor under oath at the creditors' meeting, Rule 2003(b)(1); if he gathers information impugning her exemption claims, he may ask the bankruptcy court to hold a hearing to determine valuation issues, Rule 4003(c). See Taylor, 503 U.S., at 644 ("If [the trustee] did not know the value of [a claimed exemption], he could have sought a hearing on the issue . . . or . . . asked the Bankruptcy Court for an extension of time to object."). See also NACBA Brief 19, 21-23 (listing ways trustees may enlarge the limitations period for objections). Trustees, in sum, have ample mechanisms at their disposal to gain the time and information they need to lodge objections to valuation.

B

On affording trustees fair notice of the need to object, the Court emphasizes that a debtor must list her claimed exemptions "in a manner that makes the scope of the exemption clear." If a debtor wishes to exempt property in its entirety, for example, the Court counsels her to write "full fair market value (FMV)" or "100% of FMV" in Schedule C's value-of-claimed-exemption column. See also In re Hyman, 967 F.2d 1316, 1319-1320, n. 6 (CA9 1992) (Trustees must be able to assess the validity of an exemption from the face of a debtor's schedules.). Our decision in Taylor v. Freeland & Kronz, the Court notes, is instructive. In Taylor, the debtor recorded the term "$unknown" as the value of a claimed exemption, which, the Court observes, raised a "warning fla[g]" because the value "was not plainly within the limits the Code allows."

True, a debtor's schedules must give notice sufficient to cue the trustee that an objection may be in order. But a "warning flag" is in the eye of the beholder: If a debtor lists identical amounts as the market value of exempted property and the value of her claimed exemption, she has, on the face of her schedules, reclaimed the entire asset just as surely as if she had recorded "100% of FMV" in Schedule C's value-of-claimed-exemption column. See Brief for Respondent 36. See also 9 Collier P4003.03[3], p. 4003-14 ("Only when a debtor's schedules specifically value the debtor's interest in the property at an amount higher than the amount claimed as exempt can it be argued that a part of the debtor's interest in property has not been exempted." (emphasis added)).

In this case, by specifying $10,718 as both the current market value of her kitchen equipment and the value of her claimed exemptions, Reilly gave notice that she had reclaimed the listed property in full. To borrow the Court's terminology, Reilly waved a "warning flag" that should have prompted Schwab to object if he believed the equipment could not be reclaimed in its entirety because its value exceeded the statutory cap. 534 F.3d at 179. See 4 Collier P522.05[2][b], p. 522-33 ("Normally, if a debtor lists an asset as having a particular

exempt] which [is] disallowed be turned over to the trustee herein as property of the estate, and that he have such other and further relief as is just." 13A Collier § CS17.14, p. CS 17-22 (rev. 15th ed. 2009). See also Rules 9013-9014.

value in the schedules and then exempts that value, the schedules should be read as a claim of exemption for the entire asset, to which the trustee should object if the trustee believes the asset has been undervalued.").

Training its attention on trustees' needs, moreover, the Court overlooks the debtor's plight. As just noted, the Court counsels debtors wishing to exempt an asset in full to write "100% of FMV" or "full FMV" in the value-of-claimed-exemption column. But a debtor following the instructions that accompany Schedule C would consider such a response nonsensical, for those instructions direct her to "state the dollar value of the claimed exemption in the space provided." Fed. Rule Bkrtcy. Proc. Official Form 6, Schedule C, Instruction 5 (1991) (emphasis added). Chapter 7 debtors are often unrepresented. How are they to know they must ignore Schedule C's instructions and employ the "warning flag" described today by the Court, if they wish to trigger the trustee's obligation to object to their market valuation in a timely fashion? See In re Anderson, 377 B. R. 865, 875 (Bkrtcy. App. Panel CA6 2007).[36]

C

Schwab finally urges that requiring timely objections to a debtor's market-value estimations "would give debtors a perverse incentive to game the system by undervaluing their assets." Brief for Petitioner 35; see Brief for United States as Amicus Curiae 27. The Court rejected an argument along these lines in Taylor, and should follow suit here. Multiple measures, Taylor explained, discourage undervaluation of property claimed as exempt. 503 U.S., at 644. Among those measures: The debtor files her exemption claim under penalty of perjury. See Rule 1008. She risks judicial sanction for signing documents not well grounded in fact. Rule 9011. And proof of fraud subjects her to criminal prosecution, 18 U.S.C. § 152; extends the limitations period for filing objections to Schedule C, Rule 4003(b); and authorizes denial of discharge, 11 U.S.C. § 727(a)(4)(B). See also NACBA Brief 29-33 (detailing additional checks against inadequate or inaccurate filings).

Furthermore, the objection procedure is itself a safeguard against debtor undervaluation. If a trustee suspects that the market value of property claimed as exempt may exceed a debtor's estimate, he should do just what Rule 4003(b) prescribes: "[F]ile an objection . . . within 30 days after the meeting of creditors."

For the reasons stated, I would affirm the Third Circuit's judgment.

Notes and Questions

1. The Schwab majority claims that Taylor is not overruled. Yet both cases involved monetarily limited exemptions. For the view that Schwab is absolutely inconsistent with Taylor, see David Gray Carlson, The Role of Valuation in the Federal Bankruptcy Exemption Process: The Supreme Court Reads Schedule C, 18 AM. BANKR. INST. L. REV. 461 (2010).

2. After Schwab, do judicial valuations play any role in the federal exemption process?

[36] Trustees, in contrast, are repeat players in bankruptcy court; if this Court required timely objections to market valuation, trustees would, no doubt, modify their practices in response. See 1 Collier P8.06[1][c][ii], p. 8-75 (rev. 15th ed. 2009) ("Since Taylor, trustees rarely fail to closely scrutinize vague exemption claims."). Moreover, because valuation objections are already the norm, few trustees would have to adjust their behavior.

IN RE COVINGTON

368 B.R. 44 (Bankr. E.D. Cal. 2006)

MICHAEL S. MCMANUS, J.

Cornelius F. Covington ("the debtor") is one of the joint debtors in this chapter 7 case. His petition was filed after the Bankruptcy Abuse Prevention and Consumer Protection Act of 2005 (BAPCPA) became effective.

The Madera County Child Support Department has filed a proof of claim on behalf of the debtor's daughter. The proof of claim demands $38,211.59 for past due child support.

11 U.S.C. § 101(14A) defines a domestic support obligation as:

> a debt that accrues before, on, or after the date of the order for relief in a case under this title, including interest that accrues on that debt as provided by applicable nonbankruptcy law notwithstanding any other provision of this title, that is- (A) owed to or recoverable by- (I) a spouse, former spouse, or child of the debtor or such child's parent, legal guardian, or responsible relative; or (ii) a governmental unit; (B) in the nature of alimony, maintenance, or support (including assistance provided by a governmental unit) of such spouse, former spouse, or child of the debtor or such child's parent, without regard to whether such debt is expressly so designated; (C) established or subject to establishment before, on, or after the date of the order for relief in a case under this title, by reason of applicable provisions of- (I) a separation agreement, divorce decree, or property settlement agreement; (ii) an order of a court of record; or (iii) a determination made in accordance with applicable nonbankruptcy law by a governmental unit; and (D) not assigned to a nongovernmental entity, unless that obligation is assigned voluntarily by the spouse, former spouse, child of the debtor, or such child's parent, legal guardian, or responsible relative for the purpose of collecting the debt.

Based on the information in the proof of claim, to which no objection has been filed, it is clear that the $38,211.59 is a domestic support obligation.

When a debt is a domestic support obligation, it cannot be discharged by an individual chapter 7 debtor. See 11 U.S.C. § 523(a)(5). Consequently, once an individual debtor receives a chapter 7 discharge, the holder of a domestic support obligation claim is not subject to the statutory injunction barring enforcement of the debt against the debtor as a personal liability. See 11 U.S.C. §§ 523(a)(5), 524(a)(2), & 727(b).

Moreover, a domestic support obligation may be enforced against property of the debtor, both during the chapter 7 case without violation of the automatic stay, and after entry of a discharge without violation of the discharge injunction. See 11 U.S.C. §§ 362(b)(2)(B) & 522(c)(1). This is so even when the property against which the domestic support obligation is being enforced has been exempted by the debtor in the bankruptcy case. See 11 U.S.C. §§ 522(c)(1). Section 522(c)(1) provides in pertinent part:

> Unless the case is dismissed, property exempted under this section is not liable during or after the case for any debt of the debtor that arose . . . before the commencement of the case, except-(1) a debt of a kind specified in paragraph . . . (5) of section 523(a) (in which case, notwithstanding any provision of applicable nonbankruptcy law to the contrary, such property shall be liable for a debt of a kind specified in section 523(a)(5)). . . .

Because the debtor in this chapter 7 case owes a domestic support obligation, the trustee argues that section 522(c)(1) requires the disallowance of the debtor's exemptions in a $1,000 bank deposit and an automobile to permit these assets to be liquidated and the proceeds paid to the holder of the domestic support obligation claim.

The trustee's objection to these exemptions will be overruled. Section 522(c)(1) does not provide for the disallowance of an exemption. Rather, it provides that property exempted by the debtor is nonetheless liable for a domestic support obligation. Disallowance of the exemption is not a predicate to the enforcement of a domestic support obligation against the property.

The next issue is whether, by virtue of section 522(c)(1), the trustee may liquidate the exempt property in order to pay the domestic support obligation. The court concludes that he may not. The trustee's motion to sell the automobile will therefore be denied.

A chapter 7 trustee must "collect and reduce to money property of the estate . . . ." See 11 U.S.C. § 704(a)(1). When a debtor exempts property, it is effectively removed from the estate.[1] See, e.g., In re Szekely, 936 F.2d 897 (7th Cir. 1991). Here, the automobile and the bank deposit have been removed from the estate by virtue of their exemption. There is no nonexempt value in either asset and neither has appreciated above the maximum exemption amount. Therefore, there is no "property of the estate" for the trustee to administer for the benefit of creditors in general or the holder of the domestic support obligation in particular.

An analogous situation, one that predates the enactment of BAPCPA, involves the enforcement of nondischargeable tax claims against exempt property. Like domestic support obligations, section 522(c)(1) permits the holder of a nondischargeable tax claim to enforce it against property the debtor has exempted in the bankruptcy case. See 11 U.S.C. § 523(a)(1). When taxes are owed, for example, to the Internal Revenue Service, section 522(c)(1) dovetails with 26 U.S.C. § 6334(c) which provides that "[n]otwithstanding any other law of the United States . . ., no property or rights to property shall be exempt from levy" unless 26 U.S.C. § 6334(a) provides an applicable exemption. Kieferdorf v. Commissioner, 142 F.2d 723 (9th Cir. 1944).

Even though this provision has been part of the Bankruptcy Code since 1979, the trustee has cited no authority indicating that he may liquidate otherwise exempt property because the debtor happens to owe a nondischargeable tax claim.

Also, while section 522(c)(1) permits the enforcement of domestic support obligation and tax claims against "property exempted under . . . section [522]," when such claims are enforced pursuant to applicable nonbankruptcy law, that law may provide the debtor with exemptions apart from section 522.

For instance, even though a debtor's exemptions under section 522(b) will not prevent the Internal Revenue Service from levying on property, it cannot levy against property of the type described in 26 U.S.C. § 6334(a). And, in California, the enforcement of a judgment for child, family, or spousal support (all of which would be encompassed within the definition of a domestic support obligation), is subject to some exemptions. See Cal. Civ. Proc. Code §§ 703.070,

[1] However, if the property declared exempt by the debtor has value beyond the exemption amount, or if it appreciates beyond the exemption amount after the petition is filed, the nonexempt amount or appreciation is property of the estate that may be administered by the trustee. See In re Hyman, 967 F.2d 1316 (9th Cir. 1992).

703.115.

Given the potential availability of these "nonbankruptcy" exemptions, in a chapter 7 case that would otherwise be a "no-asset" case, it makes more sense to require the holder of a domestic support obligation claim, not the bankruptcy trustee, to enforce a domestic support obligation in a nonbankruptcy forum. That forum then may deal with the availability and extent of nonbankruptcy exemptions.

Finally, a chapter 7 trustee generally will not administer an asset unless it will produce a net return for the estate. For instance, when an asset is fully encumbered by a lien, it is considered improper for a chapter 7 trustee to liquidate the asset. See e.g., In re Preston Lumber Corp., 199 B.R. 415 (Bankr. N.D. Cal. 1996).

While the trustee's motion to sell does not involve the sale of fully encumbered property, the property is being liquidated for the benefit of just one creditor - the holder of the domestic support obligation claim - rather than unsecured creditors generally. Given that the Madera County Child Support Department is collecting the claim for the benefit of the claim holder, it is clear that the assistance of the trustee, which would come at a price, is unnecessary. By enforcing the domestic support obligation in state court, the trustee's administrative expenses will be avoided. Cf. Williams v. California 1st Bank, 859 F.2d 664 (9th Cir. 1988) (holding that it is improper for a trustee to liquidate claims that benefit only select creditors with the only benefit to the estate being the recoupment of administrative costs).

For these reasons, the trustee's objections to the debtor's exemptions will be overruled and his motion to sell the automobile will be denied. . .

Notes and Questions

1. Notice that § 522(c)(1) purports to overrule state exemption law with regard to domestic support obligations. Presumably the section applies only if a debtor has filed for bankruptcy and has claimed exemptions. The implication of § 522(c)(1) is that a domestic creditor may have all of a debtor's property that has passed out of the bankruptcy estate by the debtor's claim of exemption. Presumably, § 522(c)(1) does not apply to a debtor's postpetition wages, which are not exempt but are excluded from the bankruptcy estate under § 541(a)(6). See Alan M. Ahart, The Liability of Property Exempted in Bankruptcy for Pre-Petition Domestic Support obligations After BAPCPA: Debtors Beware, 81 AM. BANKR. L.J. 233 (2007).

2. State opt-out

RICHARDSON v. SCHAFER (IN RE SCHAFER)

689 F.3d 601 (6th Cir. 2012), cert. denied, 133 S. Ct. 1244 (2013)

COLE, J.

The Constitution's Bankruptcy Clause grants Congress the power to establish "uniform Laws on the subject of Bankruptcies throughout the United States[,]" U.S. Const. art. I, § 8, cl. 4, and its Supremacy Clause makes the laws that Congress passes pursuant to that power the "supreme Law of the Land[,]" U.S. Const. art. VI, cl. 2. The question before this Court is whether, in light of those provisions, a state may enact an exemption scheme that applies only to debtors in bankruptcy. The bankruptcy trustee argues that a state may not, that such a law would violate both the Bankruptcy Clause and the Supremacy Clause. The debtor and the State of Michigan disagree. They argue that the interpretation given to the phrase "uniform Laws" by both the Supreme Court and this Court permits states to act in the arena of bankruptcy exemptions even if they do so by making certain exemptions available only to debtors in bankruptcy, and that such exemptions schemes are not invalidated by the Supremacy Clause. We agree, and thus AFFIRM the judgment of the bankruptcy court and hold that Michigan's bankruptcy-specific exemption statute, Mich. Comp. Laws § 600.5451, is constitutionally sound.

I. BACKGROUND

In March 2009, Steven Schafer, the debtor-appellant, filed a petition under Chapter 7 of the Bankruptcy Code. Richardson v. Schafer (In re Schafer), 455 B.R. 590, 592 (B.A.P. 6th Cir. 2011). Michigan law permits debtors in bankruptcy to choose their exemptions from those set forth in 11 U.S.C. § 522(d), from a set of general exemptions available to all Michigan residents irrespective of their bankruptcy status, Mich. Comp. Laws § 600.6023, or from a list of exemptions available solely to debtors in bankruptcy, Mich. Comp. Laws § 600.5451.

Schafer elected to claim a homestead exemption under the last of these, which permits bankruptcy debtors--and only bankruptcy debtors--to exempt up to $30,000 of the value of the home, or up to $45,000 if the debtor is over the age of 65 or disabled. Mich. Comp. Laws § 600.5451(1)(n). These figures are adjusted for inflation triennially, such that Schafer, who is disabled, claimed a total exemption of $44,695 in the value of his home. Schafer, 455 B.R. at 592 . . . The homestead exemption contained in § 600.5451 is substantially more generous than either its federal counterpart ($21,625), 11 U.S.C. § 522(d)(1), or the Michigan general homestead exemption ($3,500), Mich. Comp. Laws § 600.6023(1)(h).

Thomas Richardson, the trustee-appellee ("Trustee"), subsequently filed an objection to Schafer's use of § 600.5451's exemption scheme. Schafer, 455 B.R. at 592. The Trustee argued that the bankruptcy-specific exemption statute violates the Bankruptcy Clause, as well as the Supremacy Clause.

The Bankruptcy Court for the Western District of Michigan held the bankruptcy-specific exemption scheme constitutional. In re Jones, 428 B.R. 720, 721 (Bankr. W.D. Mich. 2010). In so doing, the bankruptcy court relied on Supreme Court and Sixth Circuit precedent, including our decision in Rhodes v. Stewart, 705 F.2d 159 (6th Cir. 1983), for the proposition that states have concurrent authority to promulgate laws governing exemptions applicable in bankruptcy cases. Jones, at 428 B.R. at 723 The bankruptcy court suggested that Rhodes was at odds with another of our decisions, Hood v. Tennessee Student Assistance Corp., 319 F.3d 755 (6th Cir. 2003), aff'd on other grounds, 541 U.S. 440 (2004), over whether Congress retained exclusive authority to implement bankruptcy laws. Jones, 428 B.R. at 727. After conducting a lengthy inquiry into the history of the "uniform Laws" language of the Constitution's Bankruptcy Clause , and taking into account the binding effect of Rhodes on our later decision in Hood, the bankruptcy court adopted the reasoning set forth in Rhodes to hold that Michigan's concurrent authority appropriately permitted § 600.5451's enactment. Id. The bankruptcy court also concluded that the law at issue here, § 600.5451(1)(n), was not in actual conflict with the system provided for by the Bankruptcy Code. Id. The bankruptcy court's decision, however, conflicted with other decisions from that district that had invalidated § 600.5451. See In re Pontius , 421 B.R. 814 (Bankr. W.D. Mich. 2009); In re Wallace, 347

B.R. 626 (Bankr. W.D. Mich. 2006).

The Trustee appealed to the United States Bankruptcy Appellate Panel of the Sixth Circuit ("BAP"), at which point the State of Michigan moved to intervene in support of Schafer's position. The BAP granted the motion, but nonetheless reversed the bankruptcy court and found the bankruptcy-specific exemption statute unconstitutional, Schafer, 455 B.R. at 591.

The BAP relied in part on our decision in Hood to hold that, in general, Congress has exclusive authority to promulgate bankruptcy laws. Rhodes, the BAP held, stood for the proposition that states have concurrent jurisdiction in the area of bankruptcy exemptions, but only because Congress affirmatively delegated that power; the power to create a bankruptcy-specific exemption statute was, according to the BAP, outside the scope of that delegation. Id. at 603. The BAP further held that even if such a power were within the scope of the delegation, the Constitution's Bankruptcy Clause requires "geographic uniformity" between the exemptions available to a debtor in bankruptcy and a debtor outside of bankruptcy. Id. at 606. Finding that § 600.5451 precluded such geographic uniformity, and was thus unconstitutional, the BAP declined to consider the bankruptcy court's Supremacy Clause analysis. Id. The State of Michigan timely appealed the BAP's judgment to this Court.

II. ANALYSIS . . .

A. The Power to Pass Bankruptcy Legislation

As an initial matter, the parties disagree on which entities are vested with the power to pass laws directly affecting the bankruptcy process. The Trustee argues that by virtue of its application solely to debtors in bankruptcy, Michigan's bankruptcy-specific exemption statute is a "bankruptcy law." A general exemption statute, on the other hand, is a "non-bankruptcy law" because all debtors, regardless of bankruptcy status, may take advantage of it to shield assets from creditors. The "uniform Laws" language of the Bankruptcy Clause, the Trustee contends, endows Congress with the exclusive authority to pass bankruptcy laws, and Michigan overstepped its bounds when it passed §600.5451.[2]

In support of his exclusivity argument, the Trustee directs our attention to language in Hood describing the original understanding of the Bankruptcy Clause: "As it was initially understood, the Bankruptcy Clause represented the states' total grant of their power to legislate on bankruptcy. . . . The authority was understood to be exclusive because any lesser grant would have defeated the grant's original purpose." Hood, 319 F.3d at 764. Such a system would permit the bankruptcy process to rise "above individual states' interests." Id. The Trustee, as became clear during oral argument, believes that any statutory developments since the Constitution's passage may only abrogate such exclusivity if the legislative intent to do so is manifest. What the Trustee does not do, however, is provide us with a full picture of the Hood Court's analysis of such exclusive power. In the very next paragraph, we explained that "this understanding that the federal power was exclusive eventually gave way to an acceptance that states

[2] It bears noting that the Trustee's argument here differs from his other uniformity argument, discussed below; here, the Trustee argues that the "uniform Laws" language serves as a procedural restraint that restricts states from acting at all, whereas below he argues that the language acts as a substantive standard against which to judge a bankruptcy law.

could, in the absence of federal legislation, pass laws on bankruptcy . . . ." Id. at 765. Hood, which resolved whether Congress could properly abrogate a state's sovereign immunity pursuant to § 106 of the Bankruptcy Code, does not stand as an unyielding barrier to state action in the bankruptcy field.

The bankruptcy court, as well as the debtor in this case, calls our attention to our earlier pronouncements in Rhodes, in which we stated that "[i]t is fundamental that the state and federal legislatures share concurrent authority to promulgate bankruptcy laws . . . ." Rhodes, 705 F.2d at 163. Unlike the bankruptcy court, we do not read Rhodes to conflict with Hood, which had nothing to do with the issue of exemptions and, therefore, did not discuss Rhodes. Under those precedents, the states retain the power to act where the federal government has declined to do so (Hood) or where, as in the area of exemptions, it has decided to permit the states to act (Rhodes). And perhaps presciently, for our purposes anyway, the Rhodes Court noted that "the Supremacy Clause and the doctrine of preemption will serve to invalidate state promulgations to the extent that they are inconsistent with or contrary to federal laws." Id.

Rhodes emphasizes the importance of 11 U.S.C. § 522(b)(2), the "opt-out" provision, which permits a state to preclude its citizens from utilizing the federal exemption scheme outlined in § 522(d). The decision explained that "Congress did not intend to preempt bankruptcy exemptions through promulgation of 11 U.S.C. § 522(d) since it vested in the states the ultimate authority to determine their own bankruptcy exemptions [via §522(b)(2)]."[3] Id. Rhodes, in turn, was cited approvingly in Storer v. French (In re Storer), wherein we noted that "the states are empowered to create whatever exemptions they elect . . . ." 58 F.3d 1125, 1128 (6th Cir. 1995) (quoting Rhodes, 705 F.2d at 163).

The Trustee's arguments would be better received had Congress decided to require all bankruptcy debtors to use the federal exemptions, but such a scheme was specifically considered and rejected with the enactment of the Bankruptcy Code. Sensing a need for reform of the exemption scheme in place under the Bankruptcy Act, Congress tasked a legislative commission with modernizing bankruptcy laws to address a "[l]ack of uniformity in the treatment of debtors." See Eric A. Posner, The Political Economy of the Bankruptcy Reform Act of 1978, 96 Mich. L. Rev. 47, 68 (1997) (citing Report of the Comm'n on the Bankr. Laws of the United States, H.R. Doc. No. 93-137, at 4 (1973)). That commission recommended adopting a set of uniform federal exemptions, but a "last minute compromise thwarted this attempt at uniformity." Marla D. Wells, Note, Federal Bankruptcy Exemptions: How Far Out Is Opting Out?, 37 Baylor L. Rev. 811, 814 (1985). Unfortunately, there is "scant available legislative history" that could provide an insight into what the drafters intended the scope of the opt-out provision to be. James B. Haines, Jr., Section 522's Opt-Out Clause: Debtors' Bankruptcy Exemptions in a Sorry State, 1983 Ariz. St. L.J. 1, 8 (1983).

Some have divined from such legislative tea leaves--or more accurately, from the lack of any such tea leaves--a congressional intent to prohibit states from enacting bankruptcy-specific exemption statutes. For example, in a decision relied on by the Trustee, one bankruptcy court held that "in adopting 11 U.S.C. § 522(b)(3), Congress did not intend to allow a bankruptcy debtor to claim

[3] Rhodes referred to § 522(b)(1), though the relevant language is now contained in § 522(b)(2). See Pub. L. 109-8, 119 Stat. 55.

exemptions under a state bankruptcy-specific exemption law." In re Reinhart, 460 B.R. 466, 467 (Bankr. E.D. Mich. 2011). In so holding, the Reinhart court relied in part on Hanover Nat'l Bank v. Moyses, 186 U.S. 181, 187 (1902). Based on Moyses, the bankruptcy court found that "it is clear that in adopting the 1898 Bankruptcy Act, Congress intended only that a state's exemptions from execution on a judgment would be applicable in bankruptcy, because such a constraint is necessary to meet the constitutional uniformity requirement." Reinhart, 460 B.R. at 468. That court also noted that the absence of any legislative history of the Bankruptcy Code discussing a change in the law of exemptions to permit states to enact bankruptcy-specific exemptions schemes provided support for its view that Congress did not intend such a change; if Congress had so intended, § 522(b)(3) would have been unconstitutional under the interpretation of the Bankruptcy Clause set forth in Moyses. Id. at 469.

The argument regarding congressional intent is not well taken. "In such a substantial overhaul of the system [as that made by the Bankruptcy Code], it is not appropriate or realistic to expect Congress to have explained with particularity each step it took." United States v. Ron Pair Enters., Inc., 489 U.S. 235, 240 (1989). "Rather, as long as the statutory scheme is coherent and consistent, there generally is no need for a court to inquire beyond the plain language of the statute." Id. at 240-41. The plain language of § 522(b) demonstrates unambiguously that "Congress has not seen fit to restrict the authority delegated to the states by requiring that state exemptions apply equally to bankruptcy and non-bankruptcy cases," such that "we are without authority to impose such a requirement." Sheehan v. Peveich, 574 F.3d 248, 252 (4th Cir. 2009). Statutes ought to be construed as constitutional when fairly possible, Eubanks, 937 F.2d at 1122, and, for the reasons explained below, an interpretation of § 522 that permits states to enact bankruptcy-specific exemptions schemes does not run afoul of either the Bankruptcy or Supremacy Clauses of the Constitution.

The BAP contended that reliance on Rhodes and Storer is not enough to legitimate § 600.5451, given that those cases do "not lead to the conclusion that states are allowed to take the affirmative step of enacting legislation that applies only to state residents who file for bankruptcy." Schafer, 455 B.R. at 604. Thus, the BAP asserts, the power to forbid is not the same as the power to create, id. at 604, and a bankruptcy-specific statute like § 600.5451 is outside the scope of Congress's limited delegation of power. But this interpretation misunderstands the concept of concurrent jurisdiction in the area of bankruptcy exemptions, and imputes, without a basis to do so, a limit onto a state's power to act. As the Rhodes Court explained, states are permitted to act in this arena, with the proviso that the Supremacy Clause and the doctrine of preemption will invalidate such laws if necessary. 705 F.2d at 163.

In reaching its conclusion, the BAP analyzed a number of arguments set forth by other courts that had concluded that because § 522(b)(3)(A) allowed debtors to exempt property under "[s]tate or local law that is applicable," Congress authorized states to pass statutes like § 600.5451. Schafer, 455 B.R. at 603. The BAP disagreed, finding that such arguments "conflate[] two different rights: that is, the debtor's right to exempt property under applicable state law, with the states' right to enact legislation which must satisfy Constitutional requirements." Id. at 604. Put simply, the BAP contends that Congress's enactment of § 522(b) was a grant of power to debtors, and not a general grant of power to states. Therefore, "[t]he states' 'concurrent jurisdiction' is limited to 'opting-out' or passing laws which apply to all state residents." Id.

That § 522(b)'s ambit is so cabined finds no basis in our precedent. To the contrary, Rhodes speaks to a state's power to enact particular legislation. Rhodes, 705 F.2d at 163 ("Congress . . . vested in the states the ultimate authority to determine their own bankruptcy exemptions [and § 522(b)(2)] encompasses no facial restrictions upon the states' authority to opt-out."). Other courts have found that such a construction of § 522(b)(2) is improper, given that other parts of the Bankruptcy Code refer to state or local law, yet it is without dispute that in those sections it would be improper for states to legislate:

> Throughout the Bankruptcy Code, Congress has referred to "state or local law" without the phrase "non-bankruptcy" and, by doing so, has not implicitly "permitted states to pass their own bankruptcy laws on the subject." See, e.g., 11 U.S.C. § 346(b) which requires a trustee to withhold amounts from the payment of wage claims "under applicable state or local tax law." Does this mean that a state or locality could promulgate a tax law applicable only to trustees in bankruptcy imposing a higher withholding level for bankruptcy claimants or more onerous withholding duties on trustees? Also, consider 11 U.S.C. § 506(b) which allows a secured creditor to collect "fees, costs, or charges provided for under . . . State statute." Does this authorize a state to grant or deny to a secured creditor the right to collect such fees only in federal bankruptcy cases?

In re Pontius, 421 B.R. at 818 n.9. The distinction between the statutes discussed in Pontius and § 522(b) is that § 522(b) implicitly authorizes states to preempt federal law on the subject of exemptions, Rhodes, 705 F.2d at 163, and to create their own exemption schemes. These other statutes, such as §§ 346(b) and 506(b), permit no similar act.

Our understanding of Rhodes, § 522(b), and the "uniform Laws" language of the Bankruptcy Clause supports our view that Michigan retains the power to pass a law like § 600.5451. States are afforded a wide berth in the exemptions arena. "The Bankruptcy Code allows the States to define what property a debtor may exempt from the bankruptcy estate that will be distributed among his creditors[,]" and "[n]othing in [§ 522(b)] limits a State's power to restrict the scope of its exemptions . . . ." Owen v. Owen, 500 U.S. 305, 306, 308 (1991). That Michigan has the power to pass such a law does not end the inquiry; that law must also be compliant with the substantive limitations of the Bankruptcy and Supremacy Clauses.

B. The Requirement of Uniformity

The Bankruptcy Clause of the Constitution grants Congress the authority to establish "uniform Laws on the subject of Bankruptcies throughout the United States[.]" U.S. Const. art. I, § 8, cl. 4. The "uniform Laws" language serves as a substantive limit on statutory acts, but is not meant to act as a "straightjacket that forbids" distinguishing among different classes of debtors. Ry. Labor Execs. Ass'n v. Gibbons, 455 U.S. 457, 469 (1982). We have previously rejected formalistic approaches to uniformity in bankruptcy, because doing so "overlooks the flexibility inherent in the constitutional provision . . . ." Schultz v. United States, 529 F.3d 343, 354 (6th Cir. 2008) (quoting Blanchette v. Conn. Gen. Ins. Corps., 419 U.S. 102, 158 (1974)).

The only decision by a federal court of appeals that has addressed the uniformity requirement of the Bankruptcy Clause in the context of a state's bankruptcy-specific exemption statute concluded that the statute did not violate the uniformity requirement. See Kulp v. Zeman (In re Kulp), 949 F.2d 1106, 1109 n.3 (10th Cir. 1991) ("Defendants . . . argue in the alternative that Colo. Rev. Stat. § 13-54-104 violates the constitution's uniformity requirement for bankruptcy laws because it creates a bankruptcy exemption which is not available to other Colorado debtors. This argument is meritless. [It] confuse[s] the geographical uniformity doctrine with the well-established principle that states may pass laws which do not conflict with the federal scheme. . . . In this case, we have no conflict because 11 U.S.C. § 522 expressly delegates to states the power to create bankruptcy exemptions.") (internal citations omitted). For the reasons stated below, we reach the same conclusion.

The bankruptcy court determined that the uniformity requirement applied only to federal enactments, and was thus not relevant to the instant inquiry. Jones, 428 B.R. at 729 n.9. The BAP disagreed, holding that "[a] state law which applies only to debtors in bankruptcy must be analyzed under the uniformity requirement of the Bankruptcy Clause." Schafer, 455 B.R. at 601. Implicit in this argument is the notion that § 600.5451 was passed pursuant to a delegation of Congress's Bankruptcy Clause power, so any resultant laws must be bound in the same way as if passed by the federal legislature. But any such delegation would have been pursuant to 11 U.S.C. § 522(b)(2), and we have previously, and repeatedly, held that § 522(b)(2) "is not an unconstitutional delegation of congressional legislative power but rather is merely a recognition of the concurrent legislative power of the state legislatures to enact laws governing bankruptcy exemptions." Storer, 58 F.3d at 1129 (quoting Rhodes, 705 F.2d at 164). Regardless, we need not decide whether the Bankruptcy Clause's introductory phrase applies to state enactments, because even if it does, § 600.5451 meets the requirements of the Bankruptcy Clause.

1. Development of uniformity jurisprudence

Prior to Congress's decision to adopt a uniform national framework for bankruptcy, states were understood to have power to pass insolvency legislation. "So long as there is no national bankrupt act, each state has full authority to pass insolvent laws binding persons and property within its jurisdiction . . . ." Brown v. Smart, 145 U.S. 454, 457 (1892). Upon national action, however, states lost such power. Moyses, 186 U.S. at 187. Moyses, which upheld the 1898 Bankruptcy Act, answered whether the adoption of state exemption schemes made the Bankruptcy Act invalid for want of uniformity. The Moyses Court ultimately held that a bankruptcy exemption system "is, in the constitutional sense, uniform throughout the United States, when the trustee takes in each state whatever would have been available to the creditor if the bankrupt[cy] law had not been passed." Moyses, 186 U.S. at 190. The Trustee argues, and the BAP held, that this language establishes § 600.5451's infirmity. According to the Trustee, "[t]he bankruptcy-specific exemption statute fails the 'geographic' uniformity test by not affording a trustee in bankruptcy the same opportunities as a creditor or receiver outside of bankruptcy." Schafer, 455 B.R. at 606. This argument fails on multiple levels.

First, the portion of Moyses that the BAP and the Trustee latch onto focuses on whether federal bankruptcy law may recognize exemptions permitted by the various states even though the states' exemptions schemes are not uniform with one another. Two sentences prior to the passage on which the Trustee relies, the Supreme Court stated that "[i]t is quite proper . . . to confine [federal bankruptcy law's] operation to such property as other legal process could reach."

Moyses, 186 U.S. at 190. The Moyses Court was not addressing whether bankruptcy and non-bankruptcy debtors must be treated alike, but rather whether a scheme whereby bankruptcy debtors in different states enjoy different exemptions is ultimately proper.

Second, in Moyses the Supreme Court did not hold that a bankruptcy exemption scheme is uniform in the constitutional sense only if the trustee takes in each state whatever would have been available if the bankruptcy law had not been passed. Rather, the Supreme Court held that "[t]he laws passed on the subject [of bankruptcy] must . . . be uniform throughout the United States, but that uniformity is geographical, and not personal," and further stated that "we do not think that the provision of the [Bankruptcy Act] as to exemptions is incompatible with the rule." Id. at 188. In other words, the general rule of law laid down by the Supreme Court in Moyses was that the uniformity requirement is geographical and that variations resulting from differences in state law are not unconstitutional. See Schultz, 529 F.3d at 353. Indeed, this Court has previously recognized that Moyses's interpretation of the uniformity requirement mandates geographical, as opposed to personal, uniformity, Schultz, 529 F.3d at 350-51, and that "[o]ver the last century, the Supreme Court has wrestled with the notion of geographic uniformity, ultimately concluding that it allows different effects in various states due to dissimilarities in state law, so long as the federal law applies uniformly among classes of debtors." Id. at 351. As explained below, taken together, § 522 and § 600.5451 apply no less uniformly among classes of debtors than did the exemption scheme that the Supreme Court found to be constitutional in Moyses.

Third, as the amici point out, full adherence to the language in Moyses on which the Trustee relies would call into doubt the constitutionality of the federal exemptions set forth in § 522(d)-- the amount of which exceed the exemptions available in certain states under their general exemption statutes. For example, the federal homestead exemption of $21,625 far exceeds Michigan's general homestead exemption of $3,500. If Michigan had not passed a bankruptcy-specific exemption statute, a debtor in Michigan (because Michigan has not opted out of the federal exemptions) could have elected to use either the general homestead exemption of $3,500 or the federal homestead exemption of $21,625. If the debtor were to elect the federal homestead exemption, the trustee would not take "whatever would have been available . . . if the bankrupt[cy] law had not been passed." Moyses, 186 U.S. at 190. And yet no one suggests that this would be impermissible, demonstrating the flaw in literal adherence to the language in Moyses on which the Trustee grounds his argument. See Sticka v. Applebaum (In re Applebaum), 422 B.R. 684, 693 (B.A.P. 9th Cir. 2009) ("The Trustee argues that under California's bankruptcy-only exemption scheme, creditors might not receive the same assets that otherwise might be available to them under California's generally applicable exemption statute. . . . However, that is exactly the result in a non-opt-out state when a debtor chooses the federal exemption scheme. In such instances, it may be that the bankruptcy trustee will not recover the same assets of a debtor for distribution that he or she would under state law.").

As one court recently noted in its discussion of Moyses, states and the federal government "have concurrent jurisdiction in bankruptcy, although only Congress has the power to establish a uniform system of bankruptcy. And once Congress passes one uniform act, if that system has differing effects on citizens of different states based on a particular state's laws, that result is acceptable." In re Westby, No. 11-40986, 473 B.R. 392, 2012 Bankr. LEXIS 1428, 2012 WL 1144412, at *5 (Bankr. D. Kan. Apr. 4, 2012).

2. Section 522 and Section 600.5451 Operate Uniformly

This Court has previously held that the Bankruptcy Clause shall act as "no limitation upon congress as to the classification of persons who are to be affected by such laws, provided only the laws shall have uniform operation throughout the United States." Leidigh Carriage Co. v. Stengel, 95 F. 637, 646 (6th Cir. 1899) (Taft, J.). And indeed, the uniformity provision has served as the basis for statutory invalidation by the Supreme Court only once--in upholding a challenge to a federal statute that, by its terms, applied to only one entity. See Gibbons, 455 U.S. at 472-73.

Our recent decision in Schultz provides additional insight into the contours of our uniformity jurisprudence. Schultz, which upheld the Bankruptcy Abuse Prevention and Consumer Protection Act of 2005 (BAPCPA) against a uniformity clause challenge, reiterated that a federal bankruptcy statute's incorporation of state laws may, without presenting any constitutional issue, "lead to different results in different states." 529 F.3d at 351 (quoting Stellwagen v. Clum, 245 U.S. 605, 613 (1918)), a view that is consistent with the interpretation of Moyses provided above. See Schultz, 529 F.3d at 353 ("Moyses, Stellwagen, and Blanchette cannot be read as standing for anything more than their precise holding: that Congress does not exceed its constitutional powers in enacting a bankruptcy law that permits variations based on state law or to solve geographically isolated problems."). Schultz clarified that it is not the outcome that determines the uniformity, but the uniform process by which creditors and debtors in a certain place are treated. "Congress may enact non-uniform laws to deal with geographically isolated problems as long as the law operates uniformly upon a given class of creditors and debtors." Id.; see also Gibbons, 455 U.S. at 473 ("[A] law must at least apply uniformly to a defined class of debtors.").

In Schultz, the debtors contended that the BAPCPA's means test--which applies only if a debtor's annualized current monthly income is above the median for the applicable state--violated the uniformity requirement because (1) the relief available to debtors under the Bankruptcy Code depends in part on the results of the means test and (2) the calculations required under the means test are based in part on the state and county in which the debtor resides. 529 F.3d at 353. We disagreed with the debtors' position, finding that the law applied uniformly to those debtors who were part of a "defined class" (i.e., those whose annualized current monthly income is above the family median income for the applicable state"). Id, at 352. "Congress is allowed to distinguish among classes of debtors, and to treat categories of debtors differently . . . ." Id. Such distinctions need not be subject to "heightened scrutiny," id. at 356, and it is not this Court's place "to pass judgment on the wisdom of congressional legislation," id. at 353. For our purposes, it is worth noting that, with limited exceptions, all bankruptcy debtors under § 600.5451 are treated the same, or uniformly, in contrast to those debtors discussed in Schultz.[4]

Quite simply, the Bankruptcy Clause does not require geographic

[4] Section 600.5451 applies differently if the debtor is elderly or disabled, and allows for a higher homestead exemption for those persons. That distinction is not being challenged.

uniformity between the exemptions available to debtors in bankruptcy and debtors outside of bankruptcy. Moreover, Michigan's decision to distinguish between debtors in bankruptcy and those outside of bankruptcy makes sense. As the amici point out, debtors in bankruptcy are often in more dire straits than those whose property is subject to levy by a specific creditor. And, as the State of Michigan points out, § 600.5451 more easily allows for bankrupt debtors to stay in their homes, updates the Michigan exemptions (at least for bankruptcy debtors) for inflation, and encourages debtors to take advantage of the bankruptcy process so as to allow for the orderly disposition of assets. The Trustee does not dispute these concerns.

Ultimately, the Trustee's arguments rely on a strained reading of the "uniform Laws" language of the Bankruptcy Clause--one that neither the Supreme Court, nor this Court, has adopted. It would be anomalous for us to hold that a federal statute under which the relief available to debtors depends in part on their state's median income is more compliant with the "uniform Laws" language than a federal statute and a state statute that, working together, treat all debtors in bankruptcy the same way. Given that the Bankruptcy Clause's "uniformity requirement was drafted in order to prohibit Congress from enacting private bankruptcy laws," Schultz, 529 F.3d at 352 (quoting Gibbons, 455 U.S. at 472), adoption of the Trustee's arguments would read into the Constitution's text requirements that simply have no basis in the precedent of the Supreme Court, our precedent, or the common law.

C. Section 600.5451 and the Supremacy Clause

The BAP declined to reach the issue of whether the bankruptcy court erred in holding that § 600.5451 does not violate the Supremacy Clause. See Schafer, 455 B.R. at 606. In the only decision by a federal court of appeals that has addressed whether a state's bankruptcy-specific exemption statute violated the Supremacy Clause, the United States Court of Appeals for the Fourth Circuit concluded that it did not, see Sheehan, 574 F.3d at 252,[5] as did the United States

[5] Relying on Rhodes, the Fourth Circuit held that "[t]here can be no preemption . . . where Congress expressly and concurrently authorizes state legislation on the subject." Sheehan, 574 F.3d at 252 (internal quotation marks omitted). "[Section 522(b)(1)] is an express delegation to the states of the power to create state exemptions in lieu of the federal bankruptcy exemption scheme." Id. "Congress has not seen fit to restrict the authority delegated to the states by requiring that state exemptions apply equally to bankruptcy and non-bankruptcy cases, and we are without authority to impose such a requirement." Id.; see also Kulp, 949 F.2d at 1109 n.3 (recognizing "the well-established principle that states may pass laws which do not conflict with the federal scheme" and stating that "we have no conflict [between the Bankruptcy Code and a state law providing for an exemption available only to debtors in bankruptcy] because 11 U.S.C. § 522 expressly delegates to states the power to create bankruptcy exemptions"). In a federal appellate decision relied on by the Trustee, Kanter v. Moneymaker (In re Kanter), 505 F.2d 228 (9th Cir. 1974), the issue was whether the bankruptcy estate had an interest in the debtor's prepetition personal injury lawsuit. There was no question that the estate had such an interest under the provisions of the Bankruptcy Act, while the interest would not be part of the estate pursuant to a California statute prohibiting "an assignee by operation of law of a party to a personal injury action [from] acquir[ing] any interest in or lien rights upon moneys recovered by such party for general damages." Id. at 230 n.1. The Ninth Circuit accepted the district court's construction of the state statute as applicable to bankruptcy trustees and then, affirming the district court, held that the statute was in conflict with the Bankruptcy Act, rendering it unconstitutional under the Supremacy Clause. See id. at 231. As explained below, there is no conflict between the Bankruptcy Code and § 600.5451.

Bankruptcy Appellate Panel of the Ninth Circuit, the only bankruptcy appellate panel that has yet addressed the issue. See Applebaum, 422 B.R. at 689. For the reasons explained below, we agree with those courts as well as the bankruptcy court below and thus reject the Trustee's challenge to § 600.5451 based on the Supremacy Clause.

"Deciding whether a state statute is in conflict with a federal statute and hence invalid under the Supremacy Clause is essentially a two-step process of first ascertaining the construction of the two statutes and then determining the constitutional question whether they are in conflict." Perez v. Campbell, 402 U.S. 637, 644 (1971). As all parties recognize, the purpose of § 600.5451 is to provide bankrupt debtors with the right to retain certain essential property and thereby emerge from bankruptcy with a fresh start. Similarly, "one of the primary purposes of [federal bankruptcy law] is to give debtors a new opportunity in life and a clear field for future effort, unhampered by the pressure and discouragement of pre-existing debt." Id, at 648 (internal quotation marks and alterations omitted); see also In re Guikema, 329 B.R. 607, 613 (Bankr. S.D. Ohio 2005) ("Exemptions give the debtors a so-called 'grubstake' to begin their fresh start and act as a safety net, so that the debtor and his family are not completely impoverished due to creditor collection action or bankruptcy such that they become wards of the state.") (internal quotation marks and alterations omitted). Seemingly, then, the statutes have similar objectives.

A state statute may conflict with federal law in one of three ways. Under "express preemption," the intent of Congress to preempt state law is explicit. R.R. Ventures, Inc. v. Surface Transp. Bd., 299 F.3d 523, 561 (2002). Under "field preemption," Congress's regulation in a field "is so pervasive or the federal interest is so dominant that an intent can be inferred for federal law to occupy the field exclusively." Id. And, under "conflict preemption," the laws in question conflict such that it is impossible for a party to comply with both laws simultaneously, or where the enforcement of the state law would hinder or frustrate the full purposes and objectives of the federal law. Id. Although there is an assumption that the federal law is not preemptive, such an assumption is not triggered "when the [s]tate regulates in an area where there has been a history of significant federal presence." United States v. Locke, 529 U.S. 89, 108 (2000). The parties agree that explicit preemption is not applicable in the instant inquiry.

This Court has previously held that Congress's regulation in the bankruptcy field is "pervasive," but did not indicate which type of preemption applied in that case. Pertuso v. Ford Motor Credit Co., 233 F.3d 417, 425 (6th Cir. 2000); see also MSR Exploration, Ltd. v. Meridian Oil, Inc., 74 F.3d 910, 913 (9th Cir. 1996) ("[T]he lengthy Bankruptcy Code, 11 U.S.C. §§ 101 et seq., demonstrates Congress's intent to create a whole system under federal control . . . ."). What is more, our disposition in Pertuso primarily rested upon a conflict, and not field, preemption analysis. Pertuso, 233 F.3d at 426 ("Permitting assertion of a host of state law causes of action to redress wrongs under the Bankruptcy Code would undermine the uniformity the Code endeavors to preserve and would stand as an obstacle to the accomplishment and execution of the full purposes of Congress.") (emphasis added) (quotation marks and alterations omitted).

In light of the Supreme Court's statement that "state laws are thus suspended only to the extent of actual conflict with the system provided by the Bankruptcy Act of Congress," Stellwagen, 245 U.S. at 613 (emphasis added), and our explanation in Rhodes that "Congress expressly authorize[d] the states to 'preempt' the federal legislation," 705 F.2d at 163, we question whether field preemption is applicable. See also In re Sullivan, 680 F.2d 1131, 1137 (7th Cir. 1982) (criticizing the use of preemption analysis when assessing state bankruptcy exemption law); Applebaum, 422 B.R. at 689 ("[F]ederal bankruptcy law is not so pervasive, nor is the federal interest so dominant, as to wholly preclude state legislation in the area."). And, given that bankruptcy exemptions were a creature of state law prior to the Bankruptcy Code's enactment in 1978, the case for field preemption is even more tenuous. See Wyeth v. Levine, 555 U.S. 555, 575 (2009) ("The case for federal pre-emption is particularly weak where Congress has indicated its awareness of the operation of state law in a field of federal interest, and has nonetheless decided to stand by both concepts and to tolerate whatever tension there is between them.") (alterations omitted) (quoting Bonito Boats, Inc. v. Thunder Craft Boats, Inc., 489 U.S. 141, 166-67 (1989)). Regardless, we need not answer whether Congress has occupied the field of bankruptcy law as a whole, because, given our reasoning in Rhodes, field preemption is inapplicable in the area of bankruptcy exemptions. As such, § 600.5451 need only be considered under a conflict-preemption framework.

The Trustee contends that in enacting § 522(b)(2) Congress sought to strike a proper balance between the competing interests of creditors and debtors. That may be true, but the Trustee's suggestion that a state's enactment of a bankruptcy-specific exemption statute would undermine such a balance goes too far. For this argument, the Trustee relies in part on In re Cross, 255 B.R. 25, 34 (Bankr. N.D. Ind. 2000). Cross invalidated Indiana's bankruptcy-specific exemption statute because it frustrated the full effectiveness of national bankruptcy laws. Yet none of the arguments put forth by the Cross court are specific to bankruptcy-specific exemption statutes; they can just as easily be made against general state exemption statutes. The Cross court tried to distinguish these two scenarios when it wrote:

> Recognizing otherwise applicable state exemptions in bankruptcy proceedings is not the same as allowing states to create exemptions just for those proceedings. The first situation simply recognizes non-bankruptcy entitlements. It allows debtors to protect the same property in bankruptcy that they could keep from creditors outside of bankruptcy. The second directly controls the distribution of assets between debtors and creditors and, thus, how the consequences of bankruptcy are allocated between them.

Cross, 255 B.R. at 34. While this is an arguably valid distinction, it is immaterial for purposes of determining whether § 600.5451 frustrates national bankruptcy policy. Assume that a state permits non-bankrupt debtors to exempt $10,000 of the value of their home from creditors, but allows bankruptcy debtors a homestead exemption in excess of the federal exemption--for example, $50,000. Also assume that another state permits all debtors, those in bankruptcy and those that are not, a $50,000 homestead exemption. It is unclear to us why whatever frustrations to national bankruptcy policy that exist under the first scenario do not also exist in the second; the Trustee does not dispute, however, that the second scenario is wholly appropriate under existing law.[6]

[6] "A few states--notably Texas and Florida--permit debtors to claim homestead exemptions in unlimited amounts, although both have acreage limitations." 3 William L. Norton, Jr., Norton Bankruptcy Law & Practice 3d § 56:10 n.10 (3d ed. 2011). Under 11 U.S.C. § 522(p) and (q), which were added in 2005 with the enactment of the BAPCPA, the amount of homestead exemptions

Were we to invalidate § 600.5451 on this basis, such frustration would still exist. And we are reticent to find unsurmountable obstacles that may result from § 600.5451's function when Congress, via § 522(b), expressly permitted variations in how states treat bankruptcy exemptions. Even if there were some conflict between § 600.5451 and the exemption policy purportedly reflected by the federal exemption amounts established in § 522, the Trustee does not make clear why this rises to the level of conflict necessary to trigger preemption. See Storer, 58 F.3d at 1128-29 ("[S]tates may enact different exemptions which would possibly conflict with Congress' own exemption policy as it was reflected in § 522(d).") (internal quotation marks omitted). "Simply because the exemptions differ from the federal exemptions (or from its non-bankruptcy counterpart), does not mean that such differences create a conflict that impedes the accomplishment and execution of the Bankruptcy Code." Applebaum, 422 B.R. at 691.

Perceiving a conflict between § 303 (providing for the commencement of involuntary bankruptcies) and bankruptcy-specific exemption statutes that allow exemptions higher than the general exemption laws, the Trustee argues that such an exemption scheme might provide a disincentive for creditors to file involuntary bankruptcy cases. As explained above, however, § 522 imposes no restrictions on the concurrent authority of the states to enact bankruptcy-specific exemption statutes. We will not read any such restrictions into another section of the Bankruptcy Code, such as §303, that has nothing to do with exemptions.

Indeed, on an as-applied basis, the Michigan statute actually furthers, rather than frustrates, national bankruptcy policy. As the Supreme Court has repeatedly noted, the goal of the Bankruptcy Code is to provide debtors in bankruptcy with a fresh start. Marrama v. Citizens Bank of Mass., 549 U.S. 365, 367 (2007) ("The principal purpose of the Bankruptcy Code is to grant a fresh start to the honest but unfortunate debtor.") (internal quotation marks omitted). By permitting debtors in bankruptcy a higher homestead exemption than either the general state exemption statute or the federal exemption statute allow, bankruptcy debtors in Michigan are better able to achieve a fresh start and to obtain "a new opportunity in life with a clear field for future effort, unhampered by the pressure and discouragement of preexisting debt." Grogan v. Garner, 498 U.S. 279, 286 (1991) (quotation marks omitted). Accordingly, Michigan's bankruptcy-specific exemption statute frustrates the full effectiveness of national bankruptcy policy no more than other statutory frameworks that have survived our scrutiny. See Storer, 58 F.3d at 1125; Rhodes, 705 F.2d at 159.

For the foregoing reasons, we AFFIRM the judgment of the bankruptcy court and conclude that Michigan's bankruptcy-specific exemption statute, Mich. Comp. Laws § 600.5451, is constitutional.

Notes and Questions

1. For a description of New York's complicated regulation of exemptions in bankruptcy, see David Gray Carlson, Critique of Money Judgment (Pt. 2: Liens on New York Personal Property), 83 ST. JOHNS L. REV. 43, 218-20 (2009).

2. If bankruptcy-only exemptions are constitutional, could a state pass a law stating that all property or no property in bankruptcy is exempt?

3. Individual retirement accounts (governed by Internal Revenue Code § 408) are often

available under state law is limited in certain instances to $146,450.

not excluded from the bankruptcy estate by §541(c)(2). Nevertheless, they are often made the subject of state exemptions. Dubroff v. First Nat'l Bank (In re Dubroff), 119 F.3d 75 (2d Cir. 1997); N.Y.C.P.L.R. § 5205(c)(2). Even if not, any debtor choosing state exemptions also can an IRA to be exempt, Bankruptcy Code § 522(b)(3)(C). Those choosing the federal exemptions can exempt an IRA per §522(d)(12). BAPCPA, however, limits the amount which can be exempted from an IRA account to $1 million. 11 U.S.C. § 522(n).

3. Federal Exemptions and Choice of Law

FERNANDEZ v MILLER (IN RE FERNANDEZ)
2011 U.S. Dist. LEXIS 86528 (W.D. Tex. August 5, 2011)

CARDONE, J.

On this day, the Court considered Alfred L. Fernandez's ("Debtor") appeal from a final order of the United States Bankruptcy Court for the Western District of Texas. Appellant has requested oral argument pursuant to Federal Rule of Bankruptcy Procedure 8012. However, after reviewing the briefs and the record, the Court has determined that oral argument is not needed because the briefs and record adequately present the facts and legal arguments. See Fed. R. Bankr. P. 8012.

For the reasons set forth below, the bankruptcy court's order is REVERSED and REMANDED.

I. BACKGROUND

The relevant facts of this case are undisputed. Debtor was born, raised, and educated in El Paso, Texas. He purchased a home in El Paso in 1987, and resided there while working in El Paso until 2000. At that time Debtor was laid off from his job in El Paso and moved to Nevada for work. He lived in Nevada until 2009, but never sold his El Paso home. He continued to make the payments on it, and always intended to keep it as his homestead. In January 2009, Debtor moved back to El Paso and took up residence at his El Paso home. He filed a petition for bankruptcy approximately one year later, on December 31, 2009. As of the date of filing his petition, Debtor held approximately $70,000 in equity in the home.

In his petition, Debtor claimed the unlimited homestead exemption under Texas law for his home. The trustee, J. Marshall Miller ("Trustee"), objected, and Debtor amended his petition, with the consent of Trustee, to claim the $550,000 homestead exemption under Nevada law instead. Trustee again objected, and after a hearing, the bankruptcy court sustained the objection and held that Debtor was not eligible to claim the Nevada exemptions. See In re Fernandez, 445 B.R. 790 (Bankr. W.D. Tex. 2011). Debtor now appeals the bankruptcy court's ruling. . . .

IV. DISCUSSION

The Court proceeds by first setting out as background the general operation of bankruptcy law in this area. Then, the Court examines the specific bankruptcy law provision that is at issue in this case. Because the precise meaning of that provision is unclear, the Court considers in turn the three different approaches courts have taken when interpreting the statute. After determining which interpretation best reflects Congress's intent, the Court proceeds to apply it to the facts of this case.

A. Application of State Homestead Exemptions in Bankruptcy

The estate in a bankruptcy proceeding consists of the property belonging to a debtor, which is to be distributed, or sold and the proceeds distributed, to the Debtor's creditors. See Owen v. Owen, 500 U.S. 305, 308 (1991). However, debtors may exempt certain property from the estate so that they might have the minimal resources needed to regain their financial footing and have a "fresh start." See In re Williams, 369 B.R. 470, 476 (Bankr. W.D. Ark. 2007); Owen, 500 U.S. at 308 ("An exemption is an interest withdrawn from the estate (and hence from the creditors) for the benefit of the debtor."). Congress has long allowed debtors to claim as exempt either the property listed in federal bankruptcy statutes or in state exemption laws. Camp v. Ingalls (In re Camp) (Camp II), 631 F.3d 757, 759-60 (5th Cir. 2011) (citing 11 U.S.C. § 522(b)(1)). However, bankruptcy law permits states to "opt-out" of the federal set of exemptions and thereby limit debtors governed by such states' law to the use of that state's exemptions. 11 U.S.C. § 522(b)(1)-(2) ("an individual debtor may exempt from property of the estate the property listed in [federal exemption law] . . . unless the State law that is applicable to the debtor . . . specifically does not so authorize"). Most states have in fact opted out, and restrict debtors subject to their laws to using the state exemptions. Graziadei v. Graziadei (In re Graziadei), 32 F.3d 1408, 1410 n.3 (9th Cir. 1994) (noting that most states, including Nevada, have opted out).

Prior to 2005, the bankruptcy statute specified that the applicable state exemption law was the law of the state that had been the debtor's domicile for the greater part of 180 days preceding the filing of the petition. 11 U.S.C. § 522(b)(2)(A) (2004); Stephens v. Holbrook (In re Stephens), 402 B.R. 1, 3 (B.A.P. 10th Cir. 2009). In 2005, through the Bankruptcy Abuse Prevention and Consumer Protection Act of 2005 ("BAPCPA"), Congress amended this section of the bankruptcy laws to extend the time that a debtor must live in a state before being able to claim that state's exemptions, from the greater part of 180 days to 730 days. In re Varanasi, 394 B.R. 430, 434 n.5 (Bankr. S.D. Ohio 2008) (citing In re Virissimo, 332 B.R. 201, 203 (Bankr. D. Nev. 2005)). Congress's purpose in extending the "look-back" window was to prevent debtors from forum-shopping by moving to a state with generous exemption laws, living there for 91 days (that being the greater part of 180 days), and then filing for bankruptcy. Stephens, 402 B.R. at 3 n.8; Drummond v. Urban (In re Urban), 375 B.R. 882, 889 (B.A.P. 9th Cir. 2007) (citing H.R. Rep. No. 109-31, pt. 1, at 15-16 (2005), reprinted in 2005 U.S.C.C.A.N. 88, 102) (describing BAPCPA as closing the "so-called 'mansion loophole,'" whereby debtors relocate to states where they can shield virtually all of the equity in their homes from their creditors); In re Bingham, No. 06-40990, 2008 Bankr. LEXIS 139, 2008 WL 186277, at (Bankr. D. Kan. Jan. 18, 2008) ("the changes to the domicile requirements for exemptions were primarily, if not solely, intended to prevent debtors from" forum-shopping to protect assets under certain states' more generous bankruptcy exemptions).

The amended statute, § 522(b), now reads,

> (1) . . . [A]n individual debtor may exempt from property of the estate the property listed in either paragraph (2) or, in the alternative, paragraph (3) of this subsection . . . .
>
> (2) Property listed in this paragraph is property that is specified under [the federal bankruptcy law exemptions], unless the State law that is applicable to the debtor under paragraph (3)(A) specifically does not so authorize.

> (3) Property listed in this paragraph is--
>
> (A) . . . any property that is exempt under Federal law, other than [the federal bankruptcy law exemptions], or State or local law that is applicable on the date of the filing of the petition to the place in which the debtor's domicile has been located for the 730 days immediately preceding the date of the filing of the petition or if the debtor's domicile has not been located in a single State for such 730-day period, the place in which the debtor's domicile was located for 180 days immediately preceding the 730-day period or for a longer portion of such 180-day period than in any other place;
>
> . . . .
>
> If the effect of the domiciliary requirement under subparagraph (A) is to render the debtor ineligible for any exemption, the debtor may elect to exempt property that is specified under subsection (d) [the federal exemptions].

The effect of the amended statute is that if a debtor has not lived in one state for the requisite 730 days preceding the filing of the petition, the law requires the debtor to use the exemption laws of the state where he lived for the greater part of the 180 days preceding that 730 day period. Stephens, 402 B.R. at 4. If that state's opt-out law prevents a debtor from choosing the federal exemptions and also prevents the debtor from using the state exemptions, then under the so-called "savings clause" or "hanging paragraph" at the end of the quoted language above, the debtor can use the federal exemptions as a fall-back. Urban, 375 B.R. at 889.

The application under the 730 day look-back provision of the exemption laws of a debtor's former state of domicile to the debtor and his property, which after the debtor's move are both likely located outside the state, is known as the extraterritorial application of state exemption law. Stephens, 402 B.R. at 4-5. As some authorities have recognized, extraterritoriality of exemption laws is best split into two aspects: whether a non-resident can use a state's exemption laws, and whether a state's exemption laws can apply to property outside the state. See In re Arrendondo-Smith, 436 B.R. 412, 417 (Bankr. W.D. Tex. 2010); In re Calhoun, 47 B.R. 119, 122-23 (Bankr. E.D. Va. 1985); Hon. W.H. Brown et al., Bankruptcy Exemption Manual § 4:6 (2010 ed.). Both aspects can affect the ultimate determination of whether a nonresident may claim protection of property, depending on the precise factual scenario. As one treatise has explained it,

> There are two major issues presented by the domiciliary changes in section 522(b). One is whether the applicable state's exemptions, typically the homestead, may be used on property located outside of that state . . . . A second, and separate, issue is whether a state permits use of its exemptions only by its residents or domiciliaries . . . . In other words, the domiciliary look-back presents questions not simply of which state's exemptions control but whether those exemptions may be used by a debtor who is no longer domiciled in, or a resident of, that state.

Brown et al., supra, § 4:6.

Although this treatise describes the issue as one created by BAPCPA, the issue of extraterritoriality is not a new one, and courts occasionally faced it pre-BAPCPA, either a result of moving debtors or simply from debtors trying to claim exemptions on property located in other states. See, e.g., Arrol v. Broach (In re Arrol), 170 F.3d 934, 935-36 (9th Cir. 1999); In re Schulz, 101 B.R. 301, 302

(Bankr. N.D. Fla. 1989); Calhoun, 47 B.R. at 121-22; see also In re Garrett, 435 B.R. 434, 439 n.5 (Bankr. S.D. Tex. 2010) (noting the similarity of the issue pre- and post-BAPCPA); Dale Joseph Gilsinger, Annotation, Extraterritorial Application of State's Homestead Exemption Pursuant to Bankruptcy Code § 522 §§ 4-5, 47 A.L.R. Fed. 2d 335 (2010) (listing other pre-BAPCPA cases finding both for and against extraterritoriality). However, the changes wrought by BAPCPA have caused the issue to arise much more frequently. See Fernandez, 445 B.R. at 803.

After BAPCPA, when the issue of extraterritorial application of state exemption law arises, it usually does so in one of two ways: first, a debtor seeks to use the state exemptions of his former state of domicile while he is residing in a new state or for property located out of state, see, e.g., Williams, 369 B.R. at 471; or second, the debtor seeks to use the federal exemptions but the opt-out law of his former state of domicile prevents him from doing so. See, e.g., Camp II, 631 F.3d at 759. The issue involved in this appeal relates to the first type of situation. Because Debtor had not lived in Texas for 730 days prior to filing his petition, he had to use the exemption law of the state where he lived for the 180 days preceding 730 days prior to filing his petition, that being Nevada. However, as a result Debtor was forced to claim the homestead exemption from a state where he no longer lives, and where his property is not located. Trustee objected to Debtor's claimed homestead exemption for this reason, arguing that Debtor could not use the "exemption of homestead property under Nevada exemption statutes for property located in Texas." Trustee's Objection to Debtors' Schedule-C Property Claimed as Exempt, In re Alfred L Fernandez, No. 09-32896-C (Bankr. W.D. Tex. June 11, 2010), ECF No. 15. The issue is a significant one for Debtor, because his assets include approximately $71,000 in equity in his home in El Paso, Texas, and the Nevada and federal homestead exemptions protect the value of his homestead to different degrees. The Nevada homestead exemption protected up $550,000 of home equity, while the federal homestead exemption as of the date Debtor filed his petition protected only $20,200 of home equity. Fernandez, 445 B.R. at 794.

Debtor argues that he may use the Nevada state exemptions either because any possible state law limits upon extraterritorial effects of state exemption law are preempted by federal bankruptcy law, or because as a matter of state law Nevada's exemptions are not limited to resident debtors or property located in Nevada. Trustee contends that the bankruptcy court below correctly determined that state exemption laws can never have extraterritorial effect, regardless of what any state's law may indicate.

B. Statutory Interpretation

The issue on appeal is at its core one of statutory interpretation: what was Congress's intent when it required debtors to use exemption laws of their former state of domicile? "'The objective of a court called upon to interpret a statute B is to ascertain congressional intent and give effect to legislative will.'" Cotroneo v. Shaw Env't & Infrastructure, Inc., 639 F.3d 186, 194 (5th Cir. 2011) (quoting Davis v. Johnson, 158 F.3d 806, 810 (5th Cir. 1998)). The Court begins with the language of the statute, as "[t]he Supreme Court has repeatedly counseled that in statutory interpretation, 'courts must presume that a legislature says in a statute what it means and means in a statute what it says.'" United States v. Johnson, 632 F.3d 912, 922 (5th Cir. 2011) (quoting Conn. Nat'l Bank v. Germain, 503 U.S. 249,

253-54 (1992)). "When the statutory 'language is plain, the sole function of the courts--at least where the disposition required by the text is not absurd--is to enforce it according to its terms.'" Arlington Cent. Sch. Dist. Bd. of Educ. v. Murphy, 548 U.S. 291, 296-97 (2006) (quoting Hartford Underwriters Ins. Co. v. Union Planters Bank, N. A., 530 U.S. 1, 6 (2000)). In addition, courts must read a "'statute as a whole, so as to give effect to each of its provisions without rendering any language superfluous.'" Waggoner v. Gonzales, 488 F.3d 632, 636 (5th Cir. 2007) (quoting Bustamante-Barrera v. Gonzales, 447 F.3d 388, 397 (5th Cir. 2006)).

The plain language of the statute unfortunately does not resolve the issue. The most literal interpretation of the language allows Debtor to exempt

> any property that is exempt under . . . State or local law that is applicable on the date of the filing of the petition to the place in which the debtor's domicile has been located for the 730 days immediately preceding the date of the filing of the petition, or if the debtor's domicile has not been located in a single State for such 730-day period, the place in which the debtor's domicile was located for 180 days immediately preceding the 730-day period.

11 U.S.C. § 522(b)(3)(A).

Here, that means Debtor is allowed to exempt property that is exempt under Nevada law, since that is where he lived for the 180 day period prior to the 730 day period preceding the filing of his petition. But this is ambiguous as to precisely how Nevada state law should be applied. Should the Court strictly construe the phrase "is exempt" and look to what Nevada courts would allow debtors to exempt in non-bankruptcy actions? Should the Court look to Nevada law to see if Nevada would permit out-of-state property to be exempt in bankruptcy? Or should the Court treat the subsection as a choice of law provision, and simply apply the categories and amounts of Nevada exemptions to Debtor's bankruptcy estate, paying no attention to any potential limitations Nevada law might impose on applying Nevada law outside Nevada? The statute's terse command to determine what "is exempt under . . . State" law provides no clear answer.

A split in the case law on how to apply the rule reflects this ambiguity. At present, after approximately four years of cases interpreting the statute as amended by BAPCPA, courts and commentators have split into essentially three groups of opinion on how to apply this provision. The first interpretation, which the Court terms the anti-extraterritoriality interpretation, maintains that state exemption laws can never apply extraterritorially. Therefore, in bankruptcy proceedings, to the extent that a debtor is no longer domiciled in a state or his property is no longer located there, that state's exemption laws are inapplicable to him and he must instead rely on the federal exemptions. It appears that the bankruptcy court below is currently the only federal court to interpret the statute in this manner. See Fernandez, 445 B.R. at 816. The second view, held by the majority of courts to consider the issue, holds that while states may not apply their exemption laws outside their borders, in the bankruptcy context it is the federal government giving the laws extraterritorial effect, so it is permissible to apply state exemption laws to nonresidents and out-of-state property to the extent that the state laws, by their terms, allow for it. See, e.g., Arrol, 170 F.3d at 935-36; Stephens, 402 B.R. at 4-6. The Court terms this the state-specific interpretation. Finally, the third view, which a few courts have endorsed, holds that a state's exemption laws may be applied to non-residents and to out-of-state property, regardless of whether that state's laws allow for such extraterritorial effect or not. See, e.g., Garrett, 435 B.R. at 451-52.[7] The interpretation has been termed the preemption view. See Laura B. Bartell, The Peripatetic Debtor: Choice of Law and Choice of Exemptions, 22 Emory Bankr. Dev. J. 401, 417, 420.

The bankruptcy court, establishing and following the first view, refused to allow Debtor to use Nevada exemption law, regardless of whether Nevada law allows for extraterritorial effect or not. See Fernandez, 445 B.R. at 816. The Court disagrees, and believes the state-specific approach is the correct one, finding it more persuasive than both the anti-extraterritoriality and the preemption interpretations. To explain why, the Court proceeds by examining the relative merits of each view.

1. Anti-extraterritoriality interpretation

This first view, which the bankruptcy court below is the only federal court to endorse, holds that a state cannot require another state to give effect to its exemption laws, and consequently that bankruptcy courts may not give extraterritorial effect to any state's exemption laws. In other words, when applying a former domicile state's exemption laws, the bankruptcy court should apply them as if it were a state court of the forum state where the bankruptcy court were located, giving them like effect. See Fernandez, 445 B.R. at 798. However, the Court finds the bankruptcy court's premise to be inapposite, so that its conclusion was in error.

The bankruptcy court arrived at the anti-extraterritoriality view after first examining the initial purpose served by state exemption laws. As persuasively explained by the bankruptcy judge below, that purpose was to protect assets of debtors from creditors seeking to enforce judgments:

> A state's interest in enacting exemption laws flows directly from its interest in preserving a minimum amount of property for every debtor, regardless of their level of indebtedness, so that they do not end up becoming a burden on the state, and so that they may preserve a modicum of dignity even in the depths of financial straits. In Cobbs v. Coleman, the Texas Supreme Court colorfully stated the purpose thusly:
>
>> No Creditor shall strip from the sacred body of the wife of your bosom, from the tender form of the precious child she bore you, or from your own frame, the clothing you have purchased with your earnings to hide your nakedness and that of your beloved dependents. This unnecessary humiliation shall never be visited upon you, with the consent of the law.
>
> 14 Tex. 594 (1855) . . .

To protect its citizens from suffering such indignities and prevent them from becoming dependent upon the state government, states enacted exemption

---

[7] There is a variant of the third view that would give extraterritorial effect to a state's law without regard to the state's intent, but only inasmuch as it is substituted for the exemption law of the forum state. Under this approach, the state's laws cannot apply to property located outside the state of the debtor's domicile at filing. See In re Camp (Camp I), 396 B.R. 194 (Bankr. W.D. Tex. 2008), rev'd on other grounds, 631 F.3d 757 (5th Cir. 2011). However, because this view has been advanced by only one court and the outcome under it and the stronger view of preemption would be identical here, the Court does not distinguish between the two in its analysis.

laws exempting certain property, such as homesteads, from being used to satisfy a person's debts. See id.

The bankruptcy court appears also to be correct that in carrying out these protective policies states have been free to enact whatever exemption laws they wished, and have not had to respect the exemption laws of any other state. While the Full Faith and Credit Clause requires states to give the same effect to a judgment from another state's courts the same effect it would have there, under Supreme Court jurisprudence this has never meant that states were also required to give effect to the other state's exemption laws. M'Elmoyle ex rel. Bailey v. Cohen, 38 U.S. (13 Pet.) 312, 324-25 (1839). A judgment "does not carry with it, into another state, the efficacy of a judgment upon property or persons, to be enforced by execution. To give it the force of a judgment in another state, it must be made a judgment there; and can only be executed in the latter as its laws may permit." Id. at 325; Baker ex rel. Thomas v. General Motors Corp., 522 U.S. 222, 235 (1998) ("Full faith and credit, however, does not mean that enforcement measures must travel with the sister state judgment as preclusive effects do; such measures remain subject to the evenhanded control of forum law.") (citing M'Elmoyle, 38 U.S. (13 Pet.) at 325; Restatement (Second) of Conflict of Laws ("Restatement") § 99 (1969)). A creditor cannot directly execute on a judgment from another state, but must instead "domesticate" the out-of-state judgment in some fashion before executing on it. Adar v. Smith, 639 F.3d 146, 158 (5th Cir. 2011) ("full faith and credit doctrine does not contemplate requiring an executive officer to 'execute' a foreign judgment without the intermediary of a state court"); see also Sara L. Johnson, Annotation, Validity, Construction, and Application of Uniform Enforcement of Foreign Judgments Act, 31 A.L.R.4th 706 (1984) (laying out procedure and case law relevant to enforcing foreign state judgments). Thus, because a foreign judgment when executed upon has been converted or incorporated in some sense into a local judgment, a creditor is bound by the local rules on enforcing judgments, and is not bound by the enforcement rules of the state where the judgment originated. Adar, 639 F.3d at 159 (state enforcement of foreign judgments must be "evenhanded," meaning that a foreign judgment is enforced in the same way as a local judgment of the forum). In line with these cases, it appears the majority of states have held that they are not required to give effect to another state's exemption laws. See 35 C.J.S. Exemptions § 6 (2011); Bartell, supra, at 416 & n.103 (citing DeLotel v. DeLotel (In re Marriage of DeLotel), 73 Cal. App. 3d 21, 140 Cal. Rptr. 553, 555 (Cal. Ct. App. 1977); Garrett v. Garrett, 30 Colo. App. 167, 490 P.2d 313, 315 (Colo. App. 1971); Mahl v. Aaron, 809 N.E.2d 953, 957 (Ind. Ct. App. 2004); Ferneau v. Armour & Co., 303 S.W.2d 161, 167 (Mo. Ct. App. 1957); Goodwin v. Claytor, 137 N.C. 224, 49 S.E. 173, 174 (N.C. 1904); State ex rel. Lankford v. Collins, 1918 OK 441, 70 Okla. 323, 174 P. 568, 570 (Okla. 1918); Carson v. Memphis & C.R. Co., 88 Tenn. 646, 13 S.W. 588, 589 (Tenn. 1890); Bergman v. Bergman, 888 S.W.2d 580, 582 (Tex. App. 1994); Strawn Mercantile Co. v. First Nat'l Bank of Strawn, 279 S.W. 473, 474 (Tex. App. 1925); Wm. Cameron & Co. v. Abbott, 258 S.W. 562, 564 (Tex. App. 1924); S. Pac. Co. v. I.X.L. Furniture & Carpet Installment House, 44 Utah 472, 140 P. 665, 666 (Utah 1914)).

But, and this is where the Court parts ways with the bankruptcy court's argument that state laws may never have extraterritorial effect, there is a crucial difference between a state being required to give effect to another state's exemption laws and a state being allowed to give effect to another state's exemption laws. That a state is prevented from imposing its laws on another state does not mean that a state may not offer its laws for use by another state, if that other state so wishes, or that a state may not, in actions brought in its own courts, apply its own state law to property located elsewhere. See In re McWilliams, 296 B.R. 424, 426 (Bankr. E.D. Va. 2002) (applying Virginia homestead exemption statute with procedure for application to property located outside the state).

Authorities enunciating the general principle of no required extraterritorial effect recognize this point, since it has long been the rule that a state may give effect to another state's laws when its own rules of comity require it. See, e.g., 35 C.J.S. Exemptions §§ 6-7 (2011) ("If it is determined that the exemption policies of the two states are congruous, the exercise of comity will not be defeated merely because the amount of exemption provided for by each differs."); DeLotel, 140 Cal. Rptr. at 555 ("where the exemption laws of both states are practically the same, the exemption law of the foreign state will be granted comity"); Ferneau, 303 S.W.2d at 167 ("Nor can defendant as a matter of right avail himself here of [another state's exemption laws]," but "as a voluntary act of courtesy and good will under the rule of comity, the courts of this state will recognize and enforce the exemption laws of a sister state where the general policy of the two states is the same.") (emphasis in original). Indeed, in a seeming expansion of the rule of comity, the Restatement provision dealing with choice of exemption law provisions actually requires recognition of another state's exemption laws when another state has the dominant interest:

> The local law of the forum determines what property of a debtor within the state is exempt from execution unless another state, by reason of such circumstances as the domicil of the creditor and the debtor within its territory, has the dominant interest in the question of exemption. In that event, the local law of the other state will be applied.

Restatement § 132; see also Bergman, 888 S.W.2d at 585-86 (applying the Restatement rule); In re Pederson, 105 B.R. 622, 624 (Bankr. D. Colo. 1989) (applying the Restatement rule to select exemption law in bankruptcy proceeding).

Thus, the authorities cited by the bankruptcy court do not support the proposition that state laws are always and necessarily local in nature. States have always been free to give effect to other states' exemption laws, and have occasionally done so.

This conclusion is unremarkable on its face, since it is in accord with longstanding conflict of law principles. Under contractual choice of law clauses or under a state's choice of law rules, any state can give effect to another state's laws when it chooses to do so. See, e.g., Restatement § 6 (listing factors to apply when deciding which state's substantive law should apply when there is no statutory choice of law rule); Sonat Exploration Co. v. Cudd Pressure Control, Inc., 271 S.W.3d 228, 231 (Tex. 2008) (applying Texas's choice of law rules, which follow the Restatement, and deciding Louisiana law should apply); Castro v. Budget Rent-A-Car System, Inc., 154 Cal. App. 4th 1162, 65 Cal. Rptr. 3d 430, 441-44 (Cal. Ct. App. 2007) (applying California's "governmental interest analysis" choice of law rule and deciding Alabama tort law should apply); Flint v. Liberty Ins. Corp., 613 F. Supp. 2d 899, 902-03 (E.D. Ky. 2009) (applying Kentucky's choice of law rules, which follow the Restatement, and deciding Indiana law should apply). The only limitations on the application of another state's laws are the "modest restrictions" imposed by the Due Process and Full Faith and Credit Clauses, which require only that a state "have a significant contact or significant aggregation of contacts, creating state interests, such that choice of its law is neither arbitrary nor fundamentally unfair." Phillips Petroleum Co. v. Shutts, 472 U.S. 797, 818, 105 S. Ct. 2965, 86 L. Ed. 2d 628 (1985) (quotation omitted).

The bankruptcy judge below found that an attempt to apply a state's exemption laws extraterritorially was a wild goose chase, since it would entail giving extraterritorial effect to a law that was only designed for application within a state. Fernandez, 445 B.R. at 798 n.12. As the bankruptcy judge put it, because states cannot require each other to apply their exemption laws, "it is unnecessary (perhaps even misleading) to examine whether a given state's exemption law is intended to apply extraterritorially, or whether a given state's law is silent with regard to its extraterritorial application. Courts that go down this road are on a snipe hunt, because the question itself is irrelevant." Fernandez, 445 B.R. at 798 n.12; cf. In re George, 440 B.R. 164, 166 (Bankr. E.D. Wis. 2010) (holding that it was "implied by the structure and function of the applicable statutes" that Illinois exemption laws had exclusively in-state effect). However, the same argument applies to application of any state law through a choice of law rule, and that does not prevent states from doing so. The drafters of the Restatement recognized the problem, noting, "Legislatures usually legislate, and courts usually adjudicate, only with the local situation in mind. They rarely give thought to the extent to which the laws they enact, and the common law rules they enunciate, should apply to out-of-state facts." Restatement § 6 cmt. b. But rather than viewing this as a basis for refusing to give extraterritorial effect to state laws, the drafters instead concluded that the general inattention of legislatures and courts meant a more fact-intensive inquiry was necessary for deciding which state's law should apply. Id.

Besides the flaws in the bankruptcy court's analysis of the potential extraterritorial effect of a state's laws, the Court finds three other defects in the anti-extraterritoriality interpretation. First, the analysis focuses entirely on the question of whether a state's exemption laws can apply to out-of-state property, but does not address at all the equally significant issue of whether a state's exemption laws can apply to out-of-state residents. If a state's exemption laws cannot apply to out-of-state property because only parties to a state judgment execution could invoke them, the same laws are equally inapplicable in other types of actions to out-of-state parties for the same reason. In both situations the law would have to be stretched to encompass a context never intended by the drafters, and would be applied to factual settings over which the state could not require its laws be given effect. Following this argument into the bankruptcy context, it would mean that every debtor who changed his domicile within two years of filing a petition would be forced to use state exemption laws that could by definition never apply to him or any of his property. Where a given interpretation of a statute leads to an absurd result such as this, it cannot be the correct one. See Murphy, 548 U.S. at 296-97 "When the statutory language is plain, the sole function of the courts--at least where the disposition required by the text is not absurd--is to enforce it according to its terms.") (emphasis added) (quotation omitted).

Second, this approach reads part of the language right out of the statute. If a debtor has moved from a state and is now domiciled in another state where he has been required to file his bankruptcy petition, it is likely that most if not all of his property is located in his new state of residence. However, this reading would indicate that in these types of scenarios, the most common types of scenarios, the complicated inquiry into the debtor's state of domicile up to 910 days prior to the petition would be meaningless, since the debtor would never be able to claim that state's exemptions. The only debtors who could make any use of the exemptions of their former state of domicile would be debtors who still owned property in that state. Moreover, even debtors holding property in their former state would still be non-residents, and as just explained, under the logic of the anti-extraterritoriality interpretation, it is doubtful that a state's exemption laws are any more applicable to out-of-state debtors than they are to out-of-state property. Thus, under this reading, any debtor who has not resided in his current state of domicile for at least 730 days would not be able to use any state exemptions, and would only be able to use the federal exemptions. If that were truly Congress's intent, it could have simply said as much, without this more elaborate procedure; because this interpretation seems to make so much of the statute irrelevant, it cannot be correct. See Waggoner, 488 F.3d at 636 (courts must interpret statutes "so as to give effect to each of [their] provisions without rendering any language superfluous") (quotation omitted).

Third, § 522(b)(2) requires application of state opt-out law to determine if a debtor may use the federal exemptions. Specifically, the statute states that the federal exemptions are available "unless the State law that is applicable to the debtor under paragraph (3)(A) specifically does not so authorize." 11 U.S.C. § 522(b)(2). But in the bankruptcy court's view, there is no state law that would ever be "applicable" to a debtor under paragraph (3)(A), so there is no state law to use to make this determination. With no state opt-out law to apply and with state exemptions always unavailable under the bankruptcy court's view, the debtor is left with a Hobson's choice between the federal exemptions or no exemptions at all. While this is not an absurd result, since the debtor still gets the use of the federal exemptions, it does make the hanging paragraph superfluous. After all, the hanging paragraph is designed for situations in which state opt-out law prevents a debtor from using federal exemptions, while state exemption law requirements prevent a debtor from using state exemptions because the debtor or the property is located out of state. But if opt-out laws can never apply because no state law under paragraph (3)(A) will ever be applicable, then debtors can always get the protection of the federal exemptions simply because it is the only choice available to them, and there would never be a reason to have recourse to the hanging paragraph to exempt property. Cf. George, 440 B.R. at 166 (finding a debtor entitled to federal exemptions either because an opt-out law did not apply extraterritorially or because state exemption laws did not apply extraterritorially). The Court cannot endorse a reading of the statute that makes some of its language superfluous. See Waggoner, 488 F.3d at 636 (courts must interpret statutes "so as to give effect to each of [their] provisions without rendering any language superfluous") (quotation omitted).

2. State-specific interpretation

The second interpretation holds that a state's exemption laws may be used by out-of-state debtors for out-of-state property to the extent that each state's exemption law permits. Generally, under this approach, if the state's exemption statutes or decisional authority interpreting them do not explicitly limit the use of the exemptions to in-state residents or to in-state property, then the bankruptcy court should apply the state's exemption laws to a debtor's property, wherever located. See Stephens, 402 B.R. at 6. The Court finds this is the approach Congress intended and applies it here. The Court does so for three reasons. First, the weight of authority supports this position. Second, this approach is in line with the recent decision of the Fifth Circuit on the closely analogous question of extraterritorial effect of state opt-out laws. Third, and most importantly, it is a plausible interpretation of language of the statute that gives full effect to all of the statutory language, especially when considered in light of the purpose of the BAPCPA amendments.

a. Weight of authority

The majority of courts to address the issue of extraterritorial application of state exemption laws have adopted the state-specific view, and looked to state law to determine whether the exemption may apply extraterritorially. Garrett, 435 B.R. at 439 (describing the state-specific interpretation as the majority position). The Court has reviewed the extensive case law, and it appears that this is not merely the majority position, but the majority position by a considerable margin. Of the forty bankruptcy court or district court cases that the Court has found which address whether and how to apply a state's exemption laws to out-of-state property or debtors, thirty-six of them have looked to state law to decide the question.[8] Additionally, three of the four cases decided by Circuit Courts of Appeals or Bankruptcy Panels of Circuit Courts of Appeals have taken this position. See Stephens, 402 B.R. 1; In re Drenttel, 403 F.3d 611 (8th Cir. 2005); Arrol, 170 F.3d 934.

The rationale of these courts is somewhat varied, and some, especially the earliest case, simply interpret the statute in this way without explanation. See, e.g., Cappetta, 33 B.R. at 756-757. But the most common approach is patterned after Arrol, the seminal Ninth Circuit case that first adopted this view, and Drenttel, the Eighth Circuit opinion that followed Arrol. Courts taking this approach begin with the proposition that § 522 is itself a choice of law statute, so

---

[8] See In re Stephens ("Stephens II"), No. 10-41450-JDP, 2011 Bankr. LEXIS 1689, 2011 WL 1790777 (Bankr. D. Idaho May 10, 2011); In re Roberts, 450 B.R. 159, 2011 WL 1760283 (N.D. Iowa 2011); In re Beckwith, 448 B.R. 757 (Bankr. S.D. Ohio 2011); George, 440 B.R. 164; In re Capps, 438 B.R. 668 (Bankr. D. Idaho 2010); Arrendondo-Smith, 436 B.R. 412; In re Harris, No. 09-03792, 2010 Bankr. LEXIS 2020, 2010 WL 2595294 (Bankr. D. Idaho June 23, 2010); Bierbach v. Brooks (In re Brooks), 393 B.R. 80 (Bankr. M.D. Pa. 2008); In re Jevne, 387 B.R. 301 (Bankr. S.D. Fla. 2008); Bingham, 2008 Bankr. LEXIS 139, 2008 WL 186277; In re Katseanes, No. 07-40168-JDP, 2007 Bankr. LEXIS 3475, 2007 WL 2962637 (Bankr. D. Idaho, Oct. 9, 2007); In re Adams, 375 B.R. 532 (Bankr. W.D. Mo. 2007); In re Nickerson, 375 B.R. 869 (Bankr. W.D. Mo. 2007); Williams, 369 B.R. 470; In re Schlakman, No. 05-36921-BKC-PGH, 2007 Bankr. LEXIS 1724, 2007 WL 1482011 (Bankr. S.D. Fla. Jan. 16, 2007; In re Tate, No. 06-61718 FRA7, 2007 Bankr. LEXIS 98, 2007 WL 81835 (Bankr. D. Or. Jan. 8, 2007); [*35] Battle, 366 B.R. 635; In re West, 352 B.R. 905 (Bankr. M.D. Fla. 2006); In re Jewell, 347 B.R. 120 (Bankr. W.D.N.Y. 2006); In re Crandall, 346 B.R. 220 (Bankr. M.D. Fla. 2006); Underwood, 342 B.R. 358; In re Morris, 340 B.R. 78 (Bankr. W.D. Ark. 2006); In re Woodruff, No. 04-63288, 2005 Bankr. LEXIS 832, 2005 WL 1139891 (Bankr. W.D. Mo. Apr. 28, 2005); In re Bausback, No. 02-0825-WH, 2003 Bankr. LEXIS 2337, 2003 WL 25932295 (Bankr. S.D. Iowa June 3, 2003); McWilliams, 296 B.R. 424; In re Ginther, 282 B.R. 16 (Bankr. D. Kan. 2002); In re Weza, 248 B.R. 470 (Bankr. D.N.H. 2000); In re Stratton, 269 B.R. 716 (Bankr. D. Or. 2001); In re Carter, 213 B.R. 26 (Bankr. N.D. Ala. 1997); In re Halpin, No. 93-03215, 1994 WL 594199 (Bankr. D. Idaho Nov. 1, 1994); In re Sipka, 149 B.R. 181 (D. Kan. 1992); In re Bloedon, 137 B.R. 824 (Bankr. D. Colo. 1992); Schulz, 101 B.R. 301; In re Sanders, 72 B.R. 124 (Bankr. M.D. Fla. 1987); Calhoun, 47 B.R. 119; In re Cappetta, 33 B.R. 755 (Bankr. E.D. Va. 1983).

that it is unnecessary and duplicative to look to state choice of law rules when deciding what state's exemptions to apply. Stephens, 402 B.R. at 5; Drenttel, 403 F.3d at 614; Arrol, 170 F.3d at 935; see also Calhoun, 47 B.R. at 122 (describing, pre-Arrol, § 522(b) as a choice of law statute); contra Pederson, 105 B.R. at 624-25 (looking to state choice of law principles to see which exemptions should apply). Following this, the courts then examine the state's exemption law, since that is the law the federal choice of law rule has selected.

Under this view, courts should begin with the state constitution as the primary authority of state law. Stephens, 402 B.R. at 5; Adams, 375 B.R. at 534. If the constitution is silent with regard to the availability of the claimed exemption to out-of-state debtors or property, then the courts should look to statutory law. Stephens, 402 B.R. at 6; Arrol, 170 F.3d at 936. If a court finds no answer there, it should turn to the decisions of the state's courts to see whether the exemption law should have extraterritorial effect. Stephens, 402 B.R. at 6; Drenttel, 403 F.3d at 615; Arrol, 170 F.3d at 936; Adams, 375 B.R. at 534. If, after all of these inquiries, the courts find no direct evidence of the state's position on extraterritoriality, they typically infer from the silence that the laws should have extraterritorial effect, since state law usually indicates that exemption laws are to be liberally construed. Stephens, 402 B.R. at 6-7 ("Given the fact that most, if not all, state courts generally require homestead exemptions to be liberally construed in favor of debtors, it is very likely that a state's homestead exemption will be given extraterritorial effect absent a limitation placed on the exemption by either the statute itself, or a case interpreting that statute."); Drenttel, 403 F.3d at 614; Arrol, 170 F.3d at 935; but see Jevne, 387 B.R. at 304-05 (describing some contrary authority, though ultimately concluding that silence should be construed in favor of extraterritoriality); contra George, 440 B.R. at 166 (construing silence in state law against extraterritorial interpretation, in light of the "structure and function" of the exemption laws).

Now, to be sure, many of the courts that have looked to a state's law to determine whether that state's exemptions apply to former residents or out-of-state property have concluded, based on that state's law, that they do not. See, e.g., Adams, 375 B.R. at 534-35; Jewell, 347 B.R. at 122-23; Carter, 213 B.R. at 32 n.1. In fact, it appears that the majority of states restrict their laws to in-state debtors or property. Brown et al., supra, § 4:6 (describing the extraterritoriality of most states' laws). But regardless of the exact content of the state law or how courts go about determining it, that bankruptcy courts look to state law when deciding which exemptions apply is what is significant. One prominent treatise's treatment of the issue acknowledges this, flatly stating that when a debtor is required by § 522(b) to apply the exemption law of his former state of domicile, courts "must give effect to those exemptions allowed by the law of the state" and that "it makes no difference where the property is situated or where the petition is filed, so long as the property is exempt under the law of the domiciliary state." 4 Collier on Bankruptcy ¶ 522.06 (Alan N. Resnick & Henry J. Sommer eds.-in chief, 16th ed. rev. 2007). The treatise goes on to note a split in the case law on how to precisely determine whether property located out of state would be exempt, but it does not question the fact that the inquiry should focus on the content of state law. Id.

Critics of the state-specific interpretation have argued that by "import[ing] state exemption laws wholesale, including limitations based on residency or location of property, [it] can lead to some absurd results." See Camp I, 396 B.R. at 200; Garrett, 435 B.R. at 450 (quoting Camp I). That is, if bankruptcy courts must look to state law to see whether exemptions are available extraterritorially, what happens when the state law indicates that its own exemptions do not apply, but another state's laws do? See Camp I, 396 B.R. at 200 (highlighting the issue). The question is not purely academic, as at least two states have this kind of exemption statute. See Idaho Code. Ann. § 11-602 ("Residents of this state are entitled to the exemptions provided by this act. Nonresidents are entitled to the exemptions provided by the law of the jurisdiction of their residence."); Wis. Stat. § 815.18(5) ("A resident is entitled to the exemptions provided by this section. A nonresident is entitled to the exemptions provided by the law of the jurisdiction of his or her residence."). However, this argument is disposed of by the state-specific view's approach of disregarding state choice of law rules when looking at state exemption law. Since the kind of exemption law in force in Idaho and Wisconsin is in effect a state choice of law rule, as opposed to a requirement that applies only to the availability of that state's exemption laws, bankruptcy courts should disregard this type of provision in state statutes when examining state exemption law. See Stephens, 402 B.R. at 5; Drenttel, 403 F.3d at 614; Arrol, 170 F.3d at 935.

b. In re Camp

This majority support for the state-specific interpretation is consistent with the approach the Fifth Circuit has taken on the closely analogous question of whether to give state opt-out laws extraterritorial effect. As described above, § 522 states that one must look to the debtor's former state of domicile to determine which state exemptions may apply, but also says that that state can opt out of the federal exemptions and restrict debtors to its state exemptions. 11 U.S.C. § 522(b). In several recent cases, courts have confronted the issue of whether and how to apply the opt-out laws of a debtor's former state of domicile. Just as they have on the extraterritoriality of state substantive exemption laws, they have split on the question of how to apply a state's opt-out law to a debtor who is only applying the state's exemption laws because of § 522(b). See, e.g., In re Battle, 366 B.R. 635, 636 (Bankr. W.D. Tex. 2006) (not applying a Florida opt-out statute because it was limited by its literal language to residents); Williams, 369 B.R. at 474 (applying Iowa's opt-out statute to non-residents because it was not limited by its terms to residents); Camp I, 396 B.R. at 200 (finding Florida opt-out residency restriction preempted by bankruptcy law).

The Fifth Circuit has recently taken a side in this split, holding in Camp II that one must look at the precise language of the relevant opt-out statute to see whether it "specifically" applies to former residents. Camp II, 631 F.3d at 760. The Florida statute at issue in Camp II stated, "'In accordance with the provisions of [11 U.S.C. § 522(b)], residents of this state shall not be entitled to the federal exemptions provided in [11 U.S.C. § 522(d)].'" Id. (quoting Fla. Stat. Ann. § 222.20) (alterations and emphasis in original). Based on the precise language stating that it only applied to "residents of this state," the court held that the opt-out provision was not applicable to former residents, and thus that former residents who were forced to use Florida exemption law because of the 730 day domicile requirement of § 522(b)(3)(A) could freely choose the federal exemptions if they so desired. Id.; see also In re Chandler, 362 B.R. 723, 726-27 (Bankr. N.D. W. Va. 2007) (holding similarly for Georgia opt-out statute); In re Underwood, 342 B.R. 358, 361-62 (Bankr. N.D. Fla. 2006) (same for Colorado law).

The Fifth Circuit foresaw the corollary issue of extraterritorial reach of substantive exemption laws, which faces the Court today, but explicitly reserved judgment on it. See Camp II, 631 F.3d at 761 n.3. The court specifically noted,

> We do not reach the corollary questions of (1) whether the choice-of-law provision in § 522(b)(3)(A) preempts state-law restrictions on the extraterritorial application of state-law exemption schemes, and (2) whether the "savings clause" in the hanging paragraph at the end of § 522(b) permits debtors to claim the federal exemptions when the applicable state law opts out of the federal exemption scheme and, at the same time, restricts the extraterritorial application of the state-law exemption scheme, thereby rendering both exemption schemes unavailable to the debtor through the normal operation of the Bankruptcy Code.

Id. (citations omitted).

Nonetheless, despite this reservation, the Court finds Camp II to be persuasive authority for the state-specific interpretation. The Fifth Circuit did not look at the historical reasons why states enacted opt-out laws and try to divine whether, in light of those reasons, bankruptcy courts should try to apply an opt-out law to out-of-state debtors. Nor did it find the reach of state opt-out laws to be preempted by § 522(b) and the BAPCPA amendments. Instead, the Fifth Circuit simply looked to the statutory language of Florida's opt-out law to determine its reach. The Court takes the same approach to the related issue of extraterritoriality of exemption laws.

It seems unlikely on its face that Florida purposefully legislated with an eye to how its opt-out statute would affect non-residents forced to use Florida exemption laws by § 522(b)(3)(A), just as it seems unlikely here that Nevada was considering how its exemption laws could be applied to out-of-state debtors or property when it enacted them. But the Fifth Circuit in Camp brushed aside such concerns, noting that Florida's opt-out statute was enacted in 1979, and that there had been the potential for a conflict between state residency and state opt-out laws since 1978, when Congress first set a 180 day look-back for determining a debtor's domicile. Camp II, 631 F.3d at 761. The court found that Florida's failure to amend its statute in the face of this potential conflict indicated an intent to only opt out of the federal exemptions for Florida residents. Id. This reasoning supports the approach the Court takes today, albeit with diminished force. Here, Nevada has had approximately five years after the passage of BAPCPA to amend its exemption laws to take into account the potential for them to be applied to former residents or to out-of-state property. It has not done so. Thus, it is not a "snipe hunt" to look at the language of Nevada's exemption statutes to see whether they should apply to non-residents or out-of-state property.

C. Statutory language

The Court finds the state-specific interpretation especially persuasive because it is a natural reading of the statute and gives meaning to all of the statutory language. The text of § 522(b) is not the most straightforward of statutes and is susceptible to multiple different readings:

> (1) . . . [A]n individual debtor may exempt from property of the estate the property listed in either paragraph (2) or, in the alternative, paragraph (3) of this subsection . . . .
>
> (2) Property listed in this paragraph is property that is specified under [the federal bankruptcy law exemptions], unless the State law that is applicable to the

> debtor under paragraph (3)(A) specifically does not so authorize.
> (3) Property listed in this paragraph is--
>
> > (A) . . . any property that is exempt under Federal law, other than [the federal bankruptcy law exemptions], or State or local law that is applicable on the date of the filing of the petition to the place in which the debtor's domicile has been located for the 730 days immediately preceding the date of the filing of the petition or if the debtor's domicile has not been located in a single State for such 730-day period, the place in which the debtor's domicile was located for 180 days immediately preceding the 730-day period or for a longer portion of such 180-day period than in any other place;
> > . . .
>
> If the effect of the domiciliary requirement under subparagraph (A) is to render the debtor ineligible for any exemption, the debtor may elect to exempt property that is specified under subsection (d) [the federal exemptions].

11 U.S.C. §522(b).

Reduced to the essence relevant here, the state exemption portion of the statute says that a debtor may claim as exempt, property that is exempt under state law that is applicable to the debtor's former state of domicile. The state-specific interpretation gives this language its most natural and literal effect: whatever is exempt under state law is exempt in bankruptcy. Because § 522(b) does not restrict or give a broader reach to the state exemption statutes, they retain whatever reach they have as a matter of state law. If a state wants to restrict the availability of exemptions to non-residents or to out-of-state property, then the bankruptcy law will honor that policy choice. See Jewell, 347 B.R. at 122-23 (holding that the language of the statute requires that state law be "applicable," which gives effect to state territoriality requirements preventing an exemption law from being applicable). This makes sense, since it is state law that defines the property interests in bankruptcy, see Butner v. United States, 440 U.S. 48, 55 (1979), and courts have held that to claim property as exempt under state or local laws, "'it must be claimed as exempt in the manner prescribed by those laws.'" Beckwith, 448 B.R. at 765 (quoting Zimmerman v. Morgan (In re Morgan), 689 F.2d 471, 472 (4th Cir. 1982)).

Unlike the first view, where the look-back language in § 522(b)(3)(A) is surplusage that calls for a pointless inquiry into the debtor's former state of domicile, under the second view there are many situations where a debtor could actually make use of the exemptions of his former state of domicile. The number of such situations is fluid; this interpretation means states are free to change their exemption laws to loosen or restrict the availability of their exemption laws, and the bankruptcy statute will automatically take those changes into account. See United States v. Sharpnack, 355 U.S. 286, 293-97 (1958) (holding it a constitutional delegation of Congress's power to incorporate state laws by reference, even when those laws have not yet been enacted, and citing bankruptcy law's treatment of state exemption laws as a permissible example of doing so). And for those states that choose to restrict the availability of their state exemptions for whatever reason, the hanging paragraph is there to prevent any debtors from being unable to claim any exemptions at all. Unlike the first view, through the state-specific interpretation the hanging paragraph serves the purpose it appears designed for--as a gap-filler provision, rather than the dominant exemption selection rule.

While the Court finds this interpretation of § 522 to be more persuasive than either of the alternatives, the Court acknowledges two counter-arguments cast it into some doubt. First, while the statutory language and decisional authority conclusively indicate what Congress's intent was behind the statute, they do nothing to illuminate why Congress had that intent. That is, the reasoning behind states' restrictions on extraterritorial application of exemption laws is not clear, and Congress's rationale for respecting those restrictions even less so. States could conceivably treat debtors and property located in state differently from debtors and property located out of state, since local debtors and property will in all likelihood have more effect within the state. See Camp II, 631 F.3d at 761 (finding such a concern to underlie a state opt-out law that treated residents and non-residents differently). However, given that it costs states nothing to extend the reach of their policies through bankruptcy law to property and debtors located out of state, and that other states can have no complaint when they do so because it is Congress's policy that makes it possible, it is hard to understand why states would voluntarily prevent their policies from having a slightly wider reach. With the rationale behind states' territoriality restrictions being unclear, it is doubly difficult to discern why Congress would respect those restrictions enough to give them effect in bankruptcy law, when the result is that a debtor who has moved between states in the two years prior to filing his petition will be treated differently than a debtor who has not moved. See Garrett, 435 B.R. at 449-50 (noting how, under a non-preemption interpretation, debtors who move may either receive a choice between state and federal exemptions if an opt-out law does not apply, or lose the benefit of state exemptions and be forced to rely on federal exemptions if the state exemptions have territoriality restrictions). Were the case law and language of the statute less conclusive the Court would be troubled by this absence of a clear policy justification for the state-specific interpretation. But since the statute, as written, clearly reflects the congressional intent, the Court must check its concerns and give effect to Congress's will.

Second, the Court is sensitive to the bankruptcy court's argument that looking to state law for extraterritorial effect gives outsized significance to choices of drafting language that might have been entirely unintentional. See Fernandez, 445 B.R. at 798 n.12 (characterizing the inquiry as a "snipe hunt"). However, this appears to be the result Congress intended, as set forth above. Additionally, state exemption laws are not static fixtures; state legislatures can and do change their laws in this area to take into account changes in how bankruptcy law would give them effect. See Stephens II, 2011 Bankr. LEXIS 1689, at n.6 (noting that the "Idaho legislature has on multiple occasions amended or clarified Idaho's exemption laws in obvious response to the decisions of" that court). Thus, even if states' exemption laws' allowance of or restrictions on extraterritorial effects are more the result of choices of language that seemed inconsequential at the time, states are free to amend their exemption laws to take into account the possibility of their having extraterritorial effect in bankruptcy proceedings. See Camp II, 631 F.3d at 761 (finding the absence of amendments to indicate a tacit acquiescence to the interpretation of an opt-out law as restricted to state residents). Indeed, states have been free to make such changes for many years, since the extraterritorial issue is not a new one. See Stephens II, 2011 Bankr. LEXIS 1689, at n.6 (observing that the court first confronted the issue of extraterritoriality of Idaho exemption laws in approximately 1994); Arrol, 170 F.3d 934 (decided more than ten years ago, in 1999).

3. Preemption interpretation

The third interpretation of § 522(b) is the most straightforward and facially appealing, and addresses the potential shortcoming of the state-specific interpretation mentioned above. This interpretation would hold that § 522(b) is a choice of law rule that incorporates state exemption law by reference. And because choice of law rules in general work to give extraterritorial effect to a state's laws without regard to the state's intent for them to have such effect, state exemption laws should be applied to any debtor and any property, wherever located, whenever § 522(b) calls for it. As some have phrased it, this views § 522(b) as totally preempting any state restrictions on the applicability of state exemption laws. See Bartell, supra, at 417, 420. While this view is a sensible interpretation of the statute on its face, it is the minority position, see Brown et al., supra, § 4:5, and the Court finds it ultimately unpersuasive because it is not the most reasonable interpretation of the statute and fails to give meaning to all of the statutory language.

The case for preemption is straightforward, and proceeds from the same premise as the second view, the principle that § 522(b) is a choice of law statute. See Camp I, 396 B.R. at 202. When a choice of law rule requires the application of another state's law, that law is defined as "'the body of standards, principles and rules, exclusive of its rules of Conflict of Laws, which the courts of that state apply in the decision of controversies brought before them.'" Bartell, supra, 411 (quoting Restatement § 4). States applying another state's laws generally do not apply the other state's choice of law rules, else the courts might find themselves caught in endless loops of reference to another state's laws, which refer to yet another state's laws, and so forth. Cf. Restatement § 8 (treating the issue of when and how courts should look to another state's choice of law rules). According to the preemption view, territoriality or residency requirements in a state's substantive laws are equivalent to a form of choice of law rule, and so should be equally disregarded when applying that state's law under choice of law rules. Camp I, 396 B.R. at 199.

Just as states' choice of law rules or private contracts can require the application of a certain state's laws without any issues of extraterritoriality coming into play, so too can Congress choose to have a certain state's exemptions laws apply, either as a matter of preemption under the Bankruptcy Clause or more simply as a choice of law issue. Bartell, supra, at 417. That is, if "§ 522(b)(3) gives state exemption laws extraterritorial effect, it does so as a matter of federal law." Id. Because state statutes are being incorporated by reference into the federal legislation, the exemptions being applied are ultimately federal ones. Cf. Bartlett v. Giguere (In re Bartlett), 168 B.R. 488, 494 (Bankr. D.N.H. 1994) ("the exemption right that we are dealing with in these cases is created by federal law, and is a matter of federal law as to applicability, even though the amount and items of exemption are defined and set forth in existing state statutes"). As stated by the Sixth Circuit, "[C]oncerns regarding extraterritorial effects of state law are misplaced. Section 522(b) is a federal statute which has incorporated state law into its application. Upon incorporation, state law became a part of the federal statutory scheme; so it is federal law being given effect, not state law." Farinash v. Stockburger (In re Stockburger), 106 F.3d 402, [published in full-text format at 1997 U.S. App. LEXIS 2034] (6th Cir. 1997) (table decision) .

a. Basis for preemption

This line of argument appears to be a sensible approach to the issue of state exemptions and a populace of debtors who change their domiciles with increasing frequency. See Fernandez, 445 B.R. at 814 & n.40 (citing Bartell, supra, at 401) (discussing the rising numbers of Americans who move from one state to another each year). The preemption approach can be troublesome, though, as there is no clear basis in the statute's history and purpose or general preemption analysis principles for preempting state extraterritoriality requirements.

Preemption proponents and opponents have attempted to argue in favor of or against preemption based on a perceived overarching purpose for the inclusion of state exemptions in federal bankruptcy. See, e.g., Fernandez, 445 B.R. at 799-802. They have tried to find this purpose from the history of bankruptcy legislation in the United States and from suppositions as to whether bankruptcy law in general, and the exemption laws in particular, are intended to defer to the states or take power away from them. See id.; Bartell, supra, at 402-07; Stephens, 402 B.R. at 5; Garrett, 435 B.R. at 446-50. The Court declines to wade into this morass, finding no clear answers as to whether Congress's general aim was to defer to states' exemption laws or to supplant them with federal bankruptcy law. The bankruptcy laws are, like most legislation, a balance between competing policies, and the Court cannot say that one policy dominates over the others. See Owen, 500 U.S. at 313 ("it is not inconsistent with the policy of permitting state-defined exemptions to have another policy disfavoring waiver of exemptions, whether federal- or state-created"). The Tenth Circuit's succinct conclusion in Stephens that "Congress's intent in allowing states to opt out of the federal exemption scheme is not entirely clear, since the provision was the result of a legislative compromise" is perhaps the best that can be said on this topic. 402 B.R. at 5 n.16. There is insufficient evidence of Congressional intent to either defer to or override states' exemption laws for this Court to use in favor of or against a preemption interpretation of § 522(b).

While there is clear evidence as to Congress's purpose behind the BAPCPA amendments, it is difficult to conclude from this purpose that Congress intended to preempt state law. One of the primary purposes of BAPCPA was to discourage forum-shopping. Urban, 375 B.R. at 889 (citing H.R. Rep. No. 109-31, pt. 1, at 15-16 (2005), reprinted in 2005 U.S.C.C.A.N. 88, 102). But there is no evidence of how Congress intended this to be achieved. The Garrett court and Professor Bartell ascribe to Congress the intent to return affairs to the status quo ante, by returning debtors to the exemptions that would have applied to them but for their move. See Garrett, 435 B.R. at 449; Bartell, supra, at 419-20. This purpose would argue in favor of preemption, since it would prevent the states' exemption law requirements from interfering with the process of recreating the status quo ante. However, the legislative history cited by the Garrett court to support this intended method contained the views of the dissenting members of Congress, and even the Garrett court admitted that courts do "'not usually accord much weight to the statements of a bill's opponents.'" Garrett, 435 B.R. at 447 (quoting Shell Oil Co. v. Iowa Dept. of Revenue, 488 U.S. 19, 30, 109 S. Ct. 278, 102 L. Ed. 2d 186 (1988)). Without further evidence of an intent to preempt state exemption territoriality requirements through the BAPCPA amendments, the Court does not find the argument in favor of preemption based upon BAPCPA credible.

Preemption analysis is of little help, either, in determining whether Congress intended to defer to states' definition of their exemptions or preempt any extraterritoriality limitations. Preemption can take one of three forms: express, implied from occupation of the field, and conflict. Castro v. Collecto, Inc., 634 F.3d 779, 785 (5th Cir. 2011) (citing Hillsborough Cnty., Fla. v. Automated Med. Labs., Inc., 471 U.S. 707, 713 (1985); Wyeth v. Levine, 555 U.S. 555 (2009)). Express preemption arises from explicit statutory language. Id. (citations omitted). Implied preemption from occupation of the field arises when federal law is so comprehensive as to leave no room for state law, or the federal interest is so dominant as to preclude enforcement of state law. Id. (citations omitted). Conflict preemption arises when compliance with both federal and state law is impossible, or the state law poses an unacceptable obstacle to the enforcement of the federal law. Id. (citations omitted).

The Court agrees with the bankruptcy court below that express and implied field preemption do not apply here. See Fernandez, 445 B.R. at 808. There is no language in the statute or its history that would support express preemption. As explained above, the purpose behind the BAPCPA amendment to § 522(b) was to prevent debtors from forum-shopping by requiring them to apply the exemption law of their former state of domicile. This purpose does not say anything specifically about Congress' intent to preempt extraterritoriality restrictions in state exemption laws. Regarding preemption implied from occupation of the field, Congress does not appear to have totally occupied the field. After all, even if some states were to restrict their laws, others might let them reach to out-of-state debtors or property; the Court cannot say that Congress intended to so occupy the field of exemption law as to prevent this.

The Court finds express or implied field preemption particularly unlikely because Congress has explicitly deferred to state law in the exemption law area. See Stephens, 402 B.R. at 5 ("'Rather than preempting the exemption area, Congress expressly authorizes the states to 'preempt' the federal legislation.'") (alterations omitted) (quoting Rhodes v. Stewart, 705 F.2d 159, 163 (6th Cir. 1983)). Rather than restricting debtors to certain federal exemptions, Congress allowed debtors the choice of state or federal exemptions. See 11 U.S.C. § 522(b). Moreover, Congress further deferred to state law by allowing states to opt out of the federal exemptions and restrict debtors to only state exemptions. See id. Though, as explained above, the Court cannot say this solicitude for state interests is so overwhelming as to completely defeat the preemption argument, the Court does believe that if Congress wanted to defer to state exemption laws in one way but limit them in another it would have made that intent more clear in the legislation. See Sheehan v. Peveich, 574 F.3d 248, 252 (4th Cir. 2009) (citing Rhodes, 705 F.2d at 163) ("There can be no preemption, however, where Congress "expressly and concurrently authorizes" state legislation on the subject.")). Similarly, the state-specific view, which the Court finds most persuasive, has substantial and relatively longstanding support in the case law that predates the BAPCPA amendments. The Court sees no evidence that Congress intended to overrule this line of case law. See Bingham, 2008 Bankr. LEXIS 139, 2008 WL 186277, at ("nothing in the 2005 revisions to the Bankruptcy Code suggest an intent by Congress to overrule the long line of cases providing that" bankruptcy courts should apply state exemption laws extraterritorially only when those states so permit).

The conflict preemption argument, which both the Camp I and Garrett courts advanced, is more persuasive, at least with regard to exemption law residency restrictions. Conflict preemption exists "(1) where complying with both federal law and state law is impossible; or (2) where the state law creates an unacceptable obstacle to the accomplishment and execution of the full purposes and objectives of Congress." Collecto, 634 F.3d at 785 (quotation omitted). The entire purpose behind the BAPCPA changes were to require debtors to use exemption laws of states where they necessarily no longer resided. As the Court explained above in its discussion of the anti-extraterritoriality interpretation, this purpose would be substantially thwarted if residency restrictions were allowed to stand. See Camp I, 396 B.R. at 197-99; Garrett, 435 B.R. at 451-52. If a debtor were restricted from using the exemptions of his former domicile, there would be little point to engaging in the complicated determination of where that debtor's domicile was between 730 and 910 days prior to filing his petition. But while there might be little point in engaging in the inquiry, the Camp I and Garret courts are not correct that there is no point; Congress's policy would not be entirely thwarted, as indicated by the hanging paragraph. Because that paragraph seems to make provision for just such an eventuality, the Court cannot say that compliance with both state and federal laws would be an impossibility or would be unacceptably impeded. By including that section in the statute, Congress left space for both federal bankruptcy law and state exemption law to be fully enforced to the extent of their terms, which is enough to defeat any claim of conflict preemption.

b. Hanging paragraph

The hanging paragraph is actually the most persuasive evidence against the preemption interpretation. As one might guess from the fact that the anti-extraterritoriality view gives the hanging paragraph too much emphasis and the state-specific view just enough, the preemption view gives it no role at all. If Congress intended to preempt any and all restrictions in states' exemption laws, whether they were contained in the exemption laws themselves or in the state's opt-out law, then there would be no purpose to the hanging paragraph. If states could not make former resident debtors ineligible for exemptions and unable to choose the federal exemptions, then Congress would not need to provide for exemptions to apply as a fall back. See Jewell, 347 B.R. at 122-23 (finding that the hanging paragraph would be surplusage if the statute, by requiring that the state law be "applicable," did not give effect to state exemption law territoriality requirements). Professor Bartell frankly acknowledged as much in her article that appears to have been the first authority to espouse the preemption interpretation. See Bartell, supra, at 423-24. She stated that under the preemption interpretation, the hanging paragraph is "unnecessary" and "should never be applicable." Id. at 424. It being a well-established rule of statutory construction that all words in a statute must have meaning, this is enough to sink the third interpretation. See Waggoner, 488 F.3d at 636 (courts must interpret statutes "so as to give effect to each of [their] provisions without rendering any language superfluous") (quotation omitted).

The court in Garrett, attempting to defeat the surplusage argument, set forth several scenarios in which the hanging paragraph would apply. See 435 B.R. at 450-51. For example, a debtor who recently moved to a new state before filing for bankruptcy, but who had lived in a foreign country during the 180 days preceding the 730 prior to filing, would not be eligible for any exemptions because there would be no former state of domicile to turn to. Id. Similarly, a debtor who files for bankruptcy soon after immigrating to the United States would not have a former state of domicile to look to for exemption law. Id. at

451. Finally, a separated but not divorced couple who file for bankruptcy in different states, but whose former state of domicile requires a married couple to use exemptions jointly, would not be eligible for any state exemptions. Id.

Like the Stephens court, this Court rejects this argument. See Stephens, 402 B.R. at 5 n.18. While the Court appreciates the fact that these scenarios might invoke the use of the hanging paragraph, it does not believe that these scenarios were what Congress had in mind when it enacted BAPCPA and added the hanging paragraph. See id. To begin with, debtors who recently relocated to the United States would be eligible to choose the federal exemptions without the hanging paragraph, because, just as there would be no state's exemption laws to apply, there would be no state's opt-out law to apply. See In re Arispe, 289 B.R. 245, 248 (Bankr. S.D. Fla. 2002) (prior to BAPCPA, holding a non-immigrant alien debtor eligible to elect the federal exemptions because he was not domiciled in any state during the look-back period, so no state's opt-out law could apply). Also, since the hanging paragraph was added at the same time that the extended look-back provision was introduced into § 522(b)(3)(A), the Court interprets the intent behind the hanging paragraph in light of the extended look-back provision. See id. (citing U.S. West Commc'ns, Inc. v. Hamilton, 224 F.3d 1049, 1053 (9th Cir. 2000)). Given that the extended look-back provision created an increased potential for a disconnect between current state of domicile and the exemptions available from the former state of domicile, the Court finds it likely that Congress intended the hanging paragraph to address any problems that might arise from that potential disconnect.[9] Thus, even if some of the Garrett court's scenarios work to prevent the hanging paragraph from becoming surplusage, they do not negate the Court's conclusion that Congress intended the hanging paragraph to alleviate some of the possible harsh effects of state exemption law eligibility requirements.

Finally, the Court notes that, as the Garrett court conceded, at present the hanging paragraph saves debtors formerly domiciled in one of at least seven states, who would otherwise be ineligible for any exemptions. See Garrett, 435 B.R. at 444 n.13; Brown et al., supra, App. C (listing the opt-out rules and extraterritoriality requirements for all the states). The Court finds it much more likely that Congress intended the hanging paragraph to handle the problem posed by seven states' laws than that it intended to aid foreign debtors or debtors recently returning to the United States from foreign countries. Because the hanging paragraph appears intended to assist in the event that a state restricts the extraterritorial effect of its exemptions, the Court finds that the total preemption argument is not persuasive, notwithstanding the existence of other possible

[9] The Court notes that the history of the BAPCPA legislation and the hanging paragraph also tend to support this argument. The bankruptcy court below argued that the hanging paragraph was the result of a letter from Department of Justice's Office of Legislative Affairs, who believed that "unintended gaps [would] still arise under [the proposed law] as debtors attempt to claim exemptions under the laws of another state in which they no longer reside or have property." See Fernandez, 445 B.R. at 815-16 (citing Letter to Representative Henry Hyde from Dennis K. Burke, Office of Legislative Affairs, Dept. of Justice (April 19, 1999), reprinted at H.R. Rep. No. 106-123, pt. 1, at 201 (1999)). Besides giving a basis for the inclusion of the hanging paragraph, this letter also supports the state-specific view of the effect of state exemption law eligibility requirements, as it implicitly acknowledges that some states might restrict the availability of their exemptions while others might not. However, because the letter was sent in reference to a proposed statute that predated the statute ultimately enacted by several years, and because the Court [*67] has doubts as to the persuasive power of this kind of legislative history, it does not rely on it here.

scenarios to which the hanging paragraph might apply.

c. Statutory language

Apart from making the hanging paragraph surplusage, the preemption view also runs aground on the language of the statute. As the bankruptcy court found below, if Congress intended to apply the state exemption laws without reference to their residency or territoriality requirements, it would likely have done so with different language. See Fernandez, 445 B.R. at 812. As currently written the statute uses the vague formulation that exempt property "is any property that is exempt under . . . State or local law." 11 U.S.C. § 522(b)(3)(A). A statute intended to preempt state exemption law territoriality requirements would instead likely provide that exempt property is any property that would be exempt under State or local law. See Fernandez, 445 B.R. at 812. Congress might have even been more clear and made explicit the contrary to fact condition implied in the "would be" language by stating that property exempt from the bankruptcy estate is any property that "that would be exempt if said property were located in or subject to the State or local law." Id. (emphasis in original). In fact, the Supreme Court twenty years ago held that Congress used a subjunctive construction in another part of § 522 to indicate when certain aspects of state law should be disregarded. See Owen, 500 U.S. at 311 (contrasting the phrase "is entitled" with "would have been entitled," and noting that the second phrase "denotes a state of affairs that is conceived or hypothetical, rather than actual, and requires the reader to disregard some element of reality"). The Court cannot ignore the fact that Congress used the indicative form "is" and not the subjunctive, "would be," and must interpret the statute as written. See Johnson, 632 F.3d at 922 ("courts must presume that a legislature says in a statute what it means and means in a statute what it says") (quotation omitted). If Congress intended a preemption of state law, it would have so indicated in the statute.

In sum, after considering the benefits and drawbacks of each possible interpretation, the Court finds that the second view of § 522(b) is the correct one. The bankruptcy court below erred when it decided that state exemption laws could never have extraterritorial effect and that Congress failed to appreciate this limitation when it drafted the statute. Instead, this Court finds that Congress wanted to respect limitations in state law on extraterritorial application of exemptions, and intended that debtors be allowed to use the exemptions of the state specified in § 522(b)(3)(A) to the extent that that state's law allows them to do so.

C. Extraterritoriality of Nevada's Homestead Exemption

[The court determines that nothing in Nevada law precludes the use of Nevada law to Texas real estate.-ed.]

Accordingly, the bankruptcy court's January 26, 2011, Memorandum Decision on Objection to Exemption is hereby REVERSED. Debtor is not precluded from claiming the Nevada homestead exemption on his Texas property simply because he and his property are located out of state. Debtor may claim the Nevada homestead exemption if he otherwise meets the requirements for the exemption set by Nevada law. The case is REMANDED to the bankruptcy court for further proceedings consistent with this opinion.

Notes and Questions

1. According to Bankruptcy Code § 522(b)(3), if a debtor does not or cannot choose the exemptions in § 522(d), the debtor is entitled to the exemptions under federal nonbankruptcy law and also under the

> local law that is applicable on the date of the filing of the petition at the place in which the debtor's domicile has been located for the 730 days immediately preceding the date of the filing of the petition, or if the debtor's domicile has not been located at a single State for such 730-day period, the place in which the debtor's domicile was located for 180 days immediately preceding the 730-day period or for a longer portion of such 180-day period than in any other place . . .

Bankruptcy Code § 522(b)(3)(A). Meanwhile, § 522(b)(2) provides a debtor can choose the § 522(d) exemptions, unless the State law that is applicable to the debtor under paragraph 3(A) specifically does not authorize.

According to Fla. Stat § 222.20, "residents of this state shall not be entitled to the federal exemptions provided in § 522(d) . . ."

Suppose D lives in Florida for some years but moves to Texas on April 30, 2007. D files for bankruptcy on June 10, 2008. Texas has not opted out. Can D choose the § 522(d) exemptions? Camp v. Ingalls (In re Camp), 631 F.3d 757 (5th Cir. 2011).

2. Suppose D moves to Ohio just before bankruptcy. Ohio and Florida are both opt-out states. Can D choose the federal exemptions? In re Beckwith, 448 B.R. 757 (Bankr. S.D. Ohio, 2011). Review the last sentence (the "hanging paragraph") in § 522(b) for a surprising result.

4. Judicial Lien Avoidance

EAST CAMBRIDGE SAVINGS BANK v SILVEIRA (IN RE SILVEIRA)

141 F.3d 34 (1st Cir. 1998)

STAHL, J.

. . . The Bankruptcy Code provides every debtor with a personal power to avoid certain types of liens that would impinge upon interests that the debtor would otherwise be entitled to claim as exemptions from the bankruptcy estate. 11 U.S.C. § 522(f)(1). Judicial liens are principal targets for this avoidance power:

> (f)(1). . . The debtor may avoid the fixing of a lien on an interest of the debtor in property to the extent that such lien impairs an exemption to which the debtor would have been entitled under [§ 522(b)], if such lien is--
>
> (A) a judicial lien, other than a judicial lien that secures a debt . . . .

In the years leading up to the Bankruptcy Reform Act of 1994 ("1994 Act"), a wide divergence of views developed concerning the circumstances in which a judicial lien could be deemed to "impair" an exemption within the meaning of § 522(f)(1), and the precise extent to which liens causing such impairment could be avoided. See, e.g., 2 DAVID G. EPSTEIN, STEVE H. NICKLES & JAMES J. WHITE, BANKRUPTCY § 8-28, at 560 (West 1992) (describing various approaches). In an effort to resolve this discord, Congress included in the 1994 Act an amendment to § 522(f), which added the following new subsection:

> For the purposes of this subsection, a lien shall be considered to impair an exemption to the extent that the sum of--
>
> (i) the lien;
>
> (ii) all other liens on the property; and
>
> (iii) the amount of the exemption that the debtor could claim if there

> were no liens on the property;
> exceeds the value that the debtor's interest in the property would have in the absence of any liens.

In this case, it is undisputed that the sum of the targeted judicial lien ($209,500), all other liens ($117,680) and the amount of the debtor's exemption ($15,000) exceeds the (stipulated) value of the debtor's property ($157,000), by $185,180. Thus, the Bank's judicial lien clearly does "impair" an exemption of the debtor within the meaning of § 522(f)(2)(A). The question here concerns the extent of the debtor's power under § 522(f)(1) to alleviate this "impairment."

The district court concluded that once a debtor's power of avoidance is triggered by the fact of an impairment of whatever size, that power permits the debtor to avoid the judicial lien causing the impairment in its entirety. The court thus held that Silveira was entitled to avoid the entire amount of the Bank's $209,500 lien. The Bank now argues that the district court misapplied § 522(f)(1)(A), and that Silveira is in fact entitled to avoid only so much of the Bank's lien as necessary to prevent impairment of the debtor's exemption within the meaning of § 522(f)(2)(A). We agree.

As an initial matter, we find unpersuasive Silveira's argument that the "plain language" of the statute supports the district court's view. On the contrary, the language of the relevant provisions seems to us to support the Bank's position. Section 522(f)(1) permits a debtor to "avoid the fixing of a lien on an interest of the debtor in property to the extent that such lien impairs an exemption [of the debtor]." 11 U.S.C. § 522(f)(1) (emphasis added). Section 522(f)(2)(A), similarly, provides that a judicial lien "impairs an exemption to the extent that" the targeted lien, in combination with other liens and the value of the debtor's exemption, exceeds the value of the debtor's property. 11 U.S.C. § 522(f)(2)(A) (emphasis added). If Congress intended for avoidance of judicial liens to be an "all-or-nothing" matter, one might wonder why the provisions' drafters chose to use the connective phrase "to the extent that," in lieu of the word "if," which obviously would have been a simpler construction. See In re Furkes, 65 B.R. 232, 235 (D.R.I. 1986) ("The 'to the extent that' clause cannot be seen as some sort of legislative slip of the pen. . . . Had Congress intended . . . an all-or-nothing proposition, it would have drafted the statutory language more infrangibly . . . ."). The statutory directive that a debtor may avoid a judicial lien "to the extent that" the lien impairs an exemption favors -- or is at least readily amenable to -- reading the definition of "impairment" in § 522(f)(2)(A) not only as a condition of avoidability, but also as a proportional measure of the scope of the debtor's avoidance power.

But even if the statute's language does not settle the issue, the debtor's proposed interpretation is unacceptable in view of the statute's intended purposes. Consider the following two hypothetical scenarios:

> Hypothetical A: The debtor owns a primary residence with a market value of $100,000, subject to an outstanding mortgage balance of $55,000, a judicial lien of $30,000 (not securing a debt), and no other liens. The debtor is entitled, under § 522(d)(1), to claim an exemption of $15,000 with respect to the property.
>
> Hypothetical B: Same as Hypothetical A, except that the debtor's property is subject to a judicial lien of $30,001 instead of $30,000.

In Hypothetical A, we can see that the sum of the judicial lien ($30,000), other liens ($55,000) and the debtor's exemption ($15,000) does not exceed the value of the debtor's property ($100,000). Thus the judicial lien in Hypothetical A does not impair the debtor's exemption within the meaning of § 522(f)(2)(A), and the debtor is not entitled to avoid any portion of that lien under § 522(f)(1).

In Hypothetical B, however, the sum of the judicial lien ($30,001), other liens ($55,000) and the debtor's exemption ($15,000) does exceed the property's value (by $1), and so the targeted judicial lien is deemed under § 522(f)(2)(A) to impair the debtor's exemption. Under Silveira's proposed interpretation, the fact of this impairment requires that the debtor in Hypothetical B be permitted to avoid the $30,001 judicial lien in its entirety. Thus, as Silveira would have it, a $1 increase in the amount of the (unavoidable) judicial lien in Hypothetical A would result in the debtor's acquiring the power to avoid the lien in full.[1]

We find it difficult to conceive of any reason that would counsel in favor of interpreting § 522(f)(1)(A) & (f)(2)(A) to produce such a result. The district court, in siding with Silveira, suggested that denying debtors the right to avoid in full any judicial lien that impairs an exemption would "circumvent" Congress's goal of providing debtors with a "fresh start" after bankruptcy and would thus frustrate the basic purpose of § 522(f)(1). The problem with this argument, however, is that it proves too much.

The implication of the district court's reasoning is that the statute effects a general policy against the fixing of judicial liens with respect to property in which the debtor holds an exempt interest. Clearly, however, the statute cannot be read so broadly. Section 522(f) unquestionably contemplates that in some circumstances -- see, for example, Hypothetical A above -- a judicial lien up to some calculable amount will not be deemed to impair the debtor's exemption and hence will not be subject to the debtor's avoidance power. But if, in such a circumstance, the statute would not permit the debtor to avoid any judicial lien smaller than that calculable amount, it would seem arbitrary and unfair to permit a debtor to avoid the entirety of a judicial lien that was larger than that amount. Thus, if § 522(f)(1) would permit the fixing of a $30,000 judicial lien on the facts of Hypothetical A above, then it would border on the absurd not to permit the holder of a $30,001 judicial lien, on otherwise identical facts, to pursue the fixing of its lien up to the amount of $30,000.

This reasoning compels an analogous result in this case. Here, the sum of the debtor's exemption ($15,000) and all consensual liens on his property ($117,680) is $24,320 less than the value of the property ($157,000); in other words, there is $24,320 of excess equity available. This means that if the Bank's judicial lien here had been for $24,320 or less, that lien would have been absolutely unavoidable under § 522(f)(1), because there would have been no "impairment" within the meaning of § 522(f)(2)(A).[2] The fact that the Bank's actual lien is for more than $24,320 surely provides no reason to place the Bank in a position worse than it would have been had its lien originally been limited to that amount. Fairness requires, therefore, that the Bank be permitted to pursue the fixing of its $209,500 judicial lien up to the amount of $24,320.

---

[1] The debtor in Hypothetical A would also acquire full avoidance power (according to Silveira's approach) if the value of the debtor's property or the amount of consensual liens were reduced by $1.

[2] That is, the sum of (i) the judicial lien ($24,320), (ii) other liens ($117,680), and (iii) the debtor's exemption ($15,000) would not have exceeded the value of the debtor's property ($157,000). See 11 U.S.C. § 522 (f)(2)(A).

In more intuitive terms, it is obvious that the value of the debtor's property in this case is sufficient to cover the entire amount of the debtor's mortgage ($117,680) plus his claimed exemption ($15,000), with $24,320 of equity to spare. Nothing in § 522(f)(1) or § 522(f)(2) can be read to require that this excess equity be preserved either for the debtor or the bankruptcy estate, rather than being made available for the partial satisfaction of a judicial lien. And, as shown above, the fixing of a judicial lien in an amount equal to this excess equity would not create any impairment of the debtor's $15,000 exemption. See 11 U.S.C. § 522(f)(2)(A). It follows that no legitimate purpose underlying the statute would be served by permitting Silveira to avoid so much of the Bank's lien -- $24,320 -- as could be covered by the excess equity available in the property.

In summary, we apply § 522(f)(1)(A) and § 522(f)(2)(A) to the facts of this case as follows. First, pursuant to § 522(f)(2)(A), we determine that the sum of (i) the targeted judicial lien ($209,500), (ii) all other liens ($117,680), and (iii) the amount of the debtor's exemption ($15,000) -- which sum equals $342,180 -- exceeds the value that the debtor's property would have in an unencumbered state ($157,000), and exceeds that value by $185,180. Thus, the Bank's judicial lien impairs the debtor's exemption to the extent of $185,180. Because Silveira is entitled to avoid the Bank's lien to the extent of any impairment, Silveira is entitled to avoidance in the amount of $185,180. See 11 U.S.C. § 522(f)(1)(A). The remainder of the Bank's judicial lien, in the amount of $24,320 ($209,500 minus $185,180), is not subject to avoidance by the debtor under § 522(f)(1)(A).

We note that this result follows the approach recently adopted by this Circuit's Bankruptcy Appellate Panel. See In re Finn, 211 B.R. 780 (1st Cir. BAP 1997); accord In re Ryan, 210 B.R. 7 (Bankr. D. Mass. 1997); In re Corson, 206 B.R. 17 (Bankr. D. Conn. 1997); In re Moe, 179 B.R. 654, 199 B.R. 737 (Bankr. D. Mont. 1995); see also 2 NORTON BANKRUPTCY LAW & PRACTICE 2d § 46:23, at 334-35 (Supp. 1997) (applying same approach); David G. Carlson, Security Interests on Exempt Property After the 1994 Amendments to the Bankruptcy Code, 4 AM. BANKR. INST. L. REV. 57, 65 (1996) (same).

. . . So Ordered.

Notes and Questions

1. The debtor's house was appraised at $157,000. Who gains if the value of the house is $200,000 after bankruptcy? Is this consistent with the spirit of Dewsnup v. Timm, supra?

2. Suppose JC obtains a judicial lien on D's non-exempt property. D files for bankruptcy and wrongly claims the property as exempt. The trustee fails to challenge the exemption by the deadline in Rule 4003(b). D then moves to avoid JC's lien under § 522(f)(1). Can JC challenge the exemption in light of the trustee's failure to object to the exemption? In re Schoonover, 331 F.3d 575 (7th Cir. 2003) (yes).

FARREY v. SANDERFOOT
500 U.S. 291 (1991)

WHITE, J.

In this case we consider whether § 522(f) of the Bankruptcy Code allows a debtor to avoid the fixing of a lien on a homestead, where the lien is granted to the debtor's former spouse under a divorce decree that extinguishes all previous interests the parties had in the property, and in no event secures more than the value of the nondebtor spouse's former interest. We hold that it does not.

I.

Petitioner Jeanne Farrey and respondent Gerald Sanderfoot were married on August 12, 1966. The couple eventually built a home on 27 acres of land in Hortonville, Wisconsin, where they raised their three children. On September 12, 1986, the Wisconsin Circuit Court for Outagamie County entered a bench decision granting a judgment of divorce and property division that resolved all contested issues and terminated the marriage. See Wis. Stat. § 767.37(3) (1989-1990). A written decree followed on February 5, 1987.

The decision awarded each party one-half of their net $60,600.68 marital estate. This division reflected Wisconsin's statutory presumption that the marital estate "be divided equally between the parties." § 767.255. The decree granted Sanderfoot sole title to all the real estate and the family house, which was subject to a mortgage and which was valued at $104,000, and most of the personal property. For her share, Farrey received the remaining items of personal property and the proceeds from a court-ordered auction of the furniture from the home. The judgment also allocated the couple's liabilities. Under this preliminary calculation of assets and debts, Sanderfoot stood to receive a net award of $59,508.79, while Farrey's award would otherwise have been $1,091.90. To ensure that the division of the estate was equal, the court ordered Sanderfoot to pay Farrey $29,208.44, half the difference in the value of their net assets. Sanderfoot was to pay this amount in two installments: half by January 10, 1987, and the remaining half by April 10, 1987. To secure this award, the decree provided that Farrey "shall have a lien against the real estate property of [Sanderfoot] for the total amount of money due her pursuant to this Order of the Court, i. e. $29,208.44, and the lien shall remain attached to the real estate property . . . until the total amount of money is paid in full." App. to Pet. for Cert. 57a.

Sanderfoot never made the required payments nor complied with any other order of the state court. Instead, on May 4, 1987, he voluntarily filed for Chapter 7 bankruptcy. Sanderfoot listed the marital home and real estate on the schedule of assets with his bankruptcy petition and listed it as exempt homestead property. Exercising his option to invoke the state rather than the federal homestead exemption, 11 U. S. C. § 522(b)(2)(A), Sanderfoot claimed the property as exempt "to the amount of $40,000" under Wis. Stat. § 815.20 (1989-1990).[1] He also filed a motion to avoid Farrey's lien under the provision in dispute, 11 U. S. C. § 522(f)(1), claiming that Farrey possessed a judicial lien that impaired his homestead exemption. Farrey objected to the motion, claiming that § 522(f)(1) could not divest her of her interest in the marital home. The Bankruptcy Court

---

[1] Section 815.20 provides in relevant part:

> "Homestead exemption definition.
>
> "(1) An exempt homestead as defined in s. 990.01(14) selected by a resident owner and occupied by him or her shall be exempt from execution, from the lien of every judgment and from liability for the debts of the owner to the amount of $40,000, except mortgages, laborers', mechanics' and purchase money liens and taxes and except as otherwise provided. . . . The exemption extends to the interest therein of the tenants in common, having a homestead thereon with the consent of the cotenants, and to any estate less than a fee."

denied Sanderfoot's motion, holding that the lien could not be avoided because it protected Farrey's pre-existing interest in the marital property. In re Sanderfoot, 83 B.R. 564 (ED Wis. 1988). The District Court reversed, concluding that the lien was avoidable because it "is fixed on an interest of the debtor in the property." In re Sanderfoot, 92 B.R. 802 (ED Wis. 1988).

A divided panel of the Court of Appeals affirmed. In re Sanderfoot, 899 F.2d 598 (CA7 1990). The court reasoned that the divorce proceeding dissolved any pre-existing interest Farrey had in the homestead and that her new interest, "created in the dissolution order and evidenced by her lien, attached to Mr. Sanderfoot's interest in the property." Id., at 602. Noting that the issue had caused a split among the Courts of Appeals, the court expressly relied on those decisions that it termed more "faithful to the plain language of section 522(f)." Ibid. (citing In re Pederson, 875 F.2d 781 (CA9 1989); Maus v. Maus, 837 F.2d 935 (CA10 1988); Boyd v. Robinson, 741 F.2d 1112, 1115 (CA8 1984) (Ross, J., dissenting)).

Judge Posner, in dissent, argued that to avoid a lien under § 522(f), a debtor must have an interest in the property at the time the court places the lien on that interest. Judge Posner concluded that because the same decree that gave the entire property to Sanderfoot simultaneously created the lien in favor of Farrey, the lien did not attach to a pre-existing interest of the husband. The dissent's conclusion followed the result, though not the rationale, of Boyd, supra, In re Borman, 886 F.2d 273 (CA10 1989), and In re Donahue, 862 F.2d 259 (CA10 1988).

We granted certiorari to resolve the conflict of authority. 498 U.S. 980 (1990). We now reverse the Court of Appeals' judgment and remand.

II.

Section 522(f)(1) provides in relevant part:

> "Notwithstanding any waiver of exemptions, the debtor may avoid the fixing of a lien on an interest of the debtor in property to the extent that such lien impairs an exemption to which the debtor would have been entitled under subsection (b) of this section, if such lien is --
>
> "(1) a judicial lien . . . ."

The provision establishes several conditions for a lien to be avoided, only one of which is at issue. See In re Hart, 50 B.R. 956, 960 (Bkrtcy. Ct. Nev. 1985). Farrey does not challenge the Court of Appeals' determination that her lien was a judicial lien, 899 F.2d at 603-605, nor do we address that question here. The Court of Appeals also determined that Farrey had waived any challenge as to whether Sanderfoot was otherwise entitled to a homestead exemption under state law, id., at 603, and we agree. See Owen v. Owen, 500 U.S. 305 (1991). The sole question presented in this case is whether § 522(f)(1) permits Sanderfoot to avoid the fixing of Farrey's lien on the property interest that he obtained in the divorce decree.

The key portion of § 522(f) states that "the debtor may avoid the fixing of a lien on an interest . . . in property." Sanderfoot, following several Courts of Appeals, suggests that this phrase means that a lien may be avoided so long as it is currently fixed on a debtor's interest. Farrey, following Judge Posner's lead, reads the text as permitting the avoidance of a lien only where the lien attached to the debtor's interest at some point after the debtor obtained the interest.

We agree with Farrey. No one asserts that the two verbs underlying the provision possess anything other than their standard legal meaning: "avoid" meaning "annul" or "undo," see Black's Law Dictionary 136 (6th ed. 1990); H. R. Rep. No. 95-595, pp. 126-127 (1977), and "fix" meaning to "fasten a liability upon," see Black's Law Dictionary, supra, at 637. The statute does not say that the debtor may undo a lien on an interest in property. Rather, the statute expressly states that the debtor may avoid "the fixing" of a lien on the debtor's interest in property. The gerund "fixing" refers to a temporal event. That event -- the fastening of a liability -- presupposes an object onto which the liability can fasten. The statute defines this pre-existing object as "an interest of the debtor in property." Therefore, unless the debtor had the property interest to which the lien attached at some point before the lien attached to that interest, he or she cannot avoid the fixing of the lien under the terms of § 522(f)(1).[2]

This reading fully comports with the provision's purpose and history. See United States v. Ron Pair Enterprises, Inc., 489 U.S. 235, 242 (1989). Congress enacted § 522(f) with the broad purpose of protecting the debtor's exempt property. See S. Rep. No. 95-989, p. 77 (1978); H. R. Rep. No. 95-595, supra, at 126-127. Ordinarily, liens and other secured interests survive bankruptcy. In particular, it was well settled when § 522(f) was enacted that valid liens obtained before bankruptcy could be enforced on exempt property, see Louisville Joint Stock Land Bank v. Radford, 295 U.S. 555, 582-583 (1935), including otherwise exempt homestead property, Long v. Bullard, 117 U.S. 617, 620-621 (1886). Congress generally preserved this principle when it comprehensively revised bankruptcy law with the Bankruptcy Reform Act of 1978, Pub. L. 95-598, 92 Stat. 2587, 11 U. S. C. § 522(c)(2)(A)(i). But Congress also revised the law to permit the debtor to avoid the fixing of some liens. See, e. g., 11 U. S. C. § 545 (statutory liens).

Section 522(f)(1), by its terms, extends this protection to cases involving the fixing of judicial liens onto exempt property. What specific legislative history exists suggests that a principal reason Congress singled out judicial liens was because they are a device commonly used by creditors to defeat the protection bankruptcy law accords exempt property against debts. As the House Report stated:

> "The first right [§ 522(f)(1)] allows the debtor to undo the actions of creditors

---

[2] Other provisions of the Code likewise indicate that Congress used the term "fixing" to refer to the timing of an event. Section 545(1), for example, provides:

> "The trustee may avoid the fixing of a statutory lien on property of the debtor to the extent that such lien --
> "(1) first becomes effective against the debtor --
> "(A) when a case under this title concerning the debtor is commenced;
> "(B) when an insolvency proceeding other than under this title concerning the debtor is commenced;
> "(C) when a custodian is appointed or authorized to take or takes possession;
> "(D) when the debtor become insolvent;
> "(E) when the debtor's financial condition fails to meet a specified standard; or
> "(F) at the time of an execution against property of the debtor levied at the instance of an entity other than the holder of such statutory lien." 11 U. S. C. § 545 (1) (emphasis added).

that bring legal action against the debtor shortly before bankruptcy. Bankruptcy exists to provide relief for an overburdened debtor. If a creditor beats the debtor into court, the debtor is nevertheless entitled to his exemptions." H. R. Rep. No. 95-595, supra, at 126-127.

One factor supporting the view that Congress intended § 522(f)(1) to thwart a rush to the courthouse is Congress' contemporaneous elimination of § 67a of the 1898 Bankruptcy Act, 30 Stat. 564. Prior to its repeal, § 67a invalidated any lien obtained on an exempt interest of an insolvent debtor within four months of the bankruptcy filing. The Bankruptcy Reform Act eliminated the insolvency and timing requirements. It is possible that Congress simply decided to leave exemptions exposed despite its longstanding policy against doing so. But given the legislative history's express concern over protecting exemptions, it follows instead that § 522(f)(1) was intended as a new device to handle the old provision's job by "giving the debtor certain rights not available under current law with respect to exempt property." H. R. Rep. No. 95-595, supra, at 126-127.

Conversely, the text, history, and purpose of § 522(f)(1) also indicate what the provision is not concerned with. It cannot be concerned with liens that fixed on an interest before the debtor acquired that interest. Neither party contends otherwise. Section 522(f)(1) does not state that any fixing of a lien may be avoided; instead, it permits avoidance of the "fixing of a lien on an interest of the debtor." If the fixing took place before the debtor acquired that interest, the "fixing" by definition was not on the debtor's interest. Nor could the statute apply given its purpose of preventing a creditor from beating the debtor to the courthouse, since the debtor at no point possessed the interest without the judicial lien. There would be no fixing to avoid since the lien was already there. To permit lien avoidance in these circumstances, in fact, would be to allow judicial lienholders to be defrauded through the conveyance of an encumbered interest to a prospective debtor. See In re McCormick, 18 B.R. 911, 913-914 (Bkrtcy. Ct. WD Pa. 1982). For these reasons, it is settled that a debtor cannot use § 522(f)(1) to avoid a lien on an interest acquired after the lien attached. See, e. g., In re McCormick, supra; In re Stephens, 15 B.R. 485 (Bkrtcy. Ct. WD NC 1981); In re Scott, 12 B.R. 613 (Bkrtcy. Ct. WD Okla. 1981). As before, the critical inquiry remains whether the debtor ever possessed the interest to which the lien fixed, before it fixed. If he or she did not, § 522(f)(1) does not permit the debtor to avoid the fixing of the lien on that interest.

III.

We turn to the application of § 522(f)(1) to this case.

Whether Sanderfoot ever possessed an interest to which the lien fixed, before it fixed, is a question of state law. Farrey contends that prior to the divorce judgment, she and her husband held title to the real estate in joint tenancy, each possessing an undivided one-half interest. She further asserts that the divorce decree extinguished these previous interests. At the same time and in the same transaction, she concludes, the decree created new interests in place of the old: for Sanderfoot, ownership in fee simple of the house and real estate; for Farrey, various assets and a debt of $29,208.44 secured by a lien on the Sanderfoot's new fee simple interest. Both in his briefs and at oral argument, Sanderfoot agreed on each point. Brief for Respondent 7-8; Tr. of Oral Arg. 39.

On the assumption that the parties characterize Wisconsin law correctly,

Sanderfoot must lose. Under their view, the lien could not have fixed on Sanderfoot's pre-existing undivided half interest because the divorce decree extinguished it. Instead, the only interest that the lien encumbers is debtor's wholly new fee simple interest. The same decree that awarded Sanderfoot his fee simple interest simultaneously granted the lien to Farrey. As the judgment stated, he acquired the property "free and clear" of any claim "except as expressly provided in this [decree]." App. to Pet. for Cert. 58a. Sanderfoot took the interest and the lien together, as if he had purchased an already encumbered estate from a third party. Since Sanderfoot never possessed his new fee simple interest before the lien "fixed," § 522(f)(1) is not available to void the lien.

The same result follows even if the divorce decree did not extinguish the couple's pre-existing interests but instead merely reordered them. The parties' current position notwithstanding, it may be that under Wisconsin law the divorce decree augmented Sanderfoot's previous interest by adding to it Farrey's prior interest. If the court in exchange sought to protect Farrey's previous interest with a lien, § 522(f)(1) could be used to undo the encumbrance to the extent the lien fastened to any portion of Sanderfoot's previous surviving interest. This follows because Sanderfoot would have possessed the interest to which that part of the lien fixed, before it fixed. But in this case, the divorce court did not purport to encumber any part of Sanderfoot's previous interest even on the assumption that state law would deem that interest to have survived. The decree instead transferred Farrey's previous interest to Sanderfoot and, again simultaneously, granted a lien equal to that interest minus the small amount of personal property she retained. Sanderfoot thus would still be unable to avoid the lien in this case since it fastened only to what had been Farrey's pre-existing interest, and this interest Sanderfoot would never have possessed without the lien already having fixed.[3]

The result, on either theory, accords with the provision's main purpose. As noted, the legislative history suggests that Congress primarily intended § 522(f)(1) as a device to thwart creditors who, sensing an impending bankruptcy, rush to court to obtain a judgment to defeat the debtor's exemptions. That is not what occurs in a divorce proceeding such as this. Farrey obtained the lien not to defeat Sanderfoot's pre-existing interest in the homestead but to protect her own pre-existing interest in the homestead that was fully equal to that of her spouse. The divorce court awarded the lien to secure an obligation the court imposed on the husband in exchange for the court's simultaneous award of the wife's homestead interest to the husband. We agree with Judge Posner that to permit a debtor in these circumstances to use the Code to deprive a spouse of this protection would neither follow the language of the statute nor serve the main goal it was designed to address.

IV.

We hold that § 522(f)(1) of the Bankruptcy Code requires a debtor to have possessed an interest to which a lien attached, before it attached, to avoid the fixing of the lien on that interest. Accordingly, the judgment of the Court of Appeals is reversed, and the case is remanded for further proceedings consistent with this opinion.

---

[3] JUSTICE SCALIA does not join in this paragraph.

MARINE MIDLAND BANK v. SCARPINO
113 F.3d 338 (2d Cir. 1997)

KEARSE, J.

This appeal turns on whether New York law, under which an unsatisfied money judgment automatically becomes a lien on real property thereafter acquired by the judgment debtor in the county in which the judgment has been docketed, see, e.g., Hulbert v. Hulbert, 216 N.Y. 430, 111 N.E. 70 (1916) ("Hulbert"); N.Y. C.P.L.R. 5203 Practice Commentaries, leaves a temporal interval between the acquisition of the property and the attachment of the lien. Marine Midland Bank ("Marine Midland" or the "Bank") appeals from a judgment of the United States District Court for the Western District of New York, Michael A. Telesca, Judge, affirming an order of the Bankruptcy Court for the Western District of New York that granted the motion of debtor Mark Scarpino pursuant to 11 U.S.C. § 522(f) (1994) to avoid the Bank's judgment lien on certain real property he acquired after the Bank had docketed its judgment. Both courts ruled that, under New York law, after Scarpino acquired the property there was an interval before the Bank's judgment lien attached, thereby per-mitting Scarpino to avoid attachment of the lien. On appeal, Marine Midland challenges that ruling, contending that, with respect to an interest in real property acquired by a judgment debtor after the judgment has been docketed, the judgment lien created by New York law attaches to that interest simultaneously with the debtor's acquisition of the interest. We agree, and we therefore reverse.

I. Background

In 1990, Marine Midland obtained a judgment against Scarpino in New York State Supreme Court in the amount of $16,378.56. The judgment was docketed in the office of the Monroe County Clerk on December 11, 1990, and was never satisfied. In 1994, after obtaining a mortgage in the amount of $86,540, Scarpino purchased a parcel of real property in Monroe County. In October 1995, he petitioned for bankruptcy under Chapter 7, see 11 U.S.C. §§ 701-66 (1994), of the Bankruptcy Code, 11 U.S.C. §§ 101 -1330 (the "Code").

To the extent pertinent to this appeal, New York law provides a judgment debtor with a homestead exemption to the extent of $10,000, see N.Y. C.P.L.R. 5206(a) (McKinney 1978), and the Code allows a debtor to "avoid the fixing of" a judgment lien to the extent that the lien would impair an exemption to which the debtor would otherwise be entitled, 11 U.S.C. § 522(f). In papers filed with his bankruptcy petition, Scarpino listed his Monroe County real property as an asset valued at $86,500; pursuant to 11 U.S.C. § 522(b)(2)(A), he claimed the $10,000 homestead exemption. Shortly thereafter, he moved in the bankruptcy court pursuant to § 522(f) to avoid Marine Midland's judgment lien on the property.

Marine Midland opposed Scarpino's motion. Though it acknowledged that the sum of its lien ($16,378.56), the mortgage balance ($86,061.60), and the amount of the exemption ($10,000) exceeded the value of the property ($86,500), it argued that § 522(f), as inter-preted by the Supreme Court in Farrey v. Sanderfoot, 500 U.S. 291 (1991), does not allow a debtor to avoid a lien unless the lien attached sometime after the debtor acquired the property. Relying on the New York Court of Appeals decision in Hulbert, in which the court stated that a judgment lien attaches "to the interest of [the judgment debtor] upon his acquiring title to that interest," 216 N.Y. at 433, the Bank argued that its lien attached simultaneously with Scarpino's acquisition of the property, not afterwards, and hence could not be avoided pursuant to § 522(f).

The bankruptcy court . . . granted Scarpino's motion to avoid the Bank's lien. While accepting the Bank's premise that Farrey v. Sanderfoot means that a debtor cannot under § 522(f) avoid a judgment lien that attached to exempt property simultaneously with the property's acquisition, the court rejected Marine Midland's interpretation of state law. It distinguished Hulbert on the ground that that case did not directly involve the question of the time at which a judgment lien attaches but only the question of which of several judgment creditors' liens had priority. See Bankruptcy Court Opinion at 5-7. The bankruptcy court viewed the question of the time at which a judgment lien attaches to the debtor's later-acquired property as "a matter of first impression," id. at 4, and it resolved the question in favor of Scarpino, stating that "logic and common sense would dictate that an interest would first have to be acquired before any other right, title or interest could be acquired in it or attach to it, including the attachment of a lien of a prior judgment." Id. at 7. The bankruptcy court inferred support for its conclusion from the language of another New York decision, In re Hazard's Estate, 73 Hun 22, 25 N.Y.S. 928 (Sup. Ct. 1893), aff'd, 141 N.Y. 586, 36 N.E. 739 (1894), that "until title is acquired it seems to be clear that no lien can attach," id. at 931. See Bankruptcy Court Opinion at 6-7.

The district court affirmed, agreeing with the bankruptcy court that Hulbert was dis-tinguishable on the ground that it "addressed the issue of lien priority, not the question of precisely when the liens attached to the after-acquired property interest," Stating that "con-ceptually, there could be no attachment of the pre-existing lien until the property was first transferred to the debtor," id., the district court ruled that the Bank's lien did not attach until sometime after Scarpino owned the property and that he was therefore entitled to avoid the lien pursuant to § 522(f).

This appeal followed.

II. Discussion

A bankruptcy estate generally comprises all property in which a debtor has an interest at the time the petition is filed. See 11 U.S.C. § 541. Section 522(b) of the Code, however, allows the debtor in a liquidation case to exempt from the estate certain property that would otherwise be liquidated and distributed to creditors. The effect of exemption is to immunize the exempt property from seizure or attachment for satisfaction of debts incurred prior to the bankruptcy proceeding. See id. § 522(c) (exempt property generally "is not liable during or after the case for any debt of the debtor that arose . . . before the commencement of the [bankruptcy] case"). The purpose of allowing such exemptions is to help ensure that "a debtor that [sic] goes through bankruptcy comes out with adequate possessions to begin his fresh start." H.R. Rep. No. 95-595, at 126 (1977), reprinted in, 1978 U.S.C.C.A.N. 5963, 6087.

Section 522(c), however, provides no such immunization with respect to any of the debtor's liabilities that were secured by liens on the exempt property, unless those liens are avoided during the bankruptcy case under certain sections of the Code, including § 522(f). See 11 U.S.C. § 522(c)(2); Johnson v. Home State Bank, 501 U.S. 78, 82-84 (1991) (unavoided liens survive bankruptcy, and lienholders may, pursuant to applicable state-law procedure, enforce them against the debtor's property after the bankruptcy case is closed); Farrey v. Sanderfoot, 500 U.S. at 297; S. Rep. No. 95-989, at 76 (1978), reprinted in 1978 U.S.C.C.A.N. 5787, 5862. Section 522(f) provides, to the extent pertinent here, that

> the debtor may avoid the fixing of a lien on an interest of the debtor in property to the extent that such lien impairs an exemption to which the debtor would have been entitled under subsection (b) of this section, if such lien is--
>
> (A) a judicial lien . . .

11 U.S.C. § 522(f)(1)(A), and it defines "impairment" as the amount by which the sum of (a) the lien whose avoidance is sought, (b) all other liens, and (c) the amount of the exemption "exceeds the value that the debtor's interest in the property would have in the absence of any liens," id. § (f)(2)(A). The purpose of allowing avoidance of such liens is to "protect[] the debtor's exemptions, his discharge, and thus his fresh start." S. Rep. No. 95-989, at 76, reprinted in 1978 U.S.C.C.A.N. at 5862.

In Farrey v. Sanderfoot, the Supreme Court reasoned that, by referring to the "fixing" of the lien, § 522(f) contemplates a property interest that existed before the lien attached, and the Court concluded that if the creation of the interest and the creation of the lien are simultaneous, there can be no avoidance of the lien under that section:

> The statute does not say that the debtor may undo a lien on an interest in property. Rather, the statute expressly states that the debtor may avoid "the fixing" of a lien on the debtor's interest in property. The gerund "fixing" refers to a temporal event. That event--the fastening of a liability--presupposes an object onto which the liability can fasten. The statute defines this pre-existing object as "an interest of the debtor in property." Therefore, unless the debtor had the property interest to which the lien attached at some point before the lien attached to that interest, he or she cannot avoid the fixing of the lien under the terms of § 522(f)(1).

500 U.S. at 296. The Court stated that "the critical inquiry remains whether the debtor ever possessed the interest to which the lien fixed, before it fixed." Id. at 299 In the case before it, the Farrey Court held that the debtor was not entitled under § 522(f) to avoid a judicial lien on homestead property awarded to him under a divorce decree because that lien, which was created by the same decree, attached to the property simultaneously with the debtor's acquisition of the property. See id. at 299-300.

The question before this Court, therefore, is whether, under New York law, a judgment lien attaches at the moment of the debtor's postjudgment acquisition of real property or sometime thereafter. We conclude that the lien attaches at the moment of acquisition.

Since at least 1813, New York has provided by statute for a lien that automatically attaches to a judgment debtor's real property if the judgment is docketed in the county in which the property is located. See, e.g., Hulbert, 216 N.Y. at 440; N.Y. C.P.L.R. 5203 (McKinney 1978). As to a properly docketed judgment, the present provision states that, for a 10-year period, "no transfer of an interest of the judgment debtor in real property, against which property a money judgment may be enforced, is effective against the judgment creditor . . . ." N.Y. C.P.L.R. 5203. As we read this provision, there cannot be an interval between the debtor's postjudgment acquisition of an interest and the fixing of the lien arising from a previously docketed judgment, for if there were, the debtor would logically be able to transfer his interest in that interval, defeating the lien of the judgment creditor. Since, as § 5203 indicates, the debtor would not be allowed to thus defeat the judgment creditor's interest, we conclude that there is no interval in which the lien has not attached. We need not rely on our own interpretation of the statute to reach this conclusion, however, for unlike the bankruptcy court, we do not view this case as presenting a question of first impression.

For many decades, the New York Court of Appeals, interpreting predecessors of § 5203, has construed New York law to mean (a) that the lien attaches "from the moment a judgment is duly filed and docketed," Hulbert, 216 N.Y. at 440, and (b) that the lien extends not only to real property the debtor owned at the time the judgment was docketed, but also to any real property acquired by him thereafter, see, e.g., id at 433; In re Hazard's Estate, 73 Hun 22, 25 N.Y.S. 928, 930 (Sup. Ct. 1893) ("Hazard's Estate") (citing N.Y. C.C.P. § 1251, which provided that a properly docketed judgment, for a period of 10 years, "binds, and is a charge upon . . . the real property . . . in that county, which the judgment debtor has at the time of so docketing it, or which he acquires at any time afterwards" (emphasis added)), aff'd, 141 N.Y. 586, 36 N.E. 739 (1894). As to such after-acquired property, the New York Court of Appeals in Hulbert stated that it was the "settled rule" that a judgment lien on the judgment debtor's property interest attaches "at the time of its acquisition by the debtor," i.e., "upon [the debtor's] acquiring title to that interest." 216 N.Y. at 433 (emphases added). See also In re Luftman, 245 F. Supp. 723, 725 (S.D.N.Y. 1965) (Feinberg, J.) (judgment lien attaches to subsequently acquired property at "the moment the debtor obtains the realty"). Although the precise question before the Hulbert court was which of several judgment liens, if any, had priority with respect to property that the debtor inherited after the judgments were docketed, we see no basis for disregarding that court's clear and repeated view that the docketed judgments became liens on the after-acquired property of the judgment debtor: "at the time of its acquisition by the debtor," 216 N.Y. at 433; "when [the debtor] acquired the property," 216 N.Y. at 441; "upon his acquisition of the interest," id. at 440; "upon his acquiring title to that interest," id. at 433.

The district and bankruptcy courts in the present case relied on Hazard's Estate for the proposition that the lien arises not upon the judgment debtor's acquisition of the interest but sometime thereafter. That reading of the New York Supreme Court's opinion in Hazard's Estate is not warranted, and indeed is contrary to the interpretation given Hazard's Estate by the New York Court of Appeals. The Hazard's Estate opinion merely emphasized the obvious: that a lien cannot attach to a person's interest in property before the interest is created. See 25 N.Y.S. at 931 ("until title is acquired it seems to be clear that no lien can attach"). But the court did not indicate that it equated "not before," id., with after, for it stated that the lien arises "when the debtor acquires the property," id. at 930 (emphasis added). Noting the statutory language that a judgment lien "'shall bind the lands'" acquired by the judgment debtor "'at any time thereafter,'" the Hazard's Estate court asked "Bind when? Clearly when acquired, and not before." Id. at 930-31. Thus, the Hulbert court, which had affirmed in Hazard's Estate on the basis of the Supreme Court's opinion, cited Hazard's Estate for "the settled rule" that judgments become liens on an after-acquired property interest of the judgment debtor at the time the debtor acquires his interest. Hulbert, 216 N.Y. at 433.

Given New York's "settled rule," we conclude that Marine Midland's judgment lien attached to Scarpino's Monroe County property simultaneously with his acquisition of the property. Accordingly, the lien is not avoidable pursuant to § 522(f).

Conclusion

We have considered all of Scarpino's arguments in favor of affirmance and have found them to be without merit. The judgment of the district court is reversed, and the order of the bankruptcy court avoiding the lien is vacated.

Notes

1. Not only does § 522(f)(1)(A) destroy "judicial liens" that impair exemptions, but § 522(f)(1)(B) destroys consensually created security interests on certain designated personal property. Purchase money security interests and pledges, however, may not be destroyed.

In response to § 522(f)(1)(B), lending institutions began to lobby for reworded exemption statutes, of which the following Tennessee provision is typical.

> Personal property to the aggregate value of four thousand dollars (4000.00) debtor's equity interest shall be exempt from execution, seizure or attachment . . . [The debtor] may select for exemption the items of the owned and possessed personal property . . . up to the aggregate value of four thousand dollars (4000.00) debtor's equity interest.

T.C.A. § 26-2-102. The idea of this statute is that, since only debtor equity, is exempt, a lender's consensual security interest never impairs it. Therefore, § 522(f)(1)(B) cannot possibly destroy the security interest. Courts initially agreed with this proposition. Pine v. Credithrift of America, 717 F.2d 281 (6th Cir. 1983). What does the next case have to say about such state exemption laws?

OWEN v. OWEN

500 U.S. 305 (1991)

SCALIA, J.

The Bankruptcy Code allows the States to define what property a debtor may exempt from the bankruptcy estate that will be distributed among his creditors. 11 U. S. C. § 522(b). The Code also provides that judicial liens encumbering exempt property can be eliminated. § 522(f). The question in this case is whether that elimination can operate when the State has defined the exempt property in such a way as specifically to exclude property encumbered by judicial liens.

I

In 1975, Helen Owen, the respondent, obtained a judgment against petitioner Dwight Owen, her former husband, for approximately $160,000. The judgment was recorded in Sarasota County, Florida, in July 1976. Petitioner did not at that time own any property in Sarasota County, but under Florida law, the judgment would attach to any after-acquired property recorded in the county. B. A. Lott, Inc. v. Padgett, 153 Fla. 304, 14 So. 2d 667 (1943). In 1984, petitioner purchased a condominium in Sarasota County; upon acquisition of title, the property became subject to respondent's judgment lien. Porter-Mallard Co. v. Dugger, 117 Fla. 137, 157 So. 429 (1934).

One year later, Florida amended its homestead law so that petitioner's condominium, which previously had not qualified as a homestead, thereafter did.

Under the Florida Constitution, homestead property is "exempt from forced sale . . . and no judgment, decree or execution [can] be a lien thereon . . .," Fla. Const., Art. 10, § 4(a). The Florida courts have interpreted this provision, however, as being inapplicable to pre-existing liens, i. e., liens that attached before the property acquired its homestead status. Bessemer v. Gersten, 381 So. 2d 1344, 1347, n.1 (Fla. 1980); Aetna Ins. Co. v. LaGasse, 223 So. 2d 727, 728 (Fla. 1969); Pasco v. Harley, 73 Fla. 819, 824-825, 75 So. 30, 32-33 (1917); Volpitta v. Fields, 369 So. 2d 367, 369 (Fla. App. 1979); Lyon v. Arnold, 46 F.2d 451, 452 (CA5 1931). Pre-existing liens, then, are in effect an exception to the Florida homestead exemption.

In January 1986, petitioner filed for bankruptcy under Chapter 7 of the Code, and claimed a homestead exemption in his Sarasota condominium. The condominium, valued at approximately $135,000, was his primary asset; his liabilities included approximately $350,000 owed to respondent. The Bankruptcy Court discharged petitioner's personal liability for these debts, and sustained, over respondent's objections, his claimed exemption.

The condominium, however, remained subject to respondent's pre-existing lien, and after discharge, petitioner moved to reopen his case to avoid the lien pursuant to § 522(f)(1). The Bankruptcy Court refused to decree the avoidance; the District Court affirmed, finding that the lien had attached before the property qualified for the exemption, and that Florida law therefore did not exempt the lien-encumbered property. 86 B.R. 691 (MD Fla. 1988). The Court of Appeals for the Eleventh Circuit affirmed on the same ground. 877 F.2d 44 (1989). We granted certiorari. 495 U.S. 929 (1990).

II

An estate in bankruptcy consists of all the interests in property, legal and equitable, possessed by the debtor at the time of filing, as well as those interests recovered or recoverable through transfer and lien avoidance provisions. An exemption is an interest withdrawn from the estate (and hence from the creditors) for the benefit of the debtor. Section 522 determines what property a debtor may exempt. Under § 522(b), he must select between a list of federal exemptions (set forth in § 522(d)) and the exemptions provided by his State, "unless the State law that is applicable to the debtor . . . specifically does not so authorize," § 522(b)(1) -- that is, unless the State "opts out" of the federal list. If a State opts out, then its debtors are limited to the exemptions provided by state law. Nothing in subsection (b) (or elsewhere in the Code) limits a State's power to restrict the scope of its exemptions; indeed, it could theoretically accord no exemptions at all.

Property that is properly exempted under § 522 is (with some exceptions) immunized against liability for prebankruptcy debts. § 522(c). No property can be exempted (and thereby immunized), however, unless it first falls within the bankruptcy estate. Section 522(b) provides that the debtor may exempt certain property "from property of the estate"; obviously, then, an interest that is not possessed by the estate cannot be exempted. Thus, if a debtor holds only bare legal title to his house -- if, for example, the house is subject to a purchase-money mortgage for its full value -- then only that legal interest passes to the estate; the equitable interest remains with the mortgage holder, § 541(d).[1] And since the equitable interest does not pass to the estate, neither can it pass to the debtor as an exempt interest in property. Legal title will pass, and can be the subject of an exemption; but the property will remain subject to the lien interest of the mortgage holder. This was the rule of Long v. Bullard, 117 U.S. 617 (1886), codified in § 522. Only where the Code empowers the court to avoid liens or transfers can an interest originally not within the estate be passed to the estate, and subsequently (through the claim of an exemption) to the debtor. It is such an avoidance provision that is at issue here, to which we now turn. Section 522(f) reads as follows:

> "(f) Notwithstanding any waiver of exemptions, the debtor may avoid the fixing of a lien on an interest of the debtor in property to the extent that such lien impairs an exemption to which the debtor would have been entitled under subsection (b) of this section, if such lien is --
>
> "(1) a judicial lien; or
>
> "(2) a nonpossessory, nonpurchase-money security interest . . . ."

The lien in the present case is a judicial lien, and we assume without deciding that it fixed "on an interest of the debtor in property." See Farrey v. Sanderfoot, ante, p. 291. The question presented by this case is whether it "impairs an exemption to which [petitioner] would have been entitled under subsection (b)." Since Florida has chosen to opt out of the listed federal exemptions, see Fla. Stat. § 222.20 (1989), the only subsection (b) exemption at issue is the Florida homestead exemption described above. Respondent suggests that, to resolve this case, we need only ask whether the judicial lien impairs that exemption. It obviously does not, since the Florida homestead exemption is not assertable against pre-existing judicial liens. To permit avoidance of the lien, respondent urges, would not preserve the exemption but would expand it.

At first blush, this seems entirely reasonable. Several Courts of Appeals in addition to the Eleventh Circuit here have reached this result with respect to built-in limitations on state exemptions, though others have rejected it. What must give us pause, however, is that this result has been widely and uniformly rejected with respect to built-in limitations on the federal exemptions. Most of the federally listed exemptions (set forth in § 522(d)) are explicitly restricted to the "debtor's aggregate interest" or the "debtor's interest" up to a maximum amount. See §§ 522(d)(1)-(6), (8). If respondent's approach to § 522(f) were applied, all of these exemptions (and perhaps others as well) would be limited by unavoided encumbering liens, see § 522(c). The federal homestead exemption, for example, allows the debtor to exempt from the property of the estate "the debtor's aggregate interest, not to exceed $7,500 in value, in . . . a residence." § 522(d)(1). If respondent's interpretation of § 522(f) were applied to this exemption, a debtor who owned a house worth $10,000 that was subject to a judicial lien for $9,000 would not be entitled to the full homestead exemption of $7,500. The judicial lien would not be avoidable under § 522(f), since it does not "impair" the exemption, which is limited to the debtor's "aggregate interest" of $1,000. The uniform practice of bankruptcy courts, however, is to the contrary. To determine the

[1] [This is a highly confusing characterization of the law of mortgages. Usually, a debtor (not the mortgagee) is said to have the equitable interest following the grant of a mortgage. Nor does it make any difference whether the mortgage is for purchase money or not. -Ed.]

application of § 522(f) they ask not whether the lien impairs an exemption to which the debtor is in fact entitled, but whether it impairs an exemption to which he would have been entitled but for the lien itself.

As the preceding italicized words suggest, this reading is more consonant with the text of § 522(f) -- which establishes as the baseline, against which impairment is to be measured, not an exemption to which the debtor "is entitled," but one to which he "would have been entitled." The latter phrase denotes a state of affairs that is conceived or hypothetical, rather than actual, and requires the reader to disregard some element of reality. "Would have been" but for what? The answer given, with respect to the federal exemptions, has been but for the lien at issue, and that seems to us correct.

The only other conceivable possibility is but for a waiver-harking back to the beginning phrase of § 522(f), "Notwithstanding any waiver of exemptions . . . ." The use of contrary-to-fact construction after a "notwithstanding" phrase is not, however, common usage, if even permissible. Moreover, though one might employ it when the "notwithstanding" phrase is the main point of the provision in question ("Notwithstanding any waiver, a debtor shall retain those exemptions to which he would have been entitled under subsection (b)"), it would be most strange to employ it where the "notwithstanding" phrase, as here, is an aside. The point of § 522(f) is not to exclude waivers (though that is done in passing, waivers are addressed directly in § 522(e)) but to provide that the debtor may avoid the fixing of a lien. In that context, for every instance in which "would have been entitled" may be accurate (because the incidentally mentioned waiver occurred) there will be thousands of instances in which "is entitled" should have been used. It seems to us that "would have been entitled" must refer to the generality, if not indeed the universality, of cases covered by the provision; and on that premise the only conceivable fact we are invited to disregard is the existence of the lien.

This reading must also be accepted, at least with respect to the federal exemptions, if § 522(f) is not to become an irrelevancy with respect to the most venerable, most common, and most important exemptions. The federal exemptions for homesteads (§ 522(d)(1)), for motor vehicles (§ 522(d)(2)), for household goods and wearing apparel (§ 522(d)(3)), and for tools of the trade (§ 522(d)(6)), are all defined by reference to the debtor's "interest" or "aggregate interest," so that if respondent's interpretation is accepted, no encumbrances of these could be avoided. Surely § 522(f) promises more than that -- and surely it would be bizarre for the federal scheme to prevent the avoidance of liens on those items, but to permit it for the less crucial items (for example, an "unmatured life insurance contract owned by the debtor," § 522(d)(7)) that are not described in such fashion as unquestionably to exclude liens.

We have no doubt, then, that the lower courts' unanimously agreed-upon manner of applying § 522(f) to federal exemptions-ask first whether avoiding the lien would entitle the debtor to an exemption, and if it would, then avoid and recover the lien-is correct. The question then becomes whether a different interpretation should be adopted for state exemptions. We do not see how that could be possible. Nothing in the text of § 522(f) remotely justifies treating the two categories of exemptions differently. The provision refers to the impairment of "exemption[s] to which the debtor would have been entitled under subsection (b)," and that includes federal exemptions and state exemptions alike. Nor is there any overwhelmingly clear policy impelling us, if we possessed the power, to create a distinction that the words of the statute do not contain. Respondent asserts that it is inconsistent with the Bankruptcy Code's "opt-out" policy, whereby the States may define their own exemptions, to refuse to take those exemptions with all their built-in limitations. That is plainly not true, however, since there is no doubt that a state exemption which purports to be available "unless waived" will be given full effect, even if it has been waived, for purposes of § 522(f) -- the first phrase of which, as we have noted, recites that it applies "notwithstanding any waiver of exemptions." See Dominion Bank of Cumberlands, NA v. Nuckolls, 780 F.2d 408, 412 (CA4 1985). Just as it is not inconsistent with the policy of permitting state-defined exemptions to have another policy disfavoring waiver of exemptions, whether federal-or state-created; so also it is not inconsistent to have a policy disfavoring the impingement of certain types of liens upon exemptions, whether federal- or state-created. We have no basis for pronouncing the opt-out policy absolute, but must apply it along with whatever other competing or limiting policies the statute contains.

On the basis of the analysis we have set forth above with respect to federal exemptions, and in light of the equivalency of treatment accorded to federal and state exemptions by § 522(f), we conclude that Florida's exclusion of certain liens from the scope of its homestead protection does not achieve a similar exclusion from the Bankruptcy Code's lien avoidance provision.[2]

III

The foregoing conclusion does not necessarily resolve this case. Section 522(f) permits the avoidance of the "fixing of a lien on an interest of the debtor." Some courts have held it inapplicable to a lien that was already attached to property when the debtor acquired it, since in such a case there never was a "fixing of a lien" on the debtor's interest. See In re McCormick, 18 B.R. 911, 914 (Bankr. WD Pa.), aff'd, 22 B.R. 997 (WD Pa. 1982); In re Scott, 12 B.R. 613, 615 (Bkrtcy. Ct. WD Okla. 1981). Under Florida law, the lien may have attached simultaneously with the acquisition of the property interest. If so, it could be argued that the lien did not fix "on an interest of the debtor." See Farrey v. Sanderfoot, ante, p. 291. The Court of Appeals did not pass on this issue, nor on the subsidiary question whether the Florida statute extending the homestead exemption was a taking, cf. United States v. Security Industrial Bank, 459 U.S. 70 (1982). We express no opinion on these points, and leave them to be considered by the Court of Appeals on remand.

The judgment of the Court of Appeals is reversed, and the case is remanded for proceedings consistent with this opinion. It is so ordered.

[Dissenting opinion omitted.]

Notes and Questions

1. Owen was handed down the same day that Farrey v. Sanderfoot was. Notice that Mr.

---

[2] In the dissent's view, the question is whether the lien impairs an "exemption to which the debtor would have been entitled at the time the lien 'fixed.'" Under the Code, however, the question is whether the lien impairs an "exemption to which the debtor would have been entitled under subsection (b)," and under subsection (b), exempt property is determined "on the date of the filing of the petition," not when the lien fixed. 11 U. S. C. §§ 522 (f), (b)(2)(A). We follow the language of the Code.

Owen's co-op apartment was "after-acquired," compared to Mrs. Owen's docketing of a judicial lien. On remand, the Eleventh Circuit held that, under Farrey, Mrs. Owen's judicial lien never "fixed" to Mr. Owen's co-op and could not be avoided. Owen v. Owen (In re Owen), 961 F.2d 170 (11th Cir. 1992).

2. The Owen test–"ask first whether avoiding the lien would entitle the debtor to an exemption, and if it would, then avoid . . . the lien," has been incorporated in § 522(f)(2), which Congress enacted in 1994.

4. Exempt Property and Fraudulent Conveyances

ZUBROD v DUNCAN (IN RE DUNCAN)
329 F.2d 1195 (10th Cir. 2003)

CLAIRE V. EAGAN, J.

Glenn Allen Duncan ("Debtor") declared bankruptcy after transferring his fee interest in property he used for a home and office ("Property") to himself and to his wife so as to create a tenancy by the entirety. Debtor claimed a homestead exemption, and no objections to his claim were filed. Tracy Lynne Zubrod ("Trustee") then recovered the Property for the bankruptcy estate by avoiding the transfer as fraudulent. When Trustee put the Property up for sale, Debtor moved for turnover of his homestead exemption proceeds at the conclusion of the sale.

The United States Bankruptcy Court for the District of Wyoming and the Bankruptcy Appellate Panel ("BAP") for the Tenth Circuit ruled in favor of Debtor, reasoning that Trustee actually recovered only that portion of the Property owned by Debtor's wife. Trustee appeals, claiming that Debtor is not entitled to the exemption proceeds because he voluntarily transferred the Property . . . For the following reasons, we reverse and remand.

I

Debtor is a Wyoming attorney. In 1992, he began representing Michael Gallegos, the personal representative of the Estate of Castulo Gallegos, deceased, to prosecute a wrongful death action. In 1993, he purchased the Property and took title solely in his own name, although he paid part of the purchase price by borrowing funds with his fiancee based on her credit rating. After their marriage, the couple resided in the Property, and Debtor used the Property as his law office as well.

Debtor filed the wrongful death action on behalf of the Gallegos family in 1994. The defendant moved to dismiss, arguing that the complaint was barred by the applicable statute of limitations. The court set a hearing on the motion, but before the date of the hearing, Debtor transferred title to the Property to himself and his wife as tenants by the entirety. The transfer rendered Debtor insolvent. The court dismissed the wrongful death action a few months later based on the defendant's argument that it was time-barred.

In 1996, Michael Gallegos sued Debtor for professional negligence. The judge entered summary judgment for the Gallegos estate and submitted the question of damages to a jury. A jury awarded damages in the amount of $172,000 on March 7, 1998. Debtor filed a voluntary petition for Chapter 7 relief on March 12, 1998, prior to the entry of a final judgment in the legal malpractice action. He listed the worth of the Property as $200,000, with a $95,117.94 mortgage against it, leaving approximately $105,000 equity in the Property. He claimed that the Property was completely exempt under 11 U.S.C. § 522(b)(2)(B) because he and his wife held title as tenants by the entirety; he also claimed a $10,000 homestead exemption under Wyoming law.[1] No objection was filed within the statutory 30-day period for filing objections, and Debtor was discharged on June 16, 1998.

Trustee filed an adversary proceeding on July 6, 1998, seeking to avoid the transfer as fraudulent and recover the Property for the benefit of the estate. The Bankruptcy Court granted summary judgment in Trustee's favor on June 16, 1999. When Trustee filed a notice of intent to sell the Property and sought the court's approval for the sale, Debtor objected because the notice did not include reference to Debtor's $10,000 homestead exemption, and he moved for turnover of the exemption proceeds at the time of the sale. Debtor argued that Trustee's failure to object to his claim for the homestead exemption within the 30-day period prescribed by law entitled him to the exemption proceeds after sale of the Property. Trustee argued that the Debtor's claim to a homestead exemption was invalid under 11 U.S.C. § 522(g) because he voluntarily transferred the recovered Property.

The Property ultimately sold pursuant to an order of the Bankruptcy Court, but the parties agreed to hold approximately $45,000 in proceeds from the sale pending a decision on Debtor's motion for turnover. On June 4, 2001, the Bankruptcy Court ruled that Debtor was not prevented by 11 U.S.C. § 522(g)(1) from claiming his homestead exemption. The Bankruptcy Court reasoned:

> [Debtor's] ownership and other rights in the property, including the right to possession and occupancy, were rights which were never transferred. Those interests became property of the estate at filing. Construing the exemption laws in the debtor's favor, the court concludes the transfer avoided by the trustee did not include the rights of ownership and possession to which the homestead exemption attaches, interests in property [Debtor] enjoyed on the date he filed the bankruptcy petition. The homestead exemption is valid on those rights.

Appellant's Appendix ("Aplt. App.") at 67. The Bankruptcy Court also mentioned Trustee's failure to object to the exemption claim under Fed. R. Bankr. P. 4003(b) as a possible alternative basis for its ruling. The order required Trustee to disburse the homestead exemption proceeds in the amount of $10,000 to Debtor.

Trustee timely appealed to the BAP, and the BAP affirmed on January 3, 2002. The BAP's rationale for its decision was that Debtor and his wife each held a separate, undivided interest in the Property, and Debtor's interest passed to the estate when he filed for bankruptcy protection under Chapter 7. According to the BAP, the judgment avoiding the transfer resulted in a recovery of property from Debtor's wife -- not from Debtor. Thus, section 522(g)(1) was not applicable to the exemption claimed by Debtor. Trustee timely appealed to this Court.

II

. . . The parties initially framed the issue in terms of whether the Debtor's

---

[1] Wyo. Stat. Ann. § 1-20-101 provides: "Every resident of the state is entitled to a homestead not exceeding ten thousand dollars ($10,000.00) in value, exempt from execution and attachment arising from any debt, contract or civil obligation entered into or incurred." Wyo. Stat. Ann. § 1-20-102 provides: "(a) The homestead is only exempt as provided in W.S. 1-20-101 while occupied as such by the owner or the person entitled thereto, or his or her family. (b) When two (2) or more persons jointly own and occupy the same residence, each shall be entitled to the homestead exemption."

claim to a homestead exemption was invalid notwithstanding the Trustee's failure to object within the statutory period of Fed. R. Bankr. P. 4003(b). First the Bankruptcy Court, and then the BAP, rephrased the issue in terms of whether the homestead exemption was valid notwithstanding the avoided transfer. In so doing, the Bankruptcy Court and the BAP shifted the focus of the inquiry to the character of the Property transferred.

The statutory provision at the center of this controversy is section 522(g)(1) of the Bankruptcy Code, which provides as follows:

> (g) Notwithstanding sections 550 and 551 of this title the debtor may exempt under subsection (b) of this section property that the trustee recovers under sections 510(c)(2), 542, 543, 550, 551, or 553 of this title, to the extent that the debtor could have exempted such property under subsection (b) of this section if such property had not been transferred, if–
>
> (1)(A) such transfer was not a voluntary transfer of such property by the debtor; and
>
> (B) the debtor did not conceal such property . . . .

The plain language of section 522(g)(1) provides that a debtor cannot assert any exemption in property a trustee recovers after the debtor's voluntary transfer of the property. Redmond v. Tuttle, 698 F.2d 414, 417-18 (10th Cir. 1983). The term "transfer" is broadly defined. Id. at 417 n. 8 . To avoid the import of Redman, the Bankruptcy Court and BAP focused on the term "recovers." In their analysis of what the Trustee recovered, however, they semantically negated the effect of the Debtor's transfer.

In particular, the BAP's emphasis on the phrase "property that the trustee recovers" in section 522(g)(1) led to its ultimate conclusion that the section was inapplicable. The BAP reasoned that the Trustee recovered only the interest in the Property held by the Debtor's wife because the Debtor's undivided interest in the Property passed to the estate when he filed for bankruptcy, and his wife continued to hold a "separate, undivided interest" in the Property. The BAP's repeated use of the oxymoronic phrase "separate, undivided interest" is unfortunate because, while each tenant by the entirety may have separate rights in entirety property, it is clear that, under Wyoming law, they do not have separate interests in the property. See Talbot v. United States, 850 F. Supp. 969, 972-73 (D. Wyo. 1994); Peters v. Dona, 49 Wyo. 306, 54 P.2d 817, 820 (Wyo. 1936). This distinction is critical to the Debtor's right to claim an exemption.

Relying on In re Ford, 3 B.R. 559, 570 (Bankr. D. Md. 1980), for the general proposition that a debtor's interest in property as a tenant by the entirety is property of the estate, the BAP disregarded the Ford court's specific remarks explaining that the "time-honored unities of time, title, identity of interest, and possession necessary to preserve the estate by the entireties," was not severed when the debtor's interest passed to the estate. The court observed:

> The trustee merely obtains and retains custody of the debtor's undivided interest consisting of the same unities, intact and unaltered as they existed immediately prior to the filing of the petition, until such time as that interest, still intact and unaltered, is exempted from the estate under § 522(b)(2)(B), provided such exemption is available and properly taken by the debtor.

Id. at 570.

The Ford decision did not address a situation in which fraudulent conduct is involved. The court generally recognized that a debtor is entitled to convert non-exempt property into exempt property up until the filing of the bankruptcy petition, and that this practice is not fraudulent per se. Id. at 577. "However, when the conversion is intended to defeat the interests of creditors, such exemptions may be denied to the extent of any fraudulent conduct." In re Elliott, 79 B.R. 944, 946 (Bankr. M.D. Fla. 1987). In this matter, the BAP ignored the effect of the Debtor's fraudulent, voluntary transfer on his right to claim any exemption in the Property, whether or not his interest could be characterized as "separate, yet undivided." The BAP thus erred in finding section 522(g)(1) inapplicable.

The two Wyoming decisions, In re Wenande, 107 B.R. 770 (Bankr. D. Wyo. 1989), and In re Anselmi, 52 B.R. 479 (Bankr. D. Wyo. 1985), cited by the BAP as supportive of the Ford general proposition, do not support the BAP's overall analysis. Wenande concluded that entireties property which was not exempt could be used to satisfy all of a creditor's claims, including claims against only one of two joint debtors. 107 B.R. at 774-75. In so holding, the Wenande court cited to Anselmi for the proposition that a Wyoming debtor may exempt property held as tenants by the entireties. Id. at 775 . "Bankruptcy courts and appellate courts have been nearly unanimous in holding that the debtor's interest in the entirety property is property of the estate under Section 541(a)(3),"[2] but "once all property of the debtor comes into the estate under § 541, the debtor may then exempt certain property under 11 U.S.C. § 522(b)," including any interest in property held as a tenant by the entirety. In re Anselmi, 52 B.R. at 483-84 (footnote citations omitted). Here, however, the Property is subject to execution because it was fraudulently transferred.

Absent the Bankruptcy Court's avoidance of the transfer, Debtor claimed exemption in all of the Property, not just the $10,000 homestead exemption. If his fraudulent act does not permit him to claim the tenancy by the entirety exemption under section 522(b)(2)(B), it should not permit him to claim the $10,000 Wyoming homestead exemption. Section 522(g) precludes either exemption. The decisions of the Bankruptcy Court and the BAP, however, permit the latter but not the former.

Debtor, being a Wyoming lawyer, presumably knew that "property held as a tenancy by the entireties 'is not subject to execution or other creditor's process for the separate debts of one of the spouses.'" Talbot, 850 F. Supp. at 973 (quoting Colorado Nat'l Bank v. Miles, 711 P.2d 390, 394 (Wyo. 1985)). He transferred the Property to himself and his wife during the legal malpractice action, apparently to keep the Property beyond the reach of creditors in the event he were found liable. The transfer was deemed fraudulent for that reason. (See Decision on Cross Motions for Summary Judgment, Aplt. App. at 5-21) If Debtor had not transferred the Property, or if the transfer had been involuntary, he could have claimed the homestead exemption. He cannot claim the exemption for a voluntary transfer.

Essentially, the BAP's analysis blurs the distinction between two well-established legal concepts: tenancy by the entireties and joint tenancy. Under Wyoming law, "'an estate by the entireties involves the unities of time,

[2] Section 541(a)(3) provides: "The commencement of a case under section 301 , 302 , or 303 of this title creates an estate. Such estate is comprised of all the following property, wherever located and by whomever held: . . . (3) Any interest in property that the trustee recovers under section 329(b), 363(n), 543 , 550 , 553 , or 723 of this title."

title, interest, and possession, as well as the husband and wife unity of ownership.' 26 Am. Jur. § 71, p. 698." Ward Terry & Co. v. Hensen, 75 Wyo. 444, 297 P.2d 213, 215 (Wyo. 1956) (emphasis added). This contradicts the assertion by the Bankruptcy Court that the Debtor held the rights of ownership and possession separate from the interests in the Property held by his wife. See Aplt. App. at 67.

Debtor transferred his pre-existing sole rights to ownership and possession of the Property to himself and his wife so as to share those rights with his wife. As the Trustee argues, these rights cannot be "unbundled" from the "bundle of sticks" represented by a tenancy in the entirety. See United States v. Craft, 535 U.S. 274 (2002) (explaining that the common "bundles of sticks" idiom refers to "a collection of individual rights which, in certain combinations, constitute property.")[3] The Ward Terry court explained,

> Entirety in this connection means indivisibility. The estate is owned not by one [but] by both as an indivisible entity and has the characteristics of a joint tenancy by reason of the fact that the survivor takes all. But the estates differ in the fact that joint tenants may divide the estate, but tenants by the entirety cannot do so except by the joint act of husband and wife.

297 P.2d at 214-15 . The principles of Ward Terry have consistently been upheld by the Wyoming Supreme Court and federal courts in Wyoming. E.g., Talbot, 850 F. Supp. at 973 ("the long-standing rule in Wyoming [is] that in an estate by the entireties, the husband and wife together take the whole estate as one person, and '"neither has a separate estate or interest in the land, but each has the whole estate.'"(quoting Peters, 54 P.2d at 820)); In re Anselmi, 52 B.R. at 491 (quoting Ward Terry for its emphasis on the unity of interest); see also Witzel v. Witzel, 386 P.2d 103, 106-07 (Wyo. 1963); Wambeke v. Hopkin, 372 P.2d 470, 474-75 (Wyo. 1962).[4] The BAP and Bankruptcy Court orders undermine this well-established law in Wyoming. By virtue of the unity of interest, when the Trustee recovered the Property, the Trustee recovered the interest of the Debtor and his wife.

The BAP and Bankruptcy Court orders also undermine the policy underlying section 522(g)(1). As set forth in Hitt v. Glass (In re Glass), 164 B.R. 759 (B.A.P. 9th Cir. 1994), aff'd, 60 F.3d 565 (9th Cir. 1995), "the purpose of

---

[3] The Craft court found that some of those "sticks" constitute property for federal tax lien purposes under 26 U.S.C. § 6321 . 122 S. Ct. at 1423-25 . In so holding, the Craft court examined the nature of tenancy by the entirety, recognizing that it is a "unique sort of concurrent ownership that can only exist between married persons." Id. at 1421 . The Court recognized that, under Michigan law, a taxpayer does not have a separate, individual interest in entireties property, but a tenant by the entirety may have personal rights to use, share income, and exclude third parties, among other rights, to which a federal tax lien may attach. Id. at 1422-23 . Absent this ruling, two spouses could shield their entire property from federal taxation by holding it as entireties property. Id. at 1424 . We read the Craft ruling as limited to the interest in a taxpayer's property to which a federal tax lien attaches. The Court stated as much by its recognition of state law exempting tenancy by the entirety property from claims of creditors. See id. at 1426 . The Court indicated that it was not bound by state law on the issue because its interpretation of the federal tax lien statute is a federal question. Id. at 1420, 1426 .

[4] Tader by Tader, 737 P.2d 1065 (Wyo. 1987), cited by the BAP, is inapposite. Notwithstanding the remarks of the Tader court relevant to the common law fiction of "unity" between husband and wife, the issue in Tader was the abolition of interspousal immunity -- not tenancy by the entirety.

section 522(g) is to prevent a debtor from claiming an exemption in recovered property which was transferred in a manner giving rise to the trustee's avoiding powers, where the transfer was voluntary or where the transfer or property interest was concealed." 164 B.R. at 764 (citation omitted). A debtor should not be afforded any benefit from fraudulent conduct that necessitates additional proceedings for a trustee to secure the assets for the debtor's creditors. Id. at 765. Debtor injured the creditor with the largest claim on his assets when he failed to file a lawsuit within the applicable statute of limitations. He should not be permitted to cause additional injury by claiming an exemption that would significantly diminish the funds from which that creditor may obtain some measure of relief.

The Trustee argues that affirming the BAP order would create an incentive for a debtor to fraudulently transfer property to a tenancy by the entirety because the property could be entirely exempt from creditor claims if the trustee fails to bring an avoidance action, and the debtor will be no worse off if the trustee manages to avoid the transfer. The Trustee also points out that affirmance could have other adverse implications because section 522(g)(1) embraces all "recoveries" under sections 510(c)(2), 542, 543, 550 [which incorporates sections 544, 547, 548, 559, 553(b) and 724(a)], 551, and 553 of the Bankruptcy Code. In essence, affirmance would encourage debtors to transfer to others the rights in their property that have economic value to their creditors, while retaining limited interests, and thus "open the floodgates" to further litigation.

We find these policy arguments particularly strong. The orders of the BAP and the Bankruptcy Court foster the general policy of giving a debtor an unencumbered fresh start. However, the opportunity for a fresh start is available only to the honest debtor. See Grogan v. Garner, 498 U.S. 279 (1991); Village of San Jose v. McWilliams, 284 F.3d 785, 790 (7th Cir. 2002); In re Glass, 164 B.R. at 764; Schieffler v. Beshears (In re Beshears), 182 B.R. 235, 241 (Bankr. E.D. Ark. 1995). Section 522(g)(1) is applicable to the homestead exemption claimed by Debtor. He is not entitled to the exemption proceeds.

III

The Bankruptcy Court stated that "alternative grounds may be in the debtor's favor as well," in reference to the Trustee's failure to object to the homestead exemption under Fed. R. Bankr. P. 4003(b), but the opinion did not rest on that ground. (Aplt. App. at 68.) The BAP also mentioned the Trustee's failure to object but did not rely on that failure as a basis for its affirmation. The BAP specifically stated: "We are not holding that the Trustee's objection to the Debtor's exemption under § 522(g)(1) was barred as untimely. We are merely stating that since § 522(g)(1) does not apply in this case, the Debtor's otherwise unopposed claimed exemption stands." (Aplt. App. at 78.)

Both opinions cite to Taylor v. Freeland & Kronz, 503 U.S. 638 (1992), wherein a Chapter 7 debtor claimed an exemption in potential proceeds from a pending employment discrimination suit. The Taylor court held that the trustee in that matter could not contest the validity of the claimed exemption, even though the debtor had no colorable basis for claiming it, because the 30-day period for objecting under Rule 4003(b) had expired and the trustee had not obtained an extension of time. 503 U.S. at 643-44. Taylor did not involve an adversary proceeding to avoid a fraudulent transfer, or any issue of whether section 522(g)(1) applies despite the lack of a timely objection under Rule 4003(b). Courts faced with these issues since Taylor have reached differing conclusions. Compare Levine v. Weissing (In re Levine), 134 F.3d 1046 (11th Cir. 1998) (holding that Rule 4003(b) does not bar trustee from bringing an adversary proceeding under the Bankruptcy Code to contest a transfer of funds) with In re Butler, 271 B.R. 807 (Bankr. E.D. Tenn. 2001) (holding that debtor was entitled to a homestead exemption in property that was sold by trustee because trustee failed to object within 30 days, even though a preferential transfer of property was involved that could have been avoided under the Bankruptcy Code), and Moore v. Harrell (In re Harrell), 212 B.R. 174 (Bankr. S.D. Ga. 1997) (holding that trustee's failure to object barred him from challenging an exemption claimed by debtor in proceeds paid by debtor in settlement of trustee's claim for fraudulent conveyances and concealment of estate property).

We believe the better view is that of the Levine court. The debtors in that case voluntarily and fraudulently transferred non-exempt assets to various insurance companies to purchase annuities that were exempt from creditors' claims under state law, and the court permitted the trustee to set aside the transfer notwithstanding the trustee's failure to object under Rule 4003(b). The Levine court found that the trustee's actions were subject to the two-year statute of limitations governing adversary proceedings under the trustee's avoidance powers, 11 U.S.C. § 546(a)(1)(A). The Levine court reasoned that the trustee's actions were not subject to the 30-day limitations period governing objections to claimed exemptions because the trustee was not contesting the exemptions per se; pursuant to 11 U.S.C. § 544(a), he was seeking instead to avoid the transfer of property by the debtor.[5]

We find the Levine court's rationale persuasive. Were we to hold otherwise, the two-year limitations period of section 546(a)(1)(A) would effectively become a 30-day limitations period, thereby rendering the provision meaningless. As set forth in In re Harry, 151 B.R. 735 (Bankr. W.D. Va. 1992):

> The trustee is not contesting the debtor's right to claim the section 522(b)(2)(B) exemption. Unless and until the trustee successfully avoids the transfer that created the tenancy by the entirety, the debtor is entitled to the exemption. Requiring the trustee to bring such an action within the 30 day claim objection period would defeat the purpose of the much longer limitations period on the trustee's avoiding powers provided in 11 U.S.C. 546(a).

Id. at 738 . When two statutes are capable of coexistence, it is our duty, "absent a clearly expressed congressional intention to the contrary, to regard each as effective." Pitzak v. Office of Personnel Management, 710 F.2d 1476, 1479 (10th Cir. 1983) (citations omitted). . . .

We are mindful that the basic premise of Taylor has been affirmed in this circuit. See Kwiecinski v. Community First Nat'l Bank of Powell (In re

[5] A year later, the Eleventh Circuit specifically held that the proper means of challenging a debtor's exemption claim for tenancy by the entireties property, where the challenge is based on the theory that the entireties estate was created by a fraudulent conveyance and could be avoided, was through an adversary proceeding, and not through an objection to the claimed exemption. Havoco of America, Ltd. v. Hill, 197 F.3d 1135, 1140-41 (11th Cir. 1999). The Havoco court reasoned that the nondebtor spouse's "due process rights could not be adequately preserved in a proceeding to which she is not a party and in which her property rights may effectively be terminated." Id. at 1140 .

Kwiecinski), 245 B.R. 672 (B.A.P. 10th Cir. 2000). Yet, that case did not involve an adversary proceeding to recover property voluntarily and fraudulently transferred. "An objection to exemptions is not tantamount to an action to recover exempt property." In re Page, 240 B.R. 548, 552 (Bankr. W.D. Mich. 1999).[6] Accordingly, we hold that Debtor is not entitled to claim a homestead exemption in property voluntarily transferred and recovered by the Trustee in an adversary proceeding, notwithstanding the Trustee's failure to object within the 30-day period of Fed. R. Bankr. P. 4003(b).

IV

For the foregoing reasons, the orders of the Bankruptcy Appellate Panel and the Bankruptcy Court are REVERSED, and the case is REMANDED to the Bankruptcy Court for further proceedings not inconsistent with this opinion.

Notes and Questions

1. D makes a fraudulent conveyance of his house to X. A creditor brings suit against D and also against X claiming that X has received a fraudulent conveyance. In response to this law suit, X conveys the property back to D. D files for bankruptcy. The trustee objects to the exemption of the house because it had been fraudulently conveyed. Can D claim this exemption? Stornawaye Fin Corp. v. Hill (In re Hill), 562 F.3d 29 (1st Cir. 2009).

2. D makes a left turn without yielding for a motorcycle. As a result, C's spouse is killed. D is convicted of negligent vehicle homocide and is put on one year's probation. D has owned a homesteaded house in Massachusetts for many years. Under Massachusetts law, D is entitled to a $500,000 exemption. What is her maximum exemption in light of Bankruptcy Code § 522(q)(1)(A)? Larson v. Howell (In re Larson), 513 F.3d 325 (1st Cir. 2008).

WALLACE v ROGERS (IN RE ROGERS)
13 F.3d 212 (5th Cir. 2008)

DEMOSS, J.

This case involves a question of first impression in this circuit: the statutory interpretation of the newly enacted homestead exemption cap, 11 U.S.C. § 522(p)(1), found in the Bankruptcy Abuse Prevention and Consumer Protection Act of 2005 ("BAPCPA"). The issue is whether the homestead exemption cap applies to a homestead interest established within the 1,215-day period preceding the filing of the bankruptcy petition despite the fact that the debtor acquired title to the property before that statutory period. The bankruptcy court answered this question in the negative, and the district court affirmed. For the reasons discussed below, we affirm.

I. Factual & Procedural Background

On January 17, 1994, the Appellee, Sarah K. Rogers ("Rogers" or "debtor"), inherited a 72.5 acre tract of real property known as 14849 Kelly Road, Forney,

[6] The Page court noted: "The distinction between an objection to an entireties exemption and an action to set aside a fraudulent conveyance that creates a tenancy by the entireties is particularly important in bankruptcy." 240 B.R. at 552 n. 8 . The court explained: "In effect, avoiding a transfer (as opposed to merely sustaining an objection), increases (presumptively doubles) the amount of property available to satisfy claims against the estate." Id.

Texas ("Forney Property"). Rogers was single when she inherited the Forney Property from her mother. Subsequently, Rogers married George E. Rogers, and they purchased a 5.1 acre tract of real property known as 8644 South F.M. 549, Rockwall, Texas ("Rockwall Property"). Rogers and her husband constructed a residence on the Rockwall Property and claimed it as their homestead. In January 2004, Rogers separated from her husband, moved into a mobile home on the Forney Property, and claimed the Forney Property as her homestead. On April 6, 2004, Rogers and her husband divorced. Pursuant to the divorce decree, Rogers was divested of all right, title and interest in the Rockwall Property, and no equity from the Rockwall Property was rolled-over into the Forney Property. The divorce decree awarded the Forney Property to Rogers, but this award simply affirmed the reality that the Forney Property was her separate property because she inherited it from her mother before marriage.

Prior to 2004, Rogers and her husband had borrowed money from the Appellant, Jack C. Wallace, to embark on an ultimately unsuccessful business venture. Wallace eventually sued to recover the unpaid loan balance, and on April 19, 2004, he obtained a state-court judgment against both the debtor and her then ex-husband, for the total principal amount of $316,180.95, in addition to court costs and post-judgment interest.

On September 28, 2005, the debtor filed for relief under Chapter 7 of the Bankruptcy Code. The debtor elected state law exemptions in accordance with the provisions of 11 U.S.C. § 522(b). In her Schedule C, the debtor claimed her homestead exemption on the Forney Property in the amount of $359,000. Wallace filed a timely objection to the debtor's claimed homestead exemption, arguing that 11 U.S.C. § 522(p)(1) capped the debtor's homestead exemption at the federal statutory amount of $125,000 because the debtor acquired her homestead interest in the Forney Property within the 1,215-day period preceding the filing of her bankruptcy petition.

The bankruptcy court orally denied Wallace's objection at a hearing held on January 18, 2006, and this ruling was memorialized by written order dated February 7, 2006. On October 16, 2006, the district court affirmed the bankruptcy court's order overruling Wallace's objection to the claimed homestead exemption. Wallace then perfected this timely appeal.

II. Analysis . . .

B. The debtor is entitled to her full homestead exemption.

1. 11 U.S.C. § 522(p)(1)

The bankruptcy estate is comprised of "all legal or equitable interests of the debtor in property as of the commencement of the case." 11 U.S.C. § 541(a)(1); Owen v. Owen, 500 U.S. 305, 308 (1991). Rogers elected to exempt the Forney Property as her homestead under Texas state law. See 11 U.S.C. § 522(b); see also TEX. CONST. art. XVI, § 50; see also TEX. PROP. CODE §§ 41.001-.002. "'An exemption is an interest withdrawn from the estate (and hence from the creditors) for the benefit of the debtor.'" Norris v. Thomas (In re Norris), 413 F.3d 526, 527 (5th Cir. 2005) (quoting Owen, 500 U.S. at 308).

Enacted as part of BAPCPA, 11 U.S.C. § 522(p)(1) limits the state law homestead exemption under certain circumstances.[1] Section 522(p)(1) prevents the debtor from exempting certain interests from the bankruptcy estate if they were acquired by the debtor during the statutory period and their aggregate value exceeds a certain dollar threshold. The statute reads, in relevant part:

> [A]s a result of electing . . . to exempt property under State or local law, a debtor may not exempt any amount of interest that was acquired by the debtor during the 1215-day period preceding the date of the filing of the petition that exceeds in the aggregate [$125,000][2] in value in--real or personal property that the debtor or dependent of the debtor claims as a homestead.

11 U.S.C. § 522(p)(1)(D). The statute further states that "any amount of such interest does not include any interest transferred from a debtor's previous principal residence (which was acquired prior to the beginning of such 1215-day period) into the debtor's current principal residence, if the debtor's previous and current residences are located in the same State." Id. § 522(p)(2)(B).

2. The bankruptcy court held that the term "interest" refers to title, and the district court held that the term "interest" refers to equity.

Both the bankruptcy court and the district court held that Rogers was entitled to her homestead exemption, but they gave different reasons for this holding. The bankruptcy court predominantly focused on construing the relationship between different phrases in § 522(p)(1)(D) while the district court focused on interpreting the meaning of the term "interest." Ultimately, the two courts interpreted the term "interest" differently: the bankruptcy court interpreted it to mean an unquantifiable "property interest," which presumably refers to title or fee ownership, and the district court interpreted it to mean "some legal or equitable interest that can be quantified by a monetary figure," which presumably refers to equity. Both courts reached the same conclusion regarding the applicability of § 522(p)(1)(D) because a homestead interest is not the equivalent of title or equity.

The bankruptcy court construed § 522(p)(1) to mean that a debtor "can't exempt any amount in excess of $125,000 if an interest in property was acquired by the debtor during the 1,215 day period preceding the date of the filing of the petition." Thus, the bankruptcy court concluded that the phrase "any amount" modifies the phrase "that exceeds in the aggregate $125,000." In the words of the bankruptcy court, "it's got to be the interest that's acquired, not an amount of interest." The bankruptcy court concluded that § 522(p)(1) was inapplicable because Rogers acquired her "property interest" in the Forney Property in 1994, which was outside the statutory period.

Although the Texas Supreme Court has characterized the homestead interest as a "legal interest" created by the Texas Constitution, the bankruptcy court held that this "legal interest" was not the type of "property interest" covered by § 522(p)(1). Although it did not further define the term "property interest,"

[1] Unlike most other provisions of the statute, 11 U.S.C. § 522(p) became effective immediately upon enactment of BAPCPA on April 20, 2005. See Pub. L. No. 109-8, § 1501(b)(2), 119 Stat. 23, 216 (2005).

[2] In 2007, the Judicial Conference of the United States adjusted the dollar amount from $ 125,000 to $ 136,875. See 72 Fed. Reg. 7082-01 (Feb. 14, 2007); 11 U.S.C. § 104(b). At the time the bankruptcy petition was filed in this case, the relevant dollar amount was $ 125,000.

the bankruptcy court's conclusion that the phrase "any amount" does not modify the term "interest" strongly suggests that it equated acquiring a "property interest" with acquiring title to the property. Furthermore, the only case cited by the bankruptcy court at the hearing held that the term "interest" refers to title, not equity. See In re Blair, 334 B.R. 374, 376 (Bankr. N.D. Tex. 2005).

Based on the legislative history, the bankruptcy court concluded that the purpose of the statute was to close the "mansion loophole" and prevent debtors from moving to states with more generous homestead exemptions on the eve of bankruptcy in order to avail themselves of those exemptions. After observing that Rogers did not move to Texas in anticipation of bankruptcy and that her homestead designation of the Forney Property was precipitated by divorce, the bankruptcy judge overruled Wallace's objection and held that Rogers may exempt the entirety of her homestead from the bankruptcy estate.

On appeal, the district court affirmed the bankruptcy court's order. Wallace v. Rogers (In re Rogers), 354 B.R. 792, 798 (N.D. Tex. 2006). Unlike the bankruptcy court, the district court assumed that the phrase "any amount" modifies the term "interest," so the issue was whether "the characterization of real property as a homestead qualif[ies] as an 'interest' within the phrase 'debtor may not exempt any amount of interest.'" Id. at 795. The district court held that the statutory language of § 522(p)(1) was unambiguous and that the term "'interest' refers to some legal or equitable interest that can be quantified by a monetary figure." Id. at 796. In support of its holding that "interest" refers to a quantitative measure, the district court observed that (1) the term "interest" is modified by the term "amount," which is a quantitative term; (2) the statute mandates that the "amount of interest" may not exceed in the aggregate a specified dollar amount; and (3) § 522(p)(2)(B) allows for transfer of any amount of interest from the debtor's previous principal residence that was acquired before the statutory period. Id. at 796-97. Regarding this third point, the district court noted that both § 522(p)(1) and § 522(p)(2)(B) used the term "interest," and it reasoned that only equity, which has a quantitative value, can be rolled-over into a new property, not a homestead interest. Id. at 797.

The district court observed that it is impossible "to have a 'quantity' of classification as homestead." Id. The district court disagreed with the bankruptcy court's analysis in In re Greene, 346 B.R. 835, 843 (Bankr. D. Nev. 2006), which held that § 522(p)(1) applied to a homestead interest established within the statutory period despite the fact that the debtor acquired title to the property outside that period. Rogers, 354 B.R. at 797. The district court criticized the Greene court for ignoring statutory language indicating that the term "interest" refers to a quantitative measure. Id. The district court cited approvingly to the bankruptcy court's analysis in In re Rasmussen, 349 B.R. 747, 758 (Bankr. M.D. Fla. 2006), which held that the term "interest" referred to equity in the property, not an ownership interest equivalent to a fee simple. Rogers, 354 B.R. at 798. The district court refused to consider the legislative history of § 522(p)(1) because it concluded that the statute was unambiguous, and it declined to address the meaning of the term "acquired" because its interpretation of the term "interest" was dispositive of the appeal. Id. Thus, the district court affirmed the bankruptcy court, holding that "the term 'interest' does not encompass the classification of real property as a homestead." Id.

3. Three other bankruptcy courts have addressed this same legal issue.

Two bankruptcy courts have held that § 522(p)(1) does not apply to a homestead interest established within the 1,215-day period if the debtor acquired title the property before that period. See In re Lyons, 355 B.R. 387, 390-91 (Bankr. D. Mass. 2006); see also Venn v. Reinhard (In re Reinhard), 377 B.R. 315, 321 (Bankr. N.D. Fla. 2007). One bankruptcy court has held to the contrary. See In re Greene, 346 B.R. 835, 843 (Bankr. D. Nev. 2006).[3]

In Lyons, the debtor purchased the property on April 26, 1977 and recorded a homestead declaration on August 12, 2004. 355 B.R. at 389. Two weeks after the debtor recorded the homestead designation, a creditor was granted an attachment on the property in the amount of $50,000. Id. Regarding the applicability of § 522(p)(1)(D), the Lyons court held the following:

> The plain language of Section 522(p) indicates that the debtor must have acquired an interest in the property within 1,215 days of filing. The term "interest" refers to some quantitative amount of legal or equitable value. See In re Rogers, 354 B.R. 792, 796 (N.D. Tex. 2006) (discussing at length the statutory construction of Section 522(p)). The homestead is not a quantifiable interest; it is a classification of property under state law. Id. Here, the Debtor did not acquire his interest in the Property within 1,215 days; rather, the Property "acquired" its classification as a homestead during that time. Thus, the Court finds that [Section 522(p)(1)(D)] do[es] not apply and that Debtor is entitled to the $500,000.00 homestead exemption under Massachusetts law.

355 B.R. at 390-91. Thus, the Lyons court adopted the reasoning of the district court in this case.

In Reinhard, the debtor and his wife ("the Reinhards") acquired title to a Florida property (the "Seaside Property") on February 24, 1995. 377 B.R. at 317. However, they resided in a different Florida property (the "Tallahassee Property") until June 30, 2005. Id. During the 1,215-day period before they filed for bankruptcy, the Reinhards moved into the Seaside Property and designated it as their homestead under Florida law. Id. No equity was transferred from the Tallahassee Property to the Seaside Property. Id. The Reinhards filed for bankruptcy on November 3, 2006. Id. According to the Reinhard court, the issue was whether "the Debtor acquired any amount of interest in value in the Seaside Property when it acquired homestead status under Florida law." Id.

The Reinhard court asserted that the acquisition of an interest in property and the acquisition of homestead status are distinct concepts because homestead status attaches to protect the property after it is acquired by the debtor. Id. at 319. The Reinhard court stated the following:

> Homestead is simply a status, constitutionally defined, which exempts certain property from execution and limits its alienability. It is not a property interest. When a Florida resident's property acquires homestead status, the owner does not acquire any of the rights traditionally associated with property interests: the right to possession, the right to use, the right to transfer--the owner already holds whatever of these he has. Accordingly, homestead status in Florida is not properly conceptualized as a stick in the bundle; rather, it is a

[3] The bankruptcy court decision in Greene was affirmed by the district court in an unpublished opinion, and the case is currently on appeal before the Ninth Circuit.

protective safe in which the bundle is put.

Id. Thus, the Reinhard court concurred with the conclusion of Rogers and Lyons that a homestead is a classification of property, not a "property interest" that implicates § 522(p)(1).

Relying in part on the district court's opinion in this case, the Reinhard court held that the term "interest" refers to "a quantitative or monetary value in property." Id. at 320. The Reinhard court further elaborated on this concept when it stated that "the debtor must acquire some amount of interest in the value of one of the four types of property listed during the 1215-day period in order for the cap to apply." Id. According to the Reinhard court, § 522(p)(1) refers to the acquisition of monetary value in property, not in an exemption. Id. The debtor does not acquire additional monetary value in the property when she designates it as her homestead; rather, the designation merely protects the existing monetary value that the debtor acquired in the property before filing for bankruptcy. See id. at 321 ("Homestead status simply exempts the homesteader's existing share in the property from forced sale and limits its alienability. Therefore, the Debtor did not acquire any amount of interest in value in the Seaside Property when it acquired homestead status.").

To date, only one bankruptcy court has reached a conclusion contrary to that of Rogers, Lyons, and Reinhard. In Greene, the debtor purchased a 67-acre parcel of undeveloped land (the "Sparks Property") in May 1994. 346 B.R. at 838. The debtor admitted that he lived with his girlfriend at another location until early August 2004. Id. On August 10, 2004, the debtor moved a travel trailer onto the property, and on August 11, 2004, the debtor designated the property and the travel trailer as his homestead. Id. The debtor filed his Chapter 13 petition just 16 days later, on August 27, 2004. Id. After the debtor voluntarily dismissed his Chapter 13 petition, the debtor filed his Chapter 7 petition on October 15, 2005. Id. A creditor filed a timely objection to the debtor's claimed homestead exemption, arguing that the exempted amount must be reduced from $350,000 to $125,000 pursuant to § 522(p)(1) because the homestead was an interest acquired within 1,215 days of the filing of the petition.[4] Id.

In Greene, the debtor argued that § 522(p)(1) does not apply because he purchased the property more than 1,215 days before he filed the petition. Id. at 840. In rejecting this argument, the Greene court stated that the homestead exemption is a "property interest" that "lies dormant and inactive until it is acquired by the debtor." Id. at 842. In the words of the Greene court, "[w]hat must be acquired during the 1,215 day period is the homestead exemption, not the real property. These are separate interests." Id. at 842-43. Although the Greene court recognized that the debtor's interest in the property includes title to the property, it insisted that the term "interest" refers to a broader concept. See id. at 843 ("Whatever Debtor had in his bundle of rights and interests pertaining to the Property, homestead protection was not one of them."). Thus, the Greene court concluded that the debtor's homestead interest "is a property interest acquired within 1,215 days of his bankruptcy petition and is limited to $125,000 pursuant to Section 522(p)." Id.

---

[4] In Nevada, the homestead exemption extends to the claimant's equity in the homestead property up to a maximum of $ 350,000. NEV. REV. STAT. § 115.010(2).

4. Other courts have addressed the meaning of the term "interest" in cases involving different facts.

For purposes of § 522(p)(1), other courts have generally defined "interest" as either title[5] or equity.[6] Those courts adopting the equity definition have been forced to address complex issues regarding passive and active equity appreciation during the 1,215-day period. See In re Rasmussen, 349 B.R. at 757-58 (distinguishing between active equity appreciation, which is subject to the cap, and passive equity appreciation, which is not); see In re Chouinard, 358 B.R. at 815 (holding that "passive market appreciation" resulting in increased equity is not an interest that a debtor "acquires" during the statutory period). In contrast, those courts adopting the title definition have crafted an easily-applied rule that is arguably in conflict with the statutory language indicating that the term "interest" refers to a quantitative or monetary value.[7] See In re Sainlar, 344 B.R. at 669 (holding that § 522(p)(1) "has no applicability to property in which a debtor obtained an ownership interest more than 1,215 days before the petition date, even if the property's equity increases [through market appreciation or principal debt reduction] during the 1,215-day pre-petition period"); see In re Blair, 334 B.R. at 375, 378 (same); see In re Anderson, 374 B.R. at 859-60 (same).

---

[5] See In re Anderson, 374 B.R. 848, 859 (Bankr. D. Kan. 2007) (holding that the phrase "interest that was acquired" should be construed as "applying to the actual purchase or acquisition of an ownership or fee interest in the homestead property"); see In re Sainlar, 344 B.R. 669, 673 (Bankr. M.D. Fla. 2006) ("The phrase 'interest that was acquired' as used in § 522(p)(1) means the acquisition of ownership of real property. Section 522(p), therefore, does not apply to property to which a debtor acquired title more than 1,215 days before a bankruptcy filing."); see In re Blair, 334 B.R. 374, 376-77 (Bankr. N.D. Tex. 2005) (holding that § 522(p)(1) was inapplicable because the debtors "acquired title and fee to their home" before the statutory period); see Khan v. Bankowski (In re Khan), 375 B.R. 5, 13-14 (B.A.P. 1st Cir. 2007) (holding that § 522(p)(1) applied because legal title to the property was transferred from a trust to the debtor within the statutory period); see also 4 COLLIER ON BANKRUPTCY P 522.13[2] (Alan N. Resnick & Henry J. Sommer eds., 15th ed. rev. 2007) ("[T]he phrase ["interest that was acquired"] should be construed as applying to the actual purchase or acquisition of an ownership or fee interest in the homestead property.")

[6] See In re Rasmussen, 349 B.R. 747, 756 (Bankr. M.D. Fla. 2006) (concluding that the term "interest" means "equity in the homestead acquired by a debtor during the 1,215-day period," not title or a fee simple ownership interest); see In re Chouinard, 358 B.R. 814, 815 (Bankr. M.D. Fla. 2006) (concurring with the Rasmussen court's holding that the term "interest" refers to equity); see In re Rogers, 354 B.R. at 798 (holding that interest refers to some legal or equitable interest that can be quantified by a monetary figure and stating that "[t]he court finds In re Rasmussen to [be] a better reasoned interpretation of § 522(p)"); see In re Reinhard, 377 B.R. at 320 (citing Rogers, Lyons, and Rasmussen and holding that the term "interest" refers to "a quantitative or monetary value in property"); see In re Presto, 376 B.R. 554, 577 (Bankr. S.D. Tex. 2007) (adopting the Rogers interpretation of the term "interest"); see also Shaun Mulreed, Casenote, In re Blair Misses the Mark: An Alternative Interpretation of the BAPCPA's Homestead Exemption, 43 SAN DIEGO L. REV. 1071, 1087 (2006) (arguing that the phrase "interest that was acquired" should apply "to all equity acquired within the 1,215 days preceding the filing of a bankruptcy petition").

[7] Those courts and commentators adopting the title definition of "interest" have indicated that creditors could challenge fraudulent mortgage payments or capital improvements made during the statutory period through another BAPCPA provision, 11 U.S.C. § 522(o). See In re Anderson, 374 B.R. at 858 ("The Court concludes that accumulation of equity by early payoff or substantially paying down the mortgage against the homestead property, such as debtor's $ 240,000 one-time lump sum payment during the 1,215 day period here, may be subject to challenge under § 522(o)."); see also 4 COLLIER ON BANKRUPTCY P 522.13[2] (same). Unlike § 522(p)(1), § 522(o) requires proof of "intent to hinder, delay, or defraud a creditor." See In re Anderson, 374 B.R. at 859-60.

5. A homestead interest is not the equivalent of title or equity.

We find it unnecessary at this time to pick a side in the title versus equity debate. A homestead interest is not the equivalent of title or equity. In this case, Rogers acquired title to the property when she inherited it from her mother in 1994, which was outside the statutory period. Those courts adopting the title definition of "interest" would conclude that § 522(p)(1) is inapplicable to Rogers. See In re Anderson, 374 B.R. at 861. Rogers acquired most of her equity in the Forney Property at the time she inherited it in 1994. Those courts adopting the equity definition of "interest" would also conclude that § 522(p)(1) is inapplicable to Rogers.[8] She did not actively acquire equity through making a down payment or monthly mortgage payments on the Forney Property during the statutory period. See In re Rasmussen, 349 B.R. at 757. Rogers made capital improvements to the Forney Property by spending less than $100,000 of her retirement money to construct a permanent residence, but the aggregate value of those improvements did not exceed $125,000. Rogers presumably benefitted from market appreciation during the statutory period; however, those courts adopting the equity definition of "interest" have concluded that passive equity appreciation is not "acquired" by the debtor and not covered by § 522(p)(1). Id. at 757-58.

Wallace argues that Rogers acquired an interest in the Forney Property during the 1,215-day period because the divorce decree divested the debtor's husband of "all right, title, interest, and claim" in the Forney Property and awarded it to the debtor. Recently, a bankruptcy court addressed the issue of whether acquiring an ex-spouse's community property interest in the homestead property is a form of active equity appreciation that is subject to § 522(p)(1). If the Forney Property had constituted the community property of the debtor and her husband, then Wallace's argument might have some merit. See In re Presto, 376 B.R. at 576. However, the Forney Property was the debtor's separate property because she inherited it from her mother before marriage. See TEX. FAM. CODE § 3.001. A trial court in Texas has no discretion to divest title to separate property and award that property to the other spouse in a divorce. Cameron v. Cameron, 641 S.W.2d 210, 219-20 (Tex. 1982). In this case, the divorce decree did not increase Rogers's equity share in the Forney Property because she owned it as her separate property. Rogers did not acquire "new value in a homestead through a divorce decree." See In re Presto, 376 B.R. at 580.

6. A homestead interest is not covered by § 522(p)(1) because it does not constitute a vested economic interest in property.

Wallace does not appear to quarrel with the proposition that the debtor's acquisition of title or equity during the 1,215-day period can implicate the homestead exemption cap. He is simply advocating a more expansive definition of "interest" that includes a "homestead interest." Although other courts have interpreted the term "interest" more narrowly, we must determine whether the

[8] The date of acquisition of title is irrelevant for purposes of the equity definition; however, if title is acquired during the statutory period, any lump-sum down payment made in connection with closing (i.e. the date of acquisition of title) would apply towards the $ 125,000 equity cap. In this case, Rogers inherited the Forney Property in 1994, so she did not make a down payment during the statutory period that would apply towards the cap.

term refers to a broader concept that includes a homestead interest.[9] answer to this federal question, however, largely depends upon state law." United States v. Craft, 535 U.S. 274, 278 (2002). Thus, we look initially to state law to determine what rights the debtor had in the Forney Property pursuant to Texas homestead law, then to federal law to determine whether the debtor's "state-delineated rights" qualify as an "interest" within the compass of the homestead exemption cap. Id. In Craft, which addressed whether property held as a tenant by the entirety constituted "property and rights to property" for purposes of the federal tax lien statute, the Supreme Court stated the following:

> A common idiom describes property as a "bundle of sticks"--a collection of individual rights which, in certain combinations, constitute property. State law determines only which sticks are in a person's bundle. Whether those sticks qualify as "property" for purposes of the federal tax lien statute is a question of federal law. In looking to state law, we must be careful to consider the substance of the rights state law provides, not merely the labels the State gives these rights or the conclusions it draws from them. Such state law labels are irrelevant to the federal question of which bundles of rights constitute property that may be attached by a federal tax lien.

Id. at 278-79 (internal citations omitted). In Craft, the Supreme Court held that "the statutory language authorizing the tax lien is broad and reveals on its face that Congress meant to reach every interest in property that a taxpayer might have." Id. at 283 (internal quotation marks omitted). Accordingly, the Supreme Court held that the husband's rights in the entireties property fall within this broad statutory language: "all property and rights to property." Id.; 26 U.S.C. § 6321. Based on the statutory language of 11 U.S.C. § 522(p)(1), we find that Congress did not intend the scope of the term "interest" to sweep so broadly.

Under Texas law, "[t]he homestead interest is a legal interest created by the constitution that provides prophylactic protection from all but [a few] types of constitutionally permitted liens against homesteads. This interest . . . gives protective legal security rather than vested economic rights."[10] Heggen v. Pemelton, 836 S.W.2d 145, 148 (Tex. 1992). Although the Texas Supreme Court referred to the homestead interest as a "legal interest" in Heggen, we must look

---

[9] We note the distinction between a homestead interest and a homestead designation. "To establish homestead rights, the claimant must show a combination of both overt acts of homestead usage and the intention on the part of the owner to claim the land as a homestead." Dominguez v. Castaneda, 163 S.W.3d 318, 330 (Tex. App.--El Paso 2005, pet. denied). Thus, a homestead interest is established when those two elements are satisfied. In contrast, a homestead designation refers to the ministerial act of recording a notice in the county deed records. TEX. PROP. CODE § 41.005; see id. at § 41.021 (allowing judgment debtors to record a homestead designation under § 41.005 after execution is issued). In this case, the debtor established her homestead rights and recorded her homestead designation within the statutory period. Cf. Laster v. First Huntsville Props. Co., 826 S.W.2d 125, 130-32 (Tex. 1991) (using the term "homestead right" and "homestead interest" interchangeably). If the debtor had established her homestead rights outside the statutory period and filed her homestead designation within the statutory period, then § 522(p)(1) would also be inapplicable. Even assuming that a homestead interest is "acquired" by the debtor, which we do not decide, we conclude that it is not the type of "interest" covered by § 522(p)(1).

[10] "Homesteads are protected from forced sale for the payment of debts, except for those debts specifically enumerated in the constitution, including debts incurred for purchase money on the homestead, taxes thereon, work or services performed thereon, certain extensions of credit, and certain reverse mortgages." Florey v. Estate of McConnell, 212 S.W.3d 439, 443 (Tex. App.--Austin 2006, no pet.).

beyond that label and consider the substance of the right conferred by state law. See Craft, 535 U.S. at 279. Based on our review of the statutory language, we conclude that the term "interest" as used in § 522(p)(1) refers to vested economic interests that the debtor acquires in the homestead property during the 1,215-day period preceding the filing of the petition. Thus, a homestead interest established within the statutory period, without more, does not fall within the purview of § 522(p)(1).

Unlike a homestead interest, title and equity both constitute vested economic interests in the homestead property that can be acquired during the 1,215-day period preceding the filing of the petition. These interests are vested because they have an ascertainable economic value at the moment they are acquired by the debtor. In contrast, for purposes of federal bankruptcy law, the homestead exemption is valueless until it is claimed in bankruptcy, such that any value attributable to the exemption is not realized by the debtor until after the filing of the petition. Wallace essentially argues that "interest" refers to all rights that enhance a debtor's claimed exemption on Schedule C. However, we believe that "interest" refers to property interests acquired within the statutory period that the debtor "may not exempt" from the bankruptcy estate. "Value" as used in § 522(p)(1) refers to the economic value of the property interests acquired within the statutory period, not the value of the exemption claimed by the debtor.

Although we decline to address whether the equity definition of "interest" is correct, we concur with the Reinhard court's conclusion that the debtor must acquire vested economic interests in the homestead property during the 1,215-day period. A debtor acquires an interest in property, not in an exemption. See Owen, 500 U.S. at 311 n.4 ("[T]here would be no debtor's interest in the property to which a[n] . . . exemption could attach."). "A fundamental canon of statutory construction instructs that in the absence of a statutory definition, we give terms their ordinary meaning." Hamilton v. United Healthcare of La., Inc., 310 F.3d 385, 391 (5th Cir. 2002). BLACK'S LAW DICTIONARY 828 (8th ed. 2005) defines "interest" as "a legal share in something; all or part of a legal or equitable claim to or right in property <right, title, and interest>." Similarly, WEBSTER'S THIRD NEW INTERNATIONAL DICTIONARY 1178 (1971) defines "interest" as "right, title, or legal share in something" and "something in which one has a share of ownership or control." These definitions clearly indicate that one has "interests" in the property itself, not in the exemption that protects those interests.

For purposes of federal bankruptcy law, the homestead exemption is not a separate interest, but rather the status of a withdrawn interest in property that was acquired prior to bankruptcy. See Norris v. Thomas, 215 S.W.3d 851, 856 (Tex. 2007) ("[W]e agree that the proper test for whether a residence attains homestead status . . . ."); see also Owen, 500 U.S. at 308 ("An exemption is an interest withdrawn from the estate"). The homestead interest simply gives "protective legal security" to those vested economic interests in property that were acquired by the debtor before the filing of the petition. Heggen, 836 S.W.2d at 148; see Laster, 826 S.W.2d at 131 ("[The party's] homestead interest protects the portion of the property that she owns.").

Our own precedent has recognized that a homestead interest is a legal right vested in the individual to attach an exempt status to existing property interests. See Perry v. Dearing (In re Perry), 345 F.3d 303, 314-15 (5th Cir. 2003) ("According to the Texas Supreme Court, it is a well-recognized principle of law that one's homestead right in property can never rise any higher than the right, title, or interest that he owns in the property attempted to be impressed with a homestead right.") (internal quotation marks and ellipsis omitted) (emphasis added). The homestead exemption and the property interest impressed with that exemption are discrete concepts: the former is the debtor's legal right to exempt certain property interests from the bankruptcy estate, the latter is the debtor's vested economic interests in the property itself.

Although the Texas Supreme Court has characterized the homestead interest as "an estate in land" that is "analogous to a life tenancy," this language merely describes the scope of the protective legal security afforded by the homestead interest. See Laster, 826 S.W.2d at 129-31 (discussing the analogy and concluding that one spouse's homestead designation did not affect "any property interest protected by [the other spouse's] homestead right.") (emphasis added). The homestead interest does not increase the vested economic interests that the debtor holds in the homestead property; rather, it simply protects those vested economic interests in the property that the debtor acquired before the filing of the petition.

Thus, we find that the Greene court construed the scope of the term "interest" too broadly. What must be acquired during the statutory period is vested economic interests in the homestead property.

7. Other sections of 11 U.S.C. § 522 indicate that the term "interest" refers to a vested economic interest in property.

"The starting point in discerning congressional intent is the existing statutory text." Lamie v. United States Trustee, 540 U.S. 526, 534 (2004). "[W]hen the statute's language is plain, the sole function of the courts--at least where the disposition required by the text is not absurd--is to enforce it according to its terms." Id. (internal quotation marks omitted). Only after application of the principles of statutory construction, including the canons of construction, and after a conclusion that the statute is ambiguous may the court turn to the legislative history. Carrieri v. Jobs.com, Inc., 393 F.3d 508, 518-19 (5th Cir. 2004). For the language to be considered ambiguous, however, it must be susceptible to more than one reasonable interpretation or more than one accepted meaning. Id. at 519. However, a statute is not ambiguous simply because it is inartfully drafted. See Lamie, 540 U.S. at 534 ("The statute is awkward, and even ungrammatical; but that does not make it ambiguous on the point at issue.").

The statute is not ambiguous as to whether a homestead interest is covered by § 522(p)(1). The term "interest" is used in several sections of 11 U.S.C. § 522 and consistently refers to some vested economic interest in property. For example, § 522(b)(3)(B), which addresses state exemptions, characterizes "an interest as a tenant by the entirety or joint tenant" as an "interest in property." Section 522(d)(1), which addresses federal exemptions, states that the debtor may exempt her "aggregate interest, not to exceed $20,200 in value, in real property . . . that the debtor . . . uses as a residence." Section 522(p)(2)(B) states that "any amount of interest" does not include any interest transferred from a debtor's previous principal residence that was acquired outside the statutory period. In contrast to "interests," which refer to vested economic interests in property, "exemptions" refer to those interests that are withdrawn from the estate. See 11 U.S.C. § 522(b)(1) ("[A]n individual debtor may exempt from property of the estate the property listed in either paragraph (2) [federal exemptions] or, in the alternative, paragraph (3) [state exemptions]."). Section 522(p)(1) prevents the debtor from withdrawing certain vested economic interests in property from the bankruptcy estate if they were acquired by the debtor during the statutory period and their aggregate value exceeds a certain dollar threshold.

8. The legislative history indicates that the term "interest" refers to a vested economic interest in property.

Even assuming that § 522(p)(1) is ambiguous, the legislative history makes clear that the term "interest" refers to some vested economic interest in property acquired during the statutory period, not a homestead interest. "Extrinsic materials have a role in statutory interpretation only to the extent they shed a reliable light on the enacting Legislature's understanding of otherwise ambiguous terms." Exxon Mobil Corp. v. Allapattah Servs., Inc., 545 U.S. 546, 568 (2005). The House Report specifically addressed the meaning of § 522(p):

> Sec. 322. Limitations on Homestead Exemption. Section 322(a) amends section 522 of the Bankruptcy Code to impose an aggregate monetary limitation of $125,000 . . . on the value of property that the debtor may claim as exempt under State or local law pursuant to section 522(b)(3)(A) under certain circumstances. The monetary cap applies if the debtor acquired such property within the 1,215-day period preceding the filing of the petition and the property consists of any of the following: (1) real or personal property of the debtor or that a dependent of the debtor uses as a residence . . . (4) real or personal property that the debtor or dependent of the debtor claims as a homestead . . . . In addition, the limitation does not apply to any interest transferred from a debtor's principal residence (which was acquired prior to the beginning of the specified time period) to the debtor's current principal residence, if both the previous and current residences are located in the same State.

H.R. Rep. No. 109-31(I) (2005), reprinted in 2005 U.S.C.C.A.N. 88, 148, 2005 WL 832198,This piece of legislative history has been cited approvingly by those courts adopting the title definition of interest. See, e.g., In re Sainlar, at 344 B.R. at 673-74. The legislative history indicates that Congress was concerned with the acquisition of vested economic interests in property during the statutory period.

On March 10, 2005, Senator Carper stated the following:

> Today, under current law, a wealthy individual in a State such as Florida or Texas can go out, if they are a millionaire, and take those millions of dollars and invest that money in real estate, a huge house, property, and land in the State, file for bankruptcy, and basically protect all of their assets which they own because of a provision in Florida and Texas law.

151 Cong. Rec. S2415-02 (daily ed. March 10, 2005), at *S2415.

> With the legislation we have before us, someone has to figure out that 2 1/2 years ahead of time people are going to want to file for bankruptcy and be smart enough to put the money into a home, or an estate, or into a trust--not something you can do today--and file for bankruptcy tomorrow; or this year and file for bankruptcy next year or the next 2 or 3 years, or 3 1/2 years.

Id. at *S2416. Senator Carper's statement has been cited approvingly by those courts adopting the equity definition of interest. See, e.g., In re Rasmussen, 349 B.R. at 758. Senator Carper's statement is also supported by language in the House Report, which states that "[t]he bill also restricts the so-called 'mansion loophole.'

Under current bankruptcy law, debtors living in certain states can shield from their creditors virtually all of the equity in their homes. In light of this, some debtors actually relocate to these states just to take advantage of their 'mansion loophole' laws." H.R. Rep. No. 109-31(I) (2005), 2005 WL 832198,*16. In this case, it is undisputed that Rogers did not relocate to Texas to exploit the so-called "mansion loophole."

Wallace cites to the House Report, which states that "[t]he bill further reduces the opportunity for abuse by requiring a debtor to own the homestead for at least 40 months before he or she can use state exemption law." Id. at *16. Considering the fact that one "owns" property, not a homestead interest, we do not find this piece of legislative history to be particularly probative of congressional intent.

According to Wallace, BAPCPA was intended to address fraudulent transfers in general, including conversions of non-exempt assets into exempt assets within the statutory period. Cf. In re Kane, 336 B.R. 477, 481-82 (Bankr. D. Nev. 2006). We concur with the Reinhard court's observation that "Congress could have defined all [the] debtors' exemptions to be whatever they would have been 1215 days before the filing of the petition. Instead, Congress defined the cap more narrowly." 377 B.R. at 321. We do not believe that Congress was concerned with the timing of the establishment of the homestead when it enacted § 522(p)(1). The statutory text and legislative history indicate that the term "interest" refers to vested economic interests in the property that were acquired by the debtor within the 1,215-day period preceding the filing of the petition. "If Congress enacted into law something different from what it intended, then it should amend the statute to conform it to its intent." Lamie, 540 U.S. at 542. We hold that Rogers is entitled to her full homestead exemption under Texas state law. AFFIRMED.

ADDISON v SEAVER (IN RE ADDISON)

540 F.3d 805 (8th Cir. 2008)

SMITH, J

Shortly before Lance Addison filed his bankruptcy petition, he converted a portion of his nonexempt assets into exempt assets. After the bankruptcy trustee ("Trustee") filed an objection to Addison's claimed exemptions, the bankruptcy court concluded that Addison converted the assets with the intent to hinder, delay, or defraud a creditor. As a result, the bankruptcy court reduced Addison's homestead exemption by $11,500, and denied the exemption claimed in his Roth IRA. . . . Addison appealed the bankruptcy court's decision, and the Bankruptcy Appellate Panel (BAP) affirmed.

Subsequently, the Trustee initiated an adversary proceeding objecting to Addison's discharge. The bankruptcy court denied Addison's discharge, ruling as a matter of collateral estoppel that Addison had acted with the intent to hinder, delay or defraud one or more creditors when he converted his nonexempt assets to exempt assets within one year prior to filing bankruptcy. Addison also appealed this decision to the BAP and immediately requested that the BAP transfer the appeal to this court. The BAP did so, and we now hear Addison's consolidated appeals. We affirm in part, reverse in part, and remand for further proceedings.

I. Background

Addison, a part-owner of a cable company, had personally guaranteed some of his company's debt. In early 2005 the business was unable to pay its debts, and JP Morgan Chase ("Chase"), a company creditor, began to pursue Addison on a $1.3 million personal guarantee. Around June 2005, Addison first sought the advice of bankruptcy counsel in an effort to protect himself from Chase's attempts to enforce the guarantee. On or about July 21, 2005, Addison used $4,000 of his nonexempt funds to establish a Roth IRA for himself and used another $4,000 of the nonexempt funds to establish a Roth IRA for his wife. The funds came from a brokerage account that contained $45,476.71 in nonexempt funds prior to these transfers.

On October 14, 2005, Addison instructed his wife to use $11,500 in nonexempt funds to make a voluntary principal payment on their home mortgage. Addison's wife transferred $9,000 of this payment from the brokerage account mentioned above, and $2,500 came from a bank account at U.S. Bank. Later that same day, Addison filed an individual Chapter 7 bankruptcy petition. He chose the Minnesota state exemptions and claimed his Roth IRA[11] and the equity in the house as exempt. . . .

The Trustee objected to Addison's homestead and Roth IRA exemptions, and asserted that the Section 529 accounts were property of the estate not subject to any exemption. The bankruptcy court held an evidentiary hearing on the Trustee's objection and subsequently ruled in favor of the Trustee on all three issues. The court found that Addison made the $11,500 house payment and the $4,000 Roth IRA payment with the intent to hinder, delay, or defraud his creditors, and thus denied, in full, Addison's claimed exemption in the Roth IRA and ordered that the homestead exemption be reduced by $11,500. The bankruptcy court also ruled that the Section 529 plans were property of Addison's bankruptcy estate and that they were not subject to any applicable exemption.

The BAP affirmed, ruling that the bankruptcy court's finding that Addison had the intent to hinder, delay, or defraud his creditors when he converted the nonexempt assets into exempt assets was not clearly erroneous. The BAP also affirmed the bankruptcy court's determination that the Section 529 accounts were property of the estate and not subject to exemption. Addison timely appealed to this court.

After the bankruptcy court found that Addison intended to hinder, delay, or defraud a creditor when he converted his nonexempt assets into his homestead and Roth IRA, the Trustee initiated an adversary proceeding to deny Addison's discharge under 11 U.S.C. § 727(a)(2). Because a debtor's discharge can be denied under § 727(a)(2) if "the debtor, with intent to hinder, delay, or defraud a creditor . . . has transferred . . . property of the debtor, within one year before" his bankruptcy filing, and the bankruptcy court had already concluded that Addison transferred nonexempt property to exempt property with the intent to hinder, delay, or defraud a creditor within a year before his bankruptcy filing, the court denied Addison's discharge under § 727(a)(2) on collateral estoppel grounds. Addison also appealed this ruling to the BAP, which certified the appeal directly to this court. We now consider both of Addison's appeals.

[11] The Roth IRA opened in Addison's wife's name is not at issue in this case.

II. Discussion

Addison argues that the bankruptcy court erroneously found that he converted nonexempt assets to exempt assets with the intent to hinder, delay, or defraud one or more creditors. More specifically, Addison contends that the bankruptcy court's disallowance of his Roth IRA exemption claim and its reduction of his homestead exemption should be reversed along with the denial of his discharge. Further, Addison asserts that the bankruptcy court erred in ruling that the Section 529 accounts that he established for his children are property of his bankruptcy estate and in ruling that they are not subject to any exemption. Like the BAP, we review the bankruptcy court's conclusions of law de novo and its findings of facts for clear error. Official Comm. of Unsecured Creditors v. Farmland Indus., Inc. (In re Farmland Indus., Inc.), 397 F.3d 647, 650 (8th Cir. 2005).

A. Disallowance of Claimed Exemptions

The bankruptcy court found that Addison acted with the intent to hinder, delay, or defraud one or more of his creditors. Shortly before filing for bankruptcy, Addison converted nonexempt funds from a brokerage account and a bank account to pay down the mortgage on his home thereby increasing his homestead exemption. Also, he converted nonexempt funds from his brokerage account into an exemptible Roth IRA.

Under § 522(b) of the Bankruptcy Code, "a debtor can choose to exempt from property of the bankruptcy estate that property which is exempt under the applicable state or federal law." Sholdan v. Dietz, 108 F.3d 886, 888 (8th Cir. 1997) ("Sholdan I"); 11 U.S.C. § 522(b). Here, Addison elected to use the Minnesota state exemptions, and claimed a homestead exemption of $91,250 under Minn. Stat. Ann. § 510.02[12] and claimed his $4,000 Roth IRA as exempt under Minn. Stat. Ann. § 550.37(24).[13] These claimed exemptions were within the permissible amounts as provided by Minnesota law. See In re Sholdan, 217 F.3d 1006, 1008 (8th Cir. 2000) ("Sholdan II") ("The scope of a state-created exemption is determined by state law"). However, under Minnesota's enactment of the Uniform Fraudulent Transfers Act (UFTA), a debtor may not claim an exemption in property obtained through a transfer made by the debtor "with actual intent to hinder, delay, or defraud any creditor of the debtor." Minn. Stat. Ann. § 513.44; see also Sholdan II, 217 F.3d at 1008 ("[U]nder section 513.44 of Minnesota's enactment of the Uniform Fraudulent Transfer Act (UFTA), a debtor may not claim a homestead exemption when he or she transfers the property 'with actual intent to hinder, delay, or defraud' creditors"); In re Tveten, 402 N.W.2d 551, 556 (Minn. 1987) ("[I]t clearly appears that under Minnesota law a debtor in contemplation of bankruptcy may convert nonexempt property into exempt property, so long as the conversion does not violate the Uniform

---

[12] At the time of Addison's bankruptcy filing, Minnesota law provided for a homestead exemption (in a non-agricultural homestead) up to $ 200,000 in value. Minn. Stat. § 510.02. Although it has no impact on this case, we note that the maximum homestead exemption (for non-agricultural homesteads) was increased to $ 300,000 when § 510.02 was rewritten in 2007.

[13] Minn. Stat. Ann. § 550.37(24) allows a debtor to exempt his "right to receive present or future payments, or payments received by the debtor, under a . . . Roth IRA . . . up to a present value of $ 30,000 . . . ."

Fraudulent Conveyance Act"). Section 513.44(b) "contains a lengthy list of factors or 'badges of fraud' which a court may look to for help in determining actual intent." Sholdan II, 217 F.3d at 1008 (citing Minn. Stat. Ann. § 513.44(b)). Thus, Addison's claimed exemptions in his homestead and Roth IRA are not permitted if those assets were obtained by transfers made "with actual intent to hinder, delay, or defraud any creditor." Minn. Stat. Ann. § 513.44(a).

Additionally, when Congress passed the Bankruptcy Abuse Prevention and Consumer Protection Act of 2005 (BAPCPA), it added, among other things, subsection (o) to § 522 of the Bankruptcy Code ("Code"). Under § 522(o) of the Code, the amount of a state homestead exemption is reduced to the extent that the value of the exemption is attributable to nonexempt property that the debtor converted into the homestead within 10 years of filing for bankruptcy, if the conversion was made "with the intent to hinder, delay, or defraud a creditor." 11 U.S.C. § 522(o).[14] Thus, while the exemption Addison claimed in his Roth IRA is allowable unless it violates Minn. Stat. Ann. § 513.44(a), the claimed homestead exemption is subject to both 11 U.S.C. § 522(o) and Minn. Stat. Ann. § 513.44(a).

1. Homestead Exemption

The question here is whether the $91,250.00 that Addison claimed as his homestead exemption must be reduced by $11,500, under either Minnesota law or § 522(o) of the Code, due to the day-of-filing mortgage payment. For purposes of § 522(o), the issue turns on whether Addison acted "with the intent to hinder, delay, or defraud a creditor" when he transferred nonexempt funds to reduce the mortgage on his homestead. Congress did not provide any guidance regarding the construction of the phrase "with the intent to hinder, delay, or defraud" when it enacted § 522(o), but the statutory language is similar, if not identical, to the language used in § 548 and § 727 of the Code, as well as Minn. Stat. Ann. § 513.44(a).

Section 548 of the Code provides that a trustee may avoid a pre-petition transfer of assets by the debtor if the debtor made the transfer "with actual intent to hinder, delay, or defraud" any past or future creditor. 11 U.S.C. § 548(a)(1)(A). Similarly, § 727(a)(2) bars a debtor's discharge if he takes certain actions, including transferring, concealing, or removing property of the estate within one year before filing, "with intent to hinder, delay, or defraud a creditor." 11 U.S.C. § 727(a)(2). Due to the similar wording of those statutes, numerous bankruptcy courts have looked to the body of case law construing §§ 548(a)(1) and 727(a)(2) to determine the meaning of "with intent to hinder, delay, or defraud a creditor" in § 522(o). See Maronde, 332 B.R. at 599 ("It is only logical to assume that Congress intended that by using essentially the same phrase in § 522(o), cases construing the fraudulent conveyance and discharge provisions also would apply to add body to the bare words of this new Congressional language"); In re

[14] Addison asserts that § 522(o) should not reduce the amount of a state homestead exemption because the scope of state exemptions have traditionally been determined by state law, see Sholdan II, 217 F.3d at 1008. We must reject this argument in light of the express language in § 522. See 11 U.S.C. § 522(b)(3) (providing that debtors who use a state's exemptions do so "subject to subsection (o) and (p)") (emphasis added). "The Congressional purpose is clear: debtors seeking the protection of state exemptions must meet their state exemption provision requirements as limited by § 522(o) and (p)." In re Maronde, 332 B.R. 593, 599 (Bankr. D. Minn. 2005) (emphasis added).

Fehmel, No. 07-60831, 2008 Bankr. LEXIS 2577, 2008 WL 2151797, at (Bankr. W.D. Tex. May 22, 2008) "The phrase 'with the intent to hinder, delay or defraud a creditor' contained in § 522(o) is . . . not defined in the Bankruptcy Code . . . . Therefore, in interpreting the meaning of the phrase as contained in § 522(o), it is appropriate to look to case law interpreting [§ 727(a)(2) and § 548(a)(1)(A)]"); In re Agnew, 355 B.R. 276, 284 (Bankr. D. Kan. 2006) (construing the meaning of "intent to hinder, delay, or defraud a creditor" in § 522(o) from cases construing the meaning of intent to hinder, delay, or defraud in §§ 727(a)(2) and 548(a)(1)); In re Lacounte, 342 B.R. 809, 814 (Bankr. D. Mont. 2005) (same); In re Sissom, 366 B.R. 677, 691-92 (Bankr. S.D. Tex. 2007) (same).

Because direct evidence of fraudulent intent is rarely available, our cases have used the inferential "badges of fraud" approach to determine whether a debtor acted with "intent to hinder, delay, or defraud," a creditor regardless of whether the intent language came from a state fraudulent transfer statute or applicable bankruptcy law. See Sholdan II, 217 F.3d at 1009 (approving badges of fraud approach to determine whether debtor acted with "actual intent to hinder, delay, or defraud" under Minnesota fraudulent transfer statute in ruling on objection to homestead exemption); Jackson v. Star Sprinkler Corp. of Florida, 575 F.2d 1223, 1237 (8th Cir. 1978) (using badges of fraud analysis to determine whether debtor made transfers with intent to hinder, delay, or defraud creditor under fraudulent transfer section of the then-applicable Bankruptcy Act); see also Graven v. Fink (In re Graven), 936 F.2d 378, 383 (8th Cir. 1991) (comparing § 548(a)'s "actual intent to hinder, delay, or defraud" language with "intent to hinder, delay or defraud" in Missouri's then-applicable state fraudulent conveyance statute, noting that the two statutes use the "same standard"). Given the similarity of the language among these statutes, we conclude that the badges of fraud approach should also apply to determine a debtor's intent under § 522(o).[15]

Although both § 522(o) and Minn. Stat. Ann. § 513.44, like §§ 548(a)(1) and 727(a)(2), use the disjunctive "hinder, delay, or defraud," our circuit has been reluctant to deny a homestead exemption without a finding of intent to defraud. See Sholdan I, 108 F.3d at 888 (reversing bankruptcy court's finding that debtor converted nonexempt property into exempt homestead with intent to hinder or delay, and remanding for bankruptcy court to determine whether debtor acted with intent to defraud); Panuska v. Johnson (In re Johnson), 880 F.2d 78, 80 n.1 (8th Cir. 1989) (noting that courts "generally view" the phrase "hinder, delay, or defraud" as "a single test" and refusing "to separate out the terms fraud, hinder and delay").[16] In Sholdan I, a 90-year old debtor, who had been sued for injuries caused by an automobile accident, sold substantially all of his nonexempt assets and used those proceeds to purchase a home with cash. Id. at 887. At all times while living in his new home, Sholdan had the assistance of a nurse. Id. For

[15] We reject the Trustee's position that § 522(o) provides a new standard for determining what type of evidence establishes a debtor's "intent to hinder, delay, or defraud" a creditor when the debtor converts nonexempt assets into his homestead. Rather, in our view, § 522(o) merely establishes a 10-year look-back period, from the date of the bankruptcy filing, from which such evidence may be considered.

[16] See also Coder v. Arts, 213 U.S. 223, 242, 29 S. Ct. 436, 53 L. Ed. 772 (1909) (explaining that "hinder, delay, or defraud" is a "form of expression . . . familiar to the law of fraudulent conveyances . . . and has always been held to require, in order to invalidate a conveyance, that there shall be actual fraud").

approximately a year prior to purchasing the house the debtor had been living in an assisted living facility, and on nights when a nurse was not available to stay with him in his newly purchased home, the debtor would return to the assisted living facility to spend the night. Id. Additionally, for the 13 years prior to residing at the assisted living facility, the debtor had not owned a home, but had lived in an apartment. Id.

Three months after purchasing the new home the debtor filed for bankruptcy and claimed his house as exempt. Id. The trustee objected to the homestead exemption, asserting that the debtor had purchased the home with the intent to hinder, delay or defraud a creditor. Id. The bankruptcy court sustained the trustee's objection and disallowed the claimed homestead exemption, finding that the debtor had acted with the intent to "hinder or delay" a creditor when he purchased the home. Id. The bankruptcy court did not rule on whether the debtor acted with intent to defraud a creditor. Id. at 887-88. The district court affirmed, holding that it was not necessary to find an intent to defraud. Id. at 888. We then reversed and remanded for the bankruptcy court to consider whether the debtor acted with the intent to defraud. Id. In reversing, we stated that "we do not mean to say that the test of 'hinder or delay' might not prevail under another set of facts," but ruled that the facts of that case "d[id] not support such a finding." Id.

In the instant case, the bankruptcy court found sufficient evidence to establish that Addison acted with the intent to hinder, delay, and defraud a creditor.[17] However, Addison took less aggressive actions than those present in Sholdan[18]--wherein we concluded that the facts did not support a finding of intent to hinder or delay. Applying our precedent, we conclude that the record here does not support the reduction of Addison's homestead exemption based on an intent to hinder or delay. Id.

Thus, we are left with the bankruptcy court's determination that Addison converted $11,500 in nonexempt funds into his homestead with the intent to defraud a creditor. "The question of whether an individual acted with intent to defraud in converting non-exempt property into exempt property is a question of fact, on which the bankruptcy court's finding will not be reversed unless clearly erroneous." Sholdan II, 217 F.3d at 1010 (citing Hanson v. First Nat'l Bank, 848 F.2d 866, 868 (8th Cir.1988)). "It is well settled that the mere conversion of non-exempt assets to exempt assets is not in itself fraudulent." Id.; see also Hanson, 848 F.2d at 868 ("It is well established that . . . a debtor's conversion of non-exempt property to exempt property on the eve of bankruptcy

---

[17] In granting the Trustee's motion to reduce Addison's homestead exemption the court stated:

> I find and conclude that the transfers to the mortgage holder through any reduction of the mortgage debt were transfers of property made with the intent to hinder, delay, or defraud. It doesn't have to be fraud. Everyone seems to focus on fraud, but hinder or delay is sufficient and I think all of those are present here.

Hearing Tr. at 61-62 (emphasis added).

[18] Both Sholdan and Addison took steps to protect their assets after being sued, but unlike Sholdan, Addison did not create an exempt asset by purchasing a home he did not previously have; rather, Addison made an additional lump-sum payment toward the mortgage on his existing home. Further, Addison did not convert substantially all of his nonexempt assets into the home as Sholdan had done.

for the express purpose of placing that property beyond the reach of creditors, without more, will not deprive the debtor of the exemption to which he otherwise would be entitled"); Norwest Bank Nebraska, NA v. Tveten, 848 F.2d 871, 873-74 (8th Cir. 1988) ("It is well established that under the Code the conversion of non-exempt to exempt property for the purpose of placing the property out of the reach of creditors, without more, will not deprive the debtor of the exemption to which he otherwise would be entitled"). Nevertheless, "[w]here the debtor acts with actual intent to defraud creditors, his exemptions will be denied." Hanson, 848 F.2d at 868.

"Before actual fraudulent intent can be found 'there must appear in evidence some facts or circumstances which are extrinsic to the mere facts of conversion of non-exempt assets into exempt and which are indicative of such fraudulent purpose.'" Sholdan II, 217 F.3d at 1010 (quoting Tveten, 848 F.2d at 875 (in turn quoting Forsberg v. Security State Bank, 15 F.2d 499, 502 (8th Cir. 1926))). In finding that Addison had the requisite intent to defraud, the bankruptcy court properly looked to the badges of fraud enumerated in Minn. Stat. Ann. § 513.44(b),[19] and found four badges of fraud resulting from Addison's day-of-filing mortgage payment: (1) the transfer was to an insider; (2) Addison retained control of the property after the transfer; (3) the transfer was made after Addison had been sued on his personal guarantee; and (4) Addison was insolvent at the time he transferred the funds to his homestead. Additionally, the bankruptcy court noted that Addison already had significant equity in his home before he made the transfer and that the payment only increased Addison's equity in the home, but did not reduce his monthly mortgage payment. While the bankruptcy court noted that there were badges of fraud favoring both sides, it found that the homestead transfer was made with the intent to hinder, delay, or defraud Addison's creditors, as his intent was "to keep value away from creditors."

The bankruptcy court's underlying factual findings are themselves not clearly erroneous; however, they do not identify any "extrinsic evidence of fraud." In the absence of extrinsic evidence of fraud, we find clear error in the bankruptcy court's ultimate determination of intent to defraud. As discussed

---

[19] Minn. Stat. Ann. § 513.44(b), provides a nonexclusive list of "badges of fraud" that may be considered, among other things, in determining a debtor's intent to defraud. These "badges" are whether:

(1) the transfer or obligation was to an insider;

(2) the debtor retained possession or control of the property transferred after the transfer;

(3) the transfer or obligation was disclosed or concealed;

(4) before the transfer was made or obligation was incurred, the debtor had been sued or threatened with suit;

(5) the transfer was of substantially all the debtor's assets;

(6) the debtor absconded;

(7) the debtor removed or concealed assets;

(8) the value of the consideration received by the debtor was reasonably equivalent to the value of the asset transferred or the amount of the obligation incurred;

(9) the debtor was insolvent or became insolvent shortly after the transfer was made or the obligation was incurred;

(10) the transfer occurred shortly before or shortly after a substantial debt was incurred; and

(11) the debtor transferred the essential assets of the business to a lienor who transferred the assets to an insider of the debtor.

above, "[i]t is well established that . . . a debtor's conversion of non-exempt property to exempt property on the eve of bankruptcy for the express purpose of placing that property beyond the reach of creditors, without more, will not deprive the debtor of the exemption to which he otherwise would be entitled." Hanson, 848 F.2d at 868. Rather, for fraudulent intent to be found "there must appear in evidence some facts or circumstances which are extrinsic to the mere facts of conversion of non-exempt assets into exempt and which are indicative of such fraudulent purpose." Sholdan II, 217 F.3d at 1010 (quotations and citations omitted).

Here, only the fact that Addison had been sued or threatened with suit prior to making the mortgage payment was extrinsic to the fact of conversion--all of the other facts cited relate to a debtor's simple conversion of nonexempt property to exempt property on the eve of bankruptcy, which we have long held to be permissible.[20] If these facts alone constitute extrinsic evidence of intent to defraud Hanson and Johnson would have reached that same result. See Hanson, 848 F.2d at 867-68 (rejecting argument that extrinsic evidence established debtor's intent to defraud where debtors, after defaulting on bank loans and talking to bankruptcy counsel, converted approximately $20,000 into life insurance policies a couple of weeks prior to filing and prepaid an additional $11,033 on their homestead mortgage two days before filing); Johnson, 880 F.2d at 79 ("agree[ing] that there is no fraud as to [debtor's] homestead exemption," where debtor, in contemplation of filing bankruptcy, talked to bankruptcy attorney and paid off $175,000 in debts against his home after creditors obtained judgments against him). Moreover, the bankruptcy court's finding that Addison converted his nonexempt property to exempt property with the intent "to keep value away from creditors" does not provide extrinsic evidence of fraud as such an intent is not automatically impermissible. Hanson, 848 F.2d at 868; Tveten, 848 F.2d at 873

This case resembles Hanson. The Hansons, married farmers, defaulted on several bank loans when financial difficulties arose. 848 F.2d at 867. Before they filed for bankruptcy, the Hansons consulted an attorney, and on the advice of counsel, they sold several nonexempt items to family members for fair-market value. Id. A couple of weeks before filing for bankruptcy, the Hansons took the proceeds from the sales of the nonexempt assets and bought life insurance policies on each of them with a cash-surrender value of approximately $10,000 each. Then two days prior to filing for bankruptcy they prepaid $11,033 on their homestead mortgage. Id. Upon filing for bankruptcy, the Hansons claimed their life insurance policies and their homestead as exempt. Id.

A creditor objected to these exemptions, claiming that the debtors had converted nonexempt property to exempt property on the eve of bankruptcy with intent to defraud their creditors. Id. The bankruptcy court denied the objection to the exemptions, finding that the Hansons had done what was permissible under the law and that their actions did not constitute extrinsic evidence of fraud. Id. at 868. After the district court affirmed, the creditor

---

[20] A debtor's conversion of his own nonexempt property into exempt property also owned by him could always be viewed as a transfer to an insider. Likewise, after that conversion, the debtor would continue to control the property after the conversion. And, a debtor converting nonexempt property to exempt property "on the eve of bankruptcy" will almost always be insolvent. Thus, these "badges of fraud," without more, cannot support a finding of intent to defraud.

appealed to this court. Id.

The Hanson panel focused on whether extrinsic evidence established that the Hansons converted their property with the intent to defraud their creditors and concluded that the bankruptcy court was not clearly erroneous in finding no fraudulent intent by the Hansons. Id. at 869. In reaching this conclusion, we noted that the bankruptcy court had found that the creditor did not establish any indicia of fraud and further noted that "the Hansons did not borrow money to place into exempt properties; they accounted for the cash they received from the sales; they had a preexisting homestead; and they did not obtain goods on credit, sell them, and then place the money into exempt property." Id. Concluding that the debtors "sold their [nonexempt] property for its fair market value and then used this money to take advantage of some of the limited exemptions available under South Dakota law on the advice of counsel," we held that the bankruptcy court was not clearly erroneous in finding that the debtors lacked the intent to defraud and permitting the debtors to claim their full exemptions. Id.

Similar to the Hansons, Addison became insolvent (albeit due to a personal guarantee being called rather than defaulting on loans) and prior to filing for bankruptcy he sought the advice of counsel. After discussing prebankruptcy planning with his attorney, Addison transferred some of his nonexempt assets in a brokerage account to fund Roth IRAs for himself and his wife in the amount of $4,000 each. This mirrors the Hansons' conversion of non-exempt assets into life insurance policies, except that Addison converted a lesser amount into the Roth IRAs than the Hansons did for their life insurance policies. Additionally, Addison made an $11,500 principal mortgage payment on the day he filed his bankruptcy petition--nearly identical to the $11,033 mortgage payment the Hansons made two days prior to their bankruptcy filing. As in Hanson, there has been no extrinsic evidence produced here that Addison had any indicia of fraud other than the suit or threat of suit resulting from personal liability on a defaulted loan: Addison did not borrow money to place into exempt assets; he had a preexisting homestead; he did not obtain goods on credit, sell them, then place the money into exempt property; and he did not attempt to conceal the transfers in his bankruptcy filings.

"The sort of indicia of fraud necessary to find fraudulent use on an exemption would be, inter alia, conduct intentionally designed to materially mislead or deceive creditors about the debtor's position or use of credit to buy exempt property." Matter of Armstrong, 931 F.2d 1233, 1237 (8th Cir. 1991) (citations omitted). Additionally, "[c]onverting a very great amount of property could also be an indication of fraud," as could "[t]he existence of conveyances for less than adequate consideration." Id. In the present case, the record contains no extrinsic evidence of any of these indicia of fraud. The record only indicates that Addison's intent was to convert some of his nonexempt property to exempt property on the eve of bankruptcy, something that is "well established" in this circuit that he is allowed to do. Hanson, 848 F.2d at 868 ("It is well established that . . . a debtor's conversion of non-exempt property to exempt property on the eve of bankruptcy for the express purpose of placing that property beyond the reach of creditors, without more, will not deprive the debtor of the exemption to which he otherwise would be entitled"). Accordingly, we conclude that it was clear error for the bankruptcy court to find that Addison had the requisite intent to hinder, delay, or defraud a creditor when he converted some nonexempt property into his homestead on the day he filed bankruptcy.

Additionally, circuit precedent upholding findings of fraudulent intent differ factually from this case. For example, in our most recent decision on the issue, Sholdan II, which came back before the court after our remand in Sholdan I, discussed above, we upheld the bankruptcy court's finding of intent to defraud, stating:

> It is one thing to convert non-exempt assets into exempt property for the express purpose of holding it as a homestead and thereby putting the property beyond the reach of creditors. However, it is quite another thing to acquire title to a house for no other reason than to defraud creditors.

Sholdan II, 217 F.3d at 1011.[21]

In the present case, however, Addison did not "acquire title to a house for no other reason than to defraud creditors" as Sholdan had. Addison had owned his house for years prior to his bankruptcy filing and merely converted nonexempt assets into the homestead to protect it from the reach of creditors--the exact action that we implied was permissible in upholding the finding of intent to defraud in Sholdan II. Id.

Moreover, in Tveten, we upheld the finding of intent to defraud based on the evidence surrounding the debtor's conversion of nonexempt assets to exempt assets prior to bankruptcy.[22] 848 F.2d at 876. In that case, the debtor was a physician who owed creditors nearly $19 million, mostly on personal guarantees. Id. at 872. When a number of the debtor's investments declined in value, he met with a bankruptcy attorney, and then, on counsel's advice, converted almost all of his nonexempt property (approximately $700,000) into exempt life insurance policies and annuities, through a series of 17 transactions on the eve of bankruptcy. Id. After Tveten filed for bankruptcy, the trustee objected to his claimed exemptions in the property, and a creditor moved to deny his discharge. Id. at 873. The bankruptcy court denied Tveten's discharge, prior to ruling on the objection to exemptions, finding that he had converted his nonexempt property to exempt property with the intent to defraud a creditor. Id. We affirmed the denial of discharge, ruling that the finding of intent to defraud was not clearly erroneous, noting that Tveten's attempt to shield $700,000 from creditors while attempting to discharge over $18 million in debt went well beyond the purposes for which exemptions are permitted. Id. at 876. Although not citing to specific extrinsic evidence of intent to defraud, we noted that "the entire pattern of conduct" surrounding the conversions demonstrated fraudulent intent. Id.

Tveten differs markedly from the present case. Unlike Tveten, Addison did not attempt to convert "almost his entire net worth" into exempt assets prior

---

[21] As discussed above, the debtor in Sholdan was a 90-year old who, after being sued, liquidated nearly all of his nonexempt assets and used the proceeds to purchase a home in cash, just prior to filing for bankruptcy protection, even though the debtor had been living in an assisted living facility for a year prior to the home purchase, and in an apartment for the 13 years prior to that.

[22] Although Tveten dealt with the denial of discharge under § 727(a)(2) and not the objection to exemptions, because both issues are governed by identical language--intent to hinder, delay, or defraud a creditor--the standard applied to determine whether a discharge should be denied on the basis of intent to hinder, delay, or defraud is the same as the determination in this case as to whether Addison's exemption should be allowed. See Tveten, 848 F.2d at 874 "Although the determination as to whether a discharge should be granted or denied is governed by federal law, the standard applied consistently by the courts is the same as that used to determine whether an exemption is permissible, i.e. absent extrinsic evidence of fraud, mere conversion of non-exempt property to exempt property is not fraudulent as to creditors even if the motivation behind the conversion is to place those assets beyond the reach of creditors").

to bankruptcy. Rather, Addison left substantial nonexempt assets for his creditors to recover. In fact, the Trustee-initiated auction of some of Addison's nonexempt assets brought in proceeds in excess of $10,000. Moreover, the total amount of converted assets at issue in this case is less than $20,000, only a fraction of the amount present in Tveten.

In sum, we conclude that the bankruptcy court clearly erred in finding that Addison converted nonexempt property into his homestead with the intent to hinder, delay, or defraud a creditor. On the record before us, there is no extrinsic evidence of intent to hinder, delay, or defraud a creditor sufficient to uphold that finding. The evidence only suggests that Addison was converting nonexempt assets to exempt assets to place some (but not all or substantially all) of those assets beyond the reach of creditors--something our precedent permits.

2. Roth IRA Exemption

The bankruptcy court also denied Addison's claimed exemption in his $4,000 Roth IRA, finding that Addison had transferred nonexempt funds into the Roth IRA with the intent to hinder, delay, or defraud a creditor. Again, the determination of intent is a finding of fact reviewed for clear error. Sholdan II, 217 F.3d at 1010.

The bankruptcy court found Addison acted with intent to hinder, delay, or defraud regarding the transfer of funds to the Roth IRA "for the same reasons" as it found intent to hinder, delay, or defraud regarding the payment on the home mortgage. As discussed above, that finding of intent was clearly erroneous, and thus the disallowance of the Roth IRA exemption must be reversed as well. Likewise, the bankruptcy court's additional finding that Addison's real reason[23] for converting nonexempt assets into the Roth IRA was "just [to] keep the money out of the hands of creditors," will not suffice to establish intent to hinder, delay, or defraud as a debtor may intentionally convert nonexempt assets to exempt assets for the express purpose of keeping the money out of the hands of creditors, unless there is extrinsic evidence of fraud. See Hanson, 848 F.2d at 868 ("It is well established that . . . a debtor's conversion of non-exempt property to exempt property on the eve of bankruptcy for the express purpose of placing that property beyond the reach of creditors, without more, will not deprive the debtor of the exemption to which he otherwise would be entitled").

B. Denial of Discharge

Following the bankruptcy court's ruling on the Trustee's objections to exemptions, wherein it found that Addison had converted nonexempt assets into his homestead and Roth IRA with the intent to hinder, delay, or defraud a creditor, the Trustee filed an adversary proceeding objecting to Addison's discharge under § 727(a)(2) of the Code. Section 727(a)(2) of the Bankruptcy Code states, in relevant part, that:

> (a) The court shall grant the debtor a discharge, unless--
>
> . . .
>
> (2) the debtor, with intent to hinder, delay, or defraud a creditor . . . has

[23] Addison's stated reason for converting the nonexempt funds to the Roth IRA was to provide for his retirement.

> transferred, removed, destroyed, mutilated, or concealed, or has permitted to be transferred, removed, destroyed, mutilated, or concealed--
>
> (A) property of the debtor, within one year before the date of the filing of the petition . . .

11 U.S.C. § 727(a)(2) (emphasis added).

The Trustee's objection to discharge cited, among other things, Addison's conversion of nonexempt assets into his homestead and Roth IRA. As there was no dispute that Addison had made the transfers to his homestead and the Roth IRA within one year before his bankruptcy filing and that the transfers were made from property of the debtor, the only issue before the bankruptcy court was whether these transfers had been made "with intent to hinder, delay, or defraud a creditor." Because the bankruptcy court had already determined, in ruling on the Trustee's objections to exemptions, that Addison had made the transfers to his homestead and Roth IRA with the intent to hinder, delay, or defraud a creditor, the bankruptcy court granted the Trustee's motion for summary judgment on collateral estoppel grounds and denied Addison's discharge.

In this case, the same standard applies to determine whether a discharge should be denied or whether a transfer of nonexempt property to exempt property should be voided; both require proof that the debtor acted with the intent to hinder, delay, or defraud a creditor. Tveten, 848 F.2d at 874.[24] Because we reversed the bankruptcy court's determination of intent to hinder, delay, or defraud a creditor on the exemption issues, the denial of discharge based on the collateral estoppel effect of that finding must also be reversed. . . .

III. Conclusion

Accordingly, we affirm in part, reverse in part, and remand for further proceedings consistent with this opinion.

Notes and Questions

1. BAPCPA also adds new § 522(n), which limits IRA exemptions to $1 million. Notice that this limitation does not apply to ERISA plans, which never come into the bankruptcy estate, thanks to §542(c). ERISA plans are spendthrifted. IRA accounts are not.

D. REDEMPTION

IN RE MORALES

387 B.R. 36 (Bankr. C.D. Cal. 2008)

ERNEST ROBLES, J.

This case requires the Court to determine the appropriate method for calculating the replacement value of a vehicle under the retail value standard of

---

[24] "Although the determination as to whether a discharge should be granted or denied is governed by federal law, the standard applied consistently by the courts is the same as that used to determine whether an exemption is permissible, i.e. absent extrinsic evidence of fraud, mere conversion of non-exempt property to exempt property is not fraudulent as to creditors even if the motivation behind the conversion is to place those assets beyond the reach of creditors." Tveten, 848 F.2d at 874.

the second sentence of 11 U.S.C. § 506(a)(2). For the reasons discussed infra in Part III, the Court concludes that, absent unusual circumstances, the retail value for vehicles under § 506(a)(2) should be calculated by adjusting either the Kelley Blue Book retail value or the National Automobile Dealers Association ("N.A.D.A.") Guide retail value by a reasonable amount in light of evidence presented regarding condition, the retail market, and other relevant factors. In this case, the Court sets the retail value of the Vehicle for purposes of § 506(a)(2) at $10,126.00 in consideration of the limited evidence presented. . . .

II. Statement of Facts and Procedural History

On January 25, 2008, Debtor Luis A. Morales ("Debtor") filed a voluntary Chapter 7 petition.

On March 9, 2008, the Debtor filed the Debtor's Motion for Authority to Redeem Personal Property and Approval of Associated Financing Under 11 U.S.C. § 722 ("Motion"). In the Motion, the Debtor seeks to redeem a 2006 Chrysler Sebring Touring 4D ("Vehicle") from Creditor HSBC Auto Finance ("HSBC") pursuant to § 722. The Debtor does not address directly the condition of the Vehicle and submits no declaration in support of the Motion. The information included on Exhibit 1 of the Motion suggests, however, that the Vehicle was in "fair" condition on February 18, 2008, and has mileage of approximately 47,600 miles. The Debtor asserts that redemption is allowed under § 722 because the Vehicle is personal property intended primarily for personal, family, or household use, the Debtor's interest in the Vehicle is exempt, and the debt represents a dischargeable consumer debt. See Motion at 2, PP 3, 5.

The Debtor argues that the appropriate retail value of the Vehicle under § 506(a)(2) for purposes of redemption is $8,995.00. In support of this proposed valuation, the Debtor submits two valuation reports from Collateral Valuation Services, LLC ("Collateral Valuation Services"). The valuation reports were prepared in reliance on an AutoTrader.com advertisement and a .Manheim report. The AutoTrader.com advertisement lists a purchase price of $8,995.00 for a car of the same age and model with mileage of 26,543 miles. The AutoTrader.com advertisement is dated February 18, 2008. The Manheim report lists an estimated retail price of $8,950.00 for a car of the same age and model. The retail value of the Manheim report is based on transactions from the week of February 18 to February 25, 2008.

On March 19, 2008, HSBC filed the Opposition to Debtor's Motion to Redeem Personal Property Under 11 U.S.C. § 722 ("Opposition"). In the Opposition, HSBC does not challenge the Debtor's assertion that redemption is allowed, but argues that the proposed redemption value of $8,995.00 is not an accurate retail price for purposes of § 506(a)(2). Rather, HSBC asserts that the appropriate value of the Vehicle for purposes of redemption is $13,550.00. In support of this proposed valuation, HSBC submits a Kelley Blue Book value, which lists a suggested retail value of $13,550.00 for a car of the same age and model with mileage of 35,028 miles. The Kelley Blue Book retail value presupposes that the car is in "excellent" condition. HSBC alleges that the Debtor has based his proposed value on an advertisement at the extreme low end of advertised retail prices.

HSBC argues further that the new § 506(a)(2) overturned prior caselaw interpreting § 506(a) to the extent that it permitted the value of personal property acquired for personal, family, or household use in individual Chapter 7 and 13 cases to be determined based on the property's wholesale value instead of its retail value.

On April 23, 2008, the Debtor filed the Reply Memorandum in Support of Debtor's Motion to Redeem Personal Property and Approval of Associated Financing Under 11 U.S.C. 722 ("Reply"). In the Reply, the Debtor emphasizes that the plain language of § 506(a)(2) does not require a court to select a retail value at the average or high end of the retail spectrum. Accordingly, the Debtor reasons that the original AutoTrader.com advertisement submitted with the Motion, even if at the low end of the spectrum, represents an appropriate value for purposes of § 506(a)(2).

In addition, the Debtor submits two new AutoTrader.com advertisements in support of his proposed valuation. The first additional AutoTrader.com advertisement lists a purchase price of $9,995.00 for a car of the same age and model with mileage of 32,925 miles. The advertisement is dated March 15, 2008.[1] Next, the second additional AutoTrader.com advertisement lists a purchase price of $8,999.00 for a car of the same age and model with mileage of 69,165 miles. The advertisement is dated March 18, 2008.

Finally, the Debtor further submits a Kelley Blue Book value which lists a suggested retail value of $12,515.00 for a car of the same age and model with mileage of 46,000 miles. The Debtor argues that even if the Kelley Blue Book retail value were the appropriate standard, the Kelley Blue Book value submitted by HSBC is inaccurate.

The Court held a hearing on the Motion on April 30, 2008. In advance of the hearing, the Court issued a tentative ruling as to its preliminary determination of value. The Debtor submitted on the Court's tentative ruling and did not appear at the hearing. HSBC appeared at the hearing but presented only brief arguments. At the close of the hearing, the Court adopted its tentative ruling and determined the value of the Vehicle to be $10,126.00.

The Court issues this opinion in order to explain in full its approach to vehicle valuation under the retail value standard of § 506(a)(2).

III. Discussion

A. The Bankruptcy Code Allows Individual Debtors to Redeem Certain Vehicles Intended for Personal, Family, or Household Use Under 11 U.S.C. § 722

The Bankruptcy Code authorizes individual debtors to redeem personal property intended for personal, family, or household use in certain circumstances by paying the lienholder the full amount of the allowed secured claim at the time of redemption. 11 U.S.C. § 722. Section 722 provides in full:

> An individual debtor may, whether or not the debtor has waived the right to redeem under this section, redeem tangible personal property intended

---

[1] The Debtor notes that identical vehicle identification numbers and AutoTrader.com identification numbers are listed in both the $9,995.00 advertisement and the original $8,995.00 advertisement. The Debtor acknowledges that the advertisements may be selling the same car at different prices. The advertisements, however, list different exterior colors, different interior colors, different mileage, and different sellers. As a result, the ultimate reliability of these two advertisements as distinct advertisements [*6] remains open to some doubt.

> primarily for personal, family, or household use, from a lien securing a, dischargeable consumer debt, if such property is exempted under, section 522 of this title or has been abandoned under section 554 of this title, by paying the holder of such lien the amount of the allowed secured claim of such holder that is secured by such lien in full at the time of redemption.

11 U.S.C. § 722. This Court has previously articulated its general approach to redemption under § 722 in the case of In re Lopez, 224 B.R. 439 (Bankr. C.D. Cal. 1998). Under that approach, the proper date for valuation of property under § 722 is the date of the hearing on the redemption motion. In re Lopez, 224 B.R. at 444. But see In re Eagle, 51 B.R. 959, 962 (Bankr. N.D. Ohio 1985) (date of valuation is petition date).

Here, as a general matter, the Debtor and HSBC agree that the Debtor is eligible to redeem the Vehicle under § 722. The parties do not dispute that the Debtor is an individual debtor in Chapter 7, that the Vehicle is personal property intended primarily for personal, family, or household use, and that the interest of the Debtor in the Vehicle is exempt.

B. Valuation Under 11 U.S.C. § 506(a) Generally

11 U.S.C. § 506(a) governs the valuation of allowed claims in bankruptcy cases. The current version of § 506(a) was substantially amended as part of the Bankruptcy Abuse Prevention and Consumer Protection Act of 2005 ("BAPCPA"), Pub. L. No. 109-8, 119 Stat. 23 (2005). In full, § 506(a) provides as follows:

> (a)(1) An allowed claim of a creditor secured by a lien on property in which the estate has an interest, or that is subject to setoff under section 553 of this title, is a secured claim to the extent of the value of such creditor's interest in the estate's interest in such property, or to the extent of the amount subject to setoff, as the case may be, and is an unsecured claim to the extent that the value of such creditor's interest or the amount so subject to setoff is less than the amount of such allowed claim. Such value shall be determined in light of the purpose of the valuation and of the proposed disposition or use of such property, and in conjunction with any hearing on such disposition or use or on a plan affecting such creditor's interest.
>
> (2) If the debtor is an individual in a case under chapter 7 or 13, such value with respect to personal property securing an allowed claim shall be determined based on the replacement value of such property as of the date of the filing of the petition without deduction for costs of sale or marketing. With respect to property acquired for personal, family, or household purposes, replacement value shall mean the price a retail merchant would charge for property of that kind considering the age and condition of the property at the time value is determined.

11 U.S.C. § 506(a). As of yet, the changes, if any, made by § 506(a)(2) to the method for determining the value of personal property acquired for personal, family, or household use in individual Chapter 7 and Chapter 13 cases have received only modest consideration in the published caselaw . . .

C. Pre-BAPCPA Valuation of Vehicles Under 11 U.S.C. § 506(a)

Prior to BAPCPA, the Bankruptcy Code and caselaw had established that the value of a vehicle was to be determined based on its replacement value. Cf. Associates Commer. Corp. v. Rash, 520 U.S. 953 (1997) (adopting a replacement value standard under § 506(a) for purposes of Chapter 13 cram down). In Rash, the U.S. Supreme Court adopted a replacement value standard under § 506(a), and defined replacement value as "the price a willing buyer in the debtor's trade, business, or situation would pay a willing seller to obtain property of like age and condition." Assocs. Commercial Corp. v. Rash, 520 U.S. at 959, n.2. Although the Rash Court established the general standard, the Court entrusted to bankruptcy courts the appropriate method for determining replacement value on a case-by-case basis:

> Our recognition that the replacement-value standard, not the foreclosure-value standard, governs in cram down cases leaves to bankruptcy courts, as triers of fact, identification of the best way of ascertaining replacement value on the basis of the evidence presented. Whether replacement value is the equivalent of retail value, wholesale value, or some other value will depend on the type of debtor and the nature of the property.

Assocs. Commercial Corp. v. Rash, 520 U.S. at 965 n.6 (citations omitted).

In the Ninth Circuit, bankruptcy courts have generally determined the value of vehi-cles under § 502(a) on a case-by-case basis. Taffi v. United States (In re Taffi), 96 F.3d 1190, 1193 (9th Cir. 1996) (en banc), cert. denied, 521 U.S. 1103 (1997). Previously, in the case of General Motors Acceptance Corp. v. Mitchell (In re Mitchell), 954 F.2d 557 (9th Cir. 1992), overruled by Taffi v. United States (In re Taffi), 96 F.3d 1190, 1193 (9th Cir. 1996) (en banc), cert. denied, 521 U.S. 1103 (1997), the U.S. Court of Appeals for the Ninth Circuit had concluded that a vehicle's value under § 506(a) should be calculated based on wholesale value instead of retail value. In re Mitchell, 954 F.2d at 560. The Ninth Circuit subsequently overruled In re Mitchell and established that courts were to determine value in light of the fair market value. In re Taffi, 96 F.3d at 1193. The Taffi court thereby overruled the then-existing wholesale standard for vehicle valuation under In re Mitchell, but declined to establish a set approach for vehicle valuation. See id. Rather, the Taffi court cautioned as follows: "We make no judgment whether the fair market value of an automobile is high blue book or low blue book or some other value; that value is to be determined by the facts presented to the bankruptcy court." Id. As a result, In re Taffi left the determination of value under § 506(a) to bankruptcy courts in light of the factual considerations identified in each case.

Traditionally, the date of valuation under § 502(a) depends on the particular context of the valuation. See 4 Collier on Bankruptcy P 506.03[10], p. 506-99 (rev. 15th ed. 2006). Courts disagree, however, as to the appropriate dates to be used in a variety of contexts. In the context of redemption, as noted supra in Part III.A, this Court has valued property as of the hearing date on the redemption motion. In re Lopez, 224 B.R. 439, 444 (Bankr. CD. Cal. 1998); see In re King, 75 B.R. 287, 290 (Bankr. S.D. Ohio 1987). By contrast, other courts have concluded that property should be valued as of the petition date. In re Eagle, 51 B.R. 959, 962 (Bankr. N.D. Ohio 1985).

D. Post-BAPCPA Valuation of Vehicles Under 11 U.S.C. § 506(a)(2)

In 2005, under the BAPCPA amendments, Congress refined the approach to valuation of personal property in individual Chapter 7 and Chapter 13 cases by adding the new § 506(a)(2). Section 506(a)(2) ostensibly follows the general replacement standard articulated by Rash but the second sentence provides that the "replacement value" for property acquired for personal, family, or household use is defined, as "the price a retail merchant would charge for property of that kind considering the age and condition of the property at the time value is determined." 11 U.S.C. § 506(a)(2).

The Bankruptcy Code, however, does not articulate a specific method for calculating the retail value of a vehicle or any other personal property. Similarly, the legislative history sheds little insight on the correct valuation method. See H.R. REP. No. 109-31, pt. 1 (2005); In re Carlson, No. 06-40402, 2006 WL 4811331, at (Bankr. W.D. Wash. Dec. 8, 2006). As a result, the courts are faced with the task of interpreting the meaning of retail value under § 506(a)(2) and determining the appropriate method for calculating such value for vehicles.

1. Retail Value Under 11 U.S.C. § 506(a)(2)

The appellate courts of the Ninth Circuit have not yet established a specific post-BAPCPA method for calculating the retail value of vehicles under the second sentence of § 506(a)(2). See In re Carlson, 2006 Bankr. LEXIS 4405, 2006 WL 4811331, at *2. At least two bankruptcy courts, however, have articulated approaches for valuation under § 506(a)(2). See In re Cheatham, No. 07-40509-13-abf, 2007 Bankr. LEXIS 2758, 2007 WL 2428046 (Bankr. W.D. Mo. June 19, 2007) (calculating retail value of car by reducing the N.A.D.A. Guide retail value by 5%); In re Coleman, 373 B.R. 907, 912-13 (Bankr. W.D. Mo. 2007) (decision by the same court as In re Cheatham, following its earlier decision); In re Carlson, 2006 Bankr. LEXIS 4405, 2006 WL 4811331, at *2-3 (calculating retail value of mobile home under § 506(a)(2) in reliance on N.A.D.A. Guide retail value). It is too soon to know whether these decisions herald a specific trend in the Ninth Circuit. Nonetheless, In re Carlson, In re Cheatham, and In re Coleman all rely on the N.A.D.A. Guide retail value as an appropriate starting point for determining retail value under § 506(a)(2).

In other circuits, courts interpreting the second sentence of § 506(a)(2) have adopted a variety of methods for calculating retail value. This caselaw, although still developing, offers at least some further insight on valuation under § 506(a)(2). See In re De Anda-Ramirez, 359 B.R. 794, 796 (B.A.P. 10th Cir. 2007) (holding that bankruptcy court's use of Kelley Blue Book private party value instead of Kelley Blue Book retail value not reversible error without determining appropriate method); In re Clark, No. 06-31965, 2007 Bankr. LEXIS 765, 2007 WL 671346 (Bankr. N.D. Ohio Feb. 27, 2007) (calculating retail value of car as the midpoint between two proffered retail values); In re Kidwell, No. 06-14087, 2007 Bankr. LEXIS 3438, 2007 WL 2934866, at *5 (Bankr. E.D. Tenn. Oct. 4, 2007) (calculating retail value of car based on Kelley Blue Book private party value based on appraiser testimony that private party value approximates retail price if paid in cash in full); In re Ortiz, No. 06-16243-BKC-RBR, 2007 Bankr. LEXIS 1286, 2007 WL 1176019, at *2-3 (Bankr. S.D. Fla. Fed. 27, 2007) (calculating retail value of car by deducting the hypothetical cost of repairs from the retail value established by expert testimony); In re Brown, No. 06-00197-JW, 2006 Bankr. LEXIS 713, 2006 WL 3692609, at *3 (Bankr. D.S.C. April 24, 2006) (calculating retail value of car in reliance on appraiser's report submitted by creditor); In re Eddins, 355 B.R. 849, 852 (Bankr. W.D. Okla. 2006) (calculating retail value of car by reducing N.A.D.A. Guide retail value by appropriate amount based on any evidence submitted by parties in interest); In re Mayland, No. 06-10283, 2006 Bankr. LEXIS 967, 2006 WL 1476927, at *3 (Bankr. M.D.N.C. May 26, 2006) (calculating retail value of car as 90% of N.A.D.A. Guide retail value, less cost of necessary repairs); see also In re Finnegan, 358 B.R. 644, 650 (Bankr. M.D. Pa. 2006) (discussing valuation under § 506(a)(2) generally but concluding that the vehicle at issue was not acquired for personal, family, or household use, and thus valuing the vehicle under the first sentence instead of the second sentence). These cases present a range of different, though often similar, approaches to valuation. In general, however, these cases suggest that the emergent approach to valuation under § 506(a)(2) requires bankruptcy courts to reduce the N.A.D.A. Guide retail value, or other appropriate retail value, by an amount appropriate in light of evidence concerning the vehicle's condition.

The leading appellate case on this issue is In re De Anda-Ramirez, 359 B.R. 794 (B.A.P. 10th Cir. 2007), in which the Bankruptcy Appellate Panel for the Tenth Circuit held that a bankruptcy court's use of the Kelley Blue Book private party value of a car instead of the Kelley Blue Book retail value for valuation under § 506(a)(2) was not reversible error. In re De Anda-Ramirez, 359 B.R. at 796. Although the De Anda-Ramirez court declined to establish a specific method for determining retail value, id. at 797, n.3, the court analyzed and rejected the argument that the Kelley Blue Book retail value is necessarily equivalent to the retail value of § 506(a)(2), id. at 797. Rather, the In re De Anda-Ramirez court emphasized that the Kelley Blue Book retail value should not be adopted automatically as the § 506(a)(2) retail value:

> Other than both containing the word "retail," the Code and [the Kelley Blue Book] definitions have little in common. The Bankruptcy Code's definition of "retail" includes an adjustment for the age and condition of the vehicle; KBB defines "retail" as the price for a vehicle that is in "excellent condition" with the proviso that less than 5% of vehicles for sale qualify as "excellent." Clearly, these two are not equivalent and . . . reliance on the KBB retail value is misplaced.

Id. at 797.

2. Valuation Date Under 11 U.S.C. § 506(a)(2)

The new § 506(a)(2) also requires courts to determine the correct date of valuation, i.e., the date as of which the value of the property is to be calculated. The majority of courts to consider § 506(a)(2) have not expressly addressed this issue. At first glance, the date of valuation for personal property acquired for personal, family, or household use in individual Chapter 7 or Chapter 13 cases may appear readily ascertainable based on the plain language of the statute. A second glance, by contrast, reveals that § 506(a)(2) remains open to two plausible interpretations. See In re Ortiz, 2007 Bankr. LEXIS 1286, 2007 WL 1176019, at *2-3. The first sentence of § 506(a)(2) establishes that if the property is personal property in an individual Chapter 7 or Chapter 13 case then replacement value should be calculated "as of the date of the filing of the petition." 11 U.S.C. § 506(a)(2). The second sentence, however, provides that if the property was acquired for personal, family, or household purposes, then "replacement value shall mean the price a retail merchant would charge for property of that kind considering the age and condition of the property at the time value is determined." 11 U.S.C. § 506(a)(2) (emphasis added).

The issue is whether the clause "at the time value is determined" changes the date of valuation for property valued under the second sentence of § 506(a)(2). Courts must determine the proper interaction between the two sentences and set the correct date of valuation.

On the one hand, some courts have concluded that valuation under the retail value standard of § 506(a)(2) requires valuation as of the petition date. See In re Brown, 2006 Bankr. LEXIS 713, 2006 WL 3692609, at *3 (calculating value as of the petition date); In re Mayland, 2006 Bankr. LEXIS 967, 2006 WL 1476927, at *3 (same); see also In re Kidwell, 2007 Bankr. LEXIS 3438, 2007 WL 2934866, at *4 (holding that petition date is correct date of valuation but using post-petition appraisals to determine value because only evidence available). Under this reasoning, the first sentence uniformly establishes the valuation date as "the date of the filing of the petition" for all replacement values calculated under the aegis of § 506(a)(2). Although the second sentence further specifies the retail value sub-standard for property acquired for personal, family, or household purposes, the date of valuation for the sub-standard remains controlled by the date of valuation specified in the super-standard of the first sentence. In order to give meaning to the clause "at the time value is determined" without establishing a new valuation date, this interpretation reads the clause as referring back to the petition date standard of the first sentence, i.e., "at the time as of which value is determined."

On the other hand, other courts have concluded that valuation under the retail value standard of the second sentence of § 506(a)(2) requires valuation as of the valuation hearing. See In re Cheatham, 2007 Bankr. LEXIS 2758, 2007 WL 2428046, at *2 (using the retail value "at the time the determination is being made"); In re Coleman, 373 B.R. at 912 (same court, same holding); see also 4 Collier on Bankruptcy P 506.03[10], p. 506-100 (rev. 15th ed. 2006); cf. In re Ortiz, 2007 Bankr. LEXIS 1286, 2007 WL 1176019, at *2 (calculating value as of the hearing date, without resolving the issue, because parties submitted no evidence of value at the petition date). Under this reasoning, the first sentence establishes a valuation date that applies only for personal property in individual Chapter 7 and Chapter 13 cases that was not acquired for personal, family, or household purposes. See In re Finnegan, 358 B.R. at 648 (concluding that where individual debtor in Chapter 13 purchased vehicle for her husband to use in his business the value of the vehicle was to be determined at the petition date under the first sentence of § 506(a)(2) instead of the second sentence). By contrast, when the personal property at issue was acquired for personal, family, or household purposes, then the second sentence of § 506(a)(2) displaces the valuation date of the first sentence and provides that the valuation date is "at the time value is determined." This interpretation reads the clause as referring to the date of the valuation hearing, i.e., "at the time value is determined by the court."[2]

The legislative history of BAPCPA offers only modest additional insight as to the correct date of valuation for property under § 506(a)(2). In general, the legislative discussion of the scope and effect of § 506(a) mirrors the statutory language. Some legislative guidance, however, may be available to the extent that the legislative history uses language different from the statutory language:

> Section 327 of the Act amends section 506(a) of the Bankruptcy Code to provide that the value of an allowed claim secured by personal property that is an asset

---

[2] More precisely, the retail value would be calculated as of "the time value is determined," which refers to the date on which the court makes its final value determination. In some cases, this date could be after the hearing date if the court took the matter of valuation under submission or required the parties to submit additional evidence after the hearing.

> in an individual debtor's chapter 7 or 13 case is determined based on the replacement value of such property as of the filing date of the bankruptcy case without deduction for selling or marketing costs. With respect to property acquired for personal, family, or household purposes, replacement value is the price a retail merchant would charge for property of that kind considering the age and condition of the property at the time its value is determined.

H.R. Rep. No. 109-31, pt. 1, at 83 (2005) (emphasis added to highlight differences between the legislative history and the statutory language). For courts that conclude that the statutory language of § 506(a)(2) is ambiguous, the nuances of the legislative history may suggest some limited guidance.

On the whole, § 506(a)(2) raises a variety of questions regarding the appropriate method for calculating the retail value of personal property acquired for personal, family, or household use in individual Chapter 7 and Chapter 13 cases. Neither the courts of the Ninth Circuit nor the courts of other circuits have established a uniform method for calculating the retail value of vehicles under the second sentence of § 506(a)(2).

E. This Court Concludes that the Retail Value of Vehicles Valued Under the Second Sentence of 11 U.S.C. § 506(a)(2) Should Be Calculated by Adjusting the Kelley Blue Book or N.A.D.A. Guide Retail Value By a Reasonable Amount Based on Evidence Presented Regarding the Vehicle's Condition and Other Relevant Factors

After reviewing the statute, the available caselaw, and the arguments of the parties, this Court concludes that the correct method for calculating the retail value of a vehicle under § 506(a)(2) ultimately depends on the facts presented in each case. Cf. Taffi v. United States (In re Taffi), 96 F.3d 1190, 1193 (9th Cir. 1996), cert. denied, 521 U.S. 1103 (1997). As a general principle, however, this Court further concludes that, absent unusual circumstances,[3] the retail value should be calculated by adjusting the Kelley Blue Book or N.A.D.A. Guide retail value for a like vehicle by a reasonable amount in light of any additional evidence presented regarding the condition of the vehicle and any other relevant factors. See In re Coleman, 373 B.R. 907, 912-13 (Bankr. W.D. Mo. 2007); In re Carlson, No. 06-40402, 2006 Bankr. LEXIS 4405, 2006 WL 4811331, at *2 (Bankr. W.D. Wash., Dec. 8, 2006); In re Eddins, 355 B.R. 849, 852 (Bankr. W.D. Okla. 2006). Value should be calculated as of the petition date, not the valuation hearing. The burden in proving the reasonableness of any deviation from the guide retail value rests with the debtor because the debtor has the best access to information about the condition of the vehicle. See In re Coleman, 373 B.R. at 913; In re Eddins, 355 B.R. at 852. This general approach offers the benefits of standardization and predictability to parties without automatically conflating the artificial guide retail value with the actual retail value of the vehicle.

The Court's decision brings it into line with the general approach of most bankruptcy courts interpreting § 506(a)(2) and with the bankruptcy courts of the Ninth Circuit, as well as the traditional case-by-case approach to valuation

[3] The Kelley Blue Book and the N.A.D.A. Guide retail values may be inappropriate as starting points in some cases, such as where a party in interest demonstrates that the guide retail value is "not useful in the area in which the vehicle would be sold, or . . . is not appropriate in a particular instance." In re Coleman, 373 B.R. 907, 912-13 (Bankr. W.D. Mo. 2007).

established by the Ninth Circuit in In re Taffi. Although the Court declines to adopt a set automatic reduction of the guide retail value, see, e.g., In re Coleman, 373 B.R. at 912-13 (calculating retail value of car by reducing the N.A.D.A. Guide retail value by 5%), the Court agrees with the De Anda-Ramirez court that the Kelley Blue Book retail value is rarely equivalent to the retail value of § 506(a)(2), see In re De Anda-Ramirez, 359 B.R. 794, 797 (B.A.P. 10th Cir. 2007).

In most cases, the showing necessary to justify a downward adjustment from the guide retail value will be minimal because few vehicles have been maintained in the high-quality condition contemplated by the guide retail values. Evidence in support of an adjustment of the guide retail value may include, inter alia, declarations, testimony, see In re Ortiz, No. 06-16243-BKC-RBR, 2007 Bankr. LEXIS 1286, 2007 WL 1176019, at *2-3 (Bankr. S.D. Fla., Fed. 27, 2007) (expert testimony), vehicle advertisements, see In re Clark, No. 06-31965, 2007 Bankr. LEXIS 765, 2007 WL 671346, at *4 (Bankr. N.D. Ohio, Feb. 27, 2007) (advertisements), expert or appraisal reports, see In re Brown, No. 06-00197-JW, 2006 Bankr. LEXIS 713, 2006 WL 3692609, at *3 (Bankr. D.S.C., April 24, 2006) (appraiser report), and even private party values, as appropriate. In any declaration in support of a proposed vehicle valuation under § 506(a)(2), a debtor should, if possible, include the following basic information: (1) a description of the vehicle, including any options installed and special features; (2) a description of the condition of the vehicle as of the petition date, including any damage, general deterioration, and past or necessary repairs; (3) the vehicle's mileage as of the petition date; and (4) the age of the vehicle as of the petition date. A debtor may also wish to submit photographs of the vehicle and evidence as to the retail values of other like vehicles for sale by retail merchants in the debtor's geographic area. Evidence of this nature will assist the court in determining whether an adjustment to the guide retail value is warranted.

Nonetheless, the Kelley Blue Book and N.A.D.A. Guide retail values represent the appropriate starting point in determining retail value under the second sentence of § 506(a)(2) because the plain language of the statute contemplates "the price a retail merchant would charge" instead of the price a private party would charge. The first sentence of § 506(a)(2) provides that the replacement value should be calculated "without deduction for costs of sale or marketing." 11 U.S.C. § 506(a)(2). Although the second sentence remains silent as to the costs of sale and marketing, the super-standard of the first sentence should continue to control the calculation of replacement value to the extent that the second sentence does not articulate a different sub-standard.

Unlike the private party value, the retail value better approximates a price that includes the "costs of sale and marketing," as well as other costs generally included as part of a merchant's retail price, by taking into consideration the cost of sale, the cost of marketing, and the dealer's profit.[4] the wisdom of this

[4] The Kelley Blue Book defines its retail value as follows: "The Kelley Blue Book Suggested Retail Value is representative of dealers' asking prices and is the starting point for negotiation between a consumer and a dealer. This Suggested Retail Value assumes that the vehicle has been fully reconditioned and has a clean title history. This value takes into account the dealers' profit, costs of advertising, sales commissions and other costs of doing business. The final sale price will likely be less depending on the vehicle's actual condition, popularity, type of warranty offered and local market conditions." By contrast, the Kelley Blue Book defines its private party value as follows: "Private Party Value is what a buyer can expect to pay when buying a used car from a private party. The Private Party Value assumes that the vehicle is sold "As Is" and carries no

valuation approach, compare 11 U.S.C. § 506(a)(2) with Associates Commer. Corp. v. Rash, 520 U.S. 953, 956 n.6 (1997) (discussing adjustments to retail value necessary to approximate replacement value), Congress spoke plainly in establishing a retail value standard that includes costs not necessarily associated with the private party value. Ultimately, the guide retail value represents only a starting point in determining retail value under the second sentence of § 506(a)(2), and should be adjusted routinely in light of other evidence presented to the court.

The Court further holds that the second sentence of § 506(a)(2) requires retail value to be determined as of the petition date, not the hearing date. The Court acknowledges that the statutory language is ambiguous and believes that reasonable jurists can come to different conclusions on this issue, as discussed supra in Part III.D.2. Nonetheless, the Court concludes that a full view of the interaction between the first and second sentences of § 506(a)(2) favors valuation as of the petition date. By its own terms, the second sentence only establishes a specific definition of the general term "replacement value" to be used for certain property. The second sentence thus functions to provide a definition for a single term in the first sentence. No more, no less. This definition does not alter the requirement that courts not deduct for costs of sale or marketing, nor should it alter the valuation date established in the first sentence. If Congress had intended to provide for valuation as of the hearing date, Congress could have done so with greater clarity. The ambiguity of the clause "at the time value is determined" suggests that Congress did not intend to alter the valuation date so much as to refer back to its earlier valuation date.[5] Accordingly, the clause "at the time value is determined," although ambiguous, is best understood within the context of § 506(a)(2) as a whole to mean at the time as of which value is determined, i.e., at the petition date.

The Court's approach establishes a single, static date of valuation for all personal property in individual Chapter 7 and Chapter 13 cases. This approach provides greater standardization for valuation under § 506(a)(2), and generally encourages the parties to determine value as promptly as possible. Furthermore, this approach respects the interests of creditors by fixing the value of property, and therefore the extent of any secured claims, as of the earliest date so that creditors need not worry that the secured portion of a claim will fluctuate prior to redemption and throughout the case. The Court notes, however, that in many cases this holding may have little practical effect either because the valuation hearing closely follows the petition date or because the parties provide evidence of value only as of the hearing date.

---

warranty (other than the continuing factory warranty). The final sale price may vary depending on the vehicle's actual condition and local market conditions. This value may also be used to derive Fair Market Value for insurance [*29] and vehicle donation purposes."

[5] The Court's conclusion that the statutory language is ambiguous entitles the Court to consider legislative history in determining meaning. Although the legislative history provides some nuance, as discussed supra in Part III.D.2, the Court finds the legislative history to be equally as ambiguous as the statutory language itself. See H.R. REP. No. 109-31, pt. 1, at 83 (2005). However, the fact that the legislative history does not expressly discuss valuation as of the hearing date reinforces the Court's holding that valuation is to be determined "as of the date of the filing of the petition."

F. This Court Concludes that the Retail Value of the Vehicle Should Be Set at $10,126.00 Based on the Evidence Presented

In this case, the Court will use the Kelley Blue Book retail value as the appropriate starting point for calculating the retail value of the Vehicle under the second sentence of § 506(a)(2). No unusual circumstances exist to justify a different starting point. The parties have not submitted any N.A.D.A. Guide values, and the Court need not decide how to resolve any discrepancy between the retail values of the Kelley Blue Book and the N.A.D.A. Guide, if both presented. The parties, however, have presented two different Kelley Blue Book retail values: On the one hand, the Debtor submits a Kelley Blue Book retail value of $12,515.00 for a car of the same age and model with mileage of 46,000 miles. On the other hand, HSBC submits a Kelley Blue Book retail value of $13,550.00 for a car of the same age and model with mileage of 35,028 miles. It remains unclear whether HSBC listed the lower mileage figure in error or whether HSBC believes there to be an actual dispute regarding mileage. Nonetheless, the Court has no reason to distrust the mileage figures proposed by the Debtor, which range from 46,000 to 47,600 miles. Therefore, the Court rejects the Kelley Blue Book retail value proposed by HSBC and accepts the Kelley Blue Book retail value of $12,515.00 proposed by the Debtor as the appropriate starting point for determining retail value.[6]

Next, the Court must determine the Vehicle's condition as of the petition date. The Debtor does not address directly the condition of the Vehicle as of the petition date in either the Motion or the Reply. In general, the condition of a vehicle might easily be established based predominantly on declarations submitted with the motion. The issue is less clear in this case because the Debtor did not submit any declarations in support of either the Motion or the Reply. However, Exhibit 1 of the Motion indicates that the Vehicle was in "fair" condition as of approximately February 18, 2008, less than one month after the petition date of January 25, 2008, though it remains unclear whether this conclusion is based on a visual inspection by Collateral Valuation Services, or on information provided to Collateral Valuation Services by the Debtor. In any event, the Debtor has presented at least some evidence in support of the conclusion that the Vehicle is in "fair" condition.

By contrast, HSBC argues that the retail value should be calculated based on "excellent" condition instead of "fair condition. HSBC asserts that the Vehicle was purchased approximately nine months prior to the petition date and was likely in "excellent" condition at the time. Opposition at 3. HSBC further alleges that its contract with the Debtor requires the Debtor to maintain the Vehicle in "good" condition. Opposition at 3. In the Reply, the Debtor contends that there is no reason to assume the Vehicle was in "excellent" condition at the time of purchase, and asserts that the contract included with the Opposition does not contain a specific provision requiring, the Debtor to maintain the Vehicle in "good" condition.

---

[6] The Court notes that the Kelley Blue Book retail value submitted by the Debtor assumes mileage of only 46,000 miles instead of 47,600 miles, which is the mileage listed on the Collateral Valuation Services reports attached to the Motion. Although the Court will proceed in light of the evidence presented, it appears clear that the Kelley Blue Book retail value for a vehicle [*33] with mileage of 47,600 miles would be less than the Kelley Blue Book retail value actually submitted.

For purposes of valuation and based on the limited evidence presented, the Court concludes that the Vehicle was in approximately "fair" condition as of the petition date. Although the Court agrees with HSBC that the Vehicle was likely in "excellent" or "good" condition when purchased, the former condition of the Vehicle has no bearing on the issue of valuation under § 506(a)(2). Rather, valuation is to be determined as of the petition date and in light of the existing age and condition of the vehicle at that time. Similarly, the Court agrees with the Debtor that HSBC has failed to establish that the Debtor was under a contractual obligation to maintain the Vehicle in "good" condition.[7] As a result, the only evidence presented on the issue of condition is the reports from Collateral Valuation Services, which list the Vehicle in "fair" condition.

The Debtor here bears the burden in establishing the condition of the Vehicle as of the petition date. The Court is satisfied that the Debtor has established some evidence, though minimal, that the Vehicle was not in "excellent" condition and that its condition was likely closer to "fair" condition.

As a final step, the Court must determine the reasonable adjustment to the Kelley Blue Book retail value in light of the Vehicle's age and condition as of the petition date. In support of a downward adjustment, the Debtor has submitted three AutoTrader.com advertisements, listing retail prices of $8,995.00, $8,999.00, and $9,995.00, respectively. Although the dates of these advertisements range from February 18 to March 15, 2008, they sufficiently approximate examples of retail prices as of the petition date of January 25, 2008, for purposes of valuation. By contrast, HSBC submits the Declaration of Linda Curzan, in which she declares that HSBC conducted an online search for similar vehicles and found 19 vehicles for sale within a 25-mile radius of the Debtor's residence. Curzan Declaration at 2-3, P 7. Curzan declares that "[o]f the nineteen vehicles available for sale, only one was priced at $8,900.00, while thirteen (13) were listed between $10,000.00 and $14,480.00." Curzan Declaration at 3, P 7. Curzan does not identify the retail value of the remaining five cars listed, nor explain whether the vehicles listed were of the same condition as the Vehicle. The Debtor appears to acknowledge, however, that the AutoTrader.com advertisements represent retail prices at the low end of the spectrum.

The Court ultimately sets the retail value of the Vehicle at $10,126.00 in light of the limited evidence presented by the parties. The Court reaches this value as the average of the Kelley Blue Book retail value of $12,515.00 and the AutoTrader.com retail values of $8,995.00, $8,999.00, and $9,995.00. The Court acknowledges the inherent arbitrariness created by § 506(a)(2). Other cases may require a different adjustment process based on better or worse evidence, as presented. Nonetheless, the Court believes that the Debtor has not presented

---

[7] It remains unclear whether the Debtor in fact agreed to maintain the Vehicle in "good" condition pursuant to the contract with HSBC. HSBC does not identify a specific provision that imposes such a requirement in the single page of the apparently multi-page contract submitted as Exhibit 1 to the Opposition. The Court's review of Exhibit 1 does not reveal any requirement regarding the Debtor's obligation to maintain the Vehicle in a specific condition. Because language in the contract suggests that additional terms were included as part of the contract on subsequent pages, it is possible that HSBC may be correct in its assertions. Nonetheless, in light of the evidence presented, the Court concludes that HSBC has not established the existence of a contractual obligation on the part of the Debtor to maintain the Vehicle in "good" condition. Therefore, the Court need not consider what effect, if any, such [*36] a requirement would have on valuation under § 506(a)(2) assuming the Debtor has not maintained the Vehicle in "good" condition.

sufficient evidence regarding the condition of the Vehicle so as to justify a reduction from the Kelley Blue Book retail value to the lowest of the AutoTrader.com retail values. Moreover, a retail value of $10,126.00 for the Vehicle approximates the highest AutoTrader.com retail value submitted by the Debtor and falls at the low end of the range of retail prices suggested by HSBC. Without better evidence as to the condition of the Vehicle and the full spectrum of retail values of similar vehicles, the Court concludes that $10,126.00 is an appropriate retail value for purposes of the second sentence of § 506(a)(2).

IV. Conclusion

In conclusion, the Court sets the replacement value of the Vehicle under the retail value standard of § 506(a)(2) at $10,126.00. The Debtor may redeem the Vehicle provided that he pays this amount to HSBC at the time of redemption.

Notes and Questions

1. The court decides that the petition date, not the date of the hearing, is the relevant valuation point. What difference does this make?

2. Bankruptcy Code § 722 grants D a unilateral right to redeem property from certain security interests. The redemption price is based on an appraised valuation of the collateral. D's unilateral power to retrieve collateral for its appraised value must be compared to the less generous redemption right under UCC §9-623.[1] The principal difference is that, under the Bankruptcy Code, the total claim of the secured party can remain largely unpaid, and yet the debtor may still bail out individual items of collateral by paying the appraised value of the item in question. Under the UCC, however, not the tiniest shard of collateral can be saved unless the entire claim of the secured party is paid in full.

The elements of redemption under the Bankruptcy Code are as follows: First, the collateral must be tangible. Unlike MacBeth's dagger, it must be as sensible to feeling as it is to sight.

Second, the property must be personal, not real, property.

Third, the encumbered property must be intended primarily for personal, family, or household use.

Fourth, the debt secured by the collateral to be redeemed must be a consumer debt. This is defined as a "debt incurred by an individual primarily for a personal, family, or household purpose."[2]

---

[1] Section §9-623 provides:

> (a) Persons that may redeem. A debtor, any secondary obligor, or any other secured party or lienholder may redeem collateral.
>
> (b) Requirements for redemption. To redeem collateral, a person shall tender:
>
> (1) fulfillment of all obligations secured by the collateral; and
>
> (2) the reasonable expenses and attorney's fees described in Section 9-615(a)(1).
>
> (c) When redemption may occur. A redemption may occur at any time before a secured party:
>
> (1) has collected collateral under Section 9-607;
>
> (2) has disposed of collateral or entered into a contract for its disposition under Section 9-610; or
>
> (3) has accepted collateral in full or partial satisfaction of the obligation it secures under Section 9-622.

[2] 11 U.S.C. §101(8); see Robert A. Hessling, Reaffirmation and Redemption 307-10 (1994); see also Boitnott v. United Va. Bank (In re Boitnott), 4 B.R. 122 (Bankr. W.D. Va. 1980) (consumer status survived consolidation of two debts).

Fifth, the debtor must be entitled to a discharge from any unsecured deficit claim the secured party might have against the debtor.

Sixth, the secured creditor must have an allowed secured claim. This implies that the secured party has filed a proof of claim. Bankruptcy Code § §502(a).[3]

Seventh, the property to be redeemed must be exempt or abandoned by the bankruptcy trustee.

Eighth, the debtor must pay the price in a lump sum.

3. Prior to D's bankruptcy petition, SP has repossessed D's automobile. D files for bankruptcy and moves to redeem the repossessed automobile. SP claims redemption is no longer possible after repossession. Is SP right? Karr v. General Motors Acceptance Corp. (In re Karr), 129 B.R. 498 (Bankr. S.D. Ohio 1991) (no).

4. Dischargeability. According to Bankruptcy Code § 521(a)(2)(A), D must file a statement of an intent to redeem collateral within thirty days of a chapter 7 bankruptcy petition. Meanwhile, a creditor has sixty days after a creditors' meeting to file an objection to discharge. Fed. Bankr. R. Proc. 4004(a). If no objection is filed, all debts are discharged. Id. 4004(c), 4005. Hence, D must redeem before it is known whether the underlying debt is dischargeable. To solve this contradiction, one judge has ruled that redemption can occur provisionally, even though discharge might be denied at a later time. In re Pipes, 78 B.R. 981, 983 (Bankr. W.D. Mo. 1987).

5. Agreements to redeem. Are agreements to redeem at a negotiated price enforceable? Arruda v. Sears, Roebuck & Co., 310 F.3d 13 (1st Cir. 2002) (yes; the secured creditor trades a valid postpetition right to repossess for an agreed redemption price); Sears, Roebuck & Co. v. Spivey, 265 B.R. 357 (E.D.N.Y. 2001) (yes); In re Spivey, 230 B.R. 484 (Bankr. E.D.N.Y. 1999) (no); In re Lopez, 224 B.R. 439 (Bankr. C.D. Cal. 1998) (no).

6. Exempt property. Under Bankruptcy Code § 522(d)(2), D may exempt the "debtor's interest, not to exceed $2,400 in value, in one motor vehicle." Suppose D owns a Rolls Royce worth $80,000. May D redeem this car from SP under § 722? H. Rep. No. 595, 95th Cong., 1st Sess. at 381 (1977) (yes).

When exempt property is described by quantitative dollar amount, as well as by qualitative aspect (as the car is under §522(d)(2)), the general creditors may have an interest in the exempt property, once the valid senior security interest and the exemption amount are accounted for. Returning to the Rolls Royce, suppose it is encumbered by a $70,000 purchase money security interest, as well as a $2,400 exemption. The general creditors would then enjoy an interest of $7,100. Can D redeem the car? If so, for how much? Who owns the car once redemption is completed?

7. Abandoned property. D may redeem nonexempt property if the trustee has abandoned it. In a chapter 7 case, this implies the collateral is overencumbered and D's equity in it is valueless.

The trustee or some other party in interest must have moved the court for an abandonment order, and the court must have granted it. The requirement of an accomplished abandonment solves a conceptual problem with redemption. Ordinarily, when D pays down a secured claim on property, the event tends to enrich the unsecured creditors, who now may look to the disencumbered part of the collateral for their recovery. Of course, if D's payment of a secured creditor only serves to enrich the unsecured creditors, D will never redeem. Section 722 does not expressly preclude a bankruptcy trustee from laying claim to the new debtor equity created by D's payment of the secured claim. Once the property has been abandoned, however, the estate's interest in the property no longer exists. Therefore, any disencumbrance through payment adheres solely to D personally. Under these conditions, redemption becomes economically rational for debtors.

Another puzzle arises from the terminology of §722, which does not quite work with regard to abandoned property. Section 722 requires D to pay a secured creditor "the amount of the allowed secured claim." Bankruptcy Code § 506(a)(1) implies that an "allowed secured claim . . . is a secured claim to the extent of such creditor's interest in the estate's interest in such property" (Emphasis added). If property has been abandoned, the property is no longer "of the estate." It has

[3] Courts have not really dealt with this aspect of §722. The requirement of an allowed secured claim implies that a secured party can resist redemption altogether by simply failing to file. Of course, the debtor can file for a creditor, but this debtor power is subject to a bar date thirty days after the secured party's own deadline has passsed. Federal Rules of Bankruptcy Procedure 3004. If the bar date has passed, the secured party arguably obtains a windfall--freedom from redemption.

occasionally been held that, after abandonment, the bankruptcy court has no jurisdiction to value non-estate assets.[4] Such a position, if asserted in the context of redemption, would make impossible the redemption of abandoned property, unless D presciently obtained a valuation prior to abandonment. Yet, oddly, if the property is non-exempt, D is not even entitled to redeem it until the property "has been abandoned." Hence, it is impossible to honor the exact words of the Bankruptcy Code with regard to abandoned property.

8. Valuations. The court assumes (as do most courts) that §506(a)(1) applies to redemption cases. That section states:

> An allowed claim of a creditor secured by a lien on property in which the estate has an interest . . . is a secured claim to the extent of the value of such creditor's interest in the estate's interest in such property . . . Such value shall be determined in light of the purpose of the valuation and of the proposed disposition or use of such property, and in conjunction with any hearing on such disposition or use or on a plan affecting such creditor's interest.

This provision, however, can only govern property "of the estate." Property that the trustee has abandoned or that D has exempted is not "of the estate."

The question of §506(a)(1)'s applicability is important to redemption because Congress in 2005 added new §506(a)(2), which provides:

> If the debtor is an individual in a case under chapter 7 or 13, such value with respect to personal property securing an allowed claim shall be determined based on the replacement value of such property as of the date of the filing of the petition without deduction for costs of sale or marketing. With respect to property acquired for personal, family, or household purposes, replacement value shall mean the price a retail merchant would charge for property of that kind considering the age and condition of the property at the time value is determined. (Emphasis added.)

The italicized such indicates that §506(a)(2) applies only if §506(a)(1) does. Therefore, replacement value must apply to redemption cases if and only if §506(a) applies to property not of the estate.

If §506(a) does not apply, the original legislative history of §722 points toward liquidation value:

> Under [§722], the debtor may redeem from a secured creditor property that would be exempt in the absence of the security interest, or property that the trustee abandons, if the debtor pays the secured creditor the allowed amount of the creditor's secured claim. This right amounts to a right of first refusal on a foreclosure sale of the property involved. It allows the debtor to retain his necessary property and avoid high replacement costs, and does not prevent the creditor from obtaining what he is entitled to under the terms of his contract.

H. Rep. No. 595, 95th Cong., 1st Sess. 127 (1977) (emphasis added). Prior to 2005, this legislative history provided ample excuse to think that liquidation value was the appropriate criterion.

9. Often, valuation of redeemed property is not contested by secured creditors, because the amount at stake does not warrant the lawyer's time to show up at court. Suppose D moves to value collateral at impossibly low amounts, hoping that the motion will not be contested. Must the court approve the motion? In re Ridner, 102 B.R. 247 (Bankr. W.D. Okla. 1989) (suggesting attorneys for D are subject to Rule 11 sanctions for such a tactic).

---

[4] Associates Comm'l Corp. v. Rash (In re Rash), 90 F.2d 1036, 1045-47 (5th Cir. 1996) (en banc) (§506(a)(1) does not apply to exempt property because it is not "of the estate"), rev'd on other grounds, 520 U.S. 953 (1997).

E. CLAIMS AGAINST THE BANKRUPTCY ESTATE

LAMIE v UNITED STATES TRUSTEE
540 U.S. 526 (2004)

KENNEDY, J..[1]

Section 330(a)(1) of the Bankruptcy Code . . . regulates court awards of professional fees, including fees for services rendered by attorneys in connection with bankruptcy proceedings. Petitioner, a bankruptcy attorney, sought compensation under the section for legal services he provided to a bankrupt debtor after the proceeding was converted to a chapter 7 bankruptcy. His application for fees was denied by the Bankruptcy Court, the District Court, and the United States Court of Appeals for the Fourth Circuit. Each court held that in a chapter 7 proceeding § 330(a)(1) does not authorize payment of attorney's fees unless the attorney has been appointed under § 327 of the Code. See 11 USC §§ 327 and 701 et seq. Petitioner was not so appointed, and his fee request was denied. Having granted the petition for certiorari to review this holding, we now affirm.

I

In 1994 Congress amended the Bankruptcy Code. Bankruptcy Reform Act of 1994 (Act), 108 Stat 4106. The subject of professional fees was addressed and comprehensive changes were made. See 3 Collier on Bankruptcy P 330.LH[5], pp 330-75 to 330-76 (rev. 15th ed. 2003). Most of the changes served to clarify the standards for the award of professional fees; but various courts disagree over the proper interpretation of the portion of the statute relevant to this dispute, concerning attorney's fees.

The Act replaced the predecessor section to the one in issue here. Compare 108 Stat 4130-4131 (§ 224(b) of the Act was not so appointed, amending 11 USC § 330(a), with 11 U.S.C. § 330(a) (1988 ed.) Before the 1994 Act, § 330(a) had read as follows:

> "(a) After notice to any parties in interest and to the United States trustee and a hearing, and subject to sections 326, 328, and 329 of this title, the court may award to a trustee, to an examiner, to a professional person employed under section 327 or 1103 of this title, or to the debtor's attorney--
>
> "(1) reasonable compensation for actual, necessary services rendered by such trustee, examiner, professional person, or attorney . . . and by any paraprofessional persons employed by such trustee, professional person, or attorney . . .; and
>
> "(2) reimbursement for actual, necessary expenses." Ibid. (emphasis added to highlight text later deleted).

Pursuant to the 1994 Act, 11 U.S.C. § 330(a)(1) now reads as follows:

> "(a)(1) After notice to the parties in interest and the United States Trustee and a hearing, and subject to sections 326, 328, and 329, the court may award to a trustee, an examiner, a professional person employed under section 327 or 1103--

[1] Justice Souter and Justice Breyer join this opinion in its entirety. Justice Scalia joins this opinion except for Part III

"(A) reasonable compensation for actual, necessary services rendered by the trustee, examiner, professional person, or attorney and by any paraprofessional person employed by any such person; and
"(B) reimbursement for actual, necessary expenses."

As can be noted, the 1994 enactment's principal, substantive alteration was its deletion of the five words at the end of what was § 330(a) and is now § 330(a)(1): "or to the debtor's attorney."

The deletion created apparent legislative drafting error. It left current § 330(a)(1) with a missing "or" that infects its grammar (i.e., "an examiner, [or] a professional person . . ."). Furthermore, the Act's inclusion of the word "attorney" in § 330(a)(1)(A) defeats the neat parallelism that otherwise marks the relationship between §§ 330(a)(1) and 330(a)(1)(A) (i.e., in § 330(a)(1): "trustee, . . . examiner, [or] professional person;" in § 330(a)(1)(A): "trustee, examiner, professional person, or attorney") and so casts some doubt on the proper presence of "attorney." That the pre-1994 text had no grammatical error and was parallel in its structure strengthens the sense that error exists in the new text.

The Courts of Appeals for the Fifth and Eleventh Circuits, when asked to interpret current § 330(a)(1), concluded that its language was plain irrespective of these quirks and history. Under the statutory language as written, those courts held, fees may be awarded to attorneys for services rendered only to the extent they are payments to "a professional person employed under § 327," see, e.g., § 327(a) (authorizing an appointed trustee in a chapter 7 bankruptcy action to "employ one or more attorneys . . . to represent or assist the trustee in carrying out the trustee's duties under this title"); § 327(e) (authorizing an appointed trustee in a chapter 7 bankruptcy action to "employ, for a specified special purpose, other than to represent the trustee in conducting the case, an attorney that has represented the debtor, . . ."). See In re Pro-Snax Distributors, Inc., 157 F.3d 414 (CA5 1998); In re American Steel Prod., Inc., 197 F.3d 1354 (CA11 1999). The Courts of Appeals for the Second, Third, and Ninth Circuits, in contrast, concluded that the text's apparent errors rendered the section ambiguous, requiring consideration of the provision's legislative history. That history, those courts held, shows Congress intended § 330(a)(1) to continue to allow compensation of chapter 7 debtors' attorneys, irrespective of qualification under § 327. In re Ames Dep't Stores, 76 F.3d 66 (CA2 1996); In re Top Grade Sausage, Inc., 227 F.3d 123 (CA3 2000); United States Trustee v. Garvey, Schubert & Barer (In re Century Cleaning Servs.), 195 F.3d 1053 (CA9 Cir. 1999). See also 3 Collier on Bankruptcy, supra, P 330.LH[5], at 330-75 to 330-76.

This interpretive divide became relevant to petitioner in his representation of Equipment Services, Inc. (ESI). ESI retained petitioner to prepare, file, and prosecute a chapter 11 bankruptcy proceeding on its behalf. He did so, all the while representing ESI with the approval of the court under § 327. See In re Equipment Services, Inc., 290 F.3d 739, 742 (CA4 2002) (case below). See also 11 U.S.C. § 1107(a) (authorizing debtor-in-possession to exercise the statutory rights and powers of an estate trustee, including to retain counsel under § 327). Three months into the chapter 11 reorganization, the United States Trustee (Government) filed a motion to convert the action into a chapter 7 liquidation proceeding. The court granted the Government's motion and appointed an estate trustee pursuant to § 701, 11 U.S.C. § 701(a). This terminated ESI's status as debtor-in-possession and so terminated petitioner's service under § 327 as an attorney for the debtor-in-possession. Yet petitioner continued to provide legal services to ESI, the debtor, even though he did not have the trustee's authorization to do so. He prepared reports detailing debts incurred and property acquired since the initial filing; he amended asset schedules; and he appeared at a hearing on an adversary complaint.

In due course petitioner filed an application seeking fees under § 330(a)(1) for the time he spent on ESI's behalf after the chapter 7 conversion. The Government objected to the application. It argued that § 330(a)(1) makes no provision for the estate to compensate an attorney not authorized under § 327. The court agreed and denied the fees. In re Equipment Servs., 253 B.R. 724 (Bkrtcy. Ct. WD Va. 2000). (Petitioner was paid fees for the services he provided to ESI before conversion of the proceeding to chapter 7 and when ESI was the debtor-in-possession. The parties do not contest those fees.)

Petitioner unsuccessfully sought reversal of the Bankruptcy Court's determination, first from the District Court, see In re Equipment Services, Inc., 260 B.R. 273 (WD Va. 2001), then from the Court of Appeals, see 290 F.3d 739. Both courts concluded the plain language of § 330(a)(1) controlled and that attorneys who provide services to debtors in chapter 7 proceedings must be hired by the trustee under § 327 to be eligible for compensation. The Court of Appeals acknowledged that its holding deepened the divide among the various Circuits, but held fast to the statute's plain language, "particularly because application of that plain language supports a reasonable interpretation of the Bankruptcy Code," 290 F.3d, at 745. We granted the petition for certiorari, 538 U.S. 905 (2003), and now resolve the issue.

II

Petitioner argues that the existing statutory text is ambiguous and so requires us to consult legislative history to determine whether Congress intended to allow fees for services rendered by a debtor's attorney in a chapter 7 proceeding, where that attorney is not authorized under § 327. He makes the case for ambiguity, for the most part, by comparing the present statute with its predecessor. Thus, he says the statute is ambiguous because subsection (A)'s "attorney" is "facially irreconcilable" with the section's first part since

> "[e]ither Congress inadvertently omitted the 'debtor's attorney' from the 'payees' list, on which the court of appeals relied, or it inadvertently retained the reference to the attorney in the latter, 'payees list'." Brief for Petitioner 17.

Similarly, with respect to the missing conjunction "or" he says,

> "[t]here is no apparent reason, other than a drafting error, that Congress would have rewritten the statute to produce a grammatically incorrect provision." Ibid.

This is the analysis followed by the Courts of Appeals that hold the statute is ambiguous. See In re Top Grade Sausage, supra, at 129 (noting in its search for ambiguity that "[p]rior to amendment, it was undisputed that the repetition of officers in § 330(a)(1)(A) was meant to parallel the officers previously listed in § 330(a)(1)"); see also In re Century Cleaning Servs., 195 F.3d, at 1057-1058 (engaging in same resort to previous enactment to inquire as to the current text's ambiguity). One determines ambiguity, under this contention, by relying on the grammatical soundness of the prior statute. That contention is wrong.

The starting point in discerning congressional intent is the existing statutory text, see Hughes Aircraft Co. v. Jacobson, 525 U.S. 432, 438 (1999), and not the predecessor statutes. It is well established that "when the statute's language is plain, the sole function of the courts--at least where the disposition required by the text is not absurd--is to enforce it according to its terms." Hartford Underwriters Ins. Co. v. Union Planters Bank, N. A., 530 U.S. 1, 6 (2000) (internal quotation marks omitted) (quoting United States v. Ron Pair Enterprises, Inc., 489 U.S. 235, 241 (1989) (in turn quoting Caminetti v. United States, 242 U.S. 470, 485 (1917))). So we begin with the present statute.

A

The statute is awkward, and even ungrammatical; but that does not make it ambiguous on the point at issue. In its first part, the statute authorizes an award of compensation to one of three types of persons: trustees, examiners, and § 327 professional persons. A debtor's attorney not engaged as provided by § 327 is simply not included within the class of persons eligible for compensation. In subsection (A) the statute further defines what type of compensation may be awarded: compensation that is reasonable; and for actual, necessary services; and rendered by four types of persons (the same three plus attorneys). Unless the applicant for compensation is in one of the named classes of persons in the first part, the kind of service rendered is irrelevant.

The missing conjunction "or" does not change our conclusion. The Government points to numerous federal statutes that inadvertently lack a conjunction. They are read, nonetheless, for their plain meaning. See Brief for Respondent 17, n 4. Here, the missing conjunction neither alters the text's substance nor obscures its meaning. This is not a case where a "not" is missing or where an "or" inadvertently substitutes for an "and." The sentence may be awkward; yet it is straightforward.

Subsection (A)'s nonparalleled fourth category of persons who can render compensable services does not cloud the statute's meaning. Petitioner reasons that since the section is a single sentence, and since it appears to strive for parallelism between those authorized to receive fees and those whose services are compensable, there is an ambiguity as to what "attorney" in § 330(a)(1)(A) refers to in § 330(a)(1). He also points to neighboring § 331, which provides for both debtors' attorneys and § 327 professional persons to receive interim compensation after an order for relief is entered but before an application for § 330 fees is filed. He argues that since § 331 contemplates debtors' attorneys' receiving interim compensation there is reason to conclude that "attorney" in § 330(a)(1)(A) refers to debtors' attorneys in § 330(a)(1), though they go unmentioned in that clause.

Subsection (A)'s "attorney," however, can be read in a straightforward fashion to refer to those attorneys whose fees are authorized by § 330(a)(1): attorneys qualified as § 327 professional persons, that is, in a chapter 7 context, those employed by the trustee and approved by the court. See § 327(a) (appointed trustee may "employ one or more attorneys . . . to represent or assist the trustee in carrying out the trustee's duties under this title); § 327(e) (appointed trustee may "employ, for a specified special purpose, other than to represent the trustee in conducting the case, an attorney that has represented the debtor, . . ."). Likewise, § 331's reference to interim compensation for debtors' attorneys most straightforwardly refers to debtors' attorneys authorized under § 327.

It must be acknowledged that, under our reading of the text, the word "attorney" in subsection (A) may well be surplusage. Subsection (A)'s reference to § 327 professional persons undoubtedly includes attorneys, as much as does § 330(a)(1)'s reference to professional persons. That is not controlling, however. Surplusage does not always produce ambiguity and our preference for avoiding surplusage constructions is not absolute. See Chickasaw Nation v. United States, 534 U.S. 84, 94 (2001) (the preference "is sometimes offset by the canon that permits a court to reject words 'as surplusage' if 'inadvertently inserted or if repugnant to the rest of the statute'"). Where there are two ways to read the text--either attorney is surplusage, in which case the text is plain; or attorney is nonsurplusage (i.e., it refers to an ambiguous component in § 330(a)(1)), in which case the text is ambiguous--applying the rule against surplusage is, absent other indications, inappropriate. We should prefer the plain meaning since that approach respects the words of Congress. In this manner we avoid the pitfalls that plague too quick a turn to the more controversial realm of legislative history.

B

The plain meaning that § 330(a)(1) sets forth does not lead to absurd results requiring us to treat the text as if it were ambiguous. Petitioner disagrees and argues that our interpretation will "entail an inexplicable, wholesale departure from . . . the guiding principle of the 'prompt and effectual administration' of federal bankruptcy law." Brief for Petitioner 30. He says that our reading "attribute[s] to Congress an illogical, penny-wise and pound-foolish determination to eliminate entirely--as a purportedly asset-preserving measure--compensation that is essential to debtors' receipt of legal services." Id., at 35.

These arguments overstate the effect of § 330(a)(1). Under the text's instruction compensation remains available to debtors' attorneys through various permitted means. First, while § 330(a)(1) requires proper authorization for payment to attorneys from estate funds in chapter 7 filings, it does not extend throughout all bankruptcy law. Compensation for debtors' attorneys in chapter 12 and 13 bankruptcies, for example, is not much disturbed by § 330 as a whole. See, e.g., 11 U.S.C. § 330(a)(4)(B) ("In a chapter 12 or chapter 13 case in which the debtor is an individual, the court may allow reasonable compensation to the debtor's attorney").

Compensation for debtors' attorneys working on chapter 7 bankruptcies, moreover, is not altogether prohibited. Sections 327 and 330, taken together, allow chapter 7 trustees to engage attorneys, including debtors' counsel, and allow courts to award them fees. See §§ 327(a) and (e). Section 327's limitation on debtors' incurring debts for professional services without the chapter 7 trustee's approval is not absurd. In the context of a chapter 7 liquidation it advances the trustee's responsibility for preserving the estate.

If we add to all this the apparent sound functioning of the bankruptcy system under the plain meaning approach, petitioner's arguments become unconvincing. Seeming order has attended the rule's application for five years in the Fifth Circuit and for four years in the Eleventh Circuit. See In re American Steel Prod., Inc., 197 F.3d 1354 (CA11 1999); In re Pro-Snax Distributors, Inc., 157 F.3d 414 (CA5 1998). It appears to be routine for debtors to pay reasonable fees for legal services before filing for bankruptcy to ensure compliance with statutory requirements. See generally Collier Compensation, Employment and Appointment of Trustees and Professionals in Bankruptcy Cases P 3.02[1], p 3-2 (2002) ("In the majority of cases, the debtor's counsel will accept an individual or a joint consumer chapter 7 case only after being paid a retainer that covers the 'standard fee' and the cost of filing the petition"). So our interpretation accords with common practice. Section 330(a)(1) does not prevent a debtor from engaging counsel before a chapter 7 conversion and paying reasonable compensation in advance to ensure that the filing is in order. Indeed, the Code anticipates these arrangements. See, e.g., § 329 (debtors' attorneys must disclose fees they receive from a debtor in the year prior to its bankruptcy filing and courts may order excessive payments returned to the estate).

C

Petitioner's argument stumbles on still harder ground in the face of another canon of interpretation. His interpretation of the Act--reading the word "attorney" in § 330(a)(1)(A) to refer to "debtors' attorneys" in § 330(a)(1) --would have us read an absent word into the statute. That is, his argument would result "not [in] a construction of [the] statute, but, in effect, an enlargement of it by the court, so that what was omitted, presumably by inadvertence, may be included within its scope." Iselin v. United States, 270 U.S. 245, 251 (1926). With a plain, nonabsurd meaning in view, we need not proceed in this way. "There is a basic difference between filling a gap left by Congress' silence and rewriting rules that Congress has affirmatively and specifically enacted." Mobil Oil Corp. v. Higginbotham, 436 U.S. 618, 625 (1978).

Our unwillingness to soften the import of Congress' chosen words even if we believe the words lead to a harsh outcome is longstanding. It results from "deference to the supremacy of the Legislature, as well as recognition that Congressmen typically vote on the language of a bill." United States v. Locke, 471 U.S. 84, 95 (1985) (citing Richards v. United States, 369 U.S. 1, 9 (1962)).

Adhering to conventional doctrines of statutory interpretation, we hold that § 330(a)(1) does not authorize compensation awards to debtors' attorneys from estate funds, unless they are employed as authorized by § 327. If the attorney is to be paid from estate funds under § 330(a)(1) in a chapter 7 case, he must be employed by the trustee and approved by the court.

III

Though we find it unnecessary to rely on the legislative history behind the 1994 enactment of § 330(a)(1), we find it instructive that the history creates more confusion than clarity about the congressional intent. History and policy considerations lend support both to petitioner's interpretation and to the holding we reach based on the plain language of the statute.

Petitioner, for instance, cites evidence supporting the conclusion that a scrivener's error obscures what was Congress' real intent. For over 100 years debtors' attorneys have been considered by Congress and the courts to be an integral part of the bankruptcy process. See Bankruptcy Act of 1898, ch 541, §§ 59(d) and 64(b), 30 Stat 561, 563. See also In re Kross, 96 F. 816 (SDNY 1899). It is fair to doubt that Congress would so rework their longstanding role without announcing the change in the congressional record. Cf. Cohen v. de la Cruz, 523 U.S. 213, 221 (1998) ("We . . . will not read the Bankruptcy Code to erode past bankruptcy practice absent a clear indication that Congress intended such a departure" (internal quotation marks and citation omitted)).

The legislative processes behind the change also lend some support to petitioner's claim. In 1994 the original proposed draft of new § 330(a)(1) featured two changes: stylistic changes throughout the section and the addition of a new provision giving the Government a right to object to fee applications. See S. 540, 103d Cong., 1st Sess. (1993), reprinted in S. Rep. No. 103-168 (1993). The right to object provision was added at § 330(a)(1)'s end. Thus it came immediately after the critical text "or to the debtor's attorney," which the draft edited to read "or the debtors [sic] attorney." Ibid. Before voting the Act into law, however, Congress amended the proposed draft. See 140 Cong. Rec. 8383 (1994) (setting out amendment 1645 to S. 540). Amendment 1645 made only two changes to § 330(a)(1): It deleted the Government's right to object provision and the critical words ("or the debtors [sic] attorney"). The rest of the original proposed draft remained intact. Legislative history explains the first deletion, for the provision was installed elsewhere, as new § 330(a)(2). Nothing, however, explains the second. That the Government's right to object was deleted and reinstated (i.e., reorganized), while the words at issue, which had preceded the moved provision, were deleted with no notation in the legislative history suggests the scrivener just reached too far in his deletion. These factors combined to convince a leading treatise on bankruptcy law, Collier, that the deletion was a scrivener's error and ought not have any effect. See 3 Collier on Bankruptcy P 330.LH[5], at 330-75 to 330-76.

There are other aspects of the legislative record, however, that undermine this interpretation. These considerations suggest Congress may have intended the change the scrivener worked. For example, amendment 1645 was part of a reform Act designed to curtail abuses in fee awards, according to statements by the amendment's sponsor. See 140 Cong. Rec., at 28753 (statement of Sen. Metzenbaum). These abuses were not ghosts seen only by Congress. Some bankruptcy courts had reached the same conclusion. See, e.g., In re NRG Resources, Inc., 64 B.R. 643 (Bkrtcy Ct WD La 1986). The deletion at issue furthered this reform by ensuring that chapter 7 debtors' attorneys would receive no estate compensation absent the trustee's authorization of their work. This objective is not inconsistent with the interest of involving debtors' attorneys in bankruptcy proceedings. As noted, the Act still allows debtors' attorneys to be compensated in different ways. See supra, at 536-539.

Amendment 1645, viewed in its entirety, gives further reason to think Congress may have intended the change. The amendment added a new section that authorizes fee awards to debtors' attorneys in chapter 12 and 13 bankruptcies. 140 Cong. Rec., at 8383 (setting out new 11 U.S.C. § 330(a)(4)(B). Since the amendment's deletion of "or the debtors [sic] attorney" from the original proposed draft affected chapter 12 and 13 debtors' attorneys as much as chapter 7 debtors' attorneys, § 330(a)(4)(B) shows a special intent to authorize the formers' fee awards in the face of the new, broad exclusion.

If Congress' action does not prove the point, the House of Representatives' inaction may. The House passed the Act after having the deletion, as well as its impact, called to its attention. See Bankruptcy Reform: Hearing before the Subcommittee on Economic and Commercial Law of the House Committee on the Judiciary, 103d Cong., 2d Sess., 551 (1994). The National Association of Consumer Bankruptcy Attorneys (NACBA), which represents those lawyers most likely to be affected by § 330(a)(1)'s change, declined to object to the deletion. Ibid. (noting the deletion but stating that the NACBA did "not oppose" Amendment 1645's passage). This alert, followed by the Legislature's nonresponse, should support a presumption of legislative awareness and intention. The Act may now contain surplusage, along with grammatical error;

but that may have been the result of trying to make the substantive change with the fewest possible textual alterations or of an error by the scrivener in carrying out the change.

These competing interpretations of the legislative history make it difficult to say with assurance whether petitioner or the Government lays better historical claim to the congressional intent. The alert to the change in policy was given, to be sure, before the House passed the final version, but that particular circumstance cannot bear too much weight. The alert was not the subject of testimony from any witness at the congressional hearing. It consisted of but two sentences contained within 472 pages of written statements delivered to the legislative subcommittee for its August 17, 1994, hearing day. Those 472 pages were added to 236 pages of prepared statements and testimony transcribed from the day's testifying witnesses. Within the NACBA's filing, the two relevant sentences appear on the 18th page of the 27-page report. Nothing in the legislative history confirms that this particular point bore on the congressional deliberations or was given specific consideration.

These uncertainties illustrate the difficulty of relying on legislative history here and the advantage of our determination to rest our holding on the statutory text.

* * *

If Congress enacted into law something different from what it intended, then it should amend the statute to conform it to its intent. "It is beyond our province to rescue Congress from its drafting errors, and to provide for what we might think . . . is the preferred result." United States v. Granderson, 511 U.S. 39, 68 (1994) (concurring opinion). This allows both of our branches to adhere to our respected, and respective, constitutional roles. In the meantime, we must determine intent from the statute before us. The judgment of the Court of Appeals is affirmed.

STEVENS, J., CONCURRING IN THE JUDGMENT, JOINED BY JUSTICE SOUTER AND JUSTICE BREYER. As the majority recognizes, ante, at 539-540, a leading bankruptcy law treatise concluded that the 1994 amendments to § 330(a)(1) contained an unintended error. 3 Collier on Bankruptcy P 330.LH[5], pp 330-75 to 330-76 (rev. 15th ed. 2003). Whenever there is such a plausible basis for believing that a significant change in statutory law resulted from a scrivener's error, I believe we have a duty to examine legislative history.[2] In this case, that history reveals that the National Association of Consumer Bankruptcy Attorneys (NACBA) not only called the assumed drafting error to Congress' attention in a timely fashion, but also deemed the error unworthy of objection.[3] This evidence

[2] As Chief Justice Marshall stated, "Where the mind labours to discover the design of the legislature, it seizes every thing from which aid can be derived . . . ." United States v. Fisher, 6 U.S. 358, 2 Cranch 358, 386, 2 L. Ed. 304 (1805).

[3] See ante, at 541, 157 L. Ed. 2d, at 1038. Specifically, three months after the Senate passed the relevant amendment, the NACBA submitted written comments to the House Subcommittee on Economic and Commercial Law, which was considering the change. Those comments first noted that the amended version of § 330(a)(1) "appears to have some minor drafting errors, including the apparently inadvertent removal of debtors' attorneys from the list of professionals whose compensation awards are covered." Bankruptcy Reform: Hearing on H. R. 5116 before the Subcommittee on Economic and Commercial Law of the House Committee on the Judiciary, 103d

convinces me that the Court's reading of the text, which surely is more natural than petitioner's, is correct. I therefore concur in the judgment.

Notes and Questions

1. One achievement of BAPCPA is to re-insert the missing "or" in § 330(a)(1) that the Supreme Court complains about. Congress did not, however, authorize awards to attorneys for the debtor in chapter 7 cases.

2. In chapter 13 cases, the rule is different. Bankruptcy Code § 330(a)(4)(B) specifically permits the debtor's attorney compensation. Section 503(b)(2) makes any expense under § 330(a) an administrative expense. These have the high priority described in § 507(a)(2).

3. Debtors' counsel in chapter 7 cases are regulated by Bankruptcy Code § 329, which requires them to file a statement of the compensation paid or agreed to be paid, if the payment or agreement was within a year of the bankruptcy petition. The court has power to force counsel to return compensation that exceed "reasonable value." Bankruptcy Code § 329(b).

Cong., 2d Sess., 551 (1994). With no proviso that these alleged errors be corrected, the NACBA then expressly did "not oppose" passage of the amendment. Ibid. (emphasis added).

CHAPTER 5 DISCHARGE AND REAFFIRMATION

A. DISCHARGE

1. What Does It Mean?

CHANDLER BANK v RAY
804 F.2d 577 (10th Cir. 1986)

PER CURIAM

This case involves the administration of a bankruptcy estate and the question of whether the Chandler Bank's lien in collateral survives the debtor's discharge in bankruptcy. The trial judge ruled that subsequent to the debtor's discharge the creditor who has taken no action to preserve its pre-filing lien rights in the debtor's personal property does not have an in personam right against the debtor and is subject to being enjoined from enforcing his lien against the property of the debtor.

The Bank had filed an action in the Bankruptcy Court naming the debtor and seeking to reopen the case and to obtain an order of replevin of its collateral. Following a ruling of the Bankruptcy Court the Bank appealed. It was at the time of the filing that the debtor sought to exempt from the estate the 1978 Firebird which had been purchased with the Bank's money as a means of conveyance pursuant to K.S.A. § 60-2304(3). The exemption was granted without there being any objection. . . .

It was in January 1981, following the filing of bankruptcy in December, 1980 that the Bank received notice of the Chapter 7 filing and of a projected May 28, 1981 discharge for the debtor. Soon thereafter, on February 6, 1981 the Bank filed a proof of claim which reflected a secured claim, and as collateral, a 1973 Suzuki and a 1978 Firebird. No relief was sought by the Bank from the 11 U.S.C. § 362 stay or abandonment under 11 U.S.C. § 554, or reaffirmation under 11 U.S.C. § 524. Bankruptcy Reform Act of 1978, 11 U.S.C. § 101, et seq. (hereinafter "the Code"). The Bank did not participate in any court proceeding or action to get possession of its collateral prior to the debtor's discharge of May 28, 1981. At the discharge hearing it was announced that no reaffirmation agreement had been made and that an agreement to redeem had been made with one secured creditor. The Notice of Debtor's Discharge was mailed to all creditors on June 3, 1981.

There was filed on May 13, 1981 by the Trustee of debtor's estate a no asset report and notice of intended abandonment of unadministered assets upon closing the case. Indeed the case was closed on June 3, 1981.

It is important to note that in this case after the close of Chapter 7 bankruptcy, the Bank filed a complaint in an adversary proceeding in which it sought the following relief:

(1) An order of the court allowing the case to be reopened.
(2) An order of abandonment of the automobile and motorcycle to the Bank.
(3) Replevin of the automobile and motorcycle.
(4) Reaffirmation of the indebtedness.

The Bank was simply seeking to establish in the adversary proceeding that its lien with respect to the mortgage on the property involved could be pursued by the Bank. Thus it was strictly an in rem action. It did not seek generally to proceed against the bankrupt in an in personam action. Therefore, its in rem action on the secured claim survived the bankruptcy.

It should be noted that the argument for a contrary result is advanced by Judge Pusateri in this action and by him in the better known case of In re Williams, 9 Bankr. 228 (B.C. D.Kan. 1981). However, other bankruptcy judges in Kansas have taken the position adopted by this court that an in rem action on a secured claim survives the bankruptcy although the creditor did not participate by way of urging a reaffirmation or otherwise. See 3 Collier on Bankruptcy § 524.01 [3], at 529-15, 529-16 n. 176 (15th Ed.). Judge Franklin in In re Weathers, 15 Bankr. 945 (B.C. D.Kan. 1981) and Judge Morton in In re Grimes, 6 B.R. 943 (B.C. D.Kan. 1980) ably articulated the basis for this court's ruling: that for sections in the Code which relate to automatic stays and to lien avoidance to have any substance at all necessarily leads to the conclusion that unavoided liens pass through § 506(d) without action by the lien holder. Thus the injunction on discharge under § 524 of the Code does not preclude in rem actions by secured creditors.

Specifically, Code § 524(a)(2) states in part that the discharge:

> operates as an injunction against the commencement or continuation of an action, the employment of process, or any act, to collect, recover or offset any such debt as a personal liability of the debtor, or from property of the debtor, whether or not discharge of such debt is waived; . . .[1]

There was a change in wording from § 14(f) of the former Bankruptcy Act. The trial judge in this case held that "property of the debtor" included property subject to a creditor's lien and that the injunctive portion thus precluded in rem proceedings if the creditor had not participated in the bankruptcy proceedings. He thus would require the creditor to enter the proceedings and apparently enter into proceedings or negotiations relating to reaffirmation. As stated previously, this reading is plainly contrary to the specific sections of the Code relating to automatic stays and to lien avoidance, which to have any substantive meaning must be read to allow unavoided liens to pass through § 506(d) without any action by the lien holder.

The legislative history of the Code further supports this court's ruling. Referring to the lien avoidance provisions of the Code, the legislative history reveals:

> The bankruptcy discharge will not prevent enforcement of valid liens. The rule of Long v. Bullard, 117 U.S. 617 (1886), is accepted with respect to the enforcement of valid liens on nonexempt property as well as on exempt property. Cf. Louisville Joint Stock Land Bank v. Radford, 295 U.S. 555, 583

[1] [In 1984, Congress amended §524(a)(2) to eliminate the words "or from property of the debtor."-Ed.]

(1935).

H.R. Rep. No. 595, 95th Cong., 1st Sess. 361 (1977); S. Rep. No. 989, 95th Cong., 2d Sess. 76 (1978). This indicates that the provisions for avoidance of liens contain a solution for problems in this area. The reference is made in the quotation to exempt property. It is generally held that an exemption as such does not invalidate liens. Consequently, the Congressional intent is clear that valid liens may be enforced, and the phrase "the property of the debtor" in § 524(a)(2) merely refers to property acquired by the debtor after filing of the bankruptcy petition.

We conclude that the trial court erred and that the matter should be reversed . . . .

Notes and Questions

1. Discharge affects in personam rights of creditors, not their in rem rights. It is a well know proverb that "liens pass through bankruptcy unaffected." Gradel v. Piranha Cap., L.P., 495 F.3d 729 (7th Cir. 2007). Of course, liens can be specifically avoided if they are fraudulent conveyances or voidable preferences. But discharge can never destroy a lien.

2. In this case, the secured lender filed a proof of claim, meaning that it had an "allowed secured claim." Suppose the lender never did file a proof of claim. Would it have made a difference?

McGHAN v RUTZ (IN RE McGHAN)

288 F.3d 1172 (9th Cir. 2002)

RAYMOND C. FISHER, J.

Appellee Jason Rutz was a listed creditor in his stepfather's -appellant Lon McGhan-bankruptcy proceedings. Rutz, a minor at the time, did not file a complaint of nondischargeability in those proceedings. As a result, the bankruptcy court issued an order discharging Rutz's claim and issued a permanent injunction barring Rutz from collecting on the debt. After Rutz attained maturity, he nonetheless filed a civil action against McGhan to collect on the discharged debt. Over McGhan's objections, the state court in which that action was filed ruled that Rutz's action could proceed because Rutz had inadequate notice of the earlier bankruptcy proceedings. Arguing that only the bankruptcy court had jurisdiction to resolve that question, McGhan then moved the bankruptcy court to reopen his bankruptcy case to review the state court's decision. The bankruptcy court denied the motion, reasoning that McGhan's desire to relitigate an issue already heard in state court was insufficient cause to reopen the case. We reverse. Relying on Gruntz v. County of Los Angeles (In re Gruntz), 202 F.3d 1074 (9th Cir. 2000) (en banc), we hold that state courts lack jurisdiction to determine whether a listed and scheduled creditor received adequate notice of discharge proceedings. We also hold that the state court lacked authority to modify the bankruptcy court's orders discharging Rutz's claim and permanently enjoining Rutz from collecting on the debt. In light of those holdings, we conclude that it was an abuse of discretion for the bankruptcy court to decline to reopen McGhan's bankruptcy case. The bankruptcy court was required to reopen the proceedings to protect its exclusive jurisdiction over the enforcement of its own orders.

FACTS AND PROCEDURAL BACKGROUND

In 1991, McGhan was charged with five counts of sexual molestation of

Rutz, his stepson. At the time the charges were filed, Rutz was 12 years old. McGhan pled guilty to one count of felony violation of California Penal Code § 288(a) (lewd and lascivious acts committed on a child under 14).

Shortly after his conviction, McGhan filed a voluntary petition for bankruptcy under Chapter 7 of the Bankruptcy Code. When a debtor files a Chapter 7 petition, the debtor lists each of his creditors. The appointed bankruptcy trustee convenes a meeting of these creditors pursuant to 11 U.S.C. § 341(a). All creditors must receive at least 30 days' advance notice of the creditors' meeting. Rule 4007(c). Within 60 days after the date first set for that meeting, any creditor wishing to have a debt characterized as nondischargeable must file a complaint alleging nondischargeability of the debt. Id. If the creditor has adequate notice of the meeting but fails to make a timely complaint, his claim is automatically discharged pursuant to § 523(c)(1). Although debts for intentional torts such as Rutz's claim ordinarily are not dischargeable under § 523(a)(6) of the code, which states that debts for "willful and malicious injury" are nondischargeable, such claims will be discharged automatically if the listed creditor fails to make a timely objection. When a debtor is discharged under the Bankruptcy Code, the discharge "operates as a permanent injunction against any attempt to collect or recover on a . . . debt." Irizarry v. Schmidt (In re Irizarry), 171 B.R. 874, 878 (B.A.P. 9th Cir. 1994); accord Am. Hardwoods, Inc. v. Deutsche Credit Corp. (In re Am. Hardwoods, Inc.), 885 F.2d 621, 626 (9th Cir. 1989).

A different provision of the code is implicated when the creditor was not listed o-n the bankruptcy petition. An unlisted creditor's claim ordinarily is not discharged. Under § 523(a)(3) of the code, however, the debt will be discharged if the creditor had "notice or actual knowledge "of the bankruptcy proceedings in time to permit the creditor to file a proof of claim and, if necessary, challenge its dischargeability. Under § 523(a)(3)(B), which applies to debts for "willful and malicious injury" defined by § 523(a)(6), the debt will not be discharged if the creditor (1) was neither listed nor scheduled and (2) did not have "notice or actual knowledge" of the case in time for timely filing a proof of claim and timely request for a determination of dischargeability. Federal courts have exclusive jurisdiction over §§ 523(a)(6) (nondischargeability of willful and malicious injury) and 523(c)(1) (adequacy of notice to a listed creditor) of the code, whereas state and federal courts have concurrent jurisdiction over § 523(a)(3) (unlisted or unscheduled debt) proceedings.

With respect to Rutz's claim, McGhan's bankruptcy proceedings followed the general scheme for a listed creditor rather than an unlisted one. His petition for bankruptcy listed Rutz as a creditor holding an unsecured nonpriority claim against him.[2] As Rutz's guardian, Rutz's mother received timely notice of the creditors' meeting and the deadline for creditors to file a complaint objecting to discharge of the debtor or to determine dischargeability of debts, but she did not file a nondischargeability claim on her son's behalf. Applying § 523(c)(1), the bankruptcy court issued a discharge order automatically discharging McGhan's debt to Rutz. The discharge order also stated that "any judgment . . . obtained in any court other than this court is null and void as a determination of the personal liability of the debtor with respect to" any debt under § 523(a)(6). Pursuant to § 524, the discharge order also permanently enjoined any listed creditor" from

[2] The petition described the claim as follows: "January 1989[.] Potential Civil Action for Personal Injury; Amount Unknown."

instituting or continuing any action . . . to collect such debts as personal liabilities of the above-named debtor. "The bankruptcy court closed McGhan's case.

Upon reaching adulthood, Rutz filed a civil action against McGhan in California Superior Court, seeking damages arising out of his sexual molestation at the hands of McGhan. McGhan promptly moved to dismiss the action, arguing that Rutz's claim had been discharged by the bankruptcy court's discharge order and that Rutz's civil suit was enjoined by the § 524 discharge injunction. At McGhan's request, the state court took judicial notice of numerous documents from McGhan's bankruptcy case, including McGhan's bankruptcy petition, which listed Rutz as a creditor, and the discharge order containing the permanent injunction, which showed that Rutz's claim had been automatically discharged. McGhan contended that the bankruptcy court possessed exclusive jurisdiction over the dischargeability of Rutz's claim and that Rutz was estopped from collaterally attacking the validity of the discharge order and injunction in state court. Rutz responded that neither he nor the state court should be bound by the discharge order or permanent injunction because he had not received the notice required by § 523(c)(1) as a prerequisite to automatic discharge. Because notice of the proceedings had been provided only to his mother and her interests had conflicted with his own, he contended, the bankruptcy court's orders did not apply to his action against McGhan.[3] The superior court agreed with Rutz. First, the court reasoned that it had jurisdiction pursuant to § 523(a)(3) to determine the sufficiency of Rutz's notice and the applicability of the discharge order. Second, the court agreed with Rutz that notice had been inadequate.[4] Accordingly, the court ruled that Rutz was not bound by the discharge order and allowed Rutz's case to proceed.[5]

McGhan then sought to collaterally attack the state court's ruling in federal court. He moved to reopen his Chapter 7 bankruptcy case in the bankruptcy court, seeking leave to file a complaint against Rutz for violation of the § 524 permanent discharge injunction. In denying McGhan's motion, the bankruptcy court agreed that the state court had jurisdiction to adjudicate the adequacy of Rutz's notice under § 523(a)(3)(B) and reasoned that McGhan's desire to relitigate an issue already properly decided by the state court did not constitute sufficient cause to reopen.[6] The Bankruptcy Appellate Panel ("BAP") affirmed, holding that the bankruptcy court had not abused its discretion in refusing to reopen McGhan's case. Like the state court and the bankruptcy court, the BAP assumed that the state court's jurisdiction validly rested on § 523(a)(3). The BAP also affirmed on the alternative ground that the Rooker-Feldman doctrine precluded the bankruptcy court from reversing or modifying the state court

---

[3] Rutz asserted a conflict of interest because his mother, also a listed creditor in McGhan's bankruptcy proceedings, had a competing claim for child support against McGhan.

[4] Section 523(a)(3)(B) provides that a debtor is not discharged from any debt neither listed nor scheduled in time to permit the creditor to file a claim and request that the debt be found nondischargeable, unless the creditor had notice or actual knowledge of the case in time to file a timely request for a determination of dischargeability.

[5] McGhan then filed a petition for writ of mandate with the California Court of Appeal, arguing the superior court had misapplied federal bankruptcy law; the court of appeal denied the petition.

[6] Section 350(b) states: "A case may be reopened in the court in which such case was closed to administer assets, to accord relief to the debtor, or for other cause." In its conclusions of law, the bankruptcy court stated that it would exercise its discretion to reopen McGhan's bankruptcy case only if he would stipulate to allow the bankruptcy court to hear Rutz's claims under § 523(a)(6). McGhan would not so stipulate.

decision.[7] McGhan appeals. . . .

DISCUSSION

I. State Court Jurisdiction

To assess whether the bankruptcy court abused its discretion by denying McGhan's § 350(b) motion to reopen his bankruptcy case, we first must determine whether the state court had the authority to adjudicate the adequacy of Rutz's notice and modify the bankruptcy court's discharge order and permanent discharge injunction. Relying on our en banc opinion in Gruntz v. County of Los Angeles (In re Gruntz), 202 F.3d 1074 (9th Cir. 2000), we conclude that the state court lacked that authority. In reaching a contrary conclusion, the state court asserted that it had jurisdiction pursuant to § 523(a)(3), which vests state courts with concurrent jurisdiction to adjudicate the adequacy of the notice provided to creditors who were neither listed nor scheduled. Because Rutz was a listed and scheduled creditor, § 523(a)(3) has no application here.

A. Gruntz

Gruntz involved a Chapter 13 debtor who was prosecuted by the Los Angeles County District Attorney, convicted for misdemeanor failure to support his dependent children and sentenced to 360 days in jail. Gruntz subsequently filed an adversary proceeding against the County in bankruptcy court, asking the court to declare the state proceedings void as viola-tive of the § 362(a) automatic stay on proceedings to collect debt. Reasoning that the state court's judgment included a determination that the automatic stay did not enjoin the state criminal proceeding, the bankruptcy court dismissed the complaint as collaterally estopped by the state judgment. The district court, acting in its appellate capacity, affirmed the dis-missal on the basis of the Rooker-Feldman doctrine, which prohibits direct appellate review of state court decisions by federal courts other than the Supreme Court. 202 F.3d at 1077-78. We reversed. Gruntz, as well as our later decision in Contractors' State License Bd. v. Dunbar (In re Dunbar), 245 F.3d 1058, 1063 (9th Cir. 2001), stand primarily for the proposition that federal courts are not bound by state court modifications of the automatic stay. Gruntz, 202 F.3d at 1077. Gruntz held that the Rooker-Feldman doctrine does not deprive federal courts of jurisdiction over the scope and applicability of the stay. Id. at 1083. Dunbar added that state court modifications of the automatic stay do not preclude federal relitigation of the scope and applicability of the stay under the doctrines of collateral estoppel and res judicata. Dunbar, 245 F.3d at 1060.[8]

---

[7] The Rooker-Feldman doctrine takes its name from Rooker v. Fidelity Trust Co., 263 U.S. 413, 68 L. Ed. 362, 44 S. Ct. 149 (1923), and District of Columbia Court of Appeals v. Feldman, 460 U.S. 462, 75 L. Ed. 2d 206, 103 S. Ct. 1303 (1983). Rooker held that federal statutory jurisdiction over direct appeals from state courts lies exclusively in the Supreme Court and is beyond the original jurisdiction of federal district courts. See 263 U.S. at 415-16. Feldman held that this jurisdictional bar extends to particular claims that are "inextricably intertwined" with those a state court has already decided. See 460 U.S. at 486-87.

[8] Gruntz identified three limited circumstances in which a state judgment could be given preclusive effect in subsequent bankruptcy proceedings in federal court: (1) the state judgment is prepetition; (2) the bankruptcy court affirmatively has authorized the state action, as, for example, by lifting an automatic stay; or (3) the case does not involve a core proceeding that implicates substantive rights under title 11. See Dunbar, 245 F.3d at 1063; Gruntz, 202 F.3d at

Gruntz has broader implications, however, that dictate the outcome here. First, Gruntz holds not only that a federal court may review state court decisions modifying an automatic stay, but also that state courts lack jurisdiction in the first instance to modify the stay. 202 F.3d at 1082-83. Because "bankruptcy court orders are not subject to collateral attack in other courts," "any state court modification of the automatic stay would constitute an unauthorized infringement upon the bankruptcy court's jurisdiction to enforce the stay, "and actions and judicial proceedings taken in violation of the automatic stay are void. 202 F.3d at 1082; see also Gonzales v. Parks, 830 F.2d 1033, 1035-36 (9th Cir. 1987) ("Congress' grant to the federal courts of exclusive jurisdiction over bankruptcy petitions precludes collateral attacks on such petitions in state courts.").

Second, Gruntz bars state court intrusions on all "bankruptcy court orders" (or other "core" bankruptcy proceedings), 202 F.3d at 1082, not just the automatic stay. As we stated in Gruntz, "state courts should not intrude upon the plenary power of the federal courts in administering bankruptcy cases by attempting to modify or extinguish federal court orders such as the automatic stay." Id. at 1088 (emphasis added). Thus, just as "[a] state court does not have the power to modify or dissolve the automatic stay," id. at 1087, a state court also lacks authority to modify or dissolve a discharge order or the § 524 discharge injunction.[9] See Lenke v. Tischler (In re Lenke), 249 B.R. 1, 10 (Bankr. D. Ariz. 2000) (applying Gruntz and holding that state courts lack jurisdiction to modify a bankruptcy court's discharge order); see also Pavelich v. McCormick, Barstow (In re Pavelich), 229 B.R. 777, 782 (B.A.P. 9th Cir. 1999) ("Congress has plenary authority over bankruptcy in a manner that entitles it to preclude state courts from doing anything in derogation of the discharge.").

Our extension of Gruntz to modifications of the discharge order and discharge injunction flows naturally from the policy concerns that informed our decision there. Our decision was animated by our concern that permitting a state court to modify the federal automatic stay "would undermine the principle of a unified federal bankruptcy system, as declared in the Constitution and realized through the Bankruptcy Code." 202 F.3d at 1083. "If state courts were empowered to issue binding judgments modifying the federal injunction created by the

---

1084; cf. Diamond v. Kolcum (In re Diamond), 285 F.3d 822, 2002 WL 500657 (9th Cir. 2002) (affirming bankruptcy court's decision to give preclusive effect to state court judgment where the bankruptcy court lifted the stay as to the creditors' state-court action).

[9] No matter how we characterize it, the state court's action here relates to a core bankruptcy proceeding. Dischargeability of a debt under § 523(a)(6), for instance, is a core bankruptcy proceeding, see, e.g., Sandersville Prod. Credit Ass'n v. Douthit (In re Douthit), 47 B.R. 428, 430-31 (M.D. Ga. 1985); Wurm v. Ridgway (In re Ridgway), 265 B.R. 853, 857 n.1 (Bankr. N.D. Ohio 2001); Mass. Cas. Ins. Co. v. Green (In re Green), 241 B.R. 550, 559 (Bankr. N.D. Ill. 1999); Leathem v. Volkmar (In re Von Volkmar), 218 B.R. 890, 892 (Bankr. N.D. Ill. 1998), over which federal courts possess exclusive jurisdiction. Rein v. Providian Fin. Corp., 270 F.3d 895, 904 (9th Cir. 2001). The adequacy of notice required for automatic discharge under § 523(c)(1) also is related to a core proceeding over which federal courts exercise exclusive jurisdiction. See, e.g., RTC v. McKendry (In re McKendry), 40 F.3d 331, 335 (10th Cir. 1994); Schunck v. Santos (In re Santos), 112 B.R. 1001, 1005 (B.A.P. 9th Cir. 1990). Finally, actions relating to the § 524 discharge injunction also constitute "core" proceedings. See Ins. Co. of N. Am. v. NGC Settlement Trust & Asbestos Claims Mgmt. Corp. (In re Nat'l Gypsum Co.), 118 F.3d 1056, 1064 (5th Cir. 1997); In re Kewanee Boiler Corp., 270 B.R. 912, 918 (Bankr. N.D. Ill. 2002) (action to enforce discharge injunction); Polysat, Inc. v. Union Tank Car Co. (In re Polysat), 152 B.R. 886, 888 (Bankr. E.D. Pa. 1993) (scope of discharge injunction).

automatic stay, creditors would be free to rush into friendly courthouses around the nation to garner favorable relief." Id. at 1083-84. The same concerns arise when California courts purport to modify a discharge order and to grant relief from the bankruptcy court's permanent injunction.

Accordingly, we conclude that the state court lacked authority to adjudicate the adequacy of the notice received by Rutz. By reaching that issue, the state court held that Rutz was bound by neither the discharge order nor the discharge injunction, documents that on their face plainly barred Rutz's action. The state court effectively modified both orders, and in so doing impermissibly infringed upon the bankruptcy court's jurisdiction to enforce its orders. See Gruntz, 202 F.3d at 1082.

In so deciding, we do not hold that a state court is divested of all jurisdiction to construe or determine the applicability of a discharge order when discharge in bankruptcy is raised as a defense to a state cause of action filed in state court by a listed creditor. See Pavelich, 229 B.R. at 783 (holding that "state courts have the power to construe the discharge and determine whether a particular debt is or is not within the discharge" because "discharge in bankruptcy is a recognized defense under state law").[10] It plainly was in the power of the state court to take judicial notice of McGhan's proceedings. In this case, those documents showed that Rutz was a listed creditor, that Rutz's claim was discharged and that Rutz was enjoined from taking any action to collect on the debt. The state court should have given effect to the bankruptcy court's orders. By going further, the state court exceeded its jurisdiction, even if the state court believed that Rutz had valid grounds to object to the orders. As we noted in Gruntz, "'persons subject to an injunctive order issued by a court with jurisdiction are expected to obey that decree until it is modified or reversed [by the issuing court], even if they have proper grounds to object to the order.'" 202 F.3d at 1082 (quoting Celotex Corp. v. Edwards, 514 U.S. 300, 306 (1995)).

Nor do we suggest that a listed creditor such as Rutz is without means to attack a discharge order on grounds of inadequate notice or to repel attempts to enforce the order against him if notice was insufficient. Rather, we hold that only the bankruptcy court could grant such relief. Rutz had several options, such as addressing the validity of the discharge order before proceeding in state court by petitioning the court to reopen the McGhan proceedings or by petitioning the bankruptcy court for leave to file an untimely complaint of nondischargeability. If Rutz was unaware of the existence of the bankruptcy order until after he filed his state action, he could have sought to stay the lawsuit and petitioned the bankruptcy court for relief before proceeding in state court.

---

[10] At least one out-of-circuit bankruptcy court has read Gruntz as barring a state court not only from modifying a discharge order but also from assessing the applicability of a discharge order to the action before it. See Siskin v. Complete Aircraft Services, Inc. (In re Siskin), 258 B.R. 554, 562 (Bankr. E.D.N.Y. 2001) (criticizing and refusing to follow Gruntz because it supposedly blurred the distinction between a state court's valid authority to determine the applicability of an automatic stay to the action before it and the bankruptcy court's exclusive authority to grant relief from the automatic stay). But see Lenke v. Tischler (In re Lenke), 249 B.R. 1, 8 (Bankr. D. Ariz. 2000) ("Gruntz should not be read to mean that states lack jurisdiction to determine the applicability of either the stay or the discharge, but only that they lack jurisdiction to modify either of them[.]"). However narrowly Gruntz is read, the state court's modification of the discharge order runs afoul of that decision.

B. Section 523(a)(3)

In concluding that it possessed jurisdiction to adjudicate the adequacy of Rutz's notice and to modify the discharge order and injunction, the state court erroneously relied on § 523(a)(3). State and federal courts have concurrent jurisdiction over actions brought under § 523(a)(3), which allows debtors to extend the coverage of the discharge order to creditors who were not listed but who had actual notice of the bankruptcy proceedings. See Menk v. Lapaglia (In re Menk), 241 B.R. 896, 904 (B.A.P. 9th Cir. 1999). By its plain language, however, that subsection applies only to creditors "neither listed nor scheduled" during the initial bankruptcy proceedings. See, e.g., Malandra, 206 B.R. 667, 672 (holding that a listed creditor contending that he did not receive notice of the case until after the discharge had issued did not raise a § 523(a)(3) claim because not being listed is a prerequisite to raising an issue under that subsection). Rutz offers no authority to the contrary. There is no dispute that Rutz was listed during McGhan's bankruptcy proceedings, so the state court had no jurisdiction under § 523(a)(3) and Rutz is barred from obtaining relief under that subsection.

The distinction between § 523(a)(3), pertaining to an unlisted creditor, and § 523(c)(1), relating to the adequacy of notice provided to a listed creditor, is not merely technical. A creditor who was not listed in the bankruptcy proceedings is not expressly covered by the discharge order. When a court adjudicates whether that creditor's claim nonetheless should be discharged because the creditor had actual notice of the bankruptcy proceedings in time to file a nondischargeability complaint, the state court is not entertaining a collateral attack on the bankruptcy court's order or infringing on the bankruptcy court's exclusive jurisdiction. That situation is altogether different from the one here, where a state court entertains a listed creditor's argument to void or modify a discharge order or injunction that is facially valid and that expressly covers the creditor's claim. In the latter situation, the jurisdictional and policy concerns discussed in Gruntz are paramount.

II. Abuse of Discretion

Having concluded that the bankruptcy court erroneously assumed that the state court had jurisdiction to modify the discharge order and injunction, we hold that the bankruptcy court abused its discretion by denying McGhan's § 350(b) motion to reopen proceedings. First, Gruntz and Dunbar make clear that neither Rooker-Feldman nor collateral estoppel is applicable here. To the extent that the bankruptcy court was concerned that it would have been collaterally estopped from relitigating an issue determined by the California Superior Court, therefore, that concern was misplaced. See Dunbar, 245 F.3d at 1064 (holding that the bankruptcy court erred in finding itself precluded from reviewing the judgment of a state administrative law judge modifying the automatic stay); see also Pavelich, 229 B.R. at 782 (holding that when a bankruptcy court was presented with a motion to reopen proceedings after a state court had proceeded to hear a claim on a debt discharged by a bankruptcy court order, the bankruptcy court "should not have taken the position that it could not examine the state court judgment"). For the same reason, the BAP erroneously concluded that the bankruptcy court's decision was compelled by the Rooker-Feldman doctrine. See Gruntz, 202 F.3d at 1083 (holding that Rooker-Feldman is not implicated by collateral challenges to core bankruptcy proceedings because Congress vested the federal courts with the final authority to determine such issues). Our concern that the bankruptcy court misconstrued the validity of the state court's jurisdiction and the preclusive effect of the state court's decision requires at the very least that we remand for the bankruptcy court to reconsider its decision. See Dunbar, 245 F.3d at 1064.

Given the posture of this case, however, we go further and hold that the bankruptcy court should have reopened the proceedings. It is well settled that "[a] Congressional grant of exclusive jurisdiction to the federal courts includes the implied power to protect that grant." Gonzales, 830 F.2d at 1036. A bankruptcy court may not decline to invoke this power in the face of a clearly invalid state court action infringing upon the bankruptcy court's exclusive jurisdiction. The bankruptcy court was required to reopen the proceedings to protect its exclusive jurisdiction over the enforcement of its own orders. Cf. id. (holding that the bankruptcy court properly vacates a state court judgment and properly holds that a state court's action was void from the outset when the state court proceeded with an action in violation of an automatic stay).

III. Adequacy of Rutz's Notice

We offer no opinion on the viability of Rutz's claim that he did not receive the notice required by § 523(c)(1). Because the bankruptcy court may confront that issue on remand, however, we note that in In Re Chicago, Rock Island & Pacific R.R. Co., 788 F.2d 1280 (7th Cir. 1986), the Seventh Circuit opined that notice to a minor's mother might be inadequate where a conflict of interest prevents the mother from representing the minor's interests adequately in the bankruptcy proceedings. Id. at 1283. Whether the Seventh Circuit's reasoning should be applied here, and, if so, whether Rutz can establish that a conflict of interest or other grounds prevented his interests from being adequately represented so as to vitiate notice are issues to be determined in the first instance by the bankruptcy court.

CONCLUSION

The judgment of the BAP is reversed. Under the circumstances of this case, the bankruptcy court abused its discretion by denying McGhan's motion to reopen the bankruptcy proceedings. We remand for further proceedings consistent with this opinion.

Notes and Questions

1. Under Federal Rules of Civil Procedure 8(b), bankruptcy discharge is listed as an affirmative defense that must be pleaded. Suppose a discharged defendant does not plead it and loses the case. Can the defendant then return to bankruptcy court and collaterally attack the post-discharge judgment against her?

2. In this case, Rutz was listed as a creditor. His claim was that notification was unfair because his guardian had a conflict of interest with him. Suppose Rutz had been left off the schedule altogether. Would the state court have jurisdiction to rule on the defense of discharge?

3. The McGhan case is an important shift in the law of discharge. See generally Benjamin Marguilis, The Bbankruptcy Hegemon: Section 524(a) and its Effect on State and Federal Comity, 31 CARDOZO L. REV. 905 (2010). Heretofore, it has been assumed that discharges are affirmative defense must be pleaded. If not pleaded they are waived. It remains to be seen whether other circuits will follow suit.

4. D infringes on a patent, files for bankruptcy and gets a discharge. After bankruptcy,

D infringes again. If the plaintiff sues, has the plaintiff violated the discharge injunction? Hazelquist v. Guchi Moochie Tackle Co., 437 F.3d 1178 (Fed. Cir. 2006) (no).

HENDRIX v PAGE (IN RE HENDRIX)

986 F.3d 195 (7th Cir. 1993)

POSNER, J.

This appeal concerns the effect of a discharge in bankruptcy on litigation against the debtor's liability insurer outside of bankruptcy. In re Shondel, 950 F.2d 1301 (7th Cir. 1991), decided well before the appeal briefs were filed yet cited by neither party, dooms the appeal, but we shall not stop with that observation, as there are a few new wrinkles in this case.

On April 6, 1990, an automobile driven by Daniel Hendrix injured Sara Page. Hendrix had liability insurance, but, whether because he feared that his liability to Mrs. Page might exceed his coverage or for some other reason, he and his wife (but we can ignore her) declared bankruptcy under Chapter 7 of the Bankruptcy Code on June 5, 1990. On July 13, Hendrix added to the list of creditors that he had filed in the bankruptcy court the Pages, who at some time (the date is not in the record) between April 6 and July 13 had filed a personal injury suit against Hendrix in an Indiana state court. The Pages, despite being listed and receiving notice, did not file a claim in the bankruptcy proceeding. On September 12, 1990, the bankruptcy court granted Hendrix a discharge from his debts to the listed creditors. A lawyer nominally representing Hendrix, but in fact representing the Atlanta Casualty Company, Hendrix's liability insurer, then filed a motion for summary judgment in the Pages' state court action against Hendrix. The motion was granted, and final judgment in that action was entered in favor of Hendrix on May 22, 1991. None of the motion papers is in the record, or for that matter the order granting summary judgment. But apparently the basis of the order was that any debt that Hendrix might have had to the Pages had been discharged, so that the Pages were barred from trying to collect it by means of a suit in state court.

Shortly afterward, the Pages filed a motion to reopen the bankruptcy proceeding. The motion asked the bankruptcy judge to modify Hendrix's discharge so that they could ask the Indiana state court to reopen their suit for the purpose of proceeding against Hendrix's insurer. The bankruptcy judge granted the relief sought on September 23, 1991, the district judge affirmed, and Hendrix--which is to say Atlanta Casualty Company, for Hendrix has no interest in the matter, his discharge being secure, unmodified, and unchallenged, as far as any effort by the Pages to collect a judgment against him arising from the accident is concerned--appeals. The bankruptcy judge's order terminated a stand-alone proceeding commenced by the filing of the Pages' motion to reopen a closed bankruptcy, and the district judge's order affirming it was therefore a final order appealable to this court under 28 U.S.C. § 158(d).

The discharge had by virtue of 11 U.S.C. § 524(a)(2) the force of an injunction against a suit by any holders of listed debts (such as the Pages) to collect those debts from Hendrix. But as to whether such an injunction extends to a suit only nominally against the debtor because the only relief sought is against his insurer, the cases are pretty nearly unanimous that it does not. In re Shondel, supra, 950 F.2d at 1306-09; Green v. Welsh, 956 F.2d 30 (2d Cir. 1992); In re Jet Florida Systems, Inc., 883 F.2d 970 (11th Cir. 1989) (per curiam); In re Western Real Estate Fund, Inc., 922 F.2d 592, 601 n. 7 (10th Cir. 1990) (per curiam); 3 Collier on Bankruptcy P 524.01 at pp. 524- 16 to 524-17 (Lawrence P. King ed., 15th ed. 1991); see also In re Fernstrom Storage & Van Co., 938 F.2d 731, 733-34 (7th Cir. 1991); contra, In re White Motor Credit, 761 F.2d 270, 274-75 (6th Cir. 1985). The reasoning is that a suit to collect merely the insurance proceeds and not the plaintiff's full damages (should they exceed the insurance coverage) would not create a "personal liability of the debtor," because only the insurance company would be asked to pay anything, and hence such a suit would not infringe the discharge. 11 U.S.C. § 524(a)(2). It would be like a suit against a guarantor of the bankrupt's debt. An alternative line of reasoning proceeds from the statutory reminder that a discharge "does not affect the liability of any other entity on [the debtor's] debt," 11 U.S.C. § 524 (e)--and the insurance company is the other. If this is right, the discharge did not in fact prevent the Pages from proceeding in state court against Hendrix, provided they were seeking only the proceeds of his insurance policy.

The state court, however, evidently thought that the discharge did apply to a suit effectively against Hendrix's insurer only; and we do not understand the Pages--who cite neither Shondel nor any other case which holds that the injunction automatically created by a discharge does not run in favor of the debtor's insurer--to be contesting the Indiana state court's determination; or, more precisely, to be contending that they have a shot at getting the Indiana judge to change his mind, or his judicial superiors to reverse him. If, moreover, that is all that the Pages had wanted--a chance to argue that the discharge never was applicable to their suit because it was a suit to impose liability on the insurance company rather than on the debtor--they wouldn't have had to move in the bankruptcy court. They didn't need the leave of that court to ask a state court judge to construe, or rather reconstrue, the scope of an injunction. It is not as if the bankruptcy court had impressed its own interpretation upon the injunction, so that the Pages would be risking contempt in asking a state court to interpret it differently. They accept that the injunction runs in favor of Atlanta Casualty Company as well as Hendrix but hope that if the bankruptcy court's action in lifting the injunction stands, they can induce the state court to withdraw its judgment, since the judgment was premised on the injunction or, what comes to the same thing, on the state judge's understanding of the injunction's scope.

Although the Pages never filed a claim or an appearance in the bankruptcy proceeding, as persons bound by the injunction that issued automatically upon the discharge of the listed debts they have standing to ask the bankruptcy court to lift it. "A defendant may move to dissolve an injunction if it injuriously affects his interests, although the order is not against him," Hall v. Orlikowski Construction Co., 24 Ill. App. 3d 60, 62, 321 N.E.2d 23, 25 (1974) --and it is against the Pages, because they were on the list of creditors whose claims were discharged. A bankruptcy proceeding is in rem, and its orders can therefore bind nonparties, and actually the Pages were defendants, by virtue of their being listed as creditors, of the discharge, and of the automatic injunction, created by section 524, protecting the discharge. A variety of provisions allow such a defendant to obtain a dissolution or other modification of equitable relief in a bankruptcy matter. 11 U.S.C. §§ 105(a), 350(b), 727(d); Bankr. R. 5010. No doubt it is misleading, though it is the standard parlance, to speak of the Pages' petition as one "to reopen" the bankruptcy proceeding. Discharge brought into existence a perpetual injunction, making the bankruptcy proceeding a continuous, ongoing proceeding as to anyone bound by the injunction. 11 U.S.C.

§§ 524(a)(2), (3); cf. Transgo, Inc. v. AJAC Transmission Parts Corp., 768 F.2d 1001, 1030 (9th Cir. 1985). And although the Bankruptcy Code does not expressly authorize the modification of a discharge, as distinct from its revocation, 11 U.S.C. § 727(d), which is equivalent to the dissolution of the section 524 injunction created by the discharge, any court that issues an injunction can modify it for good cause on the motion of a person adversely affected by it. Transgo, Inc. v. AJAC Transmission Parts Corp., supra, 768 F.2d at 1030; Winterland Concessions Co. v. Trela, 735 F.2d 257, 260 (7th Cir. 1984).

Until recently, however, the standard for modification of injunctions was the "grievous wrong" standard of United States v. Swift & Co., 286 U.S. 106, 119 (1932) (Cardozo, J.). Lower courts, including our own, were restive under this confining standard. See, e.g., Alliance to End Repression v. City of Chicago, 742 F.2d 1007, 1020 (7th Cir. 1984) (en banc); Duran v. Elrod, 760 F.2d 756, 758 (7th Cir. 1985); New York State Ass'n for Retarded Children, Inc. v. Carey, 706 F.2d 956, 970 (2d Cir. 1983) (Friendly, J.). Last year the Supreme Court gave it the coup de grace. Rufo v. Inmates of Suffolk County, 112 S. Ct. 748, 758-60 (1992); see also Board of Education v. Dowell, 498 U.S. 237 (1991). Although, as the Court emphasized, that case, like the lower-court cases that had expressed dissatisfaction with the standard of Swift, involved institutional reform litigation, the "flexible standard" adopted in Rufo (112 S. Ct. at 765) is no less suitable to other types of equitable case. Rufo assimilates the standard for modification to Fed. R. Civ. P. 60(b)(5), which, so far as pertinent to this case, authorizes relief from a judgment whenever "it is no longer equitable that the judgment should have prospective application." So now a court can modify an injunction that it has entered whenever the principles of equity require it do so. Of particular importance to this case, the court can, where equity requires, modify an injunction based on a misunderstanding of the applicable law. 112 S. Ct. at 763. Thus, if the section 524 injunction erroneously enjoined the Pages from proceeding against Atlanta Casualty, the court had the power, on the Pages' motion, to modify the injunction in order to correct the error. In re Shondel, supra, 950 F.2d at 1308-09; In re White Motor Credit, supra, 761 F.2d at 274.

Hendrix (that is to say, Atlanta Casualty) argues that the Pages have no standing to seek to lift the injunction, because if they succeed they will have gained nothing; they still will face an insurmountable obstacle in the form of the final judgment against them in the Indiana state court action. Of course if they really have nothing to gain one wonders why Atlanta Casualty has carried its fight against the motion through three courts. It must in fact believe that the Pages have some chance of getting the Indiana state court to vacate its final judgment, provided the premise of that judgment--the injunction against seeking to collect a discharged debt--is removed. The belief that we are imputing to Atlanta Casualty is realistic and establishes standing, which requires no more than a reasonable probability that the person seeking to maintain a legal action in federal court will gain something tangible, something akin to the kind of interest that the common law protects, if the action is successful. Village of Arlington Heights v. Metropolitan Housing Development Corp., 429 U.S. 252, 264 (1977); Warth v. Seldin, 422 U.S. 490, 504 (1975); Price v. Pierce, 823 F.2d 1114, 1118 (7th Cir. 1987).

The Pages could not, it is true, maintain in any federal court a personal-injury suit against Hendrix or its insurer arising out of the automobile accident in which Mrs. Page was injured--not because they would lack standing but because they would be barred by the final judgment in the state court action.

28 U.S.C. § 1738. That is not what they are trying to do. They are trying to modify an injunction that prevents them, or at least is thought to prevent them, from asking the state court to vacate its judgment. This is not a collateral attack on the state court judgment. The state court retains full power to refuse to vacate its judgment. Therefore the relief given by the bankruptcy judge does not constitute a refusal to accord full faith and credit to the state court judgment, as section 1738 requires. In re Shondel, supra, 950 F.2d at 1308.

We do not understand Atlanta to be arguing that if the bankruptcy judge had the power, as we think he did, to reach the merits of the Pages' motion to lift the injunction to permit them to go back into the Indiana state court, he abused it by granting the motion. The purpose of such an injunction is to protect the debtor from suits to collect debts that have been discharged in bankruptcy. Although the suit in the state court, if allowed to be reopened, will presumably still name Hendrix as the defendant, it is equally the case that the injunction, as modified, will still protect him against any effort by the Pages to collect the judgment in that suit (if they get a judgment) from him, should it exceed Atlanta Casualty's coverage or should Atlanta Casualty become insolvent. The lifting of the injunction to permit the Pages to proceed solely against Hendrix's insurer is thus not inconsistent with the purpose either of the injunction or of the statute by virtue of which it sprang into effect automatically upon Hendrix's discharge. The Pages' lawyer can be faulted for not having moved more swiftly and decisively. He could have asked the state court early on to stay its proceedings pending resolution of the bankruptcy issues, rather than suffering a final judgment to be entered against his clients. He could have asked the bankruptcy court to lift the automatic stay before discharge, and need not have waited for nine months after discharge to move in the bankruptcy court. These were considerations for the bankruptcy judge to weigh in the balance against the Pages' interest in being allowed to proceed on their tort claim without harming the debtor. They were ingredients in the judge's equitable consideration. They do not invalidate his order.

We acknowledge the oddness of an order that purports to relieve a party (the Pages) from the bar of an injunction that under the law of this circuit as set forth in the Shondel decision does not apply to them because they don't seek to impose personal liability on the party in whose favor the injunction runs. But Shondel had not yet been decided when the Pages filed, and the bankruptcy judge granted, their motion to modify the injunction to allow them to proceed against Atlanta. There was thus a danger that the injunction would, unless modified, bar an attempt to reopen the Indiana suit. Another possible bar was res judicata, in the form of collateral estoppel (issue preclusion, as distinct from claim preclusion). The state court judgment dismissing the Pages' suit might prevent them from arguing to the bankruptcy court that the injunction was inapplicable to their suit. Klingman v. Levinson, 831 F.2d 1292, 1295 (7th Cir. 1987); 18 Charles Alan Wright, Arthur R. Miller & Edward H. Cooper, Federal Practice and Procedure §§ 4419, 4425, at pp. 178-80, 253 (1981). If so--if the bankruptcy court was obliged to treat the injunction as having been authoritatively construed by the Indiana court for purposes of further litigation between these parties--still it was free to modify the injunction, as it did.

Even if there had been no good reason to suppose that the original injunction stood athwart the Pages' path--as there would not have been, if Shondel had been decided already and the Indiana court had not ruled against the Pages--a person subject to an injunction always has the right to ask the court that is administering it whether it applies to conduct in which the person proposes to engage. If this looks like a request for an "advisory opinion," it is one that even a federal court can grant, in order to prevent unwitting contempts, Regal Knitwear Co. v. NLRB, 324 U.S. 9, 15 (1945), and frequently does. Perkins v. Lukens Steel Co., 310 U.S. 113, 122 n. 6 (1940); Buckhanon v. Percy, 708 F.2d 1209, 1212 (7th Cir. 1983); Godinez v. Lane, 733 F.2d 1250, 1256 (7th Cir. 1984); Mikel v. Gourley, 951 F.2d 166, 168-69 (8th Cir. 1991); FDIC v. Gordinier, 783 F. Supp. 1181, 1184 (D. Minn. 1992) (a bankruptcy case, like this one). So here, at least if we set to one side the possible effect of the Indiana state court judgment, the bankruptcy court was free to clarify the inexplicit section 524 injunction against the Pages-- inexplicit because it did not indicate whether it applied to a suit effectively against the debtor's liability insurer alone.

Whether or not the original injunction barred the Pages from going against the insurance company--obviously the modified one does not--it is a separate question whether the insurance company is liable to its insured's victim when the insured has been discharged from his debts to that victim. Ordinarily a liability insurance policy obligates the insurance company to pay only those sums that the insured becomes legally obligated to pay as damages. If by virtue of having been discharged from his listed debts the insured has no legal obligation to pay damages, it is not obvious where the insurance company's liability comes from. In a direct-action state, the company's liability would be direct rather than derivative, but Indiana is not such a state. Martin v. Levinson, 409 N.E.2d 1239, 1243 (Ind. App. 1980). However, Indiana law requires insurance policies to contain "a provision that the insolvency or bankruptcy of the . . . insured shall not release the insurance carrier from the payment of damages" for personal injury. Ind. Code § 27-17. We assume, although the parties do not discuss the issue, that this statute entitles the Pages to collect from Atlanta Casualty a damages judgment, should they obtain one, against Hendrix. But that is an issue of state law, not bankruptcy law.

We recur in closing to the parties' failure to cite Shondel. Although the cases are not identical, this appeal could not succeed unless we overruled Shondel. Needless to say, the appellant failed to make any argument for overruling Shondel, for it failed even to cite the case. This omission by the Atlanta Casualty Company (the real appellant) disturbs us because insurance companies are sophisticated enterprises in legal matters, Shondel was an insurance case, and the law firm that handled this appeal for Atlanta is located in this circuit. The Pages' lawyer, a solo practitioner in a nonmetropolitan area, is less seriously at fault for having failed to discover Shondel--and anyway his failure could not have been a case of concealing adverse authority, because Shondel supported his position. At all events, by appealing in the face of dispositive contrary authority without making arguments for overruling it, Atlanta Casualty filed a frivolous appeal.

This conclusion may seem questionable because, given the intrinsic difficulty of the issues presented by the appeal, and the fact that Shondel is the only case on point, the appellant, although it would still have lost, would not have risked sanctions had it urged us to overrule Shondel. But that is true in a great many cases in which sanctions are imposed under Fed. R. App. P. 38 for filing a frivolous appeal. The court does not ask whether the appeal might have been nonfrivolous if presented differently, with arguments and authorities to which the appellant in fact never alluded. If the appeal is blocked by authorities that the appellant ignored, the appellant is sanctioned without inquiry into whether the authorities if acknowledged might have been contested. Brooks v. Allison Division, 874 F.2d 489 (7th Cir. 1989).

There is a further point. Although as we noted in Thompson v. Duke, 940 F.2d 192, 196 n. 2 (7th Cir. 1991), the circuits are divided (and we have not taken sides) on whether a failure to acknowledge binding adverse precedent violates Fed. R. Civ. P. 11, if Atlanta Casualty's counsel knowingly concealed dispositive adverse authority it engaged in professional misconduct. ABA Model Rules of Professional Conduct Rule 3.3(a)(3) (1983). The inference would arise that it had filed the appeal for purposes of delay, which would be an abuse of process and thus provide an additional basis for imposition of sanctions under Fed. R. App. P. 38 ("damages for delay"). A frivolous suit or appeal corresponds, at least approximately, to the tort of malicious prosecution, that is, groundless litigation; a suit or appeal that is not necessarily groundless but was filed for an improper purpose, such as delay, corresponds to-- indeed is an instance of--abuse of process. Hill v. Norfolk & Western Ry., 814 F.2d 1192, 1202 (7th Cir. 1987); Brown v. Federation of State Medical Boards, 830 F.2d 1429, 1436 (7th Cir. 1987); Grip-Pak, Inc. v. Illinois Tool Works, Inc., 694 F.2d 466, 471 (7th Cir. 1982). Both, we hold, are sanctionable under Rule 38. We direct Atlanta Casualty's counsel to submit within 14 days a statement as to why it or its client, or both, should not be sanctioned under Rule 38 for failing to cite the Shondel case to us.

We are not quite done. Rule 46(c) of the appellate rules authorizes us to discipline lawyers who practice before us. In deciding whether a lawyer has engaged in conduct sanctionable under that rule, we have looked not only to the rules of professional conduct but also to Rule 11 of the civil rules, Mays v. Chicago Sun-Times, 865 F.2d 134, 139 (7th Cir. 1989), which makes it sanctionable misconduct for a lawyer to sign a pleading or other paper, including a brief, if he has failed to make a reasonable inquiry into whether his position "is well grounded in fact and is warranted by existing law or a good faith argument for the extension, modification, or reversal of existing law." Reasonable inquiry would have turned up Shondel. The lawyer who signed Atlanta Casualty's briefs in this court is therefore directed to submit a statement within 14 days as to why he should not be sanctioned under Rule 46(c).

Affirmed, with order on sanctions.

Notes

1. Suppose X commits a tort against D. As a result, D has to file for bankruptcy. Because D is ruined, D cannot pay C. D, however, is discharged and does not have to pay C. Can the bankruptcy trustee bring an action against X? Can X argue that D was not damaged because D does not have to pay C? See Bankruptcy Code § 524(e). What is the role of § 524(f) in this? See generally David Gray Carlson, Indemnity, Liability, Insolvency, 25 CARDOZO L. REV. 1951 (2004).

B. DEBTS NOT DISCHARGEABLE UNDER §523(a)

1. Taxes

YOUNG v UNITED STATES

535 U.S. 43 (2002)

SCALIA, J.

A discharge under the Bankruptcy Code does not extinguish certain tax liabilities for which a return was due within three years before the filing of an individual debtor's petition. 11 U.S.C. §§ 523(a)(1)(A), 507(a)(8)(A)(i). We must decide whether this "three-year lookback period" is tolled during the pendency of a prior bankruptcy petition.

I

Petitioners Cornelius and Suzanne Young failed to include payment with their 1992 income tax return, due and filed on October 15, 1993 (petitioners had obtained an extension of the April 15 deadline). About $15,000 was owing. The Internal Revenue Service (IRS) assessed the tax liability on January 3, 1994, and petitioners made modest monthly payments ($40 to $300) from April 1994 until November 1995. On May 1, 1996, they sought protection under Chapter 13 of the Bankruptcy Code in the United States Bankruptcy Court for the District of New Hampshire. The bulk of their tax liability (about $13,000, including accrued interest) remained due. Before a reorganization plan was confirmed, however, the Youngs moved on October 23, 1996, to dismiss their Chapter 13 petition, pursuant to 11 U.S.C. § 1307(b). On March 12, 1997, one day before the Bankruptcy Court dismissed their Chapter 13 petition, the Youngs filed a new petition, this time under Chapter 7. This was a "no asset" petition, meaning that the Youngs had no assets available to satisfy unsecured creditors, including the IRS. A discharge was granted June 17, 1997; the case was closed September 22, 1997.

The IRS subsequently demanded payment of the 1992 tax debt. The Youngs refused and petitioned the Bankruptcy Court to reopen their Chapter 7 case and declare the debt discharged. In their view, the debt fell outside the Bankruptcy Code's "three-year lookback period," §§ 523(a)(1)(A), 507(a)(8)(A)(i), and had therefore been discharged, because it pertained to a tax return due on October 15, 1993, more than three years before their Chapter 7 filing on March 12, 1997. The Bankruptcy Court reopened the case but sided with the IRS. Although the Youngs' 1992 income tax return was due more than three years before they filed their Chapter 7 petition, it was due less than three years before they filed their Chapter 13 petition on May 1, 1996. Holding that the "three-year lookback period" is tolled during the pendency of a prior bankruptcy petition, the Bankruptcy Court concluded that the 1992 tax debt had not been discharged. The District Court for the District of New Hampshire and Court of Appeals for the First Circuit agreed. 233 F.3d 56 (2000). We granted certiorari. 533 U.S. 976 (2001).

II

Section 523(a) of the Bankruptcy Code excepts certain individual debts from discharge, including any tax "of the kind and for the periods specified in section . . . 507(a)(8) of this title, whether or not a claim for such tax was filed or allowed." § 523(a)(1)(A). Section 507(a), in turn, describes the priority of certain claims in the distribution of the debtor's assets. Subsection 507(a)(8)(A)(i) gives eighth priority to "allowed unsecured claims of governmental units, only to the extent that such claims are for-. . . a tax on or measured by income or gross receipts-. . . for a taxable year ending on or before the date of the filing of the petition for which a return, if required, is last due, including extensions, after three years before the date of the filing of the petition . . . ." (Emphasis added.) This is commonly known as the "three-year lookback period." If the IRS has a claim for taxes for which the return was due within three years before the bankruptcy petition was filed, the claim enjoys eighth priority under §

507(a)(8)(A)(i) and is nondischargeable in bankruptcy under § 523(a)(1)(A).

The terms of the lookback period appear to create a loophole: Since the Code does not prohibit back-to-back Chapter 13 and Chapter 7 filings (as long as the debtor did not receive a discharge under Chapter 13, see §§ 727(a)(8),(9)), a debtor can render a tax debt dischargeable by first filing a Chapter 13 petition, then voluntarily dismissing the petition when the lookback period for the debt has lapsed, and finally refiling under Chapter 7. During the pendency of the Chapter 13 petition, the automatic stay of § 362(a) will prevent the IRS from taking steps to collect the unpaid taxes, and if the Chapter 7 petition is filed after the lookback period has expired, the taxes remaining due will be dischargeable. Petitioners took advantage of this loophole, which, they believe, is permitted by the Bankruptcy Code.

We disagree. The three-year lookback period is a limitations period subject to tradi-tional principles of equitable tolling. Since nothing in the Bankruptcy Code precludes equi-table tolling of the lookback period, we believe the courts below properly excluded from the three-year limitation the period during which the Youngs' Chapter 13 petition was pending.

A

The lookback period is a limitations period because it prescribes a period within which certain rights (namely, priority and nondischargeability in bankruptcy) may be enforced. 1 H. Wood, Limitations of Actions § 1, p. 1 (4th D. Moore ed. 1916). Old tax claims-those pertaining to returns due more than three years before the debtor filed the bankruptcy petition-become dischargeable, so that a bankruptcy decree will relieve the debtor of the obligation to pay. The period thus encourages the IRS to protect its rights-by, say, collecting the debt, 26 U.S.C. §§ 6501, 6502 (1994 ed. and Supp. V), or perfecting a tax lien, §§ 6322, 6323(a), (f) (1994 ed.)-before three years have elapsed. If the IRS sleeps on its rights, its claim loses priority and the debt becomes dischargeable. Thus, as petitioners concede, the lookback period serves the same "basic policies [furthered by] all limitations provisions: repose, elimination of stale claims, and certainty about a plaintiff's opportunity for recovery and a defendant's potential liabilities." Rotella v. Wood, 528 U.S. 549, 555 (2000). It is true that, unlike most statutes of limitations, the lookback period bars only some, and not all legal remedies[1] for enforcing the claim (viz., priority and nondischargeability in bankruptcy); that makes it a more limited statute of limitations, but a statute of limitations nonetheless.

Petitioners argue that the lookback period is a substantive component of the Bankruptcy Code, not a procedural limitations period. The lookback period commences on the date the return for the tax debt "is last due," § 507(a)(8)(A)(i), not on the date the IRS discovers or assesses the unpaid tax. Thus, the IRS may have less than three years to protect itself against the risk that a debt will become dischargeable in bankruptcy.

To illustrate, petitioners offer the following variation on this case: Suppose

[1] Equitable remedies may still be available. Traditionally, for example, a mortgagee could sue in equity to foreclose mortgaged property even though the underlying debt was time barred. Hardin v. Boyd, 113 U.S. 756, 765-766 (1885); 2 G. Glenn, Mortgages §§ 141-142, pp. 812-818 (1943); see also Beach v. Ocwen Fed. Bank, 523 U.S. 410, 415-416 (1998) (recoupment is available after a limitations period has lapsed); United States v. Dalm, 494 U.S. 596, 611 (1990) (same).

the Youngs filed their 1992 tax return on October 15, 1993, but had not received (as they received here) an extension of the April 15, 1993, due date. Assume the remaining facts of the case are unchanged: The IRS assessed the tax on January 3, 1994; petitioners filed a Chapter 13 petition on May 1, 1996; that petition was voluntarily dismissed and the Youngs filed a new petition under Chapter 7 on March 12, 1997. In this hypothetical, petitioners argue, their tax debt would have been dischargeable in the first petition under Chapter 13. Over three years would have elapsed between the due date of their return (April 15, 1993) and their Chapter 13 petition (May 1, 1996). But the IRS-which may not have discovered the debt until petitioners filed a return on October 15, 1993-would have enjoyed less than three years to collect the debt or prevent the debt from becoming dischargeable in bankruptcy (by perfecting a tax lien). The Code even contemplates this possibility, petitioners believe. Section 523(a)(1)(B)(ii) renders a tax debt nondischargeable if it arises from an untimely return filed within two years before a bankruptcy petition. Thus, if petitioners had filed their return on April 30, 1994 (more than two years before their Chapter 13 petition), and if the IRS had been unaware of the debt until the return was filed, the IRS would have had only two years to act before the debt became dischargeable in bankruptcy. For these reasons, petitioners believe the lookback period is not a limitations period, but rather a definition of dischargeable taxes.

We disagree. In the sense in which petitioners use the term, all limitations periods are "substantive": They define a subset of claims eligible for certain remedies. And the lookback is not distinctively "substantive" merely because it commences on a date that may precede the date when the IRS discovers its claim. There is nothing unusual about a statute of limitations that commences when the claimant has a complete and present cause of action, whether or not he is aware of it. See 1 C. Corman, Limitation of Actions § 6.1, pp. 370, 378 (1991); 2 Wood, supra, § 276c(1), at 1411. As for petitioners' reliance on § 523(a)(1)(B)(ii), that section proves, at most, that Congress put different limitations periods on different kinds of tax debts. All tax debts falling within the terms of the three-year lookback period are nondischargeable in bankruptcy. §§ 523(a)(1)(A), 507(a)(8)(A)(i). Even if a tax debt falls outside the terms of the lookback period, it is nonetheless nondischargeable if it pertains to an untimely return filed within two years before the bankruptcy petition. § 523(a)(1)(B)(ii). These provisions are complementary; they do not suggest that the lookback period is something other than a limitations period.

B

It is hornbook law that limitations periods are "customarily subject to 'equitable tolling,'" Irwin v. Department of Veterans Affairs, 498 U.S. 89, 95 (1990), unless tolling would be "inconsistent with the text of the relevant statute," United States v. Beggerly, 524 U.S. 38, 48 (1998). See also American Pipe & Constr. Co. v. Utah, 414 U.S. 538, 558-559 (1974); Holmberg v. Armbrecht, 327 U.S. 392, 397 (1946); Bailey v. Glover, 88 U.S. 342 349-350 (1875). Congress must be presumed to draft limitations periods in light of this background principle. Cf. National Private Truck Council, Inc. v. Oklahoma Tax Comm'n, 515 U.S. 582, 589-590 (1995); United States v. Shabani, 513 U.S. 10, 13 (1994). That is doubly true when it is enacting limitations periods to be applied by bankruptcy courts, which are courts of equity and "apply the principles and rules of equity jurisprudence." Pepper v. Litton, 308 U.S. 295, 304 (1939); see also United States

v. Energy Resources Co., 495 U.S. 545, 549 (1990). . . .

Tolling is in our view appropriate regardless of petitioners' intentions when filing back-to-back Chapter 13 and Chapter 7 petitions -- whether the Chapter 13 petition was filed in good faith or solely to run down the lookback period. In either case, the IRS was disabled from protecting its claim during the pendency of the Chapter 13 petition, and this period of disability tolled the three-year lookback period when the Youngs filed their Chapter 7 petition.

C

Petitioners invoke several statutory provisions which they claim display an intent to preclude tolling here. First they point to § 523(b), which, they believe, explicitly permits discharge in a Chapter 7 proceeding of certain debts that were nondischargeable (as this tax debt was) in a prior Chapter 13 proceeding. Petitioners misread the provision. Section 523(b) declares that

> "a debt that was excepted from discharge under subsection (a)(1), (a)(3), or (a)(8) of this section . . . in a prior case concerning the debtor . . . is dischargeable in a case under this title unless, by the terms of subsection (a) of this section, such debt is not dischargeable in the case under this title." (Emphasis added.)

The phrase "excepted from discharge" in this provision is not synonymous (as petitioners would have it) with "nondischargeable." It envisions a prior bankruptcy proceeding that progressed to the discharge stage, from which discharge a particular debt was actually "excepted." It thus has no application to the present case; and even if it did, the very same arguments in favor of tolling that we have found persuasive with regard to § 507 would apply to § 523 as well. One might perhaps have expected an explicit tolling provision in § 523(b) if that subsection applied only to those debts "excepted from discharge" in the earlier proceeding that were subject to the three-year lookback-but in fact it also applies to excepted debts (see § 523(a)(3)) that were subject to no limitation period. And even the need for tolling as to debts that were subject to the three-year lookback is minimal, since a separate provision of the Code, § 727(a)(9), constrains successive discharges under Chapters 13 and 7: Generally speaking, six years must elapse between filing of the two bankruptcy petitions, which would make the need for tolling of the three-year limitation nonexistent. The absence of an explicit tolling provision in § 523 therefore suggests nothing.

Petitioners point to two provisions of the Code, which, in their view, do contain a tolling provision. Its presence there, and its absence in § 507, they argue, displays an intent to preclude equitable tolling of the lookback period. We disagree. Petitioners point first to § 108(c), which reads:

> "Except as provided in section 524 of this title, if applicable nonbankruptcy law . . . fixes a period for commencing or continuing a civil action in a court other than a bankruptcy court on a claim against the debtor . . .,and such period has not expired before the date of the filing of the petition, then such period does not expire until the later of -- (1) the end of such period, including any suspension of such period occurring on or after the commencement of the case; or (2) 30 days after notice of the termination or expiration of the stay . . . with respect to such claim."

Petitioners believe § 108(c)(1) contains a tolling provision. The lower courts have split over this issue, compare, e.g., Rogers v. Corrosion Products, Inc.,

42 F.3d 292, 297 (CA5), cert. denied, 515 U.S. 1160 (1995), with Garbe Iron Works, Inc. v. Priester, 99 Ill. 2d 84, 457 N.E.2d 422, 75 Ill. Dec. 428 (1983); we need not resolve it here. Even assuming petitioners are correct, we would draw no negative inference from the presence of an express tolling provision in § 108(c)(1) and the absence of one in § 507. It would be quite reasonable for Congress to instruct nonbankruptcy courts (including state courts) to toll nonbankruptcy limitations periods (including state-law limitations periods) while, at the same time, assuming that bankruptcy courts will use their inherent equitable powers to toll the federal limitations periods within the Code.

Finally, petitioners point to a tolling provision in § 507(a)(8)(A), the same subsection that sets forth the three-year lookback period. Subsection 507(a)(8)(A) grants eighth priority to tax claims pertaining to returns that were due within the three-year lookback period, § 507(a)(8)(A)(i), and to claims that were assessed within 240 days before the debtor's bankruptcy petition, § 507(a)(8)(A)(ii). Whereas the three-year lookback period contains no express tolling provision, the 240-day lookback period is tolled "any time plus 30 days during which an offer in compromise with respect to such tax that was made within 240 days after such assessment was pending." § 507(a)(8)(A)(ii). Petitioners believe this express tolling provision, appearing in the same subsection as the three-year lookback period, demonstrates a statutory intent not to toll the three-year lookback period.

If anything, § 507(a)(8)(A)(ii) demonstrates that the Bankruptcy Code incorporates traditional equitable principles. An "offer in compromise" is a settlement offer submitted by a debtor. When § 507(a)(8)(A)(ii) was enacted, it was IRS practice-though no statutory provision required it-to stay collection efforts (if the Government's interests would not be jeopardized) during the pendency of an "offer in compromise," 26 CFR § 301.7122-1(d)(2) (1978); M. Saltzman, IRS Practice and Procedure P15.07[1], p. 15-47 (1981).[2] Thus, a court would not have equitably tolled the 240-day lookback period during the pendency of an "offer in compromise," since tolling is inappropriate when a claimant has voluntarily chosen not to protect his rights within the limitations period. See, e.g., Irwin, 498 U.S. at 96. Hence the tolling provision in § 507(a)(8)(A)(ii) supplements rather than displaces principles of equitable tolling.

We conclude that the lookback period of 11 U.S.C. § 507(a)(8)(A)(i) is tolled during the pendency of a prior bankruptcy petition. The judgment of the Court of Appeals for the First Circuit is affirmed.

It is so ordered.

2. Obtaining money by false pretenses

FIELD v MANS
516 U.S. 59 (1995)

SOUTER, J.

The Bankruptcy Code's provisions for discharge stop short of certain debts resulting from "false pretenses, a false representation, or actual fraud." 11 U.S.C. § 523 (a)(2)(A). In this case we consider the level of a creditor's reliance on a fraudulent misrepresentation necessary to place a debt thus beyond release. While the Court of Appeals followed a rule requiring reasonable reliance on the

[2] The Code was amended in 1998 to prohibit collection efforts during the pendency of an offer in compromise. See 26 U.S.C. § 6331(k) (1994 ed., Supp. V).

statement, we hold the standard to be the less demanding one of justifiable reliance and accordingly vacate and remand.

I

In June 1987, petitioners William and Norinne Field sold real estate for $462,500 to a corporation controlled by respondent Philip W. Mans, who supplied $275,000 toward the purchase price and personally guaranteed a promissory note for $187,500 secured by a second mortgage on the property. The mortgage deed had a clause calling for the Fields' consent to any conveyance of the encumbered real estate during the term of the secured indebtedness, failing which the entire unpaid balance on the note would become payable upon a sale unauthorized.

On October 8, 1987, Mans's corporation triggered application of the clause by conveying the property to a newly formed partnership without the Fields' knowledge or consent. The next day, Mans wrote to the Fields asking them not for consent to the conveyance but for a waiver of their rights under the due-on-sale clause, saying that he sought to avoid any claim that the clause might apply to arrangements to add a new principal to his land development organization. The letter failed to mention that Mans had already caused the property to be conveyed. The Fields responded with an offer to waive if Mans paid them $10,500. Mans answered with a lower bid, to pay only $500, and again failed to disclose the conveyance. There were no further written communications.

The ensuing years brought a precipitous drop in real estate prices, and on December 10, 1990, Mans petitioned the United States Bankruptcy Court for the District of New Hampshire for relief under Chapter 11 of the Bankruptcy Code. On the following February 6, the Fields learned of the October 1987 conveyance, which their lawyer had discovered at the registry of deeds. In their subsequent complaint in the bankruptcy proceeding, they argued that some $150,000 had become due upon the 1987 conveyance for which Mans had become liable as guarantor, and that his obligation should be excepted from discharge under § 523(a)(2)(A) of the Bankruptcy Code, a debt resulting from fraud.[1]

The Bankruptcy Court found that Mans's letters constituted false representations on which petitioners had relied to their detriment in extending credit.[2] The court followed Circuit precedent, however, see In re Burgess, 955 F.2d 134 (CA1 1992), in requiring the Fields to make a further showing of reasonable reliance, defined as "what would be reasonable for a prudent man to do under those circumstances." App. 43-44. The court held that a reasonable person would have checked for any conveyance after the exchange of letters, and that the Fields had unreasonably ignored further reason to investigate in 1988, when Mr. Field's boss told him of a third party claiming to be the owner of the

---

[1] Although we observe the distinction between Mans and his corporations, the record before us does not indicate that the parties thought anything should turn on treating them separately. As the case comes to us, Mans is presented as the originator of both debt and misrepresentation.

[2] Here, Mans argues that neither he nor his corporation obtained any extension of credit at the time of the alleged fraud or thereafter. Since this issue was never raised previously and is not fairly subsumed within the question on which we granted certiorari, we do not reach it.

property.[3] Having found the Fields unreasonable in relying without further enquiry on Mans's implicit misrepresentation about the state of the title, the court held Mans's debt dischargeable.

The District Court affirmed, likewise following Circuit precedent in holding that § 523(a)(2)(A) requires reasonable reliance to exempt a debt from discharge, and finding the Bankruptcy Court's judgment supported by adequate indication in the record that the Fields had relied without sufficient reason. The Court of Appeals for the First Circuit affirmed judgment for the Bankruptcy Court's reasons. Judgt. order reported at 36 F.3d 1089 (1994).

We granted certiorari, 514 U.S. 1095 (1995), to resolve a conflict among the Circuits over the level of reliance that § 523(a)(2)(A) requires a creditor to demonstrate.

II

The provisions for discharge of a bankrupt's debts, 11 U.S.C. §§ 727, 1141, 1228, and 1328(b), are subject to exception under 11 U.S.C. § 523(a), which carries 16 subsections setting out categories of nondischargeable debts. Two of these are debts traceable to falsity or fraud or to a materially false financial statement, as set out in § 523(a)(2):

> "(a) A discharge under section 727, 1141, 1228(a), 1228(b), or 1328(b) of this title does not discharge an individual debtor from any debt --
>
> . . . .
>
> "(2) for money, property, services, or an extension, renewal, or refinancing of credit, to the extent obtained by-
>
> "(A) false pretenses, a false representation, or actual fraud, other than a statement respecting the debtor's or an insider's financial condition; [or]
>
> "(B) use of a statement in writing --
>
> "(i) that is materially false;
>
> "(ii) respecting the debtor's or an insider's financial condition;
>
> "(iii) on which the creditor to whom the debtor is liable for such money, property, services, or credit reasonably relied; and
>
> "(iv) that the debtor caused to be made or published with intent to deceive."

These provisions were not innovations in their most recent codification, the Bankruptcy Reform Act of 1978 (Act), Pub. L. 95-598, 92 Stat. 2590, but had obvious antecedents in the Bankruptcy Act of 1898 (1898 Act), as amended, 30 Stat. 544. The precursor to § 523(a)(2)(A) was created when § 17(a)(2) of the 1898 Act was modified by an amendment in 1903, which provided that debts that were "liabilities for obtaining property by false pretenses or false representations" would not be affected by any discharge granted to a bankrupt, who would still be required to pay them. Act of Feb. 5, 1903, ch. 487, 32 Stat. 798. This language inserted in § 17(a)(2) was changed only slightly between 1903 and 1978,[4] at which time the section was recodified as § 523(a)(2)(A) and amended to read as

[3] Mr. Field testified in the Bankruptcy Court proceeding that he asked Mans in 1988 about the report of a conveyance and that Mans indicated he had not conveyed the property, App. 14-15, but Mr. Field later testified that he had not confronted Mans on the issue, id., at 26-27. The Bankruptcy Court made no finding about any such conversation.

[4] The one intervening change to the quoted language was that "obtaining property" became "obtaining money or property." Act of June 22, 1938, 52 Stat. 851.

quoted above. Thus, since 1903 the statutory language at issue here merely progressed from "false pretenses or false representations" to "false pretenses, a false representation, or actual fraud, other than a statement respecting the debtor's or an insider's financial condition."

Section 523(a)(2)(B), however, is the product of more active evolution. The germ of its presently relevant language was also inserted into the 1898 Act by a 1903 amendment, which barred any discharge by a bankrupt who obtained property by use of a materially false statement in writing made for the purpose of obtaining the credit. Act of Feb. 5, 1903, ch. 487, 32 Stat. 797-798. The provision did not explicitly require an intent to deceive or set any level of reliance, but Congress modified its language in 1960 by adding the requirements that the debtor intend to deceive the creditor and that the creditor rely on the false statement, and by limiting its application to false financial statements. Act of July 12, 1960, 74 Stat. 409.[5] In 1978, Congress rewrote the provision as set out above and recodified it as § 523(a)(2)(B). Though the forms of the 1960 and 1978 provisions are quite different, the only distinction relevant here is that the 1978 version added a new element of reasonable reliance.

The sum of all this history is two close statutory companions barring discharge. One applies expressly when the debt follows a transfer of value or extension of credit induced by falsity or fraud (not going to financial condition), the other when the debt follows a transfer or extension induced by a materially false and intentionally deceptive written statement of financial condition upon which the creditor reasonably relied.

III

The question here is what, if any, level of justification a creditor needs to show above mere reliance in fact in order to exempt the debt from discharge under § 523(a)(2)(A). The text that we have just reviewed does not say in so many words. While § 523(a)(2)(A) speaks of debt for value "obtained by . . . false pretenses, a false representation, or actual fraud," it does not define those terms or so much as mention the creditor's reliance as such, let alone the level of reliance required. No one, of course, doubts that some degree of reliance is required to satisfy the element of causation inherent in the phrase "obtained by," but the Government, as amicus curiae (like petitioners in a portion of their brief), submits that the minimum level will do. It argues that when § 523(a)(2)(A) is understood in its statutory context, it requires mere reliance in fact, not reliance

[5] The 1960 amendments also transferred the language on false financial statements by individuals from § 14 (where it barred any discharge) to § 17(a)(2) (where it barred discharge of only the specific debt incurred as a result of the false financial statement). Thus, as of 1960 the relevant portion of § 17(a)(2) provided that discharge would not release a bankrupt from debts that

> "are liabilities for obtaining money or property by false pretenses or false representations, or for obtaining money or property on credit or obtaining an extension or renewal of credit in reliance upon a materially false statement in writing respecting [the bankrupt's] financial condition made or published or caused to be made or published in any manner whatsoever with intent to deceive."

Act of July 12, 1960, Pub. L. 86-621, 74 Stat. 409.

that is reasonable under the circumstances. Both petitioners and the Government note that § 523(a)(2)(B) expressly requires reasonable reliance, while § 523(a)(2)(A) does not. They emphasize that the precursors to §§ 523(a)(2)(A) and (B) lacked any reasonableness requirement, and that Congress added an element of reasonable reliance to § 523(a)(2)(B) in 1978, but not to § 523(a)(2)(A). They contend that the addition to § 523(a)(2)(B) alone supports an inference that, in § 523(a)(2)(A), Congress did not intend to require reasonable reliance, over and above actual reliance. But this argument is unsound.

The argument relies on the apparent negative pregnant, under the rule of construction that an express statutory requirement here, contrasted with statutory silence there, shows an intent to confine the requirement to the specified instance. See Gozlon-Peretz v. United States, 498 U.S. 395, 404 (1991) ("'Where Congress includes particular language in one section of a statute but omits it in another section of the same Act, it is generally presumed that Congress acts intentionally and purposely in the disparate inclusion or exclusion'") (quoting Russello v. United States, 464 U.S. 16, 23 (1983)). Thus the failure of § 523(a)(2)(A) to require the reasonableness of reliance demanded by § 523(a)(2)(B) shows that (A) lacks such a requirement. Without more, the inference might be a helpful one. But there is more here, showing why the negative pregnant argument should not be elevated to the level of interpretive trump card.

First, assuming the argument to be sound, the most it would prove is that the reasonableness standard was not intended. But our job does not end with rejecting reasonableness as the standard. We have to discover the correct standard, and where there are multiple contenders remaining (as there are here), the inference from the negative pregnant does not finish the job.

There is, however, a more fundamental objection to depending on a negative preg-nant argument here, for in the present circumstances there is reason to reject its soundness even as far as it goes. Quite simply, if it proves anything here, it proves too much. If the negative pregnant is the reason that § 523(a)(2)(A) has no reasonableness requirement, then the same reasoning will strip paragraph (A) of any requirement to establish a causal connection between the misrepresentation and the transfer of value or extension of credit, and it will eliminate scienter from the very notion of fraud. Section 523(a)(2)(B) expressly requires not only reasonable reliance but also reliance itself; and not only a representation but also one that is material; and not only one that is material but also one that is meant to deceive. Section 523(a)(2)(A) speaks in the language neither of reliance nor of materiality nor of intentionality. If the contrast is enough to preclude a reasonableness requirement, it will do as well to show that the debtor need not have misrepresented intentionally, the statement need not have been material, and the creditor need not have relied. But common sense would balk.[6] If Congress really had wished to bar discharge to a debtor who made

[6] The fact that § 523(a)(2) uses the term "obtained by" does not avoid this problem, for two reasons. First, "obtained by" applies to both §§ 523(a)(2)(A) and (B); if it supplies the elements of materiality, intent to deceive, and actual reliance it renders § 523(a)(2)(B)'s inclusion of materiality and intent to deceive redundant. More to the point, it renders Congress's addition of the requirements of actual reliance and intent to deceive to the precursor of § 523(a)(2)(B) (§ 17(a)(2) of the 1898 Act) in 1960 nonsensical, since that provision also had the "obtained by" language. Second, it seems impossible to construe "obtained by" as encompassing a requirement of intent to deceive; one can obtain credit by a misrepresentation even if one has no intention of doing so (for example, by unintentionally writing that one has an annual income of $100,000, rather than $10,000, in applying for a loan).

unintentional and wholly immaterial misrepresentations having no effect on a creditor's decision, it could have provided that. It would, however, take a very clear provision to convince anyone of anything so odd, and nothing so odd has ever been apparent to the courts that have previously construed this statute, routinely requiring intent, reliance, and materiality before applying § 523(a)(2)(A). See, e. g., In re Phillips, 804 F.2d 930 (CA6 1986); In re Martin, 963 F.2d 809 (CA5 1992); In re Menna, 16 F.3d 7 (CA1 1994).

The attempt to draw an inference from the inclusion of reasonable reliance in § 523(a)(2)(B), moreover, ignores the significance of a historically persistent textual difference between the substantive terms in §§ 523(a)(2)(A) and (B): the former refer to common-law torts, and the latter do not. The principal phrase in the predecessor of § 523(a)(2)(B) was "obtained property . . . upon a materially false statement in writing," Act of Feb. 5, 1903, ch. 487, 32 Stat. 797; in the current § 523(a)(2)(B) it is value "obtained by . . . use of a statement in writing." Neither phrase is apparently traceable to another context where it might have been construed to include elements that need not be set out separately. If other elements are to be added to "statement in writing," the statutory language must add them (and of course it would need to add them to keep this exception to dischargeability from swallowing most of the rule). The operative terms in § 523(a)(2)(A), on the other hand, "false pretenses, a false representation, or actual fraud," carry the acquired meaning of terms of art. They are common-law terms, and, as we will shortly see in the case of "actual fraud," which concerns us here, they imply elements that the common law has defined them to include. See Durland v. United States, 161 U.S. 306, 312 (1896); James-Dickinson Farm Mortgage Co. v. Harry, 273 U.S. 119, 121 (1927). Congress could have enumerated their elements, but Congress's contrary drafting choice did not deprive them of a significance richer than the bare statement of their terms.

IV

"It is . . . well established that 'where Congress uses terms that have accumulated settled meaning under . . . the common law, a court must infer, unless the statute otherwise dictates, that Congress means to incorporate the established meaning of these terms.'" Community for Creative Non-Violence v. Reid, 490 U.S. 730, 739 (1989) (quoting NLRB v. Amax Coal Co., 453 U.S. 322, 329 (1981)); see also Nationwide Mut. Ins. Co. v. Darden, 503 U.S. 318, 322 (1992). In this case, neither the structure of § 523(a)(2) nor any explicit statement in § 523(a)(2)(A) reveals, let alone dictates, the particular level of reliance required by § 523(a)(2)(A), and there is no reason to doubt Congress's intent to adopt a common-law understanding of the terms it used.

Since the District Court treated Mans's conduct as amounting to fraud, we will look to the concept of "actual fraud" as it was understood in 1978 when that language was added to § 523(a)(2)(A).[7] Then, as now, the most widely accepted

---

[7] Although we do not mean to suggest that the requisite level of reliance would differ if there should be a case of false pretense or representation but not of fraud, there is no need to settle that here.

distillation of the common law of torts[8] was the Restatement (Second) of Torts (1976), published shortly before Congress passed the Act. The section on point dealing with fraudulent misrepresentation states that both actual and "justifiable" reliance are required. Id., § 537. The Restatement expounds upon justifiable reliance by explaining that a person is justified in relying on a representation of fact "although he might have ascertained the falsity of the representation had he made an investigation." Id., § 540. Significantly for our purposes, the illustration is given of a seller of land who says it is free of encumbrances; according to the Restatement, a buyer's reliance on this factual representation is justifiable, even if he could have "walked across the street to the office of the register of deeds in the courthouse" and easily have learned of an unsatisfied mortgage. Id., § 540, Illustration 1. The point is otherwise made in a later section noting that contributory negligence is no bar to recovery because fraudulent misrepresentation is an intentional tort. Here a contrast between a justifiable and reasonable reliance is clear: "Although the plaintiff's reliance on the misrepresentation must be justifiable . . . this does not mean that his conduct must conform to the standard of the reasonable man. Justification is a matter of the qualities and characteristics of the particular plaintiff, and the circumstances of the particular case, rather than of the application of a community standard of conduct to all cases." Id., § 545A, Comment b. Justifiability is not without some limits, however. As a comment to § 541 explains, a person is

> "required to use his senses, and cannot recover if he blindly relies upon a misrepresentation the falsity of which would be patent to him if he had utilized his opportunity to make a cursory examination or investigation. Thus, if one induces another to buy a horse by representing it to be sound, the purchaser cannot recover even though the horse has but one eye, if the horse is shown to the purchaser before he buys it and the slightest inspection would have disclosed the defect. On the other hand, the rule stated in this Section applies only when the recipient of the misrepresentation is capable of appreciating its falsity at the time by the use of his senses. Thus a defect that any experienced horseman would at once recognize at first glance may not be patent to a person who has had no experience with horses." Id., § 541, Comment a.

A missing eye in a "sound" horse is one thing; long teeth in a "young" one, perhaps, another.

Similarly, the edition of Prosser's Law of Torts available in 1978 (as well as its current successor) states that justifiable reliance is the standard applicable to a victim's conduct in cases of alleged misrepresentation and that "it is only where, under the circumstances, the facts should be apparent to one of his knowledge and intelligence from a cursory glance, or he has discovered something which should serve as a warning that he is being deceived, that he is required to make an investigation of his own." W. PROSSER, LAW OF TORTS § 108, p. 718 (4th ed. 1971) (footnotes omitted); accord, W. KEETON, D. DOBBS, R. KEETON, & D. OWEN, PROSSER AND KEETON ON LAW OF TORTS § 108, p. 752 (5th ed. 1984) (Prosser & Keeton). Prosser represents common-law authority as rejecting the reasonable person standard here, stating that "the matter seems to turn upon an individual standard of the plaintiff's own capacity and the

[8] We construe the terms in § 523(a)(2)(A) to incorporate the general common law of torts, the dominant consensus of common-law jurisdictions, rather than the law of any particular State. See Nationwide Mut. Ins. Co. v. Darden, 503 U.S. 318, 323 n. 3 (1992); Community for Creative Non-Violence v. Reid, 490 U.S. 730, 740 (1989).

knowledge which he has, or which may fairly be charged against him from the facts within his observation in the light of his individual case." Prosser, supra, § 108, at 717; accord, Prosser & Keeton § 108, at 751; see also 1 F. HARPER & F. JAMES, LAW OF TORTS § 7.12, pp. 581-583 (1956) (rejecting reasonableness standard in misrepresentation cases in favor of justifiability and stating that "by the distinct tendency of modern cases, the plaintiff is entitled to rely upon representations of fact of such a character as to require some kind of investigation or examination on his part to discover their falsity, and a defendant who has been guilty of conscious misrepresentation can not offer as a defense the plaintiff's failure to make the investigation or examination to verify the same") (footnote omitted); accord, 2 F. HARPER, F. JAMES, & O. GRAY, LAW OF TORTS § 7.12, pp. 455-458 (2d ed. 1986).

These authoritative syntheses surely spoke (and speak today) for the prevailing view of the American common-law courts. Of the 46 States that, as of November 6, 1978 (the day the Act became law), had articulated the required level of reliance in a common-law fraud action, 5 required reasonable reliance, 5 required mere reliance in fact, and 36 required an intermediate level of reliance, most frequently referred to as justifiable reliance. Following our established practice of finding Congress's meaning in the generally shared common law when common-law terms are used without further specification, we hold that § 523(a)(2)(A) requires justifiable, but not reasonable, reliance. See In re Vann, 67 F.3d 277 (CA11 1995); In re Kirsh, 973 F.2d 1454 (CA9 1992).[9]

It should go without saying that our analysis does not relegate all reasoning from a negative pregnant to the rubbish heap, or render the reasonableness of reliance wholly irrelevant under § 523(a)(2)(A). As for the rule of construction, of course it is not illegitimate, but merely limited. The more apparently deliberate the contrast, the stronger the inference, as applied, for example, to contrasting statutory sections originally enacted simultaneously in relevant respects, see Gozlon-Peretz v. United States, 498 U.S. at 404 (noting that a single enactment created provisions with language that differed). Even then, of course, it may go no further than ruling out one of several possible readings as the wrong one. The rule is weakest when it suggests results strangely at odds with other textual pointers, like the common-law language at work in the statute here. See Alaska Airlines, Inc. v. Brock, 480 U.S. 678, 690-691 (1987).

As for the reasonableness of reliance, our reading of the Act does not leave reasonableness irrelevant, for the greater the distance between the reliance claimed and the limits of the reasonable, the greater the doubt about reliance in fact. Naifs may recover, at common law and in bankruptcy, but lots of creditors are not at all naive. The subjectiveness of justifiability cuts both ways, and reasonableness goes to the probability of actual reliance.

V

There remains a fair question that ought to be faced. It makes sense to protect a creditor even if he was not quite reasonable in relying on a fraudulent representation; fraudulence weakens the debtor's claim to consideration. And yet, why should the rule be different when fraud is carried to the point of a written financial statement? Does it not count against our reading of the statute that a

---

[9] [Many footnotes have been omitted from this paragraph-ed.]

debtor who makes a misrepresentation with the formality of a written financial statement may have less to bear than the debtor who commits his fraud by a statement, perhaps oral, about something other than his bank balance? One could answer that the question does have its force, but counter it by returning to the statutory history and asking why Congress failed to place a requirement of reasonable reliance in § 523(a)(2)(A) if it meant all debtors to be in the same boat. But there may be a better answer, tied to the peculiar potential of financial statements to be misused not just by debtors, but by creditors who know their bankruptcy law. The House Report on the Act suggests that Congress wanted to moderate the burden on individuals who submitted false financial statements, not because lies about financial condition are less blameworthy than others, but because the relative equities might be affected by practices of consumer finance companies, which sometimes have encouraged such falsity by their borrowers for the very purpose of insulating their own claims from discharge.[10] The answer softens the ostensible anomaly.

VI

In this case, the Bankruptcy Court applied a reasonable person test entailing a duty to investigate. The court stated that

> "the case law establishes an objective test, and that is what would be reasonable for a prudent man to do under those circumstances. At a minimum, a prudent man, I think, would have asked his attorney, could he transfer it without my consent? And the answer would have to be yes, and then the next question would be, well, let's see if he's done it? And those questions simply were not asked, and I don't think on balance that was reasonable reliance." App. 43-44.

Because the Bankruptcy Court's requirement of reasonableness clearly exceeds the demand of justifiable reliance that we hold to apply under § 523(a)(2)(A), we vacate the judgment and remand the case for proceedings consistent with this opinion.[11]

GINSBURG, J., CONCURRING. I concur in the Court's opinion and write separately to highlight a causation issue still open for determination on remand:

---

[10] "It is a frequent practice for consumer finance companies to take a list from each loan applicant of other loans or debts that the applicant has outstanding. While the consumer finance companies use these statements in evaluating the credit risk, very often the statements are used as a basis for a false financial statement exception to discharge. The forms that the applicant fills out often have too little space for a complete list of debts. Frequently, a loan applicant is instructed by a loan officer to list only a few or only the most important of his debts. Then, at the bottom of the form, the phrase 'I have no other debts' is either printed on the form, or the applicant is instructed to write the phrase in his own handwriting." H. R. Rep. No. 95-595, pp. 130-131 (1977) (footnote omitted).

[11] JUSTICE BREYER would not remand, for essentially two reasons: in substance the Bankruptcy Court applied the right standard, looking to the individual capacity of Mr. Field in testing whether the Fields relied at all; and the Fields do not deserve a remand, having failed to get their own terminology right below and having no real prospect of anything but needless expense even if there is a remand. The first reason takes a bit of kind reading, since the Bankruptcy Judge spoke in terms of an objective standard and expressly found that the Fields had in fact relied, however imprudently. The second may indicate that we would have been justified in denying certiorari, but after taking the case and declaring the correct standard in response to the Fields' argument in this Court, we think they are entitled to decide how Pyrrhic a victory to declare.

Was the debt in question, as the statute expressly requires, "obtained by" the alleged fraud? See 11 U.S.C. § 523 (a)(2)(A); ante, at 3, n. 3. Mans ultimately urges that the promissory note to the Fields is, in any event, a dischargeable debt because it was not "obtained by" the allegedly fraudulent letters Mans's attorney wrote to the Fields' attorney months after the debt was incurred. The Fields maintain that they relied on the letters to their detriment, in effect according Mans an extension of credit instead of invoking the due-on-sale clause.

Mans prevailed on the reliance issue before the bankruptcy, district, and appellate courts on the basis of thengoverning Circuit precedent. See In re Burgess, 955 F.2d 134, 140 (CA1 1992) (creditor required to prove that its reliance was reasonable). With the Circuit law on reliance solidly in his favor, Mans understandably did not advance in the lower courts the argument that the debt was not "obtained by" fraud. When the "reliance must be reasonable" rule solid in the Circuit was challenged in this Court, however, Mans raised the causation point as an alternate justification for the judgment in his favor. See Brief for Respondent 32-33 (argument heading V. reads: "Since the credit here was not 'obtained by' the alleged fraud, petitioners have failed to meet the [causation] requirement of 523(a)(2)(A)"); Tr. of Oral Arg. 43 ("Under the clear language of the statute, there has to be an extension of credit in connection with the fraud. It has to be obtained by the fraud . . . .").

At oral argument, the following exchange between the Court and the Fields' attorney occurred:

> "QUESTION: . . . Suppose the debtor here had simply transferred the property without saying one word to the creditor. . . . Would [the debt] then be dischargeable? There would be no representation at all, just in violation of the agreement the debtor sells the property . . . . Dischargeable, right?
>
> "MR. SEUFERT: While [those are] not the facts of this case, I would agree with you, it would be dischargeable." Id., at 8-9.

It bears consideration whether a debt that would have been dischargeable had the debtor simply transferred the property, in violation of the due-on-sale clause with never a word to the creditor, nonetheless should survive bankruptcy because the debtor wrote to the creditor of the prospect, albeit not the actuality, of the transfer. Because this Court is not positioned to provide a first view on questions of this order, I express no opinion on the appropriate resolution of the unsettled causation ("obtained by") issue.

BREYER, J., DISSENTING. I agree with the Court's holding that "actual fraud" under 11 U.S.C. § 523 (a)(2)(A) incorporates the common-law elements of intentional misrepresentation. I also agree that to recover under a common-law fraud theory, plaintiffs must do more than show that they actually relied upon the defendant's misrepresentation -- they must show that the reliance was "justifiable" in the circumstances, but they need not go so far as to show that a "reasonably prudent" person would have relied upon it similarly. See W. KEETON, D. DOBBS, R. KEETON, & D. OWEN, PROSSER AND KEETON ON LAW OF TORTS § 108, pp. 749-753 (5th ed. 1984) (hereinafter Prosser & Keeton). And, I agree that the Bankruptcy Court used the wrong words when it described the "reliance" standard as "an objective test" that asks "what would be reasonable for a prudent man to do under [the] circumstances." App. 43-44. I disagree, however, with the Court's result in this case.

First, the Bankruptcy Court, while using the wrong words, did the right thing. That court essentially found that in mid-1987, Mr. Field and his wife sold their inn for about $500,000 to Mr. Mans, a developer. To secure the $187,000 that Mans still owed them, the Fields kept a mortgage, which had a term that accelerated the debt should Mans transfer the property to anyone else without their permission. A few months later, Mans wrote to the Fields saying that he wanted to transfer the inn to a development partnership which Mans had formed with a new partner, Mr. De Felice. Mans observed that because the Fields had transferred the inn to a corporation, the stock of which was wholly owned by Mans, Mans could effectively accomplish the transfer to the new partnership by simply conveying the stock of the holding company to the partnership, thereby avoiding the "debt acceleration" clause. But, Mans said, he would prefer to transfer the inn outright, and therefore was seeking their permission to do so without accelerating the debt. The Fields did not give permission. Mans transferred the inn anyway. Nothing more was heard of the matter until 1991, when real estate values fell, Mans went bankrupt, and the Fields brought this law suit in an effort to prevent the $150,000 they were then owed from disappearing in the bankruptcy.

The Bankruptcy Judge found that Mans' mid-1987 letters implied that he had not yet transferred the inn to the partnership as of the time he wrote the letters. But this implication was false, for Mans had transferred the inn at least a few days earlier. Still, the Bankruptcy Court asked whether that false implication had made any difference, i. e., whether the Fields, during the next few years, had relied upon this false implication in not accelerating the debt (and obtaining their money before Mans' bankruptcy). The judge very much doubted any actual reliance. But, in any event, Mr. Field had visited the property fairly regularly to check on the progress of the development, he had seen Mans there fairly often, and he had been told that De Felice had been on the premises, claiming to be "the new owner." And, that being so, the judge held that at some point over the course of the next 3 1/2 years -- during which time Mr. Field was "accepting mortgage payments and looking at drawings and discussing the project with Mans" -- Mr. Field should simply have asked Mans, "What's the deal here? Who owns this thing?" Id., at 42-43. (Or, the Fields could "have simply checked the title in the . . . County Registry of Deeds which Mr. Field has demonstrated he knows very well is up in North Haverhill"). Id., at 42.

To hold this is, in my view, to apply the commentators' "justifiable reliance" standard. The court focused upon the individual circumstances and capacity of the plaintiff, Mr. Field. See Prosser & Keeton § 108, at 751. The court found that Mr. Field should have looked into the matter, not because of any general "duty to investigate," but because, in the particular circumstances, he "discovered something which should serve as a warning that he [was] being deceived." Id., § 108, at 752. That is, the court did not use the "objective" test as an improper search for "contributory negligence" -- i. e., to deny recovery to one also at fault for failing to exercise "the care of a reasonably prudent person for his own protection." Id., § 108, at 750. Rather, the court viewed the failure to investigate, in light of the clear warnings of deception, as a means of testing whether there was "some objective corroboration to plaintiff's claim that he did rely," a primary purpose of the "justifiable reliance" requirement. See id., § 108, at 750-751.

Second, the Bankruptcy Court's use of what turned out to be the wrong words ("reasonable" and "prudent man" rather than "justifiable") is not grounds for reversal, for no one brought the "correct" terminology to the lower courts' attention. The Fields did not argue in the Bankruptcy Court, or in their briefs to the District Court or the Court of Appeals, or in their petition for certiorari, that there was any difference between "reasonable reliance" and "justifiable reliance." To the contrary, the Fields took the view (which the Court now unanimously rejects) that actual reliance alone -- whether or not it meets any objective standard -- is sufficient for recovery. Indeed, it appears that the Fields did not even mention the word "justifiable" below, but, rather, used the term "reasonable" throughout to refer to any kind of objective standard. The first time the word "justifiable" appears in this case seems to be in the Fields' brief on the merits in this Court where they point to the Restatement's use of the term "justifiable," Restatement (Second) of Torts § 540 (1976), and argue that "justifiable reliance does not require that the recipient of misrepresentation investigate the underlying assertion." Brief for Petitioners 20 (emphasis in original). But see Prosser & Keeton § 108, at 752.

Third, the "correct" terminology would not have appeared obvious to a judge, certainly not to a judge who was not a special expert in the common law of misrepresentation. Prior case law was not neat in its use of the terminology. The commentaries do not refer to the old prudent person standard as a "reasonable reliance" standard, but, instead, distinguish between the "justifiable reliance" standard as it has been understood in cases now disapproved, and the "justifiable reliance" standard as it is applied in most modern cases. See id., § 108; 2 F. Harper, F. James, & O. Gray, Law of Torts § 7.12, pp. 455-464 (2d ed. 1986). Indeed, the majority's footnotes distinguish between cases in which a court (1) used a "prudent person" standard or imposed a general duty to investigate, and (2) used a plaintiff-specific standard while disavowing a general duty to investigate. Ante, 516 U.S. at 72-75, nn. 10-12. But, courts in the first category did not always use the words "reasonable reliance" to describe their standard. See, e. g., Horner v. Ahern, 207 Va. 860, 863-864, 153 S.E.2d 216, 219 (1967). Indeed, sometimes they used the word "justifiable." See, e. g., Cudemo v. Al & Lou Construction Co., 54 A.D.2d 995, 996, 387 N.Y.S.2d 929, 930 (1976). Nor did courts in the second category always use the words "justifiable reliance" to describe their standard. See, e. g., Barnes v. Lopez, 25 Ariz. App. 477, 480, 544 P.2d 694, 697 (1976). Indeed, sometimes they used the words "reasonable reliance." See, e. g., Johnson v. Owens, 263 N.C. 754, 758-759, 140 S.E.2d 311, 314 (1965). The relevant historical controversy in the law of fraud has focused not so much on labels as on the nature of the duty to investigate (e. g., whether the duty is applicable normally or only in special, suspicious circumstances) and on the extent to which the law looks to the circumstances and capacities of a particular plaintiff. See Prosser & Keeton § 108. The Bankruptcy Court, as I have just pointed out, followed modern fraud law in both respects.

Fourth, while I understand that sometimes this Court might appropriately announce a legal standard and remand the case to the lower courts for application of the chosen standard, I do not agree that it should do so here. The record below is brief (87 pages of transcript plus exhibits). The Bankruptcy Judge's findings are reasonably clear. And, further litigation is expensive. Mr. Mans is bankrupt, representing himself until this Court appointed a lawyer for him; the Fields are not wealthy and should not be encouraged to pursue what is, in my view, the impossible dream of eventually recovering the $150,000 (minus legal fees). And, the example this Court sets by not looking more closely into the details of the case is not a happy one -- particularly if it suggests that appellate courts can, or should, insist that lower courts use commentator-approved technical terminology when the parties have not argued for its use and when that use seems most unlikely to have made any difference. Doing so simply generates unnecessary appeals, creating additional delay and expense in a system that could use less of both.

For these reasons, I dissent.

Notes and Questions

1. A debtor is discharged from any claim described by subsections (2), (4) or (6) of Bankruptcy Code § 523, unless the creditor comes forward to prove that indeed her claim is described by one of those subsections. Bankruptcy Code § 523(c)(1). Any such claim must be brought within 60 days of the first date set for the meeting of creditors under § 341(a). Federal Rules of Bankruptcy Procedure 4007(c). The debtor has a rather wobbly right to attorneys' fees if the creditor fails. See Bankruptcy Code § 523(d).

2. Did the debtor (or anyone else) obtain money by false pretences in this case? Did the debtor actually make any affirmative misrepresentative at all?

3. Suppose D is a gambling addict. D receives an unsolicited credit card in the mail, with an offer to enter into a contract the mode of acceptance being actual use of the credit card. D uses the card at an ATM machine at a casino, maxes out the card and then loses all the money in the slot machines. The credit card issuer claims the debt is not dischargeable under 11 U.S.C. § 523(a)(2)(A) (credit obtained by false pretenses/representation or actual fraud). Result? AT&T Univ. Card Servs. v. Mercer (In re Mercer), 246 F.3d 391 (5th Cir. 2001) (en banc decision by 10-6 vote).

3. Unscheduled creditors

MASSA v ADDONA (IN RE MASSA)

187 F.3d 292 (2d Cir. 1999)

MINER, J.

Debtor-Appellant Louis Paul Massa appeals from a denial of his motion to hold appellees C. Donald Addona and Rebecca Addona (the "Addonas") and their attorneys in contempt for violating an injunction pursuant to an order granting discharge of Massa's bankruptcy petition and 11 U.S.C. § 524 (a). Massa contends that the appellees had knowledge of his bankruptcy petition through three letters mailed to the Addonas' attorneys and that the Addonas continued their action against Massa in the state court despite Massa's bankruptcy proceeding. The Addonas contend that the state court appropriately exercised concurrent jurisdiction over their action against Massa and that Massa is now precluded from challenging that decision.

For the reasons that follow, we affirm the denial of Massa's motion to hold the appellees in contempt.

BACKGROUND

In April of 1991, the Addonas commenced a civil action against Massa d/b/a Keseca Development Company in the New York State Supreme Court in Ontario County (James R. Harvey, Justice) (the "State Court Action") alleging fraud and false representation in connection with a contract for the development of a commercial real estate complex. On June 19, 1992, the Addonas filed a Note of Issue indicating that the State Court Action was ready for trial.

On July 1, 1992 Massa filed a petition in the United States Bankruptcy Court for the Western District of New York initiating a Chapter 13 bankruptcy proceeding. Six days later, on July 7th, Massa's attorney in the State Court Action sent a letter to Justice Harvey with a copy to the Addonas' attorney, appellee C.

Clark Cannon, stating that "we have been informed that the Defendant, Louis Massa d/b/a Keseca Development Company, has filed a Chapter 13 Bankruptcy in the Western District of New York. Accordingly, this action is now stayed and we request that the Court hold the motion [to proceed with trial] in abeyance pending the disposition of the bankruptcy filing." On July 14, 1992 Massa's attorney in the State Court Action sent another letter to Cannon which stated, in pertinent part,

> I presume that you received a copy of my letter to Judge Harvey dated [July 7, 1992], indicating that Mr. Massa has apparently filed a Chapter 13 bankruptcy. Accordingly, all proceedings before Judge Harvey are stayed.
>
> As indicated in my July 7th letter, we have filed motion papers with the Court, requesting that the Note of Issue be stricken . . . . The motion is being held in abeyance pending Mr. Massa's bankruptcy proceeding. In the event that the Chapter 13 is stricken, and a Chapter 7 is not filed, we will proceed with the motion.

The day before the July 14 letter was sent by his counsel, Massa had filed the schedules and statement required under the Bankruptcy Code (the "Schedules"). See 11 U.S.C. § 521(1). The Schedules did not list the Addonas as creditors or disclose the pending State Court Action. Massa's Chapter 13 proceeding was later converted to a Chapter 11 proceeding, then to a Chapter 7 proceeding in November of 1992 and thereafter administered as an asset case. On March 10, 1993, an Order was entered granting Massa a discharge (the "Discharge Order") and in May of 1997 the case was closed.

Meanwhile, the State Court Action continued. In a letter dated November 18, 1994 and mailed to the Addonas' attorney, Massa's attorney stated, in pertinent part, that "Mr. Massa is in bankruptcy and there is a stay of all proceedings against him; furthermore, he is in a New York State Correctional Facility and, therefore, is unable to attend a trial on November 22, 1994, unless a Court orders the State to produce him." Nevertheless, the State Court Action proceeded. On October 20, 1995, Justice Harvey entered Findings of Fact and Conclusions of Law, finding Massa liable for fraud upon the Addonas' motion for a default judgment and awarding the Addonas damages in the amount of $342,587.97 (the "State Court Judgment").

The Addonas then retained another attorney, appellee Peter J. Craig, to assist them in collecting the State Court Judgment. Craig sought a subpoena compelling Massa's attendance at a post-judgment asset deposition; Massa, however, failed to appear. Craig also sought a levy upon Massa's 1993 Cadillac. In March of 1997, prior to the Sheriff's execution sale of the Cadillac, Massa's attorney filed a Chapter 7 Amended Voluntary Petition and Amended Schedules with the bankruptcy court (the "Amended Schedules"). The Amended Schedules listed the State Court Action and claimed the Cadillac as an asset of Massa's bankruptcy estate.

In May of 1997, by Order to Show Cause and supporting papers, the Addonas moved in the State Court Action for an order adjudging Massa in contempt for his failure to appear at the asset deposition and directing the Sheriff to proceed with the execution sale of the Cadillac. Massa cross-moved to dismiss, arguing that the debt had been discharged in bankruptcy and that the Addonas' claim should be pursued in bankruptcy court. In support of his motion to dismiss, Massa submitted the November 18, 1994 letter, arguing that the Addonas were notified of the bankruptcy proceedings. The Addonas argued that because they were never listed in Massa's Schedules, they did not have an opportunity to file a claim, and therefore, pursuant to Bankruptcy Code § 523(a)(3), their claim had not been discharged by the Discharge Order.

On June 26, 1997 Justice Harvey issued a Decision and Order (the "State Court Deci-sion") determining that, by virtue of § 523(a)(2) and § 523(a)(3) (exceptions to discharge), the Addonas' claim had not been discharged. Massa's subsequent appeal to the Appellate Division of the New York State Supreme Court was dismissed for failure to perfect.

On November 24, 1997 Massa's bankruptcy case was reopened when he filed a motion requesting that the court enter an order enforcing the provisions of the Discharge Order and finding the Addonas, Cannon and Craig in contempt for violation of the Discharge Order and 11 U.S.C. § 524(a) as a consequence of their respective roles in continuing the State Court Action after the Discharge Order was entered. Bankruptcy Judge Ninfo denied Massa's motion and upheld the State Court Decision as having been validly rendered in the exercise of the New York State Supreme Court's concurrent jurisdiction over § 523(a)(3) dischargeability issues. See In re Massa, 217 B.R. 412, 420-21 (Bankr. W.D.N.Y. 1998). Bankruptcy Judge Ninfo also determined that under the Rooker-Feldman doctrine the bankruptcy court lacked jurisdiction to overturn the State Court Decision even if that decision was erroneous as a matter of bankruptcy law. See id. at 421. By Decision and Order dated July 7, 1998, Judge Siragusa of the United States District Court for the Western District of New York affirmed Bankruptcy Judge Ninfo's decision and entered judgment in accordance therewith. This appeal followed. We affirm on grounds somewhat different than those relied upon by the district court.

DISCUSSION

. . . Section 523 of the Bankruptcy Code governs the nondischargeability of debts in a Chapter 7 proceeding. A debt that is scheduled pursuant to § 521(1) and Federal Rules of Bankruptcy Procedure 1007(a) and (b)(1) is discharged unless the debt is excepted from discharge under one of the exceptions set forth in § 523(a). One such exception is a deter-mination, pursuant to 11 U.S.C. § 523(a)(2), that the debt was fraudulently incurred. Ano-ther exception to discharge is if the debt was not scheduled and the creditor lacked notice or actual knowledge of the case. See id. § 523(a)(3). If, however, an unscheduled creditor had actual knowledge of the bankruptcy proceeding and failed to act, the debt would be discharged. See GAC Enterprises, Inc. v. Medaglia (In re Medaglia), 52 F.3d 451, 455 (2d Cir. 1995) (discussing § 523(a)(3)); see also Byrd v. Alton (In re Alton), 837 F.2d 457, 460 (11th Cir. 1988) (per curiam); In re Thompson, 177 B.R. 443, 450 (Bankr. E.D.N.Y. 1995).

The notice requirement is codified at 11 U.S.C. § 342(a), which provides that "there shall be given such notice as is appropriate . . . of an order for relief in a case under this title." Conversion from one chapter to another triggers the requirement that a creditor receive notice. See 11 U.S.C. § 348 (c) ("Section[] 342 . . . applies in a case that has been converted . . . as if the conversion order were the order for relief."); Fed. R. Bankr. P. 1017(d), 2002(f)(2), 9014. The burden of establishing that a creditor has received adequate notice rests with the debtor. See Dependable Ins. Co. v. Horton (In re Horton), 149 B.R. 49, 57 (Bankr. S.D.N.Y. 1992) (Chapter 7).

Massa asserts that § 523(a)(3)(B) and In re Medaglia compel the finding that the debt was discharged because the Addonas had "actual knowledge of the case in time for such timely filing" and the bankruptcy court discharged the Addonas' claim in its March 10, 1993 Discharge Order. However, the Addonas counter that § 523(a)(2) precludes discharge because the debt was fraudulently incurred and because Massa failed to schedule the claim. Thus, the Addonas argue that the state court properly exercised concurrent jurisdiction to exclude the claim from discharge. In support of their argument, the Addonas assert that Justice Harvey never received the July 7, 1992 and July 14, 1992 letters and properly assumed jurisdiction. The Addonas acknowledge that Cannon received the July 7, 1992 and July 14, 1992 letters.

The opportunity for a creditor to participate in bankruptcy proceedings is of obvious importance. See, e.g., Capital Communications Fed. Credit Union v. Boodrow (In re Boodrow), 126 F.3d 43 (2d Cir. 1997), cert. denied, 522 U.S. 1117 (1998). Since Massa failed to schedule the debt owed to the Addonas on his original petition, no official notice of the proceeding was provided. We therefore consider whether knowledge of the proceeding can be derived from the letters sent to the Addonas' attorney. The letters sent by Massa to the Addonas on July 7, 1992, July 14, 1992 and November 18, 1994 were inadequate for the Addonas to acquire actual knowledge of Massa's Chapter 7 bankruptcy proceeding. While official notice from a bankruptcy court is not required, none of the three letters even mentioned the Chapter 7 proceeding that resulted in the Discharge Order.

Although the letters indicated that Massa had filed for bankruptcy, none indicated specifically that Massa had filed a petition pursuant to Chapter 7 or had filed for conversion to Chapter 7. The first letter, dated July 7, 1992, noted that "we have been informed that the Defendant, Louis Massa d/b/a Keseca Development Company, has filed a Chapter 13 Bankruptcy in the Western District of New York." The letter further noted that "[the State Court Action] is now stayed" due to Massa's bankruptcy. The July 14th letter similarly failed to refer to a Chapter 7 proceeding, stating only that Massa "has apparently filed a Chapter 13 bankruptcy." Like the prior letters, the November 18, 1994 letter, while stating that "Massa is in bankruptcy," failed to confer actual knowledge of the Chapter 7 proceeding or the venue for the proceeding.[1]

We look "to the totality of the circumstances" in determining whether a creditor was adequately apprised of the proceeding. Dinova v. Harris (In re Dinova), 212 B.R. 437, 443 (B.A.P. 2d Cir. 1997); see also United States v. Hairopoulos (In re Hairopoulos), 118 F.3d 1240, 1246 (8th Cir. 1997) (notice of Chapter 7 proceeding insufficient to put creditor on inquiry notice of Chapter 13 proceeding); cf. In re Medaglia, 52 F.3d at 453 (letter by creditor's counsel acknowledging debtor's Chapter 7 proceeding sufficient to establish actual knowledge of the creditor); In re Alton, 837 F.2d at 458-59 (notice of the bankruptcy pro-ceeding and of the stay mailed by debtor to the creditor sufficient to establish actual notice). Examining the content of the letters, we conclude that under the totality of the circumstances the letters were insufficient to afford the Addonas actual knowledge of Massa's Chapter 7 bankruptcy. See In re Hairopoulos, 118 F.3d at 1246 (notice of Chapter 7 proceeding insufficient to

[1] In certain instances, a post-discharge claim may entitle a creditor to payment from undistributed assets. See 11 U.S.C. § 726(a)(2)(C); In re Columbia Ribbon & Carbon Mfg. Co., 54 B.R. 714, 721 (Bankr. S.D.N.Y. 1985). In light of our conclusion that the November 18, 1994 letter, which post-dated the discharge, did not provide adequate knowledge, we need not address this issue further.

constitute actual knowledge of Chapter 13 proceeding); cf. Pioneer Inv. Servs. Co. v. Brunswick Assocs. Ltd. Partnership, 507 U.S. 380, 389 (1993) (describing differences between Chapter 7 and Chapter 11); United States Internal Revenue Serv. v. Osborne (In re Osborne), 76 F.3d 306, 310 (9th Cir. 1996) (describing differences between Chapter 13 and Chapter 7). None of the letters apprised of the conversion of Massa's bankruptcy from Chapter 13 to Chapter 11 and finally to Chapter 7. See 11 U.S.C. § 348 (c); Fed. R. Bankr. P. 2002(f)(2). The letters may have been adequate to apprise a creditor of a Chapter 13 bankruptcy; however, knowledge/notice in a Chapter 13 proceeding is insufficient to constitute knowledge/notice if the proceeding is converted to Chapter 7.

Massa's failure to notify the Addonas of the conversion from Chapter 13 to Chapter 7 is important in this case because creditors' responsibilities are completely different under each chapter. Under Chapter 7, the issue of discharge turns upon notice/knowledge and not the scheduling of the debt; under Chapter 13, it turns on scheduling (although notice may be required as well, see In re Hairopoulos, 118 F.3d at 1246). The difference is illustrated in the case of creditors such as the Addonas, who believe that the debt was induced by fraud. If they have knowledge of a Chapter 7 proceeding, they would have to act or would lose their right to collect the debt. Scheduling is irrelevant if they possessed adequate knowledge. See 11 U.S.C. § 523(a)(3). In a Chapter 13 proceeding, however, they need not act to protect their debt.

Here scheduling is critical. If the debt were scheduled in the Chapter 13 proceeding, it could be discharged even if it were grounded in fraud; i.e., the Section 523(a)(2) exception does not apply. See Ravenot v. Rimgale (In re Rimgale), 669 F.2d 426, 428 (7th Cir. 1982); Illinois Dep't of Pub. Aid v. Ellis (In re Ellis), 66 B.R. 821, 824 (N.D. Ill. 1986) ("All other debts provided for in the plan, regardless of whether they would be dischargeable in a Chapter 7 case, are covered by a Chapter 13 discharge. Therefore, the debtor can use Chapter 13 to avoid claims based on fraud, willful and malicious injuries to persons or property, drunk driving injuries, educational loans and the like.") (internal quotation marks omitted); St. Joseph Wholesale Liquor Co. v. Butler (In re Butler), 74 B.R. 106, 108 (W.D. Mo. 1985) (mem.). If the debt were not scheduled (and not provided for in the plan), however, notice/knowledge would be irrelevant. See In re Hairopoulos, 118 F.3d 1240, 1243 (8th Cir. 1997); 8 Lawrence P. King, et. al., Collier on Bankruptcy P 1328.02 (15th ed. rev. 1999). Thus, while the Addonas had knowledge of the Chapter 13 proceeding, they were not required to do anything to preserve their right to collect their unscheduled debt later; their inaction in the context of a Chapter 13 proceeding should not act to their detriment in the context of a Chapter 7 proceeding of which they had no notice or actual knowledge.

In order to permit a creditor to act upon conversion of a proceeding from Chapter 13 to Chapter 7, creditors are afforded additional time periods for filing claims, dischargeability complaints and objections to discharge. See Fed. R. Bankr. P. 1019(2), (3); see, e.g., NCNB Tex. Nat'l Bank v. Jones (In re Jones), 966 F.2d 169, 173 (5th Cir. 1992) (bank filed objection to debtors' discharge after conversion from Chapter 11 to Chapter 7). Notice of the conversion to Chapter 7 would have afforded the Addonas an opportunity to act to protect their claim by asserting that the debt was fraudulently incurred pursuant to § 523(a)(2).

Because the Addonas had neither notice nor actual knowledge of the Chapter 7 proceeding, the debt was never discharged. Accordingly, they were not precluded from continuing the State Court Action, and Massa's motion to hold the Addonas, Craig and Cannon in contempt for violations of the Discharge Order and § 524(a) is without merit.

In accordance with the foregoing, the judgment of the district court is affirmed.

Notes and Questions

1. The Court of Appeals refuses to uphold the judgment of the state court justice on res judicata grounds but instead upholds the justice on the merits. Does this imply anything about the worth of res judicata in discharge cases?

2. Soon after July 7, the Addonas knew of the chapter 13 proceeding. Successful chapter 13 proceedings end up with a confirmed plan. Prior to 2005, these plans typically lasted three years. Bankruptcy Code §1322(d) (prior to 2005). A discharge is awarded at the end of the plan, and the discharge applies to "all debts provided for by the plan or disallowed under section 502. . ." Bankruptcy Code §1328(a). Meanwhile, the automatic stay continues in a chapter 13 case until discharge. Bankruptcy Code § 362(c)

So if the facts that the Addonas believed to be true were in fact true, then the Addonas were in flagrant violation of the automatic stay. Yet because, unbeknownst to them, the case had converted to chapter 7 and culminated in a discharge, the Addonas were not in violation of the discharge injunction, because they had no knowledge of the chapter 7 case.

4. Fraud or defalcation in a fiduciary capacity

BULLOCK v BANKCHAMPAIGN, N.A.

133 S. Ct. 1754 (2013)

BREYER, J.

Section 523(a)(4) of the Federal Bankruptcy Code provides that an individual cannot obtain a bankruptcy discharge from a debt "for fraud or defalcation while acting in a fiduciary capacity, embezzlement, or larceny." 11 U. S. C. §523(a)(4). We here consider the scope of the term "defalcation." We hold that it includes a culpable state of mind requirement akin to that which accompanies application of the other terms in the same statutory phrase. We describe that state of mind as one involving knowledge of, or gross recklessness in respect to, the improper nature of the relevant fiduciary behavior.

I

In 1978, the father of petitioner Randy Bullock established a trust for the benefit of his five children. He made petitioner the (nonprofessional) trustee; and he transferred to the trust a single asset, an insurance policy on his life. 670 F. 3d 1160, 1162 (CA11 2012). The trust instrument permitted the trustee to borrow funds from the insurer against the policy's value (which, in practice, was available at an insurance-company-determined 6% interest rate).

In 1981, petitioner, at his father's request, borrowed money from the trust, paying the funds to his mother who used them to repay a debt to the father's business. In 1984, petitioner again borrowed funds from the trust, this time using the funds to pay for certificates of deposit, which he and his mother used to buy a mill. In 1990, petitioner once again borrowed funds, this time using the money to buy real property for himself and his mother. 670 F. 3d, at 1162. Petitioner saw that all of the borrowed funds were repaid to the trust along with 6% interest.

In 1999, petitioner's brothers sued petitioner in Illinois state court. The state court held that petitioner had committed a breach of fiduciary duty. It explained that petitioner "does not appear to have had a malicious motive in borrowing funds from the trust" but nonetheless "was clearly involved in self-dealing." It ordered petitioner to pay the trust "the benefits he received from his breaches" (along with costs and attorney's fees). The court imposed constructive trusts on petitioner's interests in the mill and the original trust, in order to secure petitioner's payment of its judgment, with respondent BankChampaign serving as trustee for all of the trusts. 670 F. 3d, at 1162. After petitioner tried unsuccessfully to liquidate his interests in the mill and other constructive trust assets to obtain funds to make the court-ordered payment, petitioner filed for bankruptcy in federal court.

BankChampaign opposed petitioner's efforts to obtain a bankruptcy discharge of his state-court-imposed debts to the trust. And the Bankruptcy Court granted summary judgment in the bank's favor. It held that the debts fell within §523(a)(4)'s exception "as a debt for defalcation while acting in a fiduciary capacity." Hence, they were not dischargeable.

The Federal District Court reviewed the Bankruptcy Court's determination. It said that it was "convinced" that BankChampaign was "abusing its position of trust by failing to liquidate the assets," but it nonetheless affirmed the Bankruptcy Court's decision.

In turn, the Court of Appeals affirmed the District Court. It wrote that "defalcation requires a known breach of a fiduciary duty, such that the conduct can be characterized as objectively reckless." 670 F. 3d, at 1166. And it found that petitioner's conduct satisfied this standard.

Petitioner sought certiorari. In effect he has asked us to decide whether the bankruptcy term "defalcation" applies "in the absence of any specific finding of ill intent or evidence of an ultimate loss of trust principal." The lower courts have long disagreed about whether "defalcation" includes a scienter requirement and, if so, what kind of scienter it requires. Compare In re Sherman, 658 F. 3d 1009, 1017 (CA9 2011) ("defalcation" includes "even innocent acts of failure to fully account for money received in trust" (internal quotation marks and brackets omitted)), with In re Uwimana, 274 F. 3d 806, 811 (CA4 2001) (defalcation occurs when "negligence or even an innocent mistake . . . results in misappropriation"), with 670 F. 3d, at 1166 ("defalcation requires . . . conduct [that] can be characterized as objectively reckless"), and with In re Baylis, 313 F. 3d 9, 20 (CA1 2002) ("defalcation requires something close to a showing of extreme recklessness"). In light of that disagreement, we granted the petition.

II A

Congress first included the term "defalcation" as an exception to discharge in a federal bankruptcy statute in 1867. See id., at 17. And legal authorities have disagreed about its meaning almost ever since. Dictionary definitions of "defalcation" are not particularly helpful. On the one hand, a law dictionary in use in 1867 defines the word "defalcation" as "the act of a defaulter," which, in turn, it defines broadly as one "who is deficient in his accounts, or fails in making his accounts correct." 1 J. Bouvier, Law Dictionary 387, 388 (4th ed. 1852). See also 4 Oxford English Dictionary 369 (2d ed. 1989) (quoting an 1846 definition that defines the term as "'a breach of trust by one who has charge or management of money'"). Modern dictionaries contain similarly broad definitional language. Black's Law Dictionary, for example, defines "defalcation" first as "EMBEZZLEMENT," but, second, as "[l]oosely, the failure to meet an obligation;

a nonfraudulent default." Black's Law Dictionary 479 (9th ed. 2009) (hereinafter Black's). See also American Heritage Dictionary 474 (5th ed. 2011) ("To misuse funds; embezzle"); 4 Oxford English Dictionary, supra, at 369 ("monetary deficiency through breach of trust by one who has the management or charge of funds; a fraudulent deficiency in money matters"); Webster's New International Dictionary 686 (2d ed. 1954) ("An abstraction or misappropriation of money by one, esp. an officer or agent, having it in trust"); Webster's Third New International Dictionary 590 (1986) ("misappropriation of money in one's keeping").

On the other hand, an 1842 bankruptcy treatise warns that fiduciaries "are not supposed to commit defalcation in the matter of their trust, without . . . at least such criminal negligence as admits of no excuse." G. Bicknell, Commentary on the Bankrupt Law of 1841, Showing Its Operation and Effect 12 (2d ed. 1842). Modern dictionaries often accompany their broad definitions with illustrative terms such as "embezzle," American Heritage Dictionary, supra, at 474, or "fraudulent deficiency," 4 Oxford English Dictionary, supra, at 369. And the editor of Black's Law Dictionary has written that the term should be read as limited to deficiencies that are "fraudulent" and which are "the fault of someone put in trust of the money." B. Garner, Modern American Usage 232 (3d ed. 2009) (emphasis added).

Similarly, courts of appeals have long disagreed about the mental state that must accompany the bankruptcy-related definition of "defalcation." Many years ago Judge Augustus Hand wrote that "the misappropriation must be due to a known breach of the duty, and not to mere negligence or mistake." In re Bernard, 87 F. 2d 705, 707 (CA2 1937). But Judge Learned Hand suggested that the term "may have included innocent defaults." Central Hanover Bank & Trust Co. v. Herbst, 93 F. 2d 510, 511 (CA2 1937) (emphasis added). A more modern treatise on trusts ends its discussion of the subject with a question mark. 4 A. Scott, W. Fratcher, & M. Ascher, Scott and Ascher on Trusts §24.26 p. 1797 (5th ed. 2007).

In resolving these differences, we note that this longstanding disagreement concerns state of mind, not whether "defalcation" can cover a trustee's failure (as here) to make a trust more than whole. We consequently shall assume without deciding that the statutory term is broad enough to cover the latter type of conduct and answer only the "state of mind" question.

B 1

We base our approach and our answer upon one of this Court's precedents. In 1878, this Court interpreted the related statutory term "fraud" in the portion of the Bankruptcy Code laying out exceptions to discharge. Justice Harlan wrote for the Court:

> "[D]ebts created by 'fraud' are associated directly with debts created by 'embezzlement.' Such association justifies, if it does not imperatively require, the conclusion that the 'fraud' referred to in that section means positive fraud, or fraud in fact, involving moral turpitude or intentional wrong, as does embezzlement; and not implied fraud, or fraud in law, which may exist without the imputation of bad faith or immorality." Neal v. Clark, 95 U. S. 704, 709, 24 L. Ed. 586 (1878).

We believe that the statutory term "defalcation" should be treated similarly.

Thus, where the conduct at issue does not involve bad faith, moral turpitude, or other immoral conduct, the term requires an intentional wrong. We include as intentional not only conduct that the fiduciary knows is improper but also reckless conduct of the kind that the criminal law often treats as the equivalent. Thus, we include reckless conduct of the kind set forth in the Model Penal Code. Where actual knowledge of wrongdoing is lacking, we consider conduct as equivalent if the fiduciary "consciously disregards" (or is willfully blind to) "a substantial and unjustifiable risk" that his conduct will turn out to violate a fiduciary duty. ALI, Model Penal Code §2.02(2)(c), p. 226 (1985). See id., §2.02 Comment 9, at 248 (explaining that the Model Penal Code's definition of "knowledge" was designed to include "'wilful blindness'"). That risk "must be of such a nature and degree that, considering the nature and purpose of the actor's conduct and the circumstances known to him, its disregard involves a gross deviation from the standard of conduct that a law-abiding person would observe in the actor's situation." Id., §2.02(2)(c), at 226 (emphasis added). Cf. Ernst & Ernst v. Hochfelder, 425 U. S. 185, 194, n. 12 (1976) (defining scienter for securities law purposes as "a mental state embracing intent to deceive, manipulate, or defraud").

Several considerations lead us to interpret the statutory term "defalcation" in this way. First, as Justice Harlan pointed out in Neal, statutory context strongly favors this interpretation. Applying the canon of interpretation noscitur a sociis, the Court there looked to fraud's linguistic neighbor, "embezzlement." It found that both terms refer to different forms of generally similar conduct. It wrote that both are "'ejusdem generis,'" of the same kind, and that both are "'referable to the same subject-matter.'" 95 U. S., at 709. Moreover, embezzlement requires a showing of wrongful intent. Ibid. (noting that embezzlement "involv[es] moral turpitude or intentional wrong"). See Moore v. United States, 160 U. S. 268, 269-270 (1895) (describing embezzlement and larceny as requiring "felonious intent"). See also, e.g., W. LaFave, Criminal Law §19.6(a), p. 995 (5th ed. 2010) ("intent to deprive" is part of embezzlement). Hence, the Court concluded, "fraud" must require an equivalent showing. Neal, supra, at 709. Neal has been the law for more than a century. And here, the additional neighbors ("larceny" and, as defined in Neal, "fraud") mean that the canon noscitur a sociis argues even more strongly for similarly interpreting the similar statutory term "defalcation."

Second, this interpretation does not make the word identical to its statutory neighbors. See Babbitt v. Sweet Home Chapter of Communities for a Great Or., 515 U. S. 687, 698 (1995) (noting "[a] reluctance to treat statutory terms as surplusage"). As commonly used, "embezzlement" requires conversion, and "larceny" requires taking and carrying away another's property. See LaFave, Criminal Law §§19.2, 19.5 (larceny); id., §19.6 (embezzlement). "Fraud" typically requires a false statement or omission. See id., §19.7 (discussing fraud in the context of false pretenses). "Defalcation," as commonly used (hence as Congress might have understood it), can encompass a breach of fiduciary obligation that involves neither conversion, nor taking and carrying away another's property, nor falsity. Black's 479. See, e.g., In re Frankel, 77 B. R. 401 (Bkrtcy. Ct. WDNY 1987) (finding a breach of fiduciary duty and defalcation based on an unreasonable sale of assets).

Nor are embezzlement, larceny, and fiduciary fraud simply special cases of defalcation as so defined. The statutory provision makes clear that the first two terms apply outside of the fiduciary context; and "defalcation," unlike "fraud," may be used to refer to nonfraudulent breaches of fiduciary duty. Black's 479.

Third, the interpretation is consistent with the long-standing principle that "exceptions to discharge 'should be confined to those plainly expressed.'" Kawaauhau v. Geiger, 523 U. S. 57, 62 (1998) (quoting Gleason v. Thaw, 236 U. S. 558, 562 (1915)). See Local Loan Co. v. Hunt, 292 U. S. 234, 244 (1934); Neal , supra, at 709. It is also consistent with a set of statutory exceptions that Congress normally confines to circumstances where strong, special policy considerations, such as the presence of fault, argue for preserving the debt, thereby benefiting, for example, a typically more honest creditor. See, e.g., 11 U. S. C. §§523(a)(2)(A), (a)(2)(B), (a)(6), (a)(9) (fault). See also, e.g., §§523(a)(1), (a)(7), (a)(14), (a)(14A) (taxes); §523(a)(8) (educational loans); §523(a)(15) (spousal and child support). In the absence of fault, it is difficult to find strong policy reasons favoring a broader exception here, at least in respect to those whom a scienter requirement will most likely help, namely nonprofessional trustees, perhaps administering small family trusts potentially immersed in intrafamily arguments that are difficult to evaluate in terms of comparative fault.

Fourth, as far as the briefs before us reveal, at least some Circuits have interpreted the statute similarly for many years without administrative, or other practical, difficulties. Baylis, 313 F. 3d 9. See also In re Hyman, 502 F. 3d 61, 69 (CA2 2007) ("This [scienter] standard . . . also has the virtue of ease of application since the courts and litigants have reference to a robust body of securities law examining what these terms mean").

Finally, it is important to have a uniform interpretation of federal law, the choices are limited, and neither the parties nor the Government has presented us with strong considerations favoring a different interpretation. In addition to those we have already discussed, the Government has pointed to the fact that in 1970 Congress rewrote the statute, eliminating the word "misappropriation" and placing the term "defalcation" (previously in a different exemption provision) alongside its present three neighbors. See Brief for United States as Amicus Curiae 16-17. The Government believes that these changes support reading "defalcation" without a scienter requirement. But one might argue, with equal plausibility, that the changes reflect a decision to make certain that courts would read in similar ways "defalcation," "fraud," "embezzlement," and "larceny." In fact, we believe the 1970 changes are inconclusive.

III

In this case the Court of Appeals applied a standard of "objectiv[e] reckless[ness]" to facts presented at summary judgment. 670 F. 3d, at 1166. We consequently remand the case to permit the court to determine whether further proceedings are needed and, if so, to apply the heightened standard that we have set forth. For these reasons we vacate the judgment of the Court of Appeals and remand the case for further proceedings consistent with this opinion.

5. Intentional torts

TEXAS v WALKER
142 F.3d 813 (5th Cir. 1998)

EDITH H. JONES, J.

This case presents a straightforward employment and contract dispute mired in a procedural thicket. Our task is to untangle the thicket, although, unhappily, we cannot finally resolve the merits. We conclude, first, that the case was correctly removed by University President Low, a counterclaim defendant newly-joined on a "separate and independent claim" for purposes of 28 U.S.C. § 1441 (c). Second, the court did not err in shielding the counterclaim defendants from Walker's § 1983 claims on qualified immunity grounds. Third, Walker's debt to the state for fees he owed before he filed for bankruptcy relief is dischargeable post-Seminole, although whether it is nondischargeable under 11 U.S.C. § 523(a)(6) is a question left to be addressed on remand.

I. Background

Dr. Walker was a heart surgeon and a tenured faculty member at the University of Texas Health Science Center at Houston ("UTHSC"). As a condition of his employment, Walker joined the Medical Services, Research, and Development Plan ("MSRDP") by executing the standard MSRDP contract in 1980. The MSRDP contract required Walker to remit all professional fees he earned to the University of Texas ("University"). The MSRDP's by-laws define professional fees in part as fees for all court appearances, depositions, or legal consultations. During the period of his employment at UTHSC, Walker received substantial fees for court appearances, depositions, and legal consultations, but he never remitted any of them to the University. When Walker's noncompliance with the MSRDP came to the attention of the University, it investigated Walker's and other faculty members' personal retention of professional fees. Walker and the other faculty members denied that they retained fees in violation of the MSRDP. After attempts to settle the resulting contractual disagreement failed, Walker was terminated by the Board of Regents of the University of Texas System in August 1994.

Prior to his termination, Walker filed for bankruptcy relief under Chapter 7 on September 1, 1992. His debts were discharged by the bankruptcy court on January 19, 1993. The University was not identified as a creditor in Walker's no-asset bankruptcy filing, and it did not file a proof of claim.

In February 1995, the State of Texas, by and through the Board of Regents of the University of Texas System and UTHSC ("State"), filed suit against Walker in state court. The State alleged conversion and breach of contract and sought an accounting of the fees retained by Walker. Walker counterclaimed against the State, made additional claims against the Regents in their individual capacities ("Regents"), and impleaded as an additional defendant UTHSC's president, M. David Low, in both his official and individual capacities. Walker alleged state tort and breach of contract claims, as well as substantive due process and equal protection claims pursuant to 42 U.S.C. § 1983, all of which were related to his allegedly improper termination.

The counter-defendants removed this case to federal court pursuant to 28 U.S.C. § 1441(c). The State and Walker subsequently filed motions for summary judgment. The district court granted partial summary judgment to the State, the Regents, and Low, dismissing Walker's federal § 1983 claims with prejudice based on sovereign and qualified immunity. The district court also granted partial summary judgment to Walker, holding that the fees Walker retained prior to his filing bankruptcy on September 1, 1992, were discharged. The district court remanded to state court Walker's state-law claims against the State, the Regents, and Low, as well as the State's claims against Walker for fees earned after September 1, 1992.

Walker now appeals the district court's grant of summary judgment to the

Regents and Low based on qualified immunity. The State appeals the district court's grant of summary judgment to Walker based on discharge in bankruptcy for Walker's fees earned pre-bankruptcy. . . .

IV. Discharge in Bankruptcy

The State contends that the district court erred in holding that Walker's debt to the University for professional fees earned prior to September 1, 1992, was discharged. The State makes two arguments: (1) the Eleventh Amendment barred the bankruptcy court from discharging Walker's debt to the State; and (2) Walker's debt was nondischargeable under 11 U.S.C. § 523(a)(6) because it was a "willful and malicious injury" against the State. We hold, first, that the Eleventh Amendment did not preclude the discharge of Walker's debt to the State, and second, that there exists a fact issue regarding whether Walker's debt was nondischargeable under § 523(a)(6).

A. The Eleventh Amendment and Bankruptcy Discharge

Walker's bankruptcy filing did not list the State as a creditor, and the State did not file a bankruptcy proof of claim. In fact, the State did not participate in any manner in Walker's bankruptcy case. Subsequently, in this entirely separate proceeding, the State sued Walker for conversion and breach of contract. Walker asserted the affirmative defense that his debt to the State was discharged in bankruptcy. The district court agreed with Walker, insofar as his debt to the State consists of professional fees earned prior to Walker's bankruptcy.

Consequently, the precise issue here is whether the Eleventh Amendment prevents the discharge of a debt owed to a state in a bankruptcy proceeding in which the state does not participate in any fashion. In deciding that it does not, we mean only that the discharge may be raised as a defense to the state's suit on the debt. . . .

B. The Willful and Malicious Injury Exception to Discharge

The final issue is the applicability of § 523(a)(6) to Walker's acts in breaching his contract and failing to account to UTHSC for his outside earnings.

Section 523(a)(6) bars the discharge of a debt "for willful and malicious injury by the debtor to another entity or to the property of another entity." 11 U.S.C. § 523(a)(6). A "will-ful and malicious injury" results from an act done with the actual intent to cause injury, not from an act done intentionally that causes injury. See Kawaauhau v. Geiger, 118 S. Ct. 974, 977-78 (1998). In other words, "for willfulness and malice to prevent discharge under § 523(a)(6), the debtor must have intended the actual injury that resulted." In re Delaney, 97 F.3d 800, 802 (5th Cir. 1996). "Debts arising from recklessly or negligently inflicted injuries do not fall within the compass of § 523(a)(6)." Kawaauhau, 118 S. Ct. at 978. "Intent to injure may be established by a showing that the debtor intentionally took action that neces-sarily caused, or was substantially certain to cause, the injury." In re Delaney, 97 F.3d at 802.

Neither a claim for breach of contract nor the tort of conversion necessarily involves an intentional injury. See Kawaauhau, 118 S. Ct. at 977 (negligence and breach of contract); National Union Fire Ins. Co. v. Care Flight Air Ambulance Serv., Inc., 18 F.3d 323, 325 (5th Cir. 1994) (conversion); Moody

v. Smith, 899 F.2d 383, 385 (5th Cir. 1990) (conversion). The act of conversion, however, can result in a " willful and malicious injury." See McIntyre v. Kavanaugh, 242 U.S. 138 (1916); see also Kawaauhau, 118 S. Ct. at 978 (reaffirming the holding of McIntyre). In addition, under Texas law, a claim for breach of contract and the tort of conversion may arise from the same set of facts. See Care Flight Air Ambulance Serv., 18 F.3d at 326.

Walker admits that he acted intentionally when he kept the professional fees he earned while a UTHSC faculty member. Consequently, the issue before this court is whether it is appropriate to grant Walker judgment as a matter of law that his pre-bankruptcy debt to the University is discharged and to conclude that § 523(a)(6) is inapplicable because the injury suffered by the State allegedly was not intended by Walker (i.e., was not " willful and malicious ").

The district court found that Walker's retention of his professional fees was an "innocent and technical" act rather than a " willful and malicious injury." See Davis v. Aetna Acceptance Co., 293 U.S. 328 (1934) (Cardozo, J.) ("[A] willful and malicious injury does not follow as of course from every act of conversion, without reference to the circumstances. There may be a conversion which is innocent or technical, an unauthorized assumption of dominion without willfulness or malice."); see also Kawaauhau, 118 S. Ct. at 978 (reaffirming the holding of Davis). For the following reasons, we reverse the district court's grant of judgment as a matter of law to Walker on the issue of § 523(a)(6) nondischargeability. An issue of fact exists regarding whether Walker was aware of his obligations to the University under the MSRDP and nonetheless knowingly kept his professional fees with the intent of depriving the University of money owed to it.

Walker signed his MSRDP contract in 1980. The MSRDP contract expressly states that all fees received by a faculty member for "professional services" are to be assigned to the University. The MSRDP's by-laws expressly state that "professional fees " include fees for all "court appearances, depositions, or legal consultations." The MSRDP contract and by-law language is crystal clear, and all MSRDP participants were sent a memorandum in November 1990 reminding them that " fees for all court appearances, depositions and legal consultations (including expert witness fees) shall be deposited in the departmental MSRDP account." Walker claims that he did not receive this memorandum and that he did not read the MSRDP by-laws until 1993, months after his September 1992 bankruptcy filing. He also testified that the general belief among UTHSC faculty members was that professional fees earned for legal consulting need not be remitted to the University. The UTHSC faculty tribunal that reviewed Walker's case as part of UTHSC's grievance procedures found that there was a lack of understanding among faculty members about the MSRDP's requirements. Based upon these conflicting facts alone, what Walker knew regarding his obligations under the MSRDP and when he knew it are disputed. If a factfinder were to decide that Walker knew of his obligations under the MSRDP contract and its by-laws, either at the time he signed the contract or received the November 1990 memorandum, then it might also find that Walker knowingly retained his professional fees in violation of the MSRDP, an act which he knew would necessarily cause the University's injury. This, in turn, could result in a finding of " willful and malicious injury." Such factual issues must be submitted to a trier of fact in order to determine if Walker's debt was nondischargeable under § 523(a)(6).

V. Conclusion

For the foregoing reasons, we affirm the district court's judgment upholding the Regents' and Low's qualified immunity, and we reverse the district court's judgment regarding Walker's discharge in bankruptcy.

Notes and Questions

1. Why didn't Bankruptcy Code §523(c)(1) save Dr. Walker?

6. Student loans

EDUCATIONAL CREDIT MANAGEMENT CORP. v MASON (IN RE MASON)

464 F.3d 878 (9th Cir. 2006)

A. WALLACE TASHIMA, J.

Educational Credit Management Corporation ("ECMC") appeals from the decision of the Bankruptcy Appellate Panel ("BAP"), which affirmed the bankruptcy court's partial discharge of government-insured student loans held by Debtor-Appellee Keith Mason ("Mason"). The bankruptcy court held that full repayment of the loans would cause Mason an undue hardship within the meaning of 11 U.S.C. § 523(a)(8). It therefore discharged all amounts that Mason owed to ECMC in excess of $32,400.[1] [W]e reverse.

BACKGROUND

At the time of the bankruptcy adversary proceeding, Mason was 33 years old, single, in good physical health, and had no dependents. Mason is well-educated, having earned an under-graduate degree in philosophy from Boise State University in 1995, and a law degree from Gonzaga University in 1999. Mason financed his education by acquiring federally-insured student loans from various lenders totaling approximately $193,000 in principal and accrued interest. At issue in this proceeding is approximately $100,000 owed to ECMC in its capacity as successor-in-interest to Northwest Education Loan Association.[2]

Despite his education, Mason has had difficulty putting his education to use because of a learning disability that has affected his ability to concentrate, focus on details, read, and write. Mason's mother testified that he was diagnosed with the learning disability in the third grade, and that she initially thought that he would be unable to complete high school. Mason did, however, finish high school, and then served in the Army and National Guard for eight years. Following his service, Mason enrolled at Boise State, and earned a philosophy degree in 1995. After college, Mason took the Law School Admission Test and applied to law school. Despite his low test scores and GPA, Mason was accepted at Gonzaga University Law School. Although Mason initially struggled in law school, the University provided for special testing accommodations, and Mason earned his law degree in 1999.

---

[1] Mason owed ECMC approximately $100,000.

[2] The record indicates that Mason has entered into a repayment plan with another lender, Help Services Group, Inc., in order to repay a separate $65,000 student loan obligation.

In December 1999, Mason began working for MicronPC in Boise as a "process analyst" earning $26,000 per year. Mason took the position with the hope of ultimately joining MicronPC's legal department. In 2000, Mason took the Idaho bar examination, but failed. In May 2001, Mason became a "government contracts technician" at MicronPC, earning $14.00 per hour, but was laid off in January 2002. After receiving unemployment benefits for a few months, Mason began working as an independent contractor in April 2002, installing home siding for Diamond Construction.

The bankruptcy court found that Mason is currently earning between $1,000 and $1,200 per month as a part-time contractor for Diamond Construction, and that his monthly expenses average between $1,300 and $1,340. Mason has no fixed schedule and works on an "as needed basis," which allows Mason to apply for other jobs and attend interviews. Mason has worked with an employment service counselor, and considered a variety of jobs, but has had poor results. Based on his experience, Mason has testified that he does not expect his law degree will improve his chances of securing employment. While Mason has a commercial truck driver's license, he has been unable, or unwilling, to work as a truck driver.

Mason filed a petition for relief under Chapter 7 of the Bankruptcy Code on January 16, 2003. Mason owed a total of $209,070.91 in unsecured, nonpriority claims, the majority of which were for student loan debts. Mason sought discharge of his student loan obligations pursuant to 11 U.S.C. § 523(a)(8). Applying Brunner v. New York State Higher Education Services Corp. (In re Brunner), 831 F.2d 395, 396 (2d Cir. 1987), and Saxman v. Education Credit Management Corp. (In re Saxman), 325 F.3d 1168, 1174-75 (9th Cir. 2003), the bankruptcy court partially discharged Mason's debt owed to ECMC, to the extent it exceeded $32,400. The BAP affirmed, and ECMC now appeals. . . .

DISCUSSION

An educational loan is dischargeable in bankruptcy if "excepting such debt from discharge . . . would impose an undue hardship on the debtor and the debtor's dependents." 11 U.S.C. § 523(a)(8). To determine if excepting student debt from discharge will impose an undue hardship, we apply the three-part test first enunciated in In re Brunner, 831 F.2d at 396. See United Student Aid Funds, Inc. v. Pena (In re Pena), 155 F.3d 1108, 1112 (9th Cir. 1998) (adopting the Brunner test). Under the Brunner test, the debtor must prove that: (1) he cannot maintain, based on current income and expenses, a "minimal" standard of living for himself and his dependents if required to repay the loans; (2) additional circumstances exist indicating that this state of affairs is likely to persist for a significant portion of the repayment period; and (3) the debtor has made good faith efforts to repay the loans. Id. at 1111; Brunner, 831 F.2d at 396. "[T]he burden of proving undue hardship is on the debtor, and the debtor must prove all three elements before discharge can be granted." In re Rifino, 245 F.3d at 1087-88 (citation omitted).

I. Minimal Standard of Living

The first prong of the Brunner test requires that Mason prove that he cannot maintain a minimal standard of living if he were required to repay the loans. See In re Saxman, 325 F.3d at 1173; In re Rifino, 245 F.3d at 1088. The bankruptcy court found that Mason's average monthly income generally fluctuated between $1,000 and $1,200 per month, and that in some months it was below that amount. The bankruptcy court also found that Mason's necessary average monthly expenses, excluding his loan payments, were between $1,300 and $1,340 per month. Based on these findings, the bankruptcy court concluded that Mason satisfied the first prong of the Brunner test because he would not be able to maintain a minimal standard of living if required to repay the loans.

"The method for calculating a debtor's average monthly expenses is a matter properly left to the discretion of the bankruptcy court." In re Pena, 155 F.3d at 1112. Because ECMC does not dispute the bankruptcy court's findings regarding Mason's monthly income and expenses, we will not disturb them. See id.; Pa. Higher Educ. Assistance Agency v. Birrane (In re Birrane), 287 B.R. 490, 496 (B.A.P. 9th Cir. 2002).[3]

II. Additional Circumstances

The second prong of the Brunner test requires a debtor to prove that "additional circumstances exist indicating that this state of affairs is likely to persist for a significant portion of the repayment period of the student loans." In re Brunner, 831 F.2d at 396. We recently clarified that a "debtor does not have a separate burden to prove 'additional circumstances,' beyond the inability to pay presently or in the future." Educ. Credit Mgmt. Corp. v. Nys (In re Nys), 446 F.3d 938, 945 (9th Cir. 2006) (holding that that bankruptcy court erred in requiring debtor to show exceptional circumstances beyond the inability to pay in the present and a likely inability to pay in the future).

Here, the bankruptcy court found that Mason's learning disability, and his inability to put his law degree to use, were additional circumstances indicating that Mason's financial circumstances would not improve for a significant period of time. ECMC argues that the bankruptcy court erred because: (1) Mason presented legally insufficient evidence of any disability; (2) Mason should not be permitted to rely on a pre-existing circumstance (i.e., a disability that predated his decision to take out the loans); and (3) despite Mason's learning disability, there is every indication that Mason's situation will improve.

ECMC's first argument-that Mason presented legally insufficient evidence of his disability-is being raised for the first time on appeal; heretofore, ECMC has

---

[3] ECMC argues that the bankruptcy court erred because Mason failed to establish that he maximized his income. As a preliminary matter, ECMC did not raise this argument before the bankruptcy court or the BAP, and therefore has waived it on appeal. See Burnett v. Resurgent Capital Servs. (In re Burnett), 435 F.3d 971, 975-77 (9th Cir. 2006) ("[A]n issue is waived if not presented to the BAP, unless exceptional circumstances exist to justify consideration of the issue."). Even if we were to reach the argument, however, ECMC's contention that Mason must establish that he maximized his income in order to meet the first prong of Brunner does not find support in the case law. Although ECMC claims that United Student Aid Funds, Inc. v. Nascimento (In re Nascimento), 241 B.R. 440 (B.A.P. 9th Cir. 1999), requires that Mason prove that he has maximized his income, Nascimento appears to impose no such requirement. See In re Nascimento, 241 B.R. at 444-45 . In any event, even if Nascimento could be read to require a debtor to prove that he maximized his income to meet the first prong of the Brunner test, we have not specifically imposed such a requirement. See In re Rifino, 245 F.3d at 1088 (requiring only that debtor prove she could not maintain a minimal standard of living based on her current income and expenses); In re Pena, 155 F.3d at 1112-13 (determining whether first prong of Brunner test was met by subtracting debtor's average monthly expenses from their net monthly income). Accordingly, ECMC's contention fails.

never disputed the existence of Mason's learning disability. In fact, ECMC's own vocational expert acknowledged that Mason had a learning disability that might affect his performance. See In re Burnett, 435 F.3d at 975-77 (holding that an argument is generally considered waived if not presented to the BAP). In addition, Mason testified regarding his learning disability and the impact it has had on his ability to succeed. Mason's testimony was also corroborated by his mother's testimony and the special accommodations he received in law school. Thus, sufficient evidence supports the bankruptcy court's finding that Mason has a learning disability.

ECMC further argues that even if Mason has provided corroborating evidence of the existence of his learning disability, he failed to provide any evidence of how his learning disability impaired his ability to work. While ECMC's position has some merit, see Brightful v. Pa. Higher Educ. Assistance Agency (In re Brightful), 267 F.3d 324, 330-31 (3d Cir. 2001) (holding that the bankruptcy court cannot merely assume that debtor's psychiatric problems precluded her from finding employment, and requiring some showing of how disability affected debtor's ability to earn income), the record establishes that Mason's learning disability has made it difficult for him to hold positions that require particular attention to detail or concentration. Moreover, unlike in Brightful, the bankruptcy court in this case did make specific findings that Mason's learning disability diminished his prospects of succeeding in any professional career and has placed him at a relative disadvantage compared to other job applicants. Cf. id. ("What is missing from the Bankruptcy Court's analysis, however, is any discussion of the nature of Brightful's emotional and psychiatric problems, or how these problems prevent her from being gainfully employed."). We conclude that the bankruptcy court did not clearly err in finding that Mason suffered from a learning disability that impaired his ability to earn a sufficient income now or in the future.

ECMC next argues that Mason should not be permitted to rely on an "additional circumstance" that predated his decision to take out the loans, relying on Thoms v. Educational Credit Management Corp (In re Thoms), 257 B.R. 144, 149 (Bankr. S.D.N.Y. 2001). We have never drawn such a distinction between pre-existing and later-arising "additional circumstances," and ECMC cites no binding authority supporting its position. As the BAP aptly noted:

> [N]o circuit court has held that a circumstance or condition in existence at the time the debtor obtained the educational loan in question must be excluded from consideration in the persistence analysis, or that the debtor must show a worsening or exacerbation to carry his burden on the second Brunner prong.

315 B.R. at 561. We agree with the BAP's reasoning and, consequently, reject this argument. See also Educ. Credit Mgmt. Corp. v. Nys (In re Nys), 308 B.R. 436, 446 (B.A.P. 9th Cir. 2004) (explaining that "[t]he 'additional circumstances' test does not focus on a debtor's past choices, but on currently existing circumstances and what those circumstances show with regard to the debtor's future financial situation"), aff'd, 446 F.3d 938 (9th Cir. 2006).

Finally, ECMC argues that despite Mason's learning disability, there is every indication that Mason's situation will improve. The bankruptcy court agreed, concluding that Mason would, at some point, be able to make loan payments, and thus granted Mason only a partial discharge of his loan debt. Because ECMC does not argue that these findings are erroneous, and the bankruptcy court held that Mason had satisfied the second prong of the Brunner test only with respect to a portion of his student loans, see In re Saxman, 325 F.3d at 1174 ("A debtor who wishes to obtain a discharge of his student loans must therefore meet the requirements of § 523(a)(8) as to the portion of the debt to be discharged before that portion of his or her debt can be discharged." (citation omitted), we reject this claim.

III. Good Faith

The final prong of the Brunner test requires that the debtor exhibit good faith in his efforts to repay the student loans. See In re Pena,155 F.3d at 1114. "Good faith is measured by the debtor's efforts to obtain employment, maximize income, and minimize expenses." In re Birrane, 287 B.R. at 499 (citations omitted); see also In re Pena, 155 F.3d at 1114. Courts will also consider "[a] debtor's effort -- or lack thereof -- to negotiate a repayment plan," In re Birrane, 287 B.R. at 499, although a history of making or not making payments is, by itself, not dispositive, see id. at 499-500.

The bankruptcy court concluded that Mason exhibited good faith because he attempted to maximize his income, minimize his expenses, and negotiate with his student loan creditors. The court rejected ECMC's argument that Mason has not shown good faith based on his failure to attempt the bar exam a second time, his failure to obtain a second part-time job in the evening, and his failure to sign up for the Income Contingent Repayment Plan ("ICRP"). ECMC now renews these arguments on appeal.

In In re Biranne, the Ninth Circuit BAP recently reversed the bankruptcy court, inter alia, because the debtor did not use her "best efforts to maximize her income" and failed to take steps towards re-negotiating a repayment schedule under the ICRP. See 287 B.R. at 499-500; 34 C.F.R. § 685.209.[4] There, the BAP reasoned that the debtor failed to maximize her income because she worked only part-time and provided no evidence that "she explored the possibility, or was even willing, to take a second job outside her field." Id. at 499. While the BAP recognized that the debtor had "previously made some effort in negotiating repayment of her student debt," it further reasoned that the debtor's failure to explore the ICRP option that became available to her also weighed against finding that she had met her burden of proof on the issue of good faith. Id. at 499-500.

We conclude that, like the debtor in In re Biranne, Mason has not met his burden of establishing good faith in attempting to pay back the student loans. While Mason has minimized his expenses, he has not maximized his income, nor has he made adequate efforts to obtain full-time employment. Mason works only part-time as a home siding installer, despite holding a bachelor's degree in philosophy and a law degree. Mason sought to justify his unwillingness to find a second part-time job on the ground that it would make it difficult for him to continue his ongoing search for a full-time position. The record belies this testimony, instead revealing that Mason's search for full-time employment has been inadequate in light of the significant free time his schedule provides him. See In re Birrane, 287 B.R. at 499-500 (finding lack of good faith, in part, because

[4] Under the ICRP, a debtor's monthly payments vary based on the debtor's ability to pay. After 25 years, any debt remaining on the consolidated loans is forgiven. See 34 C.F.R. § 685.209(c)(4)(iv).

debtor declined to obtain a second part-time job).

Mason also claims that he is unable to seek work as an attorney because he cannot pass the bar examination. Mason has, however, made only one attempt to pass the Idaho bar exam, without requesting special testing accommodations, despite blaming his failure on his learning disability. Mason further testified that he does not intend to take the bar exam a second time, even though he acknowledged that he has substantial free time that he could dedicate to studying. See Pobiner v. Educ. Credit Mgmt. Corp. (In re Pobiner), 309 B.R. 405, 418 (Bankr. E.D.N.Y. 2004) ("In general, courts have found that failure to pass the bar exam is not a sufficient reason for the discharge of student loans." (citations omitted)); Parks v. Graduate Loan Ctr. (In re Parks), 293 B.R. 900, 904 (Bankr. N.D. Ohio 2003) (refusing to discharge law school loans after debtor failed bar exam primarily due to insufficient effort to retake exam).

Finally, while Mason appears to have made some previous efforts to negotiate repayment of his debt, his efforts have been inadequate. The record demonstrates that Mason could have attempted renegotiation of his debt under the ICRP, but failed to pursue this option with diligence. See In re Birrane, 287 B.R. at 500 (finding lack of good faith, where debtor previously made some effort in negotiating repayment of her student debt but failed to pursue ICRP option when it became available). For the foregoing reasons, we conclude that the bankruptcy court clearly erred in finding that Mason demonstrated good faith efforts to repay his loans.

Accordingly, the BAP's decision is REVERSED and REMANDED for further proceedings consistent with this opinion.

Notes and Questions

1. May a court give a partial discharge of a student loan, on the grounds that hardship exists if the debtor had to pay back the entire loan, but no hardship exists as to paying some portion of it? Saxman v. Educational Credit Management BJR Corp (In re Saxman), 325 F.3d 1168 (9th Cir. 2003) (yes).

C. DEBTS NOT DISCHARGEABLE UNDER § 727(a)

KONTRICK v RYAN

540 U.S. 443 (2004)

GINSBURG, J.

This case concerns the duration of a right to object to a pleading on the ground that it was filed out of time. Under the Bankruptcy Rules governing Chapter 7 liquidation proceedings, a creditor has "60 days after the first date set for the meeting of creditors" to file a complaint objecting to the debtor's discharge. Fed. Rule Bkrtcy. Proc. 4004(a). That period may be extended "for cause" on motion "filed before the time has expired." Fed. Rule Bkrtcy. Proc. 4004(b). In the matter before us a creditor, in an untimely pleading, objected to the debtor's discharge. The debtor, however, did not promptly move to dismiss the creditor's plea as impermissibly late. Only after the Bankruptcy Court decided, on the merits, that the discharge should be refused did the debtor, in a motion for reconsideration, urge the untimeliness of the creditor's plea.

Bankruptcy Rule 4004's time prescription, the debtor maintains, is "jurisdictional," i.e., dispositive whenever raised in the proceedings. Rejecting the debtor's "jurisdictional" characterization, the courts below held that Rule 4004's time prescription could not be invoked to upset an adjudication on the merits.

We agree that Rule 4004 is not "jurisdictional." Affirming the judgment of the Court of Appeals for the Seventh Circuit, we hold that a debtor forfeits the right to rely on Rule 4004 if the debtor does not raise the Rule's time limitation before the bankruptcy court reaches the merits of the creditor's objection to discharge.

I

A debtor in a Chapter 7 liquidation case qualifies for an order discharging his debts if he satisfies the conditions stated in § 727(a) of the Bankruptcy Code. 11 U.S.C. § 727(a).[1] A discharge granted under § 727(a) frees the debtor from all debts existing at the commencement of the bankruptcy proceeding other than obligations § 523 of the Code excepts from discharge. § 727(b).[2]

A debtor's discharge may be opposed by the trustee, the United States trustee, or any creditor. § 727(c)(1). Adjudication of "objections to discharg[e]," Congress provided, is a "[c]ore proceedin[g]" within the jurisdiction of the bankruptcy courts. 28 U.S.C. § 157(b)(2)(J). No statute, however, specifies a time limit for filing a complaint objecting to the debtor's discharge. Instead, the controlling time prescriptions are contained in the Federal Rules of Bankruptcy Procedure, specifically, Rules 4004(a) and (b) and 9006(b)(3).

In relevant part, Bankruptcy Rule 4004(a) states: "[A] complaint objecting to the debtor's discharge under § 727(a) of the Code shall be filed no later than 60 days after the first date set for the meeting of creditors." Rule 4004(b), governing extensions of the Rule 4004(a) filing deadline, provides: "[T]he court may for cause extend the time [Rule 4004(a) allows] to file a complaint objecting to discharge" if the motion is "filed before the time has expired." Reinforcing Rule 4004(b)'s restriction on extension of the Rule 4004(a) deadline, Rule 9006(b)(3) allows enlargement of "the time for taking action" under Rule 4004(a) "only to the extent and under the conditions stated in [that rule]," i.e., only as permitted by Rule 4004(b).[3]

---

[1] Under § 727(a), the court may not grant a discharge of any debts if the debtor, inter alia: (1) is not an individual; (2) has, with intent to defraud a creditor, concealed, transferred, or destroyed property of the estate (A) in the year preceding bankruptcy or (B) during the bankruptcy case; (3) has destroyed books or records; (4) has knowingly (A) given a false oath or account, (B) presented or used a false claim, (C) attempted to obtain money by acting or forbearing to act, or (D) withheld documents relating to the debtor's property or financial affairs; or (5) has failed to explain a loss or deficiency of assets. 11 U.S.C. §§ 727(a)(1)-(5).

[2] Section 523 categorizes debts that are nondischargeable. See, e.g., 11 U.S.C. § 523(a)(1) (certain debts "for a tax or a customs duty"); § 523(a)(2)(A) (certain debts for money obtained by "false pretenses, a false representation, or actual fraud"); § 523(a)(5) (certain debts "to a spouse, former spouse, or child of the debtor" for "support of such spouse or child"); § 523(a)(6) (debts for "willful and malicious injury by the debtor").

[3] Under Bankruptcy Rule 4007(c), essentially the same time prescriptions apply to complaints targeting the discharge of a particular debt pursuant to 11 U.S.C. § 523(c). Rule 4007(c) tracks Rules 4004(a) and (b), and Rule 9006(b)(3) lists Rule 4007(c) as well as Rule 4004(a) among time prescriptions bankruptcy courts may enlarge "only to the extent and under the conditions stated [in the rules themselves]." Because of the practical identity of the time prescriptions for objections to the discharge of any debts under § 727(a) and for objections to the discharge of particular debts under § 523(c), courts have considered decisions construing Rule 4007(c) in determining whether the time limits delineated in Rules 4004(a) and (b) may be forfeited. See, e.g., In re Kontrick, 295 F.3d 724, 730, n. 3 (CA7 2002) (citing In re Santos, 112 B. R. 1001, 1004, n. 2 (BAP CA9 1990)).

II

On April 4, 1997, petitioner, Dr. Andrew J. Kontrick, filed a Chapter 7 bankruptcy petition. Respondent, Dr. Robert A. Ryan, a major creditor and Kontrick's former associate in a cosmetic and plastic surgery practice, opposed Kontrick's discharge. After gaining three successive time extensions from the Bankruptcy Court, Ryan filed an original complaint on January 13, 1998, in which he objected to the discharge of any of Kontrick's debts. Ryan alleged that Kontrick had transferred property, within one year of filing the bankruptcy petition, with intent to defraud creditors, and therefore did not qualify for a discharge under 11 U.S.C. §§ 727(a)(2)-(5).

Ryan filed an amended complaint on May 6, 1998, with leave of court, but without seeking or gaining a court-approved time extension. The amended complaint particularized for the first time the debtor's violation of § 727(a)(2)(A) in this regard: Debtor Kontrick, creditor Ryan alleged, had fraudulently transferred money to Kontrick's wife, first by removing Kontrick's own name from the family's once-joint checking account, then by continuing regularly to deposit his salary checks into the account, from which his wife routinely paid family expenses (the "family-account" claim). Id. at 52-53.[4]

Kontrick answered Ryan's amended complaint on June 10, 1998. His answer "did not raise the untimeliness of [the family-account] claim," Brief for Petitioner 4; on the merits, he admitted the transfers to the family account but denied violating § 727(a)(2)(A). In March 1999, after the parties engaged in acrimonious discovery, Ryan moved for summary judgment. As Local Bankruptcy Rule 402(M) (Bkrtcy Ct ND Ill 1994) instructs, Ryan appended to his motion "a statement of material facts as to which [he] contend[ed] there [was] no genuine issue." Kontrick cross-moved, in August 1999, to strike portions of Ryan's summary judgment filings.

Kontrick's motion to strike sought deletion of "new allegations," i.e., allegations making their first appearance in the litigation in Ryan's summary judgment submissions--Ryan's statement of facts pursuant to Local Rule 402(M), accompanying exhibits, and corresponding portions of the summary judgment motion and memorandum. Motion to Strike and Response to [Ryan's] Statement of Facts Under Local Rule 402(N) in No. 97 B 10353 (Bkrtcy Ct ND Ill), pp 2, 5, 26. Although Kontrick noted that the family-account allegations were stated only in the amended complaint and were absent from the original complaint, id., at 3-4, he did not ask the court to strike those allegations. His response, instead, and in line with Local Rule 402(N), addressed the substance of the family-account claim. He admitted taking his name off the account, but observed that he did so "over four years before bankruptcy." Id., at 13. He also acknowledged that, thereafter, he "deposited his paycheck into the account the same way he had always done." Ibid.

On February 25, 2000, the Bankruptcy Court ruled on the cross-motions, granting in part Kontrick's motion to strike, awarding summary judgment to Ryan on the family-account claim, and dismissing the remaining claims. The court used the amended complaint as its baseline; it struck as untimely

[4] Although Kontrick took his name off the family bank account some four years prior to his bankruptcy petition, his salary check deposits continued into the one-year period preceding bankruptcy specified in 11 U.S.C. §727(a)(2)(A).

"allegations not included in [that] complaint." App. to Pet. for Cert. 47; see id., at 48-50. Homing in on Kontrick's continuing deposits into the account from which he had removed his name, the court concluded that Kontrick had transferred property with intent "to hinder, delay or defraud at least [creditor] Ryan." Id., at 55. That course of conduct, coupled with Kontrick's testimony,[5] the court concluded, sufficed to prove a violation of § 727(a)(2). Accordingly, the court held, Kontrick was not entitled to a discharge of his debts.

Kontrick moved for reconsideration. He argued that the Bankruptcy Court lacked jurisdiction over the sole claim on which the court had granted summary judgment, the family-account claim. See id., at 71. The court was powerless to adjudicate the claim, Kontrick insisted, because the amended complaint containing the claim was untimely. Governing Rules 4004(a) and (b) and 9006(b)(3), Kontrick maintained, establish a mandatory, unalterable time limit of the kind he then called "jurisdictional." App. to Pet. for Cert. 71. It was the first time Kontrick appended a jurisdictional label to any pleading he filed relating to the family-account claim.

The Bankruptcy Court denied the reconsideration motion on June 8, 2000, and entered final judgment five days later. The court held that Rule 4004's complaint-filing time instructions are not "jurisdictional," and that Kontrick had waived the right to assert the untimeliness of the amended complaint by failing squarely to raise the point before the court reached the merits of Ryan's objections to discharge.

The District Court sustained the Bankruptcy Court's decision denying Kontrick's discharge. The Court of Appeals for the Seventh Circuit, in turn, affirmed the judgment of the District Court. In re Kontrick, 295 F.3d 724 (CA7 2002). Both courts relied on decisions of sister Circuits holding that "the timeliness provisions at issue here are not jurisdictional." Id., at 733 (citing In re Benedict, 90 F.3d 50, 54-55 (CA2 1996), and Farouki v. Emirates Bank Int'l Ltd., 14 F.3d 244, 248 (CA4 1994)); accord App. to Pet. for Cert. 31-32. Both courts also agreed with the Bankruptcy Court that Kontrick had waived the right to challenge Ryan's amended complaint as impermissibly late.

The Seventh Circuit found in Kontrick's papers opposing summary judgment nothing that placed in issue the timeliness of allegations in the amended complaint. 295 F.3d at 735. Instead, according to the Court of Appeals, Kontrick apparently accepted creditor Ryan's amended complaint as properly filed; Kontrick used that complaint, not the original complaint, as a baseline to object to new allegations Ryan made for the first time in his statement of facts supporting summary judgment. Ibid. The Seventh Circuit further commented that "[t]he policy concerns of expeditious administration of bankruptcy matters and the finality of the bankruptcy court's decision hardly are fostered by requiring the bankruptcy court to consider the timeliness of an issue that it already has adjudicated." Ibid.

We granted certiorari in view of the division of opinion on whether Rule 4004 is "jurisdictional," 538 U.S. 998 (2003), and we now affirm the judgment of the Seventh Circuit.

---

[5] In a prebankruptcy deposition, Kontrick admitted he transferred the once-joint bank account to his wife to prevent his creditors from attaching the funds. See App. to Pet. for Cert. 53; 295 F.3d 724, 727-728.

III

Only Congress may determine a lower federal court's subject-matter jurisdiction. U.S. Const., Art. III, § 1. Congress did so with respect to bankruptcy courts in Title 28 (Judiciary and Judicial Procedure); in cataloging core bankruptcy proceedings, Congress authorized bankruptcy courts to adjudicate, inter alia, objections to discharge. See 28 USC §§ 157(b)(1) and (b)(2)(I) and (J) Certain statutory provisions governing bankruptcy courts contain built-in time constraints. For example, § 157(c)(1) addresses de novo district court review of bankruptcy court findings and conclusions in noncore proceedings; that provision confines review to "matters to which any party has timely and specifically objected."[6] The provision conferring jurisdiction over objections to discharge, however, contains no timeliness condition. Section 157(b)(2)(J) instructs only that "objections to discharges" are "[c]ore proceedings" within the jurisdiction of the bankruptcy courts.

The time constraints applicable to objections to discharge are contained in Bankruptcy Rules prescribed by this Court for "the practice and procedure in cases under title 11." 28 USC § 2075; cf. § 2072 (similarly providing for Court-prescribed "rules of practice and procedure" for cases in the federal district courts and courts of appeals). "[I]t is axiomatic" that such rules "do not create or withdraw federal jurisdiction." Owen Equipment & Erection Co. v. Kroger, 437 U.S. 365, 370 (1978). As Bankruptcy Rule 9030 states, the Bankruptcy Rules "shall not be construed to extend or limit the jurisdiction of the courts." Rule 9030's forerunner--its counterpart in the Federal Rules of Civil Procedure, Rule 82 --similarly states: "These rules shall not be construed to extend or limit the jurisdiction of the United States district courts . . . ." See 12 C. Wright, A. Miller, & R. Marcus, Federal Practice and Procedure § 3141, pp 484-485 (2d ed. 1997) ("Rule 82 states [the] important principle" that "[t]he rules merely prescribe the method by which the jurisdiction granted the courts by Congress is to be exercised."); Schacht v. United States, 398 U.S. 58, 64 (1970) ("The procedural rules adopted by the Court for the orderly transaction of its business are not jurisdictional . . . ."). In short, the filing deadlines prescribed in Bankruptcy Rules 4004 and 9006(b)(3) are claim-processing rules that do not delineate what cases bankruptcy courts are competent to adjudicate.

This much is common ground. Kontrick does not contend in this Court that the timing rules in question affect the subject-matter jurisdiction of the bankruptcy courts. See Tr. of Oral Arg. 9 (acknowledging that "[t]his case does not deal with subject matter jurisdiction") . . . .

Courts, including this Court, it is true, have been less than meticulous in this regard; they have more than occasionally used the term "jurisdictional" to describe emphatic time prescriptions in rules of court. "Jurisdiction," the Court has aptly observed, "is a word of many, too many, meanings." Steel Co. v. Citizens for Better Environment, 523 U.S. 83, 90 (1998) (internal quotation marks

---

[6] Provisions of a similar order, with built-in time constraints, include 28 U.S.C. § 2401(b) (tort claim against United States "shall be forever barred" unless presented "to the appropriate Federal agency within two years after [the] claim accrues" or civil action "is begun within six months after . . . notice of final denial of the claim by the agency to which it was presented"); and § 2107(a) ("Except as otherwise provided in this section, no appeal shall bring any judgment, order or decree in an action, suit or proceeding of a civil nature before a court of appeals for review unless notice of appeal is filed, within thirty days after the entry of such judgment, order or decree.").

omitted). For example, we have described Federal Rule of Civil Procedure 6(b), on time enlargement, and correspondingly, Federal Rule of Criminal Procedure 45(b), on extending time, as "mandatory and jurisdictional." United States v. Robinson, 361 U.S. 220, 228-229 (1960). But see Carlisle v. United States, 517 U.S. 416, 419-433 (1996) (holding that, over the prosecutor's objection, a court may not grant a postverdict motion for a judgment of acquittal filed one day outside the time limit allowed by Fed. Rule Crim. Proc. 29(c); this Court did not characterize the Rule as "jurisdictional"); Taylor v. Freeland & Kronz, 503 U.S. 638, 642-646 (1992) (similar ruling regarding Fed. Rule Bkrtcy. Proc. 4003(b)). "[C]lassify[ing] time prescriptions, even rigid ones, under the heading 'subject matter jurisdiction'" can be confounding. Carlisle, 517 U.S. at 434 (Ginsburg, J., concurring). Clarity would be facilitated if courts and litigants used the label "jurisdictional" not for claim-processing rules, but only for prescriptions delineating the classes of cases (subject-matter jurisdiction) and the persons (personal jurisdiction) falling within a court's adjudicatory authority.

Though Kontrick concedes that Rules 4004 and 9006(b)(3) are not properly labeled "jurisdictional" in the sense of describing a court's subject-matter jurisdiction, he maintains that the Rules have the same import as provisions governing subject-matter jurisdiction. A litigant generally may raise a court's lack of subject-matter jurisdiction at any time in the same civil action, even initially at the highest appellate instance. Mansfield, C. & L. M. R. Co. v. Swan, 111 U.S. 379, 382 (1884) (challenge to a federal court's subject-matter jurisdiction may be made at any stage of the proceedings, and the court should raise the question sua sponte); Capron v. Van Noorden, 6 U.S. 126, 127 (1804) (judgment loser successfully raised lack of diversity jurisdiction for the first time before the Supreme Court); Fed. Rule Civ. Proc. 12(h)(3) ("Whenever it appears by suggestion of the parties or otherwise that the court lacks jurisdiction of the subject matter, the court shall dismiss the action.").[7] Just so, Kontrick urges, a debtor may challenge a creditor's objection to discharge as untimely under Rules 4004 and 9006(b)(3) any time in the proceedings, even initially on appeal or certiorari . . . .

The equation Kontrick advances overlooks a critical difference between a rule governing subject-matter jurisdiction and an inflexible claim-processing rule. Characteristically, a court's subject-matter jurisdiction cannot be expanded to account for the parties' litigation conduct; a claim-processing rule, on the other hand, even if unalterable on a party's application, can nonetheless be forfeited if the party asserting the rule waits too long to raise the point.

IV

We turn back now to the relevant claim-processing rules in this case. Bankruptcy Rules 4004(a) and (b) and 9006(b)(3), governing proceedings over which bankruptcy courts have subject-matter jurisdiction,[8] serve three primary

[7] Even subject-matter jurisdiction, however, may not be attacked collaterally. Des Moines Nav. & R. Co. v. Iowa Homestead Co., 123 U.S. 552, 31 L. Ed. 202, 8 S. Ct. 217 (1887) ; see Restatement (Second) of Judgments § 12 (1982).

[8] Like Federal Rule of Criminal Procedure 45(b) and Federal Rule of Appellate Procedure 26(b), Bankruptcy Rule 9006(b) is modeled on Federal Rule of Civil Procedure 6(b). See Advisory Committee's Note accompanying Rule 9006 ("Subdivision (b) is patterned after Rule 6(b) F.R.Civ.P. and Rule 26(b) F.R.App.P. " (emphasis in original)).

purposes. First, they inform the pleader, i.e., the objecting creditor, of the time he has to file a complaint. Second, they instruct the court on the limits of its discretion to grant motions for complaint-filing-time enlargements. Third, they afford the debtor an affirmative defense to a complaint filed outside the Rules 4004(a) and (b) limits. This case involves the third office of the Rules.

It is uncontested that creditor Ryan filed his complaint objecting to debtor Kontrick's discharge outside the Rules' time limits. Kontrick urges that nothing occurring thereafter counts, for the Rules' time prescriptions are unalterable, allowing no recourse to "equitable exceptions." Brief for Petitioner 13, n 4; see id., at 8, 16-18. This case, however, involves no issue of equitable tolling or any other equity-based exception. Neither at the time creditor Ryan filed the amended complaint containing the family-account claim nor anytime thereafter did he assert circumstances--equitable or otherwise--qualifying him for a time extension. Whether the Rules, despite their strict limitations, could be softened on equitable grounds[9] is therefore a question we do not reach.[10]

We can assume, arguendo, that had Kontrick timely asserted the untimeliness of Ryan's amended complaint, Kontrick would have prevailed in the litigation. The question, in that event, would have been "whether the time restrictions in th[e] Rules are in such 'emphatic form'" as to preclude equitable exceptions. Brief for United States as Amicus Curiae 16 (citation omitted). See, e.g., Carlisle, 517 U.S. at 419-433 (upholding timely challenge to one-day-late filing under Fed. Rule Crim. Proc. 29(c)); Taylor, 503 U.S. at 642-646 (similar ruling regarding Fed. Rule Bkrtcy. Proc. 4003(b)); Robinson, 361 U.S. at 222-230 (similar ruling regarding Fed. Rule Crim. Proc. 45(b)). Here, however, the sole question is whether Kontrick forfeited his right to assert the untimeliness of Ryan's amended complaint by failing to raise the issue until after that complaint was adjudicated on the merits.[11] In other words, how long did the affirmative defense Rules 4004(a) and (b) and 9006(b)(3) afforded Kontrick linger in the proceedings?

The Court of Appeals, we agree, followed the proper path on this key question. See 295 F.3d at 734-735. Time bars, that court noted, generally must be raised in an answer or responsive pleading. See Fed. Rule Civ. Proc. 8(c) (made

[9] Lower courts have divided on the question whether Bankruptcy Rules 4004 and 4007(c) allow equitable exceptions. Compare, e.g., 295 F.3d at 733 (Rules 4004 and 4007(c) "are subject to equitable defenses"); In re Benedict, 90 F.3d at 54 (same conclusion regarding Rule 4007(c)); Farouki v. Emirates Bank Int'l, Ltd., 14 F.3d 244, 248 (CA4 1994) (same conclusion regarding Rule 4004), with, e.g., In re Alton, 837 F.2d 457, 459 (CA11 1988) (Rule 4007(c) confers no discretion to grant an untimely motion to extend the time to object, even if the creditor lacked notice of the bar date); Neeley v. Murchison, 815 F.2d 345, 346-347 (CA5 1987) (same).

[10] Nor should anything in this opinion be read to suggest that a debtor and creditor may stipulate to the assertion of time-barred claims when such an accommodation would operate to the detriment of other creditors. See, e.g., In re Dollar, 257 B. R. 364, 366 (Bkrtcy. Ct. SD Ga. 2001) ("Although the defendant debtor would significantly benefit by the allowance of the amended complaint [reflecting the parties' pretrial agreement to substitute an untimely § 523(a)(6) cause of action for a timely § 727(a) (2) claim,] the defendant's other creditors would be significantly harmed.").

[11] As the Government notes, "[t]he issue in this case is more accurately described as one of forfeiture rather than waiver." Brief for United States as Amicus Curiae 7, n 5. Although jurists often use the words interchangeably, "forfeiture is the failure to make the timely assertion of a right[;] waiver is the 'intentional relinquishment or abandonment of a known right.' United States v. Olano, 507 U.S. 725, 733 (1993) (quoting Johnson v. Zerbst, 304 U.S. 458, 464 (1938))." Ibid. (some internal quotation marks omitted).

applicable to adversary proceedings in bankruptcy courts by Fed. Rule Bkrtcy. Proc. 7008(a)).[12] An answer may be amended to include an inadvertently omitted affirmative defense, and even after the time to amend "of course" has passed, "leave [to amend] shall be freely given when justice so requires." Fed. Rule Civ. Proc. 15(a); see Fed. Rule Bkrtcy. Proc. 7015 ("Rule 15 F.R.Civ.P. applies in adversary proceedings.").

Kontrick not only failed to assert the time constraints of Rules 4004(a) and (b) and 9006(b)(3) in a pleading or amended pleading responsive to Ryan's amended complaint. As earlier recounted, Kontrick moved to delete certain items from Ryan's summary judgment filings, but, even that far into the litigation, he did not ask the Bankruptcy Court to strike the family-account claim.

Ordinarily, under the Bankruptcy Rules as under the Civil Rules, a defense is lost if it is not included in the answer or amended answer. See Fed. Rule Bkrtcy. Proc. 7012(b) ("Rule 12(b)-(h) F.R.Civ.P. applies in adversary proceedings."); 5A C. Wright & A. Miller, Federal Practice and Procedure § 1347, p 184 (2d ed. 1990) ("A defense or objection that is not raised by motion or in the responsive pleading is waived unless it is protected by Rules 12(h)(2) or 12(h)(3) or by the successful invocation of the liberal amendment policy of Rule 15."). Rules 12(h)(2) and (3) prolong the life of certain defenses, but time prescriptions are not among those provisions. Even if a defense based on Bankruptcy Rule 4004 could be equated to "failure to state a claim upon which relief can be granted," the issue could be raised, at the latest, "at the trial on the merits. " Fed. Rule Civ. Proc. 12(h)(2). Only lack of subject-matter jurisdiction is preserved post-trial. Fed. Rule Civ. Proc. 12(h)(3). And, as we earlier explained, Kontrick's resistance to the family-account claim is not of that order. No reasonable construction of complaint-processing rules, in sum, would allow a litigant situated as Kontrick is to defeat a claim, as filed too late, after the party has litigated and lost the case on the merits.

Notes and Questions

1. D agrees to buy 50% of the shares in a dental corporation over time. D cannot make the payments. D uses corporate funds to prepay office and equipment rental. D resigns from her employment with the old dental corporation and forms a new corporation. The new corporation hires the same personnel that worked for the old corporation. D treats the same patients that she did before. Can D be denied a discharge under Bankruptcy Code § 727(a)(2)? Watman v. Groman (In re Watman), 458 FD.3d 26 (1st Cir. 2006) (yes).

2. Suppose D is in a partnership but has kept no business records. D relied on the other partners to keep records, which they didn't. Is D in violation of §727(a)(3)? D.A.N. Joint Venture v. Cacioli (In re Cacioli), 463 F.3d 229 (2d Cir. 2006)

3. Suppose D filed under chapter 13 five years ago. Under a confirmed plan, D paid $7,500 on unsecured prepetition claims for $20,000. D also paid $18,000 to secured creditors and administrative claims for $4,000. D then files for chapter 7 bankruptcy. Is D entitled to a discharge under §727(a)(9)? Griffin v. Banks (In re Griffin), 352 B.R. 475 (Bankr. 8th Cir. 2006) (yes).

CHAUNCEY v DZIKOWSKI (IN RE CHAUNCEY)
454 F.3d 1292 (11th Cir. 2006)

SILER, J.

In bankruptcy proceedings, Debtor Andrea Chauncey sought refuge in

[12] In fuller detail, Bankruptcy Rule 4004(d) provides that "[a] proceeding commenced by a complaint objecting to discharge is governed by Part VII of these rules." Part VII includes Bankruptcy Rule 7008(a), which states that "Rule 8 F.R.Civ.P. applies in adversary proceedings."

Florida's protection of the homestead. The bankruptcy court concluded that Chauncey forfeited discharge of her debt obligations when she fraudulently transferred the proceeds of a personal injury settlement to her mortgagee in an attempt to shield that asset from her creditors. Accordingly, the bankruptcy court imposed an equitable lien, benefitting the Trustee, Patricia Dzikowski, on Chauncey's homestead property. On appeal, the district court affirmed the bankruptcy court. For the following reasons, we REVERSE in part and AFFIRM in part.

I.

When Chauncey filed for bankruptcy in 2002, she owned a home in Lake Worth, Florida. In the late 1990s, Chauncey opened her own business called AAA Affordable Transmissions ("AAA"), and in 2000, she closed the business. She claimed that she lost all of AAA's books and records and has not been able to locate them since the move. Thus, she could not make them available to the Trustee for inspection. Furthermore, Chauncey failed to provide the Trustee with documents related to her financial accounts because she did not retain copies of bank statements or cancelled checks; she claims that due to the cost (be-tween $50.00 and $75.00) of obtaining copies of such records, she cannot afford to do so.

In March 2002, she initiated a personal injury lawsuit against Eclipse Marketing of Utah, Inc. in state court seeking to recover for personal injuries sustained in an accident which occurred between Chauncey and an agent of Eclipse.

Soon thereafter, in July 2002, American Express Centurion Bank filed suit against Chauncey. Chauncey first consulted with her bankruptcy attorney in August 2002, but she did not immediately file for bankruptcy. On October 23, 2002, a judgment in favor of American Express was entered against her.

On November 22, 2002, the personal injury lawsuit was settled for $80,000.00. After payment of attorney's fees and costs, the remaining sum of the settlement funds totaled $47,430.82. Chauncey never took possession of the settlement proceeds; rather, she directed her personal injury attorney to remit the proceeds directly from his trust account to the mortgagee (Chase).

On December 18, 2002, Chase received the payment from Chauncey's personal injury attorney and applied the settlement proceeds to the outstanding principal balance that existed on the mortgage. As a result, the principal of the mortgage was reduced from $82,486.65 to $34,950.02. Chauncey testified that she was afraid that she would lose her home and she realized that the equity in her homestead could be protected from unsecured creditors. Chauncey also denied any intent to deceive, defraud or hinder her creditors.

Chauncey filed her bankruptcy petition on December 31, 2002. She claimed her home as her homestead and as exempt under 11 U.S.C. § 522(b), Fla. Const. Art. 10, § 4(a)(1), and Florida Statute § 222.01 (2003). The filing of the bankruptcy case was intentionally delayed until after she received the settlement proceeds and the payment was made to Chase.

II.

A. Trustee is Not Entitled to an Equitable Lien on Chauncey's Home

The bankruptcy court granted, and the district court affirmed, the imposition of an equitable lien on Chauncey's home benefitting the Trustee.

Chauncey claims such an action was in error and violative of the Florida Constitution's homestead exemption. This is correct. See Havoco of Am., Ltd. v. Hill, 790 So. 2d 1018, 1020 (Fla. 2001).

The Havoco court acknowledged that "this Court has not hesitated to reach beyond the literal language of the [Florida homestead] exemption to allow the imposition of equitable liens against homestead property used as an 'instrument of fraud or imposition upon creditors.'" Havoco, 790 So. 2d at 1023 (quoting Milton v. Milton, 63 Fla. 533, 58 So. 718, 719 (Fla. 1912)). It would, however, stray only "where the equities have demanded it," having "done so rarely and always with due regard to the exceptions provided in article X, section 4." Id. at 1023-24.

The Havoco court concluded that the "transfer of nonexempt assets into an exempt homestead with the intent to hinder, delay, or defraud creditors is not one of the three exceptions to the homestead exemption . . . . We have invoked equitable principles to reach beyond the literal language of the excepts only where funds obtained through fraud or egregious conduct were used to invest in, purchase, or improve the homestead." Id. We later affirmed. Havoco of Am., Ltd. v. Hill, 255 F.3d 1321, 1322 (11th Cir. 2001).

Under Havoco, Chauncey's actions do not warrant the imposition of an equitable lien upon her homestead. She obtained funds, not through fraud, but by instituting a personal injury action against Eclipse, and received a settlement through no wrongdoing. Her decision to delay the filing of a bankruptcy petition until after she received the funds, while blatantly a move designed to deceive her creditors and one made in bad faith, does not rise to the level of fraud, nor does it constitute egregious behavior. The imposition of an equitable lien is not justified under Florida law.

B. Sufficient Evidence Supports the Bankruptcy Court's Denial of Discharge

Chauncey also appeals the district court's denial of her right to discharge her debt. Generally, pre-confirmation debts are discharged in Chapter 7 proceedings, because the debtor's fresh start is the primary objective of bankruptcy law. 11 U.S.C. § 727(b).

The bankruptcy court denied Chauncey a discharge of her debt under both 11 U.S.C. § 727(a)(2)(A) and § 727(a)(3). Its findings of fact in determining that Chauncey transferred her property within one year before filing her petition with intent to defraud creditors and in failing to keep financial records without justification are not clearly erroneous.

For the foregoing reasons, we AFFIRM the judgment of the district court denying Chauncey's discharge under 11 U.S.C. § 727(a)(2) (A) and (3), and REVERSE the judgment of the district court imposing an equitable lien on Chauncey's homestead.

Notes and Questions

1. The court's equitable lien ruling is overruled by the enactment of Bankruptcy Code §522(o).

EMERY v CITIBANK, N.A. (IN RE EMERY)
132 F.3d 892 (2d Cir. 1998)

FEINBERG, J.

Defendant Claude Emery appeals from an order of the United States District Court for the Eastern District of New York, Joanna Seybert, J., which reversed the holding of the bankruptcy court, Marvin A. Holland, J., that plaintiff-appellee Citibank, N.A. (Citibank) had failed to state a claim (based upon Emery's alleged fraud) for revocation of Emery's bankruptcy discharge. Citibank had obtained knowledge of the alleged fraud in the period after the bar date for creditors' objections to discharge, but prior to the actual grant of discharge. The principal basis of the bankruptcy court's decision was 11 U.S.C. § 727(d), which precludes a creditor from seeking revocation of a discharge if it had knowledge of the fraud before the discharge. The district court reversed, finding that § 727(d) did not bar Citibank's request for revocation under the circumstances of the case. For the reasons stated below, we affirm.

I. Background

Emery filed a petition for relief under Chapter 7 of the Bankruptcy Code on May 16, 1991. Pursuant to 11 U.S.C. § 341(a), the first scheduled meeting of his creditors commenced on July 12, 1991. Under Bankruptcy Rule 4004(a), Emery's creditors then had 60 days -- or until September 10, 1991 (the Bar Date) -- to object to Emery's discharge. Bankruptcy Rule 4004(c) requires that a discharge be granted "forthwith" after a bar date has passed. Despite this requirement, Emery did not actually receive a discharge until November 29, 1991 (the Discharge Date), or 80 days after the Bar Date.

The instant suit arises out of Citibank's claim that Emery attempted to conceal his involvement with certain partnerships and joint ventures. Citibank alleges that Emery made fraudulent representations and omissions both in the schedules filed with his petition and in his responses to creditors at his § 341 examination. Citibank claims that as a result of Emery's fraud, it did not have sufficient facts as of the Bar Date (September 10, 1991) to frame an objection to discharge.

In early September, Citibank requested Emery's consent to an extension of the Bar Date. When Emery refused, Citibank did not seek an extension from the bankruptcy court pursuant to Bankruptcy Rule 4004(b). Citibank did, however, continue to investigate. The bankruptcy court found that Citibank had at least constructive knowledge of Emery's alleged fraud on or before November 18, 1991, eleven days before the Discharge Date.

On November 25, 1992, Citibank filed a complaint to revoke Emery's discharge pursuant to § 727(d). This was within one year from the Discharge Date (November 29, 1991), which is the limitations period established for § 727(d) actions by § 727(e). This complaint was dismissed for failure to plead fraud with particularity. Citibank obtained leave to replead and thereafter filed a Second Complaint. Emery moved to dismiss the Second Complaint for failure to state a cause of action. In August 1994, the bankruptcy court granted the motion to dismiss, holding that the plain language of § 727(d), foreclosed relief because Citibank had knowledge of Emery's fraud prior to the Discharge Date, and that Citibank was not entitled to equitable relief because Citibank should have sought an extension of time pursuant to Rule 4004(b) in which to object to discharge under § 727(c).

In September 1996, the district court reversed, holding that if knowledge of fraud was obtained in the period after the Bar Date but before the Discharge Date (the Gap Period), the Discharge Date should be imputed back to the Bar Date so that the court's ministerial delay in granting a discharge did not create an unintended period of immunity for fraudulent debtors. The district court also held that for purposes of application of the one-year limitations period of § 727(e), the date that Citibank commenced its proceeding to revoke discharge should also be adjusted back by the same number of days because of the lack of clarity in this area of the law. Emery thereafter appealed to this court . . . .

II. Discussion

The issue before us is whether Citibank's proceeding to revoke discharge under § 727(d) is barred because it acquired knowledge of fraud in the Gap Period. We must also determine whether such knowledge has any effect on the time limit for suit specified by § 727(e). This appeal grows out of Emery's motion to dismiss for failure to state a claim upon which relief can be granted. Therefore, Citibank's allegations are accepted as true and Citibank is entitled to the benefit of all permissible inferences . . . .

A. The Effect of Post-Bar Date, Pre-Discharge Date Knowledge

Under § 727(c), a creditor may object to the granting of a discharge on the grounds set forth in § 727(a), which include fraud. As already indicated, however, the time in which a creditor may object to discharge is limited by Rule 4004(a). That rule specifies that a creditor has 60 days from the date set for the first examination under § 341 in which to file an objection to discharge. Once that date has passed, Rule 4004(c) provides that "the court shall forthwith grant the discharge" (emphasis added). Once a discharge has been granted, a creditor may obtain revocation under § 727(d) if a creditor can prove both that the discharge was obtained through fraud and that the creditor had no knowledge of the fraud until after the discharge was granted. See, e.g., In re Ginsberg, 164 B.R. 870, 876 (Bankr. S.D.N.Y. 1994).

The Bankruptcy Code and the Bankruptcy Rules obviously contemplate a unitary concept: If a creditor knows of a debtor's fraud before a bar date, the creditor should object to discharge. If there are no objections to discharge by the bar date, the bankruptcy court should grant discharge forthwith. A creditor then has a year to bring an action to revoke the discharge based upon knowledge of fraud obtained after the discharge date. In other words, Congress has provided the remedy of denying discharge to a fraudulent debtor from the beginning of a case until one year after discharge.

In the ordinary case, this scheme makes good sense. However, the problem with it is that a busy bankruptcy court sometimes does not grant a discharge "forthwith" after a bar date has passed and does so only after a considerable period -- here 80 days -- has gone by. The existence of such a gap period creates the situation we have in this case. The Bar Date passed on September 10, 1991. If discharge had been granted right away, Citibank would not have known of Emery's fraud until over two months after the discharge. Therefore, the stricture of § 727(d) that Citibank "not know of such fraud until after the granting of such discharge" would not have barred its action.

Emery understandably argues principally that the plain language of § 727(d) precluded Citibank's proceeding to revoke his discharge because it was aware of his alleged fraud by November 18, 1991, which was before the Discharge Date of November 29, 1991. Emery relies heavily on Powell v. First Bank of Nashville, Arkansas, 113 B.R. 512 (W.D. Ark. 1990), in which a court facing a situation similar to ours held that the plain language of Rule 4004 and § 727(d) foreclosed any remedy, stating that "it is true that it is difficult, perhaps impossible, to imagine why [Congress and the Supreme Court] would have wanted [this result] . . . but the court does not conceive it to be its job to rationalize the statute and the rule." Id. at 513.

Nonetheless, we agree with the district court that dismissal of Citibank's complaint was inappropriate in this case. It is true that the plain language of § 727(d) would ordinarily preclude a suit to revoke a discharge where a creditor had knowledge of fraud prior to the applicable discharge date. Ginsberg, 164 B.R. at 876. The Supreme Court has stated that "as long as the statutory scheme is coherent and consistent, there generally is no need for a court to inquire beyond the plain language of the statute." United States v. Ron Pair Enter-prises, Inc., 489 U.S. 235, 240-41 (1989). However, the Court also made clear in Ron Pair that a court may depart from the plain language if "literal application of the statute will pro-duce a result demonstrably at odds with the intentions of [the statute's] drafters." Id. at 242.

Emery argues to us, in effect, that because of the Gap Period of 80 days, Citibank can do nothing about the fraud it alleges and which, on a motion to dismiss, we must assume existed. Thus, according to Emery, because the discharge was not entered forthwith, Citibank had knowledge of fraud before the delayed Discharge Date (November 29, 1991) and was barred by § 727(d) from moving to revoke the discharge. However, we do not believe that Congress intentionally drafted a statute to punish fraudulent conduct by debtors that at the same time provides a period of immunity for such debtors. We agree that the literal application of § 727(d) here cannot have been intended by Congress and the Supreme Court. See, e.g., In re Dietz, 914 F.2d 161, 164 (9th Cir. 1990) (court acted "consistently with the spirit of the bankruptcy rules," which contemplate immediate discharge after a bar date); In re Stevens, 107 B.R. 702, 706 (9th Cir. BAP 1989) ("the rights of parties . . . would be unreasonably frustrated, if Rule 4004 were read to create a temporary period when no . . . complaint under § 727 could be brought"); In re Staub, 208 B.R. 602, 606-7 (Bankr. S.D. Ga. 1997) ("rational sense" requires that there be no "safe haven gap period"). Nothing in the Bankruptcy Code itself indicates an intention to create immunity during a gap period. Sections 727(c) and 727(d), taken together, clearly contemplate that diligent creditors will have a remedy against fraudulent debtors.

Emery argues that the use of "forthwith" in Bankruptcy Rule 4004(c) contemplates a period of immunity because there is always the possibility of delay in the performance of a ministerial task. This argument is unconvincing. The primary meaning of "forthwith" is "immediately, without delay." Black's Law Dictionary 654 (6th ed. 1990). Of course, delay is always a possibility. It is clear, however, that neither Congress nor the Supreme Court intended such delay. Rather, a gap period is the direct result of the inability of the bankruptcy court system to comply with Rule 4004(c)'s mandate that a discharge be entered "forthwith" after a bar date has passed. See generally In re Anwiler, 958 F.2d 925 (9th Cir. 1992) (surveying cases in which a bankruptcy court used its equitable powers under Bankruptcy Code § 105 to avoid prejudicing litigants for ministerial mistakes).

The bankruptcy court held that equitable grounds for disregarding the plain language of § 727(d) in this case were not compelling in view of Citibank's failure to seek an extension of the Bar Date. The bankruptcy court apparently reasoned that a creditor is obliged to make use of Rule 4004(b) to seek an extension of the bar date if it has suspicions of fraud, even if those suspicions do not amount to constructive or actual knowledge. We do not agree. A rule barring a creditor for failing to seek an extension of the bar date in those circumstances would pressure creditors to move for precautionary extensions of the bar date based on the slightest suspicion, and thus interfere with the Bankruptcy Code policy in favor of a prompt discharge for deserving debtors.

In sum, for the reasons stated above we hold that on this record, § 727(d) did not preclude Citibank's suit.

B. The Timeliness of the Complaint under § 727(e)

There is still the question whether Citibank complied with the one-year limitations period of § 727(e). As already indicated, the district court imputed the Discharge Date back to the Bar Date, which was September 10, 1991. Emery argues that on this theory, Citibank's action was untimely since it was not actually brought until November 28, 1992, well over a year after the imputed Discharge Date. The district court resolved this problem by making a "corresponding adjustment" (apparently 80 days, although the district court did not specify in more detail) to the date that Citibank began its adversary proceeding. The district judge's rationale was that this would "prevent a creditor, who commenced [an] adversary proceeding within one year of the nominal date of discharge, from being prejudiced through the absence of clarity in the law."

We see no need to make such an "adjustment." In II-A above, we conclude that on the facts of this case the district court correctly held that § 727(d) did not bar Citibank's action because doing so would lead to an absurd result that Congress could not have intended. Citibank did bring its action on November 25, 1992, within a year after the actual date of discharge (November 29, 1991). It could not have had notice that the district court was going to shorten the one-year limitations period by moving the Discharge Date back 80 days, and we agree with the district court that in the circumstances here Citibank should not be prejudiced by the lack of clarity with respect to the effect of the Gap Period. We therefore hold that the § 727(e) limitations period continued to run from the actual date of discharge and that Citibank's action was therefore timely. We also hold that in future cases involving a gap period this statute of limitations will run from the actual date of discharge.

We have considered all of Emery's arguments and find them to be insufficient reason for reversal. We affirm the order of the district court and remand the case for further proceedings consistent with this opinion.

E. REAFFIRMATION

IN RE GARAY

2006 Bankr. LEXIS 3372 (Bankr. W.D. Tex., November 28, 2006)

LIEF M. CLARK, J.

CAME ON for consideration the foregoing matter. The debtor filed a chapter 13 bankruptcy case on January 3, 2005. The case was converted to chapter 7 on July 24, 2006. The debtor received her discharge on October 30, 2006. On November 14, 2006, the debtor filed a reaffirmation agreement with Aaron Rents, Inc. The reaffirmation agreement was submitted by the debtor to the creditor on August 7, 2006. It was not signed by Aaron Rents, Inc. until November 7, 2006. It was then filed with the court on November 14, 2006.

It is not possible to ascertain who mailed the document to the court. However, it is clear that the document was not electronically filed, however, because the docketing was done by a member of the court's staff, confirming that court staff scanned a paper version of the document. In view of the fact that the last dated signature on the document is that of Aaron Rents, it is fair to infer that Aaron Rents either mailed it to the clerk for filing, or mailed it to the debtor's attorney, who in turn mailed it to the clerk for filing. In either event, the document could not have been forwarded for filing any earlier than November 7, 2006, the date that someone at Aaron Rents signed the document.

The point to be made here is this: Section 524(c)(1) provides that a reaffirmation agreement is enforceable only if, inter alia, "such agreement was made before the granting of the discharge . . ." 11 U.S.C. § 524(c)(1). This agreement was not made until it was signed by the creditor. The debtor's signature on the document constituted an offer. The document was then tendered to Aaron Rents for its signature, which signature would have constituted its acceptance. There cannot be an agreement unless there is both offer and acceptance. See CORBIN, CONTRACTS (One Vol. Ed.) §§ 55-56 (West 1952). On these facts, there was no "agreement" made before the granting of the debtor's discharge on October 30, 2006. The reaffirmation agreement is thus not enforceable.

The debtor is always free to perform on any debt, regardless of discharge. Discharge merely prevents the creditor from legally enforcing performance by the debtor. See 11 U.S.C. § 524(a)(2). That is appropriate in this case, in view of the creditor's failure to promptly act to protect itself.[1]

Notes and Questions

1. Can a debtor waive a discharge in order to get a court to approve a reaffirmation agreement? In re Stewart, 2006 Bankr. LEXIS 2959 (Bankr. N.D. Ohio, October 26, 2006) (no).

2. Suppose D files for bankruptcy and, pursuant to Bankruptcy Code §521(2), declares an intent to reaffirm a security agreement pertaining to her vehicle. The car lender sends D a reaffirmation agreement and requests D to sign. Has the car lender violated the automatic stay? Pertuso v. Ford Motor Credit Co., 223 F.3d 417 (Bankr. 6th Cir. 2000) (no).

IN RE CALABRESE

353 B.R. 925 (Bankr. M.D. Fla. 2006)

JERRY A. FUNK, J.

This case came before the Court upon Ford Motor Credit Company's ("Movant") Request for Hearing to Review Reaffirmation Agreement ("Request for Hearing"). Debtors filed for relief under Chapter 7 of the Bankruptcy Code on July 18, 2006. Shortly thereafter, Debtors and Movant executed two reaffirmation

---

[1] It is noted as well that the reaffirmation called for the debtors to pay over $500 in rent for a washer and dryer worth only a tad more than $100. The reaffirmation agreement was a bad deal for the debtor in any event.

agreements.

Reaffirmation agreements are governed by § 524(c) of the Bankruptcy Code, which permits debtors to reaffirm a debt owed to a creditor while excusing such creditor from the consequences of a debtor's discharge. Section 524(c)(2) states that a debtor must receive the appropriate § 524(k) disclosures at the same time or before the debtor enters into a reaffirmation agreement. 11 U.S.C. 524(c)(2) (2006). If the debtor is represented by an attorney, according to § 524(k)(5), the attorney must attest that the reaffirmation agreement is in the best interests of the debtor, and that the agreement does not impose an undue hardship on the debtor. 11 U.S.C. § 524(k)(5) (2006). If, however, there is a presumption of an undue hardship, the attorney must certify that in the attorney's opinion, the debtor is capable of making such payments as required by the reaffirmation agreement. 11 U.S.C. § 524(k)(5)(B) (2006). A presumption of undue hardship occurs when the debtor does not have sufficient funds to make the required reaffirmation payments.

In the instant case, Debtors' attorney attested that there was no presumption of undue hardship on either reaffirmation agreement. However, one reaffirmation agreement required a $333.38 monthly payment, yet Debtors acknowledged that they only had available $282.28 to make the required payments. The other agreement required a $341.90 monthly payment, yet Debtors acknowledged that they only had available $290.80 to make the required payments. With respect to both agreements, to certify that Debtors would have the needed funds to make the payments, Debtors attached a statement explaining that they obtained a new prescription drug plan which would reduce their monthly expenses, and that they anticipated an increase in projected income from an expected lump sum payment.

Given the language of § 524, the Court believes that Congress did not intend for judges to review reaffirmation agreements when the debtor has been represented by an attorney. However, if a debtor is acting on his or her own behalf, then the Court is required to examine the reaffirmation agreement and decide whether such agreement is in the best interests of the debtor, and if it presents an undue hardship that would prevent the debtor from being able to make the required payments. Such is not the case here. Debtors were represented by counsel when they entered into the reaffirmation agreement with Movant. Further, if the Court set a hearing on this matter responsibility for the reaffirmation agreement would reside with the Court, rather than the Debtors' attorney, as intended by Congress. Thus, the Court will not hold a hearing on this matter. Based on the foregoing, it is ORDERED: Movant's Request for Hearing is denied.

IN RE MENDOZA

347 B.R. 34 (Bankr. W.D. Tex. 2006)

LEIF CLARK, J.

. . . The debtor filed a reaffirmation agreement pursuant to 11 U.S.C. § 524(c). This section generally provides that a debtor may agree to reaffirm a debt, excusing the creditor from the effects of the bankruptcy discharge. Congress amended this section of the Code in BAPCPA, effective October 17, 2005. New subsection 524(c)(2) now provides, as one of the pre-conditions for the approval of such agreements, that "the debtor receive[] the disclosures required in subsection (k) at or before the time at which the debtor signed the agreement."

11 U.S.C. § 524(c)(2). New subsection (k)(4) now specifies the contents of a new reaffirmation form. See 11 U.S.C. § 524(k)(4). Subsection (k)(5) then sets out the exact language of the attorney's declaration. See 11 U.S.C. § 524(k)(5).

In "Part C: Certification by Debtor's Attorney (if any)" the attorney is to sign a certification to the following effect:

> I hereby certify that (1) this agreement represents a fully informed and voluntary agreement by the debtor; (2) this agreement does not impose an undue hardship on the debtor or any dependent of the debtor; and (3) I have fully advised the debtor of the legal effect and consequences of this agreement.

11 U.S.C. § 524(k)(5)(A) (Part C: Certification by Debtor's Attorney (If Any)). If a presumption of undue hardship has been established (at least in the opinion of the attorney making the certification, in any event), then the certification must also state that "in the opinion of the attorney, the debtor is able to make the payment."[1]

In service to this new statutory provision, the Judicial Conference adopted a new form, Form B240. The form contains a Part C, as directed by the statute. It offers two certification paragraphs that track the language of the statute exactly, and contains a direction at the top advising the attorney to "check each applicable box." The first paragraph (with a box to be checked next to it), sets out the certification in section 524(k)(5)(A) verbatim. The second paragraph (also with a box to be checked next to it), closely follows the directive in section 524(k)(5)(B), and appears in the form as follows:

> [If applicable and the creditor is not a Credit Union.] A presumption of undue hardship has been established with respect to this agreement. In my opinion, however, the debtor is able to make the required payment.

Form B240, Part C: Certification by Debtor's Attorney (If Any). To determine whether an undue hardship presumption has arisen, one consults Part D of the form. There, the form calls upon the debtor to fill out and certify the following paragraph:

> I believe this reaffirmation agreement will not impose an undue hardship on my dependents or me. I can afford to make the payments on the reaffirmed debt because my monthly income (take home pay plus any other income received) is $, and my actual current monthly expenses including monthly payments on post-bankruptcy debt and other reaffirmation agreements total $, leaving $ to make the required payments on this reaffirmed debt. I understand that if my income less my monthly expenses does not leave enough to make the payments, this reaffirmation agreement is presumed to be an undue hardship on me and must be reviewed by the court. However, this presumption may be overcome if I explain to the satisfaction of the court how I can afford to make the payments here: .

Form B240, Part D: Debtor's Statement in Support of Reaffirmation Agreement.

---

[1] Presumably, the attorney is not statutorily directed to certify to a falsehood. Thus, if a presumption of undue hardship has been established and the attorney does not believe that the debtor is able to make the payment, then, of course, the attorney should not sign a certification to the contrary. The presumption of undue hardship arises whenever the debtor's monthly income less monthly expenses does not leave enough to make the payments. See 11 U.S.C. § 524(k)(6)(A) (Part D: Debtor's Statement in Support of Reaffirmation Agreement).

Fairly obviously, if the debtor's monthly expenses exceed the debtor's total monthly income, such that there is not enough to make the reaffirmation payments, a presumption of undue hardship ought to arise.[2] The form, consistent with the language of the statute, affords the debtor an opportunity to explain how the debtor, in spite of appearances, can afford to make the payments.[3]

According to both the form and the statute, the court has the obligation to review any agreement which imposes an undue hardship, but the statute does not address how that review is expected to occur. The statute itself contemplates that reaffirmation agreements are not set for hearing before the court so long as the debtor was represented by counsel and the debtor has signed the requisite certifications. If the debtor is not represented by counsel, the statute now specifies the contents of the motion that may be used by the debtor to obtain the required hearing.[4] The form, per the directive of the statute, incorporates the language as Part E. This is what Part E says:

> I . . . affirm the following to be true and correct:
>
> I am not represented by an attorney in connection iwth this reaffirmation agreement.
>
> I believe this reaffirmation agreement is in my best interest based on the income and expenses I have disclosed in my Statement in Support of this reaffirmation agreement, and because (provide any additional relevant reasons the court should consider)
>
> Therefore, I ask the court for an order approving this reaffirmation agreement.

Form B240, Part E. Neither the form nor the statute make any provision for court review of undue hardship situations. If the debtor is represented by counsel, there will be no hearing. If the debtor is pro se, the motion incorporated in the form says nothing about undue hardship. Unless the court, on its own, undertakes to physically review every reaffirmation agreement filed, there would be no judicial review of undue hardship situations.[5] This analysis brings us to the problem that

---

[2] One could even argue that the arithmetic calculation alone confirms by a preponderance of the evidence that the reaffirmation agreement is an undue hardship. After all, the debtor certainly cannot make the payments to which the debtor is about to contractually bind herself to make. And even if the reaffirmation agreement contained no provision for monthly payment but merely stated the debtor's agreement to, in effect, waive her discharge as to that creditor, the debtor would immediately place herself directly in the line of fire of credit collection activity, including wage garnishment (in some states) that would only exacerbate the shortfall between income and living expenses.

[3] One reaffirmation agreement reviewed by the court contained, as an explanation, "financial assistance from friend." No further details were offered, though the agreement contemplated payments of nearly $1,500 a month over a period of 18 months, while the debtor's net after monthly expenses was just a little over $37.

[4] When the debtor is pro se, a reaffirmation agreement is not effective unless the debtor appears before the court pursuant to section 524(c)(6).

[5] Congress seems tacitly to have presumed that courts would review every reaffirmation agreement filed. So long as the volume of case filings remains low, that might be an option. If case filings increase, however, the option would become unrealistic. Another option would be for the clerk to review and automatically set for hearing all cases involving undue hardship. Again, so long as filings are low, that is a possibility. However, the clerk's staff would have to page to Part D to see what is the net amount available for making payments, then find in Part A the payment contemplated by the agreement. The clerk would then set every agreement in which the number in Part D is less than the number in Part A. Hopefully, the clerk's staff will know where to look for these numbers. Presumably, the clerk's staff would not be required to check the debtor's arithmetic. The clerk in this district under pre-BAPCPA procedures automatically set

has led to this decision's being issued.

If one returns to Part C, one quickly sees that the only choice afforded debtor's counsel when Part D confirms that the reaffirmation agreement imposes an undue hardship on the debtor is either to check the box (and thereby represent that, notwithstanding the obvious shortfall in income, the attorney thinks that the debtor can still make the payment), or not to check the box (thereby making no representation at all). What, if anything, is the court to make of a reaffirmation agreement in which Part C is signed, but no box is checked? What does it mean if the first box is checked, but not the second? Should any import be given to these choices? Should any presumptions be made? Are they express? Tacit? The questions are real because the potential liability for the attorney who signs the certification is real.[6]

In this case, the attorney in question did not check either box on Part C ---(i.e., the box next to the certification by the attorney that he has made the requisite disclosures to the client, that the agreement does not represent an undue hardship,[7] and that the agreement is voluntary, and the box next to the certification that, even though the agreement is an undue hardship, the attorney still thinks that the debtor can make the payments). The attorney did sign where indicated however. Because neither box was checked, the signature does not certify anything, though it does imply that neither of the statements applies.

On Part D, the debtors amended the certification, crossing out all of paragraph 1 except for the following: "I believe this reaffirmation agreement will not impose an undue hardship on my dependents or me. I can afford to make the payments on the reaffirmed debt." After that strike out, the debtors' certification in Part D does not contain a statement of the debtors' income, a statement of the debtors' monthly expenses, or a statement of an amount left to make the reaffirmation payment. Also stricken is the sentence in which the debtors represent that they will be able to make the payment in question, notwithstanding not having enough money left over. The debtors signed where indicated at the bottom of Part D. In a sense, this amendment resolves part of the

---

reaffirmation agreements in any case in which the debtor was pro se. That is a fairly routine administrative task, by comparison.

Some courts are of the view that the only matters that ought to be set for hearings are those that represent a live case and controversy, and that a matter in which there is no adversary does not fit that standard and so should not be set, absent a clear statutory directive to the contrary. Section 524(c) in its originally enacted form in 1978 did call for just such hearings on all reaffirmation agreements, without regard to circumstance or representation by counsel. The current statute, by contrast, has no specific directive to conduct a hearing -- only an assumption on the part of the drafters that some sort of review would be conducted.

[6] Section 526(a)(2) prohibits the debtor's attorney (who is, in virtually all of these cases, a "debt relief agency") from making "... any statement in a document filed in a case or proceeding under this title that is untrue or misleading, or that upon the exercise of reasonable care, should have been known by such agency to be untrue or misleading." See 11 U.S.C. § 526(a)(2) (emphasis added). Thus, even negligently certifying a debtor's ability to make reaffirmation payments could subject the attorney to the range of penalties spelled out in section 526(c). Nor, presumably, would the attorney's exposure end there, as many non-bankruptcy remedies could also come into play, ranging from suits for malpractice, through grievance actions by state bars, and class action suits by aggrieved former clients. One could comfortably argue that an attorney who certifies a debtor's ability to make a reaffirmation payment when the debtor's monthly income less expenses leaves the debtor with not enough money to make that payment has been negligent, or at the least, did not exercise reasonable care to assure that his certification was not untrue or misleading. See 11 U.S.C. § 526(a)(2).

[7] [Form 240A no longer has a box next to this certification. Ed.]

attorney's problem, because it does not contain a signed certification that would facially demonstrate that the debtors cannot afford to make the payments they are about to promise to pay. By the same token, the strikeout means that the debtors are not certifying what the statute says they must certify-Form D contains the exact language specified in the statute. See 11 U.S.C. § 524(k)(6)(A) ("The statement in support of such agreement, which the debtor shall sign and date prior to filing with the court, shall consist of the following").

Although denominated as certifications by both the bankruptcy form and the statute, neither Part C nor Part D are statements made under penalty of perjury. See 28 U.S.C. § 1746.[8] Nonetheless they are statements made in a signed pleading, and so would fall under the rubric of Rule 9011 of the Federal Rules of Bankruptcy Procedure.[9] And, as earlier noted, false or misleading statements made by an attorney who qualifies as a debt relief agency could subject that attorney to the range of enforcement mechanisms set out in section 526(c).

To date, there are no published decisions construing section 524(k)(5). Clerks of court are having to decide how to handle the varying permutations of Form B240 with which they are presented. If the attorney does not sign Part C, then clerks will set the reaffirmation agreement on the court's docket, as though the debtor were not represented by counsel.[10] If the attorney has signed Part C, but has not checked either of the boxes, then the clerk has a problem. Should the clerk set the matter, treating it as though the debtors were not represented by counsel, just as the clerk does (at least in this district) with agreements not signed by counsel even though they are represented? Should the clerk not set the matter, on the presumption that the signature, with no boxes checked, means that the agreement does not impose an undue hardship on the debtor? Should the clerk

---

[8] This statute says as follows, in pertinent part:

> Wherever, under any law of the United States ... or requirement made pursuant to law, any matter is required or permitted to be supported, evidenced, established, or proved by the sworn declaration, verification, certificate, statement, oath, or affidavit, in writing of the person making the same, such matter may, with like force and effect, be supported ... by the unsworn ... certificate ... in writing of such person which is subscribed by him, as true under penalty of perjury ...

Id.

[9] Says the rule:

> By presenting to the court (whether by signing, filing, submitting, or later advocating) a petition, pleading, written motion, or other paper, an attorney or unrepresented party is certifying that to the best of the person's knowledge, information, and belief, formed after an inquiry reasonable under the circumstances,-
>
> (3) the allegations and other factual contentions have evidentiary support or, if specifically so identified, are likely to have evidentiary support after a reasonable opportunity for further investigation or discovery;

FED.R.BANKR.P. 9011(b).

[10] Section 524(d) says that "... if the debtor desires to make an agreement of the kind specified in subsection (c) of this section [i.e., a reaffirmation agreement] and was not represented by an attorney during the course of negotiating such agreement, then the court shall hold a hearing at which the debtor shall appear in person ..." 11 U.S.C. § 524(d). This is language that was not amended by BAPCPA.

set all reaffirmation agreements, on grounds that the clerk has no business trying to interpret the legal significance of how the document has been completed?[11]

The permutations go further. Suppose the attorney checks the first box, but not the second. Further suppose that Part D reflects that the agreement imposes an undue hardship (because there is not enough money left over to make the payment proposed to be made in the reaffirmation agreement). Should the clerk set that reaffirmation agreement? If Part D does not reflect an undue hardship, and the attorney has not checked the second box on Part C, should the agreement then be approved without a hearing? Should the clerk be checking Part A (where the reaffirmation payment is reflected), Part D (where the undue hardship might be mathematically disclosed) and Part C (where the attorney is requested to make a certification regarding undue hardship)?

It seems obvious to the court that due administration of justice and insulating the clerk of court from exercising an inappropriate judicial function compel the court to set out clear rules as to how to handle these agreements. It is also vitally important to attorneys to know what their options are, given the potential liability that these certifications could impose on them. There are no guide posts, however. And the statute is stubbornly obtuse.[12] There is no choice but to come up with some sort of solution that rescues the clerk and gives lawyers clear guidance. The remainder of this opinion represents this court's attempt at that solution.

If the reaffirmation agreement is based in whole or in part on a consumer debt that is (a) not secured by real property of the debtor or (b) and is not a reaffirmation agreement with a credit union, then the debtor must complete Part D's financial information regarding total monthly income and total monthly expenses. See 11 U.S.C. § 524(c)(3)(B), (6)(A)(i), (d)(2). The information furnished in Part D is the way a presumption of undue hardship may be established, requiring an examination of other factors that might (at least theoretically) overcome the presumption. If this information is not furnished, no one will ever know whether the presumption has arisen -- impairing the court's ability to comply with the obligations imposed by section 524(m)(1).[13]

---

[11] Recall that the Judicial Conference amended Rule 5 of the Federal Rules of Civil Procedure to address what had become an increasingly common problem: clerks of court refusing documents for filing based on the clerk's determination that the pleading did not conform to a national or local rule. The 1991 comment to the amendment to Rule 5 said, with regard to the practice, "[t]his is not a suitable role for the office of the clerk, and the practice exposes litigants to the hazards of time bars ... the enforcement of [the federal rules] and of the local rules is a role for a judicial officer." See FED.R.CIV.P. 5 (Comment to 1991 Amendments). The language added to the rule reads as follows: "The clerk of court shall not refuse to accept for filing any paper presented for that purpose solely because it is not presented in proper form as required by these rules or any local rules or practices." See FED.R.CIV.P. 5(e).

[12] The major reason the form is a disaster is simple -- it tracks the statute.

[13] That subsection states that the presumption arises until 60 days after its filing with the court whenever the information on Part D of the form -- described in subsection (m) as a document required to be filed by subsection 524(k)(6)(A) -- shows that there is not enough income left over to make the payments in the agreement. If the presumption arises, and is not sufficiently rebutted by the debtor's explanation in Part D, then the court may disapprove the reaffirmation agreement -- but only on notice and a hearing, with notice given to both the debtor and the creditor, and with the hearing concluded before the debtor's discharge is entered. See 11 U.S.C. § 524(m)(1). Of course, there is no way the court would even know that the presumption of undue hardship has arisen if Form D is not completed, and thus no way the court could discharge its duty to at least review the form, much less set the matter for hearing on notice within the time frame specified by the statute.

Accordingly, if Part D of a reaffirmation agreement is not completed (unless the creditor is a credit union), the court will presume that a hardship is presented, and the reaffirmation agreement will be set for hearing. If Part D of the reaffirmation agreement is altered (as it has been in this case), the court must similarly presume that a hardship may be presented (again, because the calculations have not been furnished), and the clerk will set the reaffirmation for hearing.

If Part D of a reaffirmation agreement is completed, then the next step for the clerk of court is to look at Part C. If Part C is not signed, then the clerk will set the agreement for hearing.[14] If the second box on Part C is checked, and the attorney has signed the agreement, the clerk will not set the reaffirmation agreement for hearing. The reaffirmation agreement will be deemed approved.[15]

If the second box on Part C is not checked (regardless whether the first box has been checked or not), then the clerk shall forward the reaffirmation agreement to the judge for review.[16] The judge may decide whether to set the reaffirmation for hearing, and will promptly notify the clerk of same, so that the clerk can comply with the tight deadlines laid out in section 524(m)(1) ("No agreement shall be disapproved without notice and a hearing to the debtor and creditor, and such hearing shall be concluded before the entry of the debtor's discharge").[17]

These are the only permutations with which the clerk of court need concern itself. As for the lawyers involved, they may aid the clerk and court immensely by indicating (in those circumstances that require it) their desire that the matter be set for hearing. This can be done on Part C, below the signature of the attorney, with wording such as the following: "A hearing is requested." If this is done, then the clerk will not need to forward that reaffirmation agreement to chambers for review. Instead, the clerk can immediately set the matter for hearing, making it much easier to satisfy the notice and a hearing duties imposed by section 524(m)(1).

As for the case sub judice, the reaffirmation agreement will be set for hearing. In view of the impossibility of completing this decision prior to discharge day, the court, pursuant to section 105, hereby extends the time for

---

[14] The lack of a signature is the equivalent of the debtor being unrepresented. The statute contemplates a hearing in the event the debtor signs the agreement without the benefit of counsel. See 11 U.S.C. § 524(c)(6)(A), (d).

[15] In essence, the court is accepting the attorney's representation that, in his professional opinion, both as counsel for his client and an officer of the court, the reaffirmation is not a hardship, despite the calculations on Part D that might indicate to the contrary. The court, in accepting that representation, is not endorsing the attorney's view of the matter. In other words, if it should later turn out that the attorney improvidently checked this box, the court's approval of the agreement will not shelter the attorney from liability.

[16] This review is mandated by section 524(m)(1), because the court must examine Part D to determine whether an undue hardship is presented, and if, notwithstanding that hardship, the explanation offered by the debtor is satisfactory. See 11 U.S.C. § 524(m)(1). It is not appropriate to require the clerk to make that determination, as it requires comparison of Part D to information provided in Part A regarding the monthly payment provided for under the agreement, and examination of the debtor's explanation.

[17] If the court is not going to approve the reaffirmation agreement due to undue hardship, it can only do so on notice and a hearing, but the hearing must be conducted before the discharge date. Thus, if the debtor and creditor wait until the last minute to file their agreement, they make it very hard for the court to set the matter for hearing with proper notice to both the debtor and the creditor. The best advice to counsel (and creditors) is to file reaffirmation agreements early.

approval of this agreement to the day of the hearing. The clerk of court is directed to afford notice to the creditor and the debtor (and counsel, of course). Ten days' notice is sufficient. See 11 U.S.C. § 102(1).

Notes and Questions

1. Form 240A can easily be Googled from the internet. Please download it and consider the following question.

Suppose D's From 240A demonstrates that D's reaffirmation of a car loan constitutes a hardship and the court is convinced that reaffirmation is a bad idea. C, however, is a credit union. May the court deny approval of the reaffirmation agreement? In re Huskinson, 2008 Bankr. LEXIS 1685 (Bankr. N.D. Ohio June 5, 2008) (based on Bankruptcy Code § 524(m)).

IN RE CHIM

381 B.R. 191 (Bankr. D. Md. 2008)

THOMAS J. CATLIOTA, J.

Before the Court is a motion by Chanmoni Chim (the "Debtor") to approve a Reaffirmation Agreement (the "Reaffirmation Agreement") with American Honda Finance Corporation (the "Lender"). There is no dispute that the Reaffirmation Agreement raises a rebuttable presumption of undue hardship pursuant to Section 524(m) because the Debtor's monthly income is considerably less than her monthly expenses. The Court held a hearing on December 12, 2007, to allow the Debtor to rebut the presumption of undue hardship. For the reasons set forth herein, the Court finds and concludes that the Debtor did not rebut the presumption of undue hardship. Consequently, the Reaffirmation Agreement will not be approved.

Further, at the hearing, it became clear that one of the Debtor's primary reasons for entering into the Reaffirmation Agreement is her concern that, if the Court disapproved the Reaffirmation Agreement, the Lender could exercise the creditor-relief provisions of Sections 362(h), 521(a)(6) and 521(d) by, among other things, declaring a default under the ipso facto[1] provision of her loan contract and repossessing the vehicle notwithstanding the fact that she remains current on the loan. The Court finds and concludes that the Debtor has complied with the requirements of Section 521(a)(2) by timely stating her intention to reaffirm the loan and by timely entering into the Reaffirmation Agreement with the Lender. Therefore, the provisions of Sections 362(h), 521(a)(6) and 521(d) do not apply, and the automatic stay remains in place with respect to the vehicle, the vehicle remains property of the estate, the Debtor is not obligated to turn over possession of the vehicle, and the Lender may not exercise remedies as a result of default under the ipso facto provision under the loan agreement. Stated otherwise, where a debtor timely complies with Section 521(a)(2), the mere fact that the Court does not approve the reaffirmation agreement does not trigger the creditor relief provisions of Sections 362(h), 521(a)(6) or 521(d). Accordingly, the Debtor's concern that the Lender may invoke the creditor-relief provisions of Sections 362(h), 521(a)(6) or 521(d) if the Court disapproves the Reaffirmation

[1] An ipso facto provision is "a contract clause that specifies the consequences of a party's bankruptcy." BLACK'S LAW DICTIONARY 847 (8th ed. 2004). See also In re Margulis, 323 B.R. 130, 135 (Bankr. S.D.N.Y. 2005) (Ipso facto clauses "automatically terminate the contract or lease, or permit the other contracting party to terminate the contracts or lease, in the event of bankruptcy.")

Agreement is not warranted, and is not sufficient to overcome the presumption of undue hardship . . . .

FINDINGS OF FACT

The Debtor filed her Chapter 7 bankruptcy petition on September 24, 2007. On that date, she also filed a Chapter 7 Debtor's statement of intention. Docket No. 5. The statement of intention provides that the Debtor will reaffirm, pursuant to Section 524(c), the secured obligation on her 2007 Honda CRV.

On or about October 18, 2007, the Debtor executed the Reaffirmation Agreement with the Lender. In it, the Debtor sought to reaffirm her secured obligation on the 2007 Honda CRV. The obligation is to be paid over 71 months in the amount of $ 533.87 per month. In Part D of the Reaffirmation Agreement, the Debtor states that her monthly income is $ 2,609 and her monthly expenses are $ 2,839, leaving negative $ 230 to satisfy the monthly payment on the Reaffirmation Agreement. Part D also contained the Debtor's statement of explanation for how she will overcome the presumption of undue hardship that arises from her negative net monthly income. The Debtor wrote that "I have talked to my brother to help me reduce my expenses who I live with and be [sic] absorbing some of my expenses, which will allow me to pay this car loan." Reaffirmation Agreement at p. 8.

The meeting of creditors held pursuant to Section 341 took place on November 7, 2007. Docket No. 8. On November 14, 2007, the Debtor filed the Reaffirmation Agreement. Docket No. 21. The Court scheduled a hearing on the Reaffirmation Agreement because it raised a presumption of undue hardship that was not overcome to the satisfaction of the Court by the Debtor's statement in Part D.

The Debtor and her counsel appeared at the hearing. Counsel proffered that the Debtor anticipated receiving assistance from her younger brother to help her meet her obligations. The brother did not appear. Counsel also proffered that the Debtor is current on the loan. Counsel stated that he was concerned that if the Court rejected the Reaffirmation Agreement, the Lender could seek to exercise the ipso facto provision of the loan agreement, declare a default, and repossess the car notwithstanding that she is current on the loan.

Finally, notwithstanding that the Court rejects the Reaffirmation Agreement herein, the Court finds that the Debtor has acted in good faith in filing the statement of intention and entering into the Reaffirmation Agreement.

CONCLUSIONS OF LAW

Section 524(c) permits a debtor to reaffirm a debt that would otherwise be dischargeable in whole or in part in the debtor's bankruptcy case. A reaffirmation agreement made under Section 524(c) shall be presumed an undue hardship on a debtor if the debtor's monthly income minus the debtor's monthly expenses is less than the scheduled payments on the reaffirmed debt. 11 U.S.C. § 524(m). A debtor may rebut this presumption in writing if the statement includes an explanation that identifies additional sources of funds to make the necessary payments under the agreement. Id. The court may disapprove such agreement if the presumption is not rebutted to the satisfaction of the court, but only after notice and a hearing. Id.

In this case, the Debtor concedes that reaffirming the debt will impose an undue hardship under Section 524(m). The Debtor contends, however, that her younger brother will provide financial assistance to help her meet her obligations. No evidence was presented of the brother's financial condition, nor was he in court to testify on the scope of his commitment to provide such aid. Accordingly, the Court finds and concludes that the Debtor did not rebut the presumption of undue hardship to the satisfaction of the Court.

The Debtor, however, presses that the automatic stay of Section 362(a) may terminate and the creditor will be free to repossess the vehicle if the Reaffirmation Agreement is not approved. The Debtor proffered that although she is current on the payments on the loan, the loan agreement contains an ipso facto provision which automatically places, the Debtor in default under the agreement upon her filing of a bankruptcy proceeding. Thus, the Debtor argues that the fact that the creditor may be able to repossess the vehicle if the Court does not approve the Reaffirmation Agreement is sufficient to overcome the undue hardship implicated under Section 524(m).

The Debtor's concerns stem from certain creditor relief provisions added to Sections 362 and 521 of title 11 by the Bankruptcy Abuse Prevention and Consumer Protection Act of 2005 ("BAPCPA"). Pub. L. No. 109-8, 119 Stat. 23 (2005). As described below, these provisions, when applicable, result in the termination of the automatic stay of Section 362 with respect to certain collateral, require a debtor to deliver the collateral to the secured lender, dictate that such collateral is no longer property of the bankruptcy estate, and provide that ipso facto default provisions in loan contracts are enforceable. When applicable, these relief provisions apply whether or not a debtor is in default under the loan agreement for reasons other than the ipso facto provision.

Section 521(a)(2)(A) requires an individual Chapter 7 debtor who has secured debts to file, within 30 days after the filing of the petition or on or before the date of the meeting of creditors, whichever is earlier, a statement of whether he or she intends to retain or surrender the collateral and, if applicable, specifying that the debtor intends to redeem such collateral or reaffirm the debt secured by such collateral. In addition, Section 521(a)(2)(B) requires a debtor to perform that intention within 30 days after the first date set for the meeting of creditors under section 341(a).

As applied to this case, these provisions required the Debtor to (1) file a statement of her intention within the earlier of October 24, 2007 (30 days of the petition date) or November 7, 2007, (the date of the meeting of creditors); and (2) enter into the Reaffirmation Agreement before December 6, 2007 (within 30 days after the first date set for the meeting of creditors). The Court concludes that the Debtor met both of these deadlines by filing her statement of intention on September 24, 2007, and signing the Reaffirmation Agreement on October 18, 2007.

Notwithstanding the Debtor's compliance with these provisions, the Debtor contends that the Lender may still seek to take action under the creditor relief provisions described herein if the Court declines to approve the reaffirmation agreement.[2] The Debtor's concern is grounded in the distinction between the Debtor entering into the Reaffirmation Agreement, on the one hand, and the Court rejecting the agreement, on the other. The concern arises from the broad relief given to secured creditors under BAPCPA if the applicable

[2] The Court notes that this concern has been expressed on a number of occasions by other debtors during other reaffirmation hearings.

requirements of Section 521 are not met. That relief is contained in Sections 362(h), 521 (a)(6), and 521(d).

Section 362(h) provides that the automatic stay of Section 362(a) terminates with respect to personal property securing a claim if an individual Chapter 7 debtor fails to timely file the statement of intention pursuant to Section 521(a)(2) and then timely perform the intention made in the statement.

Section 521(a)(6) mandates that an individual Chapter 7 debtor must surrender certain collateral to the lender if he or she does not enter into the Reaffirmation Agreement within 45 days after the first meeting of creditors. Moreover, that section further provides that, if the debtor fails to act within the 45 day period, the automatic stay under section 362(a) is terminated with respect to the collateral, the collateral is no longer property of the estate, and the creditor may take whatever action is permitted against the collateral under applicable non-bankruptcy law. Id. at n.9.[3]

Finally, Section 521(d) makes an ipso facto clause in an agreement with a creditor holding a security interest in certain collateral operative if a debtor fails to take the actions enumerated in Sections 521(a)(6) and 362(h)(1).

Working in concert, these provisions provide that, where an individual debtor fails to timely file a statement of intention to reaffirm an applicable secured debt or to timely perform such intention by entering into a reaffirmation agreement, then: (1) the automatic stay of Section 362(a) is terminated with respect to the collateral; (2) the collateral ceases to be property of the estate; (3) the debtor is obligated to turn over possession of the collateral; and (4) the lender may exercise remedies as a result of default under the ipso facto clause under the loan agreement. What does not follow from these provisions, however, is the conclusion that these relief provisions of Sections 362(h), 521(a)(6) and 521(d) apply where the debtor timely enters into a reaffirmation agreement under Section 521(a)(2), but the Court declines to approve the agreement under the guidelines set forth in Section 524.

Section 362(h)(1) only requires an individual debtor to perform his or her duty under Section 521(a)(2) by timely filing a statement of intent to reaffirm a secured debt and to timely perform that intention by entering into a reaffirmation agreement under Section 524(c). It does not require that the Court approve such agreement. Thus, a debtor who has timely filed a statement of intent to reaffirm a secured debt and timely entered into a reaffirmation agreement and filed it with the court has fully performed the obligations under Section 362(h) whether or not the Court approves the reaffirmation agreement.

In the same vein, Section 521(a)(6)(A) only requires that the debtor "enter into an agreement with the creditor pursuant to section 524(c) with respect to the claim secured by such property." Id. at n. 9. Like Section 362(h)(1), it does not require that the Court approve the reaffirmation agreement. Consequently, a debtor who has timely entered into a reaffirmation agreement which the Court declines to approve, has nevertheless performed his or her duty under section 521(a)(6).

Similarly, Section 521(d) makes an ipso facto clause in an agreement with a creditor holding a security interest in certain collateral operative "if the debtor

---

[3] For purposes of this opinion, the Court assumes the Lender holds "an allowed claim for the purchase price secured in whole or in part by an interest in such personal property..." 11 U.S.C. § 521(a)(6).

fails timely to take the actions" enumerated in Sections 521(a)(6) and 362(h)(1). The provision does not make the applicability of the ipso facto clause dependent on Court approval of the agreement.

The Court finds and concludes that the Debtor fully complied with the deadlines of Sections 521(a)(2), 521(a)(6) and 362(h) by filing timely the statement of intention and by signing timely the Reaffirmation Agreement. Because the Court finds and concludes that the Debtor fully complied with all of the pertinent requirements of Sections 362(h) and 521 of the Bankruptcy Code, the automatic stay remains in place with respect to the vehicle, the vehicle remains property of the estate, the debtor is not obligated to turn over possession of the vehicle, and the lender may not exercise remedies as a result of default under the ipso facto clause under the loan agreement. This holding is in accord with several other bankruptcy courts that have addressed this issue. See e.g., In re Husain, 364 B.R. 211 (Bankr. E.D. Va. 2007); In re Stevens, 365 B.R. 610 (Bankr. E.D. Va. 2007); In re Moustafi, 371 B.R. 434 (Bankr. D. Ariz. 2007).

The foregoing rationale applies where a debtor has timely complied with Section 521(a)(2), but the Court declines to approve the reaffirmation agreement. A remaining issue is the scope of the right of the Lender to exercise remedies against the vehicle after the Debtor receives her discharge and the case is closed, but the Debtor remains current on the loan. Prior to the enactment of BAPCPA, the Court of Appeals for the Fourth Circuit held in Home Owners Funding Corp. v. Belanger (In re Belanger), 962 F.2d 345 (4th Cir. 1992) that an individual Chapter 7 debtor's actions with respect to a secured debt and its corresponding collateral were not confined to those options enumerated then in place 11 U.S.C. § 521(2). Id. at 348. Specifically, the Court held that a debtor was not required to reaffirm a debt securing property, or redeem or surrender the same. Instead, the Court agreed with those courts that follow the ride-through approach, and held that a debtor who is current on the payments under the loan agreement may retain the property without reaffirming the debt which it secures. Id. In reaching this conclusion, the Court expressly rejected the holding in In re Bell, 700 F.2d 1053 (6th Cir. 1983) which held that an ipso facto clause becomes effective when the trustee abandons the collateral. Id. at 1058. Following its own precedent, the Belanger Court held that "a default-on-filing clause in an installment loan contract was unenforceable as a matter of law." Belanger, 962 F2d at 348 (citing Riggs Nat'l Bank v. Perry, 729 F2d 982, 984-85 (4th Cir. 1984)).

There is no reason to conclude that the rationale of Belanger should not apply with equal vigor to post-BAPCPA cases where a debtor complies with Section 521(a)(2) but the Court rejects the reaffirmation agreement. To be sure, the creditor relief provisions of Sections 362(h), 521(a)(6), and 521(d) may impact upon a debtor's option of having a credit agreement ride through the bankruptcy case in certain circumstances where the debtor fails to comply with Section 521(a)(2). However, where a court rejects a reaffirmation agreement that was timely entered into by a debtor, the debtor is left in the same position as a debtor who elected to have the loan contract ride through bankruptcy prior to the adoption of the creditor relief provisions in BAPCPA, and the rationale of Belanger continues to apply. Stated otherwise, where a debtor complies with the requirements of Section 521(a)(2), the debtor may retain possession of the collateral after the entry of the discharge and the closure of the case without fear that the lender will exercise an ipso facto provision and repossess the collateral, provided that the debtor is otherwise current under the agreement. See Husain, 364 B.R. at 219 ("Once the discharge is granted, the creditors may not repossess the vehicles without violating the discharge injunction unless there is a subsequent payment or insurance default." (citing In re Riggs, No. 06-60346, 2006 Bankr. LEXIS 2732, 2006 WL 2990218, at(Bankr. W.D. Mo. Oct. 12, 2006))); Stevens, 365 B.R. at 612 ("National Auto Sales may continue to accept payments from the Debtor, 11 U.S.C. § 524(l)(1), but it may not repossess the Vehicle without violating the automatic stay and the discharge injunction unless there is a subsequent payment or insurance default.").

Accordingly, the Debtor's concern that the Lender may invoke the creditor relief provisions of Section 362(h), 521(a)(6) and 521(d) if the Court disapproves the Reaffirmation Agreement is not warranted, and is not sufficient to overcome the presumption of undue hardship.

CONCLUSION

For the forgoing reasons, the Court will decline to approve the Reaffirmation Agreement with the lender. However, the Court finds and concludes that the Debtor has complied with the applicable requirements of Sections 521 and 362(h). Accordingly, the creditor relief provisions of Sections 362(h), 521(a)(6) and 521(d) do not apply . . .

Notes and Questions

1. The Chim court also holds that Home Owners Funding Corp. v. Belanger (In re Belanger), 962 F.2d 345 (4th Cir. 1992), was still good law, under the circumstances in which D complied with § 521(a)(2) by timely executing a reaffirmation agreement which the court declined to approve. In Belanger, a secured party tried to force a debtor to declare whether the debtor, who wished to retain collateral, would redeem it or would negotiate a reaffirmation agreement with the secured party under §524(c). The bankruptcy court concluded that ipso facto clauses were not valid. The court of appeals affirmed, emphasizing that the debtor could retain the collateral if not in default.

Is Belanger good law in light of § 521(d)?

CHAPTER 6 CHAPTER 13 PLANS

A. ELIGIBILITY FOR CHAPTER 13

IN RE SIDEBOTTOM
430 F. 3d 893 (7th Cir. 2005)

WOOD, J.

This case involves a tangle of bankruptcy issues under the Code as it existed prior to the effective date of the Bankruptcy Abuse Prevention and Consumer Protection Act of 2005 (BAPCP Act), Pub. L. 109-8, 119 Stat. 23 (2005). The debtor, Mark A. Sidebottom, owned an eponymous construction company, Sidebottom Builders, Inc. (SBI). David and Jamie Broyles are two of Sidebottom's creditors, who had contracted with SBI to build their dream home, but were left high and dry when SBI ceased performance. Eventually, Sidebottom personally and SBI as a company both filed for protection under Chapter 7 of the Bankruptcy Code; a little while later, before the Chapter 7 proceeding was fully resolved, Sidebottom filed a petition for relief under Chapter 13. The bankruptcy court and district court focused on the question whether the Broyleses' claims for fraud and conversion could be considered a liquidated, noncontingent debt for purposes of the Chapter 13 proceeding--if not, then the Chapter 13 proceeding was barred under 11 U.S.C. § 109(e), because the debt exceeded $290,525. The district court concluded the bar of § 109 indeed applied and that Sidebottom was thus not eligible for Chapter 13 relief. We agree that it was correct to dismiss Sidebottom's case, for the more fundamental reason that he was not entitled in these circumstances simultaneously to pursue Chapter 7 and Chapter 13 relief.

I

On April 6, 2000, David and Jamie Broyles hired SBI to construct a new residence on their property in Indianapolis, Indiana. The cost of the project was estimated at $968,862, which was to be paid in stages according to a schedule set out in the parties' written contract. In order to receive the scheduled payments, SBI had to submit to the Broyleses an application for payment certifying that the stipulated work had been completed. The contract permitted the Broyleses to withhold payment for a variety of reasons: defective work; the filing or threatened filing of a mechanic's lien; the failure of SBI to make payments properly to subcontractors or for labor, materials, or equipment; SBI's failure to follow the plans or requirements of the contract; or nonperformance of the work for that stage.

During the course of construction, the Broyleses made four payments to

SBI totaling $678,205, or 70% of the full contract price. Their last payment was made on October 20, 2000. Shortly after that date, Sidebottom notified them that SBI could not perform the contract and that it planned to file for bankruptcy relief. Around December 29, 2000, the Broyleses began receiving notices from various subcontractors stating that the Broyleses were personally liable for payments that SBI owed to the subcontractors. The Broyleses paid $21,285.62 to one subcontractor, Frank Proctor. On January 10, 2001, the Broyleses and SBI executed a "Contract Termination Agreement" in which SBI acknowledged its breach. The Broyleses then hired another construction company, Hamilton Homes, to complete the project at an additional cost of $700,919, well in excess of the remaining $290,658 due under the contract. On April 9, 2001, the Broyleses filed a complaint against SBI and Sidebottom in the Superior Court of Marion County, Indiana, seeking damages for breach of contract, fraud, conversion, and unjust enrichment.

On April 23, 2001, hard on the heels of the Broyleses' suit, SBI filed a voluntary petition for bankruptcy under Chapter 7 of the Code. About nine months later, on January 23, 2002, Sidebottom followed with a personal Chapter 7 filing, which is the case of immedi-ate relevance to this appeal. Sidebottom's petition naturally triggered an automatic stay of the state court proceedings against him, see 11 U.S.C. § 362(a). The Broyleses filed an ad-versary complaint in the personal bankruptcy, claiming that their fraud and conversion claims against Sidebottom were nondischargeable under 11 U.S.C. § 523(a)(2)(A). The bankruptcy court scheduled an adversary proceeding on the matter for April 9, 2003, while it granted a general discharge to Sidebottom with respect to his other debts on May 31, 2002.

At this point, matters became more complicated. Less than two weeks before the adversary hearing, on March 24, 2003, Sidebottom filed an overlapping petition for relief under Chapter 13, which insofar as the Broyleses' claims were concerned covered exactly the same debts as the ongoing Chapter 7 proceeding. Along with his application, Sidebottom submitted a proposed plan and schedule of assets and liabilities. He listed the Broyleses' claim as a nonpriority, unsecured, disputed, unliquidated, and contingent claim of an "unknown" amount along with $350.14 in unsecured priority claims and $8,658.33 in other unsecured nonpriority claims in the schedule. His proposed plan represented that he would make 36 monthly payments to his creditors in the amount of $100.00, totaling $3,600.

The bankruptcy court assumed that the new Chapter 13 filing required a stay of the scheduled adversary hearing in the Chapter 7 case. On July 13, 2003, it ordered the proceedings in the Chapter 7 nondischargeability action stayed "until completion by the Debtor of all payments required under a confirmed chapter 13 plan, or dismissal or conversion of the chapter 13 case." The Broyleses moved to dismiss Sidebottom's Chapter 13 petition on two grounds: first, that it was not filed in good faith, and second, that Sidebottom's debts exceeded the $290,525 limit imposed by 11 U.S.C. § 109(e). The Broyleses alleged that Sidebottom had filed the case for the sole purpose of avoiding the trial of the pending § 523(a)(2)(A) claim in the Chapter 7 proceeding. In addition, the Broyleses alleged that their fraud and conversion claims represented a noncontingent, liquidated, unsecured debt and thus were covered by the $290,525 cap in § 109(e). At the same time, the Broyleses filed an objection to the confirmation of the Chapter 13 plan, arguing that it was not filed in good faith and that it unfairly discriminated against them.

After an evidentiary hearing, the bankruptcy court dismissed Sidebottom's Chapter 13 petition on the ground that the Broyleses' claims constituted a liquidated, noncontingent debt greater than the statutory cap for eligibility under Chapter 13. The district court summarily affirmed the dismissal.

II

Before this court, Sidebottom argues that the district and bankruptcy courts were mistaken to conclude that the Broyleses' claim was liquidated. His argument is somewhat hard to follow, but essentially he appears to be asserting that the only party that owes money to the Broyleses is his company, SBI, and that there was no reason for holding him personally liable for SBI's debts. He goes on to assert that any contractual liability he himself may have had to the Broyleses was covered by the May 31, 2002, general discharge in the Chapter 7 proceeding. The fraud and conversion claims, which he seems to concede survived that discharge, are not readily ascertainable (indeed, he goes so far as to assert that the amount due under the contract with SBI was not readily determinable either). Last, he argues that the Broyleses' claims against him are contingent, again because they depend on piercing the corporate veil. The Broyleses, as one would expect, defend the bankruptcy court's ruling.

A. Simultaneous "Chapter 20" Filings

Although the parties have focused on § 109(e), a more fundamental question is apparent on the face of these proceedings, namely, whether Sidebottom was entitled to maintain a Chapter 13 proceeding while a Chapter 7 proceeding involving the same debts was pending. A Chapter 13 case that follows a Chapter 7 case is a special form of serial or repetitive filing under the Bankruptcy Code; it has been nicknamed a "Chapter 20" filing. See Lex A. Coleman, Individual Consumer "Chapter 20" Cases After Johnson: An Introduction to Nonbusiness Serial Filings under Chapter 7 and Chapter 13 of the Bankruptcy Code, 9 BANKR. DEV. J. 357 (1992). In Johnson v. Home State Bank, 501 U.S. 78 (1991), the Supreme Court held that the Code did not expressly prohibit such filings where the Chapter 13 case was initiated after the Chapter 7 case had closed. Looking at other Code provisions governing serial filings, the Court wrote that "the absence of a like prohibition on serial filings of Chapter 7 and Chapter 13 petitions, combined with the evident care with which Congress fashioned these express prohibitions, convinces us that Congress did not intend categorically to foreclose the benefit of Chapter 13 reorganization to a debtor who previously has filed for Chapter 7 relief." Id. at 87.[1]

The facts in Johnson involved a Chapter 13 case that was begun after the conclusion of the Chapter 7 proceeding. Sidebottom's case, in contrast, involves a debtor's effort to institute a Chapter 13 proceeding during the pendency of the Chapter 7 proceeding--a move dubbed a "simultaneous Chapter 20" by the

[1] Among the other important changes affected by the BAPCP Act is one in this area. The BAPCP Act amended the Code to bar a debtor from relief under Chapter 13 within four years of receiving a discharge under Chapters 7, 11, or 12, or within two years of receiving a discharge in a previous Chapter 13 proceeding. See BAPCP Act § 312, amending 11 U.S.C. § 1328 . Because these changes apply only prospectively, however, see BAPCP Act § 1501, this statutory bar does not apply to Sidebottom's Chapter 13 case.

bankruptcy bar, to distinguish it from the Johnson-style "sequential Chapter 20." See In re Hodurski, 156 B.R. 353, 355 (Bankr. D. Mass. 1993) (finding no per se prohibition against simultaneous filings but dismissing on the basis of bad faith).

The courts are divided on the question whether a simultaneous "Chapter 20" filing is ever permissible. Unlike the bankruptcy court in Hodurski, the majority has endorsed a per se rule prohibiting a debtor from having more than one bankruptcy case open at any time. See, e.g., In re Turner, 207 B.R. 373, 378 (2d Cir. B.A.P. 1997) (at the preliminary injunction stage, holding that a Chapter 13 case filed before the debtor receives his Chapter 7 discharge is a nullity); In re Scruggs, 320 B.R. 94 (Bankr. D. S.C. 2004) (citing cases); In re Lord, 295 B.R. 16 (Bankr. E.D. N.Y. 2003) (barring a debtor from filing a Chapter 13 proceeding before the Chapter 7 case is closed even if the debtor has already received a discharge in the Chapter 7 case); In re Jackson, 108 B.R. 251, 252 (Bankr. E.D. Cal. 1989) ("once a bankruptcy case is filed, a second case which affects the same debt cannot be maintained"). The majority has relied on the Supreme Court's decision in Freshman v. Atkins, 269 U.S. 121 (1925), which involved a debtor who had been denied a discharge in one bankruptcy proceeding, and while that case was pending, had filed a second petition seeking to discharge both the debts listed in the first petition and some new debts. The Court allowed the petition only with respect to the new debts, writing that the "pendency of the first application precluded a consideration of the second in respect of the same debts." Id. at 122. It analogized this situation to the common law plea of "prior suit pending," which reflected "the general rule that the law will not tolerate two suits at the same time for the same cause." Id. at 123.

A minority of courts has refrained from adopting an absolute ban on simultaneous filings, but their rationale is not helpful to Sidebottom. They have noted that Freshman stands only for the limited proposition that a debtor may not maintain simultaneous applications relating to the same debts and thus is not wholly barred from maintaining two cases under different chapters of the Code in other situations. See, e.g., In re Kosenka, 104 B.R. 40 (Bankr. N.D. Ind. 1989). Some courts have permitted a debtor to file a Chapter 13 petition to reorganize the debts that have survived the Chapter 7 discharge, provided that the debtor has already received the Chapter 7 discharge, even if the Chapter 7 case has not been closed. See, e.g., In re Young, 237 F.3d 1168 (10th Cir. 2001) ; In re Saylors, 869 F.2d 1434 (11th Cir. 1989); In re Ragsdale, 315 B.R. 691 (Bankr. E.D. Mich. 2004); In re Hodurski, 156 B.R. 353. These decisions focus on the lack of an express prohibition on this practice (in the pre-October 2005 Code, of course), and on the rehabilitative purpose of Chapter 13. Rather than banning all Chapter 13 filings during the pendency of a Chapter 7 case, these courts assess the propriety of the Chapter 13 case in light of the good faith standard applicable to confirmations of Chapter 13 plans.

Although the courts have differed with respect to the permissibility of these "simultaneous Chapter 20" cases, there is general agreement that a debtor may not maintain two or more concurrent actions with respect to the same debts. Only the Tenth Circuit may have held otherwise, in In re Young, 237 F.3d 1168. The facts of Young are similar to those before us: the debtor received a general discharge in his Chapter 7 case, but one of his creditors had filed an adversary complaint alleging that the debt owed to it was nondischargeable. Before the bankruptcy court had a chance to resolve that dispute, the debtor "converted" his case to a Chapter 13 proceeding. Thus, as the Tenth Circuit saw it, nothing was left of the Chapter 7 proceeding. It described this course of events as a "Chapter

20" procedure and permitted the conversion. Id. at 1173. Any potential abuse on the debtor's part could be addressed, in the court's view, through the bankruptcy court's general power to ensure good faith in the creation and confirmation of the Chapter 13 plan.

The Second Circuit's Bankruptcy Appellate Panel, in contrast, apparently takes a stricter approach. In Turner, no general discharge had yet been granted at the time the Chapter 13 case involving the same debt was filed, but the BAP's language suggests to us that simultaneous proceedings over a debt that was excluded from the scope of a general discharge would be impermissible in its view. Quoting from In re Kosenka, 104 B.R. at 46, it observed that the Code is designed "to resolve a debtor's financial affairs by administration of a debtor's property as a single estate under a single chapter within the code." 207 B.R. at 378.

In our opinion, the Second Circuit's BAP and the majority of other courts have the better of this debate. It is possible, in fact, that the Tenth Circuit would not disagree about truly simultaneous proceedings, because it appears that the case before it was fully converted from a Chapter 7 proceeding to a Chapter 13 proceeding. Whether that is so or not, it seems to us that a debt like the Broyleses' claim against Sidebottom that is expressly excluded from a general discharge under Chapter 7 falls within the rule articulated by the Turner panel. As Freshman might have put it, the effort to litigate the same matter simultaneously in the Chapter 13 proceeding should have been rejected on the grounds of "same matter pending." This is not a case in which the Chapter 7 proceeding was finished except for some minor technicalities at the end, like the filing of a trustee's final report. Allowing Sidebottom to proceed with the Chapter 13 case significantly affects the Chapter 7 trustee's ability to administer the estate, because it will change how much each creditor gets paid if the Broyleses' claims are resolved through the Chapter 13 process.

B. Good Faith

Although the bankruptcy and district courts relied on § 109(e) to support dismissal of Sidebottom's Chapter 13 case, the Broyleses also argued that it should be dismissed because it was filed in bad faith. Because it ruled on the other ground, the bankruptcy court did not make findings of fact on this point. In our view, however, it would be difficult to conclude otherwise on this record.

When determining whether a Chapter 13 petition was filed in good faith, courts take into account the following nonexhaustive list of factors: (a) the nondischargeability of the debt; (b) the time of the filing of the petition; (c) how the debt arose; (d) the debtor's motive for filing the petition; (e) how the debtor's actions affected creditors; (f) the debtor's treatment of creditors both before and after the petition was filed; and (g) whether the debtor has been forthcoming with the bankruptcy court and the creditors. See Matter of Love, 957 F.2d 1350, 1357 (7th Cir. 1992). Taken as a whole, they cast serious doubt on Sidebottom's petition.

Without an adjudication of nondischargeability under 11 U.S.C. § 523(a), it is impossible to say how the first factor cuts. It does appear, however, that the Broyleses had a nonfrivolous claim that they were prepared to pursue and that Sidebottom went to some lengths to avoid the moment of truth. Looking at factor two, we note that his Chapter 13 petition was filed a mere two weeks before the scheduled adversary hearing. According to the Broyleses, at least, the debt arose as a result of Sidebottom's fraudulent activities and the conversion of their money. If the bankruptcy court had rejected the Broyleses' position in the adversary proceeding, their debt would have been discharged along with all of Sidebottom's other debts, but if it had ruled in their favor, Sidebottom would have been faced with a substantial debt that was nondischargeable. This, we assume, underlies the Broyleses' belief that Sidebottom's primary motive in filing the Chapter 13 case was to avoid a negative result in the nondischargeablity action pending in the Chapter 7 proceeding. He also had a financial incentive to use Chapter 13, if one assumes a significant risk of losing in the Chapter 7 adversary proceeding: his proposed Chapter 13 plan would have forced the Broyleses to receive a pro rata portion of the proposed $3,600 he was offering to fund the Chapter 13 plan--a plan that is less than forthcoming about the nature of the Broyleses' claim. Before Sidebottom's eleventh-hour Chapter 13 petition, the Broyleses had spent considerable time and resources preparing for trial.

The record suggests that Sidebottom used the Chapter 13 filing simply to save the expense of defending the adversary action. Addressing the question of good faith before the bankruptcy court, he reported that during the course of the Chapter 7 proceedings, there had been discussions between counsel with respect to his inability to fund the litigation and to pay the costs and fees necessary to complete it. There was also correspondence on January 15, 2003, which included an offer of settlement and indicated that Sidebottom was unable to participate in the adversary proceeding and would file a Chapter 13 petition in the event that it was necessary to do so prior to going to trial. None of this sounds like a proper use of the bankruptcy procedures to us, although in the absence of our conclusion above about the use of simultaneous "Chapter 20" filings we would probably remand this issue to the bankruptcy court for a finding of fact on good faith.

C. Eligibility under 11 U.S.C. § 109(e)

Last, we address briefly the ground on which the bankruptcy and district courts relied in their judgments dismissing Sidebottom's Chapter 13 proceeding. As the bankruptcy judge pointed out, "unlike other chapters of the Bankruptcy Code, debtors must meet specific debt requirements to be eligible for chapter 13 relief." The governing statute is § 109(e), which read as follows at the time Sidebottom filed:

> Only an individual with regular income that owes, on the date of the filing of the petition, noncontingent, liquidated, unsecured debts of less than $290,525 . . . may be a debtor under chapter 13 of this title.

(Under authority granted by 11 U.S.C. § 104, the Judicial Conference of the United States periodically revises the dollar amounts in various sections of the Bankruptcy Code, including § 109(e) ; the current amount applicable to § 109(e) is $307,675. This change does not affect our analysis of Sidebottom's case.)

The bankruptcy court began by noting that Sidebottom's Chapter 13 petition listed the Broyleses' claims as an unsecured nonpriority claim arising out of a lawsuit in an "unknown" amount. He checked the "contingent," "unliquidated," and "disputed" boxes on the form. Looking beyond Sidebottom's schedules to the complaint the Broyleses had filed in the state court, the court saw that the alleged fraud debt was $500,896.79, and the alleged converted funds were $254,156.91, representing payments made to SBI and Sidebottom that exceeded the value of the work performed. This was enough, in the bankruptcy court's view, to make the allegation that the amount was "unknown" misleading.

It went on to assess Sidebottom's eligibility under § 109(e) on the merits. The judge noted that the mere fact that a debt is disputed does not exempt it from being included in the § 109(e) calculation, citing Matter of Knight, 55 F.3d 231 (7th Cir. 1995), and In re Nicholes, 184 B.R. 82, 87 (9th Cir. B.A.P. 1995). Next, the judge decided that these debts were liquidated, because they could readily be computed by looking at the amount paid to SBI under the contract, the amount of the subcontractors' claims, the amount paid to Hamilton Homes to complete the project, and adjusting for the initial contract price. Even using conservative numbers, the court came up with a figure of $514,296.41, substantially in excess of the statutory ceiling. Importantly, Sidebottom did not contest these calculations: he argued instead that the debt could not readily be determined because his personal liability for SBI's debts was at issue. That point, however, does not address whether the debts are liquidated in amount; it focuses on who must pay them. Finally, the bankruptcy judge ruled that the debt was not contingent, as it did not depend on any future event.

Our only concern with this analysis relates to the question whether the debt was liquidated. The bankruptcy judge was certainly correct to include the disputed amounts in his overall assessment of Sidebottom's schedule. There was nothing contingent about these debts, nor did anyone argue that they were secured. The judge was also entitled to look at the Broyleses' complaint, which was a matter of public record, to see what was at stake in the litigation. Like him, we find Sidebottom's indication that the amount of the debt was "unknown" to be disingenuous; he easily could have described the amount in controversy and said that it was disputed. The liquidation requirement, however, is more problematic. In a sense, the bankruptcy judge avoided it by noting (sensibly enough) that the disputed amounts took Sidebottom's case well over the § 109(e) ceiling. But that is not the same thing as saying that the amounts were readily determinable with any precision. Because there are alternate grounds on which the district court's judgment may be affirmed, we have no need here to decide exactly how precise these computations must be in order to satisfy the statute.

III

We AFFIRM the judgment of the district court, which in turn affirmed the judgment of the bankruptcy court, dismissing Sidebottom's Chapter 13 petition.

Notes and Questions

1. In Sidebottom the debtor faced an adversary proceeding in the chapter 7 case as to whether the fraud claim was dischargeable. In the subsequent chapter 13 case, the charge was dischargeable (though BAPCPA changes this rule). Why couldn't D concede non-dischargeability and then proceed to pay the claim under chapter 13?

IN RE HAMMONDS

729 F.2d 1391 (11th Cir. 1984)

PER CURIAM

In this bankruptcy case, we examine whether a debtor can fund a chapter 13 plan from Aid to Families With Dependent Children (AFDC) checks received from the Bibb County Department of Family and Children Services

(Department). We are asked to determine whether, under 11 U.S.C.A. § 1325(b), a court may order the Department to deliver the debtors' AFDC checks directly to the bankruptcy trustee.

Background

Frances Collins and Callie Jean Hammonds filed petitions under Chapter 13 of Title 11 of the United States Code in the United States Bankruptcy Court for the Middle District of Georgia. Under chapter 13, a debtor who cannot meet monthly contract payments proposes a plan whereby the debts are to be paid over a longer period of time. A trustee is appointed to insure that the proposed payments are made and to disburse the funds pursuant to the plan. Chapter 13 is voluntary, and a debtor can dismiss his plan at anytime, for any reason. After confirmation of a plan, a court may order an entity from whom the debtor receives income to pay all or any part of such income to the trustee. 11 U.S.C.A. § 1325(b).

In this case, the sole source of income for both Collins and Hammonds is an AFDC check from the Department. The bankruptcy court, after confirmation of the debtors' plans, ordered the Department to mail each debtor's AFDC check to the chapter 13 trustee, pursuant to 11 U.S.C.A. § 1325(b). The payment would then be deducted from the check and the remaining funds returned to the debtors. The Department objected to the proposed use of AFDC checks as the basis for a chapter 13 plan. The Department contends that the bankruptcy court's order directing it to mail the debtors' AFDC checks to the trustee would defeat the purpose of the AFDC program.

An appeal ensued from the order of the United States Bankruptcy Court entered October 12, 1982, 23 B.R. 674, ordering the Department to mail the debtors' AFDC checks directly to the chapter 13 bankruptcy trustee. On September 6, 1983, the United States District Court for the Middle District of Georgia held that the bankruptcy court correctly determined that AFDC payments may be used to fund debtors' chapter 13 plans and ordered the Department to mail the checks directly to the trustee. The Department appeals this decision.

The Department asserts that the Debtors' AFDC checks do not constitute "property of the estate" and cannot be used by the debtors to fund their chapter 13 plans.

Discussion

The United States Code defines a debtor under chapter 13 in 11 U.S.C.A. § 109(e). . . . It states:

> Only an individual with regular income that owes, on the date of the filing of the petition, noncontingent, liquidated, unsecured debts of less than $[**][1] and

---

[1] [The monetary eligibility requirements have changed with successive amendments to the Bankruptcy Code. In 1984, (when the Hammonds case was decided), a Chapter 13 debtor needed noncontingent unliquidated unsecured debts of less than $100,000 and noncontingent liquidated secured debts of less than $350,000. Under the BAPCPA 2005 amendments, the limit on noncontingent unliquidated unsecured debts has been raised to $307,675 (from $290,525 for case commenced prior to 4/1/04) and the limit on noncontingent unliquidated secured debts has been

> noncontingent, liquidated, secured debts of less than $[ ], or an individual with regular income and such individual's spouse, except a stockbroker or a commodity broker, that owe, on the date of the filing of the petition, noncontingent, liquidated, unsecured debts that aggregate less than $[ ] and noncontingent, liquidated, secured debts of less than $[ ] may be a debtor under chapter 13 of this title.

An individual with regular income is defined in the Code as an individual whose income is sufficiently stable and regular to enable such individual to make payments under a plan under chapter 13, other than a stockbroker or a commodity broker. 11 U.S.C.A. § 101[(30)]. Once a chapter 13 debtor proposes a plan to meet his debts and that plan is confirmed, "the court may order any entity from whom the debtor received income to pay all or any part of such income to the trustee." 11 U.S.C.A. § 1325(b). The question here is whether an individual whose only income is AFDC checks may be considered an individual with regular income under the bankruptcy laws. If such an individual is considered a debtor, it is clear that a court may direct the Department to send his or her AFDC checks directly to the bankruptcy trustee. 11 U.S.C.A. § 1325(b).

In determining who Congress intended to be considered as an individual with regular income under the Bankruptcy Reform Act of 1978, we turn to an examination of legislative history. The Eleventh Circuit in United States v. Devall, 704 F.2d 1513 (11th Cir.1983), stated that the legislative history of the Bankruptcy Reform Act clearly indicates that the purpose of the term "individual with regular income" is to permit almost any individual with regular income to propose and to have approved a reasonable plan for debt repayment based on that individual's exact circumstances. Devall, 704 F.2d at 1516. The House Report relating to 11 U.S.C.A. § 101[(30)] reveals those individuals Congress deemed eligible for relief under chapter 13.

> The definition [individual with regular income] encompasses all individuals with incomes that are sufficiently stable and regular to enable them to make payments under a chapter 13 plan. Thus, individuals on welfare, social security, fixed pension incomes, or who live on investment incomes, will be able to work out repayment plans with their creditors rather than being forced into straight bankruptcy.

H.R.Rep. No. 95-595, 95th Cong., 1st Sess. at 313, reprinted in 1978 U.S.Code Cong. & Ad.News 5787, 5963, 6269.

An examination of the Bankruptcy Reform Act lends support to the contention that individuals receiving welfare benefits, and more specifically AFDC benefits, can use them to fund a chapter 13 plan. Title 11 U.S.C.A. § 522 analyzes what property a debtor may exempt from his or her estate. The following property may be exempted from the debtor's estate:

> (10) the debtor's right to receive --
>
> (A) a social security benefit, unemployment compensation, or local public assistance benefit; . . .
>
> (D) alimony, support, or separate maintenance, to the extent reasonably necessary for the support of the debtor and any dependent of the debtor.

---

raised to $922,975 (from $871,550 for cases commended prior to 4/1/04)--Ed.].

11 U.S.C.A. § 522.

Congress, in section 522, stated that local public assistance benefits, support reasonably necessary for the support of the debtor and any dependent of the debtor, are a part of the debtor's chapter 13 estate. Section 522 would be meaningless if we were to hold that property exempted (local public assistance benefits) was not intended to be considered as estate property. Devall, 704 F.2d at 1516. Since the Bankruptcy Reform Act specifically allows the debtor to exempt local public assistance benefits from his or her estate, we must conclude that welfare benefits are included in the debtor's chapter 13 estate and are therefore subject to 11 U.S.C.A. § 1325(b)'s provision for income deductions. Since AFDC benefits clearly fall under local public assistance, support reasonably necessary for the support of the debtor and any dependent of the debtor, we must conclude that Congress anticipated that AFDC recipients could use AFDC benefits to fund the chapter 13 plan.

The Department interprets the word welfare, as used in the House Report, to apply only to those types of welfare benefits payable to an individual solely for his own support. It contends that the AFDC program was designed to benefit dependent children, and not to enable parents to use the AFDC checks as part of their chapter 13 plan. The Department's argument is not persuasive. . . .

We are not convinced that a child is not benefited when his parent uses a portion of the AFDC check to fund a chapter 13 plan. Congress, in drafting 42 U.S.C.A. § 601, set forth no specific limitations on the use of AFDC benefits by the recipient parent. Parents, upon receiving AFDC checks, are entitled to spend the funds as they see fit, for the benefit of the family unit. It would, therefore, be anomalous to deprive them of a statutory debt payment mechanism which was enacted for their benefit. United States v. Devall, 704 F.2d at 1517 n. 5.

In addition, the standard procedures for monitoring the use of AFDC payments are not undermined by allowing a benefits recipient access to chapter 13. Title 42 U.S.C.A. § 605 sets out various steps the state agency may take if it determines that AFDC funds are not being used "in the best interests of the child." These steps include counseling and advising the parent or relative, transferring the payments to a more suitable guardian pursuant to 42 U.S.C.A. § 606(b)(2), seeking appointment of a legal guardian, or imposing state penalties. The filing of a voluntary chapter 13 plan does not thwart those remedies; in fact, by requiring the agency to send benefit checks to the trustee in bankruptcy, the bankruptcy judge gives the agency notice of a financial condition that may require monitoring.

The Department has attempted to argue that use of the AFDC funds by the parent to fund the chapter 13 plan is not in the best interest of the dependent child. The bankruptcy court is correct in holding that a chapter 13 plan is not a detrimental use of AFDC funds. Rather, it is another form of budgeting that a parent may elect for the benefit of the family unit. When the family unit is strengthened through the gradual elimination of any debt problems, the needs and desires of the children may, indeed, be satisfied and fulfilled. Moreover, the fact that AFDC benefits are "regular income" for purposes of chapter 13 does not command that a bankruptcy judge automatically approve a plan funded by such payments . . .

The supervision of the bankruptcy judge, who must insure that the payment plan is feasible given the needs of the individual debtor, is a safeguard against a voluntary chapter 13 plan operating to the detriment of the debtor's children. See In re Shebel, 22 B.R. 9 (Bkrtcy.D.Vt.1982) (even though AFDC benefits are income, bankruptcy judge rejectschapter 13 plan because payment schedule was not feasible given the needs of debtor's dependents)...

We conclude that the district court was correct when it held that an individual who receives AFDC benefits can use them to fund a chapter 13 plan. Congress specifically stated that an individual on welfare is deemed an individual having regular income under chapter 13. A parent who receives AFDC benefits could, outside of a chapter 13 plan, use a portion of the amount to repay debts. As such, it would be incomprehensible for a court to conclude that this parent would be prohibited from using the AFDC benefits to fund a chapter 13 plan. Under 11 U.S.C.A. § 1325(b), a court may order the Department to deliver the debtors' AFDC checks directly to the bankruptcy trustee. AFFIRMED.

Notes and Questions

1. The "regular income" requirement can also be found in the title of Chapter 13: "Adjustment of Debts of an Individual with Regular Income."

2. The stability and regularity of the income, rather than the source, has been the benchmark for determining whether the individual has regular income for Chapter 13 eligibility. In re Lapin, 302 B.R. 184 (Bankr. S.D. Tex. 2003) (income from IRA withdrawals sufficient) In re Widdicombe, 269 B.R. 803 (Bankr. W.D. Ark. 2001) (income from real estate commissions, varying from month to month, sufficient for "regular income.") As illustrated by Hammonds,, the debtor need not be a wage-earner. In general, gratuitous payments to a debtor by family members do not constitute regular and stable income, unless made made pursuant to a contractual or legal obligation or there is evidence of regular contributions in the past. In re Mullins, 360 B.R. 493 (Bankr. W.D. Va. 2007); In re Antoine, 208 B.R. 17, 19-20 (Bankr. E.D.N.Y. 1997). But see In re Baird, 228 B.R. 324, 41 Collier Bankr. Cas. 2d (MB) 282 (Bankr. M.D. Fla. 1999) (gratuitous payments sufficient for "regular income").

MARRAMA v CITIZENS BANK
549 U.S. 365 (2007)

STEVENS, J.

The principal purpose of the Bankruptcy Code is to grant a "'fresh start'" to the "'honest but unfortunate debtor.'" Grogan v. Garner, 498 U.S. 279, 286, 287 (1991). Both Chapter 7 and Chapter 13 of the Code permit an insolvent individual to discharge certain unpaid debts toward that end. Chapter 7 authorizes a discharge of prepetition debts following the liquidation of the debtor's assets by a bankruptcy trustee, who then distributes the proceeds to creditors. Chapter 13 authorizes an individual with regular income to obtain a discharge after the successful completion of a payment plan approved by the bankruptcy court. Under Chapter 7 the debtor's non-exempt assets are controlled by the bankruptcy trustee; under Chapter 13 the debtor retains possession of his property. A proceeding that is commenced under Chapter 7 may be converted to a Chapter 13 proceeding and vice versa. 11 U.S.C. §§ 706(a), 1307(a) and (c).

An issue that has arisen with disturbing frequency is whether a debtor who acts in bad faith prior to, or in the course of, filing a Chapter 13 petition by, for example, fraudulently concealing significant assets, thereby forfeits his right to obtain Chapter 13 relief. The issue may arise at the outset of a Chapter 13 case in response to a motion by creditors or by the United States trustee either to dismiss the case or to convert it to Chapter 7, see § 1307(c). It also may arise in a Chapter 7 case when a debtor files a motion under § 706(a) to convert to Chapter 13. In the former context, despite the absence of any statutory provision specifically addressing the issue, the federal courts are virtually unanimous that prepetition bad-faith conduct may cause a forfeiture of any right to proceed with a Chapter 13 case. In the latter context, however, some courts have suggested that even a bad-faith debtor has an absolute right to convert at least one Chapter 7 proceeding into a Chapter 13 case even though the case will thereafter be dismissed or immediately returned to Chapter 7. We granted certiorari to decide whether the Code mandates that procedural anomaly.

I

On March 11, 2003, petitioner, Robert Marrama, filed a voluntary petition under Chapter 7, thereby creating an estate consisting of all his property "wherever located and by whomever held." 11 U.S.C. § 541(a). Respondent Mark DeGiacomo is the trustee of that estate. Respondent Citizens Bank of Massachusetts (hereinafter Bank) is the principal creditor.

In verified schedules attached to his petition, Marrama made a number of statements about his principal asset, a house in Maine, that were misleading or inaccurate. For instance, while he disclosed that he was the sole beneficiary of the trust that owned the property, he listed its value as zero. He also denied that he had transferred any property other than in the ordinary course of business during the year preceding the filing of his petition. Neither statement was true. In fact, the Maine property had substantial value, and Marrama had transferred it into the newly created trust for no consideration seven months prior to filing his Chapter 13 petition. Marrama later admitted that the purpose of the transfer was to protect the property from his creditors.

After Marrama's examination at the meeting of creditors, see 11 U.S.C. § 341, the trustee advised Marrama's counsel that he intended to recover the Maine property as an asset of the estate. Thereafter, Marrama filed a "Verified Notice of Conversion to Chapter 13." Pursuant to Federal Rule of Bankruptcy Procedure 1017(c)(2), the notice of conversion was treated as a motion to convert, to which both the trustee and the Bank filed objections. Relying primarily on Marrama's attempt to conceal the Maine property from his creditors,[3] the trustee contended that the request to convert was made in bad faith and would constitute an abuse of the bankruptcy process. The Bank opposed the conversion on similar grounds.

At the hearing on the conversion issue, Marrama explained through counsel that his misstatements about the Maine property were attributable to "scrivener's error," that he had originally filed under Chapter 7 rather than Chapter 13 because he was then unemployed, and that he had recently become employed and was therefore eligible to proceed under Chapter 13.[4] The

[3]The trustee also noted that in his original verified schedules Marrama had claimed a property in Gloucester, Mass., as a homestead exemption, see 11 U.S.C. § 522(b)(2); Mass. Gen. Laws, ch. 188, § 1 (West 2005), but testified at the meeting of creditors that he did not reside at the property and was receiving rental income from it, App. 71a-72a. Moreover, when asked at the meeting whether anyone owed him any money, Marrama responded "No," id., at 50a, and in response to a similar question on Schedule B to his petition, which specifically requested a description of any "tax refunds," Marrama indicated that he had "none." Supp. App. 6. In fact, Marrama had filed an amended tax return in July 2002 in which he claimed the right to a refund, and shortly before the hearing on the motion to convert, the Internal Revenue Service informed the trustee that Marrama was entitled to a refund of $ 8,745.86, App. 30a-31a.

[4] The parties dispute the accuracy of this representation. The trustee's brief notes that Schedule I to Marrama's original petition indicates that he had been employed by a flooring company at the time the case was filed. See Brief for Respondent Mark G. DeGiacomo 10, n. 7

Bankruptcy Judge rejected these arguments, ruling that there is no "Oops" defense to the concealment of assets and that the facts established a "bad faith" case. The judge denied the request for conversion.

Marrama's principal argument on appeal to the Bankruptcy Appellate Panel for the First Circuit was that he had an absolute right to convert his case from Chapter 7 to Chapter 13 under the plain language of § 706(a) of the Code. The panel affirmed the decision of the Bankruptcy Court. It construed § 706(a), when read in connection with other provisions of the Code and the Bankruptcy Rules, as creating a right to convert a case from Chapter 7 to Chapter 13 that "is absolute only in the absence of extreme circumstances." In re Marrama, 313 B. R. 525, 531 (2004). In concluding that the record disclosed such circumstances, the panel relied on Marrama's failure to describe the transfer of the Maine residence into the revocable trust, his attempt to obtain a homestead exemption on rental property in Massachusetts, and his nondisclosure of an anticipated tax refund.

On appeal from the panel, the Court of Appeals for the First Circuit also rejected the argument that § 706(a) gives a Chapter 7 debtor an absolute right to convert to Chapter 13. In addition to emphasizing that the statute uses the word "may" rather than "shall," the court added:

> "In construing subsection 706(a), it is important to bear in mind that the bankruptcy court has unquestioned authority to dismiss a chapter 13 petition -- as distinguished from converting the case to chapter 13 -- based upon a showing of 'bad faith' on the part of the debtor. We can discern neither a theoretical nor a practical reason that Congress would have chosen to treat a first-time motion to convert a chapter 7 case to chapter 13 under subsection 706(a) differently from the filing of a chapter 13 petition in the first instance." In re Marrama, 430 F.3d 474, 479 (2005) (citations omitted).

While other Courts of Appeals and bankruptcy appellate panels have refused to recognize any "bad faith" exception to the conversion right created by § 706(a), we conclude that the courts in this case correctly held that Marrama forfeited his right to proceed under Chapter 13.

II

The two provisions of the Bankruptcy Code most relevant to our resolution of the issue are subsections (a) and (d) of 11 U.S.C. § 706, which provide:

> "(a) The debtor may convert a case under this chapter to a case under chapter 11, 12, or 13 of this title at any time, if the case has not been converted under section 1112, 1208, or 1307 of this title. Any waiver of the right to convert a case under this subsection is unenforceable.
>
> (d) Notwithstanding any other provision of this section, a case may not be converted to a case under another chapter of this title unless the debtor may be a debtor under such chapter."

(citing Supp. App. 18, 30). Marrama's counsel stated during oral argument, however, that the income listed in Schedule I represented an estimate based on employment that had not yet begun. Tr. of Oral Arg. 24. Since the sufficiency of the evidence of bad faith is not at issue, we may assume that Marrama did have more income available when he sought to convert than when he commenced the Chapter 7 case.

Petitioner contends that subsection (a) creates an unqualified right of conversion. He seeks support from language in both the House and Senate Committee Reports on the provision. The Senate Report stated:

> "Subsection (a) of this section gives the debtor the one-time absolute right of conversion of a liquidation case to a reorganization or individual repayment plan case. If the case has already once been converted from chapter 11 or 13 to chapter 7, then the debtor does not have that right. The policy of the provision is that the debtor should always be given the opportunity to repay his debts, and a waiver of the right to convert a case is unenforceable." S. Rep. No. 95-989, p. 94 (1978); see also H. R. Rep. No. 95-595, p. 380 (1977) (using nearly identical language).

The Committee Reports' reference to an "absolute right" of conversion is more equivocal than petitioner suggests. Assuming that the described debtor's "opportunity to repay his debts" is a short-hand reference to a right to proceed under Chapter 13, the statement that he should "always" have that right is inconsistent with the earlier recognition that it is only a one-time right that does not survive a previous conversion to, or filing under, Chapter 13. More importantly, the broad description of the right as "absolute" fails to give full effect to the express limitation in subsection (d). The words "unless the debtor may be a debtor under such chapter" expressly conditioned Marrama's right to convert on his ability to qualify as a "debtor" under Chapter 13.

There are at least two possible reasons why Marrama may not qualify as such a debtor, one arising under § 109(e) of the Code, and the other turning on the construction of the word "cause" in § 1307(c). The former provision imposes a limit on the amount of indebtedness that an individual may have in order to qualify for Chapter 13 relief. More pertinently, the latter provision, § 1307(c), provides that a Chapter 13 proceeding may be either dismissed or converted to a Chapter 7 proceeding "for cause" and includes a nonexclusive list of 10 causes justifying that relief. None of the specified causes mentions prepetition bad-faith conduct (although subparagraph 10 does identify one form of Chapter 7 error-which is necessarily prepetition conduct-that would justify dismissal of a Chapter 13 case). Bankruptcy courts nevertheless routinely treat dismissal for prepetition bad-faith conduct as implicitly authorized by the words "for cause." In practical effect, a ruling that an individual's Chapter 13 case should be dismissed or converted to Chapter 7 because of prepetition bad-faith conduct, including fraudulent acts committed in an earlier Chapter 7 proceeding, is tantamount to a ruling that the individual does not qualify as a debtor under Chapter 13. That individual, in other words, is not a member of the class of "'honest but unfortunate debtors'" that the bankruptcy laws were enacted to protect. See Grogan v. Garner, 498 U.S., at 287. The text of § 706(d) therefore provides adequate authority for the denial of his motion to convert.

The class of honest but unfortunate debtors who do possess an absolute right to convert their cases from Chapter 7 to Chapter 13 includes the vast majority of the hundreds of thousands of individuals who file Chapter 7 petitions each year. Congress sought to give these individuals the chance to repay their debts should they acquire the means to do so. Moreover, as the Court of Appeals observed, the reference in § 706(a) to the unenforceability of a waiver of the right to convert functions "as a consumer protection provision against adhesion contracts, whereby a debtor's creditors might be precluded from attempting to prescribe a waiver of the debtor's right to convert to chapter 13 as a non-negotiable condition of its contractual agreements." 430 F.3d at 479.

A statutory provision protecting a borrower from waiver is not a shield against forfeiture. Nothing in the text of either § 706 or § 1307(c) (or the legislative history of either provision) limits the authority of the court to take appropriate action in response to fraudulent conduct by the atypical litigant who has demonstrated that he is not entitled to the relief available to the typical debtor.[11] On the contrary, the broad authority granted to bankruptcy judges to take any action that is necessary or appropriate "to prevent an abuse of process" described in § 105(a) of the Code, is surely adequate to authorize an immediate denial of a motion to convert filed under § 706 in lieu of a conversion order that merely postpones the allowance of equivalent relief and may provide a debtor with an opportunity to take action prejudicial to creditors.

Indeed, as the Solicitor General has argued in his brief amicus curiae, even if § 105(a) had not been enacted, the inherent power of every federal court to sanction "abusive litigation practices," see Roadway Express, Inc. v. Piper, 447 U.S. 752, 765 (1980), might well provide an adequate justification for a prompt, rather than a delayed, ruling on an unmeritorious attempt to qualify as a debtor under Chapter 13.

Accordingly, the judgment of the Court of Appeals is affirmed. It is so ordered.

JUSTICE ALITO, WITH WHOM THE CHIEF JUSTICE, JUSTICE SCALIA AND JUSTICE THOMAS JOIN, DISSENTING. Under the clear terms of the Bankruptcy Code, a debtor who initially files a petition under Chapter 7 has the right to convert the case to another chapter under which the case is eligible to proceed. The Court, however, holds that a debtor's conversion right is conditioned upon a bankruptcy judge's finding of "good faith." Because the imposition of this condition is inconsistent with the Bankruptcy Code, I respectfully dissent . . .

Notes and Questions

1. Courts dismissing a Chapter 13 petition for bad faith look to the totality of the circumstances. The 9th Circuit Court of Appeals laid out the following factors:

> (1) whether the debtor misrepresented facts in his [petition or] plan, unfairly manipulated the Bankruptcy Code, or otherwise [filed] his Chapter 13 [petition or] plan in an inequitable manner, (2) the debtor's history of filings and dismissals, (3) whether the debtor only intended to defeat state court litigation, (4) whether egregious behavior is present.

Leavitt v. Soto (In re Leavitt), 171 F.3d 1219, 1224 (9th Cir. 1999) (internal citations omitted). Furthermore, a finding of bad faith does not require fraudulent intent by the debtors. Id. Other courts will also look at the nature of the debt, how the debt arose, the timing of the petition, the

[11]We have no occasion here to articulate with precision what conduct qualifies as "bad faith" sufficient to permit a bankruptcy judge to dismiss a Chapter 13 case or to deny conversion from Chapter 7. It suffices to emphasize that the debtor's conduct must, in fact, be atypical. Limiting dismissal or denial of conversion to extraordinary cases is particularly appropriate in light of the fact that lack of good faith in proposing a Chapter 13 plan is an express statutory ground for denying plan confirmation. 11 U.S.C. § 1325(a)(3); see In re Love, 957 F.2d at 1356 ("Because dismissal is harsh . . . the bankruptcy court should be more reluctant to dismiss a petition . . . for lack of good faith than to reject a plan for lack of good faith under Section 1325(a)").

debtor's motive in filing the petition, how the debtor's action affected creditors, the debtors treatment of creditors both before and after the petition was filed whether the debtor has been forthcoming with the bankruptcy court and creditors. In re Butt, 1999 Bankr. LEXIS 1820, at *18 (Bankr. S.D. Ohio 1999) ("From the foregoing factors, which are not exclusive, it is easy to see why it has been said that if a court looks hard enough, some evidence of bad faith can be found in almost every case. See William Thomas Thurman & Brett P. Johnson, Bankruptcy and the Bad Faith Filing, 10 Utah B.J. 12, 17 (1997)").

2. In Maremma, D allegedly made a fraudulent conveyance of his house. Is that prepetition act enough to justify dismissing a chapter 13 petition? If not, then how was D in bad faith for converting to chapter 13, when D could have commenced the case there? Incidentally, according to § 1325(a)(4), every creditor in chapter 13 must receive an amount "not less than the amount that would be paid onsuch claim if the estate of the debtor were lqiuidated under chapter 7." If, in a hypothetical chapter 7, there would have been a large fraudulent conveyance recovery, any unsecured creditor is entitled to have that hypothetical event reflected in the chapter 13 dividend. As a practical matter, however, creditors in chapter 13 may lack the incentive to litigate the fraudulent conveyance issue in the guise of objecting to the confirmation of the chapter 13 plan. Also, it may be observed that the standing chapter 13 trustee has the power to bring avoidance actions, but this trustee is accustomed to receiving wages from D and paying the creditors pursuant to the plan. Rarely do they perform any other function.

3. After Maremma, does D have an absolute right to convert her chapter 13 case to chapter 7? See Bankruptcy Code § 1307(a); Laughlin v. United States, 912 F.2d 197, 203 (8th Cir. 1990) ("a chapter 13 debtor has an absolute right to have the case dismissed, to convert the case to Chapter 7, or request modification of the plan") (citations omitted). In Rosson v. Fitzgerald (In re Rosson), 545 F.3d 764 (9th Cir. 2008), a debtor assured the bankruptcy court orally that proceeds of an arbitration would be paid to the chapter 13 trustee for distribution of the creditors. When the debtor won a sizable sum, the debtor used it to improve his house (which was property of the estate) instead of paying the creditors. The debtor then sought a voluntary dismissal of the case. The bankruptcy court denied the motion to dismiss and instead sua sponte converted the case to chapter 7, so that an independent trustee could pursue the money. The Ninth Circuit agreed that the debtor had no absolute right to dismiss the chapter 13 case, citing Marrema.

B. THE STANDING TRUSTEE AND THE PAYMENT MECHANISM

David Gray Carlson, Cars and Homes in Chapter 13 Under the 2005 Bankruptcy Amendments, 15 AM. BANKR. INST. L. REV. 300, 302-04 (2006).

Whether a secured lender is subject to reinstatement or cram down, the debtor is expected to fund a stream of payments out of postpetition income. In order to administer chapter 13 cases, a bankruptcy court engages a standing trustee[1] to receive these wages from the debtor.[2] Typically, the plan, which only the debtor can propose,[3] provides that every month the debtor will voluntarily write a check to the chapter 13 trustee. Upon receiving these funds, the chapter 13 trustee writes a new check to creditors listed under the plan.[4] If the debtor ceases making payments (as is usually the case) the chapter 13 trustee has authority, along with other parties in interest, to seek remedies, including conversion to chapter 7, dismissal or modification of the plan.[5]

The chapter 13 trustee obtains a fee for his services and is understandably

---

[1] 11 U.S.C. §1302(a).

[2] 11 U.S.C. §1326(a).

[3] 11 U.S.C. § 1321 ("The debtor shall file a plan"). To my knowledge, this is the shortest statute--the "Jesus wept"--of the United States Code.

[4] See In re Lee, 167 B.R. 417, 419 (Bankr. S.D. Miss. 1992), aff'd, 168 B.R. 319 (A.S. Miss. 1993), aff'd, 22 F.3d 1094 (5th Cir. 1994) (reporting that the chapter 13 trustee wrote 10-15 thousand checks a month).

[5] 11 U.S.C. §§ 1302(b)(2)(C), 1307, 1329.

jealous of it, as an institutional matter. According to 28 U.S.C. § 586(e)(1), the attorney general must fix a maximum annual salary and a percentage fee not to exceed ten percent (in non-farm cases).[6] Courts have no discretion to raise or lower the trustee's fee.[7] The fee is in fact not related to the salary. If the chapter 13 trustee gets a larger fee, it does not go into his pocket but simply defrays the salary. A surplus over salary and expenses simply allows the attorney general to lower the percentage fee, which is often less than the ten percent maximum.[8]

The fee, not technically an administrative claim,[9] is a percentage of wages that the debtor actually sends in. So one intractable issue is whether the debtor can pay the mortgage lender or other secured creditor directly, without the intercession of the chapter 13 trustee. This is often called payment "outside the plan." Of course, the plan will provide for payments "outside the plan," and therefore these are really payments "under the plan." What "outside the plan" really means is not through the chapter 13 trustee.[10]

If direct payments to creditors are permitted, the chapter 13 trustee's fee could be reduced, to the general benefit of the unsecured creditors or perhaps the debtor.[11] If this were the only concern, it would appear that the issue only involves the chapter 13 trustee's fee, and the effect direct payments have on the overall setting of the fee for all creditors.[12] But there is more to it. Many believe that supervisory efficiencies are gained if all payments go through the chapter 13 trustee.[13] The chapter 13 trustee's position is therefore not simply a matter of fees but is colorably about the community of interests involved in the chapter 13 case.

Prior to 2005, courts took every possible position on whether creditors could make payments directly to the trustee without involving the chapter 13 trustee. Some courts permitted it, citing the fact that, according to §1326(c), "[e]xcept as otherwise provided in the plan or in the order confirming the plan,

[6] But see Kathleen A. Laughlin, The Standing Chapter 13 Trustee's Percentage Fee: Solving an Algebraic Equation, 24 CREIGHTON L. REV. 823 (1991) (arguing that the amount received by the chapter 13 trustee must be augmented by the trustee's fee; the ten percent is calculated from that larger amount, with the result that the trustee takes over 11.1% from the amount the debtor pays in); compare Foulston v. BDT Farms, Inc. (In re BDT Farms, Inc.), 21 F.3d 1019 (10th Cir. 1994) (adopting Laughlin's theory in a chpater 12 case) with Pelofsky v. Wallace, 197 B.R. 82 (E.D. Mo. 1995) (rejecting it in a chapter 13 case).

[7] In re Schollett, 980 F.2d 639 (10th Cir. 1992) (chapter 12).

[8] Marianne B. Culhane & Michaela M. White, Taking the New Consumer Bankruptcy Model For a Test Drive: Means-Testing Real Chapter 7 Debtors, 7 AM. BANKR. L. REV. 27 (1999) (1995 average was 5.6%).

[9] It is excluded from §326 by virtue of subparagraph (b) and so is excluded from §330(a) and hence from §503(b) by virtue of subparagraph (2). In re Turner, 168 B.R. 882, 886 (Bankr. W.D. Tex. 1994).

[10] In re Foster, 670 F.2d 478, 485 (5th Cir. 1982); In re Venuto, 343 B.R. 120, 133 n.21 (Bankr. E.D. Pa. 2006); In re Perez, 339 B.R. 385, 390 n.4 (Bankr. S.D. Tex. 2006).

[11] Reduction of the trustee's fee cannot aid the secured creditors, who are entitled to receive the value of their collateral, irrespective of the fee. In re Turner, 168 B.R. 882 (Bankr. W.D. Tex. 1994). The debtor is helped only where she proposed a 100% payout to the unsecureds. After that point, the debtor must pay more to reimburse the trustee. Id. at 884 (precluding confirmation of plan when debtor proposed to sgift payment of administrative expenses to secured and unsecured creditors).

[12] But see In re Perez, 339 B.R. 385, 390 n.4 (Bankr. S.D. Tex. 2006) (payments outside the plan cannot be permitted solely to avoid the fee) (citing cases).

[13] Id. at 390-91, 414 (claiming efficiencies as a result of requiring payment through the trustee by local rule).

the trustee shall make payments to the creditors under the plan."[14] In addition, §1322(a)(1) requires a chapter 13 plan to

> provide for the submission of all or such portion of future earnings or other future income of the debtor to the supervision and control of the trustee as is necessary for the execution of the plan . . .[15]

The italicized language suggests that direct payment is contemplated in the Bankruptcy Code. There is no requirement that all wages must be paid to the chapter 13 trustee.[16]

A line of authority emphasizes that only where the debtor reinstates the contract going forward does the bankruptcy court have discretion to permit direct payments from the debtor to the secured creditor.[17] If the contract is reinstated, payments on that contract are supposedly not "under the plan." Rather, only cram down payments are "under the plan."[18] The fomer can be made directly, the latter not. Where a contract is resinstated going forward and curred retrospectively, the debtor may pay the contract installments directly, but the cure amounts must be paid through the chapter 13 trustee.[19]

Where direct payment is permitted, some courts (prior to 1986) insisted that the chapter 13 trustee obtain the fee that would have been generated if payments were entirely inside the plan.[20] Since the 1986 amendments to the Bankruptcy Code, courts now permit direct payment with the consequence of lower fees for the chapter 13 trustee.[21]

Meanwhile, other courts have insisted that only the chapter 13 trustee

---

[14] In re Foster, 670 F.2d 478, 486 (5th Cir. 1982); In re Vigil, 344 B.R. 624, 629 (Bankr. D.N.M. 2006).

[15] Emphasis added.

[16] Judge Carol Kenner responds to this point by asserting that the exception in §1322(a) refers to sales proceeds of prepetition property and third party gifts, which can be paid directly to creditors. Wages, however, she insists must always be paid to the chapter 13 trustee. In re Harris, 200 B.R. 745, 748 (Bankr. D. Mass. 1996). This, however, does not explain away the fact that §1322(a)(1) allows a portion of future earnings "as is necessary for the execution of the plan" can be paid to the trustee. In chapter 12, which closely resembles chapter 13, there is further evidence for direct payments. Section 1225(a)(5)(B)(ii)--chapter 12's cram down provision--refers to "property to be distributed by the trustee or the debtor under the plan. . . " (emphasis added). These words do not appear in §1325(a)(5), however. See Michel v. Beard (In re Beard), 45 F.3d 113 (6th Cir. 1995) (approving chapter 12 plan calling for direct cram down payments).

[17] In re Aberegg, 961 F.2d 1307 (7th Cir. 1992); In re Clay, 339 B.R. 784, 786 (Bankr. D. Utah 2006); In re Marriott, 161 B.R. 816 (Bankr. S.D. Ill. 1993); In re Kosmicki, 161 B.R. 828 (Bankr. D. Neb.. 1993); In re Finkbine, 94 B.R. 46 (Bankr. S.D. Ohio 1988).

[18] Telfair v. First Union Mortgage Corp., 216 F.3d 1333 (11th Cir. 2000), cert. denied, 531 U.S. 1073 (2000) (claiming regular loan payments were outside the planl In re Case, 11 B.R. 843 (Bankr. D. Utah 2006).

[19] In re Lopez, 350 B.R. 868 (Bankr. C.D. Cal. 2006).

[20] In re Foster, 670 F.2d 478, 490-91 (5th Cir. 1982) . . . . The Foster court, however, also affirmed the discretion of the court to lower the percentage fee, if appropriate. But this discretion was eliminated in favor of the attorney general in 1986. In re Gregory, 143 B.R. 424, 427 n.2 (Bankr. E.D. Tex. 1992). Also, after 1986, 28 U.S.C. §586(e) permits a percentage fee on amounts actually collected by the trustee. Wagner v. Armstrong (In re Wagner), 36 F.3d 723 (8th Cir. 1994) (chapter 12); In re Clay, 339 B.R. 784, 786 n.8, 10 (Bankr. D. Utah 2006).

[21] Wagner v. Armstrong, 36 F.3d 723 (8th Cir. 1994) ([supporting] awarding no fees to trustee for disbursements made directly to creditors; In re Venuto, 343 B.R. 120, 133 (Bankr. E.D. Pa. 2006) (allowing debtor to act as own disbursing agent when seeking cure of pre-petition default).

could be the disbursing agent for the creditors, including the home mortgage[22] and car lender.[23] Others think the bankruptcy courts have discretion to decide. Some courts insist that the debtor show significant[24] or sufficient[25] reasons for direct payment. Others disagree and require only that the plan generally meet the confirmation minima set forth in §1325(a).[26] No less than 21 factors have been listed as governing when a debtor should be permitted to make direct payments.[27] The national trend is said to be in favor of requiring all payments to be made through the chapter 13 trustee.[28]

BAPCPA provides some opaque hints that direct payment is at least permitted, perhaps required, but, being deeply imbedded in the adequate protection provisions, they are best presented in that context.

Notes and Questions

1. Under new Bankruptcy Code § 1326(a)(1), a debtor is directed to make payments not later than 30 days after the chapter 13 plan is filed by the debtor--i.e., before the plan is confirmed. The payment must be to the standing trustee, to lessors of personal property (i.e., cars) and adequate protection directly to a creditor holding an allowed claim secured by personal property . . . " Bankruptcy Code § 1326(a)(1)(C) (emphasis added). Does this mean Congress has a view about payments outside the plan?

2. The chapter 13 trustee will have debtor funds even before confirmation. What if no plan is confirmed? According to § 1326(a)(2):

> A payment made under paragraph (1)(A)[1] shall be retained by the trustee until confirmation or denial of confirmation. If a plan is confrimed, the trustee shall

---

[22] Mortgagees have protested payment via the chapter 13 trustee because there is a 45 day delay in obtaining payment. These objections to confirmation of plans have been rejected. In re Harris, 200 B.R. 745, 749 (Bankr. D. Mass. 1996) (holding mortgage payments were to be made through trustee). Sale of the mortgaged premises and surrender of the cash proceeds, however, need not take place via the trustee. In re Schneekloth, 186 B.R. 713 (Bankr. D. Mont. 1995) (chapter 12 case).

[23] See In re Fulkrod, 973 F.2d 801, 803 (9th Cir. 1992) (chapter 12 case); In re Perez, 339 B.R. 385, 390 (Bankr. S.D. Tex. 2006) (describing local rule prohibiting direct payment); In re Jackson Ranch Co., 181 B.R. 552 (Bankr. E.D. Okla. 1995) (chapter 12 case); In re Ford, 179 B.R. 821, 824 (Bankr. E.D. Tex. 1995); In re Hankins, 62 B.R. 831 (Bankr. W.D. Va. 1986) (rejecting debtors' attempts to characterize certain payments as "outside the plan" in order to avoid trustee's statutory fees).

[24] In re Barber, 191 B.R. 879, 884 (Bankr. D. Kan. 1996).

[25] In re McCann, 202 B.R. 824, 830 (Bankr. N.D.N.Y. 1996).

[26] In re Vigil, 344 B.R. 624, 630, 632 (Bankr. D.N.M. 2006) ("debtors need not demonstrate compelling circumstances" when confirming plan so long as plan meets requirements for confirmation in section 1325(a)").

[27] They are: (1) debtor's history; (2) reasons for the bankruptcy; (3) trustee's likelihood of delay; (4) whether the plan modifies the secured claim; (5) sophistication of the creditor; (6) ability of the creditor to monitor; (7) whether the debt is commercial or consumer; (8) the ability of the debtor to reorganize in the absence of direct payment; (9) whether payments can be delayed; (10) number of payments; (11) whether direct payments impair the trustee; (12) unique circumstances; (13) post-bankruptcy behavior; (15) good faith; (16) plan provisions; (17) consent; (18) ability of the trustee to monitor; (19) trustee burdens; (2) trustee's salary; (21) potential for abuse. In re Perez, 339 B.R. 385, 409 (Bankr. S.D. Tex. 2006). In Perez, Judge Jeff Bohm ruled that the debtor's history of responsibility should be the most important criterion.

[28] Id. at 414. Merely reducing the trustee's fee has been held no a ground for permitting direct payments to creditors. In re Genereux, 137 B.R. 411, 413 (Bankr. W.D. Wash. 1992); In re Harris, 107 B.R. 204, 207 (Bankr. D. Neb. 1989).

[1] This refers to payments by a debtor to the trustee pursuant to the terms of a proposed, not-yet-confirmed plan.

> distribute any such payment in accordance with the plan as soon as is practicable. If a plan is not confirmed, the trustee shall return any such payments not previously paid and not yet due and owing to creditors pursuanty to paragraph (3) to the debtor, after deducting any unpaid claim allowed under section 503(b).

The cross-reference to § 1326(a)(3) is surely an error. Subparagraph (3) grants power to the court to raise or lower the payments a debtor must make under § 1326(a). Assuming that the error is corrected, so that subparagraph (2) cross-references to subparagraph (1)(A), the provision seems to authorize the payment of administrative expenses only--i.e., a claim allowed under § 503(b).

PEREZ v PEAKE

373 B.R. 468 (S.D. Tex. 2007)

LEE H. ROSENTHAL, J.

In October 2005, the Southern District of Texas bankruptcy judges implemented a new local rule providing that home mortgage payments would be made through the Chapter 13 trustee, rather than directly by the debtor. The bankruptcy judges also approved Home Mortgage Payment Procedures adopted by the trustees and a revised form for Chapter 13 plans, the Uniform Plan. Local Rule 3015(b), (the "Local Rule"), the Home Mortgage Payment Procedures, (the "Procedures"), and the Uniform Plan apply to a home mortgage for the debtor's principal residence when there is a default and the plan deals with an arrearage. Under the Procedures, the trustee will make the payments "as soon as practicable," including, if the trustee has available funds, before the hearing on plan confirmation. The Local Rule and the Procedures state that the bankruptcy court may vary the requirements by order in a particular case. This appeal challenges the existence and application of the Local Rule, the Procedures, and the Uniform Plan provisions on the disbursement of home mortgage payments by Chapter 13 trustees as opposed to the debtors themselves.

The debtors, Mario and Maria Perez, moved in the bankruptcy court for leave to disburse their mortgage payments directly to the mortgage lender rather than through the trustee. The bankruptcy court held a hearing on their motion, heard testimony, and wrote a lengthy and thoughtful opinion analyzing the debtors' challenges to Local Rule 3015(b) and the related Procedures and Uniform Plan. The bankruptcy court entered findings of fact and conclusions of law upholding the Local Rule, Procedures, and Uniform Plan against the legal challenges raised by the debtors. The court declined to exercise its discretion to waive conduit payment based on the evidence the debtors presented. In re Perez, 339 B.R. 385 (Bankr. S.D. Tex. 2006). This appeal followed.

Based on a careful review of the record, the parties' submissions, and the applicable law, this court affirms the decision of the bankruptcy court. As analyzed below, the provisions in the Local Rule and Procedures that debtors must make their mortgage payments through the trustee unless the bankruptcy court exercises its discretion to order otherwise do not violate the Bankruptcy Code. The Local Rule and the Procedures are consistent with the long-standing general presumption that a debtor makes monthly payments to the Chapter 13 trustee for distribution, subject to the bankruptcy court's discretion to allow the debtor to pay creditors directly rather than through the trustee based on the facts of a specific case. See 11 U.S.C. § 1326(b) (2005); In re Foster, 670 F.2d 478, 486 (5th Cir. 1982) ("[T]he Chapter 13 trustee is normally to make distributions to creditors of the payments made under the plan by the 'debtor.'"). Based on the record evidence, the bankruptcy judge's decision not to allow these debtors to pay their mortgage lender directly was not an abuse of the discretion provided under the Code, the case law, or the Local Rule and Procedures. The reasons for these rulings are set out in detail below.

I. Background

Section 1326(c) of the Bankruptcy Code states: "Except as otherwise provided in the plan or in the order confirming the plan, the trustee shall make payments to creditors under the plan." 11 U.S.C. § 1326(c). Section 1322(a)(1) provides that the plan will "provide for the submission of all or such portion of future income of the debtor to the supervision and control of the trustee as is necessary for the execution of the plan." 11 U.S.C. § 1322(a)(1). Section 1325(a)(1) states that a court "shall" confirm a plan if a list of confirmation tests is met, including that the plan "complies with the provisions of this chapter." Fifth Circuit has read these provisions as creating a presumption in favor of payments through the trustee, while recognizing that the bankruptcy court has discretion to permit or deny debtors to make direct payments to their creditors, including home mortgage lenders, rather than require conduit payments through the Chapter 13 trustees. In re Foster, 670 F.2d at 486 ("[The Code] makes it clear that the Chapter 13 trustee is normally to make distributions to creditors of the payments made under the plan by the debtor"); Mendoza v. Temple-Inland Mortgage Corp. (In re Mendoza), 111 F.3d 1264, 1269 (5th Cir. 1997) ("[W]e believe that the bankruptcy court is in the better position to ascertain whether or not the debtor is capable of acting as a disbursing agent and make direct payments of either current mortgage payments or arrearage payments. The only limitation is that the bankruptcy court in making this determination 'must determine whether the debtor will be able to make those payments and . . . comply with the plan.'"); In re Gregory, 143 B.R. 424, 427 (Bankr. E.D. Tex. 1992) ("Clearly, a court must balance numerous considerations before permitting a debtor to act as a disbursing agent."); In re Reid, 179 B.R. 504, 507 (E.D. Tex. 1995) ("[T]he general rule requires that debts provided for in a Chapter 13 plan be paid through the Chapter 13 Trustee.").[1]

[1] Other courts have reached similar results, holding that the feasibility test in section 1325(a)(6) limits the extent to which a Chapter 13 debtor can make payments directly to creditors. See, e.g., In re Aberegg, 961 F.2d 1307, 1309 (7th Cir. 1992) (discussing § 1326(c) and § 1322(a)(1) and finding that the language in § 1322(a)(1) has "been uniformly interpreted as giving bankruptcy courts the discretion to permit debtors to make payment directly to some secured creditors, provided that the plan meets all the confirmability requirements set forth in § 1325(a)."); In re Slaughter, 188 B.R. 29, 31 (Bankr. D.N.D. 1995) (considering "(1) whether the creditor receiving direct payments has the economic incentive and ability to monitor future direct payments; (2) whether the creditor receiving direct payments is capable of taking the requisite action of protecting its interests in the event of a default; (3) [and] the impact of direct payments on plan feasibility and whether, in the case of a Chapter 13 debtor engaged in business, meaningful reorganization is dependent upon direct payment"). The courts have disagreed as to the showing necessary to justify a deviation from the presumption in favor of conduit rather than direct payments. Compare In re Barber, 191 B.R. 879, 885- 886 (D. Kan. 1996) (concluding that "deviation from the normal periodic payments to the trustee should only be departed from when the debtor can demonstrate a significant reason for doing so") with In re Vigil, 344 B.R. 624, 630 (D.N.M. 2006) (stating that while the Code creates a presumption in favor of payments by the trustee, the debtors "need not demonstrate compelling circumstances in order to justify confirmation of a plan that provides for direct payment according to the contract terms to a

In Perez, the court analyzed statutory challenges to the Local Rule and Procedures codifying the presumption in favor of conduit mortgage payments. Perez recognized that under the Local Rule and Procedures, the bankruptcy courts have discretion to allow particular debtors to make their mortgage payments directly rather than through the trustee. The Perez court drew on a number of factors identified in the case law to guide its decision as to whether the particular debtors should be allowed to make the payments directly. The court emphasized whether the debtors had been responsible in past dealings with creditors and the trustee. Perez, 339 B.R. at 409. The appellants challenge both the Perez court's conclusion that the Local Rule and Procedures are consistent with the Bankruptcy Code, and the conclusion that the debtors did not make the showing necessary to be allowed to pay their mortgage lender directly.

A. Local Rule 3015(b) and the Home Mortgage Payment Procedures

Local Rule 3015(b) and the Procedures were approved in 2005 to change the practice that had existed in the Southern District of Texas. Before 2003, Chapter 13 debtors were routinely allowed to make monthly mortgage payments directly to home lenders. As described in detail in Perez, this practice had resulted in a large number of motions to lift stay filed by mortgage companies. Such motions were costly and burdensome for debtors to litigate. In 2003, three of the district's seven divisions changed to the practice that mortgage payments would be presumptively paid through the Chapter 13 trustee. In those three divisions, the number of motions significantly declined, which in turn "materially reduced costs for the debtors . . . and improved the prospect for successful completion of Chapter 13 cases." Perez, 339 B.R. at 391. Based on the benefits realized in the two years of experience under the presumption in favor of conduit payments, the bankruptcy judges approved the district-wide adoption of this practice in 2005.

Local Rule 3015(b), effective October 17, 2005, states:

> Mortgage Payments Through the Chapter 13 Trustee. Home mortgage payments will be made through the chapter 13 trustee, in accordance with Home Mortgage Payment Procedures. Home Mortgage Payment Procedures shall be procedures adopted by the chapter 13 trustees and approved by the court.

The Chapter 13 trustees promulgated and the bankruptcy court adopted the Home Mortgage Payment Procedures on September 29, 2005. Under Local Rule 3015(b) and the Procedures, a debtor may seek relief from the general rule requiring disbursements to the mortgage lender through the trustee. Local Rule 1001(d) states: "A judge may modify the application of the rules in any case." Paragraph 12 of the Procedures states that "[t]hese procedures may be varied in a particular case only by order of the Court."

As noted, the change from routinely allowing debtors to use direct payment for home mortgages to a rule presuming that the trustees will make mortgage payments addressed increased litigation over the status of the payments in Chapter 13 cases. The Perez opinion explained the reasons such disputes had

---

creditor that is fully secured by personal property, provided the Debtors do not otherwise seek to modify the creditor's claim and provided that the plan otherwise meets all requirements for confirmation") (emphasis added).

increased: "As mortgages are packaged and sold in greater numbers, the record-keeping of the note holders, and their servicing agents, has deteriorated. The absence of accurate records of payment receipts, combined with the endemic failure of consumer debtors to maintain accurate records of their payments, has caused confusion and delay in the prosecution and resolution of motions to lift stay and, in some cases, has resulted in debtors losing their homes because they could not prove that payments had been made." 339 B.R. at 391. At the end of the case, the mortgage lender frequently claimed that the debtor was in default, while the debtor claimed that all payments had been made. Id. at 413. Both debtors and mortgage lenders had difficulty in presenting information as to what payments were made to the mortgage company and when they were received. Id. at 415. Presumptively requiring debtors to use the "trustee as the disbursing agent" minimized such problems, "as trustees typically keep impeccable records," in contrast to both debtors and mortgage lenders. Id.

In Perez, the judge summarized the reasons for the adoption of the Local Rule and Procedures, as follows:

> The implementation of Local Rule 3015(b) and the Home Mortgage Payment Procedures in the Southern District of Texas is an attempt to repair the damage that has been done to the system. By requiring debtors to make all of their payments through the trustee, debtors will no longer be able to play the shell game. Either the debtor will have sufficient funds to pay the trustee, or he will not have sufficient funds; and if he does not, he will not be allowed to prolong his Chapter 13 case. The trustee will be able to know immediately whether the existing plan is feasible--and this is exactly where the focus should be.
>
> This approach will not only serve to more effectively monitor debtors; it will also serve to more effectively police home lenders. In recent years, mortgages have increasingly been packaged and sold, and then resold, and then resold again. One detrimental consequence of this trend has been loss of payment records by mortgagees and servicing agents. And, a detrimental consequence of this poor record keeping has been an increasing number of motions to lift stay that contain incorrect allegations about whether the debtor is in default and, if so, by how many payments. Because many debtors themselves fail to keep accurate records of when and how much they have paid their home lenders, this Court has found itself increasingly dealing with movants and respondents who cannot prove, with any degree of accuracy, how many payments the debtor has made and when the mortgage company has received the payments. Chapter 13 trustees keep excellent records. By requiring debtors to make their mortgage payments to these trustees, and by having the trustees remit these payments to the mortgagees, there will be much fewer questions, and much greater accuracy, about how much was paid to the home lender and when payment was remitted.
>
> This clear evidence of payments also substantially benefits debtors upon completion of their cases. The procedures unanimously adopted by the bankruptcy judges of the Southern District of Texas achieve certainty, at the end of the case, that the mortgage is current because there is a record that all payments have been made during the case. Without such a record, it is quite common for the mortgage lender to assert that the mortgage is not current because of various allegedly missed payments during the case--shortages for tax and insurance escrows, late payments, penalties, and fees. Normally, the debtor cannot prove that the payments have been made because the debtor has no records. The usual result is that the debtor either loses the homestead or else the debtor is forced to file another bankruptcy case.

Id. at 415.

The bankruptcy court's analysis of the need for and benefits of a presumption in favor of conduit payments to mortgage lenders in Chapter 13 cases is supported by the existence of similar local rules in other districts, empirical data, and legal research and analysis by bankruptcy law experts. Similar local rules have been adopted by other districts. See, e.g, Bankr. E.D. Mich. R. 3070-1 (2005); Bankr. D. Kan. R. 3015(b).1(3) (2000); Bankr. S.D. Ohio R. C-3.18.17 (1989). Opinions issued by bankruptcy judges in these and other districts recognize the advantages of conduit payments of home mortgage loans. See, e.g., In re Teagardner, 98 B.R. 318, 321 (Bankr. S.D. Ohio 1989) (local rule requiring conduit mortgage payments "serves the salutary policy of facilitating performance under Chapter 13 plans by debtors who have demonstrated a questionable prepetition payment track record"); In re McLaughlin, 2007 Bankr. LEXIS 877,2007 WL 837239, at *3 (Bankr. N.D. Ohio 2007) ("In the court's experience, there have been multiple instances in which it has been impossible to determine who owned the mortgage and what the balance was."); In re Vigil, 344 B.R. 624, 628 (Bankr. D.N.M. 2006) ("Policy reasons also favor payments through the trustee."); In re Harris, 200 B.R. 745, 749 (Bank. D. Mass. 1996) (holding that mortgage payments were to be made through trustee despite delays).

Empirical data shows that the approach of the Local Rule and Procedures is in line with national practice. For the twelve-month period ending September 30, 2005, conduit payments were the practice among a majority of Chapter 13 trustees across the nation. Sixty percent of the trustees made at least some conduit payments during that period, and forty-seven percent used conduit payments "almost exclusively." See Gordon Bermant & Jean Braucher, Making Post-Petition Mortgage Payments Inside Chapter 13 Plans: Facts, Law, Policy, 80 Am. Bankr. L.J. 261, 270, 276 (2006). Trustees using conduit payments charged lower fees, both as a percentage and in dollars per case, than trustees who did not. Id.

Commentators have also recognized the reasons for a presumption in favor of conduit payments:

> There are many compelling reasons why Chapter 13 debtors with home mortgages should never make payments directly to the mortgage holder or mortgage servicer during the Chapter13 case. Most of the good reasons for paying home mortgages through the Chapter 13 trustee are practical--based on decades of experience in hundreds of thousands of Chapter 13 cases. Creative Chapter 13 trustees have responded to the problems presented by the Code, and increasingly districts across the country are pulling home mortgage payments into the regular distribution routine. Districts that do so experience a reduction in litigation between debtors and mortgage holders, and trustees report greater stability in Chapter 13 plans that include home mortgages.

Keith M. Lundin, Chapter 13 Bankruptcy, § 147.1 at 147-1 (3d ed. 2000 & Supp. 2004). The same commentator summarized problems with direct payments:

> Many courts have learned from experience that Chapter 13 plans are rarely successful that provide for direct payment of a home mortgage that is in default . . . . The feasibility of direct payment plans is threatened because the debtor has discretion to pay the mortgage before remitting to the trustee . . . . It is questionable whether a mortgage holder realizes any advantages from direct payment by the debtor. Chapter 13 debtors are not suddenly more reliable in making their monthly mortgage payments. The standing Chapter 13 trustee typically makes disbursements on the same day once each month. The mortgage holder will know within a few days of that day whether the debtor made a full payment to enable the trustee to make full payments to creditors. When all payments are made through the trustee, the mortgage holder can readily determine from the Chapter 13 trustee whether the debtor is meeting all obligations under the plan. . . .

> From the debtor's standpoint, direct payment of the home mortgage is a really bad idea, particularly if the plan also cures defaults. Direct payment may forfeit the protection of the automatic stay, may limit bankruptcy court jurisdiction over postconfirmation disputes between the debtor and a mortgage holder, and may preclude discharge of the debt. . . . [C]alculation of plan payments to cure default and maintain a mortgage is not simple. Allocation of incoming payments by the mortgage holder is even more difficult. Mortgage holders paid directly by the debtor often don't bother to file proofs of claim, leaving the debtor and the trustee no concrete starting point to account for payments during the years of the plan. Because mortgage servicing often changes several times during the years of the Chapter 13 case, the last hands holding the note won't have the whole picture. Only the Chapter 13 trustee can be counted on to have a complete and accurate record of everything paid on account of the home mortgage. And the trustee can serve this function only if all payments--regular installments and curing default--are made through the trustee.

Id., § 147.1 at 147-5 to 147-6. Other commentators observe the practical benefits conduit payments provide to debtors:

> By including post-petition payments in the monthly plan amount, debtors can more easily budget the costs of bankruptcy into their total monthly cash flow. This is especially true if the conduit payment is combined with a wage deduction order that includes the amount of the post-petition mortgage payment. The burden of record keeping, which can overwhelm some debtors, is eased. The debtors have placed a trustworthy fiduciary between themselves and their major creditor, an interposition that can become particularly valuable when the case completes or otherwise terminates because debtors are less likely to need further legal help in resolving disputes with mortgage companies and services.

Bermant & Braucher, 80 Am. Bankr. L.J. at 272-73.

In Perez, the court relied on the Code and the case law reading the Code as creating a presumption that the Chapter 13 trustee will make payments, including home mortgage payments. The court also relied on the empirical data and the results of the two-year actual experience in the Southern District of Texas in applying a presumption in favor of conduit payments rather than the prior practice of routinely allowing direct payments. The Perez court affirmed the Local Rule and Procedures against the statutory challenges raised by the debtors.

The bankruptcy judge held a hearing on the debtors' motion for relief from the requirement of making conduit payments through the trustee and, based on the evidence presented by the debtors, declined to waive the conduit-payment requirement for them. That evidence is set out below.

B. The Evidence Presented by the Debtors

The debtors, Maria and Mario Perez, filed for bankruptcy under Chapter 13 on November 1, 2005. At that time, they were over $8,000 in arrears on their mortgage payments, approximately one year of payments. The debtors sought relief from the Local Rule and Procedures on the ground that they did not want to pay the additional trustee's fee for their home mortgage payment. The debtors argued that they had the necessary ability to make timely and properly recorded mortgage payments.

The debtors had owned a home in Houston, Texas for approximately sixteen years. Their mortgage payment, to ABRO ABN, was $663.49 per month, although the proof of claim indicates that the payment was reduced to $616.69 seven months before the debtors filed for bankruptcy. (Record at 58, 867). The debtors made timely payments for fifteen years. They fell behind after Maria Perez was diagnosed with breast cancer and was unable to work for approximately two years.

The debtors' Chapter 13 plan submitted on November 16, 2005 included disbursement of their monthly- mortgage payments by the Chapter 13 trustee. (Record at 768-772) ("During the term of the plan, these payments will be made through the chapter 13 trustee and approved by the Court."). When the trustee tried to withdraw the first payment on December 1, 2005, there were insufficient funds in the account. (Docket Entry No. 11-2 at 8; Docket Entry No. 21 at 6). The debtors explain that because they intended to challenge the Local Rule, on advice of counsel they directly remitted their first postpetition mortgage payment to their mortgage lender, leaving only enough money in the account for the plan minus the mortgage payment. (Docket Entry No. 21 at 6; Record at 871-72).

On December 16, 2005, the debtors amended their proposed plan to remove the trustee as disbursing agent for the mortgage payment. (Record at 779-783). On December 19, 2005, the debtors filed a motion asking the bankruptcy court to relieve them of the obligation to pay their mortgage payment through the Chapter 13 trustee. (Id. at 735-40). The trustee responded on January 5, 2006. The bankruptcy court held an evidentiary hearing on the motion on January 30, 2006. Maria Perez testified at the hearing. She explained that the mortgage had been timely paid for fifteen years, during which both she and her husband worked. In either 2002 or early 2003, Maria Perez was diagnosed with breast cancer. (Id. at 869, 878). She did not work in 2003 and 2004 while undergoing cancer treatment. She returned to work as a nanny in January 2005. Although Maria Perez is able to work, she continues to receive medical treatment for breast cancer and diabetes, which requires out-of-pocket payments for doctors' visits and medications. Mario Perez is a delivery driver who worked in 2003 and 2004 but earned little, in part because of fuel expenses. (Id. at 869). It was primarily Maria Perez's inability to work for two years due to her illness that caused the debtors to fall behind on their mortgage payments.

At the hearing, Maria Perez stated that she wanted to pay the mortgage lender directly to avoid the payment of the trustee's fee, because "we can save money if we write the check." (Id. at 871). The parties assumed that the additional amount for disbursing the monthly mortgage payment through the trustee would be approximately $66.13 a month, based on a ten percent fee. Maria Perez did not testify that paying the trustee's fee each month would prevent her from being able to perform under the plan. Instead, she stated that "in our situation, it's a lot of money for us. If we can save, I appreciate it." (Id. at 873).

After the hearing, the trustee and the debtors filed supplemental briefs. The bankruptcy court issued a lengthy opinion upholding the Local Rule and the Procedures against the challenges raised by the debtors and finding no basis to exercise discretion to relieve the debtors from the requirement of making conduit payments through the trustee. Although the bankruptcy judge heard from several different debtors and examined each of the motions in the Perez opinion, only Mario and Maria Perez have appealed from the court's order denying the motion and the refusal to confirm the plan with a direct-payment provision. . . .

I. The Statutory Challenges to the Local Rule and Procedures

A. Do the Local Rule and Procedures Violate the Bankruptcy Code Because They Require Conduit Payments?

The debtors argue that Local Rule 3105(b) violates the Code because "the practice is not determined on a case by case basis but is, for all purposes mandatory." (Docket Entry No. 21 at 6). The debtors argue that the Local Rule and Procedures "require that a specific form of a chapter 13 plan must be used by chapter 13 debtors. . . . The Bankruptcy Code does not contain any requirement for chapter 13 debtors to make their regular long term monthly mortgage payments through the chapter 13 trustee." (Id. at 17). The amici also argue that the Local Rule is mandatory and therefore violates the Bankruptcy Code. (Docket Entry No. 27 at 9).

This argument is not supported by the language of the Local Rule and Procedures or the record. As the bankruptcy court recognized, the Local Rule and the Procedures allow a debtor to seek relief from the presumption that the trustee will make the payments to the mortgage lender. Local Rule 1001(d) states that "[a] judge may modify the application of the rules in any case." Paragraph 12 of the Procedures states that "[t]hese procedures may be varied in a particular case only by order of the Court." The bankruptcy court recognized that it had discretion under the Local Rule and the Procedures to allow direct rather than conduit payments. Perez, 339 B.R. at 392, 408-414. Because the Local Rule and Procedures provide this flexibility, they are consistent with the Bankruptcy Code and with long-standing case law.

The Bankruptcy Code states that a debtor's Chapter 13 plan must "provide for the submission of all or such portion of future income of the debtor to the supervision and control of the trustee as is necessary for the execution of the plan." 11 U.S.C. § 1322(a)(1). The Code also provides that a court "shall" confirm a plan if a list of confirmation tests is met, including that the plan "complies with the provisions of this chapter." 11 U.S.C. § 1325(a)(1) (2006). Section 1325(a)(6) requires that the debtor "be able to make all payments under the plan and to comply with the plan." Section 1326(c) states, "[e]xcept as otherwise provided in the plan or in the order confirming the plan, the trustee shall make payments to creditors under the plan." The language "except as otherwise provided . . . in the order confirming the plan" has been read to allow debtors to make payments directly to creditors. In Matter of Foster, 670 F.2d 478 (5th Cir. 1982), the court held that although Chapter 13 ordinarily provides that funds be disbursed by the Chapter 13 trustee, a bankruptcy judge has discretion to allow direct disbursement by the debtor. Other cases are consistent. See In re Gregory, 143 B.R. 424, 426-27 (Bankr. E.D. Tex. 1992) (upholding direct payment of priority IRS claim over the trustee's objection because the IRS agreed; the IRS was a sophisticated creditor that can protect itself, and because a single payment was involved rather than a series of payments that would benefit from trustee oversight and require continued work by the trustee); In re Reid, 179 B.R. 504, 508-509 (finding that the debtors' asserted interest in avoiding trustee fees was insufficient to overcome the potential abuse of the system allowed by direct payment and the Bankruptcy Code's preference for payment through a trustee); Barber, 191 B.R. at 885 (acknowledging that "numerous courts have recognized that decisions to allow a debtor to act as a disbursing agent for plan payments, thereby endangering the payment of fees and commissions necessary to the operation of the trustee program is a significant concern"); In re Slaughter, 188

B.R. 29, 31 (Bankr. D.N.D. 1995) (noting that "[a]lthough there is no express statutory prohibition preventing direct payments, the presumption has always been for distribution made by the trustee") (citing S. REP. NO. 989, 95th Cong., 2d Sess. 142 (1978), reprinted in 1978 U.S.C.C.A.N. 5787).

In Perez, the bankruptcy court interpreted section 1326(c) as consistent with the Local Rule and Procedures in presuming that most debtors will pay creditors through the trustee but recognizing that the bankruptcy court has the discretion to allow debtors to pay creditors directly. 339 B.R. at 409. The court supported the Local Rule and Procedures with the general experience of the Southern District of Texas and other districts that direct mortgage payments cause problems for debtors and for the courts. There were numerous disputes over the status of the payments. Mortgage lenders and servicers regularly make errors; both servicers and debtors are poor record-keepers, so that many debtors are not be able to make all payments on a direct basis without creating issues about whether the debtor is current on the loan. Id. at 397. The Perez court also gave reasons specific to the particular debtors for refusing to confirm their plan providing for direct payments, determining that the proposed plan was not feasible based in part on the debtors' poor record in making timely payments. Id. at 410-412.

As the Fifth Circuit made clear in Foster, while the Bankruptcy Code allows a bankruptcy court to depart from the general rule that the trustee is to make payments to creditors, the Code creates a presumption--not an absolute requirement--that most payments will be made through the trustee. 670 F.2d at 486; see also In re Aberegg, 961 F.2d 1307, 1309 (7th Cir. 1992). The Local Rule and the Procedures are consistent with the Bankruptcy Code because they allow the bankruptcy court to relieve the debtor from the presumption that home mortgage loans will be paid through the trustee.

B. Do the Local Rule and Procedures Violate the Bankruptcy Code Prohibition Against Modifying a Mortgage Contract?

The debtors argue that the Local Rule and Procedures violate the Bankruptcy Code, 11 U.S.C. § 1322(b)(2), because conduit payments through the trustee modify the terms of the mortgage loan. (Docket Entry No. 21 at 14). The debtors argue that "[i]n most cases, the chapter 13 trustee will not be able to make a debtor's first post-petition regular monthly mortgage payment on time." (Id.) . . .

The Bankruptcy Code states:

> [The plan may] modify the rights of holders of secured claims, other than a claim secured only by a security interest in real property that is the debtor's principal residence, or of holders of unsecured claims, or leave unaffected the rights of holders of any class of claims.

11 U.S.C. § 1322(b)(2). The Bankruptcy Code generally prohibits modification of the rights of secured creditors claiming the debtor's principal residence as collateral for a long-term loan. The debtor must pay the full debt amount, even if the collateral is worth less. The home mortgage exception to the power to modify secured loans typically requires a Chapter 13 debtor to cure defaults and maintain mortgage payments during the life of the plan. Section 1322(b)(5) permits plan provisions for curing defaults on mortgage loans within a

"reasonable time" and for maintaining regular payments if the last one is due after the final plan payment. 11 U.S.C.A. § 1322(b)(5) (stating that the plan may "provide for the curing of any default within a reasonable time and maintenance of payments while the case is pending on any . . . secured claim on which the last payment is due after the date on which the final payment under the plan is due."). A prefiling default may be cured, undoing acceleration and preventing foreclosure. In Nobelman v. American Savings Bank, 508 U.S. 324 (1993), the Supreme Court read the antimodification provision of section 1322(b)(5) broadly and held that section 1322(b)(2) prohibits bifurcation of an undersecured claim through a Chapter 13 plan when the only collateral is real property that is the debtor's principal residence.

In this case, the bankruptcy court carefully considered the argument that the Local Rule and Procedures worked an impermissible modification of the mortgage contract.[2] In rejecting the argument, the court carefully examined the relevant paragraphs of the Procedures and Uniform Plan. Paragraph 11 of the Procedures states:

> Amounts received by the holder of the ongoing mortgage prior to confirmation must be applied by the holder to the next payment due without penalty of the terms of the note; or the holder must notify the trustee in writing that it waives all late charges that accrue after the order for relief in this case. Amounts received by the holder of the ongoing mortgage after confirmation must be applied in accordance with the plan.

Perez, 339 B.R. at 403. The relevant section of the Uniform Plan reads in part as follows:

> The Secured Claims held by secured creditors holding a claim secured only by a security interest in real property that is the debtor(s)' residence (other than the arrearage claims set forth in the above table) and other claims treated under § 1322(b)(5) will be paid in accordance with the pre-petition contract held by the holder of the secured claim. The first such payment is due on the first payment due date under the promissory note (after the date this bankruptcy case was filed). During the term of the plan, these payments will be made through the chapter 13 trustee in accordance with procedures adopted from time to time by the chapter 13 trustee and approved by the Court. Each holder of a claim that is paid pursuant to this paragraph must elect to either (i) apply the payments received by it to the next payment due without penalty under the terms of the holder's pre-petition note; or (ii) waive all late charges that accrue after the order for relief in this case. Any holder that fails to file an affirmative election within 30 days of entry of the order confirming this plan has waived all late charges that accrue after the order for relief in this case. Notwithstanding the foregoing, the holder may impose any late charge that accrues following an event of default of a payment due under paragraph 1 of this Plan.

Id. at 403.

The amici note that the trustees' disbursement schedules might not

[2] The bankruptcy court noted that the debtors lacked standing to assert a claim under 11 U.S.C. § 1322(b)(2), which protects the rights of secured lenders, not debtors. (Docket Entry No. 11-2 at 22). Neither the debtors nor the amici discussed this aspect of the ruling. The bankruptcy court ruled on the debtors' argument on the merits, despite finding a lack of standing.

correspond to the due date set by mortgage contracts. One trustee in the district, for example, distributes on January 18, 2007, February 15, 2007, and March 22, 2007. The amici argue that they are forced either to waive late charges or apply the payment to the next payment cycle without penalty, an election that impermissibly modifies their mortgage contracts. (Id. at 15).

As thoroughly discussed by the bankruptcy court, the Procedures and Uniform Plan present the mortgagee with two options. The first allows the mortgagee to assess late charges for a missed payment if the next payment is applied to the next installment. Perez, 339 B.R. 403-04. If the mortgagee chooses this first option, the debtor will still have to pay both the missed payment and late charges on that payment, giving the mortgagee what it bargained for. Under this first option, the mortgagee is required to apply the late payment to the next payment due. The bankruptcy court held that this requirement was not an improper modification because the mortgagee would recover the late charges for the late payment. Id. at 404. The Procedures and Plan allow a second option, under which the mortgage company may apply a payment to a prior missed payment, but this choice waives postpetition late charges for the missed payment. This option was intended to prevent a mortgage company from not assessing late charges over the life of the plan and then asserting them at the end of that plan. Id. The bankruptcy court held that this option was not a modification of the mortgage payments but rather a "preventative measure" to protect debtors from facing late charges at the end of the plan even if they made all the plan payments to the trustee. Id.

The bankruptcy court held that the Local Rule and Procedures did not impermissibly modify the rights of mortgagees under section 1322(b)(5). As the Supreme Court held in Rake v. Wade, 508 U.S. 464, 473 (1993), when a plan allows for the curing of a default and reinstates payments on a claim, the plan may modify the creditor's contractual rights to the extent they arise from the default. The Court explained:

> When a plan cures a default and reinstates payments on a claim, the creditor's contractual rights arising from the default--which in this case included the right to declare all payments due and payable, accelerate the debt, possess the property, collect rents generated by the property, and foreclose on the property, are abrogated and therefore "modified." These modifications are allowed under § 1322(b)(5) "notwithstanding" the fact that § 1322(b)(2) generally prohibits the modification of the rights of home mortgage holders. Petitioners' construction of § 1322(b)(2) also leads to the incongruous result that only home mortgage claims would be denied the benefits of § 1325(a)(5).

Rake v. Wade, 508 U.S. at 473 at n.9 (citations omitted).

The bankruptcy court concluded that to the extent the Local Rule, Procedures, and Uniform Plan might result in a modification of a mortgage contract, they did so only by allowing the debtor to cure the default occurring as a result of the mortgagee receiving the first monthly payment from the trustee after the due date and grace period had passed. The mortgagee receives the payment, but not within the contractual deadline. The mortgagee is, however, allowed to assess late charges if the trustee's first payment is received after the contract date. The mortgagee is required to apply future payments to the next payment due, without penalty, curing the default as permitted by section 1322(b)(5).

To the extent the Local Rule, Procedures, and Uniform Plan allow the trustee to make mortgage payments on a different date than specified in the mortgage contract, that is not an impermissible modification under Fifth Circuit precedent. The court had held in In re Lee, 167 B.R. 417, 419 (Bankr. S.D. Miss. 1992), aff'd, 22 F.3d 1094 (5th Cir. 1994), that discrepancies caused by the timing of payments to the Chapter 13 trustee and the trustee's payments to the mortgage lenders did not impermissibly modify a mortgage contract. The court cited the Fifth Circuit's decision in Nobelman v. American Savings Bank, 968 F.2d 483 (5th Cir. 1992), aff'd, 508 U.S. 324 (1993), and Grubbs v. Houston First American Savings Ass'n, 730 F.2d 236 (5th Cir. 1984), in which the court allowed payments made through the Chapter 13 trustee with no suggestion that the payments were improper because they were made on dates different from the due dates in the contract.

The bankruptcy court properly held that the Local Rule, Procedures, and Uniform Plan did not modify the mortgage contract lien in ways prohibited by section 1322(b)(5).

C. Do the Local Rule and Procedures Violate the Bankruptcy Code by Allowing Preconfirmation Payments by the Trustee?

The appellants argue that the Local Rule and Procedures violate the Bankruptcy Code, 11 U.S.C. § 1326(a)(2), which states that "[a] payment made under paragraph (1)(A) [to the trustee by the debtor under 11 U.S.C. § 1326(a)(1)] shall be retained by the trustee until confirmation or denial of confirmation." The Procedures include a provision authorizing trustees to distribute to the mortgage lender mortgage payments received from the debtor after the petition is filed but before plan is confirmed.[3] The debtors renew the argument they made in the bankruptcy court that this provision violates section 1326(a)(2) by authorizing the trustee to distribute funds before the plan is confirmed. The debtors argue that the trustee cannot pay the home mortgage before the plan is confirmed under section 1326(a)(2), but if the trustee does not pay the mortgage until confirmation, the payment will be late. (Docket Entry No. 21 at 7).

Section 1326(a)(2) of the Bankruptcy Code section states that a trustee

---

[3] The Southern District of Texas Chapter 13 Home Mortgage Payment Procedures state in relevant part:

> The debtor's plan payments to the chapter 13 trustee shall include the amount due on the debtor's regular monthly mortgage installments for a claim secured by a security interest in real property that is the debtor's principal residence pursuant to the terms of 11 U.S.C. § 1322(b)(5)1 ("the ongoing mortgage") unless there is no default on the mortgage as of the petition date, the date of plan confirmation and the date of the filing of a plan modification. The following requirements will apply to all cases in which the Chapter 13 Plan deals with an arrearage:
>
> (3) Subject to these procedures, the trustee is authorized to disburse funds in payment of all regular contractual installment payments and other charges arising pursuant to the claim of a creditor that become due following the commencement of a case pursuant to the terms of the note and security agreement applicable to the claim. Disbursements should commence as soon as is practicable. If the trustee has available funds, the initial disbursement should precede the hearing on plan confirmation.

"shall" retain certain payments received from the debtor until the plan is confirmed:

> A payment made under paragraph (1)(A) shall be retained by the trustee until confirmation or denial of confirmation. If a plan is confirmed, the trustee shall distribute any such payment in accordance with the plan as soon as is practicable. If a plan is not confirmed, the trustee shall return any such payments not previously paid and not yet due and owing to creditors pursuant to paragraph (3) to the debtor, after deducting any unpaid claim allowed under section 503(b).

11 U.S.C. § 1326(a)(2) (emphasis added).

The bankruptcy court drew on the phrase "payment made under paragraph (1)(A)," which refers to payments the debtor makes to the trustee under section 1326(a)(1)(A). That section addresses payments "proposed by the plan to the trustee." The bankruptcy court distinguished between payments under section 1326(a)(1)(A)--which the trustee must retain until confirmation--and adequate protection payments under 11 U.S.C. §§ 1303, 363(e), and 361--which need not be retained. The bankruptcy court concluded that the Local Rule and Procedure authorizing the trustee to make postpetition, preconfirmation mortgage payments did not violate the Code because they were not "plan payments" but rather "adequate protection" payments. Id. at 397-400.

Section 1303 states that "the debtor shall have, exclusive of the trustee, the rights and powers of a trustee under section . . . 363(e) . . . of this title. Section 363(e) states that on the request of a lien holder, the court "shall prohibit or condition" the debtor's right to use property "as is necessary to provide adequate protection of such interest." Section 361 addresses adequate protection payments. Section 361 provides:

> When adequate protection is required under section 362, 363, or 364 of this title of an interest of an entity in property, such adequate protection may be provided by--
>
> (1) requiring the trustee to make a cash payment or periodic cash payments to such entity, to the extent that the stay under section 362 of this title, use, sale, or lease under section 363 of this title, or any grant of a lien under section 364 of this title results in a decrease in the value of such entity's interest in such property;
>
> (2) providing to such entity an additional or replacement lien to the extent that such stay, use, sale, lease, or grant results in a decrease in the value of such entity's interest in such property; or
>
> (3) granting such other relief, other than entitling such entity to compensation allowable under section 503(b)(1) of this title as an administrative expense, as will result in the realization by such entity of the indubitable equivalent of such entity's interest in such property.

11 U.S.C. § 361. The bankruptcy court held that "a Chapter 13 debtor (just like a Chapter 11 debtor-in-possession) makes adequate protection payments pursuant to a court order under these three sections, not pursuant to a proposed plan. Because § 1326(a)(1) refers to payments 'proposed by the plan,' and not to court-ordered adequate protection payments for real estate lien holders, it follows that § 1326(a)(2) is inapplicable to pre-confirmation adequate protection payments to real estate lien holders; and because of its inapplicability, this section may not be used to bar the trustee from making pre-confirmation adequate protection payments to mortgagees." Perez, 339 B.R. at 399.

The Bankruptcy Code does not specifically define "adequate protection payments." Section 361 recognizes three nonexclusive forms of adequate protection that may apply to the debtor's use of property in which a secured creditor has an interest: cash payments to the extent the collateral has declined in value, extra collateral to compensate for such a decline, or other relief "as will result in the realization by [the secured party] of the indubitable equivalent of such entity's interest in such property." 11 U.S.C. § 361. The bankruptcy court recognized that typically adequate protection means that the debtor must make preconfirmation payments to protect the claim holder from depreciation of its collateral pending plan confirmation. As applied to real estate, such adequate protection payments might take the form of a requirement that hazard insurance or real estate taxes be paid before confirmation. See, e.g, In re Pinto, 191 B.R. 610, 612 (Bankr. D.N.J. 1996). The bankruptcy court in Perez recognized that such adequate protection payment is different from an installment payment due under a mortgage contract. An installment payment which includes interest does not correspond to a decline in value of collateral resulting from the debtor's use before plan confirmation.

The Perez opinion properly rejected the application of sections 361(1) and (2) because they are explicitly based on protection against a decline in the collateral's value. Instead, the court relied on section 361(3), reasoning that "when a mortgagee in a Chapter 13 receives the current monthly payment, as well as payment of arrearages under the plan, this arrangement constitutes the 'indubitable equivalent' of the mortgagee's interest under § 361(3)." 339 B.R. at 400. In so doing, the court applied section 361(3) in a way that is not based on protection against depreciation.

The term "indubitable equivalent" is not defined in Bankruptcy Code but is drawn from Judge Learned Hand's opinion in In re Murel Holding Corp., 75 F.2d 941 (2d Cir. 1935). See S. REP. NO. 989 at 127 (1978), 1978 U.S.C.C.A.N. 5913 ("The indubitable equivalent language is intended to follow the strict approach taken by Judge Learned Hand in In re Murel Holding Corp."). In Murel, an insurance company held a mortgage and attempted to foreclose when the owners defaulted. The owners obtained an ex parte stay after filing a bankruptcy petition. They proposed a plan requiring the mortgage lender to forego amortization payments and extend the mortgage due date while allowing the mortgage lender to receive interest. The mortgage lender moved to vacate the stay and objected that the plan failed to provide adequate protection. Judge Hand acknowledged that the bankruptcy court had the power to confirm a plan over the creditor's objection if the plan provided "adequate protection for the realization by them of the full value of their interest, claims, or liens." Id. at 943. The court reversed the bankruptcy court's stay order because the mortgagee was entitled to its amortization payments or a "substitute of the most indubitable equivalence," and the plan did not offer "some reasonable assurance that a suitable substitute will be offered" for the scheduled amortization payments. Id. at 942-43.

The Perez court distinguished between payments under section 1326(a)(1)(A) and adequate protection payments. Under the BAPCPA, section 1326(a)(1)(A) payments fell into three categories: payments to the trustee in the amount "proposed by the plan" (§ 1326(a)(1)(A)); payments "directly to the lessor" in the amount "scheduled in a lease of personal property"(§ 1326(a)(1)(B)); and "adequate protection" payments "directly to a creditor holding an allowed claim secured by personal property . . . for that portion of the obligation that becomes due after the order for relief." (§ 1326(a)(1)(C)). The last two are forms of adequate protection payments to particular creditors--lessors of personal property and some purchase money secured creditors. While section 1326(a)(1)(C) does not govern preconfirmation adequate protection payments for holders of liens on real property, the section is labeled as an adequate protection payment. After the BAPCPA, there appears to be two kinds of "adequate protection" payments under the Code: the "classical" adequate protection addressed in section 361, which is tied to depreciation, and the types of adequate protection for the specific creditors addressed in sections 1326(a)(1)(B) and (C), which are tied to installment or contractual obligations rather than to a decline in collateral value due to the debtor's use. The Perez court relied on adequate protection under section 361, but did not limit it to protection against depreciation or decline in value. Instead, the Perez court construed it as broadly as it is used in section 1326(a)(1)(B) and (C), while recognizing that those sections do not apply to real estate mortgage loans.[4]

It is unclear that payments under section 1326(a)(1)(A) categorically exclude adequate protection payments under section 361. Because section 1326(a) requires that the Chapter 13 debtor begin making payments called for by the plan within thirty days of filing the plan, many debtors will satisfy adequate protection requirements by beginning to make payments to the trustee in the amount called for in the proposed plan. Adequate protection payments to a Chapter 13 trustee accounted for in a proposed plan have been recognized as advantageous for both debtors and creditors.[5] The difference between payments called for in the plan under section 1326(a)(1)(A) and adequate protection payments is unclear, particularly when the term "adequate protection" is used as broadly as the Perez court used it. The Perez court defined the term to include installment contract payments of prepetition contracts that included interest and was not limited to protection against the decline in the value of collateral resulting from the debtor's use before confirmation.

---

[4] The Perez court cited one case that applied section 361's "indubitable equivalent" provision to mortgage loan installment payments. The Perez court cited Commonwealth of Pennsylvania State Employee Retirement Fund v. Roane, 14 B.R. 542, 544 (D.C. Pa. 1981), which interpreted "indubitable equivalent" to include a Chapter 13 debtor's monthly mortgage payment as well as the arrearage paid under the plan. In that case, the court denied the mortgage company's motion for relief from the bankruptcy stay on the basis that the installment mortgage payments and arrearage payments under the plan were adequate protection. The court noted that there was an equity cushion of $ 7,500 but recognized that it might decrease over time. Id. at 544-545. The court found that "the proposed payment of the current monthly mortgage payments, as well as the payment of the arrearages under the Chapter 13 plan, would protect against such an adverse decline in the surplus value." Id. at 545. "Such an arrangement constitutes the "indubitable equivalent" of the mortgagee's interest under § 361(3). Therefore, the payment of the mortgage payments outside of the plan and the payment of the arrearage under the plan, together with the existing equity cushion, 'adequately protect' the mortgagee's interest." Id. This case does not hold that standing alone, installment mortgage payments are adequate protection under section 361. They are not the "indubitable equivalent" of what the mortgage lender is entitled to receive; they are what the mortgage lender is entitled to receive.

[5] Trustee disbursement of adequate protection payments outside a proposed plan may be risky for lienholders because they lose the value of the adequate protection payments until actually received from the trustee, and if the plan is not confirmed, the lienholder cannot receive the payment and often cannot show administrative expenses. Lundin, Chapter 13 Bankruptcy § 48.1 at 48-8. Direct adequate protection payments by debtors are "just not a good idea for the debtor, for the trustee or for others who may have administrative claims if the case fails before confirmation. Adequate protection payments to the Chapter 13 trustee accounted for in the proposed plan set a better pattern for the future of the case." Id.

Moreover, preconfirmation payments to the trustee under section 1326(a)(1) are subject to court review under section 1326(a)(3), which states: "Subject to section 363, the court may, upon notice and a hearing, modify, increase, or reduce the payments required under this subsection pending confirmation of a plan." The introductory cross-reference, "subject to section 363," would appear to incorporate the statutory powers and conditions on the use of property. For example, creditors often use section 363(e) to impose on debtors the duty to provide adequate protection of an interest in property the debtor proposes to use during the bankruptcy case. Section 363(e) incorporates the traditional adequate protection concepts of section 361. Adequate protection under section 1326 appears to cover both adequate protection as described in section 1326(a)(1)(C) and the traditional forms incorporated by the cross-references in section 1326(a)(3). Adequate protection under section 361 applies under section 1326(a)(3) when there is a motion to the court to modify, increase, or reduce payments required by "this subsection" pending plan confirmation. After the BAPCPA changes, even recognizing that section 1326(a)(1)(C) does not apply to preconfirmation adequate protection payments for holders of liens on real property, "payments under the plan" under section 1326(a)(1)(A) may not categorically exclude adequate protection payments.

The Perez court distinguished between payments under section 1326(a)(1)(A) and adequate protection payments because the Code makes payments under section 1326(a)(1)(A) subject to section 1326(a)(2), which states that the trustee "shall" retain such payments until plan confirmation. Section 1326(a)(2) specifically recognizes that a trustee may distribute some funds received from the debtor before plan confirmation by acknowledging that some payments will have been previously paid. Section 1326(a)(2) does not state that if a plan is not confirmed, the trustee must return all payments to the debtor. Instead, it states that the trustee must return only those payments "not previously paid and not yet due and owing to creditors pursuant to paragraph 3 to the debtor." The reference to "paragraph 3" is confusing. It apparently refers to section 1326(a)(3), which authorizes a court to modify, increase, or reduce preconfirmation plan payments required under "this subsection." Read literally, the phrase in section 1326(a)(2) stating that the obligation to return payments "not previously paid and not yet due and owing to creditors pursuant to paragraph (3)" applies only if the bankruptcy court has entered an order that modified payments otherwise required by "this subsection." If there is no such court order, then there are no payments "due and owing" under section 1326(a)(3). Commentators have questioned whether the "paragraph 3" cross-reference is a mistake. See Lundin, Chapter 13 Bankruptcy § 404.1 at 402-2; David Gray Carlson, Cars and Homes in Chapter 13 After the 2005 Amendments to the Bankruptcy Code, 14 Am. Bankr. Inst. L. Rev. 301, 325-26 (2006). One commentator has suggested that the reference to paragraph 3 was intended to be a reference to section 1326(a)(1)(C), which would permit the trustee to make payments before confirmation to the creditors listed in that paragraph. Carlson, 14 AM. BANKR. INST. L. REV. at 325-26. The Code itself does not, however, contain such a limitation. The result is a statement in section 1326(a)(1)(A) that preconfirmation payments made to the trustee as proposed by the plan "shall" be retained by the trustee, but it is unclear what preconfirmation payments may be disbursed by the trustee and not returned to the debtor if the plan is not confirmed.

In short, it is unclear whether it is proper to characterize preconfirmation payments of monthly mortgage payments as adequate protection payments.[6] But it is also unclear that section 1326(a)(2) prohibits preconfirmation conduit payments of mortgage installments to the lenders. As the bankruptcy court correctly noted, because the Southern District of Texas does not delay confirmation until after the claims-bar date, but instead reaches confirmation soon after the section 341 meeting, preconfirmation payments are a very small part of the payments addressed by the Local Rule and Procedures. Because a confirmation hearing must be held within eighty-five days after a case is filed and will often be held earlier, in most cases there will only be one or two preconfirmation mortgage payments. Perez, 339 B.R. at 397. As a result, the debtors' argument that the Code precluded the trustee from disbursing postpetition, preconfirmation mortgage payments did not support the debtors' proposed solution that the debtors rather than the trustee must make some or all of the mortgage payments, despite the risks of that approach.

In a footnote, the Perez court suggested that relying on 11 U.S.C. § 105(a) would achieve the express command of section 1322(b)(2) and the Code's presumption in favor of payments through the trustee without using the "indubitable equivalent" form of adequate protection under section 361(3). "[W]here an express statute such as § 1322(b)(2) seems to require a specific result--here, that the mortgagee receive its normal monthly payments--the use of § 105 to ensure that these payments are made during the time period between the date of the petition and the date of the plan confirmation seems quite appropriate." 339 B.R. at 401, n. 17.

Section 105(a) allows a court to issue any order "that is necessary or appropriate to carry out the provisions of this title." 11 U.S.C. § 105(a). Reliance on this provision is appropriate when an express statute (section 1322(b)(2)) requires a specific result (providing the mortgagee with its normal monthly payments after the petition and before confirmation), and when the Code presumptively favors a particular approach (payments through the Chapter 13 trustee). Since the Perez decision was issued, the Supreme Court has issued an opinion that supports the bankruptcy court's approach.

In Marrama v. Citizens National Bank of Massachusetts, 127 S.Ct. 1105 (2007), the Supreme Court directly addressed the equitable powers of the bankruptcy court under section 105(a) for the first time in over a decade. The case resolved a split in the lower courts over whether section 706(a) provides a debtor an absolute, one-time right to convert a Chapter 7 case to Chapter 13 or permits a bankruptcy court to limit the conversion right when the debtor is in bad faith. The Court followed the majority of cases that held that the right is subject to a bad-faith exception.[7] The Marrama majority held that "the broad

---

[6] See In re Brown, 348 B.R. 583 (Bankr. N.D. Ga. 2006) (preconfirmation adequate protection payments may not include an interest component because such payments compensate for depreciation in collateral and apply only to principal); In re Denton, 370 B.R. 441, 2007 Bankr. LEXIS 2014, 2007 WL 1701921 (Bankr. S.D. Ga. 2007) (preconfirmation adequate protection applies only to principal); Carlson, 14 AM. BANKR. INST. L. REV. at 332.

[7] The Court conditioned the Chapter 7 debtor's seemingly unconditional right under 11 U.S.C. § 706(a) to convert his case to a case under Chapter 13 to the extent the debtor had engaged in prepetition bad faith conduct that would establish "cause" warranting dismissal or reconversion of his Chapter 13 case and making him unqualified to be a debtor under Chapter 13. The Supreme Court ruled that what appeared to be an unfettered right under 11 U.S.C. § 707(a) was circumscribed. The Court stated, "In practical effect, a ruling that an individual's Chapter 13 case should be dismissed or converted to Chapter 7 because of prepetition bad faith conduct, including

authority granted to bankruptcy judges to take any action that is necessary or appropriate to 'prevent an abuse of process' described in § 105(a) of the Code, is surely adequate to authorize an immediate denial of a motion to convert filed under § 706." Id. at 1111-12. The dissent viewed section 706(a) as providing debtors with an absolute right to convert a Chapter 7 to a Chapter 13 and concluded that an application of section 105(a) vitiating that right would contravene the Code. The majority, however, took the view that section 706(a) is equivocal and that section 105(a) was properly applied to achieve a result consistent with the Code, taking into account the need to prevent abuses of the bankruptcy process. Id. at 1112.

Twenty years earlier, the Supreme Court decided Norwest Bank Worthington v. Ahlers, 485 U.S. 197 (1988), holding that a bankruptcy court cannot use its general equitable powers to confirm a reorganization plan in contravention of the absolute priority rule. Id. at 206. The Supreme Court stated that "whatever equitable powers remain in the bankruptcy courts must and can only be exercised within the confines of the Bankruptcy Code." Id. In Marrama, the Court did not overrule Ahlers. In Marrama, the Supreme Court recognized that Congress can restrict equitable powers by clear and unambiguous drafting of Code provisions. The Marrama majority reasoned that "nothing in the text of either §706 or § 1307(c) . . . limits the authority of the court to take appropriate action in response to fraudulent conduct by the atypical litigant who has demonstrated that he is not entitled to the relief available to the typical debtor." 127 S.Ct. at 1106. The dissenting Justices disagreed as to the conclusion that the Code sections at issue were ambiguous or unclear. Instead, they concluded that the Code sections specifically prohibited the procedure followed by the bankruptcy court in Marrama and precluded reliance on section 105(a).

Marrama upheld a pragmatic remedy fashioned by a bankruptcy judge under section 105(a) to achieve a result that the Code clearly required, despite the apparently inconsistent approach of another Code section that was unclear or ambiguous. In this case, a similar application of section 105(a) is warranted. Section 1322(b)(2) expressly requires that the mortgagee receive its normal monthly payments. Section 1326(a)(1) states that the debtor "shall" begin making payments not later than 30 days after filing the plan and provides that the court may order "otherwise," which allows the court to require conduit payments through the trustee. Section 1326(a)(2) states that the trustee "shall" retain payments "proposed by the plan" made by the debtor to the trustee before confirmation. Section 1326(c) states that the trustee "shall" make payments to creditors "under the plan." The Code prohibits modifying the rights of mortgage lenders and creates a presumption in favor of payments disbursed through the trustee. The courts recognize the many reasons that conduit payment of mortgage installments protects debtors, creditors, and the integrity of the bankruptcy process. The interplay among the provisions that protect mortgage lenders' rights, those that authorize conduit payments, and those that require the trustee to retain some--but not all--payments by the debtor is unclear. Section 105(a) properly applies to allow the trustee to disburse the one or two monthly mortgage

---

fraudulent acts committed in an earlier Chapter 7 proceeding, is tantamount to a ruling that the individual does not qualify as a debtor under Chapter 13. That individual, in other words, is not a member of the class of 'honest but unfortunate debtor[s]' that the bankruptcy laws were enacted to protect." Marrama, 127 S.Ct. at 1111 (citing Grogan v. Garner, 498 U.S. 279, 287 (1991)).

payments that are due postpetition but preconfirmation.

The critical aspect of the payments at issue is not whether they are "under the plan" or "adequate protection" payments, but rather that they are simply conduit payments. Given the clear and explicit command of section 1322(b) to preserve the rights of holders of mortgage loans on the debtor's principal residence, and given the ambiguous interplay of sections 1326(a)(1) and (2), the bankruptcy court's reasoned decision to allow the trustee to distribute mortgage payments received from the debtor in the short period between filing the petition and confirming the plan as well as after plan confirmation was an appropriate application of section 105(a), consistent with Marrama's approach.

This court affirms the bankruptcy court's conclusion that the Local Rule and Procedures authorizing the trustee to disburse preconfirmation mortgage payments made by the debtor did not make the Local Rule and Procedures invalid either facially or as applied to the debtors at issue. [8]

D. Do the Local Rule and Procedures Violate the Priority Payment Provisions of the Bankruptcy Code?

The appellants also challenge the bankruptcy court's conclusion that the Local Rule and Procedures do not violate the Code's priority scheme by allowing home mortgage payments to be made ahead of administrative claims, including--indeed, primarily consisting of--the debtors' attorney's fees. The appellants argued that under section 1326(b)(1), the debtors' attorney's fees must be fully paid before any other creditor, whether secured or unsecured, including the mortgage lender. (Docket Entry No. 21, at 15). The amici argued that a mortgagee's rights cannot be subordinated to the payment of the debtor's attorney's fees. (Docket Entry No. 27 at 19-20). The trustee argues that Chapter 13 does not require that a debtor's attorney's fees must be paid in full before each installment payment to the mortgage lender. (Docket Entry No. 26 at 11-12).

The following provisions of the Bankruptcy Code, as amended by BAPCPA, are relevant. Section 507(a) states in part:

> (a) The following expenses and claims have priority in the following order:
> (1) First:
>
> (A) Allowed unsecured claims for domestic support obligations

---

[8] The debtors filed for bankruptcy on November 1, 2005. The debtors claim that they were required to remit a mortgage payment before December 1, 2005 as well as the first plan payment (including an additional mortgage payment) on December 1, 2005. (Docket Entry No. 21 at 8-9). The record does not support this assertion. Maria Perez testified as follows before the bankruptcy court:

> Q: Ma'am, isn't it true that the first ACH payment to the trustee was returned for insufficient funds?
>
> A: Oh, this is for this year, for January, because the first payment is in December. What happened is Mr. Baker [her attorney] tell [sic] my husband and me to send directly to the mortgage, the payment, and the trustee, only we pay the trustee $ 375, and we signed papers for the trustee trying to take the money, the 20 to each month, but it's only $ 375. And the trustee trying [sic] to take $ 918, I think so, and there's not enough money because we send something, 600-and something for the mortgage.

(Record at 871-72). The record does not show that the trustee made a mortgage payment in November or December 2005 or whether the debtors made the November 2005 payment directly.

> . . .
>
> (C) If a trustee is appointed or elected under section 701, 702, 703, 1104, 1202, or 1302, the administrative expenses of the trustee allowed under paragraphs (1)(A), (2), and (6) of section 503(b) shall be paid before payment of claims under subparagraphs (A) and (B), to the extent that the trustee administers assets that are otherwise available for the payment of such claims.
>
> (2) Second, administrative expenses allowed under section 503(b) of this title, and any fees and charges assessed against the estate under chapter 123 of title 28.

11 U.S.C. § 507(a). Attorney's fees are administrative expenses allowed under section 503(b) as "reasonable compensation for professional services rendered by an attorney or an accountant of an entity whose expense is allowable." 11 U.S.C. § 503(b)(4).

Section 1322 sets forth requirements for what a Chapter 13 Plan must and may contain. That section states in relevant part:

> (a) The plan shall--
>
> (1) provide for the submission of all or such portion of future earnings or other future income of the debtor to the supervision and control of the trustee as is necessary for the execution of the plan;
>
> (2) provide for the full payment, in deferred cash payments, of all claims entitled to priority under section 507 of this title, unless the holder of a particular claim agrees to a different treatment of such claim;
>
> (3) if the plan classifies claims, provide the same treatment for each claim within a particular class; and
>
> (4) notwithstanding any other provision of this section, a plan may provide for less than full payment of all amounts owed for a claim entitled to priority under section 507(a)(1)(B) only if the plan provides that all of the debtor's projected disposable income for a 5-year period beginning on the date that the first payment is due under the plan will be applied to make payments under the plan.
>
> (b) Subject to subsections (a) and (c) of this section, the plan may . . .
>
> (4) provide for payments on any unsecured claim to be made concurrently with payments on any secured claim or any other unsecured claim; . . .

11 U.S.C. § 1322.

Section 1326 concerns the order of payments in a Chapter 13 Plan. That section states:

> (b) Before or at the time of each payment to creditors under the plan, there shall be paid--
>
> (1) any unpaid claim of the kind specified in section 507(a)(2) of this title.

11 U.S.C. § 1326(b).

Section 1326(b)(1) requires payment of administrative expenses "[b]efore or at the time of each payment to creditors under the plan." Section 507(a)(2) provides that administrative expenses allowed under section 503(b) are to be paid "[b]efore or at the time of each payment to creditors under the plan." The appellants argue that this is properly read "'before or at the time of each payment to creditors under the plan' so that the § 507(a)(2) claim is fully paid before other creditors, secured, priority, or unsecured, are paid." (Docket Entry No. 21 at 15).

The courts are divided over whether section 1326(b)(1) requires that section 507(a)(2) claims be paid in full before payment of other claims. A number of courts hold that a partial payment of section 507(a)(2) expenses is all that is required by section 1326(b)(1). See In re Balderas, 328 B.R. 707, 717 (Bankr. W.D. Tex. 2005) (recognizing that requiring full payment of allowed administrative expense claims in front of other creditors would conflict with the Code section requiring a plan to provide for full payment in deferred cash payments of all claims entitled to priority under section 507); In re Parker, 15 B.R. 980, 983 (Bankr. E. D. Tenn. 1981) (secured claims have priority over administrative expense claims); In re Pappas & Rose, P.C., 229 B.R. 815, 820 (W.D. Okla.1998); In re Cook, 205 B.R. 437, 443 (Bankr. N. D. Fla.1997); In re Aldridge, 335 B.R. 889 (Bankr. S.D. Ala. 2005). Other courts--including bankruptcy courts in the same district--disagree. See, e.g., In re DeSardi, 340 B.R. 790, 808 (Bankr. S.D. Tex. 2006) (section 1326(b)(1) requires full payment of administrative claims before or when general payments commence under a Chapter 13 plan, but adequate protection payments are senior in priority to those fees); In re Harris, 304 B.R. 751, 758 (Bankr. E.D. Mich. 2004) ("[Section] 1326(b)(1) does not require or allow the full payment of Debtors' attorney fees to be delayed in favor of payments to a secured creditor, unless Debtor's counsel has agreed to such delay.").

The Perez court explained that the Local Rule and Procedures had been designed in part to address an abuse created by prior practice. "Under prior procedures in the Houston Division of the Southern District of Texas, Chapter 13 plan confirmation often took many months. When the plan was eventually confirmed, the trustee usually paid the debtor's attorney's fees in full before he paid the other creditors." 339 B.R. at 407. As the court noted, "in many instances, upon the filing of the bankruptcy petition, debtors quit paying mortgage notes, in part if not in whole, in order to be able to pay the trustee, who would then distribute the funds first to pay fees of the debtors' counsel." Id. at 407, n.23. The Perez court emphasized that the result of accepting the debtors' argument would be to forbid the trustee from making any payment to a mortgage lienholder on the debtor's principal residence until administrative claims (specifically, the debtor's attorney's fees) were paid in full or until the trustee first began to pay a portion of an allowed administrative claim. Id. at 408. As the court noted, this is inconsistent with section 1322(b), which requires that the rights of a home mortgage lender cannot be modified or reduced under Chapter 13. The Local Rule and Procedures prevented this by requiring payment to the mortgage lender through the trustee and allowing concurrent payment of allowed administrative claims. Id.

The Perez court reconciled the conflicting Code provisions by characterizing mortgage payments made before plan confirmation as adequate protection payments that were senior in priority to attorney's fees of debtors' counsel. As to postconfirmation payments, the court relied on the cases holding that section 1326 permits concurrent payment of secured and administrative claims. 339 B.R. at 408. "The new procedures require adequate protection payments to be made pre-confirmation and also require payment of post-petition secured claims concurrently with priority and administrative claims. Contrary to the Debtors' argument, these provisions carry out the priority provisions of, and are specifically permitted by, the Bankruptcy Code." Id.

The appellants' position that administrative expenses must be paid in full before the trustee can make any postpetition mortgage installment payment to a home mortgage lender rests on an interpretation of a Code provision so unclear that bankruptcy courts have divided over its meaning. The appellants' position is in direct conflict with the clear Code command to protect the rights of home mortgage lenders. The appellant's position would also frustrate the bankruptcy court's ability to curtail the abuses and inefficiencies that had resulted from the prior practice of routinely allowing direct mortgage payments, including that mortgage payments were often delayed or jettisoned in favor of first paying debtors' attorney's fees. The bankruptcy court interpreted the Code to give full effect to the express statutory command to protect the interests of the secured home mortgage lender, concluding that under section 1322(b)(2), "mortgage payments reign supreme." 339 B.R. at 408. As in Marrama, there is an inconsistency between an express statutory directive--to protect a mortgagee's right to receive home mortgage payments--and a general statutory provision that is unclear and subject to conflicting case law interpretations. As in Marrama, a bankruptcy court presented with such an inconsistency has the authority to reach a result that achieves the express Code requirement and is necessary to curtail a specific abuse of the bankruptcy process. The bankruptcy court properly concluded that the Local Rule and Procedure presumptively requiring conduit payments of home mortgage loans did not violate the Bankruptcy Code's priorities for paying administrative claims. This conclusion does not depend on characterizing the preconfirmation mortgage payments as adequate protection payments. The bankruptcy court's conclusion that the Local Rule and Procedures did not violate the priority payment sections of the Code is affirmed.

III. The Challenges to the Bankruptcy Court's Discretionary Decision not to Allow the Debtors to Make Direct Payments to the Mortgage Lender

The bankruptcy court held a hearing to address the debtors' motion for relief from the conduit payment requirement. Citing Foster, Reid, and Genereaux, the bankruptcy court listed twenty-one factors that could bear on determining whether debtors should be allowed to be their own disbursement agents. Perez, 339 B.R. at 408-09. Those factors were:

(1) the degree of responsibility of the debtor, as evidenced by his past dealings with creditors;
(2) the reasons contributing to the debtor's need for filing a Chapter 13 petition and plan;
(3) any delays that the trustee might make in remitting the monthly payment to the targeted creditor;
(4) whether the proposed plan modifies the debt;
(5) the sophistication of the target creditor;
(6) the ability and incentive of the target creditor to monitor payments;
(7) whether the debt is a commercial or consumer debt;
(8) the ability of the debtor to reorganize absent direct payments;
(9) whether the payment can be delayed;
(10) the number of payments proposed to pay the targeted claim;
(11) whether a direct payment under the proposed plan will impair the trustee's ability to perform his standing trustee duties;
(12) unique or special circumstances of a particular case;
(13) the business acumen of the debtor;
(14) the debtor's post-filing compliance with statutory and court-imposed duties;
(15) the good faith of the debtor;

> (16) the plan treatment of each creditor to which a direct payment is proposed to be made;
> (17) the consent, or lack thereof, by the affected creditor to the proposed plan treatment;
> (18) the ability of the trustee and the court to monitor future direct payments;
> (19) the potential burden on the trustee;
> (20) the possible effect upon the trustee's salary or funding of the U.S. Trustee system;
> (21) the potential for abuse of the bankruptcy system.

Id. at 409 (citations omitted). The court noted that the first factor is given greater emphasis under Foster. Id. at 409-410.

The bankruptcy court found that Mario and Maria Perez did "not demonstrate financial responsibility." Id. They were approximately a year delinquent on their mortgage and had failed to make their first plan payment to the trustee as proposed initially in their plan. Id. at 410. The court found that "[t]he Debtors' failure to make their first plan payment to the trustee also shows a lack of post-filing compliance with statutory and court imposed duties." Id. The bankruptcy court, while sympathizing with the debtors' hardships, found that the debtors had not demonstrated that they had the financial responsibility necessary to be allowed to serve as their own disbursing agents. The court emphasized the past dealings with creditors and the trustee.

The debtors argued that the primary reason for their desire to make direct rather than conduit payments was to save the trustee's fee. But it is clear that avoiding the trustee's percentage fee cannot be the sole reason for allowing debtors to make home mortgage payments directly. See, e.g., In re Reid, 179 B.R. at 508 ("The motivation for the reaffirmation agreement appears to be to avoid the payment of the trustee's fee. In analogous cases, other courts refused to allow debtors to make periodic payments directly."); In re Genereux, 137 B.R. at 413 ("I am not persuaded that the Debtor's interest in avoiding the Trustee's fee outweighs the interest of debtors (and creditors) generally in an effective and efficient Chapter 13 system."). Although the bankruptcy court used the statutory maximum fee of 10% to gauge the effect of conduit payments, that is not the percentage that debtors in fact pay. The Southern District of Texas website reveals that since August 2006, the fees for the three trustees range from 6.25% for one trustee to 5.95% for the other two. See Southern District of Texas Forms, Fees, and Rules, Posted Chapter 13 Trustee's Fee, at http://www.txs.uscourts.gov/bankruptcy/rulesformsproc/ch13fee.htm (last visited July 19, 2007). The bankruptcy court also stated that if mortgage payments were made through the trustee, the percentage fee is reduced. 339 B.R. at 415.

The bankruptcy court pointed out that the financial burden of the trustee fees could support allowing the debtors to make direct payments of their mortgage loans if other factors also weighed in favor of that result. The other factors, however, did not do so. Although the lenders were sophisticated and did not object to direct payment, the established history of poor record-keeping by both the debtors and lenders weighed heavily in favor of using the trustee as the disbursement agent, to prevent abuses of the Chapter 13 system and a large number of unnecessary disputes and motions during bankruptcy, including unnecessary risks and burdens on debtors. 339 B.R. 413-414.

The bankruptcy court explained that under the Local Rule and Procedures, debtors could directly pay their mortgages under certain circumstances. "[I]n the Southern District of Texas, direct payments by a debtor are now the exception rather than the rule, and . . . the debtor must satisfy the various elements set forth in the applicable case law to obtain approval for direct payments." Id. at 417. Given the facts showing the debtors' lack of financial responsibility, the bankruptcy court's decision to deny the debtors permission to serve as their own disbursing agent rather than making conduit mortgage payments through the trustee was well within the court's discretion.

IV. Conclusion

The decision of the bankruptcy court is affirmed. This appeal will be dismissed by separate order.

Notes and Questions

1. The district court in Perez refuses to equate mortgage payments with adequate protection payments. Had it done so, the local rule requiring the chapter 13 trustee to receive mortgage payments and to disburse them prior to confirmation would arguably have cohered with § 1326(a)(2) and with § 1326(b)(2). Instead the court reads Marrama v. Citizens National Bank of Massachusetts, supra, as authorizing, under § 105(a), judicial amendment of the Bankruptcy Code to prevent abuse. Is this a fair use of Marrama?

C. CONTENTS OF THE PLAN

1. Best Interest of the Creditors

IN RE McCORMICK

354 B.R. 246 (Bankr. C.D. Ill. 2006)

GORMAN, J.

This matter came before the Court for trial on confirmation of the Second Amended Chapter 13 Plan ("Plan") filed on May 31, 2006 by Dennis P. McCormick and Marcia McCormick (sometimes hereinafter "Debtors"). Confirmation is opposed by U.S. Bank, a secured creditor. This case and the proposed Plan raise interesting issues regarding the use of a secured creditor's cash collateral to fund a Chapter 13 plan, the proper classification and treatment of student loan debt, and the feasibility of proposing a significant "balloon" payment at the end of a Chapter 13 plan term. Because the McCormicks have failed to properly address each of these issues, their Plan cannot be confirmed.

Debtors filed their voluntary petition under Chapter 13 of the Bankruptcy Code on October 16, 2005. The McCormicks are both 46 years of age and reside in Springfield, Ill. They have a daughter who is a junior in college and a son who is a senior in high school.

Mr. McCormick is self-employed and has been in the insurance business for 23 years. He sells insurance products and securities, and his income is derived exclusively from commissions earned from such sales. Mr. McCormick pays all of his business expenses from his commissions, including a salary and benefits for one employee . . . . Mrs. McCormick is a nurse and works part-time for the State of Illinois reviewing disability claims . . . .

The McCormicks' financial problems began with a failed home construction project several years ago. U.S. Bank advanced money for the project and held a first and second mortgage on the real estate involved. Although the details presented at trial were sketchy, it appears that there were significant cost overruns, and the home was ultimately sold at a substantial loss. After the sale, the deficiency amount owed to U.S. Bank was approximately $71,000. In January, 2003, U.S. Bank agreed to refinance that balance and lend an additional $90,000 to pay off the McCormicks' credit cards.

The McCormicks executed documents with U.S. Bank for a loan of $163,857.38. Monthly payments of $1,758.05 began in February, 2003, and were to continue until January 28, 2006, when the balance of $123,357.66 was due in full. The McCormicks secured this obligation by pledging Mr. McCormick's renewal commissions from his insurance business.

Notwithstanding the strain that the monthly payment to U.S. Bank placed on their budget, the McCormicks purchased a new home in November, 2004, incurring new debt of approximately $250,000. The McCormicks' mortgage payment, including an escrow for real estate taxes and insurance, is $1,950 per month.

During the period from January, 2003, until October, 2005, when this case was filed, the McCormicks incurred over $75,000 of credit card debt. They also borrowed more than $16,000 for their daughter's education. Further, during the same time period, they failed to pay their income taxes and, at the time of filing, had liabilities to the Internal Revenue Service in the amount of $28,598 and to the Illinois Department of Revenue in the amount of $1,550.

The McCormicks owned three vehicles at the time of filing. Each month they make a $412 payment on a 1997 Mercedes and a $169 payment on a 2000 Mazda. Their 1995 Ford Explorer is free and clear of liens and is driven by their son. After filing, they purchased a fourth vehicle to be driven by their daughter. Mr. McCormick testified that his current transportation costs for the four vehicles including the installment payments are about $2,000 per month.

The McCormicks' budget shows a $260 per month payment on the student loan debt and a $525 payment for the daughter's other monthly expenses at school. Mr. McCormick testified that they will continue to incur debt in the amount of $18,000 to $20,000 this year and next year for their daughter's education. He did not discuss their plans for their son's college education.

The McCormicks' Plan proposes to pay the IRS and the Illinois Department of Revenue in full through payments to the Trustee. The Plan also proposes a 13.4% dividend to unsecured creditors to be paid through the Trustee. The Plan proposes direct payments on the home mortgage loan and the vehicle loans. The Plan proposes a $1,023.40 per month direct payment to U.S. Bank with a balloon payment at the end of the Plan term.

The Court has considered the testimony presented at trial and all of the exhibits admitted into evidence. There are numerous reasons why the McCormicks' Plan does not comply with the requirements of the Bankruptcy Code and confirmation must be denied. Because the McCormicks will be given an opportunity to file another amended plan, the major issues which compel denial of confirmation will each be discussed.

A. Valuation of Renewal Commissions

Mr. McCormick's principal asset consists of his renewal commissions from sales of life insurance, disability insurance, and other insurance and investments products. Some of these renewal commissions secure the McCormicks' obligation to U.S. Bank. On the McCormicks' Schedule B, the renewal commissions are disclosed and valued at $150,000. At trial, Mr. McCormick testified that the gross value of the renewal commissions is $300,000 to $350,000 and that the value continues to grow with new sales. He further testified that the $150,000 scheduled value was "discounted."

Mr. McCormick did not explain how the value of $300,000 to $350,000 was calculated. The Court does not know whether Mr. McCormick simply added up every possible premium which may come in from sales he has made or whether he used a "rule of thumb" or industry formula to determine a value for expected renewals. Likewise, Mr. McCormick did not explain how he "discounted" the gross value to reach the scheduled value of $150,000. The Court originally understood Mr. McCormick to refer to the discount as being for the time value of money because the renewal commissions will only be paid to him as customers actually pay their renewal premiums. Later testimony indicated, however, that other factors were considered in the discount, such as Mr. McCormick's ability to compete for his own customers to purchase new policies rather than renew old policies in the event of a forced liquidation. How and why such factors were included in the calculation was not explained in any way.

The valuation of the renewal commissions is key to the resolution of several legal issues presented in this case. The paucity of evidence on the issue of valuation limits the ability of the Court to decide these issues.

B. Use of U.S. Bank's Cash Collateral

U.S. Bank has a secured interest in certain renewal commissions. No documents were submitted to identify the specific commissions subject to the secured interest of U.S. Bank. Mr. McCormick testified that he is authorized to write insurance and sell products through contracts with a number of different insurance companies. He did not testify that U.S. Bank had secured the renewal commissions from every company with whom he might possibly do business. Thus, the Court struggles to understand, not only the total value of Mr. McCormick's renewal commissions as set forth above, but also the value of commissions upon which U.S. Bank has a lien.

Both the attorney for U.S. Bank and the McCormicks' attorney referred to the fact that new sales continue to be generated, and both seemed to assume that expected renewal commissions from such new sales are additional collateral for U.S. Bank. Thus, both ignored the provisions Section 552 of the Bankruptcy Code which deal with the post-petition effect of a pre-petition security interest. Absent an express statutory provision or court order, pre-petition security interests do not attach to property acquired by the estate or a debtor after the commencement of a case. 11 U.S.C. § 552(a). No motion has been filed in this case to change that result. Accordingly, U.S. Bank does not have a secured interest in any commissions generated by post-petition sales and will not acquire such an interest unless the appropriate pleadings are filed and approved by the Court.

In order to use the cash collateral of U.S. Bank, Mr. McCormick must have the consent of U.S. Bank or must establish to the Court that U.S. Bank's interest in the cash collateral is adequately protected. 11 U.S.C. § 363(c)(2) & (f). The McCormicks filed this case a year ago but have not filed a Motion to Use Cash Collateral. U.S. Bank is well aware that Mr. McCormick is using the renewal commissions as they come in, but it has not filed a motion to prohibit or condition the use of the commissions. Mr. McCormick testified that he tendered payments to U.S. Bank early in the case but the payments were refused. Why U.S. Bank refused the payments is an unexplained fact in the case. Acceptance of the payments would not have waived U.S. Bank's rights in the case and, to the extent counsel for the Bank had concerns in that area, a simple cash collateral order could have resolved such concerns. This Court can only conclude that, to date, U.S. Bank has consented to Mr. McCormick's use of cash collateral without requiring any adequate protection payments or replacement liens.

U.S. Bank's Objection to Confirmation, however, makes clear that U.S. Bank will not continue indefinitely to allow the use of its cash collateral and wants this Court to deny confirmation of the proposed Chapter 13 Plan because the Plan does not provide adequate protection of its secured interest. In order to determine what payments will adequately protect U.S. Bank, the Court needs to know the value of its collateral and whether a replacement lien will be granted on future renewal commissions. Further, the Court needs to know how much of the cash collateral will be received and expended during the term of the Plan. If a replacement lien is granted, the Court needs to know the amount of new renewal commissions expected to be generated.

Mr. McCormick testified that he expected that, from the date of trial until the end of the year, a period of approximately 5 months, $25,000 in renewal commissions upon which U.S. Bank has a lien should be received. He also testified that, during the first six months of next year, another $37,000 in such commissions should be received. The Plan proposes a $1,023 per month payment to U.S. Bank. Accordingly, for the 11-month period from August, 2006, to June, 2007, the proposal is to pay $11,253 to U.S. Bank as adequate protection for the use of $62,000. Unless Mr. McCormick is generating sizeable new commissions upon which U.S. Bank will have a replacement lien, it is difficult to see how such a payment schedule provides adequate protection.

The lack of evidence on valuation has already been discussed. The McCormicks have not sought authority to grant a lien on newly-generated renewal commissions. Without such evidence or pleadings, the Court cannot find that U.S. Bank is adequately protected.

C. Liquidation Analysis

One requirement which must be satisfied in order to confirm a Chapter 13 plan is that the value of the property to be distributed under the plan to unsecured creditors must not be less than they would receive in a Chapter 7 case if the estate of the debtor were liquidated as of the effective date of the plan. 11 U.S.C. § 1325(a)(4); In re Brown, 332 B.R. 562, 568 (Bankr. N.D. Ill 2005). The lack of evidence on the value of the renewal commissions impedes the Court's analysis of this issue.

A Chapter 13 liquidation analysis is a hypothetical analysis of what a Chapter 7 trustee would do to liquidate the estate. In re Brennan, 208 B.R. 448, 451 (Bankr S.D. Ill. 1997). This Court believes that a Chapter 7 trustee would ask many of the same questions that this Court is asking. An inquiry would have to be made into exactly which renewal commissions are subject to U.S. Bank's security interest and which are not. The value of the commissions not subject to the lien would have to be determined. Further, a Chapter 7 trustee would consider whether there was value in the commissions subject to the U.S. Bank lien in excess of the amounts necessary to fully secure the Bank's claim. No evidence that such an analysis has been done was presented at trial. The Chapter

13 Plan contains no provision that requires any amounts to be paid into the Plan for the benefit of unsecured creditors by reason of a liquidation analysis.

The Debtors have proposed to pay $12,704 to unsecured creditors which they estimate will provide a 13.4% dividend. This amount does not appear to have been calculated based on a liquidation analysis. The explanation provided for the dividend is that the McCormicks wanted to do something for their unsecured creditors. Although the McCormicks may be well-meaning, a more thorough legal analysis of their obligations, if any, to unsecured creditors must be conducted. Further, because the funds which might be used to pay a dividend to unsecured creditors may be the cash collateral of U.S. Bank, this Court cannot simply accept a desire "to do something" as a basis to find such payments appropriate.

If the McCormicks have assets which would be liquidated by a Chapter 7 trustee for a dividend to unsecured creditors, then their Chapter 13 Plan must provide a base amount to be paid to those unsecured creditors in this case. If not, then, absent a disposable income calculation which leads to a required payment to unsecured creditors, unsecured creditors will receive no dividend in this case. See 11 U.S.C. § 1325(b). A straightforward, objective analysis of what the McCormicks are required to pay to unsecured creditors must be done in order for confirmation to be allowed.

D. Educational Expenses

The McCormicks' daughter is a junior in college and the McCormicks have incurred and continue to incur student loan debt to pay her educational expenses. The McCormicks also contribute to her ongoing monthly expenses. These issues raise further impediments to confirmation.

The McCormicks scheduled their pre-petition debt to the U.S. Department of Education as priority debt and proposed to pay the debt directly and in full. The Trustee did not object to the Debtors' schedules, nor to this Plan provision. The debt to the U.S. Department of Education is not, however, a priority debt. Priority debts are those specifically set forth in the Code, and student loan obligations, even those owed to the United States, are not priority debts. See 11 U.S.C. § 507.

Courts have found that Chapter 13 plans which propose to pay student loans at rates substantially higher than other unsecured debts unfairly discriminate against the other unsecured creditors and cannot be confirmed. See 11 U.S.C. § 1322(a)(3); In re Belda, 315 B.R. 477, 487 (N.D. Ill. 2004); In re Brown, 162 B.R. 506 (N.D. Ill. 1993); In re Caruso, 2001 WL 34076052 (Bankr. C.D. Ill. 2001); In re Chapman, 146 B.R. 411 (Bankr. N.D. Ill. 1992). The McCormicks' Chapter 13 Plan cannot be confirmed unless the student loan debt is treated in the same manner as other unsecured debt.

The educational expenses of their daughter raise other issues for the McCormicks. Their budget shows that, in addition to the student loan payment, they contribute $525 per month for their daughter's expenses while she is away at school. Mr. McCormick testified that, over and above that amount, he is incurring new student loan debt at the rate of $18,000 to $20,000 per year for her expenses. He also testified that he contributes additional sums for her sorority expenses and that insurance proceeds he received last summer for weather-related damage to the family home were used to purchase a vehicle for her. Although the McCormicks' desire to help their daughter is admirable, they simply cannot afford to do what they are doing for her and still honor their other obligations. Bankruptcy is not intended to create involuntary student loans whereby creditors, in essence, finance the education of the debtors' children. In re Henricksen, 131 B.R. 467, 473 (Bankr. N.D. Okla. 1991). This is not to say that no educational expenses or support for their daughter can be included in the McCormicks' budget. Rather, the amounts here are excessive in view of the McCormicks' financial situation and the fact that some of the funds they are using for the expenditures are the cash collateral of U.S. Bank . . .

F. Feasibility

U.S. Bank's principal objection to the McCormicks' Chapter 13 Plan is that it is not feasible for the McCormicks to refinance and pay off their obligation to U.S. Bank at the end of the five-year plan term. At that time, if all plan payments have been made, the balance due to U.S. Bank will be about $105,000.

Although so-called "balloon" payments at the end of a Chapter 13 plan are not prohibited, plans which provide for the "receipt of funds from unidentified and uncertain sources during the last month of a sixty month plan must be scrutinized carefully." In re Brunson, 87 B.R. 304, 312 (Bankr. D. N.J. 1988). One of the factors to be given consideration in such scrutiny is the equity in the property which will be sold or refinanced to obtain the funds. Id.

This Court has previously discussed its concerns about the lack of evidence regarding the value of Mr. McCormick's renewal commissions. The evidence is critical to determine the feasibility of any refinance in the future. The Court must be able to make an approximation of (i) the current value of the commissions, (ii) how much of the commissions will be received and spent, and (iii) how much will be replaced by new sales during the term of the Plan. Absent that information, the Court cannot find that it is feasible to expect a new lender to refinance the debt to U.S. Bank with then-existing renewal commissions as collateral.

Other issues in this case also impact on feasibility. The McCormicks' failure to pay income taxes as they become due cannot continue. It is not realistic to expect a lender to extend financing if Debtors' obligations to the Internal Revenue Service have increased rather than decreased during the term of the Plan. Likewise, the McCormicks cannot continue to increase their student loan debt by $20,000 or more per year and still expect to be able to borrow more money in a few years. If the McCormicks' financial picture is worse at the end of the Plan term than it was when they started, it is unlikely that they will find a way to make the required balloon payment. This Court must be able to find that the McCormicks will be able make all of their Plan payments including the balloon payment in order to confirm their Plan. See 11 U.S.C § 1325(a)(6).

Additionally, the McCormicks must control their spending in order to establish a likelihood of refinancing the U.S. Bank debt. Although the McCormicks' initial financial problems associated with the failed construction project may not have been all of their own making, their subsequent problems are clearly the result of regularly spending more than they earn. From February, 2003-when their $90,000 of credit card debt was paid off-until the filing of this case in October, 2005, the McCormicks ran up another $75,000 of credit card debt. During approximately that same time period, they failed to pay or escrow over $50,000 of income taxes. They apparently lived on Mr. McCormick's gross earnings rather than what should have been his net income. Over a period of about 33 months, this resulted in spending of more than $3,700 per month for living expenses over and above what was realistically available.

Since filing their petition, the McCormicks do not appear to have changed their spending habits. They have not escrowed the $1,023 per month payment for U.S. Bank or the $2,300 per month for taxes. Mr. McCormick testified that it had been tough to make ends meet since filing the Chapter 13 case and that he had no funds saved. Thus, the McCormicks are spending $3,300 per month on items not in their Chapter 13 budget and are still struggling to keep up. These funds may be going for educational expenses of their daughter, upkeep on their four cars, or unbudgeted expenses associated with their new home. The McCormicks can only succeed in their Chapter 13 case if they take a serious look at their spending and make the hard choices necessary to get control.

Finally, another factor in the scrutiny which must be given to balloon payment cases is the future earning capacity of the debtors. Id. Mr. McCormick's income is substantial, but is not enough to pay all of the McCormick's debts and their living expenses. At trial, Mrs. McCormick did not appear, but Mr. McCormick testified that she was a nurse and in good health. He further testified that her reason for working only part-time was that she needed to be home with the children. This testimony is confusing, considering that the McCormicks' daughter is away at college most of the year and works during the summers when she is home. The McCormicks' son is a senior in high school, is involved in sports after school, and also has a part-time job. Mr. McCormick's testimony about the independent activities of his children was intended to justify the expenses of four vehicles, but it also undercut his contention that his wife is able work only part-time because she must be home to care for the children. There may be other good reasons why Mrs. McCormick works on such a limited basis which were not presented at trial. The increased family income which full-time employment by Mrs. McCormick could bring would help to deal with many of the issues discussed herein. The Court will not order Mrs. McCormick to change her employment status but simply notes that it is a consideration in assessing the feasibility of the McCormicks' Chapter 13 Plan.

Based on the evidence, the Court cannot find that the McCormicks will be able to make all of their payments under the Plan. Specifically, based on their current situation, it is unlikely that they will be able to make the balloon payment to U.S. Bank as required by their Plan.

For all of the reasons set forth above, confirmation of the McCormicks' Second Amended Chapter 13 Plan is denied. The McCormicks will be granted 30 days to file a Third Amended Chapter 13 Plan.

Notes and Questions

1. Section 1325(a)(4), commonly referred to as the "best interest of creditors" test, requires that every creditor must be better off in the chapter 13 plan than in a hypothetical Chapter 7 liquidation.

2. Only holders of unsecured allowed claims can invoke the 1325(a)(4) "best interest of creditors test." For example, § 502(b)(9) clarifies that tardily filed claims are not allowed claims in Chapter 13. Thus, tardily filed claims cannot invoke the best interest of the creditors test. See In re Dennis, 230 B.R. 244, 249 (Bankr. D.N.J. 1999).

3. Suppose in a hypothetical chapter 7 case a chapter 13 debtor's assets are sufficient to pay the IRS in full. Is the IRS entitled to interest on its claim? In re Eason, 178 B.R. 908 (Bankr. M.D. Ga. 1994). Would it make a difference if all the other creditors could be paid in full?

4. Section 1325(a) sets forth a list of factors for a court to consider to confirm a plan, including, as discussed in McCormick, whether the plan is feasible. Bankruptcy Code § 1325(a)(6).

BAPCPA adds whether the petition (as opposed to the plan itself) was filed in good faith, whether the debtor is current in domestic support obligations and whether the debtor has filed applicable taxes as required by § 1308. If a debtor meets all the requirements of § 1325(a), the court must confirm.

If § 1325(a) is not met, does a bankruptcy court have some discretion to confirm? According to the court in In re Burgess, 143 Fed. Appx. 692, 695 (7th Cir. 2005):

> In [In re Escobedo, 28 F.3d 34, 35 (7th Cir. 1994)], we distinguished the mandatory nature of § 1322(a)(2) from the discretionary requirements of § 1325(a). Our analysis in Escobedo relied on the analysis of the Third Circuit in In re Szostek, 886 F.2d 1405, 1411 (3d Cir. 1989). Szostek found § 1322(a) mandatory for all plans because that provision contained unequivocal lan-guage that "the plan shall" satisfy three requirements. See id. This unequivocal language meant that "a bankruptcy court lacks the authority to confirm any plan unless it" complies with the provisions of § 1322(a). Escobedo, 28 F.3d at 35; Szostek, 886 F.2d at 1411. Szostek then consi-dered the language of § 1325(a), which provides that "'a court shall confirm a plan if certain things occur." Szostek, 886 F.2d at 1411. The proper interpretation of this provision is that if the requirements of § 1325(a) are met, the bankruptcy court must confirm the plan, but if they are not met (but § 1322(a) is satisfied), the bankruptcy court still has the discretion to confirm the plan. See id. Section 1325(a), therefore, is not mandatory, but only discretionary. As the Third Circuit noted, "if Congress had intended for § 1325(a) to be mandatory, it could have included that requirement with the requirements already listed in § 1322." Id.

Compare the equivalent chapter 11 confirmation provision. Bankruptcy Code § 1129(a) ("The court shall confirm a plan only if all the following requirements are met . . .) (emphasis added). Other than the Fourth and Seventh Circuits, courts think that § 1325(a) is mandatory; all its terms must be met before a plan can be confirmed. E.g., Shaw v. Aurgroup Fin. Credit Union, 552 F.3d 447 (6th Cir. 2009). Perhaps the Supreme Court has implicitly decided that § 1325(a) is a mandatory provision. In Associates Commercial Corp. v. Rash, 520 U.S. 681 (1997), debtors proposed to cram down a truck at wholesale value. The bankruptcy court confirmed the plan. Under Szostek, the appeal was surely a loser. Nevertheless the creditor appealed on the ground that the truck should have been valued at replacement value. The creditor proceeded to win most of the appeals, including an appeal to the Supreme Court. At the Supreme Court level, Court remarks, "To qualify for confirmation under Chapter 13, the [debtors] plan had to satisfy the requirements set forth in § 1325(a) of the Code." Id. at 956; see Universal American Mortg. Co. v. Bateman (In re Bateman), 331 F.3d 821, 832 n.7 (11th Cir. 2003) ("this question appears to be settled by [Rash]"). See also Johnson v. Home State Bank, 501 U.S. 78 (1991) ("A bankruptcy court is authorized to confirm a plan only if the court finds, inter alia, [that [various parts of § 1325(a) have been met]").

5. The Debtors in McCormick, wanted to use the renewal commissions, in which U.S. Bank had a security interest. This collateral is known as cash collateral, which is defined in § 363(a) as cash or cash equivalent that is subject to an interest held by a person other than the estate. Cash collateral is either cash (as in the renewal commissions in McCormick) or cash equivalents such as bank accounts, securities, negotiable instruments, etc. Cash collateral is treated differently from other property of the estate. The trustee cannot deal with cash collateral, even in the ordinary course of business, unless the entity that has an interest consent or the court authorizes the use of the cash collateral. 11 U.S.C. § 363(c)(2). The trustee is also required to segregate accounts for cash collateral. 11 U.S.C. § 363(c)(4). The liquid nature of cash collateral demands this strict approach as it is tempting for the debtor to spend these assets, dissipating the secured party's collateral. Requiring court authorization or consent to use this cash collateral ensures that the secured party receives adequate protection, 11 U.S.C. § 363(e), before the collateral is touched.

6. Note the date that the debtors in McCormick filed for bankruptcy -one day before the BAPCPA Amendments went into effect. The number of bankruptcies filed on that day was prodigious.

IN RE RAYNARD

354 B.R. 834 (Bankr. 6th Cir. 2006)

LATTA, J.

Bankruptcy Appellate Panel Judge. Debtors appeal an order denying confirmation of their chapter 13 plans and dismissing their case.

I. ISSUES ON APPEAL

Whether the Debtors' proposed Chapter 13 plan, prior to amendment, unfairly discriminated between joint and individual creditors even though the only property available for distribution in a hypothetical Chapter 7 case would be property held as tenants by the entireties. Whether the Debtors' proposed chapter 13 plan, as amended, meets the best interest of creditors test.

Whether the bankruptcy court abused its discretion in dismissing the bankruptcy case. . . .

III. FACTS

The Debtors, Alan and Karen Raynard, are Michigan dairy farmers. They own both their farm and their residence as tenants by the entireties. The Debtors filed their joint Chapter 13 petition on January 13, 2005. They have proposed a plan and three amendments for confirmation. The bankruptcy court twice denied confirmation of their plan and finally dismissed their case.

The Debtors' schedules list the value of their farm as $240,000 and the value of their residence as $130,000. The properties are subject to mortgage liens of $129,715 and $112,874 respectively. The bankruptcy court determined that after allowing 10% for liquidation costs, the Debtors had $86,285 in equity in their farm and $4,126 in equity in their residence. The Debtors claimed both their farm and their residence as exempt pursuant to 11 U.S. C. § 522(b)(2)(B) and Michigan Comp. Laws § 600.6018. The Chapter 13 trustee filed an objection to the Debtors' claim of exemption, but neither party requested that the objection be set for hearing.

The Debtors' original plan proposed to pay nothing to their unsecured creditors, whose claims, as listed by the Debtors, totaled $88,101. The Debtors subsequently filed a pre-confirmation amendment to their plan, in which they proposed to divide their unsecured creditors into two classes, the first consisting of creditors holding joint claims, and the second consisting of creditors holding individual claims. The Debtors proposed that the first class be paid a total of $29,443 (the total amount of the joint claims as listed by the Debtors), while the second class would be paid a total of $1,000 (against individual claims of $58,658).

The Debtors filed a second pre-confirmation amendment in which they proposed to pay joint creditors "100 percent through the debt plan," and left unchanged the $1,000 amount to be shared by all individual creditors. The bankruptcy court denied confirmation of this second amended plan by order entered July 15, 2005, on the basis that it discriminated unfairly in favor of joint creditors in violation of 11 U.S.C. § 1322(b). The bankruptcy court permitted the Debtors to file an amendment to their plan to conform to its ruling.

The Debtors filed a third pre-confirmation amendment to the plan whereby they proposed that during the first three years of their plan, all non-priority unsecured creditors would be paid pro rata after the secured creditors and priority unsecured creditors were paid. Thereafter, individual creditors were to receive nothing from the plan, unsecured priority creditors, if any, would be paid in full, and general unsecured creditors holding joint claims would likewise be paid in full.

The bankruptcy court denied confirmation of the Debtors' third amended plan in an order entered November 4, 2005, on the basis that it was not in the best interest of creditors in violation of 11 U.S.C. § 1322(a)(4). The court further ordered that the Debtors not be permitted an additional opportunity to amend their existing plan or file a new plan because they were "either unable or unwilling to propose a plan that will conform to the rulings I have made in this case." Finally, the court dismissed their Chapter 13 case because they twice failed to obtain confirmation of their plan. The court noted that while it would be in the best interest of creditors that the case be converted to Chapter 7, this was not permitted without the Debtors' consent because they were farmers. See 11 U.S.C. § 1307(e). As a result of the dismissal of the Debtors' case, both of the bankruptcy court prior orders denying confirmation of their proposed plans became final. The Debtors timely appealed the November 4, 2005, order. The titular Appellee, the Chapter 13 trustee, declined to respond and, in fact, filed a letter in support of the Debtors' position.

IV. DISCUSSION

The Debtors argue now and argued before the bankruptcy court that in a hypothetical distribution under chapter 7, their unsecured individual creditors would receive nothing because it is settled law in Michigan that only joint creditors can reach entireties property. Therefore, they argue that the equity in their entireties property is completely exempt from the claims of individual creditors, but not exempt (to the extent it exceeds their homestead exemption) from the claims of joint creditors. As a result, they contend that they should be permitted to propose a plan that discriminates between joint creditors and individual creditors on the basis that individual creditors are not entitled to be paid from entireties property.

The bankruptcy court rejected the Debtors' argument and concluded that the non-exempt equity in the Debtors' property must be administered for the benefit of all unsecured creditors, both joint and individual. That is, the court decided that under the Bankruptcy Code, any portion of the value of the Debtors' property that would be available to satisfy joint claims under state law should be used to satisfy all claims, both joint and individual, under federal bankruptcy law . . . .

Pursuant to section 522(b) of the Bankruptcy Code, debtors are permitted to exempt certain property from the claims of creditors. In those states, such as Michigan, that have not opted out of the federal bankruptcy exemptions, debtors are free to choose between two sets of exemptions provided by the Bankruptcy Code, provided that both spouses in a joint case make the same election. The Debtors elected to claim the exemptions provided by section 522(b)(2), generally those exemptions provided by state law. Regarding their real property, the Debtors claimed an exemption of $17,126 with respect to their home and $110,285 with respect to their farm, in both cases citing 11 U.S.C. § 522(b)(2)(B). These amounts represent the estimated equity in each of the parcels of real property after satisfaction of outstanding mortgages. Section 522(b)(2)(B) provides an exemption for:

> any interest in property in which the debtor had, immediately before the commencement of the case, an interest as a tenant by the entirety or joint tenant to the extent that such interest as a tenant by the entirety or joint tenant is exempt from process under applicable non-bankruptcy law.

11 U.S.C. § 522(b)(2)(B).

The Debtors assert that under Michigan law, the full value of their interests as tenants by the entireties is exempt from the claims of the individual creditors of either one of them, and therefore that this same value is exempt from the claims of individual creditors in their bankruptcy case. The Debtors are correct. The court of appeals has made this clear:

Michigan is one of a minority of states retaining the common law tenancy by the entirety. Tenants by the entirety, who must be husband and wife, hold under a single title with right of survivorship. Neither husband nor wife acting alone can alienate any interest in the property, nor can the creditors of one levy upon the property; but their joint creditors can reach entireties property. Liberty State Bank and Trust v. Grosslight (In re Grosslight), 757 F.2d 773, 775 (6th Cir. 1985) (citing Sanford v. Bertrau, 204 Mich. 244, 169 N.W. 880 (1918)). Nothing in the Bankruptcy Code changes this result. The bankruptcy court erred when it limited the language "to the extent that" in section 522(b)(2)(B) to a dollar amount. In effect, the bankruptcy court read section 522(b)(2)(B) to provide an exemption only to the extent of the amount not needed to satisfy joint claims. It then reasoned that because the amount needed to satisfy joint claims was not exempt under bankruptcy law, that amount should be available to satisfy all claims, whether joint or individual. The bankruptcy court failed to realize that entireties property is fully exempt from the claims of individual creditors under all circumstances. That is the extent to which it is exempt. Individual creditors are not entitled to a windfall as the result of the filing of a bankruptcy case. Whether outside of a bankruptcy estate or inside it, a debtor's interest in property held as a tenant by the entireties is exempt from the claims of his or her individual creditors pursuant to the common law of Michigan. The court of appeals could not have been more clear on this point:" Under Michigan law, ordinary creditors cannot reach interests in entireties property, and the entire interest will therefore be exempt if there are no joint creditors." Id.

The Debtors in this case have filed a joint case and have proposed a joint plan. That plan provides for payment to unsecured creditors, both joint and individual. The proposal of their present plan resulted from the bankruptcy court's prior incorrect conclusion that the Bankruptcy Code does not permit discrimination between joint creditors and individual creditors when the only property available for distribution in a hypothetical Chapter 7 case is property exempt from the claims of individual creditors. It appears that the Debtors' second amended plan was capable of confirmation. It did not unfairly discriminate between classes of creditors.

Denial of confirmation of the Debtors' third amended plan was based upon the putative failure of the plan to satisfy the best interest of creditors test. This determination resulted from the same error as to the effect of a tenancy by the entireties on the claims of individual and joint creditors. For purposes of making the best interest of creditors analysis in this case, it must be assumed that joint creditors would be paid in full because the value of the Debtors' real property after satisfaction of secured claims and their homestead exemption exceeds the amount of outstanding joint claims, and individual creditors would be entitled to no payment from entireties property. The Debtors' third amended plan was likewise capable of confirmation.

The bankruptcy court dismissed the Debtors's bankruptcy case after it refused to confirm the Debtors' third amended plan in the face of the Debtors' continued maintenance of the position that their joint creditors were entitled to more favorable treatment than their individual creditors. Because the bankruptcy court employed an incorrect legal standard in deciding to deny confirmation of the Debtors' plan, the resulting dismissal of their case was an abuse of discretion.

For the foregoing reasons, this decision of the bankruptcy court is REVERSED and the case is REMANDED to the bankruptcy court for entry of orders consistent with this opinion.

2. Disposable Income

HAMILTON v LANNING

130 S. Ct. 2464 (2010)

ALITO, J.

Chapter 13 of the Bankruptcy Code provides bankruptcy protection to "individual[s] with regular income" whose debts fall within statutory limits. 11 U.S.C. §§ 101(30), 109(e). Unlike debtors who file under Chapter 7 and must liquidate their nonexempt assets in order to pay creditors, see §§ 704(a)(1), 726, Chapter 13 debtors are permitted to keep their property, but they must agree to a court-approved plan under which they pay creditors out of their future income, see §§ 1306(b), 1321, 1322(a)(1), 1328(a). A bankruptcy trustee oversees the filing and execution of a Chapter 13 debtor's plan. § 1322(a)(1); see also 28 U.S.C. § 586(a)(3).

Section 1325 of Title 11 specifies circumstances under which a bankruptcy court "shall" and "may not" confirm a plan. § 1325(a),(b). If an unsecured creditor or the bankruptcy trustee objects to confirmation, § 1325(b)(1) requires the debtor either to pay unsecured creditors in full or to pay all "projected disposable income" to be received by the debtor over the duration of the plan.

We granted certiorari to decide how a bankruptcy court should calculate a debtor's "projected disposable income." Some lower courts have taken what the parties term the "mechanical approach," while most have adopted what has been called the "forward-looking approach." We hold that the "forward-looking approach" is correct.

I

As previously noted, § 1325 provides that if a trustee or an unsecured creditor objects to a Chapter 13 debtor's plan, a bankruptcy court may not approve the plan unless it provides for the full repayment of unsecured claims or "provides that all of the debtor's projected disposable income to be received" over the duration of the plan "will be applied to make payments" in accordance with the terms of the plan. 11 U.S.C. § 1325(b)(1); see also § 1325(b)(1) (2000 ed.). Before the enactment of the Bankruptcy Abuse Prevention and Consumer Protection Act of 2005 (BAPCPA), 119 Stat. 23, the Bankruptcy Code (Code) loosely defined "disposable income" as "income which is received by the debtor and which is not reasonably necessary to be expended" for the "maintenance or support of the debtor," for qualifying charitable contributions, or for business expenditures. § 1325(b)(2)(A), (B).

The Code did not define the term "projected disposable income," and in most cases, bankruptcy courts used a mechanical approach in calculating projected disposable income. That is, they first multiplied monthly income by the number of months in the plan and then determined what portion of the result was "excess" or "disposable." See 2 K. Lundin, Chapter 13 Bankruptcy § 164.1, p. 164-1, and n. 4 (3d ed. 2000) (hereinafter Lundin (2000 ed.)) (citing cases).

In exceptional cases, however, bankruptcy courts took into account foreseeable changes in a debtor's income or expenses. See In re Heath, 182 B. R. 557, 559-561 (Bkrtcy. App. Panel CA9 1995); In re Richardson, 283 B. R. 783, 799 (Bkrtcy. Ct. Kan. 2002); Tr. of Oral Arg. 7. Accord, 1 Lundin § 35.10, at 35-14 (2000 ed.) ("The debtor should take some care to project estimated future income on Schedule I to include anticipated increases or decreases [in income] so that the schedule will be consistent with any evidence of income the debtor would offer at a contested confirmation hearing").

BAPCPA left the term "projected disposable income" undefined but specified in some detail how "disposable income" is to be calculated. "Disposable income" is now defined as "current monthly income received by the debtor" less "amounts reasonably necessary to be expended" for the debtor's maintenance and support, for qualifying charitable contributions, and for business expenditures. § 1325(b)(2)(A)(i) and (ii) (2006 ed.). "Current monthly income," in turn, is calculated by averaging the debtor's monthly income during what the parties refer to as the 6-month look-back period, which generally consists of the six full months preceding the filing of the bankruptcy petition. See § 101(10A)(A)(i).[1] The phrase "amounts reasonably necessary to be expended" in § 1325(b)(2) is also newly defined. For a debtor whose income is below the median for his or her State, the phrase includes the full amount needed for "maintenance or support," see § 1325(b)(2)(A)(i), but for a debtor with income that exceeds the state median, only certain specified expenses are included,[2] see §§ 707(b)(2), 1325(b)(3)(A).

II.A.

Respondent had $36,793.36 in unsecured debt when she filed for Chapter 13 bankruptcy protection in October 2006. In the six months before her filing, she received a one-time buyout from her former employer, and this payment greatly inflated her gross income for April 2006 (to $11,990.03) and for May 2006 (to $15,356.42). App. 84, 107. As a result of these payments, respondent's current monthly income, as averaged from April through October 2006, was $5,343.70--a figure that exceeds the median income for a family of one in Kansas. See id., at 78. Respondent's monthly expenses, calculated pursuant to § 707(b)(2), were $4,228.71. Id., at 83. She reported a monthly "disposable income" of $1,114.98 on Form 22C. Id.

---

[1] However, if a debtor does not file the required schedule (Schedule I), the bankruptcy court may select a different 6-month period. See § 101(10A)(A)(ii).

[2] The formula for above-median-income debtors is known as the "means test" and is reflected in a schedule (Form 22C) that a Chapter 13 debtor must file. See Fed. Rule Bkrtcy. Proc. Official Form 22C (2009); In re Liverman, 383 B. R. 604, 606, n. 1, 608-609 (Bkrtcy. Ct. NJ 2008).

On the form used for reporting monthly income (Schedule I), she reported income from her new job of $1,922 per month--which is below the state median. Id., at 66; see also id., at 78. On the form used for reporting monthly expenses (Schedule J), she reported actual monthly expenses of $1,772.97. Id., at 68. Subtracting the Schedule J figure from the Schedule I figure resulted in monthly disposable income of $149.03.

Respondent filed a plan that would have required her to pay $144 per month for 36 months. See id., at 93. Petitioner, a private Chapter 13 trustee, objected to confirmation of the plan because the amount respondent proposed to pay was less than the full amount of the claims against her, see § 1325(b)(1)(A), and because, in petitioner's view, respondent was not committing all of her "projected disposable income" to the repayment of creditors, see § 1325(b)(1)(B). According to petitioner, the proper way to calculate projected disposable income was simply to multiply disposable income, as calculated on Form 22C, by the number of months in the commitment period. Employing this mechanical approach, petitioner calculated that creditors would be paid in full if respondent made monthly payments of $756 for a period of 60 months. Id., at 108. There is no dispute that respondent's actual income was insufficient to make payments in that amount.

B

The Bankruptcy Court endorsed respondent's proposed monthly payment of $144 but required a 60-month plan period. No. 06-41037 etc., 2007 Bankr. LEXIS 1639 (Bkrtcy. Ct. Kan. 2007). The court agreed with the majority view that the word "projected" in § 1325(b)(1)(B) requires courts "to consider at confirmation the debtor's actual income as it was reported on Schedule I." 2007 Bankr. LEXIS 1639 (emphasis added). This conclusion was warranted by the text of § 1325(b)(1), the Bankruptcy Court reasoned, and was necessary to avoid the absurd result of denying bankruptcy protection to individuals with deteriorating finances in the six months before filing. Id.

Petitioner appealed to the Tenth Circuit Bankruptcy Appellate Panel, which affirmed. 380 B. R. 17 (2007). The Panel noted that, although Congress redefined "disposable income" in 2005, it chose not to alter the pre-existing term "projected disposable income." Id., at 24. Thus, the Panel concluded, there was no reason to believe that Congress intended to alter the pre-BAPCPA practice under which bankruptcy courts determined projected disposable income by reference to Schedules I and J but considered other evidence when there was reason to believe that the schedules did not reflect a debtor's actual ability to pay. Id.

The Tenth Circuit affirmed. 545 F.3d 1269, 1270 (2008). According to the Tenth Circuit, a court, in calculating "projected disposable income," should begin with the "presumption" that the figure yielded by the mechanical approach is correct, but the Court concluded that this figure may be rebutted by evidence of a substantial change in the debtor's circumstances. Id., at 1278-1279.

This petition followed, and we granted certiorari . . . .

III.A

The parties differ sharply in their interpretation of § 1325's reference to "projected disposable income." Petitioner, advocating the mechanical approach, contends that "projected disposable income" means past average monthly disposable income multiplied by the number of months in a debtor's plan. Respondent, who favors the forward-looking approach, agrees that the method outlined by petitioner should be determinative in most cases, but she argues that in exceptional cases, where significant changes in a debtor's financial circumstances are known or virtually certain, a bankruptcy court has discretion to make an appropriate adjustment. Respondent has the stronger argument.

First, respondent's argument is supported by the ordinary meaning of the term "projected." "When terms used in a statute are undefined, we give them their ordinary meaning." Asgrow Seed Co. v. Winterboer, 513 U.S. 179, 187 (1995). Here, the term "projected" is not defined, and in ordinary usage future occurrences are not "projected" based on the assumption that the past will necessarily repeat itself. For example, projections concerning a company's future sales or the future cash flow from a license take into account anticipated events that may change past trends. See, e.g., Tellabs, Inc. v. Makor Issues & Rights, Ltd., 551 U.S. 308, 316 (2007) (describing adjustments to "projected sales" in light of falling demand); Innovair Aviation, Ltd. v. United States, 83 Fed. Cl. 498, 502, 504-506 (2008) (calculating projected cash flow and noting that past sales are "not necessarily the number of sales" that will be made in the future). On the night of an election, experts do not "project" the percentage of the votes that a candidate will receive by simply assuming that the candidate will get the same percentage as he or she won in the first few reporting precincts. And sports analysts do not project that a team's winning percentage at the end of a new season will be the same as the team's winning percentage last year or the team's winning percentage at the end of the first month of competition. While a projection takes past events into account, adjustments are often made based on other factors that may affect the final outcome. See In re Kibbe, 361 B. R. 302, 312, n. 9 (Bkrtcy. App. Panel CA1 2007) (contrasting "multiplied," which "requires only mathematical acumen," with "projected," which requires "mathematic acumen adjusted by deliberation and discretion").

Second, the word "projected" appears in many federal statutes, yet Congress rarely has used it to mean simple multiplication. For example, the Agricultural Adjustment Act of 1938 defined "projected national yield," "projected county yield," and "projected farm yield" as entailing historical averages "adjusted for abnormal weather conditions," "trends in yields," and "any significant changes in production practices." 7 U.S.C. § 1301(b)(8)(B), (13)(J), (K).[3]

By contrast, we need look no further than the Bankruptcy Code to see that when Congress wishes to mandate simple multiplication, it does so unambiguously--most commonly by using the term "multiplied." See, e.g., 11 U.S.C. § 1325(b)(3) ("current monthly income, when multiplied by 12"); §§ 704(b)(2), 707(b)(6), (7)(A) (same); § 707(b)(2)(A)(i), (B)(iv) ("multiplied by 60"). Accord, 2 U.S.C. § 58(b)(1)(B) ("multiplied by the number of months in such

[3] See also, e.g., 8 U.S.C. § 1364(a), (c)(2) (requiring the triennial immigration-impact report to include information "projected for the succeeding five-year period, based on reasonable estimates substantiated by the best available evidence"); 10 U.S.C.A. § 2433a(a)(2)(B) (2010 Cum. Supp.) ("projected cost of completing the [defense acquisition] program based on reasonable modification of [current] requirements"); 15 U.S.C. § 719c(c)(2) (2006 ed.) ("projected natural gas supply and demand"); 25 U.S.C. § 2009(c)(1), (2) (requiring the Director of the Office of Indian Education Programs to submit an annual report containing certain projections and "a description of the methods and formulas used to calculate the amounts projected").

year"); 5 U.S.C. § 8415(a) ("multiplied by such individual's total service"); 42 U.S.C. § 403(f)(3) ("multiplied by the number of months in such year").

Third, pre-BAPCPA case law points in favor of the "forward-looking" approach. Prior to BAPCPA, the general rule was that courts would multiply a debtor's current monthly income by the number of months in the commitment period as the first step in determining projected disposable income. See, e.g., In re Killough, 900 F.2d 61, 62-63 (CA5 1990) (per curiam); In re Anderson, 21 F.3d 355, 357 (CA9 1994); In re Solomon, 67 F.3d 1128, 1132 (CA4 1995). See 2 Lundin § 164.1, at 164-1 (2000 ed.) ("Most courts focus on the debtor's current income and extend current income (and expenditures) over the life of the plan to calculate projected disposable income"). But courts also had discretion to account for known or virtually certain changes in the debtor's income. See Heath, 182 B. R., at 559-561; Richardson, 283 B. R., at 799; In re James, 260 B. R. 498, 514-515 (Bkrtcy. Ct. Idaho 2001); In re Jobe, 197 B. R. 823, 826-827 (Bkrtcy. Ct. WD Tex. 1996); In re Crompton, 73 B. R. 800, 808 (Bkrtcy. Ct. ED Pa. 1987); see also In re Schyma, 68 B. R. 52, 63 (Bkrtcy. Ct. Minn. 1985) ("[T]he prospect of dividends . . . is not so certain as to require Debtors or the Court to consider them as regular or disposable income"); In re Krull, 54 B. R. 375, 378 (Bkrtcy. Ct. Colo. 1985) ("Since there are no changes in income which can be clearly foreseen, the Court must simply multiply the debtor's current disposable income by 36 in order to determine his 'projected' income").[4] This judicial discretion was well documented in contemporary bankruptcy treatises. See 8 Collier on Bankruptcy P 1325.08[4][a], p. 1325-50 (15th ed. rev. 2004) (hereinafter Collier) ("As a practical matter, unless there are changes which can be clearly foreseen, the court must simply multiply the debtor's known monthly income by 36 and determine whether the amount to be paid under the plan equals or exceeds that amount" (emphasis added)); 3 W. Norton, Bankruptcy Law and Practice § 75.10, p. 64 (1991) ("It has been held that the court should focus upon present monthly income and expenditures and, absent extraordinary circumstances, project these current amounts over the life of the plan to determine projected disposable income" (emphasis added)); 2 Lundin § 164.1, at 164-28 to 164-31 (2000 ed.) (describing how reported decisions treated anticipated changes in income, particularly where such changes were "too speculative to be projected"); see also In re Greer, 388 B. R. 889, 892 (Bkrtcy. Ct. CD Ill. 2008) ("'As a practical matter, unless there are changes which can be clearly foreseen, the court must simply multiply the debtor's current monthly income by thirty-six'" (quoting 5 Collier P 1325.08[4][a] (15th ed. rev. 1995))); James, supra, at 514 (same) (quoting 8

[4] When pre-BAPCPA courts declined to make adjustments based on possible changes in a debtor's future income or expenses, they did so because the changes were not sufficiently foreseeable, not because they concluded that they lacked discretion to depart from a strictly mechanical approach. In In re Solomon, 67 F.3d 1128 (1995), for example, the Fourth Circuit refused to make such an adjustment because it deemed disbursements from an individual retirement account during the plan period to be "speculative" and "hypothetical." Id., at 1132. There is no reason to assume that the result would have been the same if future disbursements had been more assured. That was certainly true of In re Killough, 900 F.2d 61 (1990), in which the Fifth Circuit declined to require inclusion of overtime pay in projected disposable income because it "was not definite enough." Id., at 65; see also id., at 66 ("[T]here may be instances where income obtained through working overtime can and should appropriately be included in a debtor's projected disposable income"). See also Education Assistance Corp. v. Zellner, 827 F.2d 1222, 1226 (CA8 1987) (affirming bankruptcy court's exclusion of future tax returns and salary increases from debtor's projected disposable income because they were "speculative").

Collier P 1325.08[4][a] (15th ed. rev. 2000)); Crompton, supra, at 808 (same) (citing 5 Collier P 1325.08[4][a], [b], at 1325-47 to 1325-48 (15th ed. 1986)). Accord, 8 Collier P 1325.08[4][b], at 1325-60 (15th ed. rev. 2007) ("As with the income side of the budget, the court must simply use the debtor's current expenses, unless a change in them is virtually certain" (emphasis added)). Indeed, petitioner concedes that courts possessed this discretion prior to BAPCPA. Tr. of Oral Arg. 7.

Pre-BAPCPA bankruptcy practice is telling because we "'will not read the Bankruptcy Code to erode past bankruptcy practice absent a clear indication that Congress intended such a departure.'" Travelers Casualty & Surety Co. of America v. Pacific Gas & Elec. Co., 549 U.S. 443, 454 (2007); Lamie v. United States Trustee, 540 U.S. 526, 539 (2004); Cohen v. de la Cruz, 523 U.S. 213, 221 (1998); see also Grogan v. Garner, 498 U.S. 279, 290 (1991); Kelly v. Robinson, 479 U.S. 36, 47 (1986). Congress did not amend the term "projected disposable income" in 2005, and pre-BAPCPA bankruptcy practice reflected a widely acknowledged and well-documented view that courts may take into account known or virtually certain changes to debtors' income or expenses when projecting disposable income. In light of this historical practice, we would expect that, had Congress intended for "projected" to carry a specialized--and indeed, unusual--meaning in Chapter 13, Congress would have said so expressly. Cf., e.g., 26 U.S.C. § 279(c)(3)(A), (B) (expressly defining "projected earnings" as reflecting a 3-year historical average).

B

The mechanical approach also clashes repeatedly with the terms of 11 U.S.C. § 1325.

First, § 1325(b)(1)(B)'s reference to projected disposable income "to be received in the applicable commitment period" strongly favors the forward-looking approach. There is no dispute that respondent would in fact receive far less than $756 per month in disposable income during the plan period, so petitioner's projection does not accurately reflect "income to be received" during that period. See In re Nowlin, 576 F.3d 258, 263 (CA5 2009). The mechanical approach effectively reads this phrase out of the statute when a debtor's current disposable income is substantially higher than the income that the debtor predictably will receive during the plan period. See Kawaauhau v. Geiger, 523 U.S. 57, 62 (1998) ("[W]e are hesitant to adopt an interpretation of a congressional enactment which renders superfluous another portion of that same law" (internal quotation marks omitted)).

Second, § 1325(b)(1) directs courts to determine projected disposable income "as of the effective date of the plan," which is the date on which the plan is confirmed and becomes binding, see § 1327(a). Had Congress intended for projected disposable income to be nothing more than a multiple of disposable income in all cases, we see no reason why Congress would not have required courts to determine that value as of the filing date of the plan. See Fed. Rule Bkrtcy. Proc. 3015(b) (requiring that a plan be filed within 14 days of the filing of a petition), online at http://www.uscourts.gov/RulesAndPolicies/FederalRulemaking/Overview/BankruptcyRules.aspx (all Internet materials as visited June 3, 2010). In the very next section of the Code, for example, Congress specified that a debtor shall commence payments "not later than 30 days after the date of the filing of the plan." § 1326(a)(1) (emphasis added). Congress' decision to require courts to measure projected disposable income "as of the effective date of the plan" is more consistent with the view that Congress expected courts to consider postfiling information about the debtor's financial circumstances. See 545 F.3d at 1279 ("determining whether or not a debtor has committed all projected disposable income to repayment of the unsecured creditors 'as of the effective date of the plan' suggests consideration of the debtor's actual financial circumstances as of the effective date of the plan").

Third, the requirement that projected disposable income "will be applied to make payments" is most naturally read to contemplate that the debtor will actually pay creditors in the calculated monthly amounts. § 1325(b)(1)(B). But when, as of the effective date of a plan, the debtor lacks the means to do so, this language is rendered a hollow command.

C

The arguments advanced in favor of the mechanical approach are unpersuasive. Noting that the Code now provides a detailed and precise definition of "disposable income," proponents of the mechanical approach maintain that any departure from this method leaves that definition "'with no apparent purpose.'" In re Kagenveama, 541 F.3d 868, 873 (CA9 2008). This argument overlooks the important role that the statutory formula for calculating "disposable income" plays under the forward-looking approach. As the Tenth Circuit recognized in this case, a court taking the forward-looking approach should begin by calculating disposable income, and in most cases, nothing more is required. It is only in unusual cases that a court may go further and take into account other known or virtually certain information about the debtor's future income or expenses.[5]

Petitioner faults the Tenth Circuit for referring to a rebuttable "presumption" that the figure produced by the mechanical approach accurately represents a debtor's "projected disposable income." See 545 F.3d at 1278-1279. Petitioner notes that the Code makes no reference to any such presumption but that related Code provisions expressly create other rebuttable presumptions. See § 707(b)(2)(A)(i) and (B)(i). He thus suggests that the Tenth Circuit improperly supplemented the text of the Code.

The Tenth Circuit's analysis, however, simply heeds the ordinary meaning of the term "projected." As noted, a person making a projection uses past occurrences as a starting point, and that is precisely what the Tenth Circuit prescribed. See, e.g., Nowlin, supra, at 260, 263.

Petitioner argues that only the mechanical approach is consistent with § 1129(a)(15)(B), which refers to "projected disposable income of the debtor (as defined in section 1325(b)(2))." This cross-reference, petitioner argues, shows that Congress intended for the term "projected disposable income" to incorporate, presumably in all contexts, the defined term "disposable income." It is evident that § 1129(a)(15)(B) refers to the defined term "disposable income," see § 1325(b)(2), but that fact offers no insight into the meaning of the word "projected" in §§ 1129(a)(15)(B) and 1325(b)(1)(B). We fail to see how that word acquires a specialized meaning as a result of this cross-reference -- particularly

[5] For the same reason, the phrase "[f]or purposes of this subsection" in § 1325(b)(2) is not rendered superfluous by the forward-looking approach.

where both §§ 1129(a)(15)(B) and 1325(b)(1)(B) refer to projected disposable income "to be received" during the relevant period. See supra, at 11.

Petitioner also notes that § 707 allows courts to take "special circumstances" into consideration, but that § 1325(b)(3) incorporates § 707 only with respect to calculating expenses. See In re Wilson, 397 B. R. 299, 314-315 (Bkrtcy. Ct. MDNC 2008). Thus, he argues, a "special circumstances" exception should not be inferred with respect to the debtor's income. We decline to infer from § 1325's incorporation of § 707 that Congress intended to eliminate, sub silentio, the discretion that courts previously exercised when projecting disposable income to account for known or virtually certain changes. Accord, In re Liverman, 383 B. R. 604, 613, and n. 15 (Bkrtcy. Ct. NJ 2008).

D

In cases in which a debtor's disposable income during the 6-month look-back period is either substantially lower or higher than the debtor's disposable income during the plan period, the mechanical approach would produce senseless results that we do not think Congress intended. In cases in which the debtor's disposable income is higher during the plan period, the mechanical approach would deny creditors payments that the debtor could easily make. And where, as in the present case, the debtor's disposable income during the plan period is substantially lower, the mechanical approach would deny the protection of Chapter 13 to debtors who meet the chapter's main eligibility requirements. Here, for example, respondent is an "individual whose income is sufficiently stable and regular" to allow her "to make payments under a plan," § 101(30), and her debts fall below the limits set out in § 109(e). But if the mechanical approach were used, she could not file a confirmable plan. Under § 1325(a)(6), a plan cannot be confirmed unless "the debtor will be able to make all payments under the plan and comply with the plan." And as petitioner concedes, respondent could not possibly make the payments that the mechanical approach prescribes.

In order to avoid or at least to mitigate the harsh results that the mechanical approach may produce for debtors, petitioner advances several possible escape strategies. He proposes no comparable strategies for creditors harmed by the mechanical approach, and in any event none of the maneuvers that he proposes for debtors is satisfactory.

1

Petitioner first suggests that a debtor may delay filing a petition so as to place any extraordinary income outside the 6-month look-back period. We see at least two problems with this proposal.

First, delay is often not a viable option for a debtor sliding into bankruptcy.

> "Potential Chapter 13 debtors typically find a lawyer's office when they are one step from financial Armageddon: There is a foreclosure sale of the debtor's home the next day; the debtor's only car was mysteriously repossessed in the dark of last night; a garnishment has reduced the debtor's take-home pay below the ordinary requirements of food and rent. Instantaneous relief is expected, if not necessary."

K. Lundin & W. Brown, Chapter 13 Bankruptcy § 3.1[2] (4th ed. rev. 2009), http://www.ch13online.com/Subscriber/Chapter_13_Bankruptcy_4th_Lundin_Brown.htm. See also id., § 38.1 ("Debtor's counsel often has little discretion when to file the Chapter 13 case").

Second, even when a debtor is able to delay filing a petition, such delay could be risky if it gives the appearance of bad faith. See 11 U.S.C. § 1325(a)(7) (requiring, as a condition of confirmation, that "the action of the debtor in filing the petition was in good faith"); see also, e.g., In re Myers, 491 F.3d 120, 125 (CA3 2007) (citing "'the timing of the petition'" as a factor to be considered in assessing a debtor's compliance with the good-faith requirement). Accord, Neufeld v. Freeman, 794 F.2d 149, 153 (CA4 1986) (a debtor's prepetition conduct may inform the court's good-faith inquiry).

2

Petitioner next argues that a debtor with unusually high income during the 6 months prior to the filing of a petition, could seek leave to delay filing a schedule of current income (Schedule I) and then ask the bankruptcy court to exercise its authority under § 101(10A)(A)(ii) to select a 6-month period that is more representative of the debtor's future disposable income. We see little merit in this convoluted strategy. If the Code required the use of the mechanical approach in all cases, this strategy would improperly undermine what the Code demands. And if, as we believe, the Code does not insist upon rigid adherence to the mechanical approach in all cases, this strategy is not needed. In any event, even if this strategy were allowed, it would not help all debtors whose disposable income during the plan period is sharply lower than their previous disposable income.[6]

Petitioner suggests that a debtor can dismiss the petition and refile at a later, more favorable date. But petitioner offers only the tepid assurance that courts "generally" do not find this practice to be abusive. Brief for Petitioner 53. This questionable stratagem plainly circumvents the statutory limits on a court's ability to shift the look-back period, see supra, at 16, and n. 6, and should give debtors pause.[7] Cf. In re Glenn, 288 B. R. 516, 520 (Bkrtcy. Ct. ED Tenn. 2002) (noting that courts should consider, among other factors, "whether this is the first or [a] subsequent filin[g]" when assessing a debtor's compliance with the good-faith requirement).

Petitioner argues that respondent might have been able to obtain relief by filing under Chapter 7 or by converting her Chapter 13 petition to one under Chapter 7. The availability of Chapter 7 to debtors like respondent who have above-median incomes is limited. In respondent's case, a presumption of abuse would attach under § 707(b)(2)(A)(i) because her disposable income, "multiplied by 60," exceeds the amounts specified in subclauses (I) and (II). See also § 707(b)(1) (allowing a court to dismiss a petition filed by a debtor "whose debts are

[6] Under 11 U.S.C. § 521(i)(3), a debtor seeking additional time to file a schedule of income must submit the request within 45 days after filing the petition, and the court may not grant an extension of more than 45 days.

[7] For example, a debtor otherwise eligible for Chapter 13 protection may become ineligible if "at any time in the preceding 180 days" "the case was dismissed by the court for willful failure of the debtor to abide by orders of the court, or to appear before the court in proper prosecution of the case," or "the debtor requested and obtained the voluntary dismissal of the case following the filing of a request for relief from the automatic stay provided by section 362 of this title." § 109(g).

primarily consumer debts . . . if it finds that the granting of relief would be an abuse of the provisions of this chapter"); App. 86-88 ("Notice to Individual Consumer Debtor under § 342(b) of the Bankruptcy Code") ("If your income is greater than the median income for your state of residence and family size, in some cases, creditors have the right to file a motion requesting that the court dismiss your case under § 707(b) of the Code"). Nevertheless, petitioner argues, respondent might have been able to overcome this presumption by claiming that her case involves "special circumstances" within the meaning of § 707(b)(2)(B)(i). Section 707 identifies as examples of "special circumstances" a "serious medical condition or a call or order to active duty in the Armed Forces," id., and petitioner directs us to no authority for the proposition that a prepetition decline in income would qualify as a "special circumstance." In any event, the "special circumstances" exception is available only to the extent that "there is no reasonable alternative," id., a proposition we reject with our interpretation of § 1325(b)(1) today.[8]

In sum, each of the strategies that petitioner identifies for mitigating the anomalous effects of the mechanical approach is flawed. There is no reason to think that Congress meant for any of these strategies to operate as a safety valve for the mechanical approach.

IV

We find petitioner's remaining arguments unpersuasive. Consistent with the text of § 1325 and pre-BAPCPA practice, we hold that when a bankruptcy court calculates a debtor's projected disposable income, the court may account for changes in the debtor's income or expenses that are known or virtually certain at the time of confirmation. We therefore affirm the decision of the Court of Appeals.

SCALIA, DISSENTING. [Deleted].

Notes and Questions

1. In his lengthy dissent, Justice Scalia accuses the majority of rendering superfluous the long definition of "disposable income" in § 1325(b)(2). "It would be pointless to define disposable income in such detail based on data during a specific 6-month period, if a court were free to set the resulting figure aside whenever it appears to be a poor predictor." Justice Scalia disagrees that the word "projected" in § 1325(b)(1) authorizes ignoring the definition because historically based information. Such information can serve as the basis of projecting the future--i.e., what's past is prologue. True, prognostications of this sort are poor practice. But Congress might have had good reason to impose such restrictions on projections. "Perhaps Congress concluded that other information a b court might consider is too uncertain or too easily manipulated. Or perhaps it thought the cost of considering such information outweighed the benefits."

Justice Scalia announces that the majority's other arguments are "easily dispatched." As to the point that debtors like. Lanning (who received a large one-time lump severance settlement) could not obtain confirmation of a plan. But Justice Scalia responds, so what? The statutory definition of disposable income "makes no sense only if one assumes that the debtor is entitled to confirmation in the first place; and that assumption is wrong." "Bankruptcy protection is not a birthright, and Congress could reasonably conclude that those who have just hit the skids do not

[8] Petitioner also suggests that some Chapter 13 debtors may be able to plead "special circumstances" on the expense side of the calculation by virtue of BAPCPA's incorporation of the Chapter 7 means test into Chapter 13. See § 707(b)(2)(B)(i), (ii). This is no help to debtors like respondent, whose income has changed but whose expenses are constant.

yet need a reprieve from repaying their debts, perhaps they will recover."

As to the point that a debtor with high income on Schedule I could escape paying thanks to the mechanical test, Justice Scalia points out that unsecured creditors can move to modify the plan under §1329(a) to recapture this income. "The Court offers no explanation of why modification would not be available in such instances, and sufficient to resolve the concern."

If the editor may interrupt this paraphrase, Justice Scalia assumes that the definition of disposable income which he wishes to govern in confirmation hearings somehow does not govern in motions to modify the plan. Is this a good assumption? See Section F of this chapter, where we will find this issue most cloudy indeed.

Justice Scalia also thinks the majority dismissed various strategies by which a debtor disadvantaged by the mechanical test might game the system. Debtors (such as Lanning) who have had bonuses can delay filing until the bonus no longer appears in the six-month lookback period. The majority proclaimed such gamesmanship as giving the appearance of bad faith, but Justice Scalia disagrees. Justice Scalia also thinks a bankruptcy court might excuse a debtor from filing Schedule B22C. Bankruptcy Code § 101(10A)(A)(ii) authorizes the court to recalculate income based on different dates. Justice Scalia views this possibility as proving that the bad effects of the mechanical test can be avoided. Justice Scalia further thinks a debtor might in good faith obtain dismissal of the chapter 13 case in order to permit refiling at a time when the mechanical test is more favorable to the debtor.

Finally, Justice Scalia accuses the majority of substituting its own subjective opinion for that of Congress:

> Underlying the Court's interpretation is an understandable urge: Sometimes the best reading of a text yields results that one thinks must be a mistake, and bending that reading just a little bit will allow all the pieces to fit together. But taking liberties with text in light of outcome makes sense only if we assume that we know better than Congress which outcomes are mistaken.

Again, if the editor may intrude, why may not the majority take the position that it is finding the true intent of Congress and is not claiming to know better than Congress what should be done? Justice Scalia concludes by stating, "we should faithfully apply our settled interpretive principles and trust that Congress will correct the law if what it previously prescribed is wrong." But this can be turned around against the learned Justice: the majority was trying to find the law, and, if the Court, in its interpretive effort, is incorrect, Congress can always change the law (as it often does) to inform the Supreme Court of its error.

2. Suppose D has no disposable income projected. D nevertheless proposes to pay in just enough to pay her lawyer and back taxes. The plan ends as soon as those payments are accomplished, even though the "applicable commitment period" for D is five years. Can this plan be confirmed? Danielson v. Flores (In re Flores), 2013 U.S. App. LEXIS 18413 (August 29, 2013) (no).

3. Section 1325(b) requires D to pay all disposable income into the plan for the applicable commitment period, but § 1325(b) applies only if a creditor or the trustee objects to confirmation. Where there is no objection, the court is obligated to confirm a plan that does not comply with § 1325(b). In re Jackson, 353 B.R. 849, 352 (Bankr. E.D.N.C. 2006).

4. D in chapter 13 filed a schedule I that listed his average monthly income at $7,492. This included $3,319 in Social Security benefits. D's plan provided that he would pay $525 a month for five years, enough to pay the mortgage arrears and the joint credit card debt with his wife. His own credit card debt would be paid at half a cent on the dollar. The trustee opposed confirmation because the expenses from Schedule J were inflated. The D conceded this but then said he was entitled to omit Social Security from projected disposable income, more than compensating for the inflated expenses. The trustee responded that, if Social Security benefits were omitted from income, then the plan was not feasible because disposable income (net of Social Security) was less than $525. May D omit Social Security from projected disposable income? May D add it back in to show that the plan is feasible? Ranta v. Gorman, 721 F.3d 214 (4th Cir. 2013).

5. As we shall see, chapter 13 plans can be modified. A majority of courts believes that modification must comply with § 1325(a), but not with § 1325(b). Sunahara v. Burchard (In re Sunahara), 326 B.R. 768, 781 (Bankr. 9th Cir. 2005); In re McCully, 398 B.R. 590 (Bankr. N.D. Ohio 2008) (describing this view as the "emerging majority opinion"). Yet § 1325(a)(3) requires that the plan be in good faith. Is a modification shortening the plan below the applicable commitment period a bad faith proposal?

IN RE RUSH

387 B.R. 26 (Bankr. W.D. Mo. 2008)

DENNIS R. DOW, J.

These matters are before the Court on the motion of the Chapter 13 Trustee to deny confirmation of the Debtors' Chapter 13 plans. The trustee has objected to each plan on the grounds that it fails to comply with certain provisions of § 1325(b). The Court has combined the discussion and determination of the trustee's objections in the two cases because they raise identical issues . . . For the reasons set forth below, the Court overrules the trustee's objections to confirmation. Specifically, the Court holds that below-median debtors who have, according to the applicable formula, no disposable income have no projected disposable income and no applicable commitment period and therefore no requirement to commit any particular sum of money to the payment of their unsecured creditors pursuant to the plan. The Court also holds that the appropriate method for determining projected disposable income for below-median debtors is to deduct from their current monthly income, the reasonable and necessary expenses as reflected on Schedule J, with certain adjustments described below.

I. FACTUAL AND PROCEDURAL BACKGROUND

Eunice Jean Rush

Debtor Eunice Jean Rush filed a petition for relief from under Chapter 13 of the Bankruptcy Code on November 6, 2007. Debtor filed a Schedule I, Current Income of Individual Debtor, showing net average monthly income of $2,992.00, $686.00 of which according to the detail explaining the entry on line 11, is Social Security. Her Schedule J, Current Expenditures of Individual Debtor, shows average monthly expenses of $2,727.00, leaving monthly net income of $265.00. Debtor also filed a Form 22C, Chapter 13 Statement of Current Monthly Income and Calculation of Commitment Period and Disposable Income, indicating current monthly income of $1,576.00, consisting exclusively of two retirement pensions. The Debtor's annualized current monthly income is $18, 912.00. According to Line 16 on Debtor's Form 22C, the applicable median family income in the state of Missouri for a household of the same size as the Debtor's is $36,702.00. Because the Debtor is below the applicable median, she checked the boxes indicating the applicable commitment period is three years and the disposable income is not determined under § 1325(b)(3) and did not complete the remaining portions of the form relating to calculation of expense deductions pursuant to the standards set forth in § 707(b)(2).

Debtor filed a Chapter 13 plan proposing to pay $150.00 per month to the Chapter 13 trustee. The plan provides a 0% recovery to non-priority unsecured creditors. The Chapter 13 trustee filed a motion to deny confirmation of the plan alleging that the plan violates § 1325(b) in that it runs for only 18 months rather than the 36-month applicable commitment period for a below-median debtor and because the Debtor has excess income in the budget not committed to payment to the trustee under the plan. Specifically, on the latter point, the trustee observes that the income on Schedule I exceeds the expenses on Schedule J by the sum of $265, but the Debtor proposes to pay the Chapter 13 trustee only $150.00 per month. The Debtor's response is that she has no disposable income if calculated according to the applicable statutory formula. In addition, Debtor argues that even if her projected disposable income were determined by deducting her Schedule J expenses from her Schedule I income, the amount received by her from Social Security should not be included as it is specifically excluded from the definition of current monthly income and that excluding that amount would make her disposable income negative. Finally, Debtor argues that with no disposable income, the concept of an applicable commitment period is simply not applicable to her and that she has no requirement to commit any particular sum of money to her unsecured creditors under the plan.

John Wilbur Glover

Debtor John Wilbur Glover filed a petition for relief under Chapter 13 of the Bankruptcy Code on December 6, 2007. Debtor's Schedule I shows average monthly net income of $1,268.00, $695.00 of which is Social Security income. Schedule J reflects average monthly expenses of $1,137.00 leaving monthly net income of $131.00. Debtor was apparently unemployed and had no other source of eligible income during the six-month period prior to the filing of the petition as his Form 22C shows no current monthly income. With zero annualized current monthly income, Debtor is quite obviously below the applicable median income for the Debtor's household size in Missouri which is $47,589.00. As with Ms. Rush, because the annualized current monthly income was below the applicable state median, Mr. Glover checked those boxes on Form 22C indicating that the applicable commitment period is three years and the disposable income is not determined under § 1325(b)(3) and did not complete the remaining portions of the form calculating applicable deductions. The Debtor's Chapter 13 plan proposes to pay the sum of $100.00 per month to the Chapter 13 trustee and specifies a dividend of 0% for non-priority unsecured creditors.

As with the prior case, the Chapter 13 trustee filed a motion to deny confirmation contending that the plan fails to comply with § 1325(b) in that payments would be completed in a period of approximately 12 months, less than a 36-month applicable commitment period for a below-median debtor. The Debtor responds by arguing that the appropriate method for determining projected disposable income for a below-median debtor is to subtract from his current monthly income the expenses shown on Schedule J and that completing that calculation in his case shows that his disposable income is a negative number. He argues that with no disposable income, the applicable commitment period is irrelevant and he has no requirement to commit any particular sum to the payment of his unsecured creditors under the plan.

Two issues are raised by these facts and the arguments raised by the parties: (1) How should the Court determine projected disposable income for debtors below the applicable state median? (2) If under the applicable formula, the debtor's disposable income is negative, is the concept of an applicable commitment period relevant to that debtor?

II. DISCUSSION AND ANALYSIS

A. Projected Disposable Income

Perhaps the most significant and difficult changes made to the Bankruptcy Code by the Bankruptcy Abuse Prevention and Consumer Protection Act of 2005 ("BAPCPA") are those relating to the determination of disposable income for Chapter 13 debtors. Prior to the enactment of BAPCPA, the Court determined the debtor's projected disposable income by deducting from the income shown on Schedule I, the expenses shown on Schedule J, subject to the Court's review for the necessity and reasonableness of those expenses. The resulting number constituted the amount to be paid to the Chapter 13 trustee pursuant to the plan. Upon objection by the holder of an unsecured claim or the Chapter 13 trustee, the debtor could obtain confirmation of a Chapter 13 plan only by demonstrating either that the unsecured claims were being paid in full or the debtor was committing all disposable income to make payments into the plan for a period of no less than 36 months. Plan payments could not extend beyond five years. BAPCPA made changes to many of these provisions and has ushered in an entirely different world.

Under BAPCPA, upon objection, if the debtor is not paying all unsecured creditors in full, the plan must provide that all projected disposable income received in the applicable commitment period be applied to make payments to unsecured creditors under the plan. § 1325(b)(1)(B). The applicable commitment period for debtors with incomes below the applicable median for similar household sizes is three years. § 1325(b)(4)(A)(i). Projected disposable income is not defined but BAPCPA contains a new definition of the phrase "disposable income." In § 1325(b)(2) the phrase is defined as current monthly income received by the debtor (minus certain designated payments) less amounts reasonably necessary to be expended for the maintenance or support of the debtor or dependent of the debtor. § 1325(b)(2)(A). The concept of "current monthly income" is itself a defined phrase meaning essentially, the average monthly income the debtor received from all sources during the six-month period prior to the date of the filing of the petition with certain exclusions, one of which is Social Security payments. § 101(10A). In addition, the Code now specifies that the reasonable and necessary expenses to be deducted from current monthly income to determine disposable income are, for debtors above the applicable median to be determined in accordance with § 707(b)(2). § 1325(b)(3). The statute does not specify how expenses are to be determined for below-median debtors. Presumably those expenses are to be taken, as they were prior to the amendments, from the debtor's Schedule J. See, e.g., In re Fuller, 346 B.R. 472, 483 (Bankr. S.D. Ill. 2006) ("under BAPCPA, below-median income debtors calculate their expenses the same way they did before BAPCPA -- by recording the actual expenses they incur each month on their Schedule J (and now, on their Form B22C)"); In re Schanuth, 342 B.R. 601 (Bankr. W.D. Mo. 2006).

These changes have spawned an avalanche of cases in which the courts have attempted to interpret these provisions. At least three schools of thought have developed with regard to the meaning of projected disposable income for above-median debtors. Some courts hold that the calculations resulting from the B22C form establish a presumptive figure for projected disposable income subject to being rebutted based either on the fact that it fails to reflect the debtor's actual income available to make plan payments or based on a change of circumstances occurring between the filing and consideration of plan confirmation.[1] Others

[1] See, e.g., In re Jass, 340 B.R. 411 (Bankr. D. Utah 2006) (looks forward to time of confirmation and thereafter); In re Grady, 343 B.R. 747 (Bankr. N.D. Ga. 2006)(same); In re Gress, 344 B.R. 919 (Bankr. W.D. Mo. 2006)(same); In re Fuller, 346 B.R. 472 (Bankr. S.D. Ill. 2006)(same); In re Risher, 344 B.R. 833 (Bankr. W.D. Ky. 2006)(same); In re Slusher, 359 B.R. 290 (Bankr. D. Nev. 2007); In re Devilliers, 358 B.R. 849 (Bankr. E.D. La. 2007); In re Teixeira, 358 B.R. 484 (Bankr. D.N.H. 2006) (reaffirms view of rebuttable presumption and that "disposable income" and

have opted for the traditional approach under which projected disposable income is determined by subtracting the expenses on Schedule J from the income shown on Schedule I.[2] Still others have held that the calculation resulting from the completion of the B22C form is dispositive.[3] The Eighth Circuit Bankruptcy

"projected disposable income" are identical; ordinarily below-median debtors derive disposable income by subtracting Schedule J expenses from current monthly income; above-median debtors subtract § 707(b) expenses from current monthly income; if presumption rebutted below-median debtors use Schedule I to determine income and Schedule J to determine expenses and above-median debtors use Schedule I to determine income and § 707(b) expenses); In re Gordon, 360 B.R. 679 (Bankr. S.D. Cal. 2007) (B22C not controlling; court may consider intervening changes in employment or other circumstances); In re Grant, 364 B.R. 656 (Bankr. E.D. Tenn. 2007) ("projected disposable income" and "disposable income" not synonymous; B22C calculation is starting point which court will presume is disposable income unless rebutted by change of circumstances); In re Watson, 366 B.R. 523 (Bankr. D. Md. 2007) (disposable income on B22C is presumptive projected disposable income; presumption may be rebutted by showing change of circumstances); In re Beckerle, 367 B.R. 718 (Bankr. D. Kan. 2007); In re Mullen, 369 B.R. 25 (Bankr. D. Or. 2007) (disposable income from Form B22C generally presumptive of projected disposable income; presumption rebutted by existence of excess income as reflected by proposed plan payments); In re Meek, 370 B.R. 294 (Bankr. D. Idaho 2007); In re Plumb, 373 B.R. 429 (Bankr. W.D.N.C. 2007) (Form B22C is starting point for determining projected disposable income; since income and expense components are forward looking concepts, must take Schedules I and J into consideration); In re Purdy, 373 B.R. 142 (Bankr. N.D. Fla. 2007) (projected disposable income is forward-looking concept; B22C controls unless debtor or trustee can show numbers do not reflect fair projection of debtor's budget into future based on substantial change in circumstances); In re Briscoe, 374 B.R. 1 (Bankr. D.D.C. 2007) (disposable income figure listed on Form B22C is presumptive, absent evidence of change of circumstances); In re Warren, 2007 Bankr. LEXIS 3106, 2007 WL 2683837 (Bankr. M.D. Ala.) (Form 22C calculation creates presumptive starting point for determining projected disposable income; may be rebutted by evidence of debtor's loss of a source of income); In re Chriss-Price, 376 B.R. 648 (Bankr. M.D. Tenn. 2006) (determining "projected disposable income" requires consideration of both the future and historical finances of debtor; debtor must propose to pay unsecured creditors number resulting from B22C unless evidence shows this number does not adequately represent debtor's budget projected into future); In re Pak, 378 B.R. 257 (9th Cir. B.A.P. 2007) ("disposable income" is merely starting point in determining "projected disposable income"); In re Lanning, 380 B.R. 17 (10th Cir. B.A.P. 2007) (disposable income as calculated from B22C form is only starting point in determining projected disposable income; may be modified if facts show that calculation fails accurately to predict debtor's actual ability to fund the plan); In re May, 381 B.R. 498 (Bankr. W.D. Pa. 2008) (disposable income derived from Form 22C is the starting point establishing a rebuttable presumption); In re Liverman, 383 B.R. 604, 2008 WL 768727 (Bankr. D.N.J.) (debtor's ability to pay creditors as of effective date of plan is most accurately depicted in debtor's Schedules I and J); In re French, 383 B.R. 402, 2008 WL 681684 (Bankr. W.D. Ky.) (projected disposable income is forward-looking concept; result reflected on Form B22C is starting point of analysis, a presumption subject to rebuttal).

[2] See, e.g., In re Kibbe, 342 B.R. 411 (Bankr. D.N.H. 2006), aff'd, 361 B.R. 302 (1st Cir. B.A.P. 2007) (looks forward to time of confirmation and thereafter); In re Riggs, 359 B.R. 649 (Bankr. E.D. Ky.2007) (projected disposable income must be determined by reference to Schedules I and J); In re Demonica, 345 B.R. 895 (Bankr. N.D. Ill.2006) (same as Kibbe); In re Edmunds, 350 B.R. 636 (Bankr. D. S.C. 2006); In re Hardacre, 338 B.R. 718 (Bankr. N.D. Tex.2006) (same).

[3] See, e.g., In re Alexander, 344 B.R. 742 (Bankr. E.D.N.C. 2006) (determination made on basis of B22, not Schedules I and J); In re Guzman, 345 B.R. 640 (Bankr. E.D. Wis. 2006) (same); In re Farrar-Johnson, 353 B.R. 224 (Bankr. N.D. Ill. 2006) (same); In re Girodes, 350 B.R. 31 (Bankr. M.D.N.C. 2006) ("disposable income" and "projected disposable income" are the same); In re Hanks, 362 B.R. 494 (Bankr. D. Utah 2007)(same); In re Miller, 361 B.R. 224 (Bankr. N.D. Ala. 2007) (Form B22C dispositive with respect to above-median income debtors' projected disposable income); In re Kolb, 366 B.R. 802 (Bankr. S.D. Ohio 2007); Coop v. Frederickson (In re Frederickson), 375 B.R. 829 (8th Cir. B.A.P. 2007) (projected disposable income is disposable income calculated on Form B22C extrapolated over applicable commitment period); In re Musselman, 379 B.R. 583 (Bankr. E.D.N.C. 2007) (projected disposable income required to be paid

Appellate Panel in its recent decision in Coop v. Frederickson, 375 B.R. 829 (8th Cir. B.A.P. 2007) adopted this last approach. In Frederickson, the Bankruptcy Appellate Panel adopted what it called the "plain meaning" approach holding that the Form 22C controls the determination of projected disposable income. In so doing, it rejected the notion that the court should look at the actual or anticipated (rather than historical) income or the actual (rather than objective) expenses of the debtor. Although decisions of the Bankruptcy Appellate Panel are not binding, they are considered persuasive, see In re Gakinya, 364 B.R. 366 (Bankr. W.D. Mo. 2007), and this Court has determined to follow the holding in Frederickson until such time as it receives different guidance from the Eighth Circuit.

That holding is, however, not specifically applicable to below-median debtors. According to one court, the majority of courts that have considered the question have held that projected disposable income for below-median debtors is determined by utilizing Schedules I and J. In re Cleary, 357 B.R. 369, 372 (Bankr. D.S.C. 2006). The statute, however, specifies that disposable income is to be determined by subtracting the amounts reasonably necessary to be expended for the support of the debtor and the debtor's dependents from the debtor's current monthly income. § 1325(b)(2). A number of other courts have so held. See In re Girodes, 350 B.R. 31 (Bankr. M.D.N.C. 2006); In re Linn, 2008 Bankr. LEXIS 792, 2008 WL 687448 (Bankr. N.D. W.Va.). The holdings of those courts opting for use of Schedules I and J to determine projected disposable income are predicated primarily upon the philosophy rejected by the court in Frederickson, that projected disposable income is a forward-looking concept and inconsistent with the historical and objective numbers reflected in the definition of disposable income. While the holding in Frederickson relates directly only to above-median debtors, this Court believes that the approach to the concept and to statutory construction reflected in Frederickson suggests that the Bankruptcy Appellate Panel would adhere to the straight-forward statutory language in determining disposable income for below-median debtors. The Court clearly opts for a formulaic approach to determining the concept in the context of above-median debtors. For below-median debtors, a formula also exists, it is simply different. For below-median debtors, the statute specifies that disposable income is determined based on current monthly income less amounts reasonably necessary to be expended for the support of the debtor or a dependent of the debtor. Based on the Frederickson court's rejection of the concept of departing from that definition to arrive at projected disposable income, this Court believes it would similarly reject any interpretation which departs from the definition in the context of below-median debtors. Accordingly, the Court holds that the appropriate method for determining projected disposable income for below-median debtors is to begin with their current monthly income as reflected on Form 22C and deduct the recurring living expenses on Schedule J.[4]

---

to unsecured creditors was simply disposable income as defined by Congress based on historical average projected over applicable commitment period); In re Mancl, 381 B.R. 537 (W.D. Wis. 2008) (projected disposable income is simply disposable income projected forward over term of plan).

[4] The Court's holding is based upon its extension to below-median debtors of the holding in Frederickson. The Frederickson case is currently on appeal to the Eighth Circuit Court of Appeals. Should the Eighth Circuit offer different guidance with respect to the use of a formulaic approach to the determination of projected disposable income, the Court reserves the right to rule

Applying that definition to the Debtors in these cases indicate that they have no disposable income and therefore no projected disposable income. As noted above, Glover's current monthly income as calculated on Form 22C is $0. His disposable income is, therefore, necessarily less than $0. In the Rush case, Form 22C shows that the current monthly income is $1,576.00. Expenses shown on the Schedule J which, as discussed below, would not be the only expenses which would need to be deducted to arrive at disposable income for the below-median debtor, are $2,727.00 resulting in a negative disposable income of $1,151.00.

As noted above, the exercise in which the court is engaged after the amendments effected by BAPCPA is no longer to determine what amount must be paid to the trustee pursuant to the plan, but rather what must be paid to unsecured creditors under the plan. In order to arrive at that figure, it is necessary to make certain additional adjustments, as other courts have noted. First, Schedule J makes no provision for taxes. The reason for this is that taxes are assumed to have been deducted from gross income to arrive at net income on Schedule I. Linn, 2008 Bankr. LEXIS 792, 2008 WL 687448 (must include payroll deductions shown on Schedule I). Second, Chapter 13 debtors are directed not to reflect on Schedule J payments on secured debts which they intend to satisfy pursuant to the plan. Accordingly, it is also necessary then to subtract amounts to be paid to secured creditors. In re Quarterman, 342 B.R. 647, 652 (Bankr. M.D. Fla. 2006) (must deduct payments debtor is proposing to make in plan on secured claims); In re Nevitt, 2006 Bankr. LEXIS 1763, 2006 WL 2433491 (Bankr. N.D. Ill.) ("Payment on account of secured debts must be taken into account to calculate projected disposable income. Schedule J does not list payments for secured debts, such as vehicle loans."). The resulting sum, after these adjustments, should be the amount payable to unsecured creditors under the plan.[5]

Even were this Court, however, to adopt the approach that projected disposable income for below-median debtors is determined by reference to Schedules I and J, it would still conclude that in these cases the Debtors have no disposable income and, therefore, no projected disposable income. The reason is

---

differently in another matter.

[5] The question of which creditors should share in the payment to unsecured creditors made by above-median debtors has been considered by a number of courts. The statutory language fails to distinguish between priority and nonpriority creditors. Because amounts payable to the priority creditors have already been taken into consideration in the calculation embedded in the B22C form, most courts have held that those creditors may not share in the required payment but that it must be committed solely to the payment of nonpriority unsecured creditors under the plan. See, e.g., In re Wilbur, 344 B.R. 650 (Bankr. D. Utah 2006) (above-median debtors must pay disposable income exclusively to non-priority unsecured creditors); In re McDonald, 361 B.R. 527 (Bankr. D. Mont. 2007) (in determining amount payable to unsecured creditors, debtor must add back deduction for trustee's fees on line 50 in Form B22C); In re Amato, 366 B.R. 348 (Bankr. D.N.J. 2007) (same; also, debtor's attorney's fees may not be deducted); In re Puetz, 370 B.R. 386 (Bankr. D. Kan. 2007) (agreeing with Wilbur and McDonald and rejecting Amato, court holds creditor specifically provided for under § 707(b)(2)(A) need not share in the unsecured creditors' pool under § 1325(b)(1)(B); other unsecured creditors, not so provided for, including debtor's attorney's fees, may share in this payment); In re Echeman, 378 B.R. 177 (Bankr. S.D. Ohio 2007) (debtor is not entitled to pay priority unsecured claims from projected disposable income if such claims have already been deducted on Form B22C). Because the priority creditors are not otherwise accounted for in the forms filed by a below-median debtor, such creditors may share in the payment amount determined by subtracting the identified expenses from current monthly income.

that in each case a substantial portion of the income shown on Schedule I is derived from Social Security. As noted above, the definition of current monthly income specifically excludes amounts attributable to Social Security. § 101(10A). Congress has therefore determined that debtors need not commit such income to the payment of unsecured creditors under the plan. Even those courts that have determined that reference to Schedules I and J is appropriate for determining projected disposable income have concluded that they should nonetheless exclude Social Security income. See, e.g., Schanuth, 342 B.R. at 606, n. 12; In re Ward, 359 B.R. 741 (Bankr. W.D. Mo. 2007); In re Devilliers, 358 B.R. 849 (Bankr. E.D. La. 2007); In re Upton, 363 B.R. 528 (Bankr. S.D. Ohio 2007); In re Barfknecht, 378 B.R. 154 (Bankr. W.D. Tex 2007). Performing that calculation in these cases yields negative disposable income. In the Rush case, Schedule I net income is $2,992.00. Subtracting the $686.00 of that amount that derives from Social Security and then the $2,727.00 in average monthly expenses yields a net monthly income of a negative $421.00. The result is similar in the Glover matter. Net income shown on Schedule I is $1,268.00. Subtracting the $695.00 portion attributable to Social Security and the $1,137.00 in average monthly expenses shown on Schedule J yields a net monthly disposable income of a negative $564.00. It is clear that neither of these Debtors has disposable income.

B. Applicable Commitment Period

[The court concludes that the "applicable commitment period" does not apply if a debtor has negative disposable income.] For all the reasons stated above, the trustee's motions to deny confirmation in both cases are denied.

3. Cram Down

DRIVE FINANCIAL SERVICES, LP v JORDAN
21 F.3d 343 (5th Cir. 2008)

GARWOOD, J.

Appellant Drive Financial Services, L.P. ("Drive Financial") directly appeals the bankruptcy court's October 18 and October 23, 2006 orders amending and confirming the Chapter 13 bankruptcy plan submitted by debtors-appellees Bobby and Freda Jordan (the "Jordans"), which provided for interest on Drive Financial's secured claim on the Jordans' pickup truck at a "prime-plus" interest rate. For the following reasons, we affirm.

FACTS AND PROCEEDINGS BELOW

The facts of this case are not in dispute. On July 20, 2003, the Jordans purchased a 2003 Chevrolet Silverado pickup truck (the "Truck"). In order to finance the Truck, the Jordans entered into a Texas Vehicle Retail Installment Contract with Drive Financial. The contract provided Drive Financial with a properly perfected, first-priority, purchase-money security interest in the Truck. The contract provided for an interest rate of 17.95%.

On or about December 22, 2005, the Jordans filed for protection under Chapter 13 of the Bankruptcy Code in the United States Bankruptcy Court, Eastern District of Texas. When the Jordans drafted their Chapter 13 plan, they elected to retain possession of the Truck and to pay Drive Financial's secured claim in installments with an interest rate of six percent. On January 10, 2006, Drive Financial filed an objection to the Jordans' Chapter 13 plan on the grounds that the proper interest rate to apply to its secured claim was the contract rate of 17.95%. The bankruptcy court held a hearing on Drive Financial's objection on March 8, 2006. At this hearing the bankruptcy court ordered additional briefing on the applicability of the decision in Till v. SCS Credit Corp., 541 U.S. 465 (2004), to the determination of the interest rate the Jordans were to pay on Drive Financial's secured claim.

In its October 18, 2006 "Order Regarding Confirmation of Debtor's Chapter 13 Plan," the bankruptcy court held that the Supreme Court decision in Till was binding precedent, so it calculated the Jordans' interest rate using the "prime-plus" approach adopted by the plurality of the Court in Till.[1] According to the parties' stipulation,[2] the bankruptcy court modified the interest rate payable on Drive Financial's claim in the Jordans' Chapter 13 plan to 7.5%. On October 23, 2006, the bankruptcy court confirmed the Jordans' Chapter 13 plan as modified by its October 18 order.

On December 15, 2006, Drive Financial timely filed a "Petition for Certification of Circumstances for Direct Appeal to the Court of Appeals" with respect to each bankruptcy court order in the United States District Court for the Eastern District of Texas. The district court entered orders granting the petitions on January 18, 2007. Drive Financial then petitioned this court to hear this direct appeal under 28 U.S.C. 158(d)(2). Those petitions were granted by this court on March 20, 2007.

JURISDICTION

Appellants have directly appealed to this court the October 18 and October 23 orders of the bankruptcy court pursuant to 28 U.S.C. § 158(d)(2). This statute was enacted as part of BAPCPA in order to provide for direct review of bankruptcy court judgments, orders, or decrees by the applicable court of appeals in cases where the bankruptcy court or the district court certify that there is no controlling Supreme Court or circuit court decision, the case involves a matter of public importance, there are conflicting precedents, or an immediate appeal may materially advance the progress of the bankruptcy proceeding. 28 U.S.C. § 158(d)(2). If this certification is made, the applicable court of appeals has jurisdiction if it authorizes the direct appeal of the bankruptcy court's judgment, order, or decree. Id.

In this case, Judge Schneider of the United States District Court for the Eastern District of Texas certified that this case met the criteria for direct appeal set forth in section 158(d)(2) on January 18, 2007. A motions panel of this court granted Drive Financial's petitions for direct appeal on March 20, 2007. Since all of the requirements of section 158(d)(2) are met in this case, this court has jurisdiction over this direct appeal from the bankruptcy court.

[1] The prime-plus rate is arrived at by taking the national prime lending rate, a readily reported rate at which a bank would make a loan to a very low-risk borrower, and augmenting it to account for a particular borrower's risk of default.

[2] Prior to the bankruptcy court's order, the parties stipulated that if Till were applicable, the appropriate prime-plus rate would be 7.5%, but if Till were not applicable, the proper rate under Fifth Circuit precedent would be the contract rate of 17.95%.

DISCUSSION

The central question in this case is what is the proper rate of interest to be paid on a secured claim that is paid in installments pursuant to a Chapter 13 plan. The Bankruptcy Code states that a Chapter 13 plan should only be confirmed if, for each allowed secured claim: 1) the holder of that claim accepts the plan; 2) the holder of the claim retains the lien securing the claim and the Chapter 13 plan provides that the value, as of the date of the plan, of property (generally cash) to be distributed under the plan to the holder of the claim is not less than the allowed amount of such claim;[3] or 3) the debtor surrenders the property securing the claim. See 11 U.S.C. 1325(a)(5). In this case, Drive Financial did not accept the plan and the Jordans are not surrendering the Truck, so in order for the plan to be confirmed, the Jordans' plan must provide for distribution to Drive Financial of property that has no less value than the amount of Drive Financial's secured claim.[4] The Bankruptcy Code's reference to paying value is generally understood to incorporate the principle of the time value of money, so payments made pursuant to a Chapter 13 plan must incorporate an interest rate to account for the fact that a dollar paid today is worth more than a dollar paid tomorrow. Till, 124 S. Ct. at 1966 (Thomas, J., concurring in judgment). The Bankruptcy Code, however, provides little guidance as to how the interest rate should be set, so we look to past precedent to determine whether the bankruptcy court applied the correct interest rate to Drive Financial's secured claim. . . .

II. Does BAPCPA's Hanging Paragraph Supercede Till?

The Supreme Court recently addressed what rate of interest needed to be paid to an objecting secured creditor whose claim was paid in installments under a Chapter 13 plan. See Till, 124 S. Ct. at 1962 (Stevens, J., plurality) (holding that the prime-plus approach should be used to determine the proper interest rate). After Till, Congress enacted BAPCPA, which made significant changes to the Bankruptcy Code. So before examining Till, we must determine whether it has been superceded by any provisions of BAPCPA.

BAPCPA added an unnumbered paragraph following section 1325(a)(9). This paragraph is commonly referred to as the "hanging paragraph." The hanging paragraph provides that section 506 of the Bankruptcy Code, 11 U.S.C. § 506, shall not apply if:

> "the creditor has a purchase money security interest securing the debt that is the subject of the claim, the debt was incurred within the 910-day [sic] preceding the date of the filing of the petition, and the collateral for that debt consists of

---

[3] This second option also requires that if the property distributed is in the form of periodic payments, the payments must be made in equal monthly amounts and that if the secured claim is for personal property, the amount of such payments shall not be less than an amount sufficient to provide the claim-holder with adequate protection. 11 U.S.C. 1325(a)(5)(B)(iii). There is no allegation that the Jordans' Chapter 13 plan did not provide for equal periodic payments, and Drive Financial does not assert that it should receive adequate protection on its secured claim.

[4] This option is referred to as the "cram down option" because it allows the debtor to confirm a Chapter 13 plan that modifies the terms of a creditor's claim over that creditor's objection as long as the debtor pays value on the claim. 11 U.S.C. 1325(a)(5)(B); Associates Commer. Corp. v. Rash, 520 U.S. 953 (1997).

> a motor vehicle (as defined in section 30102 of title 49) acquired for the personal use of the debtor . . . ."

11 U.S.C. 1325(a). Section 506 permits a debtor to bifurcate a secured creditor's claim into a secured and an unsecured portion if the value of the collateral is less than the amount of the claim. The portion of the claim that is greater than the value of the collateral is unsecured and the portion equal to the value is secured. This bifurcation process is known as "stripping down" a secured creditor's lien, and it is commonly used by debtors in conjunction with the cram down option to retain depreciated collateral on significantly better terms.[5] The hanging paragraph prevents this bifurcation for secured claims that meet its criteria, so the entire claim remains secured, regardless of the value of the collateral.[6]

Drive Financial argues that since the hanging paragraph makes section 506 inapplicable to its claim, the Supreme Court's opinion in Till is distinguishable because it dealt with a lien-stripped claim[7] and it was decided before the hanging paragraph was added to the Bankruptcy Code.[8] If Till is distinguishable, Drive Financial contends that this court should follow its prior precedent and mandate that the Jordans' Chapter 13 plan use the contract rate to pay off its claim. Green Tree Fin. Servicing Corp. v. Smithwick, 121 F.3d 211, 214-15 (5th Cir. 1997) (adopting the "presumptive contract rate approach"[9] to determine the interest rate to be paid on a secured Chapter 13 claim).

This argument is unpersuasive because Till did not rely upon the fact that the creditor's claim had been bifurcated using section 506. The purpose of bifurcation is to determine how much of a creditor's claim is secured; then section 1325(a)(5)(B) determines what interest rate should be applied to that secured claim. In Till, the Supreme Court decided what interest rate was required to be paid on an objecting creditor's secured claim to ensure that the creditor receives value for its crammed down claim as required by section 1325(a)(5)(B). That is the same question presented in this case. The only difference is that all of Drive Financial's claim is secured, as opposed to only a portion of the creditor's claim being secured in Till, because the hanging paragraph prohibited Drive Financial's claim from being bifurcated. Drive Financial has provided no reason for why this distinction would affect Till's holding regarding the proper rate of interest to be paid upon a secured claim.

---

[5] This occurs because the stripped down portion of the loan is paid at cents on the dollar like most unsecured claims in bankruptcy and the cram down option allows a debtor to obtain a more favorable interest rate on the remaining secured portion of the loan.

[6] The Jordans do not dispute that the hanging paragraph applies to Drive Financial's security interest in the Truck or that Drive Financial's entire claim is secured.

[7] Drive Financial uses the section 1325(a)(5)(B) cram down option interchangeably with section 506 lien stripping in its brief. This muddling of the two provisions is problematic because they are two distinct provisions of the Bankruptcy Code and they operate independently of each other, although debtors frequently employ both of them when restructuring their claims under Chapter 13. Furthermore, the text of the hanging paragraph only prohibits the application of section 506 lien stripping for certain Chapter 13 secured claims; it makes no mention of the section 1325(a)(5)(B) cram down provision.

[8] Drive Financial does not argue that BAPCPA prohibits the bankruptcy court from modifying the contract rate when it sets a rate for repayment of a claim covered by the hanging paragraph in a Chapter 13 plan.

[9] In this approach, the debtor bears the burden of rebutting the presumption that the contract rate was the correct rate by presenting evidence that his risk of default was lower now than it had been when he initially entered into the loan.

BAPCPA did not amend the definition of value under section 1325(a)(5)(B), nor did it prohibit bankruptcy courts from altering the contractual terms for secured claims.[10] Since these were the issues decided by Till, we hold that Congress did not supercede Till when it passed BAPCPA.

III. Is Till Binding Precedent?

Having held that BAPCPA has not superceded Till, we must now examine whether Till mandates that the prime-plus approach be used to determine the interest rate to be paid on Drive Financial's secured claim. The facts of Till are indistinguishable from the facts of this case, but Till was a plurality decision in which no opinion was joined by five justices. Consequently, we must determine which of these opinions, if any, controls.

The Supreme Court has stated that "[w]hen a fragmented Court decides a case and no single rationale explaining the result enjoys the assent of five Justices, 'the holding of the Court may be viewed as that position taken by those Members who concurred in the judgments on the narrowest grounds.'" Marks v. United States, 430 U.S. 188 (1976) . . .

In Till, the debtors filed for relief under Chapter 13 of the Bankruptcy Code and proposed a plan in which they retained possession of their truck and repaid the creditor's secured claim in installments. Till, 124 S. Ct. at 1956 (Stevens, J., plurality). The original contract rate of interest on the truck loan was twenty-one percent, but the Tills' plan proposed paying interest on the creditor's secured claim at a prime-plus rate of 9.5%. Id. at 1956-57. The creditor holding the secured claim on the Tills' truck objected, claiming that it was entitled to have interest paid on its claim at the contract rate. Id. at 1957. The bankruptcy court overruled the creditor's objection and approved the Tills' use of the prime-plus rate. Id. The district court overturned the bankruptcy court and held that Seventh Circuit precedent required that the "coerced loan" approach[11] be used to determine the appropriate interest rate. Id. The Seventh Circuit approved a slightly modified version of the district court's approach, but it noted that the contract rate was presumptively the rate to be used. Id. at 1957-58.

A plurality of four justices, joined by Justice Thomas who concurred in judgment, reversed the Seventh Circuit and held that the prime-plus rate was the appropriate risk-adjusted interest rate to use for installment payments to creditors holding a crammed-down secured claim in a Chapter 13 plan. Id. at 1962. In reaching this decision, the plurality stated that, in order to receive value, creditors should receive an interest rate higher than the prime rate to reflect the risk associated with lending to borrowers who had filed for bankruptcy. Id. at 1961-62. The plurality explicitly rejected the presumptive contract rate approach because it reasoned that that approach would reward inefficient lenders and had the potential to treat similarly situated debtors differently. Id. at 1960. Ultimately, the plurality held that the Seventh Circuit should be reversed and

[10] If Congress had intended to exclude the secured claims covered by the hanging paragraph from being modified in bankruptcy it could have done so explicitly as it has done with home mortgages. See 11 U.S.C. 1322(b)(2) (stating that a Chapter 13 plan may modify the rights of secured claim holders, except for those secured by a mortgage of the debtor's principle residence).

[11] Under this approach, the rate is set by determining what interest rate "the creditor could have obtained if it had foreclosed on the loan, sold the collateral, and reinvested the proceeds in loans of equivalent duration and risk." Till, 124 S. Ct. at 1957 (Stevens, J., plurality).

remanded the case to the bankruptcy court for further proceedings to determine the proper prime-plus interest rate. In his concurrence, Justice Thomas reasoned that it would be sufficient to pay secured creditors a risk-free interest rate, here the prime rate, because the statutory language of the Bankruptcy Code did not require secured creditors to receive a risk premium in order to receive value under section 1325(a)(5)(B). Id. at 1966-67 (Thomas, J., concurring in judgment). He concurred in judgment because the plurality's prime-plus approach, namely the debtor's proposed 9.5% rate, was greater than the risk free or prime rate, and hence "will sufficiently compensate respondent [creditor] for the fact that instead of receiving . . . [the principal] today, it will receive . . . [the principal] plus 9.5% interest over a period of up to 36 months." Id. at 1968. The dissent would have affirmed the Seventh Circuit's presumptive contract rate approach because it determined that the contract rate more closely approximated the true risk of default, whereas the prime-plus approach would "systematically undercompensate secured creditors." Id. at 1968, 1970 (Scalia, J., dissenting).

Drive Financial argues that this court is not bound by either the plurality or the concurrence because there is no common denominator on which the five justices agreed, so there is no narrowest grounds under the standard established in Marks. It supports this argument by pointing out that while the plurality states that creditors are entitled to a risk premium above the prime rate, Justice Thomas's concurrence reasons that a risk premium is not required by the Bankruptcy Code.[12] Drive financial believes that this difference in approach makes the two opinions irreconcilable and, therefore, not binding in future cases.[13]

Drive Financial's reliance on Marks is misplaced in this case because we are presented with essentially the same facts that the Supreme Court was presented with in Till.[14] The purpose of Marks' narrowest grounds test is to allow a lower court to derive a rationale from multiple opinions when none of them are joined by a majority of the justices so that the lower court can apply that rationale in future cases with different facts to ensure outcomes that are faithful to past precedent. Deriving a holding is unnecessary, however, when a future case presents the same facts as a past case decided by a higher court because stare decisis requires that we decide those cases in a similar manner. See United States v. Eckford, 910 F.2d 216, 220 (5th Cir. 1990) (holding that even when the Supreme Court issues an opinion in which there is no common rational, the holding of that case is still binding with regard to future cases presenting the

[12] It is worth noting that while Justice Thomas does not state that the Bankruptcy Code requires a risk premium to be paid, he does not state that it prohibits payment of such a premium. In Till the debtor was always willing to pay the prime plus rate of 9.5%; here the Jordans have not questioned the bankruptcy court's orders fixing the rate at the prime plus rate of 7.5%.

[13] We are aware of no cases where a court presented with similar facts has held that Till is not binding precedent. Drive Financial cites one bankruptcy court case that held that Till is not binding. In re Cook, 322 B.R. 336 (Bankr. N.D. Ohio 2005). That decision is not binding on this court and in any event may be distinguishable because it dealt with the rate owed to unsecured creditors under section 1325(a)(4), not secured creditors under section 1325(a)(5)(B).

[14] Both the Jordans and the Tills filed for relief under Chapter 13, and both sought to use the cram down option to approve a Chapter 13 plan over their secured creditors' objections. In both cases the creditors claimed that they should have been paid the contract rate of interest. Both bankruptcy courts held that the debtors should pay a prime-plus rate of interest on their respective secured claims, the prime-plus rate was considerably lower than the contract rate in each case, and the debtors made no appellate challenge to the prime plus rate.

same factual scenario). This case presents such a situation. Since we are presented with facts indistinguishable from Till, we need not attempt to divine a narrowest grounds under Marks. We are bound by stare decisis to apply the holding of Till by rejecting the creditor's challenge to the bankruptcy court's use of the prime-plus interest rate.

This result is also supported by an analysis of what the outcome would be if this court were to hold that Till is not binding precedent because there was no narrowest grounds under the Marks test. If Till were not binding, we would remand this case to the bankruptcy court with instructions that it recalculate the interest rate on Drive Financial's secured claim using the presumptive contract rate approach, which was the approach previously adopted by this court. See Smithwick, 121 F.3d at 214-15 (holding that the presumptive contract rate approach should be used to determine interest rates on Chapter 13 plan installment payments on secured claims).[15] Such a holding would be essentially identical to the holding of the Seventh Circuit in Till, which was reversed by five currently active justices on the Supreme Court. Such a result would be untenable at best.[16]

Furthermore, while the plurality opinion and Justice Thomas's concurrence offered different reasons for rejecting the Seventh Circuit's application of the presumptive contract rate approach, they both rejected the presumptive contract rate approach as being too generous to creditors. Therefore, if we were to apply the Marks test, the narrowest grounds would be that the coerced loan or presumptive contract rate approach cannot be used if they would yield an interest rate higher than the prime-plus approach.

CONCLUSION

For the foregoing reasons, we hold that the Till plurality's adoption of the prime-plus interest rate approach is binding precedent in cases presenting an essentially indistinguishable factual scenario. To this extent, Till is an intervening precedent from the Supreme Court that overrules this circuit's prior precedent of Smithwick. United States v. Holy Land Found. for Relief and Dev., 445 F.3d 771, 789-90 (5th Cir. 2006). Thus, the bankruptcy court did not err in rejecting Drive Financial's objections to application of the prime-plus rate to Drive Financial's secured claim in the Jordans' Chapter 13 plan. AFFIRMED.

Notes and Questions

1. Suppose a vehicle is acquired 950 days before bankruptcy. It is worth $8,000. The secured creditor with a purchase money security interest on the car claims $12,000. D wishes to

[15] See also United States v. Holy Land Found. for Relief & Dev., 445 F.3d 771, 789-90 (5th Cir. 2006) (holding that one panel may not overrule a prior decision of another panel absent an intervening precedent by this court sitting en banc or the Supreme Court).

[16] Drive Financial argues that this court would not have to direct the bankruptcy court to apply the presumptive contract rate approach in this case because the parties have stipulated that 17.5% is the appropriate rate if Till were held to be inapplicable. Drive Financial, however, has offered no evidence that this rate was chosen for any reason other than that it was the original contract rate, and at oral argument, Drive Financial argued that absent the stipulation, Smithwick would control the determination of the applicable interest rate if Till were held not to be binding precedent. Drive Financial admits that the only matter in the present record which would support or justify the 17.5% rate is the fact that it is the contract rate.

retain the car. What can a chapter 13 plan do to the secured claim?

2. Notice that Bankruptcy Code § 1325(a)(5) applies only to "allowed secured claims." This is usually taken to mean that the secured creditor has filed a proof of claim in the bankruptcy proceeding. Bankruptcy Code § 502(a). Also, under Federal Rules of Bankruptcy Procedure 3021 permits trustees to make distributions to "creditors whose claims have been allowed." The implications of these provisions has never been thoroughly explored in litigation. See generally David Gray Carlson, Cars and Homes in Chapter 13 After the 2005 Amendments to the Bankruptcy Code, 14 AM. BANKR. INST. L. REV. 301, 360-70 (2006).

AMERICREDIT FINANCIAL SERVICES, INC., v LONG (IN RE LONG)

519 F.3d 288 (6th Cir. 2008)

MERRITT, J.

This consumer bankruptcy, Chapter 13 case arises because the debtor bought a car under a typical financing arrangement in which the lender retained a lien or mortgage on the car as security for payment of the outstanding loan that enabled the debtor to buy the car. The debtor proposed to surrender the car to the finance company as part of the Chapter 13 plan. The value of the car was less than the outstanding debt. Due to a glitch or gap in a recent revision of the Bankruptcy Code intended to benefit creditors, the law is now silent on what happens to the remaining indebtedness in the surrender-of-the-car situation. The bankruptcy court below held that the congressional mistake in drafting the revision means that the remaining indebtedness is completely wiped out. We believe the gap should be filled and the Congressional mistake corrected. The law previously governing this situation should be restored until Congress can correct its mistake and fill in the gap.

I. The Issue to be Decided

The gap in the law is caused by a newly-formed inconsistency between §§ 1325(a) and 506 of the Bankruptcy Code. Congress simply overlooked providing for what happens in Chapter 13, consumer bankruptcy cases when the debtor surrenders the car to the lender instead of retaining the car and paying off the loan.

In the twelve-month period ending September 2007, there were 310,802 Chapter 13 bankruptcies. In many of these, there were secured loans for automobiles or trucks and other personal property for the bankruptcy courts and Chapter 13 trustees to deal with. Some courts have addressed the gap in the law by adopting a remedy based on state law remedies of foreclosure, repossession, sale at auction and adjudication to determine the deficiency that arises from the fact that the collateral is usually worth less than the remaining debt. These several state law contractual, foreclosure and judicial remedies vary widely from state to state.

By a mistake in drafting, the 2005 revision of the Bankruptcy Code does not provide for the situation in which a Chapter 13 debtor proposes to surrender the collateral to the creditor holding the lien, or purchase-money mortgage or other security interest. As Chief Judge Easterbrook recently wrote for the Seventh Circuit in an Illinois Chapter 13 case similar to the one before us:

> Bankruptcy judges across the nation have divided over the effect of the unnumbered hanging paragraph that the Bankruptcy Abuse Prevention and Consumer Protection Act of 2005 added to § 1325(a) of the Bankruptcy Code, 11 U.S.C. § 1325(a). Section 1325, part of Chapter 13, specifies the circumstances

> under which a consumer's plan of repayment can be confirmed. The hanging paragraph says that, for the purpose of a Chapter 13 plan, § 506 of the code, 11 U.S.C. § 506, does not apply to certain secured loans.

In re Wright, 492 F.3d 829, 830 (7th Cir. 2007).

In the absence of any clear bankruptcy law covering how to handle the surrender of cars and other collateral, we agree with the Seventh Circuit that the bankruptcy courts should not simply allow the debtor to surrender the car and then wipe out the deficiency, as the bankruptcy court in the instant case ruled. Wiping out the deficiency altogether undermines reasonable obligations created by the contract between the parties. These contractual obligations are referred to in our Constitution, see U.S. CONST. art. I, § 10, cl. 1, and normally should be enforced as a part of the Rule of Law based on concepts of freedom of contract and private property. But we do question the wisdom of the Seventh Circuit and our concurring colleague that the resulting deficiency judgment in bankruptcy should depend entirely on the vagaries of state laws as to foreclosure, repossession, sale and judicial remedy. By the adoption of § 506 and § 1325, Congress has demonstrated an intent to federalize and make uniform the treatment of purchase-money mortgages in bankruptcy. A uniform national rule should be adopted and substituted for the widely varying procedural and substantive foreclosure, repossession and deficiency judgment rules provided by the 50 states.

II. Analysis of Sections 506(a) and 1325(a) of the 2005 Revision of the Bankruptcy Code

Section 506(a)(1) and (2), as amended, which defines for bankruptcy the nature of the secured creditor's claim, reads in relevant part:

> (a)(1) An allowed claim of a creditor secured by a lien on property . . . is a secured claim to the extent of the value of such creditor's interest in the estate's interest in such property . . . and is an unsecured claim to the extent that the value of such creditor's interest . . . is less than the amount of such allowed claim. Such value shall be determined in light of the purpose of the valuation and of the proposed disposition or use of such property . . .
>
> (2) If the debtor is an individual in a case under chapter 7 or 13, such value with respect to personal property securing an allowed claim shall be determined based on the replacement value of such property as of the date of the filing of the petition without deduction for costs of sale or marketing. With respect to property acquired for personal, family, or household purposes, replacement value shall mean the price a retail merchant would charge for property of that kind considering the age and condition of the property at the time value is determined.

11 U.S.C. § 506 (2007). After establishing the "allowed secured claim" in § 506(a), section 1325(a) then provides for one of three treatments "with respect to each allowed secured claim provided for by the plan," as set out below. First, the holder of the claim can accept the debtor's proposed plan under § 1325(a)(5)(A). If the creditor does not accept the plan, the debtor can either retain the collateral subject to the requirements in § 1325(a)(5)(B), or surrender the collateral pursuant to § 1325(a)(5)(C). Prior to the 2005 revision, 11 U.S.C. §§ 506(a) and 1322(b)(2) operated to enable Chapter 13 debtors to bifurcate claims into secured and unsecured portions.

What has caused the confusion and incoherence in the law is known as the unnumbered "hanging paragraph" or "anti-cramdown paragraph" that Congress inserted immediately following section 1325(a):

> For purposes of paragraph (5), section 506 shall not apply to a claim described in that paragraph if the creditor has a purchase money security interest securing the debt that is the subject of the claim, the debt was incurred within the 910-day [sic] preceding the date of the filing of the petition, and the collateral for that debt consists of a motor vehicle (as defined in section 30102 of title 49) acquired for the personal use of the debtor, or if collateral for that debt consists of any other thing of value, if the debt was incurred during the 1-year period preceding that filing.

Courts use different terms to talk about the hanging paragraph because the provision does not have an alphanumeric designation. See In re Carver, 338 B.R. 521, 523 (Bankr. S.D. Ga. 2006), which explains two of the errors arising from negligent drafting of the revision:

> The reader immediately notices two problems. First, the provision "has no alphanumeric designation and merely dangles at the end of § 1325(a). There is no way to cite to this provision other than its proximity to other citable provisions." Dianne C. Kerns, Cram-a-lot: The Quest Continues, 24-Nov. Am. Bankr. Inst. J. 10, 10 (2005). In addition, the provision is "missing an operable word. The first sentence refers to 'the 910-day [period] preceding the date of the filing of the petition . . . .'" Id . Without the addition of "period," the provision makes little sense and could be read to apply only to debts of the type described that were incurred exactly 910 days -- no more, no less -- prior to the petition date. These two problems are mere shadows of the larger interpretation difficulties this provision presents.

(internal citation omitted). Not only must words be added to make any sense of the paragraph, but the literal meaning of the paragraph must be altered to deal with debtors who surrender the collateral instead of retaining it. (Our concurring colleague seems to be the only observer who finds no gap, mistake or incongruity in connection with the surrender of collateral under sections 506(a) and 1525.)

The bankruptcy court found and neither party disputes that all of the requirements set forth in the hanging paragraph are met in this case. Specifically, (1) the debtors purchased a car within the 910-day period set forth in the statute, (2) AmeriCredit holds a purchase money security interest in the car, and (3) the car was acquired for the debtors' personal use. Creditors falling under this paragraph are commonly referred to as "910 creditors."

1. The hanging paragraph does not make § 506 entirely inapplicable to secured claims. When the hanging paragraph applies, it purports to exempt all 910 claims from treatment under 11 U.S.C. § 506 which is titled "Determination of secured status." In addition to providing for the bifurcation of claims, section 506 is used first to determine when allowed claims become "secured" for purposes of the Bankruptcy Code. It may be argued that literally, without section 506, there cannot be an "allowed secured claim" at all under § 1325(a)(5). In his treatise, Judge Lundin explains that "[a]n allowed secured claim to which § 506 does not apply is an oxymoron" because "a lienholder must pass through § 506 to have an allowed secured claim but then § 506 'shall not apply' if the debt meets the new 910-day [rule]." KEITH M. LUNDIN, CHAPTER 13 BANKRUPTCY, 3d ed. 446-2, 3 (2000 & Supp. 2007-1). We agree with Judge Lundin and with those courts that have found that this literal interpretation makes no sense and that Congress did not intend for 910 claims to be a unique, previously unheard-of,

class of claims not governed by section 1325(a)(5). See, e.g., In re DeSardi, 340 B.R. 790, 812 (Bankr. S.D. Tex. 2006) ("Taking 910 claims out of the purview of § 506 does not mean 910 claims are a new and unique class of claims. . . . The Court finds it unlikely that Congress would create a new, undefined type of claim, and then furnish no guidance as to how such a claim should be handled.). Further, we agree with the Lundin treatise that a claim cannot be an "allowed secured claim" for purposes of § 1325(a)(5) without first coming through the § 506 gateway. Consequently, we decline to read the hanging paragraph to use state law or some unknown, federal law to create an allowed secured claim.

2. The purpose of the hanging paragraph is to change the law relating to retained collateral. The hanging paragraph is often referred to as the "anti-cramdown" or "anti-bifurcation" paragraph "because its most obvious function is to block bifurcation of a 910 Creditor's lien into secured and unsecured portions so that a debtor who wishes to retain a 910 Vehicle under Section 1325(a)(5)(B) must pay the full amount owing to the secured creditor without regard to the present value of the collateral." In re Pinti, 363 B.R. 369, 375 (Bankr. S.D.N.Y. 2007). Understanding how debtors "crammed down" their debt prior to the 2005 amendments is critical because the hanging paragraph was intended to address that simple issue -- the issue of how to treat claims when the debtor retains the collateral. On this point, an excerpt from Judge Lundin's treatise is instructive:

> Prior to BAPCPA, cramdown of secured claims at confirmation in Chapter 13 cases was uniform and well understood. Oversimplified, under § 506(a) an allowed claim was a secured claim to the extent of the value of the collateral. Undersecured claims were split into secured and unsecured components based on the value of the collateral. With or without consent of the lienholder, a Chapter 13 debtor could confirm a plan that proposed to pay the allowed secured claim in full with present value interest and to treat the balance of the debt as an unsecured claim.

KEITH M. LUNDIN, CHAPTER 13 BANKRUPTCY, 3d ed. 445-1 (2000 & Supp. 2007-1). Cramdown occurred exclusively under § 1325(a)(5)(B) when debtors elected to retain the collateral. In contrast, when debtors chose to surrender the collateral under § 1325(a)(5)(C), the present value of the collateral (the foreclosure value) was subtracted from the debt and the remaining debt was an allowed unsecured claim within the debtor's Chapter 13 plan. The surrender of the collateral satisfied the allowed secured claim in full leaving the undersecured creditor with a deficiency that could only be asserted as a general unsecured claim. The hanging paragraph eliminates the cramdown occurring under § 1325(a)(5)(B) by eliminating bifurcation under § 506. Without § 506, creditors falling within the scope of the hanging paragraph are fully secured so that when a debtor elects to retain the collateral, the debtor must propose a plan that will pay the full amount of the claim.

Although sparse, the legislative history supports the conclusion that the paragraph was only intended to prohibit debtors from cramming down debt when they elect to retain collateral under § 1325(a)(5)(B). See H.R. REP. NO. 109-31, pt. 1, at 17 and 71-72 (2005), reprinted in U.S.C.C.A.N. 88, 103, 140. Based upon the legislative history, there is little doubt that the "hanging-sentence architects intended only good things for car lenders and other lienholders." KEITH M. LUNDIN, CHAPTER 13 BANKRUPTCY, 3d ed. 451.5-1 (2000 & Supp. 2007-1); see, e.g., In re Duke, 345 B.R. 806, 809 (Bankr. W.D. Ky. 2006) ("It is interesting to note that the section of BAPCPA that added the hanging paragraph was entitled, "Section 306-Giving Secured Creditors Fair Treatment in Chapter 13... Restoring the Foundation for Secured Credit."). Perhaps most significantly, there is no legislative history that suggests that car lenders and lienholders should be negatively impacted by the hanging paragraph in situations where the debtor elects to surrender the collateral.

3. Literal Application of the hanging paragraph to surrendered collateral leaves a gap in contractual remedies. The current confusion over the effect of the hanging paragraph is created because, by its terms, the hanging paragraph applies to the several alternatives that arise under § 1325(a)(5) -- "only one of which has come to be known as 'cramdown.'" KEITH M. LUNDIN, CHAPTER 13 BANKRUPTCY, 3d ed. 451.5-1 (2000 & Supp. 2007-1). One of those alternatives is the surrender of collateral pursuant to § 1325(a)(5)(C). Before the amendment, courts interpreted section 1325(a)(5)(C) to permit a "Chapter 13 debtor to satisfy an 'allowed secured claim' by surrendering the property securing the claim. After disposition of the surrendered collateral, an undersecured creditor may only assert the deficiency as a general unsecured claim." In re Eubanks, 219 B.R. 468, 473 (B.A.P. 6th Cir. 1998). In essence, whereas § 506 created an unsecured claim to the debtor's benefit when the debtor retained the collateral, § 506 also provided a deficiency claim when the debtor surrendered the collateral.

The numerous courts that have addressed this issue have reached widely conflicting conclusions. The majority of courts conclude that debtors can surrender collateral in full satisfaction of the debt without any further deficiency claim. The first decision on point and the leading case for the majority is In re Ezell in which Judge Stair concluded:

> [i]f the property is to be retained pursuant to Revised 1325(a)(5)(B), the debtor must treat the entire claim as secured ... [and] must propose a plan that will pay the full amount of the claim as secured over the life of the plan. It only stands to reason that the same analysis is true when applied to surrender under Revised § 1325(a)(5)(C) -- the creditor is fully secured, and surrender therefore satisfies the creditor's allowed secured claim in full.

8 B.R. 330, 340 (Bankr. E.D. Tenn. 2006) (emphasis added). In his treatise, Judge Lundin appears to concur with this conclusion and acknowledges that while it may produce a nonsensical result not intended by the drafters, most likely "the hanging sentence in § 1325(a) works with surrender of collateral under § 1325(a)(5)(C) in the same manner that an undersecured creditor risks full satisfaction by surrender when it elects to be fully secured in a Chapter 11 case under 11 U.S.C. § 1111(b)." KEITH M. LUNDIN, CHAPTER 13 BANKRUPTCY, 3d ed. 446-3 (2000 & Supp. 2007-1). As much as we respect the authority of Judge Lundin's Chapter 13 treatise, we find unpersuasive the argument that because the Bankruptcy Code deals with nonrecourse secured debt in the treatment of secured creditors in Chapter 11 cases under § 1111(b), the complete elimination of a deficiency judgment in Chapter 13 cases is a rational result. The argument dispenses with a major obligation created by the contract. If Congress intended to create a similar outcome to the one that occurs under § 1111(b), it knew how to construct the language and its failure to do so or to make any suggestion whatsoever in the legislative history that it intended a similar outcome convinces us that the elimination of the deficiency judgment upon surrender is an unintended result. Eliminating a deficiency judgment would be in conflict with the apparent Congressional intent and would give to debtors the power to wipe out a legitimately incurred debt entirely. It is difficult to imagine why a debtor

would choose to retain the collateral and make payment on the entire debt, which would be considerably more than the value of the collateral, when the surrender of the collateral would fully satisfy the debt. The consumer would have an incentive to buy an expensive new car, drive it for awhile, file for Chapter 13, surrender the car, and wipe out the debt. Car dealers and finance companies would have to figure these new uncertainties into the price or financing costs of each car sold.

The United States Supreme Court in Associates Commercial Corp. v. Rash, 520 U.S. 953 (1997), explicitly recognized the obvious applicability of § 506(a) to surrender under § 1325(a)(5)(C). Specifically, Justice Ginsburg, analyzing the language in section 506(a) that specifies valuation of collateral should be based upon its "disposition or use," wrote:

> As we comprehend § 506(a), the "proposed disposition or use" of the collateral is of paramount importance to the valuation question. . . . [T]he debtor has two options for handling allowed secured claims: surrender the collateral to the creditor . . . or, under the cram down option, keep the collateral over the creditor's objection and provide the creditor . . . with the equivalent of the present value of the collateral . . . . The "disposition or use" of the collateral thus turns on the alternative the debtor chooses -- in one case the collateral will be surrendered to the creditor, and in the other, the collateral will be retained and used by the debtor.

520 U.S. at 962. Because section 506 was applicable to the surrender of collateral before the 2005 amendments, and makes the situation incoherent if no longer applicable, we believe the best solution is to regard section 506 as continuing to apply to surrender cases.

Some courts are inclined to rely on non-bankruptcy law to create the deficiency. As stated above, the Seventh Circuit concluded that state law, and the parties' underlying contract, creates and defines the deficiency judgment upon surrender of the collateral. Specifically, the Court found that "by knocking out § 506, the hanging paragraph leaves the parties to their contractual entitlements. . . ." In re Wright, 492 F.3d 829, 832 (7th Cir. 2007). The Court, relying on the Supreme Court's holding in Butner v. United States, wrote "state law determines rights and obligations when the [Bankruptcy] Code does not supply a federal rule." Id. (citing 440 U.S. 48 (1979)). The contract at issue in In re White provided that the parties enjoyed any rights they had under the Uniform Commercial Code, which further provided that the "obligor must satisfy any deficiency if the collateral's value is insufficient to cover the amount due." 492 F.3d at 832. Finding the Bankruptcy Code silent regarding creditor's rights when section 506 does not apply, the Court reasoned that the "fallback under Butner is the parties' contract . . . rather than non-recourse secured debt . . . or no security interest. . . ." Id. at 833. We agree with the Seventh Circuit's effort to reconstruct the statute to preserve the intent of the parties in a deficiency judgment. The Court's approach, however, fails even to consider that a primary, underlying purpose of the Bankruptcy Code is to provide a uniform, nationwide system by which claims are handled. As this Court has recognized,

> a mere browse through the complex, detailed, and comprehensive provisions of the lengthy Bankruptcy code, 11 U.S.C. § 101 et seq., demonstrates Congress's intent to create a whole system under federal control which is designed to bring together and adjust all of the rights and duties of creditors and embarrassed debtors alike. While it is true that bankruptcy law makes reference to state law

> at many points, the adjustment of rights and duties within the bankruptcy process itself is uniquely and exclusively federal. It is very unlikely that Congress intended to permit the superimposition of state remedies on the many activities that might be undertaken in the management of the bankruptcy process.

Pertuso v. Ford Motor Credit Co., 233 F.3d 417, 425 (6th Cir. 2000) (quoting MSR Exploration, Ltd. v. Meridian Oil, Inc., 74 F.3d 910, 914 (9th Cir. 1996)). Resorting to state law to preserve deficiency claims would "undermine the uniformity the Code endeavors to preserve and would 'stand[] as an obstacle to the accomplishment and execution of the full purposes and objectives of Congress.'" Id. (quoting Bibbo v. Dean Witter Reynolds, Inc., 151 F.3d 559, 562-63 (6th Cir. 1998)). Relying on state law to fill the gap forces bankruptcy courts to apply the states' varying foreclosure, automobile auction, and deficiency laws rather than a uniform federal law. The bankruptcy and reviewing courts would have to apply widely varying state laws to the tens of thousands of automobiles and other items of personal property dealt with each year in Chapter 13 cases. Specifically, judges would have to interpret varied state common law and statutory law that addresses debtors in default where the creditor must repossess the collateral. That case law has developed independently of the considerations that underlie bankruptcy cases which focus on a comprehensive plan for managing the debtor's estate. The state-specific laws, including the timing and procedure for foreclosure proceedings, notice requirements, the valuation of collateral, and what constitutes "commercial reasonableness" within the context of the Uniform Commercial Code (which has been adopted by most states) would provide widely disparate treatment to debtors and creditors whose rights Congress intended to be governed by the uniform Bankruptcy Code. Further, the Seventh Circuit's reliance on Butner is misplaced because while " Butner is certainly appropriate to determine that a creditor has a debt under state law; [it] does not compel allowance of the unsecured portion of that claim . . . ." KEITH M. LUNDIN, CHAPTER 13 BANKRUPTCY, 3d ed. 451.5-12, 13 (2000 & Supp. 2007-1).

4. The hanging paragraph gap should be filled by prior law. The Supreme Court, addressing amendments to the Bankruptcy Code, has determined that "[w]hen Congress amends the bankruptcy laws, it does not write 'on a clean slate,'" and, therefore, the "Court has been reluctant to accept arguments that would interpret the Code, however vague the particular language under consideration might be, to effect a major change in pre-Code practice that is not the subject of at least some discussion in the legislative history." Dewsnup v. Timm, 502 U.S. 410, 419 (1992).

Because we are unable to find any legislative history that suggests that Congress intended to eliminate all deficiency claims upon surrender of the collateral and because we conclude that a literal interpretation of the statute would create an unintended and illogical result, we decline to adopt a literal interpretation of the statute. Clearly, this is not an issue free from doubt, but where a statute cannot literally be applied without undermining Cong-ressional intent, equity requires that this Court interpret the language to produce results that conform with Congress' intent and the overriding purposes of the Bankruptcy Code.

In determining how to fill the gap left by Congress after the 2005 amendments, we employ a well-established common law principle of interpretation known as "the equity of the statute." This method of interpretation of gaps, mistakes and ambiguities in statutes has guided common law judges at least since the interpretation of the statute De Deonis in the Fourteenth Century. See THEODORE F.T. PLUCKNETT, A CONCISE HISTORY OF THE COMMON LAW 331-35 (1956); see also North Dakota v. Fredericks, 940 F.2d 333, 337 (8th Cir. 1991) (Arnold, J.). As described by Judge Richard Arnold, the principle connotes the idea that "statutes are an authoritative expression of public policy. That policy should be hospitably received by the courts, and they are free to apply it, absent good reasons to the contrary, in cases within the spirit of the enactment, but not within its letter." Id.[1] Our Court, as well, has referred favorably to interpretation according to the "equity of the statute." See Popovich v. Cuyahoga County Court of Common Pleas, 276 F.3d 808, 815 (6th Cir. 2002); United States v. Cheiman, 578 F.2d 160, 163 (6thCir. 1978). The United States Supreme Court, in Church of the Holy Trinity v. United States, 143 U.S. 457, 459 (1892), recognized the "familiar rule" that:

> a thing may be within the letter of the statute and yet not within the statute, because not within its spirit, nor within the intention of its makers. This has been often asserted, and the reports are full of cases illustrating its application. This is not the substitution of the will of the judge for that of the legislator, for frequently words of general meaning are used in a statute, words broad enough to include an act in question, and yet a consideration of the whole legislation, or of the circumstances surrounding its enactment, or of the absurd results which follow from giving such broad meaning to the words, makes it unreasonable to believe that the legislator intended to include the particular act.

In the same opinion, the Court noted that when determining how to properly interpret the statute when the literal meaning creates an unintended result a guide to the meaning "is found in the evil which it is designed to remedy." Id. at 463. As discussed above, the hanging paragraph was intended to protect secured creditors by eliminating debtors' ability to cram-down debt under § 1325(a)(5)(B). Applying the mandate of the hanging paragraph to surrender under § 1325(a)(5)(C) would require this Court to reach a result that would not serve the policy or purpose of the amendment. Rather, we believe the gap that exists in the statute -- how courts should evaluate surrender when 910 claims are involved -- should be filled by employing the pre-2005 law to these cases. We hold that claims subject to the hanging paragraph where the debtor elects to surrender the collateral pursuant to § 1325(a)(5)(C) will be governed and adjudicated the same as they were before the 2005 amendments. See Memphis

---

[1] Judge Arnold further explained the historic basis for this treatment of a gap in a statute as follows: "Sir Edward Coke put it this way:

> 'Equitie' is a construction made by the judges, that cases out of the letter of a statute, yet being within the same mischiefe, or cause of the making of the same, shall be within the same remedie that the statute provideth. . . .

Co. Litt., Lib. 1, C. 2, § 21, f. 24b. Or, as Dean Landis put it in a pioneering article, a statute can be a 'nursing mother of the law,' Landis, Statutes and the Sources of Law, in Harvard Legal Essays Written in Honor of and Presented to Joseph Henry Beale and Samuel Williston 213, 214 (R. Pound ed. 1934), reprinted in 2 Harv. J. on Legis. 7, 8 (1965). This principle enables 'judges to distill from a statute its basic purpose,' and they can 'then employ it to slough off the archaisms in their own legal structure.' Id. at 216 and 10." North Dakota v. Fredericks, 940 F.2d 333, 337 (8th Cir. 1991).

Bank & Trust Co. v. Whitman, 692 F.2d 427 (6th Cir. 1982).

For these reasons, we reverse and remand for further proceedings in accordance with this opinion.

COX, J. CONCURRING. I write separately because while I concur in the result, that the bankruptcy court's ruling should be reversed and remanded, I do not concur in the reasoning.

I do not agree with the lead opinion's holding that the "literal interpretation of [11 U.S.C. § 1325 and 11 U.S.C. § 506] would create an unintended and illogical result." Further, I do not find a "gap" in the law that must be filled by the courts. Finally, I am not aware of any legislative history that unequivocally supports the construction of a judge-made national rule allowing deficiency claims following surrender of collateral pursuant to 11 U.S.C. § 1325(a)(5)(C), as the lead opinion appears to hold.

The issue in this case is whether, in light of the "hanging paragraph," surrender of collateral in accordance with § 1325(a)(5)(C) is in full satisfaction of the debt, or if the creditor may pursue a claim for a deficiency. An analysis of the meaning of a statute begins with the language of the statute itself. In re Palmer, 219 F.3d 580, 583 (6th Cir. 2000) (citing United States v. Ron Pair Enterprises, Inc., 489 U.S. 235, 241 (1989)). "If the language of the statute is clear, this court's inquiry is at an end: 'where. . .the statute's language is plain, the sole function of the courts is to enforce it according to its terms.'" Id. (citation omitted). "Only in those rare instances in which 'the literal application of a statute will produce a result demonstrably at odds with the intentions of the drafters or when the statutory language is ambiguous' will we look beyond the statute's plain wording to divine the intent of its drafters." Id. (citation omitted).

Here, the so-called hanging paragraph of § 1325(a) is not ambiguous. Under its clear terms, for purposes of § 1325(a)(5), § 506 does not apply to claims falling within the definition set forth in the hanging paragraph, otherwise referred to as 910 claims. Section 1325(a)(5) provides that a plan can be confirmed if allowed secured claims are treated in one of three ways: (A) the holder of the allowed secured claim accepted the plan; (B) the debtor retains the collateral and pays the claim in full; or (C) the debtor surrenders the collateral. The hanging paragraph provides that:

> For purposes of paragraph (5), section 506 shall not apply to a claim described in that paragraph if the creditor has a purchase money security interest securing the debt that is the subject of the claim, the debt was incurred within the 910-day preceding the date of the filing of the petition, and the collateral for that debt consists of a motor vehicle . . . acquired for the personal use of the debtor, or if collateral for that debt consists of any other thing of value, if the debt was incurred during the 1-year period preceding that filing.

11 U.S.C. § 1325(a). The function of the hanging paragraph is to prevent the bifurcation of 910 claims allowed under 11 U.S.C. § 506(a) . . . .

Like the bankruptcy court and the dissent in this case, the majority of courts deciding the issue of the effect of the hanging paragraph hold that there is no deficiency claim because § 506 does not apply to bifurcate the claim. See In re Ezell, 338 B.R. 330 (Bankr.E.D.Tenn. 2006); In re Quick, 371 B.R. 459 (10th Cir. BAP 2007). The majority position that deficiency claims are no longer allowed for 910 claims by virtue of the hanging paragraph's elimination of § 506 effectively renders 910 secured loans non-recourse, without regard to the contractual terms.

This argument fails because § 506 is not the source for a deficiency claim when collateral is surrendered. Section 506 is not applicable to surrender of collateral because once the collateral is surrendered, the estate no longer has an interest in the property. The property is returned to the creditor, who is free to foreclose upon the security interest and seek a deficiency pursuant to its contractual entitlements. This is the holding of In re Particka, 355 B.R. 616 (E.D.Mich.Bankr. 2006), which I find persuasive. As has been held by several courts, including both of the other Circuit courts to rule on the issue, the inapplicability of § 506 to § 1325(a)(5)(C), by virtue of the hanging paragraph, does not effect a change in a creditor's ability to seek a deficiency because at surrender, the parties are left to their contractual entitlements under state law. See Capital One Auto Fin. v. Osborn, --- F.3d ----, 515 F.3d 817, 2008 U.S. App. LEXIS 2495, 2008 WL 304750 (8th Cir. 2008); In re Wright, 492 F.3d 829, 832 (7th Cir. 2007); and In re Rodriguez, 375 B.R. 535, 544 (9th Cir. BAP 2007).

This is also consistent with the Supreme Court's holding in Butner v. United States, 440 U.S. 48 (1979). The Wright court relied on Butner for the proposition that "state law determines rights and obligations when the [Bankruptcy] Code does not supply a federal rule." Wright, 492 F.3d at 832. The Supreme Court held that "[p]roperty interests are created and defined by state law. . .[u]nless some federal interest requires a different result, there is no reason why such interests should be analyzed differently simply because an interested party is involved in a bankruptcy proceeding." Butner, 440 U.S. at 55. Further, "[t]he justifications for application of state law are not limited to ownership interests; they apply with equal force to security interests. . ." Id. See also In re Terwilliger's Catering Plus, Inc., 911 F.2d 1168, 1172 (6th Cir. 1990)("the nature and extent of the debtor's interest are determined by state law"); In re Indian River Estates, Inc., 293 B.R. 429, 437 (N.D.Ohio Bankr. 2003)("it is state law, not federal which controls the debtor's interest in property").

The cases cited support the proposition that state law applies in the absence of a contrary federal bankruptcy statute and do not support the lead opinion's conclusion that whether a deficiency judgment is allowed should be determined by a "uniform national rule." A uniform national rule as urged by the lead opinion would allow a creditor to seek a deficiency following foreclosure without regard to whether the contract at issue was non-recourse under state law. There is no indication that this was the intent of Congress when it enacted the BAPCPA.

Surrender of collateral pursuant to § 1325(a)(5)(C) does not implicate § 506. Further, nothing in the Bankruptcy Code prohibits a deficiency claim under state law following sur-render of collateral pursuant to § 1325(a)(5)(C). Accordingly, I would hold that a creditor has a right to an allowed unsecured deficiency claim under § 502, to the extent the contrac-tual entitlements and state law allow a deficiency claim. See Particka, 355 B.R. at 624.

CLAY, J., DISSENTING. I respectfully dissent from the lead opinion because I believe it oversteps the bounds of judicial interpretation by essentially rewriting sections of the Bankruptcy Code. I agree with the court below that "a review of the legislative history for guidance does not provide any . . . evidence that the court's determination does not comport with Congressional intent when including the Anti-Cramdown Paragraph in Revised § 1325(a)." In re Ezell, 338 B.R. 330, 340 (Bankr. E.D. Tenn. 2006). The lead opinion would require us not simply to construe an ambiguity in the statute, but actually to rewrite the statute. I would be reluctant to do so because Congress has had two years since the enactment of the statute to correct any problems that it sees with the statute and has not seen fit to do so. I would affirm based upon the well-reasoned opinion of the bankruptcy court.

Notes and Questions

1. At least one appellate opinion thinks that surrender of the car in an asset payment completely discharges the car debt. In re Carter, 2008 U.S. Dist. LEXIS 10417 (M.D. Ga. 2008). At the court of appeals level, however, the car dealers have prevailed in surrender cases. For the latest pronouncement, see Tidewater Finance Co. v. Kenney, 531 F.3d 312 (4th Cir. 2008).

2. The hanging paragraph requires that the car be acquired for personal use. Which of the following is a personal use?

(a) Driving to work. In re Hill, 352 B.R. 69 (Bankr. W.D. La. 2006) (no); In re White, 352 B.R. 633 (Bankr. D. E.D. La. 2006) (yes).

(b) Acquiring the car for an adult child to use. In re Lewis, 347 B.R. 769, 771-73 (Bankr. D. Kan. 2006) (no).

(c) Acquiring the car for a a finacée to use. In re Ford, 2008 Bankr. LEXIS 1381 (Bankr. E.D. Wis., April 29 2008) (no).

3. Suppose D acquires a truck and makes his living hauling freight with it. Less than a year after acquisition, D files for bankruptcy. Does the hanging paragraph apply to bar bifurcation? In re Littlefield, 388 B.R. 1 (Bankr. D. Me. 2008).

FORD v FORD MOTOR CREDIT CORP.

574 F.3d 1279 (10th Cir. 2009)

MURPHY, J.

Appellants John Wesley Ford, Sr. and Cynthia Ford appeal an order of the Bankruptcy Court for the District of Kansas rejecting their proposed Chapter 13 bankruptcy plan. The Fords have an outstanding debt to Appellee Ford Motor Credit Company ("Ford Motor Credit") secured by their automobile. The debt includes the amount paid to discharge the "negative equity" on their trade-in vehicle. Negative equity is the amount owed on a loan in excess of the collateral's value. In their proposed bankruptcy plan, the Fords sought to bifurcate their automobile debt to Ford Motor Credit under 11 U.S.C. § 506(a) into secured and unsecured claims. The unsecured claim would be the portion of the debt used to discharge the negative equity in the trade-in. Ford Motor Credit objected to the proposed plan, claiming the debt bifurcation was impermissible under the "hanging paragraph" of 11 U.S.C. § 1325(a). The bankruptcy court sustained the objection, and the Fords sought an immediate appeal to this court. We conclude we have jurisdiction to hear this appeal under 28 U.S.C. § 158(d)(2) and AFFIRM the ruling of the bankruptcy court.

I. Background

The underlying facts of this case are not in dispute. The Fords purchased a 2007 Ford F-150 truck from Rusty Eck Ford on February 24, 2007. The Fords made a down payment of $1500 and received $40,168.30 in financing secured by the truck. At the same time, the Fords traded in their 2006 Ford truck. The 2006 truck was valued at $16,300, but the Fords owed $23,500 on it. $11,693.30 in financing covered "[a]mounts paid on [the Fords'] behalf." This included taxes, fees, a service contract, gap insurance, and $7200 to pay off the creditor on the 2006 truck for the amount owed on the vehicle in excess of its present value.

The Fords filed for Chapter 13 bankruptcy fewer than four months later. Under their proposed plan, they sought to reduce the secured debt on the 2007 truck by $7200, the amount of negative equity on their trade-in. That amount would be treated as an unsecured claim under the plan. Ford Motor Credit objected to the proposed treatment of its security interest.

Exercising jurisdiction pursuant to 28 U.S.C. § 157(b)(2)(K), (L), the bankruptcy court concluded the negative equity financing was part of the creditor's purchase money security interest under the "hanging paragraph" in 11 U.S.C. § 1325(a) and thus the debt could not be bifurcated and "crammed down" pursuant to 11 U.S.C. § 506(a). The bankruptcy court sustained Ford Motor Credit's objection to the proposed plan and ordered the Fords to file an amended plan treating the entire Ford Motor Credit debt as secured debt.

Both parties certified that an immediate appeal to this court was proper pursuant to 28 U.S.C. § 158(d)(2)(A) because the appeal presents a question of law as to which there is no controlling decision of this court or the Supreme Court and the question requires resolution of conflicting bankruptcy court decisions. A panel of this court then authorized the appeal to proceed, which satisfied the jurisdictional requirements of 28 U.S.C. § 158(a)(3) and 28 U.S.C. § 158(d)(2)(A) for appeals to this court of interlocutory bankruptcy orders.

II. Discussion

The bankruptcy court's interpretation of the Bankruptcy Code is a question of law to be reviewed de novo. In re Lanning, 545 F.3d 1269, 1274 (10th Cir. 2008). When consumers enter Chapter 13 bankruptcy, they are normally permitted, if they wish, to bifurcate each secured debt into two claims: (1) an amount equal to the present value of the collateral, and (2) any excess. 11 U.S.C. § 506(a)(1). The excess portion is converted into unsecured debt. Id. The plan can then be "crammed down," or confirmed over the secured creditor's objection, so long as the creditor receives a lien securing the claim and the plan provides for payments to the creditor over the life of the plan equal to the present value of the collateral. 11 U.S.C. § 1325(a)(5)(B); Assocs. Commercial Corp. v. Rash, 520 U.S. 953, 957 (1997). Whether debt is secured or unsecured is significant because secured creditors generally must be repaid in full before unsecured creditors receive anything. 11 U.S.C. § 1325(a)(5), (b)(1).

. . . One provision of BAPCPA amended the Bankruptcy Code to remove certain secured consumer debts from bifurcation and cramdown. Pub. L. No. 109-8, § 306(b), 119 Stat. 23, 80 (2005). At the end of 11 U.S.C. § 1325(a), Congress added an unnumbered paragraph, now commonly known as the "hanging paragraph," which reads, in relevant part, as follows:

> For purposes of paragraph (5), section 506 shall not apply to a claim described in that paragraph if the creditor has a purchase money security interest securing the debt that is the subject of the claim, the debt was incurred within the 910-day [sic] preceding the date of the filing of the petition, and the collateral for that debt consists of a motor vehicle (as defined in section 30102 of title 49) acquired for the personal use of the debtor . . . .

11 U.S.C. § 1325(a).

The hanging paragraph protects creditors possessing a "purchase money security interest securing the debt that is the subject of the claim" from § 506(a) bifurcation and cramdown. 11 U.S.C. § 1325(a). The parties agree the collateral in this case is a motor vehicle acquired for the personal use of the debtors and the motor vehicle was acquired within 910 days of the bankruptcy filing. The only issue in dispute is the extent to which Ford Motor Credit has a "purchase money security interest."

The issue of whether, under the hanging paragraph, a creditor has a purchase money security interest in the negative equity on a trade-in vehicle has been litigated extensively throughout the country, and the rulings have not been consistent. See In re Graupner, 537 F.3d. 1295 (11th Cir. 2008) (collecting cases). The Tenth Circuit Bankruptcy Appellate Panel recently held creditors have a purchase money security interest in negative equity. In re Padgett, 2009 Bankr. LEXIS 1900 (10th Cir. B.A.P., Jul. 20, 2009). District courts and bankruptcy courts within this circuit have reached varied results on the question. . . .

The Bankruptcy Code does not define the term purchase money security interest. Property interests referred to in the Bankruptcy Code are generally defined by state law. Butner v. United States, 440 U.S. 48, 54 (1979). This court, therefore, has looked to state law for a definition of the term as it is used elsewhere in the Bankruptcy Code. In re Billings, 838 F.2d 405, 406 (10th Cir. 1988) ("[T]he courts have uniformly looked to the law of the state in which the security interest is created."). When Congress enacts a statute using a phrase that has a settled judicial interpretation, it is presumed to be aware of the prior interpretation. Comm'r v. Keystone Consol. Indus., Inc., 508 U.S. 152, 159 (1993). When Congress drafted BAPCPA in 2005, it chose to use the term "purchase money security interest" without defining it. Under settled case law, that term, when used in the Bankruptcy Code, is interpreted with reference to state law. As a consequence, we presume Congress intended that term as used in BAPCPA to be interpreted according to state law.

Kansas has adopted the relevant portion of Revised Article 9 of the Uniform Commercial Code ("U.C.C."), and it also lists the Official U.C.C. Comment in its statutory compilation. Kan. Stat. Ann. § 84-9-103. Under Kansas law, "A security interest in goods is a purchase-money security interest: (1) To the extent that the goods are purchase-money collateral with respect to that security interest. . . ." Id. § 84-9-103(b). Purchase-money collateral is defined as "goods or software that secures a purchase-money obligation incurred with respect to that collateral." Id. § 84-9-103(a)(1). A purchase-money obligation is "an obligation of an obligor incurred as all or part of the price of the collateral or for value given to enable the debtor to acquire rights in or the use of the collateral if the value is in fact so used." Id. § 84-9-103(a)(2). Whether something is a purchase-money security interest thus depends upon whether the underlying obligation was incurred to pay "all or part of the price of the collateral" or covers "value given to enable the debtor to acquire rights in or the use of the collateral." Id. § 84-9-103(a).

The Official Comment to Kan. Stat. Ann. § 84-9-103 provides additional guidance on what constitutes a purchase-money security interest. It states:

> [T]he "price" of collateral or the "value given to enable" includes obligations for expenses incurred in connection with acquiring rights in the collateral, sales taxes, duties, finance charges, interest, freight charges, costs of storage in transit, demurrage, administrative charges, expenses of collection and enforcement, attorney's fees, and other similar obligations.
>
> The concept of "purchase-money security interest" requires a close nexus between the acquisition of collateral and the secured obligation.

Id. § 84-9-103 cmt. 3.

The issue is whether paying off negative equity in a trade-in car is part of the "price" of the new car or part of the "value given to enable" acquisition of the new car.[2] The Fords point out that it is possible to acquire rights in a new car without paying off the negative equity in the old one. The debtor's rights in the two vehicles are distinct. The Fords further argue the trade-in encompasses two separate transactions: the transfer of rights in the trade-in vehicle and the transfer of rights in the new vehicle. They claim negative equity is different than the expenses listed in the Official Comment. In opposition to this position, Ford Motor Credit emphasizes that vehicle trade-ins are commonplace. It further argues that many vehicle trade-ins involve negative equity on the old vehicle and cites a study by J.D. Power and Associates estimating that approximately thirty-eight percent of new car buyers have negative equity at trade-in. It argues the trade-in of the old vehicle is directly related to the purchase of the new vehicle, and the former would not have occurred absent the latter. The Kansas Bankers Association, as amicus curiae, argues the Fords' position artificially breaks a single, package transaction into two parts.

The Fords' position has some logic, and it is not surprising that a number of courts have adopted it. On balance, however, it is not as persuasive as the position advanced by Ford Motor Credit. It may be theoretically possible to split the exchange of vehicles into two separate transactions, but that is not how the parties treated the deal. They signed a single agreement encompassing the trade-in of the old vehicle and the sale of the new vehicle. This type of transaction, moreover, is very common in the automobile industry. The very name "trade-in" implies the two vehicle exchanges are linked. The entire exchange would undoubtedly be a single transaction if the Fords did not have negative equity on the trade-in vehicle and the two parties were simply swapping items of value. As indicated by the data cited by Ford Motor Credit, the existence of negative equity on the trade-in vehicle has not prevented consumers from continuing to trade-in old vehicles for new ones, and it should not turn the swap into two separate transactions. As the Bankruptcy Court recognized, discharging negative equity is necessary to complete the trade-in because otherwise the dealer would take the old vehicle subject to a lien exceeding the vehicle's value. In re Ford, 387 B.R. at 831.

We conclude the trade-in exchange is essentially a single transaction. The expense incurred in retiring the lien on the trade-in vehicle, therefore, is an "expense [] incurred in connection with acquiring rights" in the new car. Kan. Stat. Ann. § 84-9-103 cmt. 3. There is also the requisite "close nexus" between the

---

[2] The Official Comment does not differentiate between "price" and "value given to enable" in explaining what constitutes a purchase-money obligation. See Kan. Stat. Ann. § 84-9-103 cmt. 3. In the U.C.C.'s pre-revision Article 9, the "price" prong explicitly referred to security interests held by the seller of the item, while the "value" prong referred to security interests held by any "person" who incurred an obligation enabling a buyer to acquire collateral. U.C.C. app. O § 9-107. Thus, the "value" prong allowed third parties to acquire purchase money security interests if they advanced money to enable the acquisition of consumer goods. Id. cmt. 2. Revised Article 9 has retained the "price" and "value" prongs in its definition of a purchase-money obligation, although neither the text nor the Official Comment mention the distinction between credit granted by sellers or third parties. See Kan. Stat. Ann. § 84-9-103(a)(2), cmt. 3. Because the Official Comment gives no indication that "price" and "value given to enable" have distinct meanings, see id. cmt. 3, this court interprets the statute such that, as in the pre-revision Article 9, the two terms are equivalent and refer respectively to obligations incurred by sellers and third parties.

acquisition of the new vehicle and the secured obligation. Id. The entire debt incurred by the debtors is therefore a "purchase-money obligation," the new vehicle is "purchase-money collateral" for the entire obligation, and the security interest in the entire debt is a purchase-money security interest under Kansas law. Id. § 84-9-103(a)-(b). Because Ford Motor Credit has a purchase-money security interest in the full amount of the debt, it is entitled to the protection of the hanging paragraph. 11 U.S.C. § 1325(a). The Bankruptcy Court was correct, therefore, in sustaining Ford Motor Credit's objection to the proposed plan.

The Fords contend, as does the dissent, that the phrase "expenses incurred in connection with acquiring rights" must be interpreted in light of its proximity to the other examples listed in the Official Comment. This is undoubtedly true, but we discern no significant difference between the expense of discharging negative equity on a trade-in and some of the other examples listed in the Official Comment. The Official Comment lists "sales taxes, duties, finance charges, interest, freight charges, costs of storage in transit, demurrage, administrative charges, expenses of collection and enforcement, attorney's fees, and other similar obligations" as expenses that can be part of a purchase-money security interest. Kan. Stat. Ann. § 84-9-103 cmt. 3 (emphasis added). Collection and enforcement expenses and attorney's fees are costs incurred so that the creditor may realize the value of the security interest. The discharge of negative equity clears the title of the trade-in vehicle, permitting the creditor to realize the value of the vehicle it receives as part of the trade. Both categories of expenses allow the creditor to realize its benefit of the bargain. The dissent argues collection and enforcement expenses are distinguishable from negative equity because such expenses are transaction costs. Dissenting Op. at 7-8. The term "transaction costs," however, is entirely absent from the statute and the Official Comment. Had the drafters of the U.C.C. intended to limit a purchase-money security interest to cash price plus transaction costs, they could easily have done so. Instead, we are left with the language the drafters actually used, which we conclude is broad enough to encompass negative equity on trade-in vehicles.

The Fords also argue this result will enable predatory lending on the part of automobile dealers by encouraging them to refinance antecedent debt secured by a new vehicle. For reasons well articulated by the Fourth Circuit, this concern is overstated. See In re Price, 562 F.3d at 627. The reasons for treating the trade of an old vehicle for a newer one as a single transaction include the similarity in function between the new and old vehicles. The vehicle trade-in is a common, established transaction in the automobile industry, and it makes sense for many consumers to discard their old vehicles when they acquire new ones. The discharge of unrelated antecedent debt, however, may not bear the required "close nexus" to the acquisition of a new vehicle. Id.; Kan. Stat. Ann. § 84-9-103 cmt. 3. An automobile dealer who attempted to refinance unrelated antecedent debt and secure the new debt with the new car would present a question wholly different from the question presented here. See In re Vega, 344 B.R. 616, 617-18, 622 (Bankr. D. Kan. 2006) (refusing to apply hanging paragraph to portion of car dealer's loan used to extinguish debt on previous car loan when consumer did not trade in the old vehicle).

III. Conclusion

Under Kansas law, Ford Motor Credit holds a purchase-money security interest in the entire amount owed to it by the Fords. The debt therefore falls within the ambit of the hanging paragraph of 11 U.S.C. § 1325, and the Fords may not bifurcate the debt for the purpose of a cramdown under 11 U.S.C. § 506(a). The interlocutory order of the Bankruptcy Court is therefore AFFIRMED and the case is remanded to the Bankruptcy Court for further proceedings consistent with this opinion.

TYMKOVICH, J., DISSENTING. I respectfully dissent because I read the Kansas Uniform Commercial Code, which controls the resolution of this case, as providing a narrower definition of "purchase money security interest" (PMSI) than the majority adopts.

In my view, Kansas law prohibits lenders from using a PMSI to secure a loan for negative equity, even if the loan is bundled with a standard car loan that is itself secured with a PMSI. Therefore, Ford Motor Credit Company does not have a PMSI covering the portion of the Fords' loan attributable to the $7,200 of negative equity in their truck. And because the hanging paragraph, 11 U.S.C. § applies only to PMSIs, the $7,200 is not protected from cram down. Even so, Kansas's dual-status rule preserves PMSI status for the remaining portion of the Fords' loan and that portion is therefore immune from cram down.

I. PMSIs Under Kansas Law

As the majority recognizes, a basic tenet of bankruptcy--and the starting point of this case--is the Butner principle: "Property interests are created and defined by state law." Butner v. United States, 440 U.S. 48, 55 (1979); see also Raleigh v. Ill. Dep't of Revenue, 530 U.S. 15, 20 (2000). The principle arises because generally, bankruptcy law is not designed to fundamentally alter property rights. Instead, "a bankruptcy proceeding is principally a forum in which all of a debtor's creditors can gather, assemble the debtor's assets, and divide them among themselves, according to the rights that state law gives them." Douglas G. Baird, Bankruptcy Procedure and State-Created Rights: The Lessons of Gibbons and Marathon, 1982 Sup. Ct. Rev. 25, 35.

The validity of the Butner principle is undisputed here, but it is worth emphasizing because the hanging paragraph employs a state law term of art, PMSI, to define its scope. See 11 U.S.C. § Though "Congress of course may do what it likes with entitlements in bankruptcy," Raleigh, 530 U.S. at 21, it chose not to alter the state law definition of PMSI as it relates to the hanging paragraph. Therefore, the resolution of this case turns on whether Kansas law allows a creditor to secure a loan for negative equity with a PMSI. See Billings v. AVCO Colo. Indus. Bank (In re Billings), 838 F.2d 405, 406 (10th Cir. 1988) ("For [the definition of PMSI], the courts have uniformly looked to the law of the state in which the security interest is created."); see also In re Price, 562 F.3d 618, 624 (4th Cir. 2009); Graupner v. Nuvell Credit Corp. (In re Graupner), 537 F.3d 1295, 1298 (11th Cir. 2008).[3]

[3] While I recognize Kansas's U.C.C. provisions are similar to those in most states, that does not change the fundamental tenet that we interpret Kansas law consistent with the holdings of Kansas courts. As one judge put it, interpreting the U.C.C. to advance bankruptcy policy (assuming we can identify the correct policy at play here), "will becloud the clarity and predictability that the authors of Article 9 were seeking in enacting the statutes governing PMSIs." In re Peaslee, 2009 N.Y. LEXIS 2475 (N.Y. June 24, 2009) (Smith, J., dissenting). Congress, of course, remains free to establish a uniform definition of PMSI applicable to cases governed by the hanging paragraph.

A. PMSIs Generally

A PMSI is a "special type of security interest" that is created when a secured party (here, Ford Credit) "provides the credit that enables the debtor [the Fords] to obtain the collateral [the Fords' new truck]." Keith G. Meyer, A Primer on Purchase Money Security Interests Under Revised Article 9 of the Uniform Commercial Code, 50 Kan. L. Rev. 143, 152 (2001). In the consumer goods context, a common example of a transaction that creates a PMSI is a purchase using a store-issued credit card:

> Typical credit sales should be relatively familiar to all of us, though we may not always recognize them. Each time we use our Sears Card to buy a drill, a stereo, furniture, etc., we participate in a credit sale. Sears is granting us credit to purchase those items from the store, and we are granting the store a PMSI in that item until it is paid off.

Christopher Harry, Comment, To Be (Transformed) or Not To Be: The Transformation Versus Dual-Status Rules for Purchase-Money Security Interests Under Kansas' Former and Revised Article 9, 50 U. Kan. L. Rev. 1095, 1097 (2002). In this example, the consumer is the debtor, and Sears is the purchase-money lender.

Aside from the benefit conferred by the hanging paragraph (i.e., protection from cram down for some car loans), purchase-money lenders receive additional advantages under the U.C.C. and other law. Most importantly, a purchase-money lender has "super-priority"--the lender's claim to the purchase-money collateral trumps the claims of other secured creditors. See Matthews v. Transamerica Fin. Servs. (In re Matthews), 724 F.2d 798, 801 (9th Cir. 1984) ("Purchase money security is an exceptional category in the statutory scheme that affords priority to its holder over other creditors . . . ."). Additionally, unlike other security interests, PMSIs in household goods cannot be "avoided" (i.e., extinguished) in bankruptcy. See 11 U.S.C. § 522(f)(1)(B); see also In re Billings, 838 F.2d at 406 ("[I]f the security interest . . . retains its status as a purchase money security interest . . . then debtors may not avoid the security interest under § 522(f)."). In the household goods context, PMSIs have yet another benefit: Federal Trade Commission regulations prohibit lenders from taking "a nonpossessory security interest in household goods other than a purchase money security interest." 16 C.F.R. § 444.2(a)(4) (emphasis added).

Because of the advantages of PMSIs, lenders sometimes attempt to use them to secure obligations unrelated to purchase-money collateral. Indeed, "overloaded" PMSIs are a recurring concern in the law of secured transactions, and jurisdictions have adopted various mechanisms to prevent them. See Ann E. Conaway Stilson, The 'Overloaded' PMSI in Bankruptcy: A Problem in Search of a Resolution, 60 Temp. L. Q. 1, 16 (1987).[4]

[4] Several federal circuit cases from the 1980s addressed the treatment of overloaded PMSIs in bankruptcy, with respect to the anti-avoidance provision in § 522(f). See In re Billings, 838 F.2d at 408 (suggesting that an obligation can "be considered only partly a purchase money debt," and therefore a security interest can still be considered a PMSI with respect to the portion that is not overloaded (emphasis added)); Pristas v. Landaus of Plymouth, Inc. (In re Pristas), 742 F.2d 797, 801 (3d Cir. 1984) (adopting "pro tanto preservation of purchase-money security interests," but invalidating overloaded portions of PMSIs); In re Matthews, 724 F.2d at 801 (holding that when a creditor refinances a purchase money obligation, the PMSI is extinguished).

Some jurisdictions eliminate PMSI status if a lender attempts to secure a loan that exceeds the amount required for the debtor to obtain the collateral. See Marion W. Benfield, Jr., Consumer Provisions in Revised Article 9, 74 Chi-Kent L. Rev. 1255, 1292 (1999). Under this so-called "transformation" rule, "a security interest that was originally a purchase money interest loses that status entirely if the debt is restructured and an additional nonpurchase money advance is made." Id.; see also In re Matthews, 724 F.2d at 801 (applying the transformation rule under California law).

Other jurisdictions, including Kansas, adopt the "dual-status" rule, which preserves an overloaded PMSI "to the extent that it secured the price of the original goods even though the security agreement also secured the price of other items." Meyer, 50 Kan. L. Rev. at 155-56 & n.64; Kan. Stat. Ann. § 84-9-103(f) (2007) ("[A] purchase-money security interest does not lose its status as such, even if: . . . the purchase-money collateral also secures an obligation that is not a purchase-money obligation."); see also Snap-On Tools, Inc. v. Freeman (In re Freeman), 956 F.2d 252, 254-55 (11th Cir. 1992) ("A security interest in collateral is 'purchase money' to the extent that the item secures a debt for the money required to make the purchase. If an item of collateral secures some other type of debt, e.g., antecedent debt, it is not purchase money.").

These principles underscore that the benefits of PMSIs come with certain limitations. When Congress chose to use the state law term PMSI to confine the scope of the hanging paragraph, it adopted these state law limitations as well and made them applicable in bankruptcy.

B. The Kansas Definition of PMSI

The majority identifies the key Kansas statutory language governing whether negative equity may be secured with a PMSI. As the majority states, "[t]he issue is whether paying off negative equity in a trade-in car is part of the 'price' of the new car or part of the 'value given to enable' acquisition of the new car." Maj. Op. at 9. I agree with the majority that under the Kansas U.C.C., these terms include more than just the vehicle's sticker price. But I disagree with the majority's broad interpretation of these terms. In my view, Comment 3 to U.C.C. § 9-103 provides the limiting framework.

Notably absent from the items contained in Comment 3 is a description of negative equity. Instead, the comment lists items which are part of the "price" of a new car or the "value given to enable" the purchase of a new car. Granted, the list is nonexclusive and includes "other similar obligations." But Comment 3 tells us that a PMSI "requires a close nexus between the acquisition of collateral and the secured obligation." Under familiar principles of statutory interpretation, the other items on Comment 3's list shed light on whether negative equity bears the requisite "close nexus" to the acquisition of a new car. See Jarecki v. G.D. Searle & Co., 367 U.S. 303, 307 (1961) ("The maxim noscitur a sociis, that a word is known by the company it keeps, while not an inescapable rule, is often wisely applied where a word is capable of many meanings in order to avoid the giving of unintended breadth to the Acts of Congress."); State v. Urban, 40 Kan. App. 2d 517, 193 P.3d 515, 518 (Kan. Ct. App. 2008) (employing the maxim to interpret a Kansas statute).

The items on Comment 3's list--such as sales tax, finance charges, freight charges, costs of storage in transit, attorney's fees, and collection costs--are all expenses that will be charged uniformly to any potential purchaser of a vehicle who chooses to finance the purchase. Each item is akin to a transaction cost, a cost that adds no particular value for either the buyer or the seller but is instead simply "the cost of using the price mechanism." R.H. Coase, The Nature of the Firm, 4 Economica 386, 390 (1937); see also Black's Law Dictionary 372 (8th ed. 2004) (defining "transaction cost" as "[a] cost connected with a process transaction, such as a broker's commission, the time and effort expended to arrange a deal, or the cost involved in litigating a dispute"); Harold Demsetz, The Cost of Transacting, 82 Q.J. Econ. 33, 35 (1968) ("Transaction cost may be defined as the cost of exchanging ownership titles.").

Negative equity is different. It is not a transaction cost, but a transfer of money for value.[5] Much like a home equity loan used to pay a preexisting credit card debt, the portion of the auto loan attributed to negative equity is not used for the purchase of some new piece of collateral or the costs inherent in the purchase. It is used for another purpose altogether. See AmeriCredit Fin. Servs., Inc. v. Penrod (In re Penrod), 392 B.R. 835, 852 (9th Cir. B.A.P. 2008) ("[N]egative equity is nothing more than a refinancing of the preexisting debt owed on the trade-in. There is no necessary connection between this refinancing and the car's acquisition."). Unlike the other expenses listed in Comment 3, the amount (and even the existence) of negative equity depends upon circumstances completely unrelated to the price of the new vehicle and its financing or the costs associated with transfer of title. Indeed, negative equity differs vastly for each purchaser, depending in large part on the purchaser's past choices.

Thus, although the Fords and their dealer were free to use the new pickup as security for a loan to pay an antecedent debt, that does not mean paying the old debt was part of the "price" of the pickup. Nor does it mean the portion of a loan used to pay off the old debt was a purchase money security interest. As a Texas bankruptcy court stated:

> One may borrow money to buy something (e.g., a new vehicle), and also borrow additional money for some other purpose (e.g., to pay off the balance of a loan for the trade-in vehicle). The part used to buy something is purchase money obligation. The part used for some other purpose is not.

In re Sanders, 377 B.R. 836, 853 (Bankr. W.D. Tex. 2007), rev'd, 403 B.R. 435 (W.D. Tex. 2009). In my view, this is a more consistent interpretation of the Kansas U.C.C. than the majority's. By interpreting the term "price" in section 84-9-103 (a)(2) to mean the actual price of the vehicle plus amounts akin to transaction costs, the limits of PMSIs are easily discernible. In contrast, allowing a creditor to create a PMSI for any money advanced at the same time as a sale enables the creditor to overload the PMSI and defeats the limitations imposed by state law.

---

[5] The Fourth Circuit has suggested that negative equity is, indeed, a transaction cost because it is an expense incurred during the purchase of a new car. See In re Price, 562 F.3d at 627. I respectfully disagree. The Fourth Circuit's approach equates any secured refinancing with a transaction cost. The term cannot bear such a broad definition. See Demsetz, 82 Q.J. Econ. at 35 (noting the problems inherent in a broad definition of "transaction cost"). That a loan for negative equity usually occurs in connection with the purchase of a new vehicle does not render it a transaction cost.

C. The Dual-Status Rule

Because I would hold that Ford Credit does not have a PMSI securing its loan for the Fords' negative equity, I must answer "the question of what to do with that portion of the debt not entitled to purchase-money status." See In re Penrod, 392 B.R. at 838.

As mentioned above, Kansas has adopted the dual-status rule, which preserves a PMSI to the extent it secures a purchase-money obligation and destroys it to the extent the PMSI is overloaded. Kan. Stat. Ann. § 84-9-103(f) (2007); see also Harry, 50 U. Kan. L. Rev. at 1121-22 (noting that, unlike the standard version of Article 9, the Kansas version expressly adopted the dual-status rule for all transactions, including consumer transactions); see also In re Gibson, 16 B.R. 257, 268-69 (Bankr. D. Kan. 1981) (applying Kansas law and adopting the dual-status rule in the consumer context).[6] Consistent with the Butner principle, I would hold that the Kansas dual-status rule applies: part of Ford Credit's claim is a PMSI protected from cram down, and part is merely a standard secured claim which may be subject to cram down.

This does not resolve the case, however. Another question remains, namely how to adjust Ford Credit's claims to account for payments the Fords made on their car loan before entering bankruptcy. Should the payments be applied first to the negative equity portion of the loan, or should they be applied first to the PMSI portion of the loan? Kansas law states that payments must be applied "[i]n accordance with any reasonable method of application to which the parties agree." Kan. Stat. Ann. § 84-9-103(e)(1) (2007). In the absence of such an agreement, Kansas law requires courts to consider "any intention of the obligor manifested at or before the time of payment." Id. § 84-9-103(e)(2). Finally, if no such intent was manifested, payments go first to the PMSI, then to the non-PMSI. See id. § 84-9-103(e)(3); In re Kellerman, 377 B.R. 302, 304 (Bankr. D. Kan. 2007). I would remand this case, instructing the bankruptcy court to apply these rules to determine the amount of Ford Credit's claims.

II. Other Approaches

I recognize my conclusion is at odds with the majority's reasoning, and with the reasoning of a number of other courts that have addressed the treatment of negative equity under the hanging paragraph. These courts have made numerous arguments, and several common themes have emerged.

Some courts--including the majority--conclude that the financing of negative equity is part of a "package deal" and as such should be protected by the same PMSI that covers the sale price of a new vehicle. See, e.g., In re Graupner, 537 F.3d at 1302. Others utilize the in pari materia canon (i.e., the canon that encourages courts to construe statutes together), holding that the term "price" in the U.C.C. includes negative equity, because this is how other laws define the term "price." See, e.g., id. at 1301. Finally, some courts rely on the legislative

[6] Some courts have held that regardless of state law, federal policy requires the dual-status approach in the context of the hanging paragraph. See In re Penrod, 392 B.R. at 859 ("[W]e are persuaded that the Dual Status Rule should be applied as the federal rule." (footnote omitted)); see also In re Hargrove, 400 B.R. 616, 620 (Bankr. M.D. Tenn. 2008) (noting that the dual-status rule is "consistent with the purpose of" the hanging paragraph). But selectively applying the Butner principle, as these cases do, defeats its purpose.

history of the hanging paragraph to conclude Congress intended negative equity to be protected from cram down. See, e.g., In re Price, 562 F.3d at 628.

Though the majority does not make all of these arguments, I take this opportunity to explain why I find them unpersuasive.

A. The "Package Deal" Approach

One common line of reasoning holds that negative equity is part of a "package deal" and cannot be separated from the remainder of the PMSI. The In re Graupner court, for example, viewed the financing of negative equity as "part of the same transaction" as the purchase of the new vehicle such that it was "properly regarded as a 'package deal.'" 537 F.3d at 1302. To the Eleventh Circuit, negative equity was an "integral part" of the purchase and was "inextricably intertwined" with the transaction. Id.; see also In re Price, 562 F.3d at 625 ("All of the Prices' debt . . . was incurred at the same time, in the same contract, and for the same purpose: acquiring the new car."). The majority adopts this approach, concluding that "the trade-in exchange is essentially a single transaction." Maj. Op. at 11.

The intuitive difficulty with this position is that vehicle purchasers--even those that buy on credit--are not required to purchase the new vehicle by trading in an old one. Whether doing so is necessary or even desirable depends on their individual circumstances. Perhaps in this case it is true that the Fords could not have purchased their new pickup without trading in their old one. And perhaps financing the negative equity was "integral" to the Fords completing their purchase, because it was inconvenient or impossible for them to complete the purchase any other way.

The definition of PMSI, however, does not encompass any and every expense that might enable a particular purchaser to complete the purchase in the most convenient manner. If the Fords were unable to drive themselves to the dealership, we would not consider the cost of a taxi as part of the price of the new truck, even if the dealer were willing to pay for it and fold it into the sales contract. If the Fords did not qualify for a car loan because their resources were strained by too much credit card debt at high interest rates, they could not fold those debts into the PMSI for a new car even if the attendant lower interest rate solved their credit problem and enabled them to obtain the car loan.

Allowing a creditor to transform antecedent debt into a PMSI by refinancing the debt into a new contract amount that includes the purchase price of new collateral would convert the concept of "purchase money" from a defined term to one that can be expanded at the will of the parties. See In re Conyers, 379 B.R. 576, 582 (Bankr. M.D.N.C. 2007) ("Allowing the Debtor to rollover negative equity into the new loan was simply an accommodation. It was an arrangement made as a favor to another."); In re Westfall, 365 B.R. 755, 762 (Bankr. N.D. Ohio 2007) (providing the extreme example of a 'debtor [who] would not have made it to the dealer's lot were it not for the emergency appendectomy, [making] payment of the doctor's outstanding fee . . . an enabling expense"), rev'd in part, 376 B.R. 210.

Congress confined the hanging paragraph to PMSIs, and I cannot conclude the hanging paragraph protects any and every loan secured by an automobile.

B. The In Pari Materia Argument

Another approach is to apply the in pari materia doctrine. Courts employing this argument look to other statutes that use the term "price"--frequently, state motor vehicle financing statutes--and, when these other statutes explicitly include negative equity within the definition of price, interpret the U.C.C. in pari materia. See, e.g. In re Graupner, 537 F.3d at 1301 (finding support in the definition of "cash sale price" in Georgia's Motor Vehicle Sales Financing Act); Gen. Motors Acceptance Corp. v. Peaslee, 373 B.R. 252, 260 (W.D.N.Y. 2007) (analyzing the definition of "cash sale price" in New York's Motor Vehicle Retail Installment Sales Act).

But at least some other courts have considered this a dubious application of the in pari materia doctrine, as the vehicle financing statutes are concerned more with disclosure than regulation and therefore do not cover the same subject matter. For example, the Second Circuit disapproved of a bankruptcy court's reliance on the New York Motor Vehicle Retail Installment Sales Act in interpreting the U.C.C.'s definition of "price." Peaslee v. GMAC, LLC (In re Peaslee), 547 F.3d 177, 186 (2d Cir. 2008) ("But it is not manifest that 'price' in N.Y. U.C.C. § 9-103(a)(2), or 'expense' in Comment 3 to that provision, should be given the same meaning as 'cash sale price' in the MVRISA."). The Second Circuit noted the New York motor vehicle statute was aimed primarily at disclosure and served different purposes from the U.C.C., making an in pari materia interpretation of the term "price" suspect. Id.

I agree with the Second Circuit insofar as it views the in pari materia doctrine as inapplicable. Indeed, here the use of the in pari materia doctrine is even less helpful because the parties have pointed to no other Kansas statute defining the term "price." Ford Credit points mainly to the federal Truth in Lending Act (TILA), 15 U.S.C. § 1601 et seq.--or, more specifically, to the Federal Reserve Board's interpretation of that Act in Regulation Z, which requires disclosure of negative equity as part of the total sale price of an automobile. See 12 C.F.R. § 226.18(b)(2) & (j). But the manner in which a federal agency has interpreted the term "price" in a federal statute sheds little light on what the Kansas legislature meant when it employed the term in its version of the U.C.C. But see GMAC v. Horne, 390 B.R. 191, 202-03 (E.D. Va. 2008) (adopting TILA's definition of "total sales price" as the meaning of "price" under the Virginia U.C.C.).

I acknowledge that in its Uniform Consumer Credit Code, the Kansas legislature referred to both TILA and Regulation Z when it empowered an administrator to "adopt rules and regulations necessary to carry out the provisions and terms of the uniform consumer credit code which are consistent with or no less restrictive than the truth-in-lending act . . . and regulation Z." Kan. Stat. Ann. § 16a-6-117 (2007). Even so, there is no reason to believe that in doing so, the Kansas legislature meant to suggest the terms in its other statutes should now be interpreted as identical to an agency interpretation of a federal disclosure law. The Uniform Consumer Credit Code does not even use the word "price," and I fail to see how the in pari materia canon can be helpful in determining what the legislature meant by "price" in Kan. Stat. Ann. § 84-9-103 (2007).

Additionally, even if I were to apply the in pari materia doctrine, it does not suggest negative equity is part of the "price" of a new vehicle. Under Kansas tax law, the term "sales or selling price" does not include "the amount equal to the allowance given for the trade-in of property." Kan. Stat. Ann. § 79-3602(ll)(3)(D)

(2007). Here, the "allowance given for the trade-in of property" was the $7,200 of negative equity in the Fords' old truck. Kansas tax law excludes this amount from the sale price of the Fords' new truck, and the in pari materia doctrine would therefore suggest the negative equity was not part of the sale price under the Kansas U.C.C. I doubt Kansas tax law--like other states' motor vehicle financing statutes--tells us anything about the Kansas U.C.C. But a comparison to Kansas tax law illustrates that the in pari materia doctrine, even if applicable, does not offer much guidance in this case.

C. Legislative History

Finally, some courts examine the legislative history of the hanging paragraph and, despite its inconsistencies, find that it unambiguously supports the conclusion that negative equity is included in the state law definition of PMSI. See, e.g., In re Price, 562 F.3d at 628; In re Graupner, 537 F.3d at 1303 & n.5. This is problematic for two reasons.

First, legislative history is "often murky, ambiguous, and contradictory," and we should resort to it only when a statute's plain language is unclear. See United States v. Hinckley, 550 F.3d 926, 947 (10th Cir. 2008) (Gorsuch, J., concurring) (quoting Exxon Mobil Corp. v. Allapattah Servs., Inc., 545 U.S. 546, 568 (2005)), cert. denied, 129 S. Ct. 2383 (2009). Indeed, the Supreme Court has "repeatedly held[that] the authoritative statement is the statutory text, not the legislative history or any other extrinsic material." Exxon Mobil Corp., 545 U.S. at 568. Here, the statutory language is far from ambiguous. It expressly states that only PMSIs are protected from cram down in bankruptcy. Whether this state law term of art is itself ambiguous is another story. Case law (including this very opinion) shows that courts can reasonably disagree on the meaning of the term under various state laws. But the plain language of the hanging paragraph is clear, making resort to its legislative history unnecessary and potentially misleading.

Second, the legislative history of the hanging paragraph provides no pat answer to whether negative equity is protected from cram down. As Ford Credit explains in its brief, one legislative proposal predating the enactment of the hanging paragraph was narrow and protected from cram down only the "unpaid balance of the purchase price of the personal property." H.R. Rep. No. 105-794, at 25 (1998) (Conf. Rep.) (emphasis added). This language, if enacted, arguably would not have protected amounts such as title fees, taxes, or negative equity. But Ford Credit dismisses this language and emphasizes a competing version of the bill, which was broader and would have protected "an allowed claim that is secured under applicable non-bankruptcy law." S. Rep. No. 105-253, at 7 (1998) (emphasis added). This language seems to encompass negative equity, which is part of a lender's secured claim.

Congress ultimately settled on protecting only purchase money security interests from cram down. See 11 U.S.C. § This might have reflected a Congressional compromise to protect certain fees that are properly considered part of a purchase-money loan--i.e., fees akin to transaction costs--and not to protect negative equity. But we are not privy to Congress's internal deliberations, and this is why we ordinarily must confine our inquiry to the language of statutes as enacted. See Exxon Mobil Corp., 545 U.S. at 568.

Ford Credit argues that the legislative history supports their position and implies that Congress intended to broadly protect car lenders, regardless of how loan proceeds are used. Other courts agree with this reading, assuming that the "architects of the hanging paragraph intended only good things for car lenders and other lienholders." In re Graupner, 537 F.3d at 1303 (internal alterations and quotation marks omitted) (quoting AmeriCredit Fin. Servs. v. Long (In re Long), 519 F.3d 288, 294 (6th Cir. 2008)). These courts fail to recognize, however, that Congress must reconcile many competing interests when drafting legislation. Presuming Congress resolved all policy questions in favor of one constituency is simplistic and likely inaccurate. See Circuit City Stores, Inc. v. Adams, 532 U.S. 105, 120 (2001) ("We ought not attribute to Congress an official purpose based on the motives of a particular group that lobbied for or against a certain proposal-- even assuming the precise intent of the group can be determined, a point doubtful both as a general rule and in the instant case. It is for the Congress, not the courts, to consult political forces and then decide how best to resolve conflicts in the course of writing the objective embodiments of law we know as statutes.").

Congress specifically chose to use the term "purchase money security interest" instead of something broader. I believe the most prudent practice is to assume Congress meant what it said.

III. Conclusion

I conclude that negative equity is neither "all or part of the price of" a new car, nor "value given to enable the debtor to acquire rights in or the use of" a new car. Thus, I would hold that the Fords' negative equity is not part of Ford Credit's PMSI under Kansas law, and it is therefore not protected from bifurcation and cram down under the hanging paragraph. Under the dual-status rule, only the purchase price of the Fords' new car and related fees that are akin to transaction costs are secured by a PMSI. Though I recognize my view is at odds with the conclusions of several other courts, including the Fourth and Eleventh Circuits, I believe my interpretation comports more closely with the meaning of purchase money security interest under the Kansas U.C.C. than does the opposing view.

Notes and Questions

1. For a contrary case, see Americredit Financial Services, Inc. v. Penrod (In re Penrod), 611 F.3d 1158 (9th Cir. 2010). In Penrod, the debtor was allowed to bifurcate the secured claim of the creditor. In effect, the court applied the "transformation rule." According to this rule, one drop of non-purchase money obligation "transforms" a loan largely used for acquisition into a non-purchase money loan as to which the hanging paragraph does not apply. A different rule in light of impurity is "dual status." The loan is treated as a purchase money security interest to the extent of the purchase money obligation and non-purchase money as to the balance. How would this work in context of the hanging paragraph. Suppose D has borrowed $40 to acquire a vehicle, has paid $20 down and has agreed that the new car is security for $50 of debt with regard to the old car. Suppose further that D's 910 vehicle is worth $60. What kind of plan could D write?

2. Which of these is part of the purchase money aspect of a car loan?

(a) SP is authorized to buy insurance if D does not. Upon D's default, SP buys the insurance and adds the premiums to its secured claim. In re Townsend, 387 B.R. 817 (Bankr. D. Kan. 2008) (yes).

(b) D bought a service contract along with the car, and SP includes the service payments in the secured claim. In re Jernigan, 2008 Bankr. LEXIS 1159 (Bankr. E.D.N.C., March 31, 2008) (yes).

IN RE SANCHEZ

384 B.R. 574 (Bankr. D. Ore. 2008)

RADCLIFFE, J.

This matter comes before the court on creditor World Famous Auto's (WFA) objection to confirmation of the Debtors' Chapter 13 plan. The matter has been briefed and is ripe for decision.

The facts are largely undisputed. Debtors Paul and Deborah Sanchez filed their Chapter 13 petition, herein, on July 30, 2007. WFA is secured in a 2000 Chevrolet pickup. Debtors concede WFA's claim is a purchase money "910" claim entitled to protection under 11 U.S.C. § 1325(a)'s "hanging paragraph." Debtors' Amended plan dated July 30, 2007 proposes that Debtors make monthly payments of $288 to the trustee, along with net tax refunds received during the life of the plan. Among other claims, the trustee is to pay WFA's claim in full from these payments. Adequate protection payments to WFA are proposed at $50 monthly until attorney's fees are paid in full. Thereafter, WFA is to receive monthly payments of $250. Attorney's fees are disclosed as $3,000 with $2,863 to be paid through the plan "concurrently with adequate protection payments to secured payments [sic]." WFA objects that the plan's treatment does not comply with § 1325(a)(5)(B)(iii).

Discussion:

The Bankruptcy Abuse Prevention and Consumer Protection Act of 2005 (BAPCPA), through several provisions in Chapter 13 of the Bankruptcy Code, "adequate protection" requirements for certain types of secured debt. It also added a provision dictating how periodic payments on secured debt are to paid. The interplay between these new provisions is at issue here.

One of the provisions,[1] § 1326(a)(1)(C), protects purchase-money lenders secured in personal property.[2] Unless the court orders otherwise, it requires a

---

[1] Section 1326(a)(1)(C) provides:

> Unless the court orders otherwise, the debtor shall commence making payments not later than 30 days after the date of the filing of the plan or the order for relief, whichever is earlier, in the amount--
>
> that provides adequate protection directly to a creditor holding an allowed claim secured by personal property to the extent the claim is attributable to the purchase of such property by the debtor for that portion of the obligation that becomes due after the order for relief, reducing the payments under subparagraph (A) by the amount so paid and providing the trustee with evidence of such payment, including the amount and date of payment.

This District requires pre-confirmation payments under this section to be made through the trustee. LBR 3015-1.B.11. The trustee only disburses once the creditor has filed a proof of claim. Unless the plan provides otherwise, the amount of the payment is set out in the plan. Id.. The trustee applies these pre-confirmation payments to the creditor's allowed claim. Id.; see also, plan P 2(b)(3).

[2] Under § 1325(a) (5), there are three ways a debtor may treat a secured claim and gain confirmation. The creditor can accept the proposed treatment, § 1325(a)(5)(A); the debtor can surrender the collateral, § 1325(a)(5)(C); or the debtor may retain the collateral provided the creditor retains its lien until the earlier of payment of the entire underlying debt or entry of the debtor's discharge, § 1325(a)(5)(B)(i), and the value as of the plan's effective date, of property to

debtor to begin making adequate protection payments 30 days after the order for relief. The other provision, § 1325(a)(5)(B)(iii), relates to payments on secured claims when the debtor proposes to retain the collateral. It provides as follows:

> With respect to each allowed secured claim provided for by the plan--
> if--
> (I) property to be distributed pursuant to this subsection is in the form of periodic payments, such payments shall be in equal monthly amounts; and
> (II) the holder of the claim is secured by personal property, the amount of such payments shall not be less than an amount sufficient to provide to the holder of such claim adequate protection during the period of the plan.

One court has explained the purpose behind the statute as follows:

> Prior to BAPCPA, it was not uncommon for some Chapter 13 plans to provide for backloaded payments, such as balloon payments. Another form of backloading involved graduated or step-up payment plans, where the payments started out smaller and increased over time. Secured creditors, particularly those secured by a vehicle, viewed this as unfair, exposing them to undue risk in light of the constant depreciation of their collateral.
>
> Other plans, filed by debtors whose employment is seasonal, provided for reduced payments or no payments at all during certain months of the year, or called for payments to be made quarterly or semi-annually, rather than monthly, based upon the peculiarities of the debtor's income stream. Secured creditors had similar complaints with those plans.
>
> In response to those creditor concerns, Congress enacted the equal payment provision and a companion provision extending the concept of adequate protection, formerly a preconfirmation requirement, to postconfirmation plan payments. 11 U.S.C. § 1325(a)(5)(B)(iii)(II). The equal payment provision prevents debtors from backloading payments to secured creditors or paying them other than on a monthly basis.

In re Erwin, 376 B.R. 897, 901 (Bankr. C. D. Ill. 2007)

Under § 1325(a)(5)(B)(iii)(I) (subsection (I)), when a debtor proposes to pay a secured claim in "periodic payments,"[3] those payments must be in equal monthly amounts. If the debt is secured by personal property, § 1325(a)(5)(B)(iii)(II) (subsection (II))[4] that the periodic payments be sufficient to adequately protect the creditor "during the period of the plan." The issue here is whether the debtors' plan meets the "equal monthly payments" contemplated by § 1325(a)(5)(B)(iii).

There is a paucity of caselaw on this subject. In the few cases that have been reported, the courts are split. The slight majority view appears to side with Debtors' position that "adequate protection payments" may continue post-

---

be distributed under the plan is not less than the claim's allowed amount. § 1325(a)(5)(B)(ii). New § 1325(a)(5)(B)(iii) imposes additional requirements when periodic payments of secured claims are proposed.

[3] The term "periodic payments" is nowhere defined in the Bankruptcy Code. Here, the parties do not dispute that Debtors are attempting to pay WFA through periodic payments.

[4] The question of whether or not subsection (I) applies to creditors secured by real property is beyond the scope of this opinion. Subsection (II) does not apply to creditors secured by real property. Subsection (II) does, however, apply to all creditors secured by personal property, as distinguished from § 1326(a)(1)(C), which only applies to creditors with purchase-money security interests.

confirmation in one amount, with "equal monthly payments" replacing them at a higher amount at some later time during the plan. Compare, In re Hill, 2007 Bankr. LEXIS 502, 2007 WL 499622 (Bankr. M.D.N.C. 2007); In re DeSardi, 340 B.R. 790 (Bankr. S. D. Tex. 2006); In re Erwin, 376 B.R. 897 (Bankr. C.D. Ill. 2007), with, In re Denton, 370 BR 441 (Bankr. S.D. Ga. 2007).

The majority view allows room, in Chapter 13 plans, to pay debtors' attorneys on an expedited basis. While this court agrees that this is a salutary goal, this court cannot join in the statutory interpretations employed to reach this result.[5]

Each of the courts subscribing to the majority view reach the same result by different but strained interpretations of the statute. The DeSardi court views subsection (II)'s adequate protection requirement to be different from subsection (I)'s equal monthly payment requirement. Here, however, interpreting the statute's plain meaning and in context, it is clear that the term "such payments" appearing in both subsections applies to the periodic payments that must be made "during the period of the plan" and that subsections (I) and (II) are linked when the collateral is personal property.

DeSardi also rests largely on its interpretation of § 1326(b)(1). That section provides that "[b]efore or at the time of each payment to creditors under the plan, there shall be paid any unpaid claim of the kind specified in section 507(a)(2) . . . ."[6] DeSardi interprets this language to require full payment of attorney's fees (and other administrative expenses) before "equal monthly payments" to secured creditors under subsection (I) may begin. DeSardi, supra at 808. No such preference, however, may be found in this District, as administrative claimants may insist only on concurrent payments with, rather than full payment before, non-administrative claims. See, In re Ryan, 228 B.R. 746 (Bankr. D. Or. 1999) (interpreting analogous Chapter 12 provisions). As such, § 1326(b)(1) may be harmonized with § 1325(a)(5)(B)(iii).

The Hill court recognized that subsections (I) and (II) are linked when the collateral is personal property. The court then appears to undercut this link by holding the term "during the period of the plan" in subsection (II) modifies "adequate protection" not "such [periodic] payments" and thus "cannot be read to dictate any specific time for the equal monthly payments to begin." Hill, supra 2007 Bankr. LEXIS 502, 2007 WL 499622 at *6. In practical terms, this interpretation de-links subsections (I) and (II). Under subsection (II) adequate protection is provided only by subsection (I)'s equal monthly payments. Subsection (II) then answers when this protection must be provided, by requiring it "during the period of the plan." The statute does not provide for equal monthly payments "during part of the period of the plan" or "during some of the period of the plan." This court construes "during the period of the plan" to mean equal monthly payments must commence with confirmation and last until the secured claim is paid.[7]

---

[5] United States v. Ron Pair Enterprises, Inc., 489 U.S. 235, 241 (1989) ("where. . . the statue's language is plain, the sole function of the courts is to enforce it according to its terms" (internal quotation omitted)).

[6] Section 507(a)(2) gives administrative expense priority to those claims described in § 503(b), including a Chapter 13 debtor's attorney's fees. See, § 503(b)(2) (incorporating § 330(a)(4)(B)).

[7] This court agrees that monthly payments need not be made for the plan's entire duration. Debtor may propose to pay secured claims before their plan ends. Hill, supra 2007 Bankr. LEXIS 502, 2007 WL 499622 at *6. This conclusion is buttressed by new § 1325(a)(5)(B)(i)(I) which

Curiously, after explaining the purpose behind the statute, the Erwin court supra, reaches the same result as the majority. There debtors' plan proposed level payments into the plan from which pro rata distribution would go to secured creditors as determined by the trustee. Secured creditors were receiving pre-confirmation adequate protection payments paid by the trustee. The plan called for payment of the debtor's attorney's fees by the trustee. A local standing order provided for expedited payment of the fees, (i.e. the lesser of 50% of the funds available for distribution or $250, in any given month), which meant, that as a practical matter, the payments to secured creditors would be at one level while attorney's fees were being concurrently paid, then increased once the fees were paid in full. The court distinguished between the debtor's proposals in their plan and the way the plan was actually administered by the trustee, as determined by its standing order and § 1326(b)(1). The court held that debtors' level payments into the plan and the proposed pro rata distribution to secured creditors complied with subsection (I)'s "equal monthly payment" requirement; Erwin, supra at 902-3. It further held the trustee was not bound by subsection (I) in administering the plan. Id. at 902. Finally, it held the increase in payments, once attorney's fees were paid, was not due to debtors' plan, but rather the operation of § 1326(b)(1) and the court's standing order. Id. at 902-903.

Erwin's rationale is problematic for several reasons. Subsection (I) is part of § 1325(a)(5), which expressly pertains to "allowed secured claims provided for by the plan." Thus, subsection (I) refers to distributions by the trustee to creditors under the plan, not the debtor's payments into the plan. In re Lemieux, 347 B.R. 460, 465 (Bankr. D. Mass. 2006). Further, in sidestepping the "equal payment" statute, Erwin reposits too much discretion in the trustee in administration of the plan. Section § 1326(a)(2) requires the trustee to retain plan payments until confirmation and then upon confirmation distribute those payments in "accordance with the plan." Pursuant to § 1326(c), except as otherwise provided in the plan or the order confirming the plan, the trustee is required to make payments to creditors "under the plan." These provisions indicate that a plan's specific provisions trump the trustee's discretion in making payments to creditors.

In contrast, Denton holds that "periodic payments" under subsection (I) is not a defined term, but rather refers to all regularly recurring post-confirmation payments on an allowed secured claim, such that they all must be equal. Id. at 445 ("The word 'periodic' simply describes payments that recur at regular intervals."). Thus, pre-confirmation adequate protection payments under § 1326(a)(1)(C) may not be extended beyond confirmation when the monthly amount is less than the amount of payment on the allowed secured claim under the plan. This cuts through the majority courts' distinction between post-confirmation "adequate protection" and "equal monthly" payments. Under subsection (I) the periodic payments are "property to be distributed pursuant to this subsection." (emphasis added). "This subsection" refers to § 1325(a)(5)(B)(ii) which requires that "the value, as of the effective date of the plan, of property to be distributed under the plan on account of such claim," be not less than the allowed amount of the secured claim. (emphasis added). Denton recognizes that post-confirmation, adequate protection payments would be "property . . .

allows the creditor to retain its lien until the earlier of the time the entire debt is paid in full (e.g. a "910" or oversecured claim) or when discharge is granted.

distributed under the plan on account of the . . . [secured] claim," and not some special breed of payment divorced from the claim.[8] Denton's holding is further buttressed by subsection (II)'s "during the period of the plan" language, which as discussed above, means that equal monthly payments must start with the first payment after confirmation and continue until the secured claim is paid. This court agrees with the minority view as expressed by the court in Denton.

Conclusion:

Debtors' plan does not comply with § 1325(a)(5)(B)(iii)'s "equal monthly payment" requirement.[9] Confirmation must be denied. Debtors will be given 28 days to file an amended plan or a motion to convert. Absent such timely filing, this case will be dismissed without further notice or hearing.

4. Adequate Protection

David Gray Carlson, Cars and Homes in Chapter 13 Under the 2005 Bankruptcy Amendments, 15 AM. BANKR. INST. L. REV. 300, 302-04 (2006).

In 2005, Congress enacted Bankruptcy Abuse Prevention and Consumer Protection Act (BAPCPA), which thoroughly amends the Bankruptcy Code, as it pertains to individuals filing for bankruptcy. These amendments substantially benefit purchase money secured parties claiming personal property as collateral--that is to say, car lenders.

In rescuing car lenders from certain effects of cram down, Congress did not take the simple expedient of removing cars from the cram down table. Instead of equating car loans with home mortgages, Congress chose to reform the concepts of adequate protection and cram down, as these apply to purchase money car lenders.

Adequate protection can be defined as protection against the depreciating value of collateral prior to the confirmation of a reorganization plan. Cram down constitutes a rewriting of the security agreement, over the opposition of the car lender, modifying the schedule of payments, the amounts paid, and the interest rate.

Adequate protection and cram down, as applied to cars, now have a very intricate interrelation, due to the following eight principles. The first four are inherited from the pre-BAPCPA law:

(1) Adequate protection of collateral refers to protection against

---

[8] There is no dispute that "adequate protection" payments are credited against the secured claim.

[9] While this court's holding may appear to undercut the speed at which a Chapter 13 debtor's attorney's fees may be paid, this isn't necessarily so. The type of stepped payments Debtors propose are not per se, non-confirmable. A secured creditor may always accept its proposed treatment under § 1325(a)(5)(A). If the creditor objects to stepped payments, debtors are not precluded from making room for payment of attorney's fees by modifying the plan to amortize the secured claim at a lower (but equal) monthly payment over a longer period. All that is required under § 1325(a)(5)(B)(iii) is that the proposed equal monthly payments pay the secured claim and be sufficient to adequately protect the creditor's interest. Here, while WFA has not contested that $50 per month adequately protects its interest, that amount is insufficient to amortize its claim, even over the maximum 60 months permitted.

depreciating value of the collateral only.[1] It does not include the right to interest compensation.[2]

(2) Unlike adequate protection payments, cram down payments must include interest compensation.[3]

(3) The right to adequate protection terminates upon plan confirmation. Thereafter, the plan governs the right of the secured party.[4] It must provide cram down payments or reinstatement of security agreements.

(4) Arguably, cram down payments are subordinated to the claims of administrative creditors,[5] including the debtor's bankruptcy attorney.[6] The adequate protection right, however, is not so subordinated.[7]

Three additional principles from BAPCPA must now be added to the mix:

(5) Cram down payments are no longer necessarily tied to the value of the car. Rather, with respect to cars purchased within 910 days of bankruptcy ("910 vehicles"), the value of the car is deemed to be the amount the debtor owes the car lender.[8] Nevertheless, adequate protection is tied to the value of the car in all cases.

(6) Cram down payments must now be in equal installments.[9] This rule does not apply to the right of adequate protection. Nor does it apply to reinstatement and cure of security agreements.

(7) Cram down payments may never be less than the amount of depreciation of the collateral.[10]

In addition, there is an eighth principle which BAPCPA address only obliquely. According to this seventh principle:

(8) All payments to the creditor must (or need not) be made through the chapter 13 trustee. The debtor may not (or can) pay the creditors directly.

Prior to 2005, courts were deeply divided over whether payments had to be made through the standing chapter 13 trustee. Because BAPCPA is vague as to the eighth principle, courts will continue to be divided as to the necessity of payment via the chapter 13 trustee.

Notes and Questions

1. BAPCPA adds § 1326(a)(1)(C) to the Bankruptcy Code. This provision requires chapter 13 debtors (within 30 days of filing a plan) to make payments

that provides adequate protection directly to a creditor holding an allowed claim

---

[1] 11 U.S.C. §361(1) & (2).

[2] See generally United Sav. Ass'n of Tex v. Tuimbers of Inwood Forest Assocs, 484 U.S. 365 (1988) (intepreting the meaning of adequate protection [does not include the right to accrued interest]).

[3] 11 U.S.C. §1325(a)(5)(B)(ii).

[4] 11 U.S.C. §1327(a).

[5] 11 U.S.C. §1326(b) (providing for payments which occur prio to--or at least simultaneously--with any payment to creditors).

[6] 11 U.S.C. § 330(a)(4)(B) (allowing for reasonable compensation to debtor's attorney), 503(b)(2). Courts disagreed on the proposition in the text, however. See infra text accompanying notes 148-80.

[7] See infra text accompanying notes 148-80.

[8] 11 U.S.C. § 1325(a) (last sentence).

[9] 11 U.S.C. §1325(a)(5)(iii)(I).

[10] 11 U.S.C. §1325(a)(5)(iii)(II).

> secured by personal property to the extent that the claim is attributable to the purchase of such property by the debtor for that portion of the obligation that becomes due after the order for relief, reducing the payments under subparagraph (A) by the amount so paid and providing the trustee with evidence of such payment, including the amount and date of payment.

There are several notable points about this provision. First, it requires payment directly to the secured creditor. Yet as we have seen, some courts require payments to be made through the chapter 13 trustee.

Second, this provision applies only to "allowed claims." An allowed claim is one as to which a proof of claim is filed. Bankruptcy Code § 502(a). So, by implication, if the secured creditor does not file a proof of claim, the provision does not apply.

Third, the claim must be "attributable to the purchase of such property by the debtor for that portion of the obligation that becomes due after the order for relief." Presumably, this means purchase money debt only. Yet the language suggests only a portion of the purchase money claim is entitled to adequate protection--the portion that becomes due after the bankruptcy petition is filed. Bankruptcy has the effect of accelerating all installment payments. See Bankruptcy Code § 502(b). But if D has missed some installments prior to bankruptcy, these amounts must somehow be excluded from the adequate protection entitlement. This is odd, in that adequate protection is tied to depreciation of the collateral. It is not clear what Congress intended here.

Fourth, the provision only applies to personal property collateral. It does not apply to real property mortgages, for example.

5. Home Mortgages

NOBELMAN v AMERICAN SAVINGS BANK

508 U.S. 324 (1992)

THOMAS, J.

This case focuses on the interplay between two provisions of the Bankruptcy Code. The question is whether § 1322(b)(2) prohibits a Chapter 13 debtor from relying on § 506(a) to reduce an undersecured homestead mortgage to the fair market value of the mortgaged residence. We conclude that it does and therefore affirm the judgment of the Court of Appeals.

I

In 1984, respondent American Savings Bank loaned petitioners Leonard and Harriet Nobelman $68,250 for the purchase of their principal residence, a condominium in Dallas, Texas. In exchange, petitioners executed an adjustable rate note payable to the bank and secured by a deed of trust on the residence. In 1990, after falling behind in their mortgage payments, petitioners sought relief under Chapter 13 of the Bankruptcy Code. The bank filed a proof of claim with the Bankruptcy Court for $71,335 in principal, interest, and fees owed on the note. Petitioners' modified Chapter 13 plan valued the residence at a mere $23,500-an uncontroverted valuation-and proposed to make payments pursuant to the mortgage contract only up to that amount (plus prepetition arrearages). Relying on § 506(a) of the Bankruptcy Code, petitioners proposed to treat the remainder of the bank's claim as unsecured. Under the plan, unsecured creditors would receive nothing.

The bank and the Chapter 13 trustee, also a respondent here, objected to petitioners' plan. They argued that the proposed bifurcation of the bank's claim into a secured claim for $23,500 and an effectively worthless unsecured claim modified the bank's rights as a homestead mortgagee, in violation of 11 U.S.C. §

1322(b)(2). The Bankruptcy Court agreed with respondents and denied confirmation of the plan. The District Court affirmed, In re Nobelman, 129 B.R. 98 (ND Tex. 1991), as did the Court of Appeals, 968 F.2d 483 (CA5 1992). We granted certiorari to resolve a conflict among the Courts of Appeals.[1] 506 U.S. 1020 (1992).

II

Under Chapter 13 of the Bankruptcy Code, individual debtors may obtain adjustment of their indebtedness through a flexible repayment plan approved by a bankruptcy court. Section 1322 sets forth the elements of a confirmable Chapter 13 plan. The plan must provide, inter alia, for the submission of a portion of the debtor's future earnings and income to the control of a trustee and for supervised payments to creditors over a period not exceeding five years. See 11 U.S.C. §§ 1322(a)(1) and 1322(c). Section 1322(b)(2), the provision at issue here, allows modification of the rights of both secured and unsecured creditors, subject to special protection for creditors whose claims are secured only by a lien on the debtor's home. It provides that the plan may

> "modify the rights of holders of secured claims, other than a claim secured only by a security interest in real property that is the debtor's principal residence, or of holders of unsecured claims, or leave unaffected the rights of holders of any class of claims." 11 U.S.C. § 1322 (b)(2) (emphasis added).

The parties agree that the "other than" exception in § 1322(b)(2) proscribes modification of the rights of a homestead mortgagee. Petitioners maintain, however, that their Chapter 13 plan proposes no such modification. They argue that the protection of § 1322(b)(2) applies only to the extent the mortgagee holds a "secured claim" in the debtor's residence and that we must look first to § 506(a) to determine the value of the mortgagee's "secured claim." Section 506(a) provides that an allowed claim secured by a lien on the debtor's property "is a secured claim to the extent of the value of [the] property"; to the extent the claim exceeds the value of the property, it "is an unsecured claim."[2] Petitioners contend that the valuation provided for in § 506(a) operates automatically to adjust downward the amount of a lender's undersecured home mortgage before any disposition proposed in the debtor's Chapter 13 plan. Under this view, the bank is the holder of a "secured claim" only in the amount of $23,500-the value of the collateral property. Because the plan proposes to make $23,500 worth of payments pursuant to the monthly payment terms of the mortgage contract, petitioners argue, the plan effects no alteration of the bank's rights as the holder of that claim. Section 1322(b)(2), they assert, allows unconditional modification of the bank's leftover "unsecured claim."

This interpretation fails to take adequate account of § 1322(b)(2)'s focus on "rights." That provision does not state that a plan may modify "claims" or that

---

[1] Four Circuits have held that § 1322(b)(2) allows bifurcation of undersecured homestead mortgages. In re Bellamy, 962 F.2d 176 (CA2 1992); In re Hart, 923 F.2d 1410 (CA10 1991); Wilson v. Commonwealth Mortgage Corp., 895 F.2d 123 (CA3 1990); In re Hougland, 886 F.2d 1182 (CA9 1989).

[2] As a general provision under Chapter 5 of the Bankruptcy Code, § 506(a) applies in an individual bankruptcy case under Chapter 13. See 11 U.S.C. § 103 (a).

the plan may not modify "a claim secured only by" a home mortgage. Rather, it focuses on the modification of the "rights of holders" of such claims. By virtue of its mortgage contract with petitioners, the bank is indisputably the holder of a claim secured by a lien on petitioners' home. Petitioners were correct in looking to § 506(a) for a judicial valuation of the collateral to determine the status of the bank's secured claim. It was permissible for petitioners to seek a valuation in proposing their Chapter 13 plan, since § 506(a) states that "such value shall be determined . . . in conjunction with any hearing . . . on a plan affecting such creditor's interest." But even if we accept petitioners' valuation, the bank is still the "holder" of a "secured claim," because petitioners' home retains $23,500 of value as collateral. The portion of the bank's claim that exceeds $23,500 is an "unsecured claim component" under § 506(a), United States v. Ron Pair Enterprises, Inc., 489 U.S. 235, 239 n.3 (1989) (internal quotation marks omitted); however, that determination does not necessarily mean that the "rights" the bank enjoys as a mortgagee, which are protected by § 1322(b)(2), are limited by the valuation of its secured claim.

The term "rights" is nowhere defined in the Bankruptcy Code. In the absence of a controlling federal rule, we generally assume that Congress has "left the determination of property rights in the assets of a bankrupt's estate to state law," since such "property interests are created and defined by state law." Butner v. United States, 440 U.S. 48, 54-55 (1979). See also Barnhill v. Johnson, 503 U.S. 393, 398 (1992). Moreover, we have specifically recognized that "the justifications for application of state law are not limited to ownership interests," but "apply with equal force to security interests, including the interest of a mortgagee." Butner, supra, at 55. The bank's "rights," therefore, are reflected in the relevant mortgage instruments, which are enforceable under Texas law. They include the right to repayment of the principal in monthly installments over a fixed term at specified adjustable rates of interest, the right to retain the lien until the debt is paid off, the right to accelerate the loan upon default and to proceed against petitioners' residence by foreclosure and public sale, and the right to bring an action to recover any deficiency remaining after foreclosure. See Record 135-140 (deed of trust); id. at 147-51 (promissory note); Tex. Prop. Code Ann. §§ 51.002 -51.005 (Supp. 1993). These are the rights that were "bargained for by the mortgagor and the mortgagee," Dewsnup v. Timm, 502 U.S. 410, 417 (1992), and are rights protected from modification by § 1322(b)(2).

This is not to say, of course, that the contractual rights of a home mortgage lender are unaffected by the mortgagor's Chapter 13 bankruptcy. The lender's power to enforce its rights-and, in particular, its right to foreclose on the property in the event of default-is checked by the Bankruptcy Code's automatic stay provision. 11 U.S.C. § 362. See United Savings Assn. of Texas v. Timbers of Inwood Forest Associates, Ltd., 484 U.S. 365, 369-370 (1988). In addition, § 1322(b)(5) permits the debtor to cure prepetition defaults on a home mortgage by paying off arrearages over the life of the plan "notwithstanding" the exception in § 1322(b)(2).[3] These statutory limitations on the lender's rights, however, are independent of the debtor's plan or otherwise outside § 1322(b)(2)'s prohibition.

[3] Under § 1322(b)(5), the plan may, "notwithstanding paragraph (2) of this subsection, provide for the curing of any default within a reasonable time and maintenance of payments while the case is pending on any . . . secured claim on which the last payment is due after the date on which the final payment under the plan is due."

Petitioners urge us to apply the so-called "rule of the last antecedent," which has been relied upon by some Courts of Appeals to interpret § 1322(b)(2) the way petitioners favor. E. g., In re Bellamy, 962 F.2d 176, 180 (CA2 1992); In re Hougland, 886 F.2d 1182, 1184 (CA9 1989). According to this argument, the operative clause "other than a claim secured only by a security interest in . . . the debtor's principal residence" must be read to refer to and modify its immediate antecedent, "secured claims." Thus, § 1322(b)(2)'s protection would then apply only to that subset of allowed "secured claims," determined by application of § 506(a), that are secured by a lien on the debtor's home -- including, with respect to the mortgage involved here, the bank's secured claim for $23,500. We acknowledge that this reading of the clause is quite sensible as a matter of grammar. But it is not compelled. Congress chose to use the phrase "claim secured . . . by" in § 1322(b)(2)'s exception, rather than repeating the term of art "secured claim." The unqualified word "claim" is broadly defined under the Code to encompass any "right to payment, whether . . . secure[d] or unsecured" or any "right to an equitable remedy for breach of performance if such breach gives rise to a right to payment, whether . . . secure[d] or unsecured." 11 U.S.C. § 101(5) (1988 ed., Supp. III). It is also plausible, therefore, to read "a claim secured only by a [homestead lien]" as referring to the lienholder's entire claim, including both the secured and the unsecured components of the claim. Indeed, § 506(a) itself uses the phrase "claim . . . secured by a lien" to encompass both portions of an undersecured claim.

This latter interpretation is the more reasonable one, since we cannot discern how § 1322(b)(2) could be administered under petitioners' interpretation. Petitioners propose to reduce the outstanding mortgage principal to the fair market value of the collateral, and, at the same time, they insist that they can do so without modifying the bank's rights "as to interest rates, payment amounts, and [other] contract terms." That appears to be impossible. The bank's contractual rights are contained in a unitary note that applies at once to the bank's overall claim, including both the secured and unsecured components. Petitioners cannot modify the payment and interest terms for the unsecured component, as they propose to do, without also modifying the terms of the secured component. Thus, to preserve the interest rate and the amount of each monthly payment specified in the note after having reduced the principal to $23,500, the plan would also have to reduce the term of the note dramatically. That would be a significant modification of a contractual right. Furthermore, the bank holds an adjustable rate mortgage, and the principal and interest payments on the loan must be recalculated with each adjustment in the interest rate. There is nothing in the mortgage contract or the Code that suggests any basis for recalculating the amortization schedule -- whether by reference to the face value of the remaining principal or by reference to the unamortized value of the collateral. This conundrum alone indicates that § 1322(b)(2) cannot operate in combination with § 506(a) in the manner theorized by petitioners.

In other words, to give effect to § 506(a)'s valuation and bifurcation of secured claims through a Chapter 13 plan in the manner petitioners propose would require a modification of the rights of the holder of the security interest. Section 1322(b)(2) prohibits such a modification where, as here, the lender's claim is secured only by a lien on the debtor's principal residence.

The judgment of the Court of Appeals is therefore Affirmed.

STEVENS, J., CONCURRING. At first blush it seems somewhat strange that the Bankruptcy Code should provide less protection to an individual's interest in retaining possession of his or her home than of other assets. The anomaly is, however, explained by the legislative history indicating that favorable treatment of residential mortgagees was intended to encourage the flow of capital into the home lending market. See Grubbs v. Houston First American Savings Assn., 730 F.2d 236, 245-246 (CA5 1984) (canvassing legislative history of Chapter 13 home mortgage provisions). It therefore seems quite clear that the Court's literal reading of the text of the statute is faithful to the intent of Congress. Accordingly, I join its opinion and judgment.

Notes and Questions

1. Suppose a mortgage agreement makes a person's home collateral, but it also requires the person to pay in an amount into an escrow account that will be used by the mortgage lender to pay local property tax. Does §1322(b)(2) still apply to protect the mortgage lender? To make sure that it does, BAPCPA adds new Bankruptcy Code §§ 101(13A) and 101(27B).

2. Suppose the mortgage agreement covers the wall-to-wall carpeting installed in a house. The carpeting is not nailed down but simply lies on the floor. Does §1322(b)(2) protect the mortgage lender?

3. Starting about 2006, the subprime mortgage crisis plunged America and the world into a severe recession. Politically, a reversal of the prohibition against modifying home mortgages became a matter of presidential politics. In the spring of 2009, a legislative initiative to accomplish this campaign promise apparently died in the Senate, perhaps never to be revived. For details, see Robert M. Zinman & Novica Petrovski, The Home Mortgage and Chapter 13: An Essay on Unintended Consequences, 17 AM. BANKR. L. REV. 133 (2009).

ZIMMER v PSB LENDING CORP. (IN RE ZIMMER)

313 F.3d 1220 (9th Cir. 2002)

D.W. NELSON, J.

Appellant Sieglinde Zimmer, a Chapter 13 bankruptcy petitioner, filed suit against PSB Lending Corporation ("PSB Lending") to avoid a lien against her home. PSB Lending holds a second position deed of trust on Zimmer's primary residence, which is entirely unsecured because the value of the first deed of trust exceeds the value of the home. The district court dismissed Zimmer's complaint for failure to state a claim, finding that 11 U.S.C. § 1322(b)(2) prohibits avoidance of any lien on the debtor's primary residence, even where the lien is wholly unsecured. We reverse, joining with the majority of other jurisdictions in holding that a wholly unsecured lienholder is not entitled to the protections of 11 U.S.C. § 1322(b)(2).

FACTUAL AND PROCEDURAL BACKGROUND

On or about October 8, 1997, Zimmer executed a promissory note for a $39,000 loan, secured by a deed of trust on Zimmer's residence in San Diego. Although different in form, a deed of trust is similar to a mortgage in purpose and effect. The deed of trust was assigned to PSB Lending; the outstanding loan value was $37,411.19 when Zimmer filed this case. Zimmer's residence was already encumbered by a first deed of trust securing a loan of $123,000 that was used to purchase the property.

On December 29, 1999, Zimmer filed a petition under Chapter 13, which allows a bankrupt debtor with regular income to restructure her debts and repay or discharge them as necessary. In her petition, she stated the value of her residence as $110,000. Because the first mortgage exceeded the value of the residence, Zimmer listed PSB Lending's claim for the repayment of its loan as unsecured.

On April 21, 2000, Zimmer filed an adversary complaint with the bankruptcy court seeking to avoid PSB Lending's lien on her home. In general, Chapter 13 allows debtors to avoid liens, but there is an exception for homestead liens that attach only to the debtor's primary residence. See 11 U.S.C. § 1322(b)(2). Relying on our Bankruptcy Appellate Panel's decision in Lam v. Investors Thrift (In re Lam), 211 B.R. 36 (1997), Zimmer argued that even though PSB Lending's claim was secured by her primary residence, its lien was nonetheless avoidable because the claim was wholly unsecured.

PSB Lending filed a motion to dismiss for failure to state a claim under Federal Rule of Bankruptcy Procedure 7012(b), which makes Federal Rule of Civil Procedure 12(b)(6) applicable to adversary proceedings in bankruptcy court. Concluding that it was not bound by Lam, the bankruptcy court held that PSB Lending's claim was protected from modification under § 1322(b)(2), and granted the motion to dismiss.

After Zimmer initially filed an appeal to the Bankruptcy Appellate Panel, PSB Lending elected to transfer the appeal to the district court. In an unpublished order, the district court affirmed the bankruptcy court's dismissal of the complaint, agreeing that liens against the debtor's primary residence are protected from modification under § 1322(b)(2) even if the underlying claim is wholly unsecured. This appeal followed. . . .

DISCUSSION

The district court erred in holding that a wholly unsecured lien on a primary residence may not be avoided in a Chapter 13 proceeding. The plain language of 11 U.S.C. § 1322(b)(2) provides that antimodification protection is only available to holders of secured claims. PSB Lending is not the holder of a secured claim under the definitions provided in the Bankruptcy Code, and therefore its rights may be modified under § 1322(b)(2).

The Bankruptcy Code

This case turns on the interpretation and application of two provisions of the Bankruptcy Code, 11 U.S.C. § 506(a) and 11 U.S.C. § 1322(b)(2). Section 506(a) divides creditors' claims into "secured claims" and "unsecured claims." Although the conventional interpretation of "secured" might include any claim in which the creditor has a security interest in the debtor's property, § 506(a) makes clear that the status of a claim depends on the valuation of the property:

> An allowed claim of a creditor secured by a lien on property in which the estate has an interest . . . is a secured claim to the extent of the value of such creditor's interest in the estate's interest in such property . . . and is an unsecured claim to the extent that the value of such creditor's interest . . . is less than the amount of such allowed claim.

11 U.S.C. § 506(a). To put it more simply, a claim such as a mortgage is not a "secured claim" to the extent that it exceeds the value of the property that secures it. Under the Bankruptcy Code, "secured claim" is thus a term of art; not every claim that is secured by a lien on property will be considered a "secured claim."

Here, it is plain that PSB Lending's claim for the repayment of its loan is an unsecured claim, because its deed of trust is junior to the first deed of trust, and the value of the loan secured by the first deed of trust is greater than the value of the house.

In general, Chapter 13 allows the modification of the rights of creditors, including the avoidance of liens against the debtor's property, but protects homestead liens from modification:

> [A Chapter 13 plan may] modify the rights of holders of secured claims, other than a claim secured only by a security interest in real property that is the debtor's principal residence, or of holders of unsecured claims, or leave unaffected the rights of holders of any class of claims[.]

11 U.S.C. § 1322(b)(2). Assuming that PSB Lending holds "a claim secured only by a security interest in real property that is the debtor's principal residence," it might qualify for protection against modification. If so, its lien would survive bankruptcy and could not be avoided by Zimmer.

Although it seems paradoxical on its face, PSB Lending's claim is arguably an "unsecured claim" that is also "a claim secured only by a security interest in real property that is the debtor's principal residence." Whether the antimodification clause of § 1322(b)(2) applies to the holder of such a claim is a question of first impression in this Circuit. Numerous other jurisdictions, however, have addressed this question in dozens of published opinions. The position adopted by a majority of courts is that the antimodification clause does not apply to wholly unsecured homestead liens, but a substantial minority of courts has taken the contrary position. See, e.g., Bartee v. Tara Colony Homeowners Ass'n (In re Bartee), 212 F.3d 277, 288-89 n.15 & n.16 (5th Cir. 2000) (collecting cases). Both camps believe their preferred result to be compelled by the Supreme Court's decision in Nobelman v. American Savings Bank, 508 U.S. 324 (1993).

The Supreme Court's decision in Nobelman

In Nobelman, the Supreme Court considered the question of whether a partially-secured claim secured by a homestead lien could be bifurcated into its secured and unsecured components, and "stripped down" to the value of the secured claim. See id. at 326-27. The debtors argued that, under § 506(a), the holder of an undersecured mortgage--for which the value of the claim exceeds the value of the property--only holds a "secured claim" to the extent of the value of the property, and holds an "unsecured claim" for the excess value of the mortgage. Id. at 328. Because § 1322(b)(2) only protects the rights of "holders of secured claims," they maintained that only the secured portion of the mortgage was entitled to protection and, therefore, that the value of the mortgage could be effectively reduced to its secured value. Id.

The Supreme Court rejected this approach of bifurcation and stripping down, primarily because the debtors' argument failed to consider the fact that § 1322(b)(2) "focuses on the modification of the 'rights of holders,' " id., not the status of claims. Although the Court found that it was proper to look to § 506(a) "for a judicial valuation of the collateral to determine the status of the [creditor's] claim," id., because the creditor's claim was partially secured, the creditor was "still the 'holder' of a 'secured claim.' " Id. at 329. Therefore, it was entitled to the protections of the antimodification clause.

The Court's interpretation of § 1322(b)(2) is worth considering in detail. The Fifth Circuit, in the decision reviewed by Nobelman, had concluded that "section 1322(b)(2) appears to conflict with section 506(a)," and resolved the conflict in favor of § 1322(b)(2). Nobelman v. Am. Sav. Bank (In re Nobelman), 968 F.2d 483, 488 (5th Cir. 1992). The Supreme Court took a different approach, giving effect to both statutes in its interpretation of "claim" in the antimodification clause. The debtors argued that "claim secured only by a security interest in real property" should work to modify "secured claims" in the antecedent clause, such that the antimodification clause would only apply to a secured claim secured only by a security interest in the debtor's home. Nobelman, 508 U.S. at 330. The Supreme Court rejected this argument, finding that "claim secured only by" is not equivalent to the term of art "secured claim." Id. at 331. Instead, noting that " § 506(a) itself uses the phrase 'claim . . . secured by a lien' to encompass both portions of an undersecured claim," the Court found that the antimodification clause similarly applied to both the unsecured and secured components of the mortgage claim. Id. (emphasis added).

Finally, the Supreme Court indicated that its interpretation was reasonable because it would be impossible to administer a bifurcated claim. There was no dispute that the secured portion of the mortgage could not be modified, and under such circumstances there was no direction in the Bankruptcy Code as to how the terms of the mortgage could be readjusted by reducing its value to the secured portion without modifying the "rights" of the mortgage holder. Id. at 331-332. Justice Stevens also noted, in a brief concurrence, that the Court's result was in accordance with "legislative history indicating that favorable treatment of residential mortgagees was intended to encourage the flow of capital into the home lending market." Id. at 332 (Stevens, J., concurring) (citing Grubbs v. Houston First Am. Sav. Ass'n, 730 F.2d 236, 245-46 (1st Cir. 1984)).

The majority position

The majority position, that § 1322(b)(2) does not prohibit avoidance of liens associated with wholly unsecured claims, has been adopted by all five Courts of Appeals to consider the issue, as well as two Bankruptcy Appellate Panels. Lane v. W. Interstate Bancorp (In re Lane), 280 F.3d 663, 667-69 (6th Cir. 2002); Pond v. Farm Specialist Realty (In re Pond), 252 F.3d 122, 126 (2d Cir. 2001); Tanner v. FirstPlus Fin., Inc. (In re Tanner), 217 F.3d 1357, 1359-60 (11th Cir. 2000); Bartee, supra, 212 F.3d at 288, 295; McDonald v. Master Fin., Inc. (In re McDonald), 205 F.3d 606, 611 (3d Cir. 2000); Domestic Bank v. Mann (In re Mann), 249 B.R. 831, 840 (B.A.P. 1st Cir. 2000); Lam, supra, 211 B.R. at 40-41.

One of the earliest and most influential of these cases is our BAP's opinion in Lam. The panel gave three primary reasons for its conclusion that a wholly unsecured lien may be avoided: 1) although the Nobelman Court focused on the rights of the creditor, the "rights" of a wholly unsecured creditor are "empty rights"; 2) in order to qualify for the antimodification protections, the creditor must first be a "holder of a secured claim"; and 3) extending antimodification protection might have the unwanted effects of inducing more filings under Chapter 11 and inducing creditors to obtain mortgages on overburdened property in order to avoid modification of their rights. 211 B.R. at 40-41.

Other courts have focused primarily on the second reason cited in Lam, that a creditor that is not the holder of a secured claim simply cannot qualify for antimodification protection. The Sixth Circuit in Lane outlines this argument in near-syllogistic fashion:

> • Section 1322(b)(2) prohibits modification of the rights of a holder of a secured claim if the security consists of a lien on the debtor's principal residence;
> • Section 1322(b)(2) permits modification of the rights of an unsecured claim holder;
> • Whether a lien claimant is the holder of a "secured claim" or an "unsecured claim" depends, thanks to § 506(a), on whether the claimant's security interest has any actual "value" . . .
> • If a claimant's lien on the debtor's homestead has no value at all . . . the claimant holds an "unsecured claim" and the claimant's contractual rights are subject to modification by the plan.

280 F.3d at 669. This argument is appealing in its simplicity and reliance on the plain text of the statute. Without a secured claim, a creditor's rights may be modified. Nonetheless, the tenacity of the minority position compels us to consider whether its argument should prevail.

The minority position

The minority position holds that § 1322(b)(2) prohibits the avoidance of any homestead lien, regardless of whether the claim is secured or unsecured. Perhaps the lead case in the minority camp is American General Finance, Inc. v. Dickerson, 229 B.R. 539 (M.D. Ga. 1999) ("Dickerson I"). Although no appeals court has adopted the minority position, one panel of the Eleventh Circuit stated that it would do so were it not bound by the decision of a previous panel. See Am. Gen. Fin., Inc. v. Dickerson (In re Dickerson), 222 F.3d 924, 926 (11th Cir. 2000) (overruling the district court in Dickerson I but noting that, were it not bound by Tanner, supra, it would follow the district court's reasoning).[1]

The court in Dickerson I found that "the emphasis in the statute [§ 1322] is on the fact that a lien exists on the property, not the value of such property," 229 B.R. at 542, and faults the majority for failing to recognize "that the existence of a lien carries any rights if the lien is unsecured." Id. at 543. The court points out that the majority position leads to the result that one penny of secured value will protect the creditor's rights, id. at 542-43, and argues that such a result "places too much emphasis on the valuation process." Id. at 543.

The opinion in Dickerson I attempts to defeat the majority position's plain-language interpretation of § 1322(b)(2) by pointing to the Supreme Court's interpretation of "claims" in the antimodification clause. Dickerson I, 229 B.R. at 542. As noted above, the Court held that the language "claim secured only by a security interest in real property" encompasses both the secured and unsecured components of an undersecured claim, and so the Dickerson I court argues that it also encompasses a wholly unsecured claim. Id.

---

[1] We also note with concern that several bankruptcy courts in this circuit, including the bankruptcy court in this case, have criticized and refused to follow the BAP's holding of Lam, adhering instead to the minority position. E.g., In re Enriquez, 244 B.R. 156, 161-62 (Bankr. S.D. Cal. 2000); Ortiz v. Household Fin. Corp. (In re Ortiz), 241 B.R. 460, 461 (E.D. Cal. 1999). Although the binding nature of Bankruptcy Appellate Panel decisions--an open question in this circuit--is not squarely before us in this case, we join Judge O'Scannlain's call for the Judicial Council to consider an order clarifying whether the bankruptcy courts must follow the BAP. See Bank of Maui v. Estate Analysis, Inc., 904 F.2d 470, 472 (9th Cir. 1989) (O'Scannlain, J., specially concurring).

Section 1322(b)(2) allows modification of unsecured claims

We find ourselves in partial agreement with Dickerson I, but in greater agreement with the majority position. As Dickerson I notes, the language "claim secured only by a security interest in real property" does encompass all such claims, secured or unsecured. We agree that, in this case, PSB Lending may well be the holder of a "claim secured only by a security interest in real property that is the debtor's home." Nonetheless, because PSB Lending is still not a "holder of a secured claim," it cannot qualify for antimodification protection.

The analysis in Dickerson I ignores the order in which the Supreme Court proceeded in Nobelman. First, the Court determined that it was proper to engage in the § 506(a) valuation process. 508 U.S. at 328. Second, the Court noted that, "even if we accept [the debtors'] valuation," the creditor was still the holder of a secured claim. Id. at 329. Finally, and only after determining that the creditor was the holder of a secured claim and thus eligible for antimodification protection, the Court proceeded to the question of exactly what was entitled to such protection. Id. at 329-30. The Court found that the rights of such a creditor were protected and, therefore, in order to protect such rights, interpreted the antimodification clause to encompass the entire claim of such a creditor so long as it was secured by a homestead lien. Id. at 330-31.

The minority position attempts to jump forward to the last step in this analysis--determining what is entitled to protection from modification--without considering whether the creditor even qualifies for such protection in the first place. While it is clear that the term "claim secured only by" in the antimodification clause is not limited to "secured claims," it is equally clear that "holders of secured claims" does refer to the term of art as defined by § 506(a). The Nobelman Court recognized this when it pointed out that Congress used a different phrase in the antimodification clause "rather than repeating the term of art 'secured claim.' " Id. at 331 (emphasis added). Looking to § 506(a) to determine which creditors are the "holders of secured claims," a creditor in PSB Lending's position plainly does not qualify. By taking the contrary position, the minority "fails to appreciate the Nobelman Court's conclusion that [the] 'rights' [of the creditor] flowed first from a lien which had some collateral value." Mann, 249 B.R. at 837.[2]

While Dickerson I is correct in noting that the majority position places great emphasis on the valuation process, this emphasis is compelled by Nobelman and the statutory scheme:

> The courts in the minority too easily dismiss the role of a § 506(a) valuation. The Nobelman Court stated that, "By virtue of its mortgage contract with petitioners, the bank is indisputably the holder of a claim secured by a lien on petitioners' home." 508 U.S. at 328. In the very next sentence, the Supreme Court found that it was correct for a Chapter 13 debtor, in the context of a homestead lien, to seek a § 506(a) valuation. Id. Further, the Court stated that in this context, the valuation should be used to "determine the status of the [creditor's] secured claim." Id. These statements refute the analysis of courts that find a valuation to be irrelevant. In a § 1322(b)(2) plan, a valuation cannot be both irrelevant and necessary to determine the status of a homestead lien . . . . Therefore, the

[2] Because we conclude that the rights of a wholly unsecured creditor need not be protected under § 1322(b)(2), we need not consider the Lam panel's determination that such rights are "empty rights." See 211 B.R. at 40

> Supreme Court's acceptance of a § 506(a) valuation in the context of § 1322(b)(2) must control.

Johnson v. Asset Mgmt. Group, LLC, 226 B.R. 364, 367-68 (D. Md. 1998) (alteration in original). In order to give effect to the definitions of secured and unsecured claims under § 506(a), we must conclude that the rights of a creditor holding only an unsecured claim may be modified under § 1322(b)(2).

Finally, it is worth noting that the concerns expressed by the Supreme Court in Nobelman are largely absent here. Because PSB Lending's lien may be avoided entirely, and its lien rights abrogated as to its entire unsecured claim, we need not consider the dilemma of how to modify an unsecured component without affecting the creditor's rights with respect to the secured component. Furthermore, although Justice Stevens recognized a congressional policy in favor of promoting home lending, we join other courts in interpreting this as applying to first or purchase-money mortgages. See Lam, 211 B.R. at 41 (citing In re Plouffe, 157 B.R. 198, 200 (Bankr. D. Conn. 1993)). We have not found, nor have the parties pointed to, any evidence of a congressional policy in favor of promoting subsequent mortgages or deeds of trust that are entirely unsecured due to a lack of equity in the property.

CONCLUSION

We conclude that the district court erred in holding that a wholly unsecured lien is protected by the antimodification clause of § 1322(b)(2). We reverse the decision of the district court and remand for proceedings consistent with this opinion.

REVERSED and REMANDED.

Notes and Questions

1. Suppose D grants a mortgage to A for $100,000. D then grants a mortgage to B for $30,000. D files for bankruptcy, and the house is valued at $100,001. Can D bifurcate B? Suppose D throws a rock through the kitchen window. Can D now bifurcate B?

AMERICAN GENERAL FINANCE, INC. v PASCHEN
296 F.3d 1203 (11th Cir. 2002)

WILSON, J.

This case presents an issue of first impression in this Circuit: Does 11 U.S.C. § 1322(c)(2) permit Chapter 13 debtors to bifurcate undersecured, short-term[1] home mortgages into secured and unsecured claims, with the unsecured claim subject to "cramdown" pursuant to 11 U.S.C. § 1325(a)(5)? The bankruptcy court, in confirming Richard and Doreen Paschen's (Debtors') Chapter 13 plan, held that § 1322(c)(2) did indeed permit Debtors to modify undersecured, short-term home mortgages through bifurcation and "cramdown." The district court affirmed the bankruptcy court's confirmation of Debtors' Chapter 13 plan. For the foregoing reasons, we affirm.

---

[1] The short-term mortgages covered by the statute are those in which "the last payment on the original payment schedule . . . is due before the date on which the final payment under the [Chapter 13] plan is due." 11 U.S.C. § 1322(c)(2).

I.

Debtors purchased a home in Columbus, Georgia in May of 1997. Two years later, Debtors encountered serious financial difficulties. Needing an immediate infusion of cash to pay off their debts, Debtors sought to borrow money from American General Finance, Inc. (AGF), a financial services corporation with a specialty in consumer finance. In August of 1999 AGF approved a loan to Debtors for $12,377.08, secured by the equity Debtors held in their home.

In December of 1999 Debtors' financial situation became untenable, and they filed for protection from their creditors under Chapter 13. AGF filed a proof of claim with the bankruptcy court in the amount of $11,392. Debtors then submitted a Chapter 13 plan, which proposed modifying AGF's claim by bifurcating AGF's loan into its secured and unsecured components, with only the secured portion to be paid back in a series of monthly installments. Debtors valued the secured component at $2752, which Debtors claimed reflected the actual amount of equity they then held in their home.

AGF filed a motion to deny confirmation of the plan, arguing that the plan failed to assess the value of AGF's secured debt properly. AGF further contended that the applicable law prevented Debtors from bifurcating AGF's loan into secured and unsecured parts and cramming down the unsecured part, as AGF's lien was secured by an interest in Debtors' primary residence. Such loans, AGF argued, are excepted from the general rule permitting modification of secured claims pursuant to a Chapter 13 plan. See id. § 1322(b)(2).

In a written opinion dated August 10, 2000, the United States Bankruptcy Court for the Middle District of Georgia rejected AGF's legal argument that claims involving short-term loans secured by liens against a debtor's primary residence could not be bifurcated into secured and unsecured parts, with the unsecured part crammed down, in a Chapter 13 proceeding. The court found that § 1322(c)(2) explicitly permitted the bifurcation and "cramdown" of claims involving short-term mortgages such as the one at issue in this case. The August 10th opinion was incorporated into the court's ultimate findings of fact and conclusions of law, which, pursuant to Bankruptcy Rule 7052, were announced from the bench after a confirmation hearing on August 25, 2000. The court confirmed a modified version of Debtors' Chapter 13 plan, which valued AGF's lien at six thousand dollars and required debtors to repay that amount at twelve percent interest over a sixty-month period.

AGF appealed the bankruptcy court's confirmation of Debtors' plan to the United States District Court for the Middle District of Georgia, which rejected AGF's arguments and affirmed the bankruptcy court's decision. AGF filed a timely notice of appeal with this Court.

II.

. . . Chapter 13 debtors enjoy "broad power to modify the rights of the holders of secured claims." In re Eubanks, 219 B.R. 468, 470 (B.A.P. 6th Cir. 1998). The manner in which secured claims may be modified in an acceptable Chapter 13 plan is governed by § 1325(a)(5). Section 1325(a)(5) specifies the conditions under which Chapter 13 plans must address "allowed secured claims" if the plans are to be confirmed, essentially by ensuring that creditors receive appropriate value for each of their secured claims. The phrase "allowed secured claims" is a reference to 11 U.S.C. § 506 (a), which has been interpreted as providing that "a claim is secured only to the extent of the value of the property on which the lien is fixed; the remainder of that claim is considered unsecured." United States v. Ron Pair Enters., Inc., 489 U.S. 235, 238-39 (1989). Thus, taken together, these provisions permit the bifurcation of an undersecured claim into its secured and unsecured parts, with creditors only assured of receiving full value for the secured portion of the claim. Section 1325(a)(5) is recognized as the source of a Chapter 13 debtor's authority to bifurcate secured claims and to "strip down" the value of the claim to an amount equal to the value of the collateral. In re Young, 199 B.R. 643, 647 (Bankr. E.D. Tenn. 1996) ("The very essence of a § 1325(a)(5) modification is the write down or 'cramdown' of a secured claim to the value of the collateral securing the debt.").

In the instant case, Debtors' proposed plan included an assertion that AGF's debt was undersecured, because the value of Debtors' collateral (equity in their home) was substantially exceeded by the value of the debt. Relying upon the provisions of § 1325(a)(5), Debtors sought to bifurcate AGF's claim, with the secured portion paid back in monthly installments and the unsecured component crammed down. While the bankruptcy court disagreed with Debtors' valuation of AGF's collateral, it agreed with the premise of Debtors' proposal and permitted AGF's claim to be bifurcated, with only the value of the secured portion returned to AGF.

AGF argues that another provision of the Bankruptcy Code precludes the modification of its claim. According to AGF, § 1322(b)(2) expressly prohibits the modification of any claim in a Chapter 13 proceeding "secured only by a security interest in real property that is the debtor's principal residence." 11 U.S.C. § 1322(b)(2). The Supreme Court has interpreted this provision to exclude mortgages against a debtor's principal residence from the general rule permitting modification of secured claims in Chapter 13 proceedings. Nobelman v. Am. Savings Bank, 508 U.S. 324, 331-32 (1993), superseded by statute as stated in In re Escue, 184 B.R. 287 (Bankr. M.D. Tenn. 1995). In the instant case, AGF holds a note secured solely by a lien on the real property that constitutes Debtors' principal residence. Hence, AGF contends that its claim cannot be modified pursuant to § 1325(a)(5).

Debtors rely upon what they term "an exception to the section 1322(b)(2) exception" to support their contention that AGF's claim should be subject to modification. The relevant provision is found at § 1322(c)(2), which provides as follows:

> Notwithstanding subsection (b)(2) and applicable nonbankruptcy law-
>
> ....
>
> (2) in a case in which the last payment on the original payment schedule for a claim secured only by a security interest in real property that is the debtor's principal residence is due before the date on which the final payment under the plan is due, the plan may provide for payment of the claim as modified pursuant to section 1325(a)(5) of this title.

Debtors contend that this provision unambiguously provides that short-term mortgages that mature prior to the final payment on a Chapter 13 plan are subject to modification, notwithstanding the general prohibition on modification of claims secured by an interest in a debtor's primary residence found in § 1322(b)(2). Debtors note that the debt at issue here is a short-term mortgage that matures prior to the completion of the proposed Chapter 13 plan and thus argue that their debt to AGF is subject to modification. AGF rejects this reading of § 1322(c)(2); argues that the language of § 1322(c)(2) is ambiguous; and avers that the legislative history indicates that Congress did not intend for § 1322(c)(2) to permit the modification of claims secured by short-term mortgages, but rather intended to permit only the schedule of payments for those claims to be modified. Our task in this case is to evaluate these competing views of § 1322(c)(2) to determine which view best effects the will of Congress.

III.

"In construing a statute we must begin, and often should end as well, with the language of the statute itself." United States v. Steele, 147 F.3d 1316, 1318 (11th Cir. 1998) (en banc) (internal quotation marks omitted). When the language of a statute is unambiguous, we need go no further, because we must presume that Congress "said what it meant and meant what it said." Id. "The plain meaning of legislation should be conclusive, except in the rare cases [in which] the literal application of a statute will produce a result demonstrably at odds with the intentions of its drafters." Ron Pair Enters., Inc., 489 U.S. at 242 (alteration in original) (internal quotation marks omitted). The import of these authorities is that we need not resort to extrinsic evidence, such as legislative history, to discern a statute's meaning if the statute's language is unambiguous.

In the instant case, the plain language of the statute indicates a clear congressional intent to except certain short-term mortgages from the general rule prohibiting the modification of claims secured only by an interest in a debtor's primary residence in a Chapter 13 proceeding. Debtors' interpretation of the statute is the correct one. An assessment of the text of § 1322(c)(2) reflects its clarity.

The prefatory phrase "notwithstanding subsection (b)(2)" is the first important indicator of congressional intent with respect to this statute. The phrase is a plain statement that subsection (b)(2)'s prohibition on the modification of loans secured only by an interest in a debtor's primary residence does not have any application to the class of claims that fall under § 1322(c)(2). This interpretation of the "notwithstanding" phrase has been noted by a number of other courts charged with construing § 1322(c)(2). See, e.g., In re Eubanks, 219 B.R. at 470 ("The introductory phrase, 'notwithstanding subsection (b)(2)' clearly signals the drafter's intention that the provisions of the 'notwithstanding' section override conflicting provisions of any other section") (alteration in original) (internal quotation marks omitted).); In re Bagne, 219 B.R. 272, 277 (Bankr. E.D. Cal. 1998) ("Plainly, this [prefatory] language instructs the court to disregard § 1322(b)(2)."); In re Mattson, 210 B.R. 157, 160 (Bankr. D. Minn. 1997) (holding that the prefatory phrase meant that "we are therefore to ignore subsection (b)(2), at least to the extent that it is inconsistent with the language that follows").

In addition, the reference to § 1325(a)(5) is highly relevant to our understanding of § 1322(c)(2). As we noted earlier, § 1325(a)(5) permits writing down secured claims to the value of the collateral securing the debt. See United States v. Arnold, 878 F.2d 925, 928 (6th Cir. 1989) ("Under [§ 1325(a)(5)], the debtor can 'cramdown' a plan repaying only the 'allowed secured claim' . . . ."); In re Young, 199 B.R. at 647 ("The very essence of a § 1325(a)(5) modification is the write down or 'cramdown' of a secured claim to the value of the collateral securing the debt."). The phrase "payment of the claim as modified pursuant to section 1325(a)(5)" is an explicit statement of § 1322(c)(2)'s purpose: claims that fall within its ambit are subject to bifurcation into secured and unsecured parts, with the unsecured portion subject to "cramdown" pursuant to § 1325(a)(5). In re Eubanks, 219 B.R. at 471-72. And the claims that fall under § 1322(c)(2) are those in which "the last payment on the original payment schedule for a claim secured only by a security interest in real property that is the debtor's principal residence is due before the date on which the final payment under the plan is due"--precisely the kind of claim at issue in this case.

AGF argues that the language of the statute is subject to more than one plausible interpretation and is thus ambiguous, requiring reference to extrinsic sources to discern congressional intent. AGF relies upon the construction of § 1322(c)(2) advanced in In re Witt, 113 F.3d 508 (4th Cir. 1997), to support its argument that the statute is ambiguous.

In In re Witt, the Fourth Circuit found § 1322(c)(2)'s critical phrase "payment of the claim as modified" ambiguous, because "it [could not] be determined, merely from the statute's text, whether the words 'as modified' should apply to 'payment' or to 'claim.'" 113 F.3d at 511. If the term "as modified" modifies "payment," the Witt court found that a mortgage covered by § 1322(c)(2) could not be bifurcated and crammed down--rather, § 1322(c)(2) merely could provide for the modification of the schedule of payments made on such a claim. Id. The Fourth Circuit held that it was in fact a plausible reading of the statute to assume that the phrase "as modified" modifies "payment," rather than "claim." Id. The court stated that because the subject of "payment" was the focus of § 1322(c)(2), it is likely, "as a matter of common sense," that the modifier "as modified" was a reference to the central subject of the statute. Id. The court further noted that the phrase "payment" would be superfluous if the contrary reading of the statute were accepted; the court reasoned that if Congress had intended the phrase "as modified" to refer to "claim," there would have been no reason to include the term "payment" in the statute. 113 F.3d at 512. Congress simply could have stated that "the plan may provide for the claim to be modified" if this were its intended reading. Id. (internal quotation marks omitted).

After finding this alternative construction of § 1322(c)(2) one, though not necessarily the only, plausible reading of congressional intent, the Witt court assessed the statute's legislative history in an effort to gauge Congress's intent in the face of an ambiguous statute. The Fourth Circuit's reading of that history led the court to conclude that § 1322(c)(2) does not provide for the bifurcation and "cramdown" of undersecured, short-term home mortgages.[2] 113 F.3d at 513-14. AGF urges us to adopt the Fourth Circuit's analysis in construing § 1322(c)(2).

We are not convinced by our sister circuit's reasoning. The Witt court's view that the phrase "as modified" modifies "payment," rather than "claim," is a grammatically strained rea-ding of the statute. It contradicts the rule of the last antecedent,[3] an accepted canon of sta-tutory construction which provides that

[2] While we need not address the legislative history of this statute, as we find its plain language unambiguous, it should be noted that other courts that have assessed § 1322(c)(2) 's legislative history have come to conclusions that differ from those of the Witt court. See, e.g., In re Eubanks, 219 B.R. at 473-78; In re Mattson, 210 B.R. at 160-61.

[3] The Witt court acknowledged that its construction of the statute was contrary to the rule of the last antecedent, but noted that use of such a rule was "not compelled." 113 F.3d at 511 (internal quotation marks omitted). The court's assessment of the context in which the modifier was used led it to conclude that the rule of the last antecedent was not conclusive in this instance. While the rule of the last antecedent is hardly a mandatory rule of statutory construction, we

when construing statutes, "qualifying words, phrases, and clauses are to be applied to the words or phrase immediately preceding, and are not to be construed as extending to and including others more remote." United States v. Correa, 750 F.2d 1475, 1481 n.10 (11th Cir. 1985) (internal quotation marks omitted). Amicus Curiae points out that had Congress intended for the phrase "as modified" to modify "payment," it could have done so by placing the modifier next to the phrase to be modified, such as through "payments as modified on the claim," or "modified payments on the claim." Br. of Amicus Curiae Nat'l Ass'n of Consumer Bankr. Att'ys in support of Debtors-Appellees at 13.

Additionally, the Witt court advances no convincing explanation for the meaning of the reference to § 1325(a)(5) in the text of § 1322(c)(2). As we have noted, § 1325(a)(5) is the provision that permits the bifurcation of undersecured claims into secured and unsecured components, with the unsecured component subject to "cramdown." "Payments" cannot be modified pursuant to § 1325(a)(5); only claims are subject to § 1325(a)(5)'s modification provisions. The reference to § 1325(a)(5) could not be a plainer statement of the statute's purpose; it is an exception to the general rule preventing the modification of claims secured by home mortgages. See In re Mattson, 210 B.R. at 160 ("In certain limited circumstances which obtain [in § 1322(c)(2)], the debtor may in fact utilize the provisions of § 1325(a)(5) to cram down on the secured creditor . . . .").

We note that the great weight of persuasive authority supports debtors' interpretation of § 1322(c)(2); In re Witt appears to be the only case interpreting the statute differently. See, e.g., In re Eubanks, 219 B.R. at 472; In re Sexton, 230 B.R. 346, 349 (Bankr. E.D. Tenn. 1999); In re Reeves, 221 B.R. 756, 759 (Bankr. C.D. Ill. 1998); In re Mattson, 210 B.R. at 160; see also Collier on Bankruptcy § 1322.16, at 1322-51 (Lawrence P. King et al. eds., rev. 15th ed. 2001). Indeed, we have noted in dicta that § 1322(c)(2) was intended "to except short-term and balloon mortgages from [§ 1322(b)(2)'s] reach, thereby overruling Nobelman insofar as it applied to [those] types of mortgages." In re Tanner, 217 F.3d 1357, 1358 n.5 (11th Cir. 2000). The plain language of § 1322(c)(2) compels us to agree with the consensus of those courts that have considered the provision; § 1322(c)(2) permits the modification of claims (through bifurcation and "cramdown") secured by those short-term home mortgages that mature prior to the completion of a debtor's Chapter 13 plan.

IV.

In conclusion, we find that the bankruptcy court's interpretation of § 1322(c)(2) is the correct one. The provision plainly permits the modification of AGF's claim through the bifurcation of that claim into secured and unsecured components, with the unsecured component crammed down pursuant to § 1325(a)(5). The bankruptcy court did not err in confirming Debtors' plan, based upon such a construction of § 1322(c)(2), and the district court correctly affirmed the bankruptcy court's decision. The decision of the district court is AFFIRMED.

---

disagree with the Witt court that a compelling reason to reject it exists in this instance.

IN RE CONNORS

497 F.3d 314 (3d Cir. 2007)

BARRY, J.

This bankruptcy appeal presents a question on which New Jersey federal bankruptcy and district courts have been divided for more than ten years: whether, under 11 U.S.C. § 1322(c)(1), a Chapter 13 debtor has the right to cure a default on a mortgage secured by the debtor's principal residence between the time the residence is sold at a foreclosure sale and the time the deed is delivered. Having finally been given the opportunity to break what is a virtual tie between the New Jersey federal courts, we hold that § 1322(c)(1) does not afford the debtor that right.

I.

On August 21, 2002, Appellant Vincent J. Connors executed a $252,000 note and mortgage on his residence at 41 Lakeridge Drive, Matawan, New Jersey, in favor of the predecessor in interest of Appellee Deutsche Bank National Trust -Co. ("Deutsche Bank"). Connors subsequently defaulted on the note, causing Deutsche Bank to foreclose on March 4, 2004. At a foreclosure sale on November 10, 2004, the property was sold to Appellee 41 Lakeridge LLC ("Lakeridge") for $330,000; Lakeridge tendered the required 20% deposit.

On November 14, 2004, Connors filed a voluntary petition under Chapter 13 of the Bankruptcy Code. The filing triggered an automatic stay of proceedings under 11 U.S.C. § 362. Two weeks later, on November 30, 2004, Connors filed a Chapter 13 Plan, which proposed to cure his pre-petition arrears on the mortgage. He did not, however, exercise his statutory right to object to the foreclosure sale or redeem within 60 days of the filing of his Chapter 13 petition, as is permitted under N.J. Ct. R. 4:65-5 and 11 U.S.C. § 108(b), respectively.

On January 19, 2005, the 60-day period having expired, Lakeridge filed a motion to lift the automatic stay to permit it to tender the balance of the purchase price and receive the deed. Connors opposed the motion. The Bankruptcy Court held a hearing and granted the motion, explaining, in its March 9, 2005 letter opinion, that Connors no longer had the right to cure the default on his mortgage under 11 U.S.C. § 1322(c)(1), and that his right to redeem under state law had expired. Before Lakeridge could tender the balance and receive the deed, however, the Court granted a stay pending Connors's appeal.

The District Court affirmed. Noting a "schism" among New Jersey courts regarding whether § 1322(c)(1) creates a right to cure a default that expires upon delivery of the deed, the Court held that the right to cure expires at the foreclosure sale, and that § 1322(c)(1) "allows the debtor to exercise only what additional remedy applicable state law provides." (App. at 7.) Because Connors's state-law rights had expired, the Court held, the Bankruptcy Court appropriately granted Lakeridge's motion to lift the automatic stay. This appeal followed. . . .

III.

The sole question we must decide is whether, under 11 U.S.C. § 1322(c)(1), a Chapter 13 debtor has the right to cure a default on a mortgage secured by the debtor's principal residence between the time the residence is sold at a foreclosure sale and the time the deed is delivered.

A. The Unambiguous Language of § 1322(c)(1) Supports the "Gavel Rule"

Section 1322 of the Bankruptcy Code sets forth the minimum requirements for a mandatory Chapter 13 Plan. 11 U.S.C. § 1322; S. Rep. 95-989, at 141 (1978). Subsection (b)(3) broadly permits the plan to "provide for the curing or waiving of any default," and subsection (b)(5) permits the plan to "provide for the curing of any default within a reasonable time and maintenance of payments while the case is pending on any unsecured claim or secured claim on which the last payment is due after the date on which the final payment under the plan is due." 11 U.S.C. § 1322(b)(3), (5). Subsection (c)(1) limits the broad sweep of subsections (b)(3) and (b)(5) by providing, in relevant part, as follows:

> [A] default with respect to, or that gave rise to, a lien on the debtor's principal residence may be cured under paragraph (3) or (5) of subsection (b) until such residence is sold at a foreclosure sale that is conducted in accordance with applicable nonbankruptcy law . . . .

11 U.S.C. § 1322(c)(1).

Since the enactment of subsection (c)(1) as part of the Bankruptcy Reform Act of 1994, New Jersey bankruptcy and district courts have disagreed over whether (c)(1) gives a Chapter 13 debtor the right to cure a default on a home mortgage between the time the residence is sold at a foreclosure sale and the time the deed is delivered. One line of cases holds that § 1322(c)(1) guarantees the right to cure a default on a home mortgage only until the gavel falls at a foreclosure sale.[1] Courts frequently refer to this view as the "gavel rule." The other line of cases maintains that a residence is not "sold" within the meaning of § 1322(c)(1), and the debtor has the right to cure a default, until the deed is delivered to the winning bidder.[2] This view is commonly known as the "deed-delivery rule."

We start with the language of the statute. United States v. Ron Pair Enters., Inc., 489 U.S. 235, 241 (1989); Idahoan Fresh v. Advantage Produce, Inc., 157 F.3d 197, 202 (3d Cir. 1998). Some courts have found ambiguity in the phrase, "that is conducted in accordance with applicable nonbankruptcy law." In Simmons, for instance, the Court found the phrase ambiguous because "it is not readily apparent whether Congress intended the phrase to apply only to the event of sale, or to the entirety of the sale process, including the giving of a deed." 202 B.R. at 201. We are unpersuaded that the phrase is ambiguous; indeed, to find

[1] Connors v. Deutsche Bank Nat'l Trust Co., No. Civ. A. 05-2236, 2006 U.S. Dist. LEXIS 40876, 2006 WL 1722609, at *2 (D.N.J. June 20, 2006); [**7] In re Maricic, No. 02-37500, slip op. (Bankr. D.N.J. 2002); In re Mangano, 253 B.R. 339, 344-45 (Bankr. D.N.J. 2000); In re Veltre, No. 99-40669, 2000 Bankr. LEXIS 1409, at *4-6 (Bankr. D.N.J. May 31, 2000); In re Hric, 208 B.R. 21, 26 (Bankr. D.N.J. 1997); In re Simmons, 202 B.R. 198, 203, 205-06 (Bankr. D.N.J. 1996); In re Ziyambe, 200 B.R. 790, 794 (Bankr. D.N.J. 1996); In re Little, 201 B.R. 98, 105 (Bankr. 1996). The Sixth Circuit has also adopted this view. See In re Cain, 423 F.3d 617, 619 (6th Cir. 2005).

[2] Chisholm v. Cendant Mortgage Corp., No. Civ. 04-6398, 2005 U.S. Dist. LEXIS 32266, 2005 WL 1522232, at *1 (D.N.J. June 27, 2005); In re Randall, 263 B.R. 200, 201 (D.N.J. 2001); In re Downing, 212 B.R. 459, 467 (Bankr. D.N.J. 1997); In re Ross, 191 B.R. 615, 621 (Bankr. D.N.J. 1996); In re Macavia, No. 95-34118, 1995 Bankr. LEXIS 2103, at *7-8 (Bankr. D.N.J. 1995).

ambiguity would be to deny the words their plain meaning. The word "that" is a relative pronoun that restricts and, therefore, modifies, the preceding noun, "foreclosure sale." Thus, when the statute refers to "a foreclosure sale that is conducted in accordance with applicable nonbankruptcy law," it clearly refers to a foreclosure sale that complies with state-law procedures. See New Castle County v. Hartford Acc. & Indem. Co., 970 F.2d 1267, 1270 (3d Cir. 1992) ("[T]he question is not whether there is an ambiguity in the metaphysical sense, but whether the language has only one reasonable meaning when construed, not in a hypertechnical fashion, but in an ordinary, common sense manner."). We agree with those decisions that have reached this conclusion without resorting to legislative history. See, e.g., Cain, 423 F.3d at 620; Hric, 208 B.R. at 25; see also Simmons, 202 B.R. at 203 (finding that canons of statutory construction, as well as "common sense," mandated the same reading, but also considering legislative history).[3]

We must also determine what it means for a residence to be "sold at a foreclosure sale." Deconstructing this phrase further, we must determine the meaning of "foreclosure sale"--a term that Appellees contend is synonymous with the foreclosure auction, but that Connors insists refers to the entire foreclosure process, terminating with the delivery of a deed. The Bankruptcy Code does not define "foreclosure sale," so we must give it its ordinary meaning. Liberty Lincoln-Mercury, Inc. v. Ford Motor Co., 171 F.3d 818, 822 (3d Cir. 1999).

Outside of cases applying the deed-delivery rule, the term "foreclosure sale" is broadly understood to mean the foreclosure auction. First, the preposition "at" in "sold at a foreclosure sale" signifies a discrete event, rather than an ongoing process. See Chisholm, 2005 U.S. Dist. LEXIS 32266, 2005 WL 1522232, at *3. Second, at least one New Jersey bankruptcy court has taken judicial notice of the fact that New Jersey foreclosure practitioners refer to the foreclosure auction as the "sale." Hric, 208 B.R. at 25. Third, the New Jersey statute setting forth the procedures governing sheriffs' sales specifically refers to the auction as the "foreclosure sale." See N.J.S.A. § 2A:50-64 (requiring the successful bidder to deposit 20 percent of the purchase price "immediately upon the conclusion of the foreclosure sale"). Fourth, New Jersey rules governing sheriffs' sales treat "sale" as synonymous with the auction, and distinguish between the "sale" and the delivery of the deed. See N.J. Ct. R. 4:65-2 (requiring notice to be served "at least 10 days prior to the date set for sale"); 4:65-4 (specifying the place of the "sale"); 4:65-5 (permitting objections to be served "within 10 days after the sale," and permitting courts to dispose of such objections and direct the sheriff to deliver the deed); 4:65-6 (requiring sheriff to file with the court "a report of any sale made," and authorizing a subsequent judicial confirmation hearing at which the court may order delivery of the deed). And, fifth, the Supreme Court of New Jersey consistently refers to the foreclosure auction as the "foreclosure sale." See, e.g., Panetta v. Equity One, Inc., 190 N.J. 307, 920 A.2d 638, 648 (N.J. 2007); BTD-1996 NPC 1 L.L.C. v. 350 Warren L.P., 170 N.J. 90, 784 A.2d 1214, 1223

---

[3] Connors asks us to consider Wright v. Union Central Life Insurance Co., 304 U.S. 502 (1938), a case in which the Supreme Court upheld the constitutionality of a provision of the Bankruptcy Code that extended any state-law right of redemption that a debtor possessed at the time he or she filed a petition in bankruptcy. That holding is inapplicable here because § 1322(c)(1) does not purport to extend any state-law right; it simply recognizes a federal right to cure that extends until the property is "sold at a foreclosure sale." The provision that did extend Connors's state-law right to redeem, § 108(b), expired 60 days after he filed his petition.

(N.J. 2001); Conklin v. Hannoch Weisman, 145 N.J. 395, 678 A.2d 1060, 1063 (N.J. 1996). There is no doubt that "foreclosure sale," as it is commonly understood, signifies the foreclosure auction. See, e.g., Cain, 423 F.3d at 620; Hric, 208 B.R. at 25; Simmons, 202 B.R. at 203.

Some courts have found ambiguity arising from a perceived conflict between the terms "sold" and "foreclosure sale." These courts have reasoned that, in New Jersey, a residence is not "sold" until the deed is delivered, and the deed is not delivered until after the foreclosure sale. See, e.g., Chisholm, 2005 U.S. Dist. LEXIS 32266, 2005 WL 1522232, at *4; Randall, 263 B.R. at 203; Downing, 212 B.R. at 463; Ross, 191 B.R. at 621. The terms "sold" and "foreclosure sale" are not in conflict. In New Jersey, the successful bid at a foreclosure auction is generally irrevocable, see Simmons, 202 B.R. at 204,[4] and the bidder acquires equitable title that is not subject to defeasance except under narrow circumstances. If, for instance, within ten days of the foreclosure sale, the mortgagor files objections that are judicially sustained, N.J. Ct. R. 4:65-5, or exercises the right of redemption, Hardyston Nat'l Bank of Hamburg v. Tartamella, 56 N.J. 508, 267 A.2d 495, 498 (N.J. 1970), the purchaser may lose equitable title. Simmons, 202 B.R. at 204; see also Ziyambe, 200 B.R. at 796 ("Under New Jersey law, . . . title to the property is indefeasibly vested in the successful bidder unless objection to the sale is filed within ten days."). Although delivery of the deed conveys legal title, Randall, 263 B.R. at 203, the delivery itself has been described as "a ministerial act, routinely performed, which does not affect the redemption rights of the parties." Ziyambe, 200 B.R. at 796.[5] courts have concluded, accordingly, that a residence is "sold" at the foreclosure auction. See, e.g., In re Townsville, 268 B.R. 95, 118-19 (Bankr. E.D. Pa. 2001); In re Denny, 242 B.R. 593, 598-99 (Bankr. D. Md.1999); Hric, 208 B.R. at 25; Ziyambe, 200 B.R. at 796-97. For purposes of § 1322(c)(1), we conclude likewise.

The gavel rule does not, of course, cut off the debtor's state-law post-sale remedies. Those remedies may continue past the date of the foreclosure sale by operation of another provision of the Bankruptcy Code, 11 U.S.C. § 108(b). Section 108(b) provides, in relevant part, as follows:

> [I]f applicable nonbankruptcy law . . . fixes a period within which the debtor . . . may file any pleading, demand, notice, or proof of claim or loss, cure a default, or perform any other similar act, and such period has not expired before the date of the filing of the petition, the trustee may only file, cure, or perform, as the case may be, before the later of-
>
> (1) the end of such period, including any suspension of such period occurring on or after the commencement of the case; or
>
> (2) 60 days after the order for relief.

11 U.S.C. § 108(b). We have interpreted this provision to mean that "when a

[4] Cf. N.J.S.A. § 2A:61-16 (allowing purchaser relief from bid if defect of title renders title unmarketable, or if title is subject to lien or encumbrance).

[5] In rare circumstances, as when the mortgagor has received insufficient notice of foreclosure proceedings, the right to redeem may be asserted even after delivery of the deed. Mercury Capital Corp. v. Freehold Office Park, Ltd., 363 N.J. Super. 235, 832 A.2d 369, 378 n.10 (N.J. Sup. Ct. Ch. Div. 2003) (citing cases relying on the inherent equity power of the Chancery Court). An equity of redemption that continues beyond the delivery of the deed would undermine any suggestion that the delivery of the deed is the only true "point of finality" in the foreclosure process. Cf. Chisholm, 2005 U.S. Dist. LEXIS 32266, 2005 WL 1522232, at *5. A "finality" requirement, moreover, has no basis in the language of the statute.

bankruptcy petition is filed before the expiration of a statutory grace period, if need be § 108(b) can extend the grace period for 60 days from the date of the filing of the petition." Counties Contracting & Constr. Co. v. Constitution Life Ins. Co., 855 F.2d 1054, 1059 (3d Cir. 1988).[6] Under New Jersey law, the applicable grace period is the ten-day period to object, pursuant to N.J. Ct. R. 4:65-5, or redeem, pursuant to Hardyston. When a Chapter 13 petition is filed during the ten-day period, this period is extended to 60 days from the filing of the petition by operation of § 108(b). Connors, therefore, had 60 days from the filing of his petition to object or redeem. When he failed to do so, Lakeridge's equitable title was no longer subject to defeasance.

We hold, therefore, that under the unambiguous language of 11 U.S.C. § 1322(c)(1), a Chapter 13 debtor does not have the right to cure a default on a mortgage secured by the debtor's principal residence between the time the residence is sold at a foreclosure sale and the time the deed is delivered.

B. The Legislative History behind § 1322(c)(1) and Policy Considerations Lend Further Support for the Gavel Rule

Although, given the foregoing, it is unnecessary to examine the legislative history of § 1322(c)(1), we briefly do so here because it is consistent with the statutory language. Subsection (c)(1) was added to the Bankruptcy Code to make explicit that a debtor's right to cure a default on a mortgage secured by his or her principal residence continues at least until the "foreclosure sale," and may continue beyond that date if state law provides additional cure rights. H.R. Rep. 103-835, at 52 (1994), reprinted in 1994 U.S.S.C.A.N. 3340, 3361. Until our decision in In re Roach, 824 F.2d 1370 (3d Cir. 1987), all of the federal courts of appeals had recognized that a debtor's right to cure a default on a home mortgage continued at least until the time of the foreclosure sale. H.R. Rep. 103-835, at 52, reprinted in 1994 U.S.S.C.A.N. at 3361. In Roach, however, we held that a debtor's right to cure expired at the foreclosure judgment, an event that preceded the foreclosure sale. Roach, 824 F.2d at 1378-79. Congress added subsection (c)(1) to overrule Roach and establish a uniform time--the "foreclosure sale"--for expiration of a debtor's federal right to cure.

Proponents of the deed-delivery rule tend to place great emphasis on a statement in the legislative history suggesting Congress's intent to "allow[] the debtor to cure home mortgage defaults at least through completion of a foreclosure sale under applicable nonbankruptcy law." H.R. Rep. 103-835, at 52, reprinted in 1994 U.S.S.C.A.N. at 3361 (emphasis added). They reason that under state law, a foreclosure sale has not been "completed" until delivery of the deed. See, e.g., Chisholm, 2005 U.S. Dist. LEXIS 32266, 2005 WL 1522232, at *4-5; Randall, 263 B.R. at 203; Downing, 212 B.R. at 466; Ross, 191 B.R. at 621; Macavia, 1995 Bankr. LEXIS 2103, at *7-8. It is by no means evident from the word "completion" in this one fragment of legislative history, however, that Congress intended "foreclosure sale" to refer to the entire state-law foreclosure process. Viewed in the context of Congress's express intent to overrule the aberrant Roach holding, it is eminently more plausible that Congress intended

---

[6] Some courts suggest that § 108(b) extends the state-law grace period by an additional 60 days. See, e.g., Ross, 191 B.R. at 617-18. We are bound by our holding in Counties Contracting that the 60-day period runs from the filing of the petition.

to set the expiration of a debtor's federal right to cure at the foreclosure sale, thus restoring the uniformity that existed pre-Roach. The foreclosure sale is, thus, "completed" with the fall of the gavel and the vesting of equitable title in the winning bidder. See Cain, 423 F.3d at 621.

That the federal right to cure expires at the foreclosure sale finds support in the statement of Senator Charles Grassley when speaking on behalf of the bill that was ultimately enacted:

> Title III of the bill will assist homeowners. Some homeowners attempt to prevent their homes from being foreclosed upon, even though a bankruptcy court has ordered a foreclosure sale. There may be several months between the court order and the foreclosure sale. Section 301 will preempt conflicting State laws, and permit homeowners to present a plan to pay off their mortgage debt until the foreclosure sale actually occurs.

140 Cong. Rec. S14,462 (1994). Senator Grassley was an original co-sponsor of the Senate bill, which would have permitted the debtor to cure a default so long as he or she "possesses any legal or equitable interest, including a right of redemption," at the time the petition was filed. S. Rep. 103-168, at 21 (1993). This is precisely the interpretation that Connors now urges, and Congress's rejection of the Senate bill in favor of the current language of § 1322(c)(1) is telling.

The gavel rule also makes sense as a matter of policy. In In re McCarn, 218 B.R. 154, 160 (B.A.P. 10th Cir. 1998), a bankruptcy appellate panel in the Tenth Circuit acknowledged that the foreclosure sale, in contrast to the delivery of the deed, must be preceded by notice to the debtor. Such notice affords the debtor ample opportunity to protect his or her interests by filing a bankruptcy petition before the foreclosure sale and exercising the right to cure under § 1322(c)(1). See also Simmons, 202 B.R. at 203-04. To the extent that debtors' rights are not sufficiently protected, states remain free to provide them with additional post-sale remedies by virtue of § 108(b). See, e.g., Justice v. Valley Nat'l Bank, 849 F.2d 1078, 1082 (8th Cir. 1988). Meanwhile, the gavel rule protects purchasers by avoiding an interpretation that turns § 1322(c)(1) into a federal vehicle for divesting them of property rights acquired at foreclosure sales. Increased uncertainty of ownership may also translate to lower foreclosure bids, a factor that New Jersey courts consider when confirming foreclosure sales. See N.J. Ct. R. 4:65-5 (permitting court to confirm sale if it "is satisfied that the real estate was sold at its highest and best price at the time of the sale").

IV.

We, therefore, hold that under 11 U.S.C. § 1322(c)(1), a Chapter 13 debtor does not have the right to cure a default on a mortgage secured by the debtor's principal residence between the time the residence is sold at a foreclosure sale and the time the deed is delivered. We will, accordingly, affirm.

Notes and Questions

1. Provided the debtor has filed a bankruptcy petition before the deadline in § 1322(c)(1) ("until such residence is sold at a foreclsoure sale that is codcuted in accordance with applicable nonbankruptcy law"), a debtor can reinstate a mortgage going forward but must cure past defaults. The cure must be "within a reasonable time." Bankruptcy Code § 1322(b)(5). What is a reasonable time. Courts freequently hold cure over the length of the chapter 13 plan is reasonable. In re Capps, 836 F.2d 773 (3d Cir. 1987).

6. Tax Returns

IN RE FRENCH

354 B.R. 258 (Bankr. E.D. Wis. 2006)

PEPPER, J.

The trustee has delayed the meeting of creditors and the recommendation regarding confirmation in this matter because the debtor has not yet filed her 2005 tax returns as required by the Bankruptcy Abuse Prevention and Consumer Protection Act of 2005 ("BAPCPA"). The debtor demands confirmation, arguing that section 1308 of BAPCPA does not require her to provide a return whose filing deadline has not yet arrived. The Court finds that the trustee's interpretation of § 1308 is the correct one, and denies the debtor's motion demanding confirmation.

Factual Background

The debtor filed for Chapter 13 protection on January 9, 2006. This means that her matter is governed by the recently-enacted BAPCPA amendments. As practitioners and parties are becoming aware, BAPCPA has changed consumer bankruptcy practice in many respects. The debtor and her counsel, however, clearly were prepared for the changes. The debtor obtained the necessary credit briefing required by § 109 of BAPCPA. She moved for continuation of the "semi-automatic" stay pursuant to § 362(c)(3), and that motion was granted. She has, since January 25, 2006, had payroll deductions taken from her check for her plan payments. It appears that, to date, the debtor is successfully working her way through the Chapter 13 proceeding.

At some point, however, the trustee notified the debtor that the meeting of creditors would be re-scheduled to a later date (currently it is scheduled for March 30, 2006) to allow the debtor to file her 2005 tax return. The trustee based this decision on § 1308 of BAPCPA, a new provision that did not exist under the old Bankruptcy Code. Section 1308(a) states that "[n]ot later than the day before the date on which the meeting of the creditors is first scheduled to be held under section 341(a), if the debtor was required to file a tax return under applicable nonbankruptcy law, the debtor shall file with appropriate tax authorities all tax returns for all taxable periods ending during the 4-year period ending on the date of the filing of the petition." The provision goes on to state that if the relevant tax returns haven't been filed by the day before the § 341 meeting, the trustee "may" hold open the meeting for "a reasonable period of time" to allow the debtor to file the returns.

The debtor disagreed. She argued that, under 26 U.S.C. § 6072(a) of the tax code, the deadline for her to file her 2005 return would not occur until April 15, and therefore, "applicable nonbankruptcy law" did not "require" her to file a return. Lacking any other means of putting this issue before the Court for adjudication, the debtor took the unusual and creative step of moving the Court for an order of confirmation, in spite of the fact that no meeting of creditors has yet been held and the trustee has not yet recommended confirmation . . .

Discussion

As indicated above, in resolving this issue, the parties and the Court must interpret a new statute, section 1308 of BAPCPA . . . The issue raised by the debtor, therefore, appears to be one of first impression.

A. Legislative History

The scattered legislative history of BAPCPA seems to indicate that, from the beginning of BAPCPA's long journey to enactment, Congress intended to require debtors to file their tax returns as a condition of confirmation. The provision went through some changes over the years -- at various points, Congress considered making debtors provide anywhere from three to six years' worth of tax returns. At one point, it appears that Congress intended to include in § 1308 a provision that if the debtor failed to file the required tax returns, the Court could dismiss or convert the case. That provision ended up being added to § 1307 instead.

The legislative history sheds a bit of light on why Congress thought it important to demand that debtors file returns. First, it appears that Congress wanted to help state revenue agencies figure out whether they had claims against the debtor. In the March 18, 2003 report from the House Judiciary Committee, one finds the following statement: "Tax return filing. A number of provisions in the bill would require debtors to have filed tax returns before a bankruptcy case may continue. Those provisions would help states identify potential claims in bankruptcy cases where they may be owed delinquent taxes."

It also appears that Congress wanted to punish those debtors who were delinquent in filing tax returns, by withholding confirmation until they did so. The following comes from the April 8, 2005 House Judiciary Report, which is dated a mere two weeks prior to the passage of BAPCPA:

> § 716: Requirement to File Tax Returns to Confirm Chapter 13 Plans. Under current law, a debtor may enjoy the benefits of chapter 13 even if delinquent in the filing of tax returns. Section 716 of the Act responds to this problem. Subsection (a) amends section 1325(a) of the Bankruptcy Code to require a chapter 13 debtor to file all applicable Federal, state and local tax returns as a condition of confirmation as required by section 1308 (as added by section 716(b)). Section 716(b) adds section 1308 to chapter 13 to require a chapter 13 debtor to be current on the filing of tax returns for the four-year period preceding the filing of the case. If the returns are not filed by the date on which the meeting of creditors is first scheduled, the trustee may hold open that meeting for a reasonable period of time to allow the debtor to file any unfiled returns.

H.R. 109-31 (Pt. 1), April 8, 2005.

B. Statutory Construction

The first step in analyzing the debtor's is to look at the statutory language ... If the Court finds that language clear [of § 1308] and unambiguous ..., then there is nothing left for the Court to do but "enforce it according to its terms."

C. Review of the Language of § 1308

Subsection (a) of § 1308 reads as follows:

> Not later than the day before the date on which the meeting of the creditors is first scheduled to be held under section 341(a), if the debtor was required to file

> a tax return under applicable nonbankruptcy law, the debtor shall file with appropriate tax authorities all tax returns for all taxable periods ending during the 4-year period ending on the date of the filing of the petition.

When the Court-and apparently, the trustee-first read this provision, the above language seemed quite clear. By the day before the date the meeting of creditors was first scheduled, a debtor had to file tax returns for each of the four years prior to the year in which he or she filed for bankruptcy if the tax code or other law required such returns to be filed. Thus, if a debtor filed for bankruptcy on January 1, 2006, and the law had required that he or she file tax returns for 2002, 2003, 2004 and 2005, then the debtor had to make sure that he or she had filed tax returns for those four years by the day before the first date scheduled for the 341 meeting.

The debtor in this case, however, takes issue with the meaning of the phrase "if the debtor was required to file a tax return under applicable nonbankruptcy law." She argues that in her case, applicable non-bankruptcy law does not require her to file a tax return. She reasons that on the day before the date first scheduled for her meeting of creditors-February 8, 2006-applicable non-bankruptcy law did not require her to file her 2005 tax return, because 26 U.S.C. § 6072 holds that, when a return is required under 26 U.S.C. §§ 6012, 6013, 6017 or 6031, it must be filed "on or before the 15th day of April following the close of the calendar year. . . ." The debtor argues that, because applicable non-bankruptcy law gave her until April 15, 2006 to file her 2005 tax return, she was not-as of February 8, 2006-"required to file a tax return under applicable nonbankruptcy law."

The Court finds this reading of the relevant phrase strained for a number of reasons. First, had Congress wished for § 1308 to have the meaning the debtor gives it, it might have said, "if the debtor was required to file a tax return by that date by applicable nonbankruptcy law." That is the meaning the debtor asks the Court to read into § 1308, in spite of the fact that Congress did not draft the statute that way.

Second, section 1308 focuses on the question of whether applicable nonbankruptcy law requires the debtor to file a return at all, not on when the applicable nonbankruptcy law requirement must be met. Under 26 U.S.C. § 6012 of the tax code, a debtor who did not earn taxable gross income equal to or in excess of the exemption amount is not required to file a tax return. Neither is a debtor who is a surviving spouse and had gross taxable income less than the sum of the exemption plus the basic standard deduction. Under 26 U.S.C. § 6017 of the tax code, a self-employed person who makes less than $400 a taxable year from that self-employment isn't required to file a return. None of these debtors would be "required to file a tax return under applicable nonbankruptcy law," and therefore would not have to file returns under § 1308.

In contrast, Schedule I of this debtor's Chapter 13 petition reflects a take-home income of $2,380.67 a month from her job in the health care industry-approximately $28,500 per year-indicating that applicable non-bankruptcy law likely requires her to file a tax return. Indeed, the debtor does not argue that she is completely exempt from having to file a tax return for 2005-only that she isn't required to do it yet. Section 1308 does not speak of debtors who aren't required to file yet, only of debtors who are required to file at all.

Third, a review of subsection (b) of § 1308 makes the debtor's construction of subsec-tion (a) more puzzling. Subsection (b)(1) gives the trustee the ability to continue the § 341 meeting to give a debtor time to meet the filing requirement in subsection (a). It states as follows:

> Subject to paragraph (2), if the tax returns required by subsection (a) have not been filed by the date on which the meeting of creditors is first schedule to be held under section 341(a), the trustee may hold open that meeting for a reasonable period of time to allow the debtor an additional period of time to file any unfiled returns, but such additional period of time shall not extend beyond-
>
> (A) for any return that is past due as of the date of the filing of the petition, the date that is 120 days after the date of that meeting; or
>
> (B) for any return that is not past due as of the date of the filing of the petition, the later of --
>
> (i) the date that is 120 days after the date of that meeting; or
>
> (ii) the date on which the return is due under the last automatic extension of time for filing that return to which the debtor is entitled, and for which request is timely made, in accordance with applicable nonbankruptcy law.

Thus, Congress gives the debtor who has not filed tax returns for one of the four preceding years the opportunity to get those returns filed. If the returns are delinquent, the debtor gets 120 days, or four months, from the date first scheduled for the meeting of creditors to remedy the delinquency. If the returns aren't delinquent-exactly the situation the current debtor faces-the debtor may have either four months from the date first scheduled for the meeting of creditors or the date the return is due under the last correctly-applied-for automatic extension, whichever is later.

When one reads § 1308(b)(2)(B)-dealing with not-yet-delinquent returns-in conjunction with § 1308(a), it becomes clear that Congress intended to make the filing of tax returns a condition of confirmation. For those debtors who file for Chapter 13 protection between January 1 and April 15 of any given year, Congress intended to require them to have their return for the prior year filed by the date first scheduled for the meeting of creditors, even if the return is not yet delinquent under the tax code. Apparently realizing, however, that it is a rare human who has his or her 2005 tax return completed and in to the taxing authorities as of January 1, 2006, Congress allowed the trustee to hold the meeting of creditors open for a sufficient amount of time to allow a well-intentioned debtor to file the previous year's return.

To interpret the phrase "if the debtor was required to file a tax return under applicable bankruptcy law" in the way the debtor requests would be to render subsection 1308(b)(1)(B) meaningless. If "required to file a tax return under applicable bankruptcy law" means "if required by the date first set for the § 341 meeting to file a tax return under applicable nonbankruptcy law," then there is no reason to give a debtor who hasn't filed a non-delinquent return additional time to do so. And as the Seventh Circuit has firmly held, courts cannot "construe a statute in a way that makes words or phrases meaningless, redundant, or superfluous."

Further, enforcing the plain meaning of § 1308 does not produce a result demonstrably at odds with the intention of its drafters. While it is often difficult to discern the drafters' intent when looking at a piece of legislation, there are a few snippets of information one can collect regarding BAPCPA. First, as indicated above in the discussion of the legislative history, Congress appears to have wanted to make sure tax returns were filed in order to assist state taxing authorities in determining whether they had claims for delinquent taxes. Second, Congress wanted to create a strong incentive for. debtors who had delinquent tax returns to get them filed.

Admittedly, both of those stated intentions appear to be directed at debtors who are delinquent in filing tax returns, not to debtors whose reason for not filing by the date specified in § 1308 is because the tax code deadline has not yet arrived. But the enforcement mechanism that Congress created in § 1308 is a requirement that the returns be filed-regardless of whether they are yet due-in order to obtain confirmation. In other words, Congress bumped up the deadline for filing tax returns for those debtors who file petitions between January 1 and April 15 of a given year.

One might argue that this is harsh treatment for those debtors who are not, and haven't been, delinquent in filing their tax returns, and have the misfortune to find themselves needing to file petitions in the first 3 1/2 months of the year. But BAPCPA contains a number of provisions which some might consider harsh-the provision in § 521(i) that requires that a debtor's petition be "automatically" dismissed if certain information has not been filed within 45 days of the filing of the petition, the provision in § 109(h) that one cannot even be a debtor if one does not obtain a pre-petition credit briefing, the provisions in § 362 that truncate or abolish the automatic stay for debtors who've had cases dismissed in the prior year. Clearly, then, a provision that creates a result some might view as harsh does not appear to be at odds with the intention of the drafters.

Further, the apparent harshness of bumping up the deadline for filing one's tax returns for creditors who file bankruptcy early in the year is softened by subsection (b)(1)(B), which lets the debtor have until April 15-and beyond, if she appropriately seeks an extension-to file the previous year's returns. True, if the debtor takes that long to file, he or she will likely delay confirmation of their Chapter 13 plans. But that delay is limited. The debtor can control the delay by getting the return filed as soon as possible, and definitely by the April 15 tax code deadline.

At the hearing on this matter, the Court inquired of the debtor's counsel what the damage would be in holding off confirmation. Counsel responded that until the plan was confirmed, it could not begin to operate to pay back the creditors as proposed. Certainly it is true that expeditious confirmation of acceptable plans is the goal in reorganization cases. But this does not mean that speed of confirmation trumps making every effort to see that the plan has a likelihood of succeeding. As the trustee pointed out at the hearing on this matter, seeing the 2005 tax return will assist him in determining the feasibility of the plan. And while the debtor is no doubt anxious to have her plan confirmed (as, quite likely, are the creditors), this is an individual reorganization. The debtor does not have a business which is languishing for lack of the ability to implement a reorganization. And the delay in confirmation will be relatively short -- the debtor indicated at the hearing that she planned to have the 2005 return filed by April 15, 2006, approximately one month from the writing of this decision.

Finally, the Court notes that the debtor is asking this Court to order confirmation of a plan when there has been no meeting of creditors, and when the debtor has not complied with what the Court concludes is the clear requirement of § 1308. There are circumstances in which a court will order confirmation over the objection of parties, but that action is not appropriate in a case such as this one.

Conclusion

The Court concludes that the meaning of § 1308 of BAPCPA is clear-the debtor must have filed her 2005 tax return by the day before the date first scheduled for the meeting of creditors in order to obtain confirmation. The trustee may hold that meeting open until 120 days after that first meeting date or the date the return is due under the last appropriately-applied-for extension of time, whichever is later. In this case, the trustee has agreed to hold open the meeting, and the debtor has indicated that she plans to timely file her return. For those reasons, it is not appropriate to force confirmation.

Notes and Questions

1. Section 1308 will supply taxing authorities with the information needed to file proofs of claim. Section 502(b)(9), as amended by BAPCPA, now provides that a taxing authority's proof of claim will be considered timely if it is filed within 60 days after the filing of a tax return under § 1308. What if the debtor filed tax returns for the preceding seven years after the petition date? Will § 502(b)(9) allow the taxing authority to file proofs of claim for all seven years or only the preceding four years?

2.New § 1307(e) provides that "upon the failure of the debtor to file a tax return under section 1308, on request of a party in interest or the United States trustee and after notice and a hearing, the court shall dismiss a case or convert [to chapter 7]." New § 1325(a)(9) provides that the Court shall confirm a plan if the debtor has filed all applicable federal, state and local tax returns as required by section 1308.

3. Section 1308(a) requires the debtor file a tax return for the previous four years if required to file a tax return under applicable nonbankruptcy law. Having income below a certain level would exempt an individual from having to file tax returns. However, a debtor who is required to file a return, but owes no taxes, is still required to file under § 1308. The effort devoted to filing these tax returns will not only fail to lead to the filing of a proof of claim by a taxing authority (one of the purposes of § 1308) but is likely to generate administrative expenses if an attorney or accountant assists in the preparation of the tax returns.

4. A court can grant a debtor additional time to file the tax returns under § 1308(b)(2) if she establishes that the failure to file a return "is attributable to circumstances beyond the control of the debtor." In addition to filing the most recent four years of tax returns, § 521(e)(2)(A)(i) requires the debtor to provide a copy of the most recently filed tax return to the trustee or any requesting creditor no later than 7 days before the first meeting of creditors. If the debtor fails to comply, the court shall dismiss the case, unless the "debtor demonstrates that the failure to comply is due to circumstances beyond the control of the debtor." See In re Ring, 341 B.R. 387, 390 (Bankr. D. Me. 2006) (beyond debtor's control if not required to file returns for past 10 years and the last filed return not available from the IRS).

D. EFFECT OF CONFIRMATION

UNITED STUDENT AID FUNDS, INC. v. ESPINOSA

2010 U.S. Lexis 2750 (March 23, 2010)

THOMAS, J.

Under Chapter 13 of the Bankruptcy Code (Code), a debtor may obtain a discharge of certain government-sponsored student loan debts only if failure to discharge that debt would impose an "undue hardship" on the debtor and his dependents. 11 U.S.C. §§ 523(a)(8), 1328. The Federal Rules of Bankruptcy Procedure require bankruptcy courts to make this undue hardship determination in an adversary proceeding, see Rule 7001(6), which the party seeking the determination must initiate by serving a summons and complaint on his adversary, see Rules 7003, 7004, 7008. The debtor in this case filed a plan with the Bankruptcy Court that proposed to discharge a portion of his student loan debt, but he failed to initiate the adversary proceeding as required for such discharge. The creditor received notice of, but did not object to, the plan, and failed to file an appeal after the Bankruptcy Court subsequently confirmed the plan. Years later, the creditor filed a motion under Federal Rule of Civil Procedure 60(b)(4) asking the Bankruptcy Court to rule that its order confirming the plan was void because the order was issued in violation of the Code and Rules. We granted certiorari to resolve a disagreement among the Courts of Appeals as to whether an order that confirms the discharge of a student loan debt in the absence of an undue hardship finding or an adversary proceeding, or both, is a void judgment for Rule 60(b)(4) purposes.

I

Between 1988 and 1989, respondent Francisco Espinosa obtained four federally guaranteed student loans for a total principal amount of $ 13,250. In 1992, Espinosa filed a bankruptcy petition under Chapter 13. That Chapter permits individual debtors to develop a plan to repay all or a portion of their debts over a period of time specified in the plan. See Nobelman v. American Savings Bank, 508 U.S. 324, 327 (1993); see also §§ 301(a), 1321; Fed. Rule Bkrtcy. Proc. 3015(b). A proposed bankruptcy plan becomes effective upon confirmation, see §§ 1324, 1325, and will result in a discharge of the debts listed in the plan if the debtor completes the payments the plan requires, see § 1328(a).

Espinosa's plan listed his student loan debt as his only specific indebtedness. App. 15-18. The plan proposed to repay only the principal on that debt, stating that the remainder -- the accrued interest -- would be discharged once Espinosa repaid the principal. Id., at 26.

As the Federal Rules of Bankruptcy Procedure require, the clerk of the Bankruptcy Court mailed notice and a copy of Espinosa's plan to petitioner United Student Aid Funds, Inc. (United), the creditor to whom Espinosa owed the student loan debt.[1] Id., at 34; see Rules 2002(b), (g)(2), 3015(d). In boldface type immediately below the caption, the plan stated: "WARNING IF YOU ARE A CREDITOR YOUR RIGHTS MAY BE IMPAIRED BY THIS PLAN." Id., at 23. The plan also noted the deadlines for filing a proof of claim or an objection to the plan. Id., at 26-27.

United received this notice and, in response, filed a proof of claim for $ 17,832.15, an amount representing both the principal and the accrued interest on Espinosa's student loans. Id., at 35. United did not object to the plan's proposed discharge of Espinosa's student loan interest without a determination of undue hardship, nor did it object to Espinosa's failure to initiate an adversary proceeding to determine the dischargeability of that debt.

In May 1993, the Bankruptcy Court confirmed Espinosa's plan without holding an adversary proceeding or making a finding of undue hardship. One month later, the Chapter 13 trustee mailed United a form notice stating that "[t]he amount of the claim filed differs from the amount listed for payment in the

[1] United is a guaranty agency that administers the collection of federally guaranteed student loans in accordance with regulations promulgated by the United States Department of Education. See, e.g., 34 CFR § 682.200 et seq. (2009).

plan" and that "[y]our claim will be paid as listed in the plan." Id., at 44. The form also apprised United that if United "wishe[d] to dispute the above stated treatment of the claim," it had the "responsibility" to notify the trustee within 30 days. Ibid. United did not respond to that notice.

In May 1997, Espinosa completed the payments on his student loan principal, as required by the plan. Shortly thereafter, the Bankruptcy Court discharged Espinosa's student loan interest.[2]

In 2000, the United States Department of Education commenced efforts to collect the unpaid interest on Espinosa's student loans.[3] In response, Espinosa filed a motion in 2003 asking the Bankruptcy Court to enforce its 1997 discharge order by directing the Department and United to cease all efforts to collect the unpaid interest on his student loan debt.

United opposed that motion and filed a cross-motion under Federal Rule of Civil Procedure 60(b)(4) seeking to set aside as void the Bankruptcy Court's 1993 order confirming Espinosa's plan. United made two arguments in support of its motion. First, United claimed that the provision of Espinosa's plan authorizing the discharge of his student loan interest was inconsistent with the Code, which requires a court to find undue hardship before discharging a student loan debt, §§ 523(a)(8), 1328(a), and with the Bankruptcy Rules, which require the court to make the undue hardship finding in an adversary proceeding, see Rule 7001(6). Second, United argued that its due process rights had been violated because Espinosa failed to serve it with the summons and complaint the Bankruptcy Rules require as a prerequisite to an adversarial proceeding. See Rules 7003, 7004, 7008.

The Bankruptcy Court rejected both arguments, granted Espinosa's motion in relevant part, denied United's cross-motion, and ordered all claimants to cease and desist their collection efforts. United sought review in the District Court, which reversed. That court held that United was denied due process because the confirmation order was issued without service of the summons and complaint the Bankruptcy Rules require.

Espinosa appealed to the Court of Appeals for the Ninth Circuit, which issued an initial per curiam opinion remanding the case to the Bankruptcy Court to consider correcting an apparent clerical error in its discharge order.[4] 530 F.3d

---

[2] The discharge order contained an apparent clerical error that the courts below considered and addressed in adjudicating these proceedings. See n. 4, infra.

[3] After Espinosa completed payments under the plan, United assigned Espinosa's loans to the Department under a reinsurance agreement. After these proceedings began, United requested and received a recall of the loans from the Department. App. to Pet. for Cert. 63.

[4] The one-page discharge order contained a paragraph that purported to exclude "'any debt . . . for a student loan'" from the discharge. 530 F.3d 895, 896 (CA9 2008). That provision appeared irreconcilable with the confirmation order, which contemplated the discharge of the interest on Espinosa's student loan debt. Suggesting that the Bankruptcy Court may have automatically generated the discharge order without tailoring it to the terms of the confirmation order, the Court of Appeals remanded the case to the Bankruptcy Court to consider amending the discharge order to conform to the confirmation order. Id., at 899; see Fed. Rule Civ. Proc. 60(a) (authorizing a court to "correct a clerical mistake or a mistake arising from oversight or omission"). On remand, the Bankruptcy Court found that the text of its discharge order excepting Espinosa's student loan debt from discharge "was inserted because of a clerical mistake" and struck that language from the order. App. 48.

Although certain amici press the point, United has not challenged the substance of the Bankruptcy Court's amendment to the order or asked us to consider whether such amendment was proper under Rule 60(a). See Brief for Petitioner 42; Reply Brief for Petitioner 20. Thus, we

895, 899 (2008). The Bankruptcy Court corrected the error, after which the Court of Appeals resubmitted the case and reversed the judgment of the District Court. The Court of Appeals concluded that by confirming Espinosa's plan without first finding undue hardship in an adversary proceeding, the Bankruptcy Court at most committed a legal error that United might have successfully appealed, but that any such legal error was not a basis for setting aside the confirmation order as void under Rule 60(b). 553 F.3d 1193, 1198-1202 (2008).[5] In addition, the Court of Appeals held that although Espinosa's failure to serve United with a summons and complaint before seeking a discharge of his student loan debt violated the Bankruptcy Rules, this defect in service was not a basis upon which to declare the judgment void because United received actual notice of Espinosa's plan and failed to object. See id., at 1202-1205.[6]

We granted certiorari . . . .

II

A discharge under Chapter 13 "is broader than the discharge received in any other chapter." 8 Collier on Bankruptcy P1328.01, p. 1328-5 (rev. 15th ed. 2008). Chapter 13 nevertheless restricts or prohibits entirely the discharge of certain types of debts. As relevant here, § 1328(a) provides that when a debtor has completed the repayments required by a confirmed plan, a bankruptcy court "shall grant the debtor a discharge of all debts provided for by the plan or disallowed under section 502 of this title, except," inter alia, "any debt . . . of the kind specified in [§ 523(a)(8)]." § 1328(a)(2). Section 523(a)(8), in turn, specifies certain student loan debts "unless excepting such debt from discharge . . . would impose an undue hardship on the debtor and the debtor's dependents." As noted, the Bankruptcy Rules require a party seeking to determine the dischargeability of a student loan debt to commence an adversary proceeding by serving a summons and complaint on affected creditors. See supra, at 4. We must decide whether the Bankruptcy Court's order confirming Espinosa's plan is "void" under Federal Rule Civil Procedure 60(b)(4) because the Bankruptcy Court confirmed the plan without complying with these requirements.[7]

A

The Bankruptcy Court's order confirming Espinosa's proposed plan was a final judgment, see In re Optical Technologies, Inc., 425 F.3d 1294, 1300 (CA11 2005), from which United did not appeal. Ordinarily, "the finality of [a] Bankruptcy Court's orders following the conclusion of direct review" would

express no view on those issues. See Kamen v. Kemper Financial Services, Inc., 500 U.S. 90, 97, n. 4, 111 S. Ct. 1711, 114 L. Ed. 2d 152 (1991) (noting that "we do not ordinarily address issues raised only by amici").

[5] In so doing, the Court of Appeals disagreed with two other Courts of Appeals. See In re Mersmann, 505 F.3d 1033, 1047-1049 (CA10 2007) (en banc); Whelton v. Educational Credit Management Corp., 432 F.3d 150, 154 (CA2 2005).

[6] Three Courts of Appeals have reached the opposite conclusion on similar facts. See In re Ruehle, 412 F.3d 679, 682-684 (CA6 2005); In re Hanson, 397 F.3d 482, 486 (CA7 2005); In re Banks, 299 F.3d 296, 302-303 (CA4 2002).

[7] Because United brought this action on a motion for relief from judgment under Rule 60(b)(4), our holding is confined to that provision. We express no view on the terms upon which other provisions of the Bankruptcy Rules may entitle a debtor or creditor to postjudgment relief.

"stan[d] in the way of challenging [their] enforceability." Travelers Indemnity Co. v. Bailey, 557 U.S. 137, 140 (2009). Rule 60(b), however, provides an "exception to finality," Gonzalez v. Crosby, 545 U.S. 524, 529 (2005), that "allows a party to seek relief from a final judgment, and request reopening of his case, under a limited set of circumstances," id., at 528. Specifically, Rule 60(b)(4) -- the provision under which United brought this motion -- authorizes the court to relieve a party from a final judgment if "the judgment is void."[8]

A void judgment is a legal nullity. See Black's Law Dictionary 1822 (3d ed. 1933); see also id., at 1709 (9th ed. 2009). Although the term "void" describes a result, rather than the conditions that render a judgment unenforceable, it suffices to say that a void judgment is one so affected by a fundamental infirmity that the infirmity may be raised even after the judgment becomes final. See Restatement (Second) of Judgments 22 (1980); see generally id., § 12. The list of such infirmities is exceedingly short; otherwise, Rule 60(b)(4)'s exception to finality would swallow the rule.

"A judgment is not void," for example, "simply because it is or may have been erroneous." Hoult v. Hoult, 57 F.3d 1, 6 (CA1 1995); 12 J. Moore et al., Moore's Federal Practice § 60.44[1][a], pp. 60-150 to 60-151 (3d ed. 2007) (hereinafter Moore's). Similarly, a motion under Rule 60(b)(4) is not a substitute for a timely appeal. Kocher v. Dow Chemical Co., 132 F.3d 1225, 1229 (CA8 1997); see Moore's § 60.44[1][a], at 60-150. Instead, Rule 60(b)(4) applies only in the rare instance where a judgment is premised either on a certain type of jurisdictional error or on a violation of due process that deprives a party of notice or the opportunity to be heard. See United States v. Boch Oldsmobile, Inc., 909 F.2d 657, 661 (CA1 1990); Moore's § 60.44[1][a]; 11 C. Wright, A. Miller, & M. Kane, Federal Practice & Procedure § 2862, p. 331 (2d ed. 1995 and Supp. 2009); cf. Chicot County Drainage Dist. v. Baxter State Bank, 308 U.S. 371, 376 (1940); Stoll v. Gottlieb, 305 U.S. 165, 171-172 (1938). The error United alleges falls in neither category.

1

Federal courts considering Rule 60(b)(4) motions that assert a judgment is void because of a jurisdictional defect generally have reserved relief only for the exceptional case in which the court that rendered judgment lacked even an "arguable basis" for jurisdiction. Nemaizer v. Baker, 793 F.2d 58, 65 (CA2 1986); see, e.g., Boch Oldsmobile, supra, at 661-662 ("[T]otal want of jurisdiction must

[8] Subject to certain exceptions, Bankruptcy Rule 9024 makes Rule 60(b) applicable to Chapter 13 proceedings. One such exception provides that "a complaint to revoke an order confirming a plan may be filed only within the time allowed by" 11 U.S.C. § 1330. Fed. Rule Bkrtcy. Proc. 9024. Section 1330(a) imposes a 180-day time limit for a party to seek revocation of a confirmation order "procured by fraud." Courts of Appeals disagree as to whether a Rule 60(b)(4) motion should be treated as a "complaint to revoke" a plan subject to § 1330's time limit and substantive limitation to motions based on fraud. Compare Whelton, 432 F.3d at 156, n. 2, with In re Fesq, 153 F.3d 113, 119, and n. 8 (CA3 1998). We need not settle that question, however, because the parties did not raise it in the courts below. And even under a theory that would treat United's Rule 60(b)(4) motion as a "complaint to revoke" the plan, United's failure to file its motion within § 1330(a)'s 180-day deadline and its failure to seek relief on the basis of fraud did not deprive those courts -- and does not deprive us -- of authority to consider the motion on the merits because those limitations are not jurisdictional. See Arbaugh v. Y & H Corp., 546 U.S. 500, 515-516 (2006); Reed Elsevier, Inc. v. Muchnick, ante, at 12-13.

be distinguished from an error in the exercise of jurisdiction, and . . . only rare instances of a clear usurpation of power will render a judgment void" (brackets and internal quotation marks omitted)).

This case presents no occasion to engage in such an "arguable basis" inquiry or to define the precise circumstances in which a jurisdictional error will render a judgment void because United does not argue that the Bankruptcy Court's error was jurisdictional. Reply Brief for Petitioner 5, 11. Such an argument would fail in any event. First, § 523(a)(8)'s statutory requirement that a bankruptcy court find undue hardship before discharging a student loan debt is a precondition to obtaining a discharge order, not a limitation on the bankruptcy court's jurisdiction. See, e.g., Arbaugh v. Y & H Corp., 546 U.S. 500, 515-516 (2006). Second, the requirement that a bankruptcy court make this finding in an adversary proceeding derives from the Bankruptcy Rules, see Rule Proc. 7001(6), which are "procedural rules adopted by the Court for the orderly transaction of its business" that are "not jurisdictional." Kontrick v. Ryan, 540 U.S. 443, 454 (2004) (internal quotation marks omitted).

2

Although United concedes that the Bankruptcy Court had jurisdiction to enter the order confirming Espinosa's plan, United contends that the court's judgment is void under Rule 60(b)(4) because United did not receive adequate notice of Espinosa's proposed discharge of his student loan interest. Specifically, United argues that the Bankruptcy Court violated United's due process rights by confirming Espinosa's plan despite Espinosa's failure to serve the summons and complaint the Bankruptcy Rules require for the commencement of an adversary proceeding. We disagree.

Espinosa's failure to serve United with a summons and complaint deprived United of a right granted by a procedural rule. See Fed. Rule Bkrtcy. Proc. 7004(b)(3). United could have timely objected to this deprivation and appealed from an adverse ruling on its objection. But this deprivation did not amount to a violation of United's constitutional right to due process. Due process requires notice "reasonably calculated, under all the circumstances, to apprise interested parties of the pendency of the action and afford them an opportunity to present their objections." Mullane v. Central Hanover Bank & Trust Co., 339 U.S. 306, 314 (1950); see also Jones v. Flowers, 547 U.S. 220, 225 (2006) ("[D]ue process does not require actual notice"). Here, United received actual notice of the filing and contents of Espinosa's plan. This more than satisfied United's due process rights. Accordingly, on these facts, Espinosa's failure to serve a summons and complaint does not entitle United to relief under Rule 60(b)(4).

B

Unable to demonstrate a jurisdictional error or a due process violation, United and the Government, as amicus, urge us to expand the universe of judgment defects that support Rule 60(b)(4) relief. Specifically, they contend that the Bankruptcy Court's confirmation order is void because the court lacked statutory authority to confirm Espinosa's plan absent a finding of undue hardship. In support of this contention, they cite the text of § 523(a)(8), which provides that student loan debts guaranteed by governmental units are not dischargeable "unless" a court finds undue hardship. 11 U.S.C. § 523(a)(8) (emphasis added).

They argue that this language imposes a "'self-executing' limitation on the effect of a discharge order" that renders the order legally unenforceable, and thus void, if it is not satisfied. Brief for Petitioner 23-24; Brief for United States as Amicus Curiae 18 (quoting Tennessee Student Assistance Corporation v. Hood, 541 U.S. 440, 450 (2004)). In addition, United cites § 1325(a)(1), which instructs bankruptcy courts to confirm only those plans that comply with "the . . . applicable provisions" of the Code. Reading these provisions in tandem, United argues that an order confirming a plan that purports to discharge a student loan debt without an undue hardship finding is "doubly beyond the court's authority and therefore void." Brief for Petitioner 13.

We are not persuaded that a failure to find undue hardship in accordance with § 523(a)(8) is on par with the jurisdictional and notice failings that define void judgments that qualify for relief under Rule 60(b)(4). As noted, § 523(a)(8) does not limit the bankruptcy court's jurisdiction over student loan debts.[9] Supra, at 9-10; see Hood, 541 U.S., at 447 (noting that "[b]ankruptcy courts have exclusive jurisdiction over a debtor's property"). Nor does the provision impose requirements that, if violated, would result in a denial of due process. Instead, § 523(a)(8) requires a court to make a certain finding before confirming the discharge of a student loan debt. It is true, as we explained in Hood, that this requirement is "'self-executing.'" Id., at 450.[10] But that means only that the bankruptcy court must make an undue hardship finding even if the creditor does not request one; it does not mean that a bankruptcy court's failure to make the

---

[9] Sections 1328(a) and 523(a)(8) provide that student loan debt is dischargeable in a Chapter 13 proceeding if a court makes a finding of undue hardship. In contrast, other provisions in Chapter 13 provide that certain other debts are not dischargeable under any circumstances. See, e.g., §§ 523(a)(1)(B), (C) (specified tax debts); § 523(a)(5) (domestic support obligations); § 523(a)(9) (debts "caused by" the debtor's unlawful operation of a vehicle while intoxicated). We express no view on the conditions under which an order confirming the discharge of one of these types of debt could be set aside as void.

[10] The Government suggests that § 523(a)(8)'s "self-executing" nature derives in part from the text of § 523(a), which states that "[a] discharge under section 727 . . . or 1328(b) of this title does not discharge an individual debtor from any debt," including the student loan debts specified in paragraph (8) (emphasis added); see Brief for United States as Amicus Curiae 18; see also Reply Brief for Petitioner 1-2. That is not what we concluded in Hood and, in this case, would be irrelevant in any event.

In Hood, we described as "'self-executing'" paragraph (8)'s instruction that student loan debt not be discharged "unless" an undue hardship determination is made. 541 U.S., at 450. The "does not discharge" language in § 523(a), which applies generally to every enumerated paragraph in that section -- and to which we never referred in Hood -- was not relevant to our analysis. That is evident from the authority we cited to support our description of § 523(a)(8)'s condition as "'self-executing.'" E.g., id., at 450 (citing S. Rep. No. 95-989, p. 79 (1978), which states that "[p]aragraph (8) . . . is intended to be self-executing" insofar as "the lender or institution is not required to file a complaint to determine the nondischargeability of any student loan" (emphasis added)).

In any event, the "does not discharge" language in § 523(a) is inapplicable to this case. Section 523(a) provides that "[a] discharge under section 727, 1141, 1228(a), 1228(b), or 1328(b) of [the Code] does not discharge an individual debtor from" the debts described in § 523(a)'s enumerated paragraphs. But Espinosa did not seek a discharge under "sections 727, 1141, 1228(a), 1228(b), or 1328(b)." He sought a discharge under § 1328(a), which provides that, upon completion of a Chapter 13 plan, a bankruptcy court "shall grant the debtor a discharge of all debts provided for by the plan . . ., except any debt . . . of the kind specified in . . . paragraph . . . (5), (8), or (9) of section 523(a)." (Emphasis added). Section 1328(a) thus incorporates by reference paragraph (8) of § 523(a), including that paragraph's self-executing requirement for an undue hardship determination, but does not incorporate the "does not discharge" text of § 523(a) itself.

finding renders its subsequent confirmation order void for purposes of Rule 60(b)(4).[11]

Given the Code's clear and self-executing requirement for an undue hardship determination, the Bankruptcy Court's failure to find undue hardship before confirming Espinosa's plan was a legal error. See Part III, infra. But the order remains enforceable and binding on United because United had notice of the error and failed to object or timely appeal.

United's response -- that it had no obligation to object to Espinosa's plan until Espinosa served it with the summons and complaint the Bankruptcy Rules require, Brief for Petitioner 33 -- is unavailing. Rule 60(b)(4) does not provide a license for litigants to sleep on their rights. United had actual notice of the filing of Espinosa's plan, its contents, and the Bankruptcy Court's subsequent confirmation of the plan. In addition, United filed a proof of claim regarding Espinosa's student loan debt, thereby submitting itself to the Bankruptcy Court's jurisdiction with respect to that claim. See Langenkamp v. Culp, 498 U.S. 42, 44 (1990) (per curiam). United therefore forfeited its arguments regarding the validity of service or the adequacy of the Bankruptcy Court's procedures by failing to raise a timely objection in that court.

Rule 60(b)(4) strikes a balance between the need for finality of judgments and the importance of ensuring that litigants have a full and fair opportunity to litigate a dispute. Where, as here, a party is notified of a plan's contents and fails to object to confirmation of the plan before the time for appeal expires, that party has been afforded a full and fair opportunity to litigate, and the party's failure to avail itself of that opportunity will not justify Rule 60(b)(4) relief. We thus agree with the Court of Appeals that the Bankruptcy Court's confirmation order is not void.

III

In issuing its judgment, however, the Court of Appeals looked beyond the narrow question whether the Bankruptcy Court's order confirming Espinosa's plan was void under Rule 60(b)(4). It canvassed other bankruptcy court decisions within the Circuit that presented a different question -- whether a bankruptcy court presented with a debtor's plan that proposes to discharge a student loan debt, in the absence of an adversary proceeding to determine undue hardship, should confirm the plan despite its failure to comply with the Code and Rules. The Court of Appeals noted that some Bankruptcy Courts had declined to confirm such plans "even when the creditor fail[ed] to object to the plan." 553 F.3d at 1205. The court disapproved that practice and overruled those cases, stating that bankruptcy courts must confirm a plan proposing the discharge of a student loan debt without a determination of undue hardship in an adversary proceeding unless the creditor timely raises a specific objection. Ibid. This, we think, was a step too far.

As Espinosa concedes, Tr. of Oral Arg. 31, 36, a Chapter 13 plan that

---

[11] United relies on our decisions in United States ex rel. Wilson v. Walker, 109 U.S. 258 (1883), and Vallely v. Northern Fire & Marine Ins. Co., 254 U.S. 348 (1920), to argue otherwise. Those authorities are not controlling because they predate Rule 60(b)(4)'s enactment and because we interpreted the statutes at issue in those cases as stripping courts of jurisdiction -- either over the parties, id., at 354-56, or the res, Wilson, supra, at 265-66, and United concedes that the statutory limit in this case is not jurisdictional. See supra, at 9.

proposes to discharge a student loan debt without a determination of undue hardship violates §§ 1328(a)(2) and 523(a)(8). Failure to comply with this self-executing requirement should prevent confirmation of the plan even if the creditor fails to object, or to appear in the proceeding at all. See Hood, 541 U.S., at 450.[12] That is because § 1325(a) instructs a bankruptcy court to confirm a plan only if the court finds, inter alia, that the plan complies with the "applicable provisions" of the Code. § 1325(a) (providing that a bankruptcy court "shall confirm a plan" if the plan "complies with the provisions of" Chapter 13 and with "other applicable provisions of this title"); see Johnson v. Home State Bank, 501 U.S. 78, 87 (1991); see also § 105(a) (authorizing bankruptcy courts to issue "any order, process, or judgment that is necessary or appropriate to carry out" the Code's provisions).[13] Thus, contrary to the Court of Appeals' assertion, the Code makes plain that bankruptcy courts have the authority -- indeed, the obligation -- to direct a debtor to conform his plan to the requirements of §§ 1328(a)(2) and 523(a)(8).[14]

We are mindful that conserving assets is an important concern in a bankruptcy proceeding. We thus assume that, in some cases, a debtor and creditor may agree that payment of a student loan debt will cause the debtor an undue hardship sufficient to justify discharge. In such a case, there is no reason that compliance with the undue hardship requirement should impose significant costs on the parties or materially delay confirmation of the plan. Neither the Code nor the Rules prevent the parties from stipulating to the underlying facts of undue hardship, and neither prevents the creditor from waiving service of a summons and complaint. See Fed. Rule Bkrtcy. Proc. 7004; Fed. Rule Civ. Proc. 4(k). But, to comply with § 523(a)(8)'s directive, the bankruptcy court must make an independent determination of undue hardship before a plan is confirmed, even if the creditor fails to object or appear in the adversary proceeding. See supra, at 12.

IV

United argues that our failure to declare the Bankruptcy Court's order void will encourage unscrupulous debtors to abuse the Chapter 13 process by filing plans proposing to dispense with the undue hardship requirement in the

---

[12] This is essential to preserve the distinction between Congress' treatment of student loan debts in § 523(a)(8) and debts listed elsewhere in § 523. Section 523(a)(8) renders student loan debt presumptively nondischargeable "unless" a determination of undue hardship is made. In contrast, the debts listed in § 523(c), which include certain debts obtained by fraud or "willful and malicious injury by the debtor," § 523(a)(6), are presumptively dischargeable "unless" the creditor requests a hearing to determine the debt's dischargeability. The Court of Appeals' approach would subject student loan debt to the same rules as the debts specified in § 523(c), notwithstanding the evident differences in the statutory framework for discharging the two types of debt.

[13] In other contexts, we have held that courts have the discretion, but not the obligation, to raise on their own initiative certain nonjurisdictional barriers to suit. See Day v. McDonough, 547 U.S. 198, 202, 209 (2006) (statute of limitations); Granberry v. Greer, 481 U.S. 129, 134 (1987) (habeas corpus petitioner's exhaustion of state remedies). Section 1325(a) does more than codify this principle; it requires bankruptcy courts to address and correct a defect in a debtor's proposed plan even if no creditor raises the issue.

[14] Bankruptcy courts appear to be well aware of this statutory obligation. See, e.g., In re Mammel, 221 B. R. 238, 239 (Bkrtcy. Ct. ND Iowa 1998) ("[W]hether or not an objection is presently lodged in this case, the Court retains the authority to review this plan and deny confirmation if it fails to comply with the confirmation standards of the Code").

hopes the bankruptcy court will overlook the proposal and the creditor will not object. In the event the objectionable provision is discovered, United claims, the debtor can withdraw the plan and file another without penalty.

We acknowledge the potential for bad-faith litigation tactics. But expanding the availability of relief under Rule 60(b)(4) is not an appropriate prophylaxis. As we stated in Taylor v. Freeland & Kronz, 503 U.S. 638 (1992), "[d]ebtors and their attorneys face penalties under various provisions for engaging in improper conduct in bankruptcy proceedings," id., at 644; see Fed. Rule Bkrtcy. Proc. 9011. The specter of such penalties should deter bad-faith attempts to discharge student loan debt without the undue hardship finding Congress required. And to the extent existing sanctions prove inadequate to this task, Congress may enact additional provisions to address the difficulties United predicts will follow our decision.

The judgment of the Court of Appeals for the Ninth Circuit is affirmed. It is so ordered.

Notes and Questions

1. After Espinosa, does a student loan creditor have the right to insist that the hardship questioon be adjudicated in an adversary proceeding?

2. The Espinosa Court invites bankruptcy judges to find a hardship exists in the context of a confirmation hearing. What evidence should the judge require? See Federal Rules of Bankruptcy Procedure 3015(f).

3. In Universal American Mortgage Co. v. Bateman (In re Bateman), 331 F.3d 821 (11th Cir. 2001), the court approved a chapter 13 plan that modified a home mortgage in violation of Bankruptcy Code § 1322(b). The mortgage lender did not object. Later the lender filed a proof of claim as if the plan did not modify the mortgage. The court ruled that, inherently, the plan could not abrogate the rights of a mortgage lender who never consented to the modification. Is Bateman still good law after Espinosa?

E. CHAPTER 13 DISCHARGE

IN RE HARRELL

318 B.R. 692 (Bankr. E.D. Ark. 2005)

JAMES G. MIXON.

Before the Court is an objection to confirmation of the chapter 13 plan proposed by Bobbie Harrell ("Debtor"). The Department of Finance and Administration for the State of Arkansas ("DFA") objects to the plan's treatment of debts owed to DFA for income taxes for the tax years 1996, 1997, and 1998. DFA contends that the Debtor's plan has improperly treated its claims as general unsecured claims when they are actually entitled to priority classification as debts that must be paid in full over the life of the plan.

At the hearing on the objection on October 4, 2004, the parties stipulated to the facts in the case and subsequently submitted post-trial briefs arguing their positions on the issue of whether the tax debts are entitled to priority. . . .

FACTS

The Debtor filed her chapter 13 petition for bankruptcy relief on June 10, 2003. DFA was not originally listed as a creditor, but the plan was modified on July 6, 2004, to include DFA as a general unsecured creditor.

Returns for the taxes at issue were due more than three years prior to the bankruptcy petition filing, specifically on May 15 of the tax years 1997, 1998, and 1999. The Debtor filed the returns post-petition on August 4, 2003. The Debtor's modified plan reflects that she owes DFA $14,549.99.

DISCUSSION

In its post-trial brief, DFA argues that the taxes due for 1996-1998 are entitled to priority treatment by virtue of 11 U.S.C. § 507(a)(8)(A)(iii). The Debtor counters that under the facts of this case, the taxes at issue fail to meet any of the requirements for priority treatment of tax debt under sections 507(a)(8)(A)(i)-(iii) . . . .

The Bankruptcy Code provides that allowed, unsecured claims of governmental units are entitled to eighth priority if the claims are for a tax on income "other than a tax of a kind specified in section 523(a)(1)(B) or 523(a)(1)(C) of this title, not assessed before, but assessable, under applicable law or by agreement, after, the commencement of the case." 11 U.S.C. § 507(a)(8)(A)(iii)(2000). Section 523(a)(1)(B) refers to income taxes for which a return either was not filed or was untimely filed while section 523(a)(1)(C) deals with debts arising from fraudulent tax returns or willful evasion of taxes.

A leading treatise on bankruptcy explains that subsection 507(a)(8)(A)(iii) gives priority to income tax not assessed before but still assessable after the commencement of the case. However, unassessed but assessable taxes of a kind specified in section 523(a)(1)(B) or (C) are not entitled to priority under section 507(a)(8)(A)(iii). . .

With regard to the instant case, two issues must be determined under the statute: whether the taxes at issue were unassessed but assessable under applicable law or by agreement at the commencement of the case and if so, whether the taxes are nevertheless excluded from priority because they meet the section 523(a)(1)(B) or (C) exceptions to priority classification under section 507(a)(8)(A)(iii). . .

The Debtor does not dispute that the taxes were unassessed but assessable when the bankruptcy petition was filed. Instead, she argues that the taxes are excluded from section 507(a)(8)(A)(iii) priority because, even though the taxes were unassessed but assessable, they meet the requirements of the 523(a)(1)(B) exception.

This Code section provides:

> (a) A discharge under section 727, 1141, 1228(a), 1228(b), or 1328(b) of this title does not discharge an individual debtor from any debt-
>
> (1) for a tax or a customs duty-
>
> . . .
>
> (B) with respect to which a return, if required-
>
> (i) was not filed; or
>
> (ii) was filed after the date on which such return was last due, under applicable law or under any extension, and after two years before the date of the filing of the petition . . .

11 U.S.C. § 523(a)(1)(B)(i)-(ii) (2000).

Specifically, the Debtor argues that the debts owed to DFA are the kind described by section 523(a)(1)(B)(ii). This provision "extends nondischargeability beyond the failure to file a return at all; it makes nondischargeable taxes for which a return had been filed beyond its last permitted due date . . . if the return is filed less than two years before the bankruptcy petition." 4 Collier on Bankruptcy P 523.07[3][b].

Under chapters 7, 11, and 12 and under the chapter 13 hardship discharge provision, tax debt described by section 523(a)(1)(B)(ii) is excepted from discharge. Therefore, although such debt is not entitled to a priority classification under section 507(a)(8)(A)(iii), it survives the discharge and remains a liability of the debtor after the case is closed.

In a recent opinion from the Bankruptcy Appellate Panel for the Ninth Circuit, the court explained the legislative rationale for not granting the government priority over this nevertheless nondischargeable debt. The court stated,

> The bankruptcy policy for this treatment is that it is not fair to penalize private creditors of the debtor by paying out of the 'pot' of assets in the estate tax liabilities arising from the debtor's deliberate misconduct. On the other hand, the debtor should not be able to use bankruptcy to escape these kinds of taxes. Therefore, these taxes have no priority in payment from the estate but would survive as continuing debts after the case.

Savria v. United States (In re Savaria), 317 B.R. 395 n.1 (B.A.P. 9th Cir. 2004) (quoting S. Rep. No. 95-110622 (1978) . . .

However, such a debt will be discharged under chapter 13, the bankruptcy chapter offering a "super discharge" that eliminates most of the exceptions to discharge detailed in 11 U.S.C. § 523. See 11 U.S.C. § 1328(a) (2000)(exceptions to the section 1328(a) discharge do not include tax debts enumerated under section 523(a)(1)(A), (B) or (C)).

Thus, in a chapter 13 case, taxes that are unassessed but assessable but also of a kind described in section 523(a)(1)(B) or (C) are not entitled to priority under section 507(a)(8)(A)(iii) and will also be discharged upon completion of the plan, a result that occurs only in chapter 13. See, e.g., In re Zieg, 194 B.R. 469, 474 (Bankr. D.Neb. 1996) (ruling that debts for taxes on chapter 13 debtor's embezzled income were of a kind described in section 523(a)(1)(C) and therefore not entitled to priority under section 507(a)(8)(A)(iii) and also dischargeable under the plan as a general unsecured claim); In re Verdunn, 160 B.R. 682, 685 (Bankr. M.D. Fla. 1993) (stating that the clear language of the bankruptcy code dictates tax fraud claims are not afforded priority under section 507(a)(7)(A)(iii)). But see In re Norman, 162 B.R. 581, 582 (Bankr. M.D. Fla. 1993) (finding that a chapter 13 plan was not proposed in good faith and denying confirmation where the debtor delayed filing prepetition tax returns until after bankruptcy was filed in order to render tax debts nonpriority).

. . . In the instant case, the debts owed to DFA resulted from delinquent taxes. Returns for those taxes were filed August 4, 2003, which was after the date on which the returns were due under applicable law or under any extension. The returns were filed after June 10, 2001, which is the date that is two years before the petition date of June 10, 2003. Thus, subsection 523(a)(1)(B)(ii) applies to those taxes, and they are excluded from priority treatment under section 507(a)(8)(A)(iii).

Admittedly, the discussion of the interplay of the various sections of the Bankruptcy Code dealing with tax claim priority in chapter 13 is complicated, and the result reached here appears unjust. Because the debt is not entitled to priority classification, the Debtor will be allowed to pay her delinquent tax debt as a general unsecured claim on a pro rata basis and discharge the tax debt that remains at the conclusion of the case.

Bankruptcy courts dealing with section 507(a)(8)(A)(iii) in chapter 13 cases agree that the statute is clear in its intent and concede that only Congress may amend the Bankruptcy Code. In deciding that a chapter 13 debtor was not required to treat the tax debt on embezzled income as a priority claim because it fell within the section 523(a)(1)(C) exception to priority, Judge Timothy Mahoney stated:

> It is apparent that in the history of Chapter 13 several times a situation has arisen where the discharge of a debt in Chapter 13 resulted in an unfair or unpopular result, and Congress has acted to amend the Bankruptcy Code. Congress has not, however, acted to make claims due for a fraudulent return nondischargeable in Chapter 13. Such inaction is not necessarily inconsistent with the original congressional policy in creating a broader discharge under Chapter 13, which was to encourage debtors to select Chapter 13 and pay creditors something over a number of years, rather than selecting a Chapter 7 liquidation and pay nontax creditors nothing.

For the reasons stated above, DFA's claims are general unsecured claims not entitled to priority treatment. The objection to confirmation is overruled.

Notes and Questions

1. BAPCPA does not reverse the result in Harrell, but it does affect the dicta concerning discharge by excepting from discharge any tax claim listed in § 523(a)(1)(B) or (C). But it is still possible to say that chapter 13 offers the debtor a "super discharge," in that taxes described in § 523(a)(1)(A) may be discharged in chapter 13. These are taxes in which no default in filing and no fraud has been involved.

2. The Supreme Court has explained the broader discharge in chapter 13 as follows:

> The dischargeability of debts in chapter 13 that are not dischargeable in chapter 7 represents a policy judgment that [it] is preferable for debtors to attempt to pay such debts to the best of their abilities over three years rather than for those debtors to have those debts hanging over their heads indefinitely, perhaps for the rest of their lives.

Pennsylvania Department of Public Welfare et al. v. Davenport, 495 U.S. 552, 563 (1990).

3. According to Bankruptcy Code § 1328(a)(2), a chapter 13 discharge does not affect a claim specified in § 523(a)(8) (student loans). Section 523(a)(8) in turn permits a discharge if having to pay the student loan imposes "an undue hardship." Meanwhile, Federal Rules of Bankruptcy Procedure 7001 states that "[t]he following are adversary proceedings: . . . (6) a proceeding to determine the discharegability of a debt."

Suppose the chapter 13 plan declares that, because a student loan is an undue hardship, the loan will be discharged if the plan is completed. Section 1327(a) states that "[t]he provisions of a confirmed plan bind the debtor and each creditor." Is the student lender bound by the plan term. Compare Educational Credit Management Corp v. Mersmann (In re Mersmann), 505 F.3d 1033 (10th 2007) (no) with Espinosa v. United Student Aid Funds, Inc., 545 F.3d 1113 (9th Cir. 2008), cert. granted, 129 S. Ct. 2791 (2009) (yes).

BABIN v HAMILTON (IN RE HAMILTON)

383 B.R. 469 (Bankr. W.D. Ark. 2008)

BEN T. BARRY, J.

Before the Court is a motion for default judgment in the above captioned adversary proceeding. The chapter 13 trustee filed a complaint objecting to discharge on October 10, 2007, and served the debtor on October 11, 2007, by first class mail. The debtor has failed to answer the complaint and on November 14, 2007, the trustee filed her motion for default judgment. For the reasons stated below, the trustee's motion for default is denied as a matter of law and this adversary proceeding is dismissed.

The Court has jurisdiction over this matter under 28 U.S.C. § 1334 and 28 U.S.C. § 157, and it is a core proceeding under 28 U.S.C. § 157(b)(2)(J). The following opinion constitutes findings of fact and conclusions of law in accordance with Federal Rule of Bankruptcy Procedure 7052.

The debtor in this case filed a previous chapter 13 petition on May 28, 2004. On February 5, 2007, the case was converted to chapter 7 and the debtor received a discharge on May 16, 2007. On August 21, 2007, the debtor filed the pending chapter 13 case, within four years of filing his previous bankruptcy case. Relying on 11 U.S.C. § 1328(f)(1), the trustee argues that because the debtor converted from chapter 13 to chapter 7 and received a discharge in the chapter 7 case, the debtor is now precluded from receiving a discharge in a subsequent chapter 13 case for four years from the date of discharge in the prior case. This argument necessarily implicates two sections of the bankruptcy code: § 348(a) and § 1328(f). In re Ybarra, 359 B.R. 702, 706 (Bankr. S.D. Ill. 2007) (stating that it is necessary to examine § 1328(f) within the context of the statutory scheme, including § 348(a)).

Section 348(a) concerns the effect of conversion from one chapter to another. To give validity to the trustee's § 1328(f) argument--that the debtor's discharge in the prior case that was converted to a chapter 7 precludes him from receiving a discharge in a chapter 13 case for four years--the Court would have to determine that when the prior case was converted to a chapter 7 case, the chapter 13 case originally filed by the debtor did not exist. In support of her position, the trustee cites, among other cases, Resendez v. Lindquist, 691 F.2d 397 (8th Cir. 1982). However, the issue presented in Resendez is not related to the issue presented in this case.

The Resendez court had to decide whether a debtor who converts from a confirmed chapter 13 case to a chapter 7 liquidation case may exempt funds in the chapter 7 case that have been paid to the chapter 13 trustee but remain undistributed at the time of conversion. The relevant phrase cited by the trustee in her letter brief, and cited by other courts that agree with the trustee's position,[1] states that "when there is a conversion, the debtors are deemed to have filed a Chapter 7 case at the time the Chapter 13 case was filed." Id. at 399. This is true, and comports with § 348(a) of the bankruptcy code, which states that "[c]onversion of a case from a case under one chapter of this title to a case under another chapter of this title . . . does not effect a change in the date of the filing of the petition . . . ." 11 U.S.C. § 348(a). However, that does not mean that a petition (or, more accurately, a case[2] originally filed under chapter 13 that subsequently converted to a chapter 7 case is deemed to have been filed as a

[1] See, e.g., Grice v. We Energies (In re Grice), 373 B.R. 886, 888 (Bankr. W.D. Wis. 2007); McDow v. Sours (In re Sours), 350 B.R. 261, 268 (Bankr. E.D. Va. 2006); McDow v. Capers (In re Capers), 347 B.R. 169, 171-72 (Bankr. D.S.C. 2006).

[2] 11 U.S.C. § 301(a) states that "[a] voluntary case under a chapter of this title is commenced by the filing with the bankruptcy court of a petition under such chapter by an entity that may be a debtor under such chapter."

chapter 7 case. To so hold would ignore the history of the case as it progressed under chapter 13, and disregard any incentive a debtor may have had to attempt a chapter 13 repayment plan. Upon conversion, the date of filing does not change, nor does the fact that the case was originally filed under chapter 13.

Section 348(a) contains seemingly contradictory language and requires close reading to understand the difference between "filed under" and "filed as." Subsection (a) specifically states that three events are not effected by conversion: (1) the date of the filing of the petition, (2) the date of the commencement of the case, and (3) the date of the order for relief. 11 U.S.C. § 348(a). Beginning with the order for relief, subsection (a) states that conversion "constitutes an order for relief under the chapter to which the case is converted . . . ." Id. The subsection then goes on to state that conversion does not effect the date of the [original] order for relief. Id. To understand why conversion does not effect the date of the order for relief, and also constitutes an order for relief under the new chapter, another code provision must be examined. Under § 301, "[t]he commencement of a voluntary case under a chapter of this title constitutes an order for relief under such chapter." 11 U.S.C. § 301(b) (emphasis added). This code provision makes clear that the order for relief is specific to the chapter under which the case was filed. Because of this, when a case converts to another chapter, § 348(a) is necessary to recognize an order for relief under the chapter to which the case is converted: "Conversion . . . constitutes an order for relief under the chapter to which the case is converted . . . ." However, § 348(a) continues by recognizing that mere conversion of the case does not effect the original date of the order for relief.

The same situation occurs in relation to the commencement of the case. Section 301 states that a case "under a chapter of this title is commenced by the filing . . . of a petition under such chapter . . . ." 11 U.S.C. § 301(a) (emphasis added). Again, § 348 makes clear that upon conversion, the date of the commencement of the case is not affected. 11 U.S.C. § 348(a). Similarly, if a case is originally filed as a chapter 13 and later converts to a chapter 7, the date of filing the chapter 7 petition is deemed to be the same date that the chapter 13 case was filed. Resendez, 691 F.2d at 399. And it is on that date that both the chapter 13 and chapter 7 orders for relief were constituted and each case was commenced. That does not change the fact that the case remains a case originally filed under chapter 13.

According to the trustee, § 1328(f)(1) prohibits a debtor from receiving a discharge in a chapter 13 case filed within four years of receiving a discharge in a prior case that began as a chapter 13 case and later converted to chapter 7. Section 1328(f) establishes a look back period measured from the date of the order for relief in the most current case to the date the petition was filed in the prior case. Ybarra, 359 B.R. at 703; In re West, 352 B.R. 482, 487 (Bankr. E.D. Ark. 2006) (recognizing that H.R. 31, 109th Cong. § 312 (1st Sess. 2005) refers to the filing of the prior case, not the date the discharge was received). However, under § 1328(f)(1), the statute references a case filed under chapter 7 within four years, and § 1328(f)(2) references a case filed under chapter 13 within two years. 11 U.S.C. § 1328(f). Courts are continually reminded that "'when the statute's language is plain, the sole function of the courts--at least where the disposition required by the text is not absurd--is to enforce it according to its terms.'" Lamie v. United States Tr., 540 U.S. 526, 535 (2004) (quoting Hartford Underwriters Ins. Co. v. Union Planters Bank, N.A., 530 U.S. 1, 6 (2000) in reference to discerning congressional intent); see also McDow v. Sours (In re Sours), 350 B.R. 261, 267

(Bankr. E.D. Va. 2006) (recognizing two exceptions to the "Plain Meaning Rule": (1) when a literal interpretation leads to a result contrary to congressional intent, and (2) when a literal interpretation would produce an absurd result).

In this instance, a plain reading of the statute does not lead to an absurd result, and the Court finds it is not appropriate to discern "congressional intent." In this regard, the Court agrees with the Grydzuk court, which stated,

> Because of the political process involved in the enactment of legislation in our pluralistic republican form of government, the intent of Congressmen or Senators who voted for a particular piece of legislation may have nothing to do with the goals sought to be implemented by a drafter or sponsor of a law. This Court will thus not review legislative history in order to construe § 1328(f)(1).

In re Grydzuk, 353 B.R. 564, 567 (Bankr. N.D. Ind. 2006).[3] The Grydzuk court went on to find that § 1328(f)(1) is "an example of an ambiguity, not an example of a literal construction leading to an absurd result." Id. It also recognized that it would have been easy for the statute "to have been written in terms of the statutory provisions under which the discharge would have been entered," citing as examples § 727(a)(8) and (9), the comparable "look back" provisions found in chapter 7. Id. In those sections, Congress clearly stated that the relevant time frame related to a case commenced within either eight years or six years, respectively. However, with regard to § 1328(f), Congress stated that the relevant time frame related to a case filed under either chapter 7 during the preceding four years, or chapter 13 within the preceding two years. Because both provisions--§ 727(a)(8), (9) and § 1328(f)(1), (2)--were modified or added by BAPCPA, it seems apparent that Congress knew what it was doing when it referenced a case filed under in § 1328(f). Likewise, it would have been a simple matter for Congress to have said "filed under or converted to" had it wished to provide for the result argued by the trustee, but Congress choose not to use such language. Accordingly, this Court finds that § 1328(f) is not ambiguous and should be construed in accordance with the plain meaning of the statute.

One of the more common concerns other courts have with the result reached by this Court is the potential detrimental effect for a debtor filing a chapter 7 case and later con-verting to a chapter 13 case. In that case, the debtor "would be penalized for attempting to enter into a repayment plan because of the requirement that the debtor wait more than four years before becoming eligible to receive a discharge in the second chapter 13 case." Grice v. We Energies (In re Grice), 373 B.R. 886, 890 (Bankr. W.D. Wis. 2007); see also McDow v. Capers (In re Capers), 347 B.R. 169, 172 (Bankr. D.S.C. 2006) (same). What these courts fail to recognize is that if the debtor converted from chapter 7 to chapter 13, presumably the debtor would be in a chapter 13 plan for at least three years, possibly longer. Upon receiving a discharge in the chapter 13 case, the debtor would have less than a year to wait until she was eligible to file another chapter 13 case and receive a subsequent discharge.

Other courts have also expressed concern that a plain reading of § 1328(f)

[3] Interestingly, the Grydzuk court stated in the next paragraph that the "obligation of the United States Courts is to give effect to the intention of the legislature in enacting a particular law." Grydzuk, 353 B.R. at 567. It also recognized two schools of thought with regard to construing BAPCPA: (1) that "the law must be construed in strict accordance with statutory language," or (2) that the law "must be construed against the background of what is presumed the drafters intended to change from the prior law." Id.

as espoused by this Court may lead to abuse by some debtors. Specifically, a serial debtor who never intends to complete a chapter 13 case may file a chapter 13 and then convert to a chapter 7. In so doing, that debtor "preserve[s] the ability to later file another bankruptcy case after two years." Grice, 373 B.R. at 890; see also Sours, 350 B.R. at 269. Although the Court is aware that this situation may occur, there is still an intervening two year period the serial debtor must wait. Further, this result is similar to another provision in the code that has not been discussed by any of the courts holding otherwise: § 1328(b). Under § 1328(b), the court may grant a hardship discharge to a chapter 13 debtor who has not completed payments under the plan if three specific conditions are met. See 11 U.S.C. § 1328(b). Presumably, the debtor that receives a hardship discharge could file another chapter 13 case and receive another discharge after the two years has passed. Because a debtor filed under chapter 13 but was unable to consummate a plan is no reason to punish the unfortunate debtor that must again try to pay his creditors under a subsequent chapter 13 plan and receive a discharge. This particular provision of the code was not modified by BAPCPA. If the debtor truly is a serial filer with no intention to complete a chapter 13 case, the court may, after notice and a hearing, dismiss the case for cause under § 707(a), or not confirm a plan under § 1325(a)(7), which states that "the action of the debtor in filing the petition was in good faith."

For the reasons stated above, the Court finds that because the debtor filed his previous bankruptcy case under chapter 13 more than two years prior to the filing of the present case, the debtor is eligible for a discharge in this chapter 13 case and denies the trustee's motion for default judgment. Further, because the debtor is eligible for a discharge in this case, the Court dismisses the trustee's complaint objecting to discharge as a matter of law.

Notes and Questions

1. D files for chapter 7 bankruptcy on January 1, 2004. She receives a discharge on April 1, 2004. D files a chapter 13 petition on March 1, 2008. Under new § 1328(f), is D entitled to a discharge in the chapter 13 case? See Sanders v. Carroll, 2008 U.S. Dist. LEXIS 6994 (E.D. Mich. 2008) (yes; the four year period starts from the chapter 7 filing and ends with the chapter 13 filing).

2. What if a Debtor chooses to file Chapter 13 over Chapter 7 for the express purpose of discharging an otherwise nondischargeable debt? This issue arises in determining the good faith of filing a Chapter 13 petition or plan. While the courts agree that pursuit of a broader discharge under §1328(a) cannot, in it of itself, constitute bad faith,, the circuits are split as to whether it can be a factor in the good faith totality of circumstances test. Compare In re Smith, 286 F.3d 461 (7th Cir. 2002) (can be a factor); In re Chaffin, 816 F.2d 1070 (5th Cir. 1987) (same) with In re Lilley, 91 F.3d 491 (3d Cir. 1996) (cannot be a factor).

3. New Bankruptcy Code § 1328(g) requires the debtor to have completed an instructional course in personal financial management. This irksome provision will start to be litigated in 2008, when three-year plans of below-median debtors are finally paid out.

4. A discharge under § 1328(a) is also known as the "full compliance" discharge, under which the Debtor receives the benefit of a broader discharge after making all payments required by their Chapter 13 plan. A Chapter 13 Debtor can however, receive a "hardship discharge" under §1328(b) prior to making all payments under the plan.
This is addressed in the next case.

5. D's home is encumbered by a senior mortgage and a junior mortgage. The senior mortgage is under water. D files for bankruptcy in chapter 7 and obtainw a general discharge. In that proceeding, the deficit claims of their mortgage lenders are discharged. One week later, D files for chapter 13. D writes a plan proposing to reinstate the first mortgage and pay nothing at all to the second mortgagee--not even an unsecured creditor's dividend.

The trustee opposes confirmation. He argues that, pursuant to Bankruptcy Code §

1325(a)(5)(B)(i)(I), a holder of a lien must retain the lien until either the underlying debt is paid or "(bb) discharge under section 1328" (emphasis added). The trustee also points out that, under § 349(b)(1)(C), dismissal of a case reinstates "any lien voided under section 506(d) . . . " This, the trustee claims, shows a Congressional intent that lien stripping of underwater second liens depends on the grant of a discharge under chapter 13, and since the debtor is not entitled to a discharge under § 1328(f)(1), the debtor must treat the second mortgagee as a secured creditor.

May the plan be confirmed? Branigan v. Davis (In re Davis), 716 F.3d 331 (4th Cir. 2013).

IN RE BANDILLI

231 B.R. 836 (Bankr. 1st Cir. 1999)

PER CURIAM.

The Debtors, Francis Bandilli and Diane Bandilli, (the "Debtors") appeal from the bankruptcy court order denying the Debtors' motion for a hardship discharge. For the reasons set forth, we affirm. . . .

The Debtors filed a petition for relief under Chapter 13 on April 14, 1997 in the United States Bankruptcy Court for the District of Rhode Island. On August 5, 1997[2] an Order of Confirmation entered. Three and a half months later, the Debtors filed a motion seeking a hardship discharge pursuant to 11 U.S.C. § 1328(b). The Debtors allege that Mrs. Bandilli suffered from a serious medical condition that deteriorated shortly after confirmation and as a result of her illness, they had reduced income and could not make plan payments. The Debtors argue that they suffered changed circumstances for which they should not be held accountable.

The bankruptcy court conducted an evidentiary hearing and concluded that the Debtors failed to meet their burden of proof because, inter alia, the Debtors offered no credible evidence to support their claim that they suffered a loss of income as a result of Mrs. Bandilli's deteriorating health. It was undisputed below that Mrs. Bandilli clearly suffers from a serious medical condition, and has suffered from that condition for thirty-four years. In addition, Mrs. Bandilli testified that her condition worsened in the months just after confirmation, but has since stabilized. The bankruptcy court concluded that there was insufficient evidence under 11 U.S.C. § 1328(b)(1). There was little, if any, evidence that Mrs. Bandilli's worsened condition actually interfered with the Debtors' ability to perform their obligations under the plan.

On the basis of the Debtors' schedules, the bankruptcy court concluded that at the time the plan was proposed, Mr. Bandilli had three sources of income n3: (1) $3,200 per month as a self-employed pet groomer; (2) $500 per month from real property investments; and (3) $1,200 per month in wages from U-Haul. On direct examination, Mrs. Bandilli testified that her husband was missing work to take her to chemotherapy and as a result, had reduced hours and lower wages from U-Haul. On cross-examination, Mrs. Bandilli changed her testimony and stated that her husband's wages from U-Haul were $1,200, the income reduction was in his self-employed income from his work as a pet groomer. Other than Mrs. Bandilli's testimony, there is no evidence in the record to support their claim that they suffered any reduction in grooming income.

At the time of confirmation, the bankruptcy court was not aware that the Debtors had filed a Chapter 7 petition in 1994 in Massachusetts in which they discharged $ 340,000 in unsecured debt.

DISCUSSION

To determine whether a debtor should be allowed a hardship discharge, the bankruptcy court must look to 11 U.S.C. § 1328(b), which provides in relevant part, as follows:

> At any time after the confirmation of the plan and after notice and a hearing, the court may grant a discharge to a debtor that has not completed payments under the plan only if-
>
> (1) the debtor's failure to complete such payments is due to circumstances for which the debtor should not justly be held accountable;
>
> (2) the value, as of the effective date of the plan, of property actually distributed under the plan on account of each allowed unsecured claim is not less than the amount that would have been paid on such claim if the estate of the debtor had been liquidated under chapter 7 of this title on such date; and
>
> (3) modification of the plan under section 1329 of this title is not practicable.

The Debtors bear the burden of proof, and must satisfy the court on all three elements of 11 U.S.C. § 1328(b). In re Dark, 87 B.R. 497 (Bankr. N.D.Ohio 1988) (unsubstantiated and conclusory statements regarding inability to fund plan are insufficient). Of the three elements, the parties agree that the second element has been met. The third element is not at issue because the Debtors do not challenge the bankruptcy court's determination that the Debtors failed to offer any evidence, i.e., that plan modification would not be practical. The Debtors' failure to satisfy this single element is sufficient to support the denial of the hardship discharge. In re White, 126 B.R. 542, 544 (Bankr. N.D. Ill. 1991) (three independent conditions precedent to the granting of a hardship discharge); In re Schleppi, 103 B.R. 901, 904, (Bankr. S.D. Ohio 1989) (failure to establish impracticability of plan modification is, standing alone, fatal). The bankruptcy court could have properly denied the hardship discharge based solely on this absence of evidence.

Since the bankruptcy court weighed each of the elements of 11 U.S.C. § 1328(b), we address the Debtors' arguments that the bankruptcy court considered additional improper factors in its analysis of the first element of § 1328(b), i.e., whether there were circumstances beyond the Debtors' control that justify a hardship discharge. The issue of what qualifies as "circumstances for which the debtor should not justly be held accountable" under 11 U.S.C. § 1328(b) is one of first impression. One leading authority has noted: "hardship discharge under § 1328(b) is reserved for the truly worst of the awfuls-something more than just the temporary loss of a job or temporary physical disability." K. Lundin, Chapter 13 Bankruptcy, § 9.18 at 9-26 (1990); see also In re White, 126 B.R. at 545. Although there is no express requirement in 11 U.S.C. § 1328(b) that a debtor prove the existence of catastrophic circumstances, most bankruptcy courts that have addressed the issue have allowed a hardship discharge only when a debtor has suffered from catastrophic circumstances that directly cause the debtor to be unable to complete plan payments. In re Graham, 63 B.R. 95 (Bankr.E.D. Pa. 1986)(granted discharge upon death of the debtor); In re Bond, 36 B.R. 49 (Bankr. E.D.N.C. 1984) (discharge where debtor died). We are unwilling to read the word catastrophic into the statute.

Congress has not hesitated in several areas of the Bankruptcy Code to insert a "charged" term to better elucidate its intention. For example, in § 707(b), dismissal is only appropriate where the court finds "substantial abuse." In § 523(a)(8), discharge of a student loan is permitted only where the court finds that nondischargeability of the debt would cause an "undue hardship." And, in § 524(c), the court must determine the absence of "undue hardship" before reaffirmation of a prepetition debt by an individual debtor will be deemed enforceable or require counsel for the debtor to so certify. Yet, for the first element of § 1328(b), Congress has asked only that the Court determine whether the debtor is "justly . . . accountable" for the plan's failure. The word "accountable" is comparatively mild to the emotionally-laden term "catastrophic.[5]

Of course, we are mindful that a request for discharge under § 1328(b) merits special vigilance. Creditors do not enjoy the same participation in the Chapter 13 confirmation process as is afforded creditors in Chapter 11, and, with a § 1328(b) discharge, the debtor is deemed to have reorganized his or her financial affairs without meeting his or her postpetition obligations. A bankruptcy court asked to grant a discharge under Chapter 13, notwithstanding the debtor's failure to comply with its postpetition promises, should treat the request as a matter of some gravity and consider that granting unjustified requests will likely discourage effort by some debtors to meet their plan obligations when financial strain inevitably intrudes into their postconfirmation lives. On the other hand, when the request is justified, the insertion of additional conditions is not. See In re Edwards, 207 B.R. 728, 730 (Bankr. N.D. Fla. 1997)(no catastrophic circumstances, but discharge allowed where economic circumstances giving rise to failure to complete plan payments did not exist and were not foreseeable at the time of confirmation.)

The determination of whether a debtor is justly accountable for his or her failure to make payments under his or her Chapter 13 plan is necessarily fact-driven, with the emphasis properly focused on the nature and quality of the intervening event or events upon which the debtor relies. Considerations by the court in that regard should include:

> a) whether the debtor has presented substantial evidence that he or she had the ability and intention to perform under the plan at the time of confirmation;
>
> b) whether the debtor did materially perform under the plan from the date of confirmation until the date of the intervening event or events;
>
> c) whether the intervening event or events were reasonably foreseeable at the time of confirmation of the Chapter 13 plan;
>
> d) whether the intervening event or events are expected to continue in the reasonably foreseeable future;
>
> e) whether the debtor had control, direct or indirect, of the intervening event or events; and
>
> f) whether the intervening event or events constituted a sufficient and proximate cause for the failure to make the required payments.

In the case before us, the Debtors failed to show sufficient justification for the bankruptcy court to grant them a discharge under § 1328(b). Mrs. Bandilli's chronic condition existed at the time of confirmation and although she suffered a temporary relapse, she testified that her condition had stabilized by the time of the hearing. The Debtors offered little or no evidence of decreased income and

[5] Black's Law Dictionary defines the term "accountable" as "subject to pay; responsible; liable." Black's Law Dictionary 19 (6th ed. 1990).

no credible evidence of any correlation between the alleged decrease in income and Mrs. Bandilli's ongoing medical condition. The bankruptcy court's findings of fact are supported by the evidence and are not clearly erroneous. We have given due regard to the bankruptcy court's determination that Mrs. Bandilli lacked credibility. See Fed. R. Bankr. P. 8013. The bankruptcy court found Mrs. Bandilli's testimonial quantification of the loss in income to be "vague and unconvincing,"in part, because the Debtors failed to disclose their prior bankruptcy filing. The Debtors argue that the bankruptcy court improperly considered their failure to disclose their prior bankruptcy as a factor in denying the hardship discharge. We reject this argument. The bankruptcy court considered the truthfulness and accuracy of information contained in the Bandilli's petition and accompanying schedules as a factor in determining Mrs. Bandilli's lack of credibility. Other than medical records, the Debtors' evidence consisted solely of the testimony of Mrs. Bandilli, and they must suffer the consequences of the bankruptcy court's determination that she was not credible. The Debtors failed to prove that their inability to complete plan payments was due to circumstances for which they should not "justly be held accountable." 11 U.S.C. § 1328(b)(1).

The Debtors also argue that the bankruptcy court improperly considered and unfavorably weighed the short length of time between confirmation and the date the hardship discharge was requested. It was proper for the bankruptcy court to consider and compare the information provided at confirmation against the information being offered in support of the hardship discharge to determine if the circumstances alleged at the time of the hardship hearing were known or reasonably foreseeable at the time of confirmation. The bankruptcy court correctly considered the elements of 11 U.S.C. § 1328(b) and did not abuse its discretion when it denied the hardship discharge.

For these reasons, the order of the bankruptcy court is AFFIRMED.

Notes and Questions

1. A hardship discharge under §1328(b) allows a Debtor to discharge his debts prior to completing payments under the Chapter 13 plan. This is balanced, however, by removing the broad discharge provisions of 1328(a), subjecting the Debtor to the same set of non-dischargeable debts in a Chapter 7 case. Bankruptcy Code §1328(c).

2. Bandilli represents an emerging minority of cases, which is "unwilling to read the word catastrophic" into the hardship discharge clause. However, one court has noted, in contrast to other provisions of the Bankruptcy Code, the legislative history of §1328(b) mentions catastrophic circumstances. In Re Davis, 34 B.R. 319 (Bankr. E.D. Va. 1983).

F. MODIFICATION

IN RE NOLAN

232 F.3d 528 (6th Cir. 2000)

NORRIS, C.J.

On August 22, 1997, Sahnica Denise Nolan filed a petition for relief under Chapter 13 of the Bankruptcy Code. Chapter 13 permits a debtor with regular income to propose a repayment plan extending and/or reducing the balance of her obligations, thereby averting a loss of assets through Chapter 7 liquidation. Discharge of a portion of the debt is granted after a Chapter 13 debtor has complied with a court-confirmed repayment plan. Prior to confirmation of Nolan's proposed plan, Chrysler Financial Corporation filed a proof of claim showing that Nolan owed it $12,291.45 on an installment contract for the purchase of a 1995 Mitsubishi Mirage automobile. On September 23, 1997, the bankruptcy court confirmed Nolan's Chapter 13 plan, which took into account Chrysler's claim. Under the plan, Chrysler's secured claim on the automobile was for $8200, with interest at ten percent per annum. Of Nolan's monthly payments under the plan, $207.97 per month was to be applied toward the secured claim. The unsecured portion of Chrysler's claim, $4091.45, would be paid off on a cents-on-the-dollar basis from Nolan's installments under the plan, pursuant to 11 U.S.C. § 1329(a)(1).

On August 26, 1998, Nolan filed a motion to modify her plan and incur credit. Specifically, she sought permission to surrender her vehicle to Chrysler, reclassify the deficiency owed on the vehicle as an unsecured claim, and incur credit in the amount of $10,000 to purchase another car. According to Nolan, her current automobile no longer provided dependable transportation. Chrysler objected to the motion on the ground that section 1329 of the Bankruptcy Code does not allow a debtor to reclassify a secured claim as an unsecured debt absent a good faith showing of unanticipated substantial change in circumstances. Chrysler contended that Nolan had not acted in good faith because she had failed to properly maintain her vehicle.

On October 19, 1998, a hearing was held before the bankruptcy court in which Nolan testified that she had placed 100,000 miles on the vehicle in three years (an average of 2777.77 miles per month), and had changed the oil three times between February and August of 1998 (she could produce documentation for only two changes). Following a hearing, the bankruptcy court granted her motion, finding that she did not act in bad faith.

Chrysler appealed to the district court, which reversed. Chrysler Fin. Corp. v. Nolan, 234 B.R. 390 (M.D. Tenn. 1999). It did not disturb the bankruptcy court's factual finding as to the good faith of Nolan. Rather, it held that as a matter of law 11 U.S.C. § 1329(a) did not permit Nolan to modify the plan by surrendering collateral to a secured creditor and reclassifying any deficiency as an unsecured claim.

Nolan now appeals to this court.

I.

Chapter 13 of the Bankruptcy Code, entitled "Adjustments of debts of an individual with regular income," was originally adopted to address consumer credit loss during the Great Depression by providing a completely voluntary proceeding for consumers to amortize their debts out of future earnings. . . In its present version, Chapter 13 allows individual debtors to reorganize with a repayment plan as an alternative to seeking a complete discharge of debts through the Chapter 7 bankruptcy liquidation process. Since a repayment plan may prove to be unsatisfactory, section 1329 of the Code allows modification of a Chapter 13 plan under certain circumstances. 11 U.S.C. § 1329 (1993). Section 1329 must be interpreted in conjunction with 11 U.S.C. §§ 1322(b) [contents of a plan], 1325(a) [confirmation of a plan] and 1327(a) [effect of confirmation].

There has been a debate over whether section 1329 allows a debtor to modify a con-firmed plan to surrender collateral for a secured claim (the value of which typically will have been significantly reduced) and then reclassify any deficiency as an allowed, unsecured claim to be paid back at the general pennies-on-the-dollar rate set forth in the plan for unsecured debts. This appeal presents an issue of first impression for the Courts of Appeals, while there is a clear and fairly even split of authority amongst the federal district courts. . . .

Nolan argues for an interpretation of section 1329 that has been accepted by a sizable minority of the district courts, following the rationale of In re Jock, 95 B.R. 75 (Bankr. M.D. Tenn. 1989). Under the Jock interpretation, a debtor can modify a plan under section 1329(a) by: 1) surrendering collateral to a creditor; 2) allowing the creditor to sell the collateral and apply the proceeds toward the claim; and 3) classifying any remaining deficiency as an unsecured claim. See Jock, 95 B.R. at 76-77; see also Chrysler Fin. Corp., 234 B.R. at 394. The rationale is that the "proposed modification would 'increase or reduce the amount of payments on claims of a particular class provided for in the plan' within the meaning of § 1329(a)(1)." Jock, 95 B.R. at 76. Under Jock, "[a] Chapter 13 debtor can use the permitted [original] plan provisions described in § 1322(b), subject to the confirmation requirements of § 1325(a), to modify a confirmed Chapter 13 plan under § 1329(a)." Id.

Jock rests on four supporting principles. First, each secured claim is separately classified in a Chapter 13 case, and therefore subject to modification under section 1329(a)(1). See Jock, 95 B.R. at 76. Second, under 11 U.S.C. § 1329(b)(1), both the mandatory and permissive provisions of a Chapter 13 plan found in 11 U.S.C. §§ 1322(a) and (b) and the confirmation requirements of 11 U.S.C. § 1325(a) apply to impose limits upon any post-confirmation section 1329(a) modification of a Chapter 13 plan. See Chrysler Fin. Corp., 234 B.R. at 394 (quoting Jock, 95 B.R. at 77). Third, under section 1322(b)(8), a Chapter 13 debtor is permitted to "provide for the payment of all or part of a claim against the debtor from property of the estate or property of the debtor," while section 1325(a)(5)(C) permits the debtor to surrender the property securing a claim in order to satisfy an "allowed secured claim provided for by the plan." Jock, 95 B.R. at 77. Fourth, the incorporation of sections 1322(b)(8) and 1325(a)(5)(C) into the standards for post-confirmation modification in section 1329 empower the Chapter 13 debtor to satisfy the creditor's secured claim either by A) surrendering the collateral during the confirmation of the original plan, or B) modifying the confirmed plan to allow surrender of the collateral. See id. The distribution to a creditor can be altered by reducing the amount paid to the creditor from outside the plan, or by reclassifying a secured claim as an unsecured claim. See Chrysler Fin. Corp., 234 B.R. at 397 n.11 (quoting In re Stone, 91 B.R. 423, 425 (Bankr. N.D. Ohio 1988)).

We reject Jock's interpretation of section 1329. The district court correctly reversed the bankruptcy court under an alternative interpretation, adopted by In re Coleman,, 231 B.R. 397 (Bankr. S.D. Ga. 1999). Five fundamental deficiencies of the Jock position persuade us to reject it in this circuit.

First, section 1329(a) does not expressly allow the debtor to alter, reduce or reclassify a previously allowed secured claim. 11 U.S.C. § 1329(a) (1993). Instead, section 1329(a)(1) only affords the debtor a right to request alteration of the amount or timing of specific payments. A debtor cannot use section 1329(b)(1) to enlarge the modifications permitted by section 1329(a), since section 1329(b)(1) does not apply unless the proposed modification first complies with section 1329(a)(1). See Chrysler Fin. Corp. 234 B.R. at 394 (quoting Taylor, 99 B.R. at 904-05). A modification that reduces the claim of a secured debtor would add a claim to the class of unsecured creditors, a change prohibited by section 1329(a).[1] See 234 B.R. at 394-95 (quoting Taylor, 99 B.R. at 905 n.3). Section 1329(a)(1) should not be read so broadly as to authorize the reclassification of claims. See Coleman, 231 B.R. at 400.

Second, the proposed modification would violate section 1325(a)(5)(B), which mandates that a secured claim is fixed in amount and status and must be paid in full once it has been allowed.[2] See 11 U.S.C. § 1325(a)(5)(B)(ii) (1993). Debtors seeking modification are attempting to bifurcate a claim that has already been classified as fully secured into a secured claim as measured by the collateral's depreciated value and an unsecured claim as measured by any unpaid deficiency. This would negate the requirement of section 1325(a)(5)(B)(ii) that a plan is not to be confirmed unless the property to be distributed on account of a claim is not less than the allowed amount of the claim. See Chrysler Fin. Corp., 234 B.R. at 395 (quoting Dunlap, 215 B.R. at 870).

Third, proposed modification would contravene section 1327(a), because a contrary interpretation postulates an unlikely congressional intent to give debtors the option to shift the burden of depreciation to a secured creditor by reclassifying the claim and surrendering the collateral when the debtor no longer has any use for the devalued asset. See Coleman, 231 B.R. at 400. The court in [In re Banks, 161 B.R. 375 (Bankr. S.D. Miss. 1993)] saliently articulated the injustice of such a maneuver:

> Code § 1329(a) basically authorizes the amendment of a confirmed plan so as to change (1) the amount; or (2) the time for payments "on claims of a particular class provided for by the plan." The boldest and most frequent attempt by debtors to use the postconfirmation modification to alter the treatment of secured claims occurs when the collateral no longer appears to have a value which justifies full payment of the balance of the secured claim--in contrast with the composition percent being paid on unsecured claims. The collateral having lost its attractiveness, the debtor proposes an amendment to the plan so as (1) to surrender the now-unattractive collateral to the creditor; (2) to reduce

[1] We note that 11 U.S.C. § 1325(a)(5)(C) apparently does allow a surrender of collateral, but only pre-confirmation. For section 1325(a)(5)(B)(ii) to provide any protection to the creditor when the debtor chooses to retain her collateral, the secured claim must not be subject to modification throughout the life of the plan.

Section 1329(b)(1) references not only section 1325(a), but also sections 1322(a), 1322(b), and 1323(c). In doing so, section 1329(b)(1) indicates that a plan as modified must still comply with requirements for an original plan.

[2] Furthermore, as noted by the district court, Chrysler Fin. Corp., 234 B.R. at 396 (citations omitted):

> Under Section 1325(a)(5), "the debtor's proposed Chapter 13 plan must either provide that the secured creditor retain its lien and be paid the value of its claim over the life of the plan or, in the alternative, surrender the secured property." Because the debtor chose to keep possession of the [collateral] rather than allow [creditor] to recover [it] under Section 1325(a)(5) and was, thus, bound by that decision under Section 1327, the court found that "the interrelationship of §§ 1325(a)(5) and 1327 of the Code" compelled it to deny the debtor's proposed modification of the plan.

That the debtor is given the option to surrender prior to confirmation does not establish that she retains this right after confirmation when the collateral has significantly depreciated. Section 1325(a)(5)(C), read in conjunction with sections 1325(a)(5)(A) and (B) and 1325(a)(6), clearly permits only pre-confirmation surrenders. Once the plan is confirmed, it is impermissible to assert a continued option to surrender during the life of the plan.

> the unpaid balance of the secured claim to reflect the now-diminished value of the collateral; (3) to have that reduced secured balance satisfied by the surrender of the collateral; (4) to have the remaining balance of the secured claim converted to an unsecured claim; and (5) to have this balance of the claim satisfied by the 5%, 17%, or whatever percent payment provided for unsecured claims--all over the objection of the holder of the secured claim.

Banks, 161 B.R. at 377 (citation omitted). We join the Banks court in rejecting the notion that debtors have such wide latitude to subject the creditor to their whims throughout the life of the plan. We further note that under the Jock approach, debtors would obtain a double reduction in debt in many cases, because the creditor already experiences a cram down in valuation at the time of confirmation. See Chrysler Fin. Corp., 234 B.R. at 396 (quoting Banks, 161 B.R. at 379). There is no indication that Congress intended to allow debtors to reap a windfall by employing a subterfuge that unfairly shifts away depreciation, deficiency, and risk voluntarily assumed by the debtor through her confirmation of the Chapter 13 plan.

Fourth, only the debtor, the trustee, and holders of unsecured claims are permitted to bring a motion to modify a plan pursuant to section 1329(a). The Jock interpretation would create an inequitable situation where the secured creditor could not seek to reclassify its claim in the event that collateral appreciated, even though the debtor could revalue or reclassify the claim whenever the collateral depreciated. See Coleman, 231 B.R. at 400. Furthermore, allowing Chapter 13 modifications would permit the debtor to reclassify a secured creditor's claim while simultaneously evading the tradeoff risks and responsibilities attending conversion or dismissal under Chapter 7. See Chrysler Fin. Corp., 234 B.R. at 397 (citation omitted) (Chapter 7 alternative requires debtor to surrender nonexempt property to a trustee, and to lose opportunity for discharge for at least six years; Chapter 13 avoids these onerous burdens by allowing debtor to retain all personal and real property, to restructure debts, and to enjoy greater likelihood of future credit opportunities). These inequities are further indications Congress did not intend the resolution reached in Jock.

Fifth, Jock's interpretation is at odds with the plain language of section 1329. "This section does not state that the plan may be modified to increase or reduce the amount of claims. This is of significance in relation to secured claims." Banks, 161 B.R. at 378 (emphasis added). Jock fails to note that the terms "claim" and "payment" have two different meanings in the Bankruptcy Code.

Under the Code, "Claim" means-

> (A) right to payment, whether or not such right is reduced to judgment, liquidated, unliquidated, fixed, contingent, matured, unmatured, disputed, undisputed, legal, equitable, secured, or unsecured; or
>
> (B) right to an equitable remedy for breach of performance if such breach gives rise to a right to payment, whether or not such right to an equitable remedy is reduced to judgment, fixed, contingent, matured, unmatured, disputed, undisputed, secured, or unsecured.

See Johnson v. Home State Bank, 501 U.S. 78, 83 (1991) (quoting 11 U.S.C. § 101(5)). The term "claim" is consistently employed in the Code. See 11 U.S.C. § 101(5) (defining "claim"). Although "payment" is not defined in the Code, usage of the term is also consistent throughout the Code and reflects a meaning different from the term "claim." There is no reason to suppose that Congress intended in section 1329 to disregard the ordinary common law meaning of the term "payment," which is "the delivery of money or other value by a debtor to a creditor." Black's Law Dictionary 1129 (6th ed. 1990). Furthermore, if the term "payments" in section 1329(a) referred to the secured claim itself rather than to individual payments, the separate use of "claims" in section 1329(a)(3) would be superfluous. Read with the benefit of proper term definitions, section 1329 clearly indicates that modifications after plan confirmation cannot alter a claim (a right to a remedy or payment of a certain total amount), but can extend or compress payments and reduce or increase the amount of the delivery of value planned as an eventual satisfaction for the creditor's claim.

We hold that a debtor cannot modify a plan under section 1329(a) by: 1) surrendering the collateral to a creditor; 2) having the creditor sell the collateral and apply the proceeds toward the claim; and 3) having any deficiency classified as an unsecured claim. See Coleman, 231 B.R. at 398. Section 1329(a) only permits modification of the amount and timing of payments, not the total amount of the claim. This principle holds true as to the portion of a claim that is secured, where the claim is partially instead of fully secured.

We affirm the district court's reversal of the bankruptcy court, and remand this case to the bankruptcy court for further proceedings.

Notes and Questions

1. While many lower district courts and bankruptcy courts have weighed in on whether bifurcation can be revisited by modification, the 6th Circuit is the only Court of Appeals to decide this issue. Of the lower courts that disagree with Nolan, some interpret the term "payment" more broadly. Bank One N.A. v. Leuellen (In re Leuellen), 322 B.R. 648, 658-59 (N.D. Ind. 2005); In re Knappen, 281 B.R. 714, 717 (Bankr. D.N.M. 2002) ("The language of § 1329(a)(1) of the Code explicitly allows the debtor to 'reduce the amount of payments on claims of a particular class . . . .' Since each secured claim is general treated as a separate class, reducing to nothing the amount of payments on [the] secured [party's] claim fits within the language of the statute.").

RUSKIN v DAIMLERCHRYSLER SERVICES NORTH AMERICA, LLC (IN RE ADKINS)

425 F.3d 296 (6th Cir. 2005)

CALDWELL, DISTRICT COURT JUDGE

Plaintiff David Ruskin, Standing Chapter 13 Trustee for the Eastern District of Michigan ("Trustee"), appeals the district court's decision in favor of DaimlerChrysler Services North America, L.L.C. ("DaimlerChrysler"), in the Trustee's appeal from a decision of the bankruptcy court. The Chapter 13 debtor, Matthew Adkins, had defaulted on his car payments, and DaimlerChrysler, holder of a claim secured by Adkins's car, moved to repossess the vehicle. The Trustee argued that any debt remaining after the repossession and sale of the car at auction should be reclassified as an unsecured claim; DaimlerChrysler argued, and the bankruptcy court and the district court agreed, that this court's decision in Chrysler Financial Corp. v. Nolan (In re Nolan), 232 F.3d 528 (6th Cir. 2000), foreclosed such a reclassification. For the reasons explained below, we AFFIRM the district court's decision.

I. FACTUAL BACKGROUND

On August 17, 2001, Adkins ("Debtor") filed a Chapter 13 petition and proposed plan. On September 13, 2001, DaimlerChrysler filed a proof of claim secured by the Debtor's 1997 Plymouth Neon ("Neon") for $5,963.81 at 18.75% interest, valuing the Neon at $5,842.50. The Debtor's proposed plan valued the Neon at $5,525.00, and proposed an interest rate of 12%. DaimlerChrysler filed objections to the proposed plan based on the value and interest rate proposed by the debtor.

Following a confirmation hearing and resolution of both the Trustee's and DaimlerChrysler's objections, the bankruptcy court confirmed a plan ("the Plan") on November 8, 2001. The confirmed Plan set the value of the Neon at $5,842.00; DaimlerChrysler's secured claim was subject to "cram down" to that amount under 11 U.S.C. § 1325(a)(5)(B)(ii), with the remaining deficiency balance transformed into an unsecured claim for $121.81. The Plan provided that the $5,842.00 secured claim should be paid by 59 monthly payments of $136.00 and interest at 14% per annum. The Plan provided that these payments on the secured claim would be paid by the Trustee from payments the Debtor made to the Trustee. The Plan provided that general unsecured creditors receive no less than 100% on all filed claims.

Following confirmation, the Debtor failed to remit the payments to the Trustee as required by the Plan.[1] received no payments on its claims after December 6, 2001. After more than sixty (60) days passed without any payments from the Debtor, DaimlerChrysler moved for relief from the automatic stay to repossess and sell the Neon. As part of that motion, DaimlerChrysler requested that any deficiency balance, or the difference between the amount still owed to it on the previously allowed secured claim of $5,842.00 and the proceeds from selling the Neon at auction, should be paid to it as a secured claim as set forth in the original confirmed Plan after filing an amended Proof of Claim. The Trustee objected to the latter request, and a hearing was held.[2] The bankruptcy court granted the motion for lifting the automatic stay and held that this court's decision in Chrysler Financial Corp. v. Nolan (In re Nolan), 232 F.3d 528 (6th Cir. 2000), required that any deficiency resulting from the sale of the repossessed automobile be paid as a secured claim.[3] In re Adkins, 281 B.R. 905, 910 (Bankr. E.D. Mich. 2002).

The Trustee then appealed to the district court, which initially refused to hear the appeal because the foreclosure had not yet taken place.[4] Once "actual repossession, sale and assertion of a secured claim for the deficiency by Daimler

---

[1] There is nothing in the record before the Court that indicates why Debtor defaulted on his Plan payments. The Trustee admitted that Debtor defaulted on payments to the Trustee.

[2] Debtor did not respond in writing to DaimlerChrysler's motion. However, his attorney appeared on his behalf at a hearing before the bankruptcy court and represented to the bankruptcy court that Debtor "agreed" with the Trustee's objection. Debtor ceded advocacy of the objection to the Trustee.

[3] The bankruptcy court ruled from the bench on the deficiency issue on April 11, 2002, then issued a written order lifting the stay on April 12, 2002. The bankruptcy court issued a written opinion on the deficiency issue on June 18, 2002.

[4] According to the district court's order of dismissal, Debtor cured his original December 2001 default following the bankruptcy court's decision and continued making payments until August 2002. After missing a required payment on August 17, 2002, however, Debtor was once again in default, but DaimlerChrysler had not yet repossessed the car when the district court initially denied the Trustee's appeal. There is no evidence in the record before us as to why Debtor defaulted the second time.

Chrysler [sic]" took place,[5] the appeal was reinstated nunc pro tunc . . . .

On December 18, 2002, the district court affirmed the bankruptcy court's decision. In re Adkins, 307 B.R. 880, 888 (E.D. Mich. 2002). A timely notice of appeal was filed January 15, 2003. . . .

II. LAW AND ANALYSIS . . .

B. In re Nolan

The sole legal issue in this case is whether the bankruptcy court and district court correctly extended the principles this Court espoused in the case Chrysler Financial Corp. v. Nolan (In re Nolan), 232 F.3d 528 (6th Cir. 2000), to the present situation in which a secured creditor repossesses a debtor's vehicle post-confirmation under court-ordered relief from the automatic stay.

In the Nolan decision, a Chapter 13 debtor moved under 11 U.S.C. § 1329 to surrender her car post-confirmation and reclassify any deficiency resulting from the sale of the surrendered car as an unsecured claim. 232 F.3d at 529-30. Section 1329 allows modification of a Chapter 13 bankruptcy plan after confirmation of the plan but before completion of payments, on the motion of the debtor, the trustee, or the holder of an unsecured claim, to "increase or reduce the amount of payments on claims of a particular class provided for by the plan," to "extend or reduce the time for such payments," or to "alter the amount of the distribution to a creditor whose claim is provided for by the plan to the extent necessary to take account of any payment of such claim other than under the plan." 11 U.S.C. § 1329(a).[6] Prior to Nolan, lower federal courts were split on

---

[5] According to the record, DaimlerChrysler repossessed the Neon on September 16, 2002. The repossession took place pursuant to the bankruptcy court's April 12, 2002, order lifting the automatic stay, even though Debtor had cured the previous default that led to that order. However, the bankruptcy court's order did not limit the removal of the stay to a certain time period nor did it condition the lifting of the stay on Debtor's ability to cure default.

A written appraisal completed the day after DaimlerChrysler repossessed the Neon shows that the vehicle's front window was cracked, that the steering column was broken, and that the vehicle would not start. DaimlerChrysler sold the car at auction for $ 800. It is not evident from the record whether the vehicle was damaged before repossession, or whether it was damaged by the repossession company used by DaimlerChrysler. The Trustee asserts in his brief that the Neon was driveable before repossession.

[6] The full version of section 1329 applicable to both Nolan and the present case reads as follows:

> Modification of plan after confirmation.
>
> (a) At any time after confirmation of the plan but before the completion of payments under such plan, the plan may be modified, upon request of the debtor, the trustee, or the holder of an allowed unsecured claim, to-
>
> (1) increase or reduce the amount of payments on claims of a particular class provided for by the plan;
>
> (2) extend or reduce the time for such payments; or
>
> (3) alter the amount of the distribution to a creditor whose claim is provided for by the plan to the extent necessary to take account of any payment of such claim other than under the plan.
>
> (b)(1) Sections 1322(a), 1322(b), and 1323(c) of this title and the requirements of section 1325(a) of this title apply to any modification under subsection (a) of this section.
>
> (2) The plan as modified becomes the plan unless, after notice and

whether section 1329 allowed a debtor to modify a confirmed plan by surrendering collateral to a secured creditor (the value of which typically would have already been subjected to "cram down"), and then reclassifying any deficiency resulting from the sale of the collateral as an allowed unsecured claim to be paid back at the generally reduced rate for unsecured creditors set forth in the plan. See 232 F.3d at 531-32 (noting split). What the Nolan court termed "a sizable minority" of lower courts[7] a rationale set forth in In re Jock, 95 B.R. 75 (Bankr. M.D. Tenn. 1989), that allowed such a surrender and reclassification under section 1329.

In Nolan, however, this Court held that section 1329 did not allow reclassification as an unsecured claim of a deficiency resulting from the sale of a vehicle surrendered post-confirmation, finding five "fundamental deficiencies" in the reasoning of Jock and its progeny.

First, Nolan found that "section 1329(a) does not expressly allow a debtor to alter, reduce, or reclassify a previously allowed claim," but rather only "affords the debtor a right to request an alteration of the amount or timing of specific payments." 232 F.3d at 532 (emphasis added). Jock and its progeny had interpreted section 1329(b)'s reference to section 1325(a),[8] which allows for pre-confirmation surrender of collateral and classification of the deficiency as an unsecured claim, as allowing post-confirmation surrender and reclassification. Nolan, however, rejected this interpretation of section 1329(b). Nolan held that section 1329(b) does not apply unless the proposed modifications first comply with section 1329(a), and that section 1329(a) did not expressly allow reclassification of secured claims to unsecured claims. 232 F.3d at 535. In so holding, the Nolan court noted that while section 1325(a) allows surrender of collateral pre-confirmation, "for section 1325(a)(5)(B)(ii) to provide any protection to the creditor when the debtor chooses to retain her collateral, the secured claim must not be subject to modification throughout the life of the plan." Id. at 533 n.8.

Indeed, the second principle on which Nolan reversed the Jock line of cases was the finding that the proposed modification "would violate section 1325(a)(5)(B), which mandates that a secured claim is fixed in amount and status and must be paid in full once it has been allowed." 232 F.3d at 533. Nolan held that a post-confirmation surrender and subsequent reclassification is an attempt to bifurcate a claim that has already been classified as fully secured, and thus would negate the requirement in section 1325(a)(5)(B)(ii) that a plan is not to be confirmed unless the property to be distributed on account of a claim is not less than the allowed amount of the claim. Id.

Third, Nolan found that the proposed post-confirmation modification would violate section 1327(a),[9] which provides that a confirmed Chapter 13 plan is binding on debtor and creditor, and postulated "an unlikely congressional

---

a hearing, such modification is disapproved.

11 U.S.C. § 1329 (2000). In 2005, Congress added a subsection (a)(4) to allow modification to reduce payment amounts for the purpose of allowing the debtor to purchase health insurance. Bankruptcy Abuse Prevention and Consumer Protection Act of 2005 ("BAPCPA"), Pub. L. No. 109-8, § 102(i), 119 Stat. 23, 34 (2005).

[7] See, e.g., Day v. Systems & Servs. Techs., Inc. (In re Day), 247 B.R. 898 (Bankr. M.D. Ga. 2000); In re Anderson, 153 B.R. 527 (Bankr. M.D. Tenn. 1993); In re Rimmer, 143 B.R. 871 (Bankr. W.D. Tenn. 1992); In re Frost, 96 B.R. 804 (Bankr. S.D. Ohio 1989).

intent to give debtors the option to shift the burden of depreciation to a secured creditor by reclassifying the claim and surrendering the collateral when the debtor no longer has any use for the devalued asset." 232 F.3d at 533. Allowing the post-confirmation surrender and reclassification, Nolan reasoned, would subject secured creditors to a double reduction of a secured claim in those cases where the creditor already experienced a "cram down" in valuation at the time of confirmation. Id. at 534. Nolan found that allowing debtors to experience such a windfall was unfair and found no evidence for congressional approval of such a result. Id.

Fourth, because section 1329(a) only allows the debtor, the trustee, and the holders of unsecured creditors to move for a modification under that section, the Jock interpretation of section 1329 would create an inequitable situation where the secured creditor could not move to reclassify its claim if the collateral securing the claim appreciates in value, but others can move to shift the burden of a collateral's depreciation in value to the creditor. Id.

Fifth and finally, Nolan held that using section 1329 to reclassify claims post-confirmation was at odds with the plain language of section 1329. "This section does not state that the plan may be modified to increase or reduce the amount of claims." 232 F.3d at 534 (quoting In re Banks, 161 B.R. 375, 378 (Bankr. S.D. Miss. 1993)) (emphasis in Nolan). Nolan noted that the Bankruptcy Code uses the terms "claim" (which is specifically defined in the Code) and "payment" (which is not) differently throughout the Code, thus making it less likely that Congress intended the word "claim" to be substituted for the word "payment" in section 1329. Id.

Based on these five reasons, Nolan held that "a debtor cannot modify a plan under section 1329(a) by: (1) surrendering the collateral to a creditor; (2) having the creditor sell the collateral and apply the proceeds toward the claim; and (3) having any deficiency classified as an unsecured claim." 232 F.3d at 535 (citing In re Coleman, 231 B.R. 397, 398 (Bankr. S.D. Ga. 1999)).

C. Application of Nolan principles to Post-Confirmation Repossession of Collateral

The Trustee contends that the bankruptcy court and district court erred by applying Nolan to the present case, because Nolan is factually distinguishable. In Nolan, the debtor voluntarily sought to modify her plan by surrendering her vehicle and having the deficiency reclassified as an unsecured claim. Given that the debtor in Nolan reported having frequent mechanical trouble with the vehicle and had put many, many miles on the vehicle, the Trustee argues, it was clear in Nolan that the debtor was seeking to shift the burden of depreciation (which she likely accelerated through her use and lack of maintenance) to the secured creditor. Here, the Trustee contends, it was DaimlerChrysler's decision to move to lift the automatic stay under 11 U.S.C. § 362(d)(1) and repossess the secured collateral. The Trustee contends that under the present circumstances, Nolan should not be applied to allow the treatment of any deficiency resulting from sale of the collateral as a secured claim for purposes of future distributions from the Plan. Allowing DaimlerChrysler to affirmatively repossess the vehicle and retain secured status in the Plan, the Trustee argues, would allow DaimlerChrysler an unfair "double recovery" and would also be unfair to the other unsecured creditors. The Trustee further contends that allowing DaimlerChrysler to retain secured status in the Plan after it repossesses and sells the collateral makes no sense under the Bankruptcy Code because a claim is only a "secured claim" under section 506[8] of the Code if the claim is "secured by a lien on property in which the estate has an interest." 11 U.S.C. § 506(a). Once DaimlerChrysler repossesses and sells the vehicle, the Trustee argues, the lien on estate property is extinguished.

DaimlerChrysler defends the lower courts' application of Nolan to the present case, contending that the factual distinctions between this case and Nolan are insignificant. It argues that even though DaimlerChrysler was the moving party procedurally in this case, in actuality Debtor brought DaimlerChrysler's action upon himself when he defaulted on his payments to the Trustee. DaimlerChrysler argues that the Trustee's objection to DaimlerChrysler's request to treat any deficiency following the repossession as a secured claim was essentially a motion to reclassify the deficiency as an unsecured claim and essentially a motion to modify the Plan under section 1329. Therefore, DaimlerChrysler argues, Nolan forbids reclassification of the deficiency in this circumstance.

We believe that whether the Trustee technically made a motion under section 1329 is not the key to the question of whether reclassification of secured claims post-confirmation is allowed in Chapter 13 bankruptcies. Nolan's holding was not based solely on the language of section 1329. As discussed above, Nolan relied heavily on the language of sections 1325 and 1327. DaimlerChrysler emphasizes that section 1327 provides that once a plan is confirmed, its provisions bind the debtor and each creditor. Indeed, confirmation of a plan has been described as "res judicata of all issues that could or should have been litigated at the confirmation hearing." In re Cameron, 274 B.R. 457, 460 (Bankr. N.D. Tex 2002).

> Because all issues addressed during a plan confirmation are given preclusive effect, the bifurcation of a creditor's claim into a secured and an unsecured claim is likewise given preclusive effect. Thus if a creditor has an allowed secured claim of x dollars, which must be paid during the life of the plan, that issue has been litigated and cannot be altered.

In re Coffman, 271 B.R. 492, 495 (Bankr. N.D. Tex. 2002) (citations omitted).

The Nolan decision was also anchored on the provisions of section 1325(a)(5)(B), holding that this provision "mandates that a secured claim is fixed in amount and status and must be paid in full once it has been allowed." 232 F.3d at 533. "For section 1325(a)(5)(B)(ii) to provide any protection to the creditor when the debtor chooses to retain her collateral, the secured claim must not be subject to modification throughout the life of the plan." Id. at 533 n.8 (emphasis

---

[8] 11 U.S.C. § 506(a), prior to its amendment by BAPCPA in 2005, provided as follows:

> An allowed claim of a creditor secured by a lien on property in which the estate has an interest, or that is subject to setoff under section 553 of this title, is a secured claim to the extent of the value of such creditor's interest in the estate's interest in such property, or to the extent of the amount subject to setoff, as the case may be, and is an unsecured claim to the extent that the value of such creditor's interest or the amount so subject to setoff is less than the amount of such allowed claim. Such value shall be determined in light of the purpose of the valuation and of the proposed disposition or use of such property, and in conjunction with any hearing on such disposition or use or on a plan affecting such creditor's interest.

added). In Nolan, this Court found that the debtor's proposed surrender and reclassification did not adequately protect a secured creditor because it allowed the debtor to shift the burden of depreciation she originally accepted when she chose to retain her collateral from herself to the secured creditor. This burden-shifting is especially unfair in those cases where the secured creditor has already borne the burden of depreciation resulting from a cram down of the secured claim over the creditor's objection. "The Code's cram down option displaces a secured creditor's state-law right to obtain immediate foreclosure upon a debtor's default." Associates Commer. Corp. v. Rash, 520 U.S. 953, 964 (1997).

> "When a debtor surrenders the property, a creditor obtains it immediately, and is free to sell it and reinvest the proceeds . . . . If a debtor keeps the property and continues to use it, the creditor obtains at once neither the property nor its value and is exposed to double risks: The debtor may again default and the property may deteriorate from extended use."

Id. at 962. The "adequate protection" interest payments made to the secured creditor for retention of the collateral do not always offset these risks. See id. at 963.

In the present case, allowing a reclassification following a repossession caused by Debtor's default also would allow the Debtor to shift the burden of depreciation back to the secured creditor, and possibly lead to a double reduction of Debtor's debt. Therefore, we believe Nolan's ban against post-confirmation reclassifications equally applies to cases in which the Debtor's actions (i.e., default) have provided cause for the secured creditor to have the automatic stay lifted so the creditor may repossess the collateral.

D. Other court decisions that disagree with Nolan

We recognize that courts outside this circuit remain split on the issue following our decision in Nolan.[9] Those courts that have disagreed with Nolan have done so for differing reasons. Some courts simply disagree with Nolan's interpretation of section 1329.[10] See, e.g., Bank One, NA, v. Leuellen (In re Leuellen), 322 B.R. 648, 654-55 (S.D. Ind. 2005); In re Knappen, 281 B.R. 714, 717 (Bankr. D.N.M. 2002); In re Townley, 256 B.R. 697, 699 (Bankr. D.N.J. 2000).

[9] Courts outside this circuit that have agreed with our approach in Nolan include In re Barclay, 276 B.R. 276, 282 (Bankr. N.D. Ala. 2001); In re Coffman, 271 B.R. 492 (Bankr. N.D. Tex. 2002); and In re Wilcox, 295 B.R. 155 (Bankr. W.D. Okla. 2003).

[10] For example, in Bank One v. Leuellen, the district court found that section 1329 contemplated post-confirmation reclassifications of secured claims because section 1329(b) referenced section 1323(c). 322 B.R. at 656. Section 1323(c) addresses the procedure for a secured creditor's acceptance or rejection of a proposed pre-confirmation modification that changes the secured creditor' rights from what they were before the proposed pre-confirmation modification. In Nolan, however, we held that section 1329(b) does not apply until a proposed post-confirmation first complies with section 1329(a). Because, Nolan found, section 1329(a) does not expressly allow modifications that reclassify secured claims to unsecured claims, section 1329(b) does not apply to a proposed post-confirmation reclassification.

Other courts have interpreted the term "payment" in section 1329(a) more broadly than we did in Nolan. See Knappen, 281 B.R. at 717 ("The language of § 1329(a)(1) of the Code explicitly allows the debtor to 'reduce the amount of payments on claims of a particular class . . . .' Since each secured claim is general treated as a separate class, reducing to nothing the amount of payments on Ford's secured claim fits within the language of the statute.") (internal citations omitted).

Other courts agree that the language of section 1329 does not allow modifications that would reclassify a secured claim to an unsecured claim, but they disagreed with having a "secured claim" exist after the sale of the original collateral, pointing to section 506(a)'s characterization of an allowed claim as a "secured claim to the extent of the value of such creditor's interest in the estate's interest in such property."See, e.g., In re Zieder, 263 B.R. 114, 117 (Bankr. D. Ariz. 2001); In re Taylor, 297 B.R. 487, 491 (Bankr. E.D. Tex. 2003); In re Mason, 315 B.R. 759, 764 (Bankr. N.D. Cal. 2004). These latter decisions have thus advocated using 11 U.S.C. § 502(j) to reconsider the secured claim. Section 502(j) provides, in relevant part, "A claim that has been allowed or disallowed may be reconsidered for cause. A reconsidered claim may be allowed or disallowed according to the equities of the case." 11 U.S.C. 502(j).

These cases, along with a number of cases that preceded our decision in Nolan, see, e.g., Davis-McGraw, Inc. v. Johnson (In re Johnson), 247 B.R. 904 (Bankr. S.D. Ga. 1999), hold that the deficiency from a post-confirmation sale of collateral cannot be considered a "secured" claim and must be treated equally with other secured claims. In applying section 502(j), these cases interpret the portion of that statute which provides that "[a] claim that has been allowed or disallowed may be reconsidered for cause" as permitting the court to reconsider the classification of a claim as secured or unsecured. If the request for reconsideration was made in good faith and led to an equitable result,[11] the court will generally reclassify the deficiency remaining on a secured claim as an unsecured claim.[12] See, e.g., Johnson, 247 B.R. at 909.

However, as one bankruptcy court has noted, the literal language of section 502(j) addresses only the "allowance" or "disallowance" of claims, not the reclassification of an already-allowed claim. See Coffman, 271 B.R. at 497. Therefore, we cannot agree with the dissent's recommendation that the case be remanded for consideration under section 502(j). Furthermore, the dissent's view that § 506(a) counsels a different result is not relevant to our reasoning. The dissent's reliance on that section is made necessary only through the use of § 502(j), which we have stated is not applicable in this case.

Another case cited by the Trustee has allowed a reclassification of a secured claim following a post-confirmation sale of repossessed collateral without looking to either section 1329 or section 502(j). See In re White, 169 B.R. 526, 529 (Bankr. W.D.N.Y. 1994). Explicitly rejecting either provision and relying on what it termed as "common sense, common law, and custom and practice,"id. at 529, the White court found that "the lien that the secured creditor retains by virtue of 11 U.S.C. § 1325(a)(5)(B) is precisely what a lien is expected to be at common law." Id. at 530. "When a 11 U.S.C. § 362(d) motion [to lift the automatic stay] is properly made and granted, it is usually explicitly recognized (and always implicitly recognized) that the grant of the motion relegates the

[11] The Johnson court based the requirements of good faith and an equitable result on section 502(j)'s provision that "[a] reconsidered claim may be allowed or disallowed according to the equities of the case," section 1329(b)'s requirement that modified plans be made in good faith, and section 1325(a)(3) good-faith requirement for confirmation of proposed plan. 247 B.R. at 908-09.

[12] The Johnson court, however, recognized that reclassification under section 502(j) could unfairly allow debtors to shift unexpected depreciation of the value of the collateral to the secured creditor. Therefore, it suggested that a secured creditor could seek to have the deficiency considered as an administrative expense with priority over the other unsecured creditors. 247 B.R. at 909 (citing 11 U.S.C. § 507(a)(1), (b)).

parties to their State Law rights." Id. at 529. Therefore, the White court found that any deficiency resulting from the post-confirmation sale of repossessed collateral was automatically converted to an unsecured claim, that a creditor's claims under the confirmation plan are "deemed amended." Id. at 530.

The White court, however, cited no authority for these holdings. We do not find it "obvious" that the secured creditor who retains a lien under pre-BAPCPA section 1325(a)(5)(B)[13] the same creditor rights he did prior to the debtor's bankruptcy filing. See Rash, 520 U.S. at 964 ("In allowing Chapter 13 debtors to retain and use collateral over the objection of secured creditors, however, the Code has reshaped debtor and creditor rights in marked departure from state law."). Moreover, the White court's logic explicitly allows a secured creditor to retain any appreciated gain remaining from the sale of repossessed collateral, id. at 530, a result that no other court has recognized. See, e.g., Nolan, 232 F.3d at 534 (criticizing Jock for creating "an inequitable situation where the secured creditor could not seek to reclassify its claim in the event that collateral appreciated, even though the debtor could revalue or reclassify the claim whenever the collateral depreciated.") (emphasis in original). Therefore, we do not find White persuasive.

We recognize the frustration certain commentators have with our allowing a secured claim to remain classified as "secured" following the sale of the underlying collateral.[14] However, as explained above, we find that there exists no provision in the Code applicable to this case that would allow a reclassification of the deficiency given the "binding effect" of the confirmed plan under 11 U.S.C. § 1327. Therefore, in accordance with our prior decision in Nolan, we find that where the Debtor's actions (i.e., default) provide cause for lifting the automatic stay under section 362(d), the Debtor or Trustee generally cannot move to reclassify the deficiency resulting from the sale of the underlying repossessed collateral as an unsecured claim.[15]

For the foregoing reasons, the decision of the district court is AFFIRMED.

KAREN NELSON MOORE, J., DISSENTING. Because I do not believe that Nolan

---

[13] In 2005, Congress amended section 1325(a)(5)(B) to specifically provide that the holder of a secured claim "retains the lien securing such claim until the earlier of (aa) the payment of the underlying debt determined under nonbankruptcy law; or (bb) discharge under section 1328." The new 1325(a)(5)(B)(i) also provides that if a chapter 13 case is "dismissed or converted without completion of the plan, such lien shall also be retained by such holder to the extent recognized by applicable nonbankruptcy law." BAPCPA, Pub. L. No. 109-8, §§ 306(a), 1501, 119 Stat. 80, 216.

[14] See, e.g., 8 COLLIER ON BANKRUPTCY P 1329.04[1], 1329-8 through 1329-9 (15th ed. rev. 2004). But see 5 NORTON BANKR. L. & PRAC. 2 D § 124:3, n. 94 ("Mere dismissal of the applicability of the rule of res judicata to a secured claim dealt with by a confirmed plan is unconvincing, for it appears that both creditor and debtor should be able to rely on the confirmed plan's treatment of the claim, subject only to possible modification of the 'amount' or the 'time' of payments on the secured claim.").

[15] We share the Trustee's concern that there may be cases in which a portion of the deficiency is the result of damage done to the collateral by the creditor or its agents in the course of, or following, repossession of the collateral. The Trustee believes DaimlerChrysler's repossession of the Neon caused the broken steering column and led to the vehicle being sold at auction for only $ 800, but there is no evidence in the record before us proving this. However, secured creditors should not assume that our decision herein allows them to "run up" the amount of the remaining deficiency through the reckless or careless actions of a repossession agent. We decline to rule whether the bankruptcy court may take damage done to collateral during and after repossession by the creditor into account in reviewing a creditor's amended Proof of Claim after the collateral's sale.

is controlling in this instance, I respectfully dissent. In Nolan, we held that a Chapter 13 debtor cannot modify a confirmed plan under 11 U.S.C. § 1329(a) by voluntarily surrendering the property securing the debt to the creditor, requiring the creditor sell that collateral and apply the sale proceeds toward its secured claim, and classifying any deficiency as an unsecured claim. Chrysler Fin. Corp. v. Nolan (In re Nolan), 232 F.3d 528, 535 (6th Cir. 2000). Our decision in Nolan was motivated by our belief that debtors should not have "wide latitude to subject the creditor to their whims throughout the life of the plan" nor the ability to "reap a windfall by employing a subterfuge" by unfairly shifting the costs of depreciation to the creditor. Id. at 534. Our holding in Nolan was narrowly tailored to the particular facts and circumstances of that case, and therefore I disagree with the majority's decision to extend its holding beyond those boundaries. Because in this case the collateral was involuntarily taken from the debtor by the creditor's conscious decision to seek relief from stay and to sell the collateral to satisfy its secured claim, I must dissent from the majority's decision to extend Nolan. See In re Goos, 253 B.R. 416, 419 n.5 (Bankr. W.D. Mich. 2000)(stating that a creditor-initiated sale may require a different legal analysis than a debtor-initiated surrender).

Our decision in Nolan rejected "a sizable minority" of lower courts that followed the rationale set forth in In re Jock, 95 B.R. 75 (Bankr. M.D. Tenn. 1989), which allowed a debtor to initiate surrender of collateral and for any deficiency to be deemed an unsecured claim. In Nolan we explained five "fundamental deficiencies" of following the Jock line of cases in that situation, each of which stemmed from our concern about the debtor's manipulation of the Bankruptcy Code to surrender the collateral after the collateral has depreciated, thereby unfairly shifting the risk of depreciation to the creditor. Three of the deficiencies that necessitated our conclusion in Nolan related our disagreement with Jock's interpretation of § 1329. Nolan, 232 F.3d at 532-35. That provision of the code is not involved here. DaimlerChrysler's suggestion that a § 1329 modification is implicitly at issue here -- that the Trustee's objection to its attempt to maintain a secured claim after the sale of the collateral is essentially an attempt to modify the plan without a formal § 1329 motion -- is not persuasive. Appellee Br. at 25. This case arose not from an attempted modification brought by the debtor or Trustee through a § 1329 motion, but rather from DaimlerChrysler's § 362 motion to lift the stay and its request therein that any deficiency be classified as a secured claim. Unlike in Nolan, where the creditor would have preferred to continue to receive payments for its secured claim through the plan rather than have the collateral sold, here the creditor was the party moving to initiate the sale. Believing that its interests were not being adequately served through the plan, DaimlerChrysler moved to lift the stay preventing it from repossessing the collateral, thus enabling it to pursue its state-law remedies outside the plan.

The other two deficiencies cited in Nolan were also specific to the debtor-initiated surrender attempted in that case. There we were concerned that the debtor seeking a § 1329 modification in those circumstances may contravene the requirements in §§ 1325(a)(5)(B) and 1327(a) that govern a plan's confirmation and its res judicata effect. Nolan, 232 F.3d at 533-34. In this case, the debtor did not seek to surrender the collateral nor to disturb the confirmed plan. Instead it was the creditor who decided its interests were better served by obtaining its state-law remedies to repossess the collateral, and therefore the creditor moved to redeem its secured claim outside the plan.

In extending the holding in Nolan to allow a creditor who initiated sale of the collateral to recover any deficiency as a secured claim, the majority entirely relieves the creditor of any obligation to protect its own interests against anticipated depreciation in its pre-confirmation dealings. On the contrary, I believe that "the creditor has the obligation to ensure that as time goes by and, as in this case, payments are not made and it repossesses the collateral, the value of the collateral when liquidated will equal the amount of the remaining claim." In re Knappen, 281 B.R. 714, 719 (Bankr. D.N.M. 2002). Placing the risk of depreciation loss completely on the debtor, as the majority does:

> denies that the creditor has an obligation to look out for its own interests, and invites unscrupulous creditors to argue value at their whim after the confirmation hearing. In effect, therefore, the creditor needs to assure that the plan provides for a stream of payments such that at any time the value of the collateral, subject to normal wear and tear, when returned to it and liquidated, will equal the remaining amount of the secured claim.

Id. at 719. DaimlerChrysler had the opportunity to object to confirmation of the plan if it believed that the plan payments, coupled with the sale value of the collateral if repossession became necessary, would be insufficient to cover the costs of normal depreciation. If DaimlerChrysler incurred a loss due to normal depreciation upon the subsequent sale of its collateral, which unlike the creditor in Nolan, it instigated at the timing of its choice, that loss occurred not because the burden of depreciation had been shifted to it, but because it failed to meet its own burden of objecting to confirmation of a plan that did not provide protection from the normal depreciation of the collateral. See In re Zieder, 263 B.R. 114, 118-19 (Bankr. D. Ariz. 2001).

In addition to relieving creditors of their obligations to protect their own interests pre-confirmation, the majority's holding creates a second disincentive for creditors to act diligently. By guaranteeing creditors the payment of the entire amount deemed secured at the time of confirmation regardless of what the sale of collateral brings, the majority eliminates any incentive for creditors who force a sale of collateral to take care to protect the value of the collateral throughout the repossession process. Applying Nolan to the facts in this case allows a creditor to shift the risk of loss totally to the debtor, thereby turning the debtor into a guarantor. Debtors, not creditors, will bear the costs of reckless or careless repossession agents hired by the creditors.

Because I believe that our decision in Nolan does not require us to hold that the post-sale deficiency in this case must be a secured claim, I would instead hold that after a creditor-initiated sale of collateral, any deficiency claim should be reconsidered under 11 U.S.C. § 502(j). Section 502(j) states that "[a] claim that has been allowed or disallowed may be reconsidered for cause. A reconsidered claim may be allowed or disallowed according to the equities of the case." Bankruptcy courts have wide discretion to determine what constitutes cause for reconsideration of claims under § 502(j). Colley v. Nat'l Bank of Texas (In re Colley), 814 F.2d 1008, 1010 (5th Cir.)(calling a bankruptcy court's discretion to reconsider a claim under § 502(j) "virtually plenary"), cert. denied, 484 U.S. 898 (1987). I believe that the sale of the collateral at the instigation of the secured creditor is adequate cause to reconsider a previously allowed secured claim under § 502(j). See In re Mason, 315 B.R. 759, 761 (Bankr. N.D. Cal. 2004)("liquidation of the collateral by the secured creditor is adequate cause to reconsider a previously allowed secured claim" under § 502(j)); Baxter v. Sys. & Servs. Techs.,

Inc. (In re Dykes), 287 B.R. 298, 303 (Bankr. S.D. Ga. 2002) (granting relief from automatic stay to repossess and sell collateral is sufficient "cause" to reconsider under § 502(j)); Zieder, 263 B.R. at 117. I would therefore reverse the district court's decision, and remand to the bankruptcy court to treat as a § 502(j) motion for reconsideration the Trustee's objection to the lifting of the stay and classification of the deficiency as a secured claim.

When reconsidering a claim under § 502(j), a court may readjust the claim in any fashion that the equities of the case deem necessary. Id. Reconsideration under § 502(j) can occur even after a plan is confirmed. See International Yacht & Tennis, Inc. v. Wasserman (In re International Yacht & Tennis, Inc.), 922 F.2d 659, 662 n.5 (11th Cir. 1991)(stating that the probable intent of a 1984 amendment to § 502(j) was to allow claims to be reconsidered after a case has been closed and reopened); Dykes, 287 B.R. at 303 (stating that after confirmation, a " § 502(j) 'motion to reconsider' is the only means by which a claim's continued validity may be questioned"); In re Gomez, 250 B.R. 397, 400 (Bankr.M.D. Fla. 1999)(stating that § 502(j) creates a narrow exception to the res judicata effect of § 1327 that allows reconsideration after confirmation). A § 502(j) analysis of a deficiency can also account for a debtor who contributed to depreciation loss in bad faith. A bankruptcy court can determine that the deficiency amount can only be treated as an unsecured claim if the request is in good faith and leads to an equitable result. Zieder, 263 B.R. at 119 (stating if excess depreciation is due to fault of debtor, creditor may object to § 502(j) modification for lack of good faith); In re Johnson, 247 B.R. 904, 908-09 (Bankr. S.D. Ga. 1999). Furthermore, when a reconsideration under § 502(j) renders a deficiency as unsecured, a creditor may be entitled to an administrative-expense claim for failure of adequate protection, which "has priority over unsecured claims and is paid in full. 11 U.S.C. § 507(a)(1) & (b)." Id. at 909.

Finally, I believe that the plain language of § 506(a) necessitates the conclusion that any deficiency remaining after the secured creditor has initiated a sale of collateral must not be treated as a secured claim, and therefore must be reconsidered under § 502(j). Section 506(a) provides:

> An allowed claim of a creditor secured by a lien on property in which the estate has an interest, or that is subject to setoff under section 553 of this title, is a secured claim to the extent of the value of such creditor's interest in the estate's interest in such property, or to the extent of the amount subject to setoff, as the case may be, and is an unsecured claim to the extent that the value of such creditor's interest or the amount so subject to setoff is less than the amount of such allowed claim. Such value shall be determined in light of the purpose of the valuation and of the proposed disposition or use of such property, and in conjunction with any hearing on such disposition or use or on a plan affecting such creditor's interest.

11 U.S.C. § 506(a) (emphasis added). The Supreme Court has repeatedly cited § 506(a) as the basis for the tenet that a claim is secured only to the extent that it is secured by an interest in collateral. See, e.g., Till v. SCS Credit Corp., 541 U.S. 465, 470 n.5 (2004); Associates Commer. Corp. v. Rash, 520 U.S. 953, 956 (1997). To hold otherwise, as the majority does, would turn the definition of a secured claim on its head. The majority does not explain why § 506(a)'s definition of a secured claim can be ignored in these circumstan-ces. Here DaimlerChrysler initiated the sale of the collateral that secured its claim, and therefore by definition, its claim is no longer secured. There is no provision in the Bankruptcy Code that gives a creditor a secured claim without any collateral. See Zieder, 263

B.R. at 117. I respectfully dissent.

MEZA V TRUMAN (IN RE MEZA)

467 F.3d 874 (5th Cir. 2006)

BARKSADALE, C.J.

Chapter 13 Trustee Tim Truman appeals the district court's affirming the following bankruptcy court holding: Trustee's requested modification of the confirmed plan of debtors . . . could not be considered because it was untimely, Debtors having paid the plan balance while the modification motion was pending. VACATED and REMANDED.

I.

Debtors filed a voluntary petition for chapter 13 bankruptcy in April 2001. Truman, the standing chapter 13 Trustee for the Northern District of Texas, was appointed Trustee.

On 17 January 2002, Debtors filed their bankruptcy plan. The plan, confirmed on 2 April 2002, required Debtors to "pay the sum of $350.00, per month, . . . for 50 months . . . for a total of $17500". Debtors' unsecured creditors, owed a total of $23,181.59, were to receive "approximately .00%" for their claims.

Nearly two years later, on 26 February 2004, Trustee received Debtors' 2003 federal income-tax refund, in the amount of $3,029. Under the plan, "the Trustee [wa]s authorized to receive, endorse, and apply to any delinquent payments under the Plan, any Income Tax Refund payable to debtor(s) during the pendency of this case". Debtors, however, were not delinquent in their payments. Nevertheless, Trustee wanted the non-exempt portion of this refund, $1,545 in disposable income, applied to amounts due under the plan.

Accordingly, on 23 March, Trustee filed a motion to modify Debtors' plan; the requested modification would increase the distribution to Debtors' unsecured creditors from zero percent under the confirmed plan to "approximately 8.40 %". This would increase Debtors' total payment from $17,500 to $19,045. Trustee provided Debtors 20 days notice, as required by Federal Rule of Bankruptcy Procedure 3015(g), and set the motion for pre-trial conference before the bankruptcy court on 7 May 2004 . . . .

On 7 April, however, approximately a month before the scheduled hearing, Debtors paid Trustee $5,600, which paid in full the balance of their confirmed plan. To do so, Debtors refinanced their home, which was exempt property under the plan. On 3 May, Debtors filed an objection to Trustee's proposed modification, asserting it was untimely. Because they had already completed payments under the plan, Debtors claimed they were entitled to a discharge from bankruptcy.

Following a hearing on 7 July 2004, the bankruptcy court ruled the modification request was untimely: "By the time the Modification was presented to the Court, the Debtors had completed all payments required by the terms of the plan. Thus, in accordance with the unambiguous language of 11 U.S.C. § 1329(a), the Modification is disapproved as untimely". In re Meza, 2004 Bankr. LEXIS 1103, *14, No. 01-42612-BJH-13 (Bankr. N.D. Tex. Aug. 4, 2004) (emphasis added). The district court affirmed. Truman v. Meza, No. 4:04-CV-753-Y, slip op. (N.D. Tex. June 7, 2005).

II.

. . . Chapter 13 of the Bankruptcy Code, 11 U.S.C. § 1301, et seq., was created "to address consumer credit loss during the Great Depression by providing a completely voluntary proceeding for consumers to amortize their debts out of future earnings". In re Nolan, 232 F.3d 528, 530 (6th Cir. 2000). Chapter 13 permits wage-earning debtors "to reorganize with a repayment plan as an alternative to seeking a complete discharge of debts through the Chapter 7 bankruptcy liquidation process". Id. A confirmed chapter 13 plan is, of course, binding on all parties. 11 U.S.C. § 1327(a). Under 11 U.S.C. § 1329, however, the plan may be modified by either the debtor, trustee, or an unsecured creditor. See In re Solis, 172 B.R. 530, 533 (Bankr. S.D.N.Y. 1994) ("Although section 1327(a) binds the debtor and the creditors, a confirmed plan may be modified at any time after confirmation before payment is completed."). Section 1329 states:

> (a) At any time after confirmation of the plan but before the completion of payments under such plan, the plan may be modified, upon request of the debtor, the trustee, or the holder of an allowed unsecured claim, to -
>
> (1) increase or reduce the amount of payments on claims of a particular class provided for by the plan;
>
> (2) extend or reduce the time for such payments; or
>
> (3) alter the amount of the distribution to a creditor whose claim is provided for by the plan to the extent necessary to take account of any payment of such claim other than under the plan.
>
> (b)(1) Sections 1322(a), 1322(b), and 1323(c) of this title and the requirements of section 1325(a) of this title apply to any modification under subsection (a) of this section.
>
> (2) The plan as modified becomes the plan unless, after notice and a hearing, such modification is disapproved.

11 U.S.C. § 1329 (2004) (prior to 2005 revision, which added another basis for modification of a confirmed plan) (emphasis added). Modification is based on the premise that, during the life of the plan, circumstances may change, and parties should have the ability to modify the plan accordingly. In re Taylor, 215 B.R. 882, 883 (Bankr. S.D. Cal. 1997).

A.

Some courts have required an unanticipated, substantial change to occur before permitting such plan modification. See In re Hoggle, 12 F.3d 1008, 1011 (11th Cir. 1994) ("Congress designed § 1329 to permit modification of a plan due to changed circumstances of the debtor unforeseen at the time of confirmation."); In re Furgeson, 263 B.R. 28, 37-38 (Bankr. N.D.N.Y. 2001) (citing cases supporting this view); see also 5 NORTON BANKR. L. & PRAC. 2d § 124:2 (noting several courts require "a substantial or even unanticipated change in circumstances, or else the creditor is bound by confirmation of the original plan") (emphasis in original). A growing number of courts, however, do not require such a change. See, e.g., Barbosa v. Soloman, 235 F.3d 31, 41 (1st Cir. 2000) ("refrain[ing] from adopting the substantial and unanticipated test for seeking a modification pursuant to § 1329"); In re Witkowski, 16 F.3d 739, 742 (7th Cir. 1994) (emphasizing that, "[b]y its terms, § 1329 does not provide for any threshold requirement to modify a bankruptcy plan"); In re Sutton, 303 B.R. 510, 516 (Bankr. S.D. Ala. 2003) (citing Witkowski for the proposition that § 1329's plain language imposes no substantial change requirement); In re Sounakhene, 249 B.R. 801, 803 (Bankr. S.D. Cal. 2000) ("A showing of substantially changed circumstances is not a prerequisite to plan modification."); In re Phelps, 149 B.R. 534, 538 (Bankr. N.D. Ill. 1993) (noting "Congress specifically provided for a change in circumstances test under other provisions of the Bankruptcy Code, including at least one in Chapter 13"). Because we agree with this latter approach, we need not consider whether Debtors' income-tax refund constituted a substantial or unanticipated change.

B.

Consistent with § 1329's plain language, it is largely undisputed "that a plan cannot be modified once all payments have been made". In re Moss, 91 B.R. 563, 565 (Bankr. C.D. Cal. 1988). "[I]f a trustee could amend a Chapter 13 plan after the debtor completes his or her payments to the trustee, the mandatory nature of the discharge provision [11 U.S.C. § 1328] would be eviscerated". In re Casper, 154 B.R. 243, 247 (N.D. Ill. 1993) (emphasis added). Accordingly, if a debtor pays his plan balance and the trustee then seeks to modify the plan under § 1329 to account for newly-acquired funds, modification is not permitted. See, e.g., In re Bergolla, 232 B.R. 515, 516 (Bankr. S.D. Fla. 1999) ("lump sum payment was made from the proceeds of the sale of the Debtors' exempt homestead property" to complete payments under the plan before the trustee filed a motion to modify). In such instances, debtors typically contend a trustee's "modification is time-barred because they completed the plan before the [modification] motion was filed". In re Sounakhene, 249 B.R. at 802.

On the other hand, it appears a trustee's motion is timely if filed before payments are completed. See In re Profit, 283 B.R. 567, 572 (B.A.P. 9th Cir. 2002) (stating relevant issue as "[w]hether Trustee's motion to modify the chapter 13 plan was timely filed before all plan payments had been completed, pursuant to § 1329(a)"); In re Sounakhene, 249 B.R. at 804 ("The parties agree the Trustee must file his motion before all the payments under the plan are complete."). Therefore, if the trustee files a modification motion and the debtor then attempts to complete plan payments, the debtor appears to unfairly attempt to circumvent § 1329(b)(2)'s plain language that a "plan as modified becomes the plan unless, after notice and a hearing, such modification is disapproved". Whether a debtor may attempt to avoid increased plan payments by completing payments after a motion to modify is filed, but before any hearing on that motion can be held, does not appear, however, to have been addressed by this, or any other, court.

Plan modification often occurs in the context of debtors who cannot afford to make the monthly payments under their confirmed plans. E.g., In re Taylor, 215 B.R. at 883 (seeking to reduce monthly plan payment). Where a modification is sought because the debtor can make larger payments to creditors than those imposed by the plan, courts have still emphasized that a modification may not be filed after the debtor has completed plan payments. E.g., In re Sutton, 303 B.R. at 515-16 (asserting "an absolute right to request modification of the plan between confirmation of the plan and completion of plan payments"); In re Solis, 172 B.R. at 532 ("A confirmed chapter 13 plan may be modified . . . to increase or reduce payments after confirmation but before completion of debtor's payments." (emphasis added)). One bankruptcy court in our circuit, encountering a creditor who sought plan modification after the debtor completed payments ahead of schedule, explained: "[Section] 1329(a) clearly requires that any request for a post-confirmation modification of a confirmed chapter 13 plan must be presented. . . before the completion of payments under such plan". In re Smith, 237 B.R. 621, 625 n.7 (Bankr. E.D. Tex. 1999) (internal quotation marks omitted). That court concluded: "[W]ithout providing advance notice to any party, a Chapter 13 debtor may tender all the payments due and owing under a confirmed plan on an accelerated basis and thereby create an entitlement to discharge". Id. at 626.

This rationale does not, however, extend to a situation where, as here, the trustee files a modification motion prior to the debtor's tendering full payment. In this regard, for a debtor's filing a proposed modification under § 1329, at least one court has held it effective as of the date of filing. See In re Taylor, 215 B.R. at 884 (explaining "that the proposed modified plan becomes the controlling plan for debtor's performance upon filing"). The modified plan "remains the controlling document unless later disapproved after notice and a hearing". Id. (internal quotation marks omitted). The Taylor court noted it was not deciding whether this same approach would be followed "[w]here the trustee or an unsecured creditor moves to modify a plan to increase the amount of plan payments". Id.

Here, Trustee filed a proposed modification prior to Debtors' attempt to pay the plan balance. Obviously Debtors' making their final payment did not nunc pro tunc make untimely that modification filing. Because the modification was timely filed, and would become effective after the notice period unless disapproved, it precluded Debtors from making their final payment under the earlier confirmed plan.

Rule 3015(g) requires "not less than 20 days notice by mail of the time fixed for filing objections" to a proposed modification. FED. R. BANKR. P. 3015(g). Because documents providing the hearing notice and number of days to file an objection to Trustee's modification were provided in the record on appeal, we do not know what time period the parties fixed for objections to the modification motion. Trustee, as appellant, had the burden of providing a complete record on appeal. FED. R. APP. P. 10(b). Although they made final-plan payment within 20 days of the modification motion, Debtors did not file an objection to the modification until almost six weeks after the motion was filed. Nevertheless, the parties agree Debtors timely objected to Trustee's proposed modification. (Along that line, at oral argument, Trustee's counsel stated that Debtors timely objected within 20 days to Trustee's modification. The bankruptcy court's docket reflects, however, that the modification motion was filed on 23 March and no objection was made until 3 May.)

In sum, we cannot conclude from this record that Debtors' objection was untimely. In any event, as discussed below, instead of holding Trustee's modification motion untimely, the bankruptcy court should have considered it on its merits.

In concluding that Debtors were permitted to complete plan payments after Trustee had filed his proposed modification, but before a hearing on it was held, the bankruptcy court relied in part on a treatise which noted: "[T]he literal language of section 1329(a) would appear to permit a debtor to complete payments during the 20 days that a request to modify must be pending under Federal Rule of Bankruptcy Procedure 3015(g) and thereby deprive the court of the power to modify the plan". 8 COLLIER ON BANKRUPTCY P 1329.08 (15th ed. 2004). Section 1329(a), when viewed alone, could be interpreted in this fashion. But, when § 1329 is read in its entirety, within the context of chapter 13, it is improbable this is the correct or intended result. Section 1329(a) provides a plan may be modified "upon request" and "before the completion of payments"; but, § 1329(b)(2) provides that the modified plan "becomes the plan unless, after notice and a hearing, such modification is disapproved". Read together, both subsections show that, when a modification request is timely filed, the completion of the plan and eventual discharge of the debtor is stayed until the bankruptcy court is allowed to consider the modification on its merits. A contrary result would encourage gamesmanship on behalf of debtors and prevent them from repaying creditors "to the extent of [their] capabilit[ies]". In re Arnold, 869 F.2d 240, 242 ("Certainly Congress did not intend for debtors who experience substantially improved financial conditions after confirmation to avoid paying more to their creditors."). Therefore, rather than disapproving it as untimely, the bankruptcy court should have considered Trustee's proposed modification on its merits.

For the foregoing reasons, the judgment is VACATED and this matter is REMANDED to district court for remand to bankruptcy court for further proceedings consistent with this opinion. VACATED AND REMANDED.

Notes and Questions

1. Meza holds that prepayment is not modification, and so the debtor could pay and win a discharge before the trustee could move to modify in order to capture suprlus income not reflected in the plan. Yet according to § 1329(a)(2), one of the permitted purposes for modification is to "extend or reduce the time for [plan] payments. Many courts read this language to mean that a debtor has no right to prepay and must move to modify. E.g., Fridley v. Forsythe (In re Fridley), 380 B.R. 538 (Bankr. 9th Cir. 2007).

2. Since 1984, unsecured creditors and trustees have been given standing to seek modification of the plan. Bankruptcy Code § 1329(a) ("upon request of the debtor, the trustee, or the holder of an allowed unsecured claim"). In order to assist the creditors in capturing excess income not reflected in the plan, BAPCPA adds a new section 521(f)(3)(B), which requires the debtor to file

> annually after the plan is confirmed and until the case is closed, not later than the date that is 45 days before the anniversary of the confirmation of the plan; a statement under penalty of perjury, of the income and expenditures of the debtor during the tax year of the debtor most recently concluded before such statement is filed under this paragraph, and of the monthly income of the debtor, that shows how income, expenditures, and monthly income are calculated.

What if a chapter 13 debtor violates this requirement? Is dismissal or conversion to chapter 7 appropriate? The doctrinal materials are problematic. Section 1307(c) provides a non-exclusive list of reasons to dismiss or convert. According to § 1307(c)(9) and (10), the United States trustee (and no one else) can move to dismiss for failure to provide the information required by § 521(1) and (2). After BAPCPA, these sections were renumerated to § 521(a)(1) and (2). In any case, § 521(f) is beyond the scope of the cross-reference. A court wanting to boot a debtor from chapter 13 for failure to meet § 521(f)(3)(B) must rely on the fact that the list in § 1307(c) is non-exclusive. Still, Congress intended that only the United States trustee make the motion to dismiss or convert in case of nondisclosures. If someone other than the United States trustee were to move to dismiss or convert, the court would both have to rely on the non-exclusiveness of § 1307(c) and the lack of restriction with regard to an unlisted item. Nevertheless, given Congress's angry mood in 2005, it is pretty obvious that, had the drafters of BAPCPA had mustered the wit to contemplate the matter, they would have changed the cross-reference from § 521(1) and (2) to encompass any part of § 521. Yet they did not do so.

2. A hardship discharge is available to debtors who do not complete the plan. But the debtor must show the failure "is due to circumstances for which the debtor should not justly be held accountable." 11 U.S.C. § 1328(b)(1). In addition, the debtor must have paid enough already

to guarantee that every unsecured creditor received as much as she would received in a chapter 7 liquidation. 11 U.S.C. § 1328(b)(2). Finally, modification of the plan must be impracticable. 11 U.S.C. § 1328(b)(3).

The discharge, however, is not as broad as the discharge available if the debtor completes the plan. 11 U.S.C. § 1328(c) (no claim under § 523(a) is discharged). Suppose a debtor has become disabled and cannot work. Instead of seeking a hardship discharge suppose a debtor moves to modify the plan to provide of zero in future payments. The debtor has already paid enough to meet the "best interest of the creditors" test of § 1325(a)(4). Can the debtor hold on to the broader discharge by modifying the plan? See In re Vasquez, 261 B.R. 654 (Bankr. N.D. Tex. 2001).

WEBER v HEITKAMP (IN RE HOPSON)

324 B.R. 284 (S.D. Tex. 2005)

WERLEIN, J.

. . . On June 1, 2001, Debtors filed a Chapter 13 bankruptcy petition in this court. Appellant served as counsel for Debtors from the date of the filing of the Chapter 13 petition, through January 16, 2004, when counsel was allowed to withdraw.

On February 27, 2002, Debtors' Chapter 13 Plan was confirmed by the Bankruptcy Court. Thereafter, Appellant's first and second application for fees, neither of which was opposed, were granted on September 11, 2002, and May 18, 2003, respectively. On January 17, 2004, after Appellant was allowed to withdraw as counsel for Debtors, Appellant filed his third application for fees and a Motion to Modify the Confirmed Chapter 13 Plan to provide for the payment of such fees. Both Debtors and the Chapter 13 Trustee (William Heitkamp) opposed the motion. On March 22, 2004, the Bankruptcy Court granted Appellant's fee request, and in connection therewith, signed an order allowing the attorney's fees made the basis of Appellant's third request for fees as an administrative expense under § 503(b). The Bankruptcy Court, however, denied Appellant's motion to modify the plan. In a written order entered on April 30, 2004, the Bankruptcy Court wrote:

> The Court has considered Movant's request to modify Debtors' Chapter 13 Plan to pay the attorney's fees. The Court finds that at the time the Fee Application was filed, and on the hearing date (3/22/2004), Debtors had not agreed to the plan modification requested by Movant. The Court further finds and concludes that Movant, as the holder of an allowed priority administrative claim pursuant to BC § 503(b) and 507(a) (1), is not the holder of an "allowed unsecured claim" as contemplated by BC § 1329(a), and therefore, as a matter of law, lacks standing to seek a plan modification.

II. Issues

In this appeal, Appellant sets forth the two issues to be resolved as follows:

> 1. Does the holder of an allowed priority administrative claim pursuant to BC § 503(b) and § 507(a)(1) have standing to seek a plan modification under BC § 1329(a)?
>
> 2. Is the holder of an allowed priority administrative claim pursuant to BC § 503(b) and § 507(a)(1) the holder of an "allowed unsecured claim" as contemplated by BC § 1329(a)? . . .

IV. Discussion

. . . Confirmed Chapter 13 Plans may be modified upon motion as follows:

> (a) At any time after confirmation of the plan but before the completion of payments under such plan, the plan may be modified, upon request of the debtor, the trustee, or the holder of an allowed unsecured claim . . .

At issue here is whether Appellant had standing under § 1329(a) as the holder of an "allowed unsecured claim" to seek modification of the Plan.

Both sides agree that the Bankruptcy Code does not define who is a holder of an "allowed unsecured claim." Neither does the case law provide guidance as to who is a holder of an "allowed unsecured claim" within the meaning of § 1329(a). Appellant argues that the term "allowed unsecured claim" should be viewed expansively, to include all allowed claims that are not "secured by a lien on property in which the estate has an interest." 11 U.S.C. § 506(a) ("Determination of secured status"). So viewed, Appellant maintains that he, pursuant to the Bankruptcy Court's March 22, 2004 Order, which approved his motion for additional attorney's fees, is a holder of an "allowed unsecured claim" within the meaning of § 1329(a). In contrast, the Trustee argues that § 1329(a) should be viewed more narrowly, to include only general unsecured claims, not priority administrative expense claims, which are treated differently elsewhere in the Bankruptcy Code. Because Appellant's claim is undisputably an administrative expense claim, not a general unsecured claim, the Trustee maintains herein as he did in the Bankruptcy Court that § 1329(a) was not designed to, and therefore does not, confer standing upon Appellant to seek modification of the Chapter 13 Plan.

Although the Bankruptcy Code does not define the phrase "allowed unsecured claim," it does define the term "claim" and does provide guidance as to the meaning of the terms "secured" and "unsecured". A "claim" is the "right to payment, whether or not such right is reduced to judgment, liquidated, unliquidated, fixed, contingent, matured, unmatured, disputed, undisputed, legal, equitable, secured, or unsecured" or the "right to an equitable remedy for breach of performance if such breach gives rise to a right to payment, whether or not such right to an equitable remedy is reduced to judgment, fixed, contingent, matured, unmatured, disputed, undisputed, secured, or unsecured." 11 U.S.C. § 101(5). With respect to the meaning of the terms "secured" and "unsecured," as used throughout the Bankruptcy Code, 11 U.S.C. § 506(a) provides as follows:

> An allowed claim of a creditor secured by a lien on property in which the estate has an interest, or that is subject to setoff under section 553 of this title, is a secured claim to the extent of the value of such creditor's interest in the estate's interest in such property, or to the extent of the amount subject to setoff, as the case may be, and is an unsecured claim to the extent that the value of such creditor's interest or the amount so subject to setoff is less than the amount of such allowed claim. . . .

Here, Appellant's entitlement to attorney's fees as an administrative expense under § 503 of the Bankruptcy Code makes Appellant the holder of a "claim". 11 U.S.C. § 101(5); see also In re Jastrem, 253 F.3d 438, 442 (9th Cir. 2001); In re Reed, 312 B.R. 832, 838 n. 8 (N.D. Tex. 2004) (noting that administrative expenses are "surely" claims). Similarly, because Appellant's claim is not secured by a lien on property of the estate, it is an "unsecured" claim. 11 U.S.C. § 506(a). Neither side has any general disagreement with either of these propositions. Instead, as set forth above, the Trustee maintains that only holders of general unsecured claims, as opposed to holders of priority administrative expense claims, fall within the category of persons with standing to seek modification of a Chapter 13 plan under § 1329(a). The Trustee relies on the Bankruptcy Code's different treatment of priority claims and general unsecured claims, as well as the legislative history surrounding § 1329 to support his argument.

Because the phrase "allowed unsecured claim" in § 1329(a) is not defined in the Bankruptcy Code, and because it has not otherwise been defined in the case law, the rules of statutory construction must be employed to determine whether Appellant's claim constitutes an "allowed unsecured claim" for purposes of § 1329(a).

"In all cases involving statutory construction, our starting point must be the language employed by Congress' and we assume that the legislative purpose is expressed by the ordinary meaning of the words used.'" American Tobacco Co. v. Patterson, 456 U.S. 63 (1982) (citations omitted); see also FDIC v. Meyer, 510 U.S. 471 (1994) ("In the absence of [] a definition, we construe a statutory term in accordance with its ordinary or natural meaning."); Smith v. United States, 508 U.S. 223 (1993) ("When a word is not defined by statute, we normally construe it in accord with its ordinary or natural meaning."). Courts are to "'presume that a legislature says in a statute what it means and means in a statute what it says.'" Andrews & Kurth L.L.P. v. Family Snacks (In re Pro-Snax Distribs.), 157 F.3d 414, 425 (5th Cir. 1998) (quoting Connecticut Nat'l Bank v. Germain, 503 U.S. 249 (1992)). Only when an undefined term in a statute, applying its plain meaning, would the render the term "opaque," "translucent," or ambiguous, should the court "attempt to divine congressional intent by applying prescribed canons of statutory interpretation (including, without limitation, a resort to the rule of lenity and legislative history)." United States v. Barlow, 41 F.3d 935, 942 (5th Cir. 1994), cert. denied, 514 U.S. 1030 (1995); see also Carrieri v. Jobs.com, Inc., 393 F.3d 508, 2004 WL 2801793 at *6 (5th Cir. 2004) ("Only after application of the principles of statutory construction, including the canons of construction, and after a conclusion that the statute is ambiguous may the court turn to the legislative history."). For statutory language to be considered ambiguous, "it must be susceptible to more than one reasonable interpretation' or more than one accepted meaning.'" Carrieri, 393 F.3d 508, 2004 WL 2801793 at *6 (quoting United States v. Kay, 359 F.3d 738, 743 (5th Cir. 2004)). Here, given the Bankruptcy Code's definition of a "claim" and the guidance provided with respect to the meaning of the terms "secured" and "unsecured," the phrase "holder of an allowed unsecured claim" in § 1329(a) is susceptible to one reasonable interpretation, that is, that any person whose claim has been allowed, and whose claim is not secured by a lien on property of the estate, has standing under § 1329(a) to seek modification of the chapter 13 plan. Appellant's claim for additional attorney's fees, which was allowed by the Bankruptcy Court on March 22, 2004, and which is not secured by a lien on any property of the estate, is an allowed unsecured claim.

Although the Trustee makes much of the fact that priority administrative claims of the type held by Appellant are generally dealt with differently than general unsecured claims, particularly with respect to priority of payment, see 11 U.S.C. 507, § 1329(a) does not make such a distinction. Similarly, while the Trustee argues that legislative history supports his position that Appellant, as the holder of a priority administrative claim should not be construed a holder of an "allowed unsecured claim" within the meaning of § 1329(a), the Trustee fails to cite any legislative history that clearly so states. The only legislative history referenced by the Trustee in his Brief is "The Oversight Hearings on Personal Bankruptcy Before the Subcommittee on Monopolies and Commercial Law of the House Committee on [the] Judiciary." The Trustee, however, has not pointed to any specific aspect of the generally referenced "Oversight Hearings" and has not identified any aspect of the "Oversight Hearings" where mention was made of any intended distinction between holders of priority administrative claims and holders of general unsecured claims under § 1329(a). Moreover, given the unambiguous statutory language at issue, resort to legislative history is not appropriate. Pro-Snax, 157 F.3d at 425 ("even where one party's argument finds express support' in the legislative history to a statute, where that legislative history is clearly contrary to the statutory language,' it is unpersuasive.'") (citations omitted).

Because neither the individual terms in the phrase "allowed unsecured claim," nor the phrase itself is ambiguous, and because there is no clear legislative history that would override the plain meaning of the phrase "allowed unsecured claim," the Bankruptcy Court erred in determining that Appellant was not a holder of an allowed unsecured claim within the meaning of § 1329. Because Appellant had standing to seek modification of the plan, the Bankruptcy Court's Order of April 30, 2004, must be reversed and vacated. . . .

Notes and Questions:

1. In Hobson, the debtor's attorney was allowed to modify the plan to recover post-confirmation fees. How should the trustee react to a successful motion to modify?

2. A secured creditor cannot move to modify the plan. If the secured party disagrees with the amount of his claim listed on the debtor's schedules, he must quickly file a proof of claim and object at confirmation. By waiting to file his proof of claim, the secured party may lose his rights. In re Stewart, 247 B.R. 515 (Bankr. M.D. Fla. 2000) (secured creditor who had not timely filed a proof of claim could not move to modify Chapter 13 plan to add to the amount of the secured claim).

CHAPTER 7 CONVERSION TO CHAPTER 7

A. CHAPTER 13'S HIGH RATE OF FAILURE

TILL v SCS CREDIT CORP.
541 U.S. 465 (2004)

[The bankruptcy court had confirmed a chapter 13 plan involving the retention of a car encumbered by a security interest. The debtors proposed to pay the secured portion of the car lender's claim over time, with an interest rate equating with the prime rate plus a 1.5% risk factor. The district court affirmed, but the Seventh Circuit reversed, because the appopriate interest rate was the contract rate of 21%. A majority of the Supreme Court reversed the court of appeals. Four of the judges approved of the bankruptcy court's use of prime plus a risk factor. Justice Thomas, in a concurring opinion, opined that a risk free interest rate could be used.]

JUSTICE SCALIA, WITH WHOM THE CHIEF JUSTICE, JUSTICE O'CONNOR, AND JUSTICE KENNEDY JOIN, DISSENTING. My areas of agreement with the plurality are substantial. We agree that, although all confirmed Chapter 13 plans have been deemed feasible by a bankruptcy judge, some nevertheless fail. We agree that any deferred payments to a secured creditor must fully compensate it for the risk that such a failure will occur. Finally, we agree that adequate compensation may sometimes require an "'eye-popping'" interest rate, and that, if the rate is too high for the plan to succeed, the appropriate course is not to reduce it to a more palatable level, but to refuse to confirm the plan.

Our only disagreement is over what procedure will more often produce accurate estimates of the appropriate interest rate. The plurality would use the prime lending rate--a rate we *know* is too low--and require the judge in every case to determine an amount by which to increase it. I believe that, in practice, this approach will systematically undercompensate secured creditors for the true risks of default. I would instead adopt the contract rate--*i.e.*, the rate at which the creditor actually loaned funds to the debtor--as a presumption that the bankruptcy judge could revise on motion of either party. Since that rate is generally a good indicator of actual risk, disputes should be infrequent, and it will provide a quick and reasonably accurate standard.

I

The contract-rate approach makes two assumptions, both of which are reasonable. First, it assumes that subprime lending markets are competitive and therefore largely efficient. If so, the high interest rates lenders charge reflect not extortionate profits or excessive costs, but the actual risks of default that subprime borrowers present. Lenders with excessive rates would be undercut by their competitors, and inefficient ones would be priced out of the market. We have implicitly assumed market competitiveness in other bankruptcy contexts. See *Bank of America Nat. Trust and Sav. Assn.* v. *203 North LaSalle Street Partnership,* 526 U.S. 434, 456-458 (1999). Here the assumption is borne out by empirical evidence: One study reports that subprime lenders are nearly twice as likely to be unprofitable as banks, suggesting a fiercely competitive environment. See J. Lane, Associate Director, Division of Supervision, Federal Deposit Insurance Corporation, A Regulator's View of Subprime Lending: Address at the National Automotive Finance Association Non-Prime Auto Lending Conference 6 (June 18-19, 2002) (available in Clerk of Court's case file). By relying on the prime rate, the plurality implicitly assumes that the *prime* lending market is efficient; I see no reason not to make a similar assumption about the *sub*prime lending market.

The second assumption is that the expected costs of default in Chapter 13 are normally no less than those at the time of lending. This assumption is also reasonable. Chapter 13 plans often fail. I agree with petitioners that the relevant statistic is the percentage of *confirmed* plans that fail, but even resolving that issue in their favor, the risk is still substantial. The failure rate they offer--which we may take to be a conservative estimate, as it is doubtless the lowest one they could find--is 37%. See Girth, The Role of Empirical Data in Developing Bankruptcy Legislation for Individuals, 65 Ind. L. J. 17, 40-42 (1989) (reporting a 63.1% success rate).[1] In every one of the failed plans making up that 37%, a bankruptcy judge had found that "the debtor will be able to make all payments under the plan," 11 U.S.C. § 1325(a)(6) [11 USCS § 1325(a)(6)], and a trustee had supervised the debtor's compliance, § 1302. That so many nonetheless failed proves that bankruptcy judges are not oracles and that trustees cannot draw blood from a stone.

While court and trustee oversight may provide some marginal benefit to the creditor, it seems obviously outweighed by the fact that (1) an already-bankrupt borrower has demonstrated a financial instability and a proclivity to seek legal protection that other subprime borrowers have not, and (2) the costs of foreclosure are substantially higher in bankruptcy because the automatic stay bars repossession without judicial permission. See § 362. It does not strike me as plausible that creditors would *prefer* to lend to individuals already in bankruptcy than to those for whom bankruptcy is merely a possibility--as if Chapter 13 were widely viewed by secured creditors as some sort of godsend. Cf. Dunagan, Enforcement of Security Interests in Motor Vehicles in Bankruptcy, 52 Consumer

[1] The true rate of plan failure is almost certainly much higher. The Girth study that yielded the 37% figure was based on data for a single division (Buffalo, New York) from over 20 years ago (1980-1982). See 65 Ind. L. J., at 41. A later study concluded that "the Buffalo division ha[d] achieved extraordinary results, far from typical for the country as a whole." Whitford, The Ideal of Individualized Justice: Consumer Bankruptcy as Consumer Protection, and Consumer Protection in Consumer Bankruptcy, 68 Am. Bankr. L. J. 397, 411, n. 50 (1994). Although most of respondent's figures are based on studies that do not clearly exclude unconfirmed plans, one study includes enough detail to make the necessary correction: It finds 32% of filings successful, 18% dismissed without confirmation of a plan, and 49% dismissed after confirmation, for a postconfirmation failure rate of 60% (*i.e.*, 49%/(32% + 49%)). See Norberg, Consumer Bankruptcy's New Clothes: An Empirical Study of Discharge and Debt Collection in Chapter 13, 7 Am. Bankr. Inst. L. Rev. 415, 440-441 (1999). This 60% failure rate is far higher than the 37% reported by Girth.

Fin. L. Q. Rep. 191, 197 (1998). Certainly the record in this case contradicts that implausible proposition. See App. 48 (testimony of Craig Cook, sales manager of Instant Auto Finance) ("Q. Are you aware of how other lenders similar to Instant Auto Finance view credit applicants who appear to be candidates for Chapter 13 bankruptcy?" "A. Negative[ly] as well"). The better assumption is that bankrupt debtors are riskier than other subprime debtors--or, at the very least, not systematically *less* risky.

The first of the two assumptions means that the contract rate reasonably reflects actual risk at the time of borrowing. The second means that this risk persists when the debtor files for Chapter 13. It follows that the contract rate is a decent estimate, or at least the lower bound, for the appropriate interest rate in cramdown.[2]

The plurality disputes these two assumptions. It argues that subprime lending markets are not competitive because "vehicles are regularly sold by means of tie-in transactions, in which the price of the vehicle is the subject of negotiation, while the terms of the financing are dictated by the seller."[3] Tie-ins do not *alone* make financing markets noncompetitive; they only cause prices and interest rates to be considered *in tandem* rather than separately. The force of the plurality's argument depends entirely on its claim that "the terms of the financing are dictated by the seller." *Ibid.* This unsubstantiated assertion is contrary to common experience. Car sellers routinely advertise their interest rates, offer promotions like "zero-percent financing," and engage in other behavior that plainly assumes customers are sensitive to interest rates and not just price. . . .

As to the second assumption (that the expected costs of default in Chapter 13 are normally no less than those at the time of lending), the plurality responds, not that Chapter 13 *as currently administered* is less risky than subprime lending generally, but that it *would* be less risky, if only bankruptcy courts would confirm fewer risky plans. Of course, it is often quite difficult to predict which plans will fail. See Norberg, Consumer Bankruptcy's New Clothes: An Empirical Study of Discharge and Debt Collection in Chapter 13, 7 Am. Bankr. Inst. L. Rev. 415, 462 (1999). But even assuming the high failure rate primarily reflects judicial dereliction rather than unavoidable uncertainty, the plurality's argument fails for want of any reason to believe the dereliction will abate. While full compensation can be attained either by low-risk plans and low interest rates, or by high-risk plans and high interest rates, it cannot be attained by *high*-risk plans and *low* interest rates, which, absent cause to anticipate a change in confirmation practices, is precisely what the formula approach would yield. . . .

II

The defects of the formula approach far outweigh those of the contract-rate approach. The formula approach starts with the prime lending rate--a

---

[2] The contract rate is only a presumption, however, and either party remains free to prove that a higher or lower rate is appropriate in a particular case. For example, if market interest rates generally have risen or fallen since the contract was executed, the contract rate could be adjusted by the same amount in cases where the difference was substantial enough that a party chose to make an issue of it.

[3] To the extent the plurality argues that subprime lending markets are not "*perfectly* competitive" (emphasis added), I agree. But there is no reason to doubt they are *reasonably* competitive, so that pricing in those markets is *reasonably* efficient.

number that, while objective and easily ascertainable, is indisputably too low. It then adjusts by adding a risk premium that, unlike the prime rate, is neither objective nor easily ascertainable. If the risk premium is typically small relative to the prime rate--as the 1.5% premium added to the 8% prime rate by the court below would lead one to believe--then this subjective element of the computation might be forgiven. But in fact risk premiums, if properly computed, would typically be substantial. For example, if the 21% contract rate is an accurate reflection of risk in this case, the risk premium would be 13%--nearly two-thirds of the total interest rate. When the risk premium is the greater part of the overall rate, the formula approach no longer depends on objective and easily ascertainable numbers. The prime rate becomes the objective tail wagging a dog of unknown size.

As I explain below, the most relevant factors bearing on risk premium are (1) the probability of plan failure; (2) the rate of collateral depreciation; (3) the liquidity of the collateral market; and (4) the administrative expenses of enforcement. Under the formula approach, a risk premium must be computed in every case, so judges will invariably grapple with these imponderables. Under the contract-rate approach, by contrast, the task of assessing all these risk factors is entrusted to the entity most capable of undertaking it: the market. See *Bank of America*, 526 U.S., at 457 ("[T]he best way to determine value is exposure to a market"). All the risk factors are reflected (assuming market efficiency) in the debtor's contract rate--a number readily found in the loan document. If neither party disputes it, the bankruptcy judge's task is at an end. There are straightforward ways a debtor *could* dispute it--for example, by showing that the creditor is now substantially oversecured, or that some other lender is willing to extend credit at a lower rate. But unlike the formula approach, which requires difficult estimation in every case, the contract-rate approach requires it only when the parties choose to contest the issue. . . .

There is no better demonstration of the inadequacies of the formula approach than the proceedings in this case. Petitioners' economics expert testified that the 1.5% risk premium was "very reasonable" because Chapter 13 plans are "supposed to be financially feasible" and "the borrowers are under the supervision of the court." App. 43. Nothing in the record shows how these two platitudes were somehow manipulated to arrive at a figure of 1.5%. It bears repeating that feasibility determinations and trustee oversight do not prevent at least 37% of confirmed Chapter 13 plans from failing. On cross-examination, the expert admitted that he had only limited familiarity with the subprime auto lending market and that he was not familiar with the default rates or the costs of collection in that market. *Id.*, at 44-45. In light of these devastating concessions, it is impossible to view the 1.5% figure as anything other than a smallish number picked out of a hat.

Based on even a rudimentary financial analysis of the facts of this case, the 1.5% figure is obviously wrong--not just off by a couple percent, but probably by roughly an order of magnitude. For a risk premium to be adequate, a hypothetical, rational creditor must be indifferent between accepting (1) the proposed risky stream of payments over time and (2) immediate payment of its present value in a lump sum. Whether he is indifferent--*i.e.*, whether the risk premium added to the prime rate is adequate--can be gauged by comparing benefits and costs: on the one hand, the expected value of the extra interest, and on the other, the expected costs of default.

Respondent was offered a risk premium of 1.5% on top of the prime rate of 8%. If that premium were fully paid as the plan contemplated, it would yield about $60.[4] If the debtor defaulted, all or part of that interest would not be paid, so the expected value is only about $50.[5] The prime rate itself already includes some compensation for risk; as it turns out, about the same amount, yielding another $50.[6] Given the 1.5% risk premium, then, the total expected benefit to respondent was about $100. Against this we must weigh the expected costs of default. While precise calculations are impossible, rough estimates convey a sense of their scale.

The first cost of default involves depreciation. If the debtor defaults, the creditor can eventually repossess and sell the collateral, but by then it may be substantially less valuable than the remaining balance due--and the debtor may stop paying long before the creditor receives permission to repossess. When petitioners purchased their truck in this case, its value was almost equal to the principal balance on the loan.[7] By the time the plan was confirmed, however, the truck was worth only $4,000, while the balance on the loan was $4,895. If petitioners were to default on their Chapter 13 payments and if respondent suffered the same relative loss from depreciation, it would amount to about $550.[8]

The second cost of default involves liquidation. The $4,000 to which respondent would be entitled if paid in a lump sum reflects the *replacement* value of the vehicle, *i.e.*, the amount it would cost the debtor to purchase a similar used truck. See *Associates Commercial Corp.* v. *Rash*, 520 U.S. 953 (1997). If the debtor defaults, the creditor cannot sell the truck for that amount; it receives only a lesser *foreclosure* value because collateral markets are not perfectly liquid and there is thus a spread between what a buyer will pay and what a seller will demand. The foreclosure value of petitioners' truck is not in the record, but, using the relative liquidity figures in *Rash* as a rough guide, respondent would suffer a further loss of about $450.[9]

The third cost of default consists of the administrative expenses of foreclosure. While a Chapter 13 plan is in effect, the automatic stay prevents secured creditors from repossessing their collateral, even if the debtor fails to pay.

---

[4] Given its priority, and in light of the amended plan's reduced debtor contributions, the $4,000 secured claim would be fully repaid by about the end of the second year of the plan. The average balance over that period would be about $2,000, *i.e.*, half the initial balance. The total interest premium would therefore be 1.5% x 2 x $2,000 = $60. In this and all following calculations, I do not adjust for time value, as timing effects have no substantial effect on the conclusion.

[5] Assuming a 37% rate of default that results on average in only half the interest's being paid, the expected value is $60 x (1 - 37%/2), or about $50.

[6] According to the record in this case, the prime rate at the time of filing was 2% higher than the risk-free treasury rate, and the difference represented "mostly . . . risk [and] to some extent transaction costs." App. 42 (testimony of Professor Steve Russell); see also Federal Reserve Board, Selected Interest Rates, http://www.federalreserve.gov/releases/ h15/data.htm (as visited Apr. 19, 2004) (available in Clerk of Court's case file) (historical data showing prime rate typically exceeding 3-month constant-maturity treasury rate by 2%-3.5%). If "mostly" means about three-quarters of 2%, then the risk compensation included in the prime rate is 1.5%. Because this figure happens to be the same as the risk premium over prime, the expected value is similarly $50.

[7] The truck was initially worth $6,395; the principal balance on the loan was about $6,426.

[8] On the original loan, depreciation ($6,395 - $4,000, or $2,395) exceeded loan repayment ($6,426 - $4,895, or $1,531) by $864, *i.e.*, 14% of the original truck value of $6,395. Applying the same percentage to the new $4,000 truck value yields approximately $550.

[9] The truck in *Rash* had a replacement value of $41,000 and a foreclosure value of $31,875, *i.e.*, 22% less. 520 U.S., at 957. If the market in this case had similar liquidity and the truck were repossessed after losing half its remaining value, the loss would be 22% of $2,000, or about $450.

See 11 U.S.C. § 362 [11 USCS § 362]. The creditor's attorney must move the bankruptcy court to lift the stay. § 362(d). In the District where this case arose, the filing fee for such motions is now $150. See United States Bankruptcy Court for the Southern District of Indiana, Schedule of Bankruptcy Fees (Nov. 1, 2003) (available in Clerk of Court's case file). And the standard attorney's fee for such motions, according to one survey, is $350 in Indiana and as high as $875 in other States. See J. Cossitt, Chapter 13 Attorney Fee Survey, American Bankruptcy Institute Annual Spring Meeting (Apr. 10-13, 2003) (available in Clerk of Court's case file). Moreover, bankruptcy judges will often excuse first offenses, so foreclosure may require multiple trips to court. The total expected administrative expenses in the event of default could reasonably be estimated at $600 or more.

I have omitted several other costs of default, but the point is already adequately made. The three figures above total $1,600. Even accepting petitioners' low estimate of the plan failure rate, a creditor choosing the stream of future payments instead of the immediate lump sum would be selecting an alternative with an expected cost of about $590 ($1,600 multiplied by 37%, the chance of failure) and an expected benefit of about $100 (as computed above). No rational creditor would make such a choice. The risk premium over prime necessary to make these costs and benefits equal is in the neighborhood of 16%, for a total interest rate of 24%.[10]

Of course, many of the estimates I have made can be disputed. Perhaps the truck will depreciate more slowly now than at first, perhaps the collateral market is more liquid than the one in *Rash*, perhaps respondent can economize on attorney's fees, and perhaps there is some reason (other than judicial optimism) to think the Tills were unlikely to default. I have made some liberal assumptions,[11] but also some conservative ones.[12] When a risk premium is off by an order of magnitude, one's estimates need not be very precise to show that it cannot possibly be correct.

In sum, the 1.5% premium adopted in this case is far below anything approaching fair compensation. That result is not unusual, see, *e.g.*, *In re Valenti*, 105 F.3d 55, 64 (CA2 1997) (recommending a 1%-3% premium over the *treasury* rate--*i.e.*, approximately a 0% premium over prime); it is the entirely predictable consequence of a methodology that tells bankruptcy judges to set interest rates based on highly imponderable factors. Given the inherent uncertainty of the enterprise, what heartless bankruptcy judge can be expected to demand that the unfortunate debtor pay *triple* the prime rate as a condition of keeping his sole means of transportation? It challenges human nature. . . .

* * *

Today's judgment is unlikely to burnish the Court's reputation for reasoned decisionmaking. Eight Justices are in agreement that the rate of interest

---

[10] A 1.5% risk premium plus a 1.5% risk component in the prime rate yielded an expected benefit of about $100, so, to yield $590, the total risk compensation would have to be 5.9 times as high, *i.e.*, almost 18%, or a 16.5% risk premium over prime.

[11] For example, by ignoring the possibility that the creditor might recover some of its undersecurity as an unsecured claimant, that the plan might fail only after full repayment of secured claims, or that an oversecured creditor might recover some of its expenses under 11 U.S.C. § 506(b) [11 USCS § 506(b)].

[12] For example, by assuming a failure rate of 37%, cf. n. 1, *supra*, and by ignoring all costs of default other than the three mentioned.

set forth in the debtor's approved plan must include a premium for risk. Of those eight, four are of the view that beginning with the contract rate would most accurately reflect the actual risk, and four are of the view that beginning with the prime lending rate would do so. The ninth Justice takes no position on the latter point, since he disagrees with the eight on the former point; he would reverse because the rate proposed here, being above the risk-free rate, gave respondent no cause for complaint. Because I read the statute to require full risk compensation, and because I would adopt a valuation method that has a realistic prospect of enforcing that directive, I respectfully dissent.

B. PROPERTY OF THE ESTATE

IN RE MICHAEL

699 F.3d 305 (3d Cir. 2012)

AMBRO, J.

This appeal raises a question of first impression involving the interpretation of Chapter 13 of the Bankruptcy Code, 11 U.S.C. §§ 101 et seq., in the common circumstance of a debtor converting his or her case from a Chapter 13 adjustment of debts under a reorganization plan to a Chapter 7 liquidation of assets and distribution to creditors.[13] If at the time of conversion the Chapter 13 trustee is holding funds acquired post-petition by the debtor for eventual distribution to creditors under a confirmed Chapter 13 reorganization plan, must the trustee return the funds to the debtor or distribute them to creditors under the provisions of the plan? The District Court affirmed the Bankruptcy Court's holding that those funds are to be returned to the debtor at the time of conversion. We agree and thus affirm the District Court's decision.

I. *Facts and Procedural History*

Appellee Barry Michael filed a voluntary petition under Chapter 13 of the Bankruptcy Code in September 2005. In June 2006, the Bankruptcy Court confirmed his Chapter 13 reorganization plan (the "Plan"). The Plan provided that Michael would pay approximately $277 per month to the Chapter 13 trustee, Appellant Charles J. DeHart, III (the "Trustee"), for 53 months, and the Trustee would direct the monies received to creditors holding secured and priority claims. Among these creditors was GMAC Mortgage, which held a mortgage on Michael's residence. Michael agreed also to make regular mortgage payments to GMAC outside of the Plan. The Plan further provided that, to the extent funds

---

[13] The primary goal of a Chapter 13 case is the confirmation and completion of a reorganization plan, which results in the discharge of the Chapter 13 debtor's debts. *See* 11 U.S.C. § 1328(a) (providing for discharge "as soon as practicable after completion by the debtor of all payments under the plan"). If a debtor cannot confirm or complete a plan, his case most likely either will be converted to a Chapter 7 liquidation or dismissed. *But see id.* § 1328(b) (detailing the circumstances in which a debtor may receive a discharge despite not completing a plan). Empirical studies show that about a third of Chapter 13 debtors successfully confirm and complete a plan. *See, e.g.*, Katherine Porter, "The Pretend Solution: An Empirical Study of Bankruptcy Outcomes," *90 Tex. L. Rev. 103, 107-11 (2011)* (summarizing studies published from 1989 through 2006, all of which concluded that only one in three cases filed under Chapter 13 ended in a completed reorganization plan, and noting that the ratio of discharge to conversion or dismissal has "persisted for more than thirty years").

were available, creditors holding unsecured claims would be paid *pro rata*. To complete his bargain and fund the Plan, Michael allowed his wages to be attached and paid directly to the Trustee.

Michael, however, was unable to make mortgage payments to GMAC outside of the Plan, and in August 2006 the Bankruptcy Court granted GMAC relief from the automatic stay to allow it to foreclose on Michael's residence. Because Michael did not move to amend the Plan or modify the wage attachment order, the Trustee continued to receive automatic payments from Michael's employer. When the Trustee attempted to forward the funds to GMAC as provided by the Plan, GMAC refused to accept the payments (ostensibly because it wanted to foreclose--pun intended--an estoppel and/or waiver defense to its mortgage foreclosure). The funds continued to accumulate in the Trustee's account until Michael moved to convert his case to Chapter 7 in October 2009.

Several days after the conversion, Michael filed a motion seeking an order compelling the return to him by the Trustee of the accumulated funds, which amounted to $9,181.62. The Trustee objected, arguing that the funds should be distributed *pro rata* to unsecured creditors as provided by the Plan.

Both the Bankruptcy and District Courts noted that the Bankruptcy Code does not provide a clear answer on whether undistributed plan payments held by a Chapter 13 trustee should be returned to the debtor or distributed to creditors under a plan when a Chapter 13 case is converted to Chapter 7. Each court assessed the main arguments advanced by the parties and discussed by other (mainly bankruptcy) courts regarding statutory language, legislative intent, and the goals of the Code. They both concluded that the funds must be returned to Michael. The Trustee filed a timely notice of appeal.

The Chapter 13 Standing Trustees in our Circuit filed an *amicus* brief in support of the Trustee. The National Association of Consumer Bankruptcy Attorneys submitted an *amicus* brief in support of Michael.

II. *Discussion*

We have a pure question of law--what does the Bankruptcy Code require a Chapter 13 trustee to do with undistributed funds received pursuant to a confirmed Chapter 13 plan when that Chapter 13 case is converted to Chapter 7? Not only does the Code provide no clear answer to this question, in reading it one finds an internal tension, as separate provisions seemingly lead to divergent results.

Both the Bankruptcy and District Courts began their analyses, as do we, with the Bankruptcy Reform Act of 1994's amendments to the Bankruptcy Code. Included in those amendments was § 348(f), on which this appeal ultimately turns. That section provides that on conversion of a case from Chapter 13 to another Chapter, "property of the estate in the converted case shall consist of property of the estate, *as of the date of filing of the petition*, that remains in the possession of or is under the control of the debtor on the date of conversion." 11 U.S.C. § 348(f)(1)(A) (emphasis added). In the case of a bad faith conversion, "the property of the estate in the converted case shall consist of the property of the estate *as of the date of conversion*." Id. § 348(f)(2) (emphasis added).

Prior to the addition of § 348(f), courts considering the disposition of funds held by a Chapter 13 trustee at the time of conversion reached three different results: the funds were (i) property of the new Chapter 7 estate, (ii) property of the debtor, or (iii) property of creditors under a confirmed Chapter

13 plan . . . .

Section 348(f) removed the first result, but did not resolve explicitly whether the Chapter 13 trustee should give the funds to the debtor or distribute them to creditors under the confirmed Chapter 13 plan. As developed below, § 348(f)'s language and legislative history express Congress's preference as to what property belongs to a debtor after conversion, and ultimately direct our decision.

To understand the full import of § 348(f), we provide a brief overview of a Chapter 13 case. The filing of a Chapter 13 petition creates an estate consisting of all of the debtor's legal and equitable interests in property. 11 U.S.C. §§ 301(a), 541(a).[14] "[I]n addition to the property specified in section 541" that exists at the filing of the Chapter 13 petition, the estate includes "all property of the kind specified in [section 541] that the debtor acquires after the commencement of the case but before the case is closed, dismissed, or converted to a case under chapter 7, 11, or 12 of this title, whichever occurs first . . . ." *Id.* § 1306(a). This includes "earnings from services performed by the debtor after the commencement of the case but before the case is closed, dismissed, or converted . . . ." Id. § 1306(b). As is the case here, these earnings ordinarily fund the Chapter 13 plan. *See, e.g.*, 8 Collier on Bankruptcy ¶ 1322.01 (Alan N. Resnick & Henry J. Sommer eds., 16th ed. 2012) ("Chapter 13 was designed to facilitate adjustments of the debts of individuals with regular income through flexible repayment plans funded primarily from future income.").

A debtor must begin making payments to the Chapter 13 trustee "not later than 30 days after the date of the filing of the plan or the order for relief [defined below], whichever is earlier . . . ." 11 U.S.C. § 1326(a)(1). The trustee must retain these payments "until confirmation or denial of confirmation [of a plan]. . . . If a plan is not confirmed, the trustee shall return any such payments not previously paid . . . to the debtor, after deducting any unpaid claim allowed under section 503(b)." *Id.* § 1326(a)(2).

Confirmation of a reorganization plan under Chapter 13 affects the estate, debtor, creditors, and Chapter 13 trustee. The confirmed plan vests all of the property of the estate in the debtor, *id.* § 1327(b); binds the debtor and its creditors, *id.* § 1327(a); and obligates the trustee to distribute the debtor's payments under the plan to creditors, *id.* § 1326(a)(2), (c).[15] At any time during the Chapter 13 proceeding, the debtor has a near absolute right to convert his case. *Id.* § 1307(a) ("The debtor may convert a case under this chapter to a case under chapter 7 of this title at any time. Any waiver of the right to convert under this subsection is unenforceable."). Regardless when conversion takes place, it "does not effect a change in the date of the filing of the petition." *Id.* § 348(a).

Conversion also "terminates the services" of the Chapter 13 trustee. *Id.* §

---

[14] In pertinent part, § 301 reads: "A voluntary case under a chapter of this title is commenced by the filing with the bankruptcy court of a petition under such chapter by an entity that may be a debtor under such chapter." Section 541(a) provides that "[t]he commencement of a case under section 301 . . . creates an estate."

[15] In pertinent part, § 1326(a)(2) reads: "If a plan is confirmed, the trustee shall distribute any such payment [made under § 1326(a)(1)] in accordance with the plan as soon as is practicable." Section 1326(c) similarly states: "Except as otherwise provided in the plan or in the order confirming the plan, the trustee shall make payments to creditors under the plan." Sections 1327(a) and (b), respectively, provide that: "[t]he provisions of a confirmed plan bind the debtor and each creditor," regardless whether a creditor accepted the plan; and "[e]xcept as otherwise provided in the plan or the order confirming the plan, the confirmation of a plan vests all of the property of the estate in the debtor."

348(e). Though his services are ended after conversion, the trustee is required to account for the funds that came into his possession by filing a final report under Federal Rule of Bankruptcy Procedure 1019(5)(B)(ii). In addition, if the case is converted prior to confirmation of a plan, the trustee must return any payments held by him to the debtor after deducting adequate funds for him to pay allowed administrative expense claims. *See* 11 U.S.C. § 1326(a)(2).

Accordingly, when a debtor converts a Chapter 13 case to Chapter 7, the order converting the case is effectively backdated to the time of the order for relief under Chapter 13, which is the date of the filing of the Chapter 13 petition. *See id.* § 301(b) ("The commencement of a voluntary case under a chapter of this title constitutes an order for relief under such chapter."). Section 348(f), to repeat, states that "property of the estate in the converted case shall consist of property of the estate, *as of the date of filing of the petition*, that remains in the possession of or is under the control of the debtor as of the date of conversion." *Id.* § 348(f)(1) (emphasis added). Because under § 348(a) "the date of the filing of the petition" is the date the debtor filed the Chapter 13 petition, this suggests that property of the Chapter 13 estate acquired *post-petition* is excluded from the property of the new Chapter 7 estate. But does that property belong to the debtor or to its creditors waiting for Chapter 13 plan payments?

It is here we turn to § 1327(b), which vests all property of the Chapter 13 estate in the debtor on plan confirmation. The implication is that property held by the Chapter 13 trustee after plan confirmation is "under the control of the debtor as of the date of [a later] conversion" for purposes of § 348(f)(1). Even before the addition of § 348(f), the Ninth Circuit Court arrived at this conclusion regarding the vesting of monies received by the Chapter 13 trustee from the debtor during the Chapter 13 proceeding. Arkison v. Plata (In re Plata), 958 F.2d 918 (9th Cir. 1992).

> Confirmation . . . binds the creditors and the debtor to the provisions of the plan and vests all property of the estate in the debtor except as otherwise provided in the plan. The monies received by the Chapter 13 trustee from the debtors during the Chapter 13 proceeding became part of the Chapter 13 estate. The debtors' creditors acquired a nonvested interest in these monies by the plan and the order confirming the plan. A Chapter 13 creditor's interests do not vest until the monies are distributed. . . . The debtors' interests in the monies have not been extinguished.

Id. at 922 (*quoting* Resendez v. Lindquist, 691 F.2d 397, 399-400 (8th Cir. 1982) (Bright, J., dissenting)). Moreover, under § 348(e), after conversion the services of the Chapter 13 trustee are terminated, which seemingly renders it powerless to make payments to creditors under a Chapter 13 plan.

Nevertheless, confirmation of a plan is a significant event in a Chapter 13 case. This has led several courts, in decisions primarily written before the addition of § 348(f), to conclude that undistributed plan payments held by a Chapter 13 trustee should be disbursed to creditors after conversion. They reason that the funds should be treated as trust funds for the benefit of creditors, or that creditors held a vested interest in the funds at the time the trustee received them, because the debtor voluntarily parted with the funds and §§ 1326(a)(2) and (c) state that the trustee "shall" distribute payments as provided by the plan. See, e.g., In re Galloway, 134 B.R. 602, 603 (Bankr. W.D. Ky. 1991) (holding that after a debtor "voluntarily part[s] with wages and deliver[s] them to the custody of a trustee in performance of a confirmed Chapter 13 plan, the creditors have a vested right to receive those payments pursuant to the plan"); In re Waugh, 82 B.R. at 400 (observing that the word "shall" in § 1326(a)(2) "creates the condition of a trust. Creditors have the right to the funds in an active confirmed chapter 13 plan on payment by the debtor"); In re Rutenbeck, 78 B.R. 912, 913 (Bankr. E.D. Wis. 1987) ("[T]he undistributed funds ought to be treated as trust funds for the benefit of the creditors under the confirmed plan and distributed to those creditors in accordance with the terms of the plan."); In re Lennon, 65 B.R. 130, 137 (Bankr. N.D. Ga. 1986) (holding that the "mandatory provision" of § 1326(a)(2) "has the effect of vesting an interest in creditors provided for by a confirmed plan in all payments pursuant to such plan").

These courts also emphasize that a confirmed plan binds creditors to a new relationship with a debtor, one that requires creditors to forgo certain rights in exchange for the debtor's promise to make payments under the plan. See, e.g., Ledford v. Burns (In re Burns), 90 B.R. 301, 304 (Bankr. S.D. Ohio 1988) ("[A] Chapter 13 Plan represents a legislatively sanctioned, and judicially approved[,] new series of rights and responsibilities among the debtor and the debtor's creditors."). Thus despite the termination of the Chapter 13 trustee's services after conversion, they conclude that a "valid confirmation order of the Bankruptcy Court should not be made a nullity by a later failure of the debtor to observe a confirmed plan." Spero v. Porreco (In re Porreco), 426 B.R. 529, 537 (Bankr. W.D. Pa. 2010) (*quoting* In re Waugh, 82 B.R. at 400); see also In re Pegues, 266 B.R. 328, 336-37 (Bankr. D. Md. 2001) ("Although the service of the chapter 13 trustee is terminated by Section 348(e), it is clear that Congress intended that the chapter 13 trustee shall wind up the affairs of the chapter 13 estate, including disbursing monies on hand to the appropriate recipient."); In re Burns, 90 B.R. at 304 ("While it would be inappropriate to ignore other provisions of the Bankruptcy Code, it would be equally inappropriate to fail to judicially implement an order that the court has previously entered, particularly one in which the debtors voluntarily proposed the provisions, advocated their adoption and requested the court to order as binding upon the debtors and their creditors.").

Additionally, these courts further cite § 1326(a)(2) for its language requiring the Chapter 13 trustee to return any payments held by it to the debtor if a plan is not confirmed (after deducting funds for it to pay allowed administrative expense claims). Read alone, this section arguably indicates that if a plan is not confirmed the trustee must return accumulated funds to the debtor, and that if a plan is confirmed the trustee, by implication stemming from the absence of similar language, is required to distribute accumulated funds to creditors as provided by the plan. That is, if Congress intended for undistributed funds held by the trustee post-confirmation to be returned to a debtor, it could have included similar language regarding post-confirmation payments in § 1326(a)(2). See In re Burns, 90 B.R. at 304. Moreover, holding that the funds are to be returned to debtors produces the anomalous result that all or a portion of administrative expense claims may be paid in a Chapter 13 case converted pre-confirmation, but not in one converted post-confirmation.

In contrast, other courts, again in decisions written primarily before the addition of § 348(f), have read the same provisions of the Code and concluded that the debtor is entitled to undistributed plan payments held by the Chapter 13 trustee at the time of conversion. These courts focus on § 348(a) and the Congressional policy of encouraging debtors to attempt Chapter 13 without penalty if the attempt fails. See, e.g., In re Boggs, 137 B.R. at 411 ("[T]he Congressional policy of encouraging debtors to repay their creditors via Chapter

13 is furthered by debtors (and their counsel) knowing they will not be penalized for attempting Chapter 13."); McCullough v. Luna (In re Luna), 73 B.R. 999, 1003 (N.D. Ill. 1987) (concluding that § 348(a), "which determines the operative date for the filing of [the debtor's] Chapter 7 proceeding, protects [the debtor] from being penalized by providing that the Chapter 7 estate is deemed to have been filed at the time the Chapter 13 estate was filed"); In re Bullock, 41 B.R. 637, 640 (Bankr. E.D. Pa. 1984) ("[T]he case is deemed to have been filed as a chapter 7 proceeding and that portion of the debtor's postpetition wages, which were deducted from his salary, were deposited in the chapter 7 estate although they were not properly includable therein . . . . Since the deducted wages were not part of the chapter 7 estate, the debtor is entitled to recover such wages in full . . . .").

In response to those courts holding that undistributed funds should be paid out to creditors, contrary rulings have reasoned that conversion effectively vacates the confirmed plan. "[Section] 1307(a) gives debtors the absolute right to convert to Chapter 7 at any time. Analytically, a Chapter 13 plan has no relevance to or import in a case under any other chapter. . . . If a plan is vacated or no longer in effect, a Chapter 13 trustee has no authority for further disbursement to creditors." In re Boggs, 137 B.R. at 410; see also In re Doyle, 11 B.R. 110, 111 (Bank. E.D. Pa. 1981) (holding that, once a case is converted, the order confirming the plan is no longer effective). Other decisions simply conclude that the termination of the trustee's services "precludes the Trustee from taking any action with respect to these funds after the conversion." In re Luna, 73 B.R. at 1002; see also In re Perkins, 36 B.R. 618, 620 (Bank. M.D. Tenn. 1983) (holding that the Chapter 13 trustee loses all authority to act when the conversion becomes effective).

These courts also find nothing "unjust" in returning undistributed plan payments to a debtor. Rather, they note that creditors ultimately will receive as much, if not more, than they would have received if the debtor initially had filed under Chapter 7.

> Since § 1325(a) requires a finding that the holder of each allowed unsecured claim will receive not less than the holder would receive under Chapter 7 to confirm a plan, it is not self-evident that the dilution effect of treating pre-conversion creditors as pre-petition creditors in the converted Chapter 7 necessarily inflicts a net loss on actual pre-petition creditors. Those creditors have had the benefit of distribution from debtors' wage contributions, which would not have been available to them under Chapter 7. In all, there seems no inherent inequity in refunding undisbursed wage contributions to debtors on conversion.

In re Boggs, 137 B.R. at 410.

Notwithstanding strong arguments regarding the binding effect of plan confirmation, those courts holding that undistributed payments under a confirmed Chapter 13 plan should be disbursed to creditors after conversion overlook that no provision in the Bankruptcy Code classifies any property, including post-petition wages, as belonging to creditors. Rather, property comes into and flows out of the estate. In the context of a Chapter 13 case, § 1327(b) vests all property of the Chapter 13 estate in the debtor on confirmation of the plan. Thus when the debtor transfers funds to the Chapter 13 trustee to fulfill its obligations under a confirmed plan (or, as here, wages are assigned directly to the Chapter 13 trustee under a garnishment order), the funds become part of the estate, and the debtor retains a vested interest in them. Though creditors have a right to those payments based on the confirmed plan, the debtor does not lose his vested interest until the trustee affirmatively transfers the funds to creditors. Also, §§ 1326(a)(2) and (c) only address the obligation of the trustee to distribute payments in accordance with a confirmed plan; they do not vest creditors with any property rights.

Conversion to a Chapter 7 case necessarily ends the Chapter 13 case, which also terminates that Chapter 13 estate. Section 348(f) clarifies what becomes of property of the now nonexistent Chapter 13 estate. It provides that property of the Chapter 7 estate "consist[s] of property of the estate, *as of the date of filing of the [Chapter 7] petition, that remains in the possession of or is under the control of the debtor on the date of conversion*." 11 U.S.C. § 348(f)(1) (emphases added). Because § 1327(b) vests all property of the Chapter 13 estate in the debtor, including any post-petition property held by the Chapter 13 trustee at the time of conversion (such as funds transferred to the estate for eventual distribution to creditors), on conversion property of the Chapter 13 estate usually is "under the control of the debtor."[16] And because § 348(a) establishes that conversion does not change the effect of the Chapter 13 petition's filing, the Chapter 7 petition date is deemed to be the same date that the debtor began the Chapter 13 case. Hence property acquired post-petition that is in the Chapter 13 estate at the time of conversion is not property of the new Chapter 7 estate. Rather, the debtor retains a vested interest in the property, and thereby the property reverts to the debtor on conversion, assuming that the debtor does not convert in bad faith.[17] Moreover, absent anything to the contrary (and we know of nothing), by providing that a debtor who converts in bad faith is not entitled to this post-petition property, § 348(f)(2) logically requires that a debtor receive the property if he acts in good faith.

Moreover, if a Chapter 13 debtor is concerned about obtaining funds held by the Chapter 13 trustee, he can dismiss his case rather than convert. As noted

[16] Not all property necessarily will meet this requirement. For example, a debtor whose title to particular property is terminated by a divorce decree while his Chapter 13 case is pending no longer has control of the property when the case is converted to Chapter 7, and thus the property is not part of the Chapter 7 estate after conversion even though it was included initially in the Chapter 13 estate. See, e.g., Yoon v. Krick (In re Krick), 373 B.R. 593, 608 (Bankr. N.D. Ind. 2007) (holding that a parcel of real estate that was included in a couple's Chapter 13 estate at the time of the filing of their Chapter 13 petition, and in connection with marital dissolution proceedings was determined to be the property of the parents of the former wife debtor, was not property of that debtor's converted Chapter 7 estate because she did not have an interest in the real estate and thus it was not under her control).

[17] On the issue of vesting, the Trustee draws our attention to § 349(b)(3), which provides that the dismissal of a case under the Bankruptcy Code, including a Chapter 13 case, "revests the property of the estate in the entity in which such property was vested immediately before the commencement of the case under this title." None of the sub-sections of § 348 contains similar "revesting" language. As such, it may be argued that Congress intended to distinguish the two methods of terminating an estate (conversion and dismissal), and that if it meant for property of the estate to "revest" in the debtor on conversion, it would have included similar language in § 348. See In re Plata, 958 F.2d at 923 (Brunetti, J., dissenting) (distinguishing §§ 348 and 349). However, in the Chapter 13 context this argument overlooks that (i) under § 1326(a)(2) the trustee must return all payments held by it to the debtor if a plan is not confirmed, or (ii) under § 1327(b) property of the estate already is vested in the debtor at the time of the conversion after confirmation of a plan. Sections 348 and 349 are broad provisions applicable to every Chapter of the Bankruptcy Code. The specific provisions of Chapter 13 supersede any distinction that may be read into these proceeding general provisions.

by the Ninth Circuit Court, we can discern "no justification for requiring a debtor to dismiss, rather than convert . . . [,] in order to preserve his exemption rights. Aside from creating a trap for the unwary, such a requirement would merely elevate form over substance and inject a needless degree of extra work on the part of all concerned." In re Plata, 958 F.2d at 922; see also In re Boggs, 137 B.R. at 410 ("Debtors, whose motion was prompted in part by health problems, are willing to have their case dismissed if necessary to obtain the funds the Trustee holds.").

We also believe that returning undistributed funds to the debtor better aligns with the Chapter 13 trustee's limited duties post-conversion and the effect of conversion on a confirmed Chapter 13 plan. Though the trustee must account for the funds that came into his possession by filing a final report after conversion under Federal Rule of Bankruptcy Procedure 1019(5)(B)(ii), it does not follow that he is permitted to distribute funds under a plan that is no longer operative, particularly if those funds remain vested in the debtor until distribution. In light of § 348(e)'s termination of the trustee's services post-conversion, his duties thereafter should be narrowly construed. If a Chapter 13 case is converted to a Chapter 7 case after plan confirmation, the vested funds revert to the debtor, and their return should be considered part of the Chapter 13 trustee's short list of remaining duties.[18]

The legislative history of § 348(f) supports that Congress's intended outcome is that payments held by the Chapter 13 trustee revert to the debtor on conversion. Congress stated that it was overruling the holdings of *Matter of Lybrook* and similar cases, and "adopting the reasoning" of our decision in *Bobroff.* H.R. Rep. No. 835, 103d Cong., 2d Sess. 57 (1994). It included the following illustration of the "serious disincentive to file chapter 13 filings" it sought to eliminate with § 348(f). *Id.*

> [A] debtor who had $10,000 equity in a home at the beginning of the case, in a State with a $10,000 homestead exemption, would have to be counseled concerning the risk that after he or she paid off a $10,000 second mortgage in the chapter 13 case, creating $10,000 in equity, there would be a risk that the home could be lost if the case were converted to chapter 7 (which can occur involuntarily). If all of the debtor's property at the time of conversion is property of the chapter 7 estate, the trustee would sell the home . . . to realize the $10,000 in equity for the unsecured creditors and the debtor would lose the home.

---

[18] In the pre-confirmation context, the trustee is obligated to pay allowed administrative expenses from accumulated payments he is holding. *Id.* § 1326(a)(2). Though this creates the anomalous outcome that if a Chapter 13 proceeding is converted pre-confirmation administrative expense claims will be paid from undistributed plan payments, but if the proceeding is converted post-confirmation no administrative expense claims can be paid from undistributed plan payments, this inconsistency is addressed by the Federal Rules of Bankruptcy Procedure. Rule 1019(6) provides for the filing after conversion of pre-conversion administrative expense claims. Fed. R. Bank. P. 1019(6) ("Upon the filing of the schedule of unpaid debts incurred after commencement of the case and before conversion, the clerk, or some other person as the court may direct, shall give notice to those entities listed on the schedule of the time for filing a request for payment of an administrative expense . . . ."). In addition, if a debtor continues a Chapter 13 case until a plan is confirmed before converting merely to escape the trustee's payment of administrative expense claims under § 1326(a)(2),
the debtor should be found to have converted in bad faith under § 348(f)(2), and all post-petition property should be awarded to the Chapter 7 estate to be distributed to creditors, including those holding administrative expense claims.

Id. By analogy from this example, a debtor who contributes post-petition earnings to the Chapter 13 estate under a confirmed plan when the Chapter 13 trustee has not distributed those funds to creditors should not lose those earnings on conversion. Section 348(f)(1) provides that the earnings are not property of the new Chapter 7 estate. The Chapter 7 trustee thus cannot transfer those earnings to unsecured creditors. Holding that the Chapter 13 trustee must disburse the earnings to creditors under the Chapter 13 plan after conversion would result in creditors receiving a portion of the Chapter 13 estate when the legislative history of § 348(f) suggests that this property belongs to the debtor.

Such an outcome also would dissuade debtors from filing under Chapter 13. Encouraging them to attempt to repay their debts through a reorganization plan rather than liquidate was the reasoning underlying our decision in *Bobroff*. We noted that

> [i]f debtors must take the risk that property acquired during the course of an attempt at repayment will have to be liquidated for the benefit of creditors if chapter 13 proves unavailing, the incentive to give chapter 13 -- which must be voluntary -- a try will be greatly diminished. Conversely, when chapter 13 does prove unavailing "no reason of policy suggests itself why the creditors should not be put back in precisely the same position as they would have been had the debtor never sought to repay his debts . . . ."

Bobroff, 766 F.2d at 803 (*quoting* In re Hannan, 24 B.R. 691, 692 (Bankr. E.D.N.Y. 1982)). In this context, holding that the Chapter 13 trustee must distribute undisbursed plan payments to creditors would contravene Congress's reasoning in adopting § 348(f).

Additionally, in adding § 348(f) Congress rejected the analysis of those Courts of Appeals holding that undistributed funds after Chapter 13 plan confirmation belong to creditors. Those Courts based their decisions on fairness to creditors, concluding that "a rule of once in, always in[,] is necessary to discourage strategic, opportunistic behavior that hurts creditors . . . ." Matter of Lybrook, 951 F.2d at 137. To account for such "game-the-system" behavior, Congress included § 348(f)(2), which in effect "gives the court discretion, in a case in which the debtor has abused the right to convert and converted in bad faith, to order that all property held at the time of conversion shall constitute property of the estate in the converted [here, Chapter 7] case." H.R. Rep. No. 835, 103d Cong., 2d Sess. 57 (1994). The punishment for acting in bad faith is that property that otherwise would belong to the debtor goes instead to his Chapter 7 estate for distribution to creditors. But, as already noted, if a debtor does not act with bad faith in converting, logically the property should not go automatically to creditors; otherwise the penalty for a bad faith conversion would be diminished significantly.

Indeed, since the passage of § 348(f), all Courts of Appeals that have considered the disposition of a Chapter 13 estate's property on conversion to Chapter 7 have concluded that the policy reasoning we expressed in *Bobroff* now has become settled law.[19] See Stamm v. Morton (In re Stamm), 222 F.3d 216, 217-

[19] The Trustee argues that the reasoning of Bobroff does not apply here because it did not involve a confirmed plan. Though confirmation of a plan is a significant event in a Chapter 13 case, nothing in Bobroff suggests the pre-confirmation status of that bankruptcy case was critical to our reasoning, nor does anything in the language of § 348(f) or its legislative history indicate Congress's intent that bankruptcy courts treat undistributed post-petition property differently

18 (5th Cir. 2000) (noting that in Baker v. Rank (In re Baker), 154 F.3d 534 (5th Cir. 1998), "[w]e stated that Congress added Section 348(f) 'to resolve the circuit split,' quoted the relevant statutory language, and noted that Congress 'took issue with In re Lybrook.' The clear implication . . . is that Section 348(f)(1), where applicable, establishes that the post-petition income does not remain property of the estate upon conversion." (*quoting* In re Baker, 154 F.3d at 536 n.2)); Young v. Key Bank of Maine (In re Young), 66 F.3d 376, 378 (1st Cir. 1995) (concluding that post-petition contributions of income by the debtor pursuant to a confirmed plan were not property of the Chapter 7 estate on conversion and noting that "[t]he Bankruptcy Reform Act of 1994 answered the very question that confronts us. It essentially codified the *Bobroff* rule . . ."). See also Bell v. Bell (In re Bell), 225 F.3d 203, 217 (2d Cir. 2000) (observing that "[i]n the Bankruptcy Reform Act of 1994, Congress resolved this circuit split . . . by enacting 11 U.S.C. § 348(f)"); 8 Collier on Bankruptcy ¶ 348.07[1] ("The addition of [§ 348(f)] clarified that Congress had intended the result reached by cases that had not included in the postconversion chapter 7 estate the property acquired by the debtor during the preconversion chapter 13 case.").

Overall, a textual reading of § 348(f), particularly in light of its legislative history, leads us to conclude that undistributed plan payments held by a Chapter 13 trustee at the time of conversion must be returned to the debtor absent bad faith. This result furthers Congress's preference that on conversion to Chapter 7 a Chapter 13 debtor receive all post-petition property that is held by the Chapter 13 trustee, but still is under the control of the debtor, so that debtors are encouraged to attempt to repay their debts through reorganization rather than liquidation.

We recognize that a practical consequence of this method of encouragement is that, when a debtor converts to Chapter 7 after a Chapter 13 plan has been confirmed, the total amount of payments to creditors under the plan will depend on the timing of conversion and the practices of the Chapter 13 trustee. The Bankruptcy Code requires the Chapter 13 trustee to make disbursements "as soon as practicable." 11 U.S.C. § 1326(a)(2). In practice, the most efficient method of administering payments may be for the trustee to accumulate and distribute them to creditors at an established time. See, e.g., In re Hardin, 200 B.R. 312, 313 (Bankr. E.D. Ky. 1996) (noting that "often some accumulation will occur . . . prior to the making of a distribution to creditors"). For example, some trustees make plan disbursements twice a month, while some only once a month. Or a trustee may be holding funds for a reason particular to a case, as here. Section 348(f)(2)'s bad faith provision may correct for a debtor's opportunistic behavior, but outside a finding of bad faith it will not prevent a converting debtor receiving funds intended initially for Chapter 13 creditors. To deal with this potential happenstance, we foresee that creditors will request more frequent distributions from the Chapter 13 trustee.[20]

> (1) If a Chapter 13 trustee is accumulating funds because a creditor is refusing to receive payments under the plan, as here, creditors can move to modify the plan. *See* 11 U.S.C. § 1329(a)(1) ("At any time after confirmation of the plan but before the completion of payments under such plan, the plan may

---

depending on whether the Chapter 13 case was converted before or after confirmation of the plan.

[20] Creditors may avail themselves of other options to increase the likelihood that they will receive payments made by a debtor under a confirmed plan.

> be modified, upon request of the . . . holder of an allowed unsecured claim, to . . . increase or reduce the amount of payments on claims of a particular class provided for by the plan.").
>
> (2) Creditors can move to compel the trustee to make distributions under the plan immediately after the debtor files its motion to convert.
>
> (3) Section 1327(b) provides that "[e]xcept as otherwise provided in the plan or the order confirming the plan, the confirmation of a plan vests all of the property of the estate in the debtor."

Creditors can object to a proposed plan that does not provide that plan payments vest in creditors immediately on receipt by the Chapter 13 trustee. They likewise can request that similar language be included in the Bankruptcy Court's order confirming the plan. Though we do not rule on the issue, such language may be sufficient to remove undistributed plan payments held by the trustee from property "under the control of the debtor on the date of conversion." 11 U.S.C. § 348(f)(1).

As applied here, when the Plan was no longer feasible, Michael exercised the right to convert his case to Chapter 7 and sought the return of his post-petition earnings still in the Trustee's possession. Because there is no evidence that he converted in bad faith, those funds are his property by virtue of § 348(f), and should not be distributed to his creditors. The Bankruptcy and District Courts' decisions reflect the result that Congress contemplated in enacting § 348(f). We thus affirm.

ROTH, J, DISSENTING. Barry Michael converted his bankruptcy from Chapter 13 to Chapter 7. The question we must answer is whether Michael's undistributed post-confirmation, but pre-conversion, wages, which were paid to the Chapter 13 trustee pursuant to the confirmed reorganization plan, should be distributed to his creditors pursuant to the plan or returned to Michael. The Majority concludes that the addition of 11 U.S.C. § 348(f) to the Bankruptcy Code mandates that the funds revert to Michael. I respectfully disagree. The language of § 348(f) does not require such a result.

I turn first to the context in which this situation is most likely to occur. When a Chapter 13 plan of reorganization has been confirmed, the debtor will make regular payments to the Chapter 13 trustee. In many cases, the funds come from a wage attachment as happened here. At regular intervals -- monthly, bi-monthly -- the trustee, pursuant to § 1326(c), shall pay out the funds to the creditors as provided for in the confirmed plan. The trustee is the conduit for the funds to get to the creditors. Thus, the funds held by the trustee prior to these pay-outs do not build up significantly. If, ultimately, the debtor cannot keep up with the provisions of the plan and decides to convert to Chapter 7, the accumulated funds in the hands of the trustee are not of a sizeable amount. Thus, there has been little reason to dispute their disposition.

The reason for the accumulation of the funds here was because GMAC Mortgage refused to accept the payments pursuant to the plan after August 15, 2006, and sent the checks back to the trustee. Michael had been unable to keep up his own regular payments on the mortgage; as a result, on August 15, GMAC Mortgage obtained relief from the automatic stay in order to foreclose. Michael's wage attachment, however, continued on until October 2009 when he converted his bankruptcy to a Chapter 7. Although the plan provided for distribution to other secured and unsecured creditors, the trustee did not make payments to them. For that reason, more than $9,000 accumulated in the hands of the trustee. During this three year period, either Michael or the trustee could have requested an amendment to the plan. Neither did so. Michael continued to make payments for the benefit of his creditors. He also continued to enjoy the benefits of a Chapter 13 plan.[21]

There is little precedent to assist us in resolving this situation. There is evidence, however, that at least within the Third Circuit, the custom has been that, when a debtor converted a Chapter 13 bankruptcy to a Chapter 7, the Chapter 13 trustee paid out the accumulated funds to the creditors as provided for in the plan. In fact, in December 2011, the Third Circuit Judicial Council approved the Western District of Pennsylvania Local Bankruptcy Rule 3021-1(f), which provides that "[i]n the event of conversion or dismissal following the confirmation of a chapter 13 plan, then the chapter 13 trustee shall distribute all funds received prior to the effective date of the conversion or dismissal, in accordance with the terms of the confirmed plan." The Clerk of the Bankruptcy Court for the Western District of Pennsylvania believes that this rule codified a long time practice, going back to 2004. This rule -- or practice -- has not been challenged until, in this case, the sum held by the trustee became a sizeable one. The issue then is: Who gets the benefit of this windfall, the debtor or the creditors?

To answer this question, we must determine whether these funds -- on conduit through the trustee to the creditors in accord with the confirmed plan -- are property of the Chapter 13 estate.

As the Majority observes, prior to the Bankruptcy Reform Act of 1994 (Act), courts were sharply divided on whether post-petition and post-confirmation property, which was acquired by the debtor during a Chapter 13 case, remained property of the bankruptcy estate or was returned to the debtor upon the estate's conversion to Chapter 7. *Compare* Resendez v. Lindquist, 691 F.2d 397, 399 (8th Cir. 1982) *with* Bobroff v. Cont'l Bank (In re Bobroff), 766 F.2d 797, 803 (3d Cir. 1985). The Act sought to resolve this dispute with the amendment to § 348, which provided that "when a case under chapter 13 . . . is converted to a case under another chapter," 11 U.S.C. § 348(f)(1), the "property of the estate in the converted case shall consist of property of the estate, as of the date of filing of the petition, that remains in the possession of or is under the control of the debtor on the date of conversion," *id.* at § 348(f)(1)(A).

I agree that the amendment described what became of property or rights to property acquired by the debtor during the pendency of the Chapter 13 proceedings. I have no argument against this interpretation. Mr. Bobroff[22] keeps his potential tort recovery and Mr. Lybrook[23] keeps the farm land inherited from his father because the tort recovery and the farmland inheritance were not property of the estate as of the date of the filing of the petition.[24] To the extent that Michael's wages were not attached, the amendment also covered these

[21] Generally, the benefits available to a debtor under a Chapter 13 plan of reorganization are the saving of a residence from foreclosure, the curing a mortgage delinquency over time with more affordable payments, the maintaining of possession and use of an automobile or other personal property, and the automatic stay.

[22] Bobroff, 766 F.2d at 803.

[23] Matter of Lybrook, 951 F.2d 136 (7th Cir. 1991).

[24] I would note, however, that neither the Bobroff nor the Lybrook Chapter 13 plans were confirmed. A confirmed plan would have dealt with these property expectations during the period of reorganization. It would appear that the consideration of these additional assets may be a factor in the failure of approval of a plan of reorganization.

unattached wages earned during the course of the Chapter 13 bankruptcy. On conversion, these wages would not be transferred to the Chapter 7 estate. See Stamm v. Morton (In re Stamm), 222 F.3d 216, 217 (5th Cir. 2000) ("Section 348(f)(1), where applicable, establishes that the [debtors'] post-petition income does not remain property of the estate upon conversion"). There is simply no language that suggests otherwise. See e.g., In re Pegues, 266 B.R. 328, 331-32 (Bankr. D. Md. 2001); In re Bell, 248 B.R. 236, 239 (Bankr. W.D.N.Y. 2000); In re Hardin, 200 B.R. 312, 313 (Bankr. E.D. Ky. 1996).

However, we are not dealing simply with wages here but with that portion of the wages that had been attached under the plan and paid to the trustee for distribution to the creditors. I maintain that there is a crucial difference. It is my position that, although the debtor's unattached wages earned during the reorganization period will not be included in the Chapter 7 estate, the attached wages that have been paid to the trustee pursuant to the plan should be. Under the plan, these wages are under the supervision and control of the trustee.[25] Because these funds are under the supervision and control of the trustee, they should be paid out by the trustee in accord with the provisions of the plan. Moreover, the attached wages are the *quid pro quo* that the debtor has given up during the pendency of the reorganization in return for being permitted to stave off foreclosure and cure the mortgage default, retain the use of his automobile, and enjoy the automatic stay.

The Majority depends on *Bobroff* to support its decision. However, a careful analysis of *Bobroff* reveals that the Court's decision was motivated by its fear of potential inequities that might result when the recovery from a debtor's post-petition litigation was included in a converted Chapter 7 estate. Central to the Court's decision was the notion that creditors should not receive a windfall from funds that would not have been in the bankruptcy estate if the initial filing had been for a Chapter 7 proceeding. According to the Court, such a result would be inconsistent with the Bankruptcy Code's goal of encouraging debt repayment. See Bobroff, 766 F.2d at 803. If a debtor had to risk losing either all or a portion of the property he acquired during his repayment attempt, the incentive to try voluntary repayment would be substantially diminished. *Id.* The Court, therefore, opined that post-petition funds should revert to the debtor in order to ensure that both the creditors and debtor would be returned to "precisely the same position they were in had the debtor never sought to repay his debts . . .." *Id.*[26]

The concerns the Court expressed in *In re Bobroff*, however, are not present in Chapter 13 proceedings where a debtor derives a benefit from the confirmed bankruptcy plan. Once a reorganization plan is confirmed, the relationship between the debtors and creditors change; the provisions of the plan bind the parties, generating benefits and corresponding responsibilities. 11 U.S.C. § 1327(a); see Ledford v. Burns (Matter of Burns), 90 B.R. 301, 304 (Bankr. S.D. Ohio 1988) ("[A] Chapter 13 Plan represents a legislatively sanctioned, and

---

[25] The plan provides in paragraph 1 that "[t]he future earnings of the Debtor are submitted to the supervision and control of the trustee - Debtor's employer shall pay to the Trustee the sum of $138.62 bi-weekly, beginning in May, 2006 for a period of 53 months, plus $1,294.67 paid as of April 4, 2006."

[26] Of course, *Bobroff* is also distinguishable from this case in the fact that the Court in *Bobroff* held that because the debtor was not eligible for Chapter 13, "the conversion to that chapter was void *ab initio* and the provisions of § 1306 cannot be invoked to determine which property comprises the estate." Bobroff, 766 F.2d at 803.

judicially approved new series of rights and responsibilities among the debtor and the debtor's creditors"). In fact, under a confirmed plan, each party receives a benefit. The debtor is entitled to continue "receiving whatever benefits []he believed were significant enough for [him] to have converted to and proceeded in Chapter 13,"[27] In re Bell, 248 B.R.at 239, and the creditors receive the money paid into the Chapter 13 estate, In re Pegues, 266 B.R. at 336. Thus, the debtor makes payments in order to fulfill his obligations under the reorganization plan and in exchange for the benefits he derives from the plan.[28] In re Bell, 248 B.R. at 239; see In re Lennon, 65 B.R. 130, 136 (N.D. Ga. 1986) ("These payments are specifically earmarked and set aside for distribution to creditors provided for by the confirmed plan").

The Bankruptcy Code supports this view. Sections 1326(a)(2) & (c) affirmatively set forth the Chapter 13 trustee's obligation to distribute a debtor's payments to creditors pursuant to the terms of the confirmed plan. See 11 U.S.C. § 1326(a)(2) & (c). Although § 348(e) terminates the services of the trustee when a case is converted to chapter 7, the trustee is still required to perform certain tasks. See Fed. R. Bankr. P. 1019. Federal Rule of Bankruptcy Procedure 1019 details several of these post-conversion duties. See e.g., id. at 1019(4), 1019(5)(B)(ii). Thus, the Rule demonstrates that Congress did not intend § 348(e) to be interpreted too literally. Since Congress intended for the trustee to perform several ancillary duties to clean-up and finalize the administration of the estate, In re Parrish, 275 B.R. 424, 430 and & n.7 (Bankr. D. Colo. 2002), there is no logical reason why distribution of funds pursuant to the previously confirmed reorganization plan cannot be included as one of those administrative duties.

Here, unlike in *Bobroff*, the payments Michael made were in exchange for the benefits he derived from the plan. Therefore, if the undistributed funds revert to him, instead of being distributed to the creditors in accordance with the plan's terms, Michael would receive a windfall. See O'Quinn v. Brewer (In re O' Quinn), 143 B.R. 408, 413 (Bankr. S.D. Miss. 1992) ("It appears to this Court to be patently unfair to allow a debtor to drive and depreciate an automobile, occupy a home or use household goods based on a promise to his creditors in the form of a court approved plan, and then allow the debtor to snatch away the monies which the trustee is holding to make the payments, but has not yet disbursed, by allowing the debtor to pick an opportune time to convert"). He would obtain the benefits the confirmed plan offered without having to pay his creditors. Such a result would not only be patently unfair, but also contradict the reasoning of

---

[27] Although varied, the benefits a debtor receives may include: saving a residence from foreclosure, curing a mortgage delinquency over time with more affordable payments, maintaining possession over an automobile or other personal property, or having the benefit of the automatic bankruptcy stay remain in place for an extended period of time.

[28] Conversion does not retroactively alter this arrangement and undo the benefits the debtor received from the plan. See e.g., In re Pegues, 266 B.R. at 336; In re Galloway, 134 B.R. 602, 603 (Bankr. W.D. Ky. 1991); Waugh v. Saldamarco, (In re Waugh), 82 B.R. 394, 398-99 (W.D. Pa. 1988); In re Redick, 81 B.R. 881, 887 (E.D. Mich. 1987). The funds the debtor paid were in exchange for the benefits of the reorganization plan. Revocation of the plan only alters this dichotomy going forward; it does not "retroactively revoke the intent," In re Bell, 248 B.R. at 239, that debtors had when they initially chose to file under Chapter 13; nor does it retroactively alter the fact that a debtor made payments "to continue to enjoy the ongoing benefits of that plan," id at 240.

Bobroff.[29] Michael would be in a better position (and his creditors in a worse position) than he would have been if he had initially filed for bankruptcy under Chapter 7.

Therefore, my interpretation of § 348(f) will not discourage voluntary debt repayment under Chapter 13. It merely requires debtors to honor their obligations to creditors as was agreed under the confirmed plan. In re Bell, 248 B.R. at 240. I hope that we will not see the reversal of a Third Circuit practice that over the years has balanced the benefits to both parties under a plan of reorganization by providing that the undistributed funds held by the trustee will be distributed to the creditors pursuant to the confirmed plan. If we adopt the Majority's position, we will be permitting a windfall in this unusual case where inaction by the debtor and by the trustee has permitted funds to accumulate in a situation in which that normally would not occur.

For the above reasons, I respectfully dissent.

Notes and Questions

1. Would the result in *Michael* have changed if D converted to chapter 7 in bad faith? *See* Bankruptcy Code § 348(f)(2). What would be an example of a bad faith conversion to chapter 7?

2. Suppose *D* has a confirmed chapter 13 plan, which requires *D* to pay $500 per month to *SP*, a car lender. *SP*'s claim has been bifurcated (*i.e.*, it is not a 910 vehicle) into a $2,000 secured claim and a $3,000 unsecured claim. *D* makes four plan payments, so *D* receives $2,000. *D* then converts the case to chapter 7.

SP was entitled to receive prime plus 1.5% under the plan. Accordingly, *SP* still has not received $200 in interest under the plan at the time of conversion. The contract rate, however, was 24%.

What are *SP*'s rights in the converted chapter 7 case? *See* Bankruptcy Code § 348(f)(1)(C)?

IN RE BROWN

375 B.R. 362 (Bankr. D. Mich. 2007)

JEFFREY R. HUGHES, J.

Loren J. Brown ("Debtor") filed a petition for relief under Chapter 13 of the Bankruptcy Code on May 9, 2005. Debtor's schedules indicate that he owned a fee simple interest in his McMillan, Michigan home immediately preceding the commencement of his case. That interest, of course, became property of the estate pursuant to Section 541(a)(1).

Debtor has claimed as exempt a portion of the bankruptcy estate's interest in the McMillan residence. Debtor's first attempt to claim this exemption is set forth in the Schedule C he filed on the same date as his petition.[1] That schedule, when read in conjunction with Schedules A and D filed on the same date, indicates: 1) that, in Debtor's opinion, the bankruptcy estate's net equity in the McMillan residence was $ 50,400.00; 2) that Debtor was electing the state scheme

---

[29] Although the Majority does not explicitly state, it implies that § 348(f)'s bad faith provision, *see* 11 U.S.C. § 348(f)(2), would prevent this type of harm from befalling creditors. This argument is unconvincing. One can conjure many scenarios where a debtor files for Chapter 13 bankruptcy, with *bona fide* intentions of repaying his financial obligations, only to discover that he miscalculated his ability to repay his creditors. This type of conduct cannot be characterized as "game-the-system" behavior.

[1] Section 521 and FED.R.BANKR.P. 1007 require a debtor at the outset of the case to file schedules concerning his assets and liabilities. Schedule C is the schedule used to identify the property the debtor intends to claim as exempt. FED.R.BANKR.P. 4003(a).

of exemptions as permitted by Section 522(b)(2)(B) (pre-BAPCPA); 3) that Debtor claimed an exemption based upon MICH. COMP. LAWS § 600.6023a(1)(n); and 4) that the value of the exemption claimed was $ 30,000.00.

Debtor then amended his Schedule C on June 21, 2005. His amended Schedule C also claimed the McMillan residence as exempt under state law and continued to set the bankruptcy estate's net equity in the residence at $ 50,400.00. However, Debtor changed the exemption claimed to MICH. COMP. LAWS § 600.5451(1)(n). He also increased the amount of the claimed exemption to $ 45,000.00.

Neither the Chapter 13 trustee nor any other party in interest objected to the exemption originally claimed by Debtor or to the amended exemption. Debtor's Chapter 13 plan was then confirmed without objection at a hearing held on July 19, 2005.

Debtor performed under his confirmed plan until September 15, 2006, when Debtor himself elected to convert the case to a Chapter 7 proceeding. Conversion of the case prompted both the appointment of a Chapter 7 trustee to replace the Chapter 13 trustee and the scheduling of a new meeting of creditors under Section 341(a).[2] This "second" meeting of creditors was originally set for November 17, 2006, but was then rescheduled for December 13, 2006.[3]

The Chapter 7 trustee filed her objection to Debtor's claimed exemption in the McMillan residence on December 20, 2006. Her objection challenges the constitutionality of MICH. COMP. LAWS § 600.5451(1)(n), that being the state statute Debtor currently relies upon to claim his exemption. She cites as support In re Wallace, 347 B.R. 626 (Bankr. W.D. Mich. 2006).[4]

Debtor has not contested the substance of the Chapter 7 trustee's objection. [6] However, Debtor does contend that the Chapter 7 trustee's objection is untimely. Debtor relies upon Rule 4003(b) of the Federal Rules of Bankruptcy Procedure.

> A party in interest may file an objection to the list of property claimed as exempt only within 30 days after the meeting of creditors held under § 341(a) is concluded . . .

FED.R.BANKR.P. 4003(b).

---

[2] The United States Trustee is required to convene a meeting of creditors "[w]ithin a reasonable time after the order for relief in a case...." 11 U.S.C. § 341(a). Conversion of the case constitutes a new order for relief under that chapter. 11 U.S.C. § 348(a). Therefore, another meeting of creditors was necessary.

[3] The "first" meeting of creditors in the Chapter 13 case had been scheduled for June 15, 2005 but was adjourned to July 6, 2005. The court's records do not indicate whether that meeting concluded on July 6, 2005 or whether it was adjourned again.

[4] MICH. COMP. LAWS § 600.5451 provides a debtor a whole array of exemptions. However, those exemptions are available only in instances where the debtor has sought relief under the Bankruptcy Code.

> A debtor in bankruptcy under the bankruptcy code, 11 USC 101 to 1330, may exempt from property of the estate property that is exempt under federal law, or under 11 USC 522(b)(2), the following property:

MICH. COMP. LAWS § 600.5451(1). I determined in *Wallace* that the Michigan legislature could not limit the exemptions it had created to only instances involving bankruptcy proceedings without also violating the Supremacy Clause of the United States Constitution.

Debtor argues that the meeting of creditors referenced in this rule is the meeting of creditors that was previously held during the Chapter 13 proceeding and that, therefore, the Chapter 7 Trustee is time-barred from now filing an objection. The Chapter 7 Trustee, on the other hand, contends that another opportunity arose to object to Debtor's claimed exemptions when the subsequent meeting of creditors was scheduled upon conversion of the case to Chapter 7 and that, therefore, her objection is timely.[5]

DISCUSSION

The courts have gone back and forth for years as to whether a trustee or other party in interest in a converted Chapter 7 case may have a second opportunity to object to exemptions already claimed by the debtor in either a previous Chapter 11 or Chapter 13 case.[6] Although the division between the two camps is roughly equal, their respective positions have nonetheless been described as majority and minority views.

> Under one line of cases, designated as a "minority rule," the thirty-day period to object to a debtor's claimed exemptions recommences when a Chapter 13 case is converted to Chapter 7. Courts adopting this minority rule state it is supported by relevant Bankruptcy Code and Bankruptcy Rule provisions. In particular, under § 348(a), the conversion of a Chapter 13 to Chapter 7 "constitutes an order for relief under the chapter to which the case is converted, but ... does not effect a change in the date of the ... order for relief." Because the conversion of a Chapter 13 case to Chapter 7 constitutes an order for relief, a new meeting of creditors must be called in the converted Chapter 7 case pursuant to § 341(a) and Federal Rule of Bankruptcy Procedure 2003(a). The objection period set forth in Bankruptcy Rule 4003(b) runs within thirty days after the "meeting of creditors held under § 341(a) is concluded...." Given that there is nothing in Bankruptcy Rule 4003(b) limiting the "meeting of creditors" to the initial meeting of creditors in the Chapter 13 case, courts adopting the minority view hold that parties in interest have thirty days from the conclusion of the meeting of creditors called in the converted Chapter 7 case to object to a debtor's claimed exemption. Under this view, exemptions claimed by a debtor in his or her Chapter 13 case may be objected to within thirty days of the conclusion of the meeting of creditors in the Chapter 13 case, or within thirty days of the conclusion of the meeting of creditors in the converted Chapter 7 case. Courts adhering to the minority view also support it with policy and fairness considerations.
>
> The other line of cases, designated as the "majority view," holds that the thirty-day objection period in Bankruptcy Rule 4003(b) does not commence anew upon the conversion of a Chapter 13 case to Chapter 7. The majority view is based in part on Bankruptcy Rule 1019(2), which states, in relevant part, that: "A new time period for filing claims, a complaint objecting to discharge, or a complaint to obtain a determination of dischargeability of any debt shall commence pursuant to Rules 3002, 4004, or 4007...." Because the thirty-day

[5] Both parties seem to concede that the initial meeting of creditors held in conjunction with Debtor's prior Chapter 13 had in fact concluded and that the subsequent meeting of creditors held in the converted Chapter 7 concluded on December 13, 2006. However, as previously noted, the record is unclear as to whether the "first" meeting of creditors ever concluded and the record is also unclear whether the "second" meeting of creditors was properly adjourned from its originally scheduled date of November 16, 2006. These uncertainties, though, have no bearing on my decision. Therefore, I have simply accepted what the parties appear to concede as true.

[6] Although the issue could also arise in a converted Chapter 12 case, conversions from Chapter 12 to Chapter 7 are relatively rare.

> objection period in Bankruptcy Rule 4003(b) is not mentioned in Bankruptcy Rule 1019(2), courts adopting the majority view hold that it may not be reset upon the conversion of a case. The refusal of some courts to recommence the thirty-day period in Bankruptcy Rule 4003(b) is also based in part on the fact that § 348(a) states that conversion of a case does not change the date of the order for relief and, therefore, all deadlines, such as the exemption objection deadline, should not be affected by conversion. Additionally, some courts reason that to allow a new objection period upon conversion is not compatible with § 522(yl) because, under that section, the property in the preconverted case is exempt and it cannot be brought back into the estate. Finally, courts adhering to the majority view point to the importance of finality in exemption matters articulated in Taylor [v. Freeland & Kronz, 503 U.S. 638 (1992)].

In re Campbell, 313 B.R. 313, 318-19 (10th Cir. BAP 2004) (footnotes omitted).

In re Page, 240 B.R. 548, 551 (Bankr. W.D. Mich. 1999), adopts the majority view.

> Although the cases are not unanimous, the better reasoned decisions hold that the 30-day period for objecting to exemptions commences at the conclusion of the "first" first meeting of creditors, and not at the conclusion of any subsequent meetings that may be held as a consequence of a conversion of the case from one chapter to another. Therefore, the convening of a subsequent meeting of creditors following the conversion of the Debtor's case from chapter 13 to chapter 11 did not trigger a new 30-day period for objecting to exemptions.

See also In re Brown, 178 B.R. 722 (Bankr. E.D. Tenn. 1995); In re Halbert, 146 B.R. 185 (Bankr W.D. Tex. 1992).

However, I agree with the minority's interpretation.[7] Rule 4003(b)'s drafters could have been more specific in expressing their intention to permit further objections to exemptions already claimed whenever a case is converted. There is also no question that adopting the minority view presents issues regarding the administration of property that the debtor may have claimed as exempt months or even years before. Nonetheless, the unambiguous language of Rule 4003(b) itself allows for only one construction: that the conversion of a case and the attendant scheduling of another meeting of creditors gives the trustee and other parties in interest a new opportunity to object to the exemptions claimed.

> [T]he only reasonable construction of § [sic] 4003(b) is to allow the language to convey its plain meaning and to permit the Chapter 7 Trustee an opportunity to object to the claimed exemptions, provided that the Trustee files the objection within thirty (30) days after the § 341 meeting following conversion.

Weissman v. Carr (In re Weissman) 173 B.R. 235, 237 (Bankr. M.D. Fla. 1994) (footnote omitted). *See also* In re Mims, 249 B.R. 378 (Bankr. D. N.J. 2000).

The majority, though, contends that Rule 4003(b) is still subject to interpretation because of conflicting language in Rule 1019(2).

---

[7] My colleague, the Hon. James D. Gregg, authored *Page*. However, in a recent bench opinion, Judge Gregg stated that due process concerns have caused him to now question the majority view. Unpaid creditors in a Chapter 11, 12, or 13 case whose claims arose post-petition and who are not entitled to administrative priority are to be treated as if they were pre-petition creditors in the event the case is converted to Chapter 7. 11 U.S.C. § 348(d). Judge Gregg's reservation is that the majority interpretation of Rule 4003(b) denies such creditors the opportunity to object to pre-conversion exemptions claimed by the debtor.

> When a chapter 11, chapter 12 or chapter 13 has been converted or reconverted to a chapter 7 case: . . .
>
> (2) *New Filing Periods.* A new time period for filing claims, a complaint objecting to discharge, or a complaint to obtain a determination of dischargeability of any debt shall commence pursuant to Rules 3002, 4004, or 4007, provided that a new time period shall not commence if a chapter 7 case had been converted to a chapter 11, 12, or 13 case and thereafter reconverted to a chapter 7 case and the time for filing claims, a complaint objecting to discharge, or a complaint to obtain a determination of the dischargeability of any debt, or any extension thereof, expired in the original chapter 7 case.

FED.R.BANKR.P. 1019(2).

The majority's argument is that "meeting of creditors" as used in Rules 3002, 4003, 4004, and 4007 means only the initial meeting of creditors held whenever the conversion of the case requires another meeting of creditors and that it is only through Rule 1019(2) that a party is given an opportunity, for example, to object post-conversion to the non-dischargeability of a claim under Rule 4007. The majority then deduces that a trustee or other party in interest cannot object to an exemption previously claimed in conjunction with the converted case because Rule 1019(2) makes no reference to either objections to exemptions or Rule 4003(b). In other words, only Rule 4003(b) can be relied upon for determining when an objection to an exemption may be made in a converted case and, according to the majority, the meeting of creditors referenced in that rule is only the initial meeting held prior to the case's conversion.

However, such reasoning is problematic, for Rule 1019 is asymmetric. That is, while Rule 1019 applies to cases converted from Chapters 11, 12 or 13 to Chapter 7, the opposite is not true. Suppose, then, that a creditor who failed to file a proof of claim in the debtor's original Chapter 7 later files its claim after the debtor converts his case to Chapter 13. Would that claim be tardy? The plain language of Rule 3002(c) certainly suggests that the claim would be allowed provided that it was filed within thirty (30) days of the scheduling of the "second" meeting of creditors required in conjunction with the converted Chapter 13.

> (c) *Time for filing*
>
> In a chapter 7 liquidation, chapter 12 family farmer's debt adjustment, or chapter 13 individual's debt adjustment case, a proof of claim is timely filed if it is filed not later than 90 days after the first date set for the meeting of creditors called under § 341(a) of the Code, except as follows:

FED.R.BANKR.P. 3002(c).

Moreover, Rule 1019(2) could not be used in that instance to promote a different interpretation since that rule clearly does not apply with respect to a conversion of this type.

Similarly, a Chapter 13 trustee in a converted case would not be barred from raising his own objection to an exemption claimed by the debtor in his prior Chapter 7. Again, the plain language of Rule 4003(b) indicates that the scheduling of another meeting of creditors in the converted case would permit the Chapter 13 trustee to proceed with her objection and Rule 1019(2) would likewise be unavailable as an interpretative tool. However, if, as the majority insists, "meeting of creditors" in Rule 4003(b) means only the initial meeting of creditors when Rule 1019(2) applies, it is confronted with the difficulty of explaining what that same phrase means in converted cases when Rule 1019(2) does not apply. Its choices are either to persist with the same interpretation even though Rule 4003(b), when read without the aid of Rule 1019(2), clearly does not convey that meaning, or to take the inconsistent position that "meeting of creditors" means one thing when Rule 1019(2) applies but that it means something else when that rule does not apply.[8]

Frankly, the interplay between Rule 4003(b) and Rule 1019(2) remains a mystery. Perhaps the drafters' intention was exactly as the majority has suggested. However, it is just as likely that the drafters simply did not consider it. Or perhaps, as the court in *Havanec* has speculated:

> [T]he draftsmen of Rule 1019(2) might well have concluded that the language of Rule 4003(b) was sufficiently clear to assure that the trustee could object to claims following the conclusion of the chapter 7 creditors meeting after the case had been converted.

In re Havanec, 175 B.R. 920, 924 (Bankr. N.D. Ohio 1994).[9]

---

[8] The majority also relies upon Section 348(a) as support for its contrary interpretation of Rule 4003(b). However, that argument is easily addressed:

> Additionally, we are not compelled by the majority view's analysis of § 348(a) *as it relates to Bankruptcy Rule 4003(b).* We recognize, as do the courts adopting the majority view, that § 348(a) expressly states that the date of the order for relief is not altered by the conversion of a case, and that the purpose of that provision "is to preserve actions already taken in the case before conversion." But, the deadline in Bankruptcy Rule 4003(b) is not based on the date of the order for relief. It is based on the conclusion of a "meeting of creditors." This difference is real, and should not be ignored. If the drafters of Bankruptcy Rule 4003(b) wanted to limit the time to file objections to claimed exemptions based on the date of an order for relief, they would have expressly stated so.

In re Campbell, 313 B.R. at 320 (10th Cir. BAP 2004) (emphasis in original) (footnote omitted).

[9] Rule 1017(e) also tarnishes Rule 1019(2) as an interpretative tool. Rule 1017(e)(1) addresses when a motion to dismiss under Section 707(b) must be filed and, like Rules 3002(c), 4003(b), 4004(a) and 4007(b), Rule 1017(e)(1) measures that deadline based upon the Section 341 meeting of creditors. Indeed, Rule 1017(e)(1) uses the very same language as used in Rules 3002(c), 4004(a) and 4007(b).

> A motion to dismiss a case for substantial abuse may be filed by the United States trustee only within 60 days after the first date set for the meeting of creditors under § 341(a), unless, on request filed by the United States trustee before the time has expired, the court for cause extends the time for filing the motion to dismiss.

FED. R. BANKR. P. 1017(e)(1).

Rule 1019(2) also omits any reference to Section 707(b) motions and Rule 1017. Consequently, the majority, in order to be true to its reasoning, would necessarily have to conclude that no Section 707(b) motion to dismiss in a converted Chapter 7 may be filed if the deadline in the prior chapter has already passed. However, reaching such a conclusion is absurd, given that Section 707(b) motions are relevant only in the context of a Chapter 7 case.

I am also not persuaded that proposed Interim Rule 1019, even if ultimately adopted, offers any more insight as to how Rule 4003(b) is to be interpreted. Granted, the proposed rule's inclusion of 707(b) motions and Rule 1017, coupled with its continued exclusion of objections to exemptions and Rule 4003, would give some weight to the majority's argument should the rule be ultimately adopted. However, "weight" is the operative word, especially in light of the fact that the inconsistency I have identified as arising because of the asymmetrical application of Rule 1019(2) to only cases converted from Chapters 11, 12 and 13 to Chapter 7 still exists and the fact

What is clear, though, is that Rule 1019(2) is not, as the majority would have it, the Rosetta stone. Consequently, I am not persuaded by the majority's insistence that Rule 4003(b) is to be given an interpretation that is inconsistent with the words actually used in that rule, especially in light of the Supreme Court's admonitions in Lamie v. U.S. Trustee:

> It is well established that "when the statute's language is plain, the sole function of the courts - at least where the disposition required by the text is not absurd - is to enforce it according to its terms."

540 U.S. 526, 534 (2004).[10]

Therefore, I conclude that Rule 4003(b) must be interpreted to include a new opportunity to file an objection to exemptions whenever a new meeting of creditors is scheduled as a consequence of a case's conversion from one chapter to another.

Unfortunately, courts adopting the minority view have for the most part simply declared that the conversion of a case gives the subsequent trustee another opportunity to object to exemptions already claimed. What is lacking in those opinions is any explanation as to how other aspects of the bankruptcy estate's administration might affect such belated objections. It is ironic, then, that the explanation absent in these cases is found instead in majority view cases such as *Brown, Halbert* and *Page.*

The exemption process is complex enough without the added confusion of a case conversion. Therefore, it is helpful to first understand how exemptions are administered without this wrinkle. That understanding begins with the recognition that all of the debtor's interests in property, including whatever interests the debtor may ultimately keep as exempt, become property of the estate upon the commencement of the debtor's case. 11 U.S.C. § 541(a)(1). See also, Liberty State Bank and Trust v. Grosslight (In re Grosslight), 757 F.2d 773, 775 (6th Cir. 1985).[11] Section 522(b)(1) then empowers the debtor to choose from whatever has become property of the estate those interests the debtor is allowed under the bankruptcy laws to exempt, or "set aside,"[12] himself.

> Notwithstanding section 541 of this title, an individual debtor may exempt from property of the estate the property listed in either paragraph (2) or, in the alternative, paragraph (3) of this subsection.

11 U.S.C. § 522(b)(1).

The Chapter 7 trustee and creditors, of course, may object to what the debtor has claimed as his exempt property. However, if the exemption claimed is unchallenged, or if whatever objection made is overruled, the property selected as exempt ceases to be property of the estate by operation of Section 522(*l*).

---

that the plain language of Rule 4003(b) still suggests a contrary result.

[10] *Lamie,* of course, involved the interpretation of the Bankruptcy Code as opposed to a bankruptcy rule. However, a bankruptcy rule is of equal legal effect once it is adopted by Congress. In re Fuller, 255 B.R. 300, 305 (Bankr. W.D. Mich. 2000). *See also* 28 U.S.C. § 2075.

[11] In contrast, the former Bankruptcy Act treated the debtor's exempt property as remaining outside of the bankruptcy estate from the outset of the case. *Id.*

[12] WEBSTERS NINTH NEW COLLEGIATE DICTIONARY (1989).

Taylor v. Freeland & Kronz, 503 U.S. 638 (1992).[13] *See also* Owen v. Owen, 500 U.S. 305, 308 (1991) (Court observing that "[a]n exemption is an interest withdrawn from the estate (and hence from the creditors) for the benefit of the debtor."). Moreover, whatever the debtor recovers from the bankruptcy estate as exempt property is thereafter protected for the most part from the claims of the debtor's pre-petition creditors. 11 U.S.C. § 522(c).[14]

Exempting property from the bankruptcy estate is in some ways like shopping at a warehouse outlet. For example, the debtor might want to purchase (*i.e.,* exempt) his car from the warehouse (*i.e.,* bankruptcy estate). If the trustee refuses to accept the exemption tendered and the court agrees, then the car stays in the warehouse. On the other hand, if the trustee accepts the tender, or if the trustee refuses but the court compels acceptance, then the debtor is allowed to drive the car home.

The exemption process, though, is not always so simple. For example, the debtor himself may acknowledge in his Schedule C that the car he would like to exempt is worth more than the $ 3,225 he is permitted to expend under Section 522(d)(1) as his exemption.[15] If that were to occur, the car would remain as property of the estate notwithstanding the debtor's allowable exemption so that the bankruptcy trustee might still realize for the benefit of the bankruptcy estate's creditors the vehicle's acknowledged non-exempt value. In other words, Section 522(*l*) would not operate to remove the car from the bankruptcy estate in this hypothetical because Section 522(*l*) applies only when "the property claimed as exempt" itself is to be removed and in this hypothetical the debtor himself has agreed that he is not entitled to the actual vehicle, but instead is entitled to only a portion of what the vehicle is actually worth.[16]

---

[13] *Taylor* is most often cited for the proposition that the objection period set by Rule 4003(b) is to be strictly enforced. However, *Taylor* in fact turned on whether money that the debtor's attorneys had received post-petition from a settlement that the debtor had claimed as exempt was property of the estate or not. The court determined that the settlement had been removed from the bankruptcy estate by operation of Section 522(*l*) when the Rule 4003(b) deadline passed without a timely objection having been filed. Therefore, it followed that the trustee no longer had the authority to recover the amount transferred to the debtor's attorneys as estate property under Section 542. *See also, In re Anderson,* 357 B.R. 452 (Bankr. W.D. Mich. 2006).

[14] Section 522(c) provides in part that:

> Unless the case is dismissed, property exempted under this section is not liable during or after the case for any debt of the debtor that arose, or that is determined under section 502 of this title as if such debt had arisen, before the commencement of the case . . .

11 U.S.C. § 522(c).

The remainder of Section 522(c) then describes various exceptions to the protection afforded. For example, the exempted property is not protected from a pre-petition debt that is secured by a lien in that property provided that the lien has not been otherwise avoided. 11 U.S.C. § 522(c)(2).

[15] The debtor, of course, could exempt the remaining value of the car through the Section 522(d)(5) "catch all" exemption. However, for purposes of this hypothetical, I am assuming that the debtor has chosen to use his entire Section 522(d)(5) exemption to remove other property from the estate.

[16] It is easy to slip into referring to the property exempted as the *res* itself as opposed to only the debtor's interest in the res and, indeed, the two concepts are interchangeable when, as in the hypothetical here, the debtor was the sole owner of the vehicle pre-petition and the vehicle is unencumbered. However, it is more accurate to limit both what constitutes property of the estate

As for the trustee's ultimate disposition of the car, one of several paths might be taken. First, the trustee and the debtor might reach an agreement whereby the trustee would sell the car to the debtor for, say, $ 4,500 under Section 363(b) and then deduct from the purchase price the debtor's allowed Section 522(d)(2) exemption. The trustee might also sell the car to a third party and then account to the debtor for his $ 3,225 share of the proceeds. Or, finally the trustee might decide at some point that the non-exempt equity acknowledged by the debtor is not worth the cost of administration and, as a consequence, elect to abandon the car pursuant to 11 U.S.C. § 554.[17]

What effect, then, does a conversion from one case to another have on this basic process? Consider a few more hypotheticals. Assume again that the case was originally filed as a Chapter 7 (*i.e.,* it has not been converted from another chapter) but this time assume that the bankruptcy estate includes two unencumbered automobiles, a Honda and a Chevrolet, and that each is worth $ 3,225.00. Now assume that the debtor chooses to list the Chevrolet in his Schedule C as an in-kind Section 522(d)(2) exemption. That is, the debtor decides that he wants to keep the Chevrolet for himself rather than to have the trustee sell the Chevrolet and give him the lesser of $ 3,225 or the net proceeds realized. The trustee and any other party in interest would have until 30 days after the conclusion of the first meeting of creditors to object to the exemption. If a timely objection were to be filed, then the Chevrolet would continue to be held by the bankruptcy estate at least until the objection was resolved.[18] However, it is unlikely that any objection would be filed in this instance because the value of the Chevrolet and the exemption claimed are assumed to be equal. Therefore, the Chevrolet would automatically revest in the debtor by operation of Section 522(*l*) as soon as the Rule 4003(b) deadline had passed and Section 522(c) would thereafter protect the Chevrolet from the debtor's pre-petition creditors.

If, at some later date, the Chapter 7 trustee in this hypothetical were to change his mind about the Chevrolet (e.g., he later determined that the Chevrolet was worth $ 5,000.00, not $ 3,225.00), he would clearly be time-barred by Rule 4003(b) from then pursuing his objection to the debtor's prior in-kind exemption

---

and what is then exempted from the estate to just the debtor's interest in the res. For example, if the debtor owned only an undivided interest in Blackacre, then only that undivided interest would become property of the estate and only that undivided interest would be removed from the estate if successfully claimed as exempt. Similarly, only the debtor's equity in Blackacre that would become property of the estate if Blackacre was subject to a mortgage as of the commencement of the case and it would only be that equity interest that would be removed from the estate if Debtor was ultimately successful in claiming Blackacre as exempt. *See also* In re Talbert, 268 B.R. 811, 819 (Bankr. W.D. Mich. 2001).

[17] Chapter 11 and Chapter 13 add a further wrinkle by giving the debtor other ways of regaining control of property claimed as exempt where the acknowledged value of the property is in excess of the exemption allowed. The most obvious is through the confirmation process itself. For example, a Chapter 13 debtor can keep property with non-exempt equity as part of his plan provided that the distribution to unsecured creditors under the plan takes account of that equity. 11 U.S.C. § 1325(a)(4). *See also* In re Raynard, 333 B.R. 389, 392 n. 10 (Bankr. W.D. Mich. 2005) *rev'd on other grounds,* 354 B.R. 834 (6th Cir. BAP 2006).

[18] Section 522(*l*) could be literally read to remove exempted property from the bankruptcy estate only in those instances where no objection has been made at all. ("Unless a party in interest objects, the property claimed as exempt on such list is exempt."). Nonetheless, I interpret Section 522(*l*) as covering not only those instances where no objection has been made to the claimed exemption but also those instances where an objection has been made but the debtor has ultimately prevailed.

of that vehicle. Taylor, 503 U.S. at 642. *See also* In re Anderson, 357 B.R. 452, 460 (Bankr. W.D. Mich. 2006). However, what would be the outcome if instead it was the debtor who changed his mind (*e.g.,* he later decided that the Honda would run longer)? Could the debtor substitute the Honda for the Chevrolet?

Rule 1009(a) allows the debtor to amend a schedule as a matter of course at any time before the case is closed. Consequently, the debtor would certainly be within his rights to amend his Schedule C at a later date to change his claimed exemption from the Chevrolet to the Honda. However, Rule 4003(b) also permits the trustee a new opportunity to object whenever the debtor makes such an amendment. Therefore, the Chapter 7 trustee would also be entitled to object to the amendment on the basis that the debtor had already used his Section 522(d)(2) exemption with respect to the Chevrolet and that the Chevrolet was no longer even part of the bankruptcy estate because of Section 522(*l*).

However, debtors can be quite resourceful. What if, then, this debtor parried the trustee's objection with an offer to tender the Chevrolet back to the estate? Could the debtor compel the trustee to accept the return of the Chevrolet?

The answer is clearly no. The debtor in this hypothetical would be no less subject to the finality of Section 522(*l*) and Rule 4003(b) than was the trustee in *Taylor.* Remember, the underlying question in *Taylor* was whether the trustee could recover from the debtor's attorneys property that was no longer property of the estate by operation of Section 522(*l*). If Section 522(*l*) and Rule 4003(b) barred the *Taylor* trustee from later recovering that property, it stands to reason that the debtor's attorneys in that case would have been similarly barred from unilaterally tendering that property back to the estate were they in turn ever so inclined.[19]

Moreover, the outcome would be no different if the hypothetical arose instead in a converted Chapter 7. For example, assume that the debtor had claimed without objection his Section 522(d)(2) exemption in the Chevrolet prior to confirmation of a Chapter 13 plan and that he did not change his mind regarding that exemption until after his plan had failed and the case had

---

[19] Brown, 178 B.R. 722, and other cases espousing the majority point of view argue that the finality that the Court in *Taylor* deemed so important would be undermined if Rule 4003(b) is interpreted as providing a second or even third opportunity for objections to exemptions to be made. This concern, though, is valid only if one assumes that the property claimed as exempt must remain as property of the estate until all opportunities to object have been exhausted. However, Section 522(*l*) as well as the case law are quite clear that property is removed from the bankruptcy estate as exempt as soon as no objection to the exemption is made. Consequently, a debtor's in-kind exemption of his interest in his home in conjunction with a Chapter 13 proceeding, if unopposed, would cause that interest to transfer back to him from the bankruptcy estate by operation of Section 522(*l*). While a subsequent Chapter 7 trustee would in theory have a second opportunity to object to the exemptions the debtor had previously claimed were the case later converted to a Chapter 7, the Chapter 7 trustee would not be able to actually take advantage of that opportunity because of the debtor's already successful exemption of that interest prior to the case being converted.

Indeed, to interpret Section 522(*l*) otherwise would lead to no property claimed as exempt ever being removed from the estate by operation of Section 522(*l*) prior to the case being closed, for the possibility of the case converting to another chapter always exists. For example, Section 706(a) permits a debtor in most instances to convert his case to Chapter 11, 12 or 13 at anytime. Consequently, if Section 522(*l*) is to have any meaning, it must be interpreted as causing the removal of property claimed as exempt as soon as the first opportunity to object has passed even though a second opportunity to object under Rule 4003(b) would arise if the case were ever to convert to another chapter.

converted to Chapter 7. The debtor would still be able to amend his Schedule C to claim the Honda as exempt and the Chapter 7 trustee would still be able to file his objection to that amendment. However, more to the point, the intervening conversion would have had no effect upon Section 522(*l*)'s prior removal of the Chevrolet from the bankruptcy estate through debtor's successful exemption of that vehicle during the Chapter 13 proceeding. Consequently, the debtor could no more compel the Chapter 7 trustee to accept the return of the Chevrolet in a converted case than could he compel the Chapter 7 trustee to accept its return in an unconverted case.

In In re Wolf, 244 B.R. 754 (Bankr. E.D. Mich. 2000), the court concluded that "the rather technical arguments about when property was or is property of the estate" should not interfere with what that court considered to be Rule 4003(b)'s unambiguous provisions. *Id.* at 760. However, with all due respect, issues involving property of the estate, whether technical or not, cannot be so easily brushed aside. After all, much of the bankruptcy process, especially in the context of a Chapter 7 proceeding, is about the division of property between the bankruptcy estate, the debtor and third parties.[20] As the hypotheticals just discussed illustrate, a property's status vis-a-vis the bankruptcy estate can be crucial to deciding the outcome of a dispute.

Of course, this is not to say that Rule 4003(b) does not also have a role to play whenever the issue involved is the claimed exemption of that property. However, Rule 4003(b) does not stand by itself. Rather, it functions subject to the constraints imposed upon it by other aspects of the overall bankruptcy process. For example, due consideration must be given to whether the property targeted as exempt even remains in the bankruptcy estate. Think of property status as being like gravity and Rule 4003(b) as being a road sign. Both a road sign and Rule 4003(b) give direction. However, as helpful as a road sign may be, the traveler must still give heed to the inconvenience of gravity, especially when the road sign leads to the edge of a cliff. The same deference must be given to the

---

[20] "Bankruptcy is both a creditor's remedy and a debtor's right." In re Marchiando, 13 F.3d 1111, 1115 (7th Cir. 1994). One consequence of this duality is that bankruptcy law is simultaneously pursuing two contradictory goals. On the one hand, it seeks to provide a distribution to creditors by liquidating the debtor's property. At the same time, however, it also seeks to give the debtor a "fresh start" through the bankruptcy discharge and by allowing the debtor to keep property from creditors through exemptions. *See* Burlingham v. Crouse, 228 U.S. 459, 473 (1913). These goals compete with one another so that as we try to increase the interests of one group we cannot avoid circumscribing the interests of the other. For example, by excepting debts from the scope of any discharge, we enhance the rights of some creditors and improve the likelihood that their debts will be paid; yet, by refusing to relieve the debtor of a portion of its debt, the value of its fresh start is diminished. Conversely, if we enhance the debtor's fresh start by allowing it to exempt more property, we undermine the interests of creditors by reducing the assets that can be liquidated to satisfy their claims. Because of this inherent tension between debtors and creditors, in crafting the current Bankruptcy Code, Congress necessarily confronted their competing interests and sought to balance them when it allocated the consequences of bankruptcy between debtors and creditors. Just how it did this is reflected throughout the Bankruptcy Code. It can be found in the sections identifying what becomes property of the bankruptcy estate and what is excluded from it, how the assets of the estate are distributed among creditors, the exemptions available to a debtor and the ways in which a debtor can deal with the property it has exempted, the circumstances under which a debtor may receive a discharge and the nature of the debts that will survive discharge, as well as many more.

"*Controlling the distribution of assets between a debtor and its creditors goes to the heart of the bankruptcy process.*" In re Cross, 255 B.R. 25, 32-34 (Bankr. N.D. Ind. 2000) (emphasis added).

status of property vis-a-vis the bankruptcy estate when seeking guidance from Rule 4003(b).

The court in *Brown,* in fact, made this very point when it challenged the soundness of the minority's interpretation of Rule 4003(b).

> Therefore, unless there is some mechanism for the debtor's property to reenter the bankruptcy estate upon conversion, it would seem that exemptions in the Chapter 11, once considered final and unobjectionable under the rule in *Taylor,* must be considered final and unobjectionable in the converted case as well.
>
> Because all the viewpoint cases are subsequent to *Halbert,* and because *Halbert* directly makes this argument, it is interesting that none of the viewpoint cases attempt to answer it, even if they cite *Halbert* as a contrary case. *They seem to assume that something in the conversion process must adjust things so their preferred outcome can obtain, but they do not state what that something is or how it might operate within the Code.*

In re Brown, 178 B.R. 722, 727 (Bankr. E.D. Tenn. 1995) (emphasis added).

Where I differ with *Brown* is with respect to how the flaw it exposed is to be resolved. *Brown's* solution was to simply accept the majority's position that Rule 4003(b) permits only one round of objections. However, for the reasons I have already given, I agree with the minority that conversion of a case gives rise to a new opportunity to object to exemptions claimed. Nonetheless, the minority view cannot, as *Brown* correctly points out, just ignore the effect other aspects of the bankruptcy proceeding can have upon the exemption process and the ultimate question of how property of the estate is to be allocated between the debtor and his creditors.

Indeed, Rule 4003(b)'s relevance is not affected by Section 522(*l*) alone. For example, the doctrines of res judicata and collateral estoppel can also influence the outcome. The reported cases typically involve a converted proceeding where an objection to the exemption had not been previously made. What if, though, the prior trustee had in fact filed an objection but had lost? Would not the doctrine of res judicata bar re-litigation of the same objection in the subsequent Chapter 7 case regardless of what Rule 4003(b) might otherwise provide? Alternatively, would not the doctrine of collateral estoppel preclude a subsequent Chapter 7 trustee from objecting to the debtor's claimed exemption in a converted Chapter 7 if the exemption of that property had also been an issue in the Chapter 13 trustee's unsuccessful Section 1325(a)(4) objection to the debtor's prior plan?

Section 1327(b) offers yet another example. That section states that:

> Except as otherwise provided in the plan or the order confirming the plan, the confirmation of a plan vests all of the property of the estate in the debtor.

11 U.S.C. § 1327(b).

Return again to the hypothetical of the debtor with the Honda and the Chevrolet. However, assume this time that the debtor neglected to claim either vehicle as exempt at the outset of his Chapter 13 proceeding and that, therefore, the vehicles continued to belong to the bankruptcy estate at the time the debtor's plan was to be confirmed. May the debtor later claim either the Honda or Chevrolet as exempt in a subsequent Chapter 7?

The answer clearly would be yes if the debtor's Chapter 13 plan provided that the vehicles were to remain property of the estate post-confirmation. The debtor would simply amend his Schedule C at some point after the conversion to include either the Chevrolet or the Honda. Moreover, it is unlikely that the Chapter 7 trustee would have any objection to the amended exemption claimed because this hypothetical assumes both that the exemption is to be "in-kind" and that the value of each vehicle does not exceed the exemption allowed. Therefore, whatever vehicle the debtor chose as his exemption would thereupon pass from the bankruptcy estate to the debtor pursuant to Section 522(*l*) as part of that subsequent Chapter 7 proceeding.

Suppose, however, the debtor's Chapter 13 plan provided that both vehicles were to revest with the debtor upon confirmation. Or suppose the debtor's plan was silent regarding the vehicles' post-confirmation status. Would the debtor even need to later claim the Honda or Chevrolet as exempt if the Chapter 7 trustee were to thereafter attempt to administer one or both of the vehicles in a subsequently converted case?

The answer is no. Unless the debtor's plan provided otherwise, confirmation of the plan would have caused the two vehicles to be no longer the estate's property. In re Van Stelle, 354 B.R. 157 (Bankr W.D. Mich. 2006). Consequently, the problem here is the same as the problem exposed in *Brown.*[21] There is little question that the Chapter 7 trustee in this hypothetical would like to recover at least one of these vehicles so that it could be liquidated for the benefit of the bankruptcy estate's creditors. Unfortunately, there is no commensurate authority under the Bankruptcy Code for the Chapter 7 trustee to recover property already removed from the estate by Section 1327(b) or other lawful means.

> (a) Except as provided in subsection (b) or (c) of this section, the trustee may avoid a transfer of property of the estate--
>
> (1) that occurs after the commencement of the case; and
>
> (2)(A) that is authorized only under section 303(f) or 542(c) of this title; or
>
> (B) *that is not authorized under this title or by the court.*

11 U.S.C. § 549(a) (emphasis added). *See also, Van Stelle, Id.*[22]

However, it is also worth noting that reliance on Section 1327(b) as a substitute for the exemption process is not necessarily a commendable stratagem for a debtor seeking bankruptcy relief. Granted, it appears at first blush that the

---

[21] "Therefore, unless there is some mechanism for the debtor's property to reenter the bankruptcy estate upon conversion, it would seem that exemptions in the Chapter 11, once considered final and unobjectionable under the rule in *Taylor,* must be considered final and unobjectionable in the converted case as well." In re Brown, 178 B.R. at 727.

[22] Removal of property from a Chapter 13 or Chapter 11 estate by operation of either Section 522(*l*) or 1327(b), of course, is not inevitable. Proponents of the minority position argue that estate representatives in Chapters 11 and 13 do not have the same motivation as their Chapter 7 counterparts to object to exemptions claimed. *See, e.g., In re Campbell,* 313 B.R. at 319, In re Hopkins, 317 B.R. 726, 732-33 (Bankr. E.D. Mich. 2004). That may be so. However, there are options short of filing an objection. For example, a Chapter 13 trustee could, subject to the debtor's objection, seek the indefinite extension of the time within which to object under Rule 4003(b) in instances where it appears that there is a considerable amount of non-exempt equity. The Chapter 13 trustee might also insist that the plan provide for the retention of the subject property as estate property so as to prevent its removal under Section 1327(b). Indeed, the Chapter 13 trustee could object to confirmation of the plan altogether if the feasibility of the debtor's contemplated effort to compensate creditors for the non-exempt equity is in question.

debtor in this hypothetical would be effectively exempting two vehicles when Section 522(d)(2) in fact permits the exemption of only one. In reality, though, the debtor would be receiving the benefit of no exemption, for the protection afforded by Section 522(c) is only available to property that has actually been exempted. That is, the debtor's failure in this hypothetical to exempt the vehicles in his prior Chapter 13, coupled with his successful removal of those vehicles from the bankruptcy estate through the subsequent confirmation of his Chapter 13 plan, would have left both vehicles "liable ... for any debt ... that arose ... before the commencement of the case," 11 U.S.C. § 522(c). Indeed, this would be so even though the debtor himself would be protected from those same pre-petition debts through the separate Section 524(a)(2) injunction issued post-conversion in conjunction with his Chapter 7 discharge.

Moreover, the debtor in this hypothetical would not be able to unilaterally correct his error in the subsequent Chapter 7 proceeding by then claiming one or the other vehicle as exempt because Section 522(b)(1) is also quite clear: exempt property may be selected from only property of the bankruptcy estate. Ironically, the debtor in this hypothetical would be left to bargaining with the Chapter 7 trustee to accept the return of the vehicles to the bankruptcy estate in order to then claim his exemption if it later turned out that the protection of Section 522(c) was desired.

To summarize, the various hypotheticals I have given establish that Rule 4003(b) simply sets the time frames within which a party in interest, whether that party is a trustee or a creditor, may challenge the debtor's effort to remove property from the bankruptcy estate through the Section 522 exemption process. Moreover, the unambiguous language of the rule itself indicates that a party in interest has a new time frame within which to voice his objection to an exemption claimed in the event the debtor's case is later converted to a different chapter.[23]

However, the fact that Rule 4003(b) provides this second chance does not guarantee that an objection will be successful, for any number of pre-conversion events can render the subsequent opportunity to object moot. If, for example, the prior Chapter 13 trustee had struck an agreement with the debtor concerning an

[23] In Rogers v. Laurain (In re Laurain), 113 F.3d 595 (6th Cir. 1997), the Sixth Circuit stated that "Rule 4003(b) should be viewed as jurisdictional." *Id.* at 597. The wording chosen, though, is unfortunate, for if, as I have concluded, the minority interpretation of that rule is correct, it suggests that the court's jurisdiction concerning a challenged objection can be turned off and on again like a light switch as the debtor converts from one case to another.

However, jurisdiction addresses only a court's general authority to exercise its powers. "It [jurisdiction] is the power of the court to decide a matter in controversy and presupposes the existence of a duly constituted court with control over the subject matter and the parties." BLACK's LAW DICTIONARY, Sixth Ed. (1990). In reference to bankruptcy matters, the court's jurisdiction arises upon the commencement of a bankruptcy case and it extends thereafter without interruption to all matters falling within the scope of 28 U.S.C. § 1334 and the applicable local reference rule. *See also,* 28 U.S.C. § 157. It does not cease simply because some proscribed deadline has been missed during the course of administration.

This is not to say that *Rogers* was wrongly decided. The majority's opinion is well reasoned given the language of Rule 4003(b) at that time. *See, In re Travel 2000, Inc.,* 264 B.R. 451, 453 n. 2 (Bankr. W.D. Mich. 2001). However, I believe that the majority inadvertently referred to the issue before it as relating to the bankruptcy court's jurisdiction (*i.e.,* its general authority to adjudicate matters arising in or related to a bankruptcy case) when in fact the issue before it involved only the interpretation of a procedural rule as to when parties could request the court to exercise the jurisdiction already granted.

exemption claimed during the course of the Chapter 13, then that agreement would continue to bind the bankruptcy estate regardless of whether the case is later converted and the successor trustee disagrees with the agreement reached. Similarly, if the Chapter 13 trustee had objected to an exemption claimed and had lost, then the doctrine of res judicata would bar the Chapter 7 trustee from thereafter re-litigating the same objection. And finally, a subsequent Chapter 7 trustee's objection to a claimed exemption in a converted Chapter 7, no matter how valid, would be meaningless if the debtor had in the prior Chapter 13 already removed the subject property from the bankruptcy estate through his successful selection at that time of the property as an in-kind exemption, 11 U.S.C. § 522(*l*), or as part of a more general return of estate property to him upon plan confirmation. 11 U.S.C. § 1327(b). If there is any consolation for trustees, it is that debtors too are subject to the consequences of actions previously taken. For example, if the Chapter 13 trustee had objected to an exemption claimed and had won, it would then be the debtor who would be barred by res judicata in a converted case from again attempting to remove the property from the estate under the same claim of exemption.

In reaching these conclusions, I am not ignoring Section 348(f)(1)(A). That section states that:

> Except as provided in paragraph (2), when a case under chapter 13 of this title is converted to a case under another chapter under this title--
>
> (A) property of the estate in the converted case shall consist of property of the estate, as of the date of filing of the petition, that remains in the possession of or is under the control of the debtor on the date of conversion;

11 U.S.C. § 348(f)(1)(A).

As already discussed, the flaw that the court in *Brown* and I have both found in the minority's position regarding Rule 4003(b) is the failure to explain how property that has been removed from, for example, a Chapter 13 estate as an allowed exemption can then be returned to the bankruptcy estate for further administration in the event the case is later converted to Chapter 7. Some minority view courts have relied upon Section 348(f)(1)(A) to respond to this criticism. For example, in *Campbell,* the panel stated that

> [p]roperty claimed as exempt is property of the estate on a debtor's petition date. It revests in the debtor when the exemption is allowed, either by court order or because of the lack of a timely objection. Property of the estate also revests in the debtor upon the confirmation of a Chapter 13 plan under § 1327(b). Such revested property, being property that was property of the estate on the date that a debtor files a Chapter 13 petition, is property of the Chapter 7 estate upon conversion under § 348(f) if it is still in the debtor's possession. To allow property revested under § 522(*l*) to be excluded from the scope of § 348(f) would require that property revested under § 1327(b) to likewise be excluded. This would have the effect of rendering § 348(f) meaningless in Chapter 13 cases converted after the confirmation of a plan. The revesting of property under § 522(*l*) does not immunize it from being brought into the estate upon conversion of a Chapter 13 case. (footnotes omitted).

In re Campbell, 313 B.R. at 321. *See also* In re Wiggins, 341 B.R. 501, 505-6 (Bankr. M.D. Pa. 2006).

However, I do not agree with *Campbell* that Section 348(f) has meaning only if property previously removed from the bankruptcy estate by operation of

Sections 1327(b) or 522(*l*) "springs back" to the bankruptcy estate upon conversion of the case to Chapter 7. *Campbell* is certainly correct that Section 348(f)(1)(A) has no meaning, or more accurately, no relevance, in situations where the subject property was previously removed from the estate by either of these sections. However, Section 348(f)(1)(A) would still be relevant in those instances where the debtor's plan provided that some or all of the bankruptcy estate's property that remained at the time of confirmation was to continue as property of the estate post-confirmation. 11 U.S.C. § 1327(b). Section 348(f)(1)(A) would also continue to be relevant in those many other instances where the Chapter 13 case is converted to Chapter 7 before confirmation since Section 1327(b) applies only when a Chapter 13 plan is actually confirmed.

Moreover, *Campbell* disregards the fact that cases under Chapter 11 and Chapter 12 may also be converted to Chapter 7 and that these other chapters have the same provision as Chapter 13 regarding the vesting of property with the debtor upon plan confirmation. *Compare* 11 U.S.C. §§ 1141(b), 1227(b), and 1327(b).[24] Section 348(f), though, applies only to converted Chapter 13 cases. Consequently, if, as *Campbell* would have it, Section 348(f) is to include an implicit recovery of property previously removed from the Chapter 13 estate by operation of either Section 1327(b) or, by extension, Section 522(*l*), then one is left to wonder why Congress would not have provided for the same type of recovery when an individual Chapter 11 or Chapter 12 debtor converts his case to Chapter 7.

I am also reluctant to accept *Campbell's* interpretation of Section 348(f) because that interpretation does not protect good faith transferees. Suppose, for example, that a debtor, after successfully exempting his home in the Chapter 13 proceeding, sells the home but reserves for himself either a life estate or a leasehold. If *Campbell's* reasoning were to apply, then the entire fee interest, as opposed to just the leasehold or life estate reserved, would again become property of the estate notwithstanding the intervening good faith purchase of that fee by the third party.[25]

Finally, not even the legislative history underlying Section 348(f) offers support for the implicit right to recover that *Campbell* finds between the lines of that enactment. Conversion of a Chapter 13 case to a Chapter 7 always poses a problem because the bankruptcy estate in a Chapter 13 case, unlike the bankruptcy estate in a Chapter 7 case, includes not only the debtor's prepetition property but whatever the debtor might also have acquired during the course of the Chapter 13 proceeding. 11 U.S.C. § 1306(a).[26] Courts had been divided prior

---

[24] In fact, several of the reported cases concerning the issue at hand involved cases converted from Chapter 11. *See, e.g.,* Brown, 178 B.R. 722, Halbert, 146 B.R. 185, and Wolf, 244 B.R. 754.

[25] [The point made in this paragraph is odd. If the debtor had sold a remainder in the house and if the case converts to chapter 7, § 348(f) (as read in the way the court opposes) means that the good faith purchaser loses the remainder. The court here confuses the thing with property in the thing. The debtor possesses only a life estate/lease in the house, not "the house." Accordingly, under the defective interpretation, the chapter 7 trustee would obtain the retained life estate/lease, *not* the remainder. The court has forgotten the very point it made in n.16, *supra*.--ed.]

[26] A Chapter 13 estate will include whatever the debtor has acquired post-petition in the event the case is converted prior to confirmation of a plan. However, a post-confirmation Chapter 13 estate will not include whatever post-petition property remained with the estate at confirmation unless the plan specifically provided for the retention of that property. 11 U.S.C. § 1327(b). Nonetheless, even a post-confirmation Chapter 13 estate gutted by Section 1327(b) will still include post-petition assets not otherwise included in a Chapter 7 estate since the Chapter 13

to the enactment of Section 348(f) as to how this postpetition accumulation was to be accounted for in the event the case later converted to Chapter 7. The purpose of Section 348(f) was to resolve that division.

> This amendment would clarify the Code to resolve a split in the case of [sic] law about what property is in the bankruptcy estate when a debtor converts from chapter 13 to chapter 7. The problem arises because in chapter 13 (and chapter 12), any property acquired after the petition becomes property of the estate, at least until confirmation of a plan. Some courts have held that if the case is converted, all of this after-acquired property becomes part of the estate in the converted chapter 7 case, even though the statutory provisions making it property of the estate does not apply to chapter 7. Other courts have held that the property of the estate in a converted case is the property the debtor had when the original chapter 13 petition was filed.

H.R. Rep. No. 103-834, 103rd Cong. (2d Sess. 1994); 140 CONG. REC. H10770 (1994); 1994 WL 545773 (Cong. Rec.).[27]

Consequently, I do not interpret Section 348(f)(1)(A) as implicitly empowering Chapter 7 trustee's in converted cases to recover property lawfully removed from the estate in the prior chapter proceeding. Rather, I interpret the reference in Section 348(f)(1)(A) to "property of the estate, as of the filing of the petition" as merely an acknowledgment that, upon conversion from Chapter 13 to Chapter 7, the bankruptcy estate is to be shed of whatever it had accumulated as post-petition assets under Section 1306 so as to resemble what the converted estate would have looked like had the case been in fact administered from the outset as a Chapter 7 proceeding.

In the instant case, it is easy to see that the Chapter 7 trustee's objection to Debtor's claimed exemption in the McMillan residence would have been timely had there not been the conversion from the prior Chapter 13. The meeting of creditors in what would have then been an original Chapter 7 case concluded no earlier than December 13, 2006 and the Chapter 7 trustee's objection was filed

---

estate will continue to be augmented by whatever property the debtor might acquire post-confirmation. 11 U.S.C. § 1306. *See also, In re Van Stelle,* 354 B.R. 157, 170-171 (Bankr. W.D. Mich. 2006).

[27] The inclusion of subpart (2) in Section 348 also reinforces the conclusion that Section 348(f)(1)(A) does not include, as *Campbell* would have it, an implicit mechanism to retrieve property that had been previously removed from the bankruptcy estate by operation of either Section 522(*l*) or Section 1327(b). Section 348(f)(2) provides that the property of the estate in a converted Chapter 7 will include post-petition property added to the estate by Section 1306 to the extent that property remains in the estate at the time of conversion if the debtor converted his case from Chapter 13 in bad faith. In other words, a debtor who has converted his Chapter 13 to Chapter 7 in bad faith is not entitled to the same Section 348(f)(1)(A) "downsizing" of the bankruptcy estate upon conversion as is the debtor who has converted his case in good faith.

However, Section 348(f)(2) is quite clear that only post-petition property that remains property of the Chapter 13 estate at the time of conversion is to become property of the Chapter 7 estate as well. As such, one is hard pressed to read into this subpart an implicit mechanism to return property previously removed from the Chapter 13 estate prior to conversion by either Section 522(*l*) or Section 1327(b) even if one is otherwise inclined to join with *Campbell* in finding such an implicit mechanism between the lines of Section 348(f)(1)(A). If, though, a recovery is to take place under Section 348(f)(1)(A) but not under Section 348(f)(2), then one is certainly entitled to ask why Congress would have chosen to favor a bad faith debtor over a good faith debtor by letting the bad faith debtor keep assets that he had removed from the Chapter 13 estate prior to conversion as exempt or by operation of Section 1327(b) but by requiring the good faith creditor to return the same.

on December 20, 2007, only seven days later. Moreover, even if the objection had not been made, the Chapter 7 trustee would still have had the opportunity to administer the property because of the acknowledged non-exempt equity. In other words, the McMillan residence would have remained property of the estate notwithstanding Section 522(*l*) had Debtor's case been administered as a Chapter 7 from the outset.

Nor would conversion of this case from Chapter 13 to Chapter 7 have affected the Chapter 7 trustee's right to object to Debtor's claimed objection had the prior Chapter 13 plan provided for the bankruptcy estate's post-confirmation retention of the McMillan residence. Under that scenario, the property would have remained property of the estate upon conversion because of the acknowledged non-exempt equity and, therefore, it would have been still subject to the Chapter 7 trustee's further administration. Consequently, it stands to reason that Debtor's continuing effort to exempt $ 45,000 from whatever the Chapter 7 trustee might ultimately realize from this retained asset would also have been subject to the Chapter 7 trustee's new opportunity to object afforded under Rule 4003(b) by the conversion of the case and the attendant scheduling of another meeting of creditors.

On the other hand, had Debtor not conceded in his prior Chapter 13 that there was non-exempt equity in the McMillan residence, and had Debtor instead sought the removal of the residence itself from the bankruptcy estate as an in-kind exemption, the Chapter 7 trustee's subsequent opportunity to object under Rule 4003(b) would have been irrelevant. Put differently, Debtor's in-kind exemption of the interest during the Chapter 13 proceeding would have removed the McMillan residence from the bankruptcy estate by operation of Section 522(*l*) and, as such, the residence would not have been property of the estate in the ensuing Chapter 7 proceeding regardless of what the confirmed plan said about post-confirmation retention of estate property.[28]

However, the instant case presents a fourth scenario, that being one where the McMillan residence, albeit claimed as exempt, was not removed from the bankruptcy estate by operation of Section 522(*l*) notwithstanding the absence of any objection by the Chapter 13 trustee. Rather, the residence remained as property of the estate because of the acknowledged non-exempt equity in the same. Nonetheless, the McMillan residence was ultimately removed from the

---

[28] Making a distinction between the in-kind exemptions of estate property and a "value," if you will, exemption of property that will otherwise remain in the bankruptcy estate for further administration does not run afoul of Congress' desire to offer a fresh start to debtors. Property that a debtor wishes to keep in-kind as exempt should be returned from the bankruptcy estate as soon as possible. In re Anderson, 357 B.R. 460. Moreover, the need for certainty justifies denying a subsequent Chapter 7 trustee a second look at the property already exempted from the estate in the event of a conversion from another case.

However, a debtor's concession that there is non-exempt value in the targeted property negates the need for finality at the outset of the case. Granted, the debtor would certainly like to enjoy his share of the proceeds ultimately realized from the liquidation of the asset in question. However, consideration must also be given to the creditors' competing demand for sufficient time to maximize the non-exempt portion of whatever is realized from its liquidation. If it is that important for a Chapter 13 debtor, for example, to divest the bankruptcy estate of the non-exempt portion of property as well, the debtor may attempt to do so as part of the confirmation process. 11 U.S.C. § 1325(b).

However, if that debtor chooses not to do so, then the debtor is in no position to later complain if a subsequent Chapter 7 trustee elects to take a second look at an exemption claimed in property that remains subject to the trustee's administration.

estate during the Chapter 13 proceeding when Debtor's plan was later confirmed. 11 U.S.C. § 1327(b). Consequently, the residence was no longer subject to administration when the case was later converted to Chapter 7 and the Chapter 7 trustee filed her own objection to the exemption Debtor had previously claimed.

The good news for Debtor is that the Chapter 7 trustee can no more at this time compel the recovery of the McMillan residence than can the Chapter 7 trustee compel the recovery of any other property that was legitimately removed from the bankruptcy estate by operation of Section 1327(b) during the prior Chapter 13 proceeding. Therefore, it makes no difference that the Chapter 7 trustee now has a renewed opportunity to object to the constitutionality of the exemption Debtor had claimed in the residence more than a year and a half ago.

However, the bad news for Debtor is that the McMillan residence is not entitled to the protection afforded by Section 522(c) because the residence was not "exempted" from the bankruptcy estate by operation of Section 522(*l*), but rather was simply removed at a later date through the confirmation process. Moreover, Debtor finds himself no longer in the position to secure that protection since, as already discussed, an exemption can be accomplished only if the property targeted is removed from the bankruptcy estate by operation of Section 522(*l*) and there is nothing that Debtor on his own can do to now put the property he previously removed through the plan confirmation back into the bankruptcy estate.

CONCLUSION

Exempting property from the bankruptcy estate can be deceptive. On its face, it is simply the process of separating what the debtor is to keep from what the trustee may liquidate. However, as shown, other aspects of the bankruptcy process can have a profound impact upon the outcome in a particular case. The challenge, of course, is to step back far enough from the problem at hand so as to appreciate all of the processes at work.

In this instance, I am satisfied that the Chapter 7 trustee had the right under Rule 4003(b) to raise an objection concerning the constitutionality of the state exemption claimed in the McMillan residence even though that exemption was first asserted over two years ago. The recent conversion of this case from Chapter 13 to Chapter 7 caused a new meeting of creditors to be scheduled and, therefore, the Chapter 7 trustee had a new opportunity to object under Rule 4003(b). Indeed, the Chapter 7 trustee's objection would have been successful had Section 1327(b) not intervened since the McMillan residence would have otherwise remained as property of the estate for all of this time. However, Section 1327(b), combined with Debtor's confirmation of his plan in the prior Chapter 13 case, has rendered moot what otherwise appears to be both a timely and valid objection.

Therefore, for the reasons given, there is no reason for the Chapter 7 trustee to proceed with her objection to Debtor's claimed exemption in the McMillan residence. . . .

2

Notes and Questions

1. Did you catch the fact that, in spite of being disentitled to an exemption, the debtor got to keep the house after all? This was because the house became the debtor's property upon

confirmation. Bankruptcy Code § 1327(b). And what about § 348(f)(1), which provides

> Except as provided in paragraph (2) [governing bad faith debtors], when a case under chapter 13 of this title is converted to a case under another chapter under this title--
>
> (A) property of the estate in the converted case shall consist of property of the estate, as of the date of filing of the petition, that remains in the possession of or is under the control of the debtor on the date of conversion . . .

Why, in the opinion of Judge Hughes, did this section fail to bring the house into chapter 7?

2. Judge Hughes states that the "bad news" for the debtor is that § 522(c) does not protect the house, since the house is not actually exempt property. Why is this bad for the debtor?

Index

References are to pages

www.ingramcontent.com/pod-product-compliance
Lightning Source LLC
LaVergne TN
LVHW080616300926
849162LV00005B/1176